World Economic Forum
Geneva, Switzerland 2004

Professor Klaus Schwab
World Economic Forum

Professor Michael E. Porter
Harvard University

Co-Directors, The Global Competitiveness Report

The Global Competitiveness Report 2003–2004

Professor Xavier Sala-i-Martin
Columbia University and Universitat Pompeu Fabra
Editor

New York • Oxford
Oxford University Press
2004

The Global Competitiveness Report 2003–2004
is published by the World Economic Forum
within the framework of the Global
Competitiveness Programme.

Professor Klaus Schwab
Executive Chairman

Professor Xavier Sala-i-Martin
Editor

Dr Augusto Lopez-Claros
Director

Jennifer Blanke
Emma Loades
Maria-Angels Oliva
Fiona Paua
Catherine Vindret
Saadia Zahidi

We thank Hope Steele for her excellent editing
work and Ha Nguyen for her superb graphic
design and layout.

We are very grateful to Victor Echevarria Icaza
and Annette Heimlicher for their invaluable
research assistance.

The terms *country* and *nation* as used in this
report do not in all cases refer to a territorial
entity that is a state as understood by international law and practice. The term covers well-
defined, geographically self-contained economic
areas that may not be states but for which statistical data are maintained on a separate and
independent basis.

Oxford University Press

Oxford   New York
Auckland   Bangkok   Buenos Aires
Cape Town   Chennai   Dar es Salaam
Delhi   Hong Kong   Istanbul   Karachi
Kolkata   Kuala Lumpur   Madrid
Melbourne   Mexico City   Mumbai
Nairobi   São Paulo   Shanghai
Singapore   Taipei   Tokyo   Toronto

Copyright © 2004
by the World Economic Forum

Published by
Oxford University Press, Inc.
198 Madison Avenue
New York, New York 10016
http://www.oup.com

Oxford is a registered trademark of Oxford
University Press

ISBN 0-19-517360-0

9 8 7 6 5 4 3 2 1

Printed in the United States of America
on acid-free paper.

Contents

Partner Institutes

Algeria
Centre de Recherche en Economie Appliquée pour le
Développement (CREAD)
Professor Yassine Ferfera

Angola
SOF—Serviços de Organização e Finanças
Marcolino Meireles, Manager
Manuel José Alves Da Rocha, Consultant
Emil Moreso Grion, Consultant

Argentina
IAE—Universidad Austral
Marcelo Paladino, Research Director
Alberto Willi, Research Assistant

Australia
Business Council of Australia
Katie Lahey, Chief Executive
Melinda Cilento, Chief Economist

Austria
WIFO—Austrian Institute of Economic Research
Professor Karl Aiginger, Deputy Director

Bangladesh
Centre for Policy Dialogue (CPD)
Dr Debapriya Bhattacharya, Executive Director
Dr Uttam Kumar Deb, Research Fellow
Kazi Mahmudur Rahman, Research Associate

Belgium
Vlerick Leuven Gent Management School
Professor Dr Lutgart Van den Berghe, Executive Director, Chairman
    Competence Centre — Entrepreneurship, Governance & Strategy
Harry Bowen, Professor, Economics and International Business
Lucy Amez, Research Assistant

Bolivia
Universidad Catolica Boliviana
Lic. Marcela A. De Guzman, Directora, Depto. Economia

Botswana
Botswana Institute for Development Policy Analysis (BIDPA)
Dr N.H. Fidzani, Executive Director
Kedikilwe P. Maroba, Programme Coordinator

Brazil
Fundação Dom Cabral
Professor Carlos Arruda, Associate Dean for Development
Fabiana Santos

Bulgaria
Center for Economic Development
Anelia Damianova, PhD, Senior Expert

Cameroon
Centre d'Etudes et de Recherches en Economie et Gestion
Professor Seraphin Magloire Fouda, Director

Canada
Institute for Competitiveness and Prosperity
Roger Martin, Dean of the Rotman School of Management,
    University of Toronto and Chairman of the Institute for
    Competitiveness and Prosperity
James Milway, Executive Director of the Institute for
    Competitiveness and Prosperity

Chad
Groupe de Recherches Alternatives et de Monitoring du Projet
    Pétrole-Tchad-Cameroun (GRAMP-TC)
Professor Gilbert Maoundonodji, Director

Chile
Universidad Adolfo Ibañez
Andres Allamand Zavala, Dean of the School of Government
Victoria Hurtado Larrain, Academic Coordinator of the School of
    Government

China
Institute of Economics Systems and Management
State Council Office for Restructuring Economic Systems
Chen Li, Executive Deputy Director
Dr Gao Shi-Ji, Deputy Director for Research
Zhou Mei, Assistant Fellow

Colombia
National Planning Department
María Isabel Agudelo
Fernando J. Estupiñan V.

Croatia
National Competitiveness Council
Mira Lenardic, Secretary General
Ivana Cesljas, Advisor

Czech Republic
CMC—Graduate School of Business
Peter Loewenguth, President
Professor Jaroslav A. Jirasek, Honorary Dean

Denmark
Copenhagen Business School
Heather Alison Hazard, Associate Professor, Program Director, Vice
    President for International Affairs
Mette Reerbirk, Programme Administrator

Ecuador
Escuela Superior Politecnica del Litoral (ESPOL)
Escuela de Postgrado en Administracion de Empresas (ESPAE)
Virginia Lasio, Acting Director
Karina Astudillo, Project Assistant

Egypt
Egyptian Center for Economic Studies
Dr Ahmed Galal, Executive Director

Estonia
Estonian Chamber of Commerce and Industry
Siim Raie, Director General

Ethiopia
Ethiopian Economic Association/Ethiopian Economic Policy Research
   Institute
Berhanu Nega, Director
Kibre Moges, Senior Researcher
Worku Gebeyehu, Assistant Researcher

Finland
ETLA—The Research Institute of the Finnish Economy
Pentti Vartia, President
Pekka Ylä-Anttila, Managing Director
Petri Rouvinen, Research Director

France
HEC School of Management—Paris
Bernard Ramanantsoa, Professor, Dean of HEC School of
   Management
Bertrand Moingeon, Professor, Associate Dean for Executive
   Education

Gambia
Gambia Economic and Social Development Research Institute
   (GESDRI)
Makaireh A. Njie, Director

Germany
Wissenschaftliche Hochschule für Unternehmensführung Koblenz
WHU—Otto Beisheim Graduate School of Management
Professor Michael Frenkel

Ghana
The International Institute for IT (INIIT)
Professor Clement Dzidonu, President and Senior Research Fellow
Eliza Sam, Projects Officer

Greece
Federation of Greek Industries
Antonis Tortopidis, Co-ordinator, Research and Analysis
Theodora Aivazoglou, Economist, Research and Analysis

Haiti
SOGEBANK—Société Général Haïtienne de Banque S.A.
Claude Pierre-Louis, General Manager
Pierre-Marie Boisson, Chief Economist
Reginald Saint-Fleur, Economist

Hong Kong SAR
The Hong Kong General Chamber of Commerce
David O'Rear, Chief Economist

Federation of Hong Kong Industries
Alexandra Poon, Director

Hungary
Kopint-Datorg, Economic Research
Dr Éva Palócz, Deputy General Director
Ágnes Nagy, Project Manager

Iceland
ICETEC
Hallgrimur Jonasson, General Director

India
Confederation of Indian Industry
Tarun Das, Director General

Indonesia
LP3E-Kadin Indonesia
Dr Tulus Tambunan

Ireland
Department of Economics, University College Cork
Dr Eleanor Doyle
Rosemary Kelleher
Niall O'Sullivan
Bernadette Power

Israel
Manufacturers Association of Israel, Foreign Trade and International
   Relations Division
Moshe Nahum, Director

Italy
SDA Bocconi
Claudio Dematté, Full Professor Strategic Management and
   Entrepreneurship Bocconi University —SDA Bocconi
Paola Dubini, Associate Professor Strategic Management and
   Entrepreneurship Bocconi University—SDA Bocconi
Elena Grassi, Research Assistant, SDA Bocconi

Jamaica
Private Sector Organisation of Jamaica (PSOJ)
Greta Bogues, Chief Executive Officer
Mona School of Business at the University of the West Indies (MSB)
Gordon Shirley, Professor

Japan
Hitotsubashi University Graduate School of International Corporate
   Strategy (ICS)
Hirotaka Takeuchi, Dean

Jordan
Ministry of Planning, Competitiveness Unit
Naseem Al-Rahahleh, Director

Kenya
Institute of Policy Analysis and Research (IPAR)
Dr T. Nzioki Kibua, Executive Director
John Omiti, Senior Research Fellow and Coordinator, Real Sector
R. Njeri Chacha, Resource Centre Manager

Korea
Korea Development Institute
Dr Cho Byung-Koo, Chief of Information and Computing Center

Latvia
Institute of Economics, Latvian Academy of Sciences, Riga
Dr Raite Karnite, Director

Lithuania
Statistikos Tyrimai—Statistical Surveys, Vilnius
Benonas Miksas, Director

Luxembourg
Chamber of Commerce of the Grand Duchy of Luxembourg
Carlo Thelen, Member of the Management Committee

Macedonia, FYR
National Entrepreneurship and Competitiveness Council
Ilija Filipovski, Minister of Economy, Co-Chairman of the Council
Svetozar Janevski, CEO, "Pivara," Skopje, Co-Chairman of the Council

Madagascar
University of Antananarivo
Pépé Andrianomanana, Director, Centre of Economic Studies

Malawi
Malawi Investment Promotion Agency
Alick C. E. Sukasuka, Director of Operations

Malaysia
Institute of Strategic and International Studies (ISIS)
Tan Sri Dato' Dr Mohamed Noordin Sopiee, Chairman and Chief
   Executive Officer

Mali
Groupe de Recherche en Economie Appliquée et Théorique (GREAT)
Massa Coulibaly, Coordinator

Malta
Foundation for National Competitiveness
Dr John C. Grech, President
Adrian Said, Chief Coordinator
Wilfred Kenely, Policy & Programs Coordinator
Dr Jennifer Cassingena Harper, International Relations Coordinator

Mauritius
Joint Economic Council of Mauritius
Raj Makoond, Director

Mexico
Ministry of the Economy
Dr Eduardo J. Solis Sanchez, Chief of the Office for the Co-ordination of International Trade and Investment Promotion
Lic. Veronica Orendain De Los Santos, Assistant in the Office for the Co-ordination of International Trade and Investment Promotion

Center for Intellectual Capital and Competitiveness
Dr Rene Villarreal, President
Dra Rocio Ramos de Villarreal, Vice-President

Mexican Institute of Competitiveness (IMCO)
Valentín Díez Morodo, Chairman of the Board and President
Emilio Carrillo Gamboa, Secretary

Morocco
Université Hassan II
Fouzi Mourji, Professor of Economics

Mozambique
EconPolicy Research Group, Lda
Dr Peter Coughlin, Partner
Professor Dr Paulo N. Mole, Partner

Namibia
Namibian Economic Policy Research Unit
Dr Christoph Stork, Senior Researcher
Antony N. Masarakufa, Researcher

Netherlands
Erasmus Strategic Renewal Center, Erasmus University Rotterdam
Professor Frans A. J. van den Bosch
Professor Henk W. Volberda

New Zealand
Business New Zealand
Anne Knowles, Executive Director

Nigeria
Nigerian Economic Summit Group (NESG)
Chris Onyemenam, Director, Operations & Administration
Dr Felix Ogbera, Associate Director, Research
Mayowa Obilade, Research Consultant

Norway
Norwegian School of Management BI, Centre for Value Creation
Dr Erik W. Jakobsen, Associate Professor
Dr Torger Reve, Professor
Anne Fossum, Analyst

Pakistan
Pakistan Institute of Development Economics
Dr A. R. Kemal

Paraguay
Centro de Analisis y Difusion de Economia Paraguaya (CADEP)
Fernando Masi, Director
Dionisio Borda, Research Member
Nelson Aguilera Alfred, Research Member

Peru
Centro de Desarrollo Industrial (CDI)—Sociedad Nacional de Industrias
Luis Tenorio, Executive Director
Néstor Asto, Project Director

Philippines
Makati Business Club
Guillermo M. Luz, Executive Director
Marc P. Opulencia, Deputy Director
Michael B. Mundo, Chief Economist

Poland
Warsaw School of Economics
Professor Bogdan Radomski, Associate Professor

Portugal
PROFORUM, Associação Para o Desenvolvimento da Engenharia
Ilídio António de Ayala Serôdio, Member of the Board of Directors

Romania
Romanian Economics Society (SOREC)
Professor Daniel Daianu, President SOREC, Professor of Economics, Academy of Economic Studies Bucharest
Dr Liviu Voinea, Senior Lecturer, Romanian-American University
Dragos N. Pislaru, Research Fellow, Romanian Center for Economic Policies

Russian Federation
Bauman Technical University (BMSTU)
Dr Alexei Prazdnitchnyk, Project Coordinator, BMSTU Russian Regional Competitiveness Survey Project

Institute for Private Sector Development and Socio-Economic Analysis (IPSSA)
Irina Evseyeva

Stockholm School of Economics in Saint Petersburg
Professor Carl F. Fey, Associate Dean of Research
Dr Igor Dukeov, Research Fellow

Rwanda
Kigali Institute of Science, Technology and Management (KIST)
Eng. Albert Butare, Vice Rector (Academic)
Rajeev Aggarwal, Head of Department, Cottage Industry Technologies

Senegal
Centre de Recherches Economiques Appliquées (CREA)
Abdoulaye Diagne, Director
Dr Gaye Daffé, Scientific Coordinator

Serbia
Serbia National Competitiveness Council
Dragoljub Vukadinovic, Chairman
Goran Pitic, Member of the Executive Committee
Professor Boris Begovic, Member of the Executive Committee

Singapore
Economic Development Board
Shirley Chen, Assistant Managing Director, Corporate Services

Slovak Republic
Business Alliance of Slovakia (PAS)
Robert Kicina, Project Manager

Institute for Economic and Social Reforms (INEKO)
Eugen Jurzyca, Director

Slovenia
Institute for Economic Research
Dr Peter Stanovnik, Director
Dr Mateja Drnovšek, Faculty of Economics
Professor Aleš Vahčič, Faculty of Economics

South Africa
Business South Africa
Ben Van Der Ross, Chief Executive Officer
Friede Dowie, Secretary General

Preface

KLAUS SCHWAB

Executive Chairman, World Economic Forum

Since the release of last year's *Global Competitiveness Report*, the world economy has continued to struggle: a pickup in confidence associated with fledging signs of an upturn in activity in the United States and Japan has been tempered by an anemic growth performance in Europe, against the background of continued uncertainties in the international political and security environment.

We entered 2003 still facing many of the unresolved challenges of the previous two years. The fight against terrorism in the aftermath of the events of September 11 and the elusive search for a lasting peace in the Middle East have remained at the top of the political agenda for many of the world's top leaders, engaging everywhere the concerted attention of governments and international institutions. Business confidence has remained weak. This was initially in connection with the uncertainties created by a looming war in Iraq and the noisy political debates that preceded it and, subsequently, by continued concerns about the war's aftereffects and the perceived fragility of the mechanisms of international cooperation that are seen to have played such a crucial role in the long period of economic expansion and prosperity that have characterized the postwar period.

Recent events—from the difficult reconstruction efforts under way in Afghanistan and Iraq to efforts to deal with large humanitarian crises in various parts of Africa—have brought into focus the importance of concerted international action to safeguard and strengthen security and stability. Yet a continuing lack of public confidence in national institutions and governments and a growing awareness of institutional weaknesses at the international level risk slowing the development process down in many parts of the world.

Against this somber backdrop, one cause for some optimism is the growing recognition that the rule of law and the existence of credible and efficient public institutions are essential prerequisites for sustainable economic development. The Executive Opinion Survey carried out by the World Economic Forum, the backbone of our work on competitiveness issues, provides ample evidence of this. Without these basic elements, it is difficult to create the conditions under which local entrepreneurship will be nurtured and contribute to higher levels of national income. These "pillars of stability" seem to be essential

foundations for businesses to have the confidence to invest, to create jobs, and to innovate and look for alternative development opportunities, with positive externalities for the standards of living of broad segments of the population.

Much is at stake in 2003 concerning the creation of a more efficient and equitable world trading system. The debate on the benefits and costs of globalization has increasingly turned to the issue of international trade and its potential to boost the incomes of developing countries. There is a perception that, although the industrial democracies have not hesitated to press for market liberalization and the dismantling of barriers to trade in the developing world, they have not often followed with liberalizing measures of their own, particularly as regards agricultural exports from the developing countries. Following several missed deadlines set at the World Trade Organization 2001 Ministerial Meeting, 2003 has become a critical year for trade ministers to commit to the actions agreed upon in Doha and to act accordingly, even against the background of the setbacks in Cancun. These commitments include increasing market access, reducing government-financed export incentives, minimizing trade-distorting subsidies in agriculture, and reducing nontariff barriers to trade. Other breakthroughs needed for developing countries to grow include improvements in market access to developed countries for textiles and other manufactured goods. For their part, the developing countries should make further progress in reducing trade barriers among themselves. Trade and trade-supporting aid are one of the most effective ways to attack poverty.

Public health is also a key issue of concern worldwide. HIV/AIDS continues to exact a heavy toll on Africa and to spread to other countries, with China, India, and Russia rapidly becoming potential crisis zones. The destabilizing effects on the world economy of SARS earlier this year also sounded warning bells to health ministers and their governments of the dangers associated with delays in prompt, candid, and comprehensive responses to deal with new threats.

There is growing evidence of commitment to global economic recovery from governments, businesses, and civil society organizations. The World Economic Forum is pledged to playing a facilitating role in this process and, by providing detailed assessments of the economic conditions of nations worldwide, *The Global Competitiveness Report* contributes to enhancing our understanding of the key ingredients of economic growth and prosperity. By highlighting the strengths and weaknesses of an economy, policymakers and business leaders are assisted in their decision making, whether through the introduction of new economic measures or through institutional reforms.

Given the importance of capacity building in developing countries, particular efforts were devoted this year to increasing our country coverage of Africa, which have resulted in increasing from 8 to 25 the number of African countries featured in the *Report*. We also plan to release the third edition of *The Africa Competitiveness Report* early next year. Despite the challenges that we often face in efforts to increase our country coverage, we are committed to continuing to expand our geographic reach in coming years. Within the range of regional and special topic reports, we also plan to release new editions of *The Global Information Technology Report* late in 2003 and *The Latin America Competitiveness Report* in 2004.

Finally, we would like to thank Professor Michael E. Porter, Director of the Institute for Strategy and Competitiveness at the Harvard Business School, for his continued collaboration for and support of this project. We would also like to express our gratitude to Professor Xavier Sala-i-Martin, Columbia University and Universitat Pompeu Fabra, for his commitment to this year's *Report* in his role as Editor. Appreciation also goes to Augusto Lopez-Claros, the recently appointed Director of the Global Competitiveness Programme, and his team: Jennifer Blanke, Emma Loades, Maria-Angels Oliva, Fiona Paua, Catherine Vindret, and Saadia Zahidi. We would also like to thank FedEx and KPMG, our partners in this *Report*, for their invaluable support in this important venture. Finally, we would like to pass on our sincere thanks to all the business executives around the world who took the time to participate in our Executive Opinion Survey, without whose valued input this *Report* would not have been possible.

x

Executive Summary

XAVIER SALA-I-MARTIN, Columbia University and

Universitat Pompeu Fabra

The fundamental objective of the *Global Competitiveness Report* (GCR) is to evaluate the economic competitiveness of a large sample of countries. Traditionally, the GCR has focused on two complementary approaches to analyzing competitiveness. The first, called the *Growth Competitiveness Index (GCI)*, was developed by Jeffrey D. Sachs of Columbia University and John W. McArthur of The Earth Institute and was presented in *The Global Competitiveness Report 2001–2002*. The second index, now labeled the *Business Competitiveness Index (BCI)*, was developed by Michael Porter of Harvard University and was first introduced in *The Global Competitiveness Report 2000*.

The two indexes combine available hard data and data from the Executive Opinion Survey (Survey) conducted annually by the World Economic Forum (see Chapter 3.1 for additional analysis of Survey results and methodology). The Survey is conducted in the first half of every year. Input is contributed exclusively by leading business executives and entrepreneurs whose current perceptions of the business environment in which they work are captured in their responses to a comprehensive and scientifically constructed questionnaire. By participating, respondents are also provided with the opportunity to identify key obstacles to economic growth in their own countries and thus contribute to assessing the quality of the business environment in the countries where their companies operate. This, in turn, may help precipitate an internal debate within the country between government officials, business leaders, organizations of civil society and the academic community on key problem areas and how best to address them.

The Survey was carried out this year in collaboration with 104 Partner Institutes of the World Economic Forum's Global Competitiveness Programme. Partner Institutes are typically leading national research or academic institutes committed to contributing to the growth potential of their respective economies. Under the direction of the World Economic Forum, their collaboration involves conducting the Survey according to common guidelines in order to ensure that the sample of respondents is representative of the economies in question and that the Survey method used remains consistent across all countries.

The number of countries surveyed this year increased significantly, from 80 to 102. The countries added are mainly from the developing world, especially Africa. The coverage in that region of the world has increased from 8 to 25, and now also includes Algeria, Angola, Cameroon, Chad, Egypt, Ethiopia, Gambia, Ghana, Kenya, Madagascar, Malawi, Mali, Mozambique, Senegal, Tanzania, Uganda, and Zambia. Newly added countries also embrace non-African nations, including Luxembourg, Macedonia, Malta, Pakistan, and Serbia. The countries included in this year's *Report* account for 97.8 percent of world's GDP. *The Global Competitiveness Report 2003–2004*, therefore, provides comprehensive coverage of the global economy.

The Growth Competitiveness Index

The GCI's main goal is to analyze the potential for the world's economies to attain sustained economic growth over the medium and long term. The index is based on economists' current understanding of the determinants of the complex process of economic growth and development. It summarizes the set of institutions, policies, and structures driving the growth process of 102 heterogeneous countries.

The GCI is founded on three central ideas. The first one is that the process of economic growth can be analyzed within three important broad categories: the macroeconomic environment, the quality of public institutions, and technology.

Although it is certainly not true that macroeconomic stability alone can increase the growth rate of a nation, it is no less true that macroeconomic disarray kills its growth prospects. Informed decisions cannot be made in environments where the inflation rate is in the hundreds. The banking system cannot function if the government runs gigantic deficits. The government cannot provide services efficiently if it has to pay enormous interest rates on its past debts. And wasted taxation hurts the business sector unnecessarily. In sum, sustained growth is hard to achieve in nonfavorable macro environments.

The second pillar underlying the GCI relates to public institutions. In a market economy, wealth is ultimately created by private businesses. However, these businesses have to operate within a country and have to deal with its institutions. It is important, for example, that property rights are guaranteed by a legal and judicial system. It is hard for private companies to operate efficiently in countries where the rule of law is nonexistent or where contracts cannot be enforced. Firms may find it too expensive to do business where corruption is rampant. Thus, the GCI measures the soundness of the public institutions and it introduces this soundness as the second of the three pillars of economic growth and development.

The third channel is technological progress. Perhaps the main lesson of neoclassical growth theory is that the ultimate source of long-run economic growth is technological progress. The reason for this is that the other potential determinants of growth must run into diminishing returns. For example, institutions and the macroeconomic policy can have important effects on growth in countries with terrible environments. But once institutions are more or less right, and once the macroeconomy is more or less stable, additional improvements along these lines will probably have little or no effect on economic

growth. This is not true for technological progress: there do not seem to be good reasons that would suggest that there are diminishing returns to ideas. In fact, the contrary might be true, given that humanity seems to generate new ideas at accelerating rates.

The GCI uses both hard (publicly available) data and data from the World Economic Forum's Survey to estimate three "component indexes" that capture the three pillars of growth mentioned above. The three components are called the "technology index," the "public institutions index," and the "macroeconomic environment index." The three components are then combined to calculate the overall GCI.

The second idea underlying the GCI is that, although technological advance is the ultimate source of growth, its origin may be different across countries. In particular, for economies that are already close to the technological frontier, innovation is the main source of technological improvements. For those that are far away from the frontier, technological improvements can be achieved partly through innovation and partly by copying or adopting the knowledge previously developed in one of the leading economies.

To capture this second idea, the GCI separates the sample of countries into two groups: the "core" and the "non-core" innovators. Core innovators are those economies whose growth is largely driven by their capacity to innovate because they are close to the technological frontier. "Non-core" innovators are those that depend more on technological adoption from abroad. The threshold of 15 patents per million population was chosen to separate the countries into these two groups. Countries above this threshold are defined as the core group, and all others as non-core.

To reflect the fact that innovation is more important than adoption for core innovators, the technology index of the GCI puts a larger weight on innovation for the core innovators than for the non-core innovators. Technological adoption, on the other hand, receives a positive weight for non-core countries and zero weight for core innovators. Technological adoption is captured by the technology transfer subindex.

The third central idea underlying the GCI is that the importance of the determinants of economic competitiveness varies for core and non-core innovators. Getting the fundamentals right in terms of the macroeconomic environment and institutions is still extremely critical for the non-core innovators, whereas core innovators will have these fundamentals largely in place, and for them technological innovation has become the deciding factor for growth. Along these lines, the GCI assigns a larger weight to the technology index for core innovators than it does to the public institutions index and the macroeconomic environment index. On the other hand, equal weights are assigned to these three indexes for non-core innovators.

Although we have maintained the basic structure and overall logic of the GCI as developed by Sachs and McArthur, this year we have made one significant change to the methodology. In the macroeconomic environment index, we have replaced a previously used variable, the "government expenditure as a percentage of GDP," with a composite subindex aimed at capturing government spending waste. We decided to reconsider the role of government expenditure as a percentage of GDP because, implicitly, its inclusion assumed that economic growth would be maximized at zero government expenditures. We do not think that this is a good assumption, since many public expenditures are productive and contribute positively to the competitiveness of a nation. The index should capture public waste rather than public spending. After testing a number of candidate variables, three were selected:

- Extent of distortive government subsidies
- Diversion of public funds
- Public trust in the financial honesty of politicians

We think that this "composite waste subindex" captures waste through government favoritism and corruption. This should account for a large part of overall government wasteful spending. Statistical analysis of these variables indeed showed that they have strong explanatory power with regard to medium- to long-term growth. This solution was thus retained. The second change, less important in its implications, affects the innovation component of the technology index—the details are presented in Chapter 1.1.

Last year's rankings

Of course, altering the model as described in the section above necessarily has an impact on the rankings of the index. Table 1 compares last year's published rankings (Column 4) with those that would have been obtained using the current formula (Column 3). We see that there would have been a number of differences in last year's rankings if we had made the two substitutions described in the section above. A first notable point is that Finland, rather than the United States, would have topped the rankings. This can be traced to the fact that the US government spends a relatively low percentage of GDP compared to Finland. And although US spending is not seen as particularly wasteful, Finland's is seen as even less so. The combined effect of these two forces is that Finland is ranked ahead of the US once government expenditure is replaced by government waste.

Finland's relative improvement is indicative of a more general trend we see in the data: many western European countries would have been higher in the rankings last year using the new formula. These countries have governments that spend a high proportion of GDP (which was "penalized" by last year's formula), but that, as captured by the waste composite, are not seen as spending wastefully. In fact, all western European countries have either the same or higher rankings following the introduction of government waste to the index: not one of them is lower following this change.

The other side of the same coin is that many countries in Asia and Latin America would have had lower ranks last year if we had been using the waste variable rather than government expenditure. These are countries that have relatively low overall government spending, which pushed them higher in the rankings last year. However, once the wastefulness of the spending they do have is taken into account, many of these countries do less well, therefore coming in lower in the rankings.

Competitiveness Rankings 2003–2004

Column 1 of Table 1 reports the results of this year's 2003 Growth Competitiveness Index rankings using the full sample of 102 countries. In order to establish comparability between last year's rankings (Column 3) and this year's, we also report this year's rankings when only the countries that participated in last year's study are included. This is done in Column 2.

A quick comparison of Columns 2 and 3 reveals striking similarities with last year's top ten rankings. The first four ranks are identical, with Finland in the first place, followed by the United States, Sweden, and Denmark, respectively. Taiwan and Singapore maintain their rankings relative to each other, but both moved higher by one position, to 5th and 6th respectively, sliding Switzerland from the 5th to the 7th position. Norway declined by one rank to 9th place, making way for Iceland at the 8th place. Canada, previously at 9th place, falls off the top 10 list while Australia remains in 10th position.

The top two newcomers are Malta (19th) and Luxembourg (21st). The new countries from the developing world all lie at the bottom half of the table. Gambia (55th) is the highest rank newcomer, whereas Chad (101st) is the lowest. Egypt (58th) comes back to the rankings after being eliminated last year because of problems in the data collection process. Tanzania (69th), Ghana (71st), Pakistan (73rd) and Algeria (74th) are the next highest rank newcomers, followed by Malawi (76th), Serbia (77th), Senegal (79th), Uganda (80th), Macedonia (81st), Kenya (83rd), Zambia (88th), Cameroon (91st), Ethiopia (92nd), Mozambique (93rd), Madagascar (96th), Mali (99th), and Angola (100th).

Table 1: Growth Competitiveness Index rankings and 2002 comparisons

Country	GCI 2003 Rank (among 2003 countries)	GCI 2003 Rank (among 2002 countries)	GCI 2002 Rank (revised*)	GCI 2002 Rank (original)	Country	GCI 2003 Rank (among 2003 countries)	GCI 2003 Rank (among 2002 countries)	GCI 2002 Rank (revised*)	GCI 2002 Rank (original)
Finland	1	1	1	2	Tanzania	69	—	—	—
United States	2	2	2	1	Russian Federation	70	65	66	64
Sweden	3	3	3	5	Ghana	71	—	—	—
Denmark	4	4	4	10	Indonesia	72	66	69	67
Taiwan	5	5	6	3	Pakistan	73	—	—	—
Singapore	6	6	7	4	Algeria	74	—	—	—
Switzerland	7	7	5	6	Romania	75	67	67	66
Iceland	8	8	12	12	Malawi	76	—	—	—
Norway	9	9	8	9	Serbia	77	—	—	—
Australia	10	10	10	7	Argentina	78	68	64	63
Japan	11	11	16	13	Senegal	79	—	—	—
Netherlands	12	12	13	15	Uganda	80	—	—	—
Germany	13	13	14	14	Macedonia	81	—	—	—
New Zealand	14	14	15	16	Venezuela	82	69	68	68
United Kingdom	15	15	11	11	Kenya	83	—	—	—
Canada	16	16	9	8	Ukraine	84	70	74	77
Austria	17	17	18	18	Bolivia	85	71	71	78
Korea	18	18	25	21	Ecuador	86	72	73	73
Malta	19	—	—	—	Nigeria	87	73	72	71
Israel	20	19	17	19	Zambia	88	—	—	—
Luxembourg	21	—	—	—	Guatemala	89	74	75	70
Estonia	22	20	27	26	Nicaragua	90	75	70	75
Spain	23	21	20	22	Cameroon	91	—	—	—
Hong Kong	24	22	22	17	Ethiopia	92	—	—	—
Portugal	25	23	19	23	Mozambique	93	—	—	—
France	26	24	28	30	Honduras	94	76	78	76
Belgium	27	25	21	25	Paraguay	95	77	76	72
Chile	28	26	24	20	Madagascar	96	—	—	—
Malaysia	29	27	30	27	Zimbabwe	97	78	79	79
Ireland	30	28	23	24	Bangladesh	98	79	77	74
Slovenia	31	29	26	28	Mali	99	—	—	—
Thailand	32	30	37	31	Angola	100	—	—	—
Hungary	33	31	29	29	Chad	101	—	—	—
Jordan	34	32	44	47	Haiti	102	80	80	80
Greece	35	33	31	38					
Botswana	36	34	35	41					
Latvia	37	35	43	44					
Tunisia	38	36	32	34					
Czech Republic	39	37	36	40					
Lithuania	40	38	39	36					
Italy	41	39	33	39					
South Africa	42	40	34	32					
Slovak Republic	43	41	46	49					
China	44	42	38	33					
Poland	45	43	50	51					
Mauritius	46	44	41	35					
Mexico	47	45	53	45					
El Salvador	48	46	60	57					
Trinidad and Tobago	49	47	42	37					
Uruguay	50	48	40	42					
Costa Rica	51	49	49	43					
Namibia	52	50	47	53					
Croatia	53	51	48	58					
Brazil	54	52	45	46					
Gambia	55	—	—	—					
India	56	53	54	48					
Peru	57	54	55	54					
Egypt	58	—	—	—					
Panama	59	55	51	50					
Vietnam	60	56	62	65					
Morocco	61	57	52	55					
Dominican Republic	62	58	56	52					
Colombia	63	59	61	56					
Bulgaria	64	60	58	62					
Turkey	65	61	65	69					
Philippines	66	62	63	61					
Jamaica	67	63	57	60					
Sri Lanka	68	64	59	59					

(cont'd.)

xiv

*Applying the 2003 Formula
Source: World Economic Forum

Table 2 breaks down the GCI into its three main subcomponents: the macroeconomic environment index, the public institutions index, and the technology index. In Table 2 we see, for instance, that Finland is ranked first overall because it scored well in all areas. Unlike Finland, the United States maintained its position in the second place of the GCI amid varying levels of achievement in the different components. For instance, the country's overall performance is weakened by the quality of its public institutions. And although the United States still leads in the technology index, its overall score dropped, reflecting a reduction in the tertiary enrolment rate and a decline in the number of patents granted.

In Europe, France, at 26th place, received a boost in its rankings due to higher scores in public institutions and technology, which offset a decline in the macroeconomic environment. Unlike France, Ireland fell to the 30th position due to widespread declines in the different components of the index. Similarly, Italy, at the 41st position, also lost ground in the rankings, reflecting across-the-board declines in the major components of the index, particularly its macroeconomic environment.

Among central and eastern European countries, Estonia maintains its leadership at 22nd place in the overall rankings, enjoying the highest technology, public institutions, and macroeconomic environment scores in the region. Latvia is most notable for posting one of the most improved performances across the various components. Although Ukraine, at 84th place, has the lowest rank in Europe, the country has posted improvements in certain areas.

In Asia, Korea posted one of the most notable ascents in the GCI rankings, moving from the 25th to the 18th position. Korea's rise in the rankings was driven by improvements in its macroeconomic environment, increased public trust in politicians, a better score in the area of diversion of public funds, and a remarkable improvement in its technology performance with one of the highest increases in patent activity. Like Korea, Thailand and Vietnam registered notable improvements in overall rankings. Although Indonesia declines in the overall rankings, the country posts one of the most significant increases in its actual score. Its macroeconomic environment score is the 5th most improved, marked by significantly better scores in the area of government waste. Malaysia and India both derived gains from improvements in the area of technology. Among the most notable downward shifts in the rankings was experienced by China. The country's drop in the rankings was marked by a deterioration in the perceived quality of public institutions.

In Latin America, Chile continues to have the highest rank in the region, followed, at a considerable distance, by Mexico. Although Chile has the highest scores in the region in all three index components, the country has experienced notable deterioration in the area of government waste, exhibiting the worst decline in the indicator measuring public trust of politicians. The lowest ranking in the region is held by Haiti, which also occupies the 102nd position in the GCI. Brazil and Argentina both posted significant declines in the macroeconomic environment. Technology offers a bright spot for both countries: tertiary enrollment increased significantly and diffusion of ICT continues at a very fast pace in Brazil, while government prioritization of ICT and success of government ICT promotion both received higher ratings in Argentina. Among the countries in the region, the biggest declines in the rankings were experienced by Uruguay and Jamaica. Uruguay fell due to drastic deterioration of its macroeconomic environment as evident in the region's largest decline in credit rating. Lower scores in the macroeconomic environment also pushed Jamaica lower in the rankings. At the opposite extreme, Mexico and El Salvador experienced the most notable improvements in performance.

In the Middle East, Jordan and Turkey both post dramatic improvements in the quality of public institutions. Jordan, in particular, showed the largest score and rank increase in this area, driven by gains in control of corruption and greater independence of the judiciary. The country also posted better ratings relating to public trust in politicians, diversion of public funds, and the extent of distortive subsidies. Likewise, but to a lesser extent, Turkey exhibited significant improvements in the control of corruption and the independence of the judiciary.

In Africa, Botswana enjoys the highest ranking in the GCI. It has the highest public institutions and macroeconomic environment rankings in the region. Botswana's ranking in technology is lower than its ranking in other components; despite increases in ICT diffusion, significant drawbacks in technology remain. South Africa leads the region in the area of technology. However, South Africa's overall growth competitiveness ranking is lower than last year's because of a deterioration in some of the components that assess the quality of public institutions, particularly the prevalence of payments irregularities and the incidence of crime.

Table 2: Growth Competitiveness Index components

Growth Competitiveness Index (GCI)			
Country	Rank	Country	Rank
Finland	1	Bulgaria	64
United States	2	Turkey	65
Sweden	3	Philippines	66
Denmark	4	Jamaica	67
Taiwan	5	Sri Lanka	68
Singapore	6	Tanzania	69
Switzerland	7	Russian Federation	70
Iceland	8	Ghana	71
Norway	9	Indonesia	72
Australia	10	Pakistan	73
Japan	11	Algeria	74
Netherlands	12	Romania	75
Germany	13	Malawi	76
New Zealand	14	Serbia	77
United Kingdom	15	Argentina	78
Canada	16	Senegal	79
Austria	17	Uganda	80
Korea	18	Macedonia	81
Malta	19	Venezuela	82
Israel	20	Kenya	83
Luxembourg	21	Ukraine	84
Estonia	22	Bolivia	85
Spain	23	Ecuador	86
Hong Kong	24	Nigeria	87
Portugal	25	Zambia	88
France	26	Guatemala	89
Belgium	27	Nicaragua	90
Chile	28	Cameroon	91
Malaysia	29	Ethiopia	92
Ireland	30	Mozambique	93
Slovenia	31	Honduras	94
Thailand	32	Paraguay	95
Hungary	33	Madagascar	96
Jordan	34	Zimbabwe	97
Greece	35	Bangladesh	98
Botswana	36	Mali	99
Latvia	37	Angola	100
Tunisia	38	Chad	101
Czech Republic	39	Haiti	102
Lithuania	40		
Italy	41		
South Africa	42		
Slovak Republic	43		
China	44		
Poland	45		
Mauritius	46		
Mexico	47		
El Salvador	48		
Trinidad and Tobago	49		
Uruguay	50		
Costa Rica	51		
Namibia	52		
Croatia	53		
Brazil	54		
Gambia	55		
India	56		
Peru	57		
Egypt	58		
Panama	59		
Vietnam	60		
Morocco	61		
Dominican Republic	62		
Colombia	63		

(cont'd.)

Macroeconomic Environment Index			
Country	Rank	Country	Rank
Singapore	1	Indonesia	64
Finland	2	Sri Lanka	65
Luxembourg	3	Colombia	66
Norway	4	Senegal	67
Denmark	5	Ghana	68
Switzerland	6	Dominican Republic	69
Australia	7	Ukraine	70
Sweden	8	Uganda	71
Netherlands	9	Bangladesh	72
Austria	10	Bulgaria	73
Canada	11	Nigeria	74
United Kingdom	12	Brazil	75
New Zealand	13	Tanzania	76
United States	14	Kenya	77
Hong Kong	15	Cameroon	78
Iceland	16	Madagascar	79
Spain	17	Macedonia	80
Taiwan	18	Romania	81
Belgium	19	Turkey	82
France	20	Bolivia	83
Germany	21	Ethiopia	84
Ireland	22	Guatemala	85
Korea	23	Jamaica	86
Japan	24	Serbia	87
China	25	Honduras	88
Thailand	26	Uruguay	89
Malaysia	27	Ecuador	90
Italy	28	Mali	91
Malta	29	Paraguay	92
Botswana	30	Argentina	93
Portugal	31	Venezuela	94
Tunisia	32	Mozambique	95
Greece	33	Chad	96
Estonia	34	Zambia	97
Chile	35	Malawi	98
Latvia	36	Haiti	99
Slovenia	37	Nicaragua	100
Hungary	38	Angola	101
Czech Republic	39	Zimbabwe	102
South Africa	40		
Lithuania	41		
Jordan	42		
Morocco	43		
Israel	44		
Vietnam	45		
Gambia	46		
Trinidad and Tobago	47		
El Salvador	48		
Poland	49		
Slovak Republic	50		
Algeria	51		
India	52		
Namibia	53		
Mexico	54		
Croatia	55		
Egypt	56		
Mauritius	57		
Peru	58		
Panama	59		
Philippines	60		
Russian Federation	61		
Pakistan	62		
Costa Rica	63		

(cont'd.)

Source: World Economic Forum

Table 2: Growth Competitiveness Index components *(cont'd.)*

Public Institutions Index			
Country	Rank	Country	Rank
Denmark	1	Dominican Republic	64
Finland	2	Ghana	65
Iceland	3	Algeria	66
Australia	4	Croatia	67
New Zealand	5	Morocco	68
Singapore	6	Zambia	69
Sweden	7	Jamaica	70
Switzerland	8	Panama	71
Germany	9	Sri Lanka	72
Hong Kong	10	Ethiopia	73
Netherlands	11	Pakistan	74
United Kingdom	12	Senegal	75
Luxembourg	13	Indonesia	76
Austria	14	Serbia	77
Israel	15	Nicaragua	78
Norway	16	Bolivia	79
United States	17	Ecuador	80
Malta	18	Russian Federation	81
Chile	19	Mozambique	82
Jordan	20	Mali	83
Taiwan	21	Uganda	84
Portugal	22	Philippines	85
France	23	Romania	86
Canada	24	Guatemala	87
Ireland	25	Argentina	88
Botswana	26	Venezuela	89
Belgium	27	Zimbabwe	90
Estonia	28	Angola	91
Uruguay	29	Kenya	92
Japan	30	Macedonia	93
Spain	31	Ukraine	94
Tunisia	32	Cameroon	95
Hungary	33	Madagascar	96
Malaysia	34	Paraguay	97
Slovenia	35	Nigeria	98
Korea	36	Honduras	99
Thailand	37	Bangladesh	100
Malawi	38	Chad	101
Gambia	39	Haiti	102
El Salvador	40		
Lithuania	41		
Greece	42		
South Africa	43		
Mauritius	44		
Latvia	45		
Italy	46		
Czech Republic	47		
Namibia	48		
Costa Rica	49		
Mexico	50		
Slovak Republic	51		
China	52		
Brazil	53		
Peru	54		
India	55		
Trinidad and Tobago	56		
Egypt	57		
Poland	58		
Tanzania	59		
Colombia	60		
Vietnam	61		
Bulgaria	62		
Turkey	63		

(cont'd.)

Technology Index			
Country	Rank	Country	Rank
United States	1	India	64
Finland	2	China	65
Taiwan	3	Serbia	66
Sweden	4	El Salvador	67
Japan	5	Egypt	68
Korea	6	Russian Federation	69
Switzerland	7	Macedonia	70
Denmark	8	Morocco	71
Israel	9	Sri Lanka	72
Estonia	10	Vietnam	73
Canada	11	Kenya	74
Singapore	12	Zimbabwe	75
Norway	13	Ecuador	76
Germany	14	Uganda	77
Iceland	15	Indonesia	78
United Kingdom	16	Guatemala	79
Malta	17	Gambia	80
Netherlands	18	Tanzania	81
Australia	19	Nigeria	82
Malaysia	20	Pakistan	83
Czech Republic	21	Ukraine	84
Portugal	22	Nicaragua	85
New Zealand	23	Ghana	86
Slovenia	24	Honduras	87
Spain	25	Bolivia	88
Latvia	26	Senegal	89
Austria	27	Zambia	90
France	28	Paraguay	91
Belgium	29	Mozambique	92
Greece	30	Cameroon	93
Chile	31	Malawi	94
Hungary	32	Bangladesh	95
Slovak Republic	33	Algeria	96
Poland	34	Madagascar	97
Brazil	35	Angola	98
Lithuania	36	Mali	99
Hong Kong	37	Ethiopia	100
Ireland	38	Haiti	101
Thailand	39	Chad	102
South Africa	40		
Croatia	41		
Luxembourg	42		
Mexico	43		
Italy	44		
Argentina	45		
Costa Rica	46		
Trinidad and Tobago	47		
Jordan	48		
Mauritius	49		
Panama	50		
Uruguay	51		
Dominican Republic	52		
Jamaica	53		
Turkey	54		
Romania	55		
Philippines	56		
Tunisia	57		
Venezuela	58		
Botswana	59		
Colombia	60		
Peru	61		
Namibia	62		
Bulgaria	63		

(cont'd.)

The Business Competitiveness Index

Stable political, legal, and social institutions and sound macroeconomic policies create the potential for improving national prosperity. But wealth is actually created at the microeconomic level—in the ability of firms to create valuable goods and services using efficient methods. Only in this way can a nation support high wages and the attractive returns to capital necessary to support sustained investment. The *Business Competitiveness Index (BCI)* presented in this volume is based on a conceptual framework and statistical approach which follows that of the previous reports and the findings are fully comparable with previous Microeconomic Competitiveness Index results.

The microeconomic foundations of productivity rest on two interrelated areas: (1) the sophistication with which domestic companies or foreign subsidiaries operating in the country compete, and (2) the quality of the microeconomic business environment in which they operate. The productivity of a country is ultimately set by the productivity of its companies. An economy cannot be competitive unless companies operating there are competitive, whether they are domestic firms or subsidiaries of foreign companies. However, the sophistication and productivity of companies is inextricably intertwined with the quality of the national business environment. More productive company strategies require more highly skilled people, better information, more efficient government processes, improved infrastructure, better suppliers, more advanced research institutions, and more intense competitive pressure, among other things. This is what the BCI tries to capture.

The BCI is constructed from measures drawn primarily from the Executive Opinion Survey. Quantitative measures are utilized for patenting rates and Internet and cellular telephone penetration. For all of the other dimensions, quantitative data for many countries are unavailable. Thus, the Survey offers many unique measures and captures the informed judgments of thousands of business leaders and decision makers in the economies examined.

To derive the overall BCI, two subindexes are computed. The subindexes measure (1) the *sophistication of company operations and strategy* and (2) the *quality of the national business environment*, respectively. Many of the dimensions of company sophistication and the quality of the business environment tend to move together. Moreover, the sample of countries is relatively small and the number of relevant variables is high. Thus, the impact of individual variables is difficult to distinguish statistically. Hence common factor analysis is used to compute the subindexes. The two subindexes are then averaged to estimate the overall BCI. The weights are determined from the coefficients of a multiple regression of the subindexes on GDP per capita.

The BCI rankings for 2003 are shown in Table 3. Column 1 shows the overall rankings. Columns 2 and 3 display the two subindexes: the company operations and strategy subindex and the quality of the national business environment subindex, respectively.

In the overall BCI, Finland retakes the leading position, after dropping to second place behind the United States last year. Finland remains one of the world's most remarkable success cases over the last decade. The United States was pulled down by concerns about rising trade protection, tightening capital availability, and weakening cluster vitality. Other advanced nations improving their rankings include France, Denmark, Sweden, Australia, and New Zealand. France gained five positions, mainly due to an improving business environment, regaining its pre-2000 ranking. Heartening for France are improvements in local competition, governance, and reductions in government distortions. Denmark and New Zealand gained four ranks, mainly based on improvements in the business environment. Australia continued its upward trend, while Sweden reached the third position based on company and business environment improvements.

Advanced countries slipping in the rankings include Austria, based on a deteriorating business environment. The United Kingdom also slipped several places after strong gains last year. Other advanced nations that are slipping are Switzerland, Canada, and Japan. Japan, while still sliding, registered strong improvements in corporate governance and cluster collaboration. Germany's rank falls only one place, but the quality of its business environment dropped precipitously. Labor-management relations are a growing concern in Germany, along with creeping subsidies and a hollowing of clusters.

Middle-income nations improving their competitiveness rankings this year include Latvia, Jordan, Vietnam, Mexico, Colombia, Indonesia, Mauritius, Greece, and Thailand. One new country, Malta, entered the middle-income group, ranked at 42. Egypt reentered the rankings at 58, showing a significant decline compared with its ranking in the 1998–2001 period. Latvia jumped by a remarkable 16 ranks, driven by strong perceived across-the-board improvements in the business environment and company sophistication. Whether this large jump is a temporary event reflecting positive near-term sentiment or a sustainable trend will become more evident in subsequent years.

Middle-income countries losing rank in competitiveness include the Dominican Republic, Hungary, Sri Lanka, Trinidad and Tobago, Croatia, and China. The Dominican Republic (down 18 places) and Sri Lanka (down 9 places) fall back after strong jumps last year, signaling that last year's rankings might have been anomalies. The Dominican Republic's ranking was led down by concerns about the state of local companies. Hungary (down 10) and Croatia (down 8) appear to be suffering from increasing competition from other transition countries.

Table 3: The Business Competitiveness Index

Country	BCI ranking	Company operations and strategy ranking	Quality of the national business environment ranking
Finland	1	4	1
United States	2	2	2
Sweden	3	3	5
Denmark	4	7	3
Germany	5	1	9
United Kingdom	6	8	6
Switzerland	7	5	8
Singapore	8	12	4
Netherlands	9	10	11
France	10	9	14
Australia	11	18	7
Canada	12	14	10
Japan	13	6	20
Iceland	14	15	12
Belgium	15	11	17
Taiwan	16	16	16
Austria	17	13	18
New Zealand	18	23	13
Hong Kong SAR	19	22	15
Israel	20	20	19
Ireland	21	17	22
Norway	22	21	21
Korea	23	19	25
Italy	24	24	23
Spain	25	25	26
Malaysia	26	26	24
South Africa	27	28	28
Estonia	28	36	27
Latvia	29	29	31
Slovenia	30	27	34
Thailand	31	31	32
Chile	32	34	30
Tunisia	33	38	29
Brazil	34	30	39
Czech Republic	35	33	38
Portugal	36	46	33
India	37	40	36
Hungary	38	45	37
Greece	39	39	40
Lithuania	40	41	41
Jordan	41	59	35
Malta	42	47	42
Slovak Republic	43	44	43
Mauritius	44	35	46
Costa Rica	45	32	47
China	46	42	44
Poland	47	43	45
Mexico	48	37	51
Morocco	49	49	49
Vietnam	50	53	48
Colombia	51	50	54
Turkey	52	51	55
Trinidad and Tobago	53	54	53
Botswana	54	67	50
Namibia	55	64	52
Jamaica	56	56	56
Sri Lanka	57	52	59
Egypt	58	55	62
Panama	59	60	60
Indonesia	60	62	61
Dominican Republic	61	57	63
Croatia	62	65	58
Ghana*	63	66	57
El Salvador	64	58	65
Philippines	65	48	74
Russian Federation	66	69	64
Kenya	67	61	72
Tanzania	68	68	67
Argentina	69	63	73
Gambia*	70	80	66
Uruguay	71	77	68
Malawi	72	71	76
Ukraine	73	72	77
Uganda*	74	78	69
Pakistan	75	81	70
Romania	76	84	71
Bulgaria	77	85	75
Zimbabwe	78	70	81
Serbia	79	75	79
Nigeria	80	73	80
Peru	81	83	78
Macedonia*	82	79	83
Cameroon*	83	86	82
Zambia	84	82	85
Venezuela	85	74	87
Guatemala	86	76	88
Senegal	87	94	84
Algeria	88	93	86
Ecuador	89	87	92
Madagascar	90	88	90
Bangladesh	91	91	91
Mali*	92	98	89
Mozambique	93	90	95
Nicaragua	94	92	93
Honduras	95	89	96
Ethiopia	96	96	94
Paraguay	97	95	98
Bolivia	98	97	97
Chad	99	99	99
Haiti	100	101	100
Angola	101	100	101

(cont'd.)

xix

*Survey data for these countries have high within-country variance. Until the reliability of survey responses improves with future educational efforts and improved sampling in these countries, their rankings should be interpreted with caution.

Finally, Trinidad and Tobago has experienced declining competitiveness since its entry into the ranking in 2001. China, which showed a strong gain last year, has reverted back to its ranking of previous years. A surge in confidence about China's prospects proves not to have been sustainable. China was pulled down by concerns about red tape, corruption, judicial independence, and trade barriers, among other factors, though Chinese companies were judged to be making positive progress. Russia continues a slow downward trend, while Argentina's position seems to have stabilized.

Among low-income countries, rankings compared with last year's were quite stable. Peru slipped significantly (down 5 places), continuing a negative trend. Ecuador moved up 3 places. Of the low-income countries ranked for the first time, Ghana entered at 63, Kenya at 67, and Tanzania at 68. Pakistan entered at 75 and Serbia at 79. Angola became the lowest ranked country at 101.

The GCI and the BCI measure different dimensions of competitiveness. Figure 1 compares the two rankings for this year. Despite the different methodologies used in their construction, and although the two indexes are meant to capture different (although complementary) aspects of competitiveness, they are highly correlated. Finland ranks first on both indexes. The two indexes also coincide in the ranks of second, third, and fourth: the United States, Sweden, and Denmark, respectively. Moreover, the two indexes agree that the three lowest-ranked countries are Haiti, Chad, and Angola. Of course, the two rankings are not perfectly correlated, which means that some countries are ranked higher by one index than they are by the other. At the top, Taiwan is ranked 5th by the GCI and 16th by the BCI. Other countries that are ranked higher by the GCI than the BCI include Norway, Malta, Portugal, Botswana, El Salvador, Uruguay, Gambia, Perú, Bulgaria, Algeria, and Bolivia. Countries that are ranked lower by the GCI than the BCI include France, Germany, the United Kingdom, Italy, South Africa, India, Kenya, and Zimbabwe.

Structure of the *Report*

The first part of the *Report* includes two chapters. The first one, by Jennifer Blanke and Fiona Paua (of the World Economic Forum) and Xavier Sala-i-Martin (of Columbia University and Universitat Pompeu Fabra), describes the methodology and analyzes the various rankings behind the Growth Competitiveness Index. In the second chapter, Michael Porter (of Harvard University) presents the details of the construction and analyzes the results of the Business Competitiveness Index.

The second part of the *Report* includes five chapters describing various issues related to competitiveness and economic performance. In his chapter "The Year in Review," Martin Baily (of the Institute for International Economics in Washington, DC) looks at some of the important issues and challenges facing the world economy that have emerged or been at center stage this past year. First, there is a look at the impact of the war in Iraq and whether or not this will sour international relations. The war was the central political and military event of the past year, and it has indeed soured international relations. But, surprisingly, so far its economic consequences do not seem to have been all that large.

Next he turns to the issue of exchange rate adjustment and the rebalancing of global trade patterns. The United States has been running a massive trade deficit that continues to grow. Many policymakers have judged that at some point there would have to be a downward adjustment in the value of the dollar and in the current account deficit. This past year that adjustment seems to have started, with a substantial swing in the euro/dollar exchange rate. A particular concern now is to figure out how the world economy can return to sustainable growth while adjusting to a still lower dollar and lower US deficit, when these occur. The adjustment process must be seen in a global context, not just in a US context.

The review then looks at the steps being taken toward economic reform in Europe, where considerable momentum for a reform agenda has emerged this past year. The 2000 Lisbon EU council meeting was an important landmark. Implementation seems to be taking place, although with some resistance. The fourth topic is an examination of deflation, an issue that has been around for a while as part of Japan's economic difficulties, but has assumed increased importance over the past year, with concerns that deflation could spread to the United States, Germany, and possibly other countries.

The implications of rapid growth in China have been a hot topic for a while, but have become a much hotter topic in the past year. As the rest of the world economy turned sluggish, the Chinese surged ahead, increasing their exports at a very rapid pace. From Tokyo to Milan, from Mexico City to Chicago, everyone is wondering whether China can continue to grow so fast and how their own jobs and businesses will be affected if it does. The discussion of China is followed by a short review of the economic effects of SARS outbreak of the past year. Finally Baily turns to Africa where there have been important developments, both in the evaluation of the dangers of AIDS to the economy of the region and in the local and international response to the disease.

Figure 1: Growth and Business Competitiveness rankings

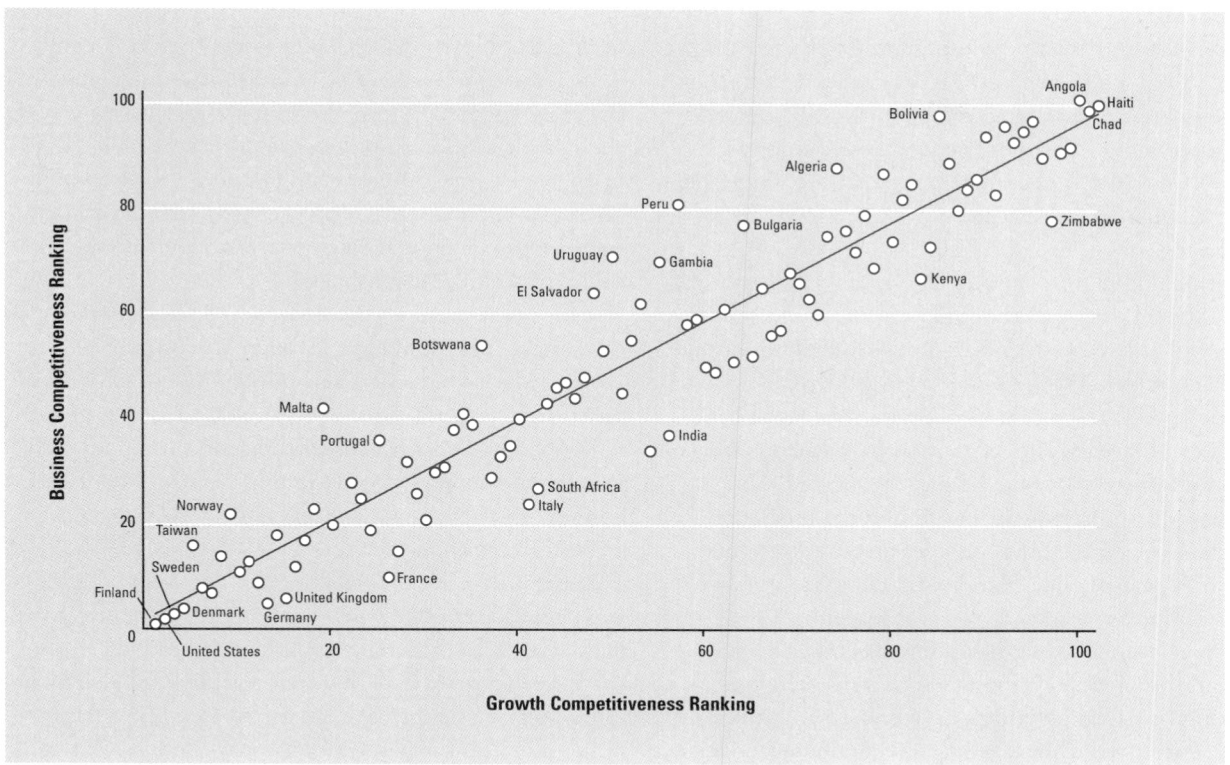

In "Varieties of Economic Experience in the Developing World," Augusto Lopez-Claros (of the World Economic Forum) outlines some of the key challenges facing policymakers in the developing world. He focuses his attention on two sets of countries, a small but representative sample of those ranked by the *Global Competitiveness Report*. The first set is made up of Argentina, Russia, and Turkey—countries that have had serious financial crises in the recent past and offer a treasure trove of insights in terms of the causes of such crises, their consequences, and the policy responses to them, to say nothing of the effectiveness of existing international institutional mechanisms to cope with them. Lopez-Claros explains that, although the causes behind the crises in these three countries have been many, there is a thread common to all three countries: the lack of fiscal discipline combined with poor public debt management. In Russia, the problem was essentially on the revenue side. A persistent output drop during much of the 1990s contributed to the erosion of the tax base and this process was made worse by tax exemptions granted by the authorities to influential lobby groups. In Turkey, the problems were largely on the expenditure side: a combination of enormous claims on the budget associated with an overly generous pension system, an extensive network of agricultural

subsidy schemes and other quasi-fiscal operations, and the fiscal burden of a public debt overhang. Argentina's crisis reflected the authorities' ultimate failure to maintain adequate control over the public finances. By end-2000 the debt-to-GDP ratio had risen to 50 percent of GDP, not unusually high by international standards, but extremely high for an economy with a very low revenue ratio, an external debt to exports ratio in excess of 400 percent, and a contracting economy.

Another common aspect of these three economies is that the currencies had been pegged in some fashion. Lopez-Claros argues that the authorities in all three countries failed to recognize that successful pegs are usually underpinned by suitably tight fiscal policies. Moreover, lack of fiscal discipline over a number of consecutive years makes the country a captive to its creditors, including bondholders. The pattern is well known: persistent fiscal deficits result in their financing at increasingly higher interest rates, which inevitably worsen the deficit. The fiscal problem then leads to an external crisis when nonresident debt holders refuse to rollover the outstanding debt. Russia and Argentina defaulted on their external obligations; Turkey did not, but only due to massive IMF financial assistance. Lopez-Claros then analyzes the role of the IMF in its various principal roles of financier, advisor, and overall crisis manager. He argues that although the Fund played—with varying degrees of success—each one of these roles in all three countries, the crisis in Argentina has forced the organization to recognize that there has to be a better way of dealing with unsustainable debt burdens than the present ad-hoc arrangements, involving a broad range of economic, social, and political dislocations. He then looks at several aspects of the ongoing debate on the need to develop formal mechanisms for sovereign debt restructuring.

The second set of countries analyzed in this paper consists of the transition economies of central and eastern Europe, eight of whose members are scheduled to join the European Union (EU) in May of 2004: the Czech Republic, Estonia, Hungary, Latvia, Lithuania, Poland, Slovakia and Slovenia. These countries have had a good growth performance during the past decade and some of its members have the potential to join in the medium-term the upper ranks of the most competitive economies in the world. Quite aside from having benefited from reasonably competent macroeconomic management, as a group they have moved farther along than virtually any other set of economies in the world in implementing broad ranging structural reforms. Lopez-Claros argues that, the impressive achievements notwithstanding, policy-makers in these countries will continue to face a number of challenges. Countries expected to grow more rapidly and to experience real appreciation of their currencies may continue to attract substantial capital inflows which could put further upward pressures on currencies, generate higher current account deficits and foreign debt accumulation by the private sectors. The question which policy-makers will want to ask is whether the above set of factors imply any particular risks as the countries join the EU and, subsequently, cope with the challenges of a much more competitive environment. One possible scenario to this policy environment sees the authorities managing the pressures identified above through a combination of cautious fiscal policies and structural reforms.

The chapter on "Ranking National Innovative Capacity: Findings from the National Innovative Capacity Index" by Michael Porter and Scott Stern (of Northwestern University) analyzes the conditions that allow countries to innovate. In this chapter, the authors use the 2003 Executive Opinion Survey to assess the innovative capacity of 78 countries for which the required data are available. They examine a wide range of national characteristics suggested by the national innovative capacity framework and available from the Survey data to construct a National Innovative Capacity Index (NICI). They then rank countries on the NICI as well as five subindexes measuring important components of innovative vitality. The statistical findings reveal the striking degree to which measures of the national environment for innovation affect

innovative output. They also find that the bar for innovation is rising; even countries with an *absolute* increase in innovative capacity over 2001 sometimes register a *relative* decline because of their inability to improve local conditions as fast as other nations. They find that some countries have aggressively invested in innovative capacity ahead of that expected given current income in an effort to enhance competitiveness and prosperity. Conversely, in other nations, innovative capacity lags overall productivity and income rankings, raising concerns about the sustainability of their competitiveness.

In "Five Puzzles in the Behavior of Productivity, Investment, and Innovation," Robert Gordon (of Northwestern University) analyzes the recent behavior of productivity growth. The behavior of productivity growth in the United States has surprised experts: instead of fading after the economy's peak in mid-2000, US nonfarm business productivity growth has actually accelerated from a 2.45 percent annual rate during 1995–2000 to a stunning 3.34 percent annual growth rate in the three years between 2000:Q2 and 2003:Q2. As US productivity performance has become even stronger over the past three years, some puzzles have emerged regarding the revival, its causes, and the performance of the United States relative to the rest of the world. Gordon's paper analyzes five of these puzzles.

The first puzzle is: *Whatever happened to the cyclical effect?* Using data through mid-2003, it is clear that there was only a negligible cyclical effect for 1995–99 but a temporary "bubble" in 2002. The author argues that this pattern of similar temporary blips was repeated in three previous business cycles.

The second puzzle is: *Why did productivity growth accelerate after 2000 when the ICT investment boom was collapsing?* Gordon analyzes a number of arguments proposed in the academic literature. He then concludes that the most persuasive argument points to "hidden" intangible investments in the late 1990s that required labor input but were not counted in measured output; after 2000, the delayed benefits of intangible investments boosted output, while much of the labor input that created them was laid off. In short, productivity growth was understated in the late 1990s but has been overstated since then.

The third puzzle reads: *What aspects of innovation caused productivity growth to take off?* To deal with this puzzle, Gordon draws an analogy between computers and electricity. In the case of electricity, miniaturization was the key step in making small electric motors practical, and complementary investments, especially roads, were necessary to reap benefits. For computers the key steps were miniaturization in the form of the PC, followed in the 1990s by the "marriage" of computer hardware with software and communication technology.

The fourth puzzle is: *How can ICT investment revive if innovations are second-rate?* First-rate inventions in the 1990s, notably the web and user-friendly business productivity software, are being followed by second-rate inventions in the current decade, such as web-enabled mobile phones, wi-fi enabled laptops, and a host of innovations providing incremental improvements in consumer entertainment but not fundamental changes in business productivity. Gordon argues that innovation is the fundamental driver of the demand for investment (rather than the other way around). Given that, the question is: what does the rise and fall of ICT investment since 1995 tell us about the pace of innovation for the near future? The author speculates about the future path of innovation in the entertainment and medical industries.

The last puzzle is: *Why has Europe failed to experience a productivity growth revival?* Gordon argues that US institutions foster creative destruction and financial markets that welcome innovation, while Europe remains under the control of corporatist institutions that dampen competition and inhibit new entry. He also argues that Europe lacks a youth culture like that of the United States, which fosters independence: US teenagers work after school and US college students must work to pay for much of their educational expense. There is a chasm of values across the Atlantic, as Americans facilitate the development of high-productivity "big-box" retail formats while Europeans are disdainful of overly dispersed American metropolitan areas with their traffic congestion, waste of energy, and starvation of public transit.

In his chapter "Governance Redux: The Empirical Challenge," Daniel Kaufmann of the World Bank Institute argues that governance is still at a crossroads, its underperformance evident in most regions and across a vast number of countries within such regions. This contrasts with the significant strides that have been made in many countries in improving the content of macroeconomic policies for well over a decade. In this sense, Kaufmann argues, there is a growing "governance gap," since improvements in governance are far from keeping pace with the progress attained in economic policy and some other areas. Such a gap implies that public governance is nowadays a central binding constraint to growth and development.

Indeed, the enterprises from developing and transition economies included in this year's Survey single out corruption and excessive bureaucracy among the top constraints to their business operations, while the respondent firms from the OECD single out excessive bureaucracy and the tax regime. Relative to these and other institutional weaknesses, high inflation and distortions in the exchange rate regime are not ranked as important constraints by the firms.

More generally, with a recently constructed worldwide governance indicators dataset, the author shows the extent to which national governance matters: a country that significantly improves key governance dimensions such as the rule of law, corruption, the regulatory regime, and voice and democratic accountability can expect in the long run a dramatic increase on its per capita incomes and in other social dimensions. Specifically, if for instance the quality of rule of law were to improve by one standard deviation, from, say the current relatively low level of Ukraine to the "middling" level of South Africa, a fourfold increase in per capita incomes can be expected in the long run. A larger increase in the quality of rule of law (by two standard deviations) in Ukraine (or in other countries in the former Soviet Union), to the much higher level in Slovenia or Spain, would further multiply such income per capita increase. Similar results emerge from other governance dimensions: a mere one standard deviation improvement in voice and accountability from the low level of Venezuela to that of South Korea, or in control of corruption from the low level of Indonesia to the middling level of Mexico, or from the level of Mexico to that of Costa Rica, would also be associated with an estimated fourfold increase in per capita incomes, as well as similar improvements in literacy and in reducing child mortality.

In contrast to the major impact that improved governance can have on incomes and development, the findings show no reverse causality or feedback mechanism: higher incomes in themselves do not get automatically translated into improved governance. The fact that there is no automatic virtuous circle means that continuous political resolve and interventions are required to attain good governance. It also implies that a country exhibiting higher incomes than would be predicted by its current levels of governance can expect downward pressure on the sustainability of such incomes—given their governance level. Such shortfall in the country's actual quality of governance, as compared with the governance level required to support the country's income level, is described as the "governance deficit." The extent of the governance deficit may constitute a warning regarding the income and growth prospects of a country. For instance, the evidence suggests that by the late 1990s most countries in Latin America had a substantial governance deficit in that their actual per capita incomes were higher than would have been predicted by the prevailing levels of governance.

The author also reviews briefly recent work anchored in the new comparative economics, which compares different capitalist systems. In particular, he discusses some of the deeper historical determinants of current governance performance, and finds that the origins of a country's legal system—particularly whether it adopted common or civil law systems—may not be a central determinant of governance outcomes nowadays, especially for lower-income countries. Further inquiry into the deeper determinants of governance, including understanding the relevance of historical patterns of settlement and of geography, seems to hold promise, however.

The empirical evidence also points to the fact that politics matter substantially in understanding good governance, and, within it, the corporate sector plays an active role in shaping such political (and thus policy) outcomes. Powerful firms are not mere passive "takers" of the overall investment climate (imposed by the public sector); instead such enterprises play a key role in shaping it. The database provided by the Survey also permits the empirical evaluation of political dimensions of governance traditionally regarded as non-measurable, such as the extent of "capture" and of undue influence by some politically connected powerful firms in shaping the regulations, laws, and policies of a country. Unequal distribution of influence on policy and regulatory outcomes (or "crony bias") are found to be closely associated with poor public and financial governance performance.

Finally, the empirical richness of the Survey data set provides a key input for the construction of an initial governance database at the city level. This database and research-in-progress is to be expanded over the coming year, yet the early results support the observation that governance performance at the city level is aided by the extent of the country's globalization and urbanization path (controlling for income levels). Further, the city's relative size and its status as a capital or a port do not appear to have a deleterious effect on the quality of city-level governance.

The findings emphasize the need to revisit conventional advice on strategies to improve public governance. Such advice has focused excessively on attempts to reform the internal functioning of public institutions, often drawing from standard templates from industrialized countries. Instead, further focus is needed on aspects that do contain a political dimension. In particular, addressing the nexus between corporate strategies and public governance (mediated by the "institution of influence") is of particular interest. And specifically, the findings on undue influence and state capture point to the limits of traditional public-sector measures (such as incessant legal drafting and codes of ethics manuals, creating new Anti-Corruption agencies, or launching another anticorruption campaign). By contrast, this chapter's findings underscore the need for far more focus on external accountability, on transparency mechanisms, and on prevention. It is emphasized that such enhanced focus on governance matters is also warranted at the subnational level.

The *Report* ends with a comprehensive section that contains country profiles for each of the individual economies covered. This part also includes data tables for the variables that are used as inputs into the calculations of the competitiveness indexes, as well as a primer on how best to glean the information contained in the country profiles and the data tables, including some of the underlying assumptions. In addition, technical notes elucidate individual variables and the results of the World Economic Forum's Executive Opinion Survey.

Part 1

The Competitiveness Indexes

The Growth Competitiveness Index: Analyzing Key Underpinnings of Sustained Economic Growth

JENNIFER BLANKE, World Economic Forum

FIONA PAUA, World Economic Forum

XAVIER SALA-I-MARTIN, Columbia University and
Universitat Pompeu Fabra

Few things matter more for the welfare of a country's citizens than the aggregate growth rate of the economy. For rich countries, positive growth rates tend to mean higher wages, larger profits, more employment, and expanded business opportunities. For poor countries, positive growth rates tend to lift people out of poverty as their incomes tend to rise along with average GDP. Indeed, a 1 percent increase in per capita GDP tends to be associated with a 1 percent increase in the incomes of the poorest 20 percent of the population.[1] Moreover, positive growth rates in the developing world tend to be associated with improvements in other dimensions: reductions in infant mortality, longer life expectancy, increased access to water and sanitation, expanded education, reduced female discrimination, declines in child labor (especially child prostitution and child soldiers), and improvement in freedom, civil liberties, and democracy. Thus, the aggregate growth rate of a nation is important, perhaps one of the most important factors affecting human welfare.

Despite its enormous importance, the determinants of the growth rate of a country remain one of economics' biggest mysteries. This is true even though the greatest economic minds of the last two centuries have tried hard to explain what can be done to increase a country's growth rate. Adam Smith thought that specialization and the division of labor was the engine of growth. The great classical economists of the 19th century (such as Thomas Malthus or David Ricardo) thought that natural resources imposed a binding limit on the growth opportunities of a nation. The law of diminishing returns to land meant that population growth would eventually require the use of low-quality land, and this would reduce production per capita and cap the potential for economic growth.

During the 20th century, economists thought that the ultimate force driving economic growth was investment in physical capital and infrastructures. This belief underlay the many plans that governed the economy of the Soviet Union and the countries under its political or intellectual influence. It was also the foundation upon which the international aid packages of institutions such as the World Bank operated for decades. The idea was that the growth rate of a country depended only on the fraction of its GDP that it invested. If the savings generated by its citizens were not enough to finance the investment required to achieve the desired growth rate, the World Bank would finance the difference (this is why this line of thought was, and still is, called the "financing gap"). The collapse of the Soviet model and the failure of many developing countries to grow, despite the aid of the Bretton Woods institutions, showed economists that investing in physical capital was not enough to improve the growth opportunities of a country. We had to look for other mechanisms. Education and training (or "human capital," as modern economists call it) became the center of economic research for a couple of decades. During this time, developing countries were advised to educate their children and to invest in the expansion of their human capital. They did . . . but economic growth failed to materialize in most of them.

Technological progress (whether created by the country or copied from the leading economies) was then thought to be a central determinant of economic growth.[2] Few people today disagree with this idea, although this merely shifts the question from "what determines the growth rate of GDP?" to "what determines the rate of technological progress?" This is why economists kept searching. Many answers have been proposed: openness, macroeconomic stability, governance, the rule of law, institutions, lack of corruption, market orientation, government waste, and many other factors have been found, at least partially, to affect the aggregate growth rate of a nation. Having confronted many failures through the years, it is increasingly clear that there is no magic solution to the problem of economic growth. The process of economic growth is rather complex and many factors are needed if a country is to succeed. It is this complexity that the World Economic Forum tried to capture when it started estimating the Growth Competitiveness Index (GCI) a few years ago.

Indeed, one of the fundamental objectives of the *Global Competitiveness Report* is to evaluate the potential for the world's economies to attain sustained economic growth over the medium and long term. With this goal in mind, the World Economic Forum developed the GCI. The index is based on economists' understanding of the determinants of the complex process of economic growth and development. Again, our understanding is far from perfect. In fact, we learn new things every year as new development experiences teach us new lessons and as new data become available.[3] But our existing knowledge can be used to evaluate the growth potential of a country by combining available data and the Executive Opinion Survey conducted annually by the WEF into an index that we call the GCI. The GCI was developed by Jeffrey Sachs and John McArthur two years ago, and it was first presented in *The Global Competitiveness Report 2001–2002*. The index summarizes the set of institutions, policies, and structures driving the growth process of many countries—102 this year—from every corner of the world.

The three pillars

The GCI is founded on three central ideas. The first one is that the process of economic growth can be summarized with three important broad mechanisms: the macroeconomic environment, the quality of public institutions, and technology. These three mechanisms are what Sachs and McArthur called the "three pillars" on which the process of economic growth rests.

Macroeconomic environment

Macroeconomic stability is important for growth. Although it is certainly not true that macroeconomic stability alone can increase the growth rate of a nation, it is no less true that macroeconomic disarray kills its growth prospects. Firms cannot make informed decisions in environments where the inflation rate is in the hundreds, typically as a result of public finances being out of control. The banking system (which is essential if an economy is to grow in the medium and long run) cannot function if the government runs gigantic deficits (especially if, as a result, it forces banks to lend it money at below-market interest rates). The government cannot provide services efficiently if it has to make enormous interest payments on its past debts. And the business sector suffers unnecessarily if the taxes they pay are wasted away by the government. In sum, the economy cannot grow unless the macro environment is favorable. This is the idea that the first pillar of the GCI is meant to capture.

Institutions

The second pillar of the GCI relates to public institutions. Although, in a market economy, wealth is largely created by private businesses, these businesses have to operate within a country and have to deal with the institutions created and maintained by the government. It is important, for example, that property rights are guaranteed by a legal and judicial system. Private companies cannot operate efficiently in environments where contracts cannot be enforced or where the rule of law is weak or nonexistent. Firms may find it too expensive (maybe prohibitive) to do business in countries where corruption is rampant. One of the most exciting areas of economic research today tries to quantify the importance of institutions for long-run economic growth.[4] As a result, the GCI measures the soundness of the public institutions and it introduces it as one of the three pillars of economic growth and development.

Technology

Finally, the third pillar is technological progress. One of the main lessons of neoclassical growth theory[5] is that, in the long run, an economy cannot grow unless technological progress occurs. The key difference between rich and poor countries is not that the citizens of rich countries have more rice, more meat, or more milk (which they do) but that they have more and better things. If we sit in a rich country and simply look around, we will notice that most of the products we see did not exist just a few years ago: from the computer to color TV to genetically modified food to the latest designer drugs. Moreover, the products that did exist are much cheaper now than they were in the past[6] or their quality has improved dramatically.[7] Technological progress is, therefore, at the heart of economic growth. And the reason for thinking that, in the long run, no growth is possible without technological improvements is that the other potential determinants of growth must run into diminishing returns. For example, institutions and the macroeconomic environment can have important consequences for growth in countries with terrible environments. But once institutions are more or less right, and once the macroeconomy is more or less stable, additional improvements along these lines will probably have little or no effect on economic growth. This contrasts with technological progress since there do not seem to be good arguments that would suggest that there are diminishing returns to ideas. And if there were, they would certainly not be empirically acceptable since worldwide technological progress does not seem to be decelerating. In fact, the contrary appears to be true.

We should note that three "pillars of growth" are not independent. In fact, they interact to support or to hinder sustained growth, as noted by Sachs and McArthur:

"... these three factors are interwoven—strong institutions, for example, are needed for technological development to occur; a sophisticated technology base will contribute greatly to macroeconomic stability—but they do each have close and statistically distinct relationships with recent trends in economic growth" (p 39).

Empirically, the GCI uses both hard (publicly available) data, and data from the World Economic Forum's Executive Opinion Survey to estimate three component indexes that capture the three pillars of growth. The three components are called the "technology index", the "public institutions index", and the "macroeconomic environment index." The three components are then combined to calculate the overall GCI.

Innovation versus imitation

The second idea underlying the GCI is that, although technological advance is generally seen as the most critical factor in driving sustained high growth for all countries (and certainly the only factor that can sustain growth in the long run), these advances may have different sources for different countries. In particular, for economies that are already close to the technological frontier, the only way to improve technology is to innovate. For countries that are far away from the frontier, on the other hand, technological improvements can be achieved partly through innovation and partly by copying or adopting the knowledge previously developed in one of the leading economies through technology transfers.

To capture this idea, the GCI separates the countries into two groups: the "core" innovators (which are those whose growth is largely driven by their capacity to inno-

Table 1: Core technology-innovating economies, 2002

Country	Average annual US utility patents granted per million population	Rank
United States	301.48	1
Japan	273.40	2
Taiwan	241.38	3
Sweden	190.34	4
Switzerland	189.44	5
Israel	165.08	6
Finland	155.58	7
Germany	137.52	8
Canada	109.62	9
Singapore	97.62	10
Netherlands	86.94	11
Luxembourg	82.59	12
Denmark	80.38	13
Korea	79.87	14
Belgium	70.10	15
France	67.59	16
Austria	65.43	17
United Kingdom	64.29	18
Norway	53.78	19
Iceland	45.94	20
Australia	44.00	21
New Zealand	36.84	22
Ireland	33.85	23
Hong Kong SAR	33.29	24
Italy	30.49	25

Source: US Patent and Trademark Office, February 2003

vate because they are close to the technological frontier), and "non-core" innovators (that is, those that depend more on technological adoption from abroad). In order to make this distinction, we used "an objective measure of their level of technological sophistication" as measured by the number of registered US utility patents (patents for innovation) per capita, per year. Based on an analysis of the data, the threshold of 15 patents per million population was chosen to separate the countries into two groups. Countries above this threshold are defined as the core group, and all others as non-core (see table 1 for a list of the core innovators).

As stressed by Sachs and McArthur, the distinction between core and non-core is for purely analytical purposes and "is not meant as a value judgment in any way. It is meant only as a useful shorthand to describe the critical division in today's world economy between the innovating and the non-innovating economies" (p 30).

More generally, the aim here is simply to acknowledge that the role of technology in the growth process differs between these two groups, and that this should be integrated into the analysis.

To reflect the fact that innovation is more important than adoption for core innovators, the technology index of the GCI puts a larger weight on innovation for the core innovators than for the non-core innovators. Technological adoption, on the other hand, receives a positive weight for non-core innovators and zero weight for core innovators. Technological adoption is captured by the *technology transfer subindex*.

Different countries are affected by different factors

The third central idea underlying the GCI is that the importance of the determinants of economic competitiveness varies for core and non-core innovators.

Sachs and McArthur argue that getting the fundamentals right in terms of the macroeconomic environment and institutions is still extremely critical for the non-core countries, whereas countries in the core will have these fundamentals largely in place, and for these countries technological innovation has become the deciding factor for growth. As the authors explained:

> "Our research has suggested that public institutions, for instance, play a more crucial role at low and middle levels of development than they do at high levels, where economies tend to have less variation in institutional quality and a satisfactory threshold of organizational efficiency has already been met. Likewise, once overall macroeconomic stability is achieved, including sustainable fiscal balances and a healthy banking system with broad access to credit, 'increased' stability becomes difficult to measure and its benefits become less pronounced" (p 38).

To capture this idea, the GCI assigns a heavier weight to the technology index for core innovators than it does to the public institutions index and the macroeconomic environment index. On the other hand, equal weights are assigned to these three indexes for noncore countries:

> "Just as the challenges of growth differ according to the stage of economic development, we have found that the explanatory power of our Growth Competitiveness Index is improved if we allow for different weightings of factors depending on the stage of development. . . . We verify through regression analysis that, as the stage of economic development changes, the relative importance of various sub-components of the GCI also changes" (p 31).

The precise weights given by Sachs and McArthur to each of the component indexes and its various subindexes can be summarized as follows:

For the core innovators:

Core GCI = 1/2 technology index
+ 1/4 public institutions index
+ 1/4 macroeconomic environment index

For the non-core innovators:

Non-core GCI = 1/3 technology index
+ 1/3 public institutions index
+ 1/3 macroeconomic environment index [8]

Specific details on the composition and construction of the GCI are found in the appendix to this chapter.

Changes to the GCI from last year

Increased coverage

The most important change to the GCI this year is the significant increase in the number of countries included in this year's analysis, from 80 to 102. An important point is that the countries added this year are mainly from the developing world, especially Africa. The coverage in that region of the world has increased from 8 to 25, and now includes Algeria, Angola, Cameroon, Chad, Egypt, Ethiopia, Gambia, Ghana, Kenya, Madagascar, Malawi, Mali, Mozambique, Senegal, Tanzania, Uganda, and Zambia. Newly added countries also include non-African nations such as Luxembourg, Macedonia, Malta, Pakistan, and Serbia. The countries included in this year's report account for 97.8 percent of world's GDP. The 2003 GCI index, therefore, analyzes almost all of the world's economic activity.

Changes to the model: innovative capacity and government waste

This year we have maintained the basic structure and overall logic of the GCI as developed by Sachs and McArthur, and as described above. However, we have made two changes to the methodology: one of these changes is minor and the other more important.

The minor change has been made to the innovation component of the technology index. We have replaced a Survey variable aimed at measuring the extent of innovative capacity in the economy with what we have found to be a better proxy. The original question was worded as follows: "Does continuous innovation play a major role in generating revenue for your business?" An analysis of the data demonstrated that this question was capturing *company*-specific, rather than *country*-specific, data, and further that the concept of "continuous innovation" was subject to a wide variety of interpretations. The Survey variable was therefore replaced with one that asks whether companies in the country are aggressive in absorbing new technology. The latter gets more to the heart of country-level technological innovation.

The second, more significant, change was made to the macroeconomic environment index. In this index we have replaced the previously used variable "government expenditure as a percentage of GDP" with a composite subindex aimed at capturing government spending waste.

According to Sachs and McArthur, the original logic behind including government expenditure was that a number of studies "have shown that high levels of government expenditure relative to GNP are associated with low economic growth" (p 48). But they acknowledged that there were fundamental problems with the use of this variable, which called for further examination:

> "We recognize that the optimal level of government expenditures is a much more complex issue than suggested by our approach. It certainly would not be correct to infer that economic growth would be maximized at zero government expenditures (though our equation has that perverse property). When government spending is too low, then governments do not meet even the core needs for education, health, and public services needed to underpin economic growth. . . . Higher levels of government spending . . . may be justified by the services provided or by the benefits for social equality even if they come at some price in terms of economic growth. . . . We hope in future studies to develop a more sophisticated evaluation of different types of government spending and their effects on competitiveness" (p 48).

This is what we have endeavored to do this year. We chose to replace government expenditure in the model precisely because it is not capturing what it was meant to capture. This became apparent upon looking at the ranking of countries for this particular variable. Since low spending is seen as a "good," the countries at the top of the ranking were those spending almost nothing, while those at the bottom spent high percentages of GDP. But this provides no indication of how well or poorly the resources are managed. One type of spending that must have a negative impact on growth is wasteful spending (or perhaps unproductive spending), as this type of spending may need to be financed with distortionary taxes (which hurt growth) while it does not provide the productive services that may enhance private productivity and, therefore, aggregate economic growth. With this in mind, we set out to find a good proxy for wasteful government spending.

Our goal, therefore, is to capture government waste. But within government expenditure, wasteful and productive spending are bundled together. The goal would therefore be to separate out public productive spending from wasteful spending in order to capture just the "bad" part. We have looked at a number of ways of doing this.

A first option considered was to introduce government expenditure into the GCI in a different way. One possibility would be to take both very low and very high spending as "bad" and moderate spending as "good": both extremes are bad for growth. The idea is that useful public spending tends to increase the productivity of private firms, which leads to larger aggregate economic growth. The down side is that public expenditures need to be financed with distortionary taxation. These distortions tend to lower the private after-tax productivity of firms, which, in turn, lowers the rate of economic growth. If the size of the government is too small, taxes are low, but the beneficial side of public spending is insufficient (for example, property rights are not well protected, infrastructures are inadequate, and so on). For the countries with governments that are "too small," an increase in the size of the government would lead to a larger growth rate as the benefits from more productive public spending would more than offset the extra costs of taxation. At the other extreme, if the size of the government is "too large," public spending may be very beneficial, but the distortions caused by all the taxes needed to finance it would more than offset the benefits. These countries could increase their growth rate by reducing overall spending. This leads to the idea that there is an "optimal size" of the government. In other words, there is a size of public spending (as a fraction of GDP) for which the growth rate of the economy is the largest.

The problem is that, in order to implement these ideas empirically, we would need to know what this "optimal size" is. And we do not. Perhaps more importantly, the optimal size may be different across countries, since a citizen's attitude toward government taxation and evasion depends on how well the government has performed historically and also on other social, structural, and cultural attributes that differ across countries. For these reasons, we decided not to try to include government spending in this year's GCI in a nonlinear fashion.

We also considered separating government consumption from government "investment." The idea here was that government consumption tends not to be productive (so it does not really increase the productivity of private firms), whereas it still needs to be financed. Thus, public consumption does not have the "positive" (productive) characteristics of public investment whereas it retains the negative effects of distortionary taxation. This solution was finally discarded because some parts of public consumption may be seen as productive by private firms, as it buys social peace and helps ease social tensions that tend to have negative effects on the overall business environment.

After having examined the potential hard data solutions above, we turned to the possibility of using data from the Executive Opinion Survey. This made intuitive sense, as what we aim to capture is a textured and qualitative measure of government spending. The idea was to replace the hard data on government expenditure with Survey data that would better capture the concept of

Box 1: Changes to last year's rankings

Of course, altering the model as described in the section above necessarily has an impact on the rankings of the index. In order to allow for better comparability between last year's and this year's rankings, this section will look at how last year's rankings would have changed if we had implemented the two changes described in the section above. Table A compares last year's published rankings with those that would have been obtained using the current formula. The section that follows will then concentrate on the changes in the rankings between last year and this year, using the current formula for both periods.

We see that there would have been a number of differences in last year's rankings if we had made the two substitutions described in the section above. Almost all of the variation can be traced to the replacement of the government spending variable by the government waste variable, since this variable is heavily weighted in the macroeconomic environment index, and thus on the overall rankings. Replacing the innovation variable,

which has a relatively low weight in the technology index, has a comparatively muted impact on the rankings. The changes can thus be primarily traced to the fact that government spending is not correlated with the new composite variable, government waste. This is as we would expect, since the two variables are in fact capturing very different things, as explained in the section above.

Turning to the rankings that would have been obtained last year using this year's formula, a first notable point is that Finland, rather than the United States, would have topped the rankings. This can be traced to the fact that the US government spends a relatively low percentage of GDP compared with Finland. And although US spending is not seen as particularly wasteful, Finland's is seen as even less so. The combined effect of these two forces is that Finland is ranked ahead of the United States once government expenditure is replaced by government waste.

Table A: GCI 2002 comparison

Country	GCI 2002 rank (revised)	GCI 2002 rank (published)
Finland	1	2
United States	2	1
Sweden	3	5
Denmark	4	10
Switzerland	5	6
Taiwan	6	3
Singapore	7	4
Norway	8	9
Canada	9	8
Australia	10	7
United Kingdom	11	11
Iceland	12	12
Netherlands	13	15
Germany	14	14
New Zealand	15	16
Japan	16	13
Israel	17	19
Austria	18	18
Portugal	19	23
Spain	20	22
Belgium	21	25
Hong Kong SAR	22	17
Ireland	23	24
Chile	24	20
Korea	25	21
Slovenia	26	28
Estonia	27	26
France	28	30
Hungary	29	29
Malaysia	30	27
Greece	31	38
Tunisia	32	34
Italy	33	39
South Africa	34	32
Botswana	35	41
Czech Republic	36	40
Thailand	37	31
China	38	33
Lithuania	39	36
Uruguay	40	42

Country	GCI 2002 rank (revised)	GCI 2002 rank (published)
Mauritius	41	35
Trinidad and Tobago	42	37
Latvia	43	44
Jordan	44	47
Brazil	45	46
Slovak Republic	46	49
Namibia	47	53
Croatia	48	58
Costa Rica	49	43
Poland	50	51
Panama	51	50
Morocco	52	55
Mexico	53	45
India	54	48
Peru	55	54
Dominican Republic	56	52
Jamaica	57	60
Bulgaria	58	62
Sri Lanka	59	59
El Salvador	60	57
Colombia	61	56
Vietnam	62	65
Philippines	63	61
Argentina	64	63
Turkey	65	69
Russian Federation	66	64
Romania	67	66
Venezuela	68	68
Indonesia	69	67
Nicaragua	70	75
Bolivia	71	78
Nigeria	72	71
Ecuador	73	73
Ukraine	74	77
Guatemala	75	70
Paraguay	76	72
Bangladesh	77	74
Honduras	78	76
Zimbabwe	79	79
Haiti	80	80

(cont'd.)

Box 1: Changes to last year's rankings *(cont'd.)*

Finland's relative improvement is indicative of a more general trend we see in the data: many western European countries would have been higher in the rankings last year using the new formula. These countries have governments that spend a high proportion of GDP (which was "penalized" by last year's formula), but that as captured by the waste composite, are not seen as spending wastefully. In fact, all western European countries have either the same or higher rankings following the introduction of government waste to the index: not one of them is lower following this change.

To reiterate, Europe's better performance can be traced to the fact that on the whole European governments spend high percentages of their GDP, which often pulled them down in the original model. However, by introducing the new waste variable, in which they are seen as spending relatively efficiently, they have necessarily been pushed higher in the rankings.

And since these are relative rankings, when some countries are higher, other countries must necessarily be lower. Turning again to Table A, we see that there are

two regions particularly affected on the downside: many countries in Asia and Latin America would have had lower ranks last year if we had been using the waste variable rather than government expenditure. These are countries that have relatively low overall government spending, which pushed them higher in the rankings last year. However, once the wastefulness of the spending is taken into account, many of these countries do less well, therefore coming in lower in the rankings.[1]

It is important to note one additional point with regard to relative rankings. It is possible for a country to do better on the government waste variable than the government expenditure variable, and to still have a lower overall ranking due to the movement of other countries in the index. This is simply due to the fact that other countries are doing even better, displacing the country in the overall rankings. Similarly, it is possible for a country to do worse in the waste variable than the government expenditure variable, but to see an improvement in their overall ranking due to the relative shifts of other countries in the index.

---

public waste. After testing a number of candidate variables, three were selected:

- Extent of distortive government subsidies
- Diversion of public funds
- Public trust in the financial honesty of politicians

The idea of this "composite waste subindex" is to capture waste through government favoritism and corruption. This should account for a large part of overall government wasteful spending. Statistical analysis of these variables indeed showed that they have strong explanatory power with regards to medium- to long-term growth. This solution was thus retained.

Competitiveness rankings 2003–2004

An immediate overview of the results of this year's 2003 Global Competitiveness Index rankings reveals striking similarities with last year's top 10 rankings. The first four ranks are identical, with Finland in the first place, followed by the United States, Sweden, and Denmark, respectively. Taiwan and Singapore maintain their rankings relative to each other, but both moved higher by one position, to 5th and 6th positions, respectively, sliding Switzerland from the 5th position to the 7th position. Norway declined by rank to 9th place, making way for Iceland in 8th place. Canada,

previously in 9th place, falls off the top 10 list while Australia stays in 10th place.

A closer study of the results, however, reflects remarkable changes underlying each country's competitive position, both in absolute as well as relative terms. Tables 2 through 7 are relevant to the rest of this chapter. **Finland**, for instance, posted improvements in its overall macroeconomic stability characterized by an increase in the government fiscal surplus, an increase in its national savings rate, and further reduction of its inflation rate and interest rate spread. Yet despite generally stable economic indicators, Finland posted the fourth worst deterioration in recession expectations (rank #69) as negative sentiment deepened over the economy's prospects in the immediate 12-month period.

Unlike Finland, which performed consistently well on the three components of the Global Competitiveness Index, the **United States** maintained its position in the second place of the GCI amid varying levels of achievement in the different components. For instance, the country's overall performance is weakened by the quality of its public institutions. Specifically, there is deterioration in the perceptions of favoritism in the decisions of government officials (rank #19) and of the extent of organized crime (rank #29). Another component that serves as a source of weakness is the macroeconomic environment characterized by a widening of the government budget deficit to 3.4 percent of GDP (rank #50) and a further decline of the national savings rate to 10.5 percent of GDP (rank #93). And although the United States still leads in the technology index, its overall score dropped, reflecting a reduction in the tertiary enrollment rate and a decline in the number of patents granted.

Significantly, **Sweden's** position in third place is unchanged, but underlying its ranking is one of the most striking improvements in scores, particularly in the area of public institutions. Sweden posted increases in the scores pertaining to the extent of organized crime and the perception of favoritism in the decisions of government officials. But like the United States, Sweden's continued leadership in the technology index (rank #4) belies a notable decline in patents granted. And like Finland, Sweden's high ranking in the macroeconomic environment (rank #8) appears in stark contrast to the heightening of recession expectations in the country (rank #68).

That **Denmark** stays in the fourth place masks notable improvements over last year's scores. Denmark, already in the top position in the quality of public institutions and the extent of government waste, achieved one of the largest gains in the perception of the extent of distortive subsidies (rank #7). Denmark's position in technology also received a boost from dramatic gains in the scores for government prioritization of ICT (rank #10) and government success in ICT promotion (rank #10).

Taiwan's ascent to the 5th place in the overall rankings also received a boost from higher scores in the quality of public institutions. The most evident improvements include more favorable perceptions of the independence of the judiciary, less favoritism in the decisions of government officials, better control of corruption and greater public trust of politicians. Taiwan's leadership in technology (rank #3) also received a further boost from increased patent activity. But the country's macroeconomic performance deteriorated, marked by a widening of the government deficit to 6.7 percent of GDP (rank #79) and an overall worsening of recession expectations (rank #57).

Moreover, **Singapore** may be ranked first in terms of the macroeconomic environment but behind the top ranking are notably lower scores in several areas: government deficit, inflation rate, savings rate and interest rate spread. In contrast, Singapore's ranking in the technology index (rank #12) may obscure the fact that the country consistently holds the number one position in terms of government prioritization of ICT and government success in ICT promotion. This year, Singapore also posted the highest increase in number of patents per capita.

Like Singapore, **Switzerland** enjoys high ranking of its macroeconomic environment (rank #6), particularly its credit rating (rank #1). Closer examination, however, reveals deterioration in the access to credit (rank #58) and a worsening of recession expectations (rank #76). Similarly, Switzerland scores quite favorably in terms of

government waste (rank #13) but its overall score is weighed down by strikingly negative perceptions of the extent of distortive government subsidies (rank #72).

Iceland, a new entrant to the top 10 rankings, received its boost from an improvement in its macroeconomic performance. Looking in further detail, however, reveals that Iceland's performance in this area is quite mixed. Indeed, the country scored well in terms of access to credit (rank #2) and recession expectations (rank #5). But its interest rate spread remained high at 10.1 percent (rank #73) while the national savings rate remains relatively low at 19.1 percent (rank #61). Similarly, in the area of technology, Iceland experienced a decline in the number of patents granted but its impact on the rankings was partly offset by the improvement in the tertiary enrollment rate.

That **Australia** stays at the 10th place in the overall rankings underplays significant improvements in the public trust in politicians and perceptions of the extent of distortive government subsidies, as well as overall quality of public institutions. What did decline is the tertiary enrollment rate from 79.8 percent to 63.3 percent, which by itself accounts for a drop of 7 positions in the technology index and 2 positions in the overall Growth Competitiveness Index.

Another notable drop is that of **Canada** (rank #16), which fell off the top 10 list. In contrast to Australia, however, Canada's fall is driven mostly by a perceived deterioration in the quality of public institutions ranging from the independence of the judiciary to the control of corruption, to a variable that captures public trust of politicians. Canada's macroeconomic environment did show improvements in some areas, with the country remaining the top performer among G-7 partners in terms of the overall stability of the macroeconomic environment. In the area of technology, Canada continues to post improvements in the diffusion of technologies, but it is significant to note that patent activity has declined.

Like Canada, the **United Kingdom** posted a significant drop in the rankings, from the 11th position to 15th, largely due to shifts in a number of variables which assess the quality of public institutions. The decline was evident across the board, particularly in the area of crime (rank #23) and business sector perceptions about possible favoritism in the decisions of government officials (rank #12). The country's macroeconomic environment showed some signs of weakness as reflected in a worsening of recession expectations (rank #73) and some erosion in the relative ranks of variables measuring the strength of the public finances and inflation. Performance in technology was mixed: there was a decline in government subsidies for R&D as well as a drop in the number of patents granted, but there were also more favorable assessments of government prioritization of ICT and government success in ICT promotion.

Table 2: Growth Competitiveness Index rankings and 2002 comparisons

Country	GCI 2003 rank (among 2003 countries)	GCI 2003 rank (among 2002 countries)	GCI 2002 rank (revised)*	GCI 2002 rank (original)
Finland	1	1	1	2
United States	2	2	2	1
Sweden	3	3	3	5
Denmark	4	4	4	10
Taiwan	5	5	6	3
Singapore	6	6	7	4
Switzerland	7	7	5	6
Iceland	8	8	12	12
Norway	9	9	8	9
Australia	10	10	10	7
Japan	11	11	16	13
Netherlands	12	12	13	15
Germany	13	13	14	14
New Zealand	14	14	15	16
United Kingdom	15	15	11	11
Canada	16	16	9	8
Austria	17	17	18	18
Korea	18	18	25	21
Malta	19	—	—	—
Israel	20	19	17	19
Luxembourg	21	—	—	—
Estonia	22	20	27	26
Spain	23	21	20	22
Hong Kong SAR	24	22	22	17
Portugal	25	23	19	23
France	26	24	28	30
Belgium	27	25	21	25
Chile	28	26	24	20
Malaysia	29	27	30	27
Ireland	30	28	23	24
Slovenia	31	29	26	28
Thailand	32	30	37	31
Hungary	33	31	29	29
Jordan	34	32	44	47
Greece	35	33	31	38
Botswana	36	34	35	41
Latvia	37	35	43	44
Tunisia	38	36	32	34
Czech Republic	39	37	36	40
Lithuania	40	38	39	36
Italy	41	39	33	39
South Africa	42	40	34	32
Slovak Republic	43	41	46	49
China	44	42	38	33
Poland	45	43	50	51
Mauritius	46	44	41	35
Mexico	47	45	53	45
El Salvador	48	46	60	57
Trinidad and Tobago	49	47	42	37
Uruguay	50	48	40	42
Costa Rica	51	49	49	43
Namibia	52	50	47	53
Croatia	53	51	48	58
Brazil	54	52	45	46
Gambia	55	—	—	—
India	56	53	54	48
Peru	57	54	55	54
Egypt	58	—	—	—
Panama	59	55	51	50
Vietnam	60	56	62	65
Morocco	61	57	52	55
Dominican Republic	62	58	56	52
Colombia	63	59	61	56
Bulgaria	64	60	58	62
Turkey	65	61	65	69
Philippines	66	62	63	61

Country	GCI 2003 rank (among 2003 countries)	GCI 2003 rank (among 2002 countries)	GCI 2002 rank (revised)*	GCI 2002 rank (original)
Jamaica	67	63	57	60
Sri Lanka	68	64	59	59
Tanzania	69	—	—	—
Russian Federation	70	65	66	64
Ghana	71	—	—	—
Indonesia	72	66	69	67
Pakistan	73	—	—	—
Algeria	74	—	—	—
Romania	75	67	67	66
Malawi	76	—	—	—
Serbia	77	—	—	—
Argentina	78	68	64	63
Senegal	79	—	—	—
Uganda	80	—	—	—
Macedonia, FYR	81	—	—	—
Venezuela	82	69	68	68
Kenya	83	—	—	—
Ukraine	84	70	74	77
Bolivia	85	71	71	78
Ecuador	86	72	73	73
Nigeria	87	73	72	71
Zambia	88	—	—	—
Guatemala	89	74	75	70
Nicaragua	90	75	70	75
Cameroon	91	—	—	—
Ethiopia	92	—	—	—
Mozambique	93	—	—	—
Honduras	94	76	78	76
Paraguay	95	77	76	72
Madagascar	96	—	—	—
Zimbabwe	97	78	79	79
Bangladesh	98	79	77	74
Mali	99	—	—	—
Angola	100	—	—	—
Chad	101	—	—	—
Haiti	102	80	80	80

*Applying the 2003 formula
Source: World Economic Forum

(cont'd.)

Table 3: Growth Competitiveness Index components

Growth Competitiveness Index (GCI)			Macroeconomic environment index			Public institutions index			Technology index		
Country	Rank	Score	Country	Rank	Score	Country	Rank	Score	Country	Rank	Score
Finland	1	6.01	Singapore	1	5.69	Denmark	1	6.56	United States	1	6.30
United States	2	5.81	Finland	2	5.54	Finland	2	6.52	Finland	2	6.00
Sweden	3	5.80	Luxembourg	3	5.44	Iceland	3	6.44	Taiwan	3	5.97
Denmark	4	5.61	Norway	4	5.43	Australia	4	6.36	Sweden	4	5.90
Taiwan	5	5.58	Denmark	5	5.38	New Zealand	5	6.36	Japan	5	5.56
Singapore	6	5.54	Switzerland	6	5.31	Singapore	6	6.28	Korea	6	5.28
Switzerland	7	5.51	Australia	7	5.15	Sweden	7	6.28	Switzerland	7	5.26
Iceland	8	5.34	Sweden	8	5.13	Switzerland	8	6.20	Denmark	8	5.25
Norway	9	5.33	Netherlands	9	5.07	Germany	9	6.10	Israel	9	5.17
Australia	10	5.33	Austria	10	5.07	Hong Kong SAR	10	6.03	Estonia	10	5.16
Japan	11	5.25	Canada	11	5.04	Netherlands	11	6.02	Canada	11	5.15
Netherlands	12	5.24	United Kingdom	12	4.99	United Kingdom	12	6.01	Singapore	12	5.09
Germany	13	5.24	New Zealand	13	4.98	Luxembourg	13	5.92	Norway	13	5.08
New Zealand	14	5.23	United States	14	4.94	Austria	14	5.83	Germany	14	5.03
United Kingdom	15	5.23	Hong Kong SAR	15	4.91	Israel	15	5.82	Iceland	15	5.01
Canada	16	5.21	Iceland	16	4.90	Norway	16	5.73	United Kingdom	16	4.96
Austria	17	5.07	Spain	17	4.83	United States	17	5.71	Malta	17	4.95
Korea	18	5.07	Taiwan	18	4.82	Malta	18	5.68	Netherlands	18	4.93
Malta	19	5.03	Belgium	19	4.82	Chile	19	5.62	Australia	19	4.90
Israel	20	5.02	France	20	4.80	Jordan	20	5.58	Malaysia	20	4.89
Luxembourg	21	4.99	Germany	21	4.78	Taiwan	21	5.55	Czech Republic	21	4.84
Estonia	22	4.96	Ireland	22	4.74	Portugal	22	5.52	Portugal	22	4.82
Spain	23	4.94	Korea	23	4.67	France	23	5.50	New Zealand	23	4.80
Hong Kong SAR	24	4.93	Japan	24	4.57	Canada	24	5.48	Slovenia	24	4.73
Portugal	25	4.92	China	25	4.56	Ireland	25	5.46	Spain	25	4.72
France	26	4.91	Thailand	26	4.54	Botswana	26	5.45	Latvia	26	4.71
Belgium	27	4.88	Malaysia	27	4.49	Belgium	27	5.41	Austria	27	4.69
Chile	28	4.86	Italy	28	4.48	Estonia	28	5.36	France	28	4.67
Malaysia	29	4.83	Malta	29	4.47	Uruguay	29	5.31	Belgium	29	4.65
Ireland	30	4.73	Botswana	30	4.44	Japan	30	5.30	Greece	30	4.64
Slovenia	31	4.70	Portugal	31	4.41	Spain	31	5.28	Chile	31	4.60
Thailand	32	4.63	Tunisia	32	4.38	Tunisia	32	5.19	Hungary	32	4.57
Hungary	33	4.61	Greece	33	4.38	Hungary	33	5.18	Slovak Republic	33	4.55
Jordan	34	4.58	Estonia	34	4.37	Malaysia	34	5.12	Poland	34	4.44
Greece	35	4.58	Chile	35	4.36	Slovenia	35	5.11	Brazil	35	4.44
Botswana	36	4.56	Latvia	36	4.31	Korea	36	5.03	Lithuania	36	4.43
Latvia	37	4.54	Slovenia	37	4.27	Thailand	37	4.97	Hong Kong SAR	37	4.40
Tunisia	38	4.49	Hungary	38	4.09	Malawi	38	4.79	Ireland	38	4.37
Czech Republic	39	4.48	Czech Republic	39	4.08	Gambia	39	4.73	Thailand	39	4.37
Lithuania	40	4.39	South Africa	40	4.08	El Salvador	40	4.72	South Africa	40	4.35
Italy	41	4.38	Lithuania	41	4.04	Lithuania	41	4.71	Croatia	41	4.32
South Africa	42	4.37	Jordan	42	4.03	Greece	42	4.71	Luxembourg	42	4.30
Slovak Republic	43	4.23	Morocco	43	3.95	South Africa	43	4.69	Mexico	43	4.26
China	44	4.19	Israel	44	3.93	Mauritius	44	4.61	Italy	44	4.24
Poland	45	4.15	Vietnam	45	3.87	Latvia	45	4.61	Argentina	45	4.22
Mauritius	46	4.12	Gambia	46	3.85	Italy	46	4.56	Costa Rica	46	4.19
Mexico	47	4.12	Trinidad and Tobago	47	3.85	Czech Republic	47	4.51	Trinidad and Tobago	47	4.13
El Salvador	48	4.07	El Salvador	48	3.84	Namibia	48	4.50	Jordan	48	4.13
Trinidad and Tobago	49	4.07	Poland	49	3.83	Costa Rica	49	4.49	Mauritius	49	4.10
Uruguay	50	4.03	Slovak Republic	50	3.82	Mexico	50	4.35	Panama	50	4.10
Costa Rica	51	4.02	Algeria	51	3.78	Slovak Republic	51	4.33	Uruguay	51	4.04
Namibia	52	3.99	India	52	3.75	China	52	4.33	Dominican Republic	52	3.98
Croatia	53	3.97	Namibia	53	3.75	Brazil	53	4.27	Jamaica	53	3.97
Brazil	54	3.95	Mexico	54	3.74	Peru	54	4.27	Turkey	54	3.96
Gambia	55	3.93	Croatia	55	3.71	India	55	4.26	Romania	55	3.93
India	56	3.90	Egypt	56	3.70	Trinidad and Tobago	56	4.21	Philippines	56	3.92
Peru	57	3.88	Mauritius	57	3.66	Egypt	57	4.18	Tunisia	57	3.90
Egypt	58	3.84	Peru	58	3.61	Poland	58	4.17	Venezuela	58	3.84
Panama	59	3.81	Panama	59	3.59	Tanzania	59	4.15	Botswana	59	3.78
Vietnam	60	3.80	Philippines	60	3.52	Colombia	60	4.13	Colombia	60	3.76
Morocco	61	3.77	Russian Federation	61	3.44	Vietnam	61	4.11	Peru	61	3.75
Dominican Republic	62	3.77	Pakistan	62	3.40	Bulgaria	62	4.10	Namibia	62	3.72
Colombia	63	3.74	Costa Rica	63	3.38	Turkey	63	4.07	Bulgaria	63	3.72
Bulgaria	64	3.67	Indonesia	64	3.37	Dominican Republic	64	4.05	India	64	3.68
Turkey	65	3.65	Sri Lanka	65	3.35	Ghana	65	3.97	China	65	3.67
Philippines	66	3.58	Colombia	66	3.33	Algeria	66	3.92	Serbia	66	3.66
Jamaica	67	3.52	Senegal	67	3.33	Croatia	67	3.87	El Salvador	67	3.64
Sri Lanka	68	3.51	Ghana	68	3.29	Morocco	68	3.86	Egypt	68	3.64
Tanzania	69	3.49	Dominican Republic	69	3.27	Zambia	69	3.86	Russian Federation	69	3.61
Russian Federation	70	3.46	Ukraine	70	3.27	Jamaica	70	3.77	Macedonia, FYR	70	3.53
Ghana	71	3.46	Uganda	71	3.20	Panama	71	3.75	Morocco	71	3.50
Indonesia	72	3.42	Bangladesh	72	3.20	Sri Lanka	72	3.70	Sri Lanka	72	3.47
		(cont'd.)			*(cont'd.)*			*(cont'd.)*			*(cont'd.)*

12

Growth Competitiveness Index (GCI)			Macroeconomic environment index			Public institutions index			Technology index		
Country	Rank	Score	Country	Rank	Score	Country	Rank	Score	Country	Rank	Score
Pakistan	73	3.41	Bulgaria	73	3.18	Ethiopia	73	3.69	Vietnam	73	3.41
Algeria	74	3.39	Nigeria	74	3.16	Pakistan	74	3.67	Kenya	74	3.36
Romania	75	3.38	Brazil	75	3.16	Senegal	75	3.64	Zimbabwe	75	3.34
Malawi	76	3.36	Tanzania	76	3.12	Indonesia	76	3.63	Ecuador	76	3.27
Serbia	77	3.36	Kenya	77	3.10	Serbia	77	3.58	Uganda	77	3.25
Argentina	78	3.35	Cameroon	78	3.10	Nicaragua	78	3.57	Indonesia	78	3.25
Senegal	79	3.34	Madagascar	79	3.04	Bolivia	79	3.51	Guatemala	79	3.23
Uganda	80	3.25	Macedonia	80	3.01	Ecuador	80	3.48	Gambia	80	3.22
Macedonia	81	3.22	Romania	81	2.93	Russian Federation	81	3.34	Tanzania	81	3.22
Venezuela	82	3.21	Turkey	82	2.93	Mozambique	82	3.33	Nigeria	82	3.16
Kenya	83	3.21	Bolivia	83	2.90	Mali	83	3.33	Pakistan	83	3.16
Ukraine	84	3.17	Ethiopia	84	2.89	Uganda	84	3.30	Ukraine	84	3.15
Bolivia	85	3.16	Guatemala	85	2.85	Philippines	85	3.29	Nicaragua	85	3.12
Ecuador	86	3.16	Jamaica	86	2.83	Romania	86	3.27	Ghana	86	3.10
Nigeria	87	3.10	Serbia	87	2.83	Guatemala	87	3.22	Honduras	87	3.08
Zambia	88	3.10	Honduras	88	2.77	Argentina	88	3.22	Bolivia	88	3.06
Guatemala	89	3.10	Uruguay	89	2.75	Venezuela	89	3.21	Senegal	89	3.04
Nicaragua	90	3.05	Ecuador	90	2.72	Zimbabwe	90	3.21	Zambia	90	2.96
Cameroon	91	2.98	Mali	91	2.67	Angola	91	3.16	Paraguay	91	2.96
Ethiopia	92	2.92	Paraguay	92	2.65	Kenya	92	3.16	Mozambique	92	2.84
Mozambique	93	2.91	Argentina	93	2.61	Macedonia	93	3.11	Cameroon	93	2.80
Honduras	94	2.90	Venezuela	94	2.59	Ukraine	94	3.09	Malawi	94	2.79
Paraguay	95	2.87	Mozambique	95	2.57	Cameroon	95	3.04	Bangladesh	95	2.68
Madagascar	96	2.85	Chad	96	2.50	Madagascar	96	3.04	Algeria	96	2.48
Zimbabwe	97	2.84	Zambia	97	2.49	Paraguay	97	3.01	Madagascar	97	2.47
Bangladesh	98	2.79	Malawi	98	2.49	Nigeria	98	2.99	Angola	98	2.43
Mali	99	2.79	Haiti	99	2.45	Honduras	99	2.85	Mali	99	2.36
Angola	100	2.60	Nicaragua	100	2.45	Bangladesh	100	2.48	Ethiopia	100	2.17
Chad	101	2.31	Angola	101	2.22	Chad	101	2.36	Haiti	101	2.17
Haiti	102	2.30	Zimbabwe	102	1.98	Haiti	102	2.28	Chad	102	2.06

Source: World Economic Forum

Table 4: GCI Component Indexes ranking comparison

Country	GCI ranking 2003 rank (among 2002 countires)	2002 rank (revised)	Change	Macroeconomic environment ranking 2003 rank (among 2002 countires)	2002 rank (revised)	Change	Public institutions ranking 2003 rank (among 2002 countires)	2002 rank (revised)	Change	Technology ranking 2003 rank (among 2002 countires)	2002 rank (revised)	Change
Algeria	—	—	—	—	—	—	—	—	—	—	—	—
Angola	—	—	—	—	—	—	—	—	—	—	—	—
Argentina	68	64	−4	76	70	−6	72	66	−6	43	44	1
Australia	10	10	0	6	12	6	4	5	1	18	9	−9
Austria	17	18	1	9	6	−3	13	11	−2	26	24	−2
Bangladesh	79	77	−2	63	62	−1	79	79	0	79	79	0
Belgium	25	21	−4	18	14	−4	25	22	−3	28	22	−6
Bolivia	71	71	0	69	67	−2	66	69	3	77	77	0
Botswana	34	35	1	28	27	−1	24	31	7	57	61	4
Brazil	52	45	−7	66	56	−10	49	45	−4	34	35	1
Bulgaria	60	58	−2	64	64	0	56	47	−9	61	56	−5
Cameroon	—	—	—	—	—	—	—	—	—	—	—	—
Canada	16	9	−7	10	7	−3	22	9	−13	11	8	−3
Chad	—	—	—	—	—	—	—	—	—	—	—	—
Chile	26	24	−2	33	26	−7	17	19	2	30	33	3
China	42	38	−4	24	24	0	48	38	−10	63	63	0
Colombia	59	61	2	60	63	3	54	54	0	58	58	0
Costa Rica	49	49	0	57	59	2	45	46	1	44	37	−7
Croatia	51	48	−3	51	47	−4	59	57	−2	40	42	2
Czech Republic	37	36	−1	37	38	1	43	50	7	20	20	0
Denmark	4	4	0	4	5	1	1	2	1	8	11	3
Dominican Republic	58	56	−2	61	60	−1	58	60	2	50	48	−2
Ecuador	72	73	1	74	75	1	67	75	8	70	70	0
Egypt	—	—	—	—	—	—	—	—	—	—	—	—
El Salvador	46	60	14	45	51	6	36	48	12	64	69	5
Estonia	20	27	7	32	36	4	26	28	2	10	14	4
Ethiopia	—	—	—	—	—	—	—	—	—	—	—	—
Finland	1	1	0	2	2	0	2	1	−1	2	3	1
France	24	28	4	19	18	−1	21	29	8	27	28	1
Gambia	—	—	—	—	—	—	—	—	—	—	—	—
Germany	13	14	1	20	13	−7	9	14	5	14	12	−2
Ghana	—	—	—	—	—	—	—	—	—	—	—	—
Greece	33	31	−2	31	29	−2	38	44	6	29	31	2
Guatemala	74	75	1	70	74	4	71	74	3	72	74	2
Haiti	80	80	0	78	79	1	80	80	0	80	80	0
Honduras	76	78	2	72	72	0	78	76	−2	76	78	2
Hong Kong SAR	22	22	0	14	15	1	10	13	3	36	32	−4
Hungary	31	29	−2	36	35	−1	31	30	−1	31	21	−10
Iceland	8	12	4	15	22	7	3	3	0	15	13	−2
India	53	54	1	48	45	−3	51	59	8	62	57	−5
Indonesia	66	69	3	58	65	7	64	77	13	71	65	−6
Ireland	28	23	−5	21	19	−2	23	18	−5	37	30	−7
Israel	19	17	−2	42	33	−9	14	17	3	9	7	−2
Italy	39	33	−6	27	21	−6	42	37	−5	42	39	−3
Jamaica	63	57	−6	71	66	−5	61	51	−10	51	46	−5
Japan	11	16	5	23	23	0	28	25	−3	5	5	0
Jordan	32	44	12	40	44	4	18	40	22	46	51	5
Kenya	—	—	—	—	—	—	—	—	—	—	—	—
Korea	18	25	7	22	30	8	34	32	−2	6	18	12
Latvia	35	43	8	34	42	8	41	52	11	25	29	4
Lithuania	38	39	1	39	43	4	37	36	−1	35	40	5
Luxembourg	—	—	—	—	—	—	—	—	—	—	—	—
Macedonia, FYR	—	—	—	—	—	—	—	—	—	—	—	—
Madagascar	—	—	—	—	—	—	—	—	—	—	—	—
Malawi	—	—	—	—	—	—	—	—	—	—	—	—
Malaysia	27	30	3	26	28	2	32	33	1	19	26	7
Mali	—	—	—	—	—	—	—	—	—	—	—	—
Malta	—	—	—	—	—	—	—	—	—	—	—	—
Mauritius	44	41	−3	52	48	−4	40	35	−5	47	45	−2
Mexico	45	53	8	50	52	2	46	58	12	41	47	6
Morocco	57	52	−5	41	39	−2	60	56	−4	66	62	−4
Mozambique	—	—	—	—	—	—	—	—	—	—	—	—
Namibia	50	47	−3	49	46	−3	44	41	−3	60	60	0
Netherlands	12	13	1	8	8	0	11	10	−1	17	19	2
New Zealand	14	15	1	12	11	−1	5	4	−1	22	27	5
Nicaragua	75	70	−5	79	78	−1	65	64	−1	75	73	−2
Nigeria	73	72	−1	65	69	4	77	78	1	73	71	−2
Norway	9	8	−1	3	3	0	15	12	−3	13	10	−3

(cont'd.)

Table 4: GCI Component Indexes ranking comparison *(cont'd.)*

Country	GCI ranking			Macroeconomic environment ranking			Public institutions ranking			Technology ranking		
	2003 rank (among 2002 countires)	2002 rank (revised)	Change	2003 rank (among 2002 countires)	2002 rank (revised)	Change	2003 rank (among 2002 countires)	2002 rank (revised)	Change	2003 rank (among 2002 countires)	2002 rank (revised)	Change
Pakistan	—	—	—	—	—	—	—	—	—	—	—	—
Panama	55	51	−4	54	50	−4	62	55	−7	48	49	1
Paraguay	77	76	−1	75	73	−2	76	71	−5	78	76	−2
Peru	54	55	1	53	54	1	50	49	−1	59	64	5
Philippines	62	63	1	55	55	0	69	70	1	54	52	−2
Poland	43	50	7	46	49	3	53	61	8	33	36	3
Portugal	23	19	−4	29	25	−4	20	21	1	21	15	−6
Romania	67	67	0	67	71	4	70	67	−3	53	55	2
Russian Federation	65	66	1	56	61	5	68	65	−3	65	66	1
Senegal	—	—	—	—	—	—	—	—	—	—	—	—
Serbia	—	—	—	—	—	—	—	—	—	—	—	—
Singapore	6	7	1	1	1	0	6	7	1	12	17	5
Slovak Republic	41	46	5	47	53	6	47	53	6	32	34	2
Slovenia	29	26	−3	35	32	−3	33	23	−10	23	25	2
South Africa	40	34	−6	38	37	−1	39	34	−5	39	38	−1
Spain	21	20	−1	16	17	1	29	26	−3	24	23	−1
Sri Lanka	64	59	−5	59	58	−1	63	42	−21	67	67	0
Sweden	3	3	0	7	9	2	7	15	8	4	4	0
Switzerland	7	5	−2	5	4	−1	8	8	0	7	6	−1
Taiwan	5	6	1	17	20	3	19	27	8	3	2	−1
Tanzania	—	—	—	—	—	—	—	—	—	—	—	—
Thailand	30	37	7	25	34	9	35	39	4	38	41	3
Trinidad and Tobago	47	42	−5	44	41	−3	52	43	−9	45	43	−2
Tunisia	36	32	−4	30	31	1	30	24	−6	55	59	4
Turkey	61	65	4	68	68	0	57	63	6	52	54	2
Uganda	—	—	—	—	—	—	—	—	—	—	—	—
Ukraine	70	74	4	62	76	14	75	72	−3	74	72	−2
United Kingdom	15	11	−4	11	10	−1	12	6	−6	16	16	0
United States	2	2	0	13	16	3	16	16	0	1	1	0
Uruguay	48	40	−8	73	57	−16	27	20	−7	49	50	1
Venezuela	69	68	−1	77	77	0	73	73	0	56	53	−3
Vietnam	56	62	6	43	40	−3	55	62	7	68	68	0
Zambia	—	—	—	—	—	—	—	—	—	—	—	—
Zimbabwe	78	79	1	80	80	0	74	68	−6	69	75	6

*Applying the 2003 formula
Source: World Economic Forum

Table 5: Macroeconomic environment index components

Country	Macroeconomic Eenvironment index		Macroeconomic stability subindex						Government waste subindex		Country credit rating	
			OVERALL		HARD DATA		SURVEY DATA					
	Rank	Score	Rank	Score	Rank	Score	Rank	Score	Rank	Score	Rank	Score
Algeria	51	3.78	5	4.91	3	5.32	51	3.88	67	2.68	68	2.60
Angola	101	2.22	100	2.73	102	2.13	33	4.24	92	2.07	95	1.35
Argentina	93	2.61	80	3.58	71	3.98	98	2.58	94	2.03	99	1.26
Australia	7	5.15	17	4.64	39	4.47	8	5.08	6	5.18	19	6.15
Austria	10	5.07	22	4.57	14	4.91	63	3.73	15	4.46	9	6.67
Bangladesh	72	3.20	55	4.19	43	4.42	68	3.62	88	2.18	75	2.24
Belgium	19	4.82	33	4.44	12	5.02	91	3.01	27	3.89	14	6.50
Bolivia	83	2.90	78	3.66	65	4.09	99	2.57	97	1.89	71	2.41
Botswana	30	4.44	23	4.57	37	4.52	13	4.70	17	4.39	38	4.23
Brazil	75	3.16	88	3.38	94	3.16	50	3.92	52	3.07	62	2.80
Bulgaria	73	3.18	76	3.70	74	3.80	77	3.43	86	2.28	57	3.04
Cameroon	78	3.10	59	4.13	50	4.30	65	3.72	74	2.47	87	1.65
Canada	11	5.04	13	4.71	18	4.81	17	4.47	21	4.11	11	6.62
Chad	96	2.50	91	3.31	95	3.14	61	3.73	90	2.08	97	1.31
Chile	35	4.36	28	4.49	24	4.62	37	4.16	36	3.64	31	4.83
China	25	4.56	4	5.05	4	5.30	18	4.44	35	3.66	34	4.49
Colombia	66	3.33	68	3.94	78	3.76	20	4.41	73	2.54	60	2.90
Costa Rica	63	3.38	82	3.50	90	3.38	59	3.78	51	3.19	52	3.36
Croatia	55	3.71	51	4.24	54	4.25	36	4.21	59	2.82	49	3.55
Czech Republic	39	4.08	27	4.49	31	4.57	24	4.31	71	2.58	32	4.76
Denmark	5	5.38	18	4.63	19	4.79	34	4.23	3	5.63	10	6.64
Dominican Republic	69	3.27	72	3.81	72	3.97	76	3.43	61	2.76	63	2.71
Ecuador	90	2.72	83	3.49	84	3.57	81	3.27	95	2.02	81	1.88
Egypt	56	3.70	63	4.02	59	4.21	74	3.53	45	3.44	53	3.34
El Salvador	48	3.84	40	4.40	52	4.29	14	4.67	47	3.40	56	3.18
Estonia	34	4.37	25	4.55	55	4.25	3	5.31	26	3.93	36	4.43
Ethiopia	84	2.89	74	3.79	60	4.18	95	2.82	66	2.71	98	1.28
Finland	2	5.54	7	4.90	7	5.16	32	4.24	2	5.75	11	6.62
France	20	4.80	36	4.43	20	4.77	69	3.58	39	3.58	8	6.78
Gambia	46	3.85	75	3.77	77	3.78	60	3.74	24	4.02	n/a	n/a
Germany	21	4.78	48	4.31	17	4.82	89	3.03	32	3.71	7	6.79
Ghana	68	3.29	70	3.87	75	3.80	40	4.06	46	3.40	79	2.02
Greece	33	4.38	45	4.34	49	4.30	19	4.42	49	3.30	23	5.53
Guatemala	85	2.85	84	3.49	81	3.63	84	3.14	98	1.83	69	2.58
Haiti	99	2.45	93	3.30	89	3.39	87	3.08	99	1.82	94	1.39
Honduras	88	2.77	85	3.49	83	3.62	85	3.14	93	2.05	77	2.07
Hong Kong SAR	15	4.91	8	4.84	8	5.16	44	4.03	9	4.86	26	5.10
Hungary	38	4.09	66	3.97	73	3.82	21	4.34	41	3.54	30	4.88
Iceland	16	4.90	30	4.48	63	4.11	1	5.42	5	5.21	25	5.43
India	52	3.75	43	4.36	69	4.02	5	5.21	72	2.56	48	3.74
Indonesia	64	3.37	65	3.98	66	4.04	56	3.83	42	3.50	80	2.01
Ireland	22	4.74	29	4.49	28	4.58	31	4.25	38	3.58	15	6.40
Israel	44	3.93	77	3.67	67	4.03	97	2.76	19	4.17	39	4.22
Italy	28	4.48	50	4.25	44	4.41	54	3.86	50	3.22	18	6.22
Jamaica	86	2.83	90	3.34	91	3.37	82	3.26	80	2.34	73	2.32
Japan	24	4.57	19	4.61	11	5.10	79	3.40	54	2.98	20	6.06
Jordan	42	4.03	39	4.40	32	4.55	41	4.05	18	4.34	59	2.97
Kenya	77	3.10	60	4.10	64	4.10	38	4.11	77	2.40	82	1.80
Korea	23	4.67	6	4.90	10	5.14	26	4.30	30	3.80	27	5.08
Latvia	36	4.31	12	4.75	27	4.58	6	5.19	28	3.85	44	3.86
Lithuania	41	4.04	14	4.71	35	4.54	7	5.13	57	2.90	46	3.83
Luxembourg	3	5.44	15	4.69	9	5.14	71	3.56	4	5.43	2	6.93
Macedonia, FYR	80	3.01	67	3.94	47	4.31	90	3.03	79	2.35	83	1.80
Madagascar	79	3.04	87	3.39	92	3.27	66	3.68	81	2.33	n/a	n/a
Malawi	98	2.49	99	2.85	99	2.75	86	3.11	68	2.65	90	1.61
Malaysia	27	4.49	11	4.77	13	4.99	35	4.21	25	3.97	35	4.44
Mali	91	2.67	89	3.36	85	3.53	93	2.94	78	2.38	91	1.58
Malta	29	4.47	38	4.41	40	4.45	23	4.32	23	4.04	28	5.01
Mauritius	57	3.66	64	4.00	70	3.99	43	4.03	58	2.83	46	3.83
Mexico	54	3.74	73	3.81	76	3.79	53	3.86	55	2.96	37	4.39
Morocco	43	3.95	37	4.42	38	4.48	28	4.27	44	3.46	50	3.51
Mozambique	95	2.57	97	3.15	98	3.05	78	3.41	82	2.33	89	1.64
Namibia	53	3.75	49	4.29	53	4.29	27	4.29	48	3.37	57	3.04
Netherlands	9	5.07	57	4.18	30	4.57	83	3.19	7	5.08	4	6.85
New Zealand	13	4.98	21	4.58	29	4.58	16	4.59	8	4.86	22	5.91
Nicaragua	100	2.45	98	3.01	97	3.06	94	2.89	87	2.26	92	1.53
Nigeria	74	3.16	32	4.45	22	4.63	45	4.00	91	2.08	87	1.65
Norway	4	5.43	3	5.15	1	5.72	64	3.73	14	4.59	5	6.82
Pakistan	62	3.40	20	4.59	48	4.31	2	5.32	63	2.73	86	1.69
Panama	59	3.59	47	4.32	21	4.73	80	3.29	83	2.32	51	3.41

(cont'd.)

Table 5: Macroeconomic environment index components *(cont'd.)*

Country	Macroeconomic Eenvironment index Rank	Score	Macroeconomic stability subindex OVERALL Rank	Score	HARD DATA Rank	Score	SURVEY DATA Rank	Score	Government waste subindex Rank	Score	Country credit rating Rank	Score
Paraguay	92	2.65	92	3.31	82	3.63	100	2.52	101	1.71	74	2.26
Peru	58	3.61	26	4.52	26	4.60	25	4.31	70	2.60	61	2.81
Philippines	60	3.52	46	4.33	36	4.52	55	3.84	89	2.11	54	3.31
Poland	49	3.83	62	4.04	57	4.24	73	3.53	65	2.71	33	4.54
Portugal	31	4.41	69	3.89	46	4.33	96	2.80	29	3.82	21	6.03
Romania	81	2.93	81	3.57	88	3.46	52	3.87	96	1.95	66	2.64
Russian Federation	61	3.44	61	4.04	68	4.03	39	4.09	76	2.46	55	3.19
Senegal	67	3.33	56	4.19	41	4.44	72	3.56	62	2.74	76	2.19
Serbia	87	2.83	86	3.47	86	3.47	75	3.48	56	2.91	93	1.48
Singapore	1	5.69	2	5.16	2	5.61	42	4.04	1	6.12	17	6.31
Slovak Republic	50	3.82	44	4.35	61	4.17	11	4.78	64	2.72	43	3.87
Slovenia	37	4.27	53	4.20	62	4.15	22	4.33	31	3.71	29	4.95
South Africa	40	4.08	41	4.38	56	4.24	12	4.71	37	3.61	40	3.95
Spain	17	4.83	35	4.44	23	4.62	46	3.99	22	4.11	16	6.35
Sri Lanka	65	3.35	71	3.85	79	3.69	30	4.26	53	2.99	65	2.70
Sweden	8	5.13	24	4.57	16	4.88	57	3.80	10	4.83	13	6.56
Switzerland	6	5.31	10	4.78	6	5.26	70	3.57	13	4.69	1	7.00
Taiwan	18	4.82	9	4.82	15	4.90	15	4.62	20	4.14	24	5.51
Tanzania	76	3.12	79	3.61	87	3.47	48	3.96	43	3.47	83	1.80
Thailand	26	4.54	1	5.28	5	5.28	4	5.30	34	3.67	41	3.94
Trinidad and Tobago	47	3.85	34	4.44	51	4.29	10	4.81	69	2.63	42	3.88
Tunisia	32	4.38	31	4.46	34	4.54	29	4.27	11	4.77	45	3.83
Turkey	82	2.93	94	3.27	96	3.09	62	3.73	75	2.47	63	2.71
Uganda	71	3.20	58	4.14	58	4.22	49	3.93	60	2.79	85	1.75
Ukraine	70	3.27	42	4.37	25	4.60	58	3.78	85	2.30	78	2.04
United Kingdom	12	4.99	54	4.20	42	4.43	67	3.62	12	4.75	5	6.82
United States	14	4.94	52	4.23	45	4.33	47	3.98	16	4.44	3	6.86
Uruguay	89	2.75	102	2.42	100	2.65	102	1.84	33	3.67	70	2.48
Venezuela	94	2.59	95	3.21	80	3.66	101	2.09	102	1.63	72	2.33
Vietnam	45	3.87	16	4.65	33	4.54	9	4.93	40	3.57	67	2.61
Zambia	97	2.49	96	3.16	93	3.20	88	3.05	84	2.32	95	1.35
Zimbabwe	102	1.98	101	2.56	101	2.41	92	2.94	100	1.78	100	1.00

Source: World Economic Forum

Table 6: Public institutions index components

Public institutions index			Contracts and law subindex			Corruption index		
Country	Rank	Score	Country	Rank	Score	Country	Rank	Score
Algeria	66	3.92	Algeria	59	3.85	Algeria	72	3.98
Angola	91	3.16	Angola	90	2.76	Angola	91	3.56
Argentina	88	3.22	Argentina	99	2.28	Argentina	65	4.15
Australia	4	6.36	Australia	3	6.10	Australia	6	6.62
Austria	14	5.83	Austria	14	5.47	Austria	16	6.20
Bangladesh	100	2.48	Bangladesh	86	2.93	Bangladesh	102	2.04
Belgium	27	5.41	Belgium	25	5.00	Belgium	29	5.82
Bolivia	79	3.51	Bolivia	85	2.93	Bolivia	70	4.10
Botswana	26	5.45	Botswana	16	5.43	Botswana	36	5.47
Brazil	53	4.27	Brazil	57	3.92	Brazil	56	4.62
Bulgaria	62	4.10	Bulgaria	92	2.71	Bulgaria	35	5.50
Cameroon	95	3.04	Cameroon	82	3.02	Cameroon	97	3.06
Canada	24	5.48	Canada	26	4.99	Canada	25	5.98
Chad	101	2.36	Chad	101	2.20	Chad	101	2.52
Chile	19	5.62	Chile	29	4.93	Chile	13	6.30
China	52	4.33	China	60	3.81	China	50	4.84
Colombia	60	4.13	Colombia	79	3.16	Colombia	44	5.10
Costa Rica	49	4.49	Costa Rica	48	4.17	Costa Rica	51	4.81
Croatia	67	3.87	Croatia	81	3.06	Croatia	54	4.68
Czech Republic	47	4.51	Czech Republic	61	3.81	Czech Republic	41	5.21
Denmark	1	6.56	Denmark	2	6.30	Denmark	1	6.82
Dominican Republic	64	4.05	Dominican Republic	53	4.02	Dominican Republic	71	4.07
Ecuador	80	3.48	Ecuador	89	2.77	Ecuador	63	4.18
Egypt	57	4.18	Egypt	47	4.23	Egypt	67	4.14
El Salvador	40	4.72	El Salvador	64	3.65	El Salvador	31	5.79
Estonia	28	5.36	Estonia	32	4.85	Estonia	27	5.86
Ethiopia	73	3.69	Ethiopia	68	3.50	Ethiopia	76	3.89
Finland	2	6.52	Finland	1	6.35	Finland	4	6.68
France	23	5.50	France	27	4.96	France	23	6.03
Gambia	39	4.73	Gambia	23	5.05	Gambia	58	4.42
Germany	9	6.10	Germany	9	5.80	Germany	10	6.39
Ghana	65	3.97	Ghana	50	4.07	Ghana	79	3.87
Greece	42	4.71	Greece	37	4.63	Greece	52	4.79
Guatemala	87	3.22	Guatemala	97	2.33	Guatemala	68	4.12
Haiti	102	2.28	Haiti	102	1.91	Haiti	100	2.64
Honduras	99	2.85	Honduras	95	2.50	Honduras	96	3.20
Hong Kong SAR	10	6.03	Hong Kong SAR	12	5.65	Hong Kong SAR	9	6.42
Hungary	33	5.18	Hungary	39	4.52	Hungary	28	5.84
Iceland	3	6.44	Iceland	4	6.08	Iceland	2	6.80
India	55	4.26	India	35	4.65	India	80	3.86
Indonesia	76	3.63	Indonesia	65	3.63	Indonesia	88	3.64
Ireland	25	5.46	Ireland	31	4.88	Ireland	22	6.03
Israel	15	5.82	Israel	19	5.39	Israel	14	6.26
Italy	46	4.56	Italy	49	4.15	Italy	47	4.96
Jamaica	70	3.77	Jamaica	72	3.38	Jamaica	64	4.15
Japan	30	5.30	Japan	38	4.57	Japan	21	6.04
Jordan	20	5.58	Jordan	15	5.44	Jordan	33	5.72
Kenya	92	3.16	Kenya	80	3.09	Kenya	95	3.22
Korea	36	5.03	Korea	34	4.72	Korea	38	5.34
Latvia	45	4.61	Latvia	44	4.37	Latvia	49	4.85
Lithuania	41	4.71	Lithuania	58	3.89	Lithuania	34	5.53
Luxembourg	13	5.92	Luxembourg	13	5.60	Luxembourg	15	6.23
Macedonia, FYR	93	3.11	Macedonia, FYR	96	2.48	Macedonia, FYR	86	3.75
Madagascar	96	3.04	Madagascar	88	2.84	Madagascar	94	3.24
Malawi	38	4.79	Malawi	42	4.44	Malawi	43	5.14
Malaysia	34	5.12	Malaysia	28	4.95	Malaysia	39	5.28
Mali	83	3.33	Mali	62	3.71	Mali	98	2.96
Malta	18	5.68	Malta	20	5.28	Malta	18	6.08
Mauritius	44	4.61	Mauritius	36	4.64	Mauritius	57	4.58
Mexico	50	4.35	Mexico	63	3.70	Mexico	46	5.00
Morocco	68	3.86	Morocco	55	3.96	Morocco	85	3.76
Mozambique	82	3.33	Mozambique	87	2.89	Mozambique	83	3.78
Namibia	48	4.50	Namibia	45	4.33	Namibia	55	4.66
Netherlands	11	6.02	Netherlands	11	5.66	Netherlands	11	6.37
New Zealand	5	6.36	New Zealand	5	6.03	New Zealand	3	6.69
Nicaragua	78	3.57	Nicaragua	84	2.94	Nicaragua	62	4.19
Nigeria	98	2.99	Nigeria	78	3.17	Nigeria	99	2.81
Norway	16	5.73	Norway	18	5.40	Norway	20	6.06
Pakistan	74	3.67	Pakistan	69	3.46	Pakistan	77	3.88
Panama	71	3.75	Panama	74	3.26	Panama	60	4.23

(cont'd)

Table 6: Public institutions index components *(cont'd.)*

Public institutions index

Country	Rank	Score
Paraguay	97	3.01
Peru	54	4.27
Philippines	85	3.29
Poland	58	4.17
Portugal	22	5.52
Romania	86	3.27
Russian Federation	81	3.34
Senegal	75	3.64
Serbia	77	3.58
Singapore	6	6.28
Slovak Republic	51	4.33
Slovenia	35	5.11
South Africa	43	4.69
Spain	31	5.28
Sri Lanka	72	3.70
Sweden	7	6.28
Switzerland	8	6.20
Taiwan	21	5.55
Tanzania	59	4.15
Thailand	37	4.97
Trinidad and Tobago	56	4.21
Tunisia	32	5.19
Turkey	63	4.07
Uganda	84	3.30
Ukraine	94	3.09
United Kingdom	12	6.01
United States	17	5.71
Uruguay	29	5.31
Venezuela	89	3.21
Vietnam	61	4.11
Zambia	69	3.86
Zimbabwe	90	3.21

Contracts and law subindex

Country	Rank	Score
Paraguay	98	2.29
Peru	76	3.19
Philippines	75	3.20
Poland	66	3.59
Portugal	21	5.22
Romania	83	2.97
Russian Federation	91	2.74
Senegal	71	3.40
Serbia	77	3.19
Singapore	7	5.89
Slovak Republic	70	3.42
Slovenia	43	4.44
South Africa	40	4.51
Spain	41	4.46
Sri Lanka	67	3.57
Sweden	6	6.00
Switzerland	8	5.87
Taiwan	24	5.03
Tanzania	46	4.31
Thailand	30	4.88
Trinidad and Tobago	51	4.03
Tunisia	22	5.20
Turkey	52	4.03
Uganda	73	3.35
Ukraine	94	2.57
United Kingdom	10	5.67
United States	17	5.42
Uruguay	33	4.74
Venezuela	100	2.27
Vietnam	54	4.00
Zambia	56	3.92
Zimbabwe	93	2.64

Corruption index

Country	Rank	Score
Paraguay	87	3.73
Peru	37	5.34
Philippines	92	3.39
Poland	53	4.75
Portugal	30	5.81
Romania	90	3.58
Russian Federation	75	3.94
Senegal	78	3.88
Serbia	74	3.96
Singapore	5	6.68
Slovak Republic	40	5.24
Slovenia	32	5.78
South Africa	48	4.87
Spain	17	6.09
Sri Lanka	81	3.84
Sweden	7	6.55
Switzerland	8	6.53
Taiwan	19	6.08
Tanzania	73	3.98
Thailand	45	5.06
Trinidad and Tobago	59	4.39
Tunisia	42	5.18
Turkey	69	4.12
Uganda	93	3.24
Ukraine	89	3.61
United Kingdom	12	6.35
United States	24	6.01
Uruguay	26	5.89
Venezuela	66	4.15
Vietnam	61	4.22
Zambia	82	3.79
Zimbabwe	84	3.77

Source: World Economic Forum

Table 7: Technology index components

Country	Technology index Rank	Technology index Score	Innovation subindex OVERALL Rank	OVERALL Score	HARD DATA Rank	HARD DATA Score	SURVEY DATA Rank	SURVEY DATA Score	ICT subindex OVERALL Rank	OVERALL Score	HARD DATA Rank	HARD DATA Score	SURVEY DATA Rank	SURVEY DATA Score	Technology transfer subindex Rank	Technology transfer subindex Score
Algeria	96	2.48	74	1.86	68	1.53	88	2.86	91	2.22	85	2.04	96	2.58	76	3.04
Angola	98	2.43	102	1.34	100	1.01	101	2.34	100	1.68	97	1.33	98	2.36	66	3.80
Argentina	45	4.22	33	2.94	33	2.74	59	3.54	47	3.96	44	4.28	75	3.32	25	5.00
Australia*	19	4.90	18	3.96	18	3.71	19	4.71	14	5.84	13	6.19	14	5.15	—	—
Austria*	27	4.69	20	3.87	17	3.73	26	4.29	22	5.51	20	5.90	26	4.73	—	—
Bangladesh	95	2.68	91	1.58	79	1.23	93	2.65	99	1.86	100	1.27	90	3.03	61	4.14
Belgium*	29	4.65	17	4.00	16	3.75	16	4.78	25	5.29	23	5.76	33	4.34	—	—
Bolivia	88	3.06	52	2.31	41	2.28	98	2.40	79	2.82	73	2.81	92	2.83	68	3.63
Botswana	59	3.78	80	1.73	84	1.16	65	3.46	65	3.37	63	3.30	70	3.49	24	5.00
Brazil	35	4.44	60	2.25	63	1.59	30	4.21	43	4.23	46	4.22	36	4.26	2	5.44
Bulgaria	63	3.72	43	2.59	36	2.47	84	2.98	49	3.94	45	4.25	73	3.33	67	3.79
Cameroon	93	2.80	85	1.68	83	1.17	77	3.22	92	2.20	90	1.70	78	3.20	65	3.97
Canada*	11	5.15	9	4.45	9	4.25	13	5.06	13	5.85	14	6.15	10	5.26	—	—
Chad	102	2.06	101	1.36	98	1.02	100	2.36	102	1.44	101	1.13	102	2.04	75	3.14
Chile	31	4.60	35	2.79	38	2.35	37	4.10	36	4.67	39	4.72	29	4.58	18	5.11
China	65	3.67	70	1.97	78	1.26	36	4.11	62	3.42	67	3.08	43	4.09	47	4.57
Colombia	60	3.76	57	2.28	56	1.83	54	3.63	57	3.63	60	3.52	51	3.85	50	4.42
Costa Rica	46	4.19	61	2.21	65	1.58	35	4.12	52	3.86	47	4.20	79	3.19	8	5.28
Croatia	41	4.32	48	2.44	48	2.06	58	3.56	39	4.54	35	4.93	59	3.76	43	4.64
Czech Republic	21	4.84	45	2.57	47	2.10	40	3.99	30	5.04	29	5.50	41	4.11	5	5.35
Denmark*	8	5.25	11	4.26	12	3.92	9	5.28	4	6.25	3	6.62	5	5.52	—	—
Dominican Republic	52	3.98	55	2.30	57	1.82	50	3.72	61	3.50	61	3.38	61	3.74	13	5.18
Ecuador	76	3.27	72	1.94	62	1.63	87	2.89	72	2.97	66	3.10	93	2.72	62	4.11
Egypt	68	3.64	39	2.71	37	2.40	56	3.62	69	3.13	76	2.63	40	4.12	44	4.63
El Salvador	67	3.64	67	2.05	61	1.65	74	3.26	68	3.20	69	3.00	67	3.59	34	4.77
Estonia	10	5.16	26	3.38	26	3.10	31	4.21	20	5.55	26	5.60	7	5.44	11	5.24
Ethiopia	100	2.17	100	1.36	96	1.05	102	2.31	101	1.50	102	1.12	100	2.27	73	3.34
Finland*	2	6.00	3	5.71	3	5.55	1	6.19	2	6.29	6	6.48	2	5.90	—	—
France*	28	4.67	19	3.92	19	3.60	15	4.89	23	5.42	24	5.74	23	4.77	—	—
Gambia	80	3.22	96	1.48	95	1.06	92	2.76	73	2.94	79	2.43	45	3.95	58	4.17
Germany*	14	5.03	10	4.36	11	4.03	8	5.35	17	5.71	16	6.11	19	4.89	—	—
Ghana	86	3.10	83	1.69	89	1.11	67	3.45	88	2.32	91	1.59	54	3.79	45	4.61
Greece	30	4.64	31	3.02	32	2.81	53	3.64	33	4.82	32	5.31	53	3.83	27	4.95
Guatemala	79	3.23	79	1.74	77	1.29	81	3.08	77	2.84	70	2.93	94	2.65	54	4.25
Haiti	101	2.17	99	1.37	97	1.03	99	2.37	96	1.96	88	1.87	101	2.15	77	2.71
Honduras	87	3.08	77	1.76	69	1.52	97	2.46	85	2.46	80	2.40	97	2.58	53	4.35
Hong Kong SAR*	37	4.40	34	2.86	39	2.31	22	4.51	8	5.94	11	6.33	12	5.15	—	—
Hungary	32	4.57	38	2.76	35	2.48	57	3.58	35	4.68	33	5.08	49	3.88	21	5.04
Iceland*	15	5.01	21	3.70	25	3.20	10	5.20	1	6.32	2	6.71	4	5.53	—	—
India	64	3.68	66	2.06	73	1.37	34	4.13	75	2.87	86	2.02	30	4.58	7	5.31
Indonesia	78	3.25	65	2.08	70	1.52	47	3.76	74	2.91	78	2.53	63	3.66	63	4.09
Ireland*	38	4.37	24	3.48	28	3.04	17	4.77	27	5.26	22	5.79	39	4.20	—	—
Israel*	9	5.17	6	4.80	7	4.54	5	5.58	21	5.54	21	5.81	16	4.99	—	—
Italy*	44	4.24	28	3.33	27	3.10	38	4.05	28	5.14	27	5.59	38	4.22	—	—
Jamaica	53	3.97	64	2.10	64	1.59	55	3.63	53	3.84	53	3.78	46	3.95	36	4.76
Japan*	5	5.56	5	5.49	4	5.43	4	5.65	18	5.63	18	5.98	17	4.94	—	—
Jordan	48	4.13	47	2.44	52	2.03	51	3.70	46	3.98	57	3.60	25	4.74	28	4.89
Kenya	74	3.36	84	1.68	90	1.10	68	3.44	86	2.46	83	2.09	80	3.19	17	5.11
Korea*	6	5.28	7	4.69	6	4.59	14	4.98	11	5.88	17	5.98	3	5.68	—	—
Latvia	26	4.71	22	3.52	22	3.27	27	4.27	34	4.73	36	4.93	32	4.35	19	5.07
Lithuania	36	4.43	30	3.14	30	2.89	42	3.88	38	4.58	37	4.83	44	4.08	42	4.65
Luxembourg*	42	4.30	40	2.68	44	2.15	25	4.30	10	5.92	7	6.43	18	4.90	—	—
Macedonia, FYR	70	3.53	63	2.12	54	1.87	89	2.85	63	3.41	59	3.52	82	3.18	59	4.16
Madagascar	97	2.47	93	1.55	93	1.07	82	3.00	94	1.99	96	1.42	84	3.14	72	3.40
Malawi	94	2.79	95	1.49	102	1.00	85	2.95	98	1.90	98	1.32	88	3.06	52	4.42
Malaysia	20	4.89	41	2.66	51	2.03	21	4.56	32	4.84	41	4.67	11	5.18	1	5.69
Mali	99	2.36	98	1.42	94	1.06	96	2.52	97	1.91	99	1.31	85	3.12	74	3.26
Malta	17	4.95	53	2.31	58	1.79	43	3.86	24	5.37	28	5.52	15	5.08	10	5.25
Mauritius	49	4.10	73	1.90	72	1.40	71	3.39	40	4.37	42	4.51	42	4.09	48	4.47
Mexico	43	4.26	59	2.25	60	1.75	48	3.76	48	3.95	50	3.98	47	3.90	6	5.35
Morocco	71	3.50	71	1.95	74	1.36	49	3.74	71	2.99	75	2.68	66	3.61	40	4.69
Mozambique	92	2.84	97	1.46	101	1.01	91	2.80	95	1.97	95	1.42	87	3.07	49	4.46
Namibia	62	3.72	76	1.82	81	1.20	52	3.66	64	3.40	64	3.24	62	3.73	33	4.78
Netherlands*	18	4.93	14	4.04	14	3.84	20	4.63	15	5.82	8	6.39	27	4.69	—	—
New Zealand*	23	4.80	16	4.02	13	3.86	23	4.49	19	5.58	19	5.97	22	4.80	—	—
Nicaragua	85	3.12	81	1.72	71	1.42	94	2.65	83	2.66	77	2.56	91	2.86	57	4.21
Nigeria	82	3.16	88	1.66	85	1.13	78	3.22	93	2.11	94	1.52	77	3.29	20	5.07
Norway*	13	5.08	12	4.23	10	4.05	18	4.76	9	5.93	4	6.52	24	4.76	—	—
Pakistan	83	3.16	94	1.54	88	1.12	90	2.81	84	2.50	89	1.80	48	3.88	46	4.58
Panama	50	4.10	42	2.64	43	2.25	45	3.80	58	3.59	58	3.56	64	3.65	9	5.26

(cont'd)

Table 7: Technology index components (cont'd.)

Country	Technology index		Innovation subindex						ICT subindex						Technology transfer subindex	
			OVERALL		HARD DATA		SURVEY DATA		OVERALL		HARD DATA		SURVEY DATA			
	Rank	Score	Rank	Score	Rank	Score	Rank	Score	Rank	Score	Rank	Score	Rank	Score	Rank	Score
Paraguay	91	2.96	89	1.65	75	1.36	95	2.53	76	2.87	65	3.15	99	2.30	70	3.52
Peru	61	3.75	54	2.30	49	2.03	80	3.12	66	3.36	62	3.32	72	3.45	37	4.75
Philippines	56	3.92	49	2.41	45	2.12	72	3.28	67	3.33	68	3.06	50	3.87	12	5.22
Poland	34	4.44	29	3.20	29	3.00	44	3.80	41	4.36	38	4.72	65	3.65	26	4.97
Portugal	22	4.82	32	2.98	31	2.81	63	3.47	29	5.04	30	5.42	35	4.29	15	5.14
Romania	55	3.93	56	2.30	53	1.98	75	3.25	54	3.75	54	3.73	55	3.78	38	4.73
Russian Federation	69	3.61	27	3.36	21	3.32	62	3.47	56	3.66	51	3.84	76	3.31	69	3.62
Senegal	89	3.04	82	1.70	87	1.12	69	3.43	81	2.67	82	2.26	69	3.49	64	3.98
Serbia	66	3.66	62	2.13	55	1.86	86	2.93	55	3.69	52	3.79	71	3.48	60	4.14
Singapore*	12	5.09	15	4.04	20	3.54	6	5.51	6	6.14	12	6.21	1	5.99	—	—
Slovak Republic	33	4.55	44	2.58	46	2.10	39	4.03	37	4.60	34	5.02	57	3.77	16	5.13
Slovenia	24	4.73	23	3.51	23	3.26	28	4.27	26	5.28	25	5.69	31	4.45	51	4.42
South Africa	40	4.35	58	2.27	66	1.57	24	4.37	44	4.09	49	4.00	37	4.26	3	5.39
Spain	25	4.72	25	3.46	24	3.21	32	4.19	31	4.99	31	5.33	34	4.32	35	4.77
Sri Lanka	72	3.47	78	1.76	82	1.18	61	3.48	78	2.83	81	2.37	58	3.76	29	4.89
Sweden*	4	5.90	4	5.52	5	5.41	3	5.85	3	6.28	1	6.76	9	5.32	—	—
Switzerland*	7	5.26	8	4.65	8	4.40	7	5.42	12	5.87	9	6.35	20	4.89	—	—
Taiwan*	3	5.97	2	5.92	2	6.18	11	5.16	7	6.01	10	6.35	8	5.33	—	—
Tanzania	81	3.22	90	1.63	99	1.01	60	3.48	90	2.27	93	1.53	60	3.76	23	5.01
Thailand	39	4.37	37	2.76	42	2.27	29	4.23	45	4.01	56	3.70	28	4.64	4	5.38
Trinidad and Tobago	47	4.13	75	1.86	80	1.22	46	3.76	50	3.93	43	4.37	89	3.05	14	5.16
Tunisia	57	3.90	50	2.38	59	1.77	33	4.19	59	3.57	71	2.92	21	4.86	31	4.85
Turkey	54	3.96	68	2.01	67	1.53	66	3.46	51	3.88	48	4.16	74	3.32	39	4.72
Uganda	77	3.25	86	1.67	91	1.10	70	3.40	89	2.31	92	1.58	56	3.77	22	5.03
Ukraine	84	3.15	36	2.79	34	2.56	64	3.46	70	3.00	72	2.91	81	3.19	71	3.46
United Kingdom*	16	4.96	13	4.11	15	3.78	12	5.08	16	5.81	15	6.15	13	5.15	—	—
United States*	1	6.30	1	6.44	1	6.61	2	5.92	5	6.16	5	6.50	6	5.48	—	—
Uruguay	51	4.04	46	2.51	40	2.30	79	3.12	42	4.30	40	4.68	68	3.53	56	4.22
Venezuela	58	3.84	51	2.34	50	2.03	73	3.27	60	3.51	55	3.71	86	3.10	32	4.78
Vietnam	73	3.41	69	1.98	76	1.34	41	3.90	82	2.67	84	2.09	52	3.83	30	4.87
Zambia	90	2.96	92	1.55	92	1.08	83	2.98	87	2.34	87	1.93	83	3.17	55	4.25
Zimbabwe	75	3.34	87	1.66	86	1.13	76	3.23	80	2.75	74	2.81	95	2.64	41	4.68

*Classified as a core technology-innovating economy
Source: World Economic Forum

Moving in the counter direction, **Japan** rose to the 11th position from the 16th, with varying levels of performance in the different component indexes. Amid a shrinking of the government deficit—to still high levels at 7.1 percent of GDP (rank #81)—the business sector remained in a gloomy mood, as reflected in a worsening of recession expectations (rank #83). Japan's macroeconomic environment performance (rank #24) has also been weakened further by a decline in the country credit rating, as well as lower scores in the area of government waste, specifically, distortive government subsidies (rank #90). Japan got a boost however, from its technology performance, particularly in light of an increase in the number of patents and a more favorable perception of government success in ICT promotion.

Likewise, **Germany's** rise by one position masks more dramatic changes in underlying performance. Notably, Germany posted widespread improvements in the quality of its public institutions, including control of corruption (rank #10) and decline in the favoritism in the decisions of government officials (rank #8). The extent of distortive government subsidies however, continues to be perceived very poorly (rank #100), a rank without peer in the developed world. Improvements in the quality of public institutions were partly offset by deterioration in the macroeconomic environment, characterized by the widening of the government deficit to 3.6 percent of GDP (rank #54) and the heightening of recession expectations (rank #91).

Israel posted one of the more notable declines in the macroeconomic environment component of the index, characterized by heightened recession expectations (rank #100), perceived tightening of access to credit (rank #66), and higher inflation. Israel's worsened macroeconomic situation (rank #44) stands in sharp contrast to its relatively high ranking (rank #15) on a broad range of indicators which reflect the quality of its public institutions. The independence of its judiciary (rank #2) is particularly noteworthy. Although Israel maintains its edge in technology, it is notable that ratings pertaining to government prioritization of ICT (rank #58) and government success in ICT promotion (rank #21) declined. Nevertheless, Israel retains a relatively high rank overall (rank #20), given its high level of technological sophistication (rank #9 in the technology index).

Western Europe

In Western Europe, new entrants **Malta** and Luxembourg hold the 19th and 21st positions, respectively, in the overall index. Malta, which holds the highest ranking among 22 new entrants, fares relatively well in the area of technology (rank #17). Specifically, the government scores highly in its prioritization of ICT (rank #6) and success in ICT promotion (rank #7) although it rates less favorably in terms of innovation (rank #53). Malta also enjoys relatively high ratings of its public institutions (rank #18), but its macroeconomic environment is a source of weakness (rank #29). Malta's overall score in the latter is weighed down by its government deficit at 5.2 percent of GDP (rank #67), and relatively low savings rate of 18.7 percent of GDP (rank #62).

Luxembourg, the second highest new entrant, performs very well in the macroeconomic environment (rank #3) and public institutions (rank #13) indexes. The country rates poorly, however, in the area of technology, and, like Malta, is weak in innovation (rank #40), particularly in terms of university/industry research collaboration (rank #64) and in tertiary enrollment (rank #76). Notably though, the country scores well in the diffusion of ICT.

France, at the 26th place, received a boost in its rankings due to higher scores in public institutions and technology, which offset a decline in the macroeconomic environment. France's macroeconomic stability score had deteriorated, marked by an expansion of government deficit to 3.2 percent of GDP (rank #47) amid heightened recession expectations (rank #80). Nonetheless, France posted significant improvements in the quality of public institutions, including in the incidence of corruption linked to property rights (rank #20) and payments irregularities. Dramatic improvements were also evident in the perceptions of corruption as well as public trust of politicians. Scores also increased in the area of technology, as reflected in the improved ranks in government prioritization of ICT (rank #26) and government success in ICT promotion (rank #26).

Unlike France, **Ireland** posted a significant decline in the rankings, falling to the 30th position due to widespread declines in the different components of the index. Perceptions of government waste deteriorated drastically, marked by lower scores for diversion of public funds (rank #26) and the extent of distortive government subsidies (rank #32). The quality of public institutions also worsened across the board, with the most notable declines evident in the assessments of the independence of the judiciary (rank #26) and favoritism in the decisions of government officials (rank #40). In the area of technology, perceptions also became less favorable toward the quality of competition in the ISP sector (rank #97), government prioritization of ICT (rank #31), and government success in ICT promotion (rank #20).

Italy, at the 41st position, also plummeted in the rankings like Ireland, reflecting across-the-board declines in the major components of the index, particularly its macroeconomic environment. The country posted low scores in macroeconomic stability (rank #50), stemming from a worsening recession expectations (rank #66), a deterioration in the government deficit to 2.5 percent of GDP (rank #39) and a decline in the national savings rate (rank #55). Italy also scored poorly in the area of government waste (rank #50). Perceptions of the quality of public institutions also deteriorated, as reflected in lower scores in the control of corruption (rank #47) and extent of organized crime (rank #76). In technology, lower scores were also recorded with regard to government prioritization of ICT (rank #65) and government success in ICT promotion (rank #58).

Central and eastern Europe

Among central and eastern European countries and CIS states, **Estonia** maintains its leadership at 22nd place in the overall rankings, enjoying the highest technology, public institutions, and macroeconomic environment scores in the region. The country's overall global rankings received a boost from better performance in technology, marked by higher tertiary enrollment scores, a sharp increase in the number of utility patents filed, and an all-around increase in the diffusion of ICT. Estonia's macroeconomic environment also received higher scores, derived from perceptions of better access to credit (rank #5) and more favorable recession expectations (rank #6). Estonia's public institutions also received higher ratings pertaining to the independence of the judiciary and safeguarding of property rights.

In the region, **Latvia** is most notable for posting one of the most improved performances across the various components. Latvia posted the 3rd most improved score in the GCI, stemming primarily from achieving the 2nd most improved in macroeconomic environment and the 5th most improved score in public institutions in the world. The former is driven by gains in the rating of government waste, specifically, strengthening of public trust in politicians as well as the perception of a decline in the extent of distortive government subsidies. In the area of public institutions, Latvia posted better ratings pertaining to the independence of the judiciary and favoritism in the decisions of government officials. The country also posted the third highest improvement in enrollment rates in the world, and the second highest improvement in the perceptions of the country's technological sophistication.

Although **Ukraine**, at 84th place, has the lowest rank in Europe, the country has posted improvements in certain areas. The country still has the worst public institutions score in the region, but its macroeconomic environment has shown signs of increasing stability, as reflected also by the rise in its credit rating score. Similarly, **Russia's** overall credit rating has also improved but the quality of public institutions continue to deteriorate particularly in terms of corruption.

Asia

In Asia, **Korea** posted one of the most notable ascents in the GCI rankings from the 25th place to the 18th position. Korea's rise in the rankings was driven by improvements in its macroeconomic environment, specifically a turnaround from a deficit position to a government surplus at 6.0 percent of GDP (rank #2). Equally important, perceptions of government waste improved, marked by increased public trust in politicians and a better score in the area of diversion of public funds. Korea also posted remarkable improvements in its technology performance, boosted by a rise in tertiary enrollment rate from 67.7 percent to 77.6 percent (rank #2) and one of the highest increases in patent activity.

Like Korea, **Thailand** and **Vietnam** registered notable improvements in overall rankings. For Thailand, the boost stemmed from its macroeconomic environment, as reflected in improved recession expectations (rank #2) and better access to credit (rank #7). For Vietnam, the rise was driven by across-the-board improvements in the quality of its public institutions.

Although **Indonesia** declines in the overall rankings, the country posts one of the most significant increases in its actual score. Its macroeconomic environment score is the 5th most improved, marked by dramatically better scores in the area of government waste: extent of distortive subsidies (rank #30), diversion of public funds (rank #45), and public trust of politicians (rank #38). Its scores pertaining to public institutions all posted significant increases, but these are not reflected in the overall rankings given the entry of many new countries to the index.

Malaysia and **India** both derived gains from improvements in the area of technology. Malaysia posted the second largest increase in technology ranks to the 20th position, driven by one of the highest jumps in tertiary enrollment rate, as well as even higher ratings in the perception of government prioritization of ICT (rank #2) and government success in ICT promotion (rank #2). Meanwhile, India posts the highest improvement in the perception of the country's technological sophistication with a decline in the ratings of the government's success in ICT promotion.

There was a notable downward shift in the ranking of **China**. The drop in the ranking was marked by a deterioration in the perceived quality of public institutions. Lower scores were posted in terms of the independence of the judiciary (rank #62) and extent of organized crime (rank #60). Perceptions of corruption worsened particularly with regard to tax collection and for connection to public utilities. Public trust of politicians, while still strong (rank #20), also fell along with scores on diversion of public funds (rank #51). And despite improvements in innovative activity and greater diffusion of Internet use and cellular phone penetration, China posted lower scores in government prioritization of ICT and government success in ICT promotion.

Like China, **Sri Lanka** and **Bangladesh** both experienced a dramatic drop in the rankings due to deterioration in the quality of public institutions. Sri Lanka posted the worst decline in scores relating to various types of corruption, judicial independence, extent of organized crime, and favoritism in the decisions of government officials. Bangladesh experienced similar declines but to a lesser degree; the country still has the worst score in the control of corruption (rank #102).

Latin America

In Latin America, **Chile** continues to have the highest rank in the region followed, with a considerable gap, by Mexico. Although Chile has the highest scores in the region in all three index components, the country has experienced notable deterioration in the area of government waste, posting the worst decline in public trust in politicians, and diversion of public funds.

Brazil and **Argentina** both posted significant declines in the macroeconomic environment. Brazil's drop was precipitated by the worsening of the government deficit to 8.7 percent of GDP in 2002, when inflation rose to 8.4 percent and the interest rate ballooned to 43.5 percent. In the case of Argentina, the government deficit expanded to 10.3 percent of GDP, while the inflation rate rose sharply as well. For both countries, the quality of public institutions also declined: for Brazil the most notable deterioration is in the area of organized crime (rank #84), while for Argentina, corruption deteriorated and the country continues to have the worst rating in terms of property rights (rank #102). But technology offers a bright spot for both countries: tertiary enrollment increased significantly and diffusion of ICT continues at a very fast pace in Brazil; while government prioritization of ICT and success of government ICT promotion both received higher ratings in Argentina.

But among the countries in the region, the biggest declines in the rankings were posted by **Uruguay** and **Jamaica**. Uruguay fell due to drastic deterioration of its macroeconomic environment as evident in the largest decline in credit rating. Lower scores in the macroeconomic environment also pushed Jamaica lower in the rankings, but not to the same extent as the decline in public institutions (rank #70), particularly corruption where the country posted the 2nd largest decline. The country also experienced a deterioration in the extent of organized crime (rank #100).

At the opposite extreme, **Mexico** and **El Salvador** experienced the most notable improvements in performance. Among other gains, Mexico registered one of the most notable improvements in the scores pertaining to independence of the judiciary, diversion of public funds, and other indicators of the quality of public institutions. Mexico's technology position also improved amid deterio-

ration in the macroeconomic environment. El Salvador posted greater gains in all components of the index, with the greatest boost stemming from improvements in the quality of the public institutions.

Ecuador and **Bolivia** are also notable performers—both benefiting from higher ratings of its public institutions. Ecuador posted improvements in contracts and law, particularly in terms of the independence of the judiciary, safeguarding of property rights, and reduction in the extent of organized crime. Meanwhile, Bolivia's gains were in the area of corruption—specifically, irregular payments in export and import permits as well as irregular payments toward connection to public utilities

Middle East and Africa

In the Middle East, **Jordan** and **Turkey** both post major improvements in the quality of public institutions. Jordan, in particular, posted the largest score and rank increase in this area, driven by gains in control of corruption and greater independence of the judiciary. The country also posted better ratings relating to public trust in politicians, diversion of public funds, and the extent of distortive subsidies. Likewise, but to a lesser extent, Turkey also posted significant improvements in the control of corruption and the independence of the judiciary.

Of the countries in Africa, **Botswana** enjoys the highest ranking in the Global Competitiveness Index. Botswana's position in the public institutions index (rank #26), the highest in the Africa region, was buoyed by perceptions of a decline in organized crime and favoritism by government officials. The country also has the highest macroeconomic environment ranking in the region, bolstered by its high savings rate (rank #5) and favorable recession expectations (rank #17). Compared with the other components, Botswana has a lower ranking in technology, where despite increases in ICT diffusion, significant drawbacks remain, including lack of competition in the ISP sector (rank #93).

But in the area of technology, **South Africa** leads the region, particularly in the field of innovation, driven by high scores in patent activity (rank #31), company spending in R&D (rank #21) and university/industry research collaboration. South Africa's overall competitiveness ranking is lower than last year's because of a deterioration in a number of factors which enter the index through its public institutions component. Noteworthy in this regard are the prevalence of crime (rank #81) and irregularities arising in connection with the payment of taxes, including on international trade.

Seventeen of the 22 new entrants to the index are from Africa. Of the region's new entrants, Gambia and Egypt occupy the highest positions at 55th and 58th, respectively. Tanzania follows at 69, while Ghana, Algeria, Malawi, and Senegal are clustered in the 70th ranks.

Box 2: Hyperinflation and deflation

Inflation has long been recognized by economists as a destabilizing factor for an economy, and thus for economic growth, by distorting the behavior of economic actors. For this reason, inflation is included in the macroeconomic stability subindex of the GCI. At present, inflation enters the index in a "linear" fashion. In other words, every increment of inflation erodes a country's overall GCI score in a parallel manner.

However, although this constitutes a good first approach to taking into account the potential destabilizing effects of inflation, it also raises two questions. The first is how to deal with the critical problem of hyperinflation. The second is how to deal with deflation, a topic that has received much attention of late.

Hyperinflation

With regards to hyperinflation, the idea of having the index punish very high inflation countries more than incrementally is very appealing. In principle this might be possible, since it has been suggested in the literature that there is a measurable point after which inflation starts to negatively affect growth strongly.[2]

However, upon further reflection, it is very difficult to actually implement this, since the standard error would have such a large range (say between 6 and 14 percent). In other words, any threshold and slope we choose would be arbitrary.[3] For this reason we have decided to explore the question further before choosing how to punish hyperinflationary countries more strongly in the index. We will come back to this issue in future editions of the GCI.

Deflation

In recent years, a great deal of attention has been paid to the potential problems associated with deflation. Of particular concern is the danger of an economy falling into a deflationary spiral out of which it is difficult to emerge (see Martin Baily's chapter elsewhere in this volume for a more detailed discussion of deflation). The question is important for our analysis, since entering inflation in the GCI where lower inflation is taken as "good" means that, by definition, deflationary countries will find themselves at the top of the ranking.

It would seem logical to somehow punish those countries that actually do become deflationary by allocating them a lower score. However, the actual implementation of any such solution raises similar questions to those related to hyperinflation raised above. If there were theoretical or empirical evidence on the negative relationship between deflation and growth, the idea would be to choose a maximum rate of inflation somewhere above 0 percent, and to punish all countries falling below that level.

However, despite all of the press attention this issue has received, it remains unclear whether deflation really is bad for growth, and to date there is no widely accepted empirical research upon which we could base our decision. This ambiguity means that any threshold selected would be arbitrary. Should the threshold be 1 percent, 0 percent, 2 percent? There would appear to be no basis at this point on which to select this cutoff. Further, even if it were possible to select a threshold inflation rate, how should the deflationary numbers be treated? For example, is −2 percent just the same as 2 percent, or is it the same as 4 percent, or even higher? There are no studies at present on which to base such a decision.

We have therefore taken the decision to leave the deflationary countries as they are for this year. We will continue to study this issue very closely, with an eye to implementing a better solution in the future.

Uganda, Kenya, and Zambia occupy positions around the 80th ranks, while Cameroon, Ethiopia, Mozambique, Madagascar, and Mali are in the 90th ranks. In the region, new entrants Angola and Chad occupy the last ranks, at 100th and 101st positions, respectively.

Conclusion

The main innovation of this year's GCI is the inclusion of 22 new countries. With a total of 102 countries now being surveyed, this year's Growth Competitiveness Index becomes the first index of its sort with such broad country coverage. This broad coverage is especially relevant because most of the additions are from the developing world and, more specifically, from Africa. This should allow readers to compare the scores, the performances, and the experiences of many more developing nations with those of the developed world. These comparisons should deliver lessons as to what can and should be done in order to induce growth and improvements in per capita income in the developing world. As we mentioned in the introduction, a better understanding of the factors underlying successful growth strategies would have far reaching consequences for human welfare.

The process of economic growth and development is a complex one. Many of its underlying mechanisms are still unknown, but economic researchers continue to make progress as new experiences and new data become available. The World Economic Forum will continue to monitor these developments and, with them, will keep improving the GCI so that it can continue to be a useful tool for economists, business leaders, and policymakers around the world.

Notes

1 Dollar and Kraay (2000). At a theoretical level, it is possible that positive growth ends up increasing poverty if the distribution of income deteriorates so much as a consequence of positive growth that the total number of people whose income is below a certain threshold (such as one dollar a day) actually increases. Although this is a theoretical possibility, empirical evidence suggests that this rarely happens in practice. In fact, there is little correlation between the per capita growth rate of an economy and measures of inequality (such as the gini coefficient). If inequality does not increase with aggregate economic growth, it must be the case that positive growth is associated with reductions in poverty rates.

2 Schumpeter (1942) and Solow (1956). See Aghion and Howitt (1992, 1998) for a technical exposition of technology-based growth theories.

3 See Barro (1991), Levine and Renelt (1992), Barro and Sala-i-Martin (1998), and Doppelhofer et al. (2003) for recent examples of cross-country empirical growth research.

4 See, for example, Acemoglu, Johnson, and Robinson (2002).

5 Solow (1956).

6 In an excellent paper, Nordhaus (1994) shows how we can purchase 45.000 times more lighting for an hour of work today than people could buy two centuries ago.

7 The rapid improvement of the quality of computers is only one example of a phenomenon that can be found in transportation, music and entertainment, medicine, drugs, food, and so on.

8 See p 39 of Sachs and McArthur (2001).

Box Notes

1 A good example is provided by Russia, a country with a relatively low expenditure-to-GDP ratio but that otherwise has fairly inefficient patterns of spending. Its overall rank fell, notwithstanding a fairly robust growth performance.

2 Fischer (1993) has established that 8 percent is the relevant threshold

3 The precise slope parameters would depend crucially on ad-hoc econometric specifications.

References

Acemoglu, D., S. Johnson, and J. Robinson. 2002.. "Reversal of Fortune: Geography and Institutions in the Making of the Modern World Income Distribution," *Quarterly Journal of Economics* 117 (4): 1231–1294.

Aghion, P. and P. Howitt. 1992. "A Model of Growth through Creative Destruction," *Econometrica* LX: 323–351.

Aghion, P. and P. Howitt. 1998. *Endogenous Economic Growth.* Cambridge, MA: MIT Press.

Barro, R. 1991. "Economic Growth in a Cross Section of Countries," *Quarterly Journal of Economics* 106: 407–444.

Barro R. J. and X. Sala-i-Martin. 1998. *Economic Growth.* Cambridge, MA: MIT Press.

Dollar, D. and A. Kraay. 2000. *Growth Is Good for the Poor.* Washington, DC: World Bank.

Doppelhofer, G., R. Miller, and X. Sala-i-Martin. 2003. "Determinants of Long-Term Growth: A Bayesian Averaging of Classical Estimates (BACE) Approach," *American Economic Review*, forthcoming.

Fischer, S. 1993. "The Role of Macroeconomic Factors in Growth," *Journal of Monetary Economics* 32: 485–512.

Levine, R. and D. Renelt. 1992. "A Sensitivity Analysis of Cross-Country Growth Regressions," *American Economic Review* 82(4): 942–963.

McArthur, J. W. and J. D. Sachs. 2002. "The Growth Competitiveness Index: Measuring Technological Advancement and the Stages of Development." In *The Global Competitiveness Report 2001–2002.* New York: Oxford University Press for the World Economic Forum.

Nordhaus, W. D. 1994. *Managing the Global Commons: The Economics of Climate Change.* Cambridge MA: MIT Press.

Schumpeter, J. A. 1942. *Capitalism, Socialism, and Democracy.* New York: Harper and Brothers.

Solow, R. 1956. "A Contribution to the Theory of Economic Growth," *Quarterly Journal of Economics*, 70: 65–94.

Appendix: Composition of the Growth Competitiveness Index

The Growth Competitiveness Index is composed of three component indexes: the technology index, the public institutions index, and the macroeconomic environment index. These indexes are calculated on the basis of both "hard data" and "Survey data."

The responses to the Executive Opinion Survey are what we refer to as *Survey data*, with responses ranging from 1 to 7 (see the chapter at the end of the Report for further information on the Executive Opinion Survey); the hard data were collected from various sources, described in the Technical Notes and Sources at the end of the *Report*. All of the data used in the calculation of the Growth Competitiveness Index can be found in the data tables section of the *Report*.

The standard formula for converting each hard data variable to the 1-to-7 scale is:

$$6 \times \frac{(\text{country value} - \text{sample minimum})}{(\text{sample maximum} - \text{sample minimum})} + 1$$

The sample minimum and sample maximum are the lowest and highest values of the overall sample, respectively. In some instances, adjustments were made to account for extreme outliers in the data.

As explained in the chapter, the sample of countries is divided into two groups: the core innovators and the non-core innovators. Core innovators are countries with more than 15 US utility patents registered per million population in 2002; non-core innovators are all other countries.

For the core innovators, we place extra emphasis on the role of innovation and technology. The weightings for the core innovators are as follows:

> Growth Competitiveness
> Index for core innovators = (1/2 technology index)
> + (1/4 public institutions index)
> + (1/4 macroeconomic environment index)

For the non-core innovators, we calculate the Growth Competitiveness Index values as a simple average of the three component indexes:

> Growth Competitiveness
> Index for non-core
> innovators = (1/3 technology index)
> + (1/3 public institutions index)
> + (1/3 macroeconomic environment index)

Technology index components

The technology index is calculated for the core and non-core innovators as follows:

> technology index for
> core innovators = (1/2 innovation subindex)
> + (1/2 information and communication technology subindex)

> technology index for
> non-core innovators = (1/8 innovation subindex)
> + (3/8 technology transfer subindex)
> + (1/2 information and communication technology subindex)

Innovation subindex

> innovation subindex = (1/4 Survey data)
> + (3/4 hard data)

Innovation Survey questions

3.01 What is your country's position in technology relative to world leaders'?

3.02 Companies in your country are not interested/aggressive in absorbing new technology?

3.06 How much do companies in your country spend on R&D relative to other countries?

3.08 What is the extent of business collaboration in R&D with local universities?

Innovation hard data

3.17 US utility patents granted per million population in 2002

3.18 Gross tertiary enrollment rate in 2000 or most recent available year

Technology transfer subindex

> technology transfer
> subindex = unweighted average of two technology transfer Survey questions

3.03 Is foreign direct investment in your country an important source of new technology?

3.04 Is foreign technology licensing in your country a common means of acquiring new technology?

Appendix: Composition of the Growth Competitiveness Index *(cont'd.)*

Information and communication technology (ICT) subindex

information and
communication
technology subindex = (1/3 information and communication
technology Survey data)
+ (2/3 information and communication
technology hard data)

Information and communication technology Survey questions

3.12 How extensive is Internet access in schools?

3.13 Is there sufficient competition among ISPs in your country to ensure high quality, infrequent interruptions and low prices?

3.14 Is ICT an overall priority for the government?

3.15 Are government programs successful in promoting the use of ICT?

3.16 Are laws relating to ICT (electronic commerce, digital signatures, consumer protection) well developed and enforced?

Information and communication technology hard data

3.19 Cellular mobile subscribers per 100 inhabitants, 2002

3.20 Internet users per 10,000 inhabitants, 2002

3.21 Internet hosts per 10,000 inhabitants, 2002

3.22 Main telephone lines per 100 inhabitants, 2002

3.23 Personal computers per 100 inhabitants, 2002

Public institutions index components

public institutions index = (1/2 contracts and law subindex)
+ (1/2 corruption subindex)

Contracts and law subindex

6.01 Is the judiciary in your country independent from political influences of members of government, citizens or firms?

6.03 Are financial assets and wealth clearly delineated and well protected by law?

6.08 Is your government neutral among bidders when deciding among public contracts?

6.17 Does organized crime impose significant costs on business?

Corruption subindex

7.01 How commonly are bribes paid in connection with import and export permits?

7.02 How commonly are bribes paid when getting connected with public utilities?

7.03 How commonly are bribes paid in connection with annual tax payments?

Macroeconomic environment index components

macroeconomic
environment index = 1/2 macroeconomic stability subindex
+ 1/4 country credit rating in March 2003
+ 1/4 government waste in 2003

Macroeconomic stability subindex

macroeconomic
stability subindex = (5/7 macroeconomic stability hard data)
+ (2/7 macroeconomic stability Survey data)

Macroeconomic stability Survey questions

2.01 Is your country's economy likely to be in a recession next year?

2.09 Has obtaining credit for your company become easier or more difficult over the past year?

Macroeconomic stability hard data

2.18 Government surplus/deficit in 2002

2.19 National savings rate in 2002

2.20 Inflation in 2002

2.21 Real exchange rate relative to the United States in 2002

2.22 Lending– borrowing interest rate spread in 2002

2.17 Institutional Investor country credit rating, March 2003

Government waste composite, 2003

2.03 Do government subsidies to business in your country keep uncompetitive industries alive artificially or do they improve the productivity of industries?

7.08 In your country, how common is the diversion of public funds to companies, individuals or groups due to corruption?

7.10 How high is the public trust in the financial honesty of politicians?

CHAPTER 1.2

Building the Microeconomic Foundations of Prosperity: Findings from the Business Competitiveness Index[1]

MICHAEL E. PORTER, Harvard University

Competitiveness has become a central preoccupation of both advanced and developing countries in an increasingly open and integrated world economy. Despite its acknowledged importance, the concept of competitiveness is often misunderstood. Here, we define *competitiveness* concretely, show its relationship to a nation's standard of living, and outline a conceptual framework for understanding its causes.

The Business Competitiveness Index (BCI), based on this conceptual framework, provides a data-rich approach to measuring and analyzing the fundamental competitiveness of a large number of countries in a comparative context. This year's BCI includes 101 countries, up from 80 last year. Our aim is to rank country competitiveness across countries, identify individual countries' competitive strengths and weaknesses, reveal the trends in competitiveness in the global economy, and extend our basic knowledge about the sources of competitiveness and the process of economic development.

Most discussion of competitiveness and economic development is still focused on the macroeconomic, political, legal, and social circumstances that underpin a successful economy. It is well understood that sound fiscal and monetary policies, a trusted and efficient legal system, a stable set of democratic institutions, and progress on social conditions contribute greatly to a healthy economy. However, these broader conditions are necessary but not sufficient. They provide the opportunity to create wealth but do not themselves create wealth. Wealth is actually created at the microeconomic level of the economy, rooted in the sophistication of actual companies as well as in the quality of the microeconomic business environment in which a nation's firms compete. Unless these microeconomic capabilities improve, macroeconomic, political, legal, and social reforms will not bear full fruit.

Beginning in 1998, we began an effort to examine statistically the microeconomic foundations of competitiveness and prosperity across a wide array of countries. This is a daunting task, given the need to measure and compare the complex array of national circumstances that support a high and sustainable level of productivity. The effort aims to move beyond the examination of broad, aggregate variables typical of most economic growth analyses, and provide a framework for countries and companies to understand their detailed competitive strengths and weaknesses. It also aims to be as rigorous as possible, verifying the importance of variables statistically and using statistical techniques to weight the contribution of individual variables. Finally, we know that improvement in competitiveness is not a simple linear process but one where nations at different levels of development face different challenges and priorities. This effort aims to highlight these differences.

The Business Competitiveness Index seeks to explore the underpinnings of a nation's prosperity measured by its level of GDP per capita. The focus of this index is on whether current prosperity is sustainable, and on the specific areas that must be addressed if GDP per capita is to achieve higher levels in the future. A separate Growth Competitiveness Index (GCI), discussed in the previous chapter of this *Report*, examines the sources of GDP per capita growth, which is more dependent on investment rates and other macroeconomic policies. The sustainable level of current GDP per capita and its rate of growth will be related in the long term, but each area requires its own distinctive policy agenda. We have renamed the BCI this year to highlight its focus on firms and productivity. However, the conceptual framework and statistical approach follow that of the previous reports, and the findings are fully comparable with previous Microeconomic Competitiveness Index results.

The analysis here is pragmatic, making use of the best available data and econometric methods even though both are far from perfect. We also confront the challenge of establishing the direction of causality, given limited time series data. However, even if definitive tests of causality are not yet possible, understanding the microeconomic correlates of prosperity remains crucial. There may be a natural tendency for some microeconomic conditions to improve as GDP per capita increases, but the large observed differences across countries, even countries at similar income levels, reveal that this improvement is far from automatic.

Despite the statistical challenges and the addition of 21 mostly low income countries, mainly from Africa, to the sample of countries, the statistical findings overall are remarkably stable and robust compared with the *Global Competitiveness Report 2002–2003* (GCR) and earlier *Reports*. We expand this year's analysis to include an analysis of natural resource endowments and their role in competitiveness, a crucial issue especially for developing countries. The results again provide strong support for the importance of microeconomic competitiveness for economic development and prosperity. Our findings also verify the striking and regular pattern of microeconomic changes that accompany economic development.

The Business Competitiveness Index proves to account for 83 percent of the variation across countries in the level GDP per capita,[2] remarkably high given the addition of so many low income countries. These findings highlight the pressing need to better incorporate microeconomic competitiveness agenda into efforts to stimulate economic growth. In advanced countries, which have largely gotten their macro policies right, it is micro reform that holds the key to reversing unemployment problems, to growing exports, and to translating economic growth into a rising standard of living.

In developing countries, microeconomic failures nullify macroeconomic and social programs again and again. By accessing global capital markets, countries can engineer spurts of growth through macroeconomic stabilization and financial reforms that bring in floods of capital and create the illusion of progress as construction cranes dot the skyline. Without microeconomic reforms, however, growth will be snuffed out as exports and jobs fail to materialize, wages stagnate, and the return on investments proves disappointing. This disappointment, and the austerity that results from such cycles, is at the heart of the backlash against globalization.

Successful economic development requires progress on multiple fronts simultaneously. Reform efforts need to be tightly connected to the country's current stage of development. As an economy progresses, the constraints to its continued advancement shift. At strategic points in the development process, the whole basis of national competitiveness must be transformed. Many aspects of company strategy must be shifted and new requirements in the national business environment must be met. Our analysis provides the conceptual framework and comparative data to define such national agendas and to measure progress.

Competitiveness and its causes

Measuring and ranking competitiveness requires a clear conceptual framework, drawing on the accumulated knowledge about competitiveness and its sources. We summarize the framework here, drawing on previous years' chapters while extending it to incorporate recent learning.

What is competitiveness?

Competitiveness remains a concept that is not well understood, despite widespread acceptance of its importance. The most intuitive definition of *competitiveness* is a country's share of world markets for its products. This makes competitiveness a zero-sum game, because one country's gain comes at the expense of others. This view of competitiveness is used to justify intervention to skew market outcomes in a nation's favor (so-called industrial policy). It also underpins policies intended to provide subsidies, hold down local wages, and devalue the nation's currency, all aimed at expanding exports. In fact, it is still often said that lower wages or devaluation "make a nation more competitive." Business leaders are drawn to the market-share view because these policies seem to address their immediate competitive concerns.

Unfortunately, the most intuitive view of competitiveness is deeply flawed, and acting on it works against national economic progress. The need for low wages reveals a lack of competitiveness and holds down prosperity. Subsidies drain national income and bias choices away from the most productive use of the nation's resources.

Devaluation results in a collective national pay cut by discounting the products and services sold in world markets while raising the cost of the goods and services purchased abroad. Exports based on low wages or a cheap currency, then, do not support an attractive standard of living.

To understand competitiveness, the starting point must be the underlying sources of prosperity. A nation's standard of living is determined by the *productivity* of its economy, which is measured by the value of goods and services produced per unit of the nation's human, capital, and natural resources. Productivity depends both on the value of a nation's products and services, measured by the prices they can command in open markets, and the efficiency with which they can be produced.

True competitiveness, then, is measured by productivity. Productivity allows a nation to support high wages, a strong currency, and attractive returns to capital—and with them a high standard of living. Productivity is the goal, not exports *per se*. Only if a nation expands exports of products or services it can produce productively will national productivity rise. Productivity is the goal, not whether firms operating in the country are domestic or foreign owned. What matters most is not ownership, but the nature and productivity of the companies' activities in a particular country. Purely local industries also matter for competitiveness because their productivity has a major influence on the cost of living and the cost of doing business, not to mention their level of wages. The productivity of the entire economy matters for the standard of living, not just the traded goods sector.

The world economy is not a zero-sum game. Many nations can improve their prosperity if they can improve productivity. The central challenge in economic development, then, is how to create the conditions for rapid and sustained productivity growth.

Microeconomic foundations of productivity

Stable political, legal, and social institutions and sound macroeconomic policies create the potential for improving national prosperity. But wealth is actually created at the microeconomic level—in the ability of firms to create valuable goods and services using efficient methods. Only in this way can a nation support high wages and the attractive returns to capital necessary to support sustained investment (see Figure 1).

The microeconomic foundations of productivity rest on two interrelated areas: (1) the sophistication with which domestic companies or foreign subsidiaries operating in the country compete, and (2) the quality of the microeconomic business environment in which they operate.

The productivity of a country is ultimately set by the productivity of its companies. An economy cannot be competitive unless companies operating there are competitive, whether they are domestic firms or subsidiaries of

Figure 1: Determinants of productivity and productivity growth

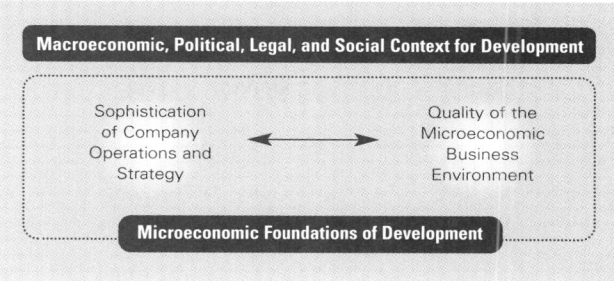

foreign companies. However, the sophistication and productivity of companies are inextricably intertwined with the quality of the national business environment. More productive company strategies require more highly skilled people, better information, more efficient government processes, improved infrastructure, better suppliers, more advanced research institutions, and more intense competitive pressure, among other things.

Companies in a nation must upgrade their ways of competing if successful economic development is to occur. Broadly, companies must shift from competing on endowments or comparative advantages (low-cost labor or natural resources) to competing on competitive advantages arising from superior or distinctive products and processes. Companies must move from tapping foreign distribution channels to building their own channels. These and other transitions in corporate strategies and operating practices required for successful economic development are shown in Figure 2.

Figure 2: Company sophistication and economic development

Low-Income Countries	Middle-Income Countries	High-Income Countries
• Competitive advantages beyond cheap inputs	• Extent of regional sales	• Capacity for innovation
• Production process sophistication	• Control of international distribution	• Breadth of international markets
• Broad value chain presence	• Extent of branding	• Extent of incentive compensation
• Reliance on professional management	• Company spending on R&D	• Willingness to delegate authority
	• Prevalence of foreign technology licensing	
	• Extent of staff training	

What were strengths in competing at earlier stages of development become weaknesses at more advanced levels of development. Extensive technology licensing works for lower- and middle-income countries, but must give way to indigenous technology development. Necessary changes are often resisted by the corporate sector because past approaches were profitable and because old habits are deeply ingrained.

Moving to more sophisticated ways of competing depends on parallel changes in the microeconomic business environment. The business environment can be understood in terms of four interrelated areas: the quality of factor (input) conditions, the context for firm strategy and rivalry, the quality of local demand conditions, and the presence of the related and supporting industries. Because of their graphical representation (see Figure 3), the four areas have collectively become referred to as the *diamond*.

As the diamond framework reveals, *almost everything matters* for competitiveness. The schools matter, the roads matter, the financial markets matter, customer sophistication matters, among many other aspects of a nation's circumstances, many of which are deeply rooted in a nation's institutions, people, and culture. This makes improving competitiveness a special challenge, because there is no single policy or grand step that can create competitiveness, only many improvements in individual areas that

inevitably take time to accomplish. Improving competitiveness is a marathon, not a sprint. How to sustain momentum in competitiveness improvements over time is among the greatest challenges facing countries.

There are distinct influences on competitiveness at *multiple geographic levels*: national, state, and local.[3] In many countries, we observe striking differences in economic performance among subnational regions. In countries such as China, India, and the United States, the benefits of decentralization of economic policy and strong initiative in individual regions is evident. The crucial need for economic strategies for subnational units such as states or regions is among the most important new directions in competitiveness thinking and practice.

National productivity can also be enhanced through coordinating policies among neighboring countries. A concerted effort to improve the business environment is needed both within countries and across countries.

Government plays an inevitable role in economic development because it affects many aspects of the business environment. Government shapes factor conditions, for example, through its training and infrastructure policies. The sophistication of home demand derives in part from regulatory standards, consumer protection laws, government purchasing practices, and openness to imports. Similar policy influences are present in all four parts of the

Figure 3: The microeconomic business environment

Context for Firm Strategy and Rivalry
- A local context and rules that encourage **investment** and **sustained upgrading** (e.g., Intellectual property protection)
- **Meritocratic** incentive systems across institutions
- Open and vigorous competition among **locally based rivals**

Factor (Input) Conditions
Presence of high quality, specialized inputs available to firms
- Human resources
- Capital resources
- Physical infrastructure
- Administrative infrastructure
- Information infrastructure
- Scientific and technological infrastructure
- Natural resources

Demand Conditions
- **Sophisticated and demanding** local customer(s)
- Local customer needs that **anticipate** those elsewhere
- Unusual local demand in **specialized segments** that can be served nationally and globally

Related and Supporting Industries
- Access to capable, locally based **suppliers** and firms in **related fields**
- Presence of **clusters** instead of isolated industries

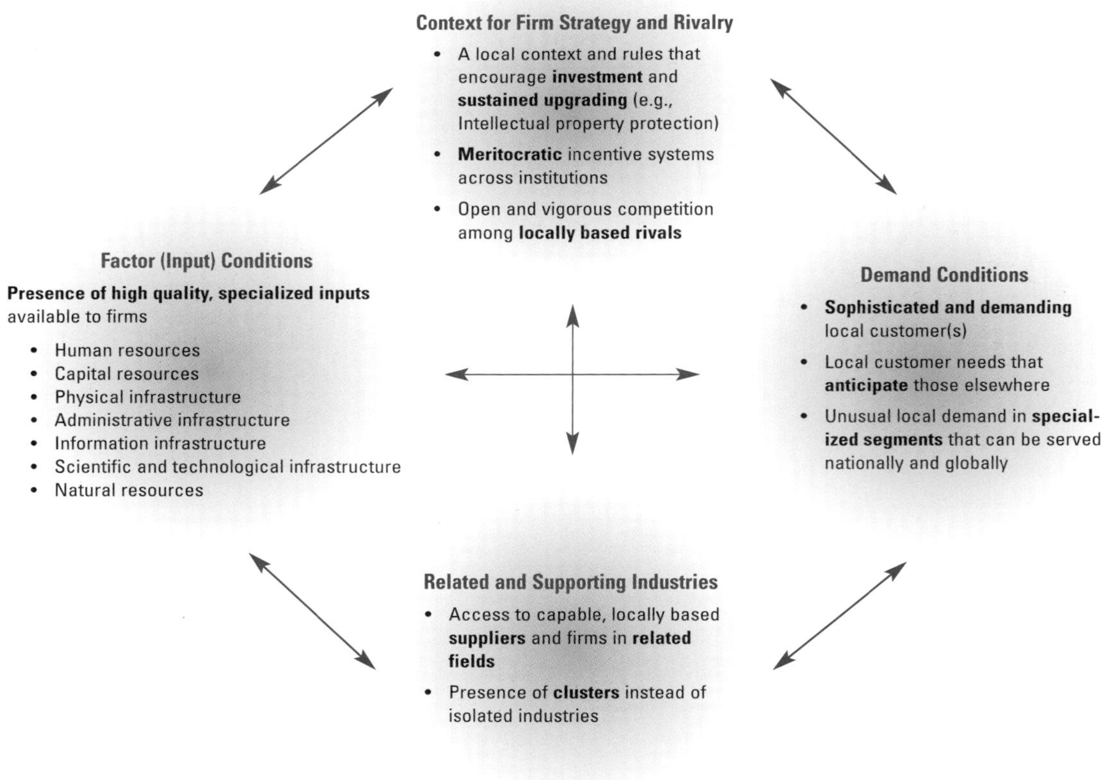

diamond. Many government departments and agencies impinge on competitiveness, as do government entities at the provincial, state, and city levels. The question is not whether government has a role, but what that role should be and how to coordinate policies across parts of government. Many countries have sought to limit the inappropriate roles of government while ignoring its positive roles. Government must set the right rules and incentives and make the public investments needed for a productive economy.

National endowments such as natural resources play a declining role in competitiveness as the resource intensity of the economy falls and as technology substitutes for resources or opens up new resource locations. The real prices of most resources or resource-intensive goods have been falling over the decades. It is the productivity with which natural resources can be utilized, not the resources themselves, that normally have the strongest influence on prosperity. Abundant natural resources also carry a risk. In countries where natural resources are abundant or dominate economic activity, forces are set in motion that limit the development of policies, skills, and attitudes enhancing competitiveness. Exploiting and redistributing resource spoils can become the dominant orientation rather than enhancing productivity. We explore the relationship between natural resource endowments and competitiveness in a later section.

Clusters and economic development

An improving business environment gives rise to the formation of clusters. *Clusters* are geographically proximate groups of interconnected companies, suppliers, service providers, and associated institutions in a particular field, linked by commonalities and complementarities. Clusters, such as software in India or high-performance cars in Germany, are often concentrated in a particular region within a larger nation, and sometimes in a single town.

Clusters affect competitiveness in three broad ways. First, they increase the productivity of constituent firms or industries. Firms with a cluster have more efficient access to specialized suppliers, employees, information, and training than isolated firms. The presence of a full range of inputs, machinery, skills, and knowledge promotes greater efficiency and flexibility than vertical integration or relationships with distant suppliers. In the Boston Life Sciences Cluster, for example, the local presence of sophisticated suppliers and research hospitals enables biotech companies to access capital and technology while operating more efficiently than in most other locations around the world.

33

Figure 4: The Boston Life Sciences Cluster

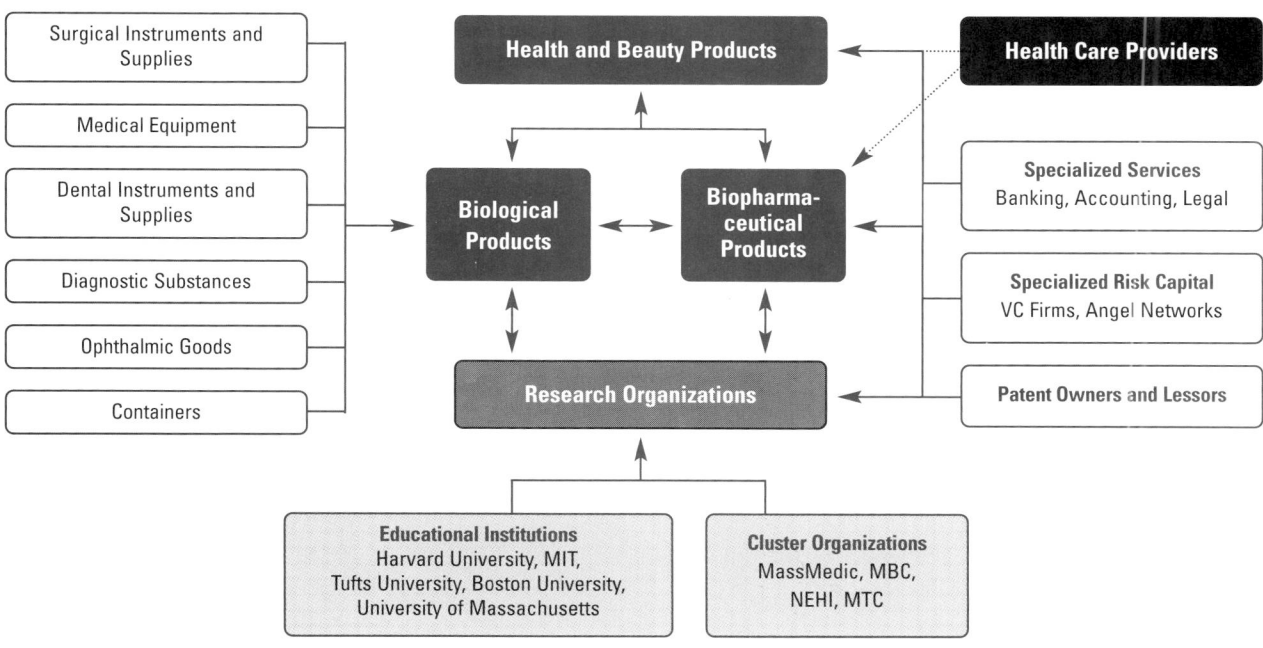

Source: Institute for Strategy and Competitiveness, Harvard Business School

Second, clusters increase the capacity for innovation and productivity growth. Opportunities for innovation can often be perceived more easily within clusters, and the assets, skills, and capital are more available to pursue them. In the Boston Life Sciences Cluster, for example, the presence of world-class research universities, teaching hospitals, competing biotech companies, and cluster institutions that facilitate interaction among them provide a fertile ground for new ideas and foster the rapid dissemination of knowledge: Between 1996 and 2000, Boston generated the highest number of life science patents of any economic area in the United States.

Third, clusters stimulate and enable new business formation that supports innovation and expands the cluster. The local presence of experienced workers and access to all the needed inputs and specialized services, for example, reduces the barriers to entry. In Boston, the availability of highly experienced managers, researchers, and technicians in the life science field; and access to specialized venture capital providers, lawyers, and suppliers all reduce the costs and risks of starting a new life sciences company. The many local options for employment in other cluster companies lower the perceived risk of failure.

National economies tend to specialize in particular clusters, which account for a disproportionate share of their output and exports. This specialization is even more evident in subnational regions. The nature and depth of clusters varies with the state of development of the economy. In developing countries, clusters are normally shallow or underdeveloped. Firms compete based on cheap labor or local natural resources, and they depend heavily on imported components, machinery, and technology. Specialized local infrastructure and institutions are absent or inefficient which limits local processing of products and limits quality. As economies advance, clusters develop and deepen to include suppliers of specialized inputs, components, machinery, and services; specialized infrastructure; and institutions providing specialized training, education, information, research, and technical support.

It is rare that there is only a single cluster in the world in a given field; usually there is an array of clusters in different locations with different levels of sophistication and specialization. In a given field, only a small number of clusters tend to be true innovation centers, such as Silicon Valley and Japan in semiconductors. These innovation centers sometimes specialize in particular market segments—the Silicon Valley cluster is unusually strong in microprocessors. Other locations may be manufacturing centers. Still other clusters can be regional assembly and service clusters.

Firms based in the most advanced clusters often seed or enhance clusters in other locations as they disperse some activities to reduce risk, access lower cost inputs, or better serve particular regional markets. Intel, for example,

has moved some assembly and testing and some wafer fabrication to a number of non-US locations that have become regional clusters. The challenge for an economy is to move from isolated firms to an array of clusters, and upgrade the sophistication of clusters to more advanced activities.

Stages of competitive development

Successful economic development is a process of successive upgrading, in which a nation's business environment evolves to support and encourage increasingly sophisticated and productive ways of competing by firms based there. Nations at different levels of development face distinctly different challenges.

Figure 5: Stages of competitive development

Source: Porter (1990)

As nations develop, they progress in terms of their competitive advantages and modes of competing.[4] In the Factor-Driven stage, basic factor conditions such as low-cost labor and unprocessed natural resources are the dominant sources of competitive advantage and exports. Firms produce commodities or relatively simple products designed in other, more-advanced countries. Technology is assimilated through imports, supply agreements, foreign direct investment, and imitation. In this stage, companies compete on price and lack direct access to consumers. They have limited roles in the value chain, focusing on assembly, labor-intensive manufacturing, and resource extraction. A Factor-Driven economy is highly sensitive to world economic cycles, commodity prices, and exchange rate fluctuations.

In the Investment-Driven stage, efficiency in producing standard products and services becomes the dominant source of competitive advantage. Heavy investment in efficient infrastructure, business-friendly government administration, strong investment incentives, and better access to capital allow major improvements in productivity. The products and services produced become more sophisticated, but technology and designs still come largely from abroad. Technology is accessed through licensing, joint ventures, foreign direct investment, and imitation. However, nations at this stage not only assimilate foreign technology but also begin to develop the capacity to improve on it. Companies serve a mix of OEM customers and end users. Firms extend capabilities more widely in the value chain. An Investment-Driven economy is concentrated on manufacturing and on outsourced service exports. It is susceptible to financial crises and external, sector-specific demand shocks.

In the Innovation-Driven stage, the ability to produce innovative products and services at the global technology frontier, using the most advanced methods, becomes the dominant source of competitive advantage. The national business environment is characterized by strengths in all areas, together with the presence of deep clusters. Institutions and incentives supporting innovation are well developed. Companies compete with unique strategies that are often global in scope. An Innovation-Driven economy has a high share of services in the economy and is resilient to external shocks. (See Chapter 2.3 for a more extensive discussion on the sources of innovative capacity at the national level and comparisons across countries.)

Seeing economic development as a sequential process of building interdependent microeconomic capabilities, shifting company strategies, improving incentives, and increasing rivalry exposes important pitfalls in economic policy. The influence of one part of the microeconomic business environment depends on the state of others. Lack of improvement in any important area can lead to a plateau in productivity growth and stalled development. Worse still, it can undermine the whole economic reform process. When well-trained college graduates cannot find appropriate jobs because companies are still competing based on cheap labor, for example, a backlash against business is created.

This analysis also begins to reveal why countries find the transition to a new stage of development so difficult. Such inflection points require wholesale transformation of many interdependent aspects of competition. The central and eastern European countries poised to join the European Union (EU) face such challenges. With a legal framework and many EU policies designed for current members of the EU, they must compete despite having economies at a different level. The strong EU focus on technological innovation rather than applying established processes, for example, is out of sync with the challenges of integrating into tougher European markets.

Institutions and roles in economic development

Although government is important to competitiveness, government alone is less and less able to build a competitive economy. Many other national and local institutions also have a role in competitiveness and economic development. The influence of universities and schools is growing as knowledge and technology become more and more central to competition. Universities and schools must not

only improve the educational and research capabilities, but become better connected to the private sector.

The private sector has also become a crucial actor in improving competitiveness and in setting economic policy. The private sector is not only a consumer of the business environment, but it also can and must play a role in shaping it. Individual firms, through steps such as establishing educational programs, attracting suppliers, or defining standards, not only benefit themselves but also improve the overall environment for competing. Collective industry bodies, such as trade associations and chambers of commerce, also have important roles to play in improving infrastructure, providing training, and developing export markets that are often overlooked. Collective efforts to enhance the capabilities of individual companies, such as quality certification programs and manufacturing assistance centers, are becoming more prominent. Engagement of the private sector in competitiveness is also important to provide the *continuity of attention* necessary to sustain progress through changes of government and to counteract the relatively short attention span of political leaders.

Finally, a whole class of institutions, which we term *Institutions for Collaboration* (IFCs), play an important role in competitiveness, though they have been largely ignored in economic development thinking.[5] Neither government agencies, educational institutions, nor firms, these organizations—trade associations, entrepreneur networks, standard setting agencies, quality centers, technology networks, and many others—are common. They are especially prevalent in the most advanced economies, but also play crucial roles in developing countries. IFCs play an essential role in connecting the parts of the diamond and fostering efficient collective activities in both advanced and developing countries.

The relationship between macroeconomic and microeconomic policy

Our analysis makes it clear why the traditional focus on macroeconomic stabilization and market opening is insufficient. Macroeconomic policies fostering high rates of capital investment, for example, will not translate into rising productivity unless the forms of investment are appropriate, the company skills and supporting industries are present to make the investments efficient, and strong competitive pressures and adequate corporate governance provide the needed market discipline. Sound monetary and fiscal policies and the removal of distortions in exchange rates and other prices will eliminate impediments to productivity, but microeconomic foundations must be in place if productivity is actually to increase.

Appropriate levels of foreign debt depend on microeconomic circumstances. The prudence of foreign debt levels depends on exactly where the foreign capital is invested, together with the microeconomic fundamentals surrounding its deployment and governance. Regulating overall debt levels is less important, in many ways, than improving the microeconomic foundations.

High rates of public investment in human capital will not pay off unless a nation's microeconomic circumstances create the demand for skills in companies. Privatization will not boost prosperity unless companies can improve efficiency and are pressured by local competition. For sound policies at the macroeconomic level to translate into an increasingly productive economy, then, parallel microeconomic improvements must take place.

The effects of trade agreements and other market opening measures, a major focus in today's international economic policymaking, also depends on microeconomic policies. Market opening is good, but its benefits in terms of prosperity depend on microeconomic progress. If the local business environment does not become more efficient and local companies do not improve their productivity and sophistication, then market opening will boost imports, while growth in exports and the attraction of foreign investment will be painfully slow. Improvement in the microeconomic business environment begins *before* market opening measures are complete.

A greater focus on microeconomic reforms will pay another essential dividend. While macro reforms almost inevitability inflict hardship in the short and medium run through raising interest rates and prices while cutting public expenditures, micro reforms can produce tangible and visible benefits for citizens. Breaking up local cartels and monopolies, for example, lowers the cost of food, housing, electricity, telephone service, and other costs of living. Regulatory reform can rapidly begin to ease inefficiencies, reduce pollution, improve product quality, and end unsafe practices. Bold steps to improve the quality of education and training are particularly important because they offer the hope of a better life for children. If citizens see businesses reforming themselves and having to confront tough competitive challenges, they themselves will be more willing to live with personal sacrifices and less likely to side with antireform interest groups. The political will and public support to make real economic change is elevated.

Ranking competitiveness

Measures of competitiveness

The Business Competitiveness Index (BCI) is constructed from measures drawn primarily from the survey of 7,707 senior business leaders in 101 countries, shown in Table 1.[6] Compared to 2002 we have added 21 countries: Algeria, Angola, Cameroon, Chad, Egypt, Ethiopia, Gambia, Ghana, Kenya, Macedonia, Madagascar, Malawi, Mali, Malta, Mozambique, Pakistan, Senegal, Serbia, Tanzania, Uganda, and Zambia. Egypt has been restored to the rankings after having been excluded last year due to the unavailability of Survey data.

Measuring competitiveness is challenging because of the sheer number and variety of influences that shape national productivity. Only through a detailed survey can textured measures of the competitive environment and company practices be assembled across many countries. The Survey questions aim to capture the state of circumstances in a nation, but do so in way that is meaningful for Survey respondents. For example, we get at the stock of basic human capital with a question on the quality of public schools because this is something that respondents can compare more readily across countries. The quality of schools, a flow measure, will be highly correlated with the stock of basic skills.

Quantitative measures are utilized for patenting rates, Internet penetration, and cellular phone penetration. For all of the other dimensions we measure, however, quantitative data are simply unavailable, especially for so many countries. The Survey not only offers many unique measures, but captures the informed judgments of thousands of actual participants in the economies examined. The Survey responses are important in their own right, because they reflect the attitudes of the decision makers that ultimately determine economic activity.

In an effort to broaden the rankings, a large number of low income countries participated in the Survey this year for the first time, many with relatively isolated economies. In view of this, we undertook additional efforts to examine the consistency of the survey data. For each Survey question we compared the standard deviation of answers within a country to the standard deviation of answers across all countries. This is a weak statistical test that the vast majority of countries easily meet. However, in those countries with high within-country variance of responses for many Survey questions, it is hard to interpret the country averages independently of the possible reasons for the variances.[7] In addition to examining all responses for each country, we further analyzed within-country consensus in the subset of responses from executives from foreign companies operating in the country. We expect these respondents to have the best perspective on how the country compares to others.

For the 80 countries ranked last year, there were few data issues.[8] We rank the 80 countries in last year's sample and compare their rankings to previous years in Table 1.

Of the new countries, 15 countries had overall survey data with a high degree of within-country consensus or foreign company responses with a high degree of within-country consensus.[9] The original 80 countries plus this group constituted a 95-country sample that was used to calculate the regression utilized to validate variables and to compute the Index model. The final 6 countries, all low-income countries, had low within-country consensus,

Table 1: The Business Competitiveness Index, constant country sample of 80 countries

Country	BCI ranking						Company operations and strategy ranking						Quality of the national business environment ranking						2002 GDP per capita rank	2002 GDP per capita (PPP-adjusted)*
	2003	2002	2001*	2000	1999	1998	2003	2002	2001	2000	1999	1998	2003	2002	2001	2000	1999	1998		
Finland	1	2	1	1	2	2	4	4	2	3	7	8	1	2	1	1	2	2	15	25,859
United States	2	1	2	2	1	1	2	1	1	2	1	2	2	1	2	2	1	1	2	35,158
Sweden	3	6	6	7	4	7	3	6	6	6	3	4	5	8	6	11	7	9	19	25,315
Denmark	4	8	8	6	7	8	7	9	9	8	9	10	3	9	10	4	6	7	3	29,975
Germany	5	4	4	3	6	4	1	2	4	1	5	1	9	4	4	6	5	8	12	26,324
United Kingdom	6	3	7	8	10	5	8	3	7	11	13	9	6	3	8	9	8	5	16	25,672
Switzerland	7	5	5	5	5	9	5	5	5	5	2	3	8	6	5	10	9	10	7	28,359
Singapore	8	9	9	9	12	10	12	14	15	15	14	12	4	5	9	5	12	6	21	23,393
Netherlands	9	7	3	4	3	3	10	8	3	7	8	5	11	10	3	3	3	4	10	27,275
France	10	15	13	15	9	11	9	10	10	9	6	6	14	21	13	15	11	13	14	26,151
Australia	11	14	14	10	13	15	18	19	24	20	19	22	7	11	7	7	10	12	8	27,756
Canada	12	10	12	11	8	6	14	13	14	16	12	15	10	7	11	8	4	3	5	28,699
Japan	13	11	10	14	14	18	6	7	8	4	4	7	20	17	16	19	19	19	17	25,650
Iceland	14	17	16	17	22	24	15	17	16	14	21	28	12	14	15	16	21	23	4	29,614
Belgium	15	13	15	12	15	19	11	11	12	10	11	13	17	15	14	13	15	18	11	26,695
Taiwan	16	16	21	21	19	20	16	16	20	18	17	16	16	13	21	21	22	21	20	23,420
Austria	17	12	11	13	11	16	13	12	11	12	10	11	18	12	12	12	13	17	6	28,611
New Zealand	18	22	20	19	16	17	23	25	19	22	16	19	13	20	20	17	14	16	23	20,455
Hong Kong SAR	19	19	18	16	21	12	22	24	21	23	24	17	15	16	17	14	18	11	13	26,235
Israel	20	18	17	18	20	21	20	20	18	13	18	21	19	18	18	20	20	20	24	19,382
Ireland	21	20	22	22	17	13	17	15	17	19	20	18	22	22	22	22	17	14	9	27,642
Norway	22	21	19	20	18	14	21	23	23	21	23	14	21	19	19	18	16	15	1	36,047
Korea	23	23	26	27	28	28	19	21	26	25	27	24	25	23	29	28	30	28	28	16,465
Italy	24	24	23	24	25	26	24	18	13	17	15	20	23	24	24	26	27	27	18	25,570
Spain	25	25	24	23	23	22	25	22	22	24	22	23	26	25	23	23	23	22	22	20,697
Malaysia	26	26	37	30	27	27	26	27	37	30	25	34	24	26	37	30	31	26	43	8,922
South Africa	27	29	25	25	26	25	28	31	25	26	28	33	28	33	27	25	25	25	37	10,132
Estonia	28	30	28	—	—	—	36	36	32	—	—	—	27	28	26	—	—	—	33	11,712
Latvia	29	45	41	—	—	—	29	48	35	—	—	—	31	42	42	—	—	—	42	8,965
Slovenia	30	27	32	—	—	—	27	26	28	—	—	—	34	27	35	—	—	—	27	17,748
Thailand	31	35	38	40	39	37	31	33	42	47	43	37	32	35	39	40	39	36	50	6,788
Chile	32	31	29	26	24	23	34	35	30	27	26	25	30	31	30	24	24	24	40	9,561
Tunisia	33	32	—	—	—	—	38	37	—	—	—	29	30	—	—	—	—	—	51	6,579
Brazil	34	33	30	31	35	35	30	28	29	29	32	27	39	36	32	32	37	39	48	7,516
Czech Republic	35	34	34	34	41	30	33	34	41	41	55	31	38	34	31	34	36	33	29	15,148
Portugal	36	36	33	28	29	33	46	41	38	35	37	48	33	32	28	27	26	30	26	17,808
India	37	37	36	37	42	44	40	40	43	40	48	50	36	37	34	37	43	42	72	2,571
Hungary	38	28	27	32	33	31	45	29	33	34	36	39	37	29	25	31	33	31	30	13,129
Greece	39	43	46	33	36	38	39	47	51	32	45	32	40	41	43	33	34	38	25	18,184
Lithuania	40	40	50	—	—	—	41	39	47	—	—	—	41	39	47	—	—	—	38	10,015
Jordan	41	53	47	35	32	32	57	59	56	46	44	42	35	48	41	35	28	32	64	4,106
Slovak Republic	42	42	40	36	48	36	44	43	57	31	51	40	42	40	36	36	47	37	31	12,426
Mauritius	43	49	51	38	30	—	35	42	49	37	29	—	45	50	50	38	29	—	35	10,530
Costa Rica	44	39	48	43	38	—	32	32	34	39	35	—	46	47	51	42	41	—	45	8,470
China	45	38	43	44	49	42	42	38	39	38	31	35	43	38	46	45	50	44	62	4,475
Poland	46	46	42	41	37	41	43	46	55	36	38	38	44	45	40	41	38	40	36	10,187
Mexico	47	55	52	42	34	39	37	45	46	42	30	29	50	60	52	43	35	41	44	8,707
Morocco	48	48	—	—	—	—	48	50	—	—	—	—	48	46	—	—	—	—	68	3,767
Vietnam	49	60	62	53	50	43	52	67	64	50	41	36	47	58	62	52	49	43	76	2,240
Colombia	50	56	57	48	52	49	49	51	52	48	40	43	53	57	59	48	53	49	56	6,068
Turkey	51	54	35	29	31	29	50	56	44	28	33	26	54	55	33	29	32	29	55	6,176
Trinidad and Tobago	52	44	31	—	—	—	53	44	27	—	—	—	52	44	38	—	—	—	41	9,114
Botswana	53	57	—	—	—	—	63	64	—	—	—	—	49	51	—	—	—	—	46	8,244
Namibia	54	51	—	—	—	—	61	58	—	—	—	—	51	49	—	—	—	—	52	6,410
Jamaica	55	59	39	—	—	—	54	60	31	—	—	—	55	59	44	—	—	—	67	3,774
Sri Lanka	56	47	58	—	—	—	51	52	58	—	—	—	57	43	56	—	—	—	69	3,447
Panama	57	50	49	—	—	—	58	54	40	—	—	—	58	52	49	—	—	—	57	5,972
Indonesia	58	64	55	47	53	51	59	55	50	51	47	52	59	65	58	47	52	51	71	3,138
Dominican Republic	59	41	60	—	—	—	55	30	59	—	—	—	60	53	61	—	—	—	54	6,197
Croatia	60	52	—	—	—	—	62	53	—	—	—	—	56	54	—	—	—	—	39	9,967
El Salvador	61	63	64	51	47	—	56	61	66	57	46	—	62	62	64	50	48	—	61	4,675
Philippines	62	61	53	46	46	45	47	49	45	43	34	41	66	67	54	46	46	45	65	4,021
Russian Federation	63	58	56	52	55	46	64	62	54	33	42	45	61	56	55	53	55	47	47	7,926
Argentina	64	65	54	45	40	34	60	57	53	45	39	30	65	68	53	44	40	34	34	10,594
Uruguay	65	62	45	—	—	—	70	63	48	—	—	—	63	61	45	—	—	—	32	12,118
Ukraine	66	69	59	56	56	52	66	66	62	52	50	51	68	69	57	56	56	52	60	4,714
Romania	67	67	61	—	—	—	72	69	63	—	—	—	64	64	60	—	—	—	53	6,326
Bulgaria	68	68	68	55	54	—	73	72	70	54	52	—	67	63	65	54	54	—	49	6,909
Zimbabwe	69	70	65	50	45	48	65	68	60	56	54	46	71	70	67	49	45	48	77	1,993
Nigeria	70	71	66	—	—	—	67	71	61	—	—	—	70	71	68	—	—	—	80	851
Peru	71	66	63	49	46	47	71	65	65	53	56	49	69	66	63	51	44	46	59	4,924
Venezuela	72	72	67	54	51	50	68	73	67	49	53	44	72	72	66	55	51	50	58	5,226
Guatemala	73	73	69	—	—	—	69	70	69	—	—	—	73	73	69	—	—	—	66	3,927
Ecuador	74	77	72	57	57	—	74	74	71	55	57	—	75	77	72	58	57	—	70	3,357
Bangladesh	75	74	73	—	—	—	76	76	72	—	—	—	74	74	73	—	—	—	78	1,736
Nicaragua	76	75	71	—	—	—	77	75	73	—	—	—	76	76	70	—	—	—	74	2,510
Honduras	77	78	74	—	—	—	75	78	74	—	—	—	77	79	75	—	—	—	73	2,520
Paraguay	78	76	70	—	—	—	78	77	68	—	—	—	79	75	71	—	—	—	63	4,419
Bolivia	79	79	75	58	58	—	79	79	75	58	58	—	78	78	74	57	58	—	75	2,360
Haiti	80	80	—	—	—	—	80	80	—	—	—	—	80	80	—	—	—	—	79	1,578

Note: GNI per capita is used for Ireland

even among units of foreign companies. We calculated Index rankings for all 101 countries shown in Table 2, with those marked with an asterisk subject to large variance in some of the Survey data.[10] The quality of Survey responses is expected to improve with future educational efforts and improved sampling in these countries. In the meantime, these rankings should be interpreted with caution.

For the 95-country sample used in the regressions and for computing the Index model, there is an average of more than 70 respondents per country. The degree of within-country consensus is striking. For all measures, the proportion of variation due to country differences is statistically significant. For most measures, between one third and one half of the overall variation in the responses is driven by country-specific differences for that measure. As expected, the within-country consensus rate is higher for cross-cutting business environment indicators, such as overall infrastructure quality, and lower for measures where there would be variation within the country across companies and clusters, such as state of cluster development. The country averages, then, capture meaningful differences across countries in competitive circumstances while limiting idiosyncratic biases that would result if there were only a handful of responses per country.

The dependent variable used to develop the BCI is the level of GDP per capita in 2002, adjusted for purchasing power parity (PPP).[11] GDP per capita is the broadest measure of national productivity and is strongly linked over time to a nation's standard of living.[12] It is the best single, summary measure of microeconomic competitiveness available across all countries.[13] GDP per capita will reflect a country's structural fundamentals over the medium and long term. However, it is also influenced by a wide array of short-term and idiosyncratic factors such as natural disasters, macroeconomic shocks, and price movements in particular export industries. The proportion of the variation in GDP per capita across all countries that can be explained by microeconomic fundamentals is interesting in its own right.

To explore differences in the sources of competitiveness across countries at different levels of development, we divided countries into three groups based on income. There is no accepted division among low-, medium-, and high-income countries, and efforts to define income cutoffs statistically have not proved fertile. Instead, we proceed pragmatically, dividing countries based on two criteria. First, we use income cutoffs that yield to logical divisions of countries in terms of aspiration and competitive position. Second, we ensure that there are enough countries in each group to allow meaningful statistical tests. This year, with the addition of many low-income countries, we were for the first time in a position to move the cutoffs down to levels that we believe are more appropriate: US$4,000

GDP per capita (PPP) for low- to middle-income countries and US$17,000 GDP per capita (PPP) for medium- to high-income countries. Hence Israel, Portugal, Greece, and Slovenia become part of the high-income group, and Thailand, Tunisia, Namibia, Romania, the Dominican Republic, Turkey, Colombia, Panama, Venezuela, Peru, the Ukraine, El Salvador, China, Paraguay, Jordan, and the Philippines become part of the middle-income group. Since there are likely to be relatively few new countries added to the sample in the future, these cutoffs should remain stable. However, differences between this year's and last year's income analysis should be interpreted with caution.

The addition of many low-income countries allows a wider separation between income groups compared to previous years. In our sample made for statistical analysis of 95 countries, there were 28 low-income countries with a purchasing power–adjusted US-dollar GDP per capita in 2002 below US$4,000, 39 middle-income countries with GDP per capita between US$4,000 and US$17,000, and 28 high-income countries with a GDP per capita above US$17,000. With the exception of Malta (high-income) and Algeria (middle-income), the new countries entering the Survey fall into the low-income group. As will be reported, these groups exhibited different patterns of influence among variables.

Sources of competitiveness

To construct an overall index of competitiveness, we first validated the statistical relationship of a wide array of measures of microeconomic competitiveness with GDP per capita that are suggested by our conceptual framework. Variables are drawn from Survey responses and available quantitative measures, and are grouped into those measuring the sophistication of company operations and strategy and those measuring the quality of the national business environment. A number of new questions were included in the Survey this year, with several addressing the context for company strategy and rivalry. A full list of Survey questions and available quantitative measures is given in Appendix A.

Table 3 gives bivariate regressions on GDP per capita that proved the most statistically significant. Included in the table is the mean response across all countries or groups of countries, the slope of the regression relationship, a measure of the statistical significance of the relationship, and the adjusted R^2 (or proportion of variation in GDP per capita explained by the variable, adjusted for statistical degrees of freedom).[14] While the bivariate regressions are not meant to represent a fully specified model, they provide a basic test of whether the variables have a meaningful relationship with the level of GDP per capita across countries. All the reported variables are highly statistically significant in the full sample of countries. A wide

Table 2: The Business Competitiveness Index, full sample of 101 countries

Country	BCI ranking, 2003	Company operations and strategy ranking, 2003	Quality of the national business environment ranking, 2003	2002 GDP per capita rank	2002 GDP per capita (PPP adjusted)
Finland	1	4	1	15	25,859
United States	2	2	2	2	35,158
Sweden	3	3	5	19	25,315
Denmark	4	7	3	3	29,975
Germany	5	1	9	12	26,324
United Kingdom	6	8	6	16	25,672
Switzerland	7	5	8	7	28,359
Singapore	8	12	4	21	23,393
Netherlands	9	10	11	10	27,275
France	10	9	14	14	26,151
Australia	11	18	7	8	27,756
Canada	12	14	10	5	28,699
Japan	13	6	20	17	25,650
Iceland	14	15	12	4	29,614
Belgium	15	11	17	11	26,695
Taiwan	16	16	16	20	23,420
Austria	17	13	18	6	28,611
New Zealand	18	23	13	23	20,455
Hong Kong SAR	19	22	15	13	26,235
Israel	20	20	19	24	19,382
Ireland	21	17	22	9	27,642
Norway	22	21	21	1	36,047
Korea	23	19	25	29	16,465
Italy	24	24	23	18	25,570
Spain	25	25	26	22	20,697
Malaysia	26	26	24	44	8,922
South Africa	27	28	28	38	10,132
Estonia	28	36	27	34	11,712
Latvia	29	29	31	43	8,965
Slovenia	30	27	34	27	17,748
Thailand	31	31	32	51	6,788
Chile	32	34	30	41	9,561
Tunisia	33	38	29	52	6,579
Brazil	34	30	39	49	7,516
Czech Republic	35	33	38	30	15,148
Portugal	36	46	33	26	17,808
India	37	40	36	77	2,571
Hungary	38	45	37	31	13,129
Greece	39	39	40	25	18,184
Lithuania	40	41	41	39	10,015
Jordan	41	59	35	67	4,106
Malta	42	47	42	28	17,344
Slovak Republic	43	44	43	32	12,426
Mauritius	44	35	46	36	10,530
Costa Rica	45	32	47	46	8,470
China	46	42	44	65	4,475
Poland	47	43	45	37	10,187
Mexico	48	37	51	45	8,707
Morocco	49	49	49	71	3,767
Vietnam	50	53	48	81	2,240
Colombia	51	50	54	58	6,068
Turkey	52	51	55	57	6,176
Trinidad and Tobago	53	54	53	42	9,114
Botswana	54	67	50	47	8,244
Namibia	55	64	52	53	6,410
Jamaica	56	56	56	70	3,774
Sri Lanka	57	52	59	73	3,447
Egypt	58	55	62	72	3,701
Panama	59	60	60	59	5,972
Indonesia	60	62	61	76	3,138
Dominican Republic	61	57	63	56	6,197
Croatia	62	65	58	40	9,967
Ghana*	63	66	57	83	2,050
El Salvador	64	58	65	64	4,675
Philippines	65	48	74	68	4,021
Russian Federation	66	69	64	48	7,926
Kenya	67	61	72	94	992
Tanzania	68	68	67	101	557
Argentina	69	63	73	35	10,594
Gambia*	70	80	66	87	1,723
Uruguay	71	77	68	33	12,118
Malawi	72	71	76	100	586
Ukraine	73	72	77	63	4,714
Uganda*	74	78	69	91	1,354
Pakistan	75	81	70	84	2,014
Romania	76	84	71	54	6,326
Bulgaria	77	85	75	50	6,909
Zimbabwe	78	70	81	85	1,993
Serbia	79	75	79	75	3,270
Nigeria	80	73	80	96	851
Peru	81	83	78	62	4,924
Macedonia*	82	79	83	55	6,262
Cameroon*	83	86	82	88	1,712
Zambia	84	82	85	97	806
Venezuela	85	74	87	61	5,226
Guatemala	86	76	88	69	3,927
Senegal	87	94	84	90	1,535
Algeria	88	93	86	60	5,536
Ecuador	89	87	92	74	3,357
Madagascar	90	88	90	98	735
Bangladesh	91	91	91	86	1,736
Mali*	92	98	89	95	878
Mozambique	93	90	95	92	1,237
Nicaragua	94	92	93	79	2,510
Honduras	95	89	96	78	2,520
Ethiopia	96	96	94	99	724
Paraguay	97	95	98	66	4,419
Bolivia	98	97	97	80	2,360
Chad	99	99	99	93	1,008
Haiti	100	101	100	89	1,578
Angola	101	100	101	82	2,053

(cont'd.)

39

* Survey data for these countries have high within-country variance. Until the reliability of Survey responses improves with future educational efforts and improved sampling in these countries, their rankings should be interpreted with caution.

range of company practices and multiple dimensions of the business environment prove strongly related to competitiveness. These findings are highly consistent with results from earlier *Global Competitiveness Reports*. While a bilateral statistical correlation to GDP per capita does not necessarily imply causation, it does refute the hypothesis that microeconomic variables have no important relation to prosperity. Interestingly, prominent macroeconomic variables such as the national savings rate and the level of investment as a percentage of GDP are either not significantly related to the level of GDP per capita in bilateral regressions or are associated with only a minor share of its variation across countries.[15]

Among the company variables, production process sophistication, the willingness to delegate authority, the extent of branding, the capacity for innovation, and the extent of staff training have the strongest bilateral association with per capita GDP. By itself, the measure of overall competitive approach—whether competitive advantage is based on cheap inputs or on unique products and processes—explains a remarkable 68 percent of the variance in GDP per capita.

All four parts of the business environment prove important, with the influences of individual variables highly stable from previous years. Among factor conditions, telecommunication access (cellular phone and Internet use), the quality of electricity supply, the quality of public schools, and university-industry research collaboration have the strongest bilateral association with GDP per capita. Many of the most important influences on GDP per capita relate to policies and institutions rather than factor stocks.

Measures of local demand conditions perform particularly strongly. The presence of demanding regulatory standards, stringent environmental regulations, and buyer sophistication, among other measures, are strongly associated with the variation in GDP per capita. These results run counter to the perceived wisdom that local demand and local market conditions are not important in a global economy.

Cluster linkages, especially the quality of local suppliers and the presence of specialized local research and training providers, also prove significant and highlight the role of clusters in competitiveness. Finally, the incentives and rules governing local competition show a strong relationship to national productivity. Intellectual property protection, the prevalence of illegal or unfair activities (corruption), the effectiveness of antitrust policy, and the openness to trade tariff and nontariff barriers are particularly potent variables.

It is important to acknowledge that causality can be argued in both directions for some of the variables, though the Survey questions were worded to avoid spurious reverse causality. The quality of scientists and engineers or the sophistication of buyers, for example, could be partly the *result* of high per capita GDP and not the cause. Note that the same causality issue applies to macroeconomic and economic growth analyses. We provide some evidence of causality from microeconomic conditions to GDP per capita later in this chapter, but more years of surveying will be required to establish definitive cause-and-effect relationships.

Competitiveness and economic development

As has been discussed, the appropriate company strategies and operating practices, as well as the influence of particular elements of the business environment will differ for countries at different levels of development. As noted earlier, the transition to entirely different stages of competitive development is particularly challenging.

To examine these issues, we explored the impact of measures of microeconomic competitiveness in the three country groups based on per capita GDP. While the reported variables are statistically significant across the entire sample and strongly distinguish countries across groups, individual variables, as expected, differ in their influence within groups. Some variables will not yet be important for low-income countries. Others may act via a threshold a country may have to reach.

The right-hand side of Table 3 presents regressions by income subgroups. We explore the differences in the mean Survey response, the differences in slope as well as the pattern of statistical significance of each variable with the caveat that limitations on subgroup sample size and the more limited variation of the dependent variable within subgroups reduce statistical power.

It is notable that for all variables the mean Survey response increases as we compare low- and high-income countries. This confirms the fact that economic development is associated with sustained improvement across many aspects of the business environment and company behavior. However, we find distinctive differences in the relative importance and trajectory of improvements of particular of the process of development.

Low-income countries

For low-income countries at the Factor-Driven stage of development, the ability to move beyond competing solely on cheap labor/natural resources is the essential challenge revealed in the regressions. At the company level, improving the sophistication of production processes, extending the presence along the value chain, and beginning to practice marketing and branding are revealed as most significant. Some progress in professionalizing the organization and widening international presence is important. At this stage, progress on other dimensions of corporate strategy and operations, especially those related to distinctive products or technology, is premature.

Low-income countries score low on most measures of the business environment, but especially on infrastructure, educational quality, cluster development, capital access, and measures related to technology and innovation. Priorities for improving the business environment in low-income countries revealed in the regressions start with upgrading the quality of infrastructure (including electricity, communications, and transportation networks) and schools. Also revealed as important are the creation of financial markets (access to risk capital and loans), the strengthening of emerging clusters (local supplier quality, local availability of machinery and components, and local availability of process machinery), and the opening of competitive processes (reduction of trade barriers and favoritism in decisions by government officials). All these steps create a foundation of efficiency, transparency, and competitive pressure that supports Factor-Driven competition. Other aspects of the business environment, such as expanding the availability of scientists and engineers, and updating regulatory standards are not yet priorities at this stage of development.

Middle-income countries

Moving into middle income, the task is to move beyond Factor-Driven competition to the Investment-Driven stage. The regressions suggest the following patterns: improving production process sophistication remains the single most important corporate priority. But companies must also begin to build brands (versus relying on commodities or products designed by foreign OEMs), expand regional and international markets, create the capacity for technology absorption and innovation, and increase the professionalism of employees and management. Their biggest challenge remains the nature of their competitive advantages, often still based solely on low cost of production inputs.

To reach the middle-income level, countries must have improved in basic factor conditions such as physical infrastructure and human resources. Continued progress in some of those areas remains important, with public schools, electricity supply, telecommunication quality, and Internet usage particularly significant, as revealed in the regressions. Success as a middle-income county also raises new challenges in the business environment. Improving university-industry research collaboration and the quality of research institutions becomes important. The quality of the judicial system becomes significant. Improving local demand conditions, for example through more stringent environmental and consumer protection laws, is needed to pressure improvements in producer quality. All aspects of cluster development become significant, with widening the supplier base and improving the availability of specialized research and training institutions registering the greatest absolute impact in statistical terms. Finally, moving

to higher levels of competition and rivalry is needed in many dimensions, including tariff and nontariff barrier liberalization, improving antitrust policy, and opening the market for corporate control.

High-income countries

To reach high-income status, improvement in quality and efficiency are no longer enough. The hurdle is to move to the Innovation-Driven stage. The patterns of regressions suggest the following priorities: companies must develop the ability to innovate at the world technology frontier, create unique product designs, become experts in marketing, build international brands, and sell their products and services globally. Reliance on foreign technology becomes a negative. In order to accomplish this transformation, a series of organizational changes such as extensive staff training, use of greater incentive compensation, and the ability to professionalize management and delegate authority becomes necessary.

High-income countries have all achieved strengths in many aspects of the business environment. Continuing to improve infrastructure, simplicity and fairness of regulation, and schools remain important. The factors that distinguish high-income countries are concentrated in areas connected to innovation and the creation of distinctive strategies: the quality of management education, availability of scientific talent, the quality of research institutions, the extent of research collaboration with universities, venture capital availability, the sophistication of demand conditions (eg, demanding regulatory standards and local buyer sophistication), deep cluster development, decentralization of corporate activity away from large business groups, and sophisticated regulatory rules on bankruptcy and corporate governance.

Trends in competitiveness in the global economy

With several years of consistent Survey data, we can examine the trends in the variables that offset competitiveness between the 1998 Survey and the 2003 Survey.[16] Table 4 identifies those variables where substantial changes in company practices and the quality of the business environment, defined as greater than 10 percent positive or negative changes in the mean Survey responses between 1998 and 2003, were registered in eight more countries, or 15 percent of the sample of 52 countries for which we have six years of data. Other measures of change (fixed absolute changes or different percentage cutoffs) produce virtually identical results.

Overall, there is clear upgrading in national business environments. The bar is rising, and improvement here is needed just to maintain position vis-à-vis other countries. In company operations and strategy, companies are progressing along some dimensions in many countries but

Table 3: Bivariate regression results, dependent variable: 2002 GDP per capita (PPP adjusted US dollars)

	All countries (N = 95)			Low-income countries GDP per capita < $4,000 (N = 28)			Middle-income countries GDP per capita > $4,000 and < $17,000 (N = 39)			High-income countries GDP per capita > $17,000 except Norway (N = 27)		
	Mean	Slope	Adj. R^2	Mean	Slope	Adj. R^2	Mean	Slope	Adj. R^2	Mean	Slope	Adj. R^2
I. COMPANY OPERATIONS & STRATEGY												
Production process sophistication	3.86	7378.6**	0.825	2.68	1198.5**	0.398	3.60	3573.9**	0.370	5.40	4282.3**	0.472
Nature of competitive advantage	3.55	7040.8**	0.678	2.82	504.3	0.026	3.06	1960.5**	0.081	4.99	2260.7**	0.254
Extent of staff training	3.91	8120.4**	0.705	3.04	660.6*	0.075	3.68	1775.5**	0.116	5.11	4583.9**	0.503
Extent of marketing	4.30	7559.3**	0.689	3.26	655.6**	0.179	4.17	2347.5**	0.211	5.54	5597.1**	0.533
Willingness to delegate authority	3.70	8250.4**	0.731	2.83	739.4*	0.080	3.45	1928.0*	0.073	4.89	3485.4**	0.432
Capacity for innovation	3.49	7617.3**	0.720	2.62	708.0*	0.087	3.17	2981.8**	0.275	4.82	2726.7**	0.293
Company spending on research and development	3.44	8196.3**	0.630	2.71	511.0	0.039	3.20	2625.6**	0.183	4.53	2877.8**	0.273
Value chain presence	3.82	6302.4**	0.669	2.78	839.3**	0.222	3.49	1713.9**	0.157	5.34	2069.4**	0.192
Breadth of international markets	3.87	6404.8**	0.661	2.81	579.3*	0.107	3.62	1624.8**	0.184	5.31	3132.5**	0.335
Degree of customer orientation	4.58	9638.3**	0.632	3.87	279.8	−0.015	4.44	1686.1*	0.058	5.50	6630.9**	0.462
Control of international distribution	3.87	10759.9**	0.637	3.28	953.3**	0.134	3.71	1787.6	0.042	4.69	5323.7**	0.473
Extent of branding	3.57	6902.7**	0.731	2.57	1094.4**	0.309	3.22	2693.0**	0.227	5.08	2629.5**	0.339
Reliance on professional management	4.69	7864.4**	0.559	4.05	−212.0	−0.019	4.44	2262.8**	0.203	5.69	3656.7**	0.348
Extent of incentive compensation	4.01	8652.5**	0.632	3.26	637.3	0.062	3.85	1803.5**	0.115	5.01	4139.8**	0.358
Extent of regional sales	4.56	5971.9**	0.515	3.47	281.0	0.012	4.57	1506.1**	0.165	5.66	2847.9**	0.276
Prevalence of foreign technology licensing	4.51	5651.7**	0.164	3.95	321.3	0.020	4.65	1322.0*	0.054	4.87	−1298.5	−0.030
II. NATIONAL BUSINESS ENVIRONMENT												
A. FACTOR (INPUT) CONDITIONS												
1. Physical Infrastructure												
Overall infrastructure quality	3.94	5428.4**	0.652	2.51	738.7**	0.182	3.81	1078.3**	0.093	5.58	2503.7**	0.308
Railroad infrastructure development	3.16	4276.0**	0.475	2.02	230.1	−0.003	2.91	929.6**	0.133	4.71	1382.5**	0.175
Port infrastructure quality	3.93	5253.6**	0.586	2.60	652.4**	0.256	3.78	813.9	0.046	5.49	1693.6*	0.082
Air transport infrastructure quality	4.58	5864.4**	0.494	3.66	287.3	0.013	4.38	443.3	−0.006	5.80	3197.4**	0.216
Quality of electricity supply	4.68	5381.3**	0.701	2.94	751.7**	0.408	4.77	2179.1**	0.377	6.29	4571.3**	0.491
Telephone/fax infrastructure quality	5.32	4917.3**	0.478	3.91	349.1**	0.148	5.43	1171.9**	0.104	6.59	5294.2*	0.094
Cellular telephones, 2002	35.98	270.9**	0.779	5.61	108.4**	0.464	27.66	124.5**	0.606	77.71	−95.3	0.065
Internet users, 2002	16.68	495.3**	0.840	1.49	436.8**	0.322	10.36	206.1**	0.499	40.32	198.2**	0.230
2. Administrative Infrastructure												
Reliability of police services	4.16	5939.4**	0.572	3.20	345.0	0.032	3.82	387.4	−0.012	5.59	3377.6**	0.212
Judicial independence	3.95	4951.1**	0.539	2.82	−3.3	−0.038	3.66	1003.7**	0.131	5.50	1801.7	0.067
Efficiency of legal framework	3.88	5823.7**	0.562	2.93	−4.3	−0.038	3.57	849.7*	0.053	5.26	2634.8**	0.205
Administrative burden for startups	4.04	5860.6**	0.312	3.46	5.4	−0.038	3.93	682.0	0.009	4.78	1815.3*	0.106
Extent of bureaucratic red tape	5.53	12876.9**	0.248	5.28	1206.0**	0.121	5.52	1429.8	0.011	5.77	5644.0	0.012
3. Human Resources												
Quality of management schools	4.28	7575.3**	0.611	3.34	553.5**	0.118	4.19	1558.9**	0.077	5.34	4016.8**	0.322
Quality of public schools	3.80	5585.4**	0.701	2.30	720.8**	0.148	3.69	1722.0**	0.364	5.46	2918.0**	0.175
Quality of the educational system	3.54	6380.4**	0.605	2.41	233.4	−0.015	3.42	1376.0**	0.113	4.85	2224.5**	0.120
Quality of math and science education	4.17	5627.1**	0.421	3.21	273.6	0.008	4.16	1382.8**	0.185	5.19	1897.2	0.053
4. Technology Infrastructure												
Utility patents, 2002	28.34	112.8**	0.483	0.07	2799.1**	0.141	2.83	121.1**	0.222	93.57	23.8**	0.181
Availability of scientists and engineers	4.70	6593.7**	0.422	3.96	204.1	−0.008	4.62	1508.1**	0.122	5.55	3507.7**	0.188
Quality of scientific research institutions	4.04	7852.2**	0.590	3.29	79.7	−0.035	3.84	2775.9**	0.285	5.07	3882.2**	0.333
University/industry research collaboration	3.33	8012.8**	0.656	2.48	458.2	0.031	3.13	2087.8**	0.164	4.46	3686.0**	0.318
5. Capital Markets												
Financial market sophistication	4.02	6189.1**	0.628	2.88	721.7**	0.198	3.85	872.4	0.036	5.43	3159.0**	0.318
Venture capital availability	3.24	8253.2**	0.610	2.51	1114.0**	0.285	3.03	1839.2**	0.148	4.24	2911.1**	0.176
Ease of access to loans	3.26	7883.5**	0.548	2.48	911.4**	0.214	3.13	947.8	0.022	4.20	2611.9*	0.109
Local equity market access	4.61	3723.5**	0.217	4.08	66.7	−0.030	4.33	278.5	−0.017	5.53	2479.7	0.064
B. DEMAND CONDITIONS												
Buyer sophistication	3.94	7604.6**	0.710	2.93	501.2*	0.073	3.72	2067.3**	0.134	5.28	5373.0**	0.414
Sophistication of local buyers' products and processes	4.49	9128.1**	0.660	3.66	402.5	0.010	4.37	2493.1**	0.175	5.47	4411.8**	0.207
Government procurment of advanced technology products	3.60	8329.1**	0.329	3.16	−23.5	−0.038	3.53	1464.4*	0.063	4.15	2807.0*	0.079
Presence of demanding regulatory standards	4.25	7178.5**	0.745	3.04	477.3	0.063	4.13	2934.4**	0.411	5.62	5273.6**	0.513
Laws relating to ICT	3.74	7647.1**	0.596	2.80	670.0*	0.102	3.67	1729.8**	0.158	4.76	3485.5**	0.199
Stringency of environmental regulations	4.03	6619.8**	0.741	2.83	363.6	−0.001	3.81	2496.4**	0.334	5.49	2679.2**	0.325

(cont'd.)

Table 3: Bivariate regression results, dependent variable: 2002 GDP per capita (PPP adjusted US dollars) *(cont'd.)*

	All countries (N = 95)			Low-income countries GDP per capita < $4,000 (N = 28)			Middle-income countries GDP per capita > $4,000 and < $17,000 (N = 39)			High-income countries GDP per capita > $17,000 except Norway (N = 27)		
	Mean	Slope	Adj. R^2	Mean	Slope	Adj. R^2	Mean	Slope	Adj. R^2	Mean	Slope	Adj. R^2
II. NATIONAL BUSINESS ENVIRONMENT *(cont'd.)*												
C. RELATED AND SUPPORTING INDUSTRIES												
Local supplier quality	4.33	8170.6**	0.719	3.33	730.2**	0.150	4.20	2312.1**	0.190	5.54	6621.8**	0.567
State of cluster development	3.27	6960.8**	0.424	2.77	397.3	0.040	3.00	1343.5*	0.051	4.14	2309.3**	0.188
Local availability of process machinery	2.87	6544.6**	0.476	2.08	746.6**	0.178	2.76	1415.6**	0.101	3.84	2295.7**	0.246
Local availability of specialized research and training services	4.10	8219.7**	0.674	3.18	674.4**	0.145	3.98	3061.8**	0.279	5.21	4512.0**	0.439
Extent of collaboration among clusters	3.60	7933.6**	0.561	2.84	705.2**	0.133	3.47	1734.5**	0.122	4.53	3550.1**	0.335
Local supplier quantity	4.68	8671.7**	0.489	4.04	179.1	−0.023	4.59	2056.2**	0.119	5.45	6349.7**	0.420
Local availability of components and parts	3.22	6594.6**	0.465	2.35	643.2**	0.155	3.19	1325.5**	0.083	4.13	2527.5**	0.226
D. CONTEXT FOR FIRM STRATEGY AND RIVALRY												
1. Incentives												
Extent of distortive government subsidies	3.37	6395.3**	0.179	3.02	490.3	0.006	3.34	1120.3	0.032	3.80	238.4	−0.039
Favoritism in decisions of government officials	3.30	7231.0**	0.494	2.61	160.1	−0.030	3.09	938.2	0.023	4.27	2051.4**	0.111
Cooperation in labor–employer relations	4.45	7573.8**	0.288	4.06	−450.2	−0.004	4.33	−116.5	−0.026	4.99	2668.7**	0.189
Efficacy of corporate boards	4.45	10674.2**	0.497	4.02	−465.3	0.009	4.29	2010.5*	0.065	5.11	4574.1**	0.293
Intellectual property protection	3.82	6818.2**	0.751	2.67	725.9**	0.109	3.53	1559.7**	0.119	5.37	3893.6**	0.411
Protection of minority shareholders' interests	4.50	7490.2**	0.439	3.99	−203.4	−0.024	4.21	101.5	−0.026	5.40	2462.1*	0.081
Regulation of securities exchanges	4.80	6933.8**	0.469	4.05	4.0	−0.038	4.66	1179.6*	0.060	5.75	4111.3**	0.207
Effectiveness of bankruptcy law	4.45	6679.7**	0.625	3.48	−134.9	−0.029	4.20	995.5	0.043	5.76	4584.6**	0.497
2. Competition												
Hidden trade barriers	4.57	8000.4**	0.597	3.73	292.0	−0.019	4.41	2354.2**	0.264	5.67	964.3	−0.024
Intensity of local competition	4.75	9526.1**	0.449	4.16	81.3	−0.036	4.71	2087.5**	0.085	5.41	6273.3**	0.125
Extent of locally based competitors	4.26	7599.2**	0.377	3.58	502.6*	0.085	4.29	982.4	0.013	4.92	4594.5**	0.252
Effectiveness of antitrust policy	3.96	7596.4**	0.654	3.05	253.1	−0.017	3.73	1742.1**	0.129	5.18	3085.4**	0.178
Decentralization of corporate activity	3.93	7606.3**	0.564	3.24	186.1	−0.023	3.66	1005.4	0.011	5.01	3609.0**	0.393
Business costs of corruption	3.92	7198.4**	0.688	3.01	567.4	0.022	3.60	1674.0**	0.127	5.28	2231.9**	0.157
Cost of importing foreign equipment	5.87	10668.5**	0.579	5.20	1050.6**	0.266	5.82	2874.5**	0.184	6.65	8374.0*	0.076
Centralization of economic policymaking	2.99	6164.9**	0.337	2.50	222.8	−0.017	2.82	1569.4**	0.077	3.72	1944.3**	0.216
Prevalence of mergers and acquisitions	3.93	8565.9**	0.525	3.28	725.4**	0.140	3.82	2304.5**	0.112	4.73	3056.3**	0.292
Foreign ownership restrictions	5.02	6102.9**	0.168	4.75	−123.5	−0.032	4.92	1864.9**	0.097	5.45	1364.9	−0.001

Note: * denotes p < 0.10, ** denotes p < 0.05

there are also signs that the growing intensity of competition is making it hard to keep up, and that greater international specialization of activity is occurring.

As shown in Table 4, companies are working to professionalize management in increasingly competitive markets, the single most widespread global development among companies. Also widespread are improvements in marketing and customer orientation plus moves to regionalize sales as regional trade opening continues.

Although companies are improving in some respects, they are struggling to cope with tough international competition. Especially in middle-income countries, companies report less presence in value chain, often accompanied by greater international specialization of activities. Companies in middle-income countries are also having difficulty defending brands and maintaining global distribution and marketing presence. Overall, these observations are consistent with a global marketplace that has, in many ways, become more sophisticated and more demanding,

especially for companies in middle-income countries that are trying to move away from dependence on cheap inputs.

Table 4 shows that governments around the world are continuing to reduce bureaucratic red tape, lower tariffs, improve corporate governance, upgrade financial markets, and improve infrastructure. Progress in these areas is increasingly becoming a given if countries are to participate fully in the world economy.

This year's data confirm a trend already noted last year: *middle-income economies have been less successful in sustaining the improvements in their business environments than high-income economies.* Hence, the competitive gap between economies at different stages of development seems to be rising again; this is a trend especially pronounced in some aspects of the context for firm rivalry and, alarmingly, in the quality of public schools. Recent worldwide economic conditions, coupled with debates about globalization, appear to have made it more difficult for less-developed

Table 4: Significant changes in competitive conditions in eight or more countries, 1998–2003

	Improving international competitive conditions				Worsening international competitive conditions			
		No. of countries				No. of countries		
		Total	L	M	H		Total	L	M	H

	Improving international competitive conditions					Worsening international competitive conditions			
Sophistication of Company Operations and Strategy	Reliance on professional management — 41	3	17	21	Value chain presence — 29	4	19	6
	Extent of marketing — 23	2	7	14	Extent of branding — 26	4	17	5
	Degree of customer orientation — 23	2	11	10	Breadth of international markets — 24	4	15	5
	Extent of regional sales — 21	2	9	10	Control of international distribution — 16	2	7	7
	Extent of staff training — 17	2	5	10	Capacity for innovation — 12	1	8	3
	Nature of competitive advantage — 12	3	6	3	Production process sophistication — 12	1	9	2
	Prevalence of foreign technology licensing — 8	2	4	2	Nature of competitive advantage — 9	1	7	1
					Prevalence of foreign technology licensing — 8	1	—	7
Quality of the Business Environment	Extent of bureaucratic red tape — 48	5	21	22	Extent of distortive government subsidies — 26	3	9	14
	Cost of importing foreign equipment — 37	5	17	15	Judicial independence — 21	2	10	9
	Efficacy of corporate boards — 33	4	14	15	Efficiency of legal framework — 21	2	13	6
	Financial market sophistication — 32	4	15	13	Venture capital availability — 20	2	12	6
	Overall infrastructure quality — 28	2	13	13	Administrative burden for startups — 18	2	10	6
	Extent of locally based competitors — 25	1	9	15	Intellectual property protection — 16	2	8	6
	Quality of scientific research institutions — 24	4	13	7	Quality of public schools — 16	4	11	1
	Railroad infrastructure development — 22	2	13	7	Buyer sophistication — 16	1	8	7
	Favoritism in decisions of government officials — 21	1	7	13	Favoritism in decisions of government officials — 14	2	9	3
	Quality of management schools — 21	1	9	11	Local equity market access — 14	1	5	8
	Air transport infrastructure quality — 18	2	12	4	University/industry research collaboration — 11	2	3	6
	Port infrastructure quality — 17	2	7	8	Reliability of police services — 9	1	3	5
	Local supplier quantity — 17	2	10	5	Railroad infrastructure development — 8	3	2	3
	Reliability of police services — 15	1	11	3	Air transport infrastructure quality — 8	3	1	4
	Presence of demanding regulatory standards — 15	3	8	4				
	Effectiveness of antitrust policy — 14	2	6	6				
	Venture capital availability — 13	1	6	6				
	Telephone/fax infrastructure quality — 12	1	10	1				
	Quality of public schools — 12	1	1	10				
	Hidden trade barriers — 12	2	4	6				
	Local equity market access — 11	2	4	5				
	University/industry research collaboration — 10	2	4	4				
	Efficiency of legal framework — 8	2	3	3				
	Administrative burden for startups — 8	1	3	4				

Note: L, M, and H refer to low-, middle-, and high-income countries, respectively. Significant change is defined as 10 percent or more change in country average score over the 5-year period from the score of year 1998. There are 5 low-, 21 middle-, and 26 high-income countries in this sample.

44

countries to sustain the investments and policies needed to improve their competitiveness, a dangerous development. Also, the data reveal the disturbing trend in high-income countries to resort to distortive government subsidies to shelter their economies from global competition.

Ranking competitiveness

To derive an overall Business Competitiveness Index (BCI), we compute subindexes measuring the sophistication of company operations and strategy and the quality of the national business environment. Because many of the dimensions of company sophistication and the quality of the business environment tend to move together, the sample of countries is relatively small, and the number of relevant variables is high, the impact of individual variables is difficult to distinguish statistically. Hence we use common factor analysis instead of multiple regressions to compute the subindexes. The first common factors defined as the

index accounts for 82.2 percent of the variation among company sophistication measures and 69.8 percent of the variation among national business environment measures.

The weighted average of the two subindexes is defined as the BCI. The weights are determined from the coefficients of a multiple regression of the subindexes on GDP per capita. This procedure results in a weight of 0.66 (2002: 0.63) for national business environment and 0.34 (2002: 0.37) for company operations and strategy, quite stable in comparison with last year's weights. When we include an interaction term in the regression on GDP per capita of the two subindexes, it proves to be positive and significant. This means that the benefits of a better business environment for prosperity are increasing with the sophistication of company operations and strategy, and vice versa. Countries that improve both the business environment and company sophistication in tandem reap disproportionate benefits, while countries where there is an imbalance bear disproportionate costs.

Figure 6 plots BCI against 2002 GDP per capita for each country in the sample of 95 countries used to develop the model. The regression line is shown, together with bands above and below the regression line that delineate the 95 percent confidence forecast region.[17] Only two countries, Norway and India, fall outside the forecast region. *Differences in BCI account for a remarkable 83 percent of variation in GDP per capita across a widely disparate group of countries.*

This year, we have modified the regression to allow for a nonlinear relationship between the BCI and GDP per capita. The resulting polynomial regression indicates a higher impact on GDP per capita of improvements in BCI for higher-income countries than for lower-income countries. This finding has a number of possible interpretations: first, improvements in microeconomic conditions should have positive spillovers; that is, an improvement in one part of the business environment has more impact if other parts of the business environment are stronger. This is consistent with the positive interaction between company sophistication and the business environment previously reported. Second, lower-income countries may reap fewer benefits for productivity from microeconomic improvements because of weaknesses in macroeconomic, political, legal, and social conditions.

We use the model along with data for each country to calculate a BCI for each country. The overall BCI rankings for 2003 for the 80 countries that were also surveyed last year are shown in Table 1, along with the rankings of the previous four years. Also included are separate subindex rankings. The rankings for all 101 countries are shown in Table 2.

Please refer to the Country Profiles section of the Report *for detailed descriptions of the competitive advantages and disadvantages of each country.* As noted earlier, competitiveness is not a zero-sum game. Many countries can improve productivity and prosperity. BCI tracks both the absolute and relative progress of countries in building a productive economy.

Finland retakes the leading position, after dropping to second place behind the United States last year. Finland remains one of the world's most remarkable success cases over the last decade. The United States was pulled down by concerns about rising trade protection, tightening capital availability, and weakening cluster vitality. Other advanced nations improving their rankings include France, Denmark, Sweden, Australia, and New Zealand. France gained five ranks, mainly due to an improving business environment, regaining its pre-2000 ranking. Heartening for France are improvements in local competition, governance, and reductions in government distortions. Denmark and New Zealand gained four ranks, mainly based on improvements in the business environment. Australia continued its upward trend, while Sweden reached the third

position based on company and business environment improvements.

Advanced countries slipping in the rankings include Austria based on a deteriorating business environment. The United Kingdom also slipped several places after strong gains last year, but remains on a long-term positive trend. Other advanced nations that are slipping are Switzerland, Canada, and Japan. Japan, while still sliding, registered strong improvements in corporate governance and cluster collaboration. Germany's rank falls only one place, but the quality of its business environment dropped precipitously. Labor-management relations are a growing concern, along with creeping subsidies and a hollowing of clusters.

Middle-income nations improving their competitiveness rankings this year include Latvia, Jordan, Vietnam, Mexico, Colombia, Indonesia, Mauritius, Greece, and Thailand. One new country, Malta, entered the middle-income group, ranked at 42. Egypt reentered the ranking at 58, showing a significant decline compared to its ranking in the 1998–2001 period. Latvia jumped by a remarkable 16 ranks, driven by strong perceived across-the-board improvements in the business environment and company sophistication. Whether this large jump is a temporary event reflecting positive near-term sentiment or sustainable will become more evident in subsequent years.

Middle-income countries losing rank in competitiveness include the Dominican Republic, Hungary, Sri Lanka, Trinidad and Tobago, Croatia, and China. The Dominican Republic (down 18 places) and Sri Lanka (down 9 places) fall back after strong jumps last year, signaling that last year's rankings might have been anomalies. The Dominican Republic's ranking was led down by concerns about the state of local companies. Hungary (down 10) and Croatia (down 8) appear to be suffering from increasing competition from other transition countries. Finally, Trinidad and Tobago has experienced declining competitiveness since its entry into the ranking in 2001. China, which showed a strong gain last year, has reverted back to its ranking of previous years. A surge in confidence about China's prospects proves not to have been sustainable. China was pulled down by concerns about red tape, corruption, judicial independence, and trade barriers, among other factors, though Chinese companies were judged to be making positive progress. Russia continues a slow downward trend, while Argentina's position seems to have stabilized.

Among low-income countries, rankings compared to last year were quite stable. Peru slipped significantly (down 5 places) continuing a negative trend. Ecuador moved up 3 places. Of the low-income countries ranked for the first time, Ghana entered at 63, Kenya at 67, and Tanzania at 68. Pakistan entered at 75 and Serbia at 79. Angola became the lowest-ranked country at 101.

Figure 6: The relationship between business competitiveness and GDP per capita

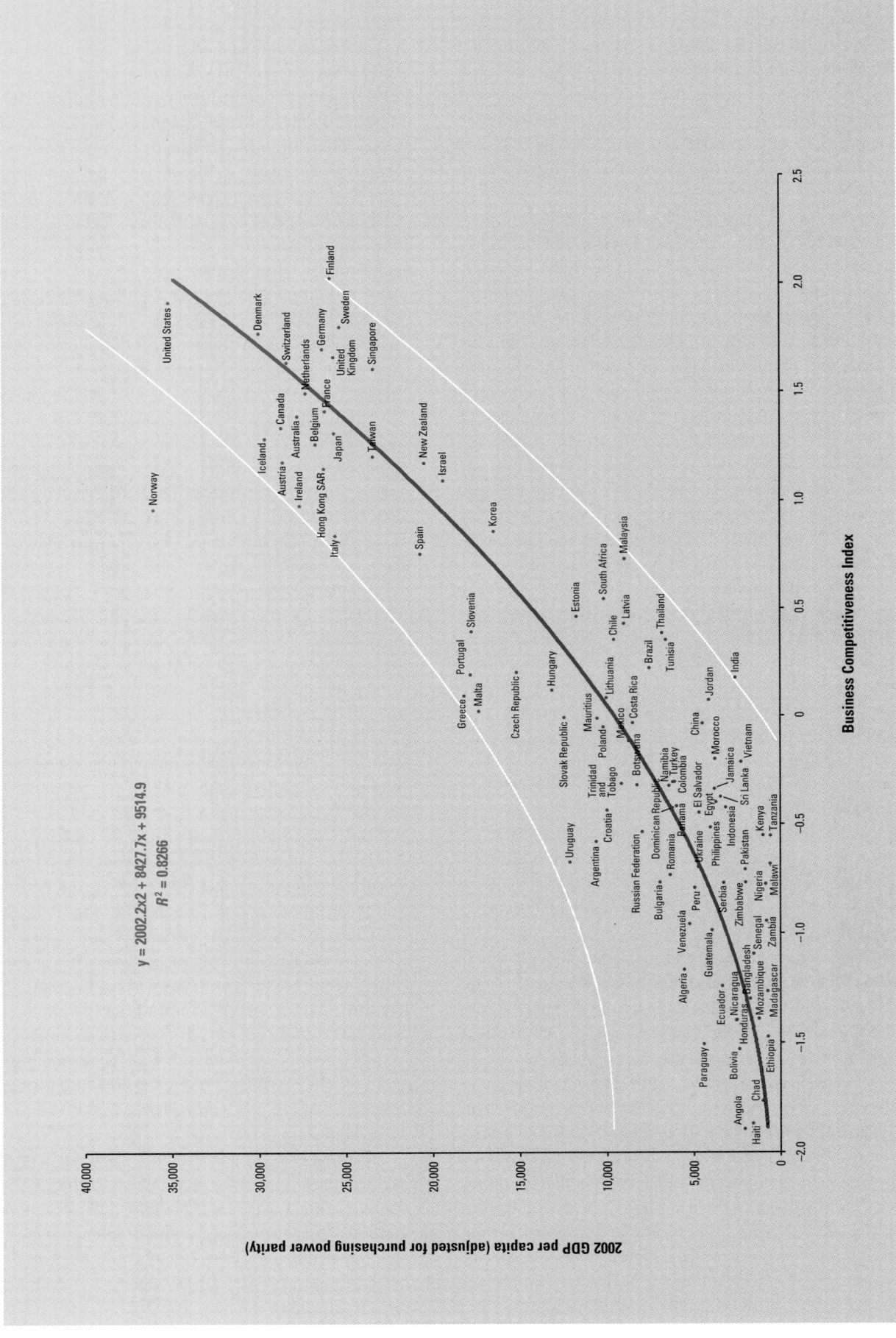

$y = 2002.2x2 + 8427.7x + 9514.9$
$R^2 = 0.8266$

Business Competitiveness Index

2002 GDP per capita (adjusted for purchasing power parity)

We also calculated the BCI for low-income countries incorporating only variables with a significant relationship to GDP per capita for this income group in order to recognize the more limited set of variables that prove significant early in development.[18] The rankings using this alternative approach turn out to be highly correlated (95 percent) to the rankings based on the general model. Honduras, Serbia, Indonesia, and Guatemala rank slightly higher based on the alternative model, while Malawi, Tanzania, and Zambia rank slightly lower.

Company competitiveness versus the quality of the business environment

To gain deeper insight into the competitive position of countries, normalized subindexes of company sophistication and the quality of the microeconomic business environment are plotted against each other in Figure 7. Countries near the line enjoy the positive interaction of the two subindexes, as noted previously. Countries lying above the 45-degree line are those whose companies are more advanced than the state of their business environment. Those below the line are countries whose business environment is more advanced than their companies.

Countries whose company development is ahead of the business environment include Japan, Germany, France, Sweden, the Philippines, Argentina, and Venezuela. With the exception of the Philippines, all these countries have reported a relative weakness in the business environment relative to company development for some years. Significant changes in public policy are necessary in these countries to improve the platform for productivity. Unless the business environment improves, companies will be prone to *move operations or make new investments outside the country*. Japan remains the advanced economy with the most glaring weaknesses in the business environment, despite strong companies. The consequences of weakness in the business environment for Japan's economic growth have been severe, as Japanese corporate investment has fled the country.[19]

Countries whose business environment ranks ahead of current company sophistication include Jordan, Estonia, Australia, Tunisia, Portugal, New Zealand, and Senegal. Many leading companies in these countries still rely on natural resource extraction (eg, Australia and New Zealand), depend heavily on OEM production, or have prevalent local subsidiaries of foreign multinationals that fail to compete with sophisticated enough strategies (eg, Portugal, Senegal, and Tunisia). In some countries, such as Australia, part of the issue is that rapid improvements in the business environment have not yet been harnessed by companies that remain focused on traditional ways of competing. Efforts to improve entrepreneurship, strategic thinking, managerial practice, and business education are high priorities in these countries.

Country overperformance and underperformance

We can gain insights into the sustainability of a country's prosperity by looking at its level of microeconomic (business) competitiveness relative to its current per capita income. Table 5 lists countries in order of the divergence between actual GDP per capita and the expected GDP given microeconomic competitiveness. Countries lying above the regression line in Figure 6 are those whose current GDP per capita *exceeds* that predicted by their microeconomic competitiveness, as measured by the BCI index. This is a danger sign, because it means that a country's per capita income may be unsustainable. Among high-income countries, Malta, Greece, Portugal, Italy, Ireland, and especially Norway all continue to enjoy a level of prosperity that exceeds their microeconomic fundamentals. Paraguay, Uruguay, Algeria, and Argentina are among a group of middle-income countries whose levels of income appear unsustainable without substantial microeconomic reform. Angola, Ecuador, and Bolivia are low-income countries in this precarious position.

Reasons for country overperformance seem to vary and can be either stable over time or transitory. Overperformance can persist for many years if it is based on natural resource endowments, as in the case of Norway, as long as the natural resources are not exhausted and commodity price levels are maintained at high enough levels. Large foreign aid inflows can also support otherwise unsustainable prosperity levels, which may explain the overperformance of a country such as Haiti. Overperformance can be more transitory if it is based on a boom in foreign investment or European Structural Fund inflows, as in Ireland, Greece, and Portugal. Overperformance can also reflect a lag in income behind deteriorating microeconomic conditions, as in Paraguay, Uruguay, Algeria, and Argentina. We find relatively few low-income countries that are overperformers. This is consistent with the higher incidence of macroeconomic, political, and social challenges among low-income countries that depresses GDP per capita levels below what could be expected given their BCI position.

Countries lying below the regression line in Figure 6 are those whose microeconomic competitiveness is *stronger* than current GDP per capita. We term them *underperformers*. Underperformance bodes well for the future, because the platform is in place to support higher GDP per capita if macro, political, or other constraints can be eased.

Finland, Sweden, Singapore, and the United Kingdom lead the advanced countries with upside potential. Jordan, China, Tunisia, Thailand, and Malaysia are among the middle-income countries that should be able to support a higher GDP per capita, given microeconomic fundamentals. India continues to head the list of low-income countries with upside potential, alongside the African countries of Tanzania, Malawi, Kenya, Nigeria, and Zambia.

Figure 7: The relative development of companies and the microeconomic business environment

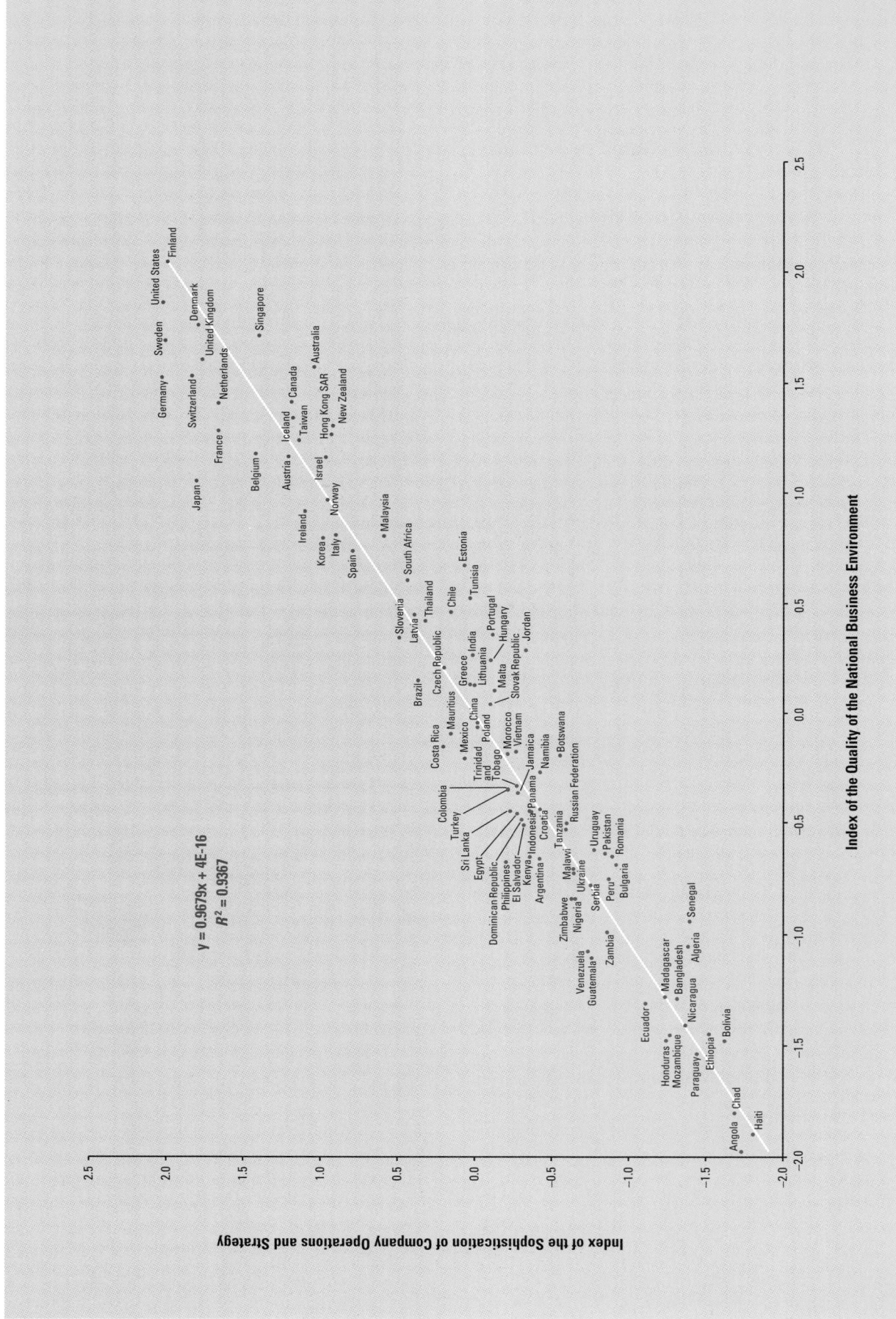

Table 5: GDP per capita relative to business competitiveness

	High-income countries	Middle-income countries	Low-income countries
	UPSIDE POTENTIAL		
Microeconomic competitiveness would support higher per capita income	Finland Sweden Singapore United Kingdom Germany	Malaysia Thailand Tunisia Jordan China South Africa Latvia Brazil Chile	India Vietnam Tanzania Kenya Morocco Malawi Nigeria Sri Lanka Indonesia Jamaica Egypt Zambia Pakistan Zimbabwe Madagascar Senegal
	NEUTRAL		
Competitiveness and income are balanced	Israel New Zealand Denmark Switzerland Netherlands France Taiwan Japan United States Australia	Estonia Korea Philippines El Salvador Colombia Turkey Costa Rica Namibia Panama Lithuania Dominican Republic Ukraine Mexico Peru Poland Mauritius Botswana Romania Venezuela Trinidad and Tobago Russian Federation	Serbia Ethiopia Mozambique Bangladesh Chad Guatemala Haiti Nicaragua Honduras
	CURRENT OVERACHIEVERS		
Per capita income is high relative to microeconomic competitiveness	Belgium Spain Canada Hong Kong SAR Slovenia Iceland Austria Portugal Italy Malta Greece Ireland Norway	Hungary Bulgaria Slovak Republic Paraguay Algeria Croatia Czech Republic Argentina Uruguay	Bolivia Ecuador Angola

Reasons for country underperformance also reflect a variety of circumstances. Chronic underperformance results from persistent structural political, governmental, or social challenges. For India and China, for example, measured underperformance on a per capita basis may well result from the sheer number of people living at the subsistence level outside the mainstream economy. In these and other countries, the Survey confirms large regional differences in business environment quality, while responses tend to come from executives in the more advanced regions. The average prosperity of such countries will remain below measured microeconomic potential until progress is spread throughout the country. More transitory underperformance can also occur in the aftermath of a macroeconomic crisis that did not lead to a deterioration of the microeconomic fundamentals, as in Thailand, Malaysia, and Singapore. Underperformance may also reflect a lag in prosperity adjusting upward to improving microeconomic conditions. This seems to be the case in Finland and the United Kingdom.

Regional disparities

This year, we included a new question on regional differences in a country's business environment. Not surprisingly, countries such as Italy, Russia, Brazil, China, and India register high regional heterogeneity. For countries such as China and India, this high degree of regional heterogeneity could help explain the low level of GDP per capita relative to the reported BCI. The Survey will tend to be completed by companies in regions better integrated into the world economy, which may not reflect average conditions in the economy.

Our data on regional differences in the business environment also hold implications for economic policy. Reducing regional disparities is revealed as one of the critical agendas in the development process. In future years, we can examine the change in regional disparity to glean lessons about policy successes and failures.

Natural resources and development

Natural resources have played a prominent role in thinking about economic development. Historically, abundant resources were seen as the source of national prosperity. In the last decade, however, the importance of natural resources has been called into question as the knowledge and skill intensity of competition has risen and technology and widening resource availability have led to generally falling real resource prices.[20]

In this year's *Report*, we set out to explore the relationship between resource abundance and competitiveness. For 85 countries in the sample we were able to assemble data on the size of minimally processed natural resources as well as overall exports.[21] The largest absolute natural resource exporters among those countries are the United

States, Canada, Norway, Russia, Nigeria, and Australia. The countries with the highest share of natural resources exports to total exports are Nigeria, Ethiopia, Paraguay, Ecuador, Venezuela, Kenya, Nicaragua, and Honduras, all with a share of greater than 50 percent. Natural resource exports per capita as a proportion of GDP per capita are plotted on Figure 8.

Natural resources result from endowments, not economic competitiveness. Countries' world market share of natural resource exports proves to be more closely related to their geographic size than to their share of world GDP, while non-natural resource exports are closely correlated to a country's share of world GDP. Natural resource exports per capita are not related to underlying competitiveness, as measured by BCI, controlling for country size (we use population density, the inverse of land area per capita). In contrast, non-natural resource exports are strongly correlated with BCI. We find that the natural resource share of a country's exports (and GDP) is decreasing in GDP per capita, again controlling for country size, as we might expect. Countries with lower levels of productivity are more dependent on natural resource exports.

Theory suggests another effect of natural resources that would counteract the positive direct effect on prosperity: abundant natural resources might bias policies toward rent seeking and redistribution and work against overall competitiveness. A crude analysis of changes in BCI supports this view: a dummy variable for countries with high natural resource exports (more than 2 percent of GDP) is negatively and significantly correlated with changes in the BCI rank between 1998 and 2003.[22]

Changing microeconomic competitiveness and prosperity growth

We also examined whether countries that are improving or worsening their competitiveness ranking register corresponding trends in growth of GDP per capita. Changes in BCI rank should affect growth in GDP per capita as per capita income responds to a new sustainable level. While macroeconomic adjustments and other shocks may also affect per capita income growth, the relationship between shifts in BCI ranking and prosperity growth provides a tentative indication of causality in the relationship between BCI and prosperity.

Regressing GDP per capita growth between 1998 and 2002 on BCI rank changes between 1999 and 2003 yields a statistically significant relationship that explains about 23 percent of the total variation in growth in GDP per capita across countries. Two outliers, Ireland and Zimbabwe, reduce the fit. Ireland's foreign direct investment inflows have been extraordinary and led to probably unsustainable growth in income; the severe political crisis for Zimbabwe has been devastating to income despite

economic fundamentals. Dropping the outliers and introducing a dummy variable for low-ranked and high-ranked countries to control for the boundedness of the ranking from above and below, the R^2 moves up to 30 percent. The relationship is highly significant. The coefficient of the relationship implies that an increase of 10 BCI ranks over the five-year time period is associated with a 1.9 percent higher growth rate in GDP per capita.

Conclusions

National prosperity is strongly affected by competitiveness, which is defined by the productivity with which a nation utilizes its human, capital, and natural resources. Competitiveness is rooted in a nation's microeconomic fundamentals, as manifested in the sophistication of its companies and the quality of its microeconomic business environment. Political stability, sound macroeconomic policies, market opening, and privatization have long been considered the cornerstones for economic development. The results here suggest that they are necessary but not sufficient. More than 80 percent of the variation of GDP per capita across countries is accounted for by microeconomic fundamentals. We find strong evidence that microeconomic upgrading is a sequential process in which countries at different levels of development face distinctly different challenges.

Importance of microeconomic reforms and other analysis results

While focus has been on macro reforms and debt relief, our findings suggest that micro reforms are equally if not more important. Without micro reforms, growth in GDP induced by sound macro policies, market opening, and privatization will be unsustainable or will not translate into improvements in GDP per capita. Appropriate micro reforms, which boost productivity and productivity growth, can greatly ease the challenge of meeting government's fiscal obligations and reducing macroeconomic distortions. Microeconomic reforms can also reduce the political pressure on governments trying to defend macroeconomic stabilization and market opening against vested interests. Citizens who see monopolies loosening their grip, businesses reforming themselves, and opportunities for employment and entrepreneurship increasing are much less likely to be seduced by the false promises of redistribution and government intervention.

Our results once again challenge the notion that microeconomic improvement is automatic if proper macroeconomic policies are instituted. Although there may be a tendency for microeconomic conditions to improve because GDP per capita rises, such improvement appears to be far from automatic. Moreover, the rate of improvement in microeconomic competitiveness can be

Figure 8: Natural resource exports share of GDP versus GDP per capita, PPP adjusted

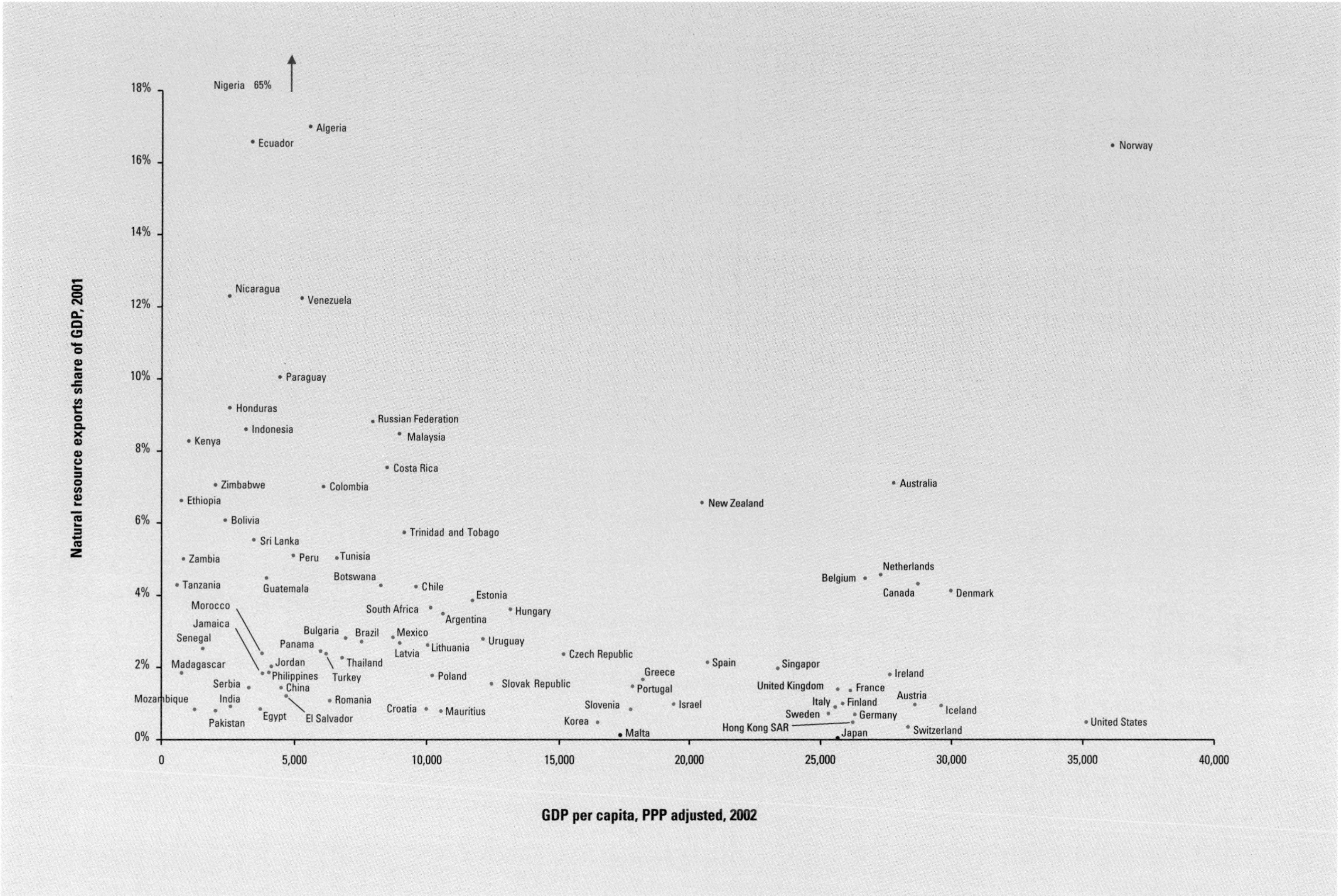

affected markedly by purposeful action in both government and the private sector. As our results reveal, microeconomic conditions can move ahead of or fall behind current GDP per capita. Shifts in competitiveness have a significant influence on future economic growth.

Our findings indicate that it is unwise to view micro reforms narrowly in terms of reducing the role of government and abolishing market distortions. Such steps remain a critical challenge that many countries still must master. Yet government has a range of positive roles that are fundamental to prosperity, such as investing in human resources, stimulating advanced demand by setting appropriate regulatory standards, and building innovative capacity. Many nations need to move beyond first-stage reforms and address these agendas. The private sector has an important role in improving a nation's competitive platform through collective activities and cluster development initiatives. Second-stage micro reforms require a new perspective on the role of the private sector.

While clusters have an important role in competitiveness as the results validate, our analysis also makes it clear that microeconomic reform is much more than cluster development. The proliferating efforts to develop and enhance clusters around the world are highly encouraging. Yet countries also need to pursue improvements throughout the business environment, or cluster initiatives will be ultimately stymied.

Finally, our results highlight the need to align a nation's economic priorities with its level of development. We describe the differing challenges for low-, medium-, and high-income countries, and the difficult transitions between broad development stages. Countries that have been very successful in one mode of competing need to recognize the multifaceted adjustments necessary for managing the transition to the next mode.

If there is to be continued momentum for economic reform in nations around the world, there is a pressing need to move to the next level of thinking and practice about economic development. Approaches centered largely on responding to international financial markets and ceding choices to impersonal global forces are producing a backlash that erodes the consensus for global economic progress and encourages populist national policies that are fundamentally self-defeating. Economic reform must move beyond now-standard approaches and embrace the textured agenda that the results here suggest.

Countries are converging on macroeconomic stabilization, trade opening, and privatization. The central challenge to much of the world economy is now microeconomic reform. Progress in improving the sophistication of companies and the quality of the business environment is the only way to produce real improvements in efficiency, product quality, and new business opportunities that support a rising standard of living for citizens.

Competitiveness and the role of international development assistance

The results presented here not only have implications for policymakers in individual countries but also offer useful guidance to international organizations active in economic development, especially in low- and middle-income countries.

A substantial number of multilateral and national aid organizations have come to play a prominent role in economic development. The World Bank, the International Monetary Fund (IMF), the United Nations, regional development banks, and single-country organizations such as the U.S. Agency for International Development (USAID) have provided, on average, over US$60 billion of development assistance annually over the last decade, or more than US$600 billion. Aid organizations have supported a wide array of agendas.

The effectiveness of this aid has, on the whole, been disappointing.[23] Our data combined with data on official development assistance (ODA) over the last decade confirm this view (see Figure 9). The level of ODA per capita provided over the last decade shows no systematic relationship to either GDP per capita or BCI. Controlling for initial GDP per capita, we find that ODA inflows over the last decade (measured either in absolute terms or relative to GDP per capita) are not positively correlated to changes in BCI or to growth in GDP per capita for the countries receiving ODA. Based on these data, then, ODA investments have not paid off. Deducting ODA inflows from GDP per capita in our model modestly increases the explanatory power of BCI for GDP per capita; this is consistent with ODA being a windfall gain in prosperity with no further effect on underlying competitiveness.

The disappointing results of development assistance are directly related to the way it has been deployed. Funding tends to be fragmented, spread over a myriad of programs that are costly for both aid organizations and recipient countries to administer. Impact is blunted by lack of concentrated and consistent spending on priority areas. The projects funded are often driven as much by donor organization priorities as by the particular needs of the recipient country. Fads and politics intrude into the giving process.

The agendas of the numerous aid organizations are largely uncoordinated in recipient countries except in rare circumstances. Recipient countries face the complex challenge of negotiating with the various organizations and adapting to donor priorities.

Recipient governments, on their side, have often failed to deliver on their commitments, spent aid money unwisely, and allowed corruption to drain resources away from meeting pressing needs. This had led to the creation of special institutional arrangements to reduce the risk of disappointments, including direct funding of projects

Figure 9: Official development assistance relative to GDP versus GDP per capita

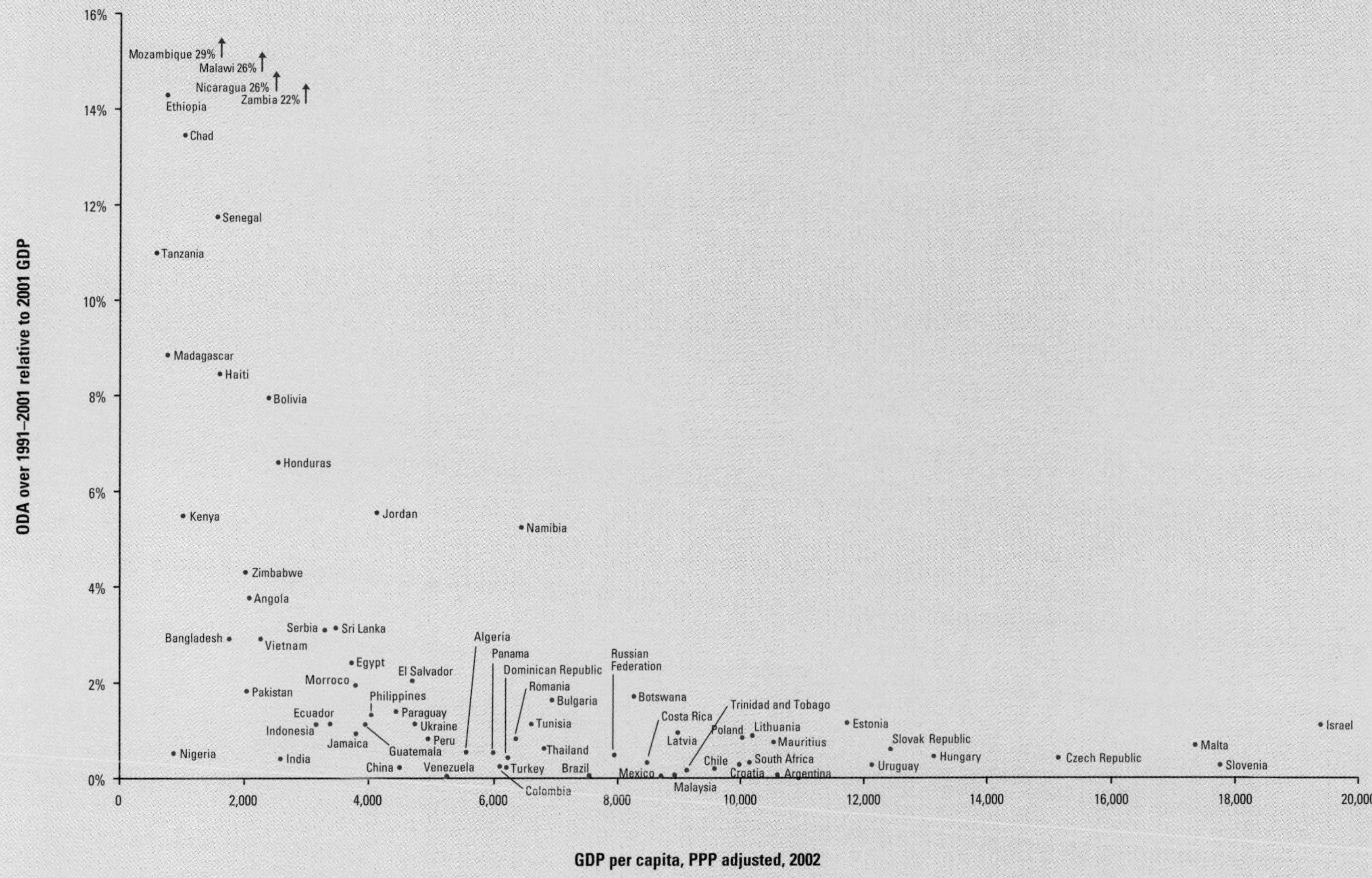

ODA over 1991–2001 relative to 2001 GDP

GDP per capita, PPP adjusted, 2002

Mozambique 29%
Malawi 26%
Nicaragua 26%
Zambia 22%
Ethiopia
Chad

Senegal

Tanzania

Madagascar
Haiti
Bolivia

Honduras

Kenya
Zimbabwe
Angola
Vietnam
Bangladesh
Serbia
Sri Lanka
Morroco
Egypt
El Salvador
Ecuador
Paraguay
Indonesia
Jamaica
Guatemala
Pakistan
India
China
Venezuela
Peru
Ukraine
Philippines

Jordan
Namibia

Algeria
Panama
Dominican Republic
Romania
Tunisia
Turkey
Colombia
Thailand
Brazil
Bulgaria

Russian Federation
Botswana
Costa Rica
Latvia
Mexico
Malaysia
Chile
Croatia
Argentina
South Africa
Poland
Trinidad and Tobago
Lithuania
Mauritius
Estonia
Slovak Republic
Uruguay
Hungary

Czech Republic

Malta
Slovenia
Israel

16% 14% 12% 10% 8% 6% 4% 2% 0%

0   2,000   4,000   6,000   8,000   10,000   12,000   14,000   16,000   18,000   20,000

outside of the government budget and strict negotiating structures. The net result is even more complexity for all the parties.

The disappointing results of past efforts suggest the need to rethink and restructure international development assistance. The aims, the institutional structure, and the process all must be redesigned.

In the context of this *Report*, we focus on the aims of development aid. The goal of poverty reduction has taken prominence among development agencies in recent years, reflecting the view that aid must benefit the poor rather than enrich the elites in developing countries. The World Bank, for example, is requiring Poverty Reduction Strategies to qualify for the Bank's concessional assistance. While this approach is laudable in many respects, it also carries a risk. Efforts to alleviate poverty that are unsustainable can gravitate to social spending and subsidies to disadvantaged groups.

A better goal is to *improve income, jobs, and wealth* that is widely shared. This places the focus where it must be: on building a viable and competitive economy. Aid agencies must step up their attention to competitiveness relative to other agendas. Improvements in macroeconomic stability, political stability, and social conditions that are sustainable all depend, in the medium and long term, on having a competitive economy. Otherwise, any progress in these areas is temporary, as we have learned over and over again.

New institutional structures will be necessary to advance competitiveness. These must include not only national governments but also need to incorporate the roles of business, educational organizations, regional governments, and other institutions. National competitiveness committees including these players should have formal responsibilities for planning and monitoring competitiveness programs. Aid must be based on objective national competitiveness assessments, not donor priorities.

The findings in this *Report* can help guide and inform such efforts. In the coming years, our aim is to work more and more closely with country leaders to improve the objectivity of the data collected in this *Report*, disseminate it more broadly, and create forums and other mechanisms to inform and catalyze local action.

54

Notes

1 I would like to thank Christian Ketels and Weifeng Weng for their major role in the analyses reported here. Lyn Pohl provided able supervision of the final production of the chapter.

2 The proportion has grown modestly over the last several years as the model has been improved.

3 See the *Clusters of Innovation* report (Porter, Council on Competitiveness, and Monitor Group, 2001); further reports on five U.S. regions are available at www.compete.org.

4 The stages were first introduced in Porter (1990).

5 The notion of institutions for collaboration has been developed further in joint work with Willis Emmons, Georgetown University. See Porter and Emmons (2003).

6 One surveyed economy, Luxembourg, was not included in the calculations because of its small size, functional concentration on a few sectors, and almost complete integration into the neighboring economies. It is better understood as a region within these economies.

7 These reasons could include larger actual heterogeneity within the country, as well as greater uncertainty by respondents about appropriate international benchmarks.

8 For Morocco, we utilized all Survey responses, and the country ranking was quite stable from last year, despite the within-country variance of responses. For Romania, we utilized the average Survey responses from foreign companies as the country average because they have a high degree of within-country consensus.

9 For Egypt, Senegal, Serbia, and Zambia, we utilized the average Survey responses from foreign subsidiaries as the country average.

10 These countries are Cameroon, Gambia, Ghana, Macedonia, Mali, and Uganda.

11 The GDP per capita (PPP adjusted) data for Norway were revised by the World Bank, leading to a 17 percent jump in the country's GDP per capita relative to the data available last year. Norway becomes an even more striking outlier due to this revision.

12 GDP per worker is employed as a productivity measure in some studies. We used the broader measure here because GDP per worker can be increased by high unemployment or low workforce participation, which do not increase wealth. Also, holders of capital, not only workers, contribute to national productivity. In comparing the United States and France, for example, the United States has absorbed a huge influx of new workers (higher workforce participation) over the last decade, while France has maintained high GDP per worker through suffering high unemployment and maintaining a large student population not counted as part of the potential workforce.

13 In the case of Ireland, we used GNP instead of GDP because of the size of dividend outflows to foreign investors. Ireland's GDP is about 20 percent higher than its GNP.

14 Statistical significance at ** = 5 percent and * = 10 percent (all two-tailed tests) is noted in the table.

15 We conducted additional bivariate regressions (not reported here) using macroeconomic indicators collected for the *Global Competitiveness Report*. These regressions show no statistical relationship between GDP per capita and individual macroeconomic indicators. See also Easterly (2001), who finds similar results.

16 This analysis covers the Survey questions that have been common over five years, which comprise the great majority of questions.

17 The forecast region has wider bands than a 95 percent mean confidence region. The mean confidence region provides a confidence interval for a given level of competitiveness over repeated observations. The forecast region method, in contrast, reflects a higher degree of inherent uncertainty in predicting a single observation. As a result, interpretation of the proximity of data points to the regression line should be undertaken with appropriate caveats. Note that the forecast region widens slightly as it moves away from the "center" of the graph. The center is the point located at the intersection of the mean GDP per capita level and mean factor score.

18 For medium- and high-income countries, most of the individual variables included in the BCI are significant.

19 For a more detailed examination of Japan's competitive situation, see Porter and Hirotaka with Sakakibara (2000).

20 See Sala-I-Martin and Subramanian (2003).

21 Data were drawn from "Trade Analysis System on Personal Computer, 1997–2001," SITC Rev.3. A list of SITC industries included can be obtained from the author.

22 The time-series data available for this analysis unfortunately include few low-income countries with high natural resource export share. The analysis will be expanded as more country data become available over time.

23 See, for example, Boone (1995), Tsikata (1998), and Lancaster (1999).

Selected References

Baumol, W. J. 2002. *The Free-Market Innovation Machine: Analyzing the Growth Miracle of Capitalism.* Princeton, NJ: Princeton University Press.

Barro, R. J. 1991. "Economic Growth in a Cross Section of Countries," *Quarterly Journal of Economics* 106 (2): 407–443.

Boone, P. 1995. "Politics and the Effectiveness of Foreign Aid," NBER Working Paper No. 5308. Cambridge, MA: National Bureau of Economic Research.

Department of Trade and Industry. 2001. *UK Competitiveness Indicators*, 2nd Edition. London: Department of Trade and Industry.

Easterly, W. 2001.*The Elusive Quest for Growth: Economists' Adventures and Misadventures in the Tropics.* Cambridge, MA: MIT Press.

Easterly, W. and R. Levine. 2002. "Tropics, Germs, and Crops: How Endowments Influence Economic Development," NBER Working Paper No. 9106. Cambridge, MA: National Bureau of Economic Research.

European Commission. 2002. *European Competitiveness Report 2002.* Brussels: European Commission.

Enright, M. J., A. Francés, and E. S. Saavadra. 1994. *Venezuela: El Reto de la Competitividad.* Caracas, Venezuela: Ediciones IESA.

Fairbanks, M. and S. Lindsay. 1997. *Plowing the Sea: The Challenge of Competitiveness in the Developing World.* Boston: Harvard Business School Press.

Hall, R. E. and C. I. Jones. 1999. "Why Do Some Countries Produce So Much More Output per Worker than Others?" *Quarterly Journal of Economics* 114 (1): 83 –116.

Hirschman, A. O. 1958. *The Strategy of Economic Development* New Haven, CT: Yale University Press.

Lancaster, C. 1999. "Aid Effectiveness in Africa: The Unfinished Agenda," *Journal of African Economics* 8(4): 487–503.

Lucas, R. E., Jr. 1988. "On the Mechanics of Economic Development," *Journal of Monetary Economics* 22 (July 1988): 3–42.

Mankiw, N. G. 1995. "The Growth of Nations," *Brookings Papers on Economic Activity* 1 (1): 275–310.

Mankiw, N. G., D. Romer, and D. N. Weil. 1992. "A Contribution to the Empirics of Economic Growth," *Quarterly Journal of Economics* 107(2): 407–437.

Nickell, S. 1996. "Competition and Corporate Performance," *Journal of Political Economy* 104 (1996): 724-746.

Nordhaus, W. D. 1994. "Climate and Economic Development." In *Proceedings of the World Bank Annual Conference on Development Economics 1993.* Washington, DC: The International Bank for Reconstruction and Development/The World Bank.

North, D. C. 1990. *Institutions, Institutional Change and Economic Performance: Political Economy of Institutions and Decisions.* Cambridge: Cambridge University Press.

Porter, M. E. 2003. "The Economic Performance of Regions," *Regional Studies* 37(6&7): 549–678.

———. 2000a. "Attitudes, Values, Beliefs, and the Microeconomic of Prosperity." In L. E. Harrison and S. P. Huntington, eds., *Culture Matters.* New York: Basic Books, 2000: 14–28.

———. 2000b. "Locations, Clusters, and Company Strategy." In G. L. Clark, M. P. Feldman, and M. S. Gertler, eds., *The Oxford Handbook of Economic Geography.* New York: Oxford University Press, 2000: 253–274.

———. 1998a. "Introduction." In *The Competitive Advantage of Nations: With a New Introduction.* New York: The Free Press.

———. 1998b. "Clusters and Competition: New Agendas for Companies, Governments, and Institutions." In *On Competition.* Boston: Harvard Business School Press.

———. 1996. "What Is Strategy?" *Harvard Business Review* 74 (6): 61–78.

———. 1995. "Comment on 'Interaction Between Regional and Industrial Policies: Evidence From Four Countries,' by J. Markusen." In *Proceedings of The World Bank Annual Conference on Development Economics 1994.* Washington, DC: The International Bank for Reconstruction and Development/The World Bank.

———. 1990. *The Competitive Advantage of Nations.* New York: The Free Press.

Porter, M. E., Council on Competitiveness, and Monitor Group. 2001. *Clusters of Innovation Initiative: Regional Foundations of U.S. Competitiveness.* Washington, DC: Council on Competitiveness.

Porter, M.E., and W. Emmons. 2003. "Institutions for Collaboration: Overview". Harvard Business School case 9-703-436.

Porter, M. E. and T. Hirotaka with M. Sakakibara. 2000. *Can Japan Compete?* Basingstoke, England, and New York: Macmillan and Basic Books.

Porter, M. E. and C. Ketels. 2003. "UK Competitiveness: Moving to the Next Stage," DTI Economics Paper No.3. London: Department of Industry and Trade & Economic and Social Research Council (ESRC).

Porter, M. E. and C. van der Linde. 1995. "Toward a New Conception of the Environment-Competitiveness Relationship," *Journal of Economic Perspectives* 9(4): 97–118.

Romer, P. M. 1990. "Endogenous Technological Change," *Journal of Political Economy* 98(5): S71–S102.

Sachs, J. D. and A. Warner. 1995. "Economic Reform and the Process of Global Integration," *Brookings Papers on Economic Activity* 1(1): 1–118.

Sakakibara, M. and M. E. Porter. 1998. "Competing at Home to Win Abroad: Evidence from Japanese Industry," Harvard Business School Working Paper No. 99-036. Cambridge, MA: Harvard Business School Press.

Sala-i-Martin, X. and A. Subramanian. 2003. "Addressing the Natural Resource Curse: An illustration from Nigeria," IMF Working Paper 03/139, Washington, DC: International Monetary Fund.

Solow, R. M. 1956. "A Contribution to the Theory of Economic Growth," *Quarterly Journal of Economics* 70(1): 65–94.

Tsikata, T.M. 1998. "Aid Effectiveness: A Survey of the Recent Empirical Literature," IMF, PPA/98/1. Washington, DC: International Monetary Fund.

Appendix A: ANOVA Analysis for Survey Responses

I. COMPANY OPERATIONS & STRATEGY	R^2
Production process sophistication	0.489
Nature of competitive advantage	0.412
Extent of staff training	0.390
Extent of marketing	0.439
Willingness to delegate authority	0.332
Capacity for innovation	0.434
Company spending on research and development	0.360
Value chain presence	0.458
Breadth of international markets	0.444
Degree of customer orientation	0.256
Control of international distribution	0.200
Extent of branding	0.456
Reliance on professional management	0.324
Extent of incentive compensation	0.290
Extent of regional sales	0.431
Prevalence of foreign technology licensing	0.190

II. NATIONAL BUSINESS ENVIRONMENT	R^2

A. FACTOR (INPUT) CONDITIONS

1. Physical Infrastructure

Overall infrastructure quality	0.638
Railroad infrastructure development	0.650
Port infrastructure quality	0.567
Air transport infrastructure quality	0.505
Quality of electricity supply	0.618
Telephone/fax infrastructure quality	0.548

2. Administrative Infrastructure

Reliability of police services	0.416
Judicial independence	0.465
Efficiency of legal framework	0.433
Administrative burden for startups	0.284
Extent of bureaucratic red tape	0.113

3. Human Resource s

Quality of management schools	0.403
Quality of public schools	0.566
Quality of the educational system	0.398
Quality of math and science education	0.435

4. Technology Infrastructure

Availability of scientists and engineers	0.338
Quality of scientific research institutions	0.335
University/industry research collaboration	0.304

5. Capital Markets

Financial market sophistication	0.512
Venture capital availability	0.278
Ease of access to loans	0.275
Local equity market access	0.402

II. NATIONAL BUSINESS ENVIRONMENT (Cont'd.)	R^2

B. DEMAND CONDITIONS

Buyer sophistication	0.365
Sophistication of local buyers' products and processes	0.285
Government procurment of advanced technology products	0.203
Presence of demanding regulatory standards	0.498
Laws relating to ICT	0.336
Stringency of environmental regulations	0.488

C. RELATED AND SUPPORTING INDUSTRIES

Local supplier quality	0.409
State of cluster development	0.266
Local availability of process machinery	0.349
Local availability of specialized research and training services	0.321
Extent of collaboration among clusters	0.301
Local supplier quantity	0.257
Local availability of components and parts	0.326

D. CONTEXT FOR FIRM STRATEGY AND RIVALRY

1. Incentives

Extent of distortive government subsidies	0.212
Favoritism in decisions of government officials	0.299
Cooperation in labor-employer relations	0.230
Efficacy of corporate boards	0.164
Intellectual property protection	0.463
Protection of minority shareholders' interests	0.254
Regulation of securities exchanges	0.374
Effectiveness of bankruptcy law	0.409

2. Competition

Hidden trade barriers	0.303
Intensity of local competition	0.202
Extent of locally based competitors	0.197
Effectiveness of antitrust policy	0.352
Decentralization of corporate activity	0.314
Business costs of corruption	0.327
Cost of importing foreign equipment	0.296
Centralization of economic policymaking	0.264
Prevalence of mergers and acquisitions	0.238
Foreign ownership restrictions	0.226

Part 2

Selected Issues of Competitiveness

CHAPTER 2.1

The Year in Review

MARTIN NEIL BAILY, The Institute for International Economics

A year ago, the economic downturn, the stock market decline, the technology slump, the revelations of corporate misdeeds, the prospects of war in Iraq, a legacy of over-investment, the possibility of another terrorist attack, and the seemingly endless series of economic crises in emerging markets had raised uncertainty about the ability of the economies of Europe, Japan, and the United States to recover from recession and sustain solid growth going forward. Without recovery in these countries, the growth prospects for the developing world were restrained.

Today, the economic outlook looks much better than a year ago, even to some extent in Europe. Some of the uncertainties hanging over the world economy have dissipated, if not all of them. The invasion of Iraq is over, and some of the worst fears about jumping oil prices have not been realized. There has not been another terrorist attack on the scale of the World Trade Center. On the economic side, the excess capacity that built up in the 1990s has been reduced or eliminated in many industries, and stock markets have made a partial recovery from their slump.

On the down side, US-led coalition forces are facing a long drawn out struggle against terrorist groups in Iraq. The task of stabilizing and rebuilding Iraq looks daunting. There have been a series of smaller but still deadly terrorist attacks around the world. Oil prices did not jump to $50 or $100 a barrel, but they did remain high. And consumer, business, and equity market confidence remain fragile, should there be more bad news ahead. To use the familiar clichés: the world economy does seem to have turned a corner, but it is not yet out of the woods.

The US economy grew at around 2 percent in the first half of 2003 and seems poised for faster growth in the second half of the year or in early 2004. Short-term macroeconomic forecasters in the United States have become very much more optimistic as new data have been released in the summer of 2003. Employment growth still lags behind the recovery, although that is because of the continuing rapid increases in productivity. In Japan, Gross Domestic Product (GDP) reportedly grew at around 3 percent in the first half of 2003, and there are clear signs of better economic performance than a year ago. However, with some skepticism about preliminary GDP numbers, and after 10 years or more of relative economic stagnation, doubts remain about Japan's ability to sustain an economic recovery. Among the developed economies, Europe seems the region that is having the most difficulty in recovering from the downturn, especially Germany. While there is significant improvement in business sentiment, the euro area economy was basically flat in the first half of 2003 and is expected to grow by only 0.6 percent for 2003 overall.

In the developing world, China's blockbuster economic growth performance has continued, apparently only modestly affected by the global slowdown and the outbreak of severe acute respiratory syndrome, SARS. The Chinese central bank is now worried about the economy overheating. Although less dynamic than China, other countries in Asia are also doing pretty well, including India. Latin America is gradually healing its wounds after a wave of crises—for example, the risk premium on sovereign debt in Brazil has dropped substantially. South Africa is growing, but it is also battling the AIDS crisis and its worsening economic effects, a topic that is discussed below.

This review considers some of the important issues and challenges facing the world economy that have emerged or been at center stage this past year. First there is a look at the impact of the war in Iraq and whether or not this will sour economic relations. The war was the central political and military event of the past year, and it has soured international relations. But so far, surprisingly, its economic consequences do not seem to have been all that large. Next is the issue of exchange rate adjustment and the rebalancing of global trade patterns. The United States has been running a massive trade deficit that continues to grow. Many policymakers have judged that at some point there would have to be a downward adjustment in the value of the dollar and in the current account deficit. This past year that adjustment seems to have started, with a substantial swing in the euro/dollar exchange rate. A particular concern now is to figure out how the world economy can return to sustainable growth while adjusting to a still lower dollar and lower US deficit, when these occur. The adjustment process must be seen in a global context, not just in a US one. The review then looks at the steps being taken toward economic reform in Europe. Considerable momentum for a reform agenda has emerged this past year in Europe. The 2000 Lisbon EU council meeting was an important landmark, but implementation now seems to be taking place, although with some resistance. The fourth topic is an examination of deflation, an issue that has been around for a while as part of Japan's economic difficulties, but has assumed increased importance over the past year, with concerns that deflation could spread to the United States, Germany, and possibly other countries. The implications of rapid growth in China have been a hot topic for a while, but have become a much hotter topic in the past year. As the rest of the world economy turned sluggish, the Chinese surged ahead, increasing their exports at a very rapid pace. From Tokyo to Milan to Chicago, everyone is wondering whether China can continue to grow so fast and how their own jobs and businesses will be affected if it does. The discussion of China is followed by a short review of the economic effects of SARS outbreak of the past year.

Finally we turn to Africa where there have been important developments, both in the evaluation of the dangers of AIDS to the economy of the region and in the local and international response to the disease. There is a short conclusion.[1]

The war in Iraq and its economic fallout

Direct economic effects of the war with Iraq were felt prior to the outbreak of war, because of the uncertainty that was created. Oil prices increased, consumer and business confidence weakened, and economic growth—which was already weak—slowed or stalled in Europe and the United States. The war itself was short, less costly in human lives than might have been expected, and not hugely expensive relative to the size of the US economy. And not all of the economic effects were negative for growth. The increase in military spending in the United States and the United Kingdom served to sustain GDP growth in the first half of 2003.

The continuation of guerilla warfare with the agony of seeing soldiers and civilians killed almost every day is a serious political and social problem. The continuing economic costs are not as devastating, but are still significant. Currently the Coalition Provisional Authority (CPA) in Iraq has allocated US$256.8 million to reconstruction in its budget for July–Dec 2003,[2] and The Emergency Wartime Supplemental Appropriations Act of 2003 granted the Bush administration an additional US$59.7 billion to Operation Iraqi Freedom and made US$2.48 billion available to an Iraqi Relief and Reconstruction Fund until September 30, 2004.[3] However, the final costs of Iraqi reconstruction are likely to be much higher. Acknowledgement by the Bush administration of rising reconstruction costs in both Iraq and Afghanistan emerged with the President's September 7th request to Congress for an additional US$87 billion in funding for fiscal year 2004. Included in this request was a US$20 billion request for Iraqi infrastructure (US$15 billion) and security provision (US$5 billion), as well as an initial medium-term estimate of US$50 to 75 billion required for Iraqi infrastructure investments alone.[4] Private estimates run even higher: Brookings scholars O'Hanlon and Brainard (2003) estimate costs borne by the United States for troop deployment in Iraq alone at US$3 billion a month in the years ahead, while US reconstruction costs range from US$5 to 120 billion a year. Much depends on the length of US deployment, therefore, but even in benign scenarios, the costs of the Iraq operation may continue to weigh on US government finances—up to 1 percent of GDP in additional spending per year if the highest figure provided by Bremer, head of the Coalition Provisional Authority (CPA) in Iraq, is correct.

Oil prices did not spike when the war started, as there was no disruption to Middle East supplies except for Iraq itself. But after the short war it seemed possible that Iraqi oil supplies would quickly be back on line and then increased rapidly compared with pre-war levels. It now seems that it will take much more time to deal with the problems of antiquated supply machinery and sabotage. As of mid-year 2003, the price of light sweet crude was still in excess of US$30 a barrel. If there had been a five or ten dollar drop in the price of oil, this would have helped the world economic recovery.

Economic frictions after the war

When the United States and Britain decided to go to war with Iraq, it was against the wishes of the United Nations and much of Europe, Russia, China, and many other countries. It is not clear yet whether the friction created by the disagreement over Iraq will spill over into the economic arena, but so far the indications are that it will not. The United States is a major market for China and Japan, and whatever misgivings these countries may have about the war have not seriously impacted economic relations. These countries have a lot to lose from economic conflict with the United States. Russia may move closer to Europe, but if so, the impact of the war itself is likely to be a minor factor in that process.

Frictions between Europe and the United States over trade and the environment were pretty strong even before the war. The European Union and the United States were engaged in a trade skirmish, if not a trade war, involving genetically modified organisms, hormone fed beef, the tax treatment of foreign sales corporations, steel tariffs, and other issues. The US government's attitude toward the European Union has not been particularly conciliatory since the war. The reactions in Europe vary by country. Germany, with huge business ties to the United States, has been more ready to try and restore good relations. Franco-American relations were never great and have suffered most.

There certainly is the potential for the trade frictions between the European Union and the United States to escalate into a damaging trade war. But the chances are good that time will ease tensions and allow the respective trade negotiators and the World Trade Organization (WTO) to find some level of compromise. Even if they do not, the disputes on the table so far, although important to specific economic constituencies within each region, are not in total terribly important relative to all trade or the economic size of the two regions.[5]

Global trade relations

In the Cancun Ministerial, progress in resolving the disputes over agriculture had seemed possible. However, the European Union, Japan, and Korea requested new investment regulations and these were rejected by the African and the Asian countries. At that point, the Mexican hosts decided to end the meeting. This seems to leave multilateral trade negotiations standing at a knife's edge, with the support of the major economies wavering. WTO negotiators are to be called together for a new meeting in December, but with the 2004 electoral cycle opening, the United States at best appears destined to pursue only bilateral free trade agreements in the medium term. The European Union which is engaging simultaneously in internal reform and enlargement, is also questioning not only its multilateral trade strategy, but also the functionality of a 146-member WTO as an effective forum for trade negotiations. Developing countries, spearheaded in Cancun by the new Group of 22, even as they celebrate their success in thwarting negotiations on the issues they opposed, have so far proven unable to formulate a coherent trade agenda for future negotiations and hence seem unable to agree on how to wield their newfound veto-power in multilateral negotiations. This is a potentially destabilizing new feature of global trade institutions, as it will likely cause negotiating partners in the developed world to refrain from fielding serious trade proposals, fearing that developing countries will be unable to reciprocate due to their internal disagreements. For most welfare gains to be achieved and to avoid a possibly prolonged stalemate, it is therefore of the utmost importance quickly to rediscover the political will required to move the Doha process forward.

Another issue coming out of the war is tensions within the European Union itself. Several countries supported the war and so did countries due to enter the European Union shortly. Efforts to strengthen political and military ties within the Union were set back by the conflict over the war. The United Kingdom in particular, which actively participated in the war and has decided to hold off on joining the euro zone, may find it is losing influence on economic decisions within the European Union.

Rebalancing exchange rates and trade flows

Sustainable world economic growth must involve a substantial trade and exchange rate rebalancing and policies in the United States and around the world should facilitate it. Importantly, the reduction of the US current account deficit is not just a US issue; it must also involve adjustments in the rest of the world. At the recent G-7 meetings in Dubai, the finance ministers agreed on the importance of the issue of rebalancing the world economy.

Looking first at the exchange rate side of the story, Figure 1 shows the movements of the euro versus the US dollar, the Japanese yen versus the US dollar, and a broad exchange rate index of the US dollar. In each case, January 1995 is set equal to 100 and an upward movement indi-

Figure 1: Real exchange movements, 1995–2003

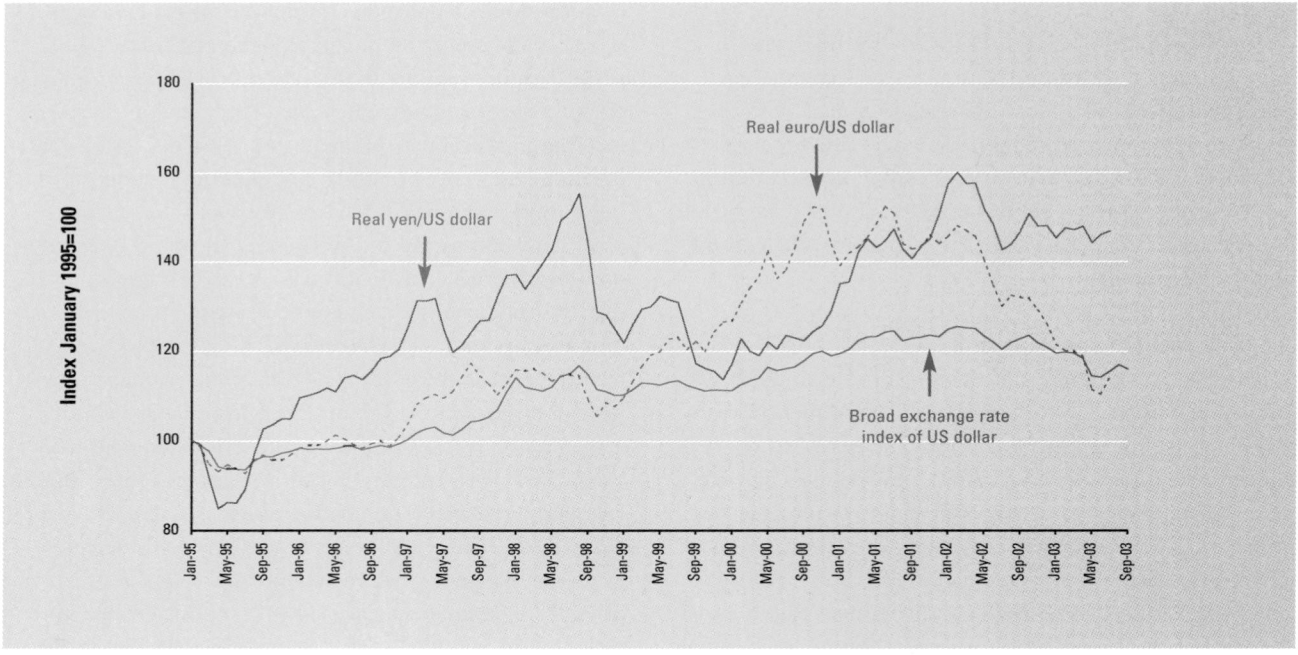

Note: Increase in value on chart equals a strengthening dollar
Sources: US Federal Reserve, Bank of Japan, European Central Bank, Pacific Exchange Rate Service, US Bureau of Labor Statistics

cates a rising value of the dollar, a downward movement a falling dollar. There are two notable implications of this figure. First, it shows the very large and sustained swings in exchange rates, with a long rise in the dollar in the 1990s and a modest decline in the dollar since early 2002. Given the continuing growth in trade and investment, large relative exchange rate movements are potentially disruptive to the business sector as it sets its investment and production decisions. Second, the figure shows that the dollar has fallen much more against the euro than against either the yen or the broad exchange rate index in recent months. This last point is of course in large part the simple averaging effect of constructing an index. But beyond this, there are many currencies that have pegged their values in relation to the dollar, either fixing exchange rates or allowing only modest movements against the dollar.

Turning to the trade and income side of the story, the United States has a current account deficit of over 5 percent of GDP, and most of this reflects a trade deficit.[6] The rest of the world, of course, is running a corresponding trade and current account surplus with the United States. There are two complementary factors that drove the long rise in the US dollar and the rising trade and current account deficits. First, as the US economy and the stock market boomed in the 1990s, Americans became richer and increased consumption. It also encouraged companies based in the United States to increase their

investments. Private sector demand in the United States increased very rapidly, outpacing the growth of supply, and Americans chose to fill the gap between what they produced and what they purchased by buying from overseas. They financed these purchases by foreign borrowing or by selling US assets. Second, the rest of the world was happy to facilitate the US spending boom. There was a huge appetite in the rest of the world for US assets.

In combination, these two forces drove the very large increases in capital inflows to the United States, which in turn pushed up the value of the dollar in the late 1990s. As a matter of arithmetic, the large capital inflow to the United States had to create a large offsetting trade deficit, which indeed it did, as the high dollar made many US goods uncompetitive in world markets and made imports cheap for Americans. As well as being willing to finance the US spending boom, the rest of the world was happy to sell their products in the United States, filling the gap between United States and the domestically available supply.

The need for rebalancing

Not everyone agrees that the large exchange rate swings and the large current account deficits and surpluses that develop around the world are a problem. After all, the flow of capital is part of the process of globalization and reflects the desire of wealth holders to seek the highest risk-adjusted returns. Mobile capital can increase efficiency as part of a market system that forces companies and policymakers around the world to ensure that capital receives a competitive return. Indeed, most economists agree with this view sufficiently to oppose capital controls and exchange rate intervention, at least for the major developed economies.

The benefits of mobile market-driven capital flows are reduced, however, by a tendency for exchange rates to overshoot. As capital flows into a country, the exchange rate rises, asset prices rise, and more capital flows in. On the down side, as capital leaves, exchange rates fall and more capital leaves. The overshooting problem is sufficiently severe that some countries intervene actively to stabilize their exchange rates. That solution can create problems of its own, of course, as the experience of Argentina has shown. Trying to prop up an overvalued exchange rate can result in a crisis with very adverse effects. But even in the large developed economies, exchange rate swings that create large trade problems can cause domestic difficulties. Specifically, the US manufacturing sector was hit hard by the rise of the US dollar and the large manufacturing trade deficit. Political pressure for protectionism becomes stronger when trade deficits increase.[7]

At the end of the day, however, the rebalancing of exchange rates and trade flows is going to happen whether it is left to the market or interventionist policies bring it about. First, large and growing US deficits will eventually result in an overweighting of US assets in world portfolios and a resulting reduction in the demand for US assets. Second, the steady increase in US net foreign indebtedness will result in an increase in the outflow of income to service that indebtedness. So even if the US current account deficit stays high, the trade deficit and the dollar will eventually decline. And third, as the rest of the world accumulates larger and larger stocks of US assets, they will eventually decide to spend some of that wealth, especially given the demographic trends in place in Europe and Japan with increasing numbers of retirees.

Facilitating the rebalancing

As noted earlier, the dollar has fallen to some extent, and for the United States a further reduction in the dollar and in the trade deficit would be helpful in the short term. Currently, there is no inflationary pressure in the United States—indeed, there is concern about the possibility of deflation. There is plenty of economic slack to accommodate a rise in exports or fall in imports or both. Manufacturing employment has fallen dramatically and would be helped by a greater dollar decline.

As the US economy reached full employment, however, the adjustment process would become harder. Even cutting the current account deficit in half would involve a shift of 2.5 percent of GDP, in the form of lower con-

sumption or investment or government spending. Simulations of a macroeconomic model have suggested that achieving the necessary reductions in the growth of private-sector spending could increase US interest rates to very high levels with adverse effects on investment, especially housing.[8] Government fiscal policy is actually making the longer-run situation much worse. To facilitate a rebalancing, the US government should be at least aiming for long-run budget balance. On the spending side, there are promises of spending restraint, but no action so far—indeed, federal spending has risen sharply with the step up in defense spending. Combined with the large tax cuts that have been passed, the result is enormous projected budget deficits. The US Congressional Budget Office predicts a federal budget deficit of US$480 billion for the 2004 fiscal year and deficits totaling US$1.4 trillion over the next decade, even with conservative assumptions. With assumptions that are probably more realistic, the US could experience deficits of US$400 to 500 billion a year over the next ten years.

US fiscal stimulus is currently helping the US and the world economic recovery by adding to aggregate demand. But the particular policies enacted will make the rebalancing of exchange rates and trade flows much more difficult by lowering US national savings, and will be harmful to long-term growth by raising interest rates not only in the United States but also in the rest of the world. The United States is on an irresponsible fiscal path.

The euro has accounted for much of the fall of the US dollar to date, and this has come at a very tough time for Europe. Germany in particular is heavily dependent on exports and is already on the verge of recession. European leaders are very concerned about the possible consequences of a further rise in the euro, with people in Germany saying that a euro at US$1.25 would be a disaster. Watch out! It is unclear where the euro will go, but the euro at US$1.40 or even US$1.50 have been suggested as possibilities.

The main thing that Europe should do to facilitate rebalancing is to use macroeconomic policies to stimulate domestic demand and to use structural reforms to expand employment and investment. Both of these aspects are considered in more detail shortly, but it is important to recognize that rebalancing is very difficult if it occurs only through exchange rate adjustments. By stimulating its own demand, Europe will increase its imports from the United States and around the world. That is actually a good thing, allowing Europeans to consume more.

The euro alone cannot carry the full burden of the downward adjustment of the US dollar and the eventual reduction of its current account deficit. Countries such as China, Japan, and Korea must reduce their accumulation of foreign exchange reserves and allow their currencies to move toward market levels. China specifically has fixed its nominal exchange rate against the US dollar while its manufactured goods prices are falling. It has experienced a modest real devaluation against the dollar and a large devaluation against the euro. Like Europe, the rest of the world will have to increase domestic demand over the future in order to offset the eventual reduction in the US trade deficit. Faulty mercantilist thinking still permeates the world economy. Creating jobs with exports is fine, but the ultimate purpose of the economy is to provide consumption and investment for the domestic economy. If the US current account deficit declines, this means more goods and services for the rest of the world. That is good for them, but the domestic demand for these goods has to be there or else the reduction of the US deficit will induce economic weakness in the rest of the world.

Increasing demand and supply in Europe[9]

Europe has shared in the slowdown in global economic growth and currently suffers from weakness in the overall demand for goods and services. Over the next year or so, the biggest contribution to growth in Europe would come from an easing of monetary policy by the European Central Bank. The biggest impediment to growth would occur if the Stability and Growth Pact were to be used to force restrictive fiscal policies. Over the longer run, structural policies to increase both productivity and employment become the most important means of spurring growth. Some structural policies, such as those intended to increase work incentives, could be helpful rather quickly.

Barriers to increased growth in Europe

Europe has a substantial unrealized potential to increase its productivity growth. There are important issues of measurement and interpretation that make comparisons tricky, but the rapid productivity growth in the United States since 1995 stands in particular contrast to the very slow growth of productivity in the core European economies in recent years. A variety of barriers discourage best-practice performance.

Banks in Germany are not able to take full advantage of investments in information technology (IT) because they cannot lay off the workers no longer needed after installing the new technology. Further, preferential treatment is given to small local banks, which discourages industry consolidation.[10] France has not privatized its electricity industry or provided effective competitive pressure in this sector. Because of the extensive use of capital intensive nuclear power, the level of productivity is quite high in the French power industry, but there is excess employment and a very slow rate of productivity increase. In retailing, Germany and France both place severe limits on the entry or expansion of the most productive companies. Zoning restrictions making it difficult or impossible

to find new store locations and create a major performance barrier in this industry and affect other industries also. Protecting green space is reasonable, but in practice such restrictions are used to protect incumbent companies from best-practice competitors. Britain has moved a long way forward in freeing up its economy, but still has many restrictive regulations. Inflexible "historic preservation" laws make it a nightmare for companies to re-model buildings. Hotel operators in Britain, for example, find it hard to expand or operate efficiently.[11]

In general, competitive intensity is the best spur to improved productivity, and the regulatory environment must encourage this. High competitive intensity is not necessarily achieved by having a large number of companies; in fact, such intensity often requires the consolidation of small traditional operations and the entry of world best-practice companies. In industries where there are natural monopolies, privatization plus a strict price cap can be an effective device to improve productivity—the electricity distribution system in Britain is an example of this approach.

Information technology has been an important driver of the increased productivity growth in the United States, and there are opportunities to use IT more effectively in Europe that would help their performance. Even the strongest companies in Europe, for example, have not developed supply chain management systems that are as good as the leading retailers in the United States. Europe also suffers a productivity growth disadvantage relative to the United States because it does not have an equivalent high-tech production sector. In general, however, better use of IT in Europe will follow from deregulation and increased competition. It is a mistake for policymakers in Europe to expect technology policy to substitute for real economic reform.

There is some good news in Europe, where deregulation and the opening of the single market have resulted in rapid increases in productivity. The electricity industry in Britain is one such example. Another is the auto industry in France, where Renault was (mostly) privatized and allowed to make layoffs. Productivity growth has been so rapid that the French industry has overtaken the German industry in output per hour. The mobile phone industry was allowed to develop in a competitive environment in Germany with regulations that encouraged strong productivity performance. In the cases where European countries have undertaken regulatory reform and/or taken advantage of the increased competition provided by a single market, the results have been good.

There are also structural barriers to employment growth. All advanced countries have social safety nets for those suffering economic reverses and most provide at least a minimum level of pension support for the elderly. But in Europe people can collect unemployment benefits

64

or welfare payments for years, and retirement benefits are largely unrelated to private saving decisions in many European countries. This means that the link between income and individual responsibility has been severely undermined and the distortions to private decisions are severe.

The labor market in much of Europe is devastating for employment. Wage rates for low-skill workers are kept high by minimum wage rates or high union wage rates. Payroll taxes are very high and inflate company employment costs (along with other employer mandates). Benefit levels paid to those who do not work are kept high relative to after-tax wages. This system discourages employers from hiring as well as discouraging workers from taking the jobs that are available.

This problem could get much worse in the future. Demographic changes already in motion will greatly increase the burden of pensions and health care for the elderly over the next decades because of the wave of upcoming retirements. In addition, people are living longer than they used to and people are retiring younger than they used to. According to the Organisation for Economic Co-operation and Development (OECD), there were two workers per retiree in 2000 in Germany and there will be only 1.3 workers per retiree in 2030. In Italy, the OECD projects only one worker per retiree in 2030! It is going to be very hard to ensure that work incentives are not crushed by the burden of supporting retirees.

What should Europe do?

Good monetary and fiscal policies are essential to sustain demand. The European Central Bank (ECB) can do more and reform of the Stability and Growth Pact is vital.

On structural reform, European governments have in principle embraced the need for change. Indeed, there are reform programs already in place in several European countries that have improved economic performance, and there are reforms being proposed throughout Europe. France achieved rapid employment growth in the late 1990s, helped by policies that increased labor market flexibility and by reductions in payroll taxes for low-wage workers enacted in 1993.

To improve the incentive to work, policymakers in Europe should now announce limits on unemployment benefits to take effect at some time in the future (such limits have been proposed and, in some countries, enacted). Companies in Europe should be able to make layoffs without the requirement of government or court permission. Companies that make layoffs should be required to make higher contributions to an unemployment fund over some period of time. There is a social cost to layoffs, and companies should be expected to offset the unemployment burden they impose, but their liability should be limited and should not be so high that it discourages needed restructuring. There should be no additional redundancy payment required beyond the experience-rated unemployment charges.[12]

Reducing the heavy burden of payroll taxes in Europe would be an important stimulus to job growth. Given the fiscal restraints faced by most European countries, there is no easy or immediate solution to this problem. Scaling back pension levels, including increases in retirement age, limiting other income support programs, and restraining other areas of government spending can create the fiscal room to support payroll tax reductions, but this process will take time.

The programs of privatization and the increased competitive pressure from the single market are working in Europe, but there remains much more to be done, especially in service sectors. There is also a danger of backsliding. Industry organizations and unions (and the regulatory bodies that have been captured by these groups) are working to prevent further progress.[13] Europe already takes advantage of the benefits of trade, especially intra-European trade, but could do more to liberalize trade with the rest of the world. In service industries that are largely nontradable, best-practice companies should be encouraged to enter and compete.

Europe must develop a virtuous cycle of macroeconomic expansion, structural reform, job growth, improved fiscal position, and further structural reform. Pension reform in particular is vital to Europe's economic viability over the next 30 years.

The dangers of deflation

Once only an issue for Japan, warnings about the possible adverse consequences from deflation have been heard all around this past year, particularly with relevance to Germany and the United States. In his testimony to the US Congress on July 15, 2003, Alan Greenspan noted that "Indeed, there is an especially pernicious, albeit remote, scenario in which inflation turns negative against a backdrop of weak aggregate demand, engendering a corrosive deflationary spiral."

Goods and services price deflation consists of a large or persistent decline in the price level, captured by broad price indexes such as the consumer price index or the GDP price index. This means that a rapid or persistent decline in the price of a single product or even a class of products does not constitute deflation. For example, the fact that computer prices have declined at around 25 percent a year over several years is not broad deflation. Goods and services deflation encourages individuals and businesses to *postpone* consumption: if prices will be lower next year, why not wait until next year before buying?

Deflation must be seen in relation to the interest rate. The interest rate is a return received for postponing purchases until next year, and it can adjust up or down in response to expectations of inflation or deflation. Changes in the rate of interest (the nominal rate of interest) can to a degree offset or compensate for expected inflation or deflation. The ability of interest rate declines to compensate for price level declines works only up to a point, however. In Japan, the rate of interest on short-term government bonds is essentially zero and cannot go lower than this, since people can always hold cash.[14]

As well as encouraging people to postpone spending, deflation affects the real value of debts. Consumers or businesses that have borrowed money find that the real value of their debt has risen and they are worse off— unexpectedly so if the deflation was not anticipated. The lenders, banks or investors in the bond market, find that the real value of their assets has risen correspondingly, so there has been a shift of wealth between borrowers and lenders. This redistribution could in principle have little effect on overall spending in an economy (one group is richer and another poorer). But in practice, borrowers may choose to default on their debts or be forced to default if their incomes also fall relative to their debt service obligations. Deflation can be disruptive to the financial system.

This argument holds much more strongly when there is not only a decline in the overall price level but also a decline in asset prices. If both occur together, the economy can get multiple hits as weak demand and excess capacity are combined with declines in equity prices and perhaps real estate prices, as well as goods and services deflation. From its peak in 2000 to its recent trough, the US stock market lost US$7 trillion of value, although— fortunately for US households—this was offset in part by a rise in residential housing prices.

Japan's prolonged economic problems of the 1990s were triggered by, or exacerbated by, massive asset price falls, and these declines have continued to affect the economy adversely. In April 2003, the Nikkei stock average was only *20 percent of its peak value* achieved in the late 1980s![15] Land prices in Japan have fallen dramatically also. Urban commercial land prices peaked in 1991 and had fallen by over half by 2002. Industrial and residential land prices also fell, although less dramatically.[16]

Asset price deflation adversely affected financial institutions in Japan. Both stocks and land had been purchased with money borrowed from banks and from the capital market. The asset price declines were large enough to reduce the value of the collateral below the value of the loan in many, many cases. As the overall economy weakened, borrowers were unable or unwilling to service the debts they had taken on,[17] so that financial institutions were left with only bad choices and often became essentially bankrupt.

The effectiveness of monetary policy in raising demand[18]

Price level deflation and asset price volatility can be serious enough for the individuals or institutions that are affected directly. Beyond this, however, deflation is much more pernicious if it accompanies a severe weakness in aggregate demand. How can monetary policy, or a combination of monetary and fiscal policy, stimulate an economy caught in a pernicious spiral when the central bank has already lowered rates close to zero?

The first answer to this question is to avoid getting into that situation to begin with. Critics of Japanese policy generally comment that it was too tentative early on when the growth bubble collapsed at the end of the 1980s. Had monetary and fiscal policy been more expansionary then, the decade-long recession in Japan and the onset of deflation could most likely have been avoided (Kuttner and Posen 2002).

But suppose the worst happens: Can monetary policy still be effective? A central bank can certainly keep expanding the money supply even after the interest rate has fallen to zero, but the question is whether it will most likely have any additional stimulative effect. One answer is to simply say, by analogy to supply and demand in any market: print enough money and the "price of money" will come down. In this analogy the price of money is interpreted to mean terms on which money is exchanged for goods and services. So a decline in the price of money implies a rise in the price of goods and services—a rise in the price level.

This simple analogy does give the right answer, but things are more complicated than it suggests. Money is not a simple commodity, and if reductions in the interest rate are the main method by which money expansion works, and if the interest rate has already fallen close to zero, then further expansion of the money supply will have little additional impact in stimulating economic growth. That is the basis for the recent concern about deflation, a fear that central banks will "run out of ammunition."

One counter argument to this "liquidity trap" view is that money is part of total wealth. Flooding the economy with money adds to household wealth, and as people feel richer they will spend more and overall demand will increase, even though the interest rate is stuck at zero. For example, a central bank could simply print enough money to mail out thousands of dollars to every household. This policy would be a combined monetary policy expansion and fiscal policy expansion (in practice it would involve something like a tax cut that was paid for by printing money).[19] Eventually this process must increase demand, although in order to be successful such a policy could well involve a money supply expansion far larger in magnitude than any that central bankers are used to making, especially Japanese central bankers. Central banks can add to total wealth only by increasing the money base, but the money base (cash and bank reserves) forms only a very modest portion of total wealth in an economy—for example, it accounted for only about 2.3 percent of total household financial assets in the United States in 2002.[20] Any significant increase in household wealth would require huge percentage increases in the money base. If self-sustaining growth were then to be achieved, there would be the possibility of a shift from a deflation problem to a serious inflation problem because the money base would have been greatly expanded. It would not be easy to calibrate monetary policy to overcome deflation and recession and then avoid inflation as growth got going.

Another way out of the liquidity trap goes back to the interest rate mechanism for stimulating demand, but it focuses on longer-term interest rates. Central banks affect or control the short-term interest rate, and this is the rate that can be driven very close to zero by monetary expansion. Even in this situation, however, long-term rates remain positive. Spending in the economy depends not only on short rates, but also on long rates such as the mortgage interest rate and the rates on auto loans or corporate bonds. One way a central bank can act to lower long-term rates is by promising to keep short-term rates low for an extended period. Or the central bank can buy long-term bonds directly, government bonds or private sector bonds, driving their prices up and the interest rates down.[21]

In summary, monetary policy does not totally lose its effectiveness in stimulating demand as the short-term interest rate falls toward zero. But clearly the policy options for a central bank become less attractive and harder to calibrate once the ability to adjust short-term interest rates is lost. It is much better to pull all the stops out before the zero interest rate bound is reached.

The miracle in China and the challenge from China and India

Except for a very brief interruption caused by SARS, economic growth and export growth have continued in China right through the global slowdown. Can this growth continue for an extended period? One question about China's growth is whether it can avoid the dangers of the "Asian development path" followed by Japan and Korea. These countries protected the largest part of their economies from competition, market forces, and foreign investment. One can make the case that China is not going down this path. It is increasingly market driven, with prices set competitively. Tariffs have come down and will drop further by 2005. Many nontariff barriers are collapsing. Foreign-based production now accounts for a larger share of manufacturing than state-owned enterprises. Banks have a mountain of bad debt, but rapid overall economic growth should allow the government to recapitalize

the banks. Rising revenues will allow for the creation of a modest social safety net and to begin the process of environmental remediation.

On the other hand, China still has major structural problems to overcome. It scores rather poorly in the Growth Competitiveness Index of the World Economic Forum, being ranked 44 in 2003, down from the previous year. It ranks particularly low on technology indicators. So far this has not proven to be a barrier to growth; in part this is because China's manufacturing production is geared to low-wage labor-intensive activities. In addition, it is because China has used foreign investment as a vehicle to introduce the technology it needs.

It is not clear at present whether this strategy can be used as effectively in the future. In consumer electronics and PCs, for example, local companies have rapidly expanded their share of the market at the expense of multinational companies. It is hard to know whether this is because they have mastered the technology and are now exploiting their superior understanding of local conditions, or whether it is because government agencies at the local or national level are favoring the local champions. If it is the latter, foreign investment will slow down and China will move closer to the traditional Asian model of growth. There are reports of popular discontent at the success of multinational companies,[22] but it is not clear whether the Chinese government is responding or will respond to this pressure by acts of favoritism. Time will tell.

How can any high-wage country compete with China? Those who are not skeptical about China's growth prospects are often fearful of the impact this growth will have on their own economies. People look at how rapidly China's manufacturing sector is growing, at how rapidly the quality of the products is increasing, and at how the combination of foreign direct investment and local initiative are raising the technological sophistication of the goods produced there (how China is moving up the value chain). People see the fact that there is an almost unlimited, industrious, and trainable workforce willing to work at very low wages. And they conclude that no one else can compete any more. Fear of China as a competitor has grown rapidly over the past year. What will limit China from taking over all (or large parts of) global manufacturing?

The basic answer is that although China is adding rapidly to the *supply* of manufactured goods in the economy, it is also adding rapidly to the *demand* for manufactured goods. China is growing rapidly and its citizens are getting richer over time. As they do so, they demand imported goods and services from the rest of the world. People in developed economies see the growth of manufacturing capacity in China and forget that there is a counterpart that makes China a fast-growing market for consumer and capital goods.

In order that China not be a drain on manufacturing jobs around the world, the Chinese currency must be set either by market forces or set by policy in close relation to a market equilibrium value. In practice, China has been adding to its foreign currency reserves, which rose by about US$170 billion over two years, reaching US$356 billion in July of 2003. This has led some policymakers in developed countries, notably in Japan and the United States, to say that China should revalue its currency.

This is not the place for an assessment of that issue in any detail. It is hard to determine what a market-determined exchange rate would be for China. The rate might rise or fall, depending on whether capital controls were fully or partially lifted and how much money would flow into and out of China.[23] However, China is actually not running a large trade surplus in manufactured goods and so it has not been a net drain on manufacturing jobs in the world economy so far.[24] Politicians in the United States look at the large bilateral deficit between China and the United States, but bilateral deficits do not indicate that the Chinese currency is overvalued.

As noted earlier, there is a need for a rebalancing of world exchange rates going forward, and China's exchange rate will likely change as that process takes place. As countries develop economically, it is often the case that their currencies appreciate in value; China should be flexible enough to allow this to happen. In short, the message to China should be that it has not been responsible for draining jobs from the developing world up until now, but it must make sure that situation continues going forward.

The real challenge from China (and India).

The impact of trade in either goods or services is to *shift production from one industry or activity to another*. The challenge from China's trade for the rest of the world is that, because it is already large and is growing so fast, it forces structural change in China's trading partners. The faster the growth in China's trade, the faster shifts have to take place among its trading partners from one economic activity to another.

India's presence in the world economy has not grown nearly as rapidly as China's. But India has a unique role in trade in services that, while still small now, is growing very fast indeed.[25] Programming and technology centers have grown up rapidly in India and this has been followed by business process off-shoring—call centers, back office work for banks and insurance companies, and so on. It used to be that service industries were largely insulated from international trade, but that seems to be changing. At this point, it remains uncertain how large the off shoring of white-collar jobs will be, but the long-term potential is large.

International trade, whether in goods or in services, increases productivity and increases incomes for both trading partners. In order to take full advantage of the gains from trade, it is necessary for production to shift. Those economies where workers who are laid off have new jobs to go to and incentives to take the new jobs will do well. Those economies that facilitate startup companies and rapid employment expansion will be able to survive and benefit from the new challenges from India and China. Those economies that are not flexible will either have to erect protectionist barriers or else face increased structural unemployment. The earlier discussion of the need for flexibility in Europe is relevant here, and the same issues apply to other countries, including the United States.[26]

That said: the size of the adjustment in developed economies caused by China and India should not be exaggerated. China's exports in 2001 were less than 4.5 percent of total world exports, so even if rapid growth continues in the years ahead, China is still going to be only a small part of total world trade. And trade in services is still in its infancy. The challenge from China and India is just a continuation of the pattern of globalization that has been going on for 50 years.

The SARS outbreak: Consequences and prospects

The first case of SARS, severe acute respiratory syndrome, was discovered in southern China in November 2002. Before it was contained at the end of June 2003, the disease had infected 5,300 people nationwide and killed more than 348. After the Chinese government realized the seriousness of the SARS outbreak in late April and informed the public, the service economy in many parts of China came to a standstill as people stayed at home for fear of contracting the disease. Once the disease was controlled, however, the economy returned to normal and SARS seems to have been only a temporary blip. The key question that remains is whether or not SARS will resurface again in the fall or winter and perhaps inflict greater costs in the future.

Short-run economic impact on China, Hong Kong, and Singapore

As a result of SARS, Chinese GDP grew at a slower rate in the second quarter of 2003 than it had been growing in the preceding period. The service and retail sectors were the worst affected by the disease as tourism and transportation expenditure contracted and private consumption was affected. In contrast, the manufacturing sector that constitutes approximately 45 percent of the total economy has escaped relatively unscathed from the SARS epidemic, and trade growth has also remained robust. As well as manufacturing output, foreign direct investment also proved resilient during the SARS outbreak, while retail sales and demand for services picked up quickly once the outbreak was contained. If SARS is contained going forward, its outbreak in the spring of 2003 is likely to be considered a temporary demand shock to the Chinese economy that will not significantly affect long-term growth. However, the fact that the Chinese authorities covered up and mishandled the outbreak could raise concerns about the openness and transparency of the Chinese economy that would adversely affect trade and investment.

Outside of China, the SARS outbreak had the largest impact in countries that have large travel-related sectors such as Hong Kong and Singapore, (as financial services centers both were also hit by the drastic decline in business travel and deal making), where preliminary estimates suggest both economies contracted during the second quarter of 2003 (by roughly 5 percent and 11 percent, respectively). Both economies are likely to recover, given that China has recovered rapidly, but this recovery also depends on whether or not SARS returns, and, if it does, how effectively it can be contained.

Possible recurrence of SARS

SARS is a seasonal virus that may resurface and establish a pattern of recurring when winter comes. So although the short-term economic impact of SARS in 2003 has been less severe than expected, the long-term effects may be more pronounced. It is unlikely that either a cure or vaccine will be developed quickly, which means that the disease will probably be around for some years, according to many medical experts. Public health measures, including effective screening, health systems, and quarantining, therefore provide the best defense against another serious outbreak. SARS need not be a major health problem or spread from the currently affected areas if appropriate measures are taken. The more effective governments are in dealing with the disease, the less severe the economic consequences will be.

The impact of AIDS in Africa

The AIDS scourge has already lowered individual life expectancy in several sub-Saharan African countries by 15 to 20 years, to the point that life expectancy is only in the thirties.[27] For the region as a whole, the estimate of the AIDS infection rate is 8.8 percent of the adult population (aged 15–49). But this overall rate masks large differences by country—38.8 percent in Botswana, 22.5 percent in Namibia, 20.1 percent in South Africa, 33.4 percent in Swaziland, 21.5 percent in Zambia, and 33.7 percent in Zimbabwe—these numbers are estimates and subject to substantial error. The extraordinarily high figures contrast with much lower rates (0.5 percent to 5 percent) in several countries including Ghana, Senegal, and Uganda. With some exceptions, West Africa has been hit less severely

than east and central Africa and South Africa, although there are signs (in Nigeria for example) that this is because West Africa is in an earlier stage of the epidemic, and not because the disease is following a different path (UNAIDS/WHO 2003).

Not only has the epidemic turned out to be as bad or worse than anticipated, but also estimates of the economic impact of the epidemic have been revised up, suggesting a much more serious impact than had previously been thought. Early studies of the macroeconomic impact of AIDS in Africa concluded that its effect would be limited, but recent research sponsored by the World Bank[28] has come to a different view and concludes, "...that the long-run economic costs of AIDS are almost certain to be much higher [than previously thought]—and possibly devastating" (Bell, Devarajan and Gersbach 2003:7). The main reason is that the AIDS virus predominantly kills young adults rather than children and the elderly, as is or was the case for other major diseases such as malaria or tuberculosis. This means its impact on human capital—the level of skills and education—in Africa is particularly harmful. AIDS not only destroys the human capital already acquired by the young adult segment of the population through their upbringing, education, and job experiences, but it also destroys the mechanisms by which parents hand on knowledge to their children. Part of this vicious cycle is that as members of the young adult population die, there will be a reduction in tax revenue to the government, making it harder to provide health care for the afflicted or education for the AIDS orphans left behind.

According to the World Bank study, South Africa is in danger of succumbing to a vicious cycle with AIDS. The infection rate is already high and the severe threat cited in the World Bank study was that it would become much higher because of a reluctance to face up to the nature of the epidemic and what will be needed to overcome it. Fortunately, this reluctance now seems to be disappearing, as policymakers in South Africa are recognizing the need for antiretroviral drugs (the standard western treatment for HIV/AIDS).

Dealing with the AIDS problem

Although there have been some encouraging private-sector and business responses to AIDS, the main responsibility for dealing with the AIDS epidemic and avoiding the economic disaster that is threatened lies with African governments and with the developed world, which can provide financial assistance. There are success stories, which indicate that a coordinated attack on the problem can succeed. This is not the place for a detailed discussion of AIDS policy, especially because data are often weak and it is hard to be sure how much of any AIDS infection outcome is the result of policy and how much other factors, such as the time when AIDS first appeared in the country. However, there are some lessons to be learned from successful approaches to AIDS within Africa, and, in addition, Brazil provides another example of a successful approach to dealing with the disease. The governments that recognized the danger from AIDS and took early aggressive steps to deal with the problem have had some success. These steps included visible campaigns to inform people about the nature of HIV/AIDS and to change behavior, conducted at the village and national levels. Increased access or free access to condoms has been helpful, together with some provision of antiretroviral drugs.

Africa faces stiff challenges on the road to sustainable economic development. Overcoming the AIDS epidemic is clearly one of the first that must be overcome. For the developed world, providing the resources to defeat or control the epidemic is a humanitarian imperative.

AIDS lessons outside Africa

This discussion has focused on Africa. However, AIDS lessons need to be learned rapidly also outside Africa. Already India, with 4.5 million people infected with HIV/AIDS, has the second-highest number of infections after South Africa, and, according to the National Aids Control Organization, the disease is spreading now into Indian rural areas and the general population.[29] Massive migration fuels the growth of the disease in China, where up to 10 million people may be infected by 2010 unless immediate action is taken.[30] AIDS could potentially threaten the progress of these two bright global economic success stories in recent years. AIDS is also a threat in Russia, where infection rates have exploded in recent years, to about 1 million in mid 2002 according to the Russian Academy of Medicine. As in Africa, the key issue for these countries is to take preventive measures and follow aggressive treatment protocols.

Conclusion

In this same review last year, I noted that the economic downturn, the collapse of the technology sector, and the recurrent economic crises in developing economies had cast doubt on the value of the economic path of liberalization and globalization. This was a pity, because even though there are indeed serious market failures and crises, the use of competitive markets remained by far the best way to achieve economic success. They generally provide the strongest incentives for work, investment, and innovation. Countries that had cut themselves off from the global economy were doing worse than those that had participated in the global economy.

How does that assessment stand today? The same conclusion still applies, and indeed the sustained economic success in China and the potentially strong recovery in the

United States strengthen the case for liberal market economics with active stabilization policies.

Regardless of whether one supported or opposed the war in Iraq, the fact that it so sharply divided the world has been a setback to global cooperation and inevitably a setback for economic cooperation and globalization. The United States easily defeated Iraq with only limited international assistance, but it is learning now, as it tries to deal with the chaos and violence of a conquered Iraq, that the United Nations and the international community are more important than it realized. The global spread of AIDS and the sudden dangers of SARS reinforce the message that worldwide cooperation is essential to continued economic success. The US administration should learn the right lessons from the past year and use economic cooperation as a way back to better political and military cooperation. Opponents of the war in Iraq, such as France, must overcome their distaste for the US administration and look for areas of mutual interest.

Economics is not a zero-sum game. Growth in China and in the United States can help Europe and Japan to recover. Recovery in the developed world will help growth in the poorer economies. The challenge for the world economy today is to overcome the divisions created this past year and push toward mutually supportive policies. Facing the AIDS epidemic is one area for cooperation; using the Doha round constructively to reduce trade barriers and help poorer countries is another.

Notes

1 I am grateful to colleagues at the Institute for International Economics for their assistance. I have also made use of the work of the McKinsey Global Institute, where I am a Senior Advisor.

2 See CPA 2003 Final Budget, available at http://www.cpa-iraq.org/budget/2003budget.pdf, accessed August 12, 2003.

3 See Emergency Wartime Supplemental Appropriations Act, 2003 (Engrossed as Agreed to or Passed by House), H.R. 1559, available at http://thomas.loc.gov/cgi-bin/query/D?c108:2:./temp/~c108OrntVo:, accessed August 12, 2003.

4 Office of the President, September 8th: Fact Sheet: Request for Additional FY 2004 Funding for the War on Terror, available at http://www.whitehouse.gov/news/releases/2003/09/iraq/20030908-1.html. Accessed September 22, 2003.

5 The European Union has a new regulatory initiative called REACH that would subject all chemicals to extensive new testing and would affect trade in any goods that contained chemicals (most trade). This initiative is potentially a very serious issue for businesses within the EU, and for all countries that either trade with the EU or have investments in the EU. As yet, it is not certain whether this initiative will be passed and, if passed, how it would be implemented in practice. But it could make all previous trade disputes look insignificant by comparison.

6 The United States is now a large net borrower from the rest of the world, but the net income flows remain relatively small.

7 See Bergsten and Williamson (2003) for a discussion of this issue.

8 See the simulation results based on the model of Macroeconomic Advisers reported in Martin Neil Baily, "Persistent Dollar Swings and the US Economy," in Bergsten and Williamson (2003).

9 This section draws on Martin Neil Baily (2004).

10 Some smaller banks are state owned and others are given credit guarantees that lower their effective cost of capital. These latter provisions are due to expire in 2005.

11 This discussion is based on analyses by the McKinsey Global Institute, including studies of France, Germany, and Britain.

12 French economists Olivier Blanchard of MIT and Jean Tirole of Toulouse have proposed reforms similar to these. See Blanchard and Tirole (2003).

13 See the discussion of the REACH initiative in note 6.

14 It is possible for governments to impose negative rates of interest on cash by forcing people to turn in their cash to a bank and get back a slightly smaller quantity of new cash. However, this would be politically difficult to do and hard and costly to implement.

15 Data are from the Tokyo stock exchange as reported by Yahoo, at http://finance.yahoo.com/q?s=^N225&d=t, accessed July 3, 2003

16 Data are from the Japan Statistics Bureau at http://www.stat.go.jp/english/, accessed July 3, 2003.

17 Goods and services price deflation can create a similar situation if wages and incomes start to decline and debt rises as a share of incomes.

18 Japan and Europe arguably suffer from structural problems that limit their economic growth as much or more than demand weakness. This section, however, is focused on demand stimulus policies that are necessary for growth.

19 Of course there could be a monetary expansion without a fiscal expansion if the central bank were to buy very large quantities of government debt outstanding: that is, open market operations, but carried out on a large scale. It is less certain that this would provide the necessary stimulus to the economy. It would be a net addition to wealth only to the extent that the household sector values money more highly than government debt. That would be the case only if households take into account the future taxes that will have to be paid to finance government debt service. So Keynesians can counter the above argument by saying that it is really the fiscal expansion that counts. The discussion here is around the feasibility of finding some policy combination that can in the limit reverse a downward deflationary spiral, not about a debate between fiscal and monetary policy.

20 As a reference point, the money base in the United States in 2002 was around US$700 billion. Households and nonprofits in the United States held around US$30 trillion in financial assets in that year. A 50 percent increase in the money base (a very large change) would add US$350 billion to wealth, but this is only a 1.1 percent addition to total wealth. By contrast, the value of US financial assets fell by US$2 trillion between 2001 and 2002.

21 This has been done in the past. It is not clear it would be effective in changing long rates unless the central bank is able to create the expectation that short rates will stay low for some time.

22 Although there are also crowds of Chinese shopping at French and US retailers Carrefour and Walmart.

23 Capital controls in China are by no means fully effective at present. The easing of controls, however, would allow wealthy Chinese who remain constrained by regulations to diversify their assets through foreign holdings.

24 The accumulation of reserves has been financed (indirectly) through the inflow of foreign investment capital.

25 This discussion draws on work being carried out by the McKinsey Global Institute, to be published in the fall of 2003.

26 Five states in the United States have introduced legislation to prohibit companies that take state contracts from providing services by outsourcing the work overseas. Only New Jersey has actually introduced such legislation, the Turner Bill, and this is stuck in committee. Legislators in Connecticut, Maryland, Missouri, and Wisconsin have "explored" similar types of legislation, but have not presented actual bills.

27 Life expectancy from 1990 to 2001 declined from 57 to 38 years in Botswana, 49 to 37 in Zambia, 56 to 39 in Zimbabwe and 62 to 47 in South Africa. Source: World Bank Development Indicators at http://devdata.worldbank.org/dataonline/.

28 See also Barnett (2002).

29 Comment by NACO Director Meenakshi Datta Ghosh, quoted in BBC On-line at http://news.bbc.co.uk/2/hi/south_asia/3098921.stm, accessed August 12, 2003.

30 UNAIDS/WHO factsheet 2003 for China.

References

Asian Development Bank, Regional Economic Monitoring Unit. 2003. *Asia Economic Monitor*, July. Available at http://aric.adb.org/aem/completereport_jul.pdf, accessed September 22, 2003.

AngloGold, 2002. *Facing the Challenge of HIV/AIDS 2001/2002*. http://www.anglogold.com/Corporate+Responsibility/HIV+Aids/, accessed September 22, 2003.

Bank of Japan Online Statistics at http://www.boj.or.jp/en/stat/stat_f.htm.

Baily, M. N. 2004. *A Radical Transformation of the European Economy*. Forthcoming, Washington, DC: Institute for International Economics.

Baily, M. N. 2003. "Persistent Dollar Swings and the US Economy." In C. F. Bergsten and J. Williamson, "Dollar Overvaluation and the World Economy," pp. 81–135, Washington, DC: Institute for International Economics.

Barnett, T. 2002 (forthcoming). "Progress Report: HIV/AIDS Impact Studies II – Some Progress Evident," *Progress in Development Studies*. Available at http://www.uea.ac.uk/dev/publink/barnett/asb02d.shtml.

Barton, D., R. Newell, and G. Wilson. 2003. *Dangerous Markets: Managing in Financial Crises*. New York: John Wiley & Sons.

BBC On-line at http://news.bbc.co.uk/2/hi/south_asia/3098921.stm, accessed August 12, 2003.

Bell, C., S. Devarajan, and H. Gersbach. 2003. "The Long-run Economic Costs of AIDS: Theory and an Application to South Africa," June. World Bank, available at http://www1.worldbank.org/hiv_aids/docs/BeDeGe_BP_total2.pdf, accessed July 28, 2003.

Bergsten C. F. and J. Williamson. 2003. "Dollar Overvaluation and the World Economy." Special Report No.16, October. Washington, DC: Institute for International Economics.

Bill and Melinda Gates Foundation at http://www.gatesfoundation.org/GlobalHealth/Announcements/Announce-030528.htm?version=print, accessed July 28, 2003.

Blanchard, O. and J. Tirole. 2003. *Contours of Employment Protection Reform*. Paris: Conseil d'Analyse Economique.

Brazilian STD AIDS Program, at http://www.aids.gov.br/indexpingl.htm, accessed July 28, 2003.

Brainerd, E. and M. V. Siegler. 2003. "The Economic Effects of the 1918 Influenza Epidemic", Centre for Economic Policy Research Discussion Paper No. 3791, London.

Bureau of Labor Statistics, CPI data online at http://www.bls.gov/cpi/home.htm, accessed August 12, 2003.

China Daily. 2003. "China's Service Industry Shakes off SARS Impact," http://www1.chinadaily.com.cn/en/doc/2003-07/10/content_244241.htm, accessed July 10, 2003.

Chinese National Bureau of Statistics, available at http://www.stats.gov.cn/english/, accessed August 12, 2003.

Coalition Provisional Authority in Iraq, 2003 Budget, available at http://www.cpa-iraq.org/budget/2003budget.pdf, accessed August 12, 2003.

The Economist. 2002. "Strategic Caring," October 3, available online at http://www.economist.com/displaystory.cfm?story_id=1373275.

European Central Bank, Online Statistics at http://www.ecb.int/.

International Monetary Fund (IMF). 2003. *International Financial Statistics*, June 2003, IMF, CD-ROM.

Kuttner, K. N. and Posen A., 2003. "The Great Recession: Lessons for Macroeconomic Policy from Japan," *Brookings Papers on Economic Activity*, 2: 2001, 93–185.

Lee, J-W. and W. J. McKibbin. 2003. "Globalization and Disease: The Case of SARS," Unpublished Working Paper presented at the Asian Economic Panel meeting in Tokyo, May 11–12.

McKinsey Global Institute studies of France and Germany and the UK, available at www.mckinsey.com.

Monico, S. M. 2003. "HIV/AIDS in Africa: What Works," *CGD HIV/AIDS in Africa: What Works conference, January 8, 2003*, Center for Global Development and John Snow Inc, available at http://www.cgdev.org/events/HIV-AIDS.html, accessed July 28, 2003.

Moss, T. 2003. *Adventure Capitalism—Globalization and the Political Economy of Stock Markets in Africa*. New York: Palgrave MacMillan.

Ndoye, I. "Senegal Experience on HIV/AIDS control," *CGD HIV/AIDS in Africa: What Works conference, January 8, 2003*, Center for Global Development and John Snow Inc, available at http://www.cgdev.org/events/HIV-AIDS.html, accessed July 28, 2003.

O'Hanlon, M. and L. Brainard. 2003. "The Heavy Price of America's Going It Alone," *Financial Times*, August 6, p. 15.

Organisation for Economic Co-operation and Development (OECD). 2003. *Sources of Economic Growth In OECD Countries*. Paris: Organisation for Economic Co-operation and Development.

Ugandan AIDS Commission, available at http://www.aidsuganda.org/aids/index.htm, accessed July 28, 2003.

UNAIDS/WHO factsheet 2003, Epidemiological Fact Sheets by Country, UNAIDS/WHO at http://www.who.int/emc-hiv/fact_sheets/All_countries.html, accessed July 28, 2003.

US Congress, Emergency Wartime Supplemental Appropriations Act, 2003 (Engrossed as Agreed to or Passed by House), H.R. 1559.

The Wall Street Journal. 2003. "China's Economic Growth Slowed to 6.7% in Quarter," http://online.wsj.com/article_print/0,,SB105843729444769400,00.html, accessed July 17, 2003.

———. 2003. "Despite SARS China's Economy Bounces Back," July 14, 2003.

World Bank Development Indicators at http://devdata.worldbank.org/dataonline/, accessed July 28, 2003.

Figure 1

http://www.federalreserve.gov/releases/, accessed July 28, 2003.

http://www.ecb.int/, accessed July 28, 2003.

http://www.boj.or.jp/en/stat/stat_f.htm, accessed July 28, 2003.

http://www.bls.gov/cpi/home.htm, accessed July 28, 2003.

Kuttner, K. N. and Posen A., 2003. "The Great Recession: Lessons for

CHAPTER 2.2

Varieties of Economic Experience in the Developing World

AUGUSTO LOPEZ-CLAROS, World Economic Forum[1]

The aim of this chapter is to provide a brief outline of some of the key challenges facing policymakers in parts of the developing world. It is not intended to be a comprehensive look at the issues. Given the large number of sovereign actors in the global economy and the variety of problems affecting their economic performance, a thorough overview is beyond the scope of this chapter. Instead, its purpose is to provide this year's *Global Competitiveness Report* with some of the flavor given to the 2002–2003 *Report* by a series of regional studies.[2]

We will focus our attention largely on two sets of countries, chosen from a variety of geographical locations and representing a broad spectrum of economic experiences. Our purpose is to highlight not only the diversity of problems that emerge during the development process, but also the different ways in which governments and policymakers have responded to those problems. As will be seen, in some cases these responses have been timely and coherent, contributing to macroeconomic stability and the growth of per capita incomes. Often, however, policy shortcomings have aggravated the consequences of macroeconomic and other imbalances. At times, delays in the implementation of corrective measures have been associated with deep crises, with serious repercussions for social welfare. The countries we have chosen are a small but representative sample of those ranked in the World Economic Forum's Growth Competitiveness Index (GCI).

The first set is made up of Argentina, Russia, and Turkey, countries that have had serious financial crises in the recent past and offer a treasure trove of insights in terms of the causes of such crises, their consequences, and the policy responses to them, to say nothing of the effectiveness of existing international institutional mechanisms to cope with them. The second set consists of the transition economies of central and eastern Europe, eight of whose members are scheduled to join the European Union (EU) in May of 2004. These countries have had a good growth performance during the past decade, and some of these transition economies have the potential to join in the medium-term the upper ranks of the most competitive economies in the world. Quite aside from having benefited from reasonably competent macroeconomic management, these countries, as a group, have moved farther along than virtually any other set of economies in the world in implementing broad-ranging structural reforms. To facilitate the discussion, our focus will be more issue-specific than country-specific; the emphasis will be less on making a thorough review of developments in the several countries chosen and more on using the experiences of these countries to illustrate policy issues in all developing countries.[3]

Table 1: Selected indicators: Argentina, Russia, and Turkey

Argentina	1998	1999	2000	2001	2002
GDP growth (annual %)	3.9	−3.4	−0.8	−4.5	−11.0
GDP per capita growth (annual %)	2.5	−4.6	−2.0	−5.6	−10.8
Inflation (end of period)	0.7	−1.8	−0.7	−1.5	41.0
Current account balance (BoP) in current US$bn	−14.5	−11.9	−8.9	−4.6	8.8
Current account balance (BoP) in % of GDP	−4.9	−4.2	−3.1	−1.7	8.1
Fiscal balance (in % of GDP)	−1.5	−2.9	−2.3	−3.3	−10.3

Russia	1998	1999	2000	2001	2002
GDP growth (annual %)	−4.6	6.4	10.0	5.0	4.3
GDP per capita growth (annual %)	−4.2	7.0	10.2	5.6	4.9
Inflation (end of period)	84.4	36.5	20.2	18.0	15.1
Current account balance (BoP) in current US$bn	2.3	24.7	46.4	35.0	30.9
Current account balance (BoP) in % of GDP	0.7	12.8	18.5	11.4	8.4
Fiscal balance (in % of GDP)	−5.9	−1.3	2.2	3.0	1.7

Turkey	1998	1999	2000	2001	2002
GDP growth (annual %)	3.1	−4.7	7.4	−7.4	6.7
GDP per capita growth (annual %)	1.6	−6.1	5.8	−8.7	0.1
Inflation (end of period)	67.4	68.8	39.0	68.5	29.7
Current account balance (BoP) in current US$bn	2.0	−1.4	−9.8	3.4	1.8
Current account balance (BoP) in % of GDP	1.0	−0.7	−4.9	2.3	−1.0
Fiscal balance (in % of GDP)	−8.4	−13.0	−11.4	−19.3	−12.5

Source: IMF, WDI, WEO, and World Bank

74

Argentina, Russia, and Turkey: meltdown and recovery

The last decade has seen a succession of financial crises in some of the key economies in the developing world. Three of the most recent crises are of particular interest on account of their intensity, the complex interaction of domestic and external factors which precipitated them, the role played along the way by the multilateral organizations, and the broader questions about international crisis management which they have raised in their wake (Table 1). We will look at some of the key issues.

The causes of the crises in Argentina, Russia, and Turkey have been many, involving in all cases different combinations of endogenous and exogenous factors, including elements of "bad luck." The crises in Asia in 1997 led to a drop in the demand for oil and other primary commodities in international markets and were, without any doubt, a precipitating factor in Russia's own crisis in 1998, given the preponderance of energy taxes in the budget and commodity exports in its balance of payments. Argentina introduced a currency board arrangement in 1991, pegging its currency against the US dollar, only to see the dollar appreciate throughout much of the 1990s. On top of this, Brazil devalued its currency in early 1999, thus gaining a major competitive advantage against Argentina, its main trade partner. Even Turkey, suffering from chronically high inflation during the past two decades, saw its fledgling efforts to set its macro house in

order in 1999 temporarily set back by a massive earthquake that put additional strains on the budget. But "bad luck" does not go very far in providing a satisfactory explanation for these crises; at best it underlines the fact that authorities everywhere have to implement economic programs against the backdrop of an uncertain external environment that, at times, can significantly reduce their room for maneuver.[4]

The advantages of fiscal discipline

A more compelling thread, common to all three countries, was the existence of very loose fiscal policies combined with poor public debt management, which compounded the effects of the public-sector deficits. The sources of the fiscal problems varied from country to country. In Russia, the problem was essentially on the revenue side. A persistent output drop during much of the 1990s—reflecting in important ways the much needed restructuring of the economy, away from activities linked to the military industrial complex—contributed to the erosion of the tax base. But the revenue-to-GDP ratio also fell, because the authorities, particularly during the long reign of Prime Minister Chernomyrdin, were prone to the granting of tax exemptions to influential lobby groups that, in turn, led to a remarkable erosion in the ability of the state to collect taxes. Tax exemptions—some of them massive, exceeding the total annual value of International Monetary Fund

(IMF) financing—deprived the budget of sizeable resources and made the task of fiscal adjustment tougher than would otherwise have been the case.

In Turkey, the problems were largely on the expenditure side: a combination of enormous claims on the budget associated with an overly generous pension system, an extensive network of agricultural subsidy schemes and other quasi-fiscal operations, and the fiscal burden of a public debt overhang had led, by 1999, to a public-sector borrowing requirement in excess of 23 percent of GDP. On the institutional side, the task of fiscal adjustment was not helped by unusually opaque fiscal accounts, in which, for instance, the military budget was approved outside the conventional channels used in working democracies. (The general staff puts together the annual budget of the armed forces and the parliament approves it "without debate and by acclamation"[see Rouleau, 2000].)

Argentina's crisis reflected the authorities' ultimate failure to maintain adequate control over the public finances. Or, as noted by Mussa (2002): "in the management of its fiscal affairs, the Argentine government is like a chronic alcoholic—once it starts to imbibe the political pleasures of deficit spending, it keeps on going until it reaches the economic equivalent of falling-down drunk." He argues that during the period 1993–98 in particular, "when the Argentine economy was receiving substantial nonrecurring revenues from privatization and enjoyed other temporary fiscal benefits, the public-sector debt-to-GDP ratio nevertheless rose by 12 percentage points." (Mussa, 2002, p 16). Indeed, in the six-year period to end-1998, Argentina's total external debt more than doubled from US$62 billion to US$142 billion, at a time when nominal GDP rose by about 26 percent. By end-2000, the debt-to-GDP ratio had risen by an additional 9 percentage points, to 50 percent of GDP, perhaps not unusually high by international standards, but extremely high for an economy with a very low revenue ratio (20 percent of GDP, including social security contributions), an external debt-to-exports ratio in excess of 400 percent, and a contracting economy.

Moreover, the authorities failed to recognize that successful currency board arrangements are always underpinned by suitably tight fiscal policies. Since the system proscribes access to central bank lending, financing of the public-sector deficit is possible only via access to the international capital markets or the domestic banking system at market rates of interest. This, however, particularly if done over a number of consecutive years, makes the country a captive to its creditors, including bondholders. The pattern is well known: persistent fiscal deficits result in their financing at increasingly higher interest rates, which inevitably worsen the deficit. The fiscal problem then leads to an external crisis when nonresident debt holders refuse to rollover the outstanding debt. Russia and

Table 2: IMF's largest debtors

Country	Total fund credit & loans outstanding (millions of SDRs)	US Dollar amounts (millions)	Percentage of quota
Turkey	16517	22749	1713
Brazil	21256	29275	700
Uruguay	1654	15068	540
Argentina	10941	2279	517
Indonesia	6454	8889	310
Pakistan	1417	1951	137
Philippines	939	1293	107
Ukraine	1318	1815	96
Russian Federation	3821	5263	64

Source: International Financial Statistics, August 2003

Argentina defaulted on their external obligations; Turkey did not, but only due to massive IMF financial assistance that rapidly turned the country into that institution's largest debtor (Table 2).

With exchange rates pegged in some form or other in all three countries, and with local interest rates much higher than those in the hard currency markets abroad, there were powerful incentives to borrow in the international capital markets. For several years leading up to the crises, borrowing short-term and in foreign currency was a booming business. This made the economies very vulnerable to shocks. In Russia and Argentina, in particular, export performance deteriorated sharply, reflecting the real appreciation of the currency and a worsening external environment. As the authorities responded to signs of a looming meltdown, higher interest rates to defend currencies put pressures on the financial position of the enterprise sector. Indeed, the sources of vulnerability associated with fixed/pegged exchange rate regimes are well known and are eloquently illustrated by the experiences of these countries.

Vulnerable pegs

Experience has shown that authorities tend to underestimate currency risk. The longer the rate has been pegged, the more likely are market players to think that it will remain so, and the frequent public appearances by central bank governors to reassure increasingly nervous markets seem to be an inseparable part of this process. The loss of price competitiveness that comes when domestic inflation rates do not fall to international levels as rapidly as was intended when the peg was introduced often brings with it a worsening balance of payments that then invites attacks on the currency. This was, with some nuances, the case in most of the emerging market crises of the past ten years, and Argentina represented perhaps the most dramatic example. A third source of vulnerability is that there is no face-saving way to exit an overvalued exchange rate.

If the market does not attack the currency, the pressure is off and there is no immediate need to devalue. By the time it does attack it, however, it is too late. More importantly, the main weapons used to defend the exchange rate are foreign exchange intervention and interest rates, but the scope for these is very limited, particularly for countries like Russia, Turkey, and Argentina that are "small," against the magnitude of resources available to the market for possible speculative attacks. If, in addition to all the above, the banking system is weak—definitely the case in Russia and Turkey—or heavily exposed (for instance to the domestic debt market in both countries), the peg is doomed.

The above is not to say that floating rate regimes are free of problems either, particularly during periods of turbulence and for economies that are quite open to international trade. Currency boards (other than in Argentina) have worked quite well in practice when accompanied by sound fiscal management. Since they cannot be easily undone, they bring with them a lower currency-risk premium. Estonia (whose currency board was introduced in 1992), Lithuania (1994), and Latvia (which has a hard peg that, in practice, operates as a quasi currency board since 1994) have all done very well, and the experience of Bulgaria in recent years has been quite encouraging. But fiscal discipline as a necessary condition of success may be more than most governments are willing or able to deliver.

The main lesson to emerge from the experience of recent emerging market crises seems to be that there is little merit in defending overvalued exchange rates, and even less in funneling large amounts of official finance—in the form of debt at market rates—on the basis of promises of fiscal rectitude. In the end, in all three countries this simply led to an intertemporal shift in debt service obligations. With the recovery of oil prices in early 1999, Russia was able to deal successfully with its external debt overhang. But Argentina has yet to fully address the consequences of its debt default and, as recently noted by the IMF (one of Argentina's most important creditors) "even with the best efforts, Argentina's medium-term outlook appears very difficult" (IMF, 2003a). As regards Turkey, the debt-to-GDP ratio is now in excess of 90 percent of GDP; much of the rise in the last two years reflects the massive inflows of IMF lending, the service of which will require primary surpluses in excess of 5 percent of GDP for the foreseeable future.

Capital inflows and the speed of the magic carpet[5]

However, poor fiscal management combined with pegged exchange rate regimes, an unhappy combination of policies at best, lethal at worst, provides only a partial explanation for the crises in these three countries. Countries seem to be able to implement irresponsible fiscal policies for a very long time without provoking domestic financial

crises or even adverse international headlines. The debt-to-GDP ratio in Turkey, for instance, rose from 30 percent in 1990 to close to 60 percent in 1999, with annual inflation throughout this period remaining chronically high at around 50 to 100 percent. What signaled the onset of the crises in Argentina, Russia, and Turkey was a reversal of capital flows, at a time when these had acquired a much greater preponderance than had been the case historically. According to the IMF, net capital inflows to emerging markets during the early 1980s—the period characterized by the recycling of petrodollars—were equivalent to about 0.7 percent of their GDP on an annual basis, compared with 2 to 2.5 percent of GDP in the 1990s. (For some countries—such as the East Asian tigers—the numbers were even more compelling, with inflows rising from 1 percent in the mid 1980s to 5 percent a decade later. In US dollar terms, they swung from an inflow of US$65 billion in 1996 to an outflow of over US$40 billion in 1998.)

There are several factors that are seen to have played a central role in the rapid rise of net capital flows to emerging economies during the past decade. These would include the removal of restrictions on capital account transactions, part of a process aimed at deregulation and economic liberalization that has also had its counterpart in the industrial world. Better policies in the developing countries have created a growing set of attractive destinations for foreign capital. A more liberal attitude to privatization has also played a role, expanding the range of investment opportunities and contributing to the rapid growth of players who are able to issue debt in the international capital markets. The increasing sophistication of financial instruments that allow investors to hedge exposure to currency and other types of risk at a time of expanding international trade have also boosted capital flows. The forces of globalization, involving a fall in the costs of transportation, communication, data processing, and transactions, have been an important additional contributing factor that suggests that the growth of international capital flows may, at least in the aggregate, be difficult to reverse. Finally, the search for higher returns and the growing risk appetite of institutional and retail investors worldwide has also been a central factor.

All of these factors, to a greater or lesser degree, played a role in the expansion of capital flows to Argentina, Russia, and Turkey. Privatization-related flows were most important in Argentina, which soon after the introduction of its currency board embarked upon an ambitious program of divestiture of state assets. Liberalization of the capital account and the search for riskier returns on the part of investors were prominent, likewise, in all three countries. In Russia and Turkey, in particular, the sky-high returns obtained in the domestic treasury bill market against the backdrop of pegged exchange rate regimes were crucial in attracting large volumes of "hot money"—the so-called moral hazard trades. Even perceptions of better policies were a factor, for instance, in Argentina during the early years of the administration of former President Menem when, as noted by Mussa (p. 1) "many of Argentina's economic policies were widely applauded and suggested as a model that other emerging-market countries should emulate." Why capital flows to these countries were reversed, whereas they have remained large and steady in the economies of central and eastern Europe, is an interesting policy question. The answer, to a large extent, lies in the fact that capital account liberalization is a tricky issue, and the governments of the central and eastern European economies have been far more adept at managing the liberalization process in an efficient way.

In particular, successful capital account liberalization seems to require a multi-layered approach with several key elements. First, it is necessary to improve the quality of information available to policymakers about possible sources of systemic risk, such as an undue accumulation of external indebtedness in the corporate sector, or the state of the nonperforming loan portfolio in the banking sector, to name a couple of issues that have arisen in several of the worst crises in recent years, beginning with Asia. Second, there is no substitute for good macroeconomic policies that contain imbalances in financial markets as well as mitigate the effects of crises when they come; Chile after the tequila crisis in 1994, or Estonia after the 1998 Russian crisis, are good examples of competent crisis management in the face of an external shock. Third, it is important to encourage adherence to internationally accepted standards of accounting, auditing, and disclosure, so as to facilitate enforcement of good rules of corporate governance that protect investors and lenders from abuse.

Fourth is the related need to make sure that financial institutions are subject to proper prudential supervision and regulation by an appropriately independent government agency, particularly since liberalization may allow banks to expand risky activities at rates that could exceed their capacity to manage them. (There seems to be broad consensus, for instance, that Argentina was able to cope reasonably well with the immediate effect of the tequila crisis because, by then, the banking system was in a much better state, having been largely sold off to large Spanish and American banks, with deep pockets that could be tapped in period of external stress.) Fifth, to contain moral hazard, it is desirable to limit government/central bank interventions to cases of systemic threat. This implies that loss-making financial institutions should absorb their losses, even if this will mean pain for shareholders, managers, and others. Following banking sector crises in the 1990s, governments in Estonia, Latvia, and Lithuania imposed a hard budget constraint on their banks. This resulted in the closure of several major banks. A process of consolidation

was set in motion that led to a quantum jump in foreign participation in the banking system. Finally, it is essential to keep public debt within sustainable levels, with appropriate maturity and currency profiles.

Russia and Turkey had serious shortcomings on all of these fronts. Weaknesses in their respective banking systems were particularly noteworthy, making them both vulnerable to currency and interest rate risk, although the impact was probably more deleterious in the case of Turkey, given the higher levels of financial intermediation relative to Russia, still largely a cash economy. Reflecting the risk premium associated with high inflation, high and volatile interest rates induced banks in both countries to concentrate on arbitrage operations, mainly involving short-term management and funding of treasury bills. Given the high dollar returns, banks financed their purchases of treasury bills by borrowing in foreign currency, leaving them vulnerable to losses in the event of devaluation. In Turkey and, to a lesser extent, in Russia, the development of an active repo market worsened the maturity mismatch of banks and increased their off-balance sheet exposure. Poor internal risk management was an additional risk factor with reporting standards falling short in both countries in several areas. Among some of the major shortcomings: overstating of reported earnings due to insufficient prevalence of mark-to-market of securities, unreliable measures of bank profitability due to a lack of inflation accounting, circumventing of prudential regulations on FX exposure through foreign subsidiaries (Turkey), and a level of non-performing loans that was much understated.

The experience of Chile is relevant in this respect because, unlike the EU accession countries that—it could be argued—have implemented, as we shall see below, largely responsible policies, because of an overriding commitment to the processes of economic and political integration, successive Chilean governments have done so without such powerful incentives. A strong commitment to sound fiscal and monetary policies, buttressed by a broad range of structural reforms, have, over time, created a friendly environment for private-sector activity with few peers in the developing world. This has been particularly the case as regards foreign investment, with the government having early on opened the country's borders and set aside undue concerns about foreign ownership of the domestic economy. The regulatory framework for foreign direct investment (FDI) has played a very positive role in the growth of investment, the authorities having long ago lifted previous restrictions on dividend remittances and on majority participation. They also streamlined authorization procedures and, more generally, created a regulatory environment characterized by well-defined, simple and stable rules. In combination with a macro framework involving low inflation, steady exchange rates, and public finances under control, the authorities contributed to create powerful incentives for investors looking for opportunities for on-site production involving economies of scale. Chile has benefited from technology transfers and know-how; although large capital inflows have at times posed problems for exchange rate management, the overall effects on the capital account have been favorable. (Chile is consistently the top performer in Latin America in the rankings of the GCI, by a significant margin.)

External support and the role of the International Monetary Fund

In all three countries, there was heavy involvement on the part of the IMF, although the nature of the Fund's interventions had certain important features that were unique to each country. In Russia, the Fund evolved from an advisory role in the early phase of Russia's transition (1991–94) in which financing was relatively limited and the focus was more on providing technical assistance (including in the area of program formulation), to becoming the principal financier of the government. This latter role was particularly intense during the three-and-a half-year period from early 1995 to July of 1998, when a total of US$17.5 billion of debt were disbursed. Interestingly, since the authorities saw IMF financing as a close substitute for tax collection, the period of most generous Fund financial support coincided with the most severe erosion in the revenue-to-GDP ratio and in the willingness of corporations and households to pay taxes. In Turkey, the Fund played a dual role: first, helping a coalition government with unusually low levels of public support and little policy credibility to formulate and implement a better set of policies. Second, providing enough volumes of finance to ensure that the country would not default on its debt obligations, a task achieved by the setting aside of all previous IMF historical parameters that linked the amount of external funding to the scale of the policy adjustment, and subverting the long-standing Fund principle of equality of treatment across its member countries.

In Argentina, the Fund found itself in the ungrateful role of trying to prop up a doomed currency regime, as discussed above. Mussa notes "the Fund did make at least two important mistakes in Argentina: (1) in failing to press the Argentine authorities much harder to have a more responsible fiscal policy, especially during the high growth years of the early through mid 1990s; and (2) in extending substantial additional financial support to Argentina during the summer of 2001, after it had become abundantly clear that the Argentine government's efforts to avoid default and maintain the exchange rate peg had no reasonable chance of success" (Mussa, 2002, p 4). That each one of these programs entailed either a financial meltdown (Russia and Argentina) or a quantum jump in the country's external indebtedness (Turkey) has raised many questions about the future role of the Fund. Given the central

role played by it in the developing world—as a source of funding and technical advice on policy formulation and implementation—it is useful to comment briefly on aspects of its evolving role.

There are at least three roles for the Fund worth highlighting.[6] One is the classical role played by the organization in those countries that, when faced with an external shock—say, a sudden drop in the demand for their exports—come to the Fund for short-term financing to ease the pain associated with "adjustment." A devaluation of the currency whose effects may take time to materialize, is the classical example; it also captures the essence of the Fund's relationship to its member countries during much of the post-war period. But not recently. Neither Russia nor Turkey nor Argentina sought or received Fund support because of a balance of payments crisis in the traditional meaning of the term.

The second role is one where the Fund is seen by the markets as that institution that provides creditors with assurances that the countries with Fund programs will fulfil their debt obligations and pursue sound policies consistent with financial sustainability. A very good example of this might be the Fund-supported program with Poland in 1990, which included the creation of a currency stabilization fund. This fund was never actually drawn, but it signaled to markets that the authorities would be able to defend the currency against speculative attacks, as it implemented an unusually ambitious program of reforms with a strong structural component. The third and most recent role concerns those countries for which there is "no feasible set of macroeconomic policies that would allow them to regain medium-term viability without a reduction in their debt" (IMF, 2003b).

The emerging markets crises of the past decade have followed a recurring pattern. In a nutshell the sequence is as follows: economic and/or political difficulties in a particular country lead to concerns on the part of creditors about the country's debt servicing capacity. This, in turn, results in creditors deciding not to rollover maturing obligations, or actually selling them in the secondary market, both leading to a widening of debt spreads and, eventually, a total shutdown of access to capital markets on terms consistent with fiscal viability. Brazil in 2002 provides an eloquent recent example: market panic reflecting investor concerns about the possibility of an "adverse" result in the presidential elections, together with heightened risk aversion in the middle of a global slowdown. With Brazilian bond yields at historically high levels, the fiscal effort that would have been necessary to bring the debt-GDP ratio to a sustainable path was so enormous as to be not politically credible (Figure 1). Argentina's default in late 2001 finally appears to have persuaded senior finance officials in creditor countries and at the international financial institutions that there has to be a better way of dealing with

Figure 1: Bond spreads

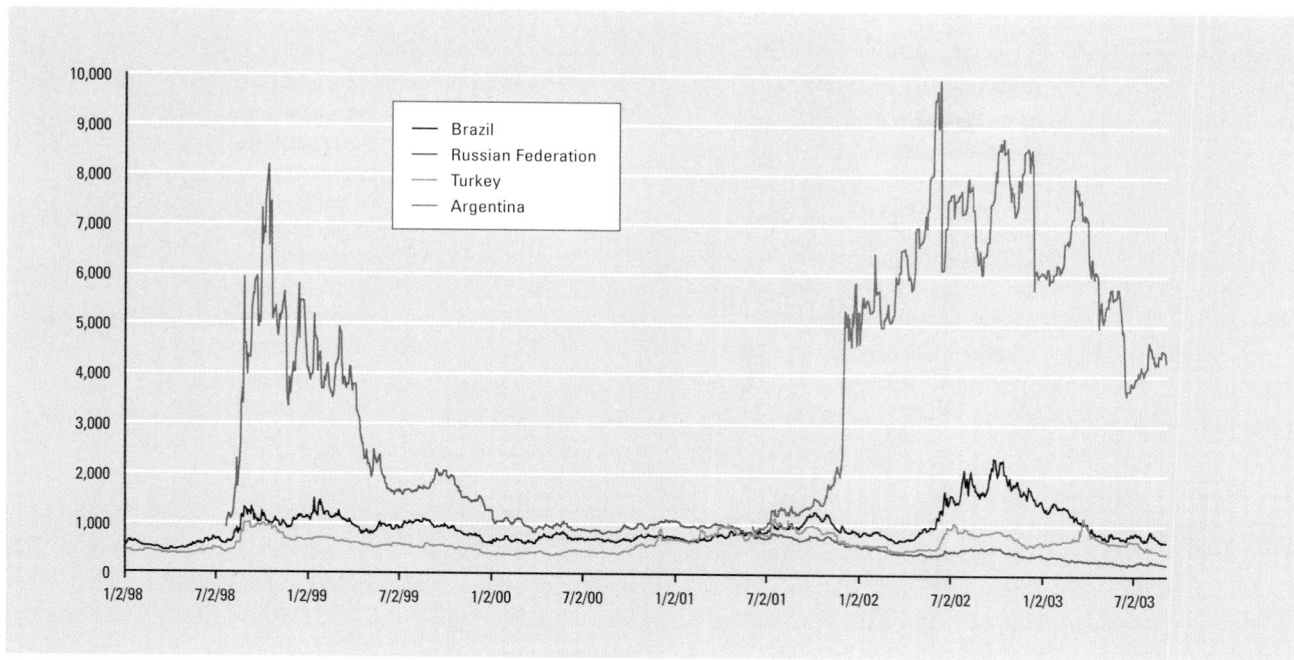

Source: Lehman Brothers

unsustainable debt burdens than the present ad-hoc arrangements, involving a disorderly combination of exploding debt spreads, uncertainty, and all the economic, social, and political dislocations associated with a sovereign debt default.[7]

The essence of the problem is that, whereas there are institutional mechanisms in place for the orderly rescheduling of public-sector debt (eg, Paris Club), there is no equivalent framework for debt instruments held by the private retail sector. The past 20 years have witnessed a dramatic shift in the structure of financing to emerging markets, with bonds and direct investment replacing syndicated bank lending and official flows. However, sovereign bond contracts are virtually impossible to restructure. Not only do they typically require near unanimous consent, but lawsuits can trigger cross-default on other securities and accelerated repayment clauses. To make matters worse, ownership of bonds is much more diffuse than in earlier times when sovereign borrowers could usually negotiate restructuring deals with a limited number of private banks, the instruments themselves have become increasingly complex, and there has been an increase as well in the number of legal jurisdictions in which they are issued.

The issue, then, is how to make sovereign debt restructuring a more predictable and orderly process. The more closely integrated nature of financial markets, reflecting a combination of trade and financial linkages and, at times, herding behavior, and the much larger volume of cross-border financial flows, have highlighted the potentially destabilizing effects of disorderly defaults, both for the defaulting country and, through contagion, for the international economy. (One aspect of this is the severe impact of a sovereign debt default on the banking system—Argentina, again, being the most recent and compelling example, with Uruguay playing the role of innocent bystander.)

A proper examination of this issue is beyond the scope of this chapter. The IMF has taken a leading role in shaping the elements of the debate and there seems to be broad agreement that "reforming the sovereign debt restructuring framework is a formidable task that will take many years to develop and implement" (IMF, 2003c). Among the issues that would need to be tackled are: what types of debt to include; determination of the debt carrying capacity of the country (by whom, on what terms); to which set of countries should the mechanism be available; what the likely effect on capital flows to developing countries would be; and what the operational mechanisms would be that would underpin the facility. The new mechanism for sovereign debt restructuring would probably not reduce the short-term pain associated with default; rather, its aim would be to put arrangements in place that reduced the span of time when debtors and creditors are forced to operate in an uncertain legal environment, making possible a quicker resumption of debt-servicing in a post-restructuring scenario.

One early line of thought against the creation of new institutional mechanisms to deal with sovereign debt restructuring is that, with the possible exception of Argentina, most of the recent cases of serious debt-servicing difficulties in emerging markets have reflected more liquidity shortfalls than actual insolvency. These have been dealt with in a variety of ways: some involving combinations of additional official finance (Asia in 1997; Russia in 1998, Brazil in 1999, Turkey during 2000/02, Argentina in 2001); some debt rollovers (Asia, Turkey); and some domestic debt default (Russia), in all cases against a background of major policy adjustments. So, the argument goes, rather than adopting new approaches to sovereign debt restructuring, the focus should be on market-based mechanisms combined with better policies. The proposals being put together by the Fund certainly do not negate the fact that better policies might well protect a country against future crises. The point rather is that, when debts become unsustainable and a sovereign default all but inevitable, financial chaos seems to be the only option available in today's international financial framework and the welfare costs of this are too onerous to be accepted with equanimity.

Governance and institutions

The above factors—fiscal adjustment (or the lack thereof), the nature of the exchange rate regime, particular approaches to the opening of the capital account and the supporting measures underpinning it—may go some way toward helping explain the meltdowns in Argentina, Russia, and Turkey. Certainly there can be no doubt that policies matter—witness the sharply different economic outcomes in Chile, a country facing a very similar external environment to that of its long-suffering neighbor but where successive governments have been far more adept at dealing with the challenges of an increasingly interdependent world. And, however mixed the results, international institutions matter a great deal as well, as the cases of all three countries eloquently show in so many different ways. But we would be remiss in not highlighting the role played by other factors, particularly those stemming from the state of the country's institutions and, more generally, the quality of its governance.

The core

At the core of good governance is the willingness of governments to open to public scrutiny the accounts and activities of public institutions and to institute reliable systems of auditing and financial management. Lack of openness, more often than not, does not serve useful public ends but has instead been used to hide unlawful practices and abuse. Transparency is particularly important in the case of the tax system, where the ability of governments to collect revenues will depend on public perceptions of the fairness of its operation as much as of the use that is made of public funds. A valuable example on the importance of transparency in public actions concerns efforts during the last decade in a number of countries to privatize hitherto publicly held assets. The process has at times run into severe difficulties as a result of public perceptions that assets were being liquidated at bargain prices and in ways that unduly favored certain groups.

The experience in Russia in this respect during the 1990s has been particularly disappointing. Corrupt privatization schemes tainted not only the reputation of the ("reform-minded") government officials that designed and implemented them, they also undermined the credibility of the donor institutions under whose tutelage such schemes were allowed to develop. Not surprisingly, they contributed to create an environment of deep cynicism among taxpayers, investors, and other economic agents. Sen (1999) notes that societies operate better under some presumption of trust and that, therefore, they will benefit from greater openness. The freedom for society's members to deal with one another under "guarantees of disclosure and honesty" are essential to prevent corruption and other abuses.

The trend seen in the past decade toward the establishment of more market-oriented systems, with a significantly reduced role for state intervention and discretion, should improve the climate for transparency in economic management. Successful and lasting economic development depends to a great extent on the government's ability to generate a broad consensus for change. A process of consultation whereby the government elicits the views of various sectors of society—trade unions, businesses, professional organizations, NGOs, and other organizations of civil society—is likely to result in greater understanding of and commitment on the part of the population to the often painful measures that accompany the implementation of various economic strategies. Dealing with the aftereffects of official corruption and/or prolonged periods of economic mismanagement is always painful, often involving fiscal retrenchment and difficult choices about the distribution of the costs of adjustment between different sectors of the population. Consultation is also likely to result in a more equitable distribution of the costs of adjustment and thereby enhance the chances of sustainable reforms. The building of consensus through consultation is at the root of participatory development and facilitates transparency and accountability.[8]

In all of these areas, the approach pursued by the authorities at various times in Argentina, Russia, and Turkey was deeply flawed. Although it may be difficult to quantify their particular relative contribution to each country's respective crises, there can be little doubt that poor governance greatly compounded the effects of bad luck and, broadly defined, "policy errors," including errors by the donor agencies supporting these countries' adjustment efforts. In all three countries malfeasance in the management of public resources was clearly a factor in setting the stage for tax avoidance and tax evasion. In all three countries this type of mismanagement—it is beyond the scope of this chapter to identify the many and sometimes inventive ways in which these were manifested—led to gross misallocation of scarce resources with a number of adverse implications.

In Russia, it sharply limited the ability of the authorities to respond to critical social needs at a time of harsh structural transformation. In Turkey, it led to the emergence of an entire political class associated with the distribution of political patronage through the state banks and a broad range of quasi-fiscal operations. In Argentina, it gradually turned tax evasion into a national pastime, leading observers such as Mussa to observe that Argentina had surpassed itself in its own "past accomplishments in the dubious domain of fiscal irresponsibility" (2002, p 10).

The potential benefits of an approach to development that seeks to incorporate the above mutually reinforcing elements should not be underestimated. To take an example: in an environment of accountability and political legitimacy, people will be far more likely to become active participants in the economy. A broadly shared sense of entitlement to economic transactions will then become an engine of economic growth. A growing economy will boost private incomes and enable the state to collect taxes out of which it will be able to finance expenditures, including in vitally important social areas such as education. Higher levels of spending on education and health care have been shown to be associated with reductions in infant mortality and a fall in birth rates. Female literacy and improved schooling change women's fertility behavior, and end up having widespread implications for the environment, the pressures on which are often linked to rapid population growth. Conversely, it is possible to interpret the heartbreakingly disappointing fruits of economic development during the last half a century in terms of the absence of the above building blocks.

Insights from the GCI and the Executive Opinion Survey

The World Economic Forum's Growth Competitiveness Index (GCI) and the Executive Opinion Survey provide strong corroboration to the above analysis. Argentina, Russia, and Turkey have relatively low scores overall, ranking 78, 70, and 65 respectively in the GCI among 102 countries surveyed.[9] Reflecting the debt default and its spillover effects, Argentina, in particular, saw its rank last year fall by several places with respect to the previous year (see detailed Tables 3–5). Lower rankings for Argentina have come not only through the macroeconomic

Table 3: Growth Competitiveness Index component ranks

Country	Argentina	Russian Federation	Turkey	Chile
GCI 2003-2004	**78**	**70**	**65**	**28**
Technology index	**45**	**69**	**54**	**31**
Innovation subindex	33	27	68	35
ICT subindex	47	56	51	36
Tech transfer subindex	25	94	57	18
Public institutions index	**88**	**81**	**63**	**19**
Contracts and law subindex	99	91	52	29
Corruption subindex	65	75	69	13
Macroeconomic environment index	**93**	**61**	**82**	**35**
Macroeconomic stability subindex	80	61	94	28
Country credit rating	99	55	63	31
Government waste	94	76	75	36

Source: Executive Opinion Survey 2003

Table 4: Macroeconomic environment index ranks

Country	Argentina	Russian Federation	Turkey	Chile
Macroeconomic stability subindex	**80**	**61**	**94**	**28**
Recession expectations	45	34	43	42
Ease of access to credit	102	49	79	37
Inflation	99	93	100	40
Interest rate spread	89	76	91	30
Real exchange rate	1	62	73	27
Government surplus/deficit	94	12	99	25
Savings rate	55	10	36	55
Country credit rating	**99**	**55**	**63**	**31**
Government waste	**94**	**76**	**75**	**36**
Macroeconomic Environment Index 2003-2004	**93**	**61**	**82**	**35**

Source: Executive Opinion Survey 2003

Table 5: Public institutions index ranks

Country	Argentina	Russian Federation	Turkey	Chile
Contracts and law subindex	**99**	**91**	**52**	**29**
Judicial independence	95	81	57	38
Property rights	102	96	66	19
Favoritism in decisions of government officials	98	81	61	32
Organized crime	84	87	42	25
Corruption subindex	**65**	**75**	**69**	**13**
Irregular payments in exports & imports	80	87	83	8
Irregular payments in public utilities	54	79	67	15
Irregular payments in tax collection	73	59	58	17
Public Institutions Index 2003-2004	**88**	**81**	**63**	**19**

Source: Executive Opinion Survey 2003

Figure 2: Protection of minority shareholders' interests

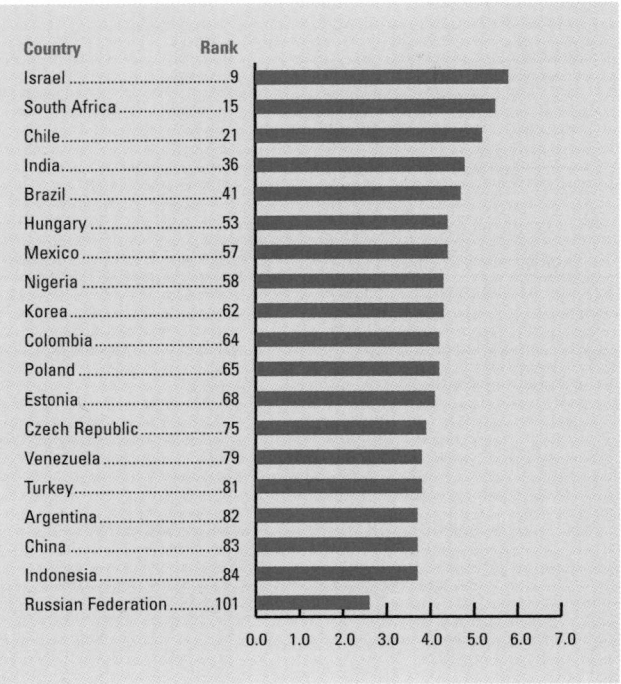

Source: Executive Opinion Survey 2003

Figure 3: Diversion of public funds

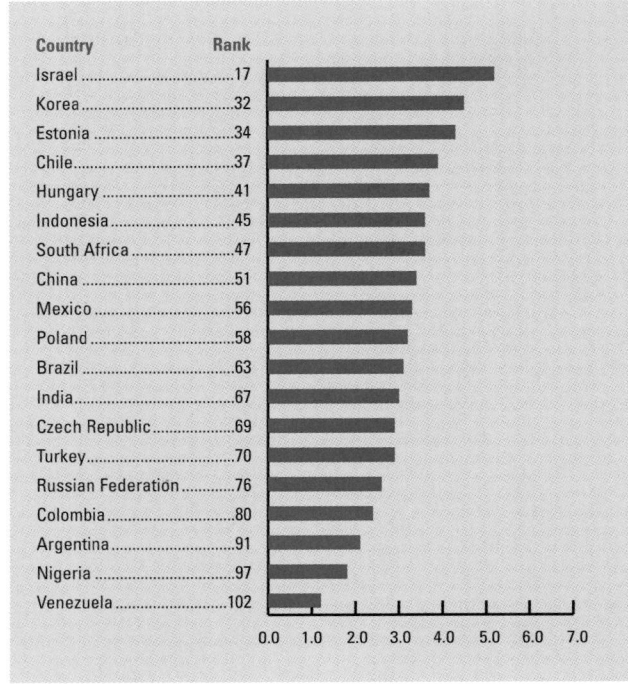

Source: Executive Opinion Survey 2003

Figure 4: Irregular payments in tax collection

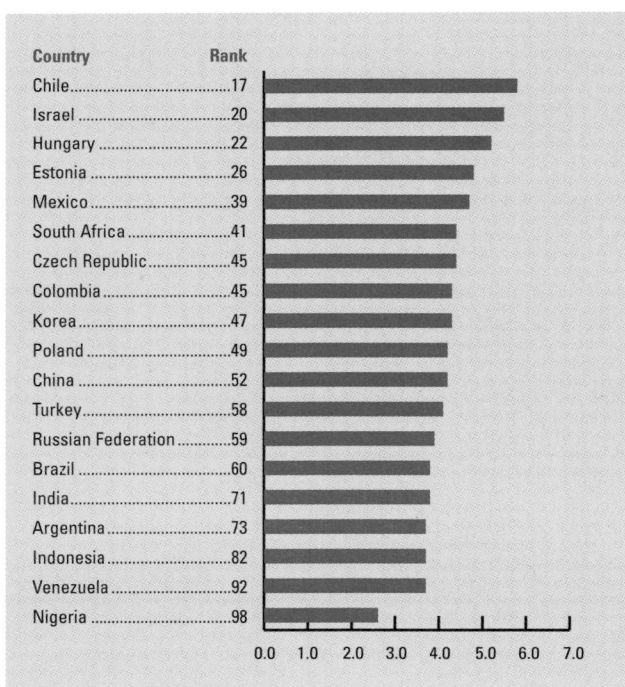

Source: Executive Opinion Survey 2003

Figure 5: Efficiency of legal framework

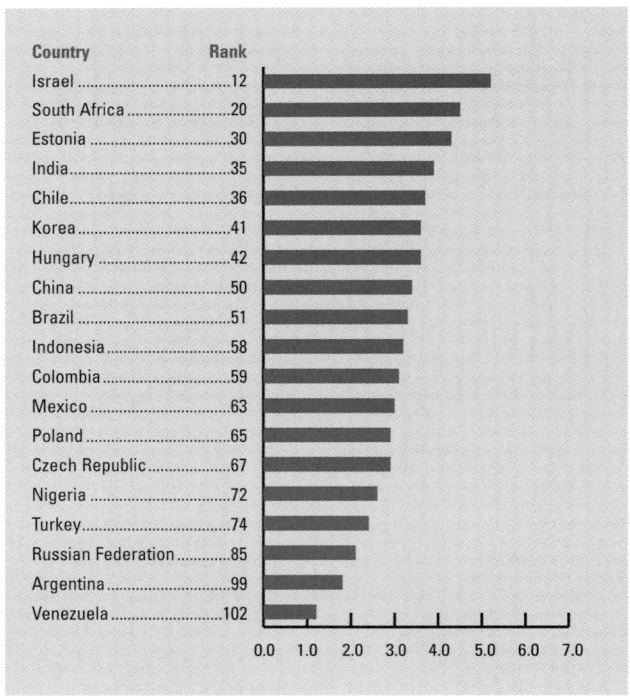

Source: Executive Opinion Survey 2003

Figure 6: Judicial independence

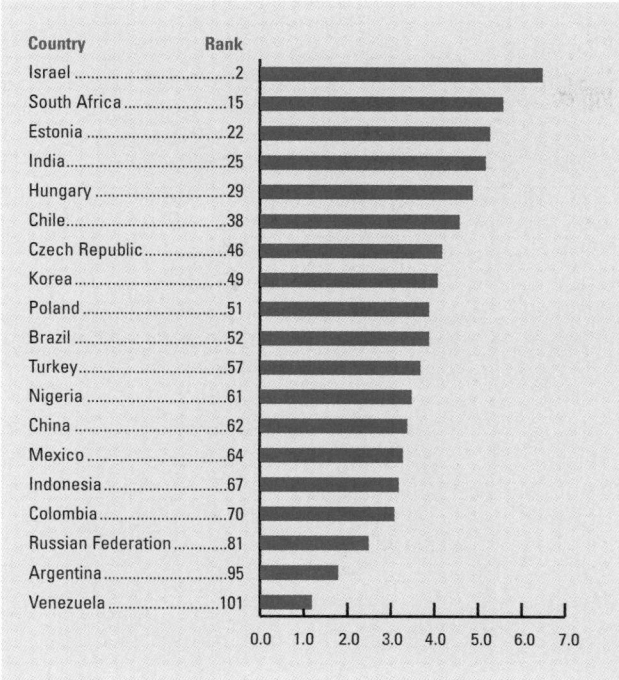

Source: Executive Opinion Survey 2003

Figure 7: Extent of distortive government intervention

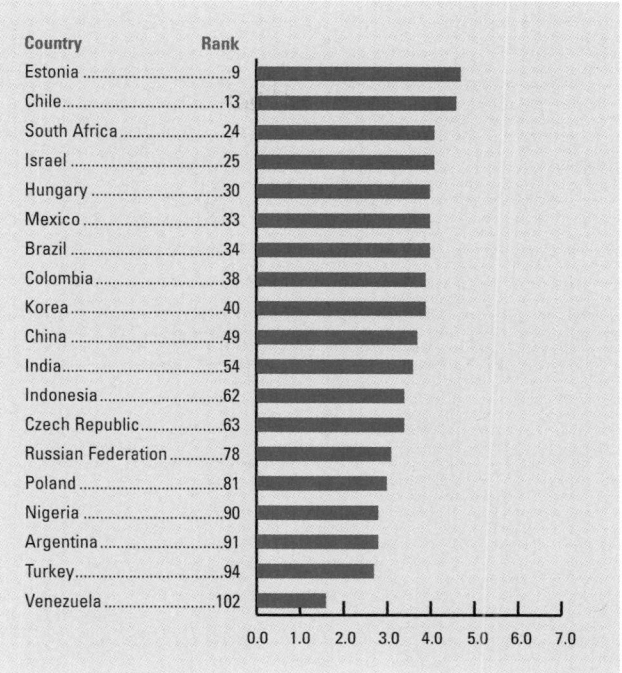

Source: Executive Opinion Survey 2003

component of the index, but also through a marked deterioration in the quality of the underlying public institutions, whether it be through indicators that attempt to capture the extent of diversion of public funds, the independence of the judicial system, or the overall efficiency of the legal framework, among others. Across a broad range of such "institutional" factors, Argentina, Russia, and Turkey score poorly—often near the bottom—in a set of 19 countries chosen from a variety of geographical regions, often in the same "neighborhood." Several questions from the Executive Opinion Survey— many of them used in the calculation of the GCI—as well as others that provide additional insights into the institutional environment, show unusually low rankings (see Figures 2 through 11). Among these are the protection of minority shareholders' interests, the strength of auditing and accounting standards, the diversion of public funds, the extent of distortive government intervention, the independence of the judiciary, and the efficiency of the legal framework.

The challenges ahead

In the period ahead, Russia has the brightest macroeconomic prospects of the three countries surveyed. The country bounced back from the 1998 crisis and has had, in the last four years, a period of robust growth. Terms of trade gains and the salutory effects of a sharp real depreciation of the ruble, combined with cautious fiscal and monetary policies, have all helped. But the authorities have not only learned the virtues of fiscal discipline, they have also started getting serious about structural reform. During the last couple of years they have approved an impressive list of legislative measures that have finally opened the way for private ownership of agricultural land (the last remaining legacy of the country's Soviet central planning past), introduced a Chilean-style private pension system, revamped the judiciary, and are now about to create a stabilization fund to reduce the economy's vulnerability to sharp changes in the price of oil. The economy is likely to expand by over 6 percent in 2003, taxes are being collected, the 2003 budget is projected to be in surplus for the fourth year running, and the days of fiscal chaos seem a thing of the past. With an unusually well educated labor force and a vast natural resource endowment, the country clearly has the inner resources for a prolonged period of high growth as it continues to open up to the beneficial effects of international trade and investment, technology transfers, and multifaceted interactions with the global economy. But although the political consensus for macroeconomic stability is, by now, broad based, the country has a long way to go in terms of the creation of a friendly environment for private-sector

Figure 8: Strength of auditing and accounting standards

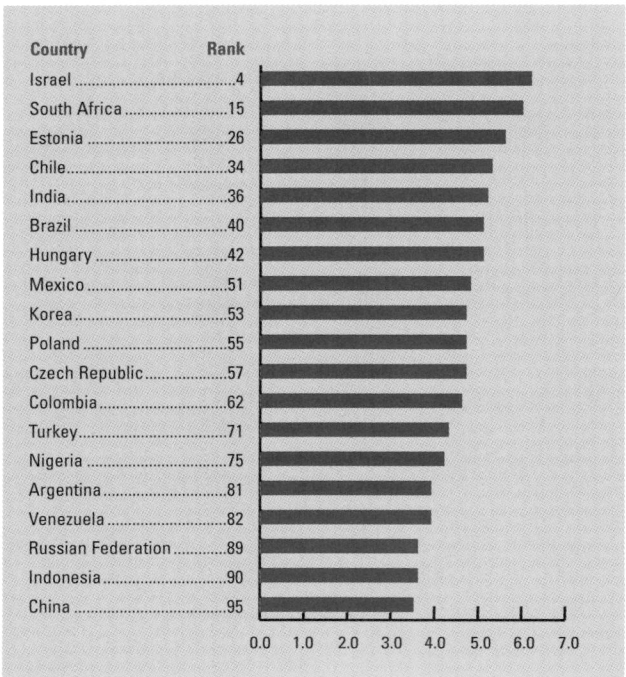

Country	Rank
Israel	4
South Africa	15
Estonia	26
Chile	34
India	36
Brazil	40
Hungary	42
Mexico	51
Korea	53
Poland	55
Czech Republic	57
Colombia	62
Turkey	71
Nigeria	75
Argentina	81
Venezuela	82
Russian Federation	89
Indonesia	90
China	95

Source: Executive Opinion Survey 2003

Figure 9: Ethical behavior of firms

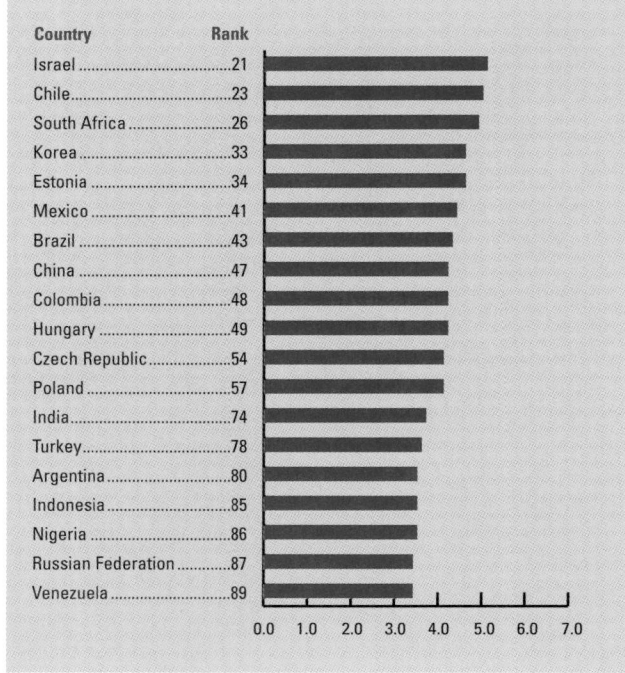

Country	Rank
Israel	21
Chile	23
South Africa	26
Korea	33
Estonia	34
Mexico	41
Brazil	43
China	47
Colombia	48
Hungary	49
Czech Republic	54
Poland	57
India	74
Turkey	78
Argentina	80
Indonesia	85
Nigeria	86
Russian Federation	87
Venezuela	89

Source: Executive Opinion Survey 2003

activity. So the challenges for this and future governments have less to do with running a tight budget and more to do with protecting minority investors' rights, improving the regulatory framework, reducing the incidence of corruption, safeguarding the progress made in the 1990s in the area of civil liberties and press freedom, and maintaining arms' length relationships with Russia's ubiquitous oligarchic structures, the bitter fruit of the corrupt privatization schemes brought into being in the mid-1990s.

The main challenge for the Argentine government and its new president, Mr Kirchner, is to learn how to run a tight fiscal ship. This is likely to be an onerous task, partly because of the historical legacy of never actually having succeeded at it for a sufficiently prolonged period of time, but also because, unlike Russia, it is difficult to envisage a positive terms of trade shock that might lift the balance of payments and the budget out of the current crisis. For the foreseeable future, Argentina will have to run, large primary surpluses on the budget to make room for sizeable payments on its soon-to-be-restructured massive eurobond external debt. At the same time the authorities will have to nurture the fledgling economic recovery under way, following the catastrophic GDP decline seen in 2002. Fiscal discipline will be particularly tough for the provinces, which have traditionally counted on the central government to pick up the tab for budgetary largesse. But, like

Russia, the country has a generous natural resource endowment and a sophisticated labor force—one of the most sophisticated in Latin America.[10] If Chile, a net energy importer facing essentially the same external environment, has managed to sustain high growth rates while simultaneously improving a broad range of social indicators, then Argentina surely has the potential to do it too.

Turkey was "saved" during the period 2000–02 from the consequences of its own poor policies by massive infusions of IMF cash. This was, as in Russia in the mid-1990s, a "strategic decision" by the Fund's largest shareholders intended to prevent an economic meltdown—reflecting over two decades of fiscal mismanagement—from turning into a political crisis, as was the case in Argentina and Russia, where debt default precipitated the fall of both governments. Turkey did not default; it bought some time for itself and, along the way, changed substantially the composition of its debt obligations, sharply increasing the share denominated in foreign currencies, including, of course, its debt obligation to the IMF. But, as in Russia, the crises of the last several years have been a sobering reminder to the Turkish political classes that runaway inflation and rising indebtedness are a recipe for disaster. Indeed, the crises of the past couple of years led to a major shift in the political landscape and the emergence of a new government in late 2002. Macroeconomic manage-

Figure 10: Foreign ownership restrictions

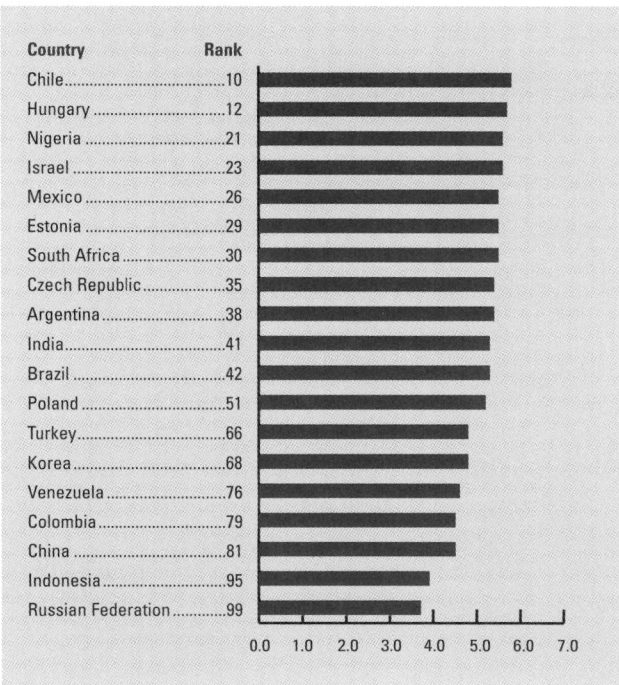

Source: Executive Opinion Survey 2003

Figure 11: Quality of the educational system

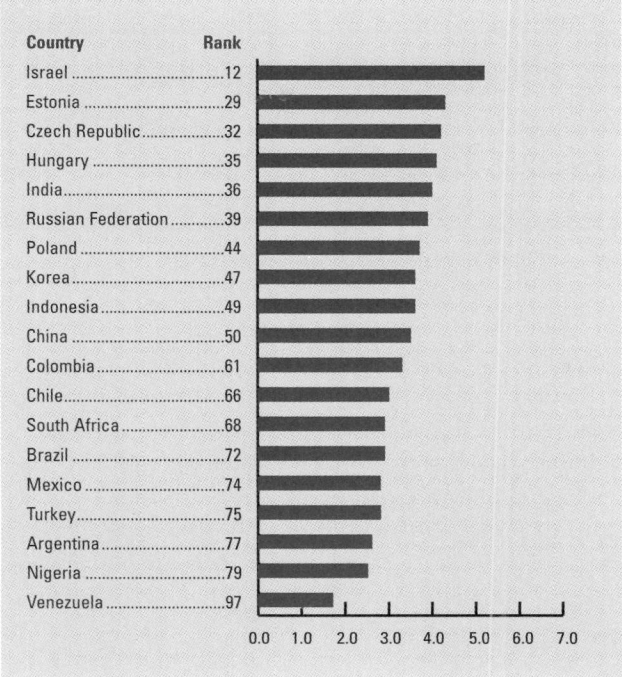

Source: Executive Opinion Survey 2003

ment has improved, GDP growth in 2003 should top 6 percent, but it is difficult to see sustainable debt dynamics. Over the longer term, this is likely to be as much a headache for the government as for the IMF. Turkey, like Russia, needs to make improvements in a number of structural areas. FDI is unusually low, reflecting an ambiguous attitude to foreign participation in the domestic economy by government and businesses alike. The treatment of minorities and the government's track record in the area of human rights remain important challenges to face if the government is going to succeed in its bid to secure the start of EU accession negotiations. Unlike Russia, however, Turkey has a thriving entrepreneurial class that has been doing business in the region for the last several hundred years and this, perhaps more than anything else, is the country's real hope for the future.

Happy families are all alike[11]

One of the most far reaching economic experiments under way today is the integration of the transition economies of eastern and central Europe into the economic, political, and institutional arrangements of the European Union. This process is expected to result in the accession of 10 new countries in May of 2004, bringing to a close an important chapter in the evolution of both

the EU and the countries concerned. The implementation of economic policies in the Czech Republic, Estonia, Hungary, Latvia, Lithuania, Poland, Slovakia, and Slovenia, in particular, has taken place against the background of the policy and institutional requirements established for each country at the time of its EU accession negotiations. These arrangements have provided a credible framework for the implementation of sound economic policies that have contributed to boost these countries' growth performance (see Table 6). Governments have largely been able to sell to their voters a combination of cautious macro policies and ambitious structural reforms—including the burdens that they often bring with them—as part of a broader strategic political objective: joining the richest trading block in the world.

The economic agenda

It is useful to separate the economic reform agenda pursued by these countries in recent years into two broad categories. First, one might identify those policies that are necessary to facilitate the transformation of these countries into "functioning market economies," able to withstand competitive pressures within a much larger economic area with well-developed private sectors. These policies would include: greater price flexibility, progress on trade and capital account liberalization, the removal of barriers to entry

Table 6: GDP growth averages for accession countries

Country	GDP growth (annual %)								Average 1995–2002
	1995	1996	1997	1998	1999	2000	2001	2002	
Czech Republic	6.4	4.8	−1.3	−1.0	0.5	3.3	3.3	2.0	2.2
Estonia	4.3	3.9	9.8	4.6	−0.6	7.1	5.0	5.0	4.9
Hungary	1.5	1.3	4.6	4.9	4.2	5.2	3.8	3.3	3.6
Latvia	−0.8	3.3	8.6	3.9	1.1	6.8	7.6	6.1	4.6
Lithuania	3.3	4.7	7.3	5.1	−3.9	3.8	5.9	5.9	4.0
Poland	7.0	6.0	6.8	4.8	4.1	4.0	1.0	1.3	4.4
Slovak Republic	6.5	5.8	5.6	4.0	1.3	2.2	3.3	4.4	4.1
Slovenia	4.1	3.5	4.6	3.8	5.2	4.6	3.0	2.9	4.0

Sources: WDI 2003 (1996–2001) and WEO 2003 (2002)

to and exit from the market place, privatization and industrial restructuring, adequate provision of social services, and legal and administrative reforms to underpin the creation of a stable macroeconomic environment, among others.[12] Progress in these areas has been tangible in all of the candidate countries, although there are important differences among them in the speed with which the reform process has moved forward.

Most noteworthy, progress has taken place even in countries that have seen frequent government changes, reflecting in many cases the early onset of experimentation with forms of democratic pluralism. Because consensus about EU entry among the political elite has been fairly widespread, the reform agenda has not fallen victim to political infighting. The overarching goal of early EU entry has been a powerful incentive to keep the politicians on track, preventing inevitable political squabbles from bringing decision making to a standstill. Latvia provides perhaps the most striking example: it has had about ten different governments in the past decade, but remains one of the top performers among the first contingent of accession countries. (Incidentally, this raises the issue of whether economic integration and the associated build-up of institutional mechanisms of cooperation could provide a useful backdrop for sustained economic and structural reforms in other parts of the world—Latin America, for instance—but this is the subject of another paper.)

Countries such as Estonia, Hungary, Slovenia, the Czech Republic, and Latvia are seen to have made the most progress; this has been reflected in their ability to attract large volumes of foreign direct investment and to access the international capital markets at tighter spreads than the vast majority of other developing countries, and in the ability of the authorities to respond effectively to changes in the international economic environment. Of these countries, Estonia has perhaps been the most impressive performer; it remains the only country among accession candidates that has actually had to *introduce* distortions as part of its EU accession negotiations. In particular, it has had to raise import tariffs to the EU's common

external tariff—having long disposed of taxes on international trade—and, most significantly, it has had to put in place the inefficient subsidies and other mechanisms of the EU's common agricultural policy, to the considerable chagrin of its politicians and civil servants.

The second category of economic reforms would include those that are not prerequisites for accession *per se*, but that are intended to ease the process of convergence with the EU. Among them, one would include those aimed at modernizing key institutions such as the pension system, boosting investment in key areas likely to enhance the economy's growth potential, and, more generally, making progress in introducing a number of "intangibles" in the economic and institutional environment that are seen to be basic elements of private-sector development.

Insights from the GCI and the Executive Opinion Survey

It is worth noting that, quite aside from the very good overall macroeconomic performance of these countries, the accession countries are among the top performers in the developing world on a broad spectrum of questions posed in the World Economic Forum's Executive Opinion Survey. In particular, a number of them score in the top third among the 102 countries surveyed. Noteworthy are: the extent of distortionary government intervention in the economy, with Estonia (9), Latvia (21), and Hungary (30) being the lead performers; irregularities in the payment of taxes and associated unethical behavior—Hungary (22), Estonia (26), Slovenia (29); the independence of the judiciary—Estonia (22), Hungary (29); restrictions to foreign ownership of local firms—Hungary (12), Slovak Republic (13), Estonia (29); quality of the educational system—Latvia (19), Slovenia (26), Estonia (29), Czech Republic (32), Lithuania (33); and public trust in the financial integrity of politicians—Latvia (31), Estonia (33).

Policy options

The above achievements notwithstanding, there are a number of factors that are likely to shape the macroeconomic environment for the accession countries in the period ahead and perhaps constrain in important ways policymakers' responses to them. EU accession candidates are expected to continue to grow fast in the next several years. The medium-term growth potential of the eight transition economies in central and eastern Europe in particular remains high, reflecting, among several other factors, the continued elimination of the distortions of their central planning past and the beneficial effects of the institutional and policy improvements associated with EU entry. The implementation of so-called second generation structural reforms are also likely to play a role, as will the fact that these countries have well-educated labor forces being exposed to a veritable flood of FDI and the benefits that it brings, a feature that should continue to boost labor productivity.

Good fundamentals mean that capital will continue to flow into these economies. These flows will take the form of FDI and portfolio flows but, with good growth prospects, the private sectors could be expected to play an even more prominent role in capital markets abroad, boosting current account deficits. A counterpart of capital inflows is high growth rates for imports, partly reflecting the import requirements of newly established firms and foreign affiliates, but also the modernization needs of existing enterprises, which, to stay competitive, must invest and upgrade. Indeed, these processes are already underway and large current account deficits have been a permanent feature of the macroeconomic landscape in virtually all of these countries during the last several years. (Deficits at times in the 10 to 15 percent of GDP range have not been unusual.)

Relative price adjustments in the transition to a market economy are among the key factors that have contributed to the persistence of higher inflation in transition countries. The prices of previously heavily subsidized goods and services (eg, food, housing, health care, and public utilities) with a large weight in the Consumer Price Index (CPI) have all increased sharply in recent years leading to upward adjustments in the price levels. Although this gap has narrowed, it is still there and will continue to put pressures on the currencies for real appreciation. Prices of nontradables have been rising faster (than the overall CPI) nearly everywhere among transition EU candidates, and this means that these economies will continue to experience real appreciation, beyond the 20 to 50 percent seen since the mid-1990s.

The above factors are likely to reinforce each other. Countries expected to grow more rapidly and to experience real appreciation of their currencies may attract even more capital inflows. Increased productivity in the tradables sector and rising relative prices in nontradables will increase the return on capital in both sectors and boost capital inflows. This, in turn, could put further upward pressures on currencies, higher current account deficits,

and foreign debt accumulation by the private sectors. The question that policymakers will want to ask is whether the above set of factors implies any particular risks as the countries join the EU and, subsequently, cope with the challenges of the new environment.

One possible scenario to this policy environment sees the authorities managing the pressures identified above through a combination of cautious fiscal policies and structural reforms. Tight budgets mitigate the pressures on the current account, while structural reforms enhance productivity and increase the level of the equilibrium exchange rate that is consistent with export competitiveness. In this scenario, some of these countries might want to continue to protect their access to international capital markets and, where needed, adapt their exchange rate regimes to changing circumstances, such as the broadening of the fluctuation bands carried out in Hungary a couple of years ago. This scenario assumes that there would be no major external shocks that might lead to capital outflows and put undue pressures on the exchange rate (particularly in those countries with fairly tight pegs), leading to possible currency crises. The main constraint in this scenario would be the need for budgetary restraint at a time when it might make more sense for governments to have a more active fiscal policy, for instance to increase capital spending for infrastructure or to upgrade the countries' health and education systems, still lagging behind those of the EU. Some countries, such as Poland and the Czech Republic, might find this quite a tall order, given the large public-sector deficits that are presently envisaged for the period 2003–04.

Given that the accession countries do not have an opt-out from European Monetary Union (EMU) and have all thus agreed to adopt the euro in due course, this scenario assumes that the authorities would be prepared to deal with the above stresses for at least several years. Those countries unable to implement a tight fiscal policy will obviously be more vulnerable and may see their adoption of the euro delayed. For those able to rise to the above challenges, however, the benefits are likely to be substantial. The main benefit of adopting the euro will stem from the elimination of currency risk, together with the capital outflows and volatility that often accompany it. Interest rates would be expected to decline and would perhaps be higher than international (euro-area) rates only in reflection of country risk. Lower interest rates would in turn bring about budgetary savings, as governments issued bonds at even lower rates. To this could be added the savings associated with monetary operations that central banks carry out to sterilize capital inflows.

The accession countries and the euro

The eventual adoption of the euro would surely strengthen financial links with the euro area and the global economy. Sustained price stability would dispel uncertainties and would improve investor sentiment as countries' commitment to financial discipline and sound fiscal policies were perceived to be irreversible. The elimination of currency risk would also reduce the collateral effects of contagion episodes, which can be quite ugly in their ramifications. Furthermore, the risk of a currency crisis precipitating a banking crisis because of currency mismatches would be greatly diminished as well. Closer integration with financial markets would encourage capital inflows and boost growth prospects, without the undesirable effects identified above, in terms of either an appreciating currency or the need to have budget surpluses to mitigate the effects of growth and capital inflows on the current account. So policymakers would be able to focus on structural reforms without immediately having to put the brakes on the economy because of concerns about external sustainability.

Enlargement will involve the integration of two sets of countries with very different levels of per capita GDP. The transition economies of central and eastern Europe have an average per capita GDP of some 35 percent of the EU average and a level of development—levels of productivity, the underlying stability of the macroeconomic and political environment, the strength of policies and institutions, the stability of the legal environment—that is seen as being still behind that of the EU's existing members. Convergence to average EU income levels will take time and a combination of sound policies in the countries joining—including a major boost to physical and human capital investment—and the transfer of technology and financial resources from the EU to the new members. How quickly this process of convergence moves will be a key indicator of the strength of domestic policies and the ability of the authorities to lay out a credible macroeconomic and legal framework: Ireland has already caught up with the EU average GDP per capita; Greece, on the other hand, more than 20 years after joining, still has not.

But the above challenges are of the "second order." They essentially involve careful management of macroeconomic policy against an otherwise favorable backdrop, involving the gradual catching up of each new EU member country to the higher levels of per capita income in the EU. This is a process that is bringing with it institutional innovation and modernization, technology transfer, increased labor mobility, and the full participation of these countries in the build up of the supranational institutional structure that is gradually emerging in Europe. For instance: to facilitate policy coordination ahead of EMU, the governors of all the central banks of countries joining the EU next year will promptly sit on the ECB's General Council. The accession countries are also expected to have fully independent central banks by end-2003, ahead of EU entry, to be able to prepare the way for EMU unencum-

bered by political pressures from their respective governments, which might impose constraints on the conduct of monetary policy.

A bright future?

The experience of the central and eastern European economies is tremendously relevant for the developing world for a number of interrelated reasons. First, it is useful to be able to point to a set of countries that, collectively, have had a fairly sustained period of relatively strong growth, reflecting the favorable consequences of good macroeconomic policies and ambitious structural reforms. Estonia, Hungary, Slovenia, and some of the other countries in the region—as Chile in Latin America—show the ample scope for good policies to affect economic outcomes, even in the context of an increasingly interdependent global economy. Second, their experience shows that when policymakers have a clearly defined vision of where the country should go, powerful domestic incentives are created for the discipline that inevitably must accompany good macro management. This "vision" was provided in the early 1990s by the political and strategic decision to join the EU by the end of the decade. Deadlines were missed, and joining the EU turned out to be a far more labyrinthine process than anyone had ever anticipated. But a legal and institutional framework was put in place that provided useful guideposts for policymakers and made it possible for politicians to credibly justify tough adjustment measures to their respective populations.

It could be argued that this situation was unique to these countries, that in the absence of a welcoming EU, Poland, a distorted economy in the early 1990s emerging out of many decades of inefficient economic management, would, most likely, have gone the way of Argentina, Venezuela, or Nigeria, squandering opportunities and ended up having a far more uneven performance. There may be an element of truth to this, but it does not take away the credit that is due to policymakers in these countries who, on the whole, seized a unique chance and made the most of it. Incidentally, there is nothing to prevent other regional groupings from creating such incentives for themselves, Latin America being the most obvious example. Clearly, political leadership will be key. Finally, the accession countries have not fully made it yet. As noted above, they will face tricky challenges surrounded, as they are, by some of the largest and most competitive economies in the world. But they will become an integral part of a community of nations engaged in a promising economic and political experiment and the benefits of this, for the countries' institutions, for the management of their respective economies, for the growth of personal incomes and the standard of living of their populations, will far outweigh the costs.

Notes

1 Augusto Lopez-Claros is the World Economic Forum's chief economist and Director of the Global Competitiveness Programme.

2 See *The Global Competitiveness Report 2002–2003* and the studies by Cook; Farrell; Ickes, von Hagen, and Traistaru; and Larrain B. therein.

3 For an interesting discussion of some of challenges faced in China and India, see the discussion by Baily elsewhere in this volume.

4 For a thorough discussion of the causes of the Asian financial crises see Petersen and Hills (1999) and Stiglitz (2002).

5 In a very readable piece on financial crises, John Cassidy (1999) quotes Keynes on the risks posed by free capital mobility in the 1940s: "nothing is more certain than the movement of capital funds must be regulated for if this did not happen money would shift with the speed of the magic carpet and these movements would have the effect of disorganizing all steady business." See Cassidy (1999).

6 For an interesting discussion on this and related issues see the excellent article by Richard Cooper (2002).

7 The IMF's First Deputy Managing Director Anne Krueger refers to "the need for better incentives to ensure the orderly and timely restructuring of unsustainable sovereign debts." See, for instance, Kreuger (2002).

8 For a fuller discussion of this and related issues see Sen (1999).

9 Russia has seen a worsening of its rank on the macroeconomic component of the index, which sits somewhat at odds with the general strengthening in some of the key macroeconomic indicators, particularly the overall improvement in the fiscal accounts and the balance of payments. The deterioration reflects a couple of distinct factors. First, the macroeconomic stability subindex incorporates variables on which Russia has not done particularly well on an international perspective. Inflation, for instance, while low by Russian historical standards, remains quite high on a cross-country basis. A 15 percent year-on-year rate of inflation in 2002 puts Russia in 93rd place among 102 countries. A similar comment can be made about the gap between lending and borrowing interest rates, a measure of the overall inefficiency of Russia's largely unreformed financial sector. The other factor is specific to changes made in the methodology of computation of the index. Whereas last year the government to GDP ratio would be used as an input into the macroeconomic component of the index (with Russia doing well overall), this year a measure of government waste in allocating expenditure is being used, on which Russia does considerably less well, with a rank of 76 among the 102 countries surveyed.

10 Latin American countries have had their share of Nobel prize winners in literature during the past several decades. However, of the three Nobel prizes awarded to Latin America in science, all three have gone to Argentine nationals (one in chemistry and two in medicine). Its scientists have shown a considerable capacity for innovation— note, for instance, the achievements of Dr Rene Favoloro, the inventor of the coronary heart by-pass and other surgical procedures.

11 "Happy families are all alike; every unhappy family is unhappy in its own way," is the starting sentence of Tolstoy's *Anna Karenina* (1875).

12 For a comprehensive discussion of these issues the reader may refer to the EU's *Enlargement Papers* issued by the European Commission's Directorate-General for Economic and Financial Affairs.

References

Cassidy, J. 1999. "The New World Disorder," *The New Yorker* November 2: 198–207.

Cook, L. D. 2003. "Africa: A Union Open for Growth, Trade, and Business?" In *The Global Competitiveness Report 2002–2003*. New York: Oxford University Press.

Cooper, R. 2002. "Chapter 11 For Countries," *Foreign Affairs*: July/August: pp 90–103.

European Commission. *Enlargement Papers*, issued by the European Commission's Directorate-General for Economic and Financial Affairs.

Farrell, D. 2003. "Asia: The Productivity Imperative." In *The Global Competitiveness Report 2002–2003*. New York: Oxford University Press.

Ickes, B. W., J. von Hagen, I. Traistaru. 2003. "Central and Eastern Europe: Economic Developments, Reforms, and Geography." In *The Global Competitiveness Report 2002–2003*. New York: Oxford University Press.

International Monetary Fund (IMF). 2003a. IMF Country Report No. 03/226, July 2003; Article IV Consultation Report for Argentina.

International Monetary Fund (IMF). 2003b. Public Information Notice (PIN) No. 03/42, April 2, 2003.

International Monetary Fund (IMF). 2003c. *Proposals for a Sovereign Debt Restructuring Mechanism (SDRM)*. Washington, DC: International Monetary Fund, January.

Krueger, A. 2002. "New Approaches to Sovereign Debt Restructuring: An Update on Our Thinking," Speech delivered on 1 April 2002 at the IIE in Washington, DC.

Larrain B., F. 2003. "Lights and Shadows of Latin American Competitiveness." In *The Global Competitiveness Report 2002–2003*. New York: Oxford University Press.

Lopez-Claros, A. and S. Alexashenko. 1998. "Fiscal Policy Issues During the Transition in Russia," Occasional Paper No. 173. Washington, DC: International Monetary Fund.

Lopez-Claros, A. and M. Zadormov. 2002. "Economic Reforms: Steady as She Goes," *The Washington Quarterly* Winter 25(1).

Mussa, M. 2002. "Argentina and the Fund: From Triumph to Tragedy," Institute for International Economics, Policy Analyses in International Economics, July 2002, 67, Washington DC.

Petersen, P. G. and C. A Hills. 1999. "The Future of the International Financial Architecture," *Foreign Affairs*: November/December.

Rouleau, E. 2000. "Turkey's Dream of Democracy," *Foreign Affairs*: November/December.

Sen, A. 1999. *Development as Freedom*. New York: Knopf.

Stiglitz, J. E. 2002. *Globalization and Its Discontents*. London: Allen Lane, The Penguin Press.

CHAPTER 2.3

Ranking National Innovative Capacity: Findings from the National Innovative Capacity Index

MICHAEL E. PORTER, Harvard University

SCOTT STERN, Northwestern University and National Bureau of Economic Research

International competitiveness increasingly depends on innovation. With continued operational improvement in education and infrastructure now a given, and with local companies able rapidly to acquire and deploy technology from around the world, producing standard products using standard methods no longer sustains competitiveness. Among high-income countries, differences in prosperity are closely related to differences in the intensity of innovation. For developing nations, low-cost inputs by themselves are no longer sufficient to maintain competitiveness. Companies must increasingly be able to access and ultimately develop global technology. With the erosion of traditional barriers to entry, enhanced prosperity flows from the ability of companies in a nation to create and then globally commercialize novel products and processes, shifting the innovation frontier as fast as rivals catch up.

A higher level of innovation in one nation need not come at the expense of others. Innovation can enhance productivity, improve consumer value, and increase prosperity in all nations, collectively speeding the rate of world economic growth. Innovation is also crucial for addressing pressing social challenges, by relaxing the tradeoffs between near-term economic growth and health, safety, and the environmental impact of development.

Over the past 15 years, an increasing number of countries have emerged as global innovators.

Although the United States and Switzerland had per capita patenting rates well in excess of those of other economies during the 1970s and 1980s, ten different countries registered per capita patenting rates greater than 100 US patents per million people in 2002, and 25 countries registered a rate of at least 30 US patents per million people (see Figure 1). Within countries, innovation tends to be dominated by geographically concentrated clusters of firms—supported by local institutions and fostered by vigorous domestic competition.

Although the number of countries capable of global innovation is growing, major differences persist among advanced economies. Whereas the Scandinavian countries and Japan have registered sharp increases in innovative output, many western European nations, such as France and Italy, continue to trail, with innovation output at roughly the same level as a generation ago. Some emerging economies, such as Singapore, Taiwan, and Israel, now outpace leading Organisation of Economic Co-operation and Development (OECD) economies, while Eastern European and Latin American countries still depend on low labor costs and imitation of foreign technology.

Why does the intensity of innovation vary across countries? How does innovation depend on locational characteristics? Innovation arises from private-sector initiative, but the R&D productivity of firms in a nation is importantly shaped by local policies and the nature of local institutions. Innovation output, then, depends on the

Figure 1: International patents per capita, leading countries, 1975–2002

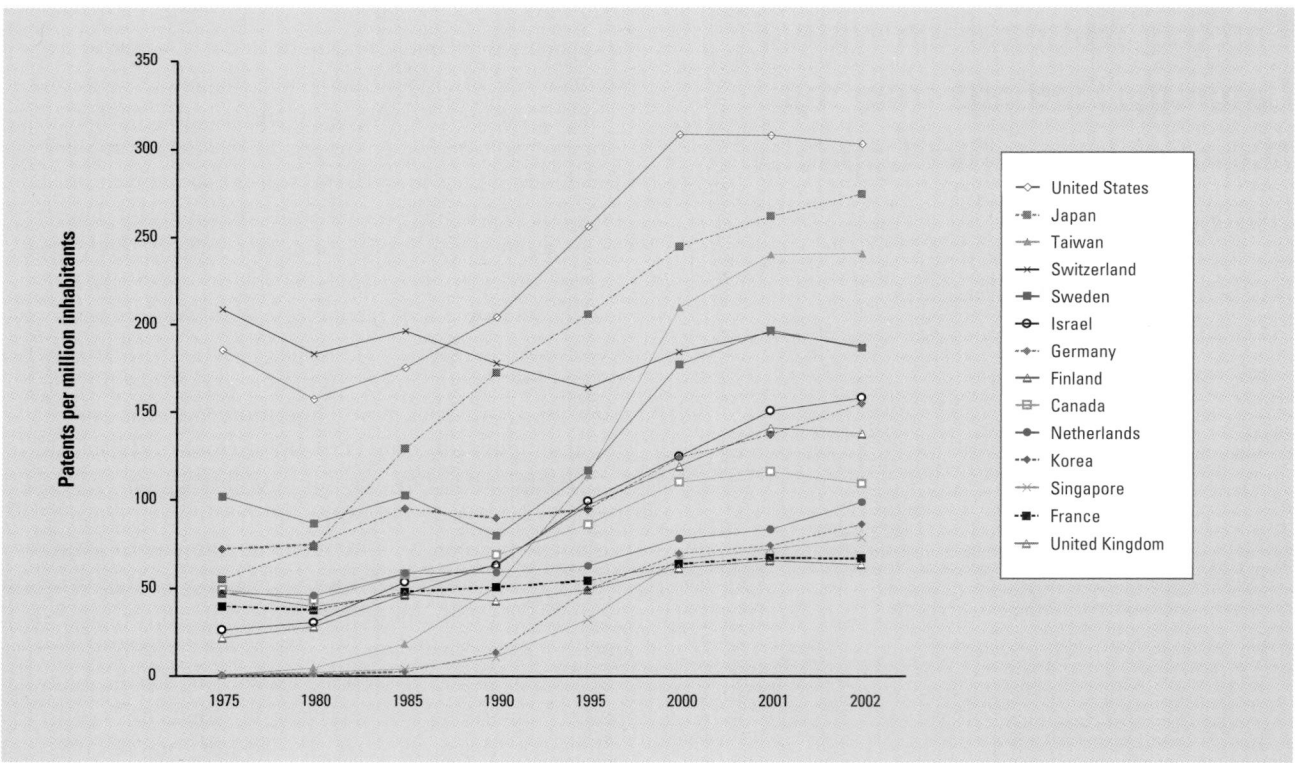

Source: US Patent and Trademark Office (www.uspto.gov); authors' analysis

interaction between private-sector strategies and public-sector policies. We term this constellation of factors *national innovative capacity*, or the degree to which a nation offers a favorable environment for innovation at the world technology frontier.[1]

This chapter extends our prior research on the role of location in innovation, using new data from the 2003 Executive Opinion Survey to assess the innovative capacity of 78 countries for which the required data are available. We examine a wide range of national characteristics suggested by the national innovative capacity framework and available from the Survey data to construct a national innovative capacity index (NICI). We rank countries on NICI as well as five subindexes measuring important components of innovative vitality (see Table 1).

Our statistical findings reveal the striking degree to which measures of the national environment for innovation affect innovative output. We also find that the bar for innovation is rising; even countries with an *absolute* increase in innovative capacity over 2001 sometimes register a *relative* decline because of their inability to improve local conditions as quickly as other nations. We find that some countries have aggressively invested in innovative capacity, ahead of that expected, given current income, in

an effort to enhance competitiveness and prosperity. Conversely, in other nations, innovative capacity lags overall productivity and income rankings, raising concerns about the sustainability of their competitiveness. Finally, there is a close connection between whether a nation's firms chose innovation-orientated strategies and the national environment in which they operate. Though our findings are subject to caveats common to any quantitative study of the causes and consequences of innovation, our results provide consistent support for the role of policy choices in enhancing the national environment for innovation and, with it, international competitiveness.

The determinants of national innovative capacity

The conceptual framework underlying our approach has been described in prior *Report*s. However, because of its importance in interpreting the results, we provide a summary here that incorporates our recent learning.

The vitality of innovation in a location is shaped by *national innovative capacity*. National innovative capacity is a country's potential—as both a political and economic entity—to produce a stream of commercially relevant innovations. National innovative capacity is distinct from

Table 1: National innovative capacity index and subindexes

Country	Innovative Capacity Index 2003 RANK	Innovative Capacity Index 2003 INDEX	Proportion of Scientists and Engineers Index RANK	Proportion of Scientists and Engineers Index INDEX	Innovation Policy Index RANK	Innovation Policy Index INDEX	Cluster Innovation Environment Index RANK	Cluster Innovation Environment Index INDEX	Innovation Linkages Index RANK	Innovation Linkages Index INDEX	Operations and Strategy Index RANK	Operations and Strategy Index INDEX	Innovative Capacity Index 2002 RANK	Business Competitiveness Index 2003 RANK	GDP per capita 2002 RANK
United States	1	36.60	4	8.44	3	5.51	2	7.59	1	7.26	1	7.80	1	2	1
Finland	2	35.96	3	8.53	2	5.58	3	7.55	2	7.02	8	7.28	3	1	15
United Kingdom	3	34.63	17	7.89	7	5.36	13	6.79	3	6.96	3	7.63	2	6	18
Japan	4	34.62	2	8.54	17	5.02	1	7.68	13	5.97	4	7.42	5	13	14
Germany	5	34.29	12	8.06	10	5.34	4	7.37	11	6.11	5	7.41	4	5	12
Singapore	6	34.19	6	8.33	1	5.96	12	6.85	14	5.91	10	7.14	10	8	20
Sweden	7	34.02	5	8.41	15	5.11	14	6.72	6	6.48	7	7.30	7	3	17
Denmark	8	33.95	10	8.15	12	5.18	7	6.99	8	6.27	6	7.36	12	4	4
Switzerland	9	33.73	8	8.19	20	4.92	10	6.89	12	6.09	2	7.65	6	7	5
France	10	33.63	15	7.91	8	5.35	9	6.96	9	6.20	9	7.22	13	10	19
Netherlands	11	33.14	18	7.85	11	5.29	17	6.61	5	6.51	13	6.87	11	9	8
Canada	12	33.11	13	8.00	6	5.37	8	6.98	7	6.39	19	6.37	9	12	6
Taiwan	13	32.84	16	7.89	5	5.39	6	7.19	20	5.63	15	6.74	8	16	n/a
Israel	14	32.64	31	7.35	9	5.35	23	6.27	4	6.62	12	7.05	15	20	23
Australia	15	32.37	11	8.14	4	5.48	21	6.42	10	6.18	22	6.14	17	11	10
Austria	16	32.05	19	7.75	13	5.16	11	6.87	24	5.53	14	6.76	14	17	9
Belgium	17	31.96	14	7.99	14	5.15	25	6.25	15	5.87	16	6.70	16	15	11
Iceland	18	31.86	1	8.65	19	4.92	24	6.25	22	5.57	17	6.47	18	14	3
Ireland	19	31.24	22	7.69	18	5.01	22	6.39	16	5.86	20	6.29	20	21	7
Korea	20	31.13	20	7.75	24	4.74	16	6.67	18	5.79	21	6.19	22	23	27
Italy	21	30.86	39	7.05	29	4.55	5	7.26	21	5.61	18	6.38	21	24	16
Norway	22	30.80	7	8.32	22	4.82	31	5.96	19	5.64	23	6.06	19	22	2
New Zealand	23	30.55	21	7.74	27	4.59	20	6.43	17	5.81	24	5.97	24	18	22
Spain	24	29.77	28	7.56	23	4.77	27	6.13	25	5.46	25	5.85	23	25	21
Hong Kong SAR	25	28.57	64	4.54	26	4.70	15	6.72	23	5.54	11	7.08	26	19	13
Estonia	26	28.42	24	7.66	33	4.42	33	5.79	26	5.37	39	5.17	29	28	33
South Africa	27	28.38	38	7.08	32	4.44	19	6.43	29	5.25	38	5.18	30	27	32
Latvia	28	28.17	40	6.98	37	4.20	32	5.81	27	5.32	26	5.85	44	29	44
Slovenia	29	28.16	23	7.69	28	4.56	41	5.40	38	4.77	27	5.74	25	30	26
Czech Republic	30	27.27	32	7.28	40	4.09	38	5.44	34	4.96	29	5.50	32	35	28
Lithuania	31	27.08	26	7.61	41	4.05	49	5.12	30	5.16	40	5.14	31	40	41
Greece	32	27.01	35	7.24	30	4.50	37	5.45	41	4.65	37	5.18	37	39	25
Portugal	33	26.90	30	7.36	25	4.73	36	5.49	35	4.90	65	4.42	27	36	24
Poland	34	26.87	33	7.28	47	3.94	35	5.50	33	4.98	36	5.18	35	47	37
Malaysia	35	26.85	59	5.07	16	5.04	18	6.47	37	4.78	31	5.48	39	26	42
Slovak Republic	36	26.12	29	7.49	44	4.00	43	5.34	53	4.40	48	4.90	40	43	31
Jordan	37	26.09	27	7.57	36	4.28	51	5.11	47	4.52	58	4.60	n/a	41	66
Tunisia	38	26.03	50	5.82	21	4.89	44	5.29	31	5.10	44	4.94	45	33	54
Hungary	39	26.00	34	7.27	31	4.45	64	4.77	43	4.58	45	4.92	28	38	30
China	40	25.86	43	6.30	45	3.99	26	6.20	40	4.65	56	4.71	36	46	65
Chile	41	25.75	47	5.91	35	4.29	42	5.36	32	4.98	34	5.20	41	32	40
Brazil	42	25.70	51	5.78	53	3.74	29	6.04	36	4.85	33	5.28	33	34	48
Russian Federation	43	25.59	9	8.16	69	3.26	48	5.13	39	4.72	72	4.32	34	65	46
India	44	25.52	60	5.06	38	4.13	28	6.12	28	5.32	50	4.89	43	37	74
Croatia	45	25.23	37	7.08	57	3.61	40	5.40	44	4.58	61	4.56	42	62	36
Costa Rica	46	25.01	44	6.28	55	3.62	52	5.10	46	4.52	30	5.49	38	45	39
Thailand	47	24.74	69	4.30	34	4.37	30	5.98	45	4.53	28	5.56	46	31	53
Mauritius	48	24.73	46	6.03	50	3.84	45	5.23	42	4.59	42	5.04	55	44	34
Ukraine	49	24.51	25	7.66	68	3.31	55	4.99	59	4.20	69	4.35	47	71	63
Indonesia	50	24.04	48	5.89	42	4.03	50	5.11	62	4.18	52	4.83	59	60	73
Mexico	51	24.00	53	5.54	43	4.01	46	5.15	55	4.38	46	4.92	51	48	43
Vietnam	52	23.99	52	5.61	48	3.91	34	5.71	54	4.38	67	4.38	53	50	77
Bulgaria	53	23.62	36	7.18	64	3.42	69	4.61	61	4.18	76	4.24	50	74	49
Turkey	54	23.23	49	5.84	56	3.62	39	5.43	74	3.79	62	4.54	54	52	56
Egypt	55	23.04	45	6.27	81	2.95	60	4.85	52	4.40	60	4.57	n/a	58	70
Argentina	56	22.98	42	6.37	73	3.17	58	4.89	66	4.03	63	4.53	52	68	35
Romania	57	22.97	41	6.82	86	2.76	59	4.87	51	4.41	80	4.11	48	73	57
Panama	58	22.68	62	4.82	52	3.75	63	4.80	49	4.44	51	4.86	57	59	58
Sri Lanka	59	22.52	57	5.25	58	3.56	57	4.97	56	4.26	64	4.49	56	57	72
Trinidad and Tobago	60	22.24	61	4.98	54	3.70	61	4.83	63	4.15	59	4.58	58	53	38
Philippines	61	21.99	58	5.19	65	3.41	54	5.03	79	3.59	55	4.76	60	64	67
Colombia	62	21.84	65	4.50	60	3.53	53	5.03	64	4.13	57	4.65	61	51	52
Dominican Republic	63	21.58	74	3.94	59	3.55	73	4.39	48	4.50	35	5.20	49	61	50
Uruguay	64	20.58	55	5.28	63	3.44	81	3.94	75	3.70	77	4.23	63	69	47

(cont'd.)

Table 1: National innovative capacity index and subindexes *(cont'd.)*

Country	Innovative Capacity Index 2003 RANK	Innovative Capacity Index 2003 INDEX	Proportion of Scientists and Engineers Index RANK	Proportion of Scientists and Engineers Index INDEX	Innovation Policy Index RANK	Innovation Policy Index INDEX	Cluster Innovation Environment Index RANK	Cluster Innovation Environment Index INDEX	Innovation Linkages Index RANK	Innovation Linkages Index INDEX	Operations and Strategy Index RANK	Operations and Strategy Index INDEX	Innovative Capacity Index 2002 RANK	Business Competitiveness Index 2003 RANK	GDP per capita 2002 RANK
Peru	65	20.58	54	5.43	80	2.96	77	4.16	76	3.69	71	4.33	62	78	62
El Salvador	66	20.52	76	3.84	66	3.40	72	4.39	72	3.83	41	5.05	65	63	59
Venezuela	67	20.34	56	5.27	82	2.92	76	4.20	77	3.68	75	4.27	64	80	60
Guatemala	68	19.71	67	4.35	77	2.99	75	4.33	70	3.85	78	4.19	67	81	64
Pakistan	69	19.60	71	4.24	70	3.20	56	4.98	85	3.14	81	4.04	n/a	72	79
Zimbabwe	70	19.47	75	3.94	72	3.18	66	4.74	68	3.92	86	3.70	69	75	80
Ecuador	71	18.78	66	4.42	79	2.97	85	3.75	80	3.52	79	4.12	68	84	71
Honduras	72	18.28	68	4.35	71	3.18	83	3.77	83	3.23	85	3.76	72	89	75
Nicaragua	73	17.80	70	4.29	76	3.08	89	3.40	84	3.16	83	3.87	66	88	n/a
Paraguay	74	17.04	63	4.64	89	2.70	88	3.45	90	2.90	90	3.36	70	91	61
Bangladesh	75	16.94	73	4.09	84	2.81	79	4.04	93	2.62	89	3.37	71	86	82
Bolivia	76	16.32	72	4.23	92	2.45	92	3.12	86	3.08	88	3.45	73	92	76
Madagascar	77	15.81	77	2.51	88	2.72	87	3.46	82	3.26	84	3.85	n/a	85	90
Senegal	78	14.81	78	0.60	83	2.82	82	3.77	78	3.67	82	3.94	n/a	82	83
Algeria	n/a	n/a	n/a	n/a	62	3.46	86	3.70	88	3.00	91	3.32	n/a	83	55
Angola	n/a	n/a	n/a	n/a	91	2.55	95	2.45	94	2.35	95	3.02	n/a	95	78
Botswana	n/a	n/a	n/a	n/a	49	3.89	71	4.42	71	3.85	53	4.82	n/a	54	45
Chad	n/a	n/a	n/a	n/a	90	2.62	90	3.20	95	2.06	94	3.07	n/a	93	85
Ethiopia	n/a	n/a	n/a	n/a	87	2.73	91	3.16	91	2.82	93	3.12	n/a	90	88
Haiti	n/a	n/a	n/a	n/a	93	2.40	94	3.05	87	3.01	87	3.50	n/a	94	81
Jamaica	n/a	n/a	n/a	n/a	61	3.47	70	4.54	57	4.22	32	5.41	n/a	56	68
Kenya	n/a	n/a	n/a	n/a	74	3.15	67	4.69	58	4.20	54	4.81	n/a	66	86
Malawi	n/a	n/a	n/a	n/a	78	2.98	80	4.00	81	3.34	74	4.28	n/a	70	91
Malta	n/a	n/a	n/a	n/a	39	4.11	62	4.83	60	4.18	43	5.02	n/a	42	29
Morocco	n/a	n/a	n/a	n/a	46	3.94	47	5.14	50	4.44	49	4.89	n/a	49	69
Mozambique	n/a	n/a	n/a	n/a	85	2.78	93	3.08	92	2.78	92	3.21	n/a	87	84
Namibia	n/a	n/a	n/a	n/a	51	3.78	68	4.66	69	3.87	47	4.92	n/a	55	51
Nigeria	n/a	n/a	n/a	n/a	75	3.11	65	4.75	67	3.94	66	4.39	n/a	77	87
Serbia	n/a	n/a	n/a	n/a	94	2.15	74	4.34	65	4.11	70	4.34	n/a	76	n/a
Tanzania	n/a	n/a	n/a	n/a	67	3.35	78	4.13	73	3.81	73	4.30	n/a	67	92
Zambia	n/a	n/a	n/a	n/a	95	2.06	84	3.76	89	2.92	68	4.35	n/a	79	89

purely scientific or technical achievements, and focuses on the economic application of new technology. Innovative capacity is not simply the realized level of innovation, but it also aims to measure the fundamental conditions that create the environment for innovation in a particular location. Innovative capacity depends in part on past technological sophistication and the size of the scientific and technical workforce, but it also reflects a series of investment and policy choices by government and the private sector that affect the incentives for research, development, and commercialization activities in a country and the productivity of these activities.

The sharp differences in innovative output across locations make clear the importance of local circumstances in R&D productivity. However, taking advantage of the local environment for innovation is far from automatic. Companies based in the same location can and do differ markedly in their success at innovation. Harnessing the local environment for innovation requires that companies pursue appropriate strategies and make appropriate investment choices.

National innovative capacity is composed of four broad elements that define how location shapes the ability of a company to innovate at the global frontier (see Figure 2). Although the framework was created for application at the national level, it can also be employed to evaluate innovative capacity at the regional or local level.

Common innovation infrastructure

A nation's common innovation infrastructure consists of the set of crosscutting factors supporting innovation throughout an entire economy, including the pool of human and financial resources devoted to scientific and technological advances, the economywide public policies bearing on innovative activity, and the economy's inherited level of technological sophistication. The foundation of a nation's common innovation infrastructure is its cadre of scientists and engineers involved in innovation. Common innovation infrastructure also includes investments in institutions engaged in basic research, which advance fundamental understanding and underpins much commercial technology. Government funding remains the mainstay of virtually every nation's investment in truly frontier research. Areas of crosscutting policy affecting innovation include the protection of intellectual property; the extent of tax-based incentives for innovation; the degree to which antitrust enforcement motivates and encourages innovation; the extent to which innovation is spurred versus impeded by the structure of safety, quality, and environmental regulations; and the openness of the economy to trade and investment. Overall, a strong common innovation infrastructure requires national investments and policy choices stretching over decades.

The cluster-specific innovation environment

Although the common innovation infrastructure sets the basic conditions for innovation, the development and commercialization of new technologies take place disproportionately in clusters—geographic concentrations of interconnected companies and institutions in a particular field. The cluster-specific innovation environment is captured in the "diamond" framework (see Figure 3).[2] Four attributes of the microeconomic environment surrounding a cluster bear on its overall competitiveness and innovative vitality—the presence of specialized and high-quality inputs, a local context in that field encouraging investment and spurred by intense rivalry, pressure and insight gleaned from sophisticated local demand for that cluster's products and services, and the local presence of high quality related and supporting industries.

The importance of clusters reflects important externalities in innovation that are contained in particular geographic areas. Presence within a cluster offers advantages to firms in perceiving both the need and the opportunity for innovation. Equally important, however, are the flexibility and capacity present in clusters to turn new ideas into reality. Within a cluster, a company can rapidly assemble the personnel, components, machinery, and services necessary for commercialization. Suppliers of essential inputs and "lead" buyers become crucial partners in the innovation process; the relationships necessary for effective innovation are more easily achieved among participants that are nearby. Reinforcing these advantages for innovation within clusters is sheer pressure—competitive pressure, peer pressure, customer pressure, and constant comparison. We focus on clusters (eg, information technology) rather than individual industries (eg, printers), then, because of powerful spillovers and externalities across discrete industries that are vital to the rate of innovation.

The innovation environment of a cluster is fundamental to its competitiveness. The recent rise of the Australian wine industry on the global stage is a good example. Though Australia's natural climate has always been conducive to wine production, the emergence of Australian firms as players in the global wine industry did not occur until the Australian wine cluster reflected

Figure 2: National innovative capacity framework

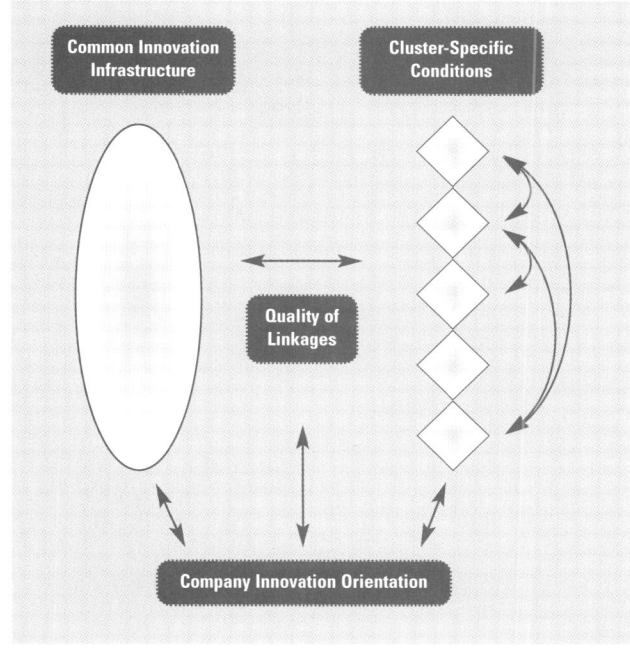

Figure 3: The microeconomic business environment

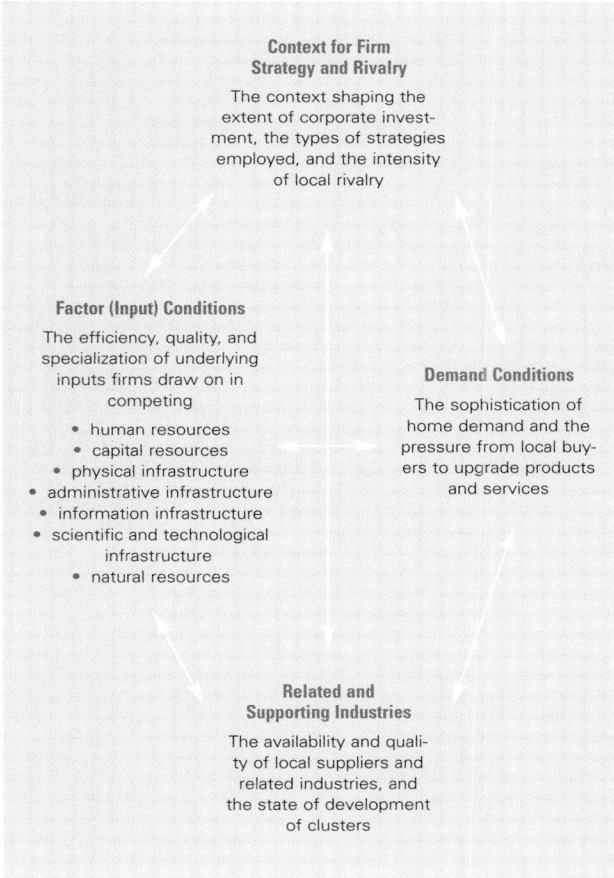

strength along each element of the diamond. The industry benefitted from the combined impact of sustained pressures from sophisticated Australian consumers, intense rivalry among domestic competitors, and a local environment supporting the use and development of advanced agricultural technologies and methods. The establishment of the Australian Wine Research Institute and domestic winemaking schools in the 1950s was crucial to the industry's takeoff decades later. Similar examples of cluster vitality in innovation occur in many fields, such as the long-term dominance of pharmaceuticals by companies whose research activities are based in the United States and global leadership by Scandinavian companies in environmental technologies.

The quality of linkages

The quality of the connections between a nation's common innovation infrastructure and individual industrial clusters is crucial to innovation. The relationship is also reciprocal: strong clusters feed the common infrastructure and also benefit from it. Without strong linkages, upstream scientific and technical advances can actually diffuse to other countries more quickly than they can be exploited at home. For example, although facsimile machine technology was developed in Britain and the United States, it was the Japanese consumer electronics optical and telecommunications firms that successfully commercialized this innovation on a global scale in the late 1970s.

Particularly important linking institutions are a nation's universities, which can play the role of bridging researchers and companies. A variety of formal and informal organizations including trade associations, standards agencies, and technology networks—which we term "institutions for collaboration"—are present in many nations, and these also build connections between research centers and firms.

Company innovation orientation

Finally, taking advantage of national innovative capacity depends on appropriate choices by companies. Even in locations with a favorable environment for innovation, many companies can be ineffective at it. Companies must embrace strategies based on innovation and choose supportive operating policies in areas such as R&D spending, customer orientation, recruiting, and training. Simply investing in R&D is not enough; advantage flows from the ability of companies to draw on specific strengths in the local innovation environment as part of an overall strategy to build a competitive advantage. In other words, appropriate corporate practices and strategy interact with the other elements of national innovative capacity in determining the propensity of firms to innovate at the global frontier.

Measuring national innovative capacity

To measure national innovative capacity, we extend our prior research by employing new data drawn from the Executive Opinion Survey. Standard governmental data sources are inadequate because they fail to capture the drivers of innovative capacity in a consistent way across a wide range of countries, including an array of innovation policy variables, the cluster-specific innovation environment, and the nature of company operations and strategy.

We employ the single best and most comparable measure of innovative output, "international" patenting, as the dependent variable in our statistical analysis. International patenting is measured by the number of patents granted to a nation's inventors in 2001 and 2002 by the United States Patent and Trademark Office (USPTO). Two years are employed to smooth out transient year-to-year variations. We employ regression analysis to evaluate the relationship between international patenting and over 30 individual Survey measures that bear on the national innovation environment and corporate practices. The regression analysis allows us to assign *relative* weights to individual variables. We use these weights to calculate subindexes of each nation's innovative capacity and combine these into an overall ranking. This procedure ensures that country-level assessment of innovative capacity is closely tied to measures that have a demonstrated statistical relationship to long-term innovative performance.

We employ USPTO patents in constructing the dependent variable for several reasons.[3] First, when a foreign inventor files for a US patent, it is a sign of the innovation's potential economic value because of the costs involved. Patents with significant economic consequences are highly likely to be filed in the United States because it is the world's largest market. Second, the US patent system tests inventions against the global technology frontier and offers a common standard comparable across innovations.[4]

The use of Survey data to measure the innovation environment raises some methodological questions. Survey data are the only alternative because there are no quantitative data at all available on most of the areas measured, much less for a meaningful number of countries, so that Survey data are the only alternative. However, it is important to establish that the Survey responses capture meaningful cross-country differences. Each country-level Executive Opinion Survey measure is computed as the *average* response by respondents within each country. To assess the reliability of this approach, we conducted an analysis of variance (ANOVA) for each Survey measure. We regressed individual Survey responses on a complete set of country-level dummy variables, calculating the share of variation across individual responses) that result from systematic country-level differences. The results are reported in Appendix A.

Considering that there is an average of more than 70 respondents per country included in the final sample, there is substantial within-country consensus. For most measures, between one-quarter and one-half of the overall variation in responses is explained by country-specific differences. For example, more than 45 percent of the dispersion across respondents from all countries on "Effectiveness of intellectual property protection in promoting innovation" reflects country-specific consensus. As a result of this substantial within-country consensus, country averages are meaningfully different from each other; for each of the 34 GCR measures employed in this chapter, the ANOVA analyses statistically rejects equality of the country-level means. By aggregating across the large number of individual respondents within each country, country-level averages isolate the meaningful differences across countries in the competitiveness environment, limiting idiosyncratic biases. Since variation in the number of Survey responses per country and the degree of consensus within countries are important concerns when conducting multivariate regression analysis, we also checked the robustness of our country rankings by weighting the key regressions by the number of respondents and the degree of consensus within each country. The results remain virtually unchanged.[5]

Determinants of innovative capacity across countries

We first regress the average level of international patenting in 2001 and 2002 in a sample of 78 countries, on three base variables: (1) total population, (2) the number of scientists and engineers employed within the nation, and (3) the "stock" of international patents generated by a country between 1981 and 1995.[6] The control for population focuses the analysis on per capita rates of international patenting; it is a nation's intensity of innovation, controlling for country size, that should matter for its international competitiveness.[7] The number of scientists and engineers is a baseline measure of the effort devoted to innovative activity. Historical patenting is a control variable for historical technological sophistication, as well as differences across countries in the propensity to patent inventions in the United States.[8] Both the number of technological personnel and the patent stock vary substantially across countries and time. For example, the percentage of the workforce represented by scientists and engineers is three times higher in Japan than in Italy or Spain, though their national living standards are similar. Over 90 percent of the total variance in international patenting across the world can be explained by the three baseline variables.

The *scientific and engineering manpower subindex*, measured as the share of total employment accounted for by scientist and engineering employment, captures the impact of the R&D workforce on innovative capacity.

Despite the explanatory power of the baseline variable, countries vary according to whether their realized level of patenting falls above or below the level predicted by the baseline variables. Figure 4 presents the "gap" between the actual level of patenting and the level predicted by the baseline model as a percentage of the predicted level. Some countries, particularly East Asian economies such as Hong Kong, Singapore, and Korea, have patenting levels well above that predicted by the baseline model. India and China also realize a level of patenting well in excess of what would have been predicted by the baseline model. Others nations, such as France and Russia, are substantially below the baseline. The largest positive deviations in absolute terms are associated with the United States, Finland, and Japan.

The remainder of our analysis focuses on explaining these gaps between predicted and realized international innovation performance. We incorporated 34 Survey measures related to innovative capacity, divided into four groupings: those bearing on innovation-related public policies (eg, the effectiveness of intellectual property protection, the effectiveness of competition policy), those assessing the cluster innovation environment (eg, the sophistication of local buyers, the quality of local suppliers), those measuring the strength of linkages, and those bearing on the degree of innovation orientation in company operations and strategies. The complete list of national innovative capacity measures and baseline regressions, including each individual measure, is reported in Appendix B.

We introduce each variable, one at a time, into the baseline specification. Out of the 34 measures, all are positive and statistically significant.[9] In other words, even after controlling for the size of a country, the aggregate level of resources devoted to innovation and the stock of past ideas to build on, a series of measures of the national innovation environment are strongly associated with the level of innovative output actually realized by countries.

To calculate an innovative capacity index, it was not feasible to include all 34 variables in a multivariate regression analysis. The reason is straightforward: nearly all of the measures are highly correlated with each other and our analysis relies on a single cross-section of 78 countries. For measures addressing similar parts of the business environment (eg, domestic competition), the correlation sometimes reaches over .9. Rather than attempt to disentangle the distinct effects associated with each measure, we create a parsimonious specification using a few key variables drawn from the range of variables relevant to each subindex. The regressions results, along with all other subindex regressions, are reported in Appendix C.

Figure 4: Actual and predicted international patenting (as a percent of predicted international patenting)

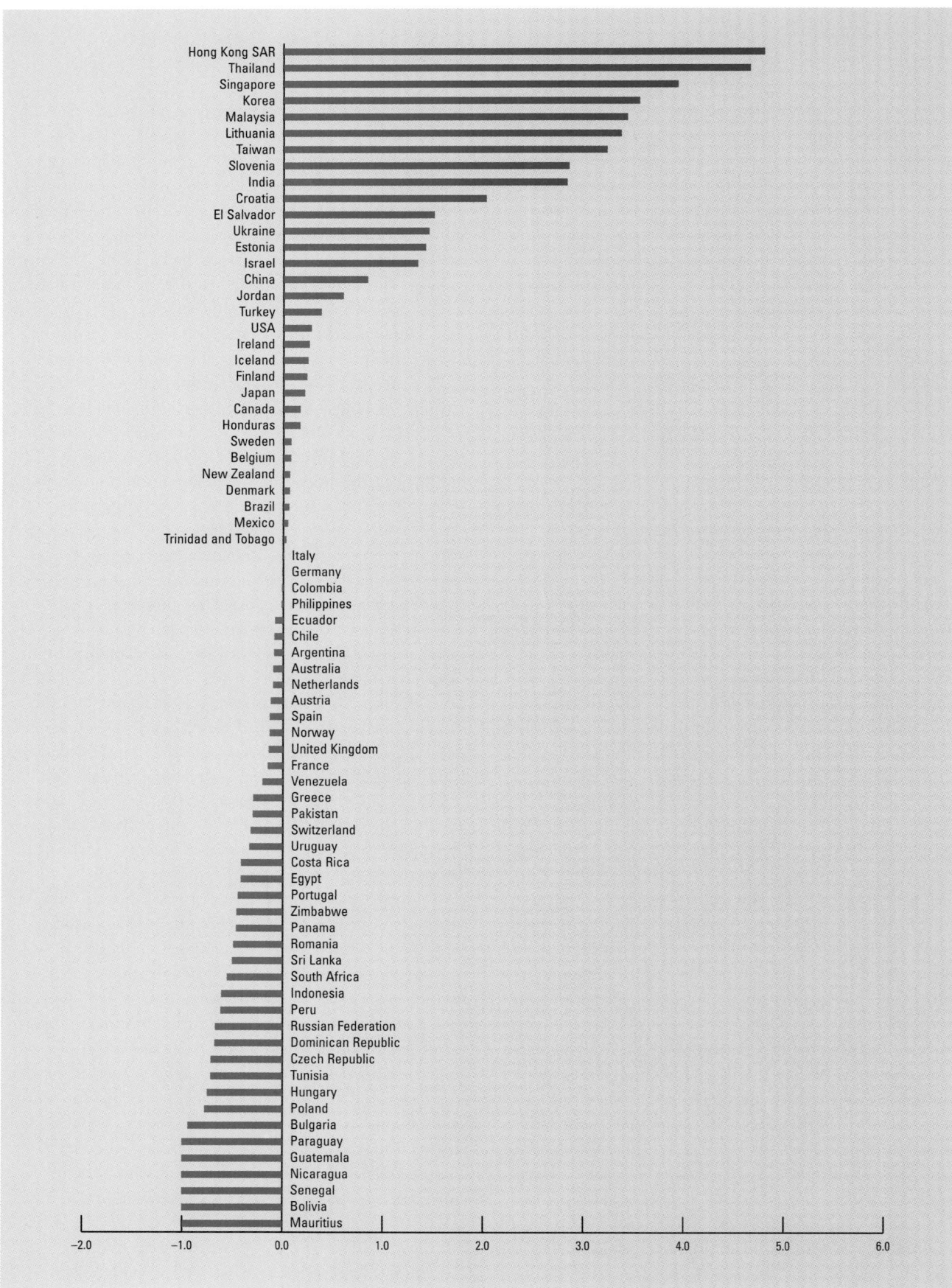

The innovation policy subindex

Three measures were selected to capture the innovation policy environment, each with a strong and robust relationship to international patenting:

- The effectiveness of intellectual property protection
- The size and availability of R&D tax credits and subsidies for the private sector
- Costs of tariff restrictions

These three variables were added to the baseline regression. The innovation policy subindex for a country is calculated as the weighted sum of the three measures, where the weights are based on the regression coefficients for each measure in the specification presented in Appendix C.

Together, these measures are highly statistically significant, and each is predicted to have a substantial impact on the level of international patenting.[10] For example, increasing the Survey response on the availability of R&D tax credits from 4 to 5 (one standard deviation) is associated with over a 35 percent increase in a country's level of international patenting.

The third column of Table 1 presents country rankings on the innovation policy subindex. Singapore registers the highest ranking, followed by Finland, the United States, and Australia. Three non-OECD economies (Singapore, Israel and Taiwan) are among the top 5. All the remaining countries in the top 10 are OECD nations, including Canada, the United Kingdom, France, and Germany. Despite weakness in the size of its science and engineering workforce, Malaysia shows particular strength in innovation policy (ranking 16th), recording well above the sample mean on each of three components of the subindex calculation.

A number of OECD economies, including Italy and New Zealand, lag substantially behind in terms of innovation policy. There is an increasing gap between countries in their willingness and ability to implement innovation-oriented policy reforms. Still other OECD countries exhibit *relative weakness* in this area, compared to their rankings on other subindexes. In particular, both Japan and Switzerland register an overall innovative capacity ranking in the top 10 but are ranked outside of the top 15 in terms of innovation policy.

The innovation policy subindex rankings also reveal substantial variation across broad geographic regions. For example, Latin American nations exhibit a weak innovation policy record relative to their overall level of competitiveness. All Latin American innovation policy rankings are below the top 35, and the innovation policy environment of even the more advanced Latin American economies, such as Argentina and Venezuela, are ranked in the bottom quartile in terms of their innovation policy ranking. Eastern European economies such as Russia and Poland also lag substantially behind in terms of implementing an effective innovation policy agenda, despite their large pools of scientific and engineering personnel. Interestingly, all of the former eastern European satellite countries rank higher in terms of innovation policy than does the Russian Federation itself. This weakness is consistent with the overall competitiveness problems continuing to plague Russia.

India and China, often cited as emerging innovation economies, register innovation policy rankings far below that of the main OECD economies (both are outside of the top 40). Both China and India are outside of the top 50 in terms of "the effectiveness of intellectual property protection," a crucial aspect of national innovation policy. Similar weaknesses are apparent in nearly all of the individual measures associated with the innovation policy environment. Both China and India have yet to establish the type of innovation policy environment found in emerging innovators such as Singapore and Israel.

The cluster innovation environment subindex

A similar methodology underlies the cluster innovation environment subindex. We selected three measures relating to the quality of the cluster environment in a nation's clusters:[11]

- The sophistication of domestic customers
- The extent of locally based competition
- The extent of product and process collaboration

Together, these measures are statistically significant and each has a quantitatively significant impact on the rate of international patenting, even after controlling for population, the historical propensity to innovate, and the size of the R&D workforce. The cluster innovation environment subindex is calculated by adding together these three factors, using the weights calculated in the regression (reported in Appendix C).

Six countries form "top tier" in terms of the cluster innovation environment, including (in order of ranking), Japan, the United States, Finland, Germany, Italy, and Taiwan. Among OECD economies, both Japan and Italy register relatively high rankings on the cluster subindex (compared with their ranking on other dimensions). The United Kingdom and Sweden record a relatively low ranking in this area.

Perhaps the most striking finding is that several emerging Asian economies demonstrate considerable strength in terms of cluster vitality. Taiwan, Korea, and Hong Kong all place within the top 20, outdistancing more mature economies such as the Netherlands. As well, a number of large Asian economies—including Malaysia, China, India, Thailand, and Vietnam—have begun to demonstrate measurable improvement in their cluster innovation environment. For example, though China's overall innovation ranking slipped from 36 to 40 from 2002 to 2003, China's cluster environment places 26th overall, ahead of some OECD economies such as Spain and Portugal. Overall, the East Asian economies are well positioned compared with most eastern European and Latin American economies, where cluster development continues at a relatively low level.

These patterns highlight meaningful and subtle differences in the sources of innovation across countries. Traditional analyses often assume that a strong innovation policy environment is a precondition for the development of dynamic clusters. However, the pattern observed in emerging Asian economies suggests that innovation-oriented cluster development can *precede* the establishment of a world-class innovation policy environment, driven in the case of China and India by inward foreign investment. Indeed, the growth of world-class clusters can itself spur the enactment of a more effective innovation policy regime, including the establishment of more effective intellectual property protection and the suspension of trade and regulatory barriers. The development of a robust innovation policy environment coevolves with cluster growth, a dynamic not captured using standard data sources.

The linkages subindex

This subindex measures the strength of linkages between the common innovation infrastructure and a country's clusters and firms. Perhaps the most difficult area to measure of the drivers of national innovative capacity, it reflects the subtle but crucial collaboration between public and private institutions and firm investments. Given the limited number of measures, this subindex is based on just two Survey measures closely associated with the process by which a country's innovation resources are directed toward the needs of individual clusters and firms:

- The local availability of specialized research and training institutions
- The availability of venture capital for innovative but risky projects

The availability of specialized research and training institutions highlights the importance of leading universities and other independent research institutions in fostering linkages. The availability of venture capital reflects the role of venture capital providers in seeking out commercializable research and moving it to the marketplace. Each measure is statistically and quantitatively significant in its predicted impact on the rate of international patenting. The linkages subindex is the weighted sum of the two linkages measures, with the weights determined by the regression coefficients reported in Appendix C.

Countries also vary widely in their ability to foster collaboration between the public and private sectors. As reported in the fifth column of Table 1, the United States stands out at the top of this ranking, followed by Finland, the United Kingdom, and Israel. Even during a period in which the Israeli economy is threatened, linkages have so far remained strong. Japan and Germany both exhibit weakness in this area, relative to their overall innovation rankings, registering outside of the top 10. Japan's weakness in fostering linkages is symptomatic of the broader failure of public-private interaction within the Japanese economy. Continued macroeconomic stagnation has its roots, in part, in the inability to leverage Japanese cluster strength as a springboard for broader microeconomic reform.

No emerging economy except Israel ranks in the top 10 on linkages. Relative weakness in this area is endemic in East Asia, Latin America, and eastern Europe. This is not surprising. Most developing countries have weak research institutions and also perhaps a history of sharp divisions across government, business, and universities. The development of linkages requires policy attention, resource investments, institution building, and attitude shifts that require patience and perseverance. This slow process contrasts with the relative speed in instituting policy choices such as R&D tax credits.

The company operations and strategy subindex

The final subindex measures the extent to which company strategies and operating practices are oriented toward innovation versus other modes of competing. The national environment shapes the opportunities and constraints that firms face when setting strategy, but managers must act on these through their choices. By choosing strategies based on innovation, companies link their competitive advantage to the innovative capacity of their local environment. We take advantage of three nuanced Survey measures to capture the impact of corporate practices on innovative capacity:

- The degree to which competitive advantage depends on introducing unique goods and services
- The extent and sophistication of marketing
- The degree to which pay is linked to productivity

At its heart, innovation-oriented strategies result from a choice by managers to seek competitive advantage from sustained introduction of unique products and services rather than rely on low-cost inputs. Premising strategy on innovation affects all aspects of a company's business, from product positioning to internal organization. The second and third measures capture other practices that support innovation-based strategies. As in the other subindexes, each measure is statistically and quantitatively linked to the rate of international patenting. As in the prior subindexes, the company operations and strategy subindex is the weighted sum of these three measures, with the weights determined by the regression coefficients reported in Appendix C.

As reported in Table 1, the United States leads this ranking, followed closely by Switzerland and the United Kingdom. A number of countries are closely bunched together in a second tier, including several European countries such as Germany and Denmark. Relative to the other subindexes, Finland and Australia register poor performance in this area, while Hong Kong achieves its strongest subindex ranking. Four emerging economies—Hong Kong, Singapore, Taiwan, and Israel—are within the top 15, suggesting that innovation-oriented firm strategies and operating practices are not limited to historically advanced economies.

Although there should be a positive relationship between the quality of the innovation environment and the innovation orientation of firm strategies, the relationship is far from automatic as firms may fail to recognize or have the skills to take advantage of national assets. To gain insight into this complex relationship, Figures 5a, b, and c show the relationship between the company operations and strategy subindex and the other subindexes.

The innovation orientation of local companies leads the innovative environment indicators in some countries. In other countries, companies do not seem to be taking full advantage of the innovative capacity of their local environment. For example, though the Swiss innovation environment ranks outside the top 10, Swiss companies remain focused on innovation-oriented strategies (and are ranked second along this dimension). In contrast, Australia's companies lag behind the quality of the local innovation environment. Similarly, in the large Asian economies of China, Vietnam, Malaysia, and India, company operations and strategy lag far behind cluster rankings. In order for such countries to move beyond low-cost manufacturing, individual firms within these countries will need to take better advantage of emerging cluster strengths.

Ranking overall innovative capacity

The national innovative capacity index, reported as the first column of Table 1, is calculated as the unweighted sum of the five subindexes:

- Science and engineering manpower subindex
- The innovation policy subindex
- The cluster innovation environment subindex
- The innovation linkages subindex
- The company operations and strategy subindex

The United States ranks first, as the result of leadership in two of the five subindexes and a position within the top 5 rankings in all of the subindexes. Finland is a close second, outperforming the United States in terms of science and engineering manpower and innovation policy subindexes. The United Kingdom and Japan round out the first tier, with almost identical overall scores. The remainder of the top 10 countries are closely bunched in terms of their absolute scores; only small differences distinguish the second tier of international innovators. The only non-OECD economies among the top 10 is Singapore, which has maintained a top 10 innovative capacity ranking for each of the last three years. A third tier, composed of another 13 countries (from the Netherlands [11th] to New Zealand [23rd]), are also closely bunched, with small differences in the absolute scores for this group of countries determining the relative positioning within the group.

These findings strongly confirm our earlier research and research by others on patterns of international innovation. Over the past quarter century, the set of leading innovator economies has expanded to include as many as 15 European economies (including nearly all the nations of Northern Europe) as well as several emerging economies, highlighted by the presence of 4 Asian nations within the top 20. Although OECD nations continue to be responsible for the great majority of global innovation, a growing number of emerging economies have achieved the conditions to support innovation. Overall, since the end of the Cold War, steady "convergence" in innovation achievement has resulted from a substantial upgrading in the innovation environment in a group of about 25 nations.

While the remainder of the world lags in innovative capacity, a number of countries are beginning to show positive signs. The large Asian economies, notably China and India, are still at an early stage of development in terms of innovation at the global frontier. Their strength in cluster development, however, has not yet been balanced with improvements in innovation policy or company behavior.

In contrast, despite improvements in macroeconomic stability over the past two decades in Latin America and positive political and economic changes in eastern Europe, these areas of the world do not yet offer environments conducive to innovation at the global frontier. In eastern Europe, a large pool of scientists and engineers has not yet led to comprehensive strategies to develop innovative capacity; as a result these nations continue to register unfulfilled promise. Similarly, African nations as yet have the ability only to absorb and develop technologies applicable to the local market; none is ranked within the top 30. Even South Africa underperforms on innovation relative to its overall level of economic development.

Figure 5a: The relation between company innovation orientation and innovation policy

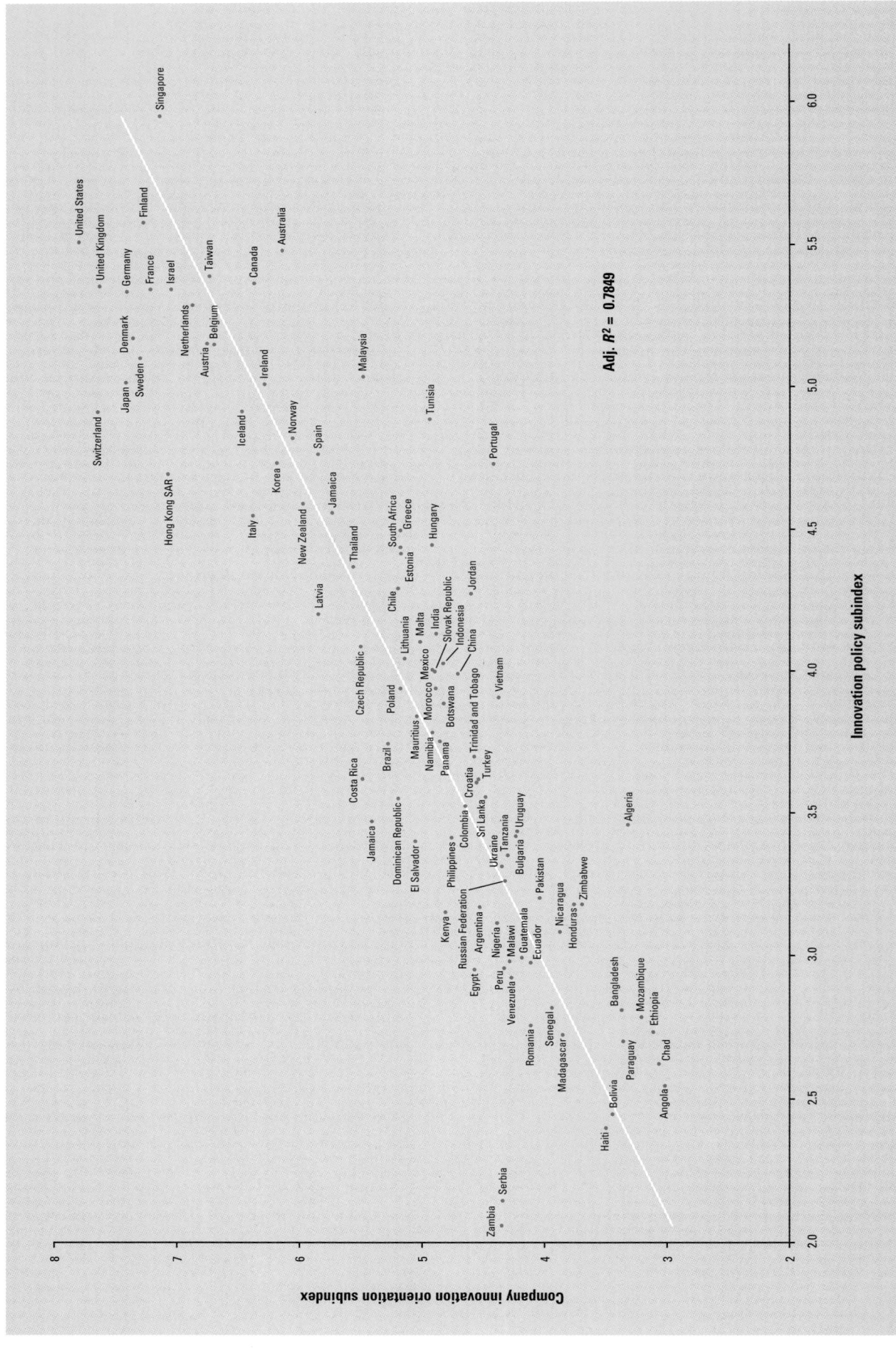

Figure 5b: The relation between company innovation orientation and cluster environment

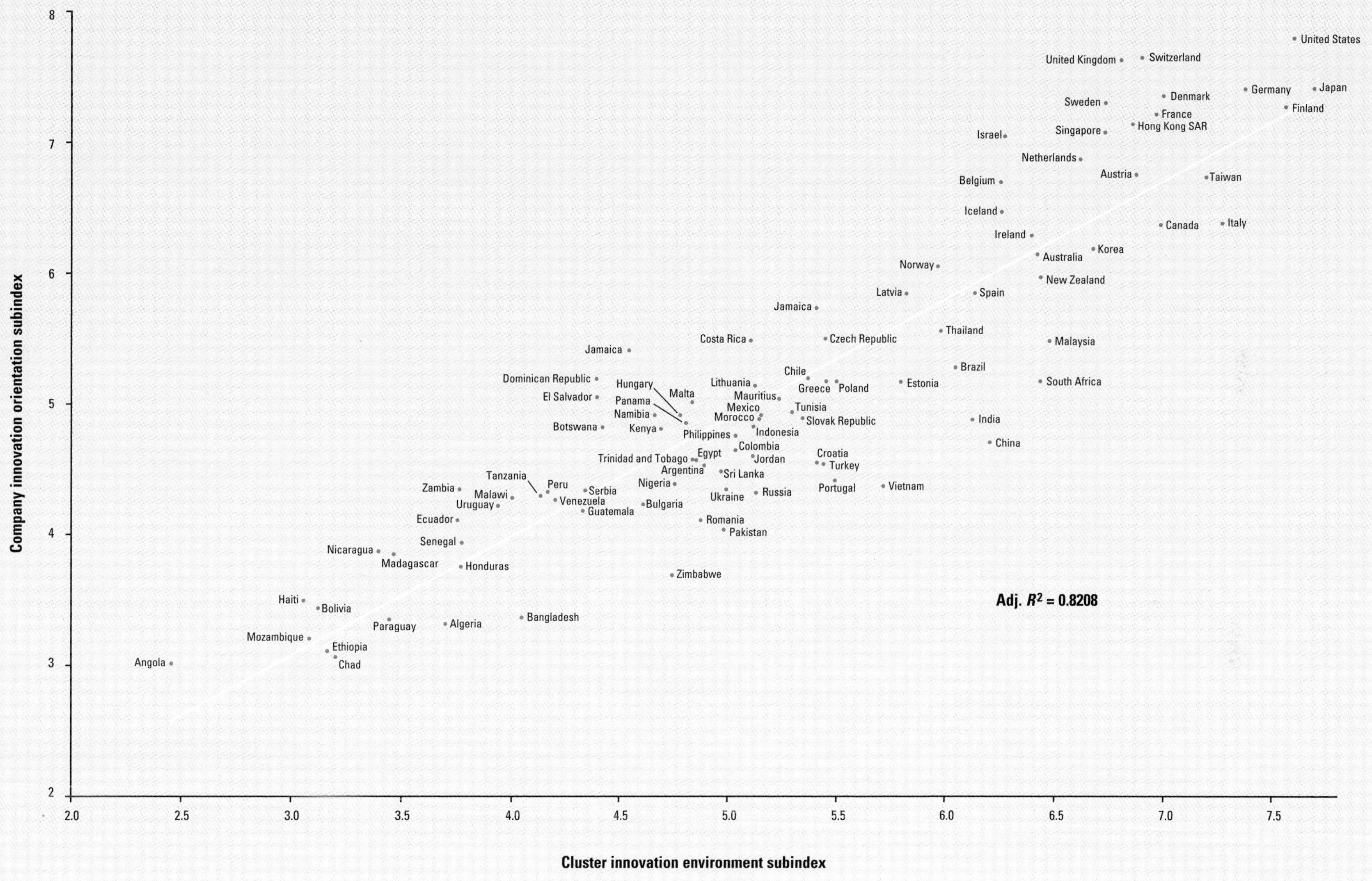

Figure 5c: The relation between company innovation orientation and innovation linkages

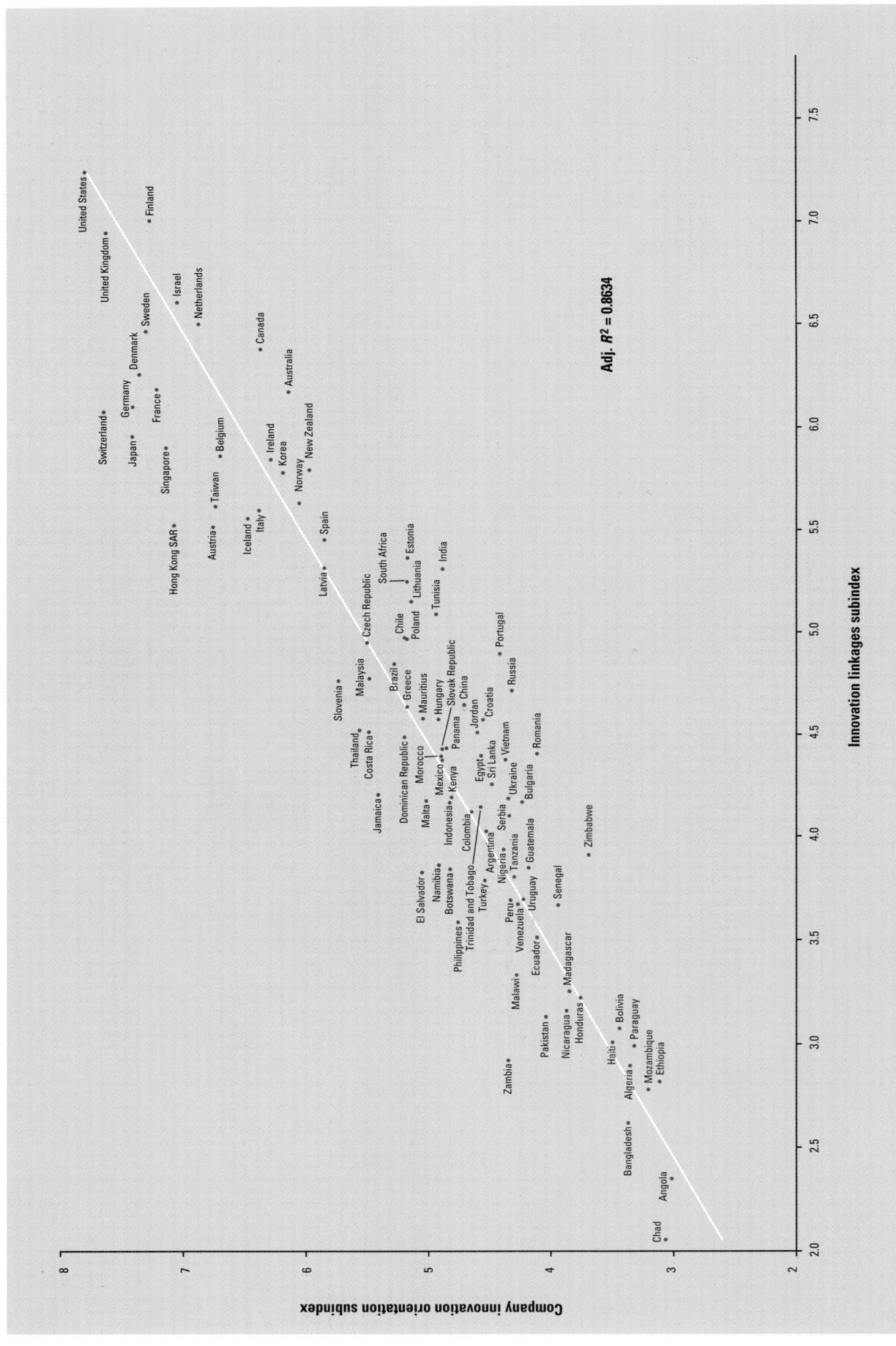

The subindexes differ in the extent of variation across countries and thus in their relative impact on the overall innovative capacity ranking. Particularly for more mature countries, the innovation policy subindex exhibits the least amount of variation: the essential elements of effective innovation policy have diffused widely, eroding the ability to achieve global innovation leadership purely through policy differentiation. In contrast, the gap in innovative capacity among top-tier countries is driven by large differences in the linkages and company operations and strategy subindexes. Differences among middle-tier innovation economies (ranking from 20th to 40th overall in innovative capacity) are more closely linked to differences in the cluster innovation environment and the science and engineering manpower subindexes.

To gain insight into how innovative capacity has shifted around the globe, Table 2 provides a comparison of the national innovative capacity index (NICI) for 2002 and 2003. To make the results comparable, we use the data for each year but impose the same model for both years. In other words, we re-calculated innovative capacity rankings for 2002 using last year's data but the model developed for this year's ranking.

Across the world, absolute innovative capacity has shown a very slight improvement. With the average rate of increase equal to 0.13 (and with a standard deviation of 0.10), the change in innovative capacity over the past year is extremely modest and statistically insignificant. In contrast to the 2002 *Report*, where nearly all countries experienced year-to-year improvement (the average level of improvement was more than 3), more than 30 countries experienced a decline in the absolute value of measured innovative capacity between 2002 and 2003 (out of 71 countries for which the comparison was feasible). For example, the level of the index for Hungary declined by more than 2, leading to a ranking decline from 28 to 39.

Overall, the relative rankings of most countries have remained relatively stable, with most OECD economies maintaining their relative standing. While the top 5 nations (the United States, Finland, the United Kingdom, Japan, and Germany) are the same for both years, three countries—the United States, the United Kingdom, and Germany—register an absolute decline in the index. Where the United States had a large lead in 2002 (the absolute level of the index for the United States is more than 2.2 units higher than it is for any other country), its lead has moderated in 2003. Since the majority of countries within the top 25 improve their absolute score, additional convergence between first-tier and second-tier innovator economies has occurred.

Innovative capacity, competitiveness, and prosperity

We are now in a position to explore the complex interplay between innovative capacity, competitiveness, and economywide prosperity. We begin, in Figures 6 and 7, by comparing the Innovative Capacity ranking with the overall Business Competitiveness Index and with GDP per Capita, a summary measure of prosperity.

The innovative capacity index is highly correlated with the overall Business Competitiveness Index (the correlation is just over 0.9). A high level of innovative capacity is integral to achieving the high levels of productivity necessary to achieve and sustain overall competitiveness.

Innovative capacity and competitiveness are related even for lower-income countries. The incentive and ability to embrace new technology is now a sine qua non of international competition. Although most countries are positioned quite close to the regression line, interesting groups of outliers stand out. Although Finland and the United States are only marginally ahead of other countries in terms of overall competitiveness, these two countries demonstrate a decided advantage with respect to innovative capacity. As well, though Japan's overall competitiveness ranks outside of the top 10, its innovative capacity remains strong. As mentioned earlier, Japan continues to suffer from an inability to leverage its strengths in science and engineering and in cluster development given financial market and other weaknesses.

The largest discrepancies between the level of innovative capacity and the level of competitiveness arise in a group of eastern European countries (Ukraine, Romaine, Bulgaria, and Russia), that score much lower on competitiveness than on innovative capacity because of their substantial science and engineering workforces. A major disappointment of the post–Cold War era has been the inability of the former Soviet bloc nations to take advantage of their legacy and upgrade innovative capacity. An even bigger disappointment has been their slow progress on overall competitiveness.

Thailand is a distinct outlier in the opposite direction, with a level of competitiveness substantially above its measured level of innovative capacity. Thailand still largely competes as a low-cost assembler. Its relative weakness in innovative capacity highlights its challenges in evolving from its low-cost position to establish a path toward long-term prosperity.

Turning to the comparison between innovative capacity and GDP per capita, the relationship is still strong but not as close as the relationship with competitiveness. A number of distinct development models seem to be present, even among leading nations. Some advanced economies, such as Finland, Israel, (and perhaps even South Korea), have developed a level of innovative capacity *ahead of the overall competitiveness of the economy*. In these countries, increases in innovative capacity reflected

Table 2: National innovative capacity index rankings, 2002 versus 2003

Country	2002 IC (Using 2003 Formula)	2003 IC	Change in Innovative Capacity (2003–2002)	Country	2002 IC (Using 2003 Formula)	2003 IC	Change in Innovative Capacity (2003–2002)
United States	37.21	36.60	–0.61	Ecuador	18.26	18.78	0.52
Finland	34.92	35.96	1.04	Honduras	17.71	18.28	0.57
United Kingdom	35.55	34.63	–0.92	Nicaragua	18.95	17.80	–1.14
Japan	33.98	34.62	0.64	Paraguay	18.13	17.04	–1.09
Germany	34.48	34.29	–0.19	Bangladesh	17.66	16.94	
Singapore	32.45	34.19	1.74	Bolivia	17.14	16.32	
Sweden	33.59	34.02	0.43	Madagascar	n/a	15.81	
Denmark	32.70	33.95	1.24	Senegal	n/a	14.81	
Switzerland	33.57	33.73	0.16	Algeria	n/a	n/a	
France	33.14	33.63	0.49	Angola	n/a	n/a	
Netherlands	33.04	33.14	0.10	Botswana	n/a	n/a	
Canada	33.23	33.11	–0.12	Chad	n/a	n/a	
Taiwan	32.34	32.84	0.50	Ethiopia	n/a	n/a	
Israel	32.56	32.64	0.08	Haiti	n/a	n/a	
Australia	32.40	32.37	–0.03	Jamaica	n/a	n/a	
Austria	32.75	32.05	–0.70	Kenya	n/a	n/a	
Belgium	33.34	31.96	–1.37	Malawi	n/a	n/a	
Iceland	30.88	31.86	0.98	Malta	n/a	n/a	
Ireland	31.14	31.24	0.10	Morocco	n/a	n/a	
Korea	30.59	31.13	0.54	Mozambique	n/a	n/a	
Italy	31.26	30.86	–0.40	Namibia	n/a	n/a	
Norway	30.93	30.80	–0.12	Nigeria	n/a	n/a	
New Zealand	29.59	30.55	0.95	Serbia	n/a	n/a	
Spain	30.16	29.77	–0.39	Tanzania	n/a	n/a	
Hong Kong SAR	28.73	28.57	–0.16	Zambia	n/a	n/a	
Estonia	27.59	28.42	0.83	**AVERAGE CHANGE**			**0.13**
South Africa	27.16	28.38	1.22				
Latvia	25.14	28.17	3.03				
Slovenia	29.00	28.16	–0.84				
Czech Republic	27.43	27.27	–0.15				
Lithuania	26.37	27.08	0.71				
Greece	26.25	27.01	0.76				
Portugal	28.06	26.90	–1.16				
Poland	26.27	26.87	0.60				
Malaysia	26.20	26.85	0.65				
Slovak Republic	26.13	26.12	–0.01				
Jordan	n/a	26.09	n/a				
Tunisia	25.05	26.03	0.98				
Hungary	28.08	26.00	–2.08				
China	26.06	25.86	–0.20				
Chile	25.84	25.75	–0.09				
Brazil	26.61	25.70	–0.91				
Russian Federation	25.32	25.59	0.27				
India	25.24	25.52	0.28				
Croatia	25.46	25.23	–0.23				
Costa Rica	25.50	25.01	–0.49				
Thailand	25.16	24.74	–0.42				
Mauritius	22.53	24.73	2.20				
Ukraine	23.89	24.51	0.62				
Indonesia	22.09	24.04	1.95				
Mexico	23.13	24.00	0.87				
Vietnam	22.82	23.99	1.17				
Bulgaria	23.28	23.62	0.35				
Turkey	22.80	23.23	0.43				
Egypt	n/a	23.04	n/a				
Argentina	22.96	22.98	0.02				
Romania	23.57	22.97	–0.60				
Panama	22.87	22.68	–0.19				
Sri Lanka	22.84	22.52	–0.32				
Trinidad and Tobago	22.92	22.24	–0.69				
Philippines	21.82	21.99	0.17				
Colombia	21.49	21.84	0.36				
Dominican Republic	23.76	21.58	–2.18				
Uruguay	20.92	20.58	–0.34				
Peru	20.95	20.58	–0.37				
El Salvador	20.34	20.52	0.18				
Venezuela	20.97	20.34	–0.64				
Guatemala	19.49	19.71	0.22				
Pakistan	n/a	19.60	n/a				
Zimbabwe	18.70	19.47	0.77				

(cont'd.)

Figure 6: The relationship between the innovative capacity index and the Business Competitiveness Index

$y = 4.6534x - 164.83$
Adj. $R^2 = 0.9156$

2003 innovative capacity index

2003 Business Competitiveness Index

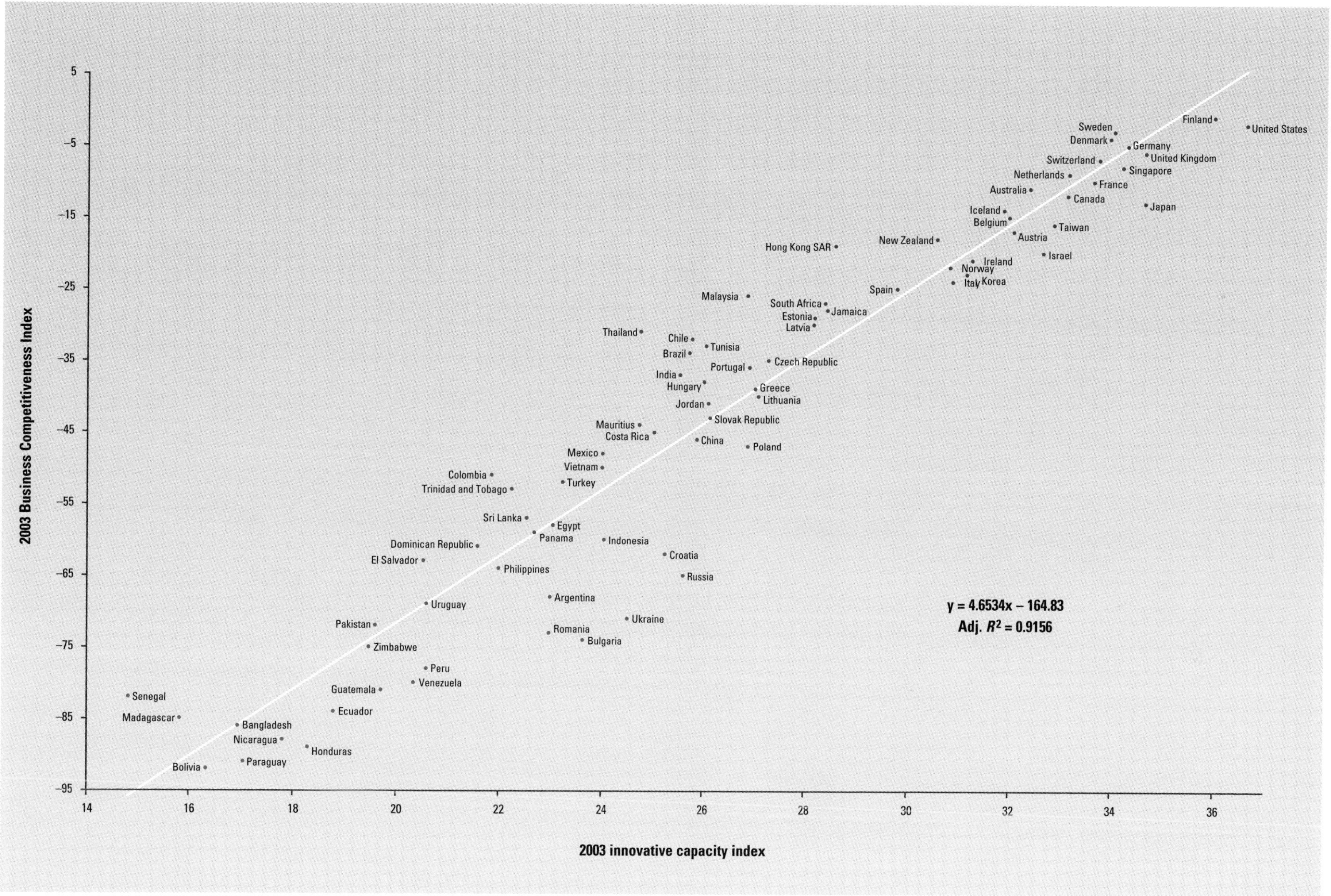

Figure 7: The relationship between the innovative capacity index and GDP per capita

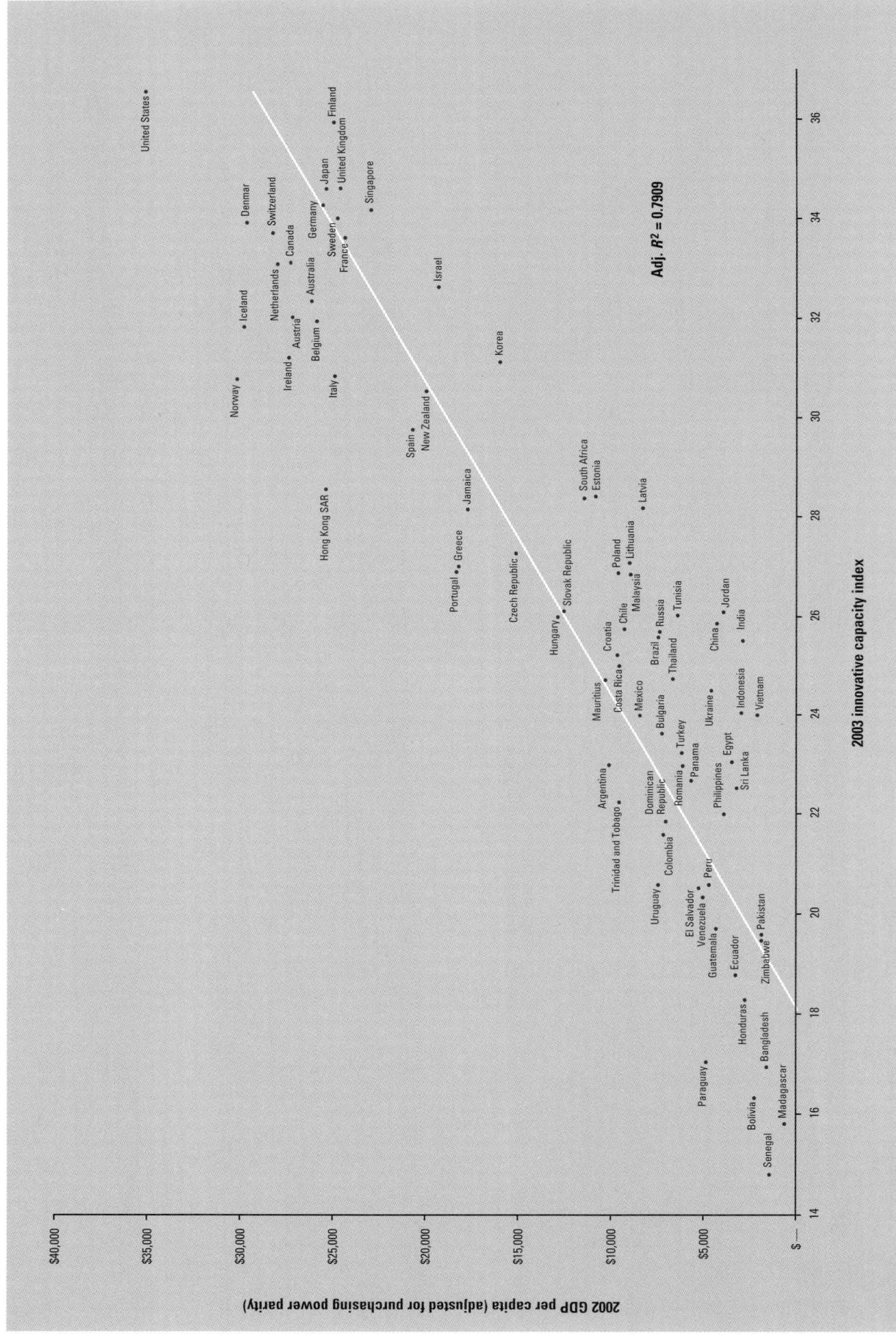

public- and private-sector consensus about the priority of innovation in driving long-term competitiveness. For example, Finland's current prosperity can be tied closely to investments from the early 1980s onward that have nurtured the development of the telecommunications cluster, stepped up investment in basic research, and improved advanced education, among other things.

In contrast, countries such as Norway, Portugal, and Greece have continued to rely on favorable natural endowments or proximity to major markets. Despite increasing evidence of the role of innovation in long-term prosperity, these countries have as yet made little change in their economic development strategies, raising the possibility of long-term stagnation. Finally, several leading nations, such as France and Germany, are located close to the regression line, suggesting a "balanced" path in which innovative capacity and the overall environment for productivity progress at roughly the same rate.

The United States continues to lead the world in innovative capacity and current GDP per capita.

Policy makers in the United States remain highly focused on innovation at both the Federal and regional levels. Although continued attention bodes well for the United States., several challenges remain. Perhaps most importantly, the pipeline of undergraduate and graduate students choosing to pursue scientific and engineering careers continues to diminish. The continued availability of a well-trained innovator workforce thus depends on the continued attractiveness of the United States to foreign scientists and engineers. However, convergence between the United States and other countries in terms of innovative capacity may reduce the viability of this strategy. The supply of scientific and technical personnel represent the greatest threat to US leadership.

Creating versus absorbing new technology

Although innovative capacity and competitiveness are correlated even among countries with low incomes, the initial challenge for developing countries is normally to access and exploit technology from elsewhere. Effective technology absorption may well be a precursor to the development of innovative capacity revealed by international patenting. Many of the same attributes affect the ability to absorb technology as affect the ability to create technology. However, it is revealing to separate the two, especially for lower-income nations.

For all countries below median income in our example (less than US$8,900 per year), we computed a "technology absorptive capacity" score by adding together Survey responses to two questions:

- The prevalence of foreign technology licensing
- The ability to absorb foreign technology

Although imperfect, these measures provide a summary of the extent of accessing foreign technology in a country. We then plot this score against the 2003 National Innovative Capacity Index in Figure 8. Perhaps not surprisingly, there is a close relationship between absorptive and innovative capacity (Figure 8). Although the ability to absorb technology typically precedes the ability to develop global innovation, countries differ in the balance among activities. Notably, among lower-income countries, Thailand and India register the highest absorptive capacity scores but a more modest level of innovative capacity, while China scores relatively high on innovative relative to absorptive capacity. Though most analyses of China and India assume that their aggressive approach to technology reflect similar strategies, these findings suggest a more subtle relationship: India's positioning is based more on *exploiting* global technology while China is making systematic investments (relative to its level of development) in *developing* global technology. However, it is important to emphasize that the source of innovation strength in both of these countries is closely tied to workforce and cluster strengths, rather than to specific government policies or the effectiveness of linkages between the public and private sector.

Figure 9 plots technology absorptive capacity against GDP per capita. The results are revealing. India, Thailand, and Brazil register an ability to exploit global technology far higher than would be predicted by their current level of economic development. Conversely, many other Latin American and Eastern European nations register a low level of technology absorptive capacity relative to income. Interestingly, while China is a bit above the regression line linking absorptive capacity and GDP per capita, China's rapid improvements in per capita income over the last decade has resulted in a position where its ability to absorb foreign technology is now roughly consistent with the level of prosperity it has achieved.

The interplay between absorptive capacity, innovative capacity, and competitiveness is subtle. For countries that have not yet emerged from a low level of economic development, improvements in competitiveness are likely to require capabilities, as well as formal policies and institutions, that facilitate access to and exploitation of the best of global technology. However, although some countries have built upon a baseline level of absorptive capacity in order to develop innovative capacity (such as those in East Asia), other countries remain focused on simply adopting and adapting the world technology frontier. For example, despite a low level of innovative capacity to the present day, Chile improved its competitiveness over the past quarter century through openness to foreign technology and investment. However, recent crises in Latin America and other regions maintaining low levels of innovative capacity highlight the fragility of this strategy. As low-cost locations

Figure 8: The relationship between technology absorptive capacity and innovative capacity, lower-income countries

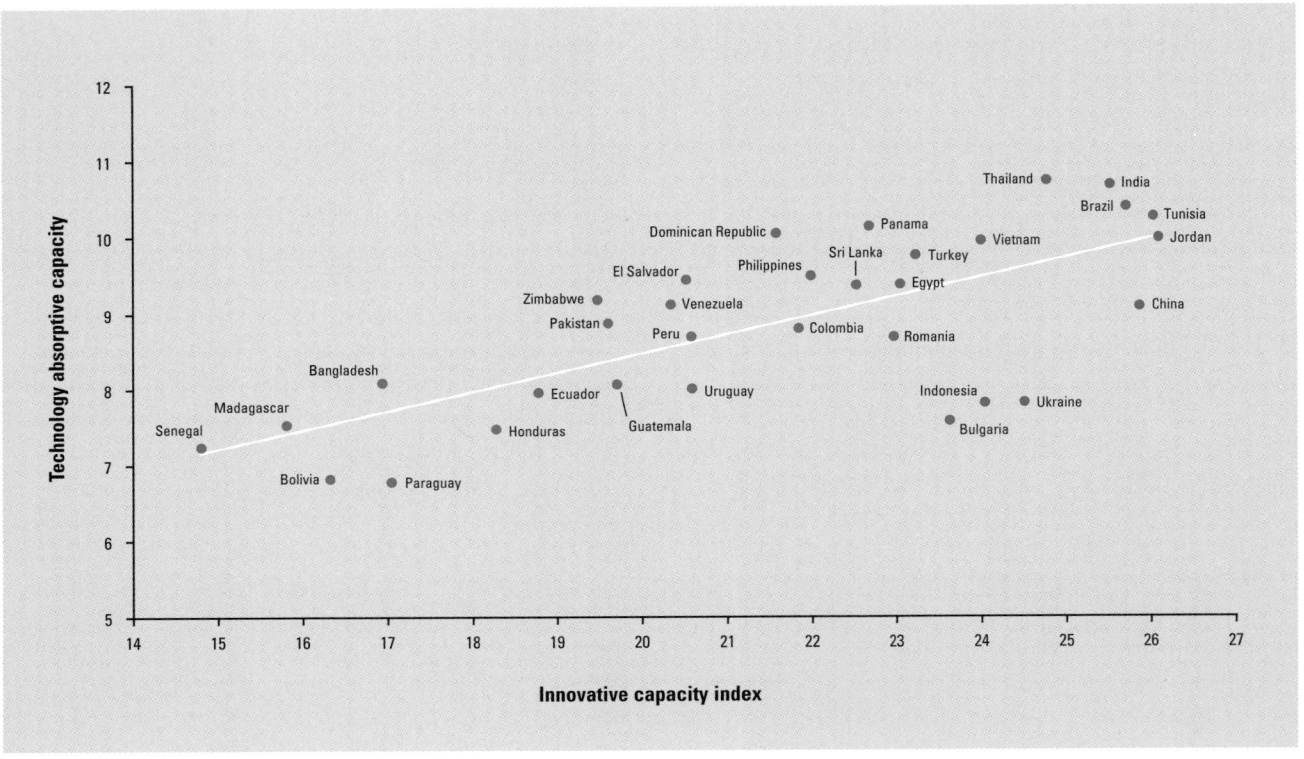

Figure 9: The relationship between technology absorptive capacity and 2002 GDP per capita, lower-income countries

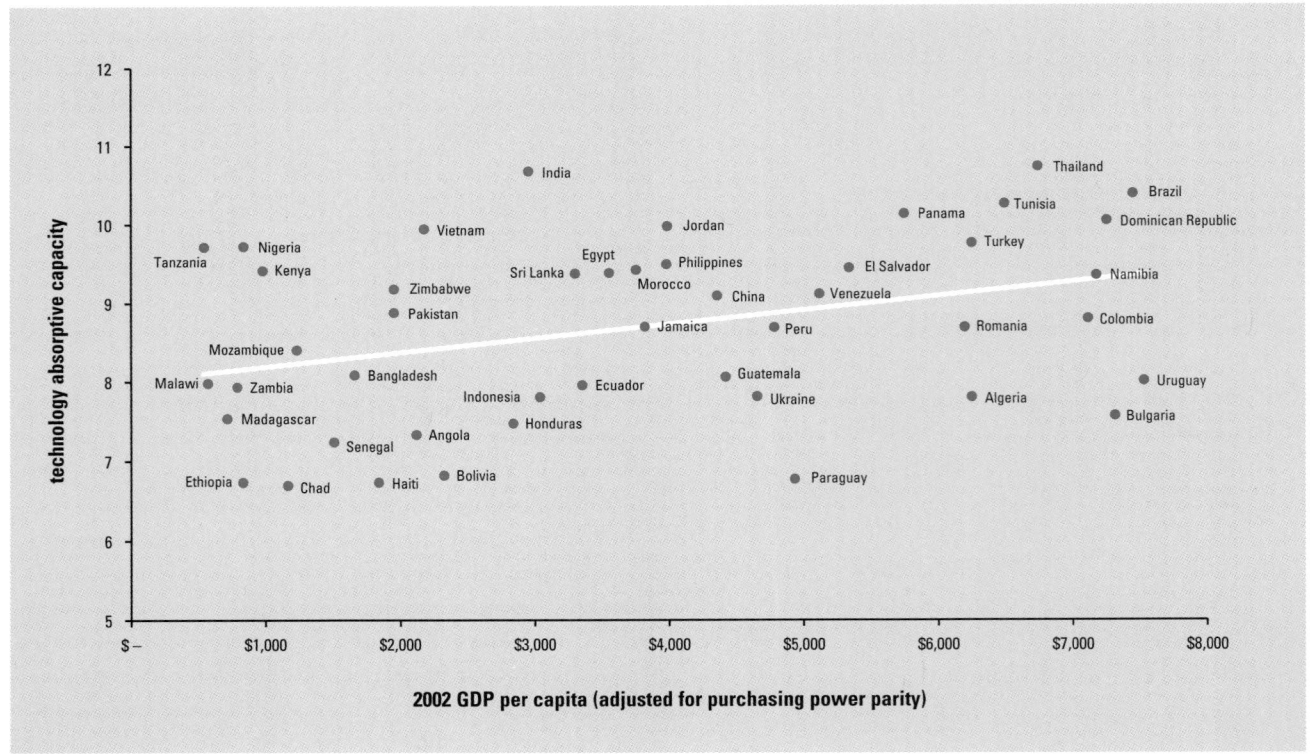

such as China invest aggressively in both absorbing and developing global technology, competitiveness in the absence of innovative capacity has become less sustainable.

Conclusions

Innovation has become perhaps the single most important source of competitiveness in advanced economies, and success in building innovative capacity has a strong relationship to a country's overall competitiveness and level of prosperity. The national innovative capacity framework allows a detailed examination of sources of the large and persistent differences across countries in innovation performance. This chapter provides an assessment of the comparative performance in national innovative capacity around the world in 2003 and provides a scorecard for national policymakers about their relative standing and priorities for policy. Although the data available and feasible statistical procedures are limited by the inherent difficulties in measuring innovation and its causes, the rankings are consistent with our knowledge about individual countries and provide insight into the strengths and challenges facing both advanced and emerging economies.

Those economies, such as Finland and Singapore, that have proactively built innovative capacity have prospered. In contrast, limited investment in innovative capacity has retarded the competitive potential of countries such as Spain and New Zealand. Recent concerns over the rapid movement of innovation-oriented employment away from traditional locations within OECD economies and toward China and India highlight the crucial importance of innovative capacity and cluster development to competitiveness, economic security and prosperity.

Notes

1 For a complete exposition of the national innovative capacity framework, see Furman, Porter, and Stern (2002) and Porter, Stern, and Council on Competitiveness (1999). The term *innovative capacity* has been used extensively in prior research in economics, geography, and innovation policy. For example, Pavitt (1980), along with co-authors at the Sussex Policy Research Unit, employed the term in the economics and innovation policy literature. Suarez-Villa (1990, 1993) provides an articulation of the concept within the geography literature, focusing on the specific linkage between invention and innovation. See Neely and Hii (1998) for a more detailed discussion of the origins and definition of innovative capacity in the academic literature.

2 For a more complete exposition of the diamond framework and its role in understanding the origins of national competitive advantage, see Porter (1990, 1998).

3 Although the systematic use of patent data can be traced back at least to Schmookler (1966), the use of patents has expanded dramatically over the past decade, building on the careful investigations and database development of, among others, Griliches (1984; 1990; 1994). For a thorough discussion of the use of patenting and international patenting data (and alternatives) in studying the causes and consequences of innovation, see Adam Jaffe and Manuel Trajtenberg, *Patents, Citations and Innovation: A Window on the Knowledge Economy*, MIT Press, 2002, as well as J. Furman, M. E. Porter, and S. Stern, "The Determinants of National Innovative Capacity," *Research Policy*, 31(6): 899–933. The use of international patents also has precedent in prior work comparing and assessing international inventive activity (see Dosi, Pavitt, and Soete, 1990; Eaton and Kortum, 1996).

4 Since no single measure of innovation output is ideal, we have explored several alternatives such as the pattern of exports in international high-technology markets and the flow of technology licensing revenues across countries. Overall, international patenting offers by far the best and most consistent measure across time and location.

5 Appendix D reports the rankings from the "weighted" regression specifications. The results for alternative weighting schemes are available by request from the authors.

6 This specification is simply the "ideas" production function, as developed in endogenous growth theory (Romer, 1990). See Porter and Stern (2000) for a full derivation of our empirical formulation.

7 Although controlling for differences in GDP per capita is feasible in this regression (and we have used this formulation in our related work), the focus here is on *explaining* the drivers of prosperity, and so we focus our analysis on measures more closely related to the underlying microeconomic environment.

8 More precisely, we first take the natural logarithm of all of these variables, to smooth out the variation in country size and also to provide for easily interpretable coefficient estimates. Science and engineering resources are drawn from several data sources, as summarized in *World Development Indicators*. Specifically, data for OECD countries are drawn from the OECD Main Science and Technology Indicators, Latin American data are drawn from the RICYT, and the Asian data are drawn primarily from the science and technology statistics from individual countries.

9 Thirty-three of the 34 measures are significant at the 95 percent confidence level; the "Quality of Math and Science Education" measure is only significant at the 90 percent level. Although each of the 34 Survey measures related to innovative capacity framework are positively correlated with the level of international patenting, Survey measures with a more remote relationship to innovation are uncorrelated with the level of patenting. For example, after controlling for the baseline variables, international patenting is uncorrelated with Survey measures such as the "availability of an independent judiciary," "the degree of press censorship," or the "rarity of insider trading."

10 In the multivariate regression, only two of the three innovation policy measures are individually statistically significant. We included these three measures for this subindex as they had the most robust and stable relationship to international patenting when combined with other measures of the innovation policy environment (as listed in Appendix A).

11 This specification differs somewhat from the specification employed in the 2002 innovative capacity index. "The extent of product and process collaboration" measure has been substituted in place of the measure for "the state of cluster development." Although the results are qualitatively similar with either measure, the current specification is more closely tied to the innovative capacity framework and incorporates a more robust and significant statistical relationship with international patenting.

111

References

Dosi, G., K. Pavitt, and L. Soete. 1990. *The Economics of Technical Change and International Trade*. New York: Columbia University Press.

Eaton, J. and S. Kortum. 1996. "Trade in Ideas: Patenting & Productivity in the OECD," *Journal of International Economics*, 40(3-4): 251–278.

Furman, J. L., M. E. Porter, and S. Stern. 2002. "The Determinants of National Innovative Capacity," *Research Policy*, 31(6): 899–933.

Griliches, Z. 1984. *R&D, Patents, and Productivity*. Chicago: University of Chicago Press.

———. 1990. "Patent Statistics as Economic Indicators: A Survey," *Journal of Economic Literature* 92: 630–653.

———. 1994. "Productivity, R&D, and the Data Constraint," *American Economic Review* 84: 1–23.

Jaffe, A. and M. Trajtenberg. 2002. *Patents, Citations and Innovation: A Window on the Knowledge Economy*. Cambridge, MA: MIT Press.

Neely, A. and J. Hii. 1998. "Innovation and Business Performance: A Literature Review," mimeo., Judge Institute of Management Studies, University of Cambridge.

Pavitt, K. 1980. "Industrial R&D and the British Economic Problem," *R&D Management* 10: 149.

Porter, M. E. 1990. *The Competitive Advantage of Nations*. New York: Free Press.

———. 1998. "Clusters and Competition: New Agendas for Companies, Governments, and Institutions," In *On Competition*. Boston, MA: Harvard Business School Press.

Porter, M. E. and S. Stern. 2000. "Measuring the 'Ideas' Production Function," NBER Working Paper WP 7891. Cambridge, MA: National Bureau of Economics Research.

Porter, M. E., S. Stern, and Council on Competitiveness. 1999. *The New Challenge to America's Prosperity: Findings from the Innovation Index*. Washington, C: Council on Competitiveness.

Romer, P. 1990. "Endogenous Technological Change," *Journal of Political Economy*, 98, S71–S102.

Schmookler, J. 1966. *Invention and Economic Growth*. Cambridge, MA: Harvard University Press.

Suarez-Villa, L. 1990. "Invention, Inventive Learning, and Innovative Capacity," *Behavioral Science* 35: 290–310.

———. 1993. "The Dynamics of Regional Invention and Innovation: Innovative Capacity and Regional Change in the Twentieth Century," *Geographical Analysis* 25 (2): 147–164.

Appendix A: ANOVA analysis for each subindex area

	Innovation Policy Subindex	Cluster Subindex	Linkages Subindex	Operations and Strategy Subindex
	Adj. R^2	Adj. R^2	Adj. R^2	Adj. R^2
Intellectual Property Protection	0.4552			
Quality of Math and Science Education	0.4267			
Attractiveness of National Environment for Retaining Talented People	0.3906			
Government R&D Tax Credits and Subsidies	0.3631			
Government Procurement of Advanced Technology Products	0.1905			
Tariff Liberalization	0.2839			
Presence of Demanding Regulatory Standards	0.4913			
Effectiveness of Anti-Trust Policy	0.3425			
Environmental Compliance Helps Long-Run Competitiveness	0.1446			
Buyer Sophistication		0.3560		
Local Supplier Quality		0.4010		
Consumer Adoption of Latest Products		0.2751		
State of Cluster Development		0.2553		
Extent of Product and Process Collaboration		0.2898		
Extent of Locally Based Competitors		0.1852		
Absorption of New Technology			0.1762	
Quality of Scientific Research Institutions			0.3260	
Local Availability of Specialized Research and Training Institutions			0.3106	
University/Industry Research Collaboration			0.2940	
Venture Capital Availability			0.2672	
Nature of Competitive Advantage				0.4034
Value Chain Presence of Exporting Firms				0.4497
Extent of Branding for Exporting Companies				0.4484
Capacity of Innovation				0.4258
Extent of Marketing				0.4312
Degree of Customer Orientation				0.2455
Control of International Distribution				0.1886
Breadth of International Markets				0.4357
Company Spending on R&D				0.3506
Extent of Staff Training				0.3807
Pay Linked to Productivity				0.2132
Willingness to Delegate Authority				0.3228
Reliance on Professional Management				0.3142
Quality of Management Schools				0.3942

Appendix B: Bilateral regressions for each of the four subindex areas

Dependent Variable — Log of U.S. Patents, 2000-2001

Independent Variables	Baseline			Innovation Policy Variables			Cluster Variables			Linkages Variables			Operations and Strategy Variables		
	Coeff	t-stat	adj. R^2	Coeff	t-stat	adj. R^2	Coeff	t-stat	adj. R^2	Coeff	t-stat	adj. R^2	Coeff	t-stat	adj. R^2
Log of Patent Stock Metric (patents issued between 1981 and 1995)	0.783	0.051	0.919												
Log of Population in 2002	0.161	0.081													
Log of Proportion of Full-time Employed Scientists and Engineers	0.351	0.092													
Intellectual Property Protection				0.627	0.119	0.918									
Quality of Math and Science Education				0.285	0.159	0.889									
Attractiveness of National Environment for Retaining Talented People				0.470	0.131	0.903									
Government R&D Tax Credits and Subsidies				0.674	0.131	0.917									
Government Procurement of Advanced Technology Products				0.843	0.167	0.916									
Tariff Liberalization				0.811	0.228	0.902									
Presence of Demanding Regulatory Standards				1.003	0.175	0.922									
Effectiveness of Anti-Trust Policy				0.601	0.155	0.905									
Environmental Compliance Helps Long-Run Competitiveness				1.157	0.222	0.917									
Buyer Sophistication							0.918	0.140	0.929						
Local Supplier Quality							0.949	0.172	0.920						
Consumer Adoption of Latest Products							1.101	0.162	0.931						
State of Cluster Development							0.829	0.143	0.923						
Extent of Product and Process Collaboration							1.092	0.178	0.925						
Extent of Locally Based Competitors							1.120	0.225	0.915						
Absorption of New Technology										1.259	0.179	0.933			
Quality of Scientific Research Institutions										1.087	0.226	0.914			
Local Availability of Specialized Research and Training Institutions										1.199	0.287	0.908			
University/Industry Research Collaboration										1.043	0.154	0.931			
Venture Capital Availability										0.709	0.156	0.911			
Nature of Competitive Advantage													0.801	0.138	0.922
Value Chain Presence of Exporting Firms													0.621	0.115	0.919
Extent of Branding for Exporting Companies													0.856	0.154	0.920
Capacity of Innovation													1.176	0.193	0.925
Extent of Marketing													0.880	0.152	0.922
Degree of Customer Orientation													1.026	0.197	0.917
Control of International Distribution													1.248	0.240	0.917
Breadth of International Markets													0.697	0.119	0.923
Company Spending on R&D													1.016	0.160	0.927
Extent of Staff Training													0.829	0.135	0.925
Pay Linked to Productivity													0.479	0.180	0.895
Willingness to Delegate Authority													0.855	0.149	0.922
Reliance on Professional Management													0.704	0.158	0.910
Quality of Management Schools													0.518	0.158	0.900

Appendix C: Regressions for each of the four subindexes

Innovation Policy Subindex

Regression Statistics

Adj. R^2	0.9227			
Observations	72			

	Coef.	Std. Error	t-stat	P-value
Intercept	−5.7469	1.3536	−4.2500	0.0000
Log (Patent Stock Metric)	0.5646	0.0600	9.4100	0.0000
Log (Population)	0.3656	0.1044	3.5000	0.0010
Log (S&E Proportion)*	0.2803	0.1030	2.7200	0.0080
Intellectual Property Protection	0.3157	0.1683	1.8800	0.0650
Government R&D Tax Credits and Subsidies	0.3685	0.1728	2.1300	0.0370
Tariff Liberalization	0.2798	0.2382	1.1700	0.2440

Cluster Innovation Environment SubIndex

Regression Statistics

Adj. R^2	0.9344			
Observations	73			

	Coef.	Std. Error	t-stat	P-value
Intercept	−6.0751	0.8223	−7.3900	0.0000
Log (Patent Stock Metric)	0.5205	0.0550	9.4700	0.0000
Log (Population)	0.2144	0.0999	2.1500	0.0350
Log (S&E Proportion)*	0.2219	0.0979	2.2700	0.0270
Buyer Sophistication	0.4283	0.2257	1.9000	0.0620
Extent of Locally Based Competitors	0.3633	0.2694	1.3500	0.1820
Extent of Product and Process Collaboration	0.5637	0.2363	2.3900	0.0200

Linkages SubIndex

Regression Statistics

Adj. R^2	0.9161			
Observations	73			

	Coef.	Std. Error	t-stat	P-value
Intercept	−5.5046	0.8331	−6.6100	0.0000
Log (Patent Stock Metric)	0.5430	0.0660	8.2300	0.0000
Log (Population)	0.3121	0.0841	3.7100	0.0020
Log (S&E Proportion)*	0.1762	0.1182	1.4900	0.1410
Local Availability of Specialized Research & Training Institutions	0.7294	0.3209	2.2700	0.0260
Venture Capital Availability	0.4971	0.1782	2.7900	0.0070

Operations and Strategy SubIndex

Regression Statistics

Adj. R^2	0.9354			
Observations	73			

	Coef.	Std. Error	t-stat	P-value
Intercept	−6.9765	0.8000	−8.7200	0.0000
Log (Patent Stock Metric)	0.4188	0.0616	6.8000	0.0000
Log (Population)	0.4765	0.0819	5.8200	0.0000
Log (S&E Proportion)*	0.3573	0.0912	3.9200	0.0000
Nature of Competitive Advantage	0.5163	0.1510	3.4200	0.0010
Extent of Marketing	0.5026	0.1692	2.9700	0.0040
Pay Linked to Productivity	0.2922	0.1449	2.0200	0.0480

* Log of Proportion of Full-Time Employed Scientists and Engineers

Appendix D: Innovative capacity rankings: unweighted versus weighted regressions

The "weighted" rankings employ a weighted regression procedure in the calculation of each subindex, where the weights reflect the degree of within-country consensus. For each question included in a given subindex, we calculated the within-country standard deviation. The regression weighting for each subindex is equal to the inverse of the average of these within-country standard deviations.

Country	Baseline IC rank	Baseline IC index	"Weighted" IC rank (by within-country SD)	"Weighted" IC index (by within-country SD)	Country	Baseline IC rank	Baseline IC index	"Weighted" IC rank (by within-country SD)	"Weighted" IC index (by within-country SD)
United States	1	36.60	1	30.91	Sri Lanka	59	22.52	58	19.02
Finland	2	35.96	2	30.32	Trinidad and Tobago	60	22.24	60	18.70
United Kingdom	3	34.63	5	29.17	Philippines	61	21.99	61	18.43
Japan	4	34.62	3	29.37	Colombia	62	21.84	62	18.22
Germany	5	34.29	6	28.73	Dominican Republic	63	21.58	63	17.95
Singapore	6	34.19	4	29.31	Uruguay	64	20.58	65	17.38
Sweden	7	34.02	8	28.60	Peru	65	20.58	64	17.42
Denmark	8	33.95	7	28.66	El Salvador	66	20.52	67	17.08
Switzerland	9	33.73	9	28.54	Venezuela	67	20.34	66	17.13
France	10	33.63	10	28.35	Guatemala	68	19.71	69	16.40
Netherlands	11	33.14	13	27.82	Pakistan	69	19.60	68	16.44
Canada	12	33.11	12	28.05	Zimbabwe	70	19.47	70	16.18
Taiwan	13	32.84	11	28.12	Ecuador	71	18.78	71	15.72
Israel	14	32.64	14	27.61	Honduras	72	18.28	72	15.37
Australia	15	32.37	15	27.44	Nicaragua	73	17.80	73	15.14
Austria	16	32.05	17	27.06	Paraguay	74	17.04	74	14.41
Belgium	17	31.96	18	27.00	Bangladesh	75	16.94	75	14.34
Iceland	18	31.86	16	27.13	Bolivia	76	16.32	76	13.85
Ireland	19	31.24	19	26.49	Madagascar	77	15.81	77	13.11
Korea	20	31.13	20	26.43	Senegal	78	14.81	78	12.08
Italy	21	30.86	22	25.86	Algeria	n/a	n/a	n/a	n/a
Norway	22	30.80	21	26.15	Angola	n/a	n/a	n/a	n/a
New Zealand	23	30.55	23	25.77	Botswana	n/a	n/a	n/a	n/a
Spain	24	29.77	24	25.13	Chad	n/a	n/a	n/a	n/a
Hong Kong SAR	25	28.57	29	23.77	Ethiopia	n/a	n/a	n/a	n/a
Estonia	26	28.42	25	24.21	Haiti	n/a	n/a	n/a	n/a
South Africa	27	28.38	28	23.90	Jamaica	n/a	n/a	n/a	n/a
Latvia	28	28.17	27	24.04	Kenya	n/a	n/a	n/a	n/a
Slovenia	29	28.16	26	24.14	Malawi	n/a	n/a	n/a	n/a
Czech Republic	30	27.27	30	23.27	Malta	n/a	n/a	n/a	n/a
Lithuania	31	27.08	31	23.11	Morocco	n/a	n/a	n/a	n/a
Greece	32	27.01	32	22.99	Mozambique	n/a	n/a	n/a	n/a
Portugal	33	26.90	34	22.81	Namibia	n/a	n/a	n/a	n/a
Poland	34	26.87	33	22.90	Nigeria	n/a	n/a	n/a	n/a
Malaysia	35	26.85	35	22.77	Serbia	n/a	n/a	n/a	n/a
Slovak Republic	36	26.12	38	22.29	Tanzania	n/a	n/a	n/a	n/a
Jordan	37	26.09	36	22.39	Zambia	n/a	n/a	n/a	n/a
Tunisia	38	26.03	39	22.20					
Hungary	39	26.00	37	22.33					
China	40	25.86	41	22.13					
Chile	41	25.75	42	21.68					
Brazil	42	25.70	43	21.60					
Russian Federation	43	25.59	40	22.18					
India	44	25.52	45	21.31					
Croatia	45	25.23	44	21.49					
Costa Rica	46	25.01	47	21.15					
Thailand	47	24.74	49	20.73					
Mauritius	48	24.73	48	20.84					
Ukraine	49	24.51	46	21.26					
Indonesia	50	24.04	51	20.51					
Mexico	51	24.00	53	20.15					
Vietnam	52	23.99	50	20.71					
Bulgaria	53	23.62	52	20.40					
Turkey	54	23.23	54	19.77					
Egypt	55	23.04	56	19.57					
Argentina	56	22.98	57	19.50					
Romania	57	22.97	55	19.68					
Panama	58	22.68	59	18.85					

(cont'd.)

Five Puzzles in the Behavior of Productivity, Investment, and Innovation

ROBERT J. GORDON, Northwestern University, National Bureau of Economic Research, and Centre for Economic Policy Research[1]

Understanding the interplay between innovation, technology, and productivity growth is the foundation for projecting the future economic growth rate of a country, a region, or the world. Because the United States has been at the frontier of productivity and living standards for at least the past century, it is understandable that so much of the productivity literature is US-centric. Studies tend to divide the issues into those that involve accelerations and slowdowns in the rate of productivity growth in the United States, that is, "at the frontier," and those that involve the catching up and falling behind of other countries or regions relative to the United States. US-centricity obviously overstates the role of the United States as a leader and innovator. There is plenty of innovation in the rest of the world, and US manufacturers have been battered by losses of market share to higher quality and more innovative products from Japan, Europe, and elsewhere, especially in such industries as automobiles and machine tools. Further, the absolute level of productivity in at least eight European countries now exceeds that of the United States.[2] Nevertheless, this chapter follows the US-centric mold by placing disproportionate emphasis on US developments and debates about their causes. Attention to Europe is secondary and mainly limited to the last section of the chapter.

Three years after the end of the boom in the US stock market and in information and communication technology (ICT) investment, initial certainties about the causes of the post-1995 US productivity growth revival are unraveling, and puzzles deepen regarding not only its causes but also its durability. For numerous policy issues in the United States and other countries, long-term forecasts not just of productivity growth but of GDP growth are essential. For instance, long-run projections of government budget deficits and exhaustion dates for entitlement funds, such as US Social Security, depend heavily on projected growth rates of productivity and the population into the far future. Over a shorter horizon of one to two decades, growth forecasts are essential to inform government policy and corporate investment decisions and to predict the evolution of world trade, savings, and investment. As of mid-2003, the US productivity growth revival has lasted for eight years, and as it persists, it deserves an increasing weight relative to the dismal 1972–95 period of slow growth when making forecasts into the distant future.

The five puzzles

It is difficult to understate the extent to which the recent behavior of US productivity growth has surprised laymen and experts alike. Instead of fading after the economy's peak in mid-2000, US nonfarm business productivity growth has actually accelerated from a 2.45 percent annual rate during 1995–2000 to a stunning 3.34 percent annual growth rate in the three years between 2000:Q2 and 2003:Q2.[3] As US productivity performance has become even stronger over the past three years, at least five puzzles have emerged regarding the revival, its causes, and the performance of the United States relative to the rest of the world.

1. Whatever happened to the cyclical effect?

Is there any remaining support for the view that part of the post-1995 US productivity revival contains a cyclical component, as I argued beginning in 1999 (Gordon, 2000)? In retrospect, was the initial decomposition of the revival, as of 2000, between cyclical and trend elements justified, based on data available at that time? Can the early-recovery upsurge in productivity growth between late 2001 and mid-2003 be interpreted as a temporary phenomenon, as were temporary early-recovery upsurges in 1975–76, 1982–83, and 1991–92?

2. Why did productivity growth accelerate after 2000 when the ICT investment boom was collapsing?

US productivity grew even more rapidly after the mid-2000 peak in ICT investment and the stock market than it did in 1995–2000 when ICT investment was strong. Yet the first round of academic research on the revival (Jorgenson and Stiroh, 2000; Oliner and Sichel, 2000) attributed most of the revival to the post-1995 explosion of ICT investment. Faster growth in ICT investment translated directly into a productivity benefit from the *production* of ICT hardware. In addition, a second, larger component came from the *use* of ICT capital across the economy, particularly in ICT-intensive industries. The continuation of relatively rapid productivity growth after the mid-2000 collapse of the ICT investment boom is puzzling and raises the question of whether previous research attributed too large a causal role to ICT investment; if so, what other factors could have contributed to the revival and its post-2000 continuation.

3. What aspects of innovation caused productivity growth to take off?

It has been argued (Gordon, 2000) that sustained rapid growth of US productivity between World War I and the mid-1960s was propelled by a set of "Great Inventions" at the end of the 19th century, of which the most important were electricity and the internal combustion engine. Simply inventing the computer did not deliver a similarly long and sustained era of rapid productivity growth; almost half of the 50 years since the first commercial application of the computer in 1954 experienced slow productivity growth in the United States. What were the key innovations that produced the post-1995 productivity revival in the United States? Have those key innovations already occurred, or can we expect a continuous pace of

innovation over several decades, equal in importance to that of the late 1990s?

4. How can ICT investment revive if innovations are second-rate?

Like any magnitude in economics, the behavior of ICT investment can be summarized by changes in forces influencing supply and demand. The demand side depends on the steady arrival of innovations that create profitable investment opportunities. Without innovation, investment would have stopped centuries ago, as it would have involved "piling wooden ploughs on top of wooden ploughs." If innovation is the fundamental driver of the demand for investment, what does the rise and fall of ICT investment since 1995 tell us about the pace of innovation over the past decade, and what are the implications for the next decade?

5. Why has Europe failed to experience a productivity growth revival?

Early interpreters of the post-1995 US productivity growth revival immediately noted that, compared with the period 1990–95, Europe did not match the US productivity growth acceleration but rather exhibited a growth slowdown. European productivity growth has remained slow in the years after 2000, while the United States has experienced yet another upsurge. Thus the puzzle deepens as to why Europe continues to slip behind, especially since Europeans use the same types of ICT hardware and software that are used in the United States. This puzzle reinforces Puzzle #2, suggesting that there is some other source of US advantage—but why should this have emerged only after 1995?

Plan of the chapter

The chapter begins with Puzzle #1, discussing the cyclical behavior of productivity and the evolution of statistical trends estimated for US productivity growth. Today's view of the underlying productivity growth trend in the 1995–99 era is much more optimistic than the view from the vantage point of the year 2000, and this helps to explain why it could be argued in 2000 that a significant component of the post-1995 revival was "cyclical," whereas today's more optimistic trend for that period does not support a cyclical interpretation. Moreover, there remains a cyclical element in post-2000 productivity behavior, in the sense that in previous recoveries, an early recovery productivity growth "bubble" has been followed by below-trend growth during the subsequent two years.

The treatment of Puzzle #2 also centers on data for the United States, in this case the evolution over time of studies of the sources of the post-1995 productivity growth revival. How do such studies explain the continua-

Figure 1: Four-quarter change in US productivity and alternative trends, 1955–2003

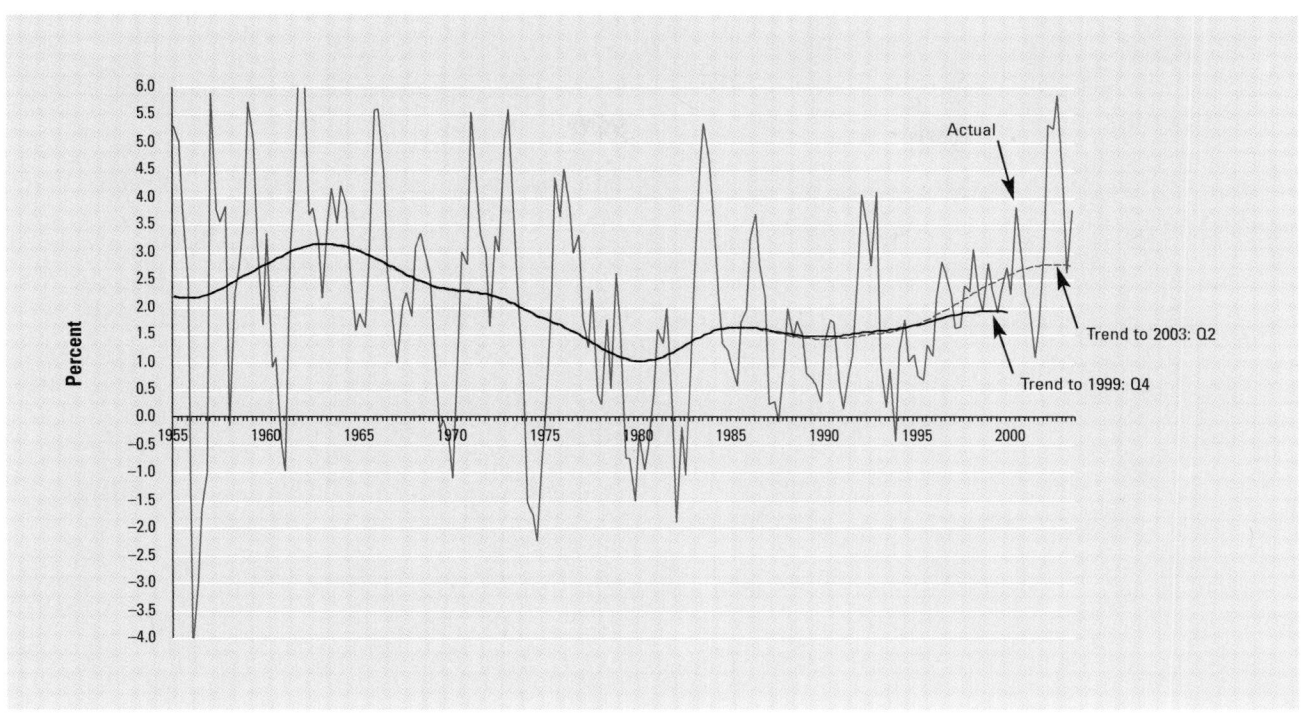

Sources: Actual changes from Bureau of Labor Statistics; trend calculations by author.

tion and acceleration of the productivity revival from the perspective of the post-2000 crash in ICT investment? Did such studies overstate the role of ICT investment in achieving the 1995–99 portion of the revival?

Examining Puzzle #3, we provide an overview of several major innovations that were important for productivity gains, including the "Great Inventions" of the late 19th century, their subsidiary and supplementary offshoots in the first half of the 20th century, the initial impact of electronic computers, and, finally, the key aspects of the post-1995 "New Economy." Our key question is why the initial impact of computers on productivity growth petered out after 1970, and why an apparently continuous stream of innovations finally brought a productivity reward only after 1995.

Our treatment of Puzzle #4 argues that traditional decompositions of the sources of growth overstate the role of the quantity and quality of capital and of improvements in the quality of labor, and understate the role of innovation in the process of economic growth. Innovation is necessary but not sufficient for investment to occur, and accelerations and decelerations of investment can be signals of changes in the pace of innovation.

Finally, Puzzle #5 leads us to examine the contrast in productivity behavior between the United States and Europe over various subintervals since 1990. Why did productivity growth slow down in Europe but accelerate in the United States?[4] To look for an answer, we provide an informal survey of explanations for the failure of Europe to join the United States in its productivity revival. We sift through a litany of complaints about European structural rigidity and overregulation in a search for convincing explanations of the differences. The final section summarizes and interrelates our proposed solutions to the five puzzles.

Puzzle #1: Whatever happened to the cyclical effect?

Over the past five decades the growth rate of productivity in the United States has been highly volatile. Displayed in Figure 1 is the four-quarter rate of change of nonfarm private business productivity, displayed as the jagged black line. Despite the appearance of random zigzags, we can pick out a few patterns in the behavior of the black line if we know the chronology of US growth and business cycles.

Decomposing cycle and trend

The growth of productivity is not uniformly high in economic expansions and low in recessions. Instead, it tends to be relatively low in the last stages of an expansion, as firms optimistically hire too many workers just when the economy's growth is slowing. This "end-of-expansion" phenomenon was first identified in Gordon (1979) and then reaffirmed with subsequent data (Gordon 1993, 2003b). Examples go back to the 1950s and include 1968–69, 1973–74, 1978–80, and 1988–90. Periods of most rapid growth are in the quarters immediately following the business cycle trough, when output begins to grow but firms are still cutting costs and laying off workers. Examples of early-recovery productivity "bubbles" include 1975–76, 1982–83, and 1991–92. In these three cases there was a sharp slowdown in productivity growth after an initial four to six quarters of the "bubble."

To interpret productivity behavior since 1995, we add to the black line in Figure 1 two different trends for the rate of change, using the methodology of the Hodrick-Prescott (H-P) filter.[5] The extent of the post-1995 revival in trend differs, depending on how much data the H-P filter is allowed to "see." The solid blue line is allowed to see data only through the end of 1999:Q4; it moves upward beginning in 1994, to reflect the sharp increase after 1995 in the average growth rate, but as of 1999:Q4 had increased only from 1.50 to 1.90 percent per annum. Allowing the trend estimation to be exposed to the full set of data through 2003:Q2 yields a much more rapid acceleration of the trend as far back as 1995. Clearly, the verdict on whether any of the post-1995 acceleration represented a cyclical effect depends on when that assessment was made and what data were available at the time. Both trend lines are identical prior to 1994, and agree that the productivity growth trend reached its maximum point in the early 1960s, and then slowed to a trough of only around 1.0 percent per year in the late 1970s, followed by a two-step revival, first between 1980 and 1985, and second after 1995.

Table 1 provides specific numbers for the actual and trend growth rates over alternative intervals. Between the 1950–72 and 1972–95 periods, the actual growth rate slowed from 2.58 to 1.43 percent per annum. Stopping the clock at 1999:Q4, the actual growth rate for 1995:Q4–1999:Q4 had accelerated to 2.52 percent, and the trend estimated at that point had accelerated to 1.90 percent, leaving a cyclical effect of 0.61 percent. The same exercise carried out by Gordon (2000, reproduced in the bottom line of Table 1) yielded somewhat higher numbers for actual and trend (because the data for that period have been revised downward since his chapter was written) but roughly the same estimate of the cyclical effect, 0.50 percent.[6]

When the trend estimator is allowed to take into account all the data through 2003:Q2, the story changes radically. Now the 1995–99 trend growth rate is 2.31 percent, not 1.90 percent, and the cyclical effect is down to 0.21 points. Further, the average actual growth rate after 1999 is up to 3.31 percent, of which 2.76 is estimated to

Table 1: Annual rate of change of US nonfarm business output per hour, actual and estimated trend, selected intervals

Interval	Actual	Trend with data to 99:Q4	Trend with data to 03:Q2	Cyclical effect trend to 99:Q4	Cyclical effect trend to 03:Q2
1950:Q2–1972:Q2	2.58	2.60	2.60	−0.02	−0.02
1972:Q2–1995:Q4	1.43	1.51	1.51	−0.09	−0.08
1995:Q4–1999:Q4	2.52	1.90	2.31	0.61	0.21
1999:Q4–2003:Q2	3.31	—	2.76	—	0.56
1995:Q4–2003:Q2	2.89	—	2.52	—	0.37
Addendum: Cyclical Effect Estimated in Gordon (2000)			256		
1995:Q4–1999:Q4	2.75	2.25	—	0.50	—

Sources: Actual data from BLS; trends estimated with H-P filter 6400 parameter; cyclical effect equals actual minus appropriate trend. Addendum source: Gordon (2000, table 2, p 55).

Table 2: Decomposition of bubble periods, alternative intervals, four-quarter rates of change

Interval	1976:Q1	1983:Q3	1992:Q4	2002:Q3
1. Deviation of Actual Change from Trend	2.90	3.90	2.57	3.03
2. Explained by Lagged Adjustment	4.14	4.79	0.70	0.86
3. Explained by End-of-Expansion Effect	−0.08	−0.57	0.75	0.26
4. Unexplained Residual (1-2-3)	−1.16	−0.32	1.12	1.91
5. Actual Change from Trend, next 2 years	−0.32	−0.06	−1.28	—
6. Deceleration in following 2 years (5–1)	−3.22	−3.96	−3.85	—

Source: Author's calculations

represent trend growth and a remaining 0.56 represents a renewed cyclical effect.

Interpreting the productivity growth "bubbles"

In view of the volatile zigzags of productivity growth evident over the postwar history displayed in Figure 1, how much of the robust post-1999 behavior is likely to persist? The H-P trend had reached 2.75 percent by mid-2003—will it level off, accelerate further, or decelerate as happened after the peak of slightly above 3.00 percent was reached between 1961 and 1964? One way to examine this question is to liken the peak growth in 2002 to three earlier "bubble" periods in the first few quarters of recoveries from recession troughs, namely 1975–76, 1982–83, and 1991–92.

We can use the regression specification developed in Gordon (1993, 2003b) to divide up productivity growth into three components: (1) a portion explained by the lag of hours adjustment behind output changes, (2) the "end-of-expansion" mechanism, and (3) an unexplained residual. The decomposition is shown in Table 2. In the two early episodes, the sharp downward and upward zigzag of output followed by hours in those sharp recessions is more than enough to explain the temporary spike of productivity growth, and in fact the model overexplains the spikes.

But in the two mild recessions of 1990–91 and 2001, there was only a mild drop in output, and so half or more of the bubble remains unexplained in the regressions.

For our purposes in trying to guesstimate what the productivity trend will look like in the future, an important precedent is that over the course of the eight quarters following the bubble, productivity growth was slower than trend by an average of −0.55 percentage points over the three previous episodes. Applying this average reaction to the current period would imply that actual productivity growth between 2002:Q3 and 2004:Q3 would fall 0.55 points short of its 2.76 percent trend, averaging 2.21 percent over this interval. However, the first three quarters of this interval have already occurred, and the average annual growth rate so far is not 2.21 percent but rather 3.15 percent, considerably above the estimated trend.

Our verdict on Puzzle #1 is that little of the initial 1995–2000 productivity growth revival was cyclical, and almost all of it it represented a fundamental shift in the trend. However, the 2001–2002 "bubble" contains a temporary element that has occurred in the early stages of the recovery in previous business cycles and deserves to be called cyclical because of its periodic repetition. The 2001–2003 economic recovery has been substantially more "jobless" than the 1991–92 recovery that gave rise to that label, and productivity in the first few quarters after the four quarter bubble period has been considerably healthier than it was in 1993–94, relative to a much more robust trend. The US economy is on track to achieving a rate of productivity growth over the decade 1995–2005 of almost 3 percent per year, raising deep questions about why this has occurred and why these causes have not been equally relevant in Europe.

Puzzle #2: Why did productivity growth accelerate after 2000 when the ICT investment boom was collapsing?

As we have seen, productivity growth was substantially more rapid after mid-2000 than during the initial revival period of 1995–2000. However, the most prominent studies by Jorgenson and Stiroh (2000) and Oliner and Sichel (2000) attributed a large fraction of the revival to the *production* and *use* of ICT equipment and software. In the case of Oliner and Sichel, the analysis included not only ICT capital, including software, but also the semiconductors that powered the hardware. This leads us to Puzzle #2, the fact that productivity growth proceeded to a second stage of acceleration during 2000–2003 just as the ICT investment boom collapsed.

Data on real investment in computers and other products with rapid relative price changes become increasingly more misleading as time extends past the base year in the national income accounts, currently 1996 in the United States. To avoid potential errors of interpretation,

the correct measure of the importance of ICT investment is the *nominal* share of that particular type of investment in *nominal* GDP. For computer hardware itself, that share averaged 0.96 percent in 1997–2000, but it then crashed to 0.71 percent in 2002 and by 2003:Q2 had recovered only to 0.77 percent. A more comprehensive measure that includes not just computer hardware but also software and "other" (mainly communications) equipment registered an average GDP share of 4.23 percent in 1997–2000, reaching 4.55 percent in the year 2000, and then falling to 3.83 percent in 2002 before recovering to 3.94 percent in 2003:Q2.

The Oliner-Sichel decomposition

The most influential research supporting a large role for ICT investment in the post-1995 productivity growth revival appears in a series of papers by Stephen Oliner and Daniel Sichel, hereafter O-S (2000, 2002). Their approach, presented in Table 3, has attracted wide attention because of the clarity with which they distinguish between the role of capital deepening of ICT capital (line 3), that is, the benefits of rapid ICT investment to the *users* of ICT capital, from the separate role of the *production* of ICT capital in raising the growth rate of multifactor productivity for the economy as a whole (line 10). It is easy to follow the evolution of the O-S results as new data emerge, because they are always presented in the same format, and because the same initial time period (growth rates from 1973 to 1995) is compared with the revival period of 1995 to the latest year for which data are available.

Table 3 compares the initial O-S (2000) decomposition with their latest unpublished results, which extend the findings to an end-date of 2002.[7] The table displays the growth rate of labor productivity in line 1, and then in lines 2 and 8 subtracts the contributions of capital deepening and improvements in labor quality (ie, education) to arrive at the growth rate of multifactor productivity (MFP). The capital deepening component is further subdivided into ICT and other capital, and into three types of ICT capital (lines 4–6). The resulting MFP growth rate is then decomposed into the role of the *production* of ICT capital and all other contributions to MFP growth (lines 10–11).

In Table 3 we add two additional lines to the standard O-S decomposition. The two types of ICT capital contribution, capital deepening (line 3) and the MFP effect (line 10), can be added together, as in line 12. Then the total ICT contribution in line 12 can be divided by the growth rate of labor productivity from line 3 to yield the total contribution of ICT capital to productivity growth and to the productivity revival, as shown in line 13. Table 3 shows three different decompositions of the post-1995 productivity growth revival, each shown in boldface and italic type. The first with data through 1999 is taken from the

Table 3: Estimates by Oliner and Sichel of the contribution of ICT capital to the post-1995 productivity revival, annual percentage rates of change

	Original O-S (2000)			Latest O-S (2003)				
	1973–1995	1995–1999	*change*	1973–1995	1995–1999	*change*	1995–2002	*change*
1. Labor productivity	1.41	2.57	*1.16*	1.41	2.36	*0.96*	2.61	*1.20*
Contributions from:								
2. Capital deepening	0.77	1.10	*0.33*	0.72	0.98	*0.26*	1.20	*0.49*
3. ICT capital	0.46	0.96	*0.50*	0.42	0.95	*0.53*	0.93	*0.51*
4. Computer hardware	0.25	0.59	*0.34*	0.22	0.52	*0.31*	0.47	*0.25*
5. Software	0.12	0.27	*0.15*	0.12	0.33	*0.20*	0.33	*0.21*
6. Communication equipment	0.08	0.10	*0.02*	0.08	0.09	*0.01*	0.13	*0.05*
7. Other capital	0.31	0.14	*-0.17*	0.30	0.03	*-0.26*	0.27	*-0.02*
8. Labor quality	0.27	0.31	*0.04*	0.27	0.30	*0.03*	0.25	*-0.02*
9. Multifactor productivity (MFP)	0.36	1.16	*0.80*	0.42	0.98	*0.56*	1.15	*0.74*
of which contributed by:								
10. ICT/semiconductor	0.22	0.66	*0.44*	0.30	0.72	*0.41*	0.70	*0.40*
11. Other nonfarm business	0.15	0.50	*0.35*	0.11	0.26	*0.15*	0.45	*0.34*
Memo: Total ICT/semiconductor Contribution to labor productivity								
12. Sum of lines 3 and 10	0.67	1.62	*0.95*	0.72	1.66	*0.94*	1.63	*0.91*
13. Share of line 1 in percent	47.9	63.0	*81.3*	51.6	70.4	*98.0*	62.6	*75.5*

Sources: Original O-S estimates from Oliner-Sichel (2000, Tables 2 and 4); Latest O-S estimates from data provided by Daniel Sichel to the author

initial O-S paper, while the second uses the latest data for the same period. Data revisions reduce the overall productivity revival in line 3 while leaving the ICT contribution intact, and this boosts the contribution of ICT capital to the 1995–99 revival from 81 to 98 percent (line 13).

When the end-point of the data is extended from 1999 to 2002, the revival in the growth rate of labor productivity (line 3) increases from 0.96 to 1.20 percentage points, while the contribution of ICT capital (line 12) shows surprisingly little response to the decline in ICT investment discussed above. As a result, the contribution of ICT capital declines from 98 percent in the period ending in 1999 to 76 percent in the period ending in 2002.[8] The spurt in productivity growth from 1999 to 2002 is more than explained by capital-deepening in "other capital" (line 7) and more rapid MFP growth contributed by sectors of the economy other than ICT and semiconductor capital. The puzzling absence of a decline in the ICT contribution, as well as the upsurge in "other" capital deepening, can both be traced to the same cause: the rapid decline in hours of labor input in 2001–2002. Since all the capital deepening terms in lines 2–7 represent the change in a capital-to-labor ratio times an income share of that type of capital, the apparent resilience of the ICT role disguises the fact that the ICT contribution by itself fell by half between 2000 and 2002, but this is dampened by the rapid decline in labor input.

Delay and intangible ("hidden") capital

Drawing back from the details of Table 3, we can take a broader view of the claim that, at least through 1999, virtually all of the productivity growth revival can be attributed to the production and use of ICT capital. This finding seems compatible with numerous studies, especially Triplett and Bosworth (2002) and Nordhaus (2002), which pinpoint wholesale and retail trade and securities trading as the industries outside of ICT manufacturing where the productivity growth revival is most evident. The largest single contribution to the revival in their work is capital-deepening in ICT capital (Table 3, line 3), and this is precisely the capital that has been used so effectively in trade and securities trading.

Nevertheless, several questions may be raised about the implication of Table 3 that the post-1995 productivity revival, at least through 1999, resulted entirely from the production and use of ICT equipment.[9] First, the Oliner-Sichel technique requires that the full productivity payoff from the use of computers occurs at the exact moment that the computer is produced.[10] Leaving aside any delay between production and installation, the computer produces its ultimate productivity benefit on the first day of use. Numerous observers, led by David (1990), argue instead that there is a substantial time delay in reorganizing business practices to take advantage of new hardware and software. If there is a substantial delay in the real world that is not taken into account by the Oliner-Sichel method, then they would exaggerate the contribution of ICT capital-deepening to the post-1995 revival during the years of peak ICT investment. Then, in the period 2001–2003 when ICT investment has declined, they would understate the leftover benefits from previous ICT investment.

David's (1990) "delay" hypothesis was based on a very general analogy between the invention of electricity and computers. We will return to this analogy in more detail below when we discuss Puzzle #3 about the fundamentals of New Economy innovation. In this section we consider a more specific and focused, albeit complementary, argument by Yang and Brynjolfsson, hereafter Y-B (2001): that the productivity revival in the late 1990s was fundamentally mismeasured, due to the exclusion of massive amounts of "intangible" or "hidden" capital from the investment and capital data in the national accounts, and hence from the growth accounting exercises such as that of O-S as summarized in Table 3.

Y-B began by treating computer hardware as the tip of the ICT iceberg, concealing a large quantity of complementary capital investment, perhaps, in their words, as much as 10 dollars of "complementary intangible capital (including software and data), new business processes, and human capital." The key distinction is between the portion of the total investment that is included as investment in the national accounts, and the remaining intangible portion that is "hidden" as a business expense rather than treated as investment. However, the Y-B 10-to-1 ratio greatly exaggerates the hidden component. We have already seen that in 2002 investment in computers and peripherals was just 0.71 percent of GDP, in contrast to investment in all ICT capital, including software, of 3.83 percent of GDP, or more than five times as much. Thus a better rule of thumb might be that each dollar of investment in computer hardware (including peripherals) generates four additional dollars of measured ICT investment in software and communications equipment, and as much as five additional hidden dollars of business process reorganization and investment in human capital—that is, retraining.

Picking up a theme discussed below in regard to Puzzle #3, we regard investment in computer hardware as automatically generating not only investment in software but also investment in communication equipment, and in fact that is why we use the abbreviation "ICT" in preference to "IT" throughout this chapter. The essence of the New Economy as it evolved in 1995–99 was the marriage of computer and communications hardware with software; the computer hardware and communications hardware interacted in so many ways that it is impossible to separate them and claim that one is at the tip of the iceberg while the other remains under water. The invention of the World Wide Web (WWW) spurred not just a massive wave of computer and peripheral purchases, along with the development of Windows 95 and 98 that incorporated integrated web browsers, but also an enormous investment in communications hardware, including not just fiber-optic cable but also everything from mundane plugs to complex electronic switching networks. Working in the opposite direction, the rapid spread of mobile phones required heavy investment in computer hardware to operate and manage the mobile phone networks. The entire computer and communications hardware component of investment, as well as software, is a portion of the iceberg that is fully visible and above water.

Whatever the ratio of hidden intangible capital—more likely 1-to-1 than 9-to-1—the implications of the Y-B argument become clear. The economy's production function for final goods depends on measured labor, measured capital input, and hidden intangible capital input. In a steady state, when new investment in open and hidden capital is balanced by depreciation and human capital, and retraining functions are at a normal level required to replace workers who quit or retire, then hidden inputs and hidden outputs offset each other and there is no mismeasurement of productivity.

But when visible ICT is growing rapidly, as during 1995–2000, then complementary hidden investments are growing rapidly as well, and the growth of unmeasured output (the present value of future benefits from business process reorganization, human capital improvements, and retraining) exceeds the growth of unmeasured inputs. Yet much of this intangible capital is being created by measured labor inputs (programmers, consultants, trainers) that appear in the denominator of productivity while their output is not counted in the numerator. Thus during 1995–2000, the "true" revival of productivity growth, including the hidden output in additional to measured output, was substantially greater than the measured revival of productivity growth that was held down both by the failure to count intangible investment and also by the counting of a temporary upsurge in labor input devoted to creating intangible hidden capital.

The period 2000–2003 has been marked by a sharp downturn in ICT investment, particularly in computer hardware but also in software and communications equipment, and by a rapid decline in employment. Output can grow despite a continuing decline in labor hours, because the benefits of the previous hidden investment in improved business processes and better-trained employees are transmitted to production, while the workers that produced the hidden output in the late 1990s (programmers, consultants, trainers) have been laid off and are walking the streets. In a sense, the US economy of 2000–2003 has been getting a "free ride" from the 1995–2000 wave of investment in hidden capital.

The Y-B analysis seems convincing, at least as a partial explanation of why US productivity growth has been so healthy during a period of relatively low *measured* ICT investment. However, its starting point is that an imbalance of measured and hidden investment is inherently temporary and depends on an acceleration or deceleration in visible, measured investment such as that which occurred on the up side during 1995–2000 and on the down side during 2000–2003. The implication is that part of the ebullient productivity performance of 2000–2003 was based on the "free ride" and is inherently temporary. This argument is in addition to the historical precedent of an early-recovery productivity growth bubble such as occurred in 2001–2002, which suggests that average measured productivity growth during 2000–2003 contains a cyclical component.

At least one obvious question is raised by the Y-B analysis, and this is why intangible capital did not produce a productivity growth upsurge during previous periods when the share of spending on computer hardware was growing rapidly, particularly in 1972–87, the interval that led Robert Solow to utter his famous quip that later became known as the Solow "computer paradox"—that "we see the computer age everywhere except in the productivity statistics." One possible answer is that the 1972–87 increase in the share of computer spending in GDP was slow and gradual, while the post-1995 upsurge was sudden and hence created a greater imbalance between measured and unmeasured ICT investment. A second possibility is that the nature of ICT innovation in the 1990s was more disruptive and required a more substantial investment in intangible capital than did earlier waves of computer innovation. We turn to this possibility in the next section.

Puzzle #3. What aspects of innovation caused productivity growth to take off?

A fundamental puzzle in the history of computers is that innovation proceeded apace throughout the 50 years after the introduction of the first commercial computer in 1951, but productivity gains in the overall economy were slow during most of the 1972–95 period when some of the most important innovations occurred. Nordhaus (2001) has documented that the rate of price decline of one standardized unit of computing power was roughly constant from the late 1940s to the present time at an annual rate of 40 to 50 percent per year, after barely declining at all from the first punch-card machines of the 1890s to the introduction of the electronic computer in the late 1940s. Thus the technology that allowed the price of one unit of computing power to decline at such a steady pace must itself have improved steadily. Why was the economy's response in terms of productivity growth so slow between 1972 and 1995, and so much more rapid after 1995? How long will the rapid response continue, or is the economy doomed to return, starting tomorrow or in several years, to an era of slow productivity growth?

The early years of computers compared with the great inventions

I have previously compared, somewhat unfavorably, the invention and development of the electronic computer with that of the "Great Inventions," of which the two most important were the heroic twin inventions of the late 19th century: electricity and the internal combustion engine. David's (1990) "delay" hypothesis provided the first suggestion that it was useful to compare the early years after the invention of electricity to the early years after the invention of the electronic computer. We may look for analogies also with the early years after the invention of the internal combustion engine.

Electricity dates from the simultaneous invention of the electric light bulb in 1879 by Thomas A. Edison in the United States and by Joseph W. Swan in England, and the first power station in 1882. As shown by Nordhaus (1997), electricity drastically reduced the price of a lumen of light. Electric motors, after a developmental period of several decades, revolutionized manufacturing by decentralizing the source of power and making possible flexible and portable tools and machines. After a somewhat longer lag, electric motors embodied in consumer appliances eliminated the greatest source of drudgery of all, manual laundry; through refrigeration virtually eliminated food spoilage; and through air conditioning made summers enjoyable and opened the southern United States for modern economic development. In fact, it has been said that the most important economic development in Asia in the 20th century was the invention of air conditioning.[11]

When comparing the importance of electricity and electronic computers, the initial and most obvious remark is that computers are one more subsidiary invention made possible by electricity and could not exist without it. More interesting is the role of size in the evolution of both electricity and computers. The upsurge in US manufacturing productivity in the 1920s has been attributed to success, after a long delay, in making electric motors small and reliable enough to be stationed at each workplace in the factory and to replace the clumsy system of belts linking a large central power source to the individual work stations (David and Wright, 1999). In turn, the miniaturization of the electric motor made possible consumer appliances and air conditioning, subsidiary inventions that were not possible in the early days (say, 1880–1910) of electric power generation.

The history of the electronic computer in similar fashion reflects the role of miniaturization. Early electronic computers were massive and required separate air conditioned rooms or even separate buildings.[12] The 1950–80 period was characterized by the gradual shrinkage of the mainframe computer and the gradual transition of its input-output interface from punch cards to "dumb" terminals that had no separate computational capability. The earliest uses of electronic computers were similar to those of the early punch-card sorting machines dating back to the 1890s, namely to count the US decennial census. Early commercial uses in the 1960s and 1970s were the production of telephone and utility bills and bank statements, and once the dumb terminal was available, prototypes of the modern airline reservation systems. Computers should have yielded major improvements in productivity by eliminating many rows of clerks sitting at desks with electro-mechanical calculators, and doubtless they did. But, as originally pointed out by Oliner and Sichel (1994) and Sichel (1997), these productivity gains barely showed above the surface in an economy where, in the 1960s, computer investment was barely 0.2 percent of GDP.

The invention of the personal computer in the early 1980s is analogous to the spread of small electric motors installed in machine tools and other factory equipment in the 1920s. Now individually controllable computational capability was available at every desk. Although main-frames were still necessary for large assembly-line functions such as bills, bank statements, and airline reservations systems, the personal computer allowed the introduction of word processing and spreadsheets. Economy-wide productivity should have surged in the 1980s as personal computers made it possible for firms to economize on secretaries who had previously been engaged in repetitive typing of legal briefs and contracts. Professors soon found that it was faster to word process their own papers from scratch than to follow the tedious previous process of end-less rounds of revising drafts typed by a secretary. Indeed, one can see a faint glimmering of an early revival in productivity growth in the 1981–85 period in Figure 1 above.

Sharing the title with electricity for the most important invention that had its main diffusion in the 20th century is the internal combustion engine, which made possible personal autos, motor transport, and air transport.[13] The early years of the internal combustion engine were also characterized by a David-type delay, but this did not involve miniaturization. Initially automobiles were quirky and unreliable, and although autos soon became capable of traveling at much faster speeds than horses, the roads required for such speeds did not exist. Only in the 1920s did automobiles become sufficiently pervasive to spell the doom of inter-urban street railways. Only in the 1950s did the full set of the automobile's complementary inventions, including supermarkets, suburbs, and superhighways, finally emerge. Similarly, more than twenty years elapsed after the Wright Brothers' first flight before the start of the commercial aviation industry in the late 1920s, and ten more years intervened before the development of the DC-3, the workhorse commercial aircraft that made possible the modern airline industry beginning in the late 1930s.

The analogy of the internal combustion engine provides the key to understanding why the productivity pay-off of the personal computer waited until the mid-1990s. Just as complementary investments in roads and suburbs were necessary to provide the full benefits of motorcars and motor transport, so complementary innovations in software and communication technology were necessary to provide the full potential benefits of the personal computer. Windows 95 and 98 provided an intuitive interface that instantly replaced DOS, with its command lines and DOS-based programs with their arcane codes. Although the replacement of DOS programs with Windows-based programs may have been little more than an annoyance for experienced DOS users in the business world, they made it possible for business firms to reduce training expenses, and also for the personal computer to penetrate the household.[14] Because we are interested in the determinants of measured business-sector productivity, it is important for us to distinguish between the benefits of computers in business firms and for consumers in the household, and we shall return to this theme below.

But the "killer application" that powered the post-1995 productivity revival was the marriage of computer hardware and Windows-type software to communications technology that made possible the WWW. Equally important were developments in hardware power and software that made it trivial to send documents as e-mail attachments, thus eliminating the need to print out many pre-liminary documents and spreadsheets and to send the printed versions via fax or courier service. Cheap communications caused a revolution in business practice such as those emphasized by Y-B in our discussion of Puzzle #2; now proprietary systems for electronic communication within firms, and between firms and suppliers, could be replaced by generic systems based on web software that combined transparent interfaces with security protection. In short, the "marriage" of computer hardware with software and communications hardware in the 1990s was as important to the development of the computer as was the development of paved roads and then superhighways to the full exploitation of the internal combustion engine.

Productivity-enhancing innovation goes beyond the ICT sector

We know that productivity growth accelerated after 1995, and we can speculate as above about the aspects of ICT innovation that helped this acceleration to occur. But the simultaneous acceleration in productivity growth and in ICT investment as a share of GDP amounts, at least in part, to circumstantial evidence. Other aspects of innovation were occurring as well, and these may be as important as ICT in explaining the outstanding productivity performance since 1995 of the retail trade sector.

This performance did not occur evenly across the board in retailing but rather was concentrated in "large stores offering a wide array of goods accompanied by low prices and relatively high use of self-service systems" (Sieling et al. 2001, p. 10). A complementary finding by Foster, Haltiwanger, and Krizan (2002) based on a study of a large set of individual retail establishments shows that *all* of retail productivity growth (not just the revival but the entire measured amount of productivity growth over the decade of the 1990s) can be attributed to more productive entering establishments which displaced much less productive existing establishments. The average establishment that continued in business exhibited zero productivity growth, and this despite the massive investment of the retail industry in ICT equipment that presumably went to both old and new establishments. In the Foster results, productivity growth reflects the greater efficiency of newly opened stores, and the Sieling comment implies that most of these highly efficient new stores were large discount operations—the proverbial "big boxes" such as Wal-Mart, Home Depot, Best Buy, Circuit City, and new large supermarkets.

The Sieling and Foster findings seem to conflict with the Oliner-Sichel implication in Table 3, at least for the period through 1999, that all of the productivity revival in retailing was achieved by purchasing new computers, software, and communications equipment. All retailers, whether new establishments of the 1990s or older establishments of the 1980s or prior decades, have adopted ICT technology. Barcode readers have become universal in new and old stores. It is likely that the productivity revival in retailing associated with newly built big-box stores involves far more than the use of computers, including large size, economies of scale, efficient design to allow large-volume unloading from delivery trucks, stacking of merchandise on tall racks with fork-lift trucks, and large-scale purchases taken by customers to vehicles in large adjacent parking lots.

In the taxonomy of Table 3, these sources of efficiency gains should count as a contribution of non-ICT capital (ie, big-box structures and fork-lift trucks) and organizational improvements that raise MFP in the non-ICT sector. In the latest results of O-S in the right column of Table 3, there has been a substantial acceleration in the contribution to MFP growth of "other nonfarm business" outside the ICT sector, and some of these innovations in retailing may be showing up there. The role of non-ICT capital and non-ICT innovations may also help us to understand the failure of Europe to experience a post-1995 productivity revival, as discussed below in connection with Puzzle #5.

Puzzle #4. How can ICT investment revive if innovations are second-rate?

Interpretations of the interplay between ICT investment and the post-1995 productivity revival are both of academic interest and also of enormous historical importance in trying to assess whether the rapid productivity growth of 1995–2003 can continue, whether it requires the "support" of a revival in ICT investment, and indeed whether that revival will occur. This section goes back to fundamentals in the economics of economic growth to argue that the contribution to productivity growth of capital deepening and MFP are not independent, as they appear to be in Table 3, but rather are both ultimately dependent on the pace of innovation. This will then lead us to speculate on the likely pace of innovation over the next few years and to distinguish between those aspects of innovation that will provide a further boost to business productivity from those that will mainly provide consumers with improved or additional entertainment options.

The pace of innovation is measured by growth in labor productivity, not MFP

Standard growth accounting exercises such as the O-S decomposition displayed in Table 3 above seem to make growth in labor productivity depend on a contribution of capital deepening and a contribution of MFP growth, as if these two were independent. Dale Jorgenson with many co-authors—originally with Zvi Griliches (Jorgenson and Griliches, 1967) and more recently with Kevin Stiroh (Jorgenson and Stiroh 2000)—has argued that the driving forces in economic growth are increases in the quantity and quality of inputs, with only a small remaining role for MFP, the residual that is usually taken to measure the importance of technical change.

In thinking about the future of productivity growth and its determinants, we need to flip the Jorgenson approach on its head. The basic argument was developed in Gordon (1968, reprinted in 2003c) and independently by Thomas K. Rymes (1971). A simple example demonstrates the deep truth that capital deepening—that is, the growth in the capital-labor ratio—must be directly attributable to innovation. If in the year 1770 all capital equipment consisted of vintage 1770 Watt-Bolton steam engines, and if technical change was all disembodied (that is, figuring out how to rearrange the Watt-Bolton steam engines to boost production) then capital accumulation would have ground to a halt within a few decades of 1770, exhausted by diminishing returns. The entire contribution of capital deepening to labor productivity growth since 1770 is attributable to trillions of dollars of investment in railroads, autos, trucks, airplanes, electrical machinery, oil refineries, computers, and much else that was invented and further developed after 1770 and would not have occurred without those post-1770 inventions.

Or, in the evocative words of Evsey Domar, without technical change capital accumulation would just amount to "wooden ploughs piled up on top of existing wooden ploughs" (Domar, 1961, p. 712).

This point applies only to capital deepening, not to all capital accumulation. Technical change is not necessary for growth in the capital stock that keeps pace with growth in labor input, maintaining a fixed capital-labor ratio; investment would then be entirely devoted to equipping the additional members of the population with additional machines of a given technology, whether wooden ploughs or personal computers. But because all capital deepening ultimately requires technical change, existing measures of multi-factor productivity (MFP) growth cannot be interpreted as measuring the pace of technical progress, since the capital-deepening effect (due also to technical change) is subtracted out in calculating MFP growth.

Standard growth analyses include corrections for changes in the "quality" of capital in addition to its quantity (included but not shown separately in Table 3), and for changes in the "quality" of labor (shown in line 8 of Table 3). Yet changes in the quality of both capital and labor require technical change, just as capital deepening does. Capital's quality improves when the composition of capital input shifts from long-lived assets like structures to short-lived assets like computers, because short-lived assets need to earn a higher marginal product in order to "pay for" their higher rate of depreciation. Yet the very shift from structures to computers reflects technical change that allows the relative price of computers to structures to decline continuously. Even the quality of labor depends on technical change. As shown in Gordon (1968), the returns to education are endogenous as well to the pace of technical change, in the sense that workers in the research sector paid to develop innovations would not be paid as much if they had no creative ideas. This point is still not widely recognized.[15]

These points can be applied to a further understanding of the productivity revival of the late 1990s in the United States. Calculations such as those of Table 3 show that after 1995 MFP growth revived, indicating an acceleration of technical change; but this understates the role of technical change, which, together with an abundant supply of capital, directly created the investment boom and hence the capital-deepening effect of the late 1990s. The post-2000 collapse of the investment boom may signal that the underlying pace of innovation began to slow. This in turn raises questions about future advances in innovation and ICT investment.

Thinking about the productivity implications of future innovation

Speculating about future innovation opens up a huge array of topics, but fortunately only a subcomponent of innovation is relevant for future changes in measured business productivity. Many ongoing innovations are providing higher quality entertainment and communication options to consumer households, but that is not relevant to business productivity. The consumer surplus created by such consumer-oriented innovations is typically missed by price indexes when new products are introduced. Although final product is understated by the omission of the benefits of these innovations, at least price indexes today are revised more often than in the past to track the price declines of new consumer products after they are introduced. Past examples of long delays in the introduction of consumer durable goods into the US Consumer Price Index include a 35-year delay for automobiles, a 12-year delay for room air conditioners, and a 9-year delay for the VCR.[16]

Between 1996 and 2000 the annual growth rate of investment in computer hardware doubled to 40 percent from around 20 percent in the previous decade. This acceleration reflected the working of both supply and demand. On the supply side, an acceleration of technical change created a faster rate of decline of computer prices per unit of performance, and this generated an increased demand for computers through a standard substitution effect. On the demand side, the demand for new computer hardware was raised by a set of five factors that were important at the time but did not persist beyond the year 2000. As argued in Gordon (2003a), the first of these factors that stimulated the demand for computers, but only for a temporary period, was that the WWW could only be invented once. By the year 2000 most firms, government agencies, and other organizations had invested in the initial construction of their web sites, and further developments and refinements required lower levels of investment in software engineers and computer hardware. Second, much of the computer hardware and software development was purchased by "dot.com" Internet startup companies that promptly went out of business, indicating that their hardware and software investment yielded a negative rate of return. Third, a new generation of user-friendly but memory-hogging business software, notably Windows 95 and 98 and Office 97, both required the purchase of new computers and also revolutionized business productivity by finally creating a universal business language that facilitated networking and electronic exchange of documents and data. But this revolution was temporary as well; since 1998 the exponential growth of computer power has far outrun the pace of innovation in business software. Today's Office XP functions almost identically to Office 97, which was introduced six years ago. Fourth, the "Y2K" crisis led to an artificial compression of the replacement cycle for computer hardware and software investment into the 1998–99 period, both boosting investment in those years and depressing investment in 2000 and beyond. Fifth, deregulation of the telecommunications industry in 1996 led to a free-for-all of investment in the late 1990s that left the United States vastly oversupplied with fiber-optic communications capacity, only a small fraction of which is being utilized.

Rapid productivity growth since 1995 combines the one-time-only aspects of the measured portion of the ICT investment boom during 1995–2000, with the disequilibrium argument of Y-B that current productivity growth is being propelled by intangible investments made during the boom years, even after the programmers-consultants-trainers who produced that intangible capital have been laid off, thus further boosting labor productivity by reducing its denominator. To project a repetition of the 1995–2003 experience, and to believe that the H-P trend of Figure 1 is actually relevant to future productivity growth over the next five to ten years, we need to look for sources of innovation that could possibly generate another ICT investment boom of the magnitude of the late 1990s.

It is useful to think of inventions as having different levels of fundamental importance, both in terms of their initial effects and in terms of their potential spin-offs and complements. Electricity and the internal combustion engine were mega-inventions, both for their direct effects and the number and importance of their spinoffs (consumer appliances, air conditioning) and complements (roads, superhighways, suburbs, supermarkets). The semiconductor, computer chip, and digitalization taken together represent a first-rate invention, if not a mega-invention. Some of the spinoffs of electricity, like television and the motion picture, were first-rate inventions, albeit nevertheless spinoffs. Down another level were products such as the VCR, at best a second-rate invention that combined motion pictures with television. The computer and personal computer are first-rate inventions that have created first-rate complements, namely the WWW and the Internet. But the PDA, Internet-accessible mobile phone, and wireless-enabled laptop are second-rate inventions at best, themselves representing spinoffs of the previous merging of computer hardware, communications hardware, and software that occurred in the 1990s.

Unfortunately, most of the excitement about current and near-term future innovations in the ICT industry involve second-rate inventions of either consumer or business products. Consumers may be thrilled about their digital cameras, camera phones, flat plasma TV screens, and ever-more-exotic game-playing machines, but these innovations are a continuation of previous incremental improvements and in any case have few if any implications for future business productivity growth.[17] For true consumer impact, none of these innovations creates the kind of quantum jump in consumer welfare that was achieved by the refrigerator, the automatic washing machine, the dishwasher, the first black-and-white televisions, the first

color televisions, the room air conditioner and then central air conditioning. Nevertheless, much of the dynamism in electronic innovation currently and in the future revolves around consumer entertainment, and it has been argued that the average home user now needs greater processing power than the average business employee working at a desk.

Innovations likely to stimulate ICT investment spending for business productivity purposes over the next few years are already known. Another round of miniaturization is at hand, with improved Internet capability of Personal Digital Assistants and cellular phones. The rush to compress e-mail and web access onto tiny screens of PDAs with tiny or nonexistent keyboards will clash head-to-head with the rapid spread of wireless hotspots that will extend the utility of laptop computers and make it easy to enjoy e-mail and web access from virtually anywhere with a full-sized screen and full-sized keyboard. The ability of business employees to hook up everywhere and anytime—whether by PDA, cell phone, or wireless-enabled laptop—raises additional issues about work hours. If travel time becomes work time, and business employees feel that they must be accessible 24/7, including while on vacation, then the productivity data may overstate the level of productivity by understating the level of hours.[18] Looking further ahead, it is easy to foresee the day when keyboards are no longer necessary for PDAs, when e-mails can be composed by voice-recognition sofware, and incoming e-mail can be automatically translated by computer voice and transmitted over tiny earphones.

One way of assessing the likely productivity impact of near-term ICT innovation is to ask whether such innovations can break through the inherent impediments to the replacement of human beings by computers. As I argued earlier (Gordon, 2000, pp. 65–66), some uses of labor are immune to replacement by computers, including airline pilots, truck drivers, doctors, nurses, dentists, lawyers, professors, investment bankers, management consultants, bartenders, wait staff, bus boys, flight attendants, barbers, lawn maintenance services, auto repair, hotel housekeepers, and almost every type of home maintenance. Innovation operates around the edges but does not change the nature of these jobs fundamentally. For the first time at a recent visit my doctor used new (at least for him) software in the examination room that allowed him to scan previous test results, current prescriptions, and to issue new prescriptions by checking a few boxes. But as a byproduct he spent most of the visit looking at his computer screen rather than examining me! Professors are on this list as a species unlikely to be replaced by computers, but professors have been affected by ICT investments. In my case, the office-productivity innovations of the 1990s, particularly Excel and e-mail attachments, have made it possible for my research assistants to send me 10 or 20 rounds of results per day without ever talking to me in person. But those innovations were all in place by 1998 and little on the horizon has appeared that remotely approaches their importance.

A different but equally skeptical view is offered by Carr (2003).[19] In his view, the failure of the dot.coms in the late 1990s reflected a pervasive tendency of ICT innovation to be easily copied, thus quickly eroding the competitive advantage for any one company that is essential for ICT investments to be profitable. Benefits for consumers and improvements in productivity come at the price of reduced or negligible corporate profitability and the erosion of incentives to undertake the next round of investment. In the past such innovations as American Airlines' Sabre reservations system provided a competitive advantage for a decade or more because they were so hard to copy, but recent developments "toward openness, toward standardization, toward greater power, toward ever more powerful hardware and software" have greatly eased the task of competitors wanting to copy a single company's initial innovation. Carr's argument comes down to diminishing returns, the same force that Gordon (2000) argued makes it ever more difficult to think up truly important innovations for business productivity. In Carr's words, "a lot of the core things that businesses do have already been automated with information technologies."[20]

Even optimists such as Intel's Andy Grove project a recovery of ICT investment, but one based on "more of the same" rather than any important new innovations. In Grove's view, the continuing exponential growth of e-commerce at those dot.com firms that survived the 1990s shake-out will inevitably require sizeable further investments to "light [presently unutilized] fiber" and to handle ever-growing e-commerce transactions. Grove agrees that the investment boom of the late 1990s was "unsustainable," and his favorite examples of the future potential growth in ICT investment seem remote from business productivity, including "digital distribution of music," "digital electronics applied to warfare," and use of ICT in the health care industry.[21]

The operation of diminishing returns makes it difficult to believe that over the next five or ten years innovation related to business productivity will be sufficiently dynamic to allow a repeat of the ICT investment boom of the late 1990s. Because innovation is the ultimate driver of the capital-deepening process, it is possible that the ebullient 2000–2003 performance of US productivity growth summarized in the H-P trend line of Figure 1 may prove to be a historical high-water mark of productivity growth.

This section of speculations must be qualified by repeated instances of pessimism in predicting the technological future. The editor of this volume reminds me that in 1844 there was serious consideration to closing the US patent office on the basis that "all useful inventions had

Table 4: Annual rate of change of output, hours, and output per hour, EU and US, selected years, 1990–2002

Interval	1990–1995	1995–2000	2000–2002	1995–2002	1995–2002 vs. 1990–1995
United States					
Output	2.38	4.00	1.28	3.22	0.84
Hours	1.24	2.03	−1.24	1.10	−0.14
Output per hour	1.14	1.97	2.52	2.13	0.99
European Union					
Output	1.61	2.63	1.28	2.24	0.63
Hours	−0.85	1.21	0.40	0.98	1.83
Output per hour	2.46	1.42	0.89	1.27	−1.19

Source: McGuckin and van Ark (2003, p 5). US hours 2000–2002 revised by author as discussed in text.

already been invented." In 1943 Thomas Watson, CEO of IBM, stated that the world needed no more than "five or six large computers." In 1985, Bill Gates is reputed to have said that "640K of memory should be enough for anyone." My arguments of techno-skepticism arrayed above are oriented rather narrowly to business uses of electronic computers and do not deny that technological breakthroughs may be just around the corner in many fields. The marriage of open web-based research access and the marriage of computers to biotechnology may make possible medical breakthroughs that achieve quantum increases in life expectancy.

Puzzle #5: Why has Europe failed to experience a productivity growth revival?

Europeans are perplexed by the failure of Europe (ie, the European Union) to experience a post-1995 productivity growth revival. In fact, Europe experienced a substantial post-1995 productivity growth slowdown, as shown in Table 4. The initial European slowdown evident in data for 1995–2000 worsened with data for 2000–2002, whereas the United States (as we saw above) experienced accelerating productivity growth at the cost of rapidly declining hours of work during 2000–2002. All the data in Table 4 are taken from a recent Conference Board pamphlet by McGuckin and van Ark (2003) except for US hours and productivity growth during 2000–2002.[22] Readers should note that international comparisons are based on data on GDP per hour for the entire economy including the government sector, and these generally display slower growth rates of productivity than the data for the nonfarm private business sector that we examined in Table 1 and Figure 1.

The right-hand column of Table 4 displays the *change* in output, hours, and output per hour between 1990–1995 and 1995–2002. Surprisingly, the post-1995 acceleration in output growth was almost the same in Europe as in the United States: 0.63 versus 0.84 percentage points, respectively. But Europe's performance in hours of work was the diametric opposite of the that of the United States, accelerating by almost two percentage points compared with pre-1995, whereas there was a slight deceleration of hours growth in the United States. As a result, the productivity change between 1990–95 and 1995–2002 was the mirror image of the hours change, with an acceleration of exactly 1 percent for the United States and a deceleration of more than 1 percent for Europe.

Most of the literature on the failure of Europe to achieve a post-1995 productivity growth acceleration treats Europe as overregulated and stuck in the mud, ignoring the turnaround from hours contraction to hours expansion before and after 1995. In this section we review recent findings on the Europe-United States difference in a search for useful conclusions. An initial reaction is that this difference appears to deny the kind of importance for ICT investment in causing the post-1995 US revival that appears in the decomposition of O-S in Table 3. Business firms, not to mention university professors, use the same PCs and Microsoft software everywhere in Europe, and Europe is widely acknowledged to be ahead in the use of mobile telephones. This reaction provides further circumstantial evidence that the O-S growth accounting exercise in Table 3 may overstate the contribution of ICT investment to the US post-1995 revival.

Aggregation, retailing, and regulation

Part of the European puzzle is resolved when we recognize that heterogeneity among European countries is more pronounced than the difference between the European Union and the United States. Numerous studies have shown a relatively strong positive correlation between MFP growth and measures of ICT intensity, for example, the ratio of ICT expenditure to GDP or the change in PC intensity per 100 inhabitants over the 1990s. In such comparisons, numerous countries achieved higher MFP growth rates than the United States over the 1990s, including Ireland, Finland, Sweden, Denmark, Norway, Canada, and Australia. Some, but not all, of these countries surpass the United States in PC intensity and/or in the share of ICT expenditure. What differs most between Europe and the United States is the low level of PC adoption and ICT expenditure in the "olive belt" ranging from Portugal and Spain on the west to Italy and Greece in the east.[23]

A comprehensive recent study by van Ark et al. (2002) provides a few answers at a more formal level. It allows us to trace the location of productivity growth accelerations and decelerations to particular industrial sectors, divided into ICT-producing, ICT-using, and non-ICT industries. The core of the US success story appears to have been in *ICT-using* industries, that is, the same wholesale, retail, and securities trading industries already

discussed above. The decomposition of van Ark et al. (2002, Figure 2a) shows that literally *all* of the productivity growth differential of the United States over Europe in the late 1990s came from these three industries, with retail contributing about 55 percent of the differential, wholesale 24 percent, and securities trade 20 percent. The remaining industries had small positive or negative differentials, netting out to zero. As might have been expected, the United States-Europe differential was negative in telecom services, reflecting US backwardness in mobile phones.

These results for Europe link to our discussion of retailing in the previous section; the retail sector was a major factor explaining Europe's poor performance in the late 1990s. Just as we argued earlier that the US retailing sector has achieved efficiency gains for reasons not directly related to computers, including physical investments in a new type of big-box organization, so we can suggest in parallel that Europe has fallen behind because European firms are much less free to develop the big-box retail formats.[24] Impediments include land use regulations that prevent the carving out of new "greenfield" sites for big-box stores in suburban and exurban locations, shop-closing regulations that restrict the revenue potential of new investments, congestion in central-city locations that are near the nodes of Europe's extensive urban public transit systems, and restrictive labor rules that limit flexibility in organizing the workplace and make it expensive to hire and fire workers with the near-total freedom to which US firms are accustomed.

A complementary interpretation is provided in a cross-country study of productivity differences in the service sector by the McKinsey Global Institute (1992). Their set of policy recommendations (Chapter 2-D, pp. 13–14) seem as relevant today as when written a decade ago, and they echo the previous paragraph by pointing to impediments to the development of modern retailing in some but not all European countries. European policymakers have adopted a set of policies that encourage high density and a concentration of retailing activity in the central city. The development of modern big-box retailing formats has been hindered by these policies and the resulting high cost of real estate and the complex and precarious process of obtaining planning approval for large plots of land.

An issue identified by McKinsey is the role of resale price maintenance policies that in the United States assure new competitors that they will be able to attain the same access to suppliers at roughly the same prices as existing retailers. In contrast, in some European countries producers refuse to discount to new, high-volume, low-cost retailing formats in order to protect smaller high-cost merchants. In some European countries, regulations directly prohibit the entry of large-scale stores and/or limit store opening days and hours, thus preventing large stores from fully amortizing their investments.

A partial survey of other cross-country studies reveals a disappointing lack of specific conclusions at the level of the van Ark et al. and McKinsey studies. The typical study conducts a growth accounting exercise, concludes that Europe has lagged behind the United States in adopting ICT technology to a greater or lesser degree, does not trace differences in behavior to specific industries, and concludes with a general plea for unspecified structural reforms. Among the studies that fit this characterization are Colecchia and Schreyer (2001), Daveri (2002), Rhine-Westphalia Institute for Economic Research (2002), and Vijselaar and Albers (2002).

Economic institutions and culture

Phelps (2003) takes a broader view of economic institutions that promote economic "dynamism" and those that suppress it. His analysis of dynamism starts from Schumpeter's concept of "creative destruction." He adds to Schumpeter's emphasis on entrepreneurship an equal if not greater emphasis on "financiership," that is, the ability of financial markets to steer finance to worthy innovations. The greater success of the United States in encouraging innovation is attributed in part to its greater emphasis on venture capital and initial public equity offerings (IPOs) than in Europe.

In Phelps' view, the relatively poor economic performance of continental Europe results *both* from the underdevelopment of capitalist institutions like venture capital and equity finance and from the overdevelopment of corporatist institutions that suppress innovation and competition. These corporatist institutions impose "penalties, impediments, prohibitions, and mandates . . . generally intended to damp down creative destruction." Among these impediments are licenses and permissions to set up a new plant or firm, the need to consult with workers on changes in the mix of products or plants, and employment protection legislation. Because these institutions are designed to dampen down the changes inherent in "unbridled capitalism," they also lead to the underdevelopment of the stock market, resulting in lower ratios of stock market valuation to GDP in continental Europe than in the United States and other less corporatist economies such as Britain, Canada, and Australia.

Phelps provides a complementary analysis of cultural differences between Europe and the United States. Europeans view with disdain the money-grubbing Americans with their out-sized rewards for CEOs and successful entrepreneurs. American children begin to work earlier than European children, earning baby-sitting money in their early teens, working in fast-food outlets while in high school, and are forced to work during college in contrast to European youth who "free ride" on government-paid college tuition and stipends. Phelps concludes that Europe has developed a culture of "dependency" that "breeds an unduly large share of young people who have little sense of independence and are unwilling to strike out on their own." He might have added that high levels of long-term youth unemployment discourage independence and encourage young adults to live with their parents in their 20s and, in Italy, into their 30s.

Caveats

Europeans do not take these criticisms lying down. Yes, they admit that high youth unemployment and low labor force participation represent an economic and social failure. But they are quick to criticize aspects of American economic and political institutions that, while making it easy for Wal-Mart and Home Depot to find the land to build thousands of big-box stores, has offsetting disadvantages.

Europeans find abhorrent the hundreds of billions, or even trillions, that Americans have spent on extra highways and extra energy to support the dispersion of the population into huge metropolitan areas spreading over hundreds or even thousands of square miles, in many cases with few transport options other than the automobile. Productivity data do not give Europe sufficient credit for the convenience benefits of frequent bus, subway, and train (including TGV) public transit. Excessive American dispersion is viewed as a response to misguided public policies, especially subsidies to interstate highways in vast amounts relative to public transport, local zoning measures in some suburbs that prohibit residential land allocations below a fixed size—for example, two acres—and the infamous and politically untouchable deduction of mortgage interest payments from income tax.

Europeans enjoy shopping at small individually owned shops on lively central city main streets and pedestrian arcades, and recoil with distaste from the ubiquitous and cheerless American strip malls and big-box retailers—although Carrefour, Ikea, and others provide American-like options in some European cities. To counter the effects of American land use regulations that create overly dispersed metropolitan areas, Europeans counter with their own brand of land use rules that preserve greenbelts and inhibit growth of suburban and exurban retailing. Even the distinction between European inner-city shopping and American exurban big-box retailing is growing increasingly obsolete. Europeans reacting to these comments point to a growing number cities that provide the same kind of suburban access to retailing as can be found in America while retaining the variety and independence of smaller shopkeepers in the central city.

A more complete consideration of these differences leads to the conclusion that GDP data understate the Europe: United States ratio of both productivity and real

GDP per capita (see Gordon, 2002). A further caveat is that these conditions, although interesting for a debate about the relationship of measured GDP and economic welfare on both sides of the Atlantic, do not appear to be particularly helpful in explaining why American productivity has grown so much faster than in most European countries since 1995.

Conclusion

This chapter began with five puzzles, and we are now prepared to provide some tentative resolutions. Puzzle #1 asked about the "cyclical effect" that was invoked in discussions of the early 1995–99 portion of the post-1995 US productivity revival to argue that the revival was in part temporary, and that unsustainably rapid growth in output had created unsustainably fast growth in productivity. The further acceleration of productivity growth in 2000–03 has laid the cyclical argument to rest insofar as it applies to the 1995–99 period. But another cyclical phenomenon has emerged more recently: the "early-recovery productivity bubble" that pushed up productivity growth in 2002 to incredible levels. This phenomenon is cyclical in the sense that it is periodic; similar "bubbles" occurred in 1975–76, 1982–83, and 1991–92, and in each case were followed by two or more years of productivity growth below trend. Data on productivity growth rates during 2000–03 are pushed up by the bubble phenomenon, as are estimated Hodrick-Prescott productivity trends that respond relatively rapidly to the evolution of the actual data.

Puzzle #2 was suggested by the paradox that productivity growth accelerated after the year 2000 despite the collapse in the ICT investment boom, suggesting that standard studies of growth accounting may exaggerate the causal role of ICT in achieving the first 1995–99 phase of the productivity revival. Three factors support the case for exaggeration. First, the growth accounting methodology unrealistically assumes that the full productivity benefits of ICT hardware and software are achieved at the instant of production, with no allowance for reorganization or training effects. Second, independent evidence for the retail trade sector finds that all of the rapid productivity growth in the 1990s was achieved by new establishments and none by old establishments, even though ICT investment has been made in both. Third, and most important, the boom in measured ICT investment in the late 1990s was accompanied by a boom of perhaps equal size in unmeasured or "hidden" improvements in intangible and human capital, as suggested by Yang and Brynjolfsson (2001). The numerator of productivity omitted the creation of the intangible capital but the denominator included the labor input, artificially holding down the magnitude of the productivity growth revival. Then after 2000 productivity growth was exaggerated, because output was supported by intangible capital input that had been created before 2000, but the labor input that had created the intangible capital had declined, as programmers, consultants, and trainers were laid off. The cyclical analysis of the 2002 productivity growth "bubble" and the intangible capital argument both suggest that observed productivity growth in 2002–03 may represent a highwater mark and cannot be expected to continue.

Puzzle #3 poses the paradox that technological change in computers has apparently proceeded at a relatively steady pace, judging by the relatively constant rate of price decline of computer power and the relatively exponential rate of increase of the performance-price ratio, yet the payoff from computer innovation in the form of productivity growth occurred in the late 1990s but not in the 1970s or 1980s. Drawing on analogies from the Great Inventions of the late 19th century, electricity and the internal combustion engine, we pointed to miniaturization and the development of complementary innovations as common threads linking the Great Inventions to the development of computers. The key development of the 1990s was the marriage of computer and communications technology with software that made possible the Internet, the WWW, and the pervasive spread of the mobile telephone. Yet some of the productivity growth revival of the 1990s was not directly attributable to this ICT marriage, but rather, especially in the retail trade sector, reflected the benefits of an organization revolution and large scale that made possible the big-box retail phenomenon.

Puzzle #4 focusses on the chicken-egg interrelationship between productivity, investment, and innovation. That major source of productivity growth, capital-deepening investment, cannot occur forever without a continuous flow of innovations, and so the post-2000 crash in ICT investment raises the question as to whether the wave of innovation in the 1990s had a one-time-only component, and whether a new wave of innovations will emerge over the next few years to create a repetition of the investment boom. We classify innovations as "mega," "first-rate," "second-rate," and beyond and argue that the marriage of computer and communications hardware with software in the 1990s was a first-rate invention, but that it had a one-time-only component because the web could be invented only once, because part of the boom consisted of demand from dot.com firms that promptly went bust, because of the mismatch between hardware and software innovation, because of the timing of Y2K, and because of the over-building of telecom infrastructure. The main areas of ICT investment in the near future are innovations that look distinctly second-rate: the further move toward mobility with Internet-enabled mobile phones and wi-fi enabled laptops that will allow e-mail, web access, Word, Excel, and Powerpoint to be accessed more conveniently, but the functions to be accessed will be the same as they were five years ago.

The final puzzle #5 is why Europe failed to exhibit any sign of a post–1995 productivity growth revival, despite its use of the same hardware and software and its evident lead in mobile telephony. References to "Europe" disguise a wide variety of performance, with Ireland and Finland exhibiting much faster productivity growth than the United States, but "olive belt" nations such as Italy and Greece scoring low on productivity and ICT investment (except for mobile phones). Disaggregated studies of industrial sectors suggest that the main difference between Europe and the United States is in ICT-using industries such as wholesale and retail trade and in securities trading, the same industries that were discussed above as leading the vanguard of computer using industries. Yet the contrast in retailing calls attention to regulatory barriers and land-use regulations in Europe that inhibit the development of the big-box retailing formats that have created many of the productivity gains in the United States

Phelps (2003) provides a unifying framework in which economic dynamism is promoted by policies that promote competition and flexible equity finance and is retarded by corporatist institutions that are designed to protect incumbent producers and inhibit new entry. He also points to European cultural attributes that inhibit the development of ambition and independence by teenagers and young adults, in contrast to their encouragement in the United States. Although competition, corporatism, and culture may help to explain the differing evolution of productivity growth on the two sides of the Atlantic since 1995, they reveal institutional flaws in both continents that are inbred and likely to persist.

Notes

1 This research has been supported in part by the National Science Foundation. I am grateful to Dan Sichel for providing the data from which I developed Table 3, and to Erik Brynjolfsson for several central ideas.

2 McGuckin and van Ark (2003), Appendix Table 1.

3 On August 7, 2003, new data from the Bureau of Labor Statistics (BLS) revised the annual rate of US productivity growth between 2001:Q1 and 2003:Q1 upward from 3.3 percent to 4.0 percent. On top of this robust rate, growth in 2003:Q2 was at an annual rate of 5.7 percent.

4 This acceleration has been made much stronger over the 2000–03 period by recent data revisions that are not yet reflected in academic and journalistic comparisons across countries.

5 We use an H-P parameter of 6400 in preference to the standard 1600, which in our view causes trends to be too volatile and to adhere too closely to the actual values.

6 Gordon (2000) estimated the trend by an alternative technique that had been used in Gordon (1993), which was to find the 1995–99 productivity trend that provided the best fit in a regression of changes in detrended hours on changes in detrended output, allowing for lags in both hours and output.

7 There have been intervening analyses of data ending in 2000 and 2001 (see Oliner and Sichel 2002); these are omitted here to simplify the table and because the most recent results are of greatest interest.

8 Data revisions released on August 7 would further reduce the ICT share of the 1995–2002 revival from the 76 percent figure shown in Table 3 to 67 percent, allowing only for the revisions in labor productivity and assuming no revisions for any other figure in the final column of Table 3. Current productivity data may exaggerate the 2002–03 productivity performance, as they reflect extensive downward revisions in aggregate hours of labor input, but they will not, until December, 2003, reflect the most important set of benchmark revisions to occur since 1999 in the national income accounts (which contribute output, investment, and capital data).

9 One of the interim versions of the O-S decomposition went through an end-point of 2001 and concluded that ICT capital *overexplains* the revival dated as 1995–2001 (see Sichel's discussion of Nordhaus, 2002).

10 Recall that the GDP statistics on which they rely measure output by production and treat any unsold goods as inventory accumulation, a part of GDP.

11 This remark was made in the discussant remarks of Tacho Bark of Seoul National University at the International Conference on Growth Engines of Korea, Seoul, July 24, 2003.

12 The first electronic computer, the ENIAC developed in the late 1940s, had only a tiny fraction of the computing power of a contemporary laptop but was 100 feet long, 10 feet high, 3 feet wide, and contained about 18,000 vacuum tubes. It was "programmed" by setting thousands of switches (Gordon, 1990, p. 191). For the early history of computing prior to 1950, see Nordhaus (2001) and the sources provided there.

13 The first internal combustion engine operating on modern principles is attributed to Julius Hock in 1870 and the first four-cycle engine to Nikolaus Otto in 1877. The first high-speed engine was built by Gottlieb Daimler in 1883 and the first three-wheeled automobile by Karl Benz in 1885. See Bunch and Hellemans (1993), pp. 268–293.

14 I am one of those experienced DOS users who still write papers like this one on Wordperfect for DOS 6.0. My fingers automatically know that CTRL+F7,1,1 creates a footnote and that SHIFT+F8,7,6,u will insert an "up" vertical advance code. But those examples underline the training cost faced by business firms ten years ago and the barriers to household adoption of PCs.

15 This is part of a broader point in the study of cross-country differences in economic growth. Many of the so-called "causes" of economic growth, such as education, are themselves in large part the consequence of growth. Countries, as they become richer, can afford to spread the bounty to education, research subsidies, better infrastructure, and better justice systems that reduce crime and corruption.

16 New price indexes and an assessment of official price indexes for consumer appliances and automobiles is provided in Gordon (1990), Chapters 7 and 8. A recent assessment of the problem of introducing new goods into price indexes is provided by Schultze and Mackie (2002), Chapter 5.

17 Consumer electronic spending could stimulate business productivity through a subtle link. Consider two classes of consumer products: electronic products with relative price declines and productivity increases, and nonelectronic products with small relative price increases and slightly below-average productivity growth. Innovations that cause consumers to shift their budget share toward more consumer electronic products could raise the growth rate of economywide productivity.

18 This point has long been made by Stephen Roach of Morgan Stanley.

19 The following discussion of Carr's views comes from [no author], "Nick Carr: The Tech Advantage is Overrated," *Business Week*, August 18–25, 2003, pp. 82–84.

20 The two quotes come from the previously cited *Business Week* article, pp. 83–84.

133

21 This paragraph and its quotes come from [no author] "Andy Grove: We Can't Even Glimpse the Potential," *Business Week*, August 18–25, 2003, pp. 86–88.

22 The McGuckin-van Ark data show a decline in hours at a rate of only –0.31 percent per annum during 2000–2002 and do not reflect the historical revisions to working hours released by the Bureau of Labor Statistics on August 7, 2003. Unfortunately, the annual series on total domestic hours of work compiled by the BEA has not been released for 2002. We based our estimate on the average growth rates of two series. The first is household survey civilian unemployment for 2000–2002 adjusted for the annual rate of decline of the BLS hours per employee series for 2000–2001. The second is the official BLS series on hours of work in the nonfarm sector, weighted together with government employment on the assumption of fixed hours per employee, weighted by the relative shares of government and private employees in total nonagricultural payroll employment in 2000.

23 Scatter plots supporting these correlations between MFP growth and computer intensity are presented in Bartelsman et al. (2002, Figures 8 and 9).

24 Any generalizations here about "Europe" must be qualified by differences across countries. The Germans until recently were notorious for restrictive shop-closing hours, while the French firm Carrefour and the Swedish firm Ikea are innovators in big box retailing formats.

References

Bartelsman, E.. A. Bassanini, J. Haltiwanger, R. Jarmin, S. Scarpetta, and T. Schank. 2002. "The Spread of ICT and Productivity Growth: Is Europe Really Lagging Behind in the New Economy," OECD draft report presented at Conference "The Information Economy: Productivity Gains and the Digital Divide," Catania, Sicily, June 15.

Bunch, B. and A. Hellemans. 1993. *The Timetables of Technology: A Chronology of the Most Important People and Events in the History of Technology.* New York: Touchstone.

Carr, N. 2003. "IT Doesn't Matter," *Harvard Business Review*, 81(5) May: 41–49.

Colecchia, A. and P. Schreyer. 2001. "ICT Investment and Economic Growth in the 1990s: Is the United States a Unique Case?" OECD, Paris, draft paper, October 7.

Daveri, F. 2002. "The New Economy in Europe (1992–2001)," IGIER Working Paper No. 213, April.

David, P. A. 1990. "The Dynamo and the Computer: An Historical Perspective on the Modern Productivity Paradox, *American Economic Review* (Papers and Proceedings) 80(2): 355–361.

David, P. A. and G. Wright. 1999. "Early Twentieth Century Productivity Growth Dynamics: An Inquiry into the Economic History of `Our Ignorance,'" Stanford Institute for Economic Policy Research Discussion Paper No. 98-3.

Domar, Evsey D. 1961. "On the Measurement of Technological Change," *Economic Journal* 71 (4, December): 709–729.

Foster, L., J. Haltiwanger, and C. J. Krizan. 2002. "The Link between Aggregate and Micro Productivity Growth: Evidence from Retail Trade," NBER Working Paper No. 9120. Cambridge, MA: National Bureau of Economic Research.

Gordon, Robert J. 1968. "The Disappearance of Productivity Change," Harvard Institute of Economic Research, Discussion Paper No. 44, September; reprinted in Gordon 2003c, pp. 90–133.

———. 1979. "The End-of-Expansion Phenomenon in Short-Run Productivity Behavior," *Brookings Papers on Economic Activity* 10 (2): 447–461.

———. 1990. *The Measurement of Durable Goods Prices.* Chicago: University of Chicago Press for NBER.

———1993. "The Jobless Recovery: Does It Signal a New Era of Productivity-Led Growth?" *Brookings Papers on Economic Activity* 24(1): 271–316.

———. 2000. "Does the New Economy Measure Up to the Great Inventions of the Past?" *Journal of Economic Perspectives* 14(4): 49–74.

———. 2002. "Two Centuries of Economic Growth: Europe Chasing the American Frontier," working paper, October.

———. 2003a. "Innovation and Future Productivity Growth: Does Supply Create Its Own Demand?" in Peter Cornelius, ed., *The Global Competitiveness Report 2002–2003.* New York and Oxford: Oxford University Press, pp. 253–275.

———. 2003b. "Cycles and Trends in the Links between Unemployment and Potential GDP," *Brookings Papers on Economic Activity,*34A(2), forthcoming.

———. 2003c. *Productivity Growth, Inflation, and Unemployment.* Cambridge, UK and New York: Cambridge University Press.

Jorgenson, D. W. and Z., Griliches.1967. "The Explanation of Productivity Change," *The Review of Economic Studies* 34 (3): 249–284.

Jorgenson, D. W. and K. J. Stiroh. 2000. "Raising the Speed Limit: U. S. Economic Growth in the Information Age," *Brookings Papers on Economic Activity* 31(1): 125–211.

McGuckin, R. H., and B. van Ark. 2003. *Performance 2002: Productivity, Employment, and Income in the World's Economies.* New York: The Conference Board.

McKinsey Global Institute 1992. *Service Sector Productivity.* Washington, DC: Author.

Oliner, S. D. and D. E. Sichel. 1994. "Computers and Output Growth Revisited: How Big is the Puzzle?" Brookings Papers on Economic Activity 25 (2): 273–317.

———. 2000. "The Resurgence of Growth in the Late 1990s: Is Information Technology the Story?" *Journal of Economic Perspectives*14 (fall): 3–22.

———. 2002. "Information Technology and Productivity: Where Are We Now and Where Are We Going?" *Atlanta Federal Reserve Bank Review*, third quarter, 15–44.

Nordhaus, W. D.. 1997. "Do Real-Output and Real-Wage Measures Capture Reality? The History of Lighting Suggests Not." In T. F. Bresnahan and R. J. Gordon, eds., *The Economics of New Goods.* Chicago: University of Chicago Press for NBER, pp. 29–66.

———. 2001. "The Progress of Computing," Cowles Foundation Discussion Paper No. 1324.

———. 2002. "Productivity Growth and the New Economy," *Brookings Papers on Economic Activity*, 33(2): 211–244.

Phelps, E. S. 2003. "Economic Underperformance in Continental Europe: A Prospering Economy Runs on the Dynamism from its Economic Institutions," lecture, Royal Institute for International Affairs, London, March 18.

Rhine-Westphalia Institute for Economic Research (RWI). 2002. *New Economy: An Assessment from a German Viewpoint.* Essen, February.

Rymes, T. K. 1971. *On Concepts of Capital and Technical Change.* Cambridge UK: Cambridge University Press.

Schultze, C. L. and C. Mackie, eds. 2002. *At What Price? Conceptualizing aand Measuring Cost-of-Living and Price Indexes.* Washington, DC: National Academy Press.

Sichel, D. E. 1997. The Computer Revolution: An Economic Perspective. Washington, DC: Brookings Institution Press.

Sieling, M. B. Friedman, and M. Dumas. 2001. "Labor Productivity in the Retail Trade Industry, 1987–99," *Monthly Labor Review* (December): 3–14.

Triplett, J. E. and B. P. Bosworth. 2002. "Baumol's Disease has been Cured: IT and Multifactor Productivity in U. S. Services Industries," paper presented at Brookings Workshop on Services Industry Productivity, Washington, DC, May 17.

van Ark, B., R. Inklaar, and R. H. McGuckin. 2002. "Changing Gear: Productivity, ICT and Service Industries: Europe and the United States," Paper presented to Brookings Workshop on Service Industry Productivity. Washington, DC, May 17.

Vijselaar, F., and R. Albers.2002. "New Technologies and Productivity Growth in the Euro Area," European Central Bank Working Paper No. 122, February.

Yang, S., and E. Brynjolfsson.2001. "Intangible Assets and Growth Accounting: Evidence from Computer Investments," MIT Working Paper, May.

Governance Redux:
The Empirical Challenge

DANIEL KAUFMANN,[1] World Bank Institute

"Brought back from imprisonment." That is the longer, Latin-rooted dictionary definition of *redux*,[2] while another refers to the return from exile. More succinctly, the English definition refers to "brought back" and cites "revived" as its synonym.[3] Indeed, core aspects of governance were taboo for international financial institutions until not long ago. By the mid 1990s, official documents would still largely avoid spelling out the word *corruption*, for instance. Thanks to a seachange at agencies such as the World Bank, as well as to the embracing of the challenge of governance by institutions such as the World Economic Forum, it is now possible to discuss openly the reality of governance worldwide, and apply such knowledge in concrete ways in countries intent on improving. Further, given the complexity of the topic, its multidisciplinary nature, and the tentative (and often subject to different interpretations) nature of the incipient lessons learnt, it is imperative to question and attempt to advance in this field by utilizing the power of empirical work—which often reveals evidence at odds with long and popularly held beliefs. Hence the title of this contribution, "Governance Redux: The Empirical Challenge," and the attempt in this chapter to cover various interrelated governance topics from an empirical perspective.

Governance remains at a crossroads

The decade of the 1970s witnessed robust economic growth around the globe, averaging well over 5 percent per year. Ever since then, economic performance has been modest, averaging less than half of this growth rate. By the end of the 1990s some acceleration in worldwide growth rates appeared to be in the offing, but disappointment set in again: growth rates declined from about 4 percent in 2000 to significantly less than 3 percent in 2002. Not surprisingly, recessionary expectations reported by the enterprises in this year's Executive Opinion Survey deepened significantly around the globe, with some exceptions. Although more than one-half of the firms expected substantial growth in their economies in 2002, this year less than one-third remained optimistic. Instead, by early 2003, the plurality of respondents expected recessionary times ahead.

To an extent, these short-term growth figures and enterprise expectations do reflect cyclical phenomena and external shocks for many countries. Yet deeper structural and productivity-related concerns also arise when taking a longer view. Has macroeconomic management deteriorated over the past decade, or do other causes explain such performance? In particular, how have countries performed on key governance dimensions? Is there a "governance reform gap" in the sense of a growing divergence between the technocratic ability of policymakers to implement traditional economic policies, as opposed to the inability or unwillingness to embark on governance reforms requiring deep-seated institutional and political change? Does it matter if a country lags behind in governance? In this sense, is there a "governance deficit" in the sense that many countries' current income level and/or their projected growth path is not attainable with their current quality of governance? What heretofore ignored factors, now subject to measurement, appear to be associated with good governance at the national and subnational levels? In this chapter we explore these and related questions.

In last year's contribution to the *Global Competitiveness Report* (GCR) on this topic, entitled "Governance Crossroads," it was suggested that there was little evidence of progress in governance in recent years, warranting a redoubling of efforts to address this complex challenge, as well as arguing for rethinking of some key premises and recommendations in the field.[4] In particular, we focused on the role of the private sector in helping shape public governance—for better or worse—challenging traditional legal and public-sector management approaches and public-policy advice.

This year, we argue that governance is still at a crossroads, its underperformance being evident in most regions and across many countries worldwide. This underperformance contrasts with the significant strides that have been made in macroeconomic policies for well over a decade. We analyze the results of this year's Survey in terms of the main constraints to the firms' operations, contrasting governance with other factors. More generally, with a recently constructed worldwide governance indicators dataset, we explore the extent to which the quality of national governance matters, quantifying the link between key governance dimensions and a country's per capita income and social progress.

We then briefly review the recent work on the deeper historical determinants of governance, focusing in particular on the origins of the country's legal system. On the basis of the governance indicators database we suggest that, for developing countries, it is imperative to analyze factors beyond whether a country's legal origins were in the common law or civil law traditions.

Furthermore, the database provided by the Survey permits the empirical evaluation of some political dimensions of governance traditionally regarded as non-measurable, such as the extent of "capture" and of undue influence by politically connected powerful firms in shaping the regulations, laws, and policies in a country. In particular, we explore the relevance of the unequal distribution of influence (or "crony bias") in a country, and its role in explaining public and financial governance performance.

The empirical richness of the Survey dataset also permits the initial construction of a governance database at the city level. On this basis, we explore potential determinants of city-level governance, such as city-level

characteristics and the country's urbanization and globalization trends.

We conclude with selected implications, further revisiting conventional advice on strategies to improve public governance, with emphasis on the need to address the nexus between corporate strategies and public governance. Methodological challenges associated with the empirical research summarized in this chapter are presented in the Appendixes.

Primacy of economic policies or of governance: A false dichotomy?

In recent writings, some authors have argued not only that governance matters significantly, but moreover that governance may dwarf the relevance of economic policies.[5] This sharply contrasts with the argument that prevailed earlier about the primacy of economic policies, and within it, the primacy of macroeconomic stabilization. Yet nowadays both extreme strands still coexist, even though there is increasing recognition among many that both governance and economic policies matter. On the macroeconomic primacy view, recent research, for instance, emphasizes the paramount importance of macroeconomic stability in attracting foreign direct investment (FDI).[6] It is by now indisputable that macroeconomic and exchange rate stability is an important precondition for FDI and growth. The question is whether macroeconomic and exchange rate stability remains a central *obstacle* to attracting FDI and economic progress, or whether its relative importance as a binding constraint may have lessened, and instead other factors have become binding. The data are indicative: they point to the fact that FDI levels (as a share of GDP) and inflation rates (or, alternatively, parallel exchange rate premia) during the last two decades have not always moved together—in Africa or elsewhere—even though there is a correlation between both sets of variables. Macroeconomic phenomena played a crucial role in the past, but the dynamics of FDI require an analysis beyond such macroeconomic variables to understand the sources and extent of the variance.

Even more important in terms of its implications for the near future is the dramatic improvement during the 1990s in the quality of macroeconomic management in the vast majority of emerging and transition economies. This resulted in a higher degree of macroeconomic and exchange rate stability, reduced inflation levels, and, notably, the virtual disappearance of parallel market premia in most countrie. And with very few exceptions, even in those few countries that still exhibit a parallel premia, it is not large. The evidence is telling: in 1983, 44 percent of the countries outside of the Organisation of Economic Co-operation and Development (OECD) had a parallel exchange rate premia exceeding 30 percent; 15 years later, by the late 1990s, a mere 11 percent of the emerging and transition economies did. By the year 2000, the number of countries with a significant parallel premia had further shrunk to such a negligible proportion that the World Bank ceased collecting data on parallel premia data altogether!

Similarly, dramatic progress has taken place in containing inflationary pressures, in even a briefer time span: 44 percent of non-OECD countries had annual inflation rates exceeding 20 percent in 1994; by the end of 2002, a mere 8 percent did.[7] Yet during the past decade this significant improvement in macroeconomic performance in itself did not automatically translate into significantly higher levels of FDI in Africa and in emerging markets more generally or into more vigorous growth and development. In fact, as reviewed below, during the recent past the gains in macroeconomic policies were not accompanied by similar advances in governance performance, which has been stagnant, thereby widening the governance reform gap between the level of effort in governance and macroeconomic policies.

Further, a simple review of the recent data suggests a much higher correlation between FDI and governance than between FDI and macroeconomic variables. In particular, using the worldwide governance indicators dataset we have constructed (described below), we find that indicators capturing various dimensions of governance, such as the quality of the regulatory regime, rule of law, and control of corruption, matter very significantly when relating it to FDI (as a share in GDP) worldwide. This is relevant in the context of recent trends: while on average macroeconomic stability is no longer a major binding constraint in emerging economies (with a few exceptions), the quality of governance has remained stagnant at a low level in many countries. Obviously, maintaining macroeconomic stability ought to continue to be regarded as a necessary precondition for growth and for FDI, yet it is far from sufficient. Particular emphasis on governance factors is warranted, since at the present juncture it appears to constitute a binding constraint.

The data from the recent Executive Opinion Survey, carried out during 2003 and covering almost 6,000 enterprises in over 100 countries, in conjunction with the comparative analysis with Survey data from earlier years, is also indicative in this context. Selected results illustrating the trend over the past five years in some key factors affecting the business climate are illustrated in Figure 1. Figure 1a suggests some progress over the years in the firms' assessment of the quality of infrastructure, contrasting the stagnant or even deteriorating trends on judicial independence (Figure 1b), and control of bribery in the judiciary (Figure 1c).[8]

Reviewing the trends of various governance variables from the Survey between 1998 and 2003 in some detail suggests the overall challenge of governance stagnation

while also bringing out some notable variation across regions. For administrative regulations,[9] a deterioration worldwide is apparent, including the rather dire assessment of OECD firms as well as the enterprises from emerging and transition economies. In the latest Survey, a mere 18 percent of enterprises worldwide rate administrative regulations as not that burdensome, while about 70 percent rate them as very or relatively burdensome. Only in East Asia's New Industrialized Countries (NICs) has a deteriorating trend not been evident, and about one-half of the enterprises there do not report such regulations as burdensome. By contrast, less than 10 percent do so in the former Soviet Union, Latin America, and Africa.

The quality of anti-monopoly policies has continued to stagnate from the levels reported last year. However, there are noteworthy differences across regions, with apparent improvement in the reports by firms in countries in the OECD, the New Industrialized Countries (NICs) in East Asia, and the Middle East and North Africa (MENA). This contrasts with the deterioration seen over the same five-year period in the former Soviet Union (Ukraine and Russia) and, in particular, in Latin America. Somewhat less deterioration was seen in South Asia, in developing East Asia, and in eastern Europe.

The extent of the independence of the judiciary has not exhibited any improvement—and may in fact have deteriorated—according to the responses by the firms (Figure 1b). It was noted in the governance chapter in last year's GCR that a drop in the assessed extent of judiciary independence worldwide took place between 2001 and 2002. This year's Survey (2003) indicates similarly low ratings compared with last year's already low levels, suggesting that the results of a year ago were not a one-year blip. The extent of bribery in the judiciary has also been subject to deteriorating ratings from 1998 to 2002, with stagnant assessments over the past year (Figure 1c). Latin American countries on average, as well as the surveyed enterprises in the former Soviet Union, rate lower than other regions in this dimension.

The Survey has also asked every year since the late 1990s whether corruption has deteriorated, has remained unchanged, or has improved over the past 3 years. The analysis of this trend of corruption variable indicates that on average the corruption trend has remained stable, but with notable regional variance. There is a significant improvement (two-thirds of the firms) reported for East Asia NIC; some modest improvement in OECD, East Asia developing countries, eastern Europe, and MENA. For each of these regions about 40 percent or so of the enterprises report an improvement, and one-quarter report a deterioration; and an overall deterioration is reported for Africa, Latin America, and the former Soviet Union (with only between one-fifth and one-quarter of the enterprises reporting an improvement).

Stagnating quality of governance in perspective: View of the firm

Figure 1a: Quality of infrastructure

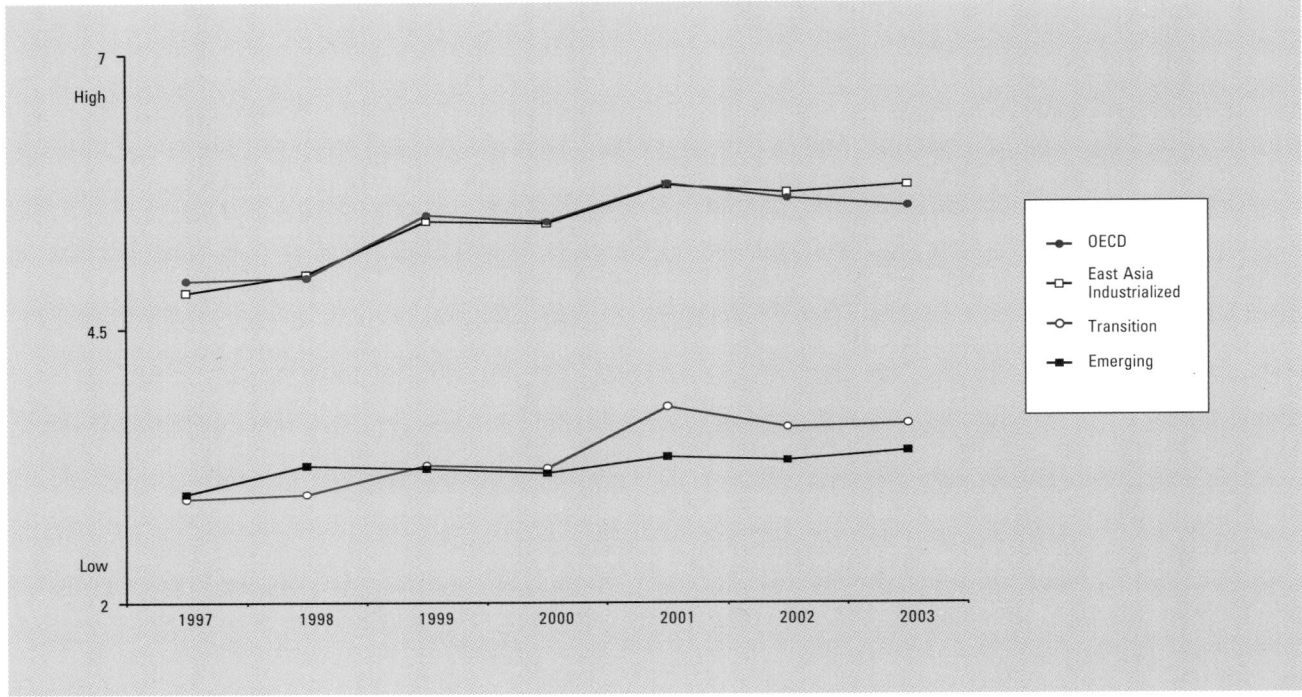

Source: Executive Opinion Surveys 1997–2003 . Question 5.01: General infrastructure in your country is (1 = poorly developed and inefficient; 7 = among the best in the world)

Figure 1b: Judicial independence

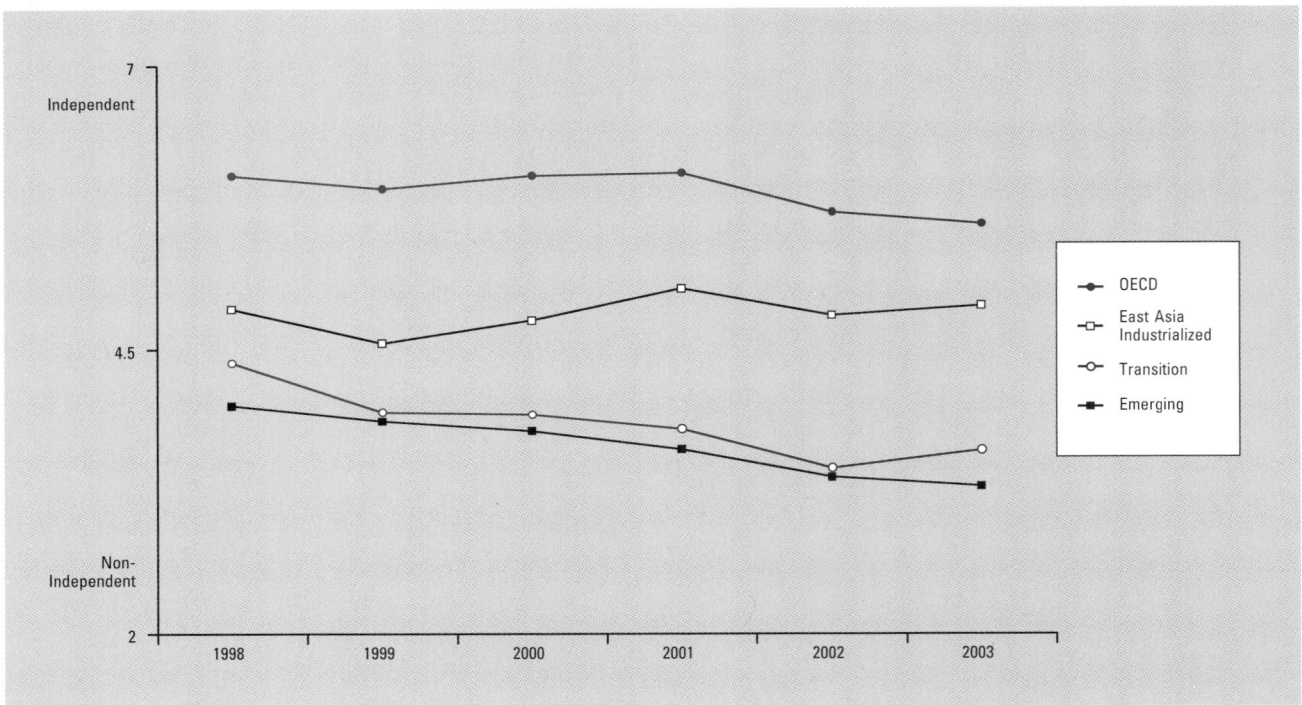

Source: Executive Opinion Surveys 1998–2003 . Question 6.01: The judiciary in your country is independent from political influences of members of government, citizens, or firms (1 = no, heavily influenced; 7 = yes, entirely independent)

Stagnating quality of governance in perspective: View of the firm *(cont'd.)*

Figure 1c: Control of judicial corruption

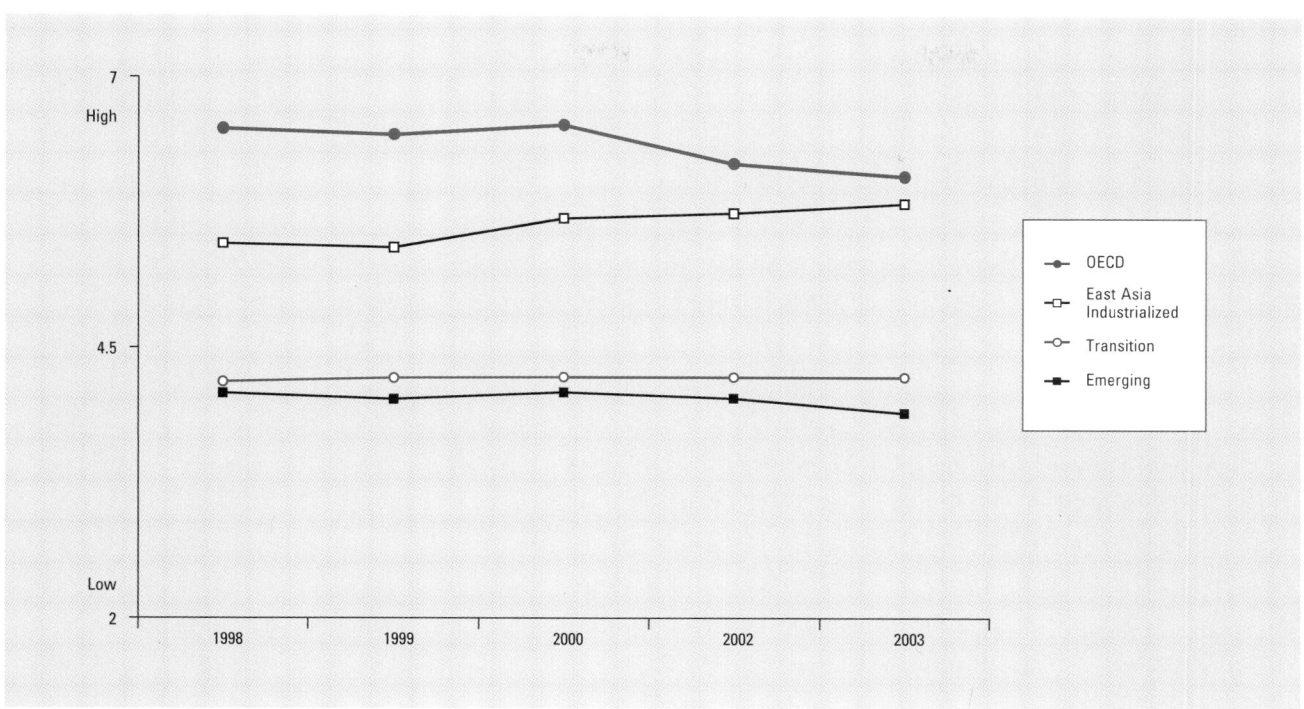

Source: Executive Opinion Surveys 1997–2003 . Question 7.07: In your industry, how commonly would you estimate that firms make undocumented extra payments or bribes connected with getting favorable judicial decisions? (1 = common; 7 = never occurs). Note: this question has been asked every year since 1998 except in the 2001 Survey.

Figure 1d: Key business environment constraint to the firm: emerging economies and OECD

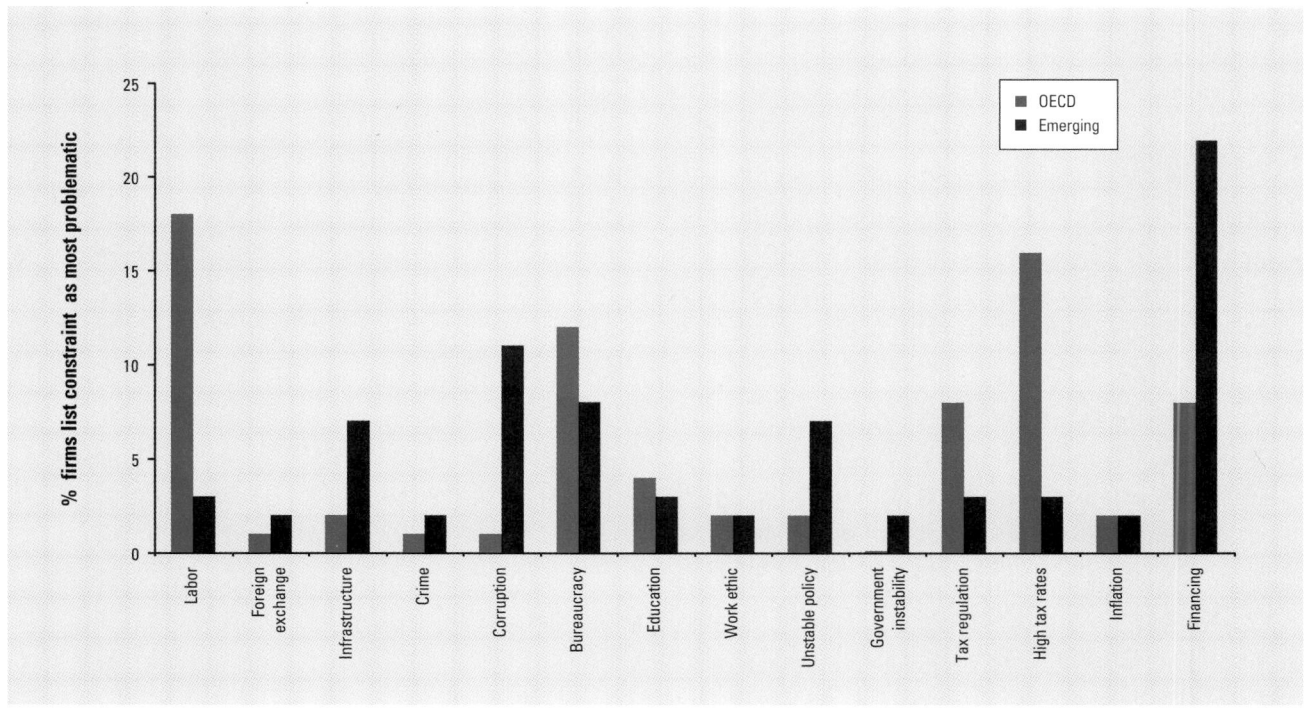

Source: Executive Opinion Survey 2003. Question 13.01. From the following list, please select the five most problematic factors for doing business in your country, and rank them between 1 (most problematic) and 5. The figure shows the percent of firms ranking the said constraint as the *most* problematic among the 14 items on the list.

Furthermore, over the past couple of years the same detailed questions on the assessment of the level of different forms of bribery has been asked in the Survey, which permits a comparison between 2003 and 2002. The findings suggest the importance of "unbundling" corruption into its different types, since the various forms of corruption can be subject to varying severity within the same country, and do not always move together over time. We find that overall there are declining levels of bribery for connection to utilities and for taxation, and in particular in eastern Europe, East Asia developing countries, and Africa. On the other hand there is an increase in bribery in procurement and in the "capture" or purchase of laws, regulations, and policies.

The reported extent of illegal party donations (not shown) remained stable on average over the past year, and at a very high level, with over one-half of all firms reporting illegal party financing to be significant. There is an apparent contrast across regions in this variable as well: East Asia (NIC) rates relatively well (better than OECD countries, in fact), with only one-fifth of the firms reporting it to be significant. In the former Soviet Union, South Asia, and Latin America between 75 and 85 percent of all enterprises indicate that illegal party financing is substantial or very substantial.[10]

In sum, the ratings reported by firms worldwide on different governance dimensions suggests a sobering picture, and points to a growing governance (policy effort) gap. Complementing the time trend analysis described above, it is of interest to review the extent to which various factors in the business environment pose a constraint to the firms and assess the relative severity of governance and other factors. This can be done by analyzing the very last question in the Survey questionnaire, which asks enterprises to provide a relative rank of obstacles to their business operations.

When asked to rate the most important constraints to their operations, businesses in emerging and transition economies rated corruption at the very top, followed closely by excessive bureaucracy (see Figure 1d). Out of a list of 14 obstacles, the only constraint that they rated higher than these governance factors, was, in fact, access to finance, a common reaction by the enterprise sector in settings usually characterized by macroeconomic stability.

Consistent with the evolution in macroeconomic policies over the past 15 years, the firms' response to this Survey question points to a lack of concern on their part about inflation as a constraint (at the very bottom of the list of 14 candidates), as well as the foreign exchange regime (see Figure 1d). This is in contrast to the severe concern reported by firms about corruption and bureaucratic red tape in emerging economies.[11]

In contrast to firms in emerging and transition economies, firms in OECD countries did not rate corruption as a major constraint. They considered the main obstacles to their operations to be focused on the extent of the bureaucracy, tax rates, and tax and labor regulations (Figure 1d). Thus even firms in OECD countries did emphasize other governance dimensions (even if they did not point to corruption in particular as a major constraint). And similar to the firms in emerging and transition economies, firms in OECD economies continued to rate inflation as a very minor constraint.

In sum, from the perspective of the firm, governance constraints appear to be more binding than the (generally improved) macroeconomic stance in most settings. At the same time, it is important to note that in the medium term the trajectory of governance and macro-economic policies cannot totally be divorced from each other, since subpar governance may undermine some of the gains attained in the macroeconomic policy arena.

Governance: Basic definitions and worldwide indicators

We recap from last year's chapter contribution to the GCR, which defined *governance* as the set traditions and formal and informal institutions that determine how authority is exercised in a particular country for the common good, thus encompassing: (1) the process of selecting, monitoring, and replacing governments; (2) the capacity to formulate and implement sound policies and deliver public services; and (3) the respect of citizens and the state for the institutions that govern economic and social interactions among them. For measurement and analysis, the three dimensions in this definition are unbundled to comprise two measurable concepts for each of the dimensions above, for a total of six governance components:

1. *voice and external accountability*, that is, the government's preparedness to be externally accountable through their own country's citizen feedback and democratic institutions, and a competitive press, thus including elements of restraint on the sovereign;
2. *political stability and lack of violence, crime, and terrorism*;
3. *government effectiveness*, including quality of policymaking, bureaucracy, and public service delivery;
4. *lack of regulatory burden*;
5. *rule of law*, protection of property rights, judiciary independence, and so on, thus including elements of law and order; and
6. *control of corruption*.

Applying the above definition of governance and gathering data from many different sources, we have analyzed hundreds of cross-country indicators as proxies for

Table 1: Worldwide governance indicators, 1996–2002 (percentile rank, regional averages)

Country	Year	Voice and accountability	Political stability and lack of violence	Government effectiveness	Regulatory quality	Rule of law	Control of corruption
Sub-Saharan Africa	2002	31	35	29	31	31	32
	2000	33	32	32	35	33	34
	1998	34	33	35	33	32	32
	1996	34	35	30	32	34	32
Middle East & North Africa	2002	29	40	50	45	54	55
	2000	30	50	56	50	59	54
	1998	29	49	53	45	62	56
	1996	29	40	53	47	55	52
South Asia	2002	30	32	48	35	42	42
	2000	27	26	45	38	37	41
	1998	32	27	44	46	40	46
	1996	33	31	50	45	36	39
East Asia	2002	50	55	51	43	48	44
	2000	49	55	51	42	45	47
	1998	50	56	50	41	46	48
	1996	52	55	57	49	54	52
OECD	2002	91	87	92	92	92	91
	2000	91	90	92	91	92	92
	1998	91	88	92	90	92	93
	1996	91	89	92	90	91	90
Latin America & Caribbean	2002	61	51	53	58	53	55
	2000	60	51	50	59	51	51
	1998	61	45	50	65	50	51
	1996	60	48	46	58	47	46
Eastern Europe	2002	65	61	58	63	57	55
	2000	63	54	56	59	57	57
	1998	56	57	52	58	55	56
	1996	55	58	59	56	54	53
Former Soviet Union	2002	23	31	22	25	20	17
	2000	28	33	20	16	21	19
	1998	28	38	22	18	22	18
	1996	25	39	23	21	22	20

Note: Data shown in percentile rank (0 is the worst-ranked country, 100 is the best), regional averages. Country coverage: 199 countries, comprising the following number of countries in each region: Sub-Saharan Africa, 47; Middle East & North Africa, 20; South Asia, 8; East Asia, 29; OECD, 29; Latin America and the Caribbean, 38; eastern Europe, 16; former Soviet Union, 12. Estimates are subject to a margin of error (a more detailed treatment is provided in Appendix B), and thus small differences in percentile ranks are not statistically significant. Presented regional average point estimates are subject to margins of error (see website for details). Figures are rounded to their closest integer.

Source: Kaufmann, Kraay, and Mastruzzi (2003). Data accessible at: http://www.worldbank.org/wbi/governance/govdata2002.

various aspects of governance.[12] These individual variables, which serve as the inputs to our aggregate governance indicators, are produced by a range of organizations. They include the perspectives of diverse observers and cover a wide range of topics: political stability and the business climate, the efficacy of public service provision, protection of property rights and judicial independence, experiences with corruption, and so on.

Imposing structure on these many available variables from diverse sources, we mapped the data to the six sub-components of governance listed above, expressed them in common units, measured the margins of error, and, thanks to a statistical methodology, aggregated into the six governance indicators—thereby improving the reliability of the resulting composite indicator and the analysis. These indicators for 1996 through 2002, for almost 200 countries,

are available online. They can assist in providing global empirical perspective on governance performance today and assess the historical and other determinants and manifestations of governance.[13] Table 1 provides the regional averages for each governance component from 1996 until 2002, and suggests the extent to which governance remains a major challenge in a number of regions in the world. The extent of the challenge varies across different components of governance within each region: note, for instance, the poor performance on control of corruption in Latin America, although the region is performing somewhat better on voice and democratic accountability to its citizenry. This is in contrast with MENA, where by far the largest governance challenge lies in the absence of voice and democratic accountability mechanisms in many settings.[14]

Figure 2: Governance indicators and income per capita, 2000–2002

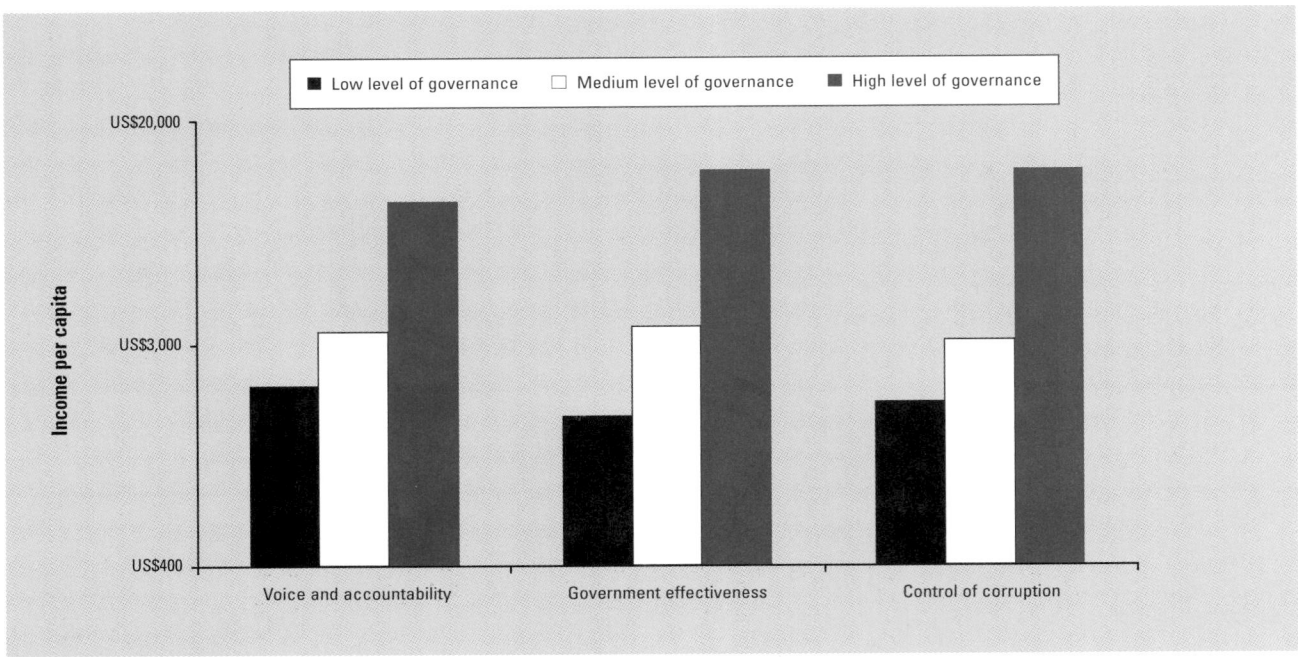

Sources: The three different indicators of governance are from Kaufmann, Kraay, and Mastruzzi (2003); income per capita (in purchasing power parity terms) is from Heston, Summers, and Aten (2002) and CIA World Factbook (2001). Vertical axis is in log scale.

Governance matters

Using the data emerging from worldwide governance indicators (and others), a number of researchers have performed systematic assessments of the benefits of good governance worldwide. Empirical studies have codified the importance of governance for development outcomes. Knack and Keefer (1997) found that the institutional environment for economic activity generally determines the ability of emerging economies to catch up to industrial country standards. Mauro (1995) studied the strong empirical link between corruption and growth. Easterly and Levine (2002) and Rodrik, Subramanian, and Trebbi (2002) have pointed to the primacy of institutions over geographical and policy determinants of growth. Sachs and Warner (1997), as well as Diamond (1999), provide evidence of the importance of geographical, ethnographic, and epidemiological factors.

In our research, we have also reviewed the link between governance quality and income growth (as well as other developmental outcomes), and attempted to address thorny issues of causality direction.

Governance and incomes are highly correlated—but causality which way?

The set of six worldwide governance research indicators, available already for the 1996–2002 period, allow systematic assessment of the benefits of good governance in a large sample of countries. At the most basic level, the data at first reveal a very high correlation between good governance and key development outcomes across countries. In summary fashion, Figure 2 depicts the very close link between various governance components (voice and democratic accountability, governance effectiveness, and control of corruption) and national income per capita.[15]

Yet these very robust correlations in themselves represent a "weak" finding in terms of policy application because such correlations do not shed light on the direction of causality or on whether an omitted ("third") correlated variable is the fundamental cause accounting for the effects on developmental outcomes. Thus, we need to probe deeper, which we do with specialized statistical techniques, unbundling each causality direction.

Logically there are three possible explanations for the strong positive correlation between incomes and governance: (1) better governance exerts a powerful effect on per capita incomes; (2) higher incomes lead to improvements in governance; and (3) there are other factors that make countries richer and are also associated with better governance. Untangling the observed high correlation between incomes and governance is important in order to ascertain whether there is an automatic "virtuous circle" where higher incomes are automatically translated into improved governance, or if such positive feedback mechanism is absent then a concerted and continuous policy intervention effort to improve governance is needed. Consequently, we need a good understanding of the effects of governance on incomes as well as of any feedback mechanisms from incomes to governance that might exist. Simply observing a strong correlation between income growth and governance does not suffice.[16]

Let us consider first the effect of governance on per capita incomes. As recently as 200 years ago, per capita incomes were not very different across countries. The wide gaps in per capita income across countries that we see today reflect the simple fact that countries that are rich today have grown rapidly over the past two centuries, while those that are poor today did not.[17]

What about causation in the opposite direction, from per capita income to the quality of governance? Conventional wisdom holds that richer countries are better able to afford the costs associated with providing a competent government bureaucracy, sound rule of law, and an environment in which corruption is not condoned. This suggests that there is positive feedback from per capita income to governance as well. Yet, to date, this conventional wisdom has not been subject to in-depth empirical scrutiny. In our research we have put such conventional wisdom through an empirical test. We implemented a novel methodology that permitted to separate out the effects of per capita income on governance, and found evidence that this effect is certainly not positive, but, if anything, is negative.[18]

This finding of an absence of (or even possibly negative) feedback from per capita income to governance has three important implications. First, a strategy of waiting for improvements to come automatically as countries become richer is unlikely to succeed. Second, in the absence of positive feedback from per capita income to governance, we are unlikely to observe virtuous circles when better governance improves incomes that *in turn* will lead to further automatic improvements in governance. Together, these two implications point to the fundamental importance of positive and sustained interventions to improve governance in countries where it is lacking. Indeed, the fact that good governance is not a "luxury good" to which a country automatically graduates when it becomes wealthier means in practical terms that leaders, policymakers, and civil society need to work hard and continuously at improving governance within their countries.

The third important implication is that, in the absence of positive feedback from per capita income to governance, it is possible to explore with the data at hand the fragility of income levels of a country for its given level of governance, or what we can label as "governance deficit," referring to the "distance" between a country's actual governance level and the level required to support and sustain its income per capita level. Such long-run

economic fragility, or governance deficit, can be approximated by the distance between a country's actual governance level (in a plotgram of incomes and governance) and the governance level that would place the country on the fitted regression line for its level of incomes.[19] Intriguingly, the vast majority of countries in Latin America in the late 1990s had levels of per capita income that were not sustainable by their actual levels of governance (rule of law, control of corruption, and so on). Particularly noteworthy was the extent of the governance deficit in countries such as Argentina, Ecuador, Guatemala, Paraguay, and Venezuela, and to a degree also Bolivia.[20] A corollary of this framework is that the extent of governance deficit can be suggestively interpreted as the additional governance reform effort required to make the prevailing per capita income levels sustainable—lest it come down if such governance effort is not present.[21]

It is important to understand the possible reasons for the absence of positive feedback from per capita income to governance when designing strategies to improve governance. Based on empirical evidence, we have advanced an explanation for this negative feedback: the phenomenon of *state capture*, defined as the undue and illicit influence of the elite in *shaping* the laws, policies, and regulations of the state.[22] When institutions of the state are "captured" by vested interests in this way, or, more subtly, when powerful vested interests exert undue influence in shaping the rules of the game for their own benefit (discussed below), entrenched elites in a country can benefit from a worsening status quo of misgovernance and can successfully resist demands for change even as per capita income rises.

Based on in-depth governance and anti-corruption country diagnostics carried out at the World Bank in countries in various regions, as well as enterprise surveys in economies in transition, we have found significant empirical evidence of the challenge of state capture (and the related "crony bias" or unequally distributed influence) in many countries. In countries with an environment that is "captured" or unduly influenced by the vested interests of the powerful few, the focus of efforts to combat corruption and improve governance needs to shift from a narrow emphasis on passing laws and rules, and on procedures within the public administration, to a much broader agenda of greater political accountability, transparency, and freedom of the press.

In contrast to the absence of positive effects from income to governance, we found a *large direct causal effect* from better governance to improved development outcomes. Consequently, the simple relationship depicted in Figure 2 in fact does approximate the causal impact of improved governance on per capita income given the lack of positive feedback in the reverse causality direction.[23]

145

Indeed, the effects of improved governance on income in the long run are found to be very large, with an estimated 400 percent improvement in per capita income associated with an improvement in governance by one standard deviation, and similar improvements in reducing child mortality and illiteracy. To illustrate, an improvement in rule of law by one standard deviation from the current levels in Ukraine to those "middling" levels prevailing in South Africa would lead to a fourfold increase in per capita income in the long run. A larger increase in the quality of rule of law (by two standard deviations) in Ukraine (or in other countries in the former Soviet Union), to the much higher level in Slovenia or Spain, would further multiply this income per capita increase. Similar results emerge from other governance dimensions: a mere one standard deviation improvement in voice and accountability from the low level of Venezuela to that of South Korea, or in control of corruption from the low level of Indonesia to the middling level of Mexico, or from the level of Mexico to that of Costa Rica, would also be associated with an estimated fourfold increase in per capita incomes, as well as similar improvements in reducing child mortality by 75 percent and major gains in literacy.

In sum, new types of surveys and statistical methodologies permit the empirical assessment of governance worldwide. These assessments in turn suggest that there are enormous differences in governance performance across the globe, and thus within different capitalist systems. Such large variation in governance matters significantly for growth and development. Income windfalls for a country do not, however, get automatically translated into improved governance, possibly due to particular political factors related to the interface between corporate strategies of the powerful, which result in unequal distribution of influence and thus of reaping the fruits from growth. With the benefit of the new database that is now available and that recognizes the enormous differences across different types of market economies, we explore next some potential historical and political determinants of governance outcomes nowadays.

On the new comparative economics and historical determinants

In recent years, comparative economics has experienced a revival, with a new focus on comparing capitalist economies. Shleifer and others have led the work on "New Comparative Economy," arguing that the transition from socialism, the Asian financial crisis, and the European economic and political integration have challenged our understanding of how capitalist economies and societies work.[24] They suggest that capitalist economies differ in important ways in how they regulate market activities,

including the extent of public ownership, regulation of social harms, and contract enforcement, as well as how they regulate political competition. And they emphasize in particular the historical origin of a country's legal system, which they suggest has proved to be a crucial factor in explaining the present quality of governance.

Although their analysis of how such systems differ in terms of legal and regulatory issues do provide further evidence of some of the negative consequences of overly interventionist measures within many capitalist systems, their central conclusion—that legal origin is the crucial determinant of performance across capitalist systems—is open to challenge, along with their particular focus on the unambiguous advantage of common law systems. A priori, we argue that a complex interplay of initial conditions, coupled with a plethora of intervening factors (throughout the development process), is likely to have a role in the substantial adaptation of governance in a country and the transformation of institutions—also within systems that have the same historical legal origins. Nonetheless, it is also valid to posit that there are considerations partly supporting the case for legal origins: the case can be made that common law is consistent with a higher degree of judiciary independence, less interventionism, and more institutional flexibility than under civil law. Indeed, statistical analysis of the worldwide dataset for OECD and developing countries suggests some advantage of common law systems in explaining governance performance today. However, the magnitude of this effect is not large, and the share of cross-country variation explained by the type of legal origins is rather low, which points to the importance of other factors as well.

Furthermore, at a basic level there is the simple empirical observation that OECD countries with vastly different legal origins perform well today, whereas some nations in Africa, Asia, Latin America, and the former Soviet Union, with different types of legal origins as well, exhibit notable cases of dysfunctional governance. Indeed, among the latter underperformers there is no clear pattern in terms of legal origins. Our own governance dataset, comprising almost 200 countries, is useful in reviewing the evidence, which we do through a matrix table (Table 2) that includes legal origins (civil versus common versus German) in the columns, and today's rule-of-law quality in the rows.

In comparing civil and common law systems (first two columns) we observe that all four cells are filled with many country illustrations. Instead of a marked diagonal pattern, many countries today exhibit subpar governance (proxied by the current indicator for the quality of rule of law indicator), across countries with common and civil law origins. And countries with very high-quality rule of law today, such as Chile, Costa Rica, France, Netherlands, and Spain, have origins in civil law. Furthermore, it is

Table 2: Quality of rule of law today versus historical legal origins (selected economies)

Governance 2002	Legal origin		
	Civil Law	Common Law	German Law
High-quality rule of law, 2002	Chile, Costa Rica, France, Italy, Netherlands, Portugal, Spain, etc.	Australia, Botswana, Canada, Ireland, United Kingdom, United States, etc.	Austria, Estonia, Germany, Hungary, Japan, Rep. of Korea, Slovenia, Switzerland, Taiwan (China), etc.
Low-quality rule of-law, 2002	Angola, Argentina, Cote d'Ivoire, Haiti, Iraq, Laos, Libya, Myanmar, Paraguay, Venezuela, etc.	Bangladesh, Liberia, Kenya, Malawi, Nigeria, Pakistan, Sierra Leone, Somalia, Sudan, Zambia, Zimbabwe, etc.	None

Source: Kaufmann (2003b).

noteworthy that countries with German legal origins (the third column of the matrix), such as Estonia, Hungary, the Republic of Korea, and Slovenia, as well as Scandinavian origins (comprising the Nordic countries, not shown), are all clustered in the good rule of law performance cell, and notably absent are any countries with dysfunctional governance. This, in turn, contrasts with ex-Socialist countries (not shown in the table).

As suggested, in reviewing econometrically the performance ratings of our six governance indicators against legal origins for the worldwide sample, controlling for other factors, on average a small advantage for countries with common law over civil law origins in a number of dimensions can be detected. Without such controls, we observe these differences between civil and common law origins in Figure 3a. Furthermore, we also see in Figure 3a that German and Scandinavian systems have performed rather well, in contrast with the legacy of the Soviet era, classified as the legal origins for the Commonwealth of Independent States.[25] Undoubtedly there are important lessons for developing countries from a comparison across legal systems that focuses on more than the (admittedly important) distinction between civil and common law systems.

Furthermore, OECD countries have done rather well in spite of their vastly different legal origins. Certain features of common code legal systems lend themselves to further adaptability and flexibility compared with civil codes (partly as a result of the relative independence of judges, the prominence of juries, and reliance on broad legal principles). There is evidence of a small but significant correlation between legal origins and governance performance today. But as we focus on the set of 75 lower-income countries, the differences between common and civil law origins essentially disappear, with minor variations in direction across different governance dimensions, as we observe in Figure 3b. It is precisely within this group of countries, many of which exhibit dysfunctional governance, that the most daunting governance challenges lie.

Consequently, drawing on the analysis of a comprehensive governance dataset for developing and transition economies, it is appropriate to probe deeper into other potential historical determinants of governance performance today. In this context, Acemoglu and others (2001) analyze the importance of historical settler mortality patterns of colonizers, while Engelman and Sokoloff (2002) address the relevance of factor endowments and educational inequality. Others, mentioned previously, focus on geographic and other related factors. Increasingly attention is also turning to political factors, even if not necessarily taking such a deep historical perspective (and thus less able to disentangle endogeneity and causality issues). A particular dimension that we have empirically studied recently is the subversion of governance in institutions, when state capture and undue influence through vested interests take place (mentioned earlier). With the benefit of empirical findings provided by the Survey, we discuss these institutions of influence next, which are at the core of the intersection between corporate strategies, politics, and public policy.

State capture and inequality of influence

The work by Glaeser and Shleifer on the theoretical underpinnings and characteristics of institutions is also part of the new comparative economics. This work is highly relevant and complements our research findings. Indeed, their argument that an important property of a successful institution is its invulnerability to capture by elite vested interests dovetails with the work on state capture we have carried out in transition economies.[26] This empirical research had antecedents in the work on influence peddling by Grossman and Helpman (2001) and on regulatory capture (Laffont and Tirole, 1991). As summarized in the governance chapter of last year's GCR, we have viewed state capture as the ability of powerful firms or interests to shape the rules of the game, often through illicit means, and thereby to affect the formulation of a country's laws, policies, and regulations. We found in

Figure 3: World governance indicators today (percentile ranks) by legal origins: Results worldwide (a) and for low-income countries (b)

Figure 3a: Worldwide

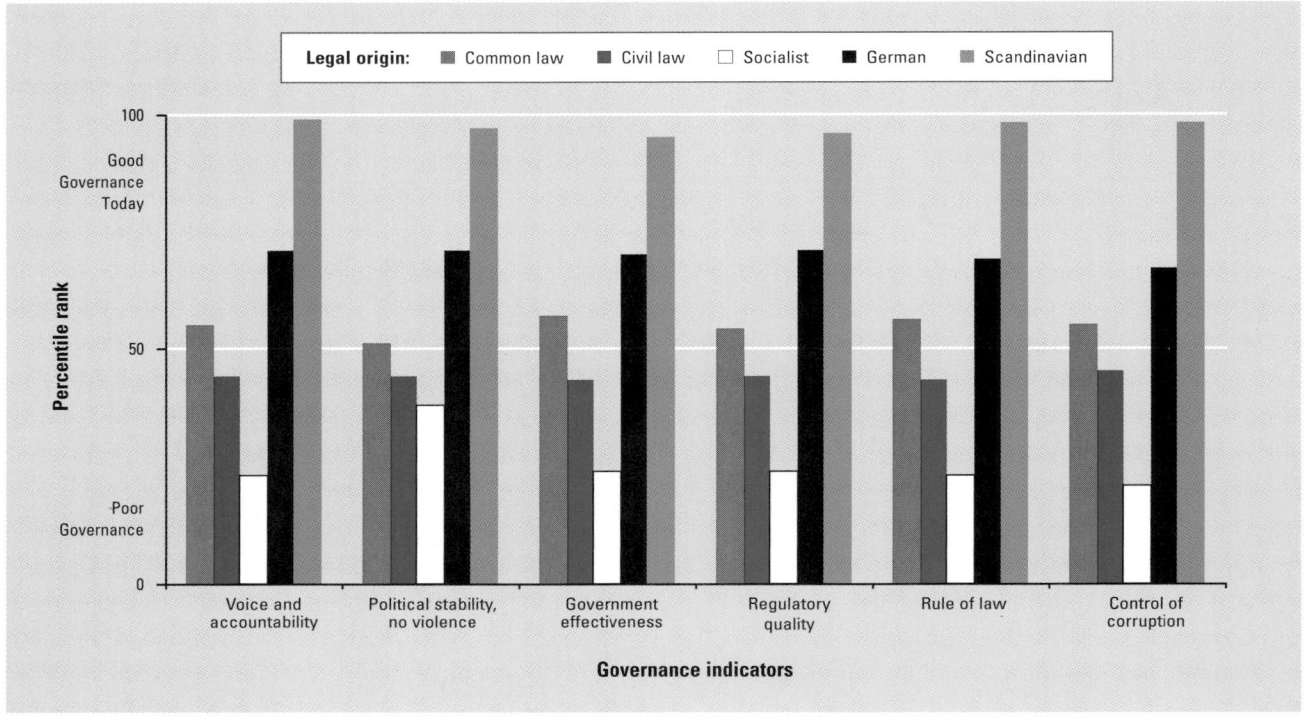

Figure 3b: Low-income countries

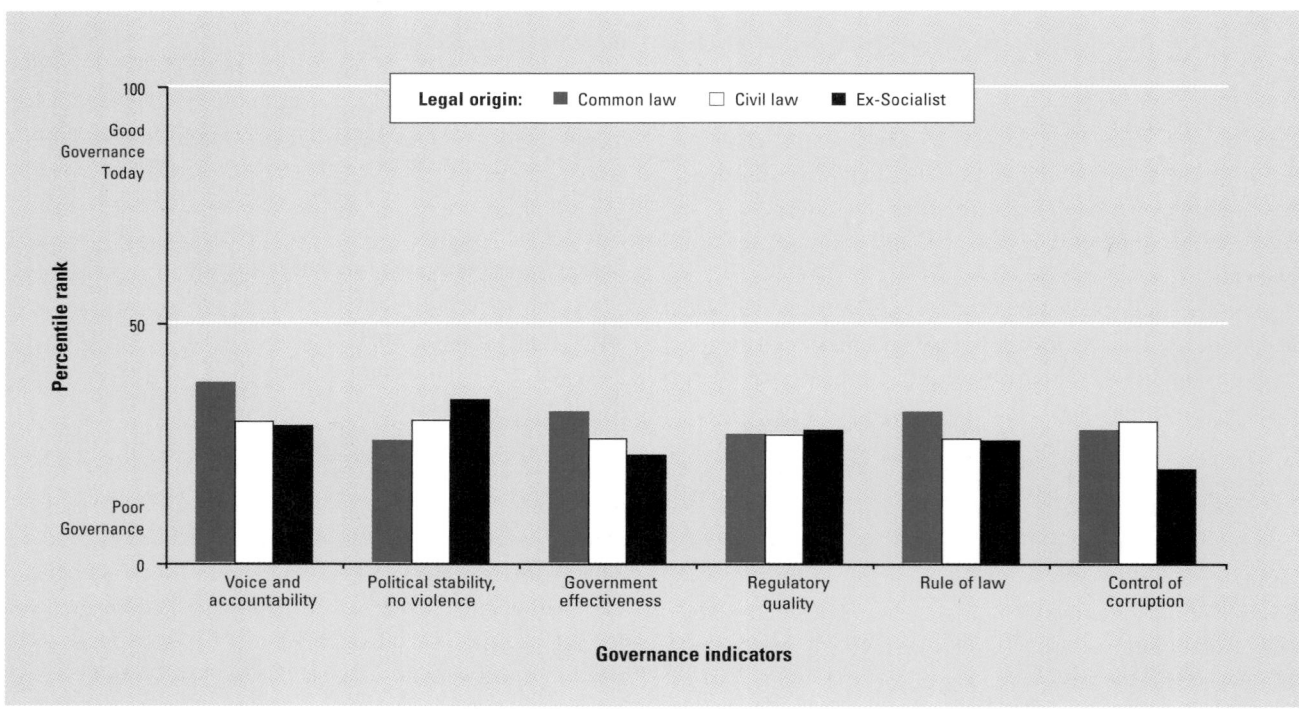

Note: Governance indicator shown as percentile rank in the world (100 being best). Worldwide (Figure 3a) includes 193 countries. The low-income country sample in Figure 3b includes all 74 low-income countries for which there are data for both variables shown. Low-income countries are defined as below GNI per capita of US$1,435 in 2001. Out of the sample of 74 low-income countries in Figure 3b, the breakdown is: common law, 25; civil law, 39; ex-Socialist, 10.

Sources: For governance indicators, Kaufmann, Kraay, and Mastruzzi (2003). For legal origin, La Porta et al. (1999) and Djankov, McLiesh, and Shleifer (2003).

Figure 4: Political influence and crony bias, regional averages, based on the 2003 Survey

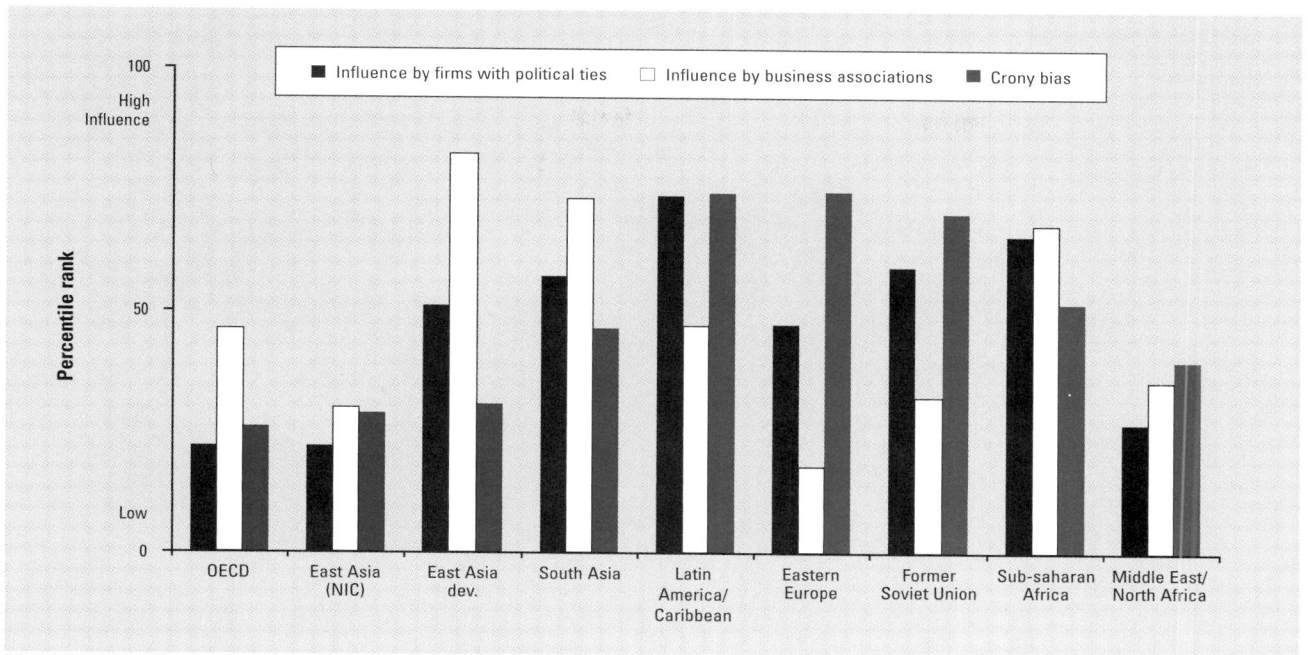

Note: *Crony bias* is defined as the difference between influence by firms with political ties and influence by firm's business association. The other two variables related to political influence refer to the Survey questions on the impact on growth produced by influence on recently enacted national laws and regulations by (1) dominant firms or conglomerates, and (2) firms or individuals with close political ties to political leaders.

Source: Executive Opinion Survey (2003).

transition economies a dichotomized reality: about half of the countries (largely those in eastern Europe and the Baltics) have made a transition to a healthy market economy, although many other countries (concentrated in the former Soviet Union) saw some of their institutions captured by vested interests. This empirical investigation into state capture is now expanded to a number of settings in Latin America, revealing the depth of the challenge in this continent as well.

Most recently, and in large measure thanks to the availability of the data from the 2003 Survey, we have expanded this line of inquiry to probe deeply into the manifestations and implications of unequal influence within countries—that is, not merely concentrating on the more extreme manifestation of capture through corrupt practices. Based on specially designed enterprise survey questions that were incorporated into the 2003 Survey, we develop proxy measures for undue influence exerted by powerful firms and analyze the impact of influence and its unequal distribution within countries. We find a consistent pattern in which the inequality of influence (or crony bias) has a strongly negative impact on assessments of public institutions that ultimately affects the behavior of firms toward those institutions. Crony bias is associated with a more negative assessment of the rule of law, as well as with lower levels of tax compliance and significantly higher lev-

els of bribery. Thus, the inequality of influence damages the credibility of institutions among weaker firms and affects the use and provision of tax resources—which in turn results in these institutions remaining weak and subject to capture by the influential. A self-reinforcing dynamic in which institutions are subverted is thus generated, further strengthening the underlying political and economic inequalities.

Specifically, the data from the World Economic Forum, which covered over 7,000 firms responding to the 2003 Survey, with its expanded coverage of 102 countries, allow us to construct a crony bias index and relate it to governance variables and regime type for this large set of countries. Such a crony bias index is the difference between two firm-level questions from the Survey: the influence exerted by politically well-connected firms in the country minus the influence exerted by the respondent firm's business association.[27] The relative percentile rank average regional ratings for these two component (of crony bias) questions, as well as the resulting crony bias itself, are depicted in Figure 4. Regions where influence by well-connected firms is not that large and/or such influence is counteracted by the influence of the individual firm's own business association will tend to exhibit lower relative levels of crony bias. Examples include East Asia NIC, OECD (where business associations tend to be

Figure 5: The unofficial economy and crony bias (data from worldwide Survey, 2003)

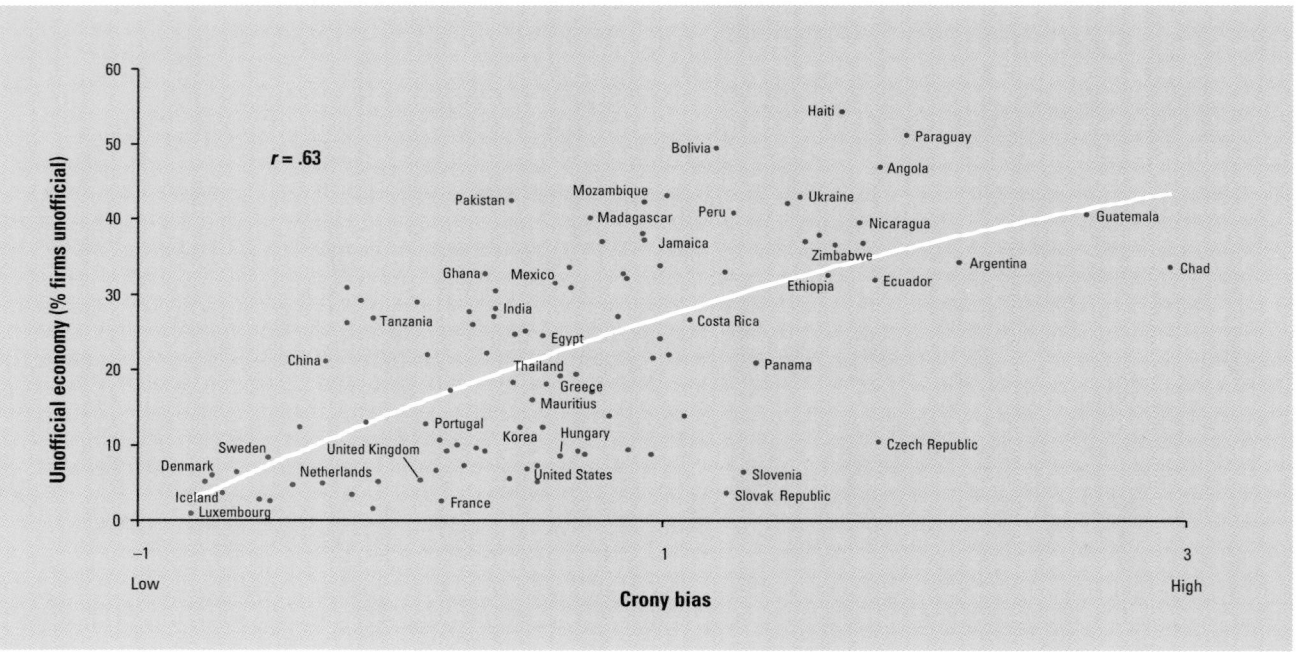

Note: Only selected countries among the 102 are labeled due to space limitations. Unofficial economy data drawn from firms' responses to following question: What percentage of business in your country would you guess are unofficial or unregistered? (categorical, converted using minimum within each range). Crony bias is constructed by authors, based on data from the 2003 Survey of firms in 102 countries, calculated as the difference between influence by firms with political ties and influence by the firm's own business association.

stronger), as well as the MENA countries participating in the Survey, in contrast with settings where some powerful vested interests exert undue influence in shaping policies, laws, and regulations without counterweight by effective or powerful business associations—such as in the case of the ex-socialist countries and Latin America.[28]

The econometric analysis of the Survey performed to ascertain the significance of crony bias (controlling for other factors), which is presented in Appendix A, indicates that crony bias is significantly associated with higher levels of corruption, misgovernance, lower institutional quality in parliament and the judiciary, and a larger unofficial economy (and thus lower tax revenues), backstopping the results found for the earlier research focused on transition economies.[29] These relatively large and rather significant effects of crony bias on governance variables and institutional informality are as robust when controlling for other potentially important explanatory variables, such as the extent of the country's globalization (which incidentally indicates a positive association between globalization and governance), the ideology of government, and the country's per capita income (proxying for level of development), as well as the recent growth rate of the country and the firm's own expectations about the economy (to control for potential "irrational exuberance" or excessive pessimism in the subjective response of the firms). Further

controlling for firm characteristics does not affect the magnitude or significance of the impact of crony bias on governance variables. The very significant relationship between the extent of crony bias and the unofficial economy is illustrated in Figure 5, consistent with the firm-level regressions of Appendix Table A1.

In reviewing the country averages for crony bias across the transition countries, an interesting pattern emerges. The lowest crony bias averages are in some of the most democratic as well as some of the least democratic regimes in the Survey sample. Indeed, Figure 6 shows a simple correlation between the average crony bias and the voice and democratic accountability indicator from our worldwide governance database, suggesting a nonlinear relationship, where there is no systematic pattern at low levels of voice and democratic accountability (where there are some market economies and some former or current socialist ones). This contrasts with the significant negative relationship between voice and accountability and crony bias for the medium and high ranges. In general, perceived inequalities of political influence are greatest on average in those countries with *partial* political reforms, what some are referring to as "semi-authoritarian regimes" or "managed democracies." Such regimes may allow some competition for political influence, but the market for influence is still highly segmented and distorted, with significant

Figure 6: Crony bias and voice and accountability

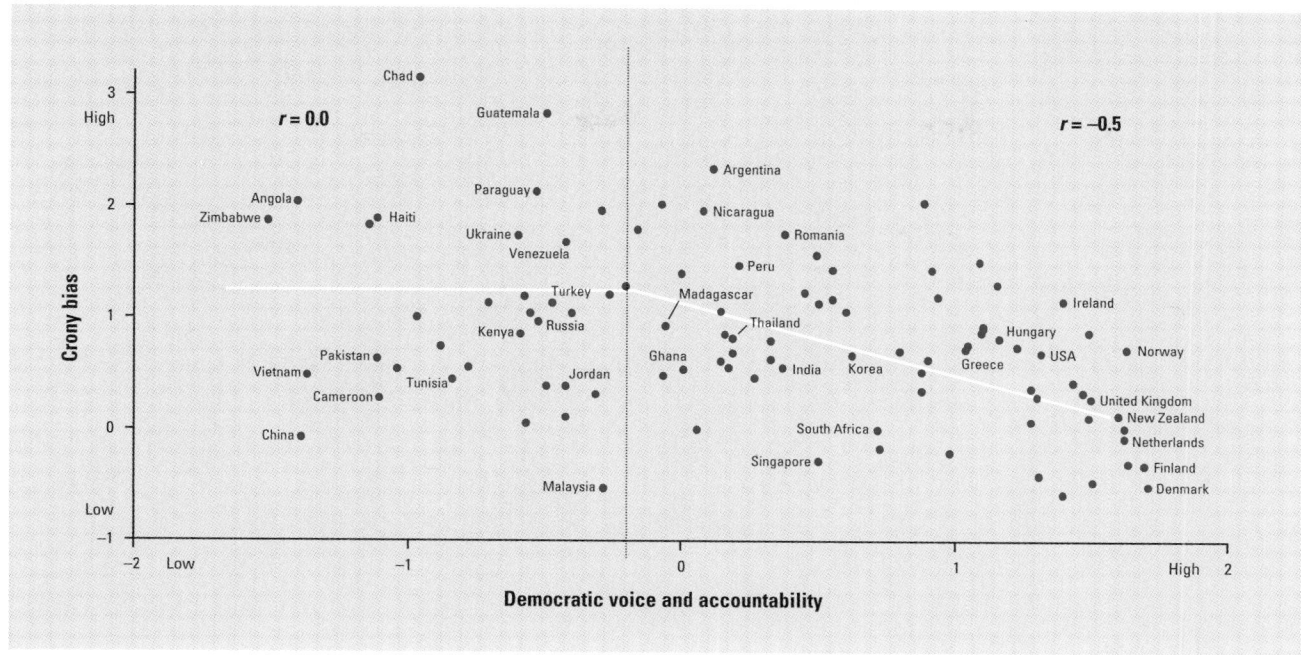

Source: 2003 Executive Opinion Survey and author's calculations. Crony bias defined in note of Figure 5 and text. Voice and accountability variable from Kaufmann, Kraay, and Mastruzzi (2003).

entry barriers and monopolistic practices (see Appendix A for details).

Governance and the city

The dramatic increase in empirical work on governance over the past few years has spearheaded a more in-depth analysis of the manifestations, causes, and consequences of misgovernance and corruption. It has drawn from cross-country data as well as in-country diagnostic perspectives. Significant inroads have been made in unbundling governance to measure and analyze its detailed components, as well as in exploring empirically (through surveys such as the World Economic Forum's Executive Opinion Survey and others) the governance performance of different institutions—such as parliament, police, customs, and the like. Furthermore, as we have illustrated in the previous section, it has become possible to gather empirical measurements of "softer" (and traditionally unquantifiable) politically related variables, such as variables measuring the extent of the unequal distribution of influence within a country's corporate sector.

At the same time important gaps remain within this broad-based empirical measurement approach to governance. An important challenge is to study governance empirically at the subnational level. In particular, given the

growing importance of the city as an economic and sociopolitical unit, it is important to undertake a world-wide cross-city analysis of governance that encompasses a large number of important cities in most countries of the world. The main limitation of carrying out this worldwide analysis of city governance has been the availability of primary data at the city level, as well as the construction of a suitable dataset for analysis. Thanks to the 2003 Survey, which collected information on the respondent's enterprise location, our current dataset can map the reported assessment of institutions and governance factors to the location of the firm. This Survey-based information, complemented by the collection of other city- and country-specific variables from sources outside of the Survey, permits us to construct a basic and initial city-based dataset of governance and related indicators for 271 cities in 101 countries.

But are differences across cities significant enough to warrant this line of empirical inquiry? And even if they are, do they matter? In this initial dataset we first assessed the extent of the within-country variance across cities among governance (and related) variables. We found that the variance is rather substantial; its orders of magnitude for different variables are not dwarfed by the extent of variation in these same variables across countries. For some variables the extent of within-country cross-city

Figure 7a: City governance and globalization

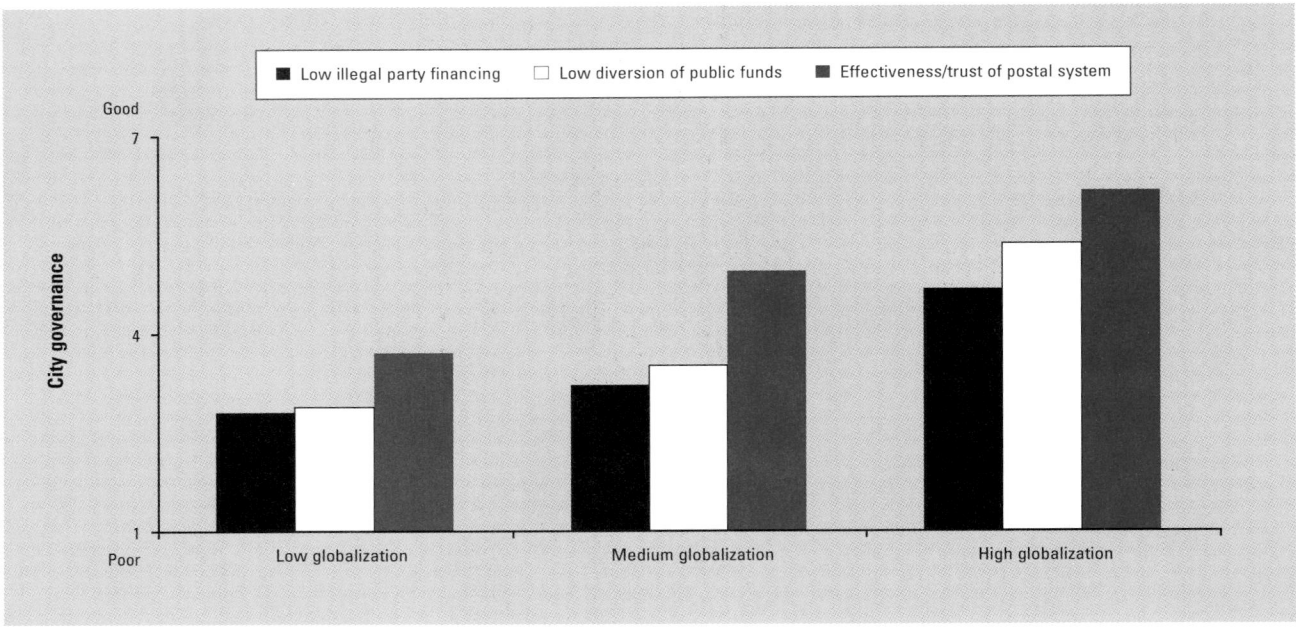

Source: Executive Opinion Survey (2003).

variance is roughly the same as the cross-country variation, while for others it is roughly one-half. Given the large cross-country variation typically found in worldwide surveys of this type, this implies a sizeable diversity of ratings at the city level—even within the same countries. Such apparent rich diversity of experiences and performance across cities within countries, likely reflecting much more than mere reporting margins of error, is worth reviewing. Thus, exploring the potential determinants of the variation in performance across cities is warranted.

In particular, aspects drawn from the Survey for this new dataset include various forms of corruption, financial governance (such as money laundering and soundness of the banking sector), public governance (such as trust in politicians, party finance, street crime, and organized crime), the regulatory regime (regional differences in the business environment and the overall burden of imports), as well as infrastructure and social variables. These governance and related performance variables are integrated and correlated against data on city characteristics (city size, capital and/or port) as well as relevant country characteristics (such as degree of urbanization, extent of globalization by the country, ideology of the government, and per capita income).[30]

We start from the urban economy perspective by focusing on the city as a key unit of analysis. Different analytical approaches have emphasized the costs and benefits of urbanization, the economies and diseconomies of agglomeration, and city governance. Such different

perspectives are subject to empirical testing, for which this initial dataset may provide (admittedly preliminary) insights.

With this dataset for over 270 cities, utilizing econometric analysis we test whether some city and country characteristics appear to affect the governance and sectoral outcomes at the city level (controlling for income). As illustrated in Figures 7a, b, and c, the data suggest that neither city nor country size negatively affect governance at the city level. Further, there is no evidence that a higher degree of urbanization within a country has a detrimental impact on the governance of cities; in fact, for some dimensions, the extent of urbanization may have a positive effect. Significantly, we also find, as depicted in Figure 7, that the extent to which the country is globalized has a significant positive impact on city governance performance (controlling for other factors, including income). The empirical importance of the extent of globalization contrasts with the evidence suggesting that whether a city is a capital city or a port is not statistically important (Figure 7c).

This early exploration suggests that some commonly held beliefs on city-level performance can be empirically challenged—such as the notions that in larger cities performance and governance will suffer due to diseconomies of agglomeration; that port cities, or the country's capital, will generally tend to be more corrupt than other cities; or that urbanization or globalization may bring about misgovernance.

Figure 7b: City governance and urbanization

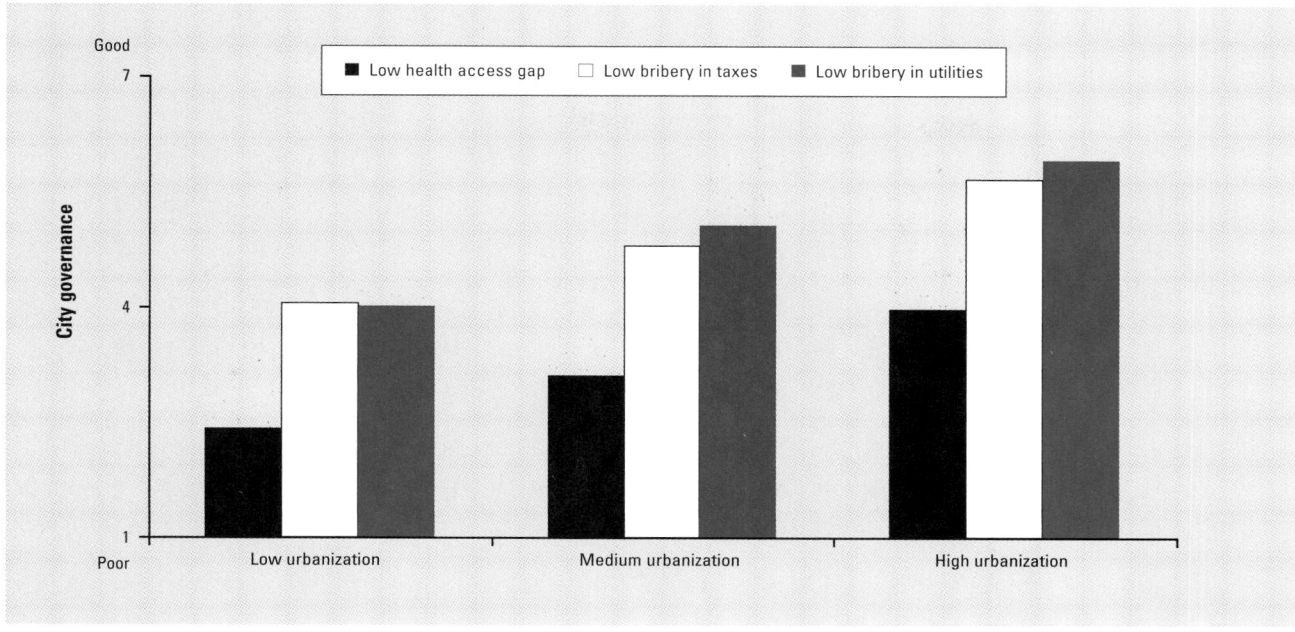

Source: Executive Opinion Survey (2003).

Figure 7c: City governance and city characteristics

153

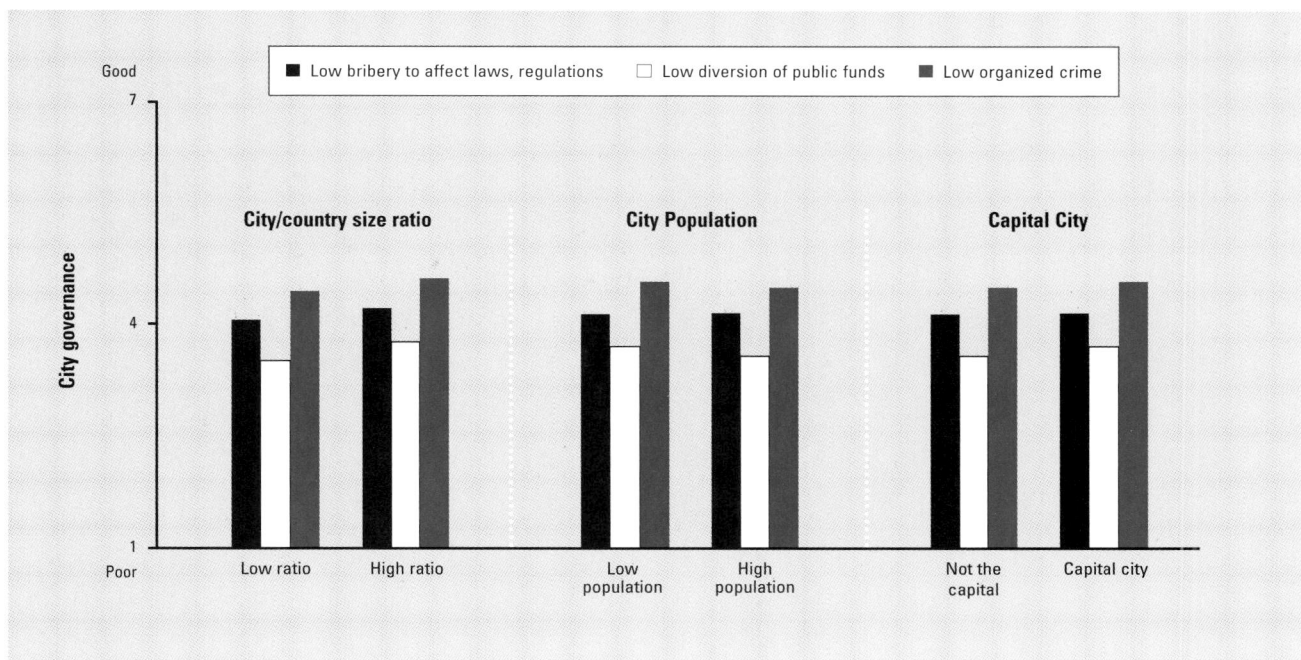

Source: Executive Opinion Survey (2003).

Conclusions and implications

Given the present global political debate and the cross-roads at which governance is at present, its "revival" as a central issue for empirical study and informed action appears justified. Hence the rationale for this chapter's heading and its content.

We started this chapter by suggesting that governance continues to be a major challenge, its underperformance evident in most regions and across a vast number of countries within these regions. This contrasts with the significant strides that have been made in many countries in improving the content of macroeconomic policies for well over a decade. There is an evident and growing "governance gap" in terms of differential policy efforts, since improvements in governance are not keeping pace with the progress attained in some areas, including economic policy. Such a gap in governance effort implies that public governance has become a central binding constraint to growth and development today in many settings. In fact the enterprises from developing and transition economies included in this year's Survey single out corruption and excessive bureaucracy among the top constraints to their business operations, while the respondent firms from the OECD countries single out excessive bureaucracy and the tax regime. Relative to these and other institutional weaknesses, high inflation and distortions in the exchange rate regime are not ranked as important constraints by the firms.

More generally, with a recently constructed world-wide governance indicators dataset, we suggested the extent to which national governance matters: a country that significantly improves key governance dimensions such as the rule of law, corruption, the regulatory regime, and voice and democratic accountability can expect, in the long run, a dramatic increase in its per capita income and in other social dimensions. An improvement in governance by only one standard deviation can result, in the long run, in up to a fourfold increase in per capita income, as discussed earlier. And a larger increase in, say, the quality of rule of law (or in control of corruption or improved voice and democratic accountability) would further multiply such income per capita increase and social gains in the long term.

In contrast to the major impact that improved governance can have on incomes and development, however, the findings show no reverse feedback mechanism: higher incomes in themselves do not get automatically translated into improved governance. The fact that there is no automatic virtuous circle means that continuous political resolve and interventions are required to attain good governance. It also implies that a country exhibiting higher incomes than would be predicted by its current levels of governance can expect downward pressure on the sustainability of such incomes—given their governance level.

Such shortfall in the country's actual quality of governance as compared with the governance level required to support the country's current (or desired) income level is described as the "governance deficit". This deficit in governance outcomes can constitute a warning regarding the income and growth prospects of a country. For instance, the evidence suggests that by the late 1990s most countries in Latin America had a substantial governance deficit: their actual per capita incomes were significantly higher than would have been predicted by the prevailing levels of governance, thereby exerting downward pressure on incomes.

We then discussed in brief recent work anchored in the new comparative economics strand of the literature, which advances concepts to compare different capitalist systems. In particular, we reviewed some of the deeper historical determinants of current governance performance, and found that the origins of a country's legal system—particularly whether it adopted common or civil law systems—may not be a central determinant of governance outcomes nowadays, especially for lower-income countries. Yet further inquiry into the deeper determinants of governance, including understanding the relevance of historical patterns of settlement and of geography, seems to hold promise.

We illustrated empirically that politics also matter substantially in understanding good governance, and found that the corporate sector plays an active role in shaping political and policy outcomes. The database provided by the Survey also permitted the empirical evaluation of political dimensions of governance traditionally regarded as non-measurable, such as the extent of "capture" and the extent of undue influence by some politically connected powerful firms in shaping the regulations, laws, and policies of a country. Unequal distribution of influence on policy and regulatory outcomes (or "crony bias") were found to be closely associated with poor public and financial governance performance.

Finally, the empirical richness of the Survey dataset provided a key input for the construction of an initial governance database at the city level. This database and research-in-progress is to be expanded over the coming year, yet the early results support the observation that governance performance at the city level is aided by the extent of the country's globalization and urbanization path (controlling for income levels). Further, the city's relative size and its status as a capital or a port do not appear to have a deleterious effect on the quality of city-level governance.

The findings described in this chapter emphasize the need to revisit conventional advice on strategies to improve public governance. Such advice has focused excessively on attempts to reform the internal functioning of public institutions, often drawing from standard templates from industrialized countries. Instead, further focus is needed on other aspects that do contain a political dimension. In particular, addressing the nexus between corporate strategies and public governance (mediated by the "institution of influence") is of particular interest. Specifically, the findings on undue influence and state capture point to the limits of traditional public-sector measures, such as incessant legal drafting and codes of ethics manuals, creating new Anti-Corruption agencies, or launching another anti-corruption campaign. By contrast, the findings here underscore the need for far more focus on external accountability, on transparency mechanisms, and on prevention within institutions.[31] These transparency mechanisms are also required to ensure a well-governed interface between the private and public sectors, inter alia providing a more level field of influence peddling consistent with a competitive enterprise sector. And such enhanced focus on governance matters is also warranted at the subnational level.

Notes

1 Daniel Kaufmann is the director of Global Governance at the World Bank Institute. The excellent assistance of Massimo Mastruzzi, Erin Hoffmann, Ha Nguyen, and Hope Steele is appreciated, as is the collaboration with Aart Kraay and Joel Hellman, whose joint research findings are reported here. I benefited by helpful feedback from Xavier Sala-I-Martin and inputs from the WEF Global Competitiveness team, whose collaboration (and major database undertaking) is noted. The views and errors are the author's, and neither those errors nor the data (which are subject to margins of error and ought not imply precise country rankings) necessarily reflect the official views of the World Bank.

2 http://latin.realdictionary.com/Latin/redux.asp.

3 "Redux." 1987. In *The Random House Dictionary of the English Language*, 2nd ed., unabridged. New York: Random House.

4 See Kaufmann 2003a.

5 See for instance Rodrik et al. (2002).

6 See, for instance, Reinhart and Rogoff (2003), focusing largely on FDI in Africa.

7 Source: WDI, World Bank. Note that OECD countries have not exhibited significant macroeconomic imbalances in the recent past, so there was no room for improvement during the period according to this "cutoff" criterion. Yet its average inflation rates also declined, albeit from a much lower initial point. It should be noted, however, that despite low inflation rates, growing concern about the rapidly growing fiscal deficit in the United States at present (and its future worldwide implications) is present—an important issue outside the purview of this chapter.

8 The evidence, based on official sources on the trends on inflation and parallel exchange rate premia, pointing to an improvement over the past 10 and 20 years, respectively, is so dramatic that it is obviously highly significant in statistical terms. By contrast, the changes in the quality of infrastructure and governance questions reported over only the past 5 years, based on the Survey responses of a multitude of firms in countries experiencing high variation in such average responses, are often not highly significant statistically (at a 90 percent confidence level). Thus any statement of improvement or deterioration for the overall sample or for a regional average over this rather limited Survey-based time span needs to be treated with caution, and requires further validation with additional data and an expanded time frame. It should be noted, however, that the main conclusion of this Survey-based over-time comparison refers to the

stagnation in governance performance (and its relatively low level in most settings), rather than claiming a definite deterioration over the past 5 years (which, where suggested by the point estimates in the trend, is not highly statistically significant). The statistical confidence in the statement that there is no evidence of a positive trend in any governance dimension is very high, based not only on the Survey evidence discussed here, but also based on other available indicators from polling agencies (see Kaufmann, Kraay, and Mastruzzi, 2003).

9 The precise wording for each question utilized to analyze variables such as the quality of infrastructure, administrative regulations, corruption, judiciary independence, and others analyzed in this chapter are included as notes in the respective Figures, as well as in the Appendix glossary and in the data tables at the end of this book.

10 The scale of the Survey questionnaire is from 1 (very poor rating) to 7 (excellent). In this chapter, whenever we indicate the percentage of firms reporting good/very good rating for a variable, it was calculated as the composite of those rating it a 5, 6, or 7; conversely, firm ratings of 1, 2, or 3 are interpreted as poor/very poor.

11 In 2003, firms reported corruption to be the top constraint at even a higher rate than the already very high rate of the previous year, while their concern about inflation declined further, from an already very low level. However, these differences (over such as short time span) are not large in magnitude or statistically significant. The main observation refers to the consistency in the ratings across both years.

12 For methodological details on the worldwide governance indicators presented here in brief, see Kaufmann, Kraay, and Mastruzzi (2003). The individual indicators used for the composites came from a variety of organizations, including commercial risk-rating agencies, multilateral organizations, think tanks, and other nongovernmental organizations. They are based on surveys of experts, firms, and citizens and cover a wide range of topics: perceptions of political stability and the business climate, views on the efficacy of public service provision, opinions on respect for the rule of law, and perceptions of the incidence of corruption. For a detailed explanation of sources and access to the full governance indicators databank see http://www.worldbank.org/wbi/governance/govdata2002. See also the appendix on methodological issues related to margins of error and interpretation for these indicators.

13 The full governance dataset for 1996–2002 is available at http://www.worldbank.org/wbi/governance/govdata2002.

14 See World Bank (2003a) and World Economic Forum (2002).

15 Not shown is the similar strong link between regulatory quality as well as rule of law on the one hand, and incomes per capita on the other (all exhibiting correlations exceeding 0.7).

16 Untangling the directions of causation underlying the strong correlations is explained in detail in "Growth Without Governance," Kaufmann and Kraay (2002).

17 A recent strand of research attributes a substantial fraction of these vast differences in very long run growth performance to deep historical differences in institutional quality. By isolating the part of current differences in governance performance that can be traced back to countries' colonial origins, these studies have identified the powerful effect of initial institutional quality on growth in the very long run. See for example Hall and Jones (1999) and Acemoglu, Johnson, and Robinson (2001). We discuss some specific historical determinants in latter sections of this chapter.

18 This of course does not mean that the simple correlation between governance and per capita income is negative, since this is dominated by the strong positive effects of governance on income. In terms of the specifics of the particular methodology used, we implemented an empirical framework allowing us to identify causal effects running in both directions between governance and per capita income. Although there is a rapidly growing literature that identifies the causation from better governance to higher per capita income, that is not the case for identifying causation in the opposite direction, from per capita income to governance. Traditionally, identification of the first direction of causality has been done with the aid of instrumental variables, such as the main language or settler mortality patterns, which we have utilized as instruments to arrive at the very large estimates of the effects of governance on income. Yet no good

instruments exist for testing the reverse causality direction, namely from per capita income to improved governance. The gathering of a major governance dataset and the construction of the aggregate indicators themselves (through the particular Unobserved Component Model) give us important additional data: the margins of error for each country estimate for the governance indicators. These additional data permit us to implement a different and rarely used strategy to estimate the effect of incomes on governance, namely the utilization of non-sample information (or the "out-of-sample" technique). Implementing this technique, we find no evidence of positive feedback from higher per capita income to better governance outcomes. See Kaufmann and Kraay (2002).

19 This is depicted in Appendix Figure B3.

20 Bolivia has lower actual income per capita, and thus the governance deficit for their levels of income is not as large as for the other countries listed above.

21 For further details and the actual plotgrams depiction, with focus on the challenge in most Latin American countries, see Kaufmann and Kraay (2002) and Appendix B of this chapter.

22 Hellman, Jones, and Kaufmann (2003, forthcoming). See also more recent evidence in some Latin American countries, emerging from the governance and anticorruption diagnostics (GAC) of the World Bank Institute (WBI) at (http://www.worldbank.org/wbi/governance/capacitybuild/).

23 In fact, due to the likelihood of a negative feedback effect from incomes per capita to governance, the actual simple correlation summarized in Figure 2 underestimates the extent (slope) of the causal link from governance to incomes per capita. In the Appendix B, see plotgram in Figure B3 where the Instrumental Variable (IV) slope is steeper than the OLS slope.

24 See Djankov et al. (2003a, 2003b).

25 *Legal origin* identifies the origin of the company law or commercial code in each country. There are five possible origins: English, French, German, Scandinavian, and Socialist. Sources are: La Porta et al. (1999); Djankov, McLiesh, and Shleifer (2003).

26 This work is summarized in Hellman, Jones, and Kaufmann (2003, forthcoming).

27 We also worked with an alternative variant for calculating a proxy for crony bias or extent of inequality of influence: instead of utilizing the variable measuring the influence of the firm's business association as the second term, we subtracted the respondent firm's own perceived influence. The firm's own influence is, on balance, less than the influence of its business association. Thus the ratings of the two crony bias variants, while highly correlated, would not be the same. At any rate, which variant is used in the statistical analysis reported here does not materially affect the results. See Hellman and Kaufmann (2003).

28 An important statistical issue often ignored is whether there are inherent biases in presenting regional averages based on partial regional samples (instead of average ratings that include all countries in each region, which is often not possible due to incomplete country coverage in individual surveys or polls). When performing cross-regional comparisons, self-selection bias may reduce comparability, given the tendency to include in the survey coverage the countries that a priori (on average) may be performing better than the countries excluded. In Appendix B we explore in brief this issue. We found that the substantial increase in country coverage by the Survey since the late 1990s (now encompassing 102 countries) has significantly reduced the sample bias, although some of it remains (as reported in Appendix B, the largest remaining estimated upward bias for governance due to the excluded set in the 2003 Survey (only 7 out of 20 countries are included) is for the MENA region, at an estimated 0.28 standard deviation units. This is, however, a fraction of the implied upward bias in smaller datasets, such as IMD's WCY, with much less regional coverage.

29 See Hellman and Kaufmann (2003) for a detailed explanation of the framework of analysis, antecedents in the literature, and specific application for transition economies (with a different firm survey dataset). In such research, in addition to the same links between crony bias and governance outcomes reported above for the Survey dataset, we also show that in transition economies higher levels of crony bias as reported by the firm is significantly associated with less use by such firms of the courts. This is another illustration of the self-reinforcing dynamics by which institutional weakening (and subversion) takes place due to highly unequal distribution of influence. Testing of the links between crony bias and the firm's utilization of some specific formal institutions, such as the courts, is not possible with the Survey dataset since such data on court usage is not collected.

30 For details, see Kaufmann, Léautier, and Mastruzzi, forthcoming, where inter alia the full set of econometric results on potential determinants of city governance (controlling for country characteristics) is presented.

31 For more detailed discussion of policy implications, see Kaufmann (2003c).

References

The word *processed* describes informally produced works that may not be available commonly through libraries.

Acemoglu, D., S. Johnson, and J. A. Robinson. 2001. "The Colonial Origins of Comparative Development: An Empirical Investigation." *American Economic Review* 91(5): 1369–1401.

Acemoglu, D. and J. A. Robinson. 1999. "A Theory of Political Transitions." Department of Economics Working Paper 99-26. Cambridge, MA: Massachusetts Institute of Technology. Online. http://papers.ssrn.com/sol3/papers.cfm?abstract id=195739.

Beck, T. G. Clarke, A. Groff, P. Keefer, and P. Walsh. 2001. "New Tools in Comparative Political Economy: The Database of Political Institutions," *World Bank Economic Review* 15(1): 165–176.

Becker, G. S. 1983. "A Theory of Competition among Pressure Groups for Political Influence." *Quarterly Journal of Economics* 98: 371–400.

Benabou, R. 2000. "Unequal Societies: Income Distribution and the Social Contract." *American Economic Review* 90: 96–129.

Diamond, J. 1999. *Guns, Germs, and Steel*. New York: W.W. Norton & Company.

Djankov, S., C. McLiesh, and A. Shleifer. 2003. "Remedial Solutions in Credit Markets." Cambridge, MA: Department of Economics, Harvard University. Processed.

Djankov, S., E. Glaeser, R. La Porta, and F. Lopez-de-Silanes. 2003a. "Appropriate Institutions." In *Annual World Bank Conference on Development Economics: The New Reform Agenda*. B. Pleskovic and N. Stern, eds. Washington, DC: World Bank and Oxford University Press.

———. 2003b. "New Comparative Economics." Working Paper 9608. Cambridge, MA: National Bureau of Economic Research. Online. http://papers.nber.org/papers/W9608.

Easterly, W. and R. Levine. 2002. "Tropics, Germs and Crops: How Endowments Influence Economic Development." Working Paper 9106. Cambridge, MA: National Bureau of Economic Research. Online. http://papers.nber.org/papers/W9106.

Engelman, S. and K. Sokoloff. 2002. "Factor Endowments, Inequality, and Paths of Development among New World Economies." *Economia* 3(1): 41–109.

Foreign Policy. 2002. 2002 A.T. Kearney/Foreign Policy Magazine Globalization Index. Online. http://www.foreignpolicy.com/www-board/g-index2.php. Released as "Globalization's Last Hurrah," *Foreign Policy* Jan/Feb: 38–51.

Glaeser, E., J. Scheinkman, and A. Shleifer. Forthcoming. "The Injustice of Inequality." *Journal of Monetary Economics: Carnegie-Rochester Series on Public Policy*. Online. http://post.economics/harvard.edu/facility/shleifer/papers/inequalityWP.pdf.

Grossman, G. M. and E. Helpman. 2001. *Special Interest Politics*. Cambridge, MA: Massachusetts Institute of Technology Press.

Hall, R., and C. Jones. 1999. "Why Do Some Countries Produce So Much More Output per Worker than Others?" *Quarterly Journal of Economics* 114: 83–116.

_____. 2002. "Far from Home: Do Foreign Investors Import Higher Standards of Governance in Transition Economies?" Draft. Washington, DC: World Bank. Online. http://www.worldbank.org/wbi/governance/pubs/farfromhome.html.

Hellman, J., G. Jones, and D. Kaufmann. 2003 (forthcoming). "Seize the State, Seize the Day: State Capture, Corruption, and Influence in Transition Economies." *Journal of Comparative Economics*. Online. http://www.worldbank.org/wbi/governance/pubs/seizestate.html.

Hellman, J., and D. Kaufmann. 2003 (forthcoming). "The Inequality of Influence." In *Trust in Transition*. J. Kornai and S. Rose-Ackerman, eds.

Heston, A., R. Summers, and B. Aten. 2002. Penn World Table Version 6.1. Philadelphia: Center for International Comparisons at the University of Pennsylvania (CICUP). Online. http://pwt.econ.upenn.edu/.

Johnston, M. 1997. "Public Officials, Private Interests, and Sustainable Democracy: When Politics and Corruption Meet." In *Corruption and the Global Economy*, K. Elliott, ed. Washington, DC: Institute for International Economics.

Kaufmann, D. 2003a. "Governance Crossroads." In *Global Competitiveness Report 2002–2003*, P. Cornelius, K. Schwab, and M. E. Porter, eds. New York: Oxford University Press.

———. 2003b. "Institutions Matter: Comment on 'Appropriate Institutions,' by S. Djankov, R. La Porta, F. Lopez-de-Silanes, and A. Shleifer and 'Foreign Direct Investment to Africa: The Role of Price Stability and Currency Instability,' by C. Reinhart and K. Rogoff." In *Annual World Bank Conference on Development Economics: The New Reform Agenda*. B. Pleskovic and N. Stern, eds. Washington, DC: The World Bank and Oxford University Press.

———. 2003c. "Rethinking Governance: Empirical Lessons Challenge Orthodoxy," World Bank mimeo, March 2003. Online. http://www.worldbank.org/wbi/governance/pubs/rethink_gov.html

Kaufmann, D. and A. Kraay. 2002. "Growth without Governance." *Economia* 3(1): 169–229. Online. http://www.worldbank.org/wbi/governance/pubs/growthgov.html.

Kaufmann, D., A. Kraay, and M. Mastruzzi. 2003. "Governance Matters III: Governance Indicators 1996–2002." Policy Research Working Paper 3106. Washington, DC: World Bank. Online. http://www.worldbank.org/wbi/governance/pubs/govmatters3.html.

Kaufmann, D., F. Léautier, and M. Mastruzzi. Forthcoming. "City Governance: A new database and empirical analysis." Washington, DC: World Bank.

Kaufmann, D., G. Mehrez, and T. Gurgur. 2002. "Voice or Public Sector Management?: An Empirical Investigation of Determinants of Public Sector Performance Based on a Survey of Public Officials." Washington, DC: World Bank. Draft. Online. http://www.worldbank.org/wbi/governance/pubs/voice_psm.html

Knack, S. and P. Keefer. 1997. "Does Social Capital Have an Economic Payoff? A Cross Country Investigation." *Quarterly Journal of Economics* 112(4): 1251–1288.

Krueger A. 1974. "The Political Economy of Rent-Seeking Society." *American Economic Review* 64(3): 291–303.

Laffont, J. J., and J. Tirole. 1991. "The Politics of Government Decision-Making: A Theory of Regulatory Capture." *Quarterly Journal of Economics* 106(4):1089–1127.

La Porta, R., F. Lopez-de-Silanes, A. Shleifer, and R. Vishny. 1998. "Law and Finance." *Journal of Political Economy* 106(6): 1113–1155. Online. http://papers.nber.org/papers/W5661.

_____. 1999. "The Quality of Government." *Journal of Law, Economics and Organization* 15(1): 222–279. Online. http://post.economics.harvard.edu/faculty/shleifer/papers/qualgov.pdf.

Lopez-Claros, A. 2003. "Redefining Governance." World Economic Forum. Mimeo note.

Mauro, Paulo. 1995. "Corruption and Growth." *Quarterly Journal of Economics* 110(3): 681–712.

Payne, J. M. et al. 2002. *Democracies in Development: Politics and Reform in Latin America*. Washington, DC: Inter-American Development Bank.

Perotti, R. 1993. "Political Equilibrium, Income Distribution, and Growth." *The Review of Economic Studies* 60: 755–776.

Rajan, R. and L. Zingales. 2002. "Property Rights and the Taming of Government." University of Chicago. Manuscript.

Reinhart, C. M., and K. S. Rogoff. 2003. "Foreign Direct Investment to Africa: The Role of Price Stability and Currency Instability." In *Annual World Bank Conference on Development Economics: The New Reform Agenda*. B. Pleskovic and N. Stern, eds. Washington, DC: The World Bank and Oxford University Press.

Rodrik, D., A. Subramanian, and E. Trebbi. 2002. "Institutions Rule: The Primacy of Institutions over Geography and Integration in Economic Development." Working Paper 97. Cambridge, MA: Center for International Development, Harvard University. Online. http://www.cid.harvard.edu/cidwp/097.htm.

Sachs, J. and A. Warner. 1997. "Natural Resource Abundance and Economic Growth." Cambridge, MA: Center for International Development and Harvard Institute for International Development. Processed.

Scott, J. C. 1972. *Comparative Political Corruption*. Englewood Cliffs, NJ: Prentice-Hall.

Slinko, I., E. Yakovlev, and E. Zhuravskaya. 2003. "Institutional Subversion: Evidence from Russian Regions." CEFIR Working Paper 31. Moscow: Centre for Economic and Financial Research.

United States Central Intelligence Agency. 2001. *The World Factbook*. Online. http://www.cia.gov/cia/publications/factbook.

World Bank. 2000. *The Quality of Growth*. New York: Oxford University Press. Online. http://www.worldbank.org/wbi/qualityofgrowth/.

———. 2003a. *Better Governance for Development in the Middle East and North Africa: Enhancing Inclusiveness and Accountability*. Washington, DC: World Bank.

———. 2003b. *World Development Indicators 2003*. Washington, DC: World Bank.

World Economic Forum. Various years. "Executive Opinion Survey." Prepared for *The Global Competitiveness Report*.

———. Various years. *The Global Competitiveness Report*. New York: Oxford University Press.

———. 2002. *Arab World Competitiveness Report 2002–2003*. New York: Oxford University Press.

Analytical considerations

In the preceding text we presented in brief the results of the research on the analysis of the inequality of influence ("crony bias"), drawn from the ongoing research project by Joel Hellman and the present author on state capture and inequality of influence.[1] This research has antecedents in the theoretical literature on influence peddling in shaping policies (in trade and related areas) by Grossman and Helpman (2001), the contributions of Laffont and Tirole on regulatory capture (1991), and it is also related to the very recent work by Glaeser, Scheinkman, and Shleifer (forthcoming) on subversion of institutions.

The results presented in the chapter text suggested a very strong association between the extent of crony bias, on the one hand, and governance outcomes, on the other. Based on new research, the chapter explored potential determinants of crony bias as well. Regarding the association between crony bias and governance variables (illustrated in Figure 5 in the text), depicting the link between a country's average crony bias indicator and the extent of unofficial activities as reported by the firms, there are a number of analytical and econometric considerations.

The first issue refers to whether the econometric model should test the potential impact of crony bias at the firm level or for country averages. A priori considerations do suggest that there are some potential advantages in performing statistical analysis at the firm level. This is the case insofar as the varying perceptions of different firms on the extent of crony bias do affect differentially each firm's perception of governance outcomes and its interaction with governance institutions (eg, the perceived unequal influence by a weaker firm may lead it to avoid utilizing the courts, to avoid paying taxes, and to engage in corrupt or unofficial activities). Conversely, if the a priori model was one where country-wide crony bias—which is assessed relatively uniformly by the many firms within each country—is a key factor associated with country-wide governance outcomes (as opposed to firm-level perceptions or behavior regarding institutions), then estimation for country averages would be warranted.

Econometric challenges

Even if a priori considerations do suggest that firm-level variance in terms of perceptions and behavior do matter, as we suggest in our framework in "Inequality of Influence" (Hellman and Kaufmann, forthcoming), caution ought to be exercised in the econometric model specification and in the interpretation of results, and a case could still be made to rely on country average econometric

estimations. We focus here on two particular challenges: the likelihood of systematic respondent perception bias (whether across firms within a country or across responses to the questions for the same firm), and the likelihood of correlated errors in firm-level regression estimations. These can result in biased coefficients and in particular in artificially inflated t-statistics (levels of significance). Further, a particular case of upward bias in t-statistics is likely to take place in firm-level regression results for country-wide independent variables that are applied uniformly across all firms for a country (such as the country's income per capita controls). However, for the reasons enumerated above, an upward bias in the estimated levels of significance is likely to take place even for firm-level independent variables in the firm-level regressions, even if not as pronounced as for country-wide independent variables.

On the econometric testing of the effects of crony bias

Consequently, our empirical strategy includes the following. First, we performed two sets of Ordinary Least Square (OLS) regressions, one at the firm level and another at the country average level. The levels of significance of the country average regressions can provide a lower bound estimate, while those at the firm level are likely to be an upper bound. In the case of country-wide variables in particular, the levels of significance of country average regressions are likely to be a better approximation. We report here this (more conservative) variant, namely the country average specifications (see Table A1 and the glossary with the variable definitions and sources below). The firm-level econometric results performed are not shown here and are available upon request. We note that the variable of interest, crony bias, is highly significant even in these country average specifications, and the magnitude of the coefficient is rather large as well.

Second, we included three sets of variables to control for possible perception biases. There are (1) the (appropriately scaled) difference between the reported perception by the firm on the Survey question about access to telephone lines in their country and the actual access to telephone lines in the country (from official statistics); (2) the firm-level assessment on recessionary expectations (possibly affecting its overall outlook and responses across the Survey), and (3) the country-level GDP growth rate over the previous three years. Notwithstanding such controls for potential perception biases, the extent of crony bias—both in terms of magnitude of the coefficient and in terms of significance levels—remains very highly associated with the governance outcomes (dependent variables) that were

Appendix A: On the role of inequality of influence ("crony bias") in determining governance outcomes: Analytical and econometric considerations *(cont'd.)*

proxied by the Survey, such as the questions about the unofficial economy, the judiciary, and parliament, as reflected in Table A1 for country-level regressions. It is also worth noting the potential importance of globalization as a likely determinant governance as well, even after controlling for per capita income, while by contrast the government ideology variable is unimportant.

On a potential explanatory factor for crony bias

In exploring the potential determinants of crony bias as depicted in Figure 6 in the chapter text—an admittedly speculative undertaking given serious endogeneity issues—we started by plotting the Survey-based crony bias in the vertical axis against a variable measuring voice and democratic accountability from a separate dataset (the aggregate governance indicators dataset). The visually evident nonlinear nature of the simple plotgram was also validated by simple regression analysis, where a kinked-linear specification performed relatively well. It suggested what

was, in effect, a zero correlation (vertical line) for lower ranges of voice and accountability; that is, countries with only partially democratic, or non-democratic, regimes can either have either a "market economy" history (some African countries), or a socialist economy history. The partially democratic or non-democratic countries can be associated with high levels of undue influence and capture by powerful corporates, but this is not necessarily the case with the countries having a socialist economy history, which have yet to emerge. Importantly, in contrast to the lower ranges of voice and accountability, there is a marked downward sloping relationship between enhanced democratic accountability and lower levels of crony bias in the higher range (as we observed in the plotgram in Figure 6 in the text).

Note

1 See Hellman, Jones, and Kaufmann (2003 forthcoming), and Hellman and Kaufmann (2003).

Table A1: The role of crony bias in affecting governance (firm-level OLS regressions)

Independent Variables	Dependent Variables					
	Diversion of public funds	Bribery in procurement	Bribery for laws, policies, and regulations	Unofficial economy	Independence of judiciary	Effectiveness of Parliament
Firm-Specific Variables						
Crony bias	0.78	0.68	0.8	0.62	−0.88	−0.83
	*6.41****	*6.04****	*8.65****	*4.24****	*7.08****	*8.74****
Firm's recessionary expectations	−0.09	−0.02	−0.01	−0.28	0.14	0.35
	1.02	*0.28*	*0.08*	*2.51***	*1.3*	*5.13****
Capital city location dummy	−0.18	−0.11	−0.03	0.05	−0.3	0.12
	1.08	*0.69*	*0.22*	*0.18*	*1.17*	*0.71*
Globalization index	−1.95	−1.24	−1.32	−2.18	1.3	1.47
	*5.23****	*3.68****	*5.40****	*5.09****	*3.35****	*5.22****
Per capita income (PPP)	−0.57	−0.6	−0.44	−0.68	0.23	0.13
	*5.01****	*7.19****	*5.34****	*5.25****	*1.94***	*1.56*
Government's ideology (left-right)	−0.01	−0.05	−0.01	0.01	−0.1	−0.07
	0.08	*0.71*	*0.12*	*0.11*	*0.99*	*0.87*
Voice and accountability	−0.01	0.12	0.06	−0.12	0.38	0.02
	0.07	*0.91*	*0.58*	*0.51*	*2.51****	*0.16*
Telephone access (bias)	−0.13	−0.08	−0.12	−0.11	0.17	0.02
	1.59	*1.27*	*2.10****	*1.05*	*1.75***	*0.27*
GDP growth rate (3-year country average)	−0.24	−0.68	−1.02	−2.75	0.59	0.49
	0.19	*0.65*	*1.04*	*1.43*	*0.38*	*0.51*
Number of Observations	102	102	102	102	102	102
Adjusted R^2	0.77	0.74	0.80	0.74	0.73	0.74

* significant at 10% level; ** significant at 5% level; *** significant at 1% level

Note: The telephone access variable was computed by taking the difference of each firm's individual rating of phone availability with the respective official country average data on telephone lines, drawn from International Telecommunications Union, 2003.

Sources: All dependent variables drawn from the 2003 Survey; ideology variable drawn from the Database of Political Institutions, 2000 (Beck et al., 2001); globalization index downloaded from *Foreign Policy* (2002), available online at http://www.foreignpolicy.com/wwwboard/g-index2.php; country population and urbanization rate drawn from WDI (2002); city population downloaded from website: www.citypopulation.de ; data on country population (PPP) drawn from Heston, Summers, and Aten (2002).

Appendix A: On the role of inequality of influence ("crony bias") in determining governance outcomes: Analytical and econometric considerations *(cont'd.)*

Table A2: Glossary of variables utilized in econometric analysis of crony bias, based on 2003 Survey in 102 countries

Variable	Source	Wording of question/detail	Variable range / Unit
Diversion of public funds	2003 Survey, WEF	In your country, diversion of public funds to companies, individuals, or groups due to corruption	(1 = is common, 7 = never occurs)
Bribery in procurement	2003 Survey, WEF	In your industry, how commonly would you estimate that firms make undocumented extra payments or bribes connected with public contracts (investment projects)?	(1 = common, 7 = never occurs)
Bribery for laws, policies, and regulations	2003 Survey, WEF	In your industry, how commonly would you estimate that firms make undocumented extra payments or bribes connected with influencing laws and policies, regulations, or decrees to favor selected business interests?	(1 = common, 7 = never occurs)
Unofficial economy	2003 Survey, WEF	What percentage of businesses in your country would you guess are unofficial or unregistered?	(1 = less than 5% of all businesses, 2 = 6–10%, 3 = 11–20%, 9 = more than 70%)
Effectiveness of parliament	2003 Survey, WEF	How effective is your national Parliament/Congress as a law-making and oversight institution?	(1 = very ineffective, 7 = very effective, equal to the best in the world)
Crony bias	2003 Survey, WEF and author's calculations	Difference between influence of firms with political ties and influence of business association	No crony bias = –6, Full crony bias = 6
Voice and accountability	KK 2002	"Voice and Accountability" Aggregate Governance Indicator (out the set of six, in Kaufmann, Kraay, and Mastruzzi "Governance Matters III: Updated Indicators for 1996–2002")	–2.5 = bad, 2.5 = good
GDP 3-year growth rate	WDI 2002	Average growth rate 1999–2001, from World Development Indicators, World Bank	% growth rate
Income per capita	Heston-Summers	Heston-Summers; *CIA World Factbook*; in Purchasing Power Parity (PPP) terms	Log US$ units
Globalization Index	A. T. Kearney; *Foreign Policy Magazine*	Composite indicator aggregating across various dimensions of globalization, for 62 countries	Rank (worst-best)
Ideology	DPI 2002	Chief Executive's Party Affiliation, from Database on Political Institutions	1=left, 3=right
Telephone access	2003 Survey and GCR database	Difference (in standardized scale) between the reported access to phone lines by the Forum's Survey respondent firms minus official data on actual number of telephone lines per 100 inhabitants.	Negative = "Pessimist Bias" Positive = "Optimist Bias"

In the chapter text we defined *governance* as the traditions and institutions that determine how authority is exercised in a particular country, and described in particular the set of six governance indicators we have constructed for about 200 countries. Further, we have made extensive use of the more disaggregated governance questions of the Executive Opinion Survey. There are a number of methodological challenges in the construction, analysis, and interpretation of these data. Succinctly, we present below seven issues, complementing the treatment in the chapter text itself (and for which further details are included in the background research referenced below and in the bibliographical references).

1. **Use of data containing elements of perception or subjectivity.** The data we utilize in constructing aggregate governance indicators has a significant element of subjectivity, as they rely on reports, assessments, and perceptions of citizens, firms (including those responding to the Forum's Survey), and experts. For measuring governance, to a large extent this is unavoidable, since only qualitative data are generally available. Moreover, stakeholders' perceptions of the quality of governance—as reflected in these qualitative ratings—matter at least as much as objective data from official statistics, and they often more accurately reflect actual outcomes. For instance, property rights are legally guaranteed in virtually all countries. Yet effective enforcement of those rights by the courts varies widely. When enterprises perceive that courts do not enforce these rights, the enterprises will look for other, less efficient ways of enforcing contracts.[2]

2. **Being precise about imprecision.** Sifting through this wealth of qualitative data, one might have several skeptical reactions. Are these data informative, coherent, comparable across countries? The answer to these questions is in the affirmative. The available indicators shed light on a fairly small number of these broad concepts of governance (voice and accountability, political instability and violence, government effectiveness, regulatory burden, rule of law, and control of corruption). The data are informative; there is surprisingly strong agreement across sources about the quality of governance. Particularly striking is the broad consensus that emerges when one compares responses of risk-rating-agency analysts with those of businesses or citizens in a country. International analysts bring a global view while businesses and citizens bring local knowledge, and generally their views coincide. And although different sources measure governance in very different units, statistical techniques are available that allow us to anchor each source in a common set of units, making them comparable. We use an "unobserved-components model" to extract a statistical consensus from the many available indicators corresponding to each of the six broad governance concepts mentioned previously. The resulting aggregate governance indicators efficiently summarize the data available and cover virtually all countries in the world. Hence, thanks to the 'unobserved components model' we have quantified the extent of precision in our indicators, which also helps in quantifying the precision of individual perception-based indicators as well as objective indicators (see below and also Figure B1). We find that in general in governance measurement, even though indicators and surveys are informative, and inferences can be made (with caution), these indicators are not very precise. Thus, particular care needs to be exercised in comparisons across countries and over time. One of the implications of the relative imprecision is that running "horse races" between countries to determine their precise rankings on governance is not useful. It is more appropriate simply to group countries into a number of broad categories along various governance dimensions, such as by using a "traffic light" approach.[3] A broad categorical approach flags vulnerabilities and points to the need for reform without encouraging fruitless debate about the precise scores or rankings assigned to particular countries.

Thus, the relative imprecision of these aggregate indicators do not severely impair their value. They can still identify the group of countries facing major governance challenges, in a statistically meaningful fashion. Furthermore, thanks to econometric techniques, margins of error notwithstanding, they can be used to systematically assess the causes and consequences of governance for a large sample of countries, as illustrated in the chapter text.

3. **Degree of precision of aggregate versus individual indicators.** Furthermore, aggregate governance indicators are more precise than any individual indicator. The caution that needs to be exercised in terms of the interpretation of governance indicators applies in fact even more strongly to individual surveys or polls. A significant advantage of the aggregation method (such as the UCM), in addition to its ability to estimate margins of error, is that it reduces significantly the margins of error as compared with any individual source. As seen in the plotgram of the country-specific

Appendix B: Governance measurement: Selected methodological issues *(cont'd.)*

Figure B1: Precision and number of sources (rule of law, 2002)

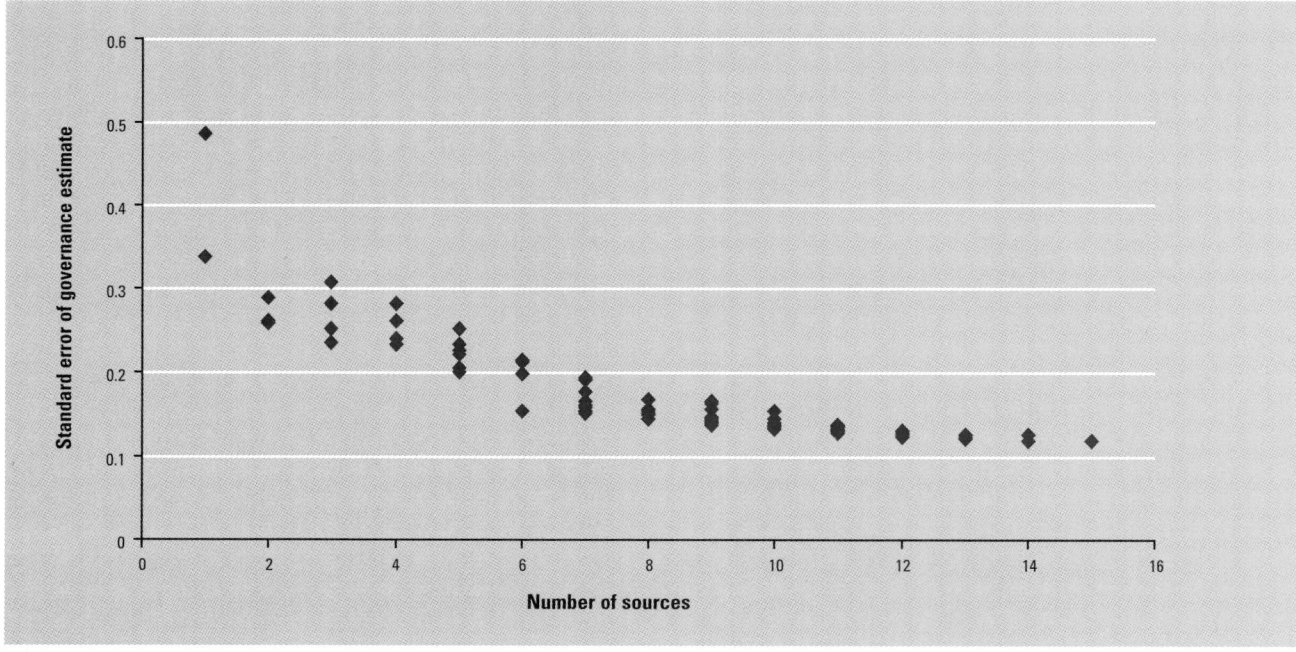

Source: Kaufmann, Kraay, and Mastruzzi (2003)

margin of error plotted against the number of sources available for such country, there is a sharp decline in the margins of error for countries with only one source as compared with those that have five or more sources. The margin of error is effectively halved when the aggregate estimate relies on numerous (five or more) sources (Figure B1). This implies that seemingly precise comparisons across countries based on a single perception survey (or expert poll, or combination of perceptions and objective data), can be misleading, particularly when the differences between countries (in rating estimates, or in ranks) are not very large. However, as in the case of the interpretation of aggregate governance indicators, it is possible to make meaningful comparisons across broad categories of countries in a worldwide sample. For instance, this can be done by indicating the countries in the top quartile in the distribution as a significantly different performance group from those countries in the bottom quartile. But comparisons within each broad category, or for relatively small changes in country ranking from one year to the next, are unlikely to be statistically significant.

4. **Imprecision varies according to indicators and country estimates.** Different individual indicators, surveys, and sources exhibit different degrees of imprecision, depending on a plethora of factors (methodology, quality of the governance questions, survey design and sampling, country coverage, how the data are gathered, quality of field work, coding, etc). Thanks to our UCM aggregation methodology, it has been possible to arrive at an estimate not only of the overall degree of (im-)precision of the aggregate indicators, but also of each one of its individual components. As discussed in the previous point, on average the margin of error of individual surveys can be about twice those of aggregate indicators. Within individual sources there can be differences as well, and across years for a particular source as well—as we see depicted in Figure B2.

5. **Margins of error of objective indicators?** Since the margins of error are large, it is at times argued that one should rely on "objective" indicators that may not have these measurement problems. We have analyzed the data, and found that where objective measures exist, such objective measures of governance also have measurement error—and hence should also have

Figure B2: Measurement error of individual sources (government effectiveness)

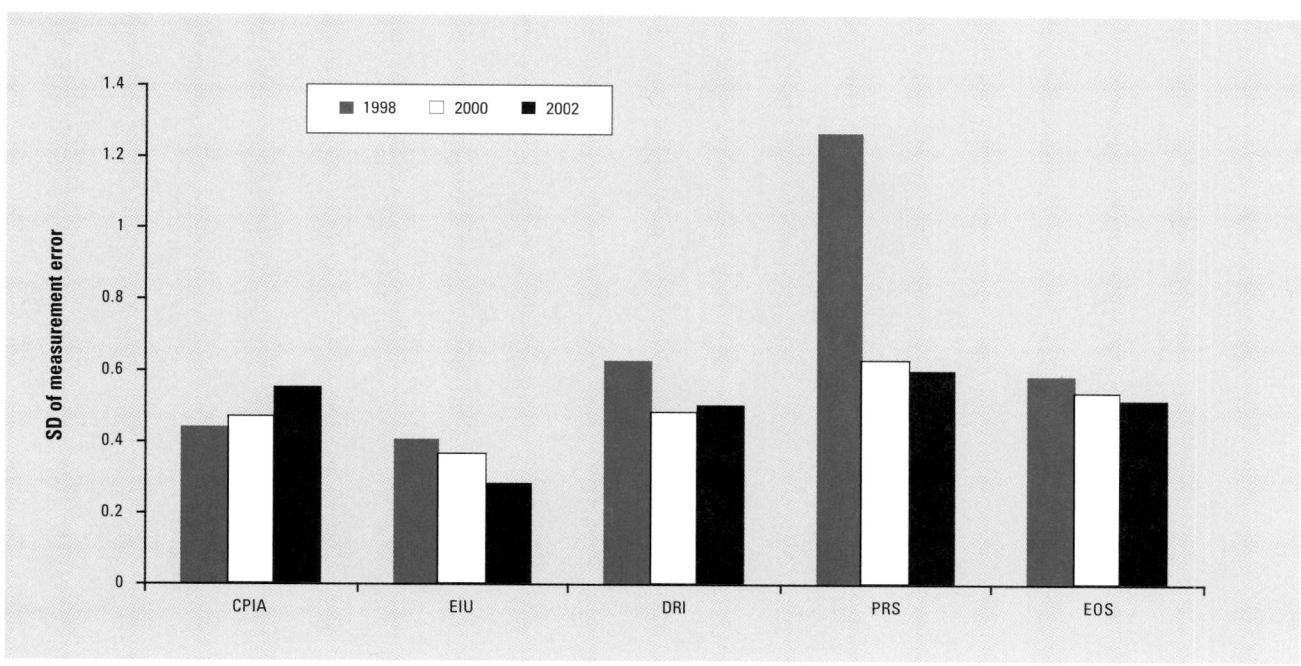

Note: Selected sources, three periods.
Source: Kaufmann, Kraay, and Mastruzzi (2003)

associated margins of error. Consider, for example, using the share of trade tax revenue in total revenues to capture the inability of a government to broaden its tax base. This measure will be a "noisy" indicator of overall government effectiveness for at least two reasons: the tax revenue itself may contain a variety of errors, and the extent of the tax base is only one dimension of government effectiveness. Our calculations suggest that measurement error in many objective sources is at least as important as measurement error in subjective governance indicators. It is important to ensure measurement of such margins of error for objective indicators as well.[4]

6. **Caution on inferences made on limited country sample.** An advantage of aggregate governance indicators is that it can effectively have full worldwide coverage (about 200 countries), while individual sources will tend to have a much more restricted coverage. On the high end, the Survey has improved its coverage dramatically over the past five years, by effectively doubling the countries surveyed to over 100. Other enterprise surveys, such as the enterprise survey conducted by IMD's World Competitiveness Yearbook, have significantly less coverage. Our

estimations, based on comparing the worldwide aggregate governance dataset with limited country samples within the same dataset, suggest that potential biases can be present due to the limited country coverage in surveys. For instance, regional average comparisons would tend to show a particular upward bias in those regions that are particularly under-represented in terms of countries participating in the survey. This is true in the case of MENA, in the Survey, as compared with East Asia NIC or OECD.[5]

7. **Defining, measuring, and (cautiously) interpreting the "governance deficit."** Per capita incomes and the quality of governance are strongly positively correlated across countries. This can be seen in Figure B3, which plots the protection of property rights or rule of law against real per capita GDP adjusted for differences in purchasing power across countries on the vertical axis. Rule of law is one of the six aggregated governance measures we have constructed, and in this case we draw from the 2000 dataset, while income in PPP terms is from the late 1990s. The best fit approximating the effects of governance on incomes in the long term is when instruments were used, as in the "IV" line in the plotgram in Figure B3.

Figure B3: Governance deficit and income fragility

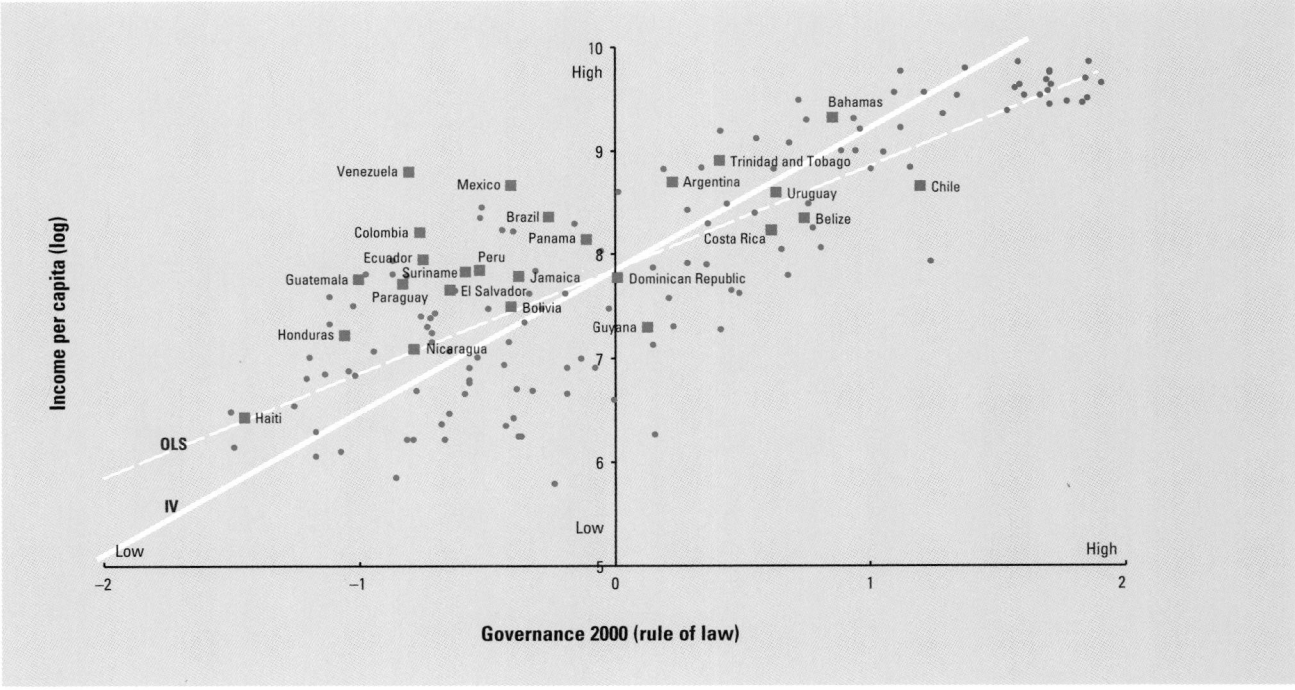

Source: Kaufmann and Kraay (2002).

Since there is no evidence of effects running from higher incomes to governance, an approximation of an estimate of the "governance deficit" for a country can be derived from this statistical device. This is because a higher actual income level than predicted by a country's governance level cannot be an indicator of potential governance gains, but instead the focus is on the reverse causality direction. Thus, the vertical distance between the actual governance estimate for the country and the "best fit" estimate for that country's income level provides such governance deficit. For instance, in the case of Venezuela, the governance deficit spanned about the equivalent of two standard deviations in governance quality (the aggregate governance indicators units are in standard deviations), which is very large. At the other extreme, Chile enjoyed a "surplus" of almost one governance standard deviation, implying that Chile's level of governance in 2002 could support higher incomes in the future.

Obviously this simplistic governance deficit exercise constitutes an approximation for illustrative purposes, and does not fully account for some other important country-specific characteristics. Nonetheless, it is striking to note that 21 out of 26 countries in the Latin American region fell above the simple line of best fit in Figure B3, implying a substantial governance deficit for the region as a whole

(with countries such as Chile, Uruguay, and Costa Rica being exceptions). Similar governance deficit analyses can be conducted for other regions and countries. For those countries saddled with a significant governance deficit, it can be suggested that their income levels (and growth paths) may be particularly fragile in the medium to long term, unless concerted efforts to improve governance are under way.

Notes

1 See Kaufmann, Kraay, and Mastruzzi, (2003).

2 See Hellman and Kaufmann (2003).

3 See further details, including a "traffic light" color-coded governance map, at http://www.worldbank.org/wbi/governance/govdata2002/.

4 See Kaufmann, Kraay, and Matruzzi (2003).

5 Fortunately, at only one-third the estimated bias level with the much more limited country coverage in 1997, such regional bias in the average regional point estimate is much lower nowadays, thanks to the increased Survey country coverage, and also significantly less than other enterprise surveys such as IMD's WCY.

Part 3

Country Profiles and Data Presentation

CHAPTER 3.1

Measuring Competitiveness with the Executive Opinion Survey

EMMA LOADES, World Economic Forum

MARIA ANGELS-OLIVA, World Economic Forum

The Executive Opinion Survey has been a major component of *The Global Competitiveness Report* since its launch in 1979, and it remains the key ingredient that turns the *Report* into a uniquely representative annual measure of a nation's economic environment and its ability to achieve sustained growth.

Sole reliance on official statistics imposes important limitations on the ability of economists, entrepreneurs, international organizations, and others to carry out serious analysis of a country's economic situation and the broad range of factors that affect its performance over time. It is the addition of the qualitative data collected through the Executive Opinion Survey, which captures the expert opinions of business leaders and entrepreneurs with their current perceptions of the business environment in which they operate, that makes the World Economic Forum's *Global Competitiveness Report* a unique source of insight into the inner workings of a particular economy. Moreover, the Survey provides valuable information on a broad range of variables for which hard data sources are scarce or, frequently, nonexistent, in areas such as public institutions, the quality and effectiveness of which are gaining increasing recognition in the academic literature as one of the key building blocks of successful development. The result is a more accurate portrayal of the current and prospective health of a nation's economic and business environment, and how it relates to the global economy.

The Executive Opinion Survey is conducted in the first half of every year in each of the economies featured in *The Global Competitiveness Report*. Input is contributed exclusively by leading business executives and entrepreneurs, whose current perceptions of the business environment in which they work are captured in their responses to a comprehensive and scientifically constructed questionnaire. By participating, respondents are also provided with the opportunity to identify key obstacles to economic growth in their own countries and thus contribute to setting the quality of the business environment in the countries where their firms operate. This, in turn, may help precipitate an internal debate within the country between government officials, business leaders, organizations of civil society, and the academic community on key problem areas and how best to address them.

The Survey process

The Executive Opinion Survey is carried out in collaboration with 104 Partner Institutes of the World Economic Forum's Global Competitiveness Programme. Each Partner Institute covers one economy, or a group[1] of economies, featured in *The Global Competitiveness Report*. Partner Institutes are typically leading national research or academic institutes committed to contributing to the growth potential of their respective economies. Under the

167

guidance of the World Economic Forum, their collaboration involves conducting the Executive Opinion Survey, according to the guidelines described below, in order to ensure that the sample of respondents is representative of the economies in question and that the Survey method used remains consistent across all countries.

Enterprises should represent the main sectors of the economy in proportion to the sector share of overall employment in the country according to the employment distribution presented in *The Yearbook of Labour Statistics* of the International Labour Office. Survey respondents should be CEOs or senior managers with an international perspective. Depending on the structure of a given economy, the sample of respondents can include:

- Domestic firms that sell in foreign markets
- Units of foreign firms that operate in the domestic market
- Enterprises with significant government ownership

In the interest of obtaining responses from the desired sample, it is the Partner Institutes that determine the best method of administering the Survey in their respective settings. In the more advanced economies, the Survey questionnaire tends to be distributed to participants by mail and followed up with a telephone call to those who fail to respond. In other economies, where the infrastructure does not lend itself to this particular method or where there are time constraints, a considerable amount of extra effort is often required to collect the responses to the Survey. This may even involve Partner Institutes having to train and assign teams of researchers to conduct the Survey in the field, even to the extent of traveling to firms across the country and interviewing participants in person.

In addition to the participation resulting from the efforts of Partner Institutes, the World Economic Forum also invites CEOs and senior management of company headquarters and subsidiaries of its members worldwide to participate in the Executive Opinion Survey.

All completed Survey questionnaires are gathered in centrally by the World Economic Forum, which carries out all data entry and analysis. Participation in the Survey is entirely voluntary and responses remain strictly confidential.

Geographic coverage

Over the years, *The Global Competitiveness Report* has increased its geographic coverage to become, in terms of country reporting, one of the most extensive studies of its kind today. Coverage has increased significantly again this year, from 80 to 102 economies (as illustrated in Figure 1).

Figure 1: Geographic coverage of the Executive Opinion Survey 2003

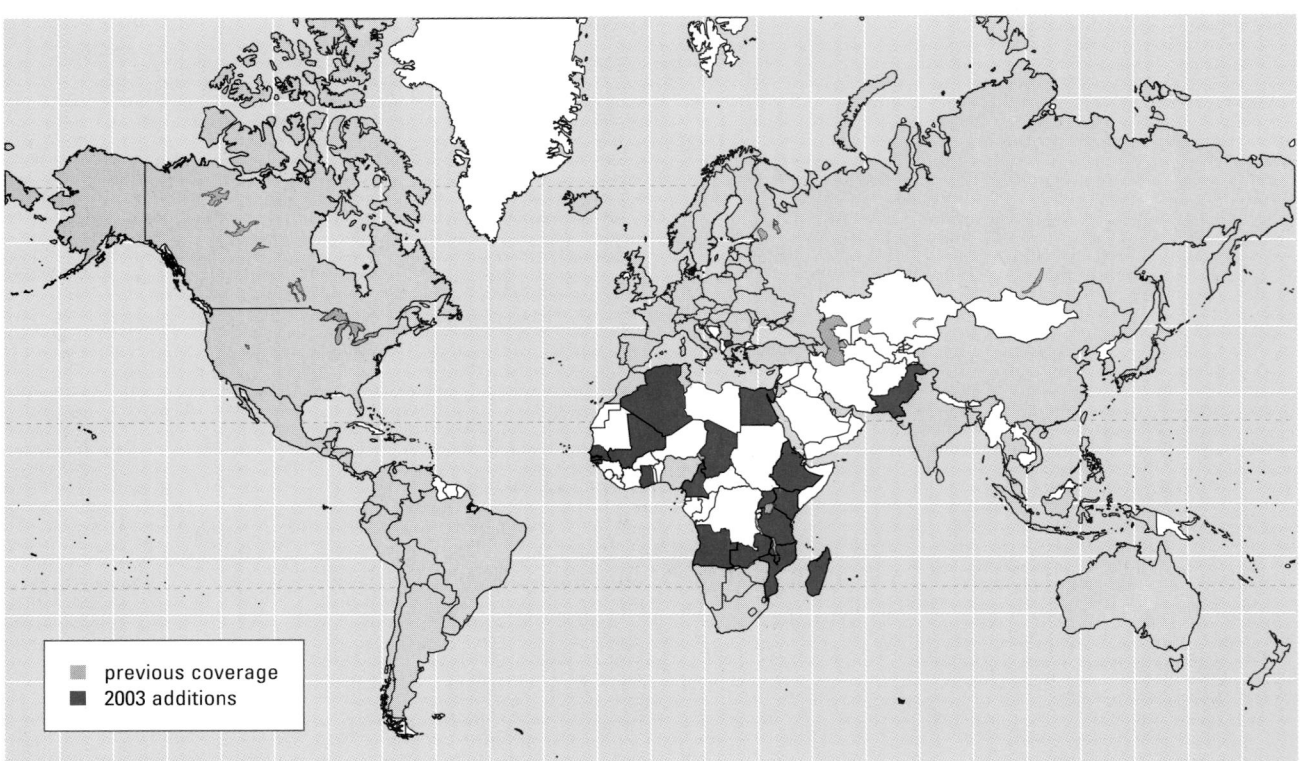

previous coverage
2003 additions

This increase in coverage is mainly the result of the special efforts devoted to increasing participation by developing countries, mainly in Africa. African countries now include Algeria, Angola, Cameroon, Chad, Egypt,[2] Ethiopia, Gambia, Ghana, Kenya, Madagascar, Malawi, Mali, Mozambique, Senegal, Tanzania, Uganda, and Zambia—increasing from 8 to 25 the total number of countries in this region featured in this year's *Report*. Other newly participating economies are Luxembourg,[3] Macedonia, Malta, Pakistan, and Serbia. Combined, the economies covered by this year's *Global Competitiveness Report* account for 97.8 percent of the world's Gross Domestic Product (GDP). Our intention is to continue to expand in coming years the geographic coverage of the *Global Competitiveness Report* to as many of the present members of the large multilateral international financial institutions as our resources will allow, with a view to enhancing the usefulness of the Survey to policymakers, the business community, civil society organizations working in these countries, the academic world, and other users of our results.[4]

Sample quality

Largely as a result of increased geographic coverage, but due also to a higher level of response from the majority of countries already featured in last year's *Report*, a record number of 8,110 responses were received this year. The purpose of the Executive Opinion Survey is to capture as true a picture of an economy's business environment as possible. This is why participation in the Survey is restricted to CEOs and senior management in the economy's business sector, whether they be domestic firms, foreign firms, or partially government owned firms. Given the extent of the Survey, however, it is inevitable that a number of responses received do not satisfy the criteria provided. We therefore carry out a careful analysis of the quality of responses to ensure that the sample of responses received from each economy is in accordance with the Survey guidelines. Excluded are questionnaires that are less than 76 percent complete or where there is evidence that answers have been provided by government bodies. The majority of exclusions this year were responses received from ministries and other national institutions. After this elimination process, the net total number of responses in this year's Executive Opinion Survey was 7,741.

Survey structure

The Executive Opinion Survey questionnaire is divided into 13 sections covering a wide range of issues related to the state of the economy in which the respondent's firm operates. Sections include overall perceptions of the macroeconomic environment, national technology levels,

the government and the public sector, public institutions, infrastructure, human resources, finance and openness, domestic competition structures, company operations and strategies, environmental policies, and international institutions. Each year, the questionnaire is tailored to capture respondents' perceptions of the most significant issues affecting the business environment at the time. This year, for example, new questions were included on health, education, trade, labor policies, and corporate governance, bringing the total number of questions in the Survey, for the first time, to over 200. To enhance the international comparability of the Survey questions, these are formulated by benchmarking the underlying concepts to internationally accepted norms.

The typical Survey question has been designed to facilitate optimal analysis of the data collected. An example of a typical Survey question is shown in Box 1 below. Participants are asked to rate their economic environment on a number of issues using a 1 to 7 bipolar scale, with 1 representing the worst possible situation and 7 representing the best. The country-level average score for each Survey question is then calculated. This year, in addition to showing the mean response for each question, the standard deviation per country is also provided (see Section 3.3: Data Tables). This gives an indication of the dispersion of responses to each question in each country, revealing the extent to which respondents agree or disagree on a particular issue. A review of the standard deviations for all questions across all countries shows that respondents in high-income countries tend to be more in agreement among themselves than those in lower-income ones. This is, perhaps, not surprising, given the greater variability likely to be seen in the overall quality of economic policies, the strength of the underlying institutions, the levels of human capital investment, technological heterogeneity, and other structural features (see Figure 2 for an interesting example).

Box 1: Example of a Typical Survey Question

In your country, diversion of public funds to companies, individuals, or groups due to corruption:

Is common   **1 2 3 4 5 6 7**   Never occurs

Circling 1.....means you agree wholeheartedly with the answer on the left-hand side

Circling 7.....means you agree wholeheartedly with the answer on the right-hand side

Circling 2.....means you largely agree with the left-hand side

Circling 3.....means you agree somewhat with left-hand side

Circling 4.....means your opinion is indifferent between the two answers

Circling 5.....means you agree somewhat with the right-hand side

Circling 6.....means you largely agree with the right-hand side

Figure 2. Country means and standard deviations for a typical Survey question

Mobile or cellular telephones for your business are (1 = not available, 7 = as accessible and affordable as in the world's most technologically advanced countries)

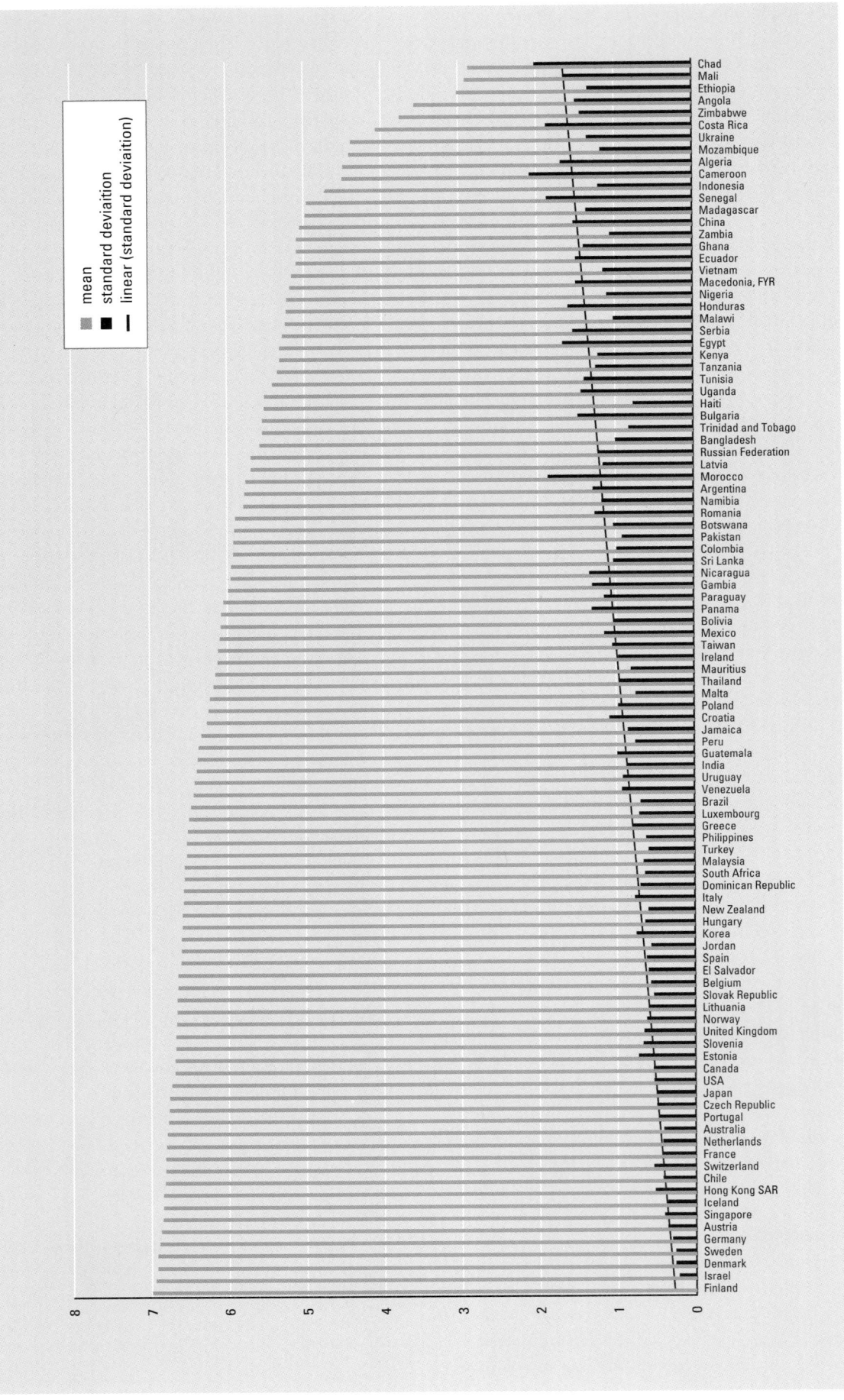

This year's Survey was made available in four different languages: English, French, German, and Spanish. It was then translated into a further 15 languages under the direction of our Partner Institutes to facilitate administration of the Survey in particular countries. These additional languages were Chinese, Croatian, Czech, Estonian, Japanese, Latvian, Lithuanian, Macedonian, Maltese, Portuguese, Russian, Serbian, Slovakian, Slovenian, and Ukrainian.

An innovation this year, designed to further facilitate the response process and to attract more participants, was the option for respondents to complete the Survey questionnaire online. The online Survey questionnaire was available in both English and Spanish. A total of 465 completed questionnaires were collected by this method, which attracted a particularly strong response from business leaders in Brazil, India, Ireland, Italy, Mexico, Singapore, South Africa, and the United States. Attempts will continue to be made in coming years to increase the share of online responses to the questionnaire.

Characteristics of respondents

Table 1 illustrates the distribution of respondents by size and type of firm. As previously mentioned, the total sample size across all countries combined was 7,741, which translates to an average of 75 responses per country, well above last year's average of 60 responses per country.

The following points may be drawn from Table 1 and are worthy of note: in exactly half of all the countries participating, more than 70 firms completed the Survey in each; in almost three-quarters of the 102 participating countries, more than 50 firms responded.

Size of firm

In terms of distribution of respondents by size of firm, Table 1 shows that over 50 percent of all responses are from firms with between 101 and 5,001 employees. When comparing responses from core innovators with those from non-core innovators,[5] it is interesting to note that core innovators tend to show a more even distribution of responses across firm size, consistent with the more homogeneous structure of the business sector in higher-income economies.

In examining the different firm size categories in further detail, the United States and Sweden had country samples where 30 percent of the companies had between 5,000 and 20,000 employees. Germany, France, and the United States are among those countries with the greatest participation of firms with over 20,000 employees (up to 17 percent of the overall number of responding firms).

With many of our new entrants to this year's competitiveness analysis being African countries, participation in this year's Executive Opinion Survey has been particularly strong among small firms, with fewer than 101 employees (33 percent of all responses). Chad, Gambia, Ghana, and Morocco are the four countries with the majority of responses from this category of firms. Furthermore, Table 1 shows that countries with over 50 percent of responses from firms with fewer than 500 employees are all non-core innovators.

Firm ownership and market orientation

Table 1 also provides an interesting picture of the ownership structure of the firms that took part in the Survey. Half of the answers obtained through the Survey process correspond to firms that are private and domestic in origin. That is, about 50 percent of respondents are CEOs working for private firms that are under local control. A full 23 percent of the sample corresponds to foreign private firms, and 10 percent of the answers were provided by CEOs of corporations that are under government control. This pattern applies independently of economic development and technological positioning.

The distinction made in the Survey between domestic and foreign firms casts some light on the issue of the extent of foreign participation in domestic economic activity across the countries in the sample. For instance, in Argentina and Brazil, the central core of Mercosur, more than 50 percent of Survey respondents indicated that ownership of their firms was foreign in its majority. This is an interesting result, consistent with the remarkable expansion of trade in these countries, which has been associated with the liberalization of cross-border flows of goods and capital during the past decade. The case of Ireland is similar, with 43 percent of respondents claiming to be majority foreign owned, the highest such share in the European Union.

The Survey provides information on the extent of government ownership of the enterprise sector—for those countries in which this share is particularly large—that is largely consistent with other well-known characteristics of such countries, including the degree of market orientation of economic policies, the prevalence of rigidities in the allocation of resources, and the levels of per-capita income. Of note is the extent to which the transition economies of central and eastern Europe—particularly those slated to join the European Union in the forth coming wave of expansion—have witnessed a remarkable reduction in the role of the state in domestic economic activity. Countries such as the Czech Republic, Estonia, Hungary, and Slovenia have levels of state ownership of the enterprise sector that are well on their way to reaching the levels seen in the more mature industrial economies.

Table 1: Distribution of respondents by size and type of firm

	Sample size	Surveys per million population	Distribution of respondents by firm size (# employees in country)						Distribution of respondents by firm type				
			<101	101–500	501–5,000	5,001–20,000	>20,000	No response	Dom[1] ≥50%	Gov[2] ≥50%	Fgn[3] ≥50%	D, G, F[4] ≤50%	No response
Algeria	71	2.3	35%	37%	24%	4%	0%	0%	35%	52%	8%	3%	1%
Angola	47	3.4	51%	34%	15%	0%	0%	0%	57%	17%	6%	6%	13%
Argentina	61	1.6	39%	18%	38%	5%	0%	0%	40%	5%	40%	10%	5%
Australia	20	1.0	0%	10%	55%	20%	10%	5%	42%	11%	36%	8%	2%
Austria	83	10.2	7%	43%	39%	10%	0%	1%	42%	11%	36%	8%	2%
Bangladesh	76	0.5	22%	22%	50%	3%	3%	0%	80%	1%	14%	0%	4%
Belgium	46	4.5	7%	41%	46%	4%	0%	2%	52%	2%	37%	2%	7%
Bolivia	79	9.1	59%	25%	13%	0%	0%	3%	62%	14%	19%	0%	5%
Botswana	56	35.0	59%	25%	14%	0%	0%	2%	39%	18%	29%	4%	11%
Brazil	63	0.4	8%	10%	49%	24%	8%	2%	38%	3%	51%	6%	2%
Bulgaria	167	21.4	57%	25%	11%	1%	0%	6%	66%	14%	11%	1%	8%
Cameroon	56	3.6	64%	18%	16%	0%	0%	2%	66%	14%	14%	2%	4%
Canada	75	2.4	45%	27%	13%	4%	11%	0%	71%	15%	8%	3%	4%
Chad	84	10.0	94%	4%	1%	0%	0%	1%	69%	2%	14%	1%	13%
Chile	170	10.9	26%	31%	36%	4%	0%	2%	62%	5%	28%	4%	2%
China	110	0.1	14%	25%	52%	5%	4%	0%	27%	50%	12%	9%	2%
Colombia	63	1.4	25%	37%	33%	5%	0%	0%	52%	3%	40%	3%	2%
Costa Rica	70	16.7	31%	49%	19%	1%	0%	0%	61%	7%	29%	1%	1%
Croatia	111	23.6	41%	39%	14%	7%	0%	0%	52%	39%	8%	1%	0%
Czech Republic	109	10.6	34%	10%	44%	6%	1%	6%	44%	6%	39%	6%	4%
Denmark	42	7.9	17%	19%	48%	14%	2%	0%	57%	12%	21%	10%	0%
Dominican Republic	35	4.1	31%	29%	31%	3%	0%	6%	66%	11%	17%	0%	6%
Ecuador	98	7.5	37%	43%	18%	2%	0%	0%	64%	13%	19%	3%	0%
Egypt	104	1.5	38%	28%	30%	1%	0%	3%	63%	1%	22%	9%	5%
El Salvador	48	7.4	27%	40%	33%	0%	0%	0%	65%	10%	23%	2%	0%
Estonia	65	46.4	62%	25%	11%	0%	0%	3%	51%	14%	29%	3%	3%
Ethiopia	85	1.3	51%	28%	14%	1%	0%	6%	65%	19%	5%	0%	12%
Finland	36	6.9	25%	19%	31%	22%	3%	0%	50%	14%	28%	6%	3%
France	93	1.6	25%	14%	28%	17%	16%	0%	59%	4%	29%	3%	4%
Gambia	79	56.4	77%	14%	1%	0%	0%	8%	63%	3%	14%	5%	15%
Germany	72	0.9	13%	13%	26%	29%	18%	1%	58%	6%	21%	8%	7%
Ghana	174	8.6	65%	24%	6%	1%	1%	4%	53%	7%	21%	3%	16%
Greece	98	9.2	21%	29%	40%	4%	2%	4%	60%	3%	29%	5%	3%
Guatemala	61	5.1	46%	33%	21%	0%	0%	0%	87%	0%	10%	2%	2%
Haiti	25	3.0	60%	32%	8%	0%	0%	0%	100%	0%	0%	0%	0%
Honduras	82	12.2	46%	32%	17%	2%	0%	2%	71%	5%	16%	2%	6%
Hong Kong SAR	60	8.6	22%	28%	35%	12%	3%	0%	43%	8%	45%	3%	2%
Hungary	106	10.7	19%	41%	33%	5%	0%	3%	47%	11%	36%	0%	6%
Iceland	27	95.4	33%	48%	19%	0%	0%	0%	74%	11%	11%	0%	4%
India	63	0.1	17%	14%	51%	6%	11%	0%	49%	2%	29%	11%	10%
Indonesia	38	0.2	24%	45%	11%	8%	3%	11%	61%	0%	13%	5%	21%
Ireland	40	10.3	38%	25%	25%	10%	3%	0%	35%	13%	43%	3%	8%
Israel	21	3.3	14%	43%	33%	10%	0%	0%	62%	14%	14%	5%	5%
Italy	48	0.8	23%	10%	31%	25%	8%	2%	50%	6%	29%	6%	8%
Jamaica	58	22.3	60%	22%	16%	0%	0%	2%	62%	3%	22%	3%	9%
Japan	72	0.6	13%	14%	35%	24%	14%	1%	71%	0%	19%	3%	7%
Jordan	85	16.3	35%	32%	29%	2%	1%	2%	62%	16%	7%	5%	9%
Kenya	75	2.4	48%	28%	20%	0%	0%	1%	59%	12%	23%	1%	5%
Korea	103	2.2	9%	27%	50%	9%	3%	2%	70%	3%	11%	11%	6%
Latvia	184	76.7	63%	23%	7%	1%	0%	7%	63%	8%	22%	3%	5%
Lithuania	134	36.2	7%	66%	25%	1%	0%	1%	46%	39%	14%	1%	0%
Luxembourg	34	75.9	29%	21%	38%	6%	0%	6%	53%	3%	38%	3%	3%
Macedonia, FYR	114	54.3	41%	37%	19%	1%	0%	2%	69%	9%	18%	3%	1%
Madagascar	93	5.5	54%	26%	15%	1%	1%	3%	66%	5%	17%	5%	6%
Malawi	34	2.9	41%	44%	15%	0%	0%	0%	38%	21%	32%	3%	6%
Malaysia	96	4.2	18%	39%	38%	4%	2%	0%	55%	4%	35%	3%	3%
Mali	37	3.1	57%	27%	14%	0%	0%	3%	46%	35%	11%	3%	5%
Malta	78	198.5	42%	38%	18%	0%	1%	0%	46%	12%	32%	8%	3%
Mauritius	32	26.7	25%	38%	31%	3%	0%	3%	59%	3%	19%	13%	6%
Mexico	105	1.0	14%	17%	31%	16%	17%	4%	58%	8%	27%	1%	7%
Morocco	101	3.3	67%	19%	10%	0%	0%	4%	79%	5%	9%	6%	2%
Mozambique	75	3.9	45%	31%	21%	0%	0%	3%	40%	9%	28%	9%	13%
Namibia	47	26.1	47%	26%	19%	2%	0%	6%	51%	9%	26%	6%	11%
Netherlands	84	5.3	11%	18%	43%	15%	11%	2%	43%	18%	26%	7%	6%
New Zealand	70	18.4	14%	36%	40%	9%	1%	0%	50%	11%	34%	3%	1%
Nicaragua	71	13.4	42%	32%	23%	0%	0%	3%	58%	17%	15%	7%	3%
Nigeria	198	1.7	41%	24%	22%	3%	1%	10%	74%	4%	12%	3%	8%
Norway	27	6.0	41%	33%	19%	7%	0%	0%	67%	4%	22%	4%	4%
Pakistan	49	0.3	10%	12%	59%	12%	0%	6%	39%	16%	33%	2%	10%
Panama	75	25.9	57%	25%	16%	0%	0%	1%	61%	3%	25%	1%	9%
Paraguay	65	11.2	46%	42%	9%	0%	0%	3%	85%	0%	12%	3%	0%
Peru	79	3.0	20%	41%	34%	3%	1%	1%	59%	6%	29%	0%	5%

(cont'd.)

Table 1: Distribution of respondents by size and type of firm *(cont'd.)*

| | Sample size | Surveys per million population | Distribution of respondents by firm size (# employees in country) | | | | | | Distribution of respondents by firm type | | | | |
			<101	101–500	501–5,000	5,001–20,000	>20,000	No response	Dom[1] ≥ 50%	Gov[2] ≥ 50%	Fgn[3] ≥ 50%	D, G, F[4] ≤ 50%	No response
Philippines	47	0.6	13%	40%	34%	9%	2%	2%	57%	2%	32%	4%	4%
Poland	92	2.4	40%	23%	27%	3%	3%	3%	33%	8%	43%	8%	9%
Portugal	46	4.6	17%	22%	43%	11%	4%	2%	67%	13%	9%	7%	4%
Romania	96	4.3	64%	20%	16%	0%	0%	1%	81%	2%	17%	0%	0%
Russian Federation	264	1.8	34%	30%	29%	4%	1%	2%	69%	16%	9%	3%	4%
Senegal	27	2.7	56%	33%	11%	0%	0%	0%	74%	7%	15%	0%	4%
Serbia	100	9.5	39%	33%	25%	1%	1%	1%	38%	36%	27%	1%	0%
Singapore	120	28.6	28%	39%	28%	3%	1%	1%	11%	4%	78%	2%	5%
Slovak Republic	71	13.1	18%	30%	45%	6%	0%	1%	49%	4%	42%	1%	3%
Slovenia	87	43.5	40%	18%	34%	3%	0%	3%	66%	9%	20%	1%	5%
South Africa	62	1.4	13%	19%	37%	16%	15%	0%	44%	5%	52%	0%	0%
Spain	70	1.8	24%	26%	37%	7%	6%	0%	71%	1%	24%	1%	1%
Sri Lanka	86	4.5	34%	29%	30%	6%	0%	1%	77%	2%	8%	3%	10%
Sweden	28	3.2	14%	21%	21%	32%	7%	4%	36%	11%	39%	4%	11%
Switzerland	73	10.1	41%	37%	14%	5%	3%	0%	71%	3%	21%	1%	4%
Taiwan	43	1.9	9%	28%	49%	9%	5%	0%	65%	16%	9%	5%	5%
Tanzania	69	1.9	43%	41%	9%	0%	0%	7%	52%	20%	20%	4%	3%
Thailand	45	0.7	0%	29%	49%	16%	7%	0%	42%	13%	31%	7%	7%
Trinidad and Tobago	61	46.9	30%	36%	30%	2%	2%	2%	56%	16%	18%	3%	7%
Tunisia	75	7.7	63%	24%	12%	0%	0%	1%	75%	3%	16%	5%	1%
Turkey	46	0.7	28%	26%	37%	4%	2%	2%	61%	0%	30%	2%	7%
Uganda	148	6.0	63%	22%	8%	0%	2%	5%	49%	11%	14%	10%	16%
Ukraine	67	1.4	43%	39%	16%	1%	0%	0%	75%	24%	0%	1%	0%
United Kingdom	65	1.1	8%	17%	43%	18%	12%	2%	55%	5%	28%	2%	11%
Uruguay	65	19.1	66%	26%	2%	0%	0%	6%	66%	5%	22%	5%	2%
USA	52	0.2	10%	12%	31%	31%	17%	0%	56%	0%	35%	0%	10%
Venezuela	34	1.4	38%	35%	21%	3%	0%	3%	50%	3%	41%	0%	6%
Vietnam	118	1.5	56%	31%	10%	1%	1%	2%	34%	29%	30%	8%	0%
Zambia	59	5.4	49%	39%	10%	0%	2%	0%	37%	29%	27%	3%	3%
Zimbabwe	33	2.5	9%	12%	67%	12%	0%	0%	48%	12%	36%	0%	6%
TOTAL	**7741**												

1 Companies majority-owned by the domestic private sector (more than 50%)
2 Companies majority-owned by the government (more than 50%)
3 Companies majority-owned by foreign groups (more than 50%)
4 Mixed companies (not more than 50% owned by any one of the three sectors)

Survey data and robustness

The data from the Executive Opinion Survey are at the heart of both competitiveness indexes calculated in this *Report*. They are thus a key input into the analysis and policy prescriptions contained in a number of its chapters. Given the central role played by the Survey data, it is important to examine the statistical robustness of the results. This is done in a number of ways, including the random drop method, which entails eliminating 50 percent of the per-country and per-variable observations using random sampling techniques and re-estimating mean responses for the variables under the smaller sample.

Random drop tests

As a first check, we provide the so-called random drop test for two questions included in the Executive Opinion Survey and the Competitiveness Indexes: the questions on foreign direct investment as a technology transfer mechanism (ie, foreign investment in your country 1 = brings little new technology, to 7 = is an important source of new technology) and on company spending levels on research and development (companies in your country 1 = do not spend money on research and development, to

7 = spend heavily on research and development relative to international peers). The results are illustrated in Figures 3a and 3b. On the axis we include the means obtained using 100 percent of individual responses and the means based on 50 percent of individual answers chosen randomly.

With relatively little dispersion, all the countries lie along a narrow corridor around the 45-degree line, meaning that the country averages obtained for these two Survey questions based either on the entire sample or on just 50 percent of the per-country observations are broadly similar. In other words, for our Survey data, halving the sample does not generate any significant differences in the responses when compared with those derived from the whole sample, highlighting the robustness of the Survey results. Although some countries do show some dispersion with respect to the 45-degree line—Slovak Republic, Pakistan, and Croatia for the question pertaining to the impact of foreign investment as a source of new technology transfers—and Indonesia and Tanzania for the question on spending on R&D—the dispersion is not nearly high enough to alter significantly the overall thrust of the random drop test results.

Figure 3a: Robustness test of Survey data: Results from random drop test FDI as source of technology

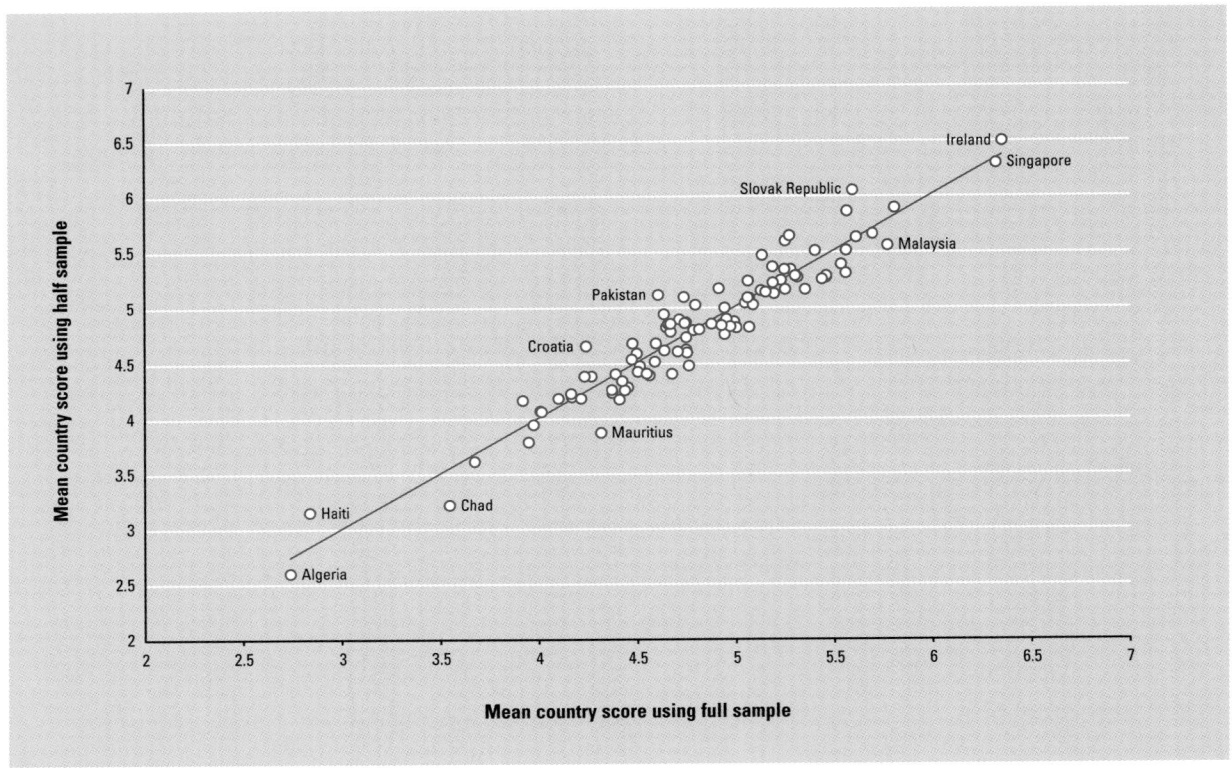

Figure 3b: Robustness test of Survey data: Results from random drop test company spending on R&D

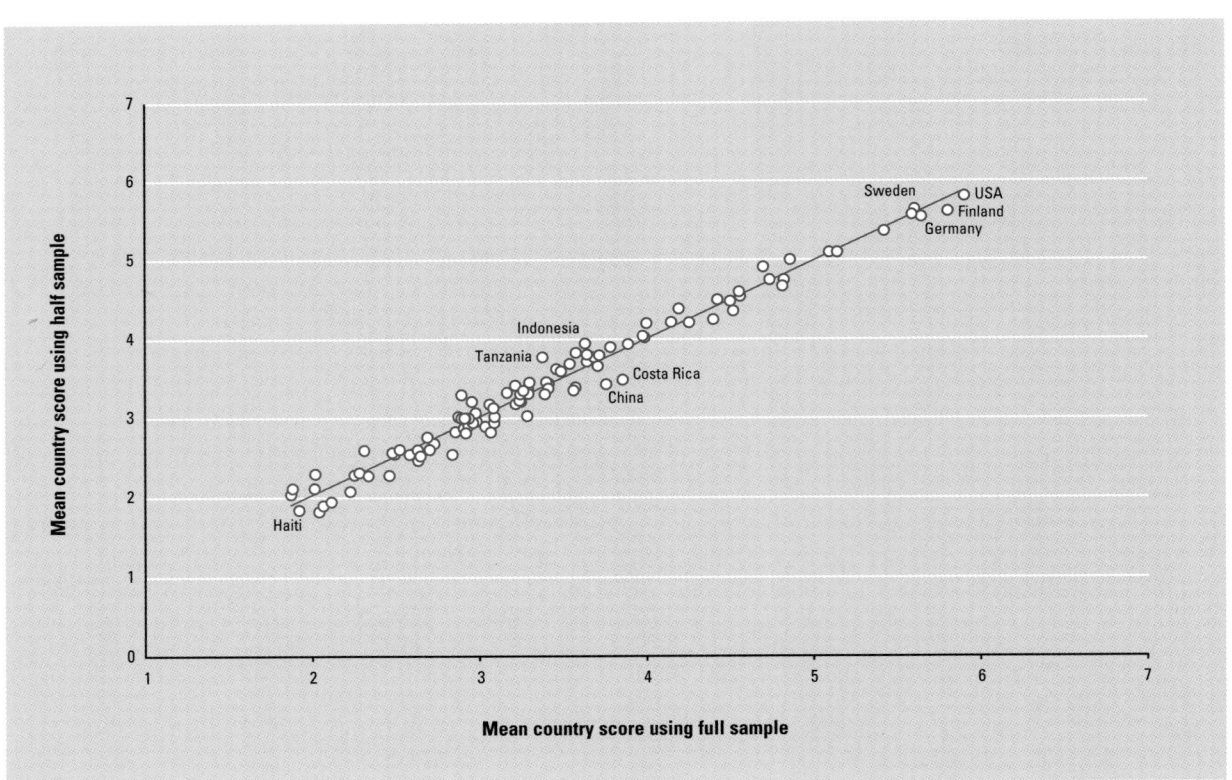

The correlation coefficients obtained from the country means, based on all individual responses and on 50 percent of the responses, are 0.96 (for the question on foreign direct investment) and 0.98 (for the question on research and development). In other words, for the two variables depicted on FDI technology transfers and R&D, which enter into the technology index of the Growth Competitiveness Index (GCI), the close relationship between the country means obtained from the full-country sample and the half-country sample shows that the results are robust.

This robustness applies throughout the Survey results. Table 2 reports the ordinary least squares (OLS) coefficients resulting from regressing the country means based on the whole sample against the country means based on half of the country samples chosen under a random sampling method. The questions shown are those that display higher average cross-economy dispersion among those Survey questions included in the *Report*. The lowest slope coefficient is 0.90 and corresponds to the question on "influence of illegal contributions on public policy." Countries falling slightly apart from the average are Norway and Haiti. The highest accuracy is obtained for the question "frequency of Internet access in schools." The goodness of fit for all these regressions is also very high (ie, the lowest adjusted R^2 statistic is 0.94). This result implies that, even for those questions that presented higher dispersion at the respondent level per country, 50 percent of the sample selected randomly is able to explain over 90 percent of the variation of the whole sample means (used as our dependent variable).

Not surprisingly, the stability properties with respect to sample size highlighted by the above tests are preserved when examining composites of the Survey data. Figure 4 shows the results of the random drop test for the corruption subindex, created on the basis of qualitative information obtained from the Survey. This index is a composite of three Survey questions about bribes affecting public utilities, annual tax payments, and the awarding of export and import permits. As with the individual variables reported in Table 2, the regression coefficient associated with this composite indicator is close to 1, as is the adjusted R^2 statistic.

Comparing hard data and Survey data

Yet another way to look at the robustness of the Survey is to examine whether, for those questions for which there are also "hard" data available, the Survey responses corroborate the information provided by the hard data. Figures 5a and 5b compare data on the perceived availability of cellular phones and telephone lines obtained from the Survey with actual data on cellular phones and telephone lines per 100 inhabitants compiled by the International Technology Union (ITU). The figures confirm the existence of a strong positive relationship between both variables, although with a significant number of outliers.

As Figure 5a illustrates, business community perceptions on the availability of cellular phones in Costa Rica, Ukraine, and some African countries such as Angola and Zimbabwe appear to be on the "pessimistic" side, with actual penetration rates for cellular phones being much higher in some cases than recorded in the Survey. In contrast, perceptions of mobile telephone penetration turn out to be more positive in India, Malawi, and Bangladesh than warranted by the actual data. It is perhaps not surprising that such discrepancies between perceptions in the business community and actual data on technology variables and infrastructure should be more pronounced in developing countries, where deficiencies in the quality of services are likely to be more common. Similar remarks apply to Figure 5b.

Table 2: Regression analysis on random drop method

Questions	Threat of terrorism	Foreign technology licensing usage	Influence of illegal contributions on public policy	Bribes for awarding of public contracts	Frequency of Internet access in schools	Impact of HIV/AIDS on company	Ease of obtaining credit for company	Competition in local markets from imports or local firms	Handling of international distribution and marketing	Priority given to compliance with international environment agreements
Dispersion*	1.7	1.5	1.5	1.6	1.3	1.6	1.5	1.6	1.4	1.4
Slope	0.91	0.97	0.9	0.96	0.99	0.96	0.92	0.905	0.973	0.968
SD	0.022	0.025	0.23	0.017	0.009	0.013	0.023	0.02	0.025	0.017
Adj. R^2	0.94	0.94	0.94	0.97	0.99	0.98	0.94	0.95	0.94	0.97
Obs	102	102	102	102	102	102	102	102	102	102

* Average dispersion per question among the 102 economies using the whole sample
Source: Authors' calculations

Figure 4: Random drop test on the corruption subindex

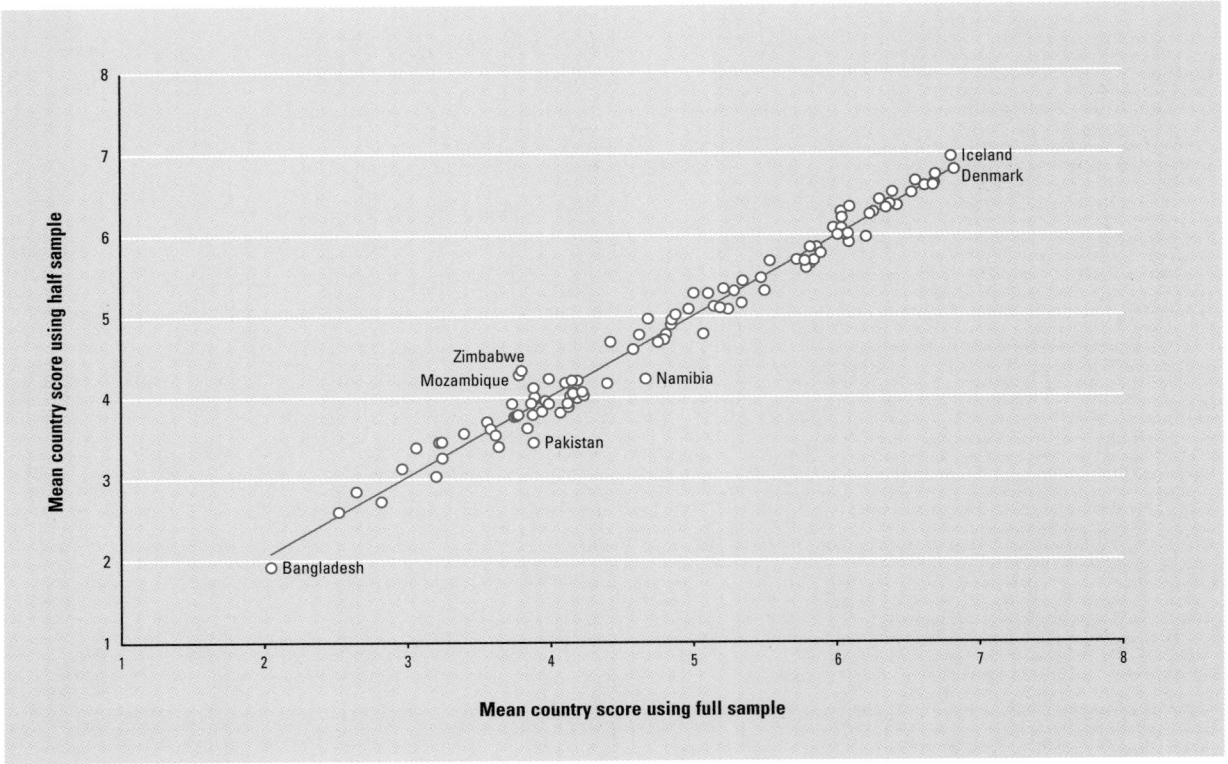

Summary

The information made available by the Executive Opinion Survey provides a large body of relevant data of a complementary nature to that captured by hard data sources. By soliciting the expert opinions of leading business executives from a representative cross-section of sectors and firms of different sizes, the aim of the Survey is to provide an unbiased reading of the multiplicity of factors that make up the environment in which firms operate. Some of these factors are economic, others are legal and/or institutional; many of them are difficult to quantify but are no less important than those captured in official statistics. Carried out in more than 100 countries worldwide, the Survey provides a treasure trove of insights and information, allowing policy makers and others to see competitiveness and the obstacles to sustained growth in an international perspective.

From the tests described in this chapter, we note that despite some variation in the responses to Survey questions, the results are fairly robust with respect to changes in sample size; in particular, when half of the sample is randomly dropped the results remain quite stable. Furthermore, we find that in those cases where hard data are available (say on the availability of some important technology to the firm), the Survey results tend to strongly corroborate the information being provided by the hard data. More importantly, over a broad range of issues, many of them at the heart of the development agenda, the Survey provides information that goes well beyond that available from hard data sources.

The Executive Opinion Survey remains a key source for the construction of the Growth Competitiveness Index and the Business Competitiveness Index. It also provides valuable information on a variety of other research topics featured in this *Report*—for instance, the many questions associated with good governance and the impediments to growth that emanate from weaknesses in public institutions. The Survey is also a fundamental building block in the development of other regional and topical reports produced by the World Economic Forum's Global Competitiveness Programme, such as *The Africa Competitiveness Report*, *The Latin America Competitiveness Report*, and *The Global Information Technology Report*.

Notes

1 The Stockholm School of Economics in Riga conducts the Survey in Estonia, Latvia, and Lithuania; The Latin American Center for Competitiveness and Sustainable Development (INCAE) conducts the Survey in Bolivia, Costa Rica, Dominican Republic, Ecuador, El Salvador, Guatemala, Honduras, Nicaragua, and Panama.

Figure 5a: Soft versus hard data on cellular telephones

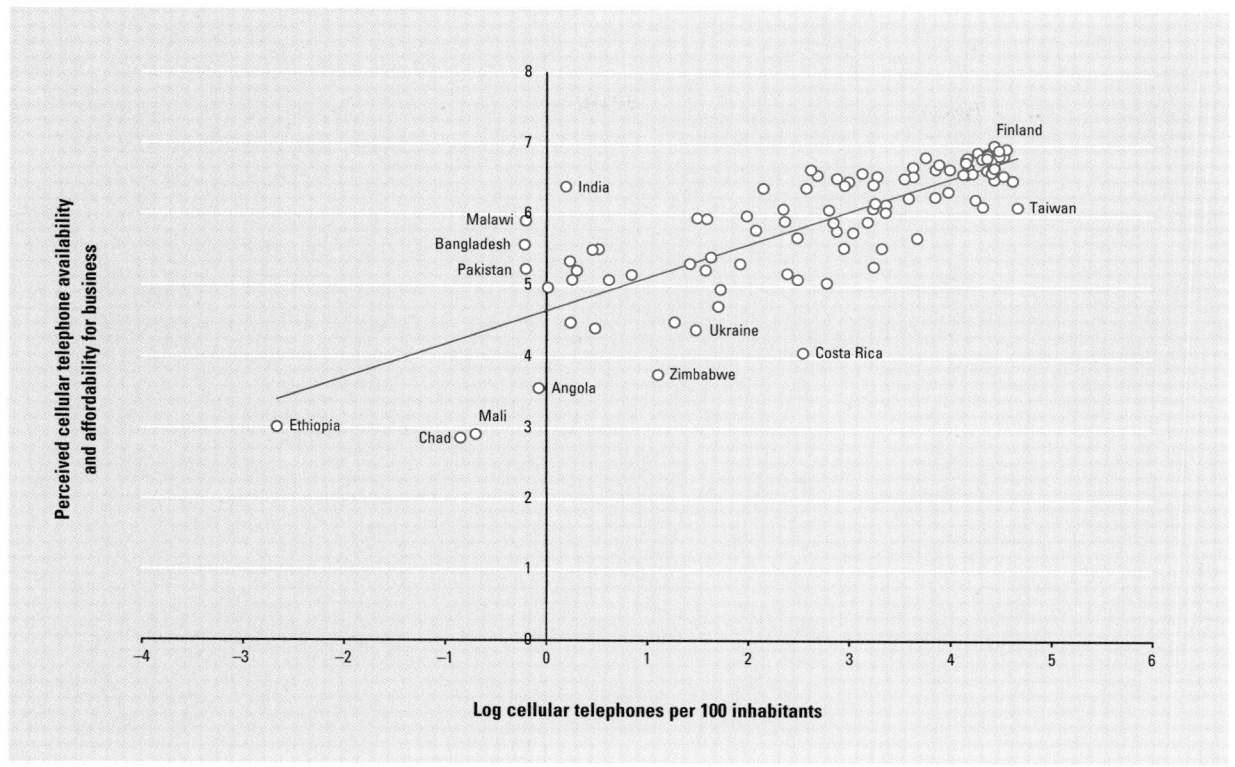

Figure 5b: Soft versus hard data on telephone lines

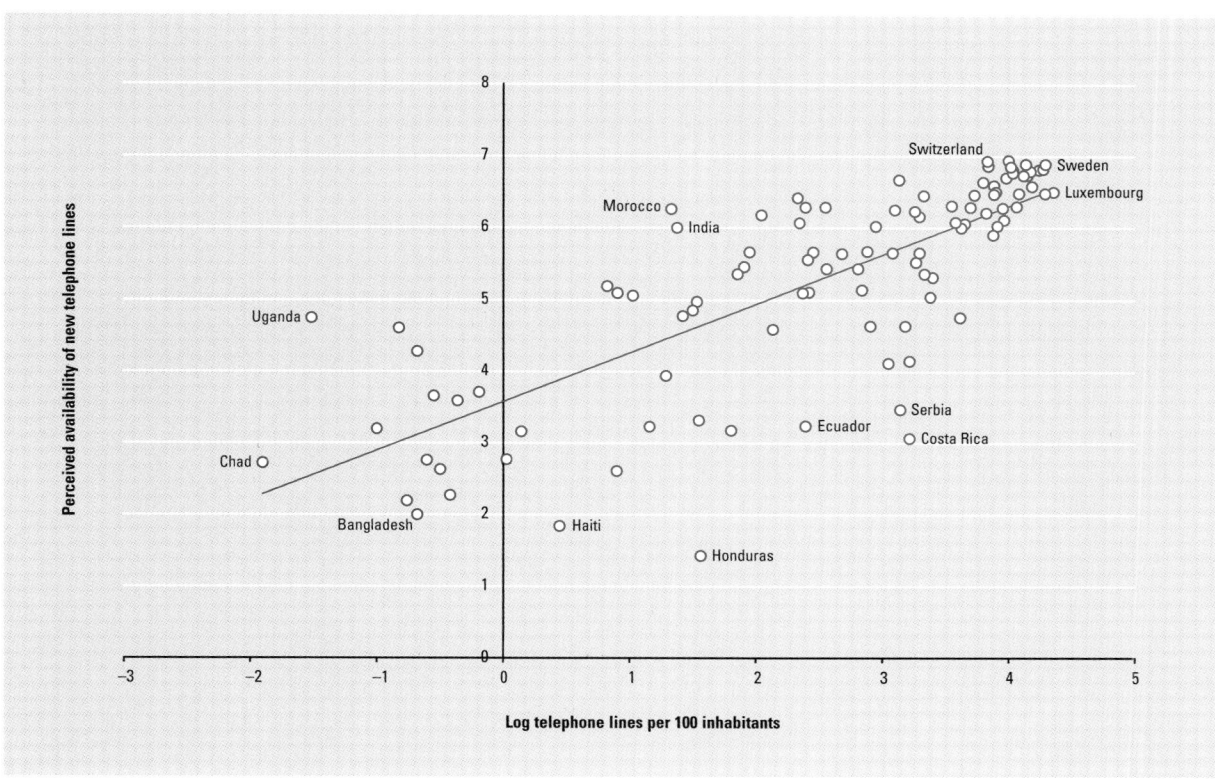

2 Egypt featured annually in our competitiveness analyses from 1995 to 2001, but was excluded from *The Global Competitiveness Report 2002–2003*.

3 Luxembourg featured annually in our competitiveness analyses from 1996 to 2000, but was excluded from the 2001–2002 and 2002–2003 *Reports*.

4 Since the World Bank has 189 members, we would regard this as our medium-term goal for expansion of the GCR's country coverage.

5 *Core innovators* are defined as those economies with an annual number of US utility patents per million population exceeding 15 in year 2002.

Reference

International Labour Organization. 2001. *Yearbook of Labour Statistics 2001*. Geneva: International Labour Organization.

3.2: Country Profiles

How country profiles work

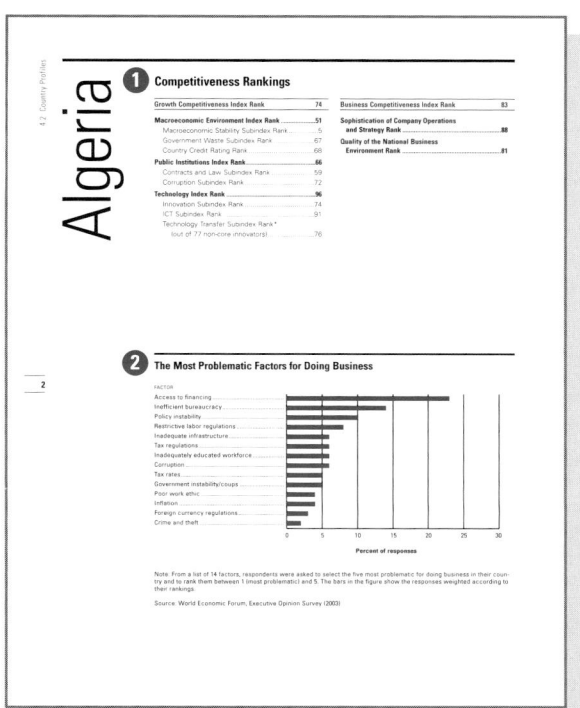

The Country Profiles section presents a two-page profile with selected data for each individual economy included in the *Global Competitiveness Report 2003–2004*.

Left-hand page

The **left-hand page** gives each country's ranks in the *Global Competitiveness Report* indexes (the GCI and the BCI), as well as information on the issues perceived as most problematic for doing business in each country. The page is divided into the following two sections:

❶ Competitiveness rankings

The Growth Competitiveness Index (GCI) rankings (out of 102 countries) and the Business Competitiveness Index (BCI) rankings (out of 95 countries) are listed in the upper right-hand side of the page, along with results for the respective subindex rankings.

❷ Most problematic factors for doing business

The chart summarizes those factors seen by CEOs and top executives as the most problematic for doing business in their country. The information is drawn from a question in the Executive Opinion Survey 2003 in which respondents were presented with 14 different factors and asked to rank from 1 (most problematic) to 5 those they considered the most problematic. The responses were tabulated and weighted according to the rank assigned by the respondents.

(continued on next page)

181

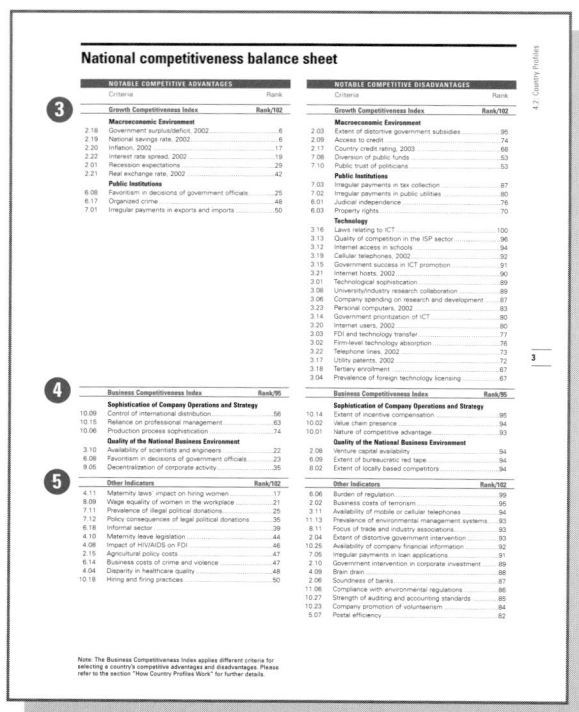

Right-hand page

The **right-hand page** of each profile forms a country competitiveness balance sheet, providing detailed information on the relative strengths and weaknesses of each economy. The balance sheet is broken into three main sections: one on growth competitiveness and one on business competitiveness, reflecting the complementary perspectives on competitiveness as presented in Chapters 1.1 and 1.2 respectively. The final section provides a list of other noteworthy indicators about the economic environment of each specific country.

The criteria used to calculate the advantages and disadvantages differ between the GCI and the BCI. The GCI balance sheet highlights strengths and weaknesses of a country relative to its global position. For the BCI balance sheet, a relative benchmark is used, reflecting the way a country's priorities shift through the process of economic development.

3 Growth Competitiveness Index section

Variable rankings for the GCI section are based on data from 102 countries; the details of these variables and their associated rankings can be found in the data tables in Section 3.3 of the *Report*.

For top-ranked countries in the GCI, such as Finland and the United States, variables ranked between 1 and 10 are considered an advantage. For those countries ranked from 11 to 51 overall in the GCI, any variables ranked better than the country's own rank are considered to be advantages. For those countries with an overall GCI rank worse than 51, any variables ranked equal to or better than 51 are considered as advantages.

4 Business Competitiveness Index section

Variable rankings for the BCI section are based on the data set for the 95 countries used for calculating the BCI; see Chapter 1.2 for further information regarding the coverage of this index.

For each subindex, variables with the top three rankings are selected as advantages, and variables with the bottom three rankings are selected as disadvantages. However, if any of the three variables in the disadvantages list rank better than 15 they are excluded. Conversely, if any of the variables in the advantages list are ranked worse than 85 they are likewise excluded. This explains why some countries may have fewer than three advantages or disadvantages.

Note that the BCI analysis indicates that "3.04 Prevalence of Foreign Technology Licensing" is not an advantage for high-income countries, since at their stage of development, innovation is more important than the transfer of technology from abroad. Therefore, "Prevalence of Foreign Technology Licensing" is not reported on the balance sheet for high-income countries.

⑤ Other indicators section

Variable rankings for the other indicators section are based on data from 102 countries; the details of these variables and their associated rankings can be found in the data tables in Section 3.3 of the *Report*. The variables are selected as advantages or disadvantages using the same decision rule described in the Growth Competitiveness Index section above.

Algeria

Competitiveness Rankings

Growth Competitiveness Index Rank	74

Macroeconomic Environment Index Rank	**51**
Macroeconomic Stability Subindex Rank	5
Government Waste Subindex Rank	67
Country Credit Rating Rank	68
Public Institutions Index Rank	**66**
Contracts and Law Subindex Rank	59
Corruption Subindex Rank	72
Technology Index Rank	**96**
Innovation Subindex Rank	74
ICT Subindex Rank	91
Technology Transfer Subindex Rank (out of 77 non-core innovators)	76

Business Competitiveness Index Rank	83

Sophistication of Company Operations and Strategy Rank	**88**
Quality of the National Business Environment Rank	**81**

The Most Problematic Factors for Doing Business

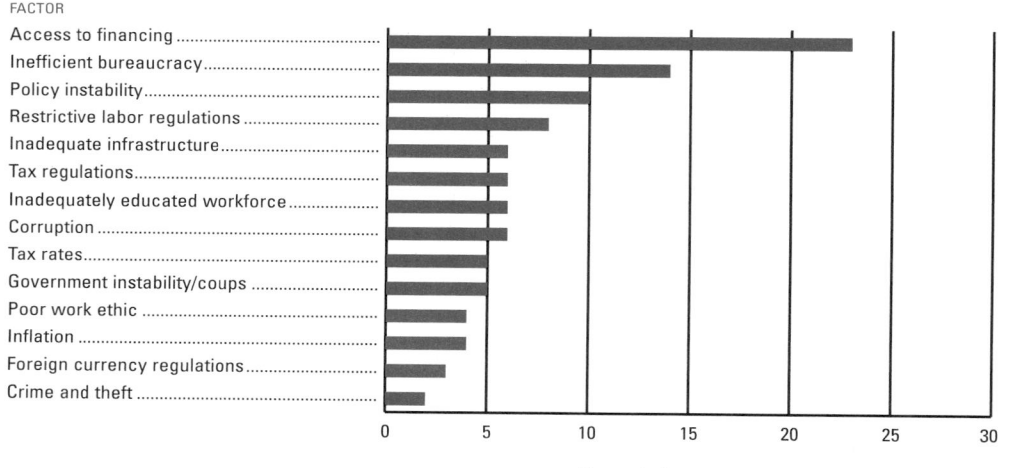

FACTOR

Access to financing
Inefficient bureaucracy
Policy instability
Restrictive labor regulations
Inadequate infrastructure
Tax regulations
Inadequately educated workforce
Corruption
Tax rates
Government instability/coups
Poor work ethic
Inflation
Foreign currency regulations
Crime and theft

Percent of responses

Note: From a list of 14 factors, respondents were asked to select the five most problematic for doing business in their country and to rank them between 1 (most problematic) and 5. The bars in the figure show the responses weighted according to their rankings.

Source: World Economic Forum, Executive Opinion Survey (2003)

National competitiveness balance sheet

NOTABLE COMPETITIVE ADVANTAGES		
Growth Competitiveness Index		**Rank/102**
	Macroeconomic Environment	
2.18	Government surplus/deficit, 2002	6
2.19	National savings rate, 2002	6
2.20	Inflation, 2002	17
2.22	Interest rate spread, 2002	19
2.01	Recession expectations	29
2.21	Real exchange rate, 2002	42
	Public Institutions	
6.08	Favoritism in decisions of government officials	25
6.17	Organized crime	48
7.01	Irregular payments in exports and imports	50

NOTABLE COMPETITIVE DISADVANTAGES		
Growth Competitiveness Index		**Rank/102**
	Macroeconomic Environment	
2.03	Extent of distortive government subsidies	95
2.09	Access to credit	74
2.17	Country credit rating, 2003	68
7.08	Diversion of public funds	53
7.10	Public trust of politicians	53
	Public Institutions	
7.03	Irregular payments in tax collection	87
7.02	Irregular payments in public utilities	80
6.01	Judicial independence	76
6.03	Property rights	70
	Technology	
3.16	Laws relating to ICT	100
3.13	Quality of competition in the ISP sector	96
3.12	Internet access in schools	94
3.19	Cellular telephones, 2002	92
3.15	Government success in ICT promotion	91
3.21	Internet hosts, 2002	90
3.01	Technological sophistication	89
3.08	University/industry research collaboration	89
3.06	Company spending on research and development	87
3.23	Personal computers, 2002	83
3.14	Government prioritization of ICT	80
3.20	Internet users, 2002	80
3.03	FDI and technology transfer	77
3.02	Firm-level technology absorption	76
3.22	Telephone lines, 2002	73
3.17	Utility patents, 2002	72
3.18	Tertiary enrollment	67
3.04	Prevalence of foreign technology licensing	67

185

Business Competitiveness Index		Rank/95
	Sophistication of Company Operations and Strategy	
10.09	Control of international distribution	56
10.15	Reliance on professional management	63
10.06	Production process sophistication	74
	Quality of the National Business Environment	
3.10	Availability of scientists and engineers	22
6.08	Favoritism in decisions of government officials	23
9.05	Decentralization of corporate activity	35

Business Competitiveness Index		Rank/95
	Sophistication of Company Operations and Strategy	
10.14	Extent of incentive compensation	95
10.02	Value chain presence	94
10.01	Nature of competitive advantage	93
	Quality of the National Business Environment	
2.08	Venture capital availability	94
6.09	Extent of bureaucratic red tape	94
8.02	Extent of locally based competitors	94

Other Indicators		Rank/102
4.11	Maternity laws' impact on hiring women	17
8.09	Wage equality of women in the workplace	21
7.11	Prevalence of illegal political donations	25
7.12	Policy consequences of legal political donations	35
6.18	Informal sector	39
4.10	Maternity leave legislation	44
4.08	Impact of HIV/AIDS on FDI	46
2.15	Agricultural policy costs	47
6.14	Business costs of crime and violence	47
4.04	Disparity in healthcare quality	48
10.18	Hiring and firing practices	50

Other Indicators		Rank/102
6.06	Burden of regulation	99
2.02	Business costs of terrorism	95
3.11	Availability of mobile or cellular telephones	94
11.13	Prevalence of environmental management systems	93
8.11	Focus of trade and industry associations	93
2.04	Extent of distortive government intervention	93
10.25	Availability of company financial information	92
7.05	Irregular payments in loan applications	91
2.10	Government intervention in corporate investment	89
4.09	Brain drain	88
2.06	Soundness of banks	87
11.06	Compliance with environmental regulations	86
10.27	Strength of auditing and accounting standards	85
10.23	Company promotion of volunteerism	84
5.07	Postal efficiency	82

Note: The Business Competitiveness Index applies different criteria for selecting a country's competitive advantages and disadvantages.
Please refer to the section "How Country Profiles Work" for further details.

Angola

Competitiveness Rankings

Growth Competitiveness Index Rank	100

Macroeconomic Environment Index Rank **101**
   Macroeconomic Stability Subindex Rank 100
   Government Waste Subindex Rank 92
   Country Credit Rating Rank 95

Public Institutions Index Rank **91**
   Contracts and Law Subindex Rank 90
   Corruption Subindex Rank....................................91

Technology Index Rank **98**
   Innovation Subindex Rank..................................102
   ICT Subindex Rank 100
   Technology Transfer Subindex Rank
   (out of 77 non-core innovators) 66

Business Competitiveness Index Rank	95

**Sophistication of Company Operations
and Strategy Rank** **94**

**Quality of the National Business
Environment Rank** **95**

The Most Problematic Factors for Doing Business

FACTOR

Factor	
Access to financing	
Inflation	
Corruption	
Inadequate infrastructure	
Inadequately educated workforce	
Inefficient bureaucracy	
Policy instability	
Foreign currency regulations	
Poor work ethic	
Tax rates	
Tax regulations	
Government instability/coups	
Crime and theft	
Restrictive labor regulations	

Percent of responses

Note: From a list of 14 factors, respondents were asked to select the five most problematic for doing business in their country and to rank them between 1 (most problematic) and 5. The bars in the figure show the responses weighted according to their rankings.

Source: World Economic Forum, Executive Opinion Survey (2003)

National competitiveness balance sheet

NOTABLE COMPETITIVE ADVANTAGES	
Growth Competitiveness Index	**Rank/102**

Macroeconomic Environment

2.01	Recession expectations	8

NOTABLE COMPETITIVE DISADVANTAGES	
Growth Competitiveness Index	**Rank/102**

Macroeconomic Environment

2.20	Inflation, 2002	101
2.22	Interest rate spread, 2002	101
2.21	Real exchange rate, 2002	99
2.03	Extent of distortive government subsidies	98
2.17	Country credit rating, 2003	95
7.10	Public trust of politicians	88
2.09	Access to credit	84
7.08	Diversion of public funds	83
2.18	Government surplus/deficit, 2002	62

Public Institutions

6.03	Property rights	95
6.01	Judicial independence	91
7.01	Irregular payments in exports and imports	90
7.02	Irregular payments in public utilities	90
6.08	Favoritism in decisions of government officials	89
7.03	Irregular payments in tax collection	79
6.17	Organized crime	63

Technology

3.06	Company spending on research and development	102
3.08	University/industry research collaboration	102
3.12	Internet access in schools	101
3.18	Tertiary enrollment	100
3.21	Internet hosts, 2002	100
3.01	Technological sophistication	99
3.14	Government prioritization of ICT	97
3.16	Laws relating to ICT	97
3.19	Cellular telephones, 2002	96
3.13	Quality of competition in the ISP sector	95
3.23	Personal computers, 2002	95
3.20	Internet users, 2002	93
3.22	Telephone lines, 2002	93
3.15	Government success in ICT promotion	90
3.02	Firm-level technology absorption	85
3.17	Utility patents, 2002	72
3.04	Prevalence of foreign technology licensing	71
3.03	FDI and technology transfer	54

187

Business Competitiveness Index	Rank/95

Sophistication of Company Operations and Strategy

10.06	Production process sophistication	75
10.14	Extent of incentive compensation	76

Quality of the National Business Environment

10.26	Foreign ownership restrictions	55
6.13	Reliability of police services	59
10.20	Cooperation in labor-employer relations	60

Business Competitiveness Index	Rank/95

Sophistication of Company Operations and Strategy

10.02	Value chain presence	95
10.03	Extent of branding	95
10.10	Extent of regional sales	95

Quality of the National Business Environment

8.01	Intensity of local competition	95
8.02	Extent of locally based competitors	95
9.03	Local supplier quality	95

Other Indicators	Rank/102

6.06	Burden of regulation	35

Other Indicators	Rank/102

11.13	Prevalence of environmental management systems	102
11.04	Chemical waste regulations	102
11.03	Toxic waste disposal regulations	102
11.06	Compliance with environmental regulations	101
10.27	Strength of auditing and accounting standards	101
11.09	Flexibility of regulations	101
11.02	Water pollution regulations	101
11.01	Air pollution regulations	101
10.05	Ethical behavior of firms	101
11.11	Effects of compliance on business	101
8.09	Wage equality of women in the workplace	101
2.04	Extent of distortive government intervention	100
11.08	Clarity and stability of regulations	100
11.10	Consistency of regulation enforcement	100
4.05	Business impact of malaria	100

Note: The Business Competitiveness Index applies different criteria for selecting a country's competitive advantages and disadvantages.
Please refer to the section "How Country Profiles Work" for further details.

Argentina

Competitiveness Rankings

Growth Competitiveness Index Rank	78

Macroeconomic Environment Index Rank **93**
    Macroeconomic Stability Subindex Rank 80
    Government Waste Subindex Rank 94
    Country Credit Rating Rank.................................99

Public Institutions Index Rank...**88**
    Contracts and Law Subindex Rank 99
    Corruption Subindex Rank.....................................65

Technology Index Rank **45**
    Innovation Subindex Rank.....................................33
    ICT Subindex Rank 47
    Technology Transfer Subindex Rank
    (out of 77 non-core innovators).........................25

Business Competitiveness Index Rank	68

**Sophistication of Company Operations
and Strategy Rank** **63**
**Quality of the National Business
Environment Rank** **70**

The Most Problematic Factors for Doing Business

FACTOR

| Access to financing |
| Policy instability |
| Corruption |
| Inefficient bureaucracy |
| Restrictive labor regulations |
| Tax rates |
| Tax regulations |
| Inadequately educated workforce |
| Crime and theft |
| Poor work ethic |
| Government instability/coups |
| Inflation |
| Foreign currency regulations |
| Inadequate infrastructure |

Percent of responses

Note: From a list of 14 factors, respondents were asked to select the five most problematic for doing business in their country and to rank them between 1 (most problematic) and 5. The bars in the figure show the responses weighted according to their rankings.

Source: World Economic Forum, Executive Opinion Survey (2003)

National competitiveness balance sheet

NOTABLE COMPETITIVE ADVANTAGES	
Growth Competitiveness Index	**Rank/102**

Macroeconomic Environment

2.21	Real exchange rate, 2002	1
2.01	Recession expectations	45

Technology

3.03	FDI and technology transfer	14
3.13	Quality of competition in the ISP sector	28
3.18	Tertiary enrollment	28
3.04	Prevalence of foreign technology licensing	33
3.17	Utility patents, 2002	37
3.21	Internet hosts, 2002	38
3.20	Internet users, 2002	42
3.23	Personal computers, 2002	44
3.01	Technological sophistication	46
3.22	Telephone lines, 2002	50

NOTABLE COMPETITIVE DISADVANTAGES	
Growth Competitiveness Index	**Rank/102**

Macroeconomic Environment

2.09	Access to credit	102
2.17	Country credit rating, 2003	99
2.20	Inflation, 2002	99
7.10	Public trust of politicians	98
2.18	Government surplus/deficit, 2002	94
7.08	Diversion of public funds	91
2.22	Interest rate spread, 2002	89
2.03	Extent of distortive government subsidies	76
2.19	National savings rate, 2002	55

Public Institutions

6.03	Property rights	102
6.08	Favoritism in decisions of government officials	98
6.01	Judicial independence	95
6.17	Organized crime	84
7.01	Irregular payments in exports and imports	80
7.03	Irregular payments in tax collection	73
7.02	Irregular payments in public utilities	54

Technology

3.14	Government prioritization of ICT	98
3.15	Government success in ICT promotion	96
3.16	Laws relating to ICT	71
3.02	Firm-level technology absorption	70
3.08	University/industry research collaboration	69
3.06	Company spending on research and development	63
3.12	Internet access in schools	60
3.19	Cellular telephones, 2002	58

Business Competitiveness Index	**Rank/95**

Sophistication of Company Operations and Strategy

10.06	Production process sophistication	41
10.10	Extent of regional sales	42
10.15	Reliance on professional management	42

Quality of the National Business Environment

10.16	Quality of management schools	25
6.09	Extent of bureaucratic red tape	27
8.02	Extent of locally based competitors	30

Business Competitiveness Index	**Rank/95**

Sophistication of Company Operations and Strategy

10.01	Nature of competitive advantage	85
10.09	Control of international distribution	78
10.02	Value chain presence	75

Quality of the National Business Environment

2.07	Ease of access to loans	92
6.02	Efficiency of legal framework	92
2.08	Venture capital availability	91

189

Other Indicators	**Rank/102**

2.02	Business costs of terrorism	15
2.15	Agricultural policy costs	31
4.06	Business impact of tuberculosis	31
4.05	Business impact of malaria	31
10.23	Company promotion of volunteerism	38
4.08	Impact of HIV/AIDS on FDI	41
4.07	Business impact of HIV/AIDS	44
8.08	Private sector employment of women	48
10.22	Charitable causes involvement	49

Other Indicators	**Rank/102**

8.11	Focus of trade and industry associations	102
6.07	Transparency of government policymaking	101
2.06	Soundness of banks	101
7.06	Irregular payments in government policymaking	100
2.10	Government intervention in corporate investment	99
10.18	Hiring and firing practices	99
6.10	Effectiveness of law-making bodies	99
6.11	Efficiency of the tax system	99
6.16	Government effectiveness in reducing income inequality	96
7.11	Prevalence of illegal political donations	96
6.06	Burden of regulation	95
6.14	Business costs of crime and violence	93
7.04	Irregular payments in public contracts	93
2.04	Extent of distortive government intervention	91
11.07	Compliance with international agreements	91

Note: The Business Competitiveness Index applies different criteria for selecting a country's competitive advantages and disadvantages. Please refer to the section "How Country Profiles Work" for further details.

Australia

Competitiveness Rankings

Growth Competitiveness Index Rank	10

Macroeconomic Environment Index Rank 7
    Macroeconomic Stability Subindex Rank 17
    Government Waste Subindex Rank 6
    Country Credit Rating Rank 19

Public Institutions Index Rank 4
    Contracts and Law Subindex Rank 3
    Corruption Subindex Rank....................................6

Technology Index Rank **19**
    Innovation Subindex Rank....................................18
    ICT Subindex Rank 14

Business Competitiveness Index Rank	11

**Sophistication of Company Operations
  and Strategy Rank** 18
**Quality of the National Business
  Environment Rank** 7

The Most Problematic Factors for Doing Business

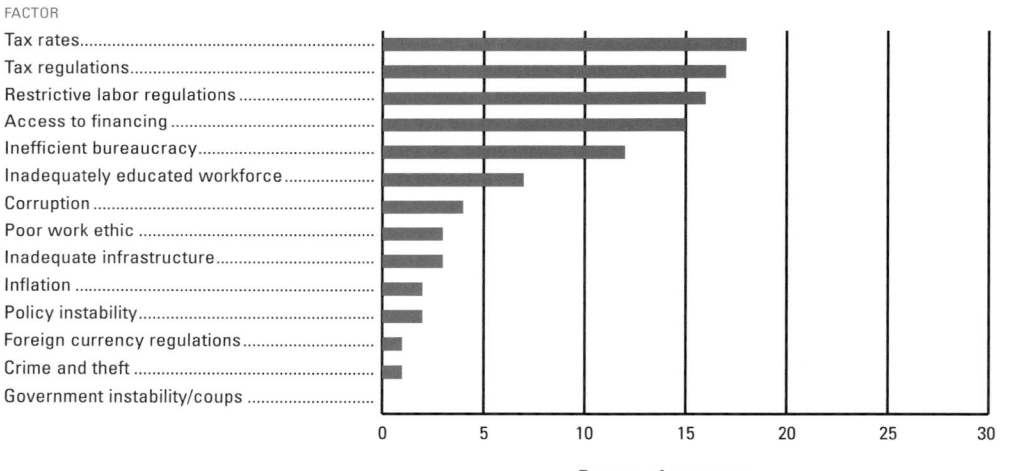

Note: From a list of 14 factors, respondents were asked to select the five most problematic for doing business in their country and to rank them between 1 (most problematic) and 5. The bars in the figure show the responses weighted according to their rankings.

Source: World Economic Forum, Executive Opinion Survey (2003)

National competitiveness balance sheet

NOTABLE COMPETITIVE ADVANTAGES			NOTABLE COMPETITIVE DISADVANTAGES		
Growth Competitiveness Index		**Rank/102**	**Growth Competitiveness Index**		**Rank/102**
	Macroeconomic Environment			**Macroeconomic Environment**	
2.01	Recession expectations	4	2.19	National savings rate, 2002	63
7.08	Diversion of public funds	4	2.20	Inflation, 2002	46
7.10	Public trust of politicians	8	2.21	Real exchange rate, 2002	44
2.03	Extent of distortive government subsidies	9	2.22	Interest rate spread, 2002	44
	Public Institutions		2.17	Country credit rating, 2003	19
6.01	Judicial independence	3	2.18	Government surplus/deficit, 2002	19
7.03	Irregular payments in tax collection	5	2.09	Access to credit	13
6.08	Favoritism in decisions of government officials	6		**Technology**	
6.03	Property rights	7	3.15	Government success in ICT promotion	45
6.17	Organized crime	7	3.14	Government prioritization of ICT	30
7.01	Irregular payments in exports and imports	7	3.19	Cellular telephones, 2002	29
7.02	Irregular payments in public utilities	8	3.06	Company spending on research and development	23
	Technology		3.08	University/industry research collaboration	22
3.16	Laws relating to ICT	3	3.17	Utility patents, 2002	21
3.21	Internet hosts, 2002	6	3.22	Telephone lines, 2002	17
3.12	Internet access in schools	7	3.02	Firm-level technology absorption	16
3.23	Personal computers, 2002	7	3.13	Quality of competition in the ISP sector	16
3.18	Tertiary enrollment	9	3.20	Internet users, 2002	14
			3.01	Technological sophistication	12

Business Competitiveness Index		**Rank/95**	**Business Competitiveness Index**		**Rank/95**
	Sophistication of Company Operations and Strategy			**Sophistication of Company Operations and Strategy**	
10.15	Reliance on professional management	1	10.02	Value chain presence	66
10.14	Extent of incentive compensation	4	10.03	Extent of branding	51
10.07	Extent of marketing	6	10.01	Nature of competitive advantage	37
	Quality of the National Business Environment			**Quality of the National Business Environment**	
2.11	Local equity market access	1	9.09	Local availability of process machinery	49
10.24	Protection of minority shareholders' interests	1	10.20	Cooperation in labor-employer relations	37
2.12	Regulation of securities exchanges	1	10.26	Foreign ownership restrictions	36

Other Indicators		**Rank/102**	**Other Indicators**		**Rank/102**
2.06	Soundness of banks	1	2.02	Business costs of terrorism	82
10.25	Availability of company financial information	2	8.11	Focus of trade and industry associations	61
10.27	Strength of auditing and accounting standards	2	10.19	Flexibility of wage determination	60
6.18	Informal sector	2	4.10	Maternity leave legislation	56
6.10	Effectiveness of law-making bodies	2	8.03	Extent of market dominance	41
6.07	Transparency of government policymaking	2	6.11	Efficiency of the tax system	40
4.08	Impact of HIV/AIDS on FDI	3	11.07	Compliance with international agreements	40
7.05	Irregular payments in loan applications	4	4.11	Maternity laws' impact on hiring women	40
2.15	Agricultural policy costs	5	8.08	Private sector employment of women	39
10.22	Charitable causes involvement	5	10.18	Hiring and firing practices	38
6.05	Freedom of the press	5	4.09	Brain drain	30
7.14	Pervasiveness of money laundering through non-bank channels	5	6.06	Burden of regulation	22
7.13	Pervasiveness of money laundering through banks	5	11.08	Clarity and stability of regulations	20
7.11	Prevalence of illegal political donations	5	7.12	Policy consequences of legal political donations	19
4.06	Business impact of tuberculosis	6	6.16	Government effectiveness in reducing income inequality	17

191

Note: The Business Competitiveness Index applies different criteria for selecting a country's competitive advantages and disadvantages. Please refer to the section "How Country Profiles Work" for further details.

Austria

Competitiveness Rankings

Growth Competitiveness Index Rank	17

Macroeconomic Environment Index Rank **10**
   Macroeconomic Stability Subindex Rank 22
   Government Waste Subindex 15
   Country Credit Rating Rank....................................9

Public Institutions Index Rank..**14**
   Contracts and Law Subindex Rank 14
   Corruption Subindex Rank.....................................16

Technology Index Rank **27**
   Innovation Subindex Rank.....................................20
   ICT Subindex Rank 22

Business Competitiveness Index Rank	17

**Sophistication of Company Operations
and Strategy Rank** **13**

**Quality of the National Business
Environment Rank** **18**

The Most Problematic Factors for Doing Business

FACTOR

Factor	
Tax rates	
Tax regulations	
Restrictive labor regulations	
Inefficient bureaucracy	
Access to financing	
Inadequately educated workforce	
Inadequate infrastructure	
Poor work ethic	
Inflation	
Crime and theft	
Foreign currency regulations	
Policy instability	
Government instability/coups	
Corruption	

Percent of responses

Note: From a list of 14 factors, respondents were asked to select the five most problematic for doing business in their country and to rank them between 1 (most problematic) and 5. The bars in the figure show the responses weighted according to their rankings.

Source: World Economic Forum, Executive Opinion Survey (2003)

National competitiveness balance sheet

NOTABLE COMPETITIVE ADVANTAGES	
Growth Competitiveness Index	**Rank/102**

Macroeconomic Environment

| 2.17 | Country credit rating, 2003 | 9 |
| 7.08 | Diversion of public funds | 14 |

Public Institutions

6.03	Property rights	3
7.02	Irregular payments in public utilities	13
7.03	Irregular payments in tax collection	14
6.17	Organized crime	15

Technology

| 3.12 | Internet access in schools | 12 |
| 3.18 | Tertiary enrollment | 16 |

NOTABLE COMPETITIVE DISADVANTAGES	
Growth Competitiveness Index	**Rank/102**

Macroeconomic Environment

2.01	Recession expectations	72
2.19	National savings rate, 2002	50
2.09	Access to credit	45
2.03	Extent of distortive government subsidies	36
2.22	Interest rate spread, 2002	28
2.18	Government surplus/deficit, 2002	23
2.21	Real exchange rate, 2002	21
2.20	Inflation, 2002	20
7.10	Public trust of politicians	17

Public Institutions

6.08	Favoritism in decisions of government officials	28
7.01	Irregular payments in exports and imports	20
6.01	Judicial independence	19

Technology

3.14	Government prioritization of ICT	56
3.15	Government success in ICT promotion	40
3.02	Firm-level technology absorption	37
3.01	Technological sophistication	32
3.06	Company spending on research and development	31
3.16	Laws relating to ICT	31
3.08	University/industry research collaboration	23
3.22	Telephone lines, 2002	22
3.13	Quality of competition in the ISP sector	21
3.19	Cellular telephones, 2002	20
3.23	Personal computers, 2002	20
3.21	Internet hosts, 2002	18
3.17	Utility patents, 2002	17
3.20	Internet users, 2002	17

Business Competitiveness Index	Rank/95

Sophistication of Company Operations and Strategy

10.15	Reliance on professional management	9
10.09	Control of international distribution	11
10.01	Nature of competitive advantage	13

Quality of the National Business Environment

6.12	Centralization of economic policymaking	5
4.02	Quality of public schools	5
11.05	Stringency of environmental regulations	5

Business Competitiveness Index	Rank/95

Sophistication of Company Operations and Strategy

3.06	Company spending on research and development	30
10.11	Breadth of international markets	24
10.13	Willingness to delegate authority	20

Quality of the National Business Environment

2.08	Venture capital availability	46
8.04	Sophistication of local buyers' products and processes	43
5.03	Port infrastructure quality	41

Other Indicators	Rank/102

11.12	Political context of environmental gains	2
11.09	Flexibility of regulations	2
4.07	Business impact of HIV/AIDS	2
11.08	Clarity and stability of regulations	5
3.11	Availability of mobile or cellular telephones	6
4.05	Business impact of malaria	6
11.03	Toxic waste disposal regulations	7
11.02	Water pollution regulations	7
4.06	Business impact of tuberculosis	8
8.10	Regional disparities in quality of business environment	8
11.06	Compliance with environmental regulations	8
11.01	Air pollution regulations	8
11.04	Chemical waste regulations	9
11.10	Consistency of regulation enforcement	9
11.07	Compliance with international agreements	9

Other Indicators	Rank/102

8.09	Wage equality of women in the workplace	102
10.19	Flexibility of wage determination	100
4.11	Maternity laws' impact on hiring women	81
8.08	Private sector employment of women	74
6.11	Efficiency of the tax system	69
4.10	Maternity leave legislation	54
10.18	Hiring and firing practices	51
10.21	Pay and productivity	45
6.07	Transparency of government policymaking	45
8.11	Focus of trade and industry associations	43
10.25	Availability of company financial information	42
2.04	Extent of distortive government intervention	41
10.23	Company promotion of volunteerism	41
5.07	Postal efficiency	40
7.13	Pervasiveness of money laundering through banks	40

193

Note: The Business Competitiveness Index applies different criteria for selecting a country's competitive advantages and disadvantages. Please refer to the section "How Country Profiles Work" for further details.

Bangladesh

Competitiveness Rankings

Growth Competitiveness Index Rank	98

Macroeconomic Environment Index Rank **72**
    Macroeconomic Stability Subindex Rank.............55
    Government Waste Subindex Rank 88
    Country Credit Rating Rank.................................75

Public Institutions Index Rank.......................................**100**
    Contracts and Law Subindex Rank 86
    Corruption Subindex Rank.................................102

Technology Index Rank **95**
    Innovation Subindex Rank...................................91
    ICT Subindex Rank 99
    Technology Transfer Subindex Rank
    (out of 77 non-core innovators).........................61

Business Competitiveness Index Rank	86

**Sophistication of Company Operations
and Strategy Rank** **86**
**Quality of the National Business
Environment Rank** **85**

The Most Problematic Factors for Doing Business

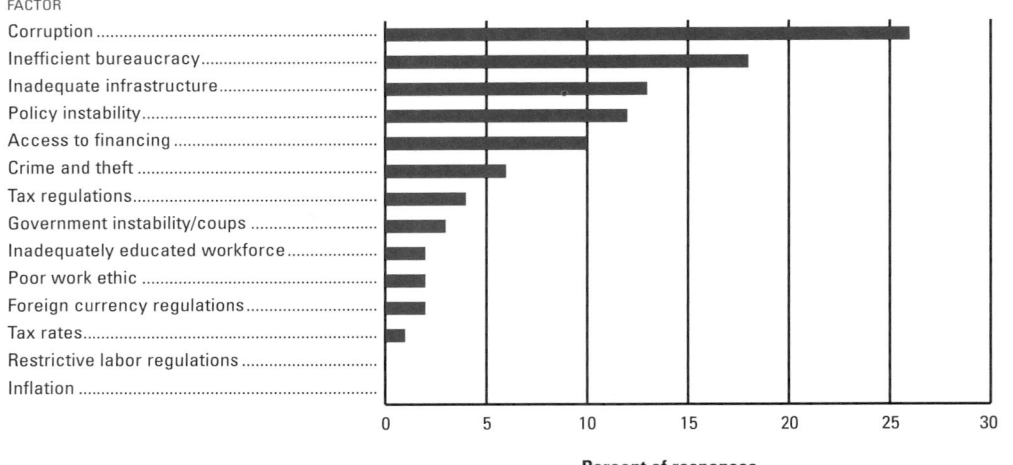

FACTOR

Corruption
Inefficient bureaucracy
Inadequate infrastructure
Policy instability
Access to financing
Crime and theft
Tax regulations
Government instability/coups
Inadequately educated workforce
Poor work ethic
Foreign currency regulations
Tax rates
Restrictive labor regulations
Inflation

Percent of responses

Note: From a list of 14 factors, respondents were asked to select the five most problematic for doing business in their country and to rank them between 1 (most problematic) and 5. The bars in the figure show the responses weighted according to their rankings.

Source: World Economic Forum, Executive Opinion Survey (2003)

National competitiveness balance sheet

NOTABLE COMPETITIVE ADVANTAGES	
Growth Competitiveness Index	**Rank/102**

Macroeconomic Environment

2.19	National savings rate, 2002	34
2.20	Inflation, 2002	37
2.09	Access to credit	46

Technology

3.14	Government prioritization of ICT	43

NOTABLE COMPETITIVE DISADVANTAGES	
Growth Competitiveness Index	**Rank/102**

Macroeconomic Environment

2.03	Extent of distortive government subsidies	92
7.10	Public trust of politicians	90
2.01	Recession expectations	81
7.08	Diversion of public funds	78
2.17	Country credit rating, 2003	75
2.22	Interest rate spread, 2002	63
2.18	Government surplus/deficit, 2002	60
2.21	Real exchange rate, 2002	55

Public Institutions

7.02	Irregular payments in public utilities	102
7.03	Irregular payments in tax collection	102
7.01	Irregular payments in exports and imports	101
6.17	Organized crime	94
6.08	Favoritism in decisions of government officials	88
6.01	Judicial independence	74
6.03	Property rights	74

Technology

3.20	Internet users, 2002	101
3.16	Laws relating to ICT	99
3.19	Cellular telephones, 2002	99
3.22	Telephone lines, 2002	96
3.08	University/industry research collaboration	94
3.06	Company spending on research and development	93
3.12	Internet access in schools	93
3.01	Technological sophistication	91
3.23	Personal computers, 2002	91
3.15	Government success in ICT promotion	88
3.02	Firm-level technology absorption	83
3.18	Tertiary enrollment	79
3.17	Utility patents, 2002	72
3.13	Quality of competition in the ISP sector	63
3.04	Prevalence of foreign technology licensing	58
3.03	FDI and technology transfer	56

Business Competitiveness Index	
	Rank/95

Sophistication of Company Operations and Strategy

10.08	Degree of customer orientation	60
10.02	Value chain presence	70
3.04	Prevalence of foreign technology licensing	79

Quality of the National Business Environment

2.11	Local equity market access	35
9.06	State of cluster development	48
8.01	Intensity of local competition	52

Other Indicators	
	Rank/102

10.18	Hiring and firing practices	22
2.15	Agricultural policy costs	23
10.19	Flexibility of wage determination	37
4.08	Impact of HIV/AIDS on FDI	42

Business Competitiveness Index	
	Rank/95

Sophistication of Company Operations and Strategy

10.01	Nature of competitive advantage	94
10.13	Willingness to delegate authority	93
10.12	Extent of staff training	92

Quality of the National Business Environment

8.07	Prevalence of mergers and acquisitions	95
6.13	Reliability of police services	94
5.06	Telephone infrastructure quality	93

Other Indicators	
	Rank/102

7.04	Irregular payments in public contracts	102
7.05	Irregular payments in loan applications	102
8.08	Private sector employment of women	101
7.11	Prevalence of illegal political donations	101
8.11	Focus of trade and industry associations	100
10.05	Ethical behavior of firms	100
8.09	Wage equality of women in the workplace	99
6.06	Burden of regulation	96
2.04	Extent of distortive government intervention	95
4.09	Brain drain	95
7.14	Pervasiveness of money laundering through non-bank channels	94
3.07	Subsidies and tax credits for firm-level research and development	94
11.04	Chemical waste regulations	94
10.27	Strength of auditing and accounting standards	93
11.03	Toxic waste disposal regulations	93

195

Note: The Business Competitiveness Index applies different criteria for selecting a country's competitive advantages and disadvantages. Please refer to the section "How Country Profiles Work" for further details.

Belgium

Competitiveness Rankings

The Most Problematic Factors for Doing Business

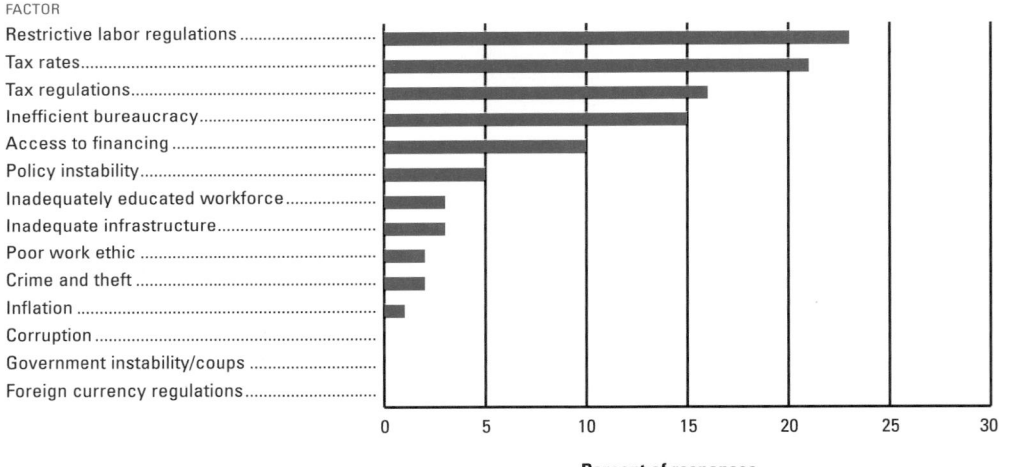

Note: From a list of 14 factors, respondents were asked to select the five most problematic for doing business in their country and to rank them between 1 (most problematic) and 5. The bars in the figure show the responses weighted according to their rankings.

Source: World Economic Forum, Executive Opinion Survey (2003)

National competitiveness balance sheet

NOTABLE COMPETITIVE ADVANTAGES	
Growth Competitiveness Index	**Rank/102**

Macroeconomic Environment

2.17	Country credit rating, 2003	14
2.18	Government surplus/deficit, 2002	16
2.20	Inflation, 2002	18
7.08	Diversion of public funds	22
2.21	Real exchange rate, 2002	23

Public Institutions

6.08	Favoritism in decisions of government officials	22
6.03	Property rights	24
7.02	Irregular payments in public utilities	26

Technology

3.08	University/industry research collaboration	12
3.17	Utility patents, 2002	15
3.06	Company spending on research and development	17
3.18	Tertiary enrollment	18
3.19	Cellular telephones, 2002	19
3.01	Technological sophistication	20
3.21	Internet hosts, 2002	20
3.22	Telephone lines, 2002	21
3.20	Internet users, 2002	23
3.12	Internet access in schools	25
3.23	Personal computers, 2002	25

Business Competitiveness Index	**Rank/95**

Sophistication of Company Operations and Strategy

10.10	Extent of regional sales	4
10.08	Degree of customer orientation	7
10.06	Production process sophistication	9

Quality of the National Business Environment

4.03	Quality of math and science education	2
6.12	Centralization of economic policymaking	4
4.01	Quality of the educational system	5

Other Indicators	**Rank/102**

4.05	Business impact of malaria	2
4.07	Business impact of HIV/AIDS	3
4.06	Business impact of tuberculosis	5
8.03	Extent of market dominance	7
4.08	Impact of HIV/AIDS on FDI	9
6.05	Freedom of the press	9
11.03	Toxic waste disposal regulations	9
11.01	Air pollution regulations	10
4.04	Disparity in healthcare quality	10
11.04	Chemical waste regulations	10
6.16	Government effectiveness in reducing income inequality	11
4.10	Maternity leave legislation	13
11.06	Compliance with environmental regulations	13
7.13	Pervasiveness of money laundering through banks	14
11.02	Water pollution regulations	14

NOTABLE COMPETITIVE DISADVANTAGES	
Growth Competitiveness Index	**Rank/102**

Macroeconomic Environment

2.01	Recession expectations	89
2.09	Access to credit	85
2.03	Extent of distortive government subsidies	50
2.22	Interest rate spread, 2002	47
7.10	Public trust of politicians	30

Public Institutions

6.17	Organized crime	33
7.03	Irregular payments in tax collection	33
7.01	Irregular payments in exports and imports	29
6.01	Judicial independence	28

Technology

3.15	Government success in ICT promotion	61
3.14	Government prioritization of ICT	60
3.02	Firm-level technology absorption	41
3.16	Laws relating to ICT	39
3.13	Quality of competition in the ISP sector	31

Business Competitiveness Index	**Rank/95**

Sophistication of Company Operations and Strategy

10.09	Control of international distribution	22
10.11	Breadth of international markets	18
3.06	Company spending on research and development	17

Quality of the National Business Environment

2.11	Local equity market access	57
10.20	Cooperation in labor-employer relations	56
3.09	Government procurement of advanced technology products	51

Other Indicators	**Rank/102**

10.18	Hiring and firing practices	98
10.19	Flexibility of wage determination	97
6.06	Burden of regulation	93
6.11	Efficiency of the tax system	86
10.21	Pay and productivity	71
11.11	Effects of compliance on business	71
11.09	Flexibility of regulations	70
10.22	Charitable causes involvement	69
2.15	Agricultural policy costs	66
11.12	Political context of environmental gains	63
8.09	Wage equality of women in the workplace	58
11.08	Clarity and stability of regulations	53
6.07	Transparency of government policymaking	53
4.11	Maternity laws' impact on hiring women	52
2.04	Extent of distortive government intervention	45

197

Note: The Business Competitiveness Index applies different criteria for selecting a country's competitive advantages and disadvantages. Please refer to the section "How Country Profiles Work" for further details.

Bolivia

Competitiveness Rankings

Growth Competitiveness Index Rank	85

Macroeconomic Environment Index Rank **83**
    Macroeconomic Stability Subindex Rank 78
    Government Waste Subindex Rank 97
    Country Credit Rating Rank 71

Public Institutions Index Rank..**79**
    Contracts and Law Subindex Rank 85
    Corruption Subindex Rank....................................70

Technology Index Rank **88**
    Innovation Subindex Rank 52
    ICT Subindex Rank 79
    Technology Transfer Subindex Rank
    (out of 77 non-core innovators).........................68

Business Competitiveness Index Rank	92

**Sophistication of Company Operations
  and Strategy Rank** **92**
**Quality of the National Business
  Environment Rank** **91**

The Most Problematic Factors for Doing Business

FACTOR

Corruption ....
Access to financing ....
Inefficient bureaucracy....................................
Policy instability...
Inadequate infrastructure................................
Inadequately educated workforce....................
Tax rates...
Tax regulations...
Government instability/coups ....
Restrictive labor regulations ....
Poor work ethic ....
Crime and theft ....
Inflation ....
Foreign currency regulations...........................

0   5   10   15   20   25   30

Percent of responses

Note: From a list of 14 factors, respondents were asked to select the five most problematic for doing business in their country and to rank them between 1 (most problematic) and 5. The bars in the figure show the responses weighted according to their rankings.

Source: World Economic Forum, Executive Opinion Survey (2003)

National competitiveness balance sheet

NOTABLE COMPETITIVE ADVANTAGES

Growth Competitiveness Index	Rank/102

Macroeconomic Environment

| 2.20 | Inflation, 2002 | 13 |

Technology

| 3.18 | Tertiary enrollment | 40 |

Business Competitiveness Index	Rank/95

Quality of the National Business Environment

6.12	Centralization of economic policymaking	52
5.06	Telephone infrastructure quality	55
5.05	Quality of electricity supply	60

Other Indicators	Rank/102

| 10.19 | Flexibility of wage determination | 20 |
| 6.11 | Efficiency of the tax system | 42 |

NOTABLE COMPETITIVE DISADVANTAGES

Growth Competitiveness Index	Rank/102

Macroeconomic Environment

7.08	Diversion of public funds	99
7.10	Public trust of politicians	99
2.01	Recession expectations	98
2.19	National savings rate, 2002	96
2.09	Access to credit	93
2.18	Government surplus/deficit, 2002	87
2.22	Interest rate spread, 2002	78
2.03	Extent of distortive government subsidies	75
2.17	Country credit rating, 2003	71
2.21	Real exchange rate, 2002	58

Public Institutions

6.01	Judicial independence	98
6.08	Favoritism in decisions of government officials	95
7.03	Irregular payments in tax collection	90
6.03	Property rights	77
7.01	Irregular payments in exports and imports	71
6.17	Organized crime	54
7.02	Irregular payments in public utilities	52

Technology

3.02	Firm-level technology absorption	102
3.06	Company spending on research and development	97
3.08	University/industry research collaboration	95
3.16	Laws relating to ICT	95
3.01	Technological sophistication	94
3.14	Government prioritization of ICT	94
3.15	Government success in ICT promotion	93
3.12	Internet access in schools	80
3.21	Internet hosts, 2002	74
3.17	Utility patents, 2002	72
3.22	Telephone lines, 2002	71
3.04	Prevalence of foreign technology licensing	70
3.19	Cellular telephones, 2002	70
3.20	Internet users, 2002	70
3.23	Personal computers, 2002	69
3.03	FDI and technology transfer	66
3.13	Quality of competition in the ISP sector	57

Business Competitiveness Index	Rank/95

Sophistication of Company Operations and Strategy

10.08	Degree of customer orientation	95
10.12	Extent of staff training	94
10.15	Reliance on professional management	92

Quality of the National Business Environment

6.04	Intellectual property protection	95
3.09	Government procurement of advanced technology products	94
9.02	Local supplier quantity	93

Other Indicators	Rank/102

10.22	Charitable causes involvement	100
6.18	Informal sector	100
7.07	Irregular payments in judicial decisions	100
10.05	Ethical behavior of firms	99
3.07	Subsidies and tax credits for firm-level research and development	99
11.04	Chemical waste regulations	99
11.11	Effects of compliance on business	98
8.09	Wage equality of women in the workplace	98
8.08	Private sector employment of women	98
7.11	Prevalence of illegal political donations	98
11.02	Water pollution regulations	98
11.06	Compliance with environmental regulations	98

199

Note: The Business Competitiveness Index applies different criteria for selecting a country's competitive advantages and disadvantages. Please refer to the section "How Country Profiles Work" for further details.

Botswana

Competitiveness Rankings

Growth Competitiveness Index Rank	36

Macroeconomic Environment Index Rank **30**
  Macroeconomic Stability Subindex Rank 23
  Government Waste Subindex Rank 17
  Country Credit Rating Rank 38

Public Institutions Index Rank **26**
  Contracts and Law Subindex Rank 16
  Corruption Subindex Rank....................................36

Technology Index Rank **59**
  Innovation Subindex Rank.....................................80
  ICT Subindex Rank 65
  Technology Transfer Subindex Rank
    (out of 77 non-core innovators)........................24

Business Competitiveness Index Rank	54

**Sophistication of Company Operations
  and Strategy Rank** **66**
**Quality of the National Business
  Environment Rank** **50**

The Most Problematic Factors for Doing Business

FACTOR

Poor work ethic
Inadequately educated workforce
Access to financing
Inefficient bureaucracy
Restrictive labor regulations
Inadequate infrastructure
Inflation
Crime and theft
Tax rates
Policy instability
Tax regulations
Foreign currency regulations
Government instability/coups
Corruption

Percent of responses

Note: From a list of 14 factors, respondents were asked to select the five most problematic for doing business in their country and to rank them between 1 (most problematic) and 5. The bars in the figure show the responses weighted according to their rankings.

Source: World Economic Forum, Executive Opinion Survey (2003)

National competitiveness balance sheet

NOTABLE COMPETITIVE ADVANTAGES	
Growth Competitiveness Index	**Rank/102**

Macroeconomic Environment

2.19	National savings rate, 2002 5
7.10	Public trust of politicians 9
2.01	Recession expectations 17
2.21	Real exchange rate, 2002 17
2.09	Access to credit 20
7.08	Diversion of public funds 24

Public Institutions

6.01	Judicial independence...11
6.08	Favoritism in decisions of government officials.............17
6.03	Property rights...21
6.17	Organized crime 24
7.03	Irregular payments in tax collection 30

Technology

3.04	Prevalence of foreign technology licensing 10
3.15	Government success in ICT promotion 29

Business Competitiveness Index	Rank/95

Sophistication of Company Operations and Strategy

3.04	Prevalence of foreign technology licensing 12
10.15	Reliance on professional management..........................22
10.01	Nature of competitive advantage..................................29

Quality of the National Business Environment

6.01	Judicial independence...11
6.02	Efficiency of legal framework 16
6.08	Favoritism in decisions of government officials.............16

Other Indicators	Rank/102

4.11	Maternity laws' impact on hiring women 1
8.09	Wage equality of women in the workplace 2
6.11	Efficiency of the tax system 3
4.10	Maternity leave legislation 8
10.22	Charitable causes involvement 11
6.07	Transparency of government policymaking....................12
6.10	Effectiveness of law-making bodies 15
2.06	Soundness of banks 16
7.12	Policy consequences of legal political donations 16
4.09	Brain drain 17
11.12	Political context of environmental gains 17
7.07	Irregular payments in judicial decisions 17
2.10	Government intervention in corporate investment.........20
7.06	Irregular payments in government policymaking............21
2.04	Extent of distortive government intervention 22

NOTABLE COMPETITIVE DISADVANTAGES	
Growth Competitiveness Index	**Rank/102**

Macroeconomic Environment

2.20	Inflation, 2002 70
2.18	Government surplus/deficit, 2002....................................56
2.22	Interest rate spread, 2002 51
2.03	Extent of distortive government subsidies 38
2.17	Country credit rating, 2003 38

Public Institutions

7.02	Irregular payments in public utilities 41
7.01	Irregular payments in exports and imports 38

Technology

3.13	Quality of competition in the ISP sector 93
3.18	Tertiary enrollment 84
3.12	Internet access in schools 76
3.16	Laws relating to ICT 73
3.17	Utility patents, 2002 72
3.20	Internet users, 2002 72
3.02	Firm-level technology absorption 69
3.08	University/industry research collaboration 68
3.22	Telephone lines, 2002 68
3.06	Company spending on research and development 64
3.21	Internet hosts, 2002 63
3.23	Personal computers, 2002 59
3.01	Technological sophistication...53
3.19	Cellular telephones, 2002...51
3.03	FDI and technology transfer...39
3.14	Government prioritization of ICT 36

Business Competitiveness Index	Rank/95

Sophistication of Company Operations and Strategy

10.09	Control of international distribution 86
10.10	Extent of regional sales 84
10.11	Breadth of international markets....................................83

Quality of the National Business Environment

9.02	Local supplier quantity 89
6.09	Extent of bureaucratic red tape.....................................85
9.08	Local availability of components and parts 83

Other Indicators	Rank/102

4.08	Impact of HIV/AIDS on FDI 99
4.07	Business impact of HIV/AIDS 98
8.03	Extent of market dominance...94
4.06	Business impact of tuberculosis 85
10.21	Pay and productivity 83
4.05	Business impact of malaria 74
11.13	Prevalence of environmental management systems......70
10.18	Hiring and firing practices 65
3.11	Availability of mobile or cellular telephones 64
11.01	Air pollution regulations..60
3.07	Subsidies and tax credits for firm-level research and development 58
11.06	Compliance with environmental regulations...................56
6.05	Freedom of the press 55
11.10	Consistency of regulation enforcement..........................53
11.04	Chemical waste regulations 52

201

Note: The Business Competitiveness Index applies different criteria for selecting a country's competitive advantages and disadvantages. Please refer to the section "How Country Profiles Work" for further details.

Brazil

Competitiveness Rankings

Growth Competitiveness Index Rank	54

Macroeconomic Environment Index Rank **75**
    Macroeconomic Stability Subindex Rank 88
    Government Waste Subindex Rank 52
    Country Credit Rating Rank 62

Public Institutions Index Rank..........................**53**
    Contracts and Law Subindex Rank 57
    Corruption Subindex Rank 56

Technology Index Rank **35**
    Innovation Subindex Rank 60
    ICT Subindex Rank 43
    Technology Transfer Subindex Rank
    (out of 77 non-core innovators) 2

Business Competitiveness Index Rank	34

**Sophistication of Company Operations
and Strategy Rank** **30**
**Quality of the National Business
Environment Rank** **39**

The Most Problematic Factors for Doing Business

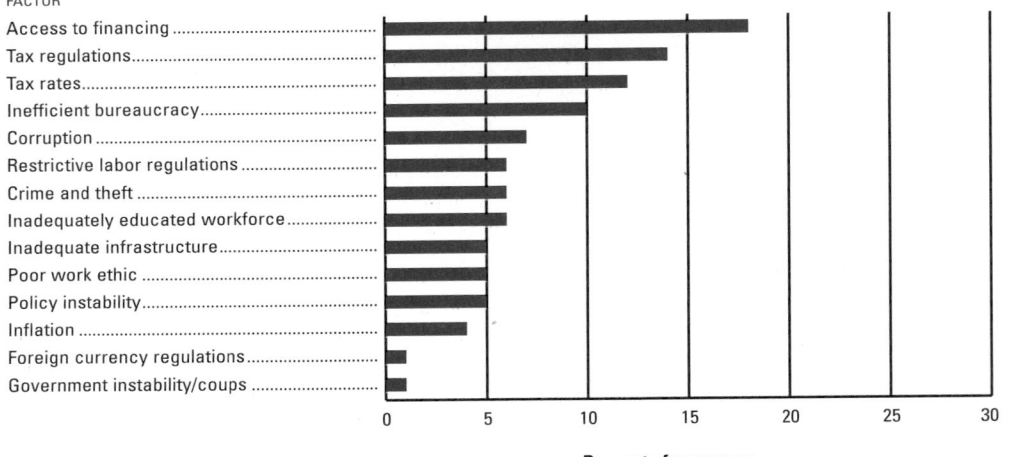

FACTOR

Access to financing
Tax regulations
Tax rates
Inefficient bureaucracy
Corruption
Restrictive labor regulations
Crime and theft
Inadequately educated workforce
Inadequate infrastructure
Poor work ethic
Policy instability
Inflation
Foreign currency regulations
Government instability/coups

Percent of responses

Note: From a list of 14 factors, respondents were asked to select the five most problematic for doing business in their country and to rank them between 1 (most problematic) and 5. The bars in the figure show the responses weighted according to their rankings.

Source: World Economic Forum, Executive Opinion Survey (2003)

National competitiveness balance sheet

NOTABLE COMPETITIVE ADVANTAGES	
Growth Competitiveness Index	**Rank/102**

Macroeconomic Environment

2.21	Real exchange rate, 2002	3
2.03	Extent of distortive government subsidies	25
2.01	Recession expectations	31

Public Institutions

6.08	Favoritism in decisions of government officials	39
6.03	Property rights	44
7.02	Irregular payments in public utilities	50

Technology

3.04	Prevalence of foreign technology licensing	5
3.03	FDI and technology transfer	8
3.06	Company spending on research and development	26
3.13	Quality of competition in the ISP sector	26
3.08	University/industry research collaboration	29
3.16	Laws relating to ICT	37
3.15	Government success in ICT promotion	38
3.01	Technological sophistication	40
3.02	Firm-level technology absorption	40
3.12	Internet access in schools	40
3.21	Internet hosts, 2002	40
3.20	Internet users, 2002	47
3.23	Personal computers, 2002	47
3.17	Utility patents, 2002	48
3.22	Telephone lines, 2002	49

Business Competitiveness Index	**Rank/95**

Sophistication of Company Operations and Strategy

3.04	Prevalence of foreign technology licensing	7
10.14	Extent of incentive compensation	21
10.07	Extent of marketing	22

Quality of the National Business Environment

8.02	Extent of locally based competitors	8
2.05	Financial market sophistication	18
9.08	Local availability of components and parts	20

Other Indicators	**Rank/102**

10.23	Company promotion of volunteerism	8
2.15	Agricultural policy costs	9
6.05	Freedom of the press	17
2.02	Business costs of terrorism	21
4.09	Brain drain	22
11.13	Prevalence of environmental management systems	22
2.06	Soundness of banks	25
11.06	Compliance with environmental regulations	25
5.07	Postal efficiency	30
10.18	Hiring and firing practices	31
8.03	Extent of market dominance	31
2.04	Extent of distortive government intervention	34
11.10	Consistency of regulation enforcement	34
11.12	Political context of environmental gains	35
3.07	Subsidies and tax credits for firm-level research and development	35

NOTABLE COMPETITIVE DISADVANTAGES	
Growth Competitiveness Index	**Rank/102**

Macroeconomic Environment

2.22	Interest rate spread, 2002	100
2.18	Government surplus/deficit, 2002	87
2.20	Inflation, 2002	80
2.19	National savings rate, 2002	75
2.09	Access to credit	70
7.08	Diversion of public funds	63
2.17	Country credit rating, 2003	62
7.10	Public trust of politicians	62

Public Institutions

6.17	Organized crime	85
7.03	Irregular payments in tax collection	60
7.01	Irregular payments in exports and imports	56
6.01	Judicial independence	52

Technology

3.14	Government prioritization of ICT	66
3.18	Tertiary enrollment	62
3.19	Cellular telephones, 2002	54

Business Competitiveness Index	**Rank/95**

Sophistication of Company Operations and Strategy

10.01	Nature of competitive advantage	64
10.02	Value chain presence	44
10.03	Extent of branding	41

Quality of the National Business Environment

2.16	Cost of importing foreign equipment	94
10.17	Efficacy of corporate boards	76
4.02	Quality of public schools	73

Other Indicators	**Rank/102**

6.11	Efficiency of the tax system	101
8.10	Regional disparities in quality of business environment	99
8.09	Wage equality of women in the workplace	95
4.04	Disparity in healthcare quality	91
6.14	Business costs of crime and violence	91
4.11	Maternity laws' impact on hiring women	88
10.19	Flexibility of wage determination	75
7.11	Prevalence of illegal political donations	70
7.12	Policy consequences of legal political donations	68
6.18	Informal sector	66
7.14	Pervasiveness of money laundering through non-bank channels	66
4.10	Maternity leave legislation	66
6.16	Government effectiveness in reducing income inequality	65
6.07	Transparency of government policymaking	65
7.13	Pervasiveness of money laundering through banks	64

203

Note: The Business Competitiveness Index applies different criteria for selecting a country's competitive advantages and disadvantages. Please refer to the section "How Country Profiles Work" for further details.

Bulgaria

Competitivenss Rankings

Growth Competitiveness Index Rank	64

Macroeconomic Environment Index Rank	**73**
Macroeconomic Stability Subindex Rank	76
Government Waste Subindex Rank	86
Country Credit Rating Rank	57
Public Institutions Index Rank	**62**
Contracts and Law Subindex Rank	92
Corruption Subindex Rank	35
Technology Index Rank	**63**
Innovation Subindex Rank	43
ICT Subindex Rank	49
Technology Transfer Subindex Rank (out of 77 non-core innovators)	67

Business Competitiveness Index Rank	74

Sophistication of Company Operations and Strategy Rank	**81**
Quality of the National Business Environment Rank	**72**

The Most Problematic Factors for Doing Business

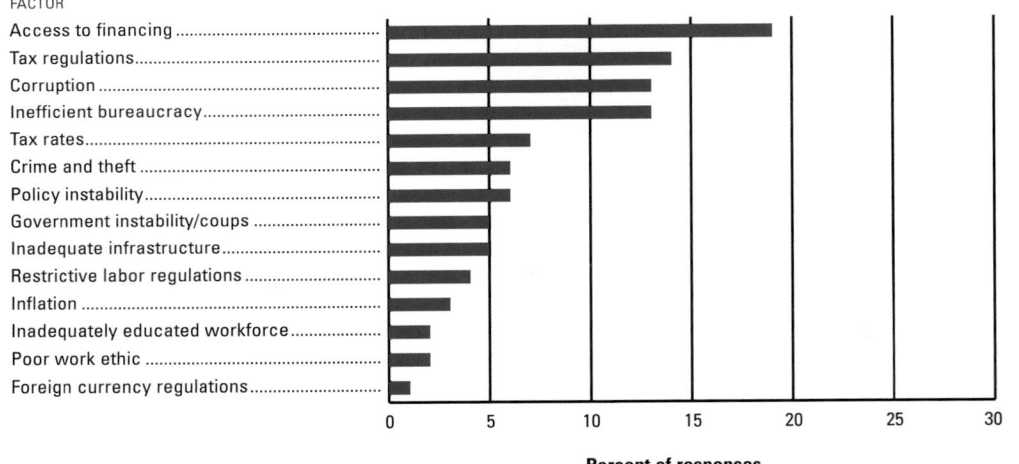

Note: From a list of 14 factors, respondents were asked to select the five most problematic for doing business in their country and to rankthem between 1 (most problematic) and 5. The bars in the figure show the responses weighted according to their rankings.

Source: World Economic Forum, Executive Opinion Survey (2003)

National competitiveness balance sheet

NOTABLE COMPETITIVE ADVANTAGES	
Growth Competitiveness Index	**Rank/102**

Macroeconomic Environment

2.18	Government surplus/deficit, 2002	24

Public Institutions

7.03	Irregular payments in tax collection	31
7.01	Irregular payments in exports and imports	35
7.02	Irregular payments in public utilities	44

Technology

3.22	Telephone lines, 2002	33
3.18	Tertiary enrollment	35
3.20	Internet users, 2002	46
3.21	Internet hosts, 2002	47
3.17	Utility patents, 2002	50

NOTABLE COMPETITIVE DISADVANTAGES	
Growth Competitiveness Index	**Rank/102**

Macroeconomic Environment

2.21	Real exchange rate, 2002	91
2.03	Extent of distortive government subsidies	89
2.19	National savings rate, 2002	80
7.10	Public trust of politicians	79
7.08	Diversion of public funds	79
2.09	Access to credit	75
2.01	Recession expectations	75
2.20	Inflation, 2002	72
2.17	Country credit rating, 2003	57
2.22	Interest rate spread, 2002	55

Public Institutions

6.17	Organized crime	93
6.03	Property rights	92
6.08	Favoritism in decisions of government officials	87
6.01	Judicial independence	78

Technology

3.02	Firm-level technology absorption	95
3.14	Government prioritization of ICT	88
3.15	Government success in ICT promotion	85
3.08	University/industry research collaboration	80
3.01	Technological sophistication	79
3.06	Company spending on research and development	79
3.03	FDI and technology transfer	70
3.13	Quality of competition in the ISP sector	70
3.16	Laws relating to ICT	70
3.04	Prevalence of foreign technology licensing	66
3.12	Internet access in schools	59
3.19	Cellular telephones, 2002	56
3.23	Personal computers, 2002	52

Business Competitiveness Index	
Business Competitiveness Index	**Rank/95**

Sophistication of Company Operations and Strategy

10.08	Degree of customer orientation	56
10.09	Control of international distribution	61
10.02	Value chain presence	67

Quality of the National Business Environment

9.09	Local availability of process machinery	27
4.03	Quality of math and science education	29
3.10	Availability of scientists and engineers	30

Business Competitiveness Index	
Business Competitiveness Index	**Rank/95**

Sophistication of Company Operations and Strategy

10.15	Reliance on professional management	88
10.12	Extent of staff training	85
3.04	Prevalence of foreign technology licensing	84

Quality of the National Business Environment

8.05	Administrative burden for startups	95
5.04	Air transport infrastructure quality	92
10.24	Protection of minority shareholders' interests	91

Other Indicators	
Other Indicators	**Rank/102**

10.19	Flexibility of wage determination	22
10.18	Hiring and firing practices	24
8.03	Extent of market dominance	28
10.21	Pay and productivity	31
7.04	Irregular payments in public contracts	34
7.06	Irregular payments in government policymaking	34
4.07	Business impact of HIV/AIDS	36
8.08	Private sector employment of women	37
8.09	Wage equality of women in the workplace	39
7.05	Irregular payments in loan applications	40
4.05	Business impact of malaria	43
4.08	Impact of HIV/AIDS on FDI	44
7.07	Irregular payments in judicial decisions	47

Other Indicators	
Other Indicators	**Rank/102**

10.22	Charitable causes involvement	102
10.23	Company promotion of volunteerism	101
4.10	Maternity leave legislation	96
2.15	Agricultural policy costs	94
4.11	Maternity laws' impact on hiring women	93
6.15	Government effectiveness in reducing poverty	93
11.09	Flexibility of regulations	91
4.09	Brain drain	91
6.07	Transparency of government policymaking	90
6.11	Efficiency of the tax system	89
6.16	Government effectiveness in reducing income inequality	88
6.14	Business costs of crime and violence	86
7.14	Pervasiveness of money laundering through non-bank channels	86
2.04	Extent of distortive government intervention	86
6.10	Effectiveness of law-making bodies	85

Note: The Business Competitiveness Index applies different criteria for selecting a country's competitive advantages and disadvantages. Please refer to the section "How Country Profiles Work" for further details.

Cameroon

Competitiveness Rankings

Growth Competitiveness Index Rank	**91**

Macroeconomic Environment Index Rank **78**
    Macroeconomic Stability Subindex Rank 59
    Government Waste Subindex Rank 74
    Country Credit Rating Rank 87

Public Institutions Index Rank..**95**
    Contracts and Law Subindex Rank 82
    Corruption Subindex Rank...................................97

Technology Index Rank **93**
    Innovation Subindex Rank...................................85
    ICT Subindex Rank 92
    Technology Transfer Subindex Rank
    (out of 77 non-core innovators).........................65

Business Competitiveness Index Rank	n/a

**Sophistication of Company Operations
and Strategy Rank** ....n/a

**Quality of the National Business
Environment Rank**..n/a

The Most Problematic Factors for Doing Business

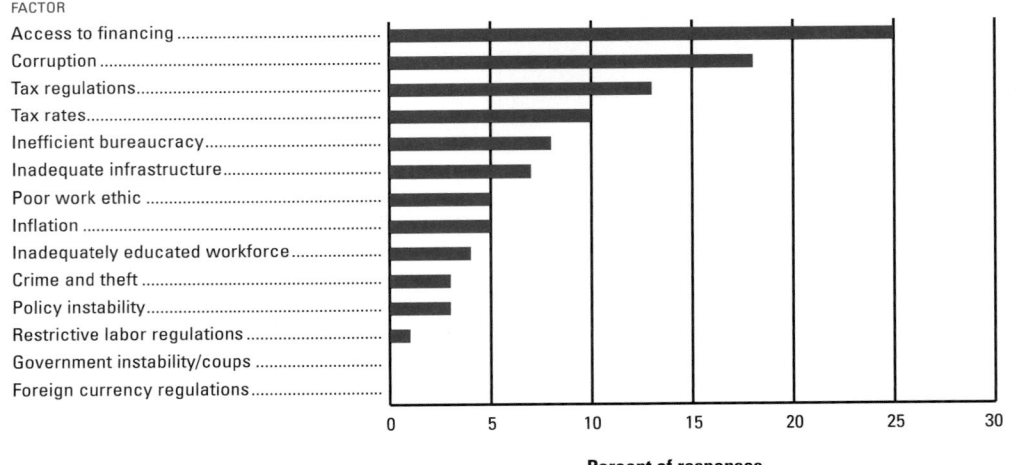

FACTOR

Note: From a list of 14 factors, respondents were asked to select the five most problematic for doing business in their country and to rank them between 1 (most problematic) and 5. The bars in the figure show the responses weighted according to their rankings.

Source: World Economic Forum, Executive Opinion Survey (2003)

National competitiveness balance sheet

NOTABLE COMPETITIVE ADVANTAGES

Growth Competitiveness Index	Rank/102
Macroeconomic Environment	
2.18 Government surplus/deficit, 2002	4
2.01 Recession expectations	18
2.19 National savings rate, 2002	43
2.21 Real exchange rate, 2002	48
Technology	
3.08 University/industry research collaboration	39
3.14 Government prioritization of ICT	46

Other Indicators	Rank/102
8.09 Wage equality of women in the workplace	4
2.15 Agricultural policy costs	17
4.11 Maternity laws' impact on hiring women	19
6.07 Transparency of government policymaking	26
4.10 Maternity leave legislation	29
11.11 Effects of compliance on business	31
11.12 Political context of environmental gains	38
10.18 Hiring and firing practices	46
3.07 Subsidies and tax credits for firm-level research and development	49

NOTABLE COMPETITIVE DISADVANTAGES

Growth Competitiveness Index	Rank/102
Macroeconomic Environment	
2.09 Access to credit	96
7.08 Diversion of public funds	95
2.17 Country credit rating, 2003	87
2.22 Interest rate spread, 2002	84
2.03 Extent of distortive government subsidies	61
2.20 Inflation, 2002	60
7.10 Public trust of politicians	54
Public Institutions	
7.02 Irregular payments in public utilities	99
6.17 Organized crime	95
7.03 Irregular payments in tax collection	95
7.01 Irregular payments in exports and imports	92
6.03 Property rights	88
6.01 Judicial independence	72
6.08 Favoritism in decisions of government officials	59
Technology	
3.12 Internet access in schools	95
3.20 Internet users, 2002	94
3.22 Telephone lines, 2002	92
3.01 Technological sophistication	90
3.21 Internet hosts, 2002	89
3.23 Personal computers, 2002	89
3.16 Laws relating to ICT	87
3.02 Firm-level technology absorption	84
3.19 Cellular telephones, 2002	83
3.18 Tertiary enrollment	83
3.06 Company spending on research and development	75
3.15 Government success in ICT promotion	73
3.17 Utility patents, 2002	72
3.13 Quality of competition in the ISP sector	68
3.03 FDI and technology transfer	65
3.04 Prevalence of foreign technology licensing	63

Other Indicators	Rank/102
10.21 Pay and productivity	100
4.06 Business impact of tuberculosis	99
4.05 Business impact of malaria	99
7.05 Irregular payments in loan applications	98
4.07 Business impact of HIV/AIDS	97
3.11 Availability of mobile or cellular telephones	93
10.25 Availability of company financial information	93
6.05 Freedom of the press	92
8.03 Extent of market dominance	92
6.14 Business costs of crime and violence	90
4.04 Disparity in healthcare quality	90
5.07 Postal efficiency	88
7.04 Irregular payments in public contracts	88
11.02 Water pollution regulations	86
11.03 Toxic waste disposal regulations	85

Note: This country is not included in the coverage of the Business Competitiveness Index 2003–2004.

Canada

Competitiveness Rankings

Growth Competitiveness Index Rank	16

Macroeconomic Environment Index Rank **11**
   Macroeconomic Stability Subindex Rank 13
   Government Waste Subindex Rank 21
   Country Credit Rating Rank 11

Public Institutions Index Rank **24**
   Contracts and Law Subindex Rank 26
   Corruption Subindex Rank...................................25

Technology Index Rank **11**
   Innovation Subindex Rank....................................9
   ICT Subindex Rank 13

Business Competitiveness Index Rank	12

**Sophistication of Company Operations
and Strategy Rank** **14**

**Quality of the National Business
Environment Rank** **10**

The Most Problematic Factors for Doing Business

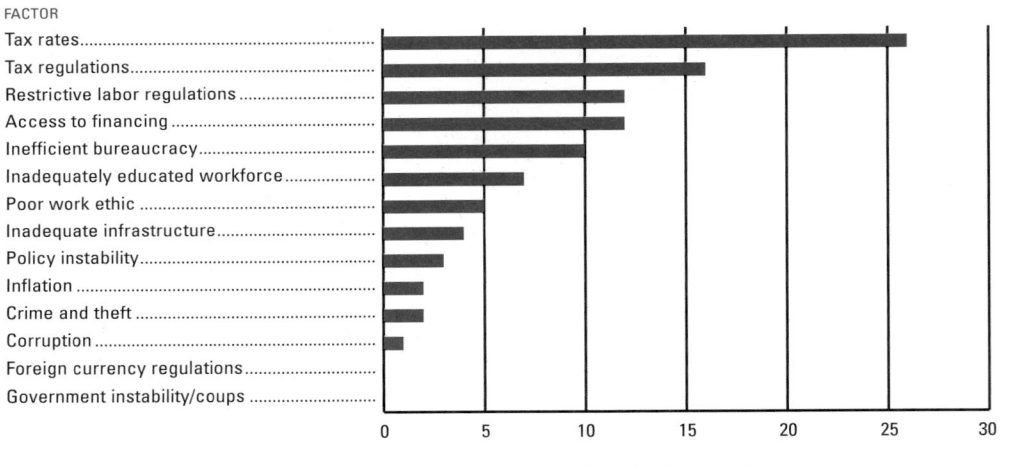

Note: From a list of 14 factors, respondents were asked to select the five most problematic for doing business in their country and to rank them between 1 (most problematic) and 5. The bars in the figure show the responses weighted according to their rankings.

Source: World Economic Forum, Executive Opinion Survey (2003)

National competitiveness balance sheet

NOTABLE COMPETITIVE ADVANTAGES

Growth Competitiveness Index	Rank/102

Macroeconomic Environment
2.22	Interest rate spread, 2002	4
2.18	Government surplus/deficit, 2002	8
2.17	Country credit rating, 2003	11

Technology
3.12	Internet access in schools	6
3.08	University/industry research collaboration	7
3.21	Internet hosts, 2002	8
3.22	Telephone lines, 2002	8
3.17	Utility patents, 2002	9
3.13	Quality of competition in the ISP sector	10
3.20	Internet users, 2002	10
3.23	Personal computers, 2002	10
3.01	Technological sophistication	11
3.18	Tertiary enrollment	12
3.06	Company spending on research and development	14

Business Competitiveness Index	Rank/95

Sophistication of Company Operations and Strategy
10.14	Extent of incentive compensation	6
10.07	Extent of marketing	9
10.10	Extent of regional sales	9

Quality of the National Business Environment
10.16	Quality of management schools	3
3.10	Availability of scientists and engineers	5
2.05	Financial market sophistication	6

Other Indicators	Rank/102

4.10	Maternity leave legislation	2
10.22	Charitable causes involvement	2
2.06	Soundness of banks	3
8.08	Private sector employment of women	4
10.23	Company promotion of volunteerism	4
3.07	Subsidies and tax credits for firm-level research and development	5
10.27	Strength of auditing and accounting standards	6
4.04	Disparity in healthcare quality	6
4.11	Maternity laws' impact on hiring women	7
10.25	Availability of company financial information	8
11.06	Compliance with environmental regulations	10
11.09	Flexibility of regulations	10
10.05	Ethical behavior of firms	10
11.08	Clarity and stability of regulations	10
11.11	Effects of compliance on business	12

NOTABLE COMPETITIVE DISADVANTAGES

Growth Competitiveness Index	Rank/102

Macroeconomic Environment
2.21	Real exchange rate, 2002	63
2.03	Extent of distortive government subsidies	48
2.19	National savings rate, 2002	46
2.09	Access to credit	31
2.20	Inflation, 2002	28
7.10	Public trust of politicians	21
2.01	Recession expectations	19
7.08	Diversion of public funds	19

Public Institutions
6.08	Favoritism in decisions of government officials	37
6.17	Organized crime	35
6.03	Property rights	27
7.01	Irregular payments in exports and imports	26
7.03	Irregular payments in tax collection	25
6.01	Judicial independence	20
7.02	Irregular payments in public utilities	20

Technology
3.19	Cellular telephones, 2002	40
3.14	Government prioritization of ICT	19
3.02	Firm-level technology absorption	18
3.15	Government success in ICT promotion	17
3.16	Laws relating to ICT	16

Business Competitiveness Index	Rank/95

Sophistication of Company Operations and Strategy
10.11	Breadth of international markets	31
10.02	Value chain presence	29
10.01	Nature of competitive advantage	23

Quality of the National Business Environment
6.09	Extent of bureaucratic red tape	53
10.26	Foreign ownership restrictions	50
2.03	Extent of distortive government subsidies	43

Other Indicators	Rank/102

2.02	Business costs of terrorism	66
6.11	Efficiency of the tax system	53
2.04	Extent of distortive government intervention	50
4.07	Business impact of HIV/AIDS	49
2.10	Government intervention in corporate investment	39
6.06	Burden of regulation	34
7.12	Policy consequences of legal political donations	32
7.05	Irregular payments in loan applications	31
6.14	Business costs of crime and violence	29
10.19	Flexibility of wage determination	28
6.18	Informal sector	27
4.09	Brain drain	26
2.15	Agricultural policy costs	25
7.04	Irregular payments in public contracts	24
4.08	Impact of HIV/AIDS on FDI	24

Note: The Business Competitiveness Index applies different criteria for selecting a country's competitive advantages and disadvantages. Please refer to the section "How Country Profiles Work" for further details.

Chad

Competitiveness Rankings

Growth Competitiveness Index Rank	**101**

Macroeconomic Environment Index Rank **96**
    Macroeconomic Stability Subindex Rank 91
    Government Waste Subindex Rank 90
    Country Credit Rating Rank 97

Public Institutions Index Rank.......................**101**
    Contracts and Law Subindex Rank 101
    Corruption Subindex Rank.................................101

Technology Index Rank **102**
    Innovation Subindex Rank.................................101
    ICT Subindex Rank 102
    Technology Transfer Subindex Rank
    (out of 77 non-core innovators) 75

Business Competitiveness Index Rank	**93**

**Sophistication of Company Operations
and Strategy Rank** **93**
**Quality of the National Business
Environment Rank** **93**

The Most Problematic Factors for Doing Business

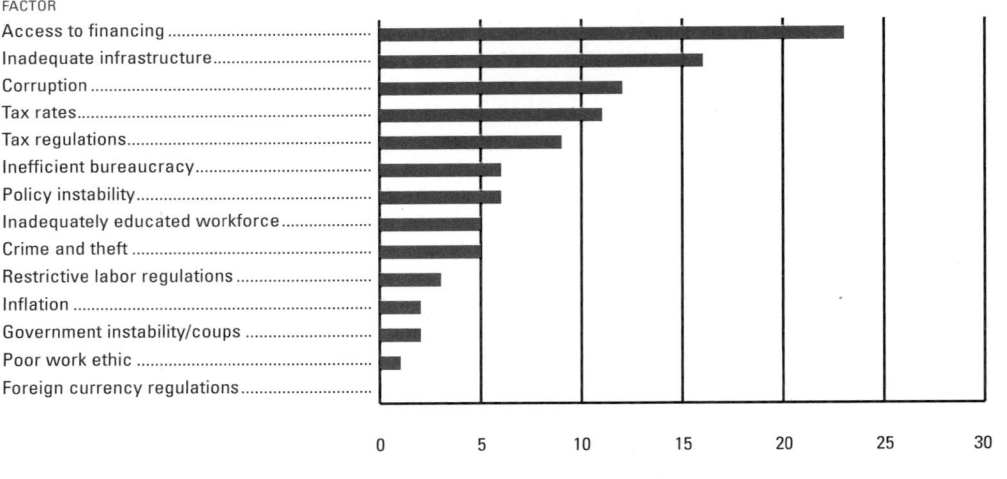

FACTOR

Note: From a list of 14 factors, respondents were asked to select the five most problematic for doing business in their country and to rank them between 1 (most problematic) and 5. The bars in the figure show the responses weighted according to their rankings.

Source: World Economic Forum, Executive Opinion Survey (2003)

National competitiveness balance sheet

NOTABLE COMPETITIVE ADVANTAGES	
Growth Competitiveness Index	**Rank/102**

Macroeconomic Environment

2.01	Recession expectations	14

NOTABLE COMPETITIVE DISADVANTAGES	
Growth Competitiveness Index	**Rank/102**

Macroeconomic Environment

2.19	National savings rate, 2002	101
2.09	Access to credit	97
2.17	Country credit rating, 2003	97
2.18	Government surplus/deficit, 2002	97
7.08	Diversion of public funds	96
7.10	Public trust of politicians	87
2.22	Interest rate spread, 2002	84
2.03	Extent of distortive government subsidies	82
2.21	Real exchange rate, 2002	75
2.20	Inflation, 2002	60

Public Institutions

7.01	Irregular payments in exports and imports	102
7.02	Irregular payments in public utilities	100
7.03	Irregular payments in tax collection	99
6.03	Property rights	98
6.08	Favoritism in decisions of government officials	97
6.17	Organized crime	97
6.01	Judicial independence	96

Technology

3.12	Internet access in schools	102
3.22	Telephone lines, 2002	102
3.13	Quality of competition in the ISP sector	101
3.19	Cellular telephones, 2002	101
3.01	Technological sophistication	100
3.02	Firm-level technology absorption	99
3.06	Company spending on research and development	99
3.20	Internet users, 2002	98
3.18	Tertiary enrollment	98
3.15	Government success in ICT promotion	98
3.21	Internet hosts, 2002	97
3.08	University/industry research collaboration	97
3.23	Personal computers, 2002	96
3.14	Government prioritization of ICT	96
3.16	Laws relating to ICT	93
3.03	FDI and technology transfer	75
3.04	Prevalence of foreign technology licensing	75
3.17	Utility patents, 2002	72

Business Competitiveness Index	
Business Competitiveness Index	**Rank/95**

Sophistication of Company Operations and Strategy

10.13	Willingness to delegate authority	78
10.14	Extent of incentive compensation	79

Quality of the National Business Environment

10.20	Cooperation in labor-employer relations	33
6.09	Extent of bureaucratic red tape	45
9.02	Local supplier quantity	53

Business Competitiveness Index	**Rank/95**

Sophistication of Company Operations and Strategy

10.07	Extent of marketing	95
10.09	Control of international distribution	95
10.11	Breadth of international markets	94

Quality of the National Business Environment

2.14	Hidden trade barriers	95
5.05	Quality of electricity supply	95
9.10	Local availability of specialized research and training	95

Other Indicators	**Rank/102**

10.19	Flexibility of wage determination	4
8.09	Wage equality of women in the workplace	9
10.18	Hiring and firing practices	10
4.11	Maternity laws' impact on hiring women	32
6.06	Burden of regulation	43
11.11	Effects of compliance on business	50

Other Indicators	**Rank/102**

7.06	Irregular payments in government policymaking	102
3.11	Availability of mobile or cellular telephones	102
7.07	Irregular payments in judicial decisions	102
10.25	Availability of company financial information	102
10.27	Strength of auditing and accounting standards	102
4.07	Business impact of HIV/AIDS	101
4.05	Business impact of malaria	101
7.05	Irregular payments in loan applications	100
4.06	Business impact of tuberculosis	100
11.03	Toxic waste disposal regulations	100
11.02	Water pollution regulations	100
11.04	Chemical waste regulations	100
11.06	Compliance with environmental regulations	100

211

Note: The Business Competitiveness Index applies different criteria for selecting a country's competitive advantages and disadvantages. Please refer to the section "How Country Profiles Work" for further details.

Chile

Competitiveness Rankings

The Most Problematic Factors for Doing Business

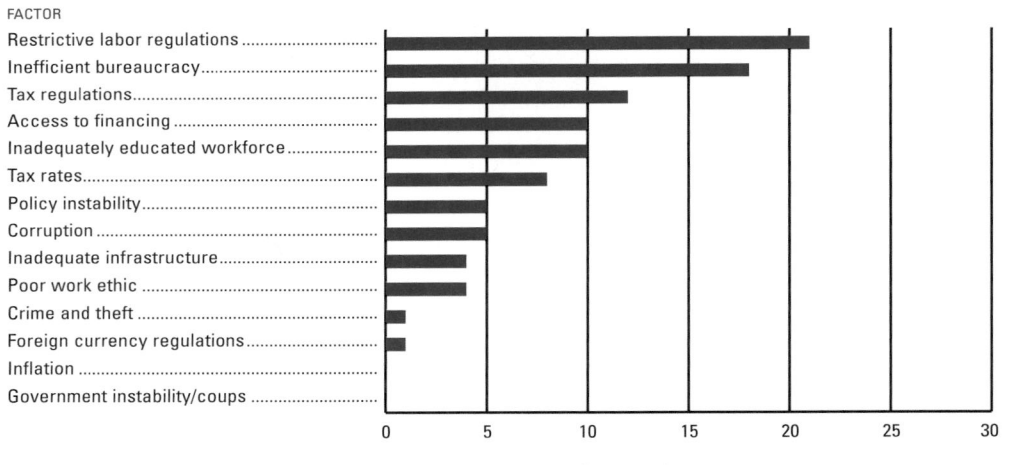

FACTOR

Note: From a list of 14 factors, respondents were asked to select the five most problematic for doing business in their country and to rank them between 1 (most problematic) and 5. The bars in the figure show the responses weighted according to their rankings.

Source: World Economic Forum, Executive Opinion Survey (2003)

National competitiveness balance sheet

NOTABLE COMPETITIVE ADVANTAGES

Growth Competitiveness Index		Rank/102
Macroeconomic Environment		
2.03	Extent of distortive government subsidies	10
2.18	Government surplus/deficit, 2002	25
2.21	Real exchange rate, 2002	27
Public Institutions		
7.01	Irregular payments in exports and imports	8
7.02	Irregular payments in public utilities	15
7.03	Irregular payments in tax collection	17
6.03	Property rights	19
6.17	Organized crime	25
Technology		
3.13	Quality of competition in the ISP sector	13
3.03	FDI and technology transfer	16
3.04	Prevalence of foreign technology licensing	20
3.02	Firm-level technology absorption	24

Business Competitiveness Index		Rank/95
Sophistication of Company Operations and Strategy		
10.11	Breadth of international markets	17
10.15	Reliance on professional management	25
10.06	Production process sophistication	26
Quality of the National Business Environment		
2.14	Hidden trade barriers	7
8.01	Intensity of local competition	7
2.03	Extent of distortive government subsidies	9

Other Indicators		Rank/102
4.09	Brain drain	3
10.19	Flexibility of wage determination	7
4.06	Business impact of tuberculosis	9
3.11	Availability of mobile or cellular telephones	10
2.02	Business costs of terrorism	11
2.15	Agricultural policy costs	12
2.04	Extent of distortive government intervention	13
8.11	Focus of trade and industry associations	16
7.14	Pervasiveness of money laundering through non-bank channels	17
2.06	Soundness of banks	17
7.05	Irregular payments in loan applications	18
4.07	Business impact of HIV/AIDS	18
10.25	Availability of company financial information	18
6.11	Efficiency of the tax system	19
7.13	Pervasiveness of money laundering through banks	20

NOTABLE COMPETITIVE DISADVANTAGES

Growth Competitiveness Index		Rank/102
Macroeconomic Environment		
2.19	National savings rate, 2002	55
7.10	Public trust of politicians	48
2.01	Recession expectations	42
2.20	Inflation, 2002	40
2.09	Access to credit	37
7.08	Diversion of public funds	37
2.17	Country credit rating, 2003	31
2.22	Interest rate spread, 2002	30
Public Institutions		
6.01	Judicial independence	38
6.08	Favoritism in decisions of government officials	32
Technology		
3.06	Company spending on research and development	49
3.22	Telephone lines, 2002	48
3.17	Utility patents, 2002	45
3.08	University/industry research collaboration	44
3.21	Internet hosts, 2002	42
3.15	Government success in ICT promotion	41
3.18	Tertiary enrollment	38
3.19	Cellular telephones, 2002	37
3.12	Internet access in schools	36
3.23	Personal computers, 2002	36
3.14	Government prioritization of ICT	33
3.20	Internet users, 2002	32
3.16	Laws relating to ICT	30
3.01	Technological sophistication	29

Business Competitiveness Index		Rank/95
Sophistication of Company Operations and Strategy		
10.01	Nature of competitive advantage	71
10.03	Extent of branding	61
10.02	Value chain presence	60
Quality of the National Business Environment		
4.03	Quality of math and science education	63
4.02	Quality of public schools	62
5.02	Railroad infrastructure development	61

Other Indicators		Rank/102
8.09	Wage equality of women in the workplace	97
4.11	Maternity laws' impact on hiring women	94
10.18	Hiring and firing practices	76
8.08	Private sector employment of women	73
7.11	Prevalence of illegal political donations	71
4.04	Disparity in healthcare quality	67
11.13	Prevalence of environmental management systems	66
4.10	Maternity leave legislation	60
11.11	Effects of compliance on business	58
11.09	Flexibility of regulations	55
6.10	Effectiveness of law-making bodies	53
11.08	Clarity and stability of regulations	49
5.07	Postal efficiency	48
6.16	Government effectiveness in reducing income inequality	47
8.10	Regional disparities in quality of business environment	47

213

Note: The Business Competitiveness Index applies different criteria for selecting a country's competitive advantages and disadvantages. Please refer to the section "How Country Profiles Work" for further details.

China

Competitiveness Rankings

Growth Competitiveness Index Rank	44

Macroeconomic Environment Index Rank **25**
    Macroeconomic Stability Subindex Rank 4
    Government Waste Subindex Rank 35
    Country Credit Rating Rank 34

Public Institutions Index Rank..........................**52**
    Contracts and Law Subindex Rank 60
    Corruption Subindex Rank...................................50

Technology Index Rank **65**
    Innovation Subindex Rank 70
    ICT Subindex Rank 62
    Technology Transfer Subindex Rank
        (out of 77 non-core innovators).......................47

Business Competitiveness Index Rank	46

**Sophistication of Company Operations
and Strategy Rank** **42**

**Quality of the National Business
Environment Rank** **44**

The Most Problematic Factors for Doing Business

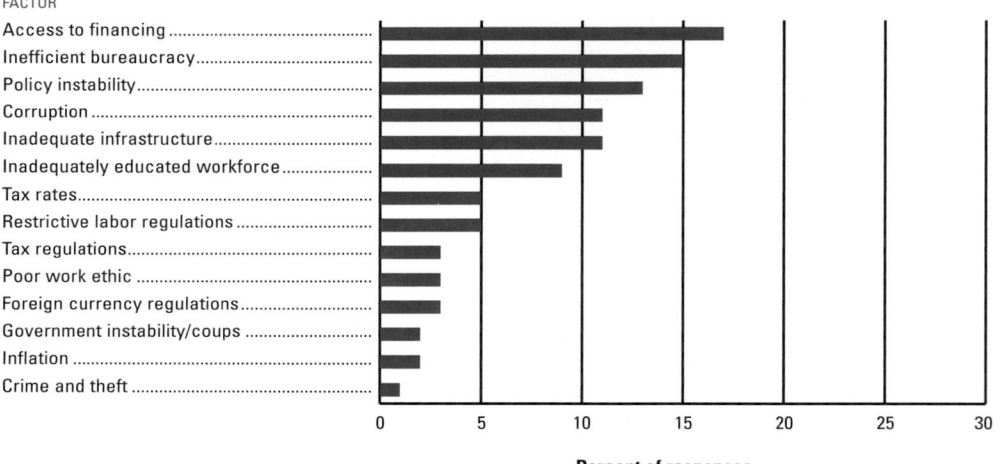

FACTOR

Access to financing
Inefficient bureaucracy
Policy instability
Corruption
Inadequate infrastructure
Inadequately educated workforce
Tax rates
Restrictive labor regulations
Tax regulations
Poor work ethic
Foreign currency regulations
Government instability/coups
Inflation
Crime and theft

Percent of responses

Note: From a list of 14 factors, respondents were asked to select the five most problematic for doing business in their country and to rank them between 1 (most problematic) and 5. The bars in the figure show the responses weighted according to their rankings.

Source: World Economic Forum, Executive Opinion Survey (2003)

National competitiveness balance sheet

NOTABLE COMPETITIVE ADVANTAGES			NOTABLE COMPETITIVE DISADVANTAGES		
Growth Competitiveness Index		**Rank/102**	**Growth Competitiveness Index**		**Rank/102**

Macroeconomic Environment (advantages)

2.19	National savings rate, 2002	2
2.20	Inflation, 2002	5
2.01	Recession expectations	7
2.22	Interest rate spread, 2002	20
7.10	Public trust of politicians	20
2.03	Extent of distortive government subsidies	29
2.17	Country credit rating, 2003	34

Public Institutions (advantages)

6.08	Favoritism in decisions of government officials	43
7.01	Irregular payments in exports and imports	43

Technology (advantages)

3.08	University/industry research collaboration	20
3.15	Government success in ICT promotion	24
3.06	Company spending on research and development	29
3.14	Government prioritization of ICT	32
3.03	FDI and technology transfer	42

Macroeconomic Environment (disadvantages)

2.21	Real exchange rate, 2002	94
2.09	Access to credit	63
7.08	Diversion of public funds	51
2.18	Government surplus/deficit, 2002	48

Public Institutions (disadvantages)

6.03	Property rights	64
6.01	Judicial independence	62
6.17	Organized crime	60
7.02	Irregular payments in public utilities	60
7.03	Irregular payments in tax collection	52

Technology (disadvantages)

3.21	Internet hosts, 2002	84
3.18	Tertiary enrollment	78
3.23	Personal computers, 2002	72
3.19	Cellular telephones, 2002	61
3.02	Firm-level technology absorption	58
3.20	Internet users, 2002	58
3.22	Telephone lines, 2002	56
3.17	Utility patents, 2002	55
3.12	Internet access in schools	54
3.13	Quality of competition in the ISP sector	52
3.16	Laws relating to ICT	51
3.01	Technological sophistication	48
3.04	Prevalence of foreign technology licensing	46

Business Competitiveness Index		**Rank/95**	**Business Competitiveness Index**		**Rank/95**

Sophistication of Company Operations and Strategy (advantages)

10.04	Capacity for innovation	25
10.09	Control of international distribution	25
3.06	Company spending on research and development	28

Quality of the National Business Environment (advantages)

9.08	Local availability of components and parts	6
9.09	Local availability of process machinery	6
8.02	Extent of locally based competitors	7

Sophistication of Company Operations and Strategy (disadvantages)

10.07	Extent of marketing	73
3.04	Prevalence of foreign technology licensing	67
10.01	Nature of competitive advantage	56

Quality of the National Business Environment (disadvantages)

6.09	Extent of bureaucratic red tape	95
2.13	Effectiveness of bankruptcy law	81
2.12	Regulation of securities exchanges	80

Other Indicators		**Rank/102**	**Other Indicators**		**Rank/102**

2.15	Agricultural policy costs	11
10.23	Company promotion of volunteerism	11
6.16	Government effectiveness in reducing income inequality	15
10.21	Pay and productivity	17
7.12	Policy consequences of legal political donations	17
7.11	Prevalence of illegal political donations	18
6.15	Government effectiveness in reducing poverty	20
6.06	Burden of regulation	21
8.03	Extent of market dominance	22
3.07	Subsidies and tax credits for firm-level research and development	22
8.11	Focus of trade and industry associations	24
6.10	Effectiveness of law-making bodies	26
10.18	Hiring and firing practices	26
11.11	Effects of compliance on business	27
6.11	Efficiency of the tax system	29

6.05	Freedom of the press	99
11.12	Political context of environmental gains	95
10.22	Charitable causes involvement	95
10.27	Strength of auditing and accounting standards	95
2.06	Soundness of banks	93
8.08	Private sector employment of women	91
4.10	Maternity leave legislation	91
4.08	Impact of HIV/AIDS on FDI	90
3.11	Availability of mobile or cellular telephones	89
4.05	Business impact of malaria	80
4.06	Business impact of tuberculosis	77
4.07	Business impact of HIV/AIDS	73
10.25	Availability of company financial information	71
2.02	Business costs of terrorism	65
7.05	Irregular payments in loan applications	64

215

Note: The Business Competitiveness Index applies different criteria for selecting a country's competitive advantages and disadvantages. Please refer to the section "How Country Profiles Work" for further details.

Colombia

Competitiveness Rankings

Growth Competitiveness Index Rank	**63**

Macroeconomic Environment Index Rank **66**
    Macroeconomic Stability Subindex Rank 68
    Government Waste Subindex Rank 73
    Country Credit Rating Rank 60

Public Institutions Index Rank **60**
    Contracts and Law Subindex Rank 79
    Corruption Subindex Rank 44

Technology Index Rank **60**
    Innovation Subindex Rank 57
    ICT Subindex Rank 57
    Technology Transfer Subindex Rank
        (out of 77 non-core innovators) 50

Business Competitiveness Index Rank	**51**

**Sophistication of Company Operations
   and Strategy Rank** **50**
**Quality of the National Business
   Environment Rank** **54**

The Most Problematic Factors for Doing Business

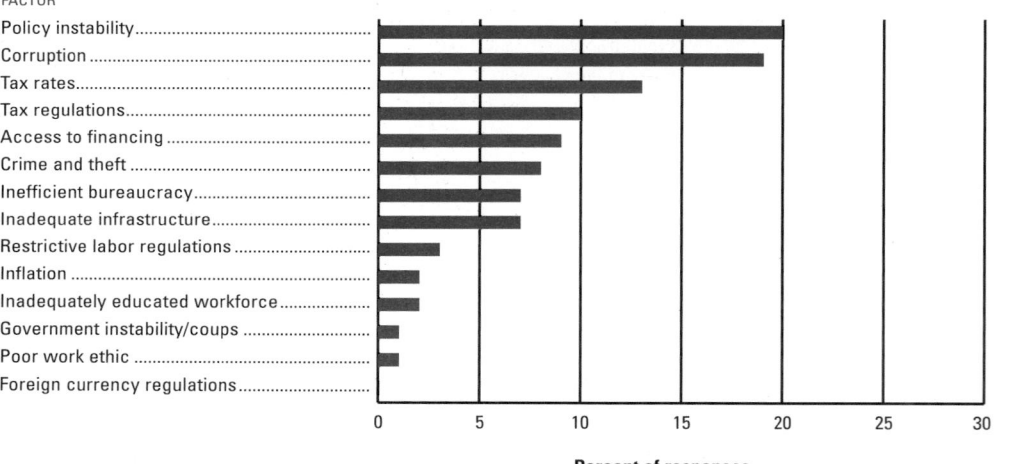

Note: From a list of 14 factors, respondents were asked to select the five most problematic for doing business in their country and to rank them between 1 (most problematic) and 5. The bars in the figure show the responses weighted according to their rankings.

Source: World Economic Forum, Executive Opinion Survey (2003)

National competitiveness balance sheet

NOTABLE COMPETITIVE ADVANTAGES

Growth Competitiveness Index	Rank/102
Macroeconomic Environment	
2.09 Access to credit	23
2.01 Recession expectations	27
2.21 Real exchange rate, 2002	40
2.03 Extent of distortive government subsidies	47
Public Institutions	
7.01 Irregular payments in exports and imports	42
7.02 Irregular payments in public utilities	45
7.03 Irregular payments in tax collection	45
6.03 Property rights	49
Technology	
3.16 Laws relating to ICT	41
3.03 FDI and technology transfer	45
3.13 Quality of competition in the ISP sector	45
3.04 Prevalence of foreign technology licensing	50
3.06 Company spending on research and development	50

Business Competitiveness Index	Rank/95
Sophistication of Company Operations and Strategy	
10.08 Degree of customer orientation	30
10.13 Willingness to delegate authority	42
10.10 Extent of regional sales	43
Quality of the National Business Environment	
8.02 Extent of locally based competitors	25
2.13 Effectiveness of bankruptcy law	30
6.09 Extent of bureaucratic red tape	34

Other Indicators	Rank/102
7.05 Irregular payments in loan applications	32
8.08 Private sector employment of women	36
10.25 Availability of company financial information	37
2.04 Extent of distortive government intervention	38
11.09 Flexibility of regulations	39
10.23 Company promotion of volunteerism	40
4.06 Business impact of tuberculosis	43
8.03 Extent of market dominance	45
6.07 Transparency of government policymaking	48
10.05 Ethical behavior of firms	48
4.08 Impact of HIV/AIDS on FDI	48
11.01 Air pollution regulations	49
6.05 Freedom of the press	49
11.06 Compliance with environmental regulations	50

NOTABLE COMPETITIVE DISADVANTAGES

Growth Competitiveness Index	Rank/102
Macroeconomic Environment	
2.19 National savings rate, 2002	88
7.08 Diversion of public funds	80
7.10 Public trust of politicians	77
2.20 Inflation, 2002	74
2.17 Country credit rating, 2003	60
2.22 Interest rate spread, 2002	59
2.18 Government surplus/deficit, 2002	56
Public Institutions	
6.17 Organized crime	101
6.08 Favoritism in decisions of government officials	72
6.01 Judicial independence	70
Technology	
3.19 Cellular telephones, 2002	69
3.12 Internet access in schools	65
3.02 Firm-level technology absorption	59
3.17 Utility patents, 2002	59
3.20 Internet users, 2002	59
3.01 Technological sophistication	58
3.21 Internet hosts, 2002	58
3.14 Government prioritization of ICT	57
3.15 Government success in ICT promotion	56
3.18 Tertiary enrollment	55
3.23 Personal computers, 2002	55
3.22 Telephone lines, 2002	54
3.08 University/industry research collaboration	52

Business Competitiveness Index	Rank/95
Sophistication of Company Operations and Strategy	
3.04 Prevalence of foreign technology licensing	74
10.09 Control of international distribution	65
10.14 Extent of incentive compensation	64
Quality of the National Business Environment	
5.02 Railroad infrastructure development	80
8.05 Administrative burden for startups	79
9.05 Decentralization of corporate activity	77

Other Indicators	Rank/102
2.02 Business costs of terrorism	101
7.14 Pervasiveness of money laundering through non-bank channels	98
7.13 Pervasiveness of money laundering through banks	92
7.12 Policy consequences of legal political donations	88
11.11 Effects of compliance on business	81
6.14 Business costs of crime and violence	80
5.07 Postal efficiency	79
4.11 Maternity laws' impact on hiring women	79
6.10 Effectiveness of law-making bodies	78
8.09 Wage equality of women in the workplace	77
10.18 Hiring and firing practices	77
8.10 Regional disparities in quality of business environment	73
6.11 Efficiency of the tax system	72
7.11 Prevalence of illegal political donations	72
10.21 Pay and productivity	72

Note: The Business Competitiveness Index applies different criteria for selecting a country's competitive advantages and disadvantages. Please refer to the section "How Country Profiles Work" for further details.

Costa Rica

Competitiveness Rankings

Growth Competitiveness Index Rank	51

Macroeconomic Environment Index Rank	**63**
Macroeconomic Stability Subindex Rank	82
Government Waste Subindex Rank	51
Country Credit Rating Rank	52

Public Institutions Index Rank	**49**
Contracts and Law Subindex Rank	48
Corruption Subindex Rank	51

Technology Index Rank	**46**
Innovation Subindex Rank	61
ICT Subindex Rank	52
Technology Transfer Subindex Rank (out of 77 non-core innovators)	8

Business Competitiveness Index Rank	45
Sophistication of Company Operations and Strategy Rank	32
Quality of the National Business Environment Rank	47

The Most Problematic Factors for Doing Business

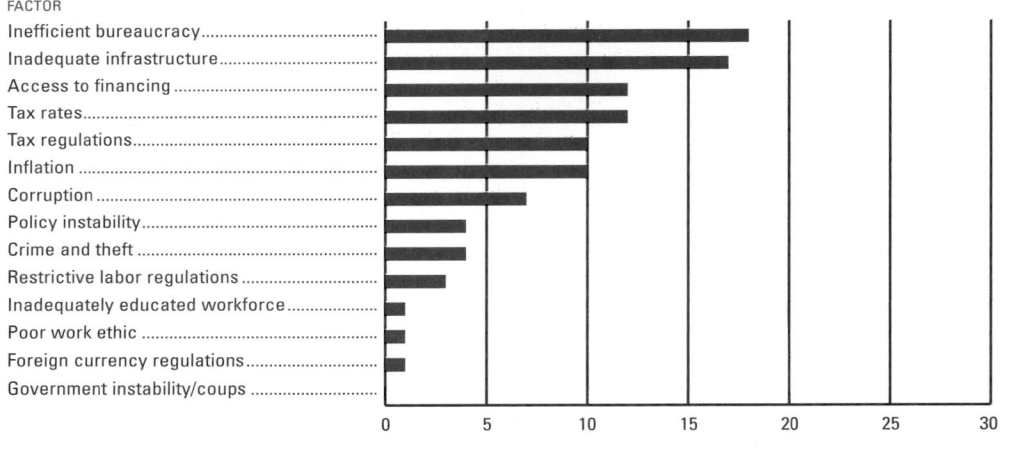

FACTOR

Note: From a list of 14 factors, respondents were asked to select the five most problematic for doing business in their country and to rank them between 1 (most problematic) and 5. The bars in the figure show the responses weighted according to their rankings.

Source: World Economic Forum, Executive Opinion Survey (2003)

National competitiveness balance sheet

NOTABLE COMPETITIVE ADVANTAGES		
Growth Competitiveness Index		**Rank/102**

Macroeconomic Environment

7.08	Diversion of public funds	40
2.03	Extent of distortive government subsidies	46
7.10	Public trust of politicians	50

Public Institutions

| 6.03 | Property rights | 38 |
| 7.02 | Irregular payments in public utilities | 48 |

Technology

3.04	Prevalence of foreign technology licensing	9
3.03	FDI and technology transfer	13
3.02	Firm-level technology absorption	17
3.06	Company spending on research and development	27
3.23	Personal computers, 2002	31
3.01	Technological sophistication	34
3.17	Utility patents, 2002	44
3.22	Telephone lines, 2002	44
3.20	Internet users, 2002	45

NOTABLE COMPETITIVE DISADVANTAGES		
Growth Competitiveness Index		**Rank/102**

Macroeconomic Environment

2.22	Interest rate spread, 2002	92
2.20	Inflation, 2002	83
2.19	National savings rate, 2002	82
2.21	Real exchange rate, 2002	76
2.01	Recession expectations	62
2.18	Government surplus/deficit, 2002	56
2.17	Country credit rating, 2003	52
2.09	Access to credit	51

Public Institutions

6.08	Favoritism in decisions of government officials	58
6.17	Organized crime	55
7.01	Irregular payments in exports and imports	55
6.01	Judicial independence	54
7.03	Irregular payments in tax collection	51

Technology

3.13	Quality of competition in the ISP sector	100
3.14	Government prioritization of ICT	77
3.19	Cellular telephones, 2002	65
3.18	Tertiary enrollment	64
3.15	Government success in ICT promotion	63
3.16	Laws relating to ICT	62
3.12	Internet access in schools	58
3.08	University/industry research collaboration	58
3.21	Internet hosts, 2002	54

Business Competitiveness Index		**Rank/95**

Sophistication of Company Operations and Strategy

3.04	Prevalence of foreign technology licensing	11
3.06	Company spending on research and development	26
10.13	Willingness to delegate authority	27

Quality of the National Business Environment

10.20	Cooperation in labor-employer relations	10
4.01	Quality of the educational system	24
10.16	Quality of management schools	26

Business Competitiveness Index		**Rank/95**

Sophistication of Company Operations and Strategy

10.09	Control of international distribution	53
10.03	Extent of branding	50
10.11	Breadth of international markets	47

Quality of the National Business Environment

5.02	Railroad infrastructure development	88
5.06	Telephone infrastructure quality	86
5.03	Port infrastructure quality	84

Other Indicators		**Rank/102**

4.09	Brain drain	9
2.02	Business costs of terrorism	20
6.05	Freedom of the press	21
4.06	Business impact of tuberculosis	25
8.11	Focus of trade and industry associations	25
8.09	Wage equality of women in the workplace	25
11.06	Compliance with environmental regulations	26
4.10	Maternity leave legislation	28
6.06	Burden of regulation	28
10.23	Company promotion of volunteerism	30
8.08	Private sector employment of women	32
11.07	Compliance with international agreements	32
11.12	Political context of environmental gains	32
2.15	Agricultural policy costs	33
4.04	Disparity in healthcare quality	34

Other Indicators		**Rank/102**

3.11	Availability of mobile or cellular telephones	97
6.10	Effectiveness of law-making bodies	84
7.13	Pervasiveness of money laundering through banks	76
7.14	Pervasiveness of money laundering through non-bank channels	75
3.07	Subsidies and tax credits for firm-level research and development	75
10.19	Flexibility of wage determination	74
5.07	Postal efficiency	72
10.18	Hiring and firing practices	72
6.14	Business costs of crime and violence	70
7.12	Policy consequences of legal political donations	69
7.11	Prevalence of illegal political donations	69
7.06	Irregular payments in government policymaking	68
6.18	Informal sector	63
6.15	Government effectiveness in reducing poverty	57
2.10	Government intervention in corporate investment	55

219

Note: The Business Competitiveness Index applies different criteria for selecting a country's competitive advantages and disadvantages. Please refer to the section "How Country Profiles Work" for further details.

Croatia

Competitiveness Rankings

Growth Competitiveness Index Rank	53

Macroeconomic Environment Index Rank **55**
    Macroeconomic Stability Subindex Rank 51
    Government Waste Subindex Rank 59
    Country Credit Rating Rank 49

Public Institutions Index Rank.........................**67**
    Contracts and Law Subindex Rank 81
    Corruption Subindex Rank...................................54

Technology Index Rank **41**
    Innovation Subindex Rank...................................48
    ICT Subindex Rank 39
    Technology Transfer Subindex Rank
    (out of 77 non-core innovators).......................43

Business Competitiveness Index Rank	62

**Sophistication of Company Operations
  and Strategy Rank** **65**

**Quality of the National Business
  Environment Rank** **57**

The Most Problematic Factors for Doing Business

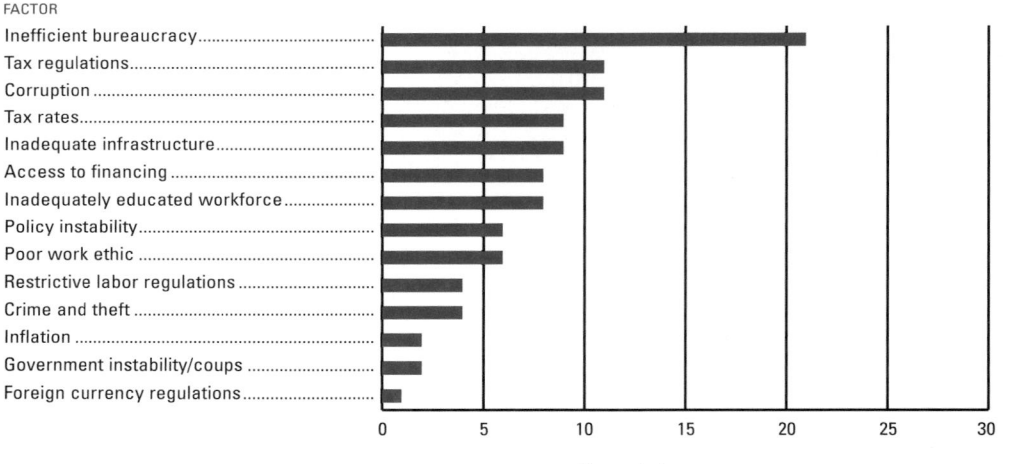

FACTOR

Note: From a list of 14 factors, respondents were asked to select the five most problematic for doing business in their country and to rank them between 1 (most problematic) and 5. The bars in the figure show the responses weighted according to their rankings.

Source: World Economic Forum, Executive Opinion Survey (2003)

National competitiveness balance sheet

NOTABLE COMPETITIVE ADVANTAGES	
Growth Competitiveness Index	**Rank/102**

Macroeconomic Environment

2.09	Access to credit	15
2.20	Inflation, 2002	32
7.08	Diversion of public funds	44
2.17	Country credit rating, 2003	49

Technology

3.04	Prevalence of foreign technology licensing	14
3.22	Telephone lines, 2002	31
3.17	Utility patents, 2002	32
3.23	Personal computers, 2002	33
3.20	Internet users, 2002	34
3.02	Firm-level technology absorption	35
3.19	Cellular telephones, 2002	36
3.12	Internet access in schools	43
3.21	Internet hosts, 2002	43
3.08	University/industry research collaboration	46
3.18	Tertiary enrollment	46
3.14	Government prioritization of ICT	49

Business Competitiveness Index	Rank/95
Business Competitiveness Index	**Rank/95**

Sophistication of Company Operations and Strategy

3.04	Prevalence of foreign technology licensing	21
10.09	Control of international distribution	33
10.01	Nature of competitive advantage	42

Quality of the National Business Environment

6.09	Extent of bureaucratic red tape	9
9.07	Extent of collaboration among clusters	14
3.17	Utility patents, 2002	30

Other Indicators	Rank/102
Other Indicators	**Rank/102**

8.09	Wage equality of women in the workplace	15
4.08	Impact of HIV/AIDS on FDI	34
4.04	Disparity in healthcare quality	35
4.07	Business impact of HIV/AIDS	38
6.11	Efficiency of the tax system	38
7.13	Pervasiveness of money laundering through banks	39
11.11	Effects of compliance on business	41
5.07	Postal efficiency	42
4.05	Business impact of malaria	44
11.02	Water pollution regulations	44
4.06	Business impact of tuberculosis	46
11.06	Compliance with environmental regulations	47
8.08	Private sector employment of women	47
11.07	Compliance with international agreements	48
11.03	Toxic waste disposal regulations	48

NOTABLE COMPETITIVE DISADVANTAGES	
Growth Competitiveness Index	**Rank/102**

Macroeconomic Environment

2.03	Extent of distortive government subsidies	83
2.18	Government surplus/deficit, 2002	78
2.22	Interest rate spread, 2002	77
7.10	Public trust of politicians	63
2.01	Recession expectations	59
2.19	National savings rate, 2002	51
2.21	Real exchange rate, 2002	51

Public Institutions

6.03	Property rights	90
6.01	Judicial independence	79
6.08	Favoritism in decisions of government officials	73
6.17	Organized crime	71
7.01	Irregular payments in exports and imports	57
7.03	Irregular payments in tax collection	54
7.02	Irregular payments in public utilities	53

Technology

3.13	Quality of competition in the ISP sector	83
3.01	Technological sophistication	80
3.03	FDI and technology transfer	64
3.15	Government success in ICT promotion	64
3.16	Laws relating to ICT	61
3.06	Company spending on research and development	57

Business Competitiveness Index	Rank/95
Business Competitiveness Index	**Rank/95**

Sophistication of Company Operations and Strategy

10.11	Breadth of international markets	82
10.10	Extent of regional sales	77
10.08	Degree of customer orientation	73

Quality of the National Business Environment

10.20	Cooperation in labor-employer relations	90
10.26	Foreign ownership restrictions	86
10.24	Protection of minority shareholders' interests	85

Other Indicators	Rank/102
Other Indicators	**Rank/102**

4.10	Maternity leave legislation	102
4.11	Maternity laws' impact on hiring women	98
10.22	Charitable causes involvement	96
2.15	Agricultural policy costs	91
10.23	Company promotion of volunteerism	89
2.10	Government intervention in corporate investment	85
6.06	Burden of regulation	85
8.11	Focus of trade and industry associations	84
10.05	Ethical behavior of firms	82
6.07	Transparency of government policymaking	81
7.12	Policy consequences of legal political donations	80
6.15	Government effectiveness in reducing poverty	80
10.25	Availability of company financial information	77
10.21	Pay and productivity	75
6.05	Freedom of the press	74

221

Note: The Business Competitiveness Index applies different criteria for selecting a country's competitive advantages and disadvantages. Please refer to the section "How Country Profiles Work" for further details.

Czech Republic

Competitiveness Rankings

Growth Competitiveness Index Rank	39

Macroeconomic Environment Index Rank	**39**
Macroeconomic Stability Subindex Rank	27
Government Waste Subindex Rank	71
Country Credit Rating Rank	32
Public Institutions Index Rank	**47**
Contracts and Law Subindex Rank	61
Corruption Subindex Rank	41
Technology Index Rank	**21**
Innovation Subindex Rank	45
ICT Subindex Rank	30
Technology Transfer Subindex Rank (out of 77 non-core innovators)	5

Business Competitiveness Index Rank	35

Sophistication of Company Operations and Strategy Rank	**33**
Quality of the National Business Environment Rank	**38**

The Most Problematic Factors for Doing Business

FACTOR

Factor	Percent of responses
Access to financing	19
Inefficient bureaucracy	17
Tax rates	16
Corruption	14
Tax regulations	8
Poor work ethic	8
Inadequate infrastructure	4
Policy instability	4
Inadequately educated workforce	3
Restrictive labor regulations	3
Crime and theft	2
Foreign currency regulations	1
Inflation	1
Government instability/coups	0

Percent of responses

Note: From a list of 14 factors, respondents were asked to select the five most problematic for doing business in their country and to rank them between 1 (most problematic) and 5. The bars in the figure show the responses weighted according to their rankings.

Source: World Economic Forum, Executive Opinion Survey (2003)

National competitiveness balance sheet

NOTABLE COMPETITIVE ADVANTAGES		
Growth Competitiveness Index		**Rank/102**
	Macroeconomic Environment	
2.20	Inflation, 2002	20
2.09	Access to credit	26
2.22	Interest rate spread, 2002	27
2.17	Country credit rating, 2003	32
2.01	Recession expectations	35
	Technology	
3.03	FDI and technology transfer	4
3.19	Cellular telephones, 2002	8
3.04	Prevalence of foreign technology licensing	12
3.21	Internet hosts, 2002	24
3.12	Internet access in schools	29
3.17	Utility patents, 2002	30
3.20	Internet users, 2002	31
3.22	Telephone lines, 2002	32
3.08	University/industry research collaboration	34
3.16	Laws relating to ICT	35
3.23	Personal computers, 2002	35
3.01	Technological sophistication	38

Business Competitiveness Index		Rank/95
	Sophistication of Company Operations and Strategy	
3.04	Prevalence of foreign technology licensing	17
10.02	Value chain presence	27
10.10	Extent of regional sales	28
	Quality of the National Business Environment	
3.19	Cellular telephones, 2002	7
4.03	Quality of math and science education	17
6.12	Centralization of economic policymaking	18

Other Indicators		Rank/102
4.05	Business impact of malaria	11
10.21	Pay and productivity	11
4.04	Disparity in healthcare quality	15
3.11	Availability of mobile or cellular telephones	16
4.08	Impact of HIV/AIDS on FDI	22
4.07	Business impact of HIV/AIDS	22
11.01	Air pollution regulations	22
11.02	Water pollution regulations	25
11.07	Compliance with international agreements	26
11.03	Toxic waste disposal regulations	27
11.08	Clarity and stability of regulations	27
2.10	Government intervention in corporate investment	27
4.06	Business impact of tuberculosis	28
11.04	Chemical waste regulations	29
10.18	Hiring and firing practices	29

NOTABLE COMPETITIVE DISADVANTAGES		
Growth Competitiveness Index		**Rank/102**
	Macroeconomic Environment	
2.21	Real exchange rate, 2002	85
2.03	Extent of distortive government subsidies	80
7.08	Diversion of public funds	69
7.10	Public trust of politicians	65
2.18	Government surplus/deficit, 2002	61
2.19	National savings rate, 2002	40
	Public Institutions	
6.03	Property rights	72
6.08	Favoritism in decisions of government officials	68
6.17	Organized crime	62
6.01	Judicial independence	46
7.03	Irregular payments in tax collection	45
7.01	Irregular payments in exports and imports	41
7.02	Irregular payments in public utilities	39
	Technology	
3.15	Government success in ICT promotion	77
3.14	Government prioritization of ICT	62
3.02	Firm-level technology absorption	53
3.13	Quality of competition in the ISP sector	47
3.18	Tertiary enrollment	45
3.06	Company spending on research and development	42

Business Competitiveness Index		Rank/95
	Sophistication of Company Operations and Strategy	
10.09	Control of international distribution	66
10.13	Willingness to delegate authority	54
10.12	Extent of staff training	49
	Quality of the National Business Environment	
2.11	Local equity market access	79
2.03	Extent of distortive government subsidies	73
10.24	Protection of minority shareholders' interests	71

Other Indicators		Rank/102
8.09	Wage equality of women in the workplace	93
10.22	Charitable causes involvement	87
8.11	Focus of trade and industry associations	83
10.23	Company promotion of volunteerism	80
10.25	Availability of company financial information	78
2.06	Soundness of banks	78
7.14	Pervasiveness of money laundering through non-bank channels	76
6.11	Efficiency of the tax system	75
11.12	Political context of environmental gains	73
6.07	Transparency of government policymaking	71
7.04	Irregular payments in public contracts	71
7.13	Pervasiveness of money laundering through banks	71
6.10	Effectiveness of law-making bodies	67
7.05	Irregular payments in loan applications	66
4.10	Maternity leave legislation	65

Note: The Business Competitiveness Index applies different criteria for selecting a country's competitive advantages and disadvantages. Please refer to the section "How Country Profiles Work" for further details.

Denmark

Competitiveness Rankings

Growth Competitiveness Index Rank	**4**

Macroeconomic Environment Index Rank **5**
    Macroeconomic Stability Subindex Rank 18
    Government Waste Subindex Rank 3
    Country Credit Rating Rank 10

Public Institutions Index Rank **1**
    Contracts and Law Subindex Rank 2
    Corruption Subindex Rank.....................................1

Technology Index Rank **8**
    Innovation Subindex Rank 11
    ICT Subindex Rank 4

Business Competitiveness Index Rank	**4**

**Sophistication of Company Operations
   and Strategy Rank** 7

**Quality of the National Business
   Environment Rank** 3

The Most Problematic Factors for Doing Business

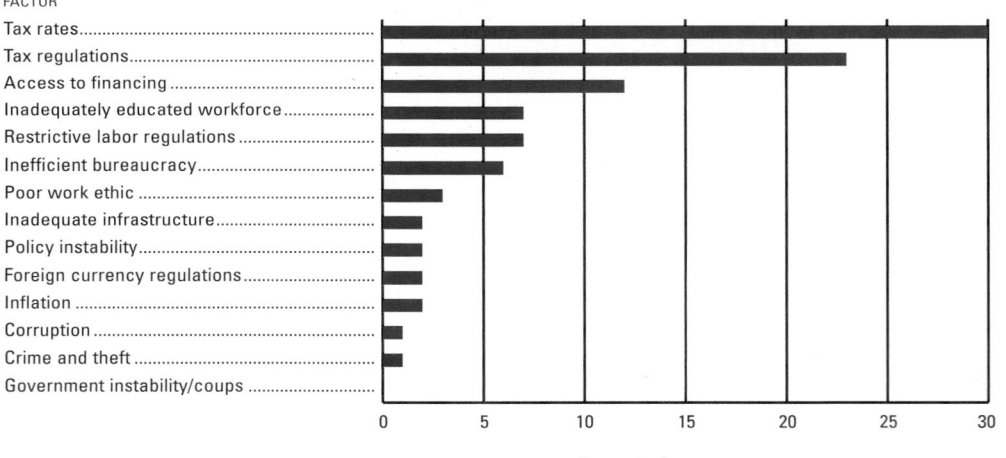

Note: From a list of 14 factors, respondents were asked to select the five most problematic for doing business in their country and to rank them between 1 (most problematic) and 5. The bars in the figure show the responses weighted according to their rankings.

Source: World Economic Forum, Executive Opinion Survey (2003)

National competitiveness balance sheet

NOTABLE COMPETITIVE ADVANTAGES		
Growth Competitiveness Index		**Rank/102**

Macroeconomic Environment

7.08	Diversion of public funds	1
7.10	Public trust of politicians	2
2.18	Government surplus/deficit, 2002	7
2.03	Extent of distortive government subsidies	7
2.17	Country credit rating, 2003	10

Public Institutions

6.08	Favoritism in decisions of government officials	1
7.01	Irregular payments in exports and imports	1
7.02	Irregular payments in public utilities	1
6.17	Organized crime	2
7.03	Irregular payments in tax collection	2
6.01	Judicial independence	4
6.03	Property rights	6

Technology

3.23	Personal computers, 2002	2
3.16	Laws relating to ICT	4
3.21	Internet hosts, 2002	5
3.22	Telephone lines, 2002	5
3.01	Technological sophistication	7
3.06	Company spending on research and development	8
3.12	Internet access in schools	8
3.13	Quality of competition in the ISP sector	9
3.14	Government prioritization of ICT	10
3.15	Government success in ICT promotion	10

Business Competitiveness Index		Rank/95

Sophistication of Company Operations and Strategy

10.12	Extent of staff training	1
10.13	Willingness to delegate authority	2
10.01	Nature of competitive advantage	4

Quality of the National Business Environment

7.09	Business costs of corruption	1
2.13	Effectiveness of bankruptcy law	1
6.08	Favoritism in decisions of government officials	1

Other Indicators		Rank/102

4.08	Impact of HIV/AIDS on FDI	1
6.05	Freedom of the press	1
6.16	Government effectiveness in reducing income inequality	1
6.15	Government effectiveness in reducing poverty	1
7.06	Irregular payments in government policymaking	1
7.05	Irregular payments in loan applications	1
4.04	Disparity in healthcare quality	2
4.06	Business impact of tuberculosis	2
7.07	Irregular payments in judicial decisions	2
10.05	Ethical behavior of firms	2
2.04	Extent of distortive government intervention	2
7.11	Prevalence of illegal political donations	2
7.04	Irregular payments in public contracts	2
4.05	Business impact of malaria	3
3.11	Availability of mobile or cellular telephones	3

NOTABLE COMPETITIVE DISADVANTAGES		
Growth Competitiveness Index		**Rank/102**

Macroeconomic Environment

2.19	National savings rate, 2002	41
2.21	Real exchange rate, 2002	38
2.22	Interest rate spread, 2002	38
2.20	Inflation, 2002	37
2.09	Access to credit	34
2.01	Recession expectations	32

Technology

3.18	Tertiary enrollment	15
3.19	Cellular telephones, 2002	14
3.02	Firm-level technology absorption	13
3.08	University/industry research collaboration	13
3.17	Utility patents, 2002	13
3.20	Internet users, 2002	11

Business Competitiveness Index		Rank/95

Sophistication of Company Operations and Strategy

10.14	Extent of incentive compensation	17
10.07	Extent of marketing	16

Quality of the National Business Environment

2.11	Local equity market access	50
6.09	Extent of bureaucratic red tape	41
4.03	Quality of math and science education	28

Other Indicators		Rank/102

10.22	Charitable causes involvement	97
6.11	Efficiency of the tax system	80
10.19	Flexibility of wage determination	76
10.23	Company promotion of volunteerism	56
2.15	Agricultural policy costs	34
8.09	Wage equality of women in the workplace	32
3.07	Subsidies and tax credits for firm-level research and development	32
4.11	Maternity laws' impact on hiring women	31
4.09	Brain drain	24
11.12	Political context of environmental gains	18
6.18	Informal sector	16
10.21	Pay and productivity	16
6.06	Burden of regulation	14
8.03	Extent of market dominance	13

225

Note: The Business Competitiveness Index applies different criteria for selecting a country's competitive advantages and disadvantages. Please refer to the section "How Country Profiles Work" for further details.

Dominican Republic

Competitiveness Rankings

Growth Competitiveness Index Rank	62

Macroeconomic Environment Index Rank **69**
    Macroeconomic Stability Subindex Rank 72
    Government Waste Subindex Rank 61
    Country Credit Rating Rank 63

Public Institutions Index Rank...**64**
    Contracts and Law Subindex Rank 53
    Corruption Subindex Rank....................................71

Technology Index Rank **52**
    Innovation Subindex Rank....................................55
    ICT Subindex Rank 61
    Technology Transfer Subindex Rank
    (out of 77 non-core innovators).........................13

Business Competitiveness Index Rank	61

**Sophistication of Company Operations
  and Strategy Rank** **57**
**Quality of the National Business
  Environment Rank** **62**

The Most Problematic Factors for Doing Business

Note: From a list of 14 factors, respondents were asked to select the five most problematic for doing business in their country and to rank them between 1 (most problematic) and 5. The bars in the figure show the responses weighted according to their rankings.

Source: World Economic Forum, Executive Opinion Survey (2003)

National competitiveness balance sheet

NOTABLE COMPETITIVE ADVANTAGES	
Growth Competitiveness Index	**Rank/102**

Macroeconomic Environment

2.18	Government surplus/deficit, 2002	15

Public Institutions

6.17	Organized crime	40

Technology

3.03	FDI and technology transfer	10
3.04	Prevalence of foreign technology licensing	21
3.02	Firm-level technology absorption	33
3.16	Laws relating to ICT	40
3.13	Quality of competition in the ISP sector	42
3.01	Technological sophistication	43
3.21	Internet hosts, 2002	46

NOTABLE COMPETITIVE DISADVANTAGES	
Growth Competitiveness Index	**Rank/102**

Macroeconomic Environment

2.21	Real exchange rate, 2002	79
2.01	Recession expectations	78
7.10	Public trust of politicians	74
2.09	Access to credit	71
2.22	Interest rate spread, 2002	70
2.20	Inflation, 2002	68
2.17	Country credit rating, 2003	63
2.03	Extent of distortive government subsidies	59
7.08	Diversion of public funds	59
2.19	National savings rate, 2002	54

Public Institutions

7.03	Irregular payments in tax collection	84
6.08	Favoritism in decisions of government officials	74
7.01	Irregular payments in exports and imports	73
6.01	Judicial independence	60
7.02	Irregular payments in public utilities	58
6.03	Property rights	54

Technology

3.20	Internet users, 2002	75
3.14	Government prioritization of ICT	74
3.15	Government success in ICT promotion	74
3.08	University/industry research collaboration	73
3.12	Internet access in schools	66
3.22	Telephone lines, 2002	64
3.19	Cellular telephones, 2002	62
3.17	Utility patents, 2002	61
3.06	Company spending on research and development	59
3.18	Tertiary enrollment	56

Business Competitiveness Index	Rank/95

Sophistication of Company Operations and Strategy

10.14	Extent of incentive compensation	29
3.04	Prevalence of foreign technology licensing	31
10.08	Degree of customer orientation	36

Quality of the National Business Environment

10.20	Cooperation in labor-employer relations	16
10.26	Foreign ownership restrictions	20
5.06	Telephone infrastructure quality	30

Business Competitiveness Index	Rank/95

Sophistication of Company Operations and Strategy

10.11	Breadth of international markets	78
10.15	Reliance on professional management	75
10.10	Extent of regional sales	72

Quality of the National Business Environment

5.05	Quality of electricity supply	90
3.10	Availability of scientists and engineers	84
9.07	Extent of collaboration among clusters	81

Other Indicators	Rank/102

2.02	Business costs of terrorism	7
4.11	Maternity laws' impact on hiring women	12
10.21	Pay and productivity	26
2.06	Soundness of banks	29
8.08	Private sector employment of women	33
4.09	Brain drain	33
3.11	Availability of mobile or cellular telephones	34
4.10	Maternity leave legislation	34
2.15	Agricultural policy costs	37
4.06	Business impact of tuberculosis	39
10.23	Company promotion of volunteerism	42
6.14	Business costs of crime and violence	43
6.11	Efficiency of the tax system	44
8.11	Focus of trade and industry associations	46
6.06	Burden of regulation	46

Other Indicators	Rank/102

5.07	Postal efficiency	98
7.06	Irregular payments in government policymaking	90
11.08	Clarity and stability of regulations	86
11.07	Compliance with international agreements	85
11.11	Effects of compliance on business	82
3.07	Subsidies and tax credits for firm-level research and development	80
11.10	Consistency of regulation enforcement	80
8.03	Extent of market dominance	79
10.25	Availability of company financial information	79
6.10	Effectiveness of law-making bodies	77
6.07	Transparency of government policymaking	76
7.12	Policy consequences of legal political donations	74
7.07	Irregular payments in judicial decisions	74
11.13	Prevalence of environmental management systems	73
4.04	Disparity in healthcare quality	73

227

Note: The Business Competitiveness Index applies different criteria for selecting a country's competitive advantages and disadvantages. Please refer to the section "How Country Profiles Work" for further details.

Ecuador

Competitiveness Rankings

Growth Competitiveness Index Rank	86

Macroeconomic Environment Index Rank **90**
    Macroeconomic Stability Subindex Rank 83
    Government Waste Subindex Rank 95
    Country Credit Rating Rank 81

Public Institutions Index Rank **80**
    Contracts and Law Subindex Rank 89
    Corruption Subindex Rank 63

Technology Index Rank **76**
    Innovation Subindex Rank 72
    ICT Subindex Rank 72
    Technology Transfer Subindex Rank
    (out of 77 non-core innovators) 62

Business Competitiveness Index Rank	84

**Sophistication of Company Operations
   and Strategy Rank** 82
**Quality of the National Business
   Environment Rank** 86

The Most Problematic Factors for Doing Business

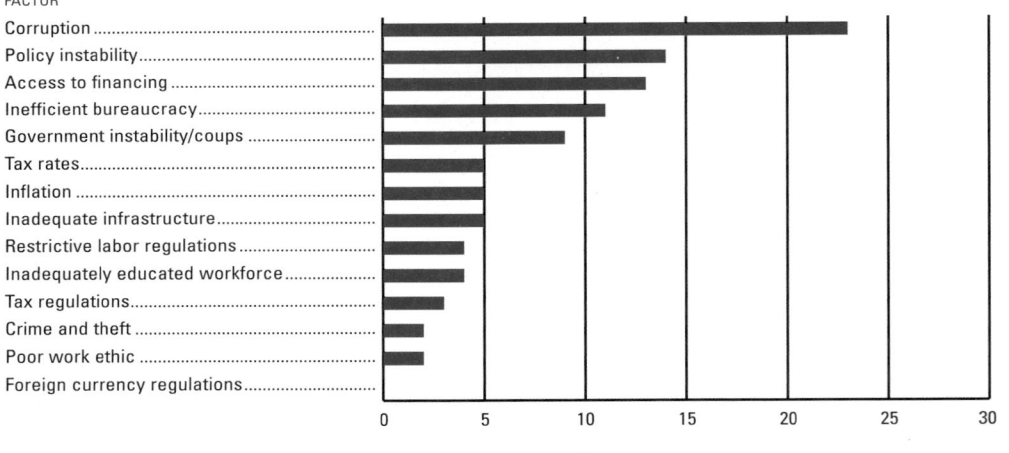

FACTOR
Corruption
Policy instability
Access to financing
Inefficient bureaucracy
Government instability/coups
Tax rates
Inflation
Inadequate infrastructure
Restrictive labor regulations
Inadequately educated workforce
Tax regulations
Crime and theft
Poor work ethic
Foreign currency regulations

0   5   10   15   20   25   30

Percent of responses

Note: From a list of 14 factors, respondents were asked to select the five most problematic for doing business in their country and to rank them between 1 (most problematic) and 5. The bars in the figure show the responses weighted according to their rankings.

Source: World Economic Forum, Executive Opinion Survey (2003)

National competitiveness balance sheet

NOTABLE COMPETITIVE ADVANTAGES	
Growth Competitiveness Index	**Rank/102**

Macroeconomic Environment

2.19	National savings rate, 2002 44

NOTABLE COMPETITIVE DISADVANTAGES	
Growth Competitiveness Index	**Rank/102**

Macroeconomic Environment

7.10	Public trust of politicians 95
2.09	Access to credit 91
7.08	Diversion of public funds 89
2.03	Extent of distortive government subsidies 88
2.20	Inflation, 2002 88
2.17	Country credit rating, 2003 81
2.18	Government surplus/deficit, 2002 80
2.01	Recession expectations 71
2.21	Real exchange rate, 2002 68
2.22	Interest rate spread, 2002..68

Public Institutions

6.08	Favoritism in decisions of government officials.............96
6.01	Judicial independence..94
6.03	Property rights..85
7.02	Irregular payments in public utilities 70
7.01	Irregular payments in exports and imports 68
6.17	Organized crime 66
7.03	Irregular payments in tax collection 65

Technology

3.14	Government prioritization of ICT 95
3.15	Government success in ICT promotion 94
3.02	Firm-level technology absorption 90
3.13	Quality of competition in the ISP sector........................90
3.06	Company spending on research and development 88
3.08	University/industry research collaboration 87
3.12	Internet access in schools 83
3.16	Laws relating to ICT 81
3.01	Technological sophistication..77
3.17	Utility patents, 2002 72
3.21	Internet hosts, 2002 72
3.19	Cellular telephones, 2002 66
3.20	Internet users, 2002 65
3.23	Personal computers, 2002 64
3.22	Telephone lines, 2002 63
3.18	Tertiary enrollment 61
3.03	FDI and technology transfer..60
3.04	Prevalence of foreign technology licensing 55

Business Competitiveness Index	Rank/95

Sophistication of Company Operations and Strategy

10.01	Nature of competitive advantage.....................................60
10.07	Extent of marketing..74
10.10	Extent of regional sales...75

Quality of the National Business Environment

6.09	Extent of bureaucratic red tape.......................................43
3.20	Internet users, 2002...63
3.19	Cellular telephones, 2002...64

Other Indicators	Rank/102

Business Competitiveness Index	Rank/95

Sophistication of Company Operations and Strategy

10.08	Degree of customer orientation.......................................91
10.15	Reliance on professional management............................89
10.12	Extent of staff training 84

Quality of the National Business Environment

9.05	Decentralization of corporate activity.............................93
2.13	Effectiveness of bankruptcy law.....................................92
5.02	Railroad infrastructure development...............................92

Other Indicators	Rank/102
7.12	Policy consequences of legal political donations 100
11.08	Clarity and stability of regulations 99
8.03	Extent of market dominance..99
11.12	Political context of environmental gains 99
11.10	Consistency of regulation enforcement..........................98
11.09	Flexibility of regulations...98
2.06	Soundness of banks...98
11.11	Effects of compliance on business 97
6.10	Effectiveness of law-making bodies 97
11.04	Chemical waste regulations...96
6.15	Government effectiveness in reducing poverty.............96
11.07	Compliance with international agreements 95
7.07	Irregular payments in judicial decisions 95

229

Note: The Business Competitiveness Index applies different criteria for selecting a country's competitive advantages and disadvantages. Please refer to the section "How Country Profiles Work" for further details.

Egypt

Competitiveness Rankings

Growth Competitiveness Index Rank	58

Macroeconomic Environment Index Rank **56**
  Macroeconomic Stability Subindex Rank 63
  Government Waste Subindex Rank 45
  Country Credit Rating Rank 53

Public Institutions Index Rank...**57**
  Contracts and Law Subindex Rank 47
  Corruption Subindex Rank....................................67

Technology Index Rank **68**
  Innovation Subindex Rank 39
  ICT Subindex Rank 69
  Technology Transfer Subindex Rank
    (out of 77 non-core innovators).........................44

Business Competitiveness Index Rank	58

**Sophistication of Company Operations
  and Strategy Rank** **55**

**Quality of the National Business
  Environment Rank** **61**

The Most Problematic Factors for Doing Business

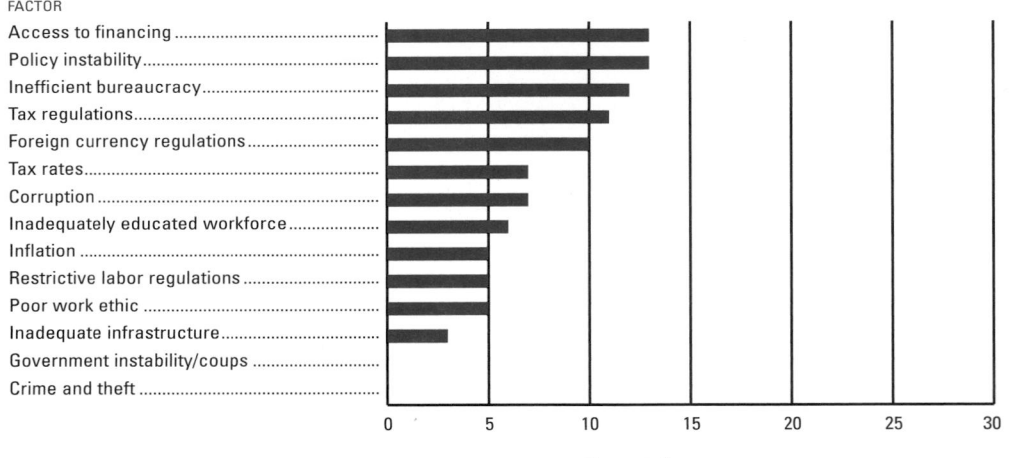

FACTOR

Access to financing
Policy instability
Inefficient bureaucracy
Tax regulations
Foreign currency regulations
Tax rates
Corruption
Inadequately educated workforce
Inflation
Restrictive labor regulations
Poor work ethic
Inadequate infrastructure
Government instability/coups
Crime and theft

Percent of responses

Note: From a list of 14 factors, respondents were asked to select the five most problematic for doing business in their country and to rank them between 1 (most problematic) and 5. The bars in the figure show the responses weighted according to their rankings.

Source: World Economic Forum, Executive Opinion Survey (2003)

National competitiveness balance sheet

NOTABLE COMPETITIVE ADVANTAGES

Growth Competitiveness Index	Rank/102

Macroeconomic Environment

2.22	Interest rate spread, 2002	35
7.08	Diversion of public funds	39
2.03	Extent of distortive government subsidies	40
2.20	Inflation, 2002	40
7.10	Public trust of politicians	41

Public Institutions

6.08	Favoritism in decisions of government officials	26
6.17	Organized crime	45

Technology

3.13	Quality of competition in the ISP sector	33
3.15	Government success in ICT promotion	35
3.18	Tertiary enrollment	37
3.04	Prevalence of foreign technology licensing	40
3.12	Internet access in schools	42
3.14	Government prioritization of ICT	42
3.03	FDI and technology transfer	46

Business Competitiveness Index	Rank/95

Sophistication of Company Operations and Strategy

10.09	Control of international distribution	27
10.08	Degree of customer orientation	33
10.06	Production process sophistication	36

Quality of the National Business Environment

8.07	Prevalence of mergers and acquisitions	26
9.09	Local availability of process machinery	29
9.06	State of cluster development	30

Other Indicators	Rank/102

8.03	Extent of market dominance	17
7.11	Prevalence of illegal political donations	27
7.04	Irregular payments in public contracts	35
8.11	Focus of trade and industry associations	36
8.10	Regional disparities in quality of business environment	38
7.14	Pervasiveness of money laundering through non-bank channels	39
8.09	Wage equality of women in the workplace	40
2.15	Agricultural policy costs	40
6.10	Effectiveness of law-making bodies	40
7.12	Policy consequences of legal political donations	41
10.19	Flexibility of wage determination	42
10.22	Charitable causes involvement	43
11.13	Prevalence of environmental management systems	43
7.13	Pervasiveness of money laundering through banks	43
7.07	Irregular payments in judicial decisions	43

NOTABLE COMPETITIVE DISADVANTAGES

Growth Competitiveness Index	Rank/102

Macroeconomic Environment

2.09	Access to credit	78
2.18	Government surplus/deficit, 2002	73
2.19	National savings rate, 2002	73
2.01	Recession expectations	61
2.21	Real exchange rate, 2002	61
2.17	Country credit rating, 2003	53

Public Institutions

7.02	Irregular payments in public utilities	84
7.03	Irregular payments in tax collection	66
6.01	Judicial independence	59
6.03	Property rights	58
7.01	Irregular payments in exports and imports	54

Technology

3.21	Internet hosts, 2002	86
3.19	Cellular telephones, 2002	74
3.20	Internet users, 2002	74
3.23	Personal computers, 2002	74
3.02	Firm-level technology absorption	71
3.17	Utility patents, 2002	64
3.16	Laws relating to ICT	63
3.22	Telephone lines, 2002	61
3.08	University/industry research collaboration	54
3.01	Technological sophistication	52
3.06	Company spending on research and development	52

Business Competitiveness Index	Rank/95

Sophistication of Company Operations and Strategy

10.10	Extent of regional sales	79
3.06	Company spending on research and development	77
10.14	Extent of incentive compensation	70

Quality of the National Business Environment

3.09	Government procurement of advanced technology products	85
3.08	University/industry research collaboration	84
6.09	Extent of bureaucratic red tape	84

Other Indicators	Rank/102

6.05	Freedom of the press	90
2.02	Business costs of terrorism	89
2.06	Soundness of banks	88
11.12	Political context of environmental gains	84
6.07	Transparency of government policymaking	79
3.11	Availability of mobile or cellular telephones	79
4.11	Maternity laws' impact on hiring women	72
4.06	Business impact of tuberculosis	71
4.05	Business impact of malaria	70
10.27	Strength of auditing and accounting standards	68
7.05	Irregular payments in loan applications	68
11.08	Clarity and stability of regulations	67
11.07	Compliance with international agreements	66
2.10	Government intervention in corporate investment	66
11.09	Flexibility of regulations	63

231

Note: The Business Competitiveness Index applies different criteria for selecting a country's competitive advantages and disadvantages. Please refer to the section "How Country Profiles Work" for further details.

El Salvador

Competitiveness Rankings

Growth Competitiveness Index Rank	48

Macroeconomic Environment Index Rank **48**
   Macroeconomic Stability Subindex Rank 40
   Government Waste Subindex Rank 47
   Country Credit Rating Rank 56

Public Institutions Index Rank **40**
   Contracts and Law Subindex Rank 64
   Corruption Subindex Rank 31

Technology Index Rank **67**
   Innovation Subindex Rank 67
   ICT Subindex Rank 68
   Technology Transfer Subindex Rank
   (out of 77 non-core innovators) 34

Business Competitiveness Index Rank	63

**Sophistication of Company Operations
  and Strategy Rank** **58**
**Quality of the National Business
  Environment Rank** **64**

The Most Problematic Factors for Doing Business

FACTOR

Crime and theft
Inefficient bureaucracy
Inadequately educated workforce
Inadequate infrastructure
Access to financing
Policy instability
Tax rates
Corruption
Tax regulations
Restrictive labor regulations
Poor work ethic
Foreign currency regulations
Inflation
Government instability/coups

Percent of responses

Note: From a list of 14 factors, respondents were asked to select the five most problematic for doing business in their country and to rank them between 1 (most problematic) and 5. The bars in the figure show the responses weighted according to their rankings.

Source: World Economic Forum, Executive Opinion Survey (2003)

National competitiveness balance sheet

NOTABLE COMPETITIVE ADVANTAGES

Growth Competitiveness Index	Rank/102

Macroeconomic Environment

2.09	Access to credit	6
2.20	Inflation, 2002	24
2.22	Interest rate spread, 2002	24
7.08	Diversion of public funds	33
2.03	Extent of distortive government subsidies	44
2.01	Recession expectations	46
2.18	Government surplus/deficit, 2002	46

Public Institutions

7.02	Irregular payments in public utilities	29
7.01	Irregular payments in exports and imports	32
7.03	Irregular payments in tax collection	32
6.03	Property rights	42
6.08	Favoritism in decisions of government officials	46

Technology

3.03	FDI and technology transfer	36
3.04	Prevalence of foreign technology licensing	37
3.13	Quality of competition in the ISP sector	43

Business Competitiveness Index	Rank/95

Sophistication of Company Operations and Strategy

10.01	Nature of competitive advantage	35
10.10	Extent of regional sales	40
10.02	Value chain presence	43

Quality of the National Business Environment

6.09	Extent of bureaucratic red tape	10
10.20	Cooperation in labor-employer relations	18
5.06	Telephone infrastructure quality	25

Other Indicators	Rank/102

6.11	Efficiency of the tax system	9
10.19	Flexibility of wage determination	11
2.04	Extent of distortive government intervention	15
2.10	Government intervention in corporate investment	18
10.22	Charitable causes involvement	20
7.05	Irregular payments in loan applications	22
7.04	Irregular payments in public contracts	25
7.13	Pervasiveness of money laundering through banks	27
10.21	Pay and productivity	27
3.11	Availability of mobile or cellular telephones	27
7.11	Prevalence of illegal political donations	29
6.06	Burden of regulation	29
6.05	Freedom of the press	29
2.06	Soundness of banks	32
7.14	Pervasiveness of money laundering through non-bank channels	37

NOTABLE COMPETITIVE DISADVANTAGES

Growth Competitiveness Index	Rank/102

Macroeconomic Environment

2.21	Real exchange rate, 2002	93
2.19	National savings rate, 2002	85
2.17	Country credit rating, 2003	56
7.10	Public trust of politicians	52

Public Institutions

6.17	Organized crime	89
6.01	Judicial independence	75

Technology

3.08	University/industry research collaboration	99
3.21	Internet hosts, 2002	81
3.06	Company spending on research and development	77
3.16	Laws relating to ICT	74
3.14	Government prioritization of ICT	72
3.17	Utility patents, 2002	72
3.23	Personal computers, 2002	70
3.12	Internet access in schools	67
3.22	Telephone lines, 2002	67
3.19	Cellular telephones, 2002	63
3.15	Government success in ICT promotion	62
3.18	Tertiary enrollment	60
3.20	Internet users, 2002	57
3.02	Firm-level technology absorption	52
3.01	Technological sophistication	49

Business Competitiveness Index	Rank/95

Sophistication of Company Operations and Strategy

3.06	Company spending on research and development	70
10.04	Capacity for innovation	70
10.11	Breadth of international markets	70

Quality of the National Business Environment

3.08	University/industry research collaboration	93
5.02	Railroad infrastructure development	93
3.10	Availability of scientists and engineers	91

Other Indicators	Rank/102

3.07	Subsidies and tax credits for firm-level research and development	100
11.13	Prevalence of environmental management systems	97
6.14	Business costs of crime and violence	92
11.11	Effects of compliance on business	88
6.10	Effectiveness of law-making bodies	87
11.10	Consistency of regulation enforcement	82
2.02	Business costs of terrorism	80
5.07	Postal efficiency	80
11.07	Compliance with international agreements	78
4.10	Maternity leave legislation	76
11.08	Clarity and stability of regulations	75
11.09	Flexibility of regulations	75
11.06	Compliance with environmental regulations	75
10.25	Availability of company financial information	73
6.18	Informal sector	72

233

Note: The Business Competitiveness Index applies different criteria for selecting a country's competitive advantages and disadvantages. Please refer to the section "How Country Profiles Work" for further details.

Estonia

Competitiveness Rankings

Growth Competitiveness Index Rank	**22**

Macroeconomic Environment Index Rank **34**
   Macroeconomic Stability Subindex Rank 25
   Government Waste Subindex Rank 26
   Country Credit Rating Rank 36

Public Institutions Index Rank **28**
   Contracts and Law Subindex Rank 32
   Corruption Subindex Rank....................................27

Technology Index Rank **10**
   Innovation Subindex Rank.....................................26
   ICT Subindex Rank 20
   Technology Transfer Subindex Rank
   (out of 77 non-core innovators) 11

Business Competitiveness Index Rank	**28**

**Sophistication of Company Operations
and Strategy Rank** **36**

**Quality of the National Business
Environment Rank** **27**

The Most Problematic Factors for Doing Business

FACTOR

Percent of responses

Note: From a list of 14 factors, respondents were asked to select the five most problematic for doing business in their country and to rank them between 1 (most problematic) and 5. The bars in the figure show the responses weighted according to their rankings.

Source: World Economic Forum, Executive Opinion Survey (2003)

National competitiveness balance sheet

<table>
<tr><td colspan="3">NOTABLE COMPETITIVE ADVANTAGES</td></tr>
<tr><td colspan="2">Growth Competitiveness Index</td><td>Rank/102</td></tr>
</table>

Macroeconomic Environment

2.09	Access to credit	5
2.01	Recession expectations	6
2.18	Government surplus/deficit, 2002	10
2.03	Extent of distortive government subsidies	11

Technology

3.03	FDI and technology transfer	3
3.13	Quality of competition in the ISP sector	5
3.16	Laws relating to ICT	6
3.15	Government success in ICT promotion	12
3.12	Internet access in schools	13
3.20	Internet users, 2002	16
3.18	Tertiary enrollment	17
3.21	Internet hosts, 2002	17
3.14	Government prioritization of ICT	18
3.02	Firm-level technology absorption	19

Business Competitiveness Index — **Rank/95**

Sophistication of Company Operations and Strategy

10.15	Reliance on professional management	27
10.06	Production process sophistication	29
10.13	Willingness to delegate authority	29

Quality of the National Business Environment

8.05	Administrative burden for startups	4
3.16	Laws relating to ICT	6
2.16	Cost of importing foreign equipment	10

Other Indicators — **Rank/102**

10.19	Flexibility of wage determination	2
2.02	Business costs of terrorism	3
6.11	Efficiency of the tax system	4
6.06	Burden of regulation	6
2.04	Extent of distortive government intervention	9
4.05	Business impact of malaria	9
10.21	Pay and productivity	10
8.03	Extent of market dominance	12
6.10	Effectiveness of law-making bodies	12
2.10	Government intervention in corporate investment	17
2.15	Agricultural policy costs	19
3.11	Availability of mobile or cellular telephones	20
6.05	Freedom of the press	20
11.08	Clarity and stability of regulations	21
11.07	Compliance with international agreements	21

<table>
<tr><td colspan="3">NOTABLE COMPETITIVE DISADVANTAGES</td></tr>
<tr><td colspan="2">Growth Competitiveness Index</td><td>Rank/102</td></tr>
</table>

Macroeconomic Environment

2.21	Real exchange rate, 2002	84
2.19	National savings rate, 2002	58
2.20	Inflation, 2002	57
2.17	Country credit rating, 2003	36
7.08	Diversion of public funds	34
7.10	Public trust of politicians	33
2.22	Interest rate spread, 2002	31

Public Institutions

6.17	Organized crime	41
6.03	Property rights	32
7.02	Irregular payments in public utilities	31
6.08	Favoritism in decisions of government officials	29
7.01	Irregular payments in exports and imports	27
7.03	Irregular payments in tax collection	26
6.01	Judicial independence	22

Technology

3.06	Company spending on research and development	44
3.08	University/industry research collaboration	41
3.22	Telephone lines, 2002	35
3.17	Utility patents, 2002	29
3.23	Personal computers, 2002	28
3.04	Prevalence of foreign technology licensing	27
3.19	Cellular telephones, 2002	26
3.01	Technological sophistication	24

Business Competitiveness Index — **Rank/95**

Sophistication of Company Operations and Strategy

10.09	Control of international distribution	67
10.01	Nature of competitive advantage	66
10.03	Extent of branding	65

Quality of the National Business Environment

9.06	State of cluster development	67
10.24	Protection of minority shareholders' interests	65
9.09	Local availability of process machinery	59

235

Other Indicators — **Rank/102**

4.10	Maternity leave legislation	99
10.22	Charitable causes involvement	99
11.12	Political context of environmental gains	88
4.11	Maternity laws' impact on hiring women	84
8.10	Regional disparities in quality of business environment	82
10.23	Company promotion of volunteerism	64
8.11	Focus of trade and industry associations	63
8.09	Wage equality of women in the workplace	59
6.16	Government effectiveness in reducing income inequality	57
6.15	Government effectiveness in reducing poverty	56
3.07	Subsidies and tax credits for firm-level research and development	55
4.08	Impact of HIV/AIDS on FDI	55
4.07	Business impact of HIV/AIDS	54
4.06	Business impact of tuberculosis	53
7.12	Policy consequences of legal political donations	50

Note: The Business Competitiveness Index applies different criteria for selecting a country's competitive advantages and disadvantages. Please refer to the section "How Country Profiles Work" for further details.

Ethiopia

Competitiveness Rankings

Growth Competitiveness Index Rank	92

Macroeconomic Environment Index Rank **84**
    Macroeconomic Stability Subindex Rank 74
    Government Waste Subindex Rank 66
    Country Credit Rating Rank 98

Public Institutions Index Rank **73**
    Contracts and Law Subindex Rank 68
    Corruption Subindex Rank.....................................76

Technology Index Rank **100**
    Innovation Subindex Rank.....................................100
    ICT Subindex Rank 101
    Technology Transfer Subindex Rank
    (out of 77 non-core innovators) 73

Business Competitiveness Index Rank	90

**Sophistication of Company Operations
  and Strategy Rank** **91**
**Quality of the National Business
  Environment Rank** **88**

The Most Problematic Factors for Doing Business

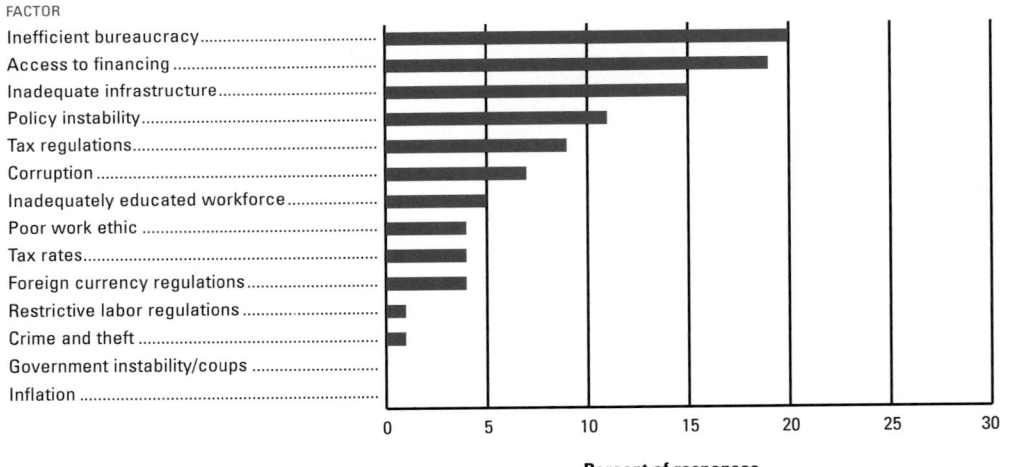

FACTOR

Inefficient bureaucracy
Access to financing
Inadequate infrastructure
Policy instability
Tax regulations
Corruption
Inadequately educated workforce
Poor work ethic
Tax rates
Foreign currency regulations
Restrictive labor regulations
Crime and theft
Government instability/coups
Inflation

Percent of responses

Note: From a list of 14 factors, respondents were asked to select the five most problematic for doing business in their country and to rank them between 1 (most problematic) and 5. The bars in the figure show the responses weighted according to their rankings.

Source: World Economic Forum, Executive Opinion Survey (2003)

National competitiveness balance sheet

NOTABLE COMPETITIVE ADVANTAGES

Growth Competitiveness Index	Rank/102
Macroeconomic Environment	
2.20 Inflation, 2002	1
2.21 Real exchange rate, 2002	14
2.22 Interest rate spread, 2002	37
Public Institutions	
6.17 Organized crime	39

NOTABLE COMPETITIVE DISADVANTAGES

Growth Competitiveness Index	Rank/102
Macroeconomic Environment	
2.18 Government surplus/deficit, 2002	101
2.19 National savings rate, 2002	100
2.17 Country credit rating, 2003	98
2.09 Access to credit	95
2.03 Extent of distortive government subsidies	91
2.01 Recession expectations	86
7.10 Public trust of politicians	58
7.08 Diversion of public funds	52
Public Institutions	
6.01 Judicial independence	87
7.03 Irregular payments in tax collection	86
6.03 Property rights	83
7.02 Irregular payments in public utilities	81
6.08 Favoritism in decisions of government officials	66
7.01 Irregular payments in exports and imports	61
Technology	
3.01 Technological sophistication	102
3.13 Quality of competition in the ISP sector	102
3.19 Cellular telephones, 2002	102
3.20 Internet users, 2002	102
3.06 Company spending on research and development	101
3.16 Laws relating to ICT	101
3.12 Internet access in schools	99
3.21 Internet hosts, 2002	99
3.02 Firm-level technology absorption	98
3.23 Personal computers, 2002	97
3.18 Tertiary enrollment	96
3.22 Telephone lines, 2002	95
3.08 University/industry research collaboration	92
3.14 Government prioritization of ICT	86
3.15 Government success in ICT promotion	84
3.04 Prevalence of foreign technology licensing	74
3.03 FDI and technology transfer	73
3.17 Utility patents, 2002	72

237

Business Competitiveness Index	Rank/95
Sophistication of Company Operations and Strategy	
10.09 Control of international distribution	68
10.08 Degree of customer orientation	77
10.01 Nature of competitive advantage	80
Quality of the National Business Environment	
5.04 Air transport infrastructure quality	37
6.13 Reliability of police services	50
10.17 Efficacy of corporate boards	52

Business Competitiveness Index	Rank/95
Sophistication of Company Operations and Strategy	
10.12 Extent of staff training	95
10.07 Extent of marketing	94
10.14 Extent of incentive compensation	94
Quality of the National Business Environment	
3.19 Cellular telephones, 2002	95
10.26 Foreign ownership restrictions	95
8.04 Sophistication of local buyers' products and processes	94

Other Indicators	Rank/102
10.19 Flexibility of wage determination	21
8.03 Extent of market dominance	25
4.11 Maternity laws' impact on hiring women	32
7.13 Pervasiveness of money laundering through banks	36
7.14 Pervasiveness of money laundering through non-bank channels	40
7.11 Prevalence of illegal political donations	40
7.12 Policy consequences of legal political donations	42
4.10 Maternity leave legislation	42
6.14 Business costs of crime and violence	45
8.09 Wage equality of women in the workplace	45
11.11 Effects of compliance on business	48

Other Indicators	Rank/102
3.11 Availability of mobile or cellular telephones	100
11.09 Flexibility of regulations	99
11.03 Toxic waste disposal regulations	99
2.15 Agricultural policy costs	99
2.04 Extent of distortive government intervention	99
4.08 Impact of HIV/AIDS on FDI	98
10.21 Pay and productivity	98
4.06 Business impact of tuberculosis	97
8.08 Private sector employment of women	97
2.10 Government intervention in corporate investment	97
8.10 Regional disparities in quality of business environment	96
11.01 Air pollution regulations	96
11.06 Compliance with environmental regulations	95
11.02 Water pollution regulations	95
11.04 Chemical waste regulations	95

Note: The Business Competitiveness Index applies different criteria for selecting a country's competitive advantages and disadvantages. Please refer to the section "How Country Profiles Work" for further details.

Finland

Competitiveness Rankings

Growth Competitiveness Index Rank	1

Macroeconomic Environment Index Rank 2
    Macroeconomic Stability Subindex Rank 7
    Government Waste Subindex Rank 2
    Country Credit Rating Rank 11

Public Institutions Index Rank 2
    Contracts and Law Subindex Rank 1
    Corruption Subindex Rank......................................4

Technology Index Rank 2
    Innovation Subindex Rank.....................................3
    ICT Subindex Rank 2

Business Competitiveness Index Rank	1

**Sophistication of Company Operations
and Strategy Rank** 4

**Quality of the National Business
Environment Rank** 1

The Most Problematic Factors for Doing Business

FACTOR

Tax rates..
Restrictive labor regulations ....
Tax regulations...
Inefficient bureaucracy......................................
Access to financing ....
Poor work ethic ....
Policy instability..
Inadequately educated workforce....................
Foreign currency regulations............................
Inadequate infrastructure..................................
Inflation ....
Crime and theft ....
Corruption...
Government instability/coups ....

0   5   10   15   20   25   30

Percent of responses

Note: From a list of 14 factors, respondents were asked to select the five most problematic for doing business in their country and to rank them between 1 (most problematic) and 5. The bars in the figure show the responses weighted according to their rankings.

Source: World Economic Forum, Executive Opinion Survey (2003)

National competitiveness balance sheet

NOTABLE COMPETITIVE ADVANTAGES

Growth Competitiveness Index	Rank/102
Macroeconomic Environment	
7.08 Diversion of public funds	2
2.03 Extent of distortive government subsidies	3
2.18 Government surplus/deficit, 2002	3
7.10 Public trust of politicians	3
Public Institutions	
6.01 Judicial independence	1
6.03 Property rights	2
6.08 Favoritism in decisions of government officials	2
6.17 Organized crime	3
7.03 Irregular payments in tax collection	3
7.02 Irregular payments in public utilities	4
7.01 Irregular payments in exports and imports	5
Technology	
3.01 Technological sophistication	1
3.02 Firm-level technology absorption	1
3.08 University/industry research collaboration	1
3.16 Laws relating to ICT	1
3.18 Tertiary enrollment	1
3.12 Internet access in schools	1
3.06 Company spending on research and development	2
3.14 Government prioritization of ICT	3
3.21 Internet hosts, 2002	3
3.15 Government success in ICT promotion	5
3.17 Utility patents, 2002	7
3.20 Internet users, 2002	7
3.19 Cellular telephones, 2002	10

Business Competitiveness Index	Rank/95
Sophistication of Company Operations and Strategy	
10.04 Capacity for innovation	1
10.06 Production process sophistication	1
10.02 Value chain presence	1
Quality of the National Business Environment	
9.07 Extent of collaboration among clusters	1
9.06 State of cluster development	1
3.08 University/industry research collaboration	1

Other Indicators	Rank/102
7.13 Pervasiveness of money laundering through banks	1
10.05 Ethical behavior of firms	1
11.13 Prevalence of environmental management systems	1
4.07 Business impact of HIV/AIDS	1
2.10 Government intervention in corporate investment	1
3.11 Availability of mobile or cellular telephones	1
7.14 Pervasiveness of money laundering through non-bank channels	2
6.14 Business costs of crime and violence	2
11.11 Effects of compliance on business	2
5.07 Postal efficiency	2
2.02 Business costs of terrorism	2
6.16 Government effectiveness in reducing income inequality	2
11.10 Consistency of regulation enforcement	2
4.09 Brain drain	2
11.04 Chemical waste regulations	2

NOTABLE COMPETITIVE DISADVANTAGES

Growth Competitiveness Index	Rank/102
Macroeconomic Environment	
2.01 Recession expectations	69
2.20 Inflation, 2002	32
2.21 Real exchange rate, 2002	22
2.22 Interest rate spread, 2002	21
2.19 National savings rate, 2002	18
2.17 Country credit rating, 2003	11
2.09 Access to credit	11
Technology	
3.22 Telephone lines, 2002	16
3.23 Personal computers, 2002	12

Business Competitiveness Index	Rank/95
Quality of the National Business Environment	
6.09 Extent of bureaucratic red tape	64
8.02 Extent of locally based competitors	26
2.11 Local equity market access	20

Other Indicators	Rank/102
10.19 Flexibility of wage determination	101
10.22 Charitable causes involvement	77
10.23 Company promotion of volunteerism	50
2.15 Agricultural policy costs	38
10.21 Pay and productivity	30
8.03 Extent of market dominance	30
10.18 Hiring and firing practices	27
8.09 Wage equality of women in the workplace	27
4.11 Maternity laws' impact on hiring women	24
4.05 Business impact of malaria	20
8.10 Regional disparities in quality of business environment	19
6.15 Government effectiveness in reducing poverty	13
6.11 Efficiency of the tax system	12

Note: The Business Competitiveness Index applies different criteria for selecting a country's competitive advantages and disadvantages. Please refer to the section "How Country Profiles Work" for further details.

France

Competitiveness Rankings

Growth Competitiveness Index Rank	**26**

Macroeconomic Environment Index Rank **20**
    Macroeconomic Stability Subindex Rank 36
    Government Waste Subindex Rank 39
    Country Credit Rating Rank 8

Public Institutions Index Rank..**23**
    Contracts and Law Subindex Rank 27
    Corruption Subindex Rank....................................23

Technology Index Rank **28**
    Innovation Subindex Rank 19
    ICT Subindex Rank 23

Business Competitiveness Index Rank	**10**

**Sophistication of Company Operations
and Strategy Rank** 9

**Quality of the National Business
Environment Rank** 14

The Most Problematic Factors for Doing Business

FACTOR

Restrictive labor regulations
Tax regulations
Tax rates
Inefficient bureaucracy
Access to financing
Inadequately educated workforce
Policy instability
Poor work ethic
Foreign currency regulations
Inflation
Crime and theft
Corruption
Inadequate infrastructure
Government instability/coups

Percent of responses

Note: From a list of 14 factors, respondents were asked to select the five most problematic for doing business in their country and to rank them between 1 (most problematic) and 5. The bars in the figure show the responses weighted according to their rankings.

Source: World Economic Forum, Executive Opinion Survey (2003)

National competitiveness balance sheet

NOTABLE COMPETITIVE ADVANTAGES		NOTABLE COMPETITIVE DISADVANTAGES	
Growth Competitiveness Index	**Rank/102**	**Growth Competitiveness Index**	**Rank/102**

	Macroeconomic Environment				Macroeconomic Environment	
2.17	Country credit rating, 2003	8		2.01	Recession expectations	80
2.22	Interest rate spread, 2002	22		2.03	Extent of distortive government subsidies	65
2.20	Inflation, 2002	24		2.09	Access to credit	52
	Public Institutions			2.18	Government surplus/deficit, 2002	47
7.02	Irregular payments in public utilities	16		2.19	National savings rate, 2002	47
6.03	Property rights	20		7.10	Public trust of politicians	37
6.08	Favoritism in decisions of government officials	21		7.08	Diversion of public funds	31
7.01	Irregular payments in exports and imports	23		2.21	Real exchange rate, 2002	28
	Technology				**Public Institutions**	
3.06	Company spending on research and development	9		6.01	Judicial independence	42
3.16	Laws relating to ICT	13		7.03	Irregular payments in tax collection	28
3.22	Telephone lines, 2002	13		6.17	Organized crime	26
3.01	Technological sophistication	14			**Technology**	
3.17	Utility patents, 2002	16		3.12	Internet access in schools	31
3.08	University/industry research collaboration	19		3.02	Firm-level technology absorption	27
3.18	Tertiary enrollment	21		3.19	Cellular telephones, 2002	27
3.23	Personal computers, 2002	22		3.14	Government prioritization of ICT	26
3.21	Internet hosts, 2002	23		3.15	Government success in ICT promotion	26
3.13	Quality of competition in the ISP sector	24				
3.20	Internet users, 2002	25				

Business Competitiveness Index	**Rank/95**	**Business Competitiveness Index**	**Rank/95**

	Sophistication of Company Operations and Strategy				Sophistication of Company Operations and Strategy	
10.09	Control of international distribution	1		10.13	Willingness to delegate authority	21
10.03	Extent of branding	4		10.08	Degree of customer orientation	20
10.07	Extent of marketing	4			**Quality of the National Business Environment**	
	Quality of the National Business Environment			10.20	Cooperation in labor-employer relations	91
10.16	Quality of management schools	2		8.05	Administrative burden for startups	75
4.03	Quality of math and science education	3		2.03	Extent of distortive government subsidies	61
5.02	Railroad infrastructure development	3				

	Other Indicators	**Rank/102**			Other Indicators	**Rank/102**
6.18	Informal sector	4		10.18	Hiring and firing practices	97
11.09	Flexibility of regulations	5		8.09	Wage equality of women in the workplace	96
10.27	Strength of auditing and accounting standards	7		6.06	Burden of regulation	90
11.11	Effects of compliance on business	8		6.11	Efficiency of the tax system	79
3.07	Subsidies and tax credits for firm-level research and development	8		10.23	Company promotion of volunteerism	76
7.13	Pervasiveness of money laundering through banks	11		10.22	Charitable causes involvement	65
11.08	Clarity and stability of regulations	11		10.19	Flexibility of wage determination	63
3.11	Availability of mobile or cellular telephones	12		2.02	Business costs of terrorism	52
4.10	Maternity leave legislation	12		2.15	Agricultural policy costs	48
4.04	Disparity in healthcare quality	13		10.21	Pay and productivity	43
7.14	Pervasiveness of money laundering through non-bank channels	14		2.04	Extent of distortive government intervention	43
11.01	Air pollution regulations	15		4.09	Brain drain	40
10.05	Ethical behavior of firms	16		2.10	Government intervention in corporate investment	36
11.04	Chemical waste regulations	16		8.08	Private sector employment of women	35
11.03	Toxic waste disposal regulations	16		6.14	Business costs of crime and violence	35

241

Note: The Business Competitiveness Index applies different criteria for selecting a country's competitive advantages and disadvantages. Please refer to the section "How Country Profiles Work" for further details.

Gambia

Competitiveness Rankings

Growth Competitiveness Index Rank	**55**

Macroeconomic Environment Index Rank **46**
    Macroeconomic Stability Subindex Rank 75
    Government Waste Subindex Rank 24
    Country Credit Rating Rank ....n/a

Public Institutions Index Rank..**39**
    Contracts and Law Subindex Rank 23
    Corruption Subindex Rank...................................58

Technology Index Rank **80**
    Innovation Subindex Rank 96
    ICT Subindex Rank 73
    Technology Transfer Subindex Rank
    (out of 77 non-core innovators)........................58

Business Competitiveness Index Rank	**n/a**

**Sophistication of Company Operations
  and Strategy Rank** ....**n/a**

**Quality of the National Business
  Environment Rank**...**n/a**

The Most Problematic Factors for Doing Business

FACTOR

Access to financing
Inflation
Inadequate infrastructure
Inadequately educated workforce
Foreign currency regulations
Tax rates
Poor work ethic
Tax regulations
Inefficient bureaucracy
Policy instability
Corruption
Government instability/coups
Crime and theft
Restrictive labor regulations

0   5   10   15   20   25   30

Percent of responses

Note: From a list of 14 factors, respondents were asked to select the five most problematic for doing business in their country and to rank them between 1 (most problematic) and 5. The bars in the figure show the responses weighted according to
their rankings.

Source: World Economic Forum, Executive Opinion Survey (2003)

National competitiveness balance sheet

NOTABLE COMPETITIVE ADVANTAGES	
Growth Competitiveness Index	**Rank/102**

Macroeconomic Environment

2.21	Real exchange rate, 2002	5
2.03	Extent of distortive government subsidies	19
7.10	Public trust of politicians	28
7.08	Diversion of public funds	29

Public Institutions

6.17	Organized crime	18
6.08	Favoritism in decisions of government officials	20
6.01	Judicial independence	30
6.03	Property rights	34
7.01	Irregular payments in exports and imports	46

Technology

3.15	Government success in ICT promotion	9
3.14	Government prioritization of ICT	13
3.02	Firm-level technology absorption	42
3.03	FDI and technology transfer	44
3.13	Quality of competition in the ISP sector	46

Other Indicators	**Rank/102**

4.11	Maternity laws' impact on hiring women	6
2.10	Government intervention in corporate investment	8
6.06	Burden of regulation	8
11.08	Clarity and stability of regulations	9
10.22	Charitable causes involvement	9
11.09	Flexibility of regulations	13
6.11	Efficiency of the tax system	13
10.18	Hiring and firing practices	15
11.11	Effects of compliance on business	16
7.13	Pervasiveness of money laundering through banks	16
7.14	Pervasiveness of money laundering through non-bank channels	16
6.15	Government effectiveness in reducing poverty	16
2.02	Business costs of terrorism	16
8.09	Wage equality of women in the workplace	16
4.10	Maternity leave legislation	17

NOTABLE COMPETITIVE DISADVANTAGES	
Growth Competitiveness Index	**Rank/102**

Macroeconomic Environment

2.18	Government surplus/deficit, 2002	91
2.22	Interest rate spread, 2002	82
2.19	National savings rate, 2002	81
2.20	Inflation, 2002	77
2.01	Recession expectations	59
2.09	Access to credit	56

Public Institutions

7.02	Irregular payments in public utilities	73
7.03	Irregular payments in tax collection	61

Technology

3.08	University/industry research collaboration	101
3.06	Company spending on research and development	96
3.18	Tertiary enrollment	95
3.01	Technological sophistication	87
3.16	Laws relating to ICT	83
3.20	Internet users, 2002	83
3.22	Telephone lines, 2002	83
3.23	Personal computers, 2002	78
3.12	Internet access in schools	78
3.19	Cellular telephones, 2002	73
3.17	Utility patents, 2002	72
3.21	Internet hosts, 2002	69
3.04	Prevalence of foreign technology licensing	65

Other Indicators	**Rank/102**

4.05	Business impact of malaria	102
4.06	Business impact of tuberculosis	91
4.09	Brain drain	89
3.07	Subsidies and tax credits for firm-level research and development	89
4.07	Business impact of HIV/AIDS	83
5.07	Postal efficiency	74
6.05	Freedom of the press	71
4.08	Impact of HIV/AIDS on FDI	69
7.05	Irregular payments in loan applications	61
3.11	Availability of mobile or cellular telephones	59
10.27	Strength of auditing and accounting standards	56
8.08	Private sector employment of women	54
11.04	Chemical waste regulations	53
11.02	Water pollution regulations	52
11.03	Toxic waste disposal regulations	51

243

Note: This country is not included in the coverage of the Business Competitiveness Index 2003–2004.

Germany

Competitiveness Rankings

Growth Competitiveness Index Rank	13

Macroeconomic Environment Index Rank **21**
    Macroeconomic Stability Subindex Rank 48
    Government Waste Subindex Rank 32
    Country Credit Rating Rank 7

Public Institutions Index Rank............................**9**
    Contracts and Law Subindex Rank 9
    Corruption Subindex Rank 10

Technology Index Rank **14**
    Innovation Subindex Rank 10
    ICT Subindex Rank 17

Business Competitiveness Index Rank	5

**Sophistication of Company Operations
and Strategy Rank** **1**

**Quality of the National Business
Environment Rank** **9**

The Most Problematic Factors for Doing Business

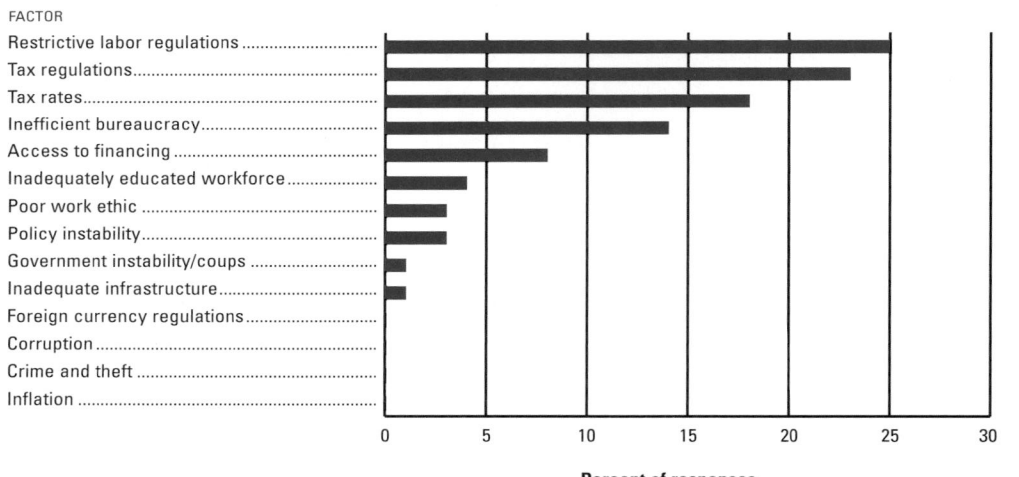

Note: From a list of 14 factors, respondents were asked to select the five most problematic for doing business in their country and to rank them between 1 (most problematic) and 5. The bars in the figure show the responses weighted according to their rankings.

Source: World Economic Forum, Executive Opinion Survey (2003)

National competitiveness balance sheet

NOTABLE COMPETITIVE ADVANTAGES

Growth Competitiveness Index	Rank/102

Macroeconomic Environment

2.17 Country credit rating, 2003 7

Public Institutions

7.02 Irregular payments in public utilities 5
6.01 Judicial independence..8
6.08 Favoritism in decisions of government officials...............8
6.03 Property rights...11

Technology

3.08 University/industry research collaboration 5
3.06 Company spending on research and development 6
3.22 Telephone lines, 2002 7
3.17 Utility patents, 2002 8
3.02 Firm-level technology absorption 11
3.13 Quality of competition in the ISP sector 11

Business Competitiveness Index	Rank/95

Sophistication of Company Operations and Strategy

10.03 Extent of branding...1
10.10 Extent of regional sales..1
10.11 Breadth of international markets.......................................2

Quality of the National Business Environment

9.05 Decentralization of corporate activity...............................1
9.04 Presence of demanding regulatory standards 1
11.05 Stringency of environmental regulations 1

Other Indicators	Rank/102

11.10 Consistency of regulation enforcement...........................1
8.03 Extent of market dominance..1
11.01 Air pollution regulations...1
11.03 Toxic waste disposal regulations.....................................1
11.02 Water pollution regulations 1
11.04 Chemical waste regulations 1
11.07 Compliance with international agreements 2
11.06 Compliance with environmental regulations....................2
4.06 Business impact of tuberculosis 3
11.09 Flexibility of regulations..4
11.13 Prevalence of environmental management systems........4
11.12 Political context of environmental gains 4
6.05 Freedom of the press 4
7.07 Irregular payments in judicial decisions 5
3.11 Availability of mobile or cellular telephones....................5

NOTABLE COMPETITIVE DISADVANTAGES

Growth Competitiveness Index	Rank/102

Macroeconomic Environment

2.03 Extent of distortive government subsidies 100
2.01 Recession expectations 91
2.09 Access to credit 82
2.22 Interest rate spread, 2002..57
2.18 Government surplus/deficit, 2002....................................54
2.19 National savings rate, 2002..42
2.21 Real exchange rate, 2002 18
2.20 Inflation, 2002...15
7.08 Diversion of public funds 15

Public Institutions

6.17 Organized crime..19
7.01 Irregular payments in exports and imports.....................13
7.03 Irregular payments in tax collection 13

Technology

3.14 Government prioritization of ICT......................................38
3.15 Government success in ICT promotion 37
3.18 Tertiary enrollment...31
3.12 Internet access in schools 23
3.19 Cellular telephones, 2002..23
3.21 Internet hosts, 2002...21
3.01 Technological sophistication..16
3.20 Internet users, 2002...15
3.16 Laws relating to ICT 14
3.23 Personal computers, 2002 13

Business Competitiveness Index	Rank/95

Quality of the National Business Environment

2.03 Extent of distortive government subsidies 93
4.03 Quality of math and science education...........................51
4.01 Quality of the educational system 44

Other Indicators	Rank/102

10.19 Flexibility of wage determination 102
6.11 Efficiency of the tax system 102
10.18 Hiring and firing practices 101
4.11 Maternity laws' impact on hiring women 97
2.15 Agricultural policy costs 90
2.02 Business costs of terrorism...86
2.04 Extent of distortive government intervention 73
2.10 Government intervention in corporate investment.........68
10.21 Pay and productivity...63
8.09 Wage equality of women in the workplace 61
2.06 Soundness of banks...55
8.08 Private sector employment of women 54
6.10 Effectiveness of law-making bodies 42
7.11 Prevalence of illegal political donations.........................38
8.11 Focus of trade and industry associations.......................38

245

Note: The Business Competitiveness Index applies different criteria for selecting a country's competitive advantages and disadvantages. Please refer to the section "How Country Profiles Work" for further details.

Ghana

Competitiveness Rankings

Growth Competitiveness Index Rank	**71**

Macroeconomic Environment Index Rank **68**
    Macroeconomic Stability Subindex Rank 70
    Government Waste Subindex Rank 46
    Country Credit Rating Rank 79

Public Institutions Index Rank **65**
    Contracts and Law Subindex Rank 50
    Corruption Subindex Rank 79

Technology Index Rank **86**
    Innovation Subindex Rank 83
    ICT Subindex Rank 88
    Technology Transfer Subindex Rank
       (out of 77 non-core innovators) 45

Business Competitiveness Index Rank	n/a

**Sophistication of Company Operations
  and Strategy Rank** ....n/a

**Quality of the National Business
  Environment Rank** ....n/a

The Most Problematic Factors for Doing Business

FACTOR

Factor	
Access to financing	
Inflation	
Inadequate infrastructure	
Inefficient bureaucracy	
Corruption	
Poor work ethic	
Tax rates	
Foreign currency regulations	
Government instability/coups	
Inadequately educated workforce	
Policy instability	
Tax regulations	
Crime and theft	
Restrictive labor regulations	

Percent of responses

Note: From a list of 14 factors, respondents were asked to select the five most problematic for doing business in their country and to rank them between 1 (most problematic) and 5. The bars in the figure show the responses weighted according to their rankings.

Source: World Economic Forum, Executive Opinion Survey (2003)

National competitiveness balance sheet

NOTABLE COMPETITIVE ADVANTAGES		NOTABLE COMPETITIVE DISADVANTAGES	
Growth Competitiveness Index	**Rank/102**	**Growth Competitiveness Index**	**Rank/102**

Macroeconomic Environment		**Macroeconomic Environment**	
2.21	Real exchange rate, 2002 13	2.20	Inflation, 2002 92
2.03	Extent of distortive government subsidies 20	2.22	Interest rate spread, 2002........................81
2.01	Recession expectations 22	2.17	Country credit rating, 2003 79
2.19	National savings rate, 2002.............................37	2.18	Government surplus/deficit, 2002.....................75
7.10	Public trust of politicians 46	2.09	Access to credit 71
7.08	Diversion of public funds 50	**Public Institutions**	
Public Institutions		7.02	Irregular payments in public utilities 87
6.01	Judicial independence....................................50	7.01	Irregular payments in exports and imports 69
6.17	Organized crime 50	7.03	Irregular payments in tax collection 69
Technology		6.03	Property rights..61
3.14	Government prioritization of ICT 17	6.08	Favoritism in decisions of government officials.............55
3.15	Government success in ICT promotion 22	**Technology**	
3.03	FDI and technology transfer............................34	3.20	Internet users, 2002......................................97
3.04	Prevalence of foreign technology licensing 47	3.21	Internet hosts, 2002.......................................93
		3.23	Personal computers, 2002 92
		3.18	Tertiary enrollment 89
		3.22	Telephone lines, 2002 88
		3.19	Cellular telephones, 2002...............................86
		3.12	Internet access in schools 85
		3.01	Technological sophistication...........................74
		3.17	Utility patents, 2002.......................................72
		3.13	Quality of competition in the ISP sector........................65
		3.02	Firm-level technology absorption 57
		3.08	University/industry research collaboration 57
		3.06	Company spending on research and development 56
		3.16	Laws relating to ICT 53

Other Indicators	Rank/102	Other Indicators	Rank/102
2.15	Agricultural policy costs 10	4.09	Brain drain 96
6.10	Effectiveness of law-making bodies 14	4.05	Business impact of malaria 90
8.09	Wage equality of women in the workplace 14	3.11	Availability of mobile or cellular telephones 87
10.18	Hiring and firing practices 18	4.07	Business impact of HIV/AIDS 86
11.13	Prevalence of environmental management systems......20	10.21	Pay and productivity......................................84
2.04	Extent of distortive government intervention 20	4.06	Business impact of tuberculosis 84
11.11	Effects of compliance on business 22	4.08	Impact of HIV/AIDS on FDI 83
6.11	Efficiency of the tax system 22	7.05	Irregular payments in loan applications........................82
10.22	Charitable causes involvement 23	10.19	Flexibility of wage determination 81
11.12	Political context of environmental gains 24	8.08	Private sector employment of women 75
2.10	Government intervention in corporate investment.........26	6.18	Informal sector 75
11.09	Flexibility of regulations..................................27	10.25	Availability of company financial information 68
6.06	Burden of regulation.......................................27	10.27	Strength of auditing and accounting standards 66
11.08	Clarity and stability of regulations 28	7.11	Prevalence of illegal political donations.........................62
6.07	Transparency of government policymaking....................29	3.07	Subsidies and tax credits for firm-level research and development 62

247

Note: This country is not included in the coverage of the Business Competitiveness Index 2003–2004.

Greece

Competitiveness Rankings

Growth Competitiveness Index Rank	**35**

Macroeconomic Environment Index Rank **33**
    Macroeconomic Stability Subindex Rank 45
    Government Waste Subindex Rank 49
    Country Credit Rating Rank 23

Public Institutions Index Rank **42**
    Contracts and Law Subindex Rank 37
    Corruption Subindex Rank 52

Technology Index Rank **30**
    Innovation Subindex Rank 31
    ICT Subindex Rank 33
    Technology Transfer Subindex Rank
    (out of 77 non-core innovators) 27

Business Competitiveness Index Rank	**39**

**Sophistication of Company Operations
  and Strategy Rank** **39**
**Quality of the National Business
  Environment Rank** **40**

The Most Problematic Factors for Doing Business

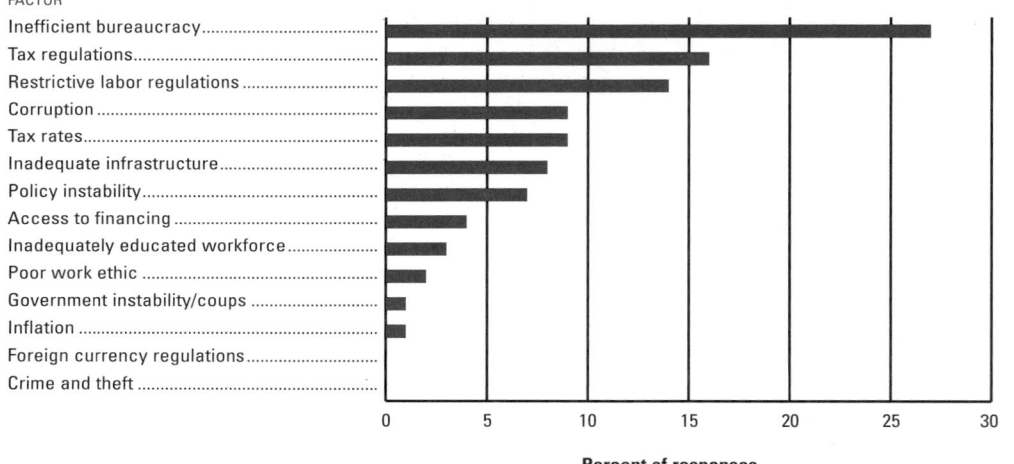

FACTOR

Inefficient bureaucracy
Tax regulations
Restrictive labor regulations
Corruption
Tax rates
Inadequate infrastructure
Policy instability
Access to financing
Inadequately educated workforce
Poor work ethic
Government instability/coups
Inflation
Foreign currency regulations
Crime and theft

Percent of responses

Note: From a list of 14 factors, respondents were asked to select the five most problematic for doing business in their country and to rank them between 1 (most problematic) and 5. The bars in the figure show the responses weighted according to their rankings.

Source: World Economic Forum, Executive Opinion Survey (2003)

National competitiveness balance sheet

NOTABLE COMPETITIVE ADVANTAGES

Growth Competitiveness Index		Rank/102
Macroeconomic Environment		
2.09	Access to credit	17
2.17	Country credit rating, 2003	23
2.18	Government surplus/deficit, 2002	30
Public Institutions		
6.17	Organized crime	22
Technology		
3.04	Prevalence of foreign technology licensing	8
3.19	Cellular telephones, 2002	9
3.22	Telephone lines, 2002	18
3.18	Tertiary enrollment	26

Business Competitiveness Index		Rank/95
Sophistication of Company Operations and Strategy		
10.07	Extent of marketing	30
10.10	Extent of regional sales	32
10.14	Extent of incentive compensation	34
Quality of the National Business Environment		
3.19	Cellular telephones, 2002	11
3.10	Availability of scientists and engineers	19
2.16	Cost of importing foreign equipment	19

Other Indicators		Rank/102
4.08	Impact of HIV/AIDS on FDI	19
6.05	Freedom of the press	24
6.14	Business costs of crime and violence	24
4.05	Business impact of malaria	25
3.07	Subsidies and tax credits for firm-level research and development	26
4.06	Business impact of tuberculosis	26
10.25	Availability of company financial information	28
4.07	Business impact of HIV/AIDS	29

NOTABLE COMPETITIVE DISADVANTAGES

Growth Competitiveness Index		Rank/102
Macroeconomic Environment		
2.19	National savings rate, 2002	71
2.20	Inflation, 2002	54
2.03	Extent of distortive government subsidies	49
2.21	Real exchange rate, 2002	45
7.10	Public trust of politicians	44
7.08	Diversion of public funds	42
2.22	Interest rate spread, 2002	38
2.01	Recession expectations	38
Public Institutions		
7.03	Irregular payments in tax collection	75
6.08	Favoritism in decisions of government officials	70
7.02	Irregular payments in public utilities	42
6.03	Property rights	41
7.01	Irregular payments in exports and imports	39
6.01	Judicial independence	35
Technology		
3.02	Firm-level technology absorption	78
3.15	Government success in ICT promotion	72
3.14	Government prioritization of ICT	68
3.16	Laws relating to ICT	64
3.01	Technological sophistication	63
3.03	FDI and technology transfer	47
3.06	Company spending on research and development	47
3.12	Internet access in schools	47
3.23	Personal computers, 2002	45
3.13	Quality of competition in the ISP sector	39
3.20	Internet users, 2002	37
3.21	Internet hosts, 2002	36
3.08	University/industry research collaboration	35
3.17	Utility patents, 2002	35

Business Competitiveness Index		Rank/95
Sophistication of Company Operations and Strategy		
10.15	Reliance on professional management	69
10.13	Willingness to delegate authority	60
10.04	Capacity for innovation	47
Quality of the National Business Environment		
3.09	Government procurement of advanced technology products	68
8.05	Administrative burden for startups	66
6.08	Favoritism in decisions of government officials	63

Other Indicators		Rank/102
10.19	Flexibility of wage determination	91
6.11	Efficiency of the tax system	88
10.18	Hiring and firing practices	81
4.11	Maternity laws' impact on hiring women	78
6.06	Burden of regulation	75
6.07	Transparency of government policymaking	67
7.04	Irregular payments in public contracts	65
11.11	Effects of compliance on business	65
10.21	Pay and productivity	62
7.12	Policy consequences of legal political donations	62
10.23	Company promotion of volunteerism	62
10.22	Charitable causes involvement	62
2.15	Agricultural policy costs	62
2.10	Government intervention in corporate investment	61
10.05	Ethical behavior of firms	60

Note: The Business Competitiveness Index applies different criteria for selecting a country's competitive advantages and disadvantages. Please refer to the section "How Country Profiles Work" for further details.

Guatemala

Competitiveness Rankings

Growth Competitiveness Index Rank	89

Macroeconomic Environment Index Rank **85**
Macroeconomic Stability Subindex Rank 84
Government Waste Subindex Rank 98
Country Credit Rating Rank 69

Public Institutions Index Rank **87**
Contracts and Law Subindex Rank 97
Corruption Subindex Rank...................................68

Technology Index Rank **79**
Innovation Subindex Rank 79
ICT Subindex Rank 77
Technology Transfer Subindex Rank
(out of 77 non-core innovators).......................54

Business Competitiveness Index Rank	81

**Sophistication of Company Operations
and Strategy Rank** **75**
**Quality of the National Business
Environment Rank** **83**

The Most Problematic Factors for Doing Business

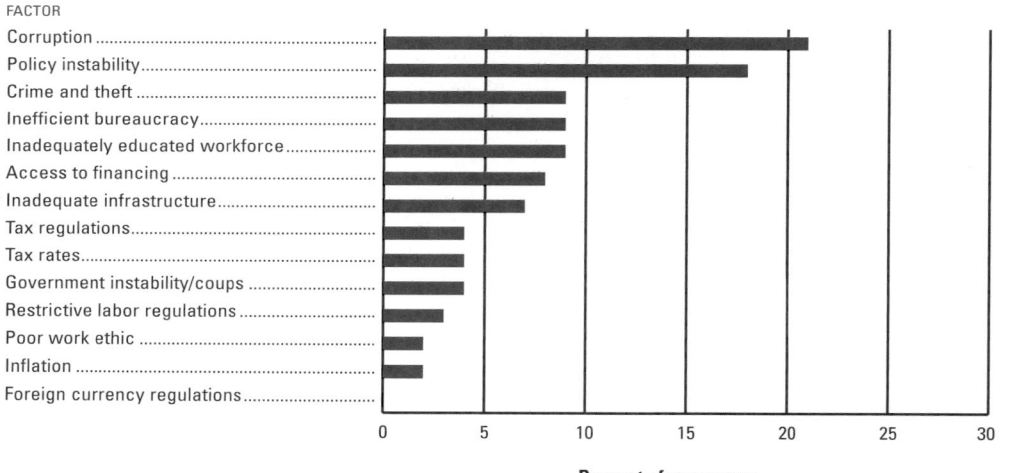

FACTOR
Corruption
Policy instability
Crime and theft
Inefficient bureaucracy
Inadequately educated workforce
Access to financing
Inadequate infrastructure
Tax regulations
Tax rates
Government instability/coups
Restrictive labor regulations
Poor work ethic
Inflation
Foreign currency regulations

Percent of responses

Note: From a list of 14 factors, respondents were asked to select the five most problematic for doing business in their country and to rank them between 1 (most problematic) and 5. The bars in the figure show the responses weighted according to their rankings.

Source: World Economic Forum, Executive Opinion Survey (2003)

National competitiveness balance sheet

NOTABLE COMPETITIVE ADVANTAGES	
Growth Competitiveness Index	**Rank/102**

Macroeconomic Environment

2.18	Government surplus/deficit, 2002	18

Technology

3.03	FDI and technology transfer	43

NOTABLE COMPETITIVE DISADVANTAGES	
Growth Competitiveness Index	**Rank/102**

Macroeconomic Environment

7.08	Diversion of public funds	101
7.10	Public trust of politicians	100
2.01	Recession expectations	94
2.19	National savings rate, 2002	90
2.21	Real exchange rate, 2002	89
2.20	Inflation, 2002	74
2.22	Interest rate spread, 2002	72
2.03	Extent of distortive government subsidies	70
2.17	Country credit rating, 2003	69
2.09	Access to credit	61

Public Institutions

6.17	Organized crime	102
6.08	Favoritism in decisions of government officials	100
6.01	Judicial independence	90
6.03	Property rights	84
7.03	Irregular payments in tax collection	81
7.01	Irregular payments in exports and imports	66
7.02	Irregular payments in public utilities	63

Technology

3.14	Government prioritization of ICT	102
3.15	Government success in ICT promotion	101
3.16	Laws relating to ICT	92
3.08	University/industry research collaboration	81
3.02	Firm-level technology absorption	81
3.12	Internet access in schools	79
3.06	Company spending on research and development	78
3.18	Tertiary enrollment	77
3.23	Personal computers, 2002	77
3.01	Technological sophistication	76
3.17	Utility patents, 2002	72
3.22	Telephone lines, 2002	70
3.20	Internet users, 2002	69
3.19	Cellular telephones, 2002	64
3.21	Internet hosts, 2002	64
3.04	Prevalence of foreign technology licensing	62
3.13	Quality of competition in the ISP sector	51

251

Business Competitiveness Index	Rank/95

Sophistication of Company Operations and Strategy

10.10	Extent of regional sales	53
10.01	Nature of competitive advantage	61
10.02	Value chain presence	63

Quality of the National Business Environment

6.09	Extent of bureaucratic red tape	4
5.06	Telephone infrastructure quality	49
10.20	Cooperation in labor-employer relations	50

Other Indicators	Rank/102

3.11	Availability of mobile or cellular telephones	45
8.11	Focus of trade and industry associations	47
4.06	Business impact of tuberculosis	49

Business Competitiveness Index	Rank/95

Sophistication of Company Operations and Strategy

10.15	Reliance on professional management	86
3.04	Prevalence of foreign technology licensing	82
10.08	Degree of customer orientation	76

Quality of the National Business Environment

4.02	Quality of public schools	95
4.03	Quality of math and science education	94
6.13	Reliability of police services	93

Other Indicators	Rank/102

6.07	Transparency of government policymaking	102
6.14	Business costs of crime and violence	102
2.10	Government intervention in corporate investment	101
11.08	Clarity and stability of regulations	101
7.14	Pervasiveness of money laundering through non-bank channels	101
7.13	Pervasiveness of money laundering through banks	101
11.11	Effects of compliance on business	100
11.07	Compliance with international agreements	99
7.06	Irregular payments in government policymaking	99
6.15	Government effectiveness in reducing poverty	99
7.04	Irregular payments in public contracts	98
6.16	Government effectiveness in reducing income inequality	98

Note: The Business Competitiveness Index applies different criteria for selecting a country's competitive advantages and disadvantages. Please refer to the section "How Country Profiles Work" for further details.

Haiti

Competitiveness Rankings

Growth Competitiveness Index Rank	102

Macroeconomic Environment Index Rank **99**
    Macroeconomic Stability Subindex Rank 93
    Government Waste Subindex Rank 99
    Country Credit Rating Rank 94

Public Institutions Index Rank.......................................**102**
    Contracts and Law Subindex Rank 102
    Corruption Subindex Rank..................................100

Technology Index Rank **101**
    Innovation Subindex Rank 99
    ICT Subindex Rank 96
    Technology Transfer Subindex Rank
    (out of 77 non-core innovators).......................77

Business Competitiveness Index Rank	94

**Sophistication of Company Operations
  and Strategy Rank** **95**

**Quality of the National Business
  Environment Rank** **94**

The Most Problematic Factors for Doing Business

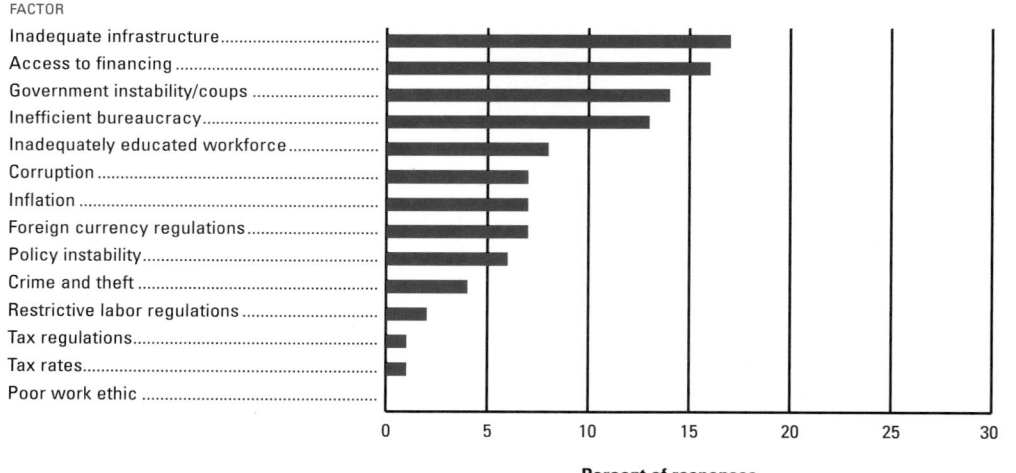

Note: From a list of 14 factors, respondents were asked to select the five most problematic for doing business in their country and to rank them between 1 (most problematic) and 5. The bars in the figure show the responses weighted according to their rankings.

Source: World Economic Forum, Executive Opinion Survey (2003)

National competitiveness balance sheet

NOTABLE COMPETITIVE ADVANTAGES	
Growth Competitiveness Index	**Rank/102**

Macroeconomic Environment

2.09	Access to credit	33

NOTABLE COMPETITIVE DISADVANTAGES	
Growth Competitiveness Index	**Rank/102**

Macroeconomic Environment

7.10	Public trust of politicians	102
2.01	Recession expectations	99
7.08	Diversion of public funds	98
2.21	Real exchange rate, 2002	95
2.22	Interest rate spread, 2002	95
2.17	Country credit rating, 2003	94
2.03	Extent of distortive government subsidies	86
2.20	Inflation, 2002	81
2.19	National savings rate, 2002	65
2.18	Government surplus/deficit, 2002	51

Public Institutions

6.01	Judicial independence	102
6.03	Property rights	101
6.08	Favoritism in decisions of government officials	101
7.02	Irregular payments in public utilities	101
7.03	Irregular payments in tax collection	101
6.17	Organized crime	98
7.01	Irregular payments in exports and imports	96

Technology

3.16	Laws relating to ICT	102
3.01	Technological sophistication	101
3.06	Company spending on research and development	100
3.08	University/industry research collaboration	100
3.14	Government prioritization of ICT	100
3.15	Government success in ICT promotion	100
3.18	Tertiary enrollment	97
3.12	Internet access in schools	96
3.02	Firm-level technology absorption	89
3.13	Quality of competition in the ISP sector	88
3.20	Internet users, 2002	88
3.19	Cellular telephones, 2002	87
3.22	Telephone lines, 2002	87
3.03	FDI and technology transfer	76
3.04	Prevalence of foreign technology licensing	76
3.17	Utility patents, 2002	72

Business Competitiveness Index	**Rank/95**

Sophistication of Company Operations and Strategy

10.02	Value chain presence	74

Quality of the National Business Environment

6.09	Extent of bureaucratic red tape	19
10.20	Cooperation in labor-employer relations	42
2.14	Hidden trade barriers	64

Business Competitiveness Index	**Rank/95**

Sophistication of Company Operations and Strategy

10.06	Production process sophistication	95
10.11	Breadth of international markets	95
10.15	Reliance on professional management	95

Quality of the National Business Environment

3.05	Quality of scientific research institutions	95
3.16	Laws relating to ICT	95
9.04	Presence of demanding regulatory standards	95

Other Indicators	**Rank/102**

10.18	Hiring and firing practices	12
7.12	Policy consequences of legal political donations	14
10.19	Flexibility of wage determination	18
8.08	Private sector employment of women	27
2.06	Soundness of banks	39
6.11	Efficiency of the tax system	43
4.11	Maternity laws' impact on hiring women	49

Other Indicators	**Rank/102**

11.08	Clarity and stability of regulations	102
11.07	Compliance with international agreements	102
6.10	Effectiveness of law-making bodies	102
11.06	Compliance with environmental regulations	102
11.02	Water pollution regulations	102
11.10	Consistency of regulation enforcement	102
11.01	Air pollution regulations	102
11.09	Flexibility of regulations	102
6.18	Informal sector	102
8.10	Regional disparities in quality of business environment	102
4.08	Impact of HIV/AIDS on FDI	102
10.23	Company promotion of volunteerism	102
4.09	Brain drain	102
7.06	Irregular payments in government policymaking	101
6.15	Government effectiveness in reducing poverty	101

253

Note: The Business Competitiveness Index applies different criteria for selecting a country's competitive advantages and disadvantages.
Please refer to the section "How Country Profiles Work" for further details.

Honduras

Competitiveness Rankings

Growth Competitiveness Index Rank	**94**

Macroeconomic Environment Index Rank **88**
    Macroeconomic Stability Subindex Rank 85
    Government Waste Subindex Rank 93
    Country Credit Rating Rank 77

Public Institutions Index Rank **99**
    Contracts and Law Subindex Rank 95
    Corruption Subindex Rank 96

Technology Index Rank **87**
    Innovation Subindex Rank 77
    ICT Subindex Rank 85
    Technology Transfer Subindex Rank
        (out of 77 non-core innovators) 53

Business Competitiveness Index Rank	**89**

**Sophistication of Company Operations
  and Strategy Rank** **84**
**Quality of the National Business
  Environment Rank** **90**

The Most Problematic Factors for Doing Business

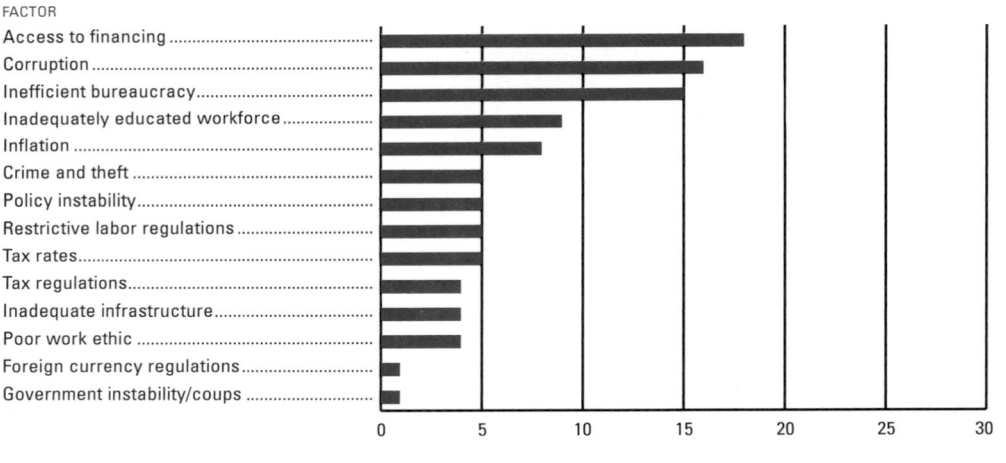

FACTOR

Note: From a list of 14 factors, respondents were asked to select the five most problematic for doing business in their country and to rank them between 1 (most problematic) and 5. The bars in the figure show the responses weighted according to their rankings.

Source: World Economic Forum, Executive Opinion Survey (2003)

National competitiveness balance sheet

NOTABLE COMPETITIVE ADVANTAGES	
Growth Competitiveness Index	**Rank/102**

Macroeconomic Environment
2.19 National savings rate, 2002 27

Technology
3.03 FDI and technology transfer 31

NOTABLE COMPETITIVE DISADVANTAGES	
Growth Competitiveness Index	**Rank/102**

Macroeconomic Environment
2.21 Real exchange rate, 2002 97
2.03 Extent of distortive government subsidies 94
7.10 Public trust of politicians 92
2.01 Recession expectations 88
7.08 Diversion of public funds 85
2.09 Access to credit 81
2.20 Inflation, 2002 79
2.17 Country credit rating, 2003 77
2.18 Government surplus/deficit, 2002 76
2.22 Interest rate spread, 2002 66

Public Institutions
7.01 Irregular payments in exports and imports 97
6.17 Organized crime 96
7.02 Irregular payments in public utilities 95
6.01 Judicial independence 93
7.03 Irregular payments in tax collection 91
6.08 Favoritism in decisions of government officials..............90
6.03 Property rights..86

Technology
3.02 Firm-level technology absorption 101
3.01 Technological sophistication 97
3.15 Government success in ICT promotion 95
3.08 University/industry research collaboration 93
3.14 Government prioritization of ICT 92
3.06 Company spending on research and development 91
3.12 Internet access in schools 91
3.16 Laws relating to ICT 91
3.13 Quality of competition in the ISP sector 89
3.21 Internet hosts, 2002 85
3.19 Cellular telephones, 2002 79
3.23 Personal computers, 2002 79
3.22 Telephone lines, 2002 74
3.20 Internet users, 2002 71
3.18 Tertiary enrollment 68
3.04 Prevalence of foreign technology licensing 64
3.17 Utility patents, 2002 52

Business Competitiveness Index	**Rank/95**

Sophistication of Company Operations and Strategy
10.10 Extent of regional sales...70
10.02 Value chain presence 72
10.07 Extent of marketing..79

Quality of the National Business Environment
6.09 Extent of bureaucratic red tape......................................37
2.16 Cost of importing foreign equipment..............................44
3.17 Utility patents, 2002 52

Other Indicators	**Rank/102**
8.10 Regional disparities in quality of business environment ...40

Business Competitiveness Index	**Rank/95**

Sophistication of Company Operations and Strategy
10.15 Reliance on professional management...........................93
10.08 Degree of customer orientation.....................................88
10.11 Breadth of international markets....................................88

Quality of the National Business Environment
5.06 Telephone infrastructure quality 95
8.06 Effectiveness of antitrust policy.....................................94
2.11 Local equity market access..93

Other Indicators	**Rank/102**
7.12 Policy consequences of legal political donations 101
7.07 Irregular payments in judicial decisions 99
6.14 Business costs of crime and violence 99
5.07 Postal efficiency 99
7.06 Irregular payments in government policymaking............98
10.27 Strength of auditing and accounting standards 98
10.05 Ethical behavior of firms 98
11.12 Political context of environmental gains 97
2.06 Soundness of banks..96
11.08 Clarity and stability of regulations 95
8.03 Extent of market dominance...95
11.11 Effects of compliance on business 93
10.21 Pay and productivity 93
10.18 Hiring and firing practices 92
2.10 Government intervention in corporate investment 90

Note: The Business Competitiveness Index applies different criteria for selecting a country's competitive advantages and disadvantages. Please refer to the section "How Country Profiles Work" for further details.

Hong Kong SAR

Competitiveness Rankings

Growth Competitiveness Index Rank	24

Macroeconomic Environment Index Rank **15**
    Macroeconomic Stability Subindex Rank 8
    Government Waste Subindex Rank 9
    Country Credit Rating Rank 26

Public Institutions Index Rank..**10**
    Contracts and Law Subindex Rank 12
    Corruption Subindex Rank.....................................9

Technology Index Rank **37**
    Innovation Subindex Rank 34
    ICT Subindex Rank 8

Business Competitiveness Index Rank	19

**Sophistication of Company Operations
and Strategy Rank** **22**
**Quality of the National Business
Environment Rank** **15**

The Most Problematic Factors for Doing Business

FACTOR

Percent of responses

Note: From a list of 14 factors, respondents were asked to select the five most problematic for doing business in their country and to rank them between 1 (most problematic) and 5. The bars in the figure show the responses weighted according to their rankings.

Source: World Economic Forum, Executive Opinion Survey (2003)

National competitiveness balance sheet

NOTABLE COMPETITIVE ADVANTAGES

Growth Competitiveness Index	Rank/102

Macroeconomic Environment

2.20	Inflation, 2002	2
2.19	National savings rate, 2002	3
7.08	Diversion of public funds	9
2.03	Extent of distortive government subsidies	12
7.10	Public trust of politicians	13
2.09	Access to credit	22

Public Institutions

6.03	Property rights	4
7.01	Irregular payments in exports and imports	9
7.03	Irregular payments in tax collection	11
7.02	Irregular payments in public utilities	12
6.17	Organized crime	13
6.08	Favoritism in decisions of government officials	15
6.01	Judicial independence	17

Technology

3.19	Cellular telephones, 2002	4
3.13	Quality of competition in the ISP sector	4
3.12	Internet access in schools	9
3.21	Internet hosts, 2002	12
3.20	Internet users, 2002	13
3.22	Telephone lines, 2002	14
3.16	Laws relating to ICT	18
3.23	Personal computers, 2002	18
3.01	Technological sophistication	19
3.14	Government prioritization of ICT	22

Business Competitiveness Index	Rank/95

Sophistication of Company Operations and Strategy

10.11	Breadth of international markets	8
10.02	Value chain presence	10
10.07	Extent of marketing	12

Quality of the National Business Environment

8.05	Administrative burden for startups	1
2.16	Cost of importing foreign equipment	1
10.26	Foreign ownership restrictions	2

Other Indicators	Rank/102

6.11	Efficiency of the tax system	1
10.19	Flexibility of wage determination	1
8.08	Private sector employment of women	1
10.18	Hiring and firing practices	1
6.06	Burden of regulation	2
2.10	Government intervention in corporate investment	2
10.21	Pay and productivity	2
8.10	Regional disparities in quality of business environment	3
6.07	Transparency of government policymaking	4
6.14	Business costs of crime and violence	5
8.11	Focus of trade and industry associations	6
7.12	Policy consequences of legal political donations	6
2.15	Agricultural policy costs	7
7.11	Prevalence of illegal political donations	7
8.09	Wage equality of women in the workplace	8

NOTABLE COMPETITIVE DISADVANTAGES

Growth Competitiveness Index	Rank/102

Macroeconomic Environment

2.18	Government surplus/deficit, 2002	70
2.01	Recession expectations	65
2.21	Real exchange rate, 2002	64
2.22	Interest rate spread, 2002	40
2.17	Country credit rating, 2003	26

Technology

3.18	Tertiary enrollment	51
3.15	Government success in ICT promotion	31
3.02	Firm-level technology absorption	28
3.06	Company spending on research and development	28
3.08	University/industry research collaboration	24
3.17	Utility patents, 2002	24

Business Competitiveness Index	Rank/95

Sophistication of Company Operations and Strategy

10.04	Capacity for innovation	42
10.15	Reliance on professional management	33
3.06	Company spending on research and development	27

Quality of the National Business Environment

8.06	Effectiveness of antitrust policy	55
9.08	Local availability of components and parts	51
3.10	Availability of scientists and engineers	50

Other Indicators	Rank/102

3.07	Subsidies and tax credits for firm-level research and development	53
6.10	Effectiveness of law-making bodies	48
4.05	Business impact of malaria	46
11.06	Compliance with environmental regulations	44
4.06	Business impact of tuberculosis	42
6.16	Government effectiveness in reducing income inequality	42
8.03	Extent of market dominance	42
11.02	Water pollution regulations	42
11.07	Compliance with international agreements	42
11.01	Air pollution regulations	41
11.13	Prevalence of environmental management systems	40
4.07	Business impact of HIV/AIDS	39
6.05	Freedom of the press	39
11.12	Political context of environmental gains	34
7.13	Pervasiveness of money laundering through banks	33

Note: The Business Competitiveness Index applies different criteria for selecting a country's competitive advantages and disadvantages. Please refer to the section "How Country Profiles Work" for further details.

Hungary

Competitiveness Rankings

Growth Competitiveness Index Rank	33

Macroeconomic Environment Index Rank **38**
    Macroeconomic Stability Subindex Rank 66
    Government Waste Subindex Rank 41
    Country Credit Rating Rank 30

Public Institutions Index Rank............................**33**
    Contracts and Law Subindex Rank 39
    Corruption Subindex Rank...................................28

Technology Index Rank **32**
    Innovation Subindex Rank...................................38
    ICT Subindex Rank 35
    Technology Transfer Subindex Rank
    (out of 77 non-core innovators) 21

Business Competitiveness Index Rank	38

**Sophistication of Company Operations
and Strategy Rank** **45**

**Quality of the National Business
Environment Rank** **37**

The Most Problematic Factors for Doing Business

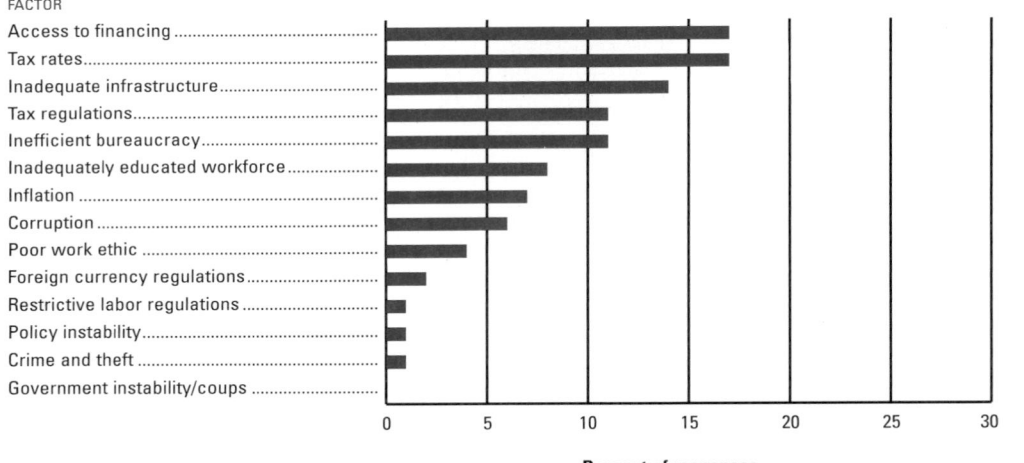

FACTOR
Access to financing
Tax rates
Inadequate infrastructure
Tax regulations
Inefficient bureaucracy
Inadequately educated workforce
Inflation
Corruption
Poor work ethic
Foreign currency regulations
Restrictive labor regulations
Policy instability
Crime and theft
Government instability/coups

Percent of responses

Note: From a list of 14 factors, respondents were asked to select the five most problematic for doing business in their country and to rank them between 1 (most problematic) and 5. The bars in the figure show the responses weighted according to their rankings.

Source: World Economic Forum, Executive Opinion Survey (2003)

National competitiveness balance sheet

NOTABLE COMPETITIVE ADVANTAGES		
Growth Competitiveness Index		**Rank/102**

Macroeconomic Environment
2.22	Interest rate spread, 2002	12
2.03	Extent of distortive government subsidies	14
2.09	Access to credit	25
2.17	Country credit rating, 2003	30

Public Institutions
7.03	Irregular payments in tax collection	22
6.01	Judicial independence	29
7.02	Irregular payments in public utilities	30

Technology
3.03	FDI and technology transfer	6
3.12	Internet access in schools	27
3.21	Internet hosts, 2002	27
3.17	Utility patents, 2002	28
3.19	Cellular telephones, 2002	28

NOTABLE COMPETITIVE DISADVANTAGES		
Growth Competitiveness Index		**Rank/102**

Macroeconomic Environment
2.18	Government surplus/deficit, 2002	86
2.21	Real exchange rate, 2002	78
2.20	Inflation, 2002	69
2.19	National savings rate, 2002	52
7.10	Public trust of politicians	47
7.08	Diversion of public funds	41
2.01	Recession expectations	37

Public Institutions
6.08	Favoritism in decisions of government officials	67
6.17	Organized crime	46
6.03	Property rights	37
7.01	Irregular payments in exports and imports	33

Technology
3.13	Quality of competition in the ISP sector	94
3.02	Firm-level technology absorption	68
3.06	Company spending on research and development	67
3.15	Government success in ICT promotion	65
3.08	University/industry research collaboration	61
3.14	Government prioritization of ICT	50
3.16	Laws relating to ICT	49
3.01	Technological sophistication	47
3.04	Prevalence of foreign technology licensing	41
3.23	Personal computers, 2002	40
3.18	Tertiary enrollment	36
3.20	Internet users, 2002	36
3.22	Telephone lines, 2002	34

Business Competitiveness Index		**Rank/95**

Sophistication of Company Operations and Strategy
10.03	Extent of branding	28
10.04	Capacity for innovation	32
10.02	Value chain presence	36

Quality of the National Business Environment
6.09	Extent of bureaucratic red tape	2
4.03	Quality of math and science education	7
10.26	Foreign ownership restrictions	12

Business Competitiveness Index		**Rank/95**

Sophistication of Company Operations and Strategy
10.08	Degree of customer orientation	64
10.12	Extent of staff training	64
10.13	Willingness to delegate authority	64

Quality of the National Business Environment
5.03	Port infrastructure quality	76
5.04	Air transport infrastructure quality	74
9.07	Extent of collaboration among clusters	66

Other Indicators		**Rank/102**
4.07	Business impact of HIV/AIDS	5
2.02	Business costs of terrorism	8
10.21	Pay and productivity	20
4.05	Business impact of malaria	21
11.07	Compliance with international agreements	24
6.18	Informal sector	25
4.06	Business impact of tuberculosis	27
11.01	Air pollution regulations	28
4.08	Impact of HIV/AIDS on FDI	29
11.02	Water pollution regulations	29
2.04	Extent of distortive government intervention	30
3.11	Availability of mobile or cellular telephones	31

Other Indicators		**Rank/102**
11.12	Political context of environmental gains	102
10.23	Company promotion of volunteerism	92
8.10	Regional disparities in quality of business environment	92
8.09	Wage equality of women in the workplace	91
8.11	Focus of trade and industry associations	91
4.10	Maternity leave legislation	83
10.22	Charitable causes involvement	81
10.25	Availability of company financial information	69
8.08	Private sector employment of women	67
11.09	Flexibility of regulations	65
2.15	Agricultural policy costs	65
11.11	Effects of compliance on business	64
2.06	Soundness of banks	64
4.11	Maternity laws' impact on hiring women	64
6.15	Government effectiveness in reducing poverty	61

259

Note: The Business Competitiveness Index applies different criteria for selecting a country's competitive advantages and disadvantages. Please refer to the section "How Country Profiles Work" for further details.

Iceland

Competitiveness Rankings

Growth Competitiveness Index Rank	8

Macroeconomic Environment Index Rank **16**
    Macroeconomic Stability Subindex Rank 30
    Government Waste Subindex Rank 5
    Country Credit Rating Rank 25

Public Institutions Index Rank **3**
    Contracts and Law Subindex Rank 4
    Corruption Subindex Rank 2

Technology Index Rank **15**
    Innovation Subindex Rank 21
    ICT Subindex Rank 1

Business Competitiveness Index Rank	14

**Sophistication of Company Operations
and Strategy Rank** **15**

**Quality of the National Business
Environment Rank** **12**

The Most Problematic Factors for Doing Business

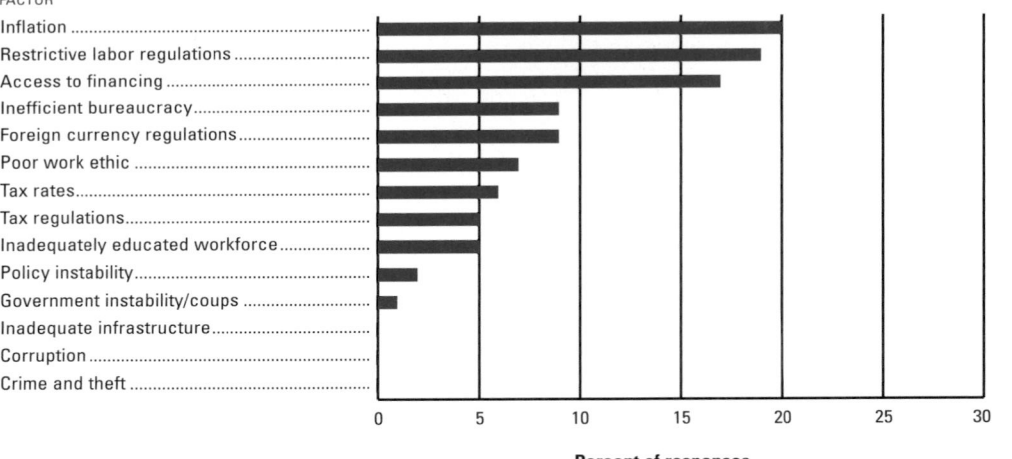

Note: From a list of 14 factors, respondents were asked to select the five most problematic for doing business in their country and to rank them between 1 (most problematic) and 5. The bars in the figure show the responses weighted according to their rankings.

Source: World Economic Forum, Executive Opinion Survey (2003)

260

National competitiveness balance sheet

NOTABLE COMPETITIVE ADVANTAGES

Growth Competitiveness Index	Rank/102

Macroeconomic Environment
2.09	Access to credit	2
2.01	Recession expectations	5
7.10	Public trust of politicians	5
7.08	Diversion of public funds	7

Public Institutions
6.17	Organized crime	1
7.03	Irregular payments in tax collection	1
7.01	Irregular payments in exports and imports	2
7.02	Irregular payments in public utilities	2
6.01	Judicial independence	6
6.08	Favoritism in decisions of government officials	7
6.03	Property rights	10

Technology
3.20	Internet users, 2002	1
3.21	Internet hosts, 2002	2
3.12	Internet access in schools	3
3.13	Quality of competition in the ISP sector	3
3.19	Cellular telephones, 2002	6
3.02	Firm-level technology absorption	7
3.01	Technological sophistication	8
3.16	Laws relating to ICT	9
3.22	Telephone lines, 2002	9

Business Competitiveness Index	Rank/95

Sophistication of Company Operations and Strategy
10.09	Control of international distribution	6
10.08	Degree of customer orientation	9
10.10	Extent of regional sales	10

Quality of the National Business Environment
3.20	Internet users, 2002	1
5.05	Quality of electricity supply	1
8.04	Sophistication of local buyers' products and processes	1

Other Indicators	Rank/102

7.07	Irregular payments in judicial decisions	1
5.07	Postal efficiency	1
7.04	Irregular payments in public contracts	1
4.04	Disparity in healthcare quality	1
7.14	Pervasiveness of money laundering through non-bank channels	1
7.06	Irregular payments in government policymaking	2
7.05	Irregular payments in loan applications	2
7.13	Pervasiveness of money laundering through banks	2
4.11	Maternity laws' impact on hiring women	2
8.11	Focus of trade and industry associations	2
11.11	Effects of compliance on business	3
4.06	Business impact of tuberculosis	4
4.08	Impact of HIV/AIDS on FDI	4
2.10	Government intervention in corporate investment	4
6.16	Government effectiveness in reducing income inequality	4

NOTABLE COMPETITIVE DISADVANTAGES

Growth Competitiveness Index	Rank/102

Macroeconomic Environment
2.22	Interest rate spread, 2002	73
2.20	Inflation, 2002	65
2.19	National savings rate, 2002	61
2.21	Real exchange rate, 2002	53
2.17	Country credit rating, 2003	25
2.03	Extent of distortive government subsidies	16
2.18	Government surplus/deficit, 2002	14

Technology
3.18	Tertiary enrollment	27
3.14	Government prioritization of ICT	20
3.17	Utility patents, 2002	20
3.06	Company spending on research and development	16
3.08	University/industry research collaboration	14
3.15	Government success in ICT promotion	11
3.23	Personal computers, 2002	11

Business Competitiveness Index	Rank/95

Sophistication of Company Operations and Strategy
10.11	Breadth of international markets	30
10.14	Extent of incentive compensation	27
10.02	Value chain presence	24

Quality of the National Business Environment
10.26	Foreign ownership restrictions	87
5.02	Railroad infrastructure development	54
9.08	Local availability of components and parts	54

Other Indicators	Rank/102

2.15	Agricultural policy costs	84
8.03	Extent of market dominance	76
10.19	Flexibility of wage determination	73
8.09	Wage equality of women in the workplace	41
3.07	Subsidies and tax credits for firm-level research and development	31
2.06	Soundness of banks	23
11.13	Prevalence of environmental management systems	23
10.23	Company promotion of volunteerism	22
11.12	Political context of environmental gains	21
8.10	Regional disparities in quality of business environment	18
10.27	Strength of auditing and accounting standards	17
11.06	Compliance with environmental regulations	15
10.25	Availability of company financial information	14
11.10	Consistency of regulation enforcement	14
11.04	Chemical waste regulations	13

261

Note: The Business Competitiveness Index applies different criteria for selecting a country's competitive advantages and disadvantages. Please refer to the section "How Country Profiles Work" for further details.

India

Competitiveness Rankings

Growth Competitiveness Index Rank	56

Macroeconomic Environment Index Rank **52**
   Macroeconomic Stability Subindex Rank 43
   Government Waste Subindex Rank 72
   Country Credit Rating Rank 48

Public Institutions Index Rank...**55**
   Contracts and Law Subindex Rank 35
   Corruption Subindex Rank...................................80

Technology Index Rank **64**
   Innovation Subindex Rank....................................66
   ICT Subindex Rank 75
   Technology Transfer Subindex Rank
   (out of 77 non-core innovators).........................7

Business Competitiveness Index Rank	37

**Sophistication of Company Operations
and Strategy Rank** **40**

**Quality of the National Business
Environment Rank** **36**

The Most Problematic Factors for Doing Business

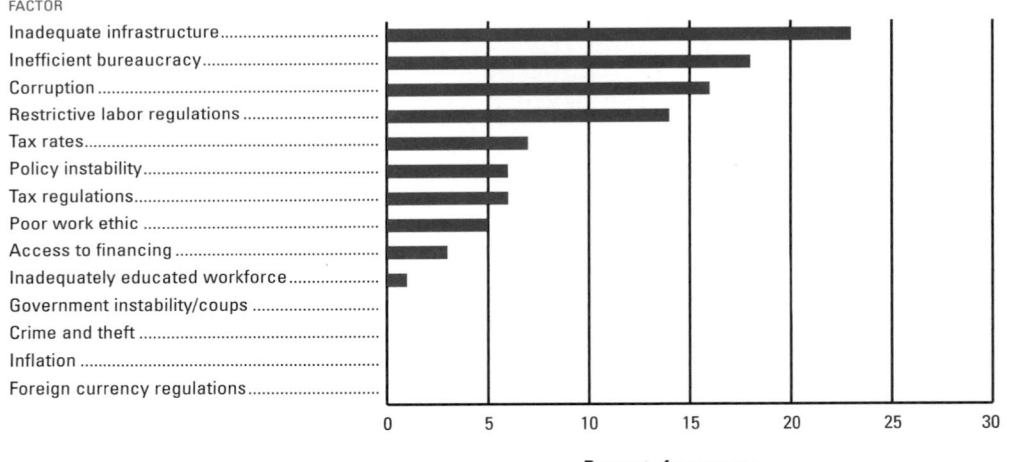

FACTOR

Inadequate infrastructure
Inefficient bureaucracy
Corruption
Restrictive labor regulations
Tax rates
Policy instability
Tax regulations
Poor work ethic
Access to financing
Inadequately educated workforce
Government instability/coups
Crime and theft
Inflation
Foreign currency regulations

Percent of responses

Note: From a list of 14 factors, respondents were asked to select the five most problematic for doing business in their country and to rank them between 1 (most problematic) and 5. The bars in the figure show the responses weighted according to their rankings.

Source: World Economic Forum, Executive Opinion Survey (2003)

National competitiveness balance sheet

NOTABLE COMPETITIVE ADVANTAGES

Growth Competitiveness Index		Rank/102

Macroeconomic Environment
2.09	Access to credit	4
2.01	Recession expectations	13
2.22	Interest rate spread, 2002	13
2.19	National savings rate, 2002	35
2.17	Country credit rating, 2003	48

Public Institutions
6.01	Judicial independence	25
6.03	Property rights	43
6.17	Organized crime	44

Technology
3.04	Prevalence of foreign technology licensing	4
3.14	Government prioritization of ICT	12
3.15	Government success in ICT promotion	16
3.01	Technological sophistication	25
3.13	Quality of competition in the ISP sector	26
3.03	FDI and technology transfer	27
3.02	Firm-level technology absorption	31
3.16	Laws relating to ICT	36
3.06	Company spending on research and development	39
3.12	Internet access in schools	48

Business Competitiveness Index		Rank/95

Sophistication of Company Operations and Strategy
3.04	Prevalence of foreign technology licensing	6
10.02	Value chain presence	26
10.07	Extent of marketing	29

Quality of the National Business Environment
8.02	Extent of locally based competitors	1
3.10	Availability of scientists and engineers	3
10.16	Quality of management schools	8

Other Indicators		Rank/102

8.03	Extent of market dominance	16
10.22	Charitable causes involvement	21
3.07	Subsidies and tax credits for firm-level research and development	21
4.11	Maternity laws' impact on hiring women	25
6.14	Business costs of crime and violence	25
6.05	Freedom of the press	26
10.25	Availability of company financial information	29
6.10	Effectiveness of law-making bodies	31
2.10	Government intervention in corporate investment	34
10.27	Strength of auditing and accounting standards	36
7.12	Policy consequences of legal political donations	37
11.13	Prevalence of environmental management systems	37
6.07	Transparency of government policymaking	41
4.08	Impact of HIV/AIDS on FDI	43
3.11	Availability of mobile or cellular telephones	44

NOTABLE COMPETITIVE DISADVANTAGES

Growth Competitiveness Index		Rank/102

Macroeconomic Environment
2.18	Government surplus/deficit, 2002	93
7.10	Public trust of politicians	82
2.03	Extent of distortive government subsidies	67
2.21	Real exchange rate, 2002	67
7.08	Diversion of public funds	67
2.20	Inflation, 2002	57

Public Institutions
7.02	Irregular payments in public utilities	83
7.01	Irregular payments in exports and imports	72
7.03	Irregular payments in tax collection	71
6.08	Favoritism in decisions of government officials	57

Technology
3.19	Cellular telephones, 2002	94
3.23	Personal computers, 2002	85
3.20	Internet users, 2002	82
3.21	Internet hosts, 2002	80
3.22	Telephone lines, 2002	79
3.18	Tertiary enrollment	72
3.17	Utility patents, 2002	54
3.08	University/industry research collaboration	51

Business Competitiveness Index		Rank/95

Sophistication of Company Operations and Strategy
10.01	Nature of competitive advantage	69
10.08	Degree of customer orientation	68
10.10	Extent of regional sales	61

Quality of the National Business Environment
3.19	Cellular telephones, 2002	86
5.05	Quality of electricity supply	82
3.20	Internet users, 2002	79

Other Indicators		Rank/102

10.18	Hiring and firing practices	96
7.11	Prevalence of illegal political donations	94
8.10	Regional disparities in quality of business environment	91
2.15	Agricultural policy costs	85
11.09	Flexibility of regulations	83
7.04	Irregular payments in public contracts	82
11.12	Political context of environmental gains	81
8.08	Private sector employment of women	81
2.02	Business costs of terrorism	79
7.06	Irregular payments in government policymaking	78
4.04	Disparity in healthcare quality	78
4.05	Business impact of malaria	77
11.07	Compliance with international agreements	75
4.07	Business impact of HIV/AIDS	74
10.05	Ethical behavior of firms	74

263

Note: The Business Competitiveness Index applies different criteria for selecting a country's competitive advantages and disadvantages. Please refer to the section "How Country Profiles Work" for further details.

Indonesia

Competitiveness Rankings

Growth Competitiveness Index Rank	72

Macroeconomic Environment Index Rank 64
    Macroeconomic Stability Subindex Rank 65
    Government Waste Subindex Rank 42
    Country Credit Rating Rank 80

Public Institutions Index Rank 76
    Contracts and Law Subindex Rank 65
    Corruption Subindex Rank 88

Technology Index Rank 78
    Innovation Subindex Rank 65
    ICT Subindex Rank 74
    Technology Transfer Subindex Rank
    (out of 77 non-core innovators) 63

Business Competitiveness Index Rank	60

**Sophistication of Company Operations
   and Strategy Rank** 62

**Quality of the National Business
   Environment Rank** 60

The Most Problematic Factors for Doing Business

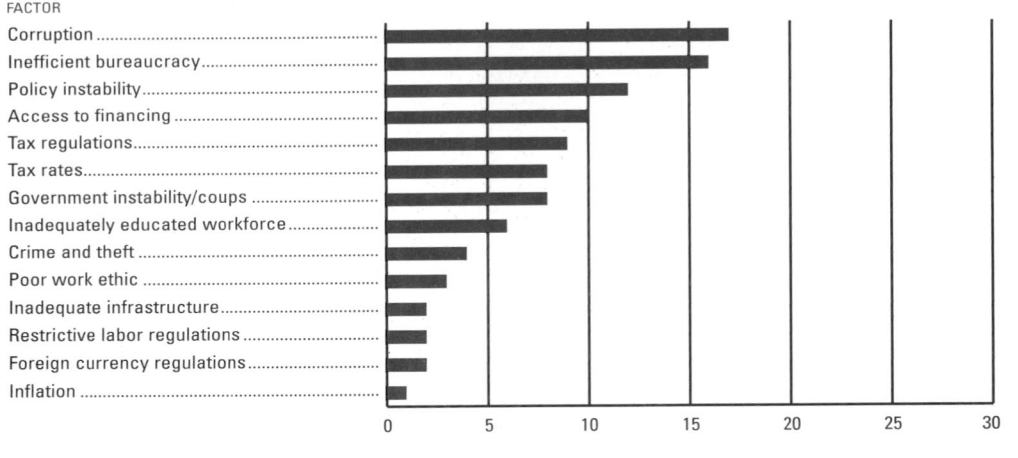

FACTOR

Corruption
Inefficient bureaucracy
Policy instability
Access to financing
Tax regulations
Tax rates
Government instability/coups
Inadequately educated workforce
Crime and theft
Poor work ethic
Inadequate infrastructure
Restrictive labor regulations
Foreign currency regulations
Inflation

Percent of responses

Note: From a list of 14 factors, respondents were asked to select the five most problematic for doing business in their country and to rank them between 1 (most problematic) and 5. The bars in the figure show the responses weighted according to their rankings.

Source: World Economic Forum, Executive Opinion Survey (2003)

National competitiveness balance sheet

NOTABLE COMPETITIVE ADVANTAGES

Growth Competitiveness Index		Rank/102

Macroeconomic Environment

2.22	Interest rate spread, 2002	13
2.21	Real exchange rate, 2002	20
2.03	Extent of distortive government subsidies	30
2.18	Government surplus/deficit, 2002	34
7.10	Public trust of politicians	38
7.08	Diversion of public funds	45

Public Institutions

| 6.08 | Favoritism in decisions of government officials | 33 |

Technology

3.08	University/industry research collaboration	28
3.06	Company spending on research and development	35
3.16	Laws relating to ICT	48

Business Competitiveness Index		Rank/95

Sophistication of Company Operations and Strategy

10.04	Capacity for innovation	30
3.06	Company spending on research and development	34
10.01	Nature of competitive advantage	38

Quality of the National Business Environment

6.12	Centralization of economic policymaking	14
3.09	Government procurement of advanced technology products	24
9.09	Local availability of process machinery	25

Other Indicators		Rank/102

8.03	Extent of market dominance	14
6.06	Burden of regulation	15
10.23	Company promotion of volunteerism	22
3.07	Subsidies and tax credits for firm-level research and development	28
6.11	Efficiency of the tax system	36
8.10	Regional disparities in quality of business environment	36
11.13	Prevalence of environmental management systems	38
4.04	Disparity in healthcare quality	38
6.18	Informal sector	43
10.18	Hiring and firing practices	43
6.16	Government effectiveness in reducing income inequality	45
4.09	Brain drain	45
7.11	Prevalence of illegal political donations	45
7.12	Policy consequences of legal political donations	46
11.06	Compliance with environmental regulations	46

NOTABLE COMPETITIVE DISADVANTAGES

Growth Competitiveness Index		Rank/102

Macroeconomic Environment

2.20	Inflation, 2002	87
2.17	Country credit rating, 2003	80
2.19	National savings rate, 2002	67
2.09	Access to credit	59
2.01	Recession expectations	52

Public Institutions

7.02	Irregular payments in public utilities	88
7.03	Irregular payments in tax collection	82
7.01	Irregular payments in exports and imports	81
6.03	Property rights	73
6.17	Organized crime	70
6.01	Judicial independence	67

Technology

3.02	Firm-level technology absorption	96
3.14	Government prioritization of ICT	83
3.22	Telephone lines, 2002	81
3.23	Personal computers, 2002	80
3.19	Cellular telephones, 2002	76
3.21	Internet hosts, 2002	73
3.13	Quality of competition in the ISP sector	69
3.15	Government success in ICT promotion	69
3.17	Utility patents, 2002	69
3.18	Tertiary enrollment	69
3.20	Internet users, 2002	67
3.03	FDI and technology transfer	61
3.04	Prevalence of foreign technology licensing	56
3.01	Technological sophistication	54
3.12	Internet access in schools	52

Business Competitiveness Index		Rank/95

Sophistication of Company Operations and Strategy

10.08	Degree of customer orientation	85
10.15	Reliance on professional management	84
3.04	Prevalence of foreign technology licensing	78

Quality of the National Business Environment

6.09	Extent of bureaucratic red tape	91
10.17	Efficacy of corporate boards	89
10.26	Foreign ownership restrictions	89

Other Indicators		Rank/102

4.08	Impact of HIV/AIDS on FDI	100
4.11	Maternity laws' impact on hiring women	100
4.10	Maternity leave legislation	98
2.06	Soundness of banks	97
8.09	Wage equality of women in the workplace	94
8.08	Private sector employment of women	93
11.11	Effects of compliance on business	92
3.11	Availability of mobile or cellular telephones	92
10.27	Strength of auditing and accounting standards	90
7.05	Irregular payments in loan applications	89
6.05	Freedom of the press	89
10.19	Flexibility of wage determination	88
10.05	Ethical behavior of firms	85
2.02	Business costs of terrorism	84
4.05	Business impact of malaria	82

265

Note: The Business Competitiveness Index applies different criteria for selecting a country's competitive advantages and disadvantages. Please refer to the section "How Country Profiles Work" for further details.

Ireland

Competitiveness Rankings

Growth Competitiveness Rank	**30**

Macroeconomic Environment Index Rank **22**
    Macroeconomic Stability Subindex Rank 29
    Government Waste Subindex 38
    Country Credit Rating Rank..................................15

Public Institutions Index Rank..**25**
    Contracts and Law Subindex Rank 31
    Corruption Subindex Rank....................................22

Technology Index Rank **38**
    Innovation Subindex Rank....................................24
    ICT Subindex Rank 27

Business Competitiveness Index Rank	**21**

**Sophistication of Company Operations
  and Strategy Rank** **17**

**Quality of the National Business
  Environment Rank** **22**

The Most Problematic Factors for Doing Business

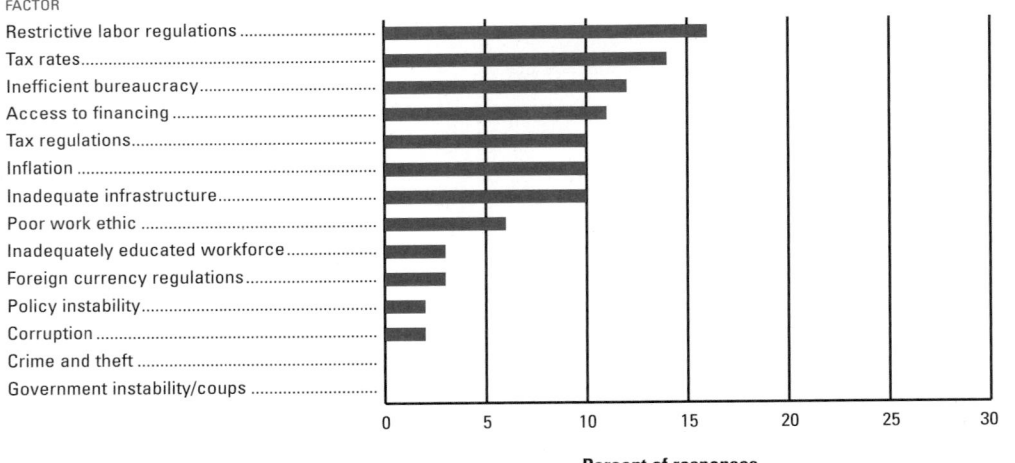

FACTOR

Restrictive labor regulations
Tax rates
Inefficient bureaucracy
Access to financing
Tax regulations
Inflation
Inadequate infrastructure
Poor work ethic
Inadequately educated workforce
Foreign currency regulations
Policy instability
Corruption
Crime and theft
Government instability/coups

Percent of responses

Note: From a list of 14 factors, respondents were asked to select the five most problematic for doing business in their country and to rank them between 1 (most problematic) and 5. The bars in the figure show the responses weighted according to their rankings.

Source: World Economic Forum, Executive Opinion Survey (2003)

National competitiveness balance sheet

NOTABLE COMPETITIVE ADVANTAGES

Growth Competitiveness Index		Rank/102

Macroeconomic Environment

2.21	Real exchange rate, 2002	10
2.17	Country credit rating, 2003	15
2.09	Access to credit	18
2.18	Government surplus/deficit, 2002	20
2.22	Interest rate spread, 2002	25
7.08	Diversion of public funds	26

Public Institutions

7.01	Irregular payments in exports and imports	17
7.02	Irregular payments in public utilities	22
7.03	Irregular payments in tax collection	24
6.01	Judicial independence	26
6.03	Property rights	26

Technology

3.08	University/industry research collaboration	11
3.23	Personal computers, 2002	17
3.06	Company spending on research and development	19
3.21	Internet hosts, 2002	19
3.15	Government success in ICT promotion	20
3.01	Technological sophistication	21
3.19	Cellular telephones, 2002	21
3.16	Laws relating to ICT	22
3.17	Utility patents, 2002	23
3.02	Firm-level technology absorption	29
3.20	Internet users, 2002	29
3.22	Telephone lines, 2002	20

Business Competitiveness Index		Rank/95

Sophistication of Company Operations and Strategy

10.10	Extent of regional sales	5
10.15	Reliance on professional management	12
10.14	Extent of incentive compensation	14

Quality of the National Business Environment

10.26	Foreign ownership restrictions	2
2.07	Ease of access to loans	4
8.07	Prevalence of mergers and acquisitions	6

Other Indicators		Rank/102

2.06	Soundness of banks	6
10.22	Charitable causes involvement	8
3.07	Subsidies and tax credits for firm-level research and development	11
4.08	Impact of HIV/AIDS on FDI	14
10.27	Strength of auditing and accounting standards	16
4.05	Business impact of malaria	17
6.06	Burden of regulation	18
6.11	Efficiency of the tax system	20
4.09	Brain drain	20
5.07	Postal efficiency	21
8.08	Private sector employment of women	21
10.25	Availability of company financial information	22
7.14	Pervasiveness of money laundering through non-bank channels	23
10.05	Ethical behavior of firms	24
11.12	Political context of environmental gains	25

NOTABLE COMPETITIVE DISADVANTAGES

Growth Competitiveness Index		Rank/102

Macroeconomic Environment

2.20	Inflation, 2002	63
7.10	Public trust of politicians	57
2.01	Recession expectations	50
2.19	National savings rate, 2002	45
2.03	Extent of distortive government subsidies	32

Public Institutions

6.08	Favoritism in decisions of government officials	40
6.17	Organized crime	38

Technology

3.13	Quality of competition in the ISP sector	97
3.12	Internet access in schools	34
3.14	Government prioritization of ICT	31
3.18	Tertiary enrollment	30

Business Competitiveness Index		Rank/95

Sophistication of Company Operations and Strategy

10.08	Degree of customer orientation	29
10.07	Extent of marketing	23
10.09	Control of international distribution	23

Quality of the National Business Environment

6.12	Centralization of economic policymaking	88
5.02	Railroad infrastructure development	64
5.01	Overall infrastructure quality	62

Other Indicators		Rank/102

10.19	Flexibility of wage determination	96
2.15	Agricultural policy costs	89
7.12	Policy consequences of legal political donations	78
8.11	Focus of trade and industry associations	70
2.10	Government intervention in corporate investment	60
10.23	Company promotion of volunteerism	59
7.11	Prevalence of illegal political donations	57
3.11	Availability of mobile or cellular telephones	53
6.14	Business costs of crime and violence	51
4.10	Maternity leave legislation	50
11.11	Effects of compliance on business	50
6.05	Freedom of the press	48
11.07	Compliance with international agreements	47
2.04	Extent of distortive government intervention	44
4.04	Disparity in healthcare quality	44

Note: The Business Competitiveness Index applies different criteria for selecting a country's competitive advantages and disadvantages. Please refer to the section "How Country Profiles Work" for further details.

Israel

Competitiveness Rankings

Growth Competitiveness Index Rank	20

Macroeconomic Environment Index Rank **44**
   Macroeconomic Stability Subindex Rank 77
   Government Waste Subindex Rank 19
   Country Credit Rating Rank 39

Public Institutions Index Rank...**15**
   Contracts and Law Subindex Rank 19
   Corruption Subindex Rank...................................14

Technology Index Rank **9**
   Innovation Subindex Rank 6
   ICT Subindex Rank 21

Business Competitiveness Index Rank	20

**Sophistication of Company Operations
   and Strategy Rank** **20**

**Quality of the National Business
   Environment Rank** **19**

The Most Problematic Factors for Doing Business

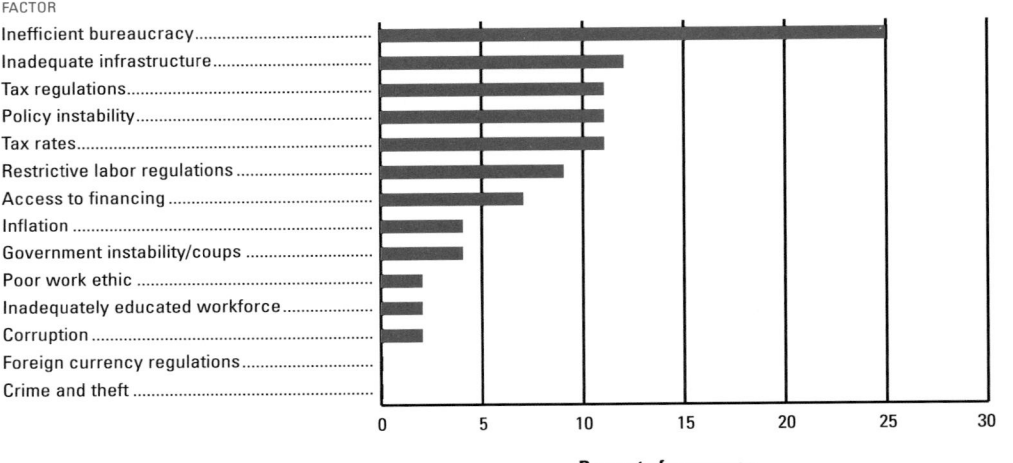

FACTOR
Inefficient bureaucracy
Inadequate infrastructure
Tax regulations
Policy instability
Tax rates
Restrictive labor regulations
Access to financing
Inflation
Government instability/coups
Poor work ethic
Inadequately educated workforce
Corruption
Foreign currency regulations
Crime and theft

0   5   10   15   20   25   30

Percent of responses

Note: From a list of 14 factors, respondents were asked to select the five most problematic for doing business in their country and to rank them between 1 (most problematic) and 5. The bars in the figure show the responses weighted according to their rankings.

Source: World Economic Forum, Executive Opinion Survey (2003)

National competitiveness balance sheet

NOTABLE COMPETITIVE ADVANTAGES			NOTABLE COMPETITIVE DISADVANTAGES		
Growth Competitiveness Index		**Rank/102**	**Growth Competitiveness Index**		**Rank/102**
	Macroeconomic Environment			**Macroeconomic Environment**	
2.03	Extent of distortive government subsidies	13	2.01	Recession expectations	100
7.08	Diversion of public funds	17	2.20	Inflation, 2002	71
	Public Institutions		2.09	Access to credit	66
6.01	Judicial independence	2	2.19	National savings rate, 2002	66
6.17	Organized crime	11	2.18	Government surplus/deficit, 2002	56
7.01	Irregular payments in exports and imports	11	2.21	Real exchange rate, 2002	46
7.02	Irregular payments in public utilities	11	7.10	Public trust of politicians	39
	Technology		2.17	Country credit rating, 2003	39
3.19	Cellular telephones, 2002	3	2.22	Interest rate spread, 2002	29
3.01	Technological sophistication	4		**Public Institutions**	
3.02	Firm-level technology absorption	4	6.08	Favoritism in decisions of government officials	53
3.17	Utility patents, 2002	6	6.03	Property rights	29
3.06	Company spending on research and development	7	7.03	Irregular payments in tax collection	20
3.13	Quality of competition in the ISP sector	7		**Technology**	
3.08	University/industry research collaboration	9	3.14	Government prioritization of ICT	58
3.12	Internet access in schools	15	3.20	Internet users, 2002	27
			3.21	Internet hosts, 2002	25
			3.22	Telephone lines, 2002	25
			3.23	Personal computers, 2002	24
			3.18	Tertiary enrollment	22
			3.15	Government success in ICT promotion	21
			3.16	Laws relating to ICT	21

Business Competitiveness Index		**Rank/95**	**Business Competitiveness Index**		**Rank/95**
	Sophistication of Company Operations and Strategy			**Sophistication of Company Operations and Strategy**	
3.06	Company spending on research and development	7	10.10	Extent of regional sales	93
10.01	Nature of competitive advantage	8	10.09	Control of international distribution	30
10.04	Capacity for innovation	10	10.08	Degree of customer orientation	26
	Quality of the National Business Environment			**Quality of the National Business Environment**	
3.10	Availability of scientists and engineers	1	6.12	Centralization of economic policymaking	66
3.19	Cellular telephones, 2002	2	6.08	Favoritism in decisions of government officials	51
3.05	Quality of scientific research institutions	2	8.02	Extent of locally based competitors	51

Other Indicators		**Rank/102**	**Other Indicators**		**Rank/102**
3.11	Availability of mobile or cellular telephones	2	2.02	Business costs of terrorism	102
3.07	Subsidies and tax credits for firm-level research and development	4	11.12	Political context of environmental gains	80
10.27	Strength of auditing and accounting standards	4	6.11	Efficiency of the tax system	77
6.14	Business costs of crime and violence	4	6.15	Government effectiveness in reducing poverty	76
7.07	Irregular payments in judicial decisions	7	10.19	Flexibility of wage determination	71
4.07	Business impact of HIV/AIDS	7	11.07	Compliance with international agreements	61
4.05	Business impact of malaria	8	6.16	Government effectiveness in reducing income inequality	61
5.07	Postal efficiency	9	2.15	Agricultural policy costs	55
8.10	Regional disparities in quality of business environment	10	6.10	Effectiveness of law-making bodies	54
4.11	Maternity laws' impact on hiring women	10	8.09	Wage equality of women in the workplace	53
10.25	Availability of company financial information	11	2.10	Government intervention in corporate investment	52
7.05	Irregular payments in loan applications	14	2.06	Soundness of banks	42
7.04	Irregular payments in public contracts	14	11.04	Chemical waste regulations	41
4.06	Business impact of tuberculosis	14	11.02	Water pollution regulations	39
8.11	Focus of trade and industry associations	14	11.01	Air pollution regulations	39

269

Note: The Business Competitiveness Index applies different criteria for selecting a country's competitive advantages and disadvantages. Please refer to the section "How Country Profiles Work" for further details.

Competitiveness Rankings

Growth Competitiveness Index Rank	41

Macroeconomic Environment Index Rank **28**
    Macroeconomic Stability Subindex Rank 50
    Government Waste Subindex Rank 50
    Country Credit Rating Rank 18

Public Institutions Index Rank..**46**
    Contracts and Law Subindex Rank 49
    Corruption Subindex Rank....................................47

Technology Index Rank **44**
    Innovation Subindex Rank 28
    ICT Subindex Rank 28

Business Competitiveness Index Rank	24

**Sophistication of Company Operations
and Strategy Rank** **24**

**Quality of the National Business
Environment Rank** **23**

The Most Problematic Factors for Doing Business

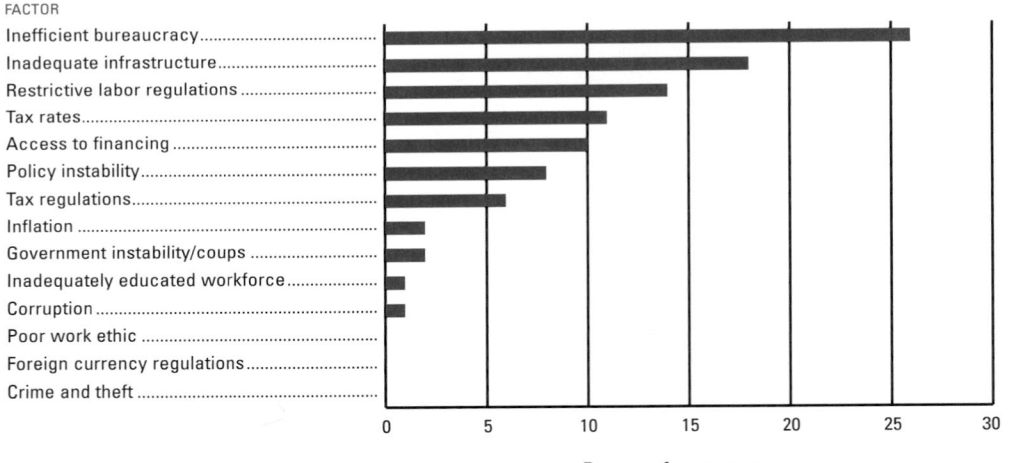

Note: From a list of 14 factors, respondents were asked to select the five most problematic for doing business in their country and to rank them between 1 (most problematic) and 5. The bars in the figure show the responses weighted according to their rankings.

Source: World Economic Forum, Executive Opinion Survey (2003)

National competitiveness balance sheet

NOTABLE COMPETITIVE ADVANTAGES

Growth Competitiveness Index		Rank/102
Macroeconomic Environment		
2.17	Country credit rating, 2003	18
2.22	Interest rate spread, 2002	32
2.03	Extent of distortive government subsidies	37
2.09	Access to credit	39
2.18	Government surplus/deficit, 2002	39
Public Institutions		
6.03	Property rights	35
Technology		
3.19	Cellular telephones, 2002	5
3.13	Quality of competition in the ISP sector	20
3.22	Telephone lines, 2002	24
3.17	Utility patents, 2002	25
3.18	Tertiary enrollment	25
3.23	Personal computers, 2002	26
3.20	Internet users, 2002	28
3.08	University/industry research collaboration	30
3.16	Laws relating to ICT	34
3.01	Technological sophistication	35
3.06	Company spending on research and development	37
3.21	Internet hosts, 2002	39

Business Competitiveness Index		Rank/95
Sophistication of Company Operations and Strategy		
10.03	Extent of branding	11
10.02	Value chain presence	12
10.11	Breadth of international markets	13
Quality of the National Business Environment		
9.08	Local availability of components and parts	2
9.09	Local availability of process machinery	2
9.06	State of cluster development	2

Other Indicators		Rank/102
11.13	Prevalence of environmental management systems	6
4.06	Business impact of tuberculosis	20
11.11	Effects of compliance on business	20
11.06	Compliance with environmental regulations	22
11.03	Toxic waste disposal regulations	22
4.07	Business impact of HIV/AIDS	23
11.09	Flexibility of regulations	23
11.04	Chemical waste regulations	23
11.01	Air pollution regulations	24
11.02	Water pollution regulations	24
6.16	Government effectiveness in reducing income inequality	25
4.05	Business impact of malaria	27
11.07	Compliance with international agreements	28
10.05	Ethical behavior of firms	29
8.03	Extent of market dominance	29

NOTABLE COMPETITIVE DISADVANTAGES

Growth Competitiveness Index		Rank/102
Macroeconomic Environment		
2.01	Recession expectations	66
2.21	Real exchange rate, 2002	59
2.19	National savings rate, 2002	55
7.10	Public trust of politicians	49
7.08	Diversion of public funds	46
2.20	Inflation, 2002	42
Public Institutions		
6.17	Organized crime	76
7.03	Irregular payments in tax collection	53
6.08	Favoritism in decisions of government officials	51
7.02	Irregular payments in public utilities	46
7.01	Irregular payments in exports and imports	45
6.01	Judicial independence	43
Technology		
3.14	Government prioritization of ICT	65
3.02	Firm-level technology absorption	61
3.15	Government success in ICT promotion	58
3.12	Internet access in schools	44

Business Competitiveness Index		Rank/95
Sophistication of Company Operations and Strategy		
10.15	Reliance on professional management	55
3.06	Company spending on research and development	36
10.12	Extent of staff training	32
Quality of the National Business Environment		
10.20	Cooperation in labor-employer relations	76
10.26	Foreign ownership restrictions	66
8.05	Administrative burden for startups	61

Other Indicators		Rank/102
10.19	Flexibility of wage determination	98
8.08	Private sector employment of women	87
8.09	Wage equality of women in the workplace	86
4.11	Maternity laws' impact on hiring women	86
8.10	Regional disparities in quality of business environment	85
6.11	Efficiency of the tax system	84
10.18	Hiring and firing practices	74
6.06	Burden of regulation	73
10.21	Pay and productivity	70
7.12	Policy consequences of legal political donations	67
10.22	Charitable causes involvement	66
7.06	Irregular payments in government policymaking	61
7.11	Prevalence of illegal political donations	59
2.02	Business costs of terrorism	57
6.10	Effectiveness of law-making bodies	57

271

Note: The Business Competitiveness Index applies different criteria for selecting a country's competitive advantages and disadvantages. Please refer to the section "How Country Profiles Work" for further details.

Jamaica

Competitiveness Rankings

Growth Competitiveness Index Rank	67

Macroeconomic Environment Index Rank	**86**
Macroeconomic Stability Subindex Rank	90
Government Waste Subindex Rank	80
Country Credit Rating Rank	73
Public Institutions Index Rank	**70**
Contracts and Law Subindex Rank	72
Corruption Subindex Rank	64
Technology Index Rank	**53**
Innovation Subindex Rank	64
ICT Subindex Rank	53
Technology Transfer Subindex Rank (out of 77 non-core innovators)	36

Business Competitiveness Index Rank	56

Sophistication of Company Operations and Strategy Rank	**56**
Quality of the National Business Environment Rank	**56**

The Most Problematic Factors for Doing Business

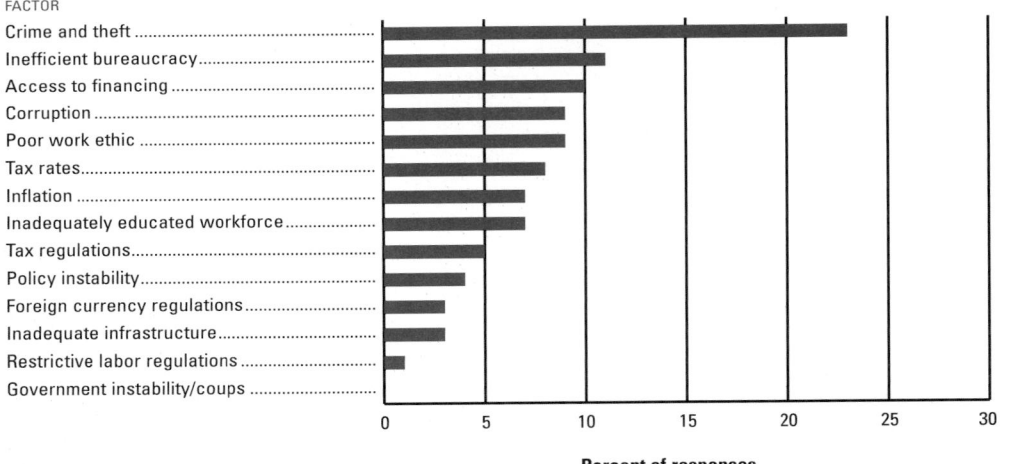

FACTOR
- Crime and theft
- Inefficient bureaucracy
- Access to financing
- Corruption
- Poor work ethic
- Tax rates
- Inflation
- Inadequately educated workforce
- Tax regulations
- Policy instability
- Foreign currency regulations
- Inadequate infrastructure
- Restrictive labor regulations
- Government instability/coups

Percent of responses

Note: From a list of 14 factors, respondents were asked to select the five most problematic for doing business in their country and to rank them between 1 (most problematic) and 5. The bars in the figure show the responses weighted according to their rankings.

Source: World Economic Forum, Executive Opinion Survey (2003)

National competitiveness balance sheet

NOTABLE COMPETITIVE ADVANTAGES		NOTABLE COMPETITIVE DISADVANTAGES	

Growth Competitiveness Index — Rank/102

Macroeconomic Environment

2.09	Access to credit	50

Public Institutions

6.01	Judicial independence	48

Technology

3.03	FDI and technology transfer	15
3.14	Government prioritization of ICT	27
3.13	Quality of competition in the ISP sector	32
3.19	Cellular telephones, 2002	33
3.17	Utility patents, 2002	43
3.06	Company spending on research and development	48
3.08	University/industry research collaboration	48
3.04	Prevalence of foreign technology licensing	49

Growth Competitiveness Index — Rank/102

Macroeconomic Environment

2.21	Real exchange rate, 2002	98
2.01	Recession expectations	93
2.18	Government surplus/deficit, 2002	89
2.03	Extent of distortive government subsidies	84
7.10	Public trust of politicians	84
7.08	Diversion of public funds	77
2.20	Inflation, 2002	76
2.17	Country credit rating, 2003	73
2.22	Interest rate spread, 2002	71
2.19	National savings rate, 2002	64

Public Institutions

6.17	Organized crime	100
6.08	Favoritism in decisions of government officials	85
7.01	Irregular payments in exports and imports	77
7.02	Irregular payments in public utilities	66
7.03	Irregular payments in tax collection	62
6.03	Property rights	55

Technology

3.02	Firm-level technology absorption	73
3.20	Internet users, 2002	66
3.21	Internet hosts, 2002	65
3.12	Internet access in schools	64
3.18	Tertiary enrollment	63
3.15	Government success in ICT promotion	60
3.16	Laws relating to ICT	59
3.01	Technological sophistication	55
3.22	Telephone lines, 2002	55
3.23	Personal computers, 2002	54

Business Competitiveness Index — Rank/95

Sophistication of Company Operations and Strategy

10.01	Nature of competitive advantage	22
10.15	Reliance on professional management	35
10.03	Extent of branding	44

Quality of the National Business Environment

2.11	Local equity market access	13
10.26	Foreign ownership restrictions	15
6.09	Extent of bureaucratic red tape	21

Business Competitiveness Index — Rank/95

Sophistication of Company Operations and Strategy

10.10	Extent of regional sales	78
10.11	Breadth of international markets	73
3.04	Prevalence of foreign technology licensing	70

Quality of the National Business Environment

5.02	Railroad infrastructure development	86
9.08	Local availability of components and parts	85
8.02	Extent of locally based competitors	81

Other Indicators — Rank/102

4.10	Maternity leave legislation	16
10.22	Charitable causes involvement	19
4.11	Maternity laws' impact on hiring women	23
8.10	Regional disparities in quality of business environment	25
8.08	Private sector employment of women	28
10.27	Strength of auditing and accounting standards	29
11.11	Effects of compliance on business	32
10.18	Hiring and firing practices	34
10.19	Flexibility of wage determination	34
10.25	Availability of company financial information	35
2.02	Business costs of terrorism	37
11.12	Political context of environmental gains	39
10.05	Ethical behavior of firms	44
3.11	Availability of mobile or cellular telephones	47
11.09	Flexibility of regulations	49

Other Indicators — Rank/102

6.14	Business costs of crime and violence	100
6.06	Burden of regulation	92
7.14	Pervasiveness of money laundering through non-bank channels	90
6.18	Informal sector	87
7.11	Prevalence of illegal political donations	85
4.07	Business impact of HIV/AIDS	84
5.07	Postal efficiency	83
6.15	Government effectiveness in reducing poverty	83
7.12	Policy consequences of legal political donations	79
4.09	Brain drain	79
7.04	Irregular payments in public contracts	78
6.16	Government effectiveness in reducing income inequality	78
10.21	Pay and productivity	74
6.07	Transparency of government policymaking	74
7.13	Pervasiveness of money laundering through banks	74

273

Note: The Business Competitiveness Index applies different criteria for selecting a country's competitive advantages and disadvantages. Please refer to the section "How Country Profiles Work" for further details.

Japan

Competitiveness Rankings

Growth Competitiveness Index Rank	11
Macroeconomic Environment Index Rank **24**	
Macroeconomic Stability Subindex Rank 19	
Government Waste Subindex Rank 54	
Country Credit Rating Rank 20	
Public Institutions Index Rank...........................**30**	
Contracts and Law Subindex Rank 38	
Corruption Subindex Rank...................................21	
Technology Index Rank **5**	
Innovation Subindex Rank 5	
ICT Subindex Rank 18	

Business Competitiveness Index Rank	13
Sophistication of Company Operations and Strategy Rank 6	
Quality of the National Business Environment Rank 20	

The Most Problematic Factors for Doing Business

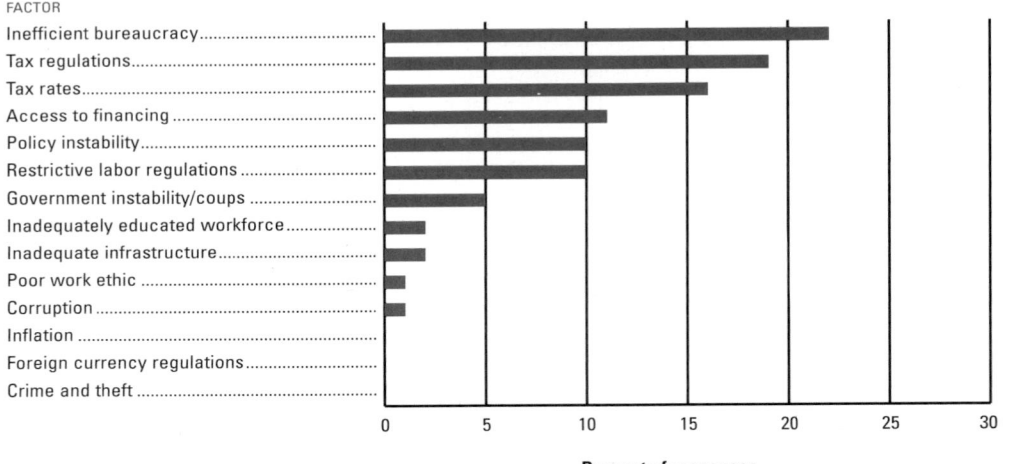

Note: From a list of 14 factors, respondents were asked to select the five most problematic for doing business in their country and to rank them between 1 (most problematic) and 5. The bars in the figure show the responses weighted according to their rankings.

Source: World Economic Forum, Executive Opinion Survey (2003)

National competitiveness balance sheet

NOTABLE COMPETITIVE ADVANTAGES	
Growth Competitiveness Index	**Rank/102**

Macroeconomic Environment
2.22	Interest rate spread, 2002	3
2.20	Inflation, 2002	4

Technology
3.02	Firm-level technology absorption	2
3.17	Utility patents, 2002	2
3.06	Company spending on research and development	3
3.01	Technological sophistication	5
3.14	Government prioritization of ICT	9

NOTABLE COMPETITIVE DISADVANTAGES	
Growth Competitiveness Index	**Rank/102**

Macroeconomic Environment
2.03	Extent of distortive government subsidies	90
2.01	Recession expectations	83
2.18	Government surplus/deficit, 2002	81
2.09	Access to credit	67
7.10	Public trust of politicians	51
7.08	Diversion of public funds	36
2.19	National savings rate, 2002	20
2.17	Country credit rating, 2003	20
2.21	Real exchange rate, 2002	16

Public Institutions
6.17	Organized crime	49
6.03	Property rights	39
6.01	Judicial independence	36
6.08	Favoritism in decisions of government officials	36
7.02	Irregular payments in public utilities	25
7.03	Irregular payments in tax collection	23
7.01	Irregular payments in exports and imports	18

Technology
3.15	Government success in ICT promotion	30
3.19	Cellular telephones, 2002	30
3.18	Tertiary enrollment	29
3.16	Laws relating to ICT	27
3.12	Internet access in schools	24
3.23	Personal computers, 2002	19
3.08	University/industry research collaboration	15
3.22	Telephone lines, 2002	15
3.13	Quality of competition in the ISP sector	14
3.21	Internet hosts, 2002	14
3.20	Internet users, 2002	12

Business Competitiveness Index	**Rank/95**

Sophistication of Company Operations and Strategy
10.11	Breadth of international markets	1
10.08	Degree of customer orientation	1
10.01	Nature of competitive advantage	1

Quality of the National Business Environment
9.08	Local availability of components and parts	1
9.09	Local availability of process machinery	1
9.02	Local supplier quantity	1

Other Indicators	**Rank/102**

11.13	Prevalence of environmental management systems	3
5.07	Postal efficiency	3
11.12	Political context of environmental gains	5
8.03	Extent of market dominance	5
4.09	Brain drain	8
11.11	Effects of compliance on business	9
6.18	Informal sector	9
3.07	Subsidies and tax credits for firm-level research and development	10

Business Competitiveness Index	**Rank/95**

Sophistication of Company Operations and Strategy
10.14	Extent of incentive compensation	54
10.15	Reliance on professional management	21
10.13	Willingness to delegate authority	19

Quality of the National Business Environment
2.03	Extent of distortive government subsidies	83
6.12	Centralization of economic policymaking	82
8.05	Administrative burden for startups	80

Other Indicators	**Rank/102**

2.06	Soundness of banks	102
2.15	Agricultural policy costs	100
8.08	Private sector employment of women	94
4.10	Maternity leave legislation	94
2.04	Extent of distortive government intervention	88
10.18	Hiring and firing practices	87
2.02	Business costs of terrorism	85
8.09	Wage equality of women in the workplace	82
6.11	Efficiency of the tax system	81
10.22	Charitable causes involvement	79
4.11	Maternity laws' impact on hiring women	73
6.07	Transparency of government policymaking	55
4.08	Impact of HIV/AIDS on FDI	52
4.05	Business impact of malaria	52
4.07	Business impact of HIV/AIDS	51

275

Note: The Business Competitiveness Index applies different criteria for selecting a country's competitive advantages and disadvantages. Please refer to the section "How Country Profiles Work" for further details.

Jordan

Competitiveness Rankings

Growth Competitiveness Index Rank	34

Macroeconomic Environment Index Rank **42**
  Macroeconomic Stability Subindex Rank 39
  Government Waste Subindex Rank 18
  Country Credit Rating Rank 59

Public Institutions Index Rank **20**
  Contracts and Law Subindex Rank 15
  Corruption Subindex Rank....................................33

Technology Index Rank **48**
  Innovation Subindex Rank 47
  ICT Subindex Rank 46
  Technology Transfer Subindex Rank
  (out of 77 non-core innovators).........................28

Business Competitiveness Index Rank	41

**Sophistication of Company Operations
  and Strategy Rank** **59**
**Quality of the National Business
  Environment Rank** **35**

The Most Problematic Factors for Doing Business

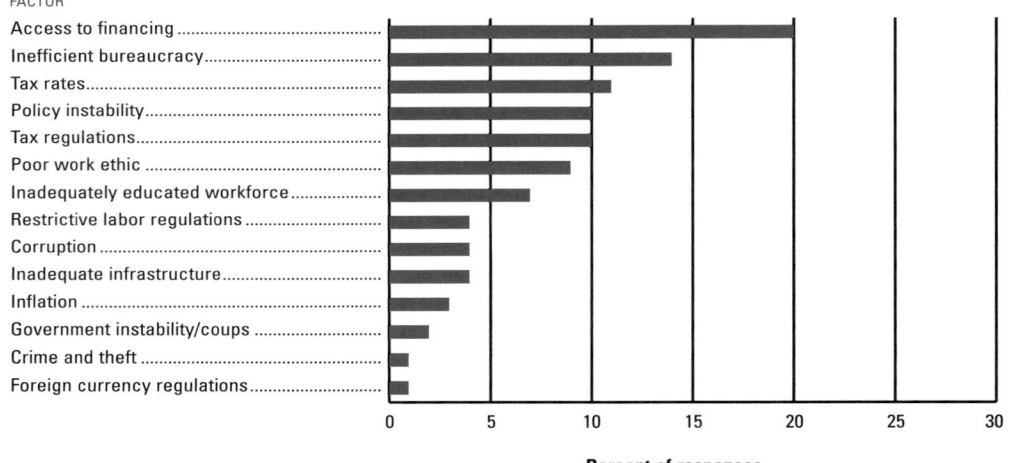

FACTOR

Access to financing
Inefficient bureaucracy
Tax rates
Policy instability
Tax regulations
Poor work ethic
Inadequately educated workforce
Restrictive labor regulations
Corruption
Inadequate infrastructure
Inflation
Government instability/coups
Crime and theft
Foreign currency regulations

Percent of responses

Note: From a list of 14 factors, respondents were asked to select the five most problematic for doing business in their country and to rank them between 1 (most problematic) and 5. The bars in the figure show the responses weighted according to their rankings.

Source: World Economic Forum, Executive Opinion Survey (2003)

National competitiveness balance sheet

NOTABLE COMPETITIVE ADVANTAGES

	Growth Competitiveness Index	Rank/102
	Macroeconomic Environment	
2.19	National savings rate, 2002	14
7.08	Diversion of public funds	18
7.10	Public trust of politicians	18
2.20	Inflation, 2002	20
2.03	Extent of distortive government subsidies	28
	Public Institutions	
6.17	Organized crime	6
6.03	Property rights	16
6.08	Favoritism in decisions of government officials	22
6.01	Judicial independence	23
7.01	Irregular payments in exports and imports	28
	Technology	
3.15	Government success in ICT promotion	8
3.04	Prevalence of foreign technology licensing	11
3.14	Government prioritization of ICT	11
3.13	Quality of competition in the ISP sector	19

	Business Competitiveness Index	Rank/95
	Sophistication of Company Operations and Strategy	
3.04	Prevalence of foreign technology licensing	13
10.09	Control of international distribution	36
10.10	Extent of regional sales	36
	Quality of the National Business Environment	
6.13	Reliability of police services	7
3.10	Availability of scientists and engineers	12
8.05	Administrative burden for startups	16

	Other Indicators	Rank/102
6.14	Business costs of crime and violence	6
7.13	Pervasiveness of money laundering through banks	8
8.03	Extent of market dominance	9
7.14	Pervasiveness of money laundering through non-bank channels	9
6.06	Burden of regulation	9
4.07	Business impact of HIV/AIDS	10
8.11	Focus of trade and industry associations	11
7.12	Policy consequences of legal political donations	11
7.11	Prevalence of illegal political donations	13
2.04	Extent of distortive government intervention	17
7.04	Irregular payments in public contracts	19
6.11	Efficiency of the tax system	20
2.10	Government intervention in corporate investment	21
7.06	Irregular payments in government policymaking	22
6.18	Informal sector	24

NOTABLE COMPETITIVE DISADVANTAGES

	Growth Competitiveness Index	Rank/102
	Macroeconomic Environment	
2.18	Government surplus/deficit, 2002	84
2.21	Real exchange rate, 2002	81
2.17	Country credit rating, 2003	59
2.22	Interest rate spread, 2002	56
2.01	Recession expectations	44
2.09	Access to credit	42
	Public Institutions	
7.02	Irregular payments in public utilities	35
7.03	Irregular payments in tax collection	35
	Technology	
3.06	Company spending on research and development	65
3.21	Internet hosts, 2002	62
3.23	Personal computers, 2002	61
3.08	University/industry research collaboration	59
3.22	Telephone lines, 2002	59
3.17	Utility patents, 2002	57
3.20	Internet users, 2002	54
3.19	Cellular telephones, 2002	52
3.03	FDI and technology transfer	49
3.02	Firm-level technology absorption	48
3.18	Tertiary enrollment	48
3.01	Technological sophistication	44
3.12	Internet access in schools	41
3.16	Laws relating to ICT	38

	Business Competitiveness Index	Rank/95
	Sophistication of Company Operations and Strategy	
10.14	Extent of incentive compensation	84
10.15	Reliance on professional management	78
10.07	Extent of marketing	71
	Quality of the National Business Environment	
6.09	Extent of bureaucratic red tape	73
5.02	Railroad infrastructure development	67
8.02	Extent of locally based competitors	64

	Other Indicators	Rank/102
6.05	Freedom of the press	85
4.09	Brain drain	63
3.07	Subsidies and tax credits for firm-level research and development	54
11.13	Prevalence of environmental management systems	51
10.22	Charitable causes involvement	47
2.06	Soundness of banks	45
10.23	Company promotion of volunteerism	45
11.01	Air pollution regulations	45
8.10	Regional disparities in quality of business environment	43
11.04	Chemical waste regulations	42
11.12	Political context of environmental gains	42
8.08	Private sector employment of women	41
10.18	Hiring and firing practices	41
6.10	Effectiveness of law-making bodies	41
11.03	Toxic waste disposal regulations	41

277

Note: The Business Competitiveness Index applies different criteria for selecting a country's competitive advantages and disadvantages. Please refer to the section "How Country Profiles Work" for further details.

Kenya

Competitiveness Rankings

Growth Competitiveness Index Rank	83

Macroeconomic Environment Index Rank **77**
    Macroeconomic Stability Subindex Rank 60
    Government Waste Subindex Rank 77
    Country Credit Rating Rank 82

Public Institutions Index Rank **92**
    Contracts and Law Subindex Rank 80
    Corruption Subindex Rank....................................95

Technology Index Rank **74**
    Innovation Subindex Rank....................................84
    ICT Subindex Rank 86
    Technology Transfer Subindex Rank
    (out of 77 non-core innovators) 17

Business Competitiveness Index Rank	66

**Sophistication of Company Operations
and Strategy Rank** **61**

**Quality of the National Business
Environment Rank** **69**

The Most Problematic Factors for Doing Business

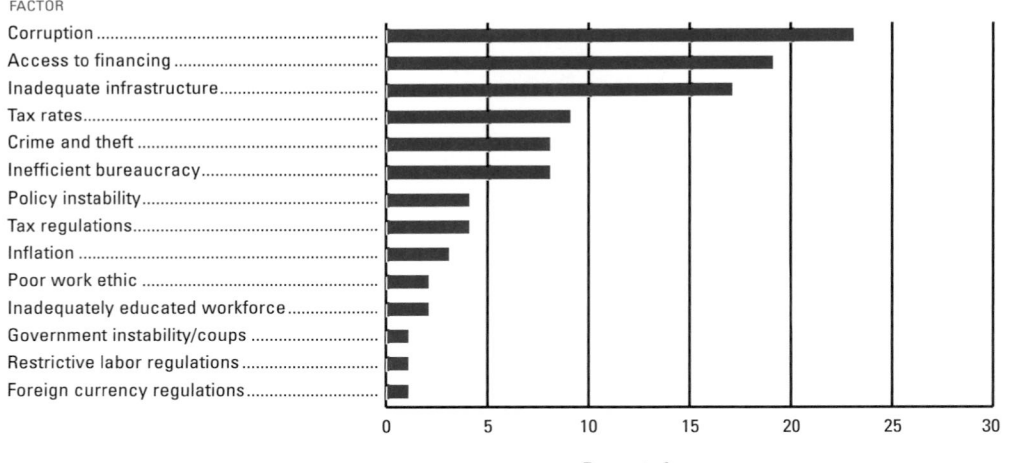

FACTOR

Corruption
Access to financing
Inadequate infrastructure
Tax rates
Crime and theft
Inefficient bureaucracy
Policy instability
Tax regulations
Inflation
Poor work ethic
Inadequately educated workforce
Government instability/coups
Restrictive labor regulations
Foreign currency regulations

Percent of responses

Note: From a list of 14 factors, respondents were asked to select the five most problematic for doing business in their country and to rank them between 1 (most problematic) and 5. The bars in the figure show the responses weighted according to their rankings.

Source: World Economic Forum, Executive Opinion Survey (2003)

National competitiveness balance sheet

NOTABLE COMPETITIVE ADVANTAGES	
Growth Competitiveness Index	**Rank/102**

Macroeconomic Environment

2.01	Recession expectations	15
2.20	Inflation, 2002	28

Technology

3.03	FDI and technology transfer	19
3.04	Prevalence of foreign technology licensing	18
3.06	Company spending on research and development	41

NOTABLE COMPETITIVE DISADVANTAGES	
Growth Competitiveness Index	**Rank/102**

Macroeconomic Environment

7.08	Diversion of public funds	93
2.19	National savings rate, 2002	87
2.22	Interest rate spread, 2002	83
2.17	Country credit rating, 2003	82
2.09	Access to credit	80
2.21	Real exchange rate, 2002	70
7.10	Public trust of politicians	67
2.03	Extent of distortive government subsidies	60
2.18	Government surplus/deficit, 2002	51

Public Institutions

7.02	Irregular payments in public utilities	96
7.03	Irregular payments in tax collection	93
7.01	Irregular payments in exports and imports	88
6.01	Judicial independence	84
6.17	Organized crime	83
6.08	Favoritism in decisions of government officials	77
6.03	Property rights	67

Technology

3.18	Tertiary enrollment	90
3.22	Telephone lines, 2002	89
3.12	Internet access in schools	86
3.23	Personal computers, 2002	86
3.19	Cellular telephones, 2002	82
3.14	Government prioritization of ICT	81
3.20	Internet users, 2002	80
3.02	Firm-level technology absorption	77
3.21	Internet hosts, 2002	77
3.15	Government success in ICT promotion	75
3.13	Quality of competition in the ISP sector	73
3.01	Technological sophistication	72
3.17	Utility patents, 2002	70
3.16	Laws relating to ICT	67
3.08	University/industry research collaboration	60

Business Competitiveness Index	Rank/95

Sophistication of Company Operations and Strategy

3.04	Prevalence of foreign technology licensing	28
10.10	Extent of regional sales	30
3.06	Company spending on research and development	40

Quality of the National Business Environment

3.05	Quality of scientific research institutions	27
8.01	Intensity of local competition	29
2.11	Local equity market access	31

Other Indicators	Rank/102

10.18	Hiring and firing practices	14
8.11	Focus of trade and industry associations	31
10.22	Charitable causes involvement	31
6.10	Effectiveness of law-making bodies	39
6.11	Efficiency of the tax system	49

Business Competitiveness Index	Rank/95

Sophistication of Company Operations and Strategy

10.06	Production process sophistication	78
10.14	Extent of incentive compensation	77
10.09	Control of international distribution	74

Quality of the National Business Environment

7.09	Business costs of corruption	90
5.06	Telephone infrastructure quality	88
10.20	Cooperation in labor-employer relations	87

Other Indicators	Rank/102

4.08	Impact of HIV/AIDS on FDI	97
6.14	Business costs of crime and violence	97
4.04	Disparity in healthcare quality	96
2.02	Business costs of terrorism	96
7.04	Irregular payments in public contracts	96
4.07	Business impact of HIV/AIDS	91
11.02	Water pollution regulations	90
4.05	Business impact of malaria	89
5.07	Postal efficiency	89
7.07	Irregular payments in judicial decisions	89
11.09	Flexibility of regulations	88
7.13	Pervasiveness of money laundering through banks	88
4.06	Business impact of tuberculosis	87
11.01	Air pollution regulations	86
11.04	Chemical waste regulations	86

Note: The Business Competitiveness Index applies different criteria for selecting a country's competitive advantages and disadvantages. Please refer to the section "How Country Profiles Work" for further details.

Korea

Competitiveness Rankings

Growth Competitiveness Rank	**18**

Macroeconomic Environment Index Rank **23**
    Macroeconomic Stability Subindex Rank 6
    Government Waste Subindex 30
    Country Credit Rating Rank.................................27

Public Institutions Index Rank...**36**
    Contracts and Law Subindex Rank 34
    Corruption Subindex Rank...................................38

Technology Index Rank **6**
    Innovation Subindex Rank 7
    ICT Subindex Rank 11

Business Competitiveness Index Rank	**23**

**Sophistication of Company Operations
  and Strategy Rank** **19**

**Quality of the National Business
  Environment Rank** **25**

The Most Problematic Factors for Doing Business

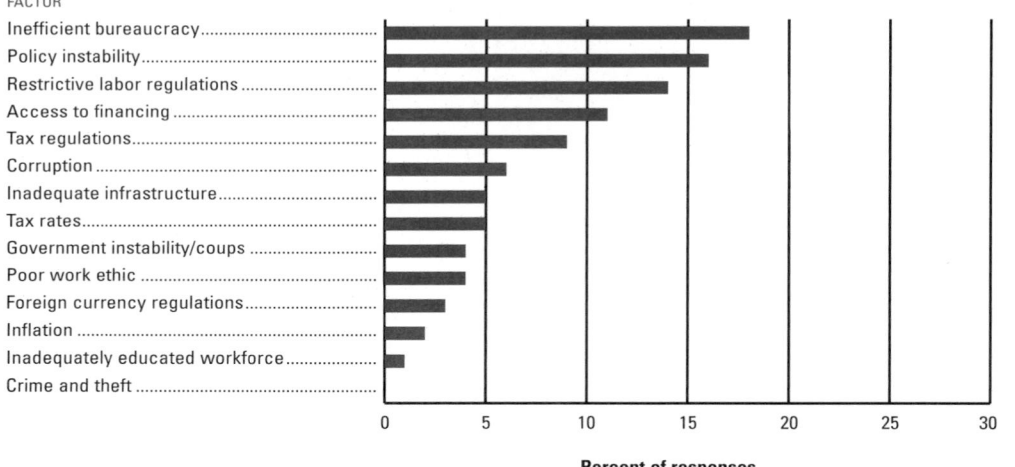

FACTOR

Note: From a list of 14 factors, respondents were asked to select the five most problematic for doing business in their country and to rank them between 1 (most problematic) and 5. The bars in the figure show the responses weighted according to their rankings.

Source: World Economic Forum, Executive Opinion Survey (2003)

National competitiveness balance sheet

NOTABLE COMPETITIVE ADVANTAGES	
Growth Competitiveness Index	**Rank/102**

Macroeconomic Environment
2.18	Government surplus/deficit, 2002	2
2.22	Interest rate spread, 2002	8
2.19	National savings rate, 2002	13
2.09	Access to credit	16

Technology
3.13	Quality of competition in the ISP sector	1
3.18	Tertiary enrollment	2
3.20	Internet users, 2002	3
3.12	Internet access in schools	4
3.15	Government success in ICT promotion	4
3.23	Personal computers, 2002	4
3.14	Government prioritization of ICT	8
3.02	Firm-level technology absorption	10
3.06	Company spending on research and development	12
3.16	Laws relating to ICT	12
3.17	Utility patents, 2002	14
3.01	Technological sophistication	15

NOTABLE COMPETITIVE DISADVANTAGES	
Growth Competitiveness Index	**Rank/102**

Macroeconomic Environment
2.01	Recession expectations	49
2.20	Inflation, 2002	44
7.10	Public trust of politicians	42
2.21	Real exchange rate, 2002	32
7.08	Diversion of public funds	32
2.17	Country credit rating, 2003	27
2.03	Extent of distortive government subsidies	23

Public Institutions
6.01	Judicial independence	49
7.03	Irregular payments in tax collection	47
7.02	Irregular payments in public utilities	38
6.03	Property rights	36
6.17	Organized crime	34
7.01	Irregular payments in exports and imports	34
6.08	Favoritism in decisions of government officials	18

Technology
3.21	Internet hosts, 2002	35
3.19	Cellular telephones, 2002	25
3.22	Telephone lines, 2002	23
3.08	University/industry research collaboration	18

Business Competitiveness Index	
Business Competitiveness Index	**Rank/95**

Sophistication of Company Operations and Strategy
3.06	Company spending on research and development	12
10.09	Control of international distribution	13
10.11	Breadth of international markets	15

Quality of the National Business Environment
3.20	Internet users, 2002	3
9.09	Local availability of process machinery	8
9.06	State of cluster development	8

Business Competitiveness Index	
Business Competitiveness Index	**Rank/95**

Sophistication of Company Operations and Strategy
10.15	Reliance on professional management	43
10.14	Extent of incentive compensation	26
10.07	Extent of marketing	25

Quality of the National Business Environment
10.20	Cooperation in labor-employer relations	86
10.26	Foreign ownership restrictions	63
10.24	Protection of minority shareholders' interests	60

Other Indicators	
Other Indicators	**Rank/102**

8.11	Focus of trade and industry associations	8
11.13	Prevalence of environmental management systems	12
10.23	Company promotion of volunteerism	14
3.07	Subsidies and tax credits for firm-level research and development	15

Other Indicators	
Other Indicators	**Rank/102**

8.08	Private sector employment of women	100
4.10	Maternity leave legislation	97
4.11	Maternity laws' impact on hiring women	95
8.09	Wage equality of women in the workplace	90
4.08	Impact of HIV/AIDS on FDI	71
2.06	Soundness of banks	70
10.22	Charitable causes involvement	70
2.15	Agricultural policy costs	60
6.05	Freedom of the press	58
6.10	Effectiveness of law-making bodies	56
10.18	Hiring and firing practices	56
2.02	Business costs of terrorism	55
10.19	Flexibility of wage determination	54
10.27	Strength of auditing and accounting standards	53
2.10	Government intervention in corporate investment	49

281

Note: The Business Competitiveness Index applies different criteria for selecting a country's competitive advantages and disadvantages. Please refer to the section "How Country Profiles Work" for further details.

Latvia

Competitiveness Rankings

Growth Competitiveness Index Rank	37

Macroeconomic Environment Index Rank **36**
    Macroeconomic Stability Subindex Rank 12
    Government Waste Subindex Rank 28
    Country Credit Rating Rank 44

Public Institutions Index Rank **45**
    Contracts and Law Subindex Rank 44
    Corruption Subindex Rank....................................49

Technology Index Rank **26**
    Innovation Subindex Rank....................................22
    ICT Subindex Rank 34
    Technology Transfer Subindex Rank
    (out of 77 non-core innovators) 19

Business Competitiveness Index Rank	29

**Sophistication of Company Operations
and Strategy Rank** **29**
**Quality of the National Business
Environment Rank** **31**

The Most Problematic Factors for Doing Business

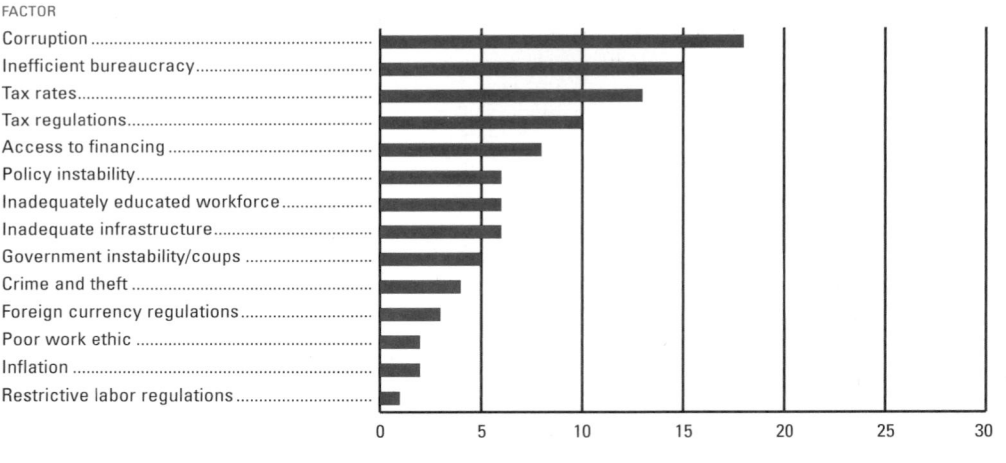

FACTOR

Corruption
Inefficient bureaucracy
Tax rates
Tax regulations
Access to financing
Policy instability
Inadequately educated workforce
Inadequate infrastructure
Government instability/coups
Crime and theft
Foreign currency regulations
Poor work ethic
Inflation
Restrictive labor regulations

Percent of responses

Note: From a list of 14 factors, respondents were asked to select the five most problematic for doing business in their country and to rank them between 1 (most problematic) and 5. The bars in the figure show the responses weighted according to their rankings.

Source: World Economic Forum, Executive Opinion Survey (2003)

National competitiveness balance sheet

NOTABLE COMPETITIVE ADVANTAGES

Growth Competitiveness Index	Rank/102

Macroeconomic Environment

2.01	Recession expectations	3
2.03	Extent of distortive government subsidies	5
2.09	Access to credit	10
2.20	Inflation, 2002	24
7.10	Public trust of politicians	31
2.19	National savings rate, 2002	32

Public Institutions

6.08	Favoritism in decisions of government officials	24

Technology

3.18	Tertiary enrollment	10
3.04	Prevalence of foreign technology licensing	13
3.06	Company spending on research and development	24
3.12	Internet access in schools	28
3.16	Laws relating to ICT	28
3.03	FDI and technology transfer	29
3.23	Personal computers, 2002	30
3.01	Technological sophistication	31
3.08	University/industry research collaboration	32
3.21	Internet hosts, 2002	34
3.22	Telephone lines, 2002	36

Business Competitiveness Index	Rank/95

Sophistication of Company Operations and Strategy

3.04	Prevalence of foreign technology licensing	18
3.06	Company spending on research and development	23
10.13	Willingness to delegate authority	25

Quality of the National Business Environment

2.03	Extent of distortive government subsidies	4
6.12	Centralization of economic policymaking	12
2.07	Ease of access to loans	13

Other Indicators	Rank/102

8.03	Extent of market dominance	3
10.21	Pay and productivity	7
8.11	Focus of trade and industry associations	13
10.23	Company promotion of volunteerism	13
6.06	Burden of regulation	13
10.18	Hiring and firing practices	16
2.15	Agricultural policy costs	16
2.04	Extent of distortive government intervention	21
6.11	Efficiency of the tax system	24
2.02	Business costs of terrorism	26
8.08	Private sector employment of women	26
3.07	Subsidies and tax credits for firm-level research and development	27
11.09	Flexibility of regulations	28
2.10	Government intervention in corporate investment	28
6.16	Government effectiveness in reducing income inequality	29

NOTABLE COMPETITIVE DISADVANTAGES

Growth Competitiveness Index	Rank/102

Macroeconomic Environment

2.21	Real exchange rate, 2002	88
2.17	Country credit rating, 2003	44
2.18	Government surplus/deficit, 2002	41
2.22	Interest rate spread, 2002	41
7.08	Diversion of public funds	38

Public Institutions

6.17	Organized crime	51
7.01	Irregular payments in exports and imports	51
7.03	Irregular payments in tax collection	50
7.02	Irregular payments in public utilities	49
6.03	Property rights	48
6.01	Judicial independence	47

Technology

3.17	Utility patents, 2002	72
3.14	Government prioritization of ICT	52
3.15	Government success in ICT promotion	43
3.20	Internet users, 2002	40
3.13	Quality of competition in the ISP sector	40
3.19	Cellular telephones, 2002	38
3.02	Firm-level technology absorption	38

Business Competitiveness Index	Rank/95

Sophistication of Company Operations and Strategy

10.10	Extent of regional sales	51
10.09	Control of international distribution	39
10.11	Breadth of international markets	39

Quality of the National Business Environment

6.09	Extent of bureaucratic red tape	78
3.17	Utility patents, 2002	71
5.06	Telephone infrastructure quality	60

Other Indicators	Rank/102

4.10	Maternity leave legislation	84
3.11	Availability of mobile or cellular telephones	69
4.11	Maternity laws' impact on hiring women	66
4.08	Impact of HIV/AIDS on FDI	64
11.13	Prevalence of environmental management systems	62
10.22	Charitable causes involvement	61
6.05	Freedom of the press	59
7.13	Pervasiveness of money laundering through banks	58
7.07	Irregular payments in judicial decisions	56
4.06	Business impact of tuberculosis	52
6.14	Business costs of crime and violence	50
7.05	Irregular payments in loan applications	49
10.25	Availability of company financial information	48
2.06	Soundness of banks	46
6.18	Informal sector	46

283

Note: The Business Competitiveness Index applies different criteria for selecting a country's competitive advantages and disadvantages. Please refer to the section "How Country Profiles Work" for further details.

Lithuania

Competitiveness Rankings

Growth Competitiveness Index Rank	**40**

Macroeconomic Environment Index Rank **41**
    Macroeconomic Stability Subindex Rank 14
    Government Waste Subindex Rank 57
    Country Credit Rating Rank 46

Public Institutions Index Rank..**41**
    Contracts and Law Subindex Rank 58
    Corruption Subindex Rank 34

Technology Index Rank **36**
    Innovation Subindex Rank 30
    ICT Subindex Rank 38
    Technology Transfer Subindex Rank
       (out of 77 non-core innovators).......................42

Business Competitiveness Index Rank	**40**

**Sophistication of Company Operations
  and Strategy Rank** **41**
**Quality of the National Business
  Environment Rank** **41**

The Most Problematic Factors for Doing Business

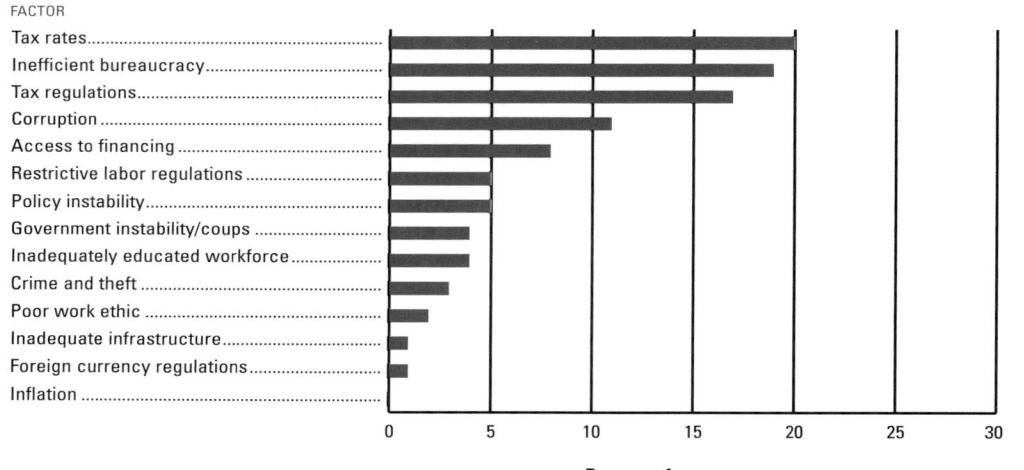

Note: From a list of 14 factors, respondents were asked to select the five most problematic for doing business in their country and to rank them between 1 (most problematic) and 5. The bars in the figure show the responses weighted according to their rankings.

Source: World Economic Forum, Executive Opinion Survey (2003)

National competitiveness balance sheet

NOTABLE COMPETITIVE ADVANTAGES		NOTABLE COMPETITIVE DISADVANTAGES	
Growth Competitiveness Index	Rank/102	**Growth Competitiveness Index**	Rank/102

Growth Competitiveness Index — Rank/102

	Macroeconomic Environment	
2.09	Access to credit	8
2.20	Inflation, 2002	9
2.01	Recession expectations	11
2.18	Government surplus/deficit, 2002	29
	Public Institutions	
7.02	Irregular payments in public utilities	32
7.03	Irregular payments in tax collection	36
6.08	Favoritism in decisions of government officials	38
	Technology	
3.18	Tertiary enrollment	23
3.02	Firm-level technology absorption	25
3.21	Internet hosts, 2002	33
3.12	Internet access in schools	35
3.19	Cellular telephones, 2002	35
3.20	Internet users, 2002	39
3.23	Personal computers, 2002	39

Growth Competitiveness Index — Rank/102

	Macroeconomic Environment	
2.21	Real exchange rate, 2002	100
2.19	National savings rate, 2002	70
7.08	Diversion of public funds	61
7.10	Public trust of politicians	60
2.03	Extent of distortive government subsidies	53
2.22	Interest rate spread, 2002	48
2.17	Country credit rating, 2003	46
	Public Institutions	
6.01	Judicial independence	65
6.17	Organized crime	65
6.03	Property rights	51
7.01	Irregular payments in exports and imports	40
	Technology	
3.13	Quality of competition in the ISP sector	58
3.01	Technological sophistication	56
3.14	Government prioritization of ICT	54
3.15	Government success in ICT promotion	52
3.17	Utility patents, 2002	49
3.08	University/industry research collaboration	47
3.16	Laws relating to ICT	45
3.04	Prevalence of foreign technology licensing	42
3.03	FDI and technology transfer	40
3.06	Company spending on research and development	40
3.22	Telephone lines, 2002	40

Business Competitiveness Index — Rank/95

	Sophistication of Company Operations and Strategy	
10.02	Value chain presence	25
10.08	Degree of customer orientation	28
10.09	Control of international distribution	31
	Quality of the National Business Environment	
2.07	Ease of access to loans	8
9.02	Local supplier quantity	20
2.08	Venture capital availability	21

Business Competitiveness Index — Rank/95

	Sophistication of Company Operations and Strategy	
10.14	Extent of incentive compensation	73
10.12	Extent of staff training	65
3.04	Prevalence of foreign technology licensing	64
	Quality of the National Business Environment	
10.24	Protection of minority shareholders' interests	86
6.13	Reliability of police services	64
9.01	Buyer sophistication	64

Other Indicators — Rank/102

10.19	Flexibility of wage determination	10
2.02	Business costs of terrorism	13
10.21	Pay and productivity	22
3.11	Availability of mobile or cellular telephones	24
11.10	Consistency of regulation enforcement	26
6.18	Informal sector	28
2.04	Extent of distortive government intervention	29
8.03	Extent of market dominance	32
11.01	Air pollution regulations	32
11.02	Water pollution regulations	33
7.05	Irregular payments in loan applications	35
11.13	Prevalence of environmental management systems	35
11.07	Compliance with international agreements	36
6.05	Freedom of the press	37
11.06	Compliance with environmental regulations	39

Other Indicators — Rank/102

4.11	Maternity laws' impact on hiring women	102
4.10	Maternity leave legislation	87
10.22	Charitable causes involvement	82
6.11	Efficiency of the tax system	82
2.15	Agricultural policy costs	80
4.08	Impact of HIV/AIDS on FDI	77
8.11	Focus of trade and industry associations	77
10.23	Company promotion of volunteerism	73
6.15	Government effectiveness in reducing poverty	72
8.08	Private sector employment of women	72
7.12	Policy consequences of legal political donations	71
11.12	Political context of environmental gains	71
6.16	Government effectiveness in reducing income inequality	70
4.09	Brain drain	69
11.09	Flexibility of regulations	68

285

Note: The Business Competitiveness Index applies different criteria for selecting a country's competitive advantages and disadvantages. Please refer to the section "How Country Profiles Work" for further details.

Luxembourg

Competitiveness Rankings

Growth Competitiveness Index Rank	21

Macroeconomic Environment Index Rank **3**
    Macroeconomic Stability Subindex Rank 15
    Government Waste Subindex Rank 4
    Country Credit Rating Rank....................................2

Public Institutions Index Rank..**13**
    Contracts and Law Subindex Rank 13
    Corruption Subindex Rank....................................15

Technology Index Rank **42**
    Innovation Subindex Rank 40
    ICT Subindex Rank 10

Business Competitiveness Index Rank	n/a

Sophistication of Company Operations
  and Strategy Rank ....**n/a**

Quality of the National Business
  Environment Rank..**n/a**

The Most Problematic Factors for Doing Business

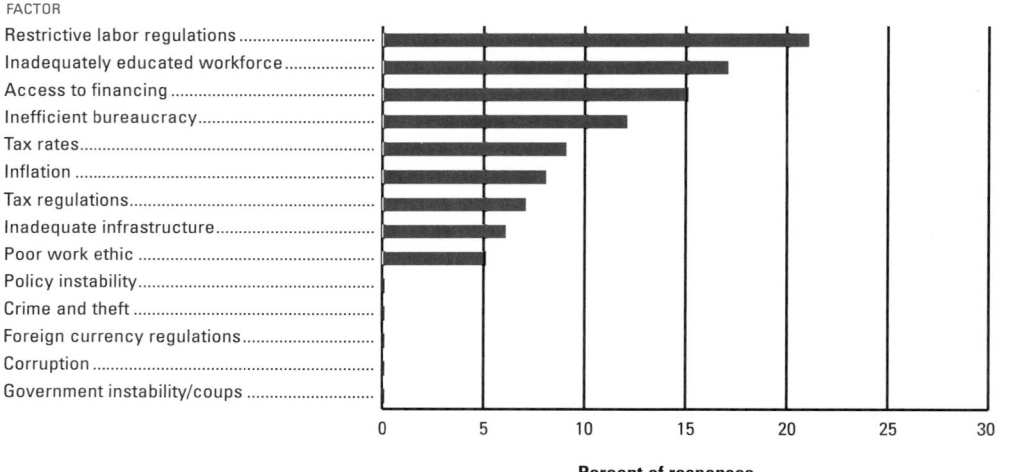

FACTOR

Restrictive labor regulations
Inadequately educated workforce
Access to financing
Inefficient bureaucracy
Tax rates
Inflation
Tax regulations
Inadequate infrastructure
Poor work ethic
Policy instability
Crime and theft
Foreign currency regulations
Corruption
Government instability/coups

Percent of responses

Note: From a list of 14 factors, respondents were asked to select the five most problematic for doing business in their country and to rank them between 1 (most problematic) and 5. The bars in the figure show the responses weighted according to their rankings.

Source: World Economic Forum, Executive Opinion Survey (2003)

National competitiveness balance sheet

NOTABLE COMPETITIVE ADVANTAGES

Growth Competitiveness Index		Rank/102
Macroeconomic Environment		
2.03	Extent of distortive government subsidies	2
2.17	Country credit rating, 2003	2
7.10	Public trust of politicians	4
2.18	Government surplus/deficit, 2002	5
2.22	Interest rate spread, 2002	9
7.08	Diversion of public funds	13
2.19	National savings rate, 2002	15
Public Institutions		
6.03	Property rights	12
7.03	Irregular payments in tax collection	12
6.08	Favoritism in decisions of government officials	13
6.17	Organized crime	14
7.02	Irregular payments in public utilities	14
6.01	Judicial independence	18
7.01	Irregular payments in exports and imports	19
Technology		
3.22	Telephone lines, 2002	1
3.19	Cellular telephones, 2002	2
3.23	Personal computers, 2002	6
3.17	Utility patents, 2002	12
3.06	Company spending on research and development	18
3.02	Firm-level technology absorption	20
3.12	Internet access in schools	20
3.16	Laws relating to ICT	20

Other Indicators		Rank/102
6.18	Informal sector	1
2.04	Extent of distortive government intervention	1
8.03	Extent of market dominance	2
3.07	Subsidies and tax credits for firm-level research and development	3
4.04	Disparity in healthcare quality	3
8.10	Regional disparities in quality of business environment	5
8.11	Focus of trade and industry associations	5
4.10	Maternity leave legislation	5
6.07	Transparency of government policymaking	6
11.10	Consistency of regulation enforcement	7
6.15	Government effectiveness in reducing poverty	7
6.11	Efficiency of the tax system	7
2.02	Business costs of terrorism	9
11.01	Air pollution regulations	9
7.06	Irregular payments in government policymaking	9

NOTABLE COMPETITIVE DISADVANTAGES

Growth Competitiveness Index		Rank/102
Macroeconomic Environment		
2.01	Recession expectations	84
2.09	Access to credit	40
2.20	Inflation, 2002	31
2.21	Real exchange rate, 2002	24
Technology		
3.18	Tertiary enrollment	76
3.08	University/industry research collaboration	64
3.13	Quality of competition in the ISP sector	30
3.01	Technological sophistication	26
3.14	Government prioritization of ICT	23
3.15	Government success in ICT promotion	23
3.21	Internet hosts, 2002	22
3.20	Internet users, 2002	21

Other Indicators		Rank/102
10.19	Flexibility of wage determination	69
4.11	Maternity laws' impact on hiring women	47
8.09	Wage equality of women in the workplace	47
10.18	Hiring and firing practices	47
3.11	Availability of mobile or cellular telephones	40
7.13	Pervasiveness of money laundering through banks	34
10.25	Availability of company financial information	31
11.13	Prevalence of environmental management systems	28
10.22	Charitable causes involvement	24
11.11	Effects of compliance on business	21

Note: This country is not included in the coverage of the Business Competitiveness Index 2003–2004.

Macedonia FYR

Competitiveness Rankings

Growth Competitiveness Index Rank	81

Macroeconomic Environment Index Rank **80**
  Macroeconomic Stability Subindex Rank 67
  Government Waste Subindex Rank 79
  Country Credit Rating Rank.................................83

Public Institutions Index Rank..........................**93**
  Contracts and Law Subindex Rank 96
  Corruption Subindex Rank...................................86

Technology Index Rank **70**
  Innovation Subindex Rank 63
  ICT Subindex Rank 63
  Technology Transfer Subindex Rank
    (out of 77 non-core innovators).......................59

Business Competitiveness Index Rank	n/a

**Sophistication of Company Operations
  and Strategy Rank** ....**n/a**
**Quality of the National Business
  Environment Rank**...**n/a**

The Most Problematic Factors for Doing Business

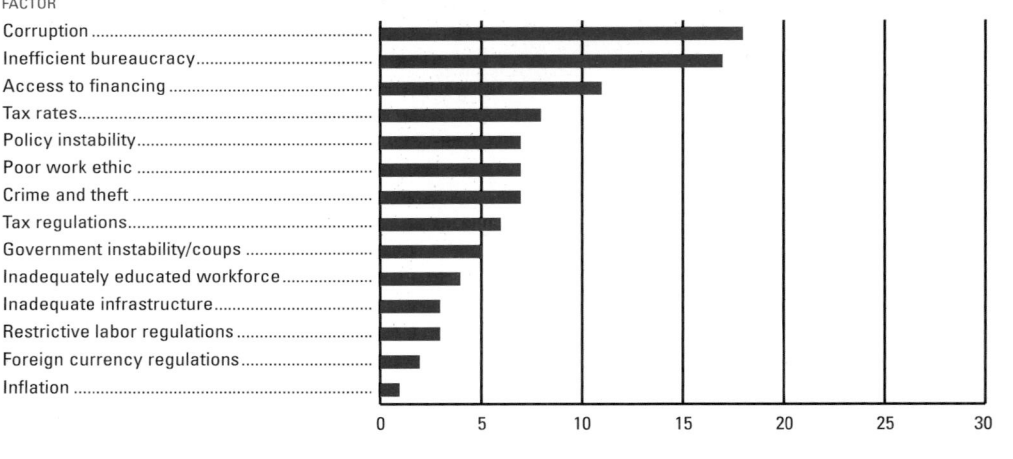

FACTOR

Corruption
Inefficient bureaucracy
Access to financing
Tax rates
Policy instability
Poor work ethic
Crime and theft
Tax regulations
Government instability/coups
Inadequately educated workforce
Inadequate infrastructure
Restrictive labor regulations
Foreign currency regulations
Inflation

Percent of responses

Note: From a list of 14 factors, respondents were asked to select the five most problematic for doing business in their country and to rank them between 1 (most problematic) and 5. The bars in the figure show the responses weighted according to their rankings.

Source: World Economic Forum, Executive Opinion Survey (2003)

National competitiveness balance sheet

NOTABLE COMPETITIVE ADVANTAGES	
Growth Competitiveness Index	**Rank/102**
Macroeconomic Environment	
2.21 Real exchange rate, 2002	6
2.20 Inflation, 2002	37
Technology	
3.22 Telephone lines, 2002	42

NOTABLE COMPETITIVE DISADVANTAGES	
Growth Competitiveness Index	**Rank/102**
Macroeconomic Environment	
2.03 Extent of distortive government subsidies	99
2.19 National savings rate, 2002	97
2.09 Access to credit	89
2.01 Recession expectations	85
2.17 Country credit rating, 2003	83
7.10 Public trust of politicians	75
7.08 Diversion of public funds	71
2.22 Interest rate spread, 2002	65
2.18 Government surplus/deficit, 2002	66
Public Institutions	
6.17 Organized crime	99
6.03 Property rights	99
7.01 Irregular payments in exports and imports	91
6.01 Judicial independence	88
6.08 Favoritism in decisions of government officials	78
7.02 Irregular payments in public utilities	76
7.03 Irregular payments in tax collection	74
Technology	
3.02 Firm-level technology absorption	93
3.15 Government success in ICT promotion	89
3.01 Technological sophistication	88
3.14 Government prioritization of ICT	85
3.16 Laws relating to ICT	84
3.06 Company spending on research and development	83
3.08 University/industry research collaboration	82
3.13 Quality of competition in the ISP sector	76
3.17 Utility patents, 2002	72
3.19 Cellular telephones, 2002	68
3.20 Internet users, 2002	68
3.12 Internet access in schools	63
3.03 FDI and technology transfer	59
3.21 Internet hosts, 2002	59
3.04 Prevalence of foreign technology licensing	53
3.18 Tertiary enrollment	53

Other Indicators		Rank/102
8.09	Wage equality of women in the workplace	1
8.08	Private sector employment of women	13
4.07	Business impact of HIV/AIDS	24
4.05	Business impact of malaria	28
4.10	Maternity leave legislation	32
10.19	Flexibility of wage determination	33
8.10	Regional disparities in quality of business environment	34
4.06	Business impact of tuberculosis	34
4.04	Disparity in healthcare quality	41
4.08	Impact of HIV/AIDS on FDI	47
6.11	Efficiency of the tax system	48
10.21	Pay and productivity	48

Other Indicators		Rank/102
10.22	Charitable causes involvement	101
2.02	Business costs of terrorism	99
4.09	Brain drain	98
10.05	Ethical behavior of firms	94
7.05	Irregular payments in loan applications	94
2.06	Soundness of banks	94
11.06	Compliance with environmental regulations	92
11.12	Political context of environmental gains	92
11.01	Air pollution regulations	91
11.08	Clarity and stability of regulations	90
11.04	Chemical waste regulations	90
11.03	Toxic waste disposal regulations	89
11.02	Water pollution regulations	88
7.04	Irregular payments in public contracts	87
8.11	Focus of trade and industry associations	87

289

Note: This country is not included in the coverage of the Business Competitiveness Index 2003–2004.

Madagascar

Competitiveness Rankings

Growth Competitiveness Index Rank	96

Macroeconomic Environment Index Rank **79**
   Macroeconomic Stability Subindex Rank 87
   Government Waste Subindex Rank 81
   Country Credit Rating Rank ....n/a

Public Institutions Index Rank..**96**
   Contracts and Law Subindex Rank 88
   Corruption Subindex Rank....................................94

Technology Index Rank **97**
   Innovation Subindex Rank....................................93
   ICT Subindex Rank 94
   Technology Transfer Subindex Rank
   (out of 77 non-core innovators) 72

Business Competitiveness Index Rank	85

**Sophistication of Company Operations
and Strategy Rank** **83**
**Quality of the National Business
Environment Rank** **84**

The Most Problematic Factors for Doing Business

FACTOR

Access to financing ....
Inadequate infrastructure...................................
Corruption ....
Inefficient bureaucracy.......................................
Policy instability..
Tax regulations...
Inflation ....
Tax rates..
Government instability/coups ....
Inadequately educated workforce...................
Poor work ethic ....
Restrictive labor regulations.............................
Foreign currency regulations............................
Crime and theft ....

Percent of responses

Note: From a list of 14 factors, respondents were asked to select the five most problematic for doing business in their country and to rank them between 1 (most problematic) and 5. The bars in the figure show the responses weighted according to their rankings.

Source: World Economic Forum, Executive Opinion Survey (2003)

National competitiveness balance sheet

NOTABLE COMPETITIVE ADVANTAGES		
Growth Competitiveness Index		**Rank/102**
	Macroeconomic Environment	
2.01	Recession expectations	21
	Technology	
3.14	Government prioritization of ICT	44
3.15	Government success in ICT promotion	50

NOTABLE COMPETITIVE DISADVANTAGES		
Growth Competitiveness Index		**Rank/102**
	Macroeconomic Environment	
2.19	National savings rate, 2002	98
2.09	Access to credit	94
2.21	Real exchange rate, 2002	90
2.22	Interest rate spread, 2002	87
7.08	Diversion of public funds	87
2.18	Government surplus/deficit, 2002	83
7.10	Public trust of politicians	80
2.03	Extent of distortive government subsidies	62
2.20	Inflation, 2002	60
	Public Institutions	
6.03	Property rights	97
7.03	Irregular payments in tax collection	96
7.02	Irregular payments in public utilities	94
6.01	Judicial independence	86
7.01	Irregular payments in exports and imports	86
6.08	Favoritism in decisions of government officials	80
6.17	Organized crime	72
	Technology	
3.22	Telephone lines, 2002	100
3.12	Internet access in schools	98
3.19	Cellular telephones, 2002	95
3.16	Laws relating to ICT	94
3.23	Personal computers, 2002	94
3.18	Tertiary enrollment	93
3.21	Internet hosts, 2002	91
3.20	Internet users, 2002	90
3.06	Company spending on research and development	86
3.08	University/industry research collaboration	85
3.01	Technological sophistication	85
3.13	Quality of competition in the ISP sector	79
3.04	Prevalence of foreign technology licensing	73
3.17	Utility patents, 2002	72
3.03	FDI and technology transfer	69
3.02	Firm-level technology absorption	56

Business Competitiveness Index		Rank/95
	Sophistication of Company Operations and Strategy	
10.03	Extent of branding	69
10.15	Reliance on professional management	70
10.02	Value chain presence	73
	Quality of the National Business Environment	
2.03	Extent of distortive government subsidies	56
3.10	Availability of scientists and engineers	58
4.03	Quality of math and science education	60

Business Competitiveness Index		Rank/95
	Sophistication of Company Operations and Strategy	
3.04	Prevalence of foreign technology licensing	91
10.06	Production process sophistication	89
10.14	Extent of incentive compensation	89
	Quality of the National Business Environment	
2.16	Cost of importing foreign equipment	95
2.07	Ease of access to loans	94
8.02	Extent of locally based competitors	93

Other Indicators		Rank/102
2.06	Soundness of banks	33
2.02	Business costs of terrorism	34
11.11	Effects of compliance on business	40
10.18	Hiring and firing practices	42
8.09	Wage equality of women in the workplace	44
8.08	Private sector employment of women	44
10.19	Flexibility of wage determination	45
11.12	Political context of environmental gains	48

Other Indicators		Rank/102
6.06	Burden of regulation	101
8.10	Regional disparities in quality of business environment	101
10.23	Company promotion of volunteerism	100
4.04	Disparity in healthcare quality	100
11.13	Prevalence of environmental management systems	99
10.25	Availability of company financial information	99
8.03	Extent of market dominance	97
7.04	Irregular payments in public contracts	94
5.07	Postal efficiency	93
11.01	Air pollution regulations	92
7.07	Irregular payments in judicial decisions	92
6.18	Informal sector	91
3.11	Availability of mobile or cellular telephones	90
11.02	Water pollution regulations	89
7.11	Prevalence of illegal political donations	88

Note: The Business Competitiveness Index applies different criteria for selecting a country's competitive advantages and disadvantages. Please refer to the section "How Country Profiles Work" for further details.

Malawi

Competitiveness Rankings

Growth Competitiveness Index Rank	76

Macroeconomic Environment Index Rank **98**
    Macroeconomic Stability Subindex Rank 99
    Government Waste Subindex Rank 68
    Country Credit Rating Rank 90

Public Institutions Index Rank **38**
    Contracts and Law Subindex Rank 42
    Corruption Subindex Rank....................................43

Technology Index Rank **94**
    Innovation Subindex Rank 95
    ICT Subindex Rank 98
    Technology Transfer Subindex Rank
        (out of 77 non-core innovators).......................52

Business Competitiveness Index Rank	70

**Sophistication of Company Operations
  and Strategy Rank** **70**
**Quality of the National Business
  Environment Rank** **73**

The Most Problematic Factors for Doing Business

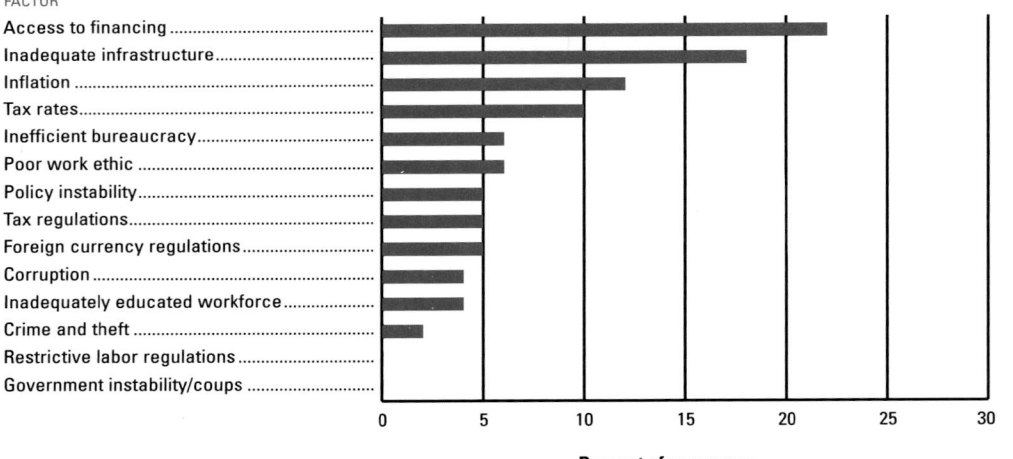

Note: From a list of 14 factors, respondents were asked to select the five most problematic for doing business in their country and to rank them between 1 (most problematic) and 5. The bars in the figure show the responses weighted according to their rankings.

Source: World Economic Forum, Executive Opinion Survey (2003)

National competitiveness balance sheet

NOTABLE COMPETITIVE ADVANTAGES	
Growth Competitiveness Index	**Rank/102**

Public Institutions

6.17	Organized crime	32
7.01	Irregular payments in exports and imports	36
6.01	Judicial independence	40
7.03	Irregular payments in tax collection	43
6.03	Property rights	50

Technology

3.03	FDI and technology transfer	35

NOTABLE COMPETITIVE DISADVANTAGES	
Growth Competitiveness Index	**Rank/102**

Macroeconomic Environment

2.19	National savings rate, 2002	99
2.22	Interest rate spread, 2002	97
2.01	Recession expectations	95
2.18	Government surplus/deficit, 2002	92
2.20	Inflation, 2002	91
2.17	Country credit rating, 2003	90
2.03	Extent of distortive government subsidies	79
2.21	Real exchange rate, 2002	69
7.10	Public trust of politicians	68
2.09	Access to credit	62
7.08	Diversion of public funds	62

Public Institutions

6.08	Favoritism in decisions of government officials	65
7.02	Irregular payments in public utilities	56

Technology

3.18	Tertiary enrollment	102
3.23	Personal computers, 2002	99
3.19	Cellular telephones, 2002	97
3.21	Internet hosts, 2002	96
3.20	Internet users, 2002	95
3.01	Technological sophistication	93
3.02	Firm-level technology absorption	92
3.12	Internet access in schools	92
3.22	Telephone lines, 2002	91
3.16	Laws relating to ICT	90
3.14	Government prioritization of ICT	89
3.08	University/industry research collaboration	83
3.15	Government success in ICT promotion	76
3.17	Utility patents, 2002	72
3.06	Company spending on research and development	62
3.13	Quality of competition in the ISP sector	55
3.04	Prevalence of foreign technology licensing	54

Business Competitiveness Index	Rank/95

Sophistication of Company Operations and Strategy

10.15	Reliance on professional management	28
10.01	Nature of competitive advantage	49
10.09	Control of international distribution	55

Quality of the National Business Environment

10.20	Cooperation in labor-employer relations	15
10.26	Foreign ownership restrictions	16
2.12	Regulation of securities exchanges	18

Business Competitiveness Index	Rank/95

Sophistication of Company Operations and Strategy

10.06	Production process sophistication	83
10.10	Extent of regional sales	81
10.11	Breadth of international markets	81

Quality of the National Business Environment

2.08	Venture capital availability	92
2.16	Cost of importing foreign equipment	91
3.19	Cellular telephones, 2002	91

Other Indicators	Rank/102

10.22	Charitable causes involvement	3
4.11	Maternity laws' impact on hiring women	8
4.10	Maternity leave legislation	9
11.12	Political context of environmental gains	10
7.13	Pervasiveness of money laundering through banks	15
2.06	Soundness of banks	20
6.06	Burden of regulation	20
10.18	Hiring and firing practices	25
10.27	Strength of auditing and accounting standards	25
2.15	Agricultural policy costs	26
8.09	Wage equality of women in the workplace	28
7.14	Pervasiveness of money laundering through non-bank channels	30
7.06	Irregular payments in government policymaking	30
6.11	Efficiency of the tax system	32
10.19	Flexibility of wage determination	36

Other Indicators	Rank/102

4.06	Business impact of tuberculosis	98
4.07	Business impact of HIV/AIDS	95
3.07	Subsidies and tax credits for firm-level research and development	93
4.05	Business impact of malaria	91
4.08	Impact of HIV/AIDS on FDI	87
8.03	Extent of market dominance	86
10.23	Company promotion of volunteerism	82
3.11	Availability of mobile or cellular telephones	81
8.08	Private sector employment of women	78
6.05	Freedom of the press	73
4.09	Brain drain	72
6.18	Informal sector	68
6.16	Government effectiveness in reducing income inequality	68
10.21	Pay and productivity	68
5.07	Postal efficiency	65

293

Note: The Business Competitiveness Index applies different criteria for selecting a country's competitive advantages and disadvantages. Please refer to the section "How Country Profiles Work" for further details.

Malaysia

Competitiveness Rankings

Growth Competitiveness Index Rank	29

Macroeconomic Environment Index Rank **27**
    Macroeconomic Stability Subindex Rank 11
    Government Waste Subindex Rank 25
    Country Credit Rating Rank 35

Public Institutions Index Rank..**34**
    Contracts and Law Subindex Rank 28
    Corruption Subindex Rank....................................39

Technology Index Rank **20**
    Innovation Subindex Rank 41
    ICT Subindex Rank 32
    Technology Transfer Subindex Rank
    (out of 77 non-core innovators)..........................1

Business Competitiveness Index Rank	26

**Sophistication of Company Operations
and Strategy Rank** **26**

**Quality of the National Business
Environment Rank** **24**

The Most Problematic Factors for Doing Business

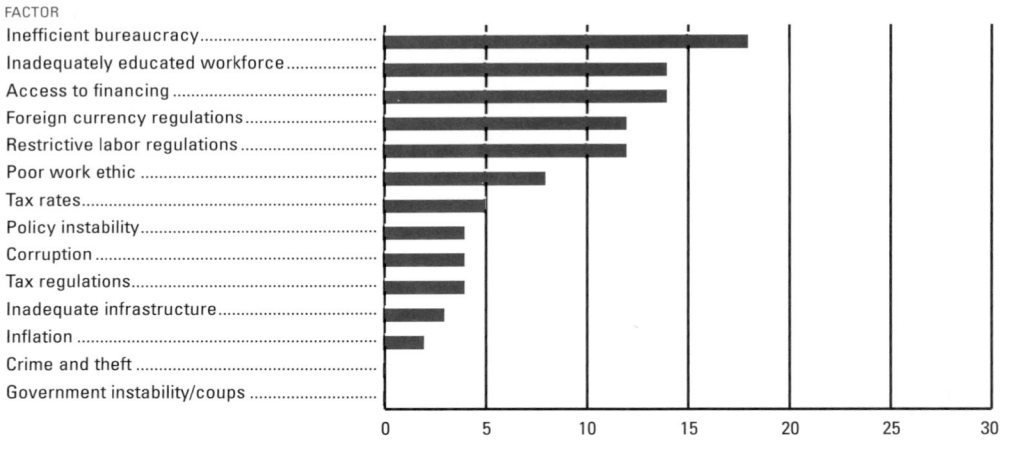

FACTOR

Inefficient bureaucracy
Inadequately educated workforce
Access to financing
Foreign currency regulations
Restrictive labor regulations
Poor work ethic
Tax rates
Policy instability
Corruption
Tax regulations
Inadequate infrastructure
Inflation
Crime and theft
Government instability/coups

Percent of responses

Note: From a list of 14 factors, respondents were asked to select the five most problematic for doing business in their country and to rank them between 1 (most problematic) and 5. The bars in the figure show the responses weighted according to their rankings.

Source: World Economic Forum, Executive Opinion Survey (2003)

National competitiveness balance sheet

NOTABLE COMPETITIVE ADVANTAGES

Growth Competitiveness Index	Rank/102

Macroeconomic Environment

2.19	National savings rate, 2002	11
2.22	Interest rate spread, 2002	18
7.10	Public trust of politicians	19
2.20	Inflation, 2002	20
2.03	Extent of distortive government subsidies	24

Public Institutions

6.17	Organized crime	16
6.03	Property rights	17
7.03	Irregular payments in tax collection	27

Technology

3.04	Prevalence of foreign technology licensing	1
3.03	FDI and technology transfer	2
3.14	Government prioritization of ICT	2
3.15	Government success in ICT promotion	2
3.16	Laws relating to ICT	7
3.02	Firm-level technology absorption	14
3.01	Technological sophistication	22
3.06	Company spending on research and development	25
3.08	University/industry research collaboration	26
3.20	Internet users, 2002	26

Business Competitiveness Index	Rank/95

Sophistication of Company Operations and Strategy

3.04	Prevalence of foreign technology licensing	2
10.12	Extent of staff training	17
10.15	Reliance on professional management	17

Quality of the National Business Environment

3.09	Government procurement of advanced technology products	2
3.16	Laws relating to ICT	7
5.03	Port infrastructure quality	7

Other Indicators	Rank/102

2.15	Agricultural policy costs	2
6.10	Effectiveness of law-making bodies	3
10.23	Company promotion of volunteerism	3
4.11	Maternity laws' impact on hiring women	4
6.11	Efficiency of the tax system	5
6.15	Government effectiveness in reducing poverty	5
10.21	Pay and productivity	6
8.08	Private sector employment of women	7
6.16	Government effectiveness in reducing income inequality	9
3.07	Subsidies and tax credits for firm-level research and development	9
4.10	Maternity leave legislation	10
10.22	Charitable causes involvement	12
11.11	Effects of compliance on business	12
11.09	Flexibility of regulations	12
8.09	Wage equality of women in the workplace	13

NOTABLE COMPETITIVE DISADVANTAGES

Growth Competitiveness Index	Rank/102

Macroeconomic Environment

2.18	Government surplus/deficit, 2002	67
2.01	Recession expectations	36
2.09	Access to credit	35
2.17	Country credit rating, 2003	35
7.08	Diversion of public funds	35
2.21	Real exchange rate, 2002	29

Public Institutions

7.01	Irregular payments in exports and imports	49
6.08	Favoritism in decisions of government officials	48
7.02	Irregular payments in public utilities	43
6.01	Judicial independence	41

Technology

3.22	Telephone lines, 2002	52
3.18	Tertiary enrollment	50
3.21	Internet hosts, 2002	48
3.19	Cellular telephones, 2002	39
3.12	Internet access in schools	37
3.13	Quality of competition in the ISP sector	36
3.17	Utility patents, 2002	34
3.23	Personal computers, 2002	34

Business Competitiveness Index	Rank/95

Sophistication of Company Operations and Strategy

10.01	Nature of competitive advantage	48
10.04	Capacity for innovation	45
10.02	Value chain presence	39

Quality of the National Business Environment

6.12	Centralization of economic policymaking	70
3.10	Availability of scientists and engineers	64
10.26	Foreign ownership restrictions	62

Other Indicators	Rank/102

6.05	Freedom of the press	98
8.03	Extent of market dominance	67
2.10	Government intervention in corporate investment	58
10.18	Hiring and firing practices	57
8.11	Focus of trade and industry associations	52
4.05	Business impact of malaria	49
7.04	Irregular payments in public contracts	49
7.05	Irregular payments in loan applications	46
7.11	Prevalence of illegal political donations	44
11.10	Consistency of regulation enforcement	40
11.02	Water pollution regulations	38
4.09	Brain drain	37
3.11	Availability of mobile or cellular telephones	36
5.07	Postal efficiency	36
2.06	Soundness of banks	36

Note: The Business Competitiveness Index applies different criteria for selecting a country's competitive advantages and disadvantages. Please refer to the section "How Country Profiles Work" for further details.

Mali

Competitiveness Rankings

Growth Competitiveness Index Rank	99

Macroeconomic Environment Index Rank **91**
    Macroeconomic Stability Subindex Rank 89
    Government Waste Subindex Rank 78
    Country Credit Rating Rank 91

Public Institutions Index Rank..**83**
    Contracts and Law Subindex Rank 62
    Corruption Subindex Rank....................................98

Technology Index Rank **99**
    Innovation Subindex Rank....................................98
    ICT Subindex Rank 97
    Technology Transfer Subindex Rank
    (out of 77 non-core innovators).........................74

Business Competitiveness Index Rank	n/a

**Sophistication of Company Operations
and Strategy Rank** ....n/a

**Quality of the National Business
Environment Rank**..n/a

The Most Problematic Factors for Doing Business

FACTOR

Access to financing
Inadequate infrastructure
Inadequately educated workforce
Inefficient bureaucracy
Corruption
Tax regulations
Tax rates
Poor work ethic
Foreign currency regulations
Policy instability
Restrictive labor regulations
Inflation
Crime and theft
Government instability/coups

Percent of responses

Note: From a list of 14 factors, respondents were asked to select the five most problematic for doing business in their country and to rank them between 1 (most problematic) and 5. The bars in the figure show the responses weighted according to their rankings.

Source: World Economic Forum, Executive Opinion Survey (2003)

National competitiveness balance sheet

NOTABLE COMPETITIVE ADVANTAGES

Growth Competitiveness Index		Rank/102
Macroeconomic Environment		
2.21	Real exchange rate, 2002	43
Public Institutions		
6.17	Organized crime	28
Technology		
3.14	Government prioritization of ICT	21

NOTABLE COMPETITIVE DISADVANTAGES

Growth Competitiveness Index		Rank/102
Macroeconomic Environment		
2.09	Access to credit	99
2.18	Government surplus/deficit, 2002	95
7.08	Diversion of public funds	92
2.17	Country credit rating, 2003	91
2.19	National savings rate, 2002	85
2.22	Interest rate spread, 2002	80
2.01	Recession expectations	74
2.03	Extent of distortive government subsidies	66
2.20	Inflation, 2002	66
7.10	Public trust of politicians	66
Public Institutions		
7.03	Irregular payments in tax collection	100
7.02	Irregular payments in public utilities	97
6.03	Property rights	94
7.01	Irregular payments in exports and imports	89
6.01	Judicial independence	63
6.08	Favoritism in decisions of government officials	63
Technology		
3.12	Internet access in schools	100
3.19	Cellular telephones, 2002	100
3.01	Technological sophistication	98
3.22	Telephone lines, 2002	98
3.23	Personal computers, 2002	98
3.16	Laws relating to ICT	96
3.06	Company spending on research and development	95
3.02	Firm-level technology absorption	94
3.18	Tertiary enrollment	94
3.21	Internet hosts, 2002	92
3.20	Internet users, 2002	91
3.08	University/industry research collaboration	90
3.13	Quality of competition in the ISP sector	84
3.04	Prevalence of foreign technology licensing	77
3.03	FDI and technology transfer	72
3.17	Utility patents, 2002	72
3.15	Government success in ICT promotion	71

Other Indicators		Rank/102
8.09	Wage equality of women in the workplace	11
11.12	Political context of environmental gains	14
11.11	Effects of compliance on business	26
6.14	Business costs of crime and violence	31
6.05	Freedom of the press	36
10.18	Hiring and firing practices	39
2.06	Soundness of banks	41
2.15	Agricultural policy costs	43
2.02	Business costs of terrorism	45
4.10	Maternity leave legislation	49
7.11	Prevalence of illegal political donations	50

Other Indicators		Rank/102
10.21	Pay and productivity	102
7.05	Irregular payments in loan applications	101
3.11	Availability of mobile or cellular telephones	101
10.25	Availability of company financial information	101
4.05	Business impact of malaria	98
7.07	Irregular payments in judicial decisions	98
11.02	Water pollution regulations	96
11.01	Air pollution regulations	95
11.13	Prevalence of environmental management systems	95
10.23	Company promotion of volunteerism	95
4.09	Brain drain	94
11.03	Toxic waste disposal regulations	94
11.04	Chemical waste regulations	92
10.27	Strength of auditing and accounting standards	91
11.10	Consistency of regulation enforcement	89

Note: This country is not included in the coverage of the Business Competitiveness Index 2003–2004.

Malta

Competitiveness Rankings

Growth Competitiveness Index Rank	19

Macroeconomic Environment Index Rank **29**
    Macroeconomic Stability Subindex Rank 38
    Government Waste Subindex Rank 23
    Country Credit Rating Rank 28

Public Institutions Index Rank **18**
    Contracts and Law Subindex Rank 20
    Corruption Subindex Rank 18

Technology Index Rank **17**
    Innovation Subindex Rank 53
    ICT Subindex Rank 24
    Technology Transfer Subindex Rank
    (out of 77 non-core innovators) 10

Business Competitiveness Index Rank	42

**Sophistication of Company Operations
  and Strategy Rank** **47**

**Quality of the National Business
  Environment Rank** **42**

The Most Problematic Factors for Doing Business

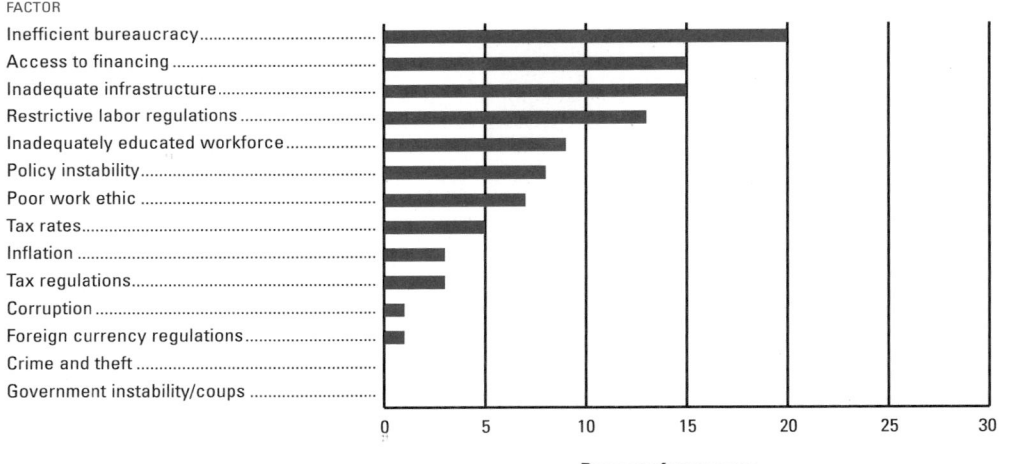

FACTOR
Inefficient bureaucracy
Access to financing
Inadequate infrastructure
Restrictive labor regulations
Inadequately educated workforce
Policy instability
Poor work ethic
Tax rates
Inflation
Tax regulations
Corruption
Foreign currency regulations
Crime and theft
Government instability/coups

Percent of responses

Note: From a list of 14 factors, respondents were asked to select the five most problematic for doing business in their country and to rank them between 1 (most problematic) and 5. The bars in the figure show the responses weighted according to their rankings.

Source: World Economic Forum, Executive Opinion Survey (2003)

National competitiveness balance sheet

NOTABLE COMPETITIVE ADVANTAGES	
Growth Competitiveness Index	**Rank/102**

Macroeconomic Environment

2.22	Interest rate spread, 2002	6
2.01	Recession expectations	16

Public Institutions

6.17	Organized crime	8
7.03	Irregular payments in tax collection	16
6.03	Property rights	18
7.02	Irregular payments in public utilities	18

Technology

3.03	FDI and technology transfer	1
3.14	Government prioritization of ICT	6
3.15	Government success in ICT promotion	7

NOTABLE COMPETITIVE DISADVANTAGES	
Growth Competitiveness Index	**Rank/102**

Macroeconomic Environment

2.18	Government surplus/deficit, 2002	67
2.19	National savings rate, 2002	62
2.21	Real exchange rate, 2002	60
2.09	Access to credit	57
2.03	Extent of distortive government subsidies	41
2.20	Inflation, 2002	32
7.08	Diversion of public funds	23
7.10	Public trust of politicians	22
2.17	Country credit rating, 2003	28

Public Institutions

6.08	Favoritism in decisions of government officials	34
7.01	Irregular payments in exports and imports	25
6.01	Judicial independence	21

Technology

3.08	University/industry research collaboration	62
3.18	Tertiary enrollment	58
3.06	Company spending on research and development	55
3.02	Firm-level technology absorption	45
3.13	Quality of competition in the ISP sector	34
3.17	Utility patents, 2002	33
3.04	Prevalence of foreign technology licensing	31
3.01	Technological sophistication	30
3.20	Internet users, 2002	30
3.16	Laws relating to ICT	29
3.21	Internet hosts, 2002	28
3.23	Personal computers, 2002	27
3.19	Cellular telephones, 2002	24
3.12	Internet access in schools	19
3.22	Telephone lines, 2002	19

Business Competitiveness Index	Rank/95

Sophistication of Company Operations and Strategy

10.06	Production process sophistication	27
10.01	Nature of competitive advantage	30
10.02	Value chain presence	31

Quality of the National Business Environment

2.11	Local equity market access	12
4.01	Quality of the educational system	16
6.01	Judicial independence	20

Other Indicators	Rank/102

8.10	Regional disparities in quality of business environment	2
6.15	Government effectiveness in reducing poverty	4
10.22	Charitable causes involvement	4
4.08	Impact of HIV/AIDS on FDI	5
6.16	Government effectiveness in reducing income inequality	6
6.11	Efficiency of the tax system	8
6.10	Effectiveness of law-making bodies	10
4.06	Business impact of tuberculosis	11
4.04	Disparity in healthcare quality	12
4.07	Business impact of HIV/AIDS	12
7.06	Irregular payments in government policymaking	16
6.14	Business costs of crime and violence	17
6.07	Transparency of government policymaking	17
7.05	Irregular payments in loan applications	17
8.09	Wage equality of women in the workplace	18

Business Competitiveness Index	Rank/95

Sophistication of Company Operations and Strategy

10.09	Control of international distribution	75
10.14	Extent of incentive compensation	68
10.15	Reliance on professional management	64

Quality of the National Business Environment

11.05	Stringency of environmental regulations	85
8.07	Prevalence of mergers and acquisitions	83
9.08	Local availability of components and parts	81

Other Indicators	Rank/102

11.06	Compliance with environmental regulations	91
11.01	Air pollution regulations	88
11.13	Prevalence of environmental management systems	87
11.03	Toxic waste disposal regulations	83
11.10	Consistency of regulation enforcement	81
11.02	Water pollution regulations	76
11.04	Chemical waste regulations	71
10.18	Hiring and firing practices	66
11.08	Clarity and stability of regulations	62
11.07	Compliance with international agreements	62
10.21	Pay and productivity	61
8.08	Private sector employment of women	59
11.09	Flexibility of regulations	59
8.03	Extent of market dominance	57
11.11	Effects of compliance on business	56

Note: The Business Competitiveness Index applies different criteria for selecting a country's competitive advantages and disadvantages. Please refer to the section "How Country Profiles Work" for further details.

Mauritius

Competitiveness Rankings

Growth Competitiveness Index Rank	46

Macroeconomic Environment Index Rank **57**
    Macroeconomic Stability Subindex Rank 64
    Government Waste Subindex Rank 58
    Country Credit Rating Rank 46

Public Institutions Index Rank **44**
    Contracts and Law Subindex Rank 36
    Corruption Subindex Rank 57

Technology Index Rank **49**
    Innovation Subindex Rank 73
    ICT Subindex Rank 40
    Technology Transfer Subindex Rank
    (out of 77 non-core innovators) 48

Business Competitiveness Index Rank	44

**Sophistication of Company Operations
and Strategy Rank** **35**
**Quality of the National Business
Environment Rank** **46**

The Most Problematic Factors for Doing Business

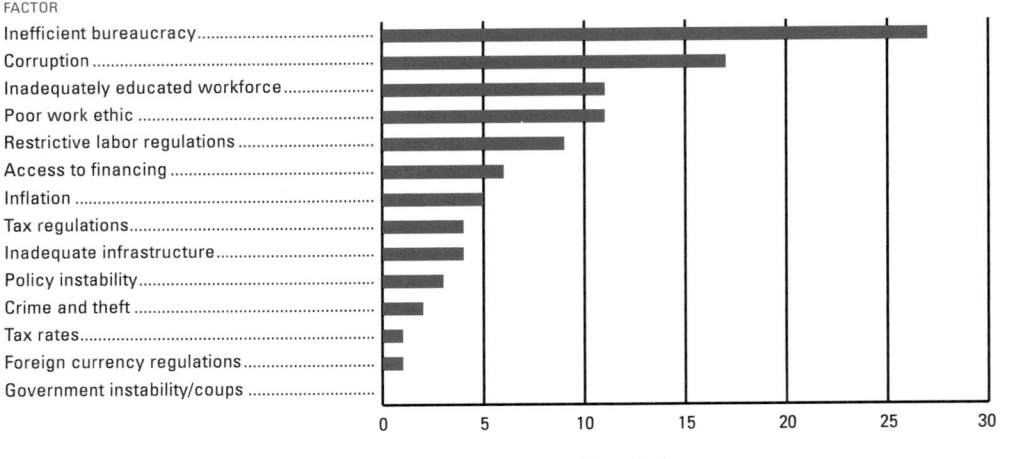

FACTOR

Inefficient bureaucracy
Corruption
Inadequately educated workforce
Poor work ethic
Restrictive labor regulations
Access to financing
Inflation
Tax regulations
Inadequate infrastructure
Policy instability
Crime and theft
Tax rates
Foreign currency regulations
Government instability/coups

Percent of responses

Note: From a list of 14 factors, respondents were asked to select the five most problematic for doing business in their country and to rank them between 1 (most problematic) and 5. The bars in the figure show the responses weighted according to their rankings.

Source: World Economic Forum, Executive Opinion Survey (2003)

National competitiveness balance sheet

NOTABLE COMPETITIVE ADVANTAGES

Growth Competitiveness Index		Rank/102
Macroeconomic Environment		
2.19	National savings rate, 2002	16
2.01	Recession expectations	40
2.03	Extent of distortive government subsidies	45
Public Institutions		
6.17	Organized crime	27
6.03	Property rights	40
6.08	Favoritism in decisions of government officials	42
7.03	Irregular payments in tax collection	42
6.01	Judicial independence	44
Technology		
3.14	Government prioritization of ICT	4
3.15	Government success in ICT promotion	13
3.16	Laws relating to ICT	32
3.04	Prevalence of foreign technology licensing	35
3.20	Internet users, 2002	38
3.22	Telephone lines, 2002	41
3.23	Personal computers, 2002	41
3.19	Cellular telephones, 2002	43

Business Competitiveness Index		Rank/95
Sophistication of Company Operations and Strategy		
10.09	Control of international distribution	16
10.02	Value chain presence	21
10.03	Extent of branding	26
Quality of the National Business Environment		
5.03	Port infrastructure quality	21
2.07	Ease of access to loans	23
5.04	Air transport infrastructure quality	26

Other Indicators		Rank/102
6.11	Efficiency of the tax system	10
8.10	Regional disparities in quality of business environment	16
11.12	Political context of environmental gains	19
4.06	Business impact of tuberculosis	22
6.07	Transparency of government policymaking	22
6.10	Effectiveness of law-making bodies	23
2.15	Agricultural policy costs	24
6.16	Government effectiveness in reducing income inequality	27
8.11	Focus of trade and industry associations	27
2.10	Government intervention in corporate investment	30
2.02	Business costs of terrorism	31
11.02	Water pollution regulations	31
4.05	Business impact of malaria	32
6.15	Government effectiveness in reducing poverty	33
4.08	Impact of HIV/AIDS on FDI	33

NOTABLE COMPETITIVE DISADVANTAGES

Growth Competitiveness Index		Rank/102
Macroeconomic Environment		
2.22	Interest rate spread, 2002	79
2.18	Government surplus/deficit, 2002	76
7.10	Public trust of politicians	75
2.20	Inflation, 2002	73
7.08	Diversion of public funds	59
2.09	Access to credit	54
2.21	Real exchange rate, 2002	49
2.17	Country credit rating, 2003	46
Public Institutions		
7.01	Irregular payments in exports and imports	79
7.02	Irregular payments in public utilities	59
Technology		
3.13	Quality of competition in the ISP sector	99
3.08	University/industry research collaboration	77
3.06	Company spending on research and development	73
3.17	Utility patents, 2002	72
3.18	Tertiary enrollment	71
3.02	Firm-level technology absorption	63
3.03	FDI and technology transfer	62
3.01	Technological sophistication	60
3.12	Internet access in schools	49
3.21	Internet hosts, 2002	49

Business Competitiveness Index		Rank/95
Sophistication of Company Operations and Strategy		
3.06	Company spending on research and development	68
10.10	Extent of regional sales	58
10.15	Reliance on professional management	56
Quality of the National Business Environment		
5.02	Railroad infrastructure development	87
9.05	Decentralization of corporate activity	83
10.26	Foreign ownership restrictions	80

Other Indicators		Rank/102
10.19	Flexibility of wage determination	94
7.11	Prevalence of illegal political donations	91
6.06	Burden of regulation	87
10.18	Hiring and firing practices	81
8.09	Wage equality of women in the workplace	81
10.21	Pay and productivity	79
7.12	Policy consequences of legal political donations	77
8.03	Extent of market dominance	71
7.04	Irregular payments in public contracts	69
2.04	Extent of distortive government intervention	68
7.13	Pervasiveness of money laundering through banks	63
4.09	Brain drain	62
8.08	Private sector employment of women	61
10.05	Ethical behavior of firms	61
11.11	Effects of compliance on business	57

Note: The Business Competitiveness Index applies different criteria for selecting a country's competitive advantages and disadvantages. Please refer to the section "How Country Profiles Work" for further details.

Mexico

Competitiveness Rankings

Growth Competitiveness Index Rank	47

Macroeconomic Environment Index Rank **54**
    Macroeconomic Stability Subindex Rank 73
    Government Waste Subindex Rank 55
    Country Credit Rating Rank 37

Public Institutions Index Rank **50**
    Contracts and Law Subindex Rank 63
    Corruption Subindex Rank...................................46

Technology Index Rank **43**
    Innovation Subindex Rank...................................59
    ICT Subindex Rank 48
    Technology Transfer Subindex Rank
    (out of 77 non-core innovators).........................6

Business Competitiveness Index Rank	48

**Sophistication of Company Operations
    and Strategy Rank** **37**
**Quality of the National Business
    Environment Rank** **51**

The Most Problematic Factors for Doing Business

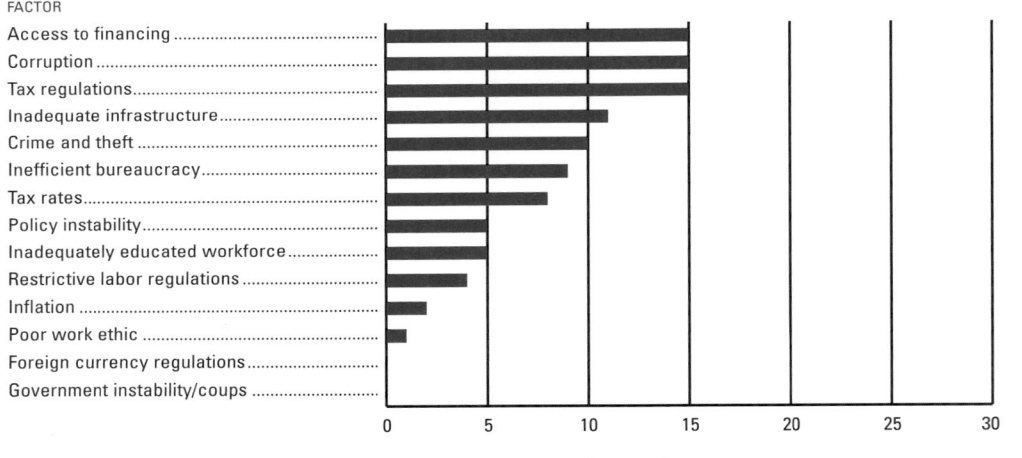

Note: From a list of 14 factors, respondents were asked to select the five most problematic for doing business in their country and to rank them between 1 (most problematic) and 5. The bars in the figure show the responses weighted according to their rankings.

Source: World Economic Forum, Executive Opinion Survey (2003)

National competitiveness balance sheet

NOTABLE COMPETITIVE ADVANTAGES

Growth Competitiveness Index		Rank/102
Macroeconomic Environment		
2.18	Government surplus/deficit, 2002	28
2.17	Country credit rating, 2003	37
Public Institutions		
7.03	Irregular payments in tax collection	39
Technology		
3.04	Prevalence of foreign technology licensing	6
3.03	FDI and technology transfer	11
3.14	Government prioritization of ICT	41
3.17	Utility patents, 2002	41
3.21	Internet hosts, 2002	41
3.02	Firm-level technology absorption	44
3.08	University/industry research collaboration	45

Business Competitiveness Index		Rank/95
Sophistication of Company Operations and Strategy		
10.10	Extent of regional sales	6
3.04	Prevalence of foreign technology licensing	8
10.03	Extent of branding	29
Quality of the National Business Environment		
10.26	Foreign ownership restrictions	25
9.08	Local availability of components and parts	30
2.05	Financial market sophistication	31

Other Indicators		Rank/102
4.11	Maternity laws' impact on hiring women	28
4.06	Business impact of tuberculosis	29
4.09	Brain drain	31
2.04	Extent of distortive government intervention	33
4.05	Business impact of malaria	34
7.05	Irregular payments in loan applications	36
2.10	Government intervention in corporate investment	37
4.08	Impact of HIV/AIDS on FDI	40
6.05	Freedom of the press	40
11.01	Air pollution regulations	40
10.05	Ethical behavior of firms	41
11.08	Clarity and stability of regulations	42
2.02	Business costs of terrorism	43
7.04	Irregular payments in public contracts	43
11.04	Chemical waste regulations	44

NOTABLE COMPETITIVE DISADVANTAGES

Growth Competitiveness Index		Rank/102
Macroeconomic Environment		
2.21	Real exchange rate, 2002	101
2.19	National savings rate, 2002	67
2.20	Inflation, 2002	67
7.08	Diversion of public funds	56
7.10	Public trust of politicians	55
2.22	Interest rate spread, 2002	54
2.01	Recession expectations	53
2.09	Access to credit	53
2.03	Extent of distortive government subsidies	52
Public Institutions		
6.17	Organized crime	88
6.01	Judicial independence	64
7.02	Irregular payments in public utilities	51
6.03	Property rights	47
6.08	Favoritism in decisions of government officials	47
7.01	Irregular payments in exports and imports	47
Technology		
3.20	Internet users, 2002	60
3.18	Tertiary enrollment	59
3.06	Company spending on research and development	58
3.22	Telephone lines, 2002	57
3.12	Internet access in schools	56
3.16	Laws relating to ICT	56
3.01	Technological sophistication	51
3.15	Government success in ICT promotion	51
3.19	Cellular telephones, 2002	50
3.13	Quality of competition in the ISP sector	49
3.23	Personal computers, 2002	49

Business Competitiveness Index		Rank/95
Sophistication of Company Operations and Strategy		
10.01	Nature of competitive advantage	63
10.15	Reliance on professional management	60
10.11	Breadth of international markets	56
Quality of the National Business Environment		
8.05	Administrative burden for startups	83
2.07	Ease of access to loans	78
3.10	Availability of scientists and engineers	77

Other Indicators		Rank/102
6.11	Efficiency of the tax system	90
8.03	Extent of market dominance	89
6.14	Business costs of crime and violence	89
8.08	Private sector employment of women	88
5.07	Postal efficiency	87
8.10	Regional disparities in quality of business environment	86
8.09	Wage equality of women in the workplace	85
6.06	Burden of regulation	82
6.10	Effectiveness of law-making bodies	82
7.14	Pervasiveness of money laundering through non-bank channels	79
10.18	Hiring and firing practices	75
7.13	Pervasiveness of money laundering through banks	75
6.16	Government effectiveness in reducing income inequality	75
7.11	Prevalence of illegal political donations	73
6.18	Informal sector	73

303

Note: The Business Competitiveness Index applies different criteria for selecting a country's competitive advantages and disadvantages. Please refer to the section "How Country Profiles Work" for further details.

Morocco

Competitiveness Rankings

Growth Competitiveness Index Rank	61

Macroeconomic Environment Index Rank **43**
  Macroeconomic Stability Subindex Rank 37
  Government Waste Subindex Rank 44
  Country Credit Rating Rank 50

Public Institutions Index Rank **68**
  Contracts and Law Subindex Rank 55
  Corruption Subindex Rank....................................85

Technology Index Rank **71**
  Innovation Subindex Rank 71
  ICT Subindex Rank 71
  Technology Transfer Subindex Rank
    (out of 77 non-core innovators).........................40

Business Competitiveness Index Rank	49

**Sophistication of Company Operations
  and Strategy Rank** **49**
**Quality of the National Business
  Environment Rank** **49**

The Most Problematic Factors for Doing Business

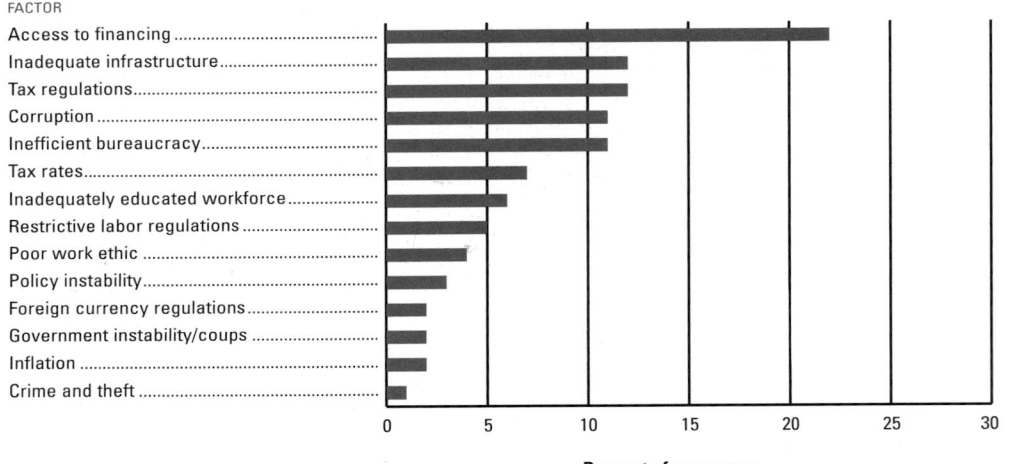

FACTOR
Access to financing
Inadequate infrastructure
Tax regulations
Corruption
Inefficient bureaucracy
Tax rates
Inadequately educated workforce
Restrictive labor regulations
Poor work ethic
Policy instability
Foreign currency regulations
Government instability/coups
Inflation
Crime and theft

0   5   10   15   20   25   30

Percent of responses

Note: From a list of 14 factors, respondents were asked to select the five most problematic for doing business in their country and to rank them between 1 (most problematic) and 5. The bars in the figure show the responses weighted according to their rankings.

Source: World Economic Forum, Executive Opinion Survey (2003)

National competitiveness balance sheet

NOTABLE COMPETITIVE ADVANTAGES

Growth Competitiveness Index	Rank/102

Macroeconomic Environment

2.03	Extent of distortive government subsidies	22
2.19	National savings rate, 2002	24
2.09	Access to credit	27
2.18	Government surplus/deficit, 2002	35
7.10	Public trust of politicians	36
2.01	Recession expectations	41
2.20	Inflation, 2002	44
2.17	Country credit rating, 2003	50
2.21	Real exchange rate, 2002	50

Public Institutions

6.17	Organized crime	47

Technology

3.15	Government success in ICT promotion	32
3.03	FDI and technology transfer	33
3.06	Company spending on research and development	38
3.02	Firm-level technology absorption	43
3.04	Prevalence of foreign technology licensing	45

Business Competitiveness Index	Rank/95

Sophistication of Company Operations and Strategy

10.09	Control of international distribution	31
3.06	Company spending on research and development	37
10.03	Extent of branding	40

Quality of the National Business Environment

2.03	Extent of distortive government subsidies	18
8.07	Prevalence of mergers and acquisitions	20
10.26	Foreign ownership restrictions	30

Other Indicators	Rank/102

8.08	Private sector employment of women	10
10.22	Charitable causes involvement	14
10.23	Company promotion of volunteerism	24
8.09	Wage equality of women in the workplace	24
6.15	Government effectiveness in reducing poverty	31
6.11	Efficiency of the tax system	31
10.05	Ethical behavior of firms	32
5.07	Postal efficiency	32
6.14	Business costs of crime and violence	33
7.11	Prevalence of illegal political donations	35
2.04	Extent of distortive government intervention	36
3.07	Subsidies and tax credits for firm-level research and development	36
6.16	Government effectiveness in reducing income inequality	36
6.06	Burden of regulation	36
10.19	Flexibility of wage determination	38

NOTABLE COMPETITIVE DISADVANTAGES

Growth Competitiveness Index	Rank/102

Macroeconomic Environment

2.22	Interest rate spread, 2002	69
7.08	Diversion of public funds	54

Public Institutions

7.03	Irregular payments in tax collection	85
7.01	Irregular payments in exports and imports	82
7.02	Irregular payments in public utilities	75
6.01	Judicial independence	71
6.03	Property rights	56
6.08	Favoritism in decisions of government officials	56

Technology

3.22	Telephone lines, 2002	80
3.21	Internet hosts, 2002	79
3.20	Internet users, 2002	78
3.23	Personal computers, 2002	75
3.13	Quality of competition in the ISP sector	74
3.12	Internet access in schools	73
3.18	Tertiary enrollment	73
3.17	Utility patents, 2002	72
3.01	Technological sophistication	64
3.14	Government prioritization of ICT	63
3.16	Laws relating to ICT	57
3.08	University/industry research collaboration	53
3.19	Cellular telephones, 2002	53

Business Competitiveness Index	Rank/95

Sophistication of Company Operations and Strategy

10.15	Reliance on professional management	68
10.01	Nature of competitive advantage	67
3.04	Prevalence of foreign technology licensing	66

Quality of the National Business Environment

2.16	Cost of importing foreign equipment	82
3.20	Internet users, 2002	75
2.14	Hidden trade barriers	72

Other Indicators	Rank/102

7.05	Irregular payments in loan applications	96
6.05	Freedom of the press	91
4.09	Brain drain	90
8.10	Regional disparities in quality of business environment	89
11.09	Flexibility of regulations	87
11.08	Clarity and stability of regulations	82
11.11	Effects of compliance on business	80
4.04	Disparity in healthcare quality	76
4.06	Business impact of tuberculosis	76
4.05	Business impact of malaria	75
4.08	Impact of HIV/AIDS on FDI	74
7.04	Irregular payments in public contracts	73
11.06	Compliance with environmental regulations	72
4.07	Business impact of HIV/AIDS	72
11.10	Consistency of regulation enforcement	70

305

Note: The Business Competitiveness Index applies different criteria for selecting a country's competitive advantages and disadvantages. Please refer to the section "How Country Profiles Work" for further details.

Mozambique

Competitiveness Rankings

The Most Problematic Factors for Doing Business

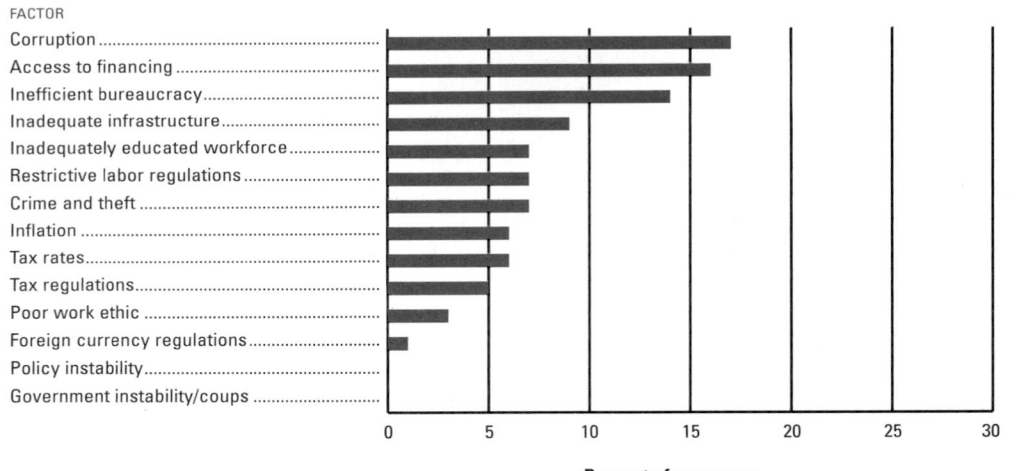

FACTOR

Corruption
Access to financing
Inefficient bureaucracy
Inadequate infrastructure
Inadequately educated workforce
Restrictive labor regulations
Crime and theft
Inflation
Tax rates
Tax regulations
Poor work ethic
Foreign currency regulations
Policy instability
Government instability/coups

Percent of responses

Note: From a list of 14 factors, respondents were asked to select the five most problematic for doing business in their country and to rank them between 1 (most problematic) and 5. The bars in the figure show the responses weighted according to their rankings.

Source: World Economic Forum, Executive Opinion Survey (2003)

National competitiveness balance sheet

NOTABLE COMPETITIVE ADVANTAGES	
Growth Competitiveness Index	**Rank/102**

Technology

3.03	FDI and technology transfer	26

NOTABLE COMPETITIVE DISADVANTAGES	
Growth Competitiveness Index	**Rank/102**

Macroeconomic Environment

2.18	Government surplus/deficit, 2002	102
2.20	Inflation, 2002	94
2.17	Country credit rating, 2003	89
2.09	Access to credit	87
7.08	Diversion of public funds	84
7.10	Public trust of politicians	78
2.19	National savings rate, 2002	75
2.03	Extent of distortive government subsidies	69
2.01	Recession expectations	58
2.22	Interest rate spread, 2002	58
2.21	Real exchange rate, 2002	57

Public Institutions

7.01	Irregular payments in exports and imports	93
6.17	Organized crime	86
6.01	Judicial independence	85
6.08	Favoritism in decisions of government officials	83
6.03	Property rights	78
7.03	Irregular payments in tax collection	78
7.02	Irregular payments in public utilities	72

Technology

3.18	Tertiary enrollment	101
3.20	Internet users, 2002	99
3.21	Internet hosts, 2002	98
3.12	Internet access in schools	97
3.22	Telephone lines, 2002	97
3.01	Technological sophistication	95
3.06	Company spending on research and development	92
3.13	Quality of competition in the ISP sector	92
3.16	Laws relating to ICT	89
3.08	University/industry research collaboration	88
3.19	Cellular telephones, 2002	88
3.23	Personal computers, 2002	88
3.17	Utility patents, 2002	72
3.02	Firm-level technology absorption	64
3.04	Prevalence of foreign technology licensing	59
3.14	Government prioritization of ICT	55
3.15	Government success in ICT promotion	53

307

Business Competitiveness Index	**Rank/95**

Sophistication of Company Operations and Strategy

10.15	Reliance on professional management	72
10.14	Extent of incentive compensation	74
10.08	Degree of customer orientation	78

Quality of the National Business Environment

6.12	Centralization of economic policymaking	57
10.26	Foreign ownership restrictions	57
8.07	Prevalence of mergers and acquisitions	61

Other Indicators	**Rank/102**

4.09	Brain drain	39
2.02	Business costs of terrorism	41
11.12	Political context of environmental gains	47

Business Competitiveness Index	**Rank/95**

Sophistication of Company Operations and Strategy

10.06	Production process sophistication	91
10.07	Extent of marketing	91
10.11	Breadth of international markets	89

Quality of the National Business Environment

3.10	Availability of scientists and engineers	94
8.01	Intensity of local competition	93
9.07	Extent of collaboration among clusters	93

Other Indicators	**Rank/102**

7.14	Pervasiveness of money laundering through non-bank channels	102
8.10	Regional disparities in quality of business environment	100
10.21	Pay and productivity	99
11.04	Chemical waste regulations	98
6.18	Informal sector	98
7.13	Pervasiveness of money laundering through banks	98
11.03	Toxic waste disposal regulations	97
10.27	Strength of auditing and accounting standards	97
10.05	Ethical behavior of firms	97
5.07	Postal efficiency	96
8.08	Private sector employment of women	96
4.04	Disparity in healthcare quality	95

Note: The Business Competitiveness Index applies different criteria for selecting a country's competitive advantages and disadvantages. Please refer to the section "How Country Profiles Work" for further details.

Namibia

Competitiveness Rankings

The Most Problematic Factors for Doing Business

FACTOR
- Inadequately educated workforce
- Poor work ethic
- Access to financing
- Crime and theft
- Inefficient bureaucracy
- Inflation
- Corruption
- Restrictive labor regulations
- Tax rates
- Tax regulations
- Government instability/coups
- Inadequate infrastructure
- Foreign currency regulations
- Policy instability

Percent of responses

Note: From a list of 14 factors, respondents were asked to select the five most problematic for doing business in their country and to rank them between 1 (most problematic) and 5. The bars in the figure show the responses weighted according to their rankings.

Source: World Economic Forum, Executive Opinion Survey (2003)

308

National competitiveness balance sheet

NOTABLE COMPETITIVE ADVANTAGES			NOTABLE COMPETITIVE DISADVANTAGES		
Growth Competitiveness Index		**Rank/102**	**Growth Competitiveness Index**		**Rank/102**
Macroeconomic Environment			**Macroeconomic Environment**		
2.21	Real exchange rate, 2002	7	2.20	Inflation, 2002	86
2.19	National savings rate, 2002	24	2.17	Country credit rating, 2003	57
2.01	Recession expectations	25	2.22	Interest rate spread, 2002	53
7.10	Public trust of politicians	34	2.03	Extent of distortive government subsidies	51
2.09	Access to credit	41	**Public Institutions**		
2.18	Government surplus/deficit, 2002	45	6.17	Organized crime	58
7.08	Diversion of public funds	48	7.02	Irregular payments in public utilities	55
Public Institutions			7.03	Irregular payments in tax collection	55
6.01	Judicial independence	32	6.08	Favoritism in decisions of government officials	54
6.03	Property rights	45	7.01	Irregular payments in exports and imports	53
Technology			**Technology**		
3.04	Prevalence of foreign technology licensing	22	3.18	Tertiary enrollment	81
3.01	Technological sophistication	41	3.02	Firm-level technology absorption	75
3.06	Company spending on research and development	43	3.20	Internet users, 2002	73
3.12	Internet access in schools	46	3.19	Cellular telephones, 2002	72
3.03	FDI and technology transfer	48	3.22	Telephone lines, 2002	72
3.23	Personal computers, 2002	50	3.17	Utility patents, 2002	72
			3.08	University/industry research collaboration	71
			3.14	Government prioritization of ICT	70
			3.16	Laws relating to ICT	68
			3.15	Government success in ICT promotion	66
			3.13	Quality of competition in the ISP sector	61
			3.21	Internet hosts, 2002	52

Business Competitiveness Index		**Rank/95**	**Business Competitiveness Index**		**Rank/95**
Sophistication of Company Operations and Strategy			**Sophistication of Company Operations and Strategy**		
10.01	Nature of competitive advantage	32	10.08	Degree of customer orientation	80
3.04	Prevalence of foreign technology licensing	33	10.03	Extent of branding	73
10.13	Willingness to delegate authority	36	10.02	Value chain presence	71
Quality of the National Business Environment			**Quality of the National Business Environment**		
5.01	Overall infrastructure quality	19	3.10	Availability of scientists and engineers	87
6.02	Efficiency of legal framework	25	10.16	Quality of management schools	85
8.05	Administrative burden for startups	26	9.02	Local supplier quantity	82

Other Indicators		**Rank/102**	**Other Indicators**		**Rank/102**
6.11	Efficiency of the tax system	17	4.08	Impact of HIV/AIDS on FDI	92
11.12	Political context of environmental gains	27	4.07	Business impact of HIV/AIDS	92
11.11	Effects of compliance on business	28	4.06	Business impact of tuberculosis	89
2.15	Agricultural policy costs	29	4.05	Business impact of malaria	85
10.22	Charitable causes involvement	29	6.14	Business costs of crime and violence	78
7.11	Prevalence of illegal political donations	30	8.03	Extent of market dominance	77
7.12	Policy consequences of legal political donations	30	10.18	Hiring and firing practices	69
10.27	Strength of auditing and accounting standards	30	3.07	Subsidies and tax credits for firm-level research and development	68
6.10	Effectiveness of law-making bodies	32	5.07	Postal efficiency	66
10.25	Availability of company financial information	33	3.11	Availability of mobile or cellular telephones	66
8.11	Focus of trade and industry associations	33	6.05	Freedom of the press	65
2.06	Soundness of banks	35	8.08	Private sector employment of women	63
7.13	Pervasiveness of money laundering through banks	35	7.05	Irregular payments in loan applications	63
6.16	Government effectiveness in reducing income inequality	37	11.10	Consistency of regulation enforcement	61
6.06	Burden of regulation	37	4.11	Maternity laws' impact on hiring women	60

309

Note: The Business Competitiveness Index applies different criteria for selecting a country's competitive advantages and disadvantages. Please refer to the section "How Country Profiles Work" for further details.

Netherlands

Competitiveness Rankings

Growth Competitiveness Index Rank	12

Macroeconomic Environment Index Rank **9**
Macroeconomic Stability Subindex Rank 57
Government Waste Subindex Rank 7
Country Credit Rating Rank 4

Public Institutions Index Rank..**11**
Contracts and Law Subindex Rank 11
Corruption Subindex Rank....................................11

Technology Index Rank **18**
Innovation Subindex Rank....................................14
ICT Subindex Rank 15

Business Competitiveness Index Rank	9

**Sophistication of Company Operations
and Strategy Rank** **10**
**Quality of the National Business
Environment Rank** **11**

The Most Problematic Factors for Doing Business

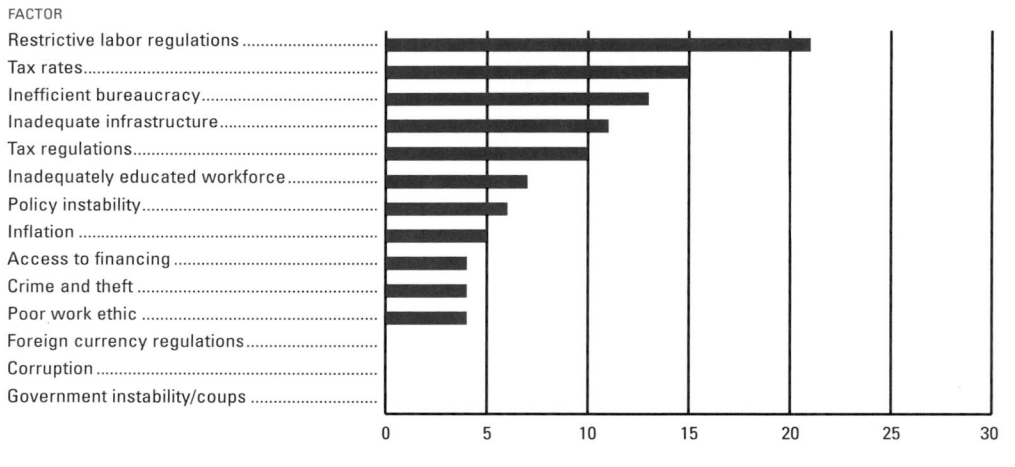

FACTOR
Restrictive labor regulations
Tax rates
Inefficient bureaucracy
Inadequate infrastructure
Tax regulations
Inadequately educated workforce
Policy instability
Inflation
Access to financing
Crime and theft
Poor work ethic
Foreign currency regulations
Corruption
Government instability/coups

Percent of responses

Note: From a list of 14 factors, respondents were asked to select the five most problematic for doing business in their country and to rank them between 1 (most problematic) and 5. The bars in the figure show the responses weighted according to their rankings.

Source: World Economic Forum, Executive Opinion Survey (2003)

National competitiveness balance sheet

NOTABLE COMPETITIVE ADVANTAGES	
Growth Competitiveness Index	**Rank/102**

Macroeconomic Environment

2.22	Interest rate spread, 2002	2
2.17	Country credit rating, 2003	4
7.10	Public trust of politicians	7
2.03	Extent of distortive government subsidies	8

Public Institutions

6.01	Judicial independence	5
7.02	Irregular payments in public utilities	9
7.03	Irregular payments in tax collection	9
6.08	Favoritism in decisions of government officials	10

Technology

3.21	Internet hosts, 2002	4
3.20	Internet users, 2002	6
3.22	Telephone lines, 2002	10
3.17	Utility patents, 2002	11

NOTABLE COMPETITIVE DISADVANTAGES	
Growth Competitiveness Index	**Rank/102**

Macroeconomic Environment

2.01	Recession expectations	87
2.09	Access to credit	76
2.20	Inflation, 2002	54
2.19	National savings rate, 2002	37
2.21	Real exchange rate, 2002	36
2.18	Government surplus/deficit, 2002	27
7.08	Diversion of public funds	12

Public Institutions

6.17	Organized crime	30
6.03	Property rights	14
7.01	Irregular payments in exports and imports	14

Technology

3.14	Government prioritization of ICT	64
3.15	Government success in ICT promotion	54
3.02	Firm-level technology absorption	51
3.16	Laws relating to ICT	26
3.01	Technological sophistication	23
3.19	Cellular telephones, 2002	22
3.18	Tertiary enrollment	20
3.12	Internet access in schools	18
3.13	Quality of competition in the ISP sector	17
3.08	University/industry research collaboration	16
3.06	Company spending on research and development	15
3.23	Personal computers, 2002	14

Business Competitiveness Index	**Rank/95**

Sophistication of Company Operations and Strategy

10.10	Extent of regional sales	3
10.14	Extent of incentive compensation	5
10.13	Willingness to delegate authority	5

Quality of the National Business Environment

5.03	Port infrastructure quality	2
6.01	Judicial independence	5
2.08	Venture capital availability	5

Business Competitiveness Index	**Rank/95**

Quality of the National Business Environment

3.10	Availability of scientists and engineers	48
6.09	Extent of bureaucratic red tape	38
8.07	Prevalence of mergers and acquisitions	38

Other Indicators	**Rank/102**

7.12	Policy consequences of legal political donations	2
6.05	Freedom of the press	3
7.11	Prevalence of illegal political donations	4
11.06	Compliance with environmental regulations	4
11.07	Compliance with international agreements	4
2.06	Soundness of banks	5
6.16	Government effectiveness in reducing income inequality	5
4.04	Disparity in healthcare quality	5
11.02	Water pollution regulations	6
4.09	Brain drain	6
2.04	Extent of distortive government intervention	6
11.03	Toxic waste disposal regulations	6
11.04	Chemical waste regulations	6
11.01	Air pollution regulations	6
8.03	Extent of market dominance	6

Other Indicators	**Rank/102**

10.19	Flexibility of wage determination	92
10.18	Hiring and firing practices	83
8.09	Wage equality of women in the workplace	68
6.06	Burden of regulation	56
10.21	Pay and productivity	52
6.14	Business costs of crime and violence	46
2.15	Agricultural policy costs	46
8.08	Private sector employment of women	43
2.02	Business costs of terrorism	40
10.22	Charitable causes involvement	36
4.10	Maternity leave legislation	27
4.07	Business impact of HIV/AIDS	25
7.14	Pervasiveness of money laundering through non-bank channels	25
6.11	Efficiency of the tax system	23
4.05	Business impact of malaria	22

311

Note: The Business Competitiveness Index applies different criteria for selecting a country's competitive advantages and disadvantages. Please refer to the section "How Country Profiles Work" for further details.

New Zealand

Competitiveness Rankings

Growth Competitiveness Index Rank	14

Macroeconomic Environment Index Rank **13**
    Macroeconomic Stability Subindex Rank 21
    Government Waste Subindex Rank 8
    Country Credit Rating Rank 22

Public Institutions Index Rank..**5**
    Contracts and Law Subindex Rank 5
    Corruption Subindex Rank....................................3

Technology Index Rank **23**
    Innovation Subindex Rank 16
    ICT Subindex Rank 19

Business Competitiveness Index Rank	18

**Sophistication of Company Operations
and Strategy Rank** **23**

**Quality of the National Business
Environment Rank** **13**

The Most Problematic Factors for Doing Business

FACTOR

Percent of responses

Note: From a list of 14 factors, respondents were asked to select the five most problematic for doing business in their country and to rank them between 1 (most problematic) and 5. The bars in the figure show the responses weighted according to their rankings.

Source: World Economic Forum, Executive Opinion Survey (2003)

National competitiveness balance sheet

NOTABLE COMPETITIVE ADVANTAGES	
Growth Competitiveness Index	**Rank/102**

Macroeconomic Environment

7.08	Diversion of public funds	6
2.18	Government surplus/deficit, 2002	9
7.10	Public trust of politicians	12

Public Institutions

7.01	Irregular payments in exports and imports	3
7.03	Irregular payments in tax collection	4
6.08	Favoritism in decisions of government officials	5
7.02	Irregular payments in public utilities	6
6.01	Judicial independence	7
6.17	Organized crime	10
6.03	Property rights	13

Technology

3.18	Tertiary enrollment	7
3.21	Internet hosts, 2002	7
3.20	Internet users, 2002	9
3.16	Laws relating to ICT	10

Business Competitiveness Index	**Rank/95**

Sophistication of Company Operations and Strategy

10.15	Reliance on professional management	5
10.13	Willingness to delegate authority	10
10.08	Degree of customer orientation	17

Quality of the National Business Environment

10.17	Efficacy of corporate boards	3
2.14	Hidden trade barriers	3
7.09	Business costs of corruption	4

Other Indicators	**Rank/102**

2.15	Agricultural policy costs	1
2.06	Soundness of banks	2
7.04	Irregular payments in public contracts	3
7.14	Pervasiveness of money laundering through non-bank channels	3
7.07	Irregular payments in judicial decisions	4
7.13	Pervasiveness of money laundering through banks	4
11.07	Compliance with international agreements	5
10.05	Ethical behavior of firms	5
10.27	Strength of auditing and accounting standards	5
7.05	Irregular payments in loan applications	5
7.06	Irregular payments in government policymaking	5
10.25	Availability of company financial information	6
7.12	Policy consequences of legal political donations	7
4.05	Business impact of malaria	7
7.11	Prevalence of illegal political donations	8

NOTABLE COMPETITIVE DISADVANTAGES	
Growth Competitiveness Index	**Rank/102**

Macroeconomic Environment

2.19	National savings rate, 2002	74
2.20	Inflation, 2002	43
2.03	Extent of distortive government subsidies	34
2.22	Interest rate spread, 2002	34
2.21	Real exchange rate, 2002	31
2.01	Recession expectations	26
2.17	Country credit rating, 2003	22

Technology

3.15	Government success in ICT promotion	59
3.14	Government prioritization of ICT	51
3.06	Company spending on research and development	34
3.19	Cellular telephones, 2002	31
3.22	Telephone lines, 2002	28
3.08	University/industry research collaboration	27
3.02	Firm-level technology absorption	22
3.13	Quality of competition in the ISP sector	22
3.17	Utility patents, 2002	22
3.01	Technological sophistication	18
3.12	Internet access in schools	16
3.23	Personal computers, 2002	16

Business Competitiveness Index	**Rank/95**

Sophistication of Company Operations and Strategy

10.02	Value chain presence	40
3.06	Company spending on research and development	33
10.01	Nature of competitive advantage	28

Quality of the National Business Environment

3.10	Availability of scientists and engineers	49
3.09	Government procurement of advanced technology products	45
9.06	State of cluster development	43

Other Indicators	**Rank/102**

3.07	Subsidies and tax credits for firm-level research and development	72
11.11	Effects of compliance on business	63
6.06	Burden of regulation	60
10.18	Hiring and firing practices	55
4.09	Brain drain	55
10.23	Company promotion of volunteerism	51
8.09	Wage equality of women in the workplace	46
2.02	Business costs of terrorism	42
8.03	Extent of market dominance	37
4.11	Maternity laws' impact on hiring women	35
3.11	Availability of mobile or cellular telephones	32
2.04	Extent of distortive government intervention	27
4.04	Disparity in healthcare quality	27
11.13	Prevalence of environmental management systems	25
11.12	Political context of environmental gains	23

313

Note: The Business Competitiveness Index applies different criteria for selecting a country's competitive advantages and disadvantages. Please refer to the section "How Country Profiles Work" for further details.

Nicaragua

Competitiveness Rankings

Growth Competitiveness Index Rank	90

Macroeconomic Environment Index Rank **100**
    Macroeconomic Stability Subindex Rank 98
    Government Waste Subindex Rank 87
    Country Credit Rating Rank.................................92

Public Institutions Index Rank..**78**
    Contracts and Law Subindex Rank 84
    Corruption Subindex Rank...................................62

Technology Index Rank **85**
    Innovation Subindex Rank...................................81
    ICT Subindex Rank 83
    Technology Transfer Subindex Rank
    (out of 77 non-core innovators).........................57

Business Competitiveness Index Rank	88

**Sophistication of Company Operations
  and Strategy Rank** 87
**Quality of the National Business
  Environment Rank** 87

314

The Most Problematic Factors for Doing Business

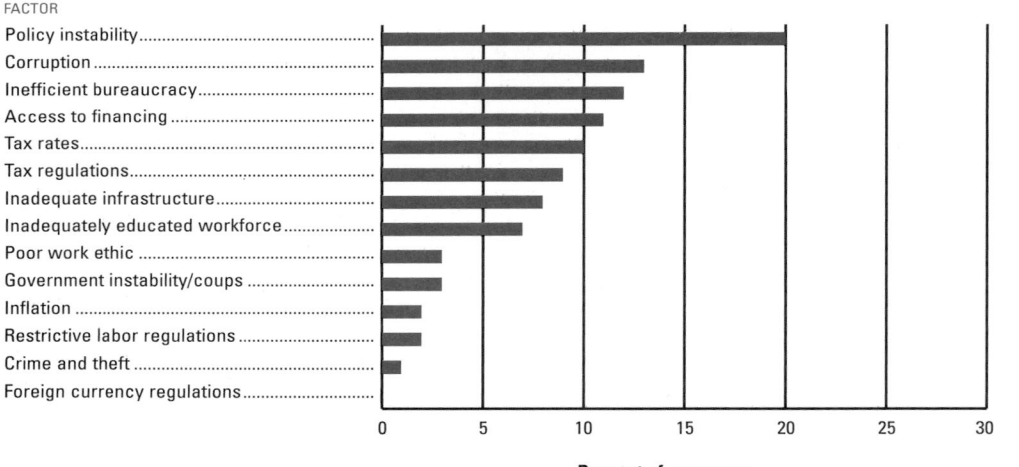

FACTOR

- Policy instability
- Corruption
- Inefficient bureaucracy
- Access to financing
- Tax rates
- Tax regulations
- Inadequate infrastructure
- Inadequately educated workforce
- Poor work ethic
- Government instability/coups
- Inflation
- Restrictive labor regulations
- Crime and theft
- Foreign currency regulations

Percent of responses

Note: From a list of 14 factors, respondents were asked to select the five most problematic for doing business in their country and to rank them between 1 (most problematic) and 5. The bars in the figure show the responses weighted according to their rankings.

Source: World Economic Forum, Executive Opinion Survey (2003)

National competitiveness balance sheet

NOTABLE COMPETITIVE ADVANTAGES	
Growth Competitiveness Index	**Rank/102**

Technology

3.03	FDI and technology transfer	50

NOTABLE COMPETITIVE DISADVANTAGES	
Growth Competitiveness Index	**Rank/102**

Macroeconomic Environment

2.19	National savings rate, 2002	102
2.22	Interest rate spread, 2002	93
7.10	Public trust of politicians	93
2.01	Recession expectations	92
2.17	Country credit rating, 2003	92
2.18	Government surplus/deficit, 2002	89
2.09	Access to credit	88
7.08	Diversion of public funds	82
2.21	Real exchange rate, 2002	65
2.03	Extent of distortive government subsidies	63
2.20	Inflation, 2002	59

Public Institutions

6.01	Judicial independence	99
6.08	Favoritism in decisions of government officials	86
6.03	Property rights	80
7.02	Irregular payments in public utilities	68
7.03	Irregular payments in tax collection	68
7.01	Irregular payments in exports and imports	63
6.17	Organized crime	57

Technology

3.06	Company spending on research and development	94
3.01	Technological sophistication	92
3.15	Government success in ICT promotion	92
3.02	Firm-level technology absorption	91
3.08	University/industry research collaboration	91
3.16	Laws relating to ICT	88
3.12	Internet access in schools	87
3.14	Government prioritization of ICT	87
3.13	Quality of competition in the ISP sector	82
3.19	Cellular telephones, 2002	80
3.20	Internet users, 2002	79
3.17	Utility patents, 2002	72
3.18	Tertiary enrollment	70
3.21	Internet hosts, 2002	68
3.23	Personal computers, 2002	66
3.22	Telephone lines, 2002	82
3.04	Prevalence of foreign technology licensing	60

315

Business Competitiveness Index	Rank/95
Sophistication of Company Operations and Strategy	

10.01	Nature of competitive advantage	79

Quality of the National Business Environment

10.20	Cooperation in labor-employer relations	45
2.16	Cost of importing foreign equipment	56
6.13	Reliability of police services	56

Business Competitiveness Index	Rank/95
Sophistication of Company Operations and Strategy	

10.09	Control of international distribution	90
10.11	Breadth of international markets	90
10.15	Reliance on professional management	90

Quality of the National Business Environment

9.05	Decentralization of corporate activity	95
5.02	Railroad infrastructure development	94
8.01	Intensity of local competition	94

Other Indicators	Rank/102

10.19	Flexibility of wage determination	9
6.05	Freedom of the press	38
10.21	Pay and productivity	41

Other Indicators	Rank/102

8.03	Extent of market dominance	102
8.09	Wage equality of women in the workplace	100
11.08	Clarity and stability of regulations	98
7.12	Policy consequences of legal political donations	98
11.10	Consistency of regulation enforcement	97
11.13	Prevalence of environmental management systems	96
11.09	Flexibility of regulations	96
6.10	Effectiveness of law-making bodies	96
11.06	Compliance with environmental regulations	96
11.07	Compliance with international agreements	96
3.07	Subsidies and tax credits for firm-level research and development	95
11.11	Effects of compliance on business	95

Note: The Business Competitiveness Index applies different criteria for selecting a country's competitive advantages and disadvantages. Please refer to the section "How Country Profiles Work" for further details.

Nigeria

Competitiveness Rankings

Growth Competitiveness Index Rank	87

Macroeconomic Environment Index Rank **74**
    Macroeconomic Stability Subindex Rank 32
    Government Waste Subindex Rank 91
    Country Credit Rating Rank 87

Public Institutions Index Rank..**98**
    Contracts and Law Subindex Rank 78
    Corruption Subindex Rank...................................99

Technology Index Rank **82**
    Innovation Subindex Rank 88
    ICT Subindex Rank 93
    Technology Transfer Subindex Rank
    (out of 77 non-core innovators)........................20

Business Competitiveness Index Rank	77

**Sophistication of Company Operations
  and Strategy Rank**...**72**

**Quality of the National Business
  Environment Rank** **77**

The Most Problematic Factors for Doing Business

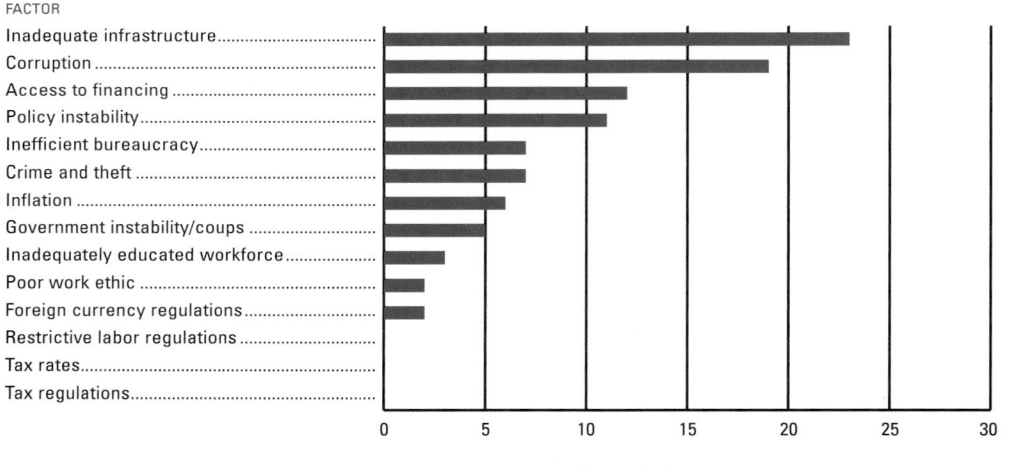

Note: From a list of 14 factors, respondents were asked to select the five most problematic for doing business in their country and to rank them between 1 (most problematic) and 5. The bars in the figure show the responses weighted according to their rankings.

Source: World Economic Forum, Executive Opinion Survey (2003)

National competitiveness balance sheet

NOTABLE COMPETITIVE ADVANTAGES

Growth Competitiveness Index	Rank/102
Macroeconomic Environment	
2.21 Real exchange rate, 2002	2
2.19 National savings rate, 2002	19
2.01 Recession expectations	28
Technology	
3.03 FDI and technology transfer	18
3.04 Prevalence of foreign technology licensing	23
3.15 Government success in ICT promotion	39
3.02 Firm-level technology absorption	49

Business Competitiveness Index	Rank/95
Sophistication of Company Operations and Strategy	
3.04 Prevalence of foreign technology licensing	34
10.15 Reliance on professional management	41
10.01 Nature of competitive advantage	57
Quality of the National Business Environment	
2.11 Local equity market access	17
10.26 Foreign ownership restrictions	20
9.06 State of cluster development	22

Other Indicators	Rank/102
8.09 Wage equality of women in the workplace	6
10.18 Hiring and firing practices	7
4.11 Maternity laws' impact on hiring women	37
4.10 Maternity leave legislation	39
8.08 Private sector employment of women	42
2.02 Business costs of terrorism	44
11.13 Prevalence of environmental management systems	47
10.19 Flexibility of wage determination	49

NOTABLE COMPETITIVE DISADVANTAGES

Growth Competitiveness Index	Rank/102
Macroeconomic Environment	
7.08 Diversion of public funds	97
2.20 Inflation, 2002	89
7.10 Public trust of politicians	89
2.17 Country credit rating, 2003	87
2.03 Extent of distortive government subsidies	73
2.09 Access to credit	65
2.22 Interest rate spread, 2002	64
2.18 Government surplus/deficit, 2002	53
Public Institutions	
7.01 Irregular payments in exports and imports	100
7.02 Irregular payments in public utilities	98
7.03 Irregular payments in tax collection	98
6.08 Favoritism in decisions of government officials	91
6.03 Property rights	82
6.17 Organized crime	75
6.01 Judicial independence	61
Technology	
3.20 Internet users, 2002	100
3.21 Internet hosts, 2002	94
3.22 Telephone lines, 2002	94
3.12 Internet access in schools	90
3.19 Cellular telephones, 2002	90
3.18 Tertiary enrollment	85
3.01 Technological sophistication	84
3.23 Personal computers, 2002	84
3.13 Quality of competition in the ISP sector	77
3.08 University/industry research collaboration	76
3.16 Laws relating to ICT	75
3.06 Company spending on research and development	69
3.17 Utility patents, 2002	68
3.14 Government prioritization of ICT	67

Business Competitiveness Index	Rank/95
Sophistication of Company Operations and Strategy	
10.02 Value chain presence	84
10.03 Extent of branding	82
10.06 Production process sophistication	82
Quality of the National Business Environment	
2.14 Hidden trade barriers	93
10.20 Cooperation in labor-employer relations	93
5.05 Quality of electricity supply	92

Other Indicators	Rank/102
5.07 Postal efficiency	100
7.04 Irregular payments in public contracts	100
11.01 Air pollution regulations	97
4.09 Brain drain	97
7.11 Prevalence of illegal political donations	95
7.05 Irregular payments in loan applications	95
11.02 Water pollution regulations	94
6.18 Informal sector	94
7.13 Pervasiveness of money laundering through banks	93
6.15 Government effectiveness in reducing poverty	91
11.04 Chemical waste regulations	91
11.07 Compliance with international agreements	90
11.03 Toxic waste disposal regulations	90
2.04 Extent of distortive government intervention	90
11.08 Clarity and stability of regulations	89

317

Note: The Business Competitiveness Index applies different criteria for selecting a country's competitive advantages and disadvantages. Please refer to the section "How Country Profiles Work" for further details.

Norway

Competitiveness Rankings

Growth Competitiveness Index Rank	9

Macroeconomic Environment Index Rank	**4**
Macroeconomic Stability Subindex Rank	3
Government Waste Subindex Rank	14
Country Credit Rating Rank	5
Public Institutions Index Rank	**16**
Contracts and Law Subindex Rank	18
Corruption Subindex Rank	20
Technology Index Rank	**13**
Innovation Subindex Rank	12
ICT Subindex Rank	9

Business Competitiveness Index Rank	22

Sophistication of Company Operations and Strategy Rank	**21**
Quality of the National Business Environment Rank	**21**

The Most Problematic Factors for Doing Business

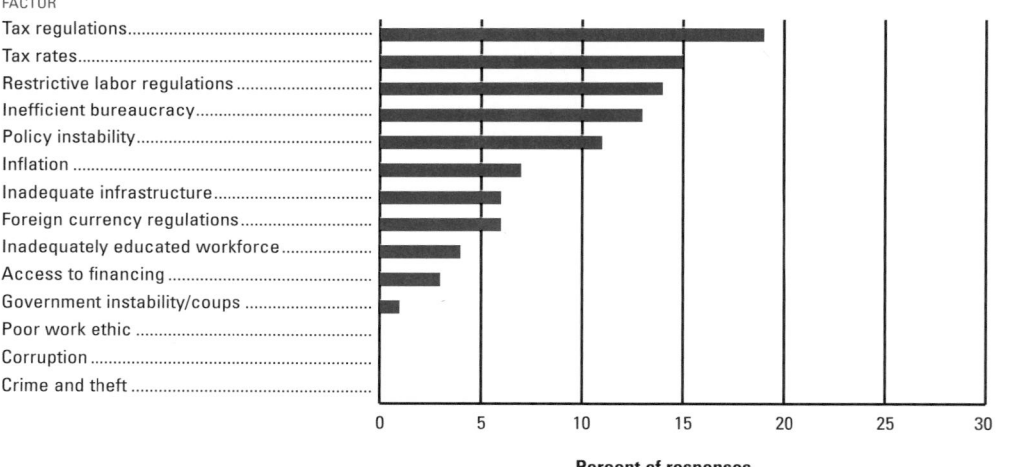

FACTOR

Tax regulations
Tax rates
Restrictive labor regulations
Inefficient bureaucracy
Policy instability
Inflation
Inadequate infrastructure
Foreign currency regulations
Inadequately educated workforce
Access to financing
Government instability/coups
Poor work ethic
Corruption
Crime and theft

Percent of responses

Note: From a list of 14 factors, respondents were asked to select the five most problematic for doing business in their country and to rank them between 1 (most problematic) and 5. The bars in the figure show the responses weighted according to their rankings.

Source: World Economic Forum, Executive Opinion Survey (2003)

National competitiveness balance sheet

NOTABLE COMPETITIVE ADVANTAGES			NOTABLE COMPETITIVE DISADVANTAGES		
Growth Competitiveness Index		**Rank/102**	**Growth Competitiveness Index**		**Rank/102**

Macroeconomic Environment

2.18	Government surplus/deficit, 2002	1
2.17	Country credit rating, 2003	5
2.22	Interest rate spread, 2002	5
2.19	National savings rate, 2002	8
7.10	Public trust of politicians	10

Technology

3.22	Telephone lines, 2002	3
3.18	Tertiary enrollment	6
3.20	Internet users, 2002	8
3.23	Personal computers, 2002	9

Macroeconomic Environment

2.01	Recession expectations	70
2.03	Extent of distortive government subsidies	57
2.21	Real exchange rate, 2002	56
2.09	Access to credit	47
2.20	Inflation, 2002	15
7.08	Diversion of public funds	11

Public Institutions

7.01	Irregular payments in exports and imports	24
6.03	Property rights	22
6.17	Organized crime	20
7.02	Irregular payments in public utilities	19
7.03	Irregular payments in tax collection	18
6.01	Judicial independence	16
6.08	Favoritism in decisions of government officials	16

Technology

3.14	Government prioritization of ICT	48
3.15	Government success in ICT promotion	42
3.13	Quality of competition in the ISP sector	25
3.06	Company spending on research and development	22
3.12	Internet access in schools	22
3.02	Firm-level technology absorption	21
3.17	Utility patents, 2002	19
3.08	University/industry research collaboration	17
3.16	Laws relating to ICT	15
3.01	Technological sophistication	13
3.21	Internet hosts, 2002	13
3.19	Cellular telephones, 2002	12

Business Competitiveness Index		**Rank/95**	**Business Competitiveness Index**		**Rank/95**

Sophistication of Company Operations and Strategy

10.13	Willingness to delegate authority	8
10.14	Extent of incentive compensation	16
10.01	Nature of competitive advantage	17

Quality of the National Business Environment

6.09	Extent of bureaucratic red tape	8
3.20	Internet users, 2002	8
2.07	Ease of access to loans	9

Sophistication of Company Operations and Strategy

10.10	Extent of regional sales	29
10.07	Extent of marketing	26
10.11	Breadth of international markets	26

Quality of the National Business Environment

10.26	Foreign ownership restrictions	64
4.03	Quality of math and science education	53
2.03	Extent of distortive government subsidies	52

Other Indicators		**Rank/102**	**Other Indicators**		**Rank/102**

4.04	Disparity in healthcare quality	4
4.09	Brain drain	5
4.10	Maternity leave legislation	6
4.08	Impact of HIV/AIDS on FDI	7
11.06	Compliance with environmental regulations	7
6.16	Government effectiveness in reducing income inequality	7
11.04	Chemical waste regulations	7
11.01	Air pollution regulations	7
11.03	Toxic waste disposal regulations	8
11.07	Compliance with international agreements	8
11.02	Water pollution regulations	8
7.11	Prevalence of illegal political donations	9

10.19	Flexibility of wage determination	95
10.18	Hiring and firing practices	94
2.15	Agricultural policy costs	92
10.21	Pay and productivity	76
6.07	Transparency of government policymaking	57
6.11	Efficiency of the tax system	56
10.22	Charitable causes involvement	54
8.03	Extent of market dominance	49
2.10	Government intervention in corporate investment	44
2.04	Extent of distortive government intervention	41
2.02	Business costs of terrorism	35
8.09	Wage equality of women in the workplace	34
6.06	Burden of regulation	32
2.06	Soundness of banks	31
4.11	Maternity laws' impact on hiring women	29

Note: The Business Competitiveness Index applies different criteria for selecting a country's competitive advantages and disadvantages. Please refer to the section "How Country Profiles Work" for further details.

Pakistan

Competitiveness Rankings

Growth Competitiveness Index Rank	**73**

Macroeconomic Environment Index Rank **62**
  Macroeconomic Stability Subindex Rank 20
  Government Waste Subindex Rank 63
  Country Credit Rating Rank 86

Public Institutions Index Rank **74**
  Contracts and Law Subindex Rank 69
  Corruption Subindex Rank....................................77

Technology Index Rank **83**
  Innovation Subindex Rank.....................................94
  ICT Subindex Rank 84
  Technology Transfer Subindex Rank
    (out of 77 non-core innovators).........................46

Business Competitiveness Index Rank	**72**

**Sophistication of Company Operations
  and Strategy Rank** **77**
**Quality of the National Business
  Environment Rank** **67**

The Most Problematic Factors for Doing Business

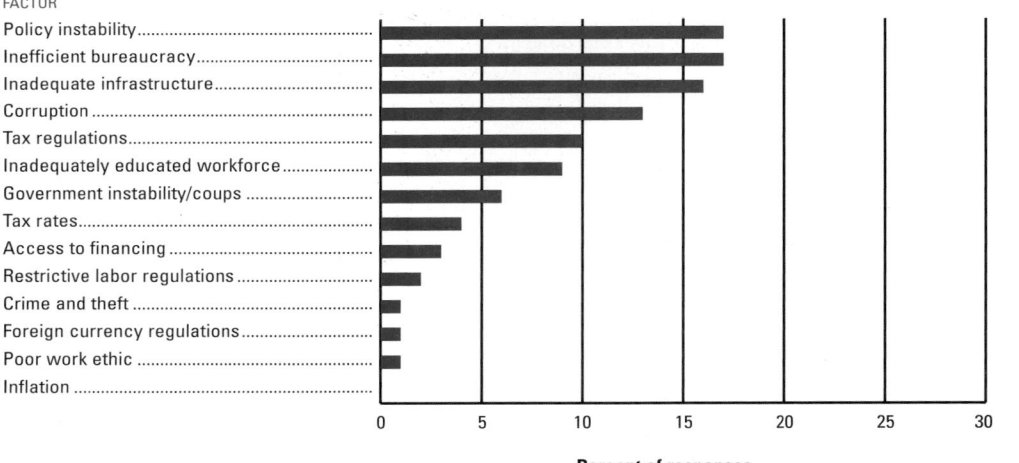

Note: From a list of 14 factors, respondents were asked to select the five most problematic for doing business in their country and to rank them between 1 (most problematic) and 5. The bars in the figure show the responses weighted according to their rankings.

Source: World Economic Forum, Executive Opinion Survey (2003)

National competitiveness balance sheet

NOTABLE COMPETITIVE ADVANTAGES

Growth Competitiveness Index	Rank/102

Macroeconomic Environment

2.09	Access to credit	1
2.01	Recession expectations	12
2.21	Real exchange rate, 2002	25
2.20	Inflation, 2002	47

Technology

3.14	Government prioritization of ICT	29
3.15	Government success in ICT promotion	33
3.13	Quality of competition in the ISP sector	38
3.04	Prevalence of foreign technology licensing	39

NOTABLE COMPETITIVE DISADVANTAGES

Growth Competitiveness Index	Rank/102

Macroeconomic Environment

2.17	Country credit rating, 2003	86
7.10	Public trust of politicians	72
7.08	Diversion of public funds	64
2.18	Government surplus/deficit, 2002	62
2.19	National savings rate, 2002	60
2.22	Interest rate spread, 2002	60
2.03	Extent of distortive government subsidies	58

Public Institutions

7.02	Irregular payments in public utilities	91
6.01	Judicial independence	77
7.03	Irregular payments in tax collection	77
6.17	Organized crime	73
6.03	Property rights	71
7.01	Irregular payments in exports and imports	58
6.08	Favoritism in decisions of government officials	52

Technology

3.19	Cellular telephones, 2002	98
3.08	University/industry research collaboration	96
3.06	Company spending on research and development	90
3.18	Tertiary enrollment	88
3.23	Personal computers, 2002	87
3.20	Internet users, 2002	87
3.22	Telephone lines, 2002	84
3.02	Firm-level technology absorption	82
3.21	Internet hosts, 2002	82
3.16	Laws relating to ICT	77
3.01	Technological sophistication	73
3.17	Utility patents, 2002	71
3.12	Internet access in schools	67
3.03	FDI and technology transfer	51

Business Competitiveness Index	Rank/95

Sophistication of Company Operations and Strategy

10.11	Breadth of international markets	60
3.04	Prevalence of foreign technology licensing	60
10.09	Control of international distribution	62

Quality of the National Business Environment

2.11	Local equity market access	5
9.06	State of cluster development	13
2.12	Regulation of securities exchanges	29

Other Indicators	Rank/102

8.03	Extent of market dominance	20
7.12	Policy consequences of legal political donations	22
10.25	Availability of company financial information	23
7.11	Prevalence of illegal political donations	31
10.19	Flexibility of wage determination	40
10.27	Strength of auditing and accounting standards	41
10.22	Charitable causes involvement	41
4.08	Impact of HIV/AIDS on FDI	45
7.13	Pervasiveness of money laundering through banks	46
10.18	Hiring and firing practices	48

Business Competitiveness Index	Rank/95

Sophistication of Company Operations and Strategy

10.13	Willingness to delegate authority	85
3.06	Company spending on research and development	84
10.10	Extent of regional sales	83

Quality of the National Business Environment

3.19	Cellular telephones, 2002	93
3.08	University/industry research collaboration	90
6.13	Reliability of police services	89

Other Indicators	Rank/102

8.08	Private sector employment of women	102
6.18	Informal sector	96
10.23	Company promotion of volunteerism	94
6.11	Efficiency of the tax system	93
8.11	Focus of trade and industry associations	90
11.09	Flexibility of regulations	90
11.11	Effects of compliance on business	89
2.02	Business costs of terrorism	88
11.10	Consistency of regulation enforcement	87
11.07	Compliance with international agreements	87
11.12	Political context of environmental gains	86
4.10	Maternity leave legislation	85
6.06	Burden of regulation	83
5.07	Postal efficiency	81
3.07	Subsidies and tax credits for firm-level research and development	81

Note: The Business Competitiveness Index applies different criteria for selecting a country's competitive advantages and disadvantages. Please refer to the section "How Country Profiles Work" for further details.

Panama

Competitiveness Rankings

Growth Competitiveness Index Rank	59

Macroeconomic Environment Index Rank **59**
    Macroeconomic Stability Subindex Rank 47
    Government Waste Subindex Rank 83
    Country Credit Rating Rank 51

Public Institutions Index Rank **71**
    Contracts and Law Subindex Rank 74
    Corruption Subindex Rank 60

Technology Index Rank **50**
    Innovation Subindex Rank 42
    ICT Subindex Rank 58
    Technology Transfer Subindex Rank
      (out of 77 non-core innovators) 9

Business Competitiveness Index Rank	59

**Sophistication of Company Operations
and Strategy Rank** **60**
**Quality of the National Business
Environment Rank** **59**

The Most Problematic Factors for Doing Business

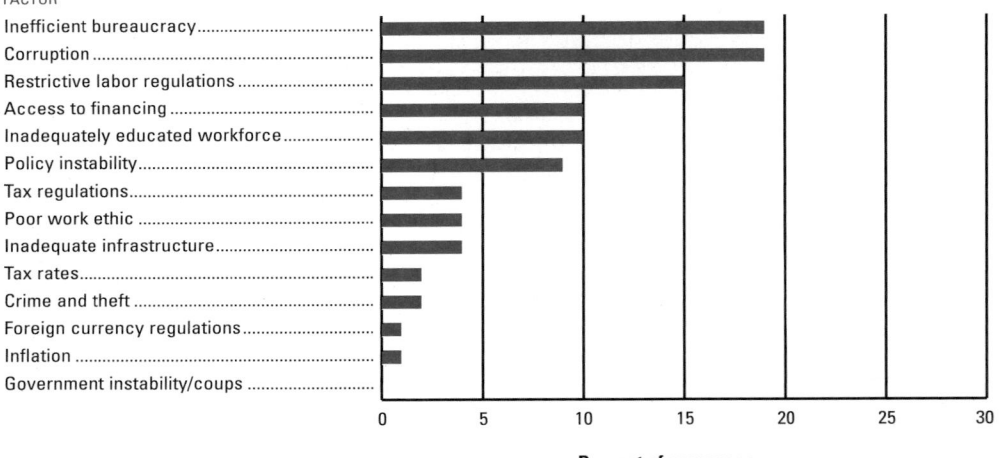

FACTOR

Note: From a list of 14 factors, respondents were asked to select the five most problematic for doing business in their country and to rank them between 1 (most problematic) and 5. The bars in the figure show the responses weighted according to their rankings.

Source: World Economic Forum, Executive Opinion Survey (2003)

National competitiveness balance sheet

NOTABLE COMPETITIVE ADVANTAGES		
Growth Competitiveness Index		**Rank/102**

Macroeconomic Environment

2.20	Inflation, 2002	14
2.19	National savings rate, 2002	31
2.18	Government surplus/deficit, 2002	48
2.22	Interest rate spread, 2002	49

Technology

3.03	FDI and technology transfer	9
3.04	Prevalence of foreign technology licensing	17
3.01	Technological sophistication	27
3.02	Firm-level technology absorption	32
3.13	Quality of competition in the ISP sector	37
3.16	Laws relating to ICT	42
3.18	Tertiary enrollment	42

Business Competitiveness Index		**Rank/95**

Sophistication of Company Operations and Strategy

3.04	Prevalence of foreign technology licensing	26
10.14	Extent of incentive compensation	39
10.01	Nature of competitive advantage	39

Quality of the National Business Environment

6.09	Extent of bureaucratic red tape	3
5.03	Port infrastructure quality	17
2.07	Ease of access to loans	21

Other Indicators		**Rank/102**

8.08	Private sector employment of women	14
10.22	Charitable causes involvement	15
4.09	Brain drain	25
2.06	Soundness of banks	27
10.23	Company promotion of volunteerism	34
4.10	Maternity leave legislation	35
8.10	Regional disparities in quality of business environment	44
4.11	Maternity laws' impact on hiring women	48
6.11	Efficiency of the tax system	50

NOTABLE COMPETITIVE DISADVANTAGES		
Growth Competitiveness Index		**Rank/102**

Macroeconomic Environment

7.10	Public trust of politicians	91
2.09	Access to credit	83
2.03	Extent of distortive government subsidies	81
2.01	Recession expectations	79
7.08	Diversion of public funds	74
2.21	Real exchange rate, 2002	72
2.17	Country credit rating, 2003	51

Public Institutions

6.08	Favoritism in decisions of government officials	92
6.01	Judicial independence	89
7.03	Irregular payments in tax collection	67
7.01	Irregular payments in exports and imports	65
7.02	Irregular payments in public utilities	65
6.03	Property rights	59
6.17	Organized crime	56

Technology

3.14	Government prioritization of ICT	91
3.15	Government success in ICT promotion	80
3.08	University/industry research collaboration	79
3.06	Company spending on research and development	66
3.20	Internet users, 2002	63
3.19	Cellular telephones, 2002	60
3.23	Personal computers, 2002	60
3.22	Telephone lines, 2002	58
3.12	Internet access in schools	57
3.17	Utility patents, 2002	51
3.21	Internet hosts, 2002	51

Business Competitiveness Index		**Rank/95**

Sophistication of Company Operations and Strategy

10.15	Reliance on professional management	83
10.10	Extent of regional sales	80
10.04	Capacity for innovation	72

Quality of the National Business Environment

6.08	Favoritism in decisions of government officials	86
7.09	Business costs of corruption	84
3.09	Government procurement of advanced technology products	83

Other Indicators		**Rank/102**

7.12	Policy consequences of legal political donations	96
6.10	Effectiveness of law-making bodies	92
6.07	Transparency of government policymaking	89
10.18	Hiring and firing practices	89
7.06	Irregular payments in government policymaking	88
2.10	Government intervention in corporate investment	87
11.11	Effects of compliance on business	86
11.07	Compliance with international agreements	86
11.09	Flexibility of regulations	82
7.13	Pervasiveness of money laundering through banks	82
6.16	Government effectiveness in reducing income inequality	81
10.21	Pay and productivity	81
7.07	Irregular payments in judicial decisions	80
8.03	Extent of market dominance	80
5.07	Postal efficiency	78

323

Note: The Business Competitiveness Index applies different criteria for selecting a country's competitive advantages and disadvantages. Please refer to the section "How Country Profiles Work" for further details.

Paraguay

Competitiveness Rankings

Growth Competitiveness Index Rank	95

Macroeconomic Environment Index Rank **92**
    Macroeconomic Stability Subindex Rank 92
    Government Waste Subindex Rank 101
    Country Credit Rating Rank 74

Public Institutions Index Rank...**97**
    Contracts and Law Subindex Rank 98
    Corruption Subindex Rank....................................87

Technology Index Rank **91**
    Innovation Subindex Rank.....................................89
    ICT Subindex Rank 76
    Technology Transfer Subindex Rank
    (out of 77 non-core innovators).........................70

Business Competitiveness Index Rank	91

**Sophistication of Company Operations
  and Strategy Rank** **90**

**Quality of the National Business
  Environment Rank** **92**

The Most Problematic Factors for Doing Business

FACTOR

Percent of responses

Note: From a list of 14 factors, respondents were asked to select the five most problematic for doing business in their country and to rank them between 1 (most problematic) and 5. The bars in the figure show the responses weighted according to their rankings.

Source: World Economic Forum, Executive Opinion Survey (2003)

National competitiveness balance sheet

NOTABLE COMPETITIVE ADVANTAGES

Critieria	Rank
Growth Competitiveness Index	**Rank/102**

Macroeconomic Environment

2.21	Real exchange rate, 2002	8
2.18	Government surplus/deficit, 2002	37
2.19	National savings rate, 2002	49

Technology

3.19	Cellular telephones, 2002	44

NOTABLE COMPETITIVE DISADVANTAGES

Critieria	Rank
Growth Competitiveness Index	**Rank/102**

Macroeconomic Environment

7.10	Public trust of politicians	101
2.09	Access to credit	100
7.08	Diversion of public funds	100
2.22	Interest rate spread, 2002	99
2.03	Extent of distortive government subsidies	93
2.01	Recession expectations	90
2.20	Inflation, 2002	85
2.17	Country credit rating, 2003	74

Public Institutions

6.08	Favoritism in decisions of government officials	102
6.01	Judicial independence	100
6.03	Property rights	91
6.17	Organized crime	90
7.03	Irregular payments in tax collection	88
7.02	Irregular payments in public utilities	85
7.01	Irregular payments in exports and imports	70

Technology

3.15	Government success in ICT promotion	102
3.14	Government prioritization of ICT	101
3.02	Firm-level technology absorption	100
3.06	Company spending on research and development	98
3.08	University/industry research collaboration	98
3.16	Laws relating to ICT	98
3.12	Internet access in schools	89
3.01	Technological sophistication	81
3.13	Quality of competition in the ISP sector	81
3.20	Internet users, 2002	77
3.22	Telephone lines, 2002	75
3.18	Tertiary enrollment	74
3.04	Prevalence of foreign technology licensing	72
3.17	Utility patents, 2002	72
3.03	FDI and technology transfer	68
3.21	Internet hosts, 2002	67
3.23	Personal computers, 2002	63

Business Competitiveness Index	Rank/95

Sophistication of Company Operations and Strategy

10.10	Extent of regional sales	55
10.08	Degree of customer orientation	75

Quality of the National Business Environment

6.09	Extent of bureaucratic red tape	13
3.19	Cellular telephones, 2002	42
2.16	Cost of importing foreign equipment	67

Business Competitiveness Index	Rank/95

Sophistication of Company Operations and Strategy

10.03	Extent of branding	94
10.15	Reliance on professional management	94
10.09	Control of international distribution	93

Quality of the National Business Environment

3.09	Government procurement of advanced technology products	95
5.02	Railroad infrastructure development	95
6.08	Favoritism in decisions of government officials	95

Other Indicators	Rank/102

2.02	Business costs of terrorism	24
6.11	Efficiency of the tax system	34
6.06	Burden of regulation	44
2.15	Agricultural policy costs	49

Other Indicators	Rank/102

11.11	Effects of compliance on business	102
3.07	Subsidies and tax credits for firm-level research and development	102
7.11	Prevalence of illegal political donations	102
10.05	Ethical behavior of firms	102
6.16	Government effectiveness in reducing income inequality	101
5.07	Postal efficiency	101
11.10	Consistency of regulation enforcement	101
4.04	Disparity in healthcare quality	101
6.18	Informal sector	101
6.10	Effectiveness of law-making bodies	100
11.07	Compliance with international agreements	100
11.09	Flexibility of regulations	100

Note: The Business Competitiveness Index applies different criteria for selecting a country's competitive advantages and disadvantages. Please refer to the section "How Country Profiles Work" for further details.

Peru

Competitiveness Rankings

Growth Competitiveness Index Rank	57

Macroeconomic Environment Index Rank **58**
    Macroeconomic Stability Subindex Rank 26
    Government Waste Subindex Rank 70
    Country Credit Rating Rank 61

Public Institutions Index Rank **54**
    Contracts and Law Subindex Rank 76
    Corruption Subindex Rank 37

Technology Index Rank **61**
    Innovation Subindex Rank 54
    ICT Subindex Rank 66
    Technology Transfer Subindex Rank
        (out of 77 non-core innovators) 37

Business Competitiveness Index Rank	78

**Sophistication of Company Operations
and Strategy Rank** **79**

**Quality of the National Business
Environment Rank** **75**

The Most Problematic Factors for Doing Business

FACTOR

Factor	
Policy instability	
Access to financing	
Inefficient bureaucracy	
Restrictive labor regulations	
Corruption	
Tax rates	
Tax regulations	
Inadequate infrastructure	
Inadequately educated workforce	
Poor work ethic	
Government instability/coups	
Crime and theft	
Inflation	
Foreign currency regulations	

Percent of responses

Note: From a list of 14 factors, respondents were asked to select the five most problematic for doing business in their country and to rank them between 1 (most problematic) and 5. The bars in the figure show the responses weighted according to their rankings.

Source: World Economic Forum, Executive Opinion Survey (2003)

National competitiveness balance sheet

NOTABLE COMPETITIVE ADVANTAGES			NOTABLE COMPETITIVE DISADVANTAGES		
Growth Competitiveness Index		**Rank/102**	**Growth Competitiveness Index**		**Rank/102**

	Macroeconomic Environment			**Macroeconomic Environment**	
2.20	Inflation, 2002	8	7.10	Public trust of politicians	86
2.01	Recession expectations	20	2.19	National savings rate, 2002	78
2.18	Government surplus/deficit, 2002	38	2.22	Interest rate spread, 2002	75
2.09	Access to credit	48	7.08	Diversion of public funds	68
	Public Institutions		2.17	Country credit rating, 2003	61
7.02	Irregular payments in public utilities	37	2.03	Extent of distortive government subsidies	56
7.03	Irregular payments in tax collection	40	2.21	Real exchange rate, 2002	54
7.01	Irregular payments in exports and imports	44		**Public Institutions**	
	Technology		6.01	Judicial independence	92
3.03	FDI and technology transfer	22	6.08	Favoritism in decisions of government officials	71
3.18	Tertiary enrollment	47	6.17	Organized crime	69
3.04	Prevalence of foreign technology licensing	48	6.03	Property rights	63
3.20	Internet users, 2002	50		**Technology**	
			3.08	University/industry research collaboration	86
			3.06	Company spending on research and development	85
			3.14	Government prioritization of ICT	82
			3.15	Government success in ICT promotion	82
			3.02	Firm-level technology absorption	79
			3.19	Cellular telephones, 2002	71
			3.22	Telephone lines, 2002	69
			3.01	Technological sophistication	67
			3.17	Utility patents, 2002	67
			3.13	Quality of competition in the ISP sector	66
			3.21	Internet hosts, 2002	66
			3.12	Internet access in schools	62
			3.16	Laws relating to ICT	60
			3.23	Personal computers, 2002	56

327

Business Competitiveness Index		**Rank/95**	**Business Competitiveness Index**		**Rank/95**
	Sophistication of Company Operations and Strategy			**Sophistication of Company Operations and Strategy**	
10.07	Extent of marketing	64	10.14	Extent of incentive compensation	85
10.06	Production process sophistication	64	10.09	Control of international distribution	83
10.08	Degree of customer orientation	67	3.06	Company spending on research and development	80
	Quality of the National Business Environment			**Quality of the National Business Environment**	
6.09	Extent of bureaucratic red tape	30	4.03	Quality of math and science education	86
5.06	Telephone infrastructure quality	36	5.04	Air transport infrastructure quality	85
2.14	Hidden trade barriers	40	6.01	Judicial independence	85

Other Indicators		**Rank/102**	**Other Indicators**		**Rank/102**
10.19	Flexibility of wage determination	5	3.07	Subsidies and tax credits for firm-level research and development	97
7.05	Irregular payments in loan applications	38	8.10	Regional disparities in quality of business environment	95
6.05	Freedom of the press	45	6.18	Informal sector	93
3.11	Availability of mobile or cellular telephones	46	11.10	Consistency of regulation enforcement	91
7.04	Irregular payments in public contracts	48	6.10	Effectiveness of law-making bodies	91
2.04	Extent of distortive government intervention	48	7.12	Policy consequences of legal political donations	91
2.06	Soundness of banks	50	7.07	Irregular payments in judicial decisions	91
			8.03	Extent of market dominance	91
			6.06	Burden of regulation	91
			10.22	Charitable causes involvement	90
			11.07	Compliance with international agreements	89
			11.12	Political context of environmental gains	87
			11.08	Clarity and stability of regulations	87
			11.09	Flexibility of regulations	85
			6.15	Government effectiveness in reducing poverty	85

Note: The Business Competitiveness Index applies different criteria for selecting a country's competitive advantages and disadvantages. Please refer to the section "How Country Profiles Work" for further details.

Philippines

Competitiveness Rankings

Growth Competitiveness Index Rank	66

Macroeconomic Environment Index Rank **60**
    Macroeconomic Stability Subindex Rank 46
    Government Waste Subindex Rank 89
    Country Credit Rating Rank 54

Public Institutions Index Rank........................**85**
    Contracts and Law Subindex Rank 75
    Corruption Subindex Rank...................................92

Technology Index Rank **56**
    Innovation Subindex Rank 49
    ICT Subindex Rank 67
    Technology Transfer Subindex Rank
    (out of 77 non-core innovators) 12

Business Competitiveness Index Rank	64

**Sophistication of Company Operations
  and Strategy Rank** **48**
**Quality of the National Business
  Environment Rank** **71**

The Most Problematic Factors for Doing Business

Note: From a list of 14 factors, respondents were asked to select the five most problematic for doing business in their country and to rank them between 1 (most problematic) and 5. The bars in the figure show the responses weighted according to their rankings.

Source: World Economic Forum, Executive Opinion Survey (2003)

National competitiveness balance sheet

NOTABLE COMPETITIVE ADVANTAGES	
Growth Competitiveness Index	**Rank/102**

Macroeconomic Environment

2.21	Real exchange rate, 2002	19
2.19	National savings rate, 2002	28
2.22	Interest rate spread, 2002	36
2.09	Access to credit	43
2.20	Inflation, 2002	47

Technology

3.03	FDI and technology transfer	12
3.04	Prevalence of foreign technology licensing	15
3.13	Quality of competition in the ISP sector	41
3.18	Tertiary enrollment	43

NOTABLE COMPETITIVE DISADVANTAGES	
Growth Competitiveness Index	**Rank/102**

Macroeconomic Environment

7.10	Public trust of politicians	94
7.08	Diversion of public funds	88
2.03	Extent of distortive government subsidies	78
2.18	Government surplus/deficit, 2002	64
2.01	Recession expectations	63
2.17	Country credit rating, 2003	54

Public Institutions

7.01	Irregular payments in exports and imports	99
7.03	Irregular payments in tax collection	97
6.08	Favoritism in decisions of government officials	84
6.17	Organized crime	80
6.01	Judicial independence	73
7.02	Irregular payments in public utilities	69
6.03	Property rights	68

Technology

3.22	Telephone lines, 2002	78
3.02	Firm-level technology absorption	72
3.08	University/industry research collaboration	72
3.01	Technological sophistication	70
3.21	Internet hosts, 2002	70
3.06	Company spending on research and development	68
3.15	Government success in ICT promotion	68
3.23	Personal computers, 2002	67
3.14	Government prioritization of ICT	61
3.20	Internet users, 2002	61
3.17	Utility patents, 2002	58
3.19	Cellular telephones, 2002	57
3.12	Internet access in schools	53
3.16	Laws relating to ICT	52

329

Business Competitiveness Index	Rank/95

Sophistication of Company Operations and Strategy

3.04	Prevalence of foreign technology licensing	23
10.14	Extent of incentive compensation	37
10.13	Willingness to delegate authority	37

Quality of the National Business Environment

6.09	Extent of bureaucratic red tape	19
10.16	Quality of management schools	32
2.16	Cost of importing foreign equipment	41

Business Competitiveness Index	Rank/95

Sophistication of Company Operations and Strategy

10.09	Control of international distribution	72
10.06	Production process sophistication	67
3.06	Company spending on research and development	64

Quality of the National Business Environment

6.13	Reliability of police services	87
2.14	Hidden trade barriers	84
5.01	Overall infrastructure quality	83

Other Indicators	Rank/102

4.10	Maternity leave legislation	14
6.05	Freedom of the press	16
4.11	Maternity laws' impact on hiring women	18
8.09	Wage equality of women in the workplace	19
8.08	Private sector employment of women	19
3.11	Availability of mobile or cellular telephones	38
10.22	Charitable causes involvement	48

Other Indicators	Rank/102

7.04	Irregular payments in public contracts	101
7.11	Prevalence of illegal political donations	100
2.02	Business costs of terrorism	100
7.13	Pervasiveness of money laundering through banks	99
6.06	Burden of regulation	98
5.07	Postal efficiency	97
11.08	Clarity and stability of regulations	96
11.11	Effects of compliance on business	96
7.06	Irregular payments in government policymaking	95
7.07	Irregular payments in judicial decisions	94
11.09	Flexibility of regulations	94
7.12	Policy consequences of legal political donations	93
11.07	Compliance with international agreements	92
8.10	Regional disparities in quality of business environment	90
11.10	Consistency of regulation enforcement	90

Note: The Business Competitiveness Index applies different criteria for selecting a country's competitive advantages and disadvantages. Please refer to the section "How Country Profiles Work" for further details.

Poland

Competitiveness Rankings

Growth Competitiveness Index Rank	45

Macroeconomic Environment Index Rank **49**
    Macroeconomic Stability Subindex Rank 62
    Government Waste Subindex Rank 65
    Country Credit Rating Rank 33

Public Institutions Index Rank **58**
    Contracts and Law Subindex Rank 66
    Corruption Subindex Rank 53

Technology Index Rank **34**
    Innovation Subindex Rank 29
    ICT Subindex Rank 41
    Technology Transfer Subindex Rank
    (out of 77 non-core innovators) 26

Business Competitiveness Index Rank	47

**Sophistication of Company Operations
and Strategy Rank** 43

**Quality of the National Business
Environment Rank** 45

The Most Problematic Factors for Doing Business

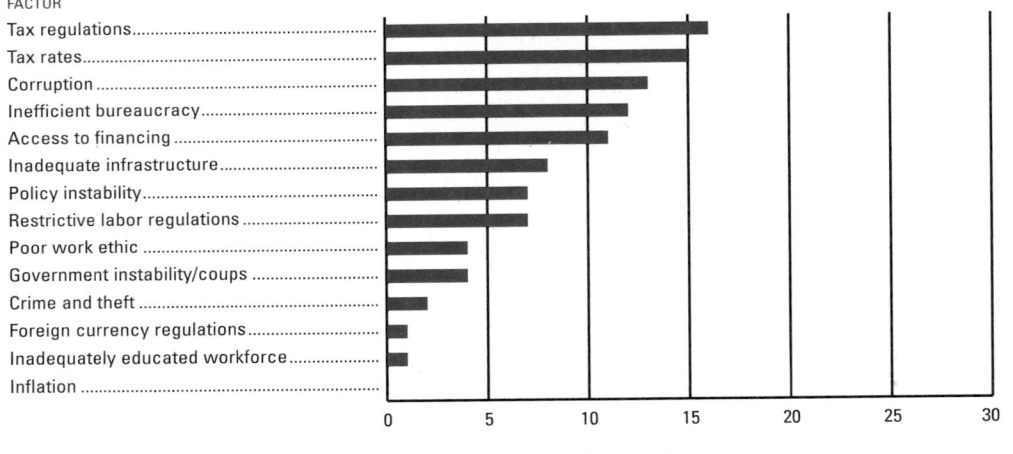

Note: From a list of 14 factors, respondents were asked to select the five most problematic for doing business in their country and to rank them between 1 (most problematic) and 5. The bars in the figure show the responses weighted according to their rankings.

Source: World Economic Forum, Executive Opinion Survey (2003)

National competitiveness balance sheet

NOTABLE COMPETITIVE ADVANTAGES

Growth Competitiveness Index	Rank/102

Macroeconomic Environment

2.20	Inflation, 2002	24
2.17	Country credit rating, 2003	33

Technology

3.18	Tertiary enrollment	19
3.03	FDI and technology transfer	24
3.04	Prevalence of foreign technology licensing	29
3.21	Internet hosts, 2002	30
3.22	Telephone lines, 2002	37
3.12	Internet access in schools	39
3.19	Cellular telephones, 2002	41
3.08	University/industry research collaboration	42
3.23	Personal computers, 2002	43
3.20	Internet users, 2002	44

Business Competitiveness Index	Rank/95

Sophistication of Company Operations and Strategy

10.03	Extent of branding	33
10.14	Extent of incentive compensation	33
10.02	Value chain presence	35

Quality of the National Business Environment

9.09	Local availability of process machinery	24
8.07	Prevalence of mergers and acquisitions	25
6.12	Centralization of economic policymaking	27

Other Indicators	Rank/102

10.21	Pay and productivity	32
8.03	Extent of market dominance	35
11.10	Consistency of regulation enforcement	37
11.09	Flexibility of regulations	40
11.06	Compliance with environmental regulations	43
11.04	Chemical waste regulations	43
10.19	Flexibility of wage determination	43
3.07	Subsidies and tax credits for firm-level research and development	43
11.01	Air pollution regulations	44
11.03	Toxic waste disposal regulations	44
4.09	Brain drain	44

NOTABLE COMPETITIVE DISADVANTAGES

Growth Competitiveness Index	Rank/102

Macroeconomic Environment

2.03	Extent of distortive government subsidies	85
2.21	Real exchange rate, 2002	80
2.19	National savings rate, 2002	79
2.09	Access to credit	73
2.18	Government surplus/deficit, 2002	72
2.01	Recession expectations	67
7.10	Public trust of politicians	59
7.08	Diversion of public funds	58
2.22	Interest rate spread, 2002	52

Public Institutions

6.17	Organized crime	74
6.03	Property rights	69
6.08	Favoritism in decisions of government officials	69
7.02	Irregular payments in public utilities	57
7.01	Irregular payments in exports and imports	52
6.01	Judicial independence	51
7.03	Irregular payments in tax collection	49

Technology

3.14	Government prioritization of ICT	84
3.15	Government success in ICT promotion	81
3.13	Quality of competition in the ISP sector	71
3.02	Firm-level technology absorption	54
3.17	Utility patents, 2002	53
3.01	Technological sophistication	50
3.16	Laws relating to ICT	46
3.06	Company spending on research and development	45

Business Competitiveness Index	Rank/95

Sophistication of Company Operations and Strategy

10.15	Reliance on professional management	59
10.08	Degree of customer orientation	53
10.12	Extent of staff training	53

Quality of the National Business Environment

10.20	Cooperation in labor-employer relations	88
2.03	Extent of distortive government subsidies	78
5.01	Overall infrastructure quality	71

Other Indicators	Rank/102

4.11	Maternity laws' impact on hiring women	99
2.15	Agricultural policy costs	93
4.10	Maternity leave legislation	93
8.09	Wage equality of women in the workplace	89
6.07	Transparency of government policymaking	88
6.11	Efficiency of the tax system	87
6.15	Government effectiveness in reducing poverty	81
2.04	Extent of distortive government intervention	81
8.11	Focus of trade and industry associations	79
11.12	Political context of environmental gains	77
7.12	Policy consequences of legal political donations	75
10.22	Charitable causes involvement	75
11.11	Effects of compliance on business	74
7.13	Pervasiveness of money laundering through banks	72
6.10	Effectiveness of law-making bodies	70

331

Note: The Business Competitiveness Index applies different criteria for selecting a country's competitive advantages and disadvantages. Please refer to the section "How Country Profiles Work" for further details.

Portugal

Competitiveness Rankings

Growth Competitiveness Index Rank	25

Macroeconomic Environment Index Rank **31**
   Macroeconomic Stability Subindex Rank 69
   Government Waste Subindex Rank 29
   Country Credit Rating Rank 21

Public Institutions Index Rank...**22**
   Contracts and Law Subindex Rank 21
   Corruption Subindex Rank....................................30

Technology Index Rank **22**
   Innovation Subindex Rank....................................32
   ICT Subindex Rank...29
   Technology Transfer Subindex Rank
   (out of 77 non-core innovators)........................15

Business Competitiveness Index Rank	36

**Sophistication of Company Operations
and Strategy Rank** **46**
**Quality of the National Business
Environment Rank** **33**

The Most Problematic Factors for Doing Business

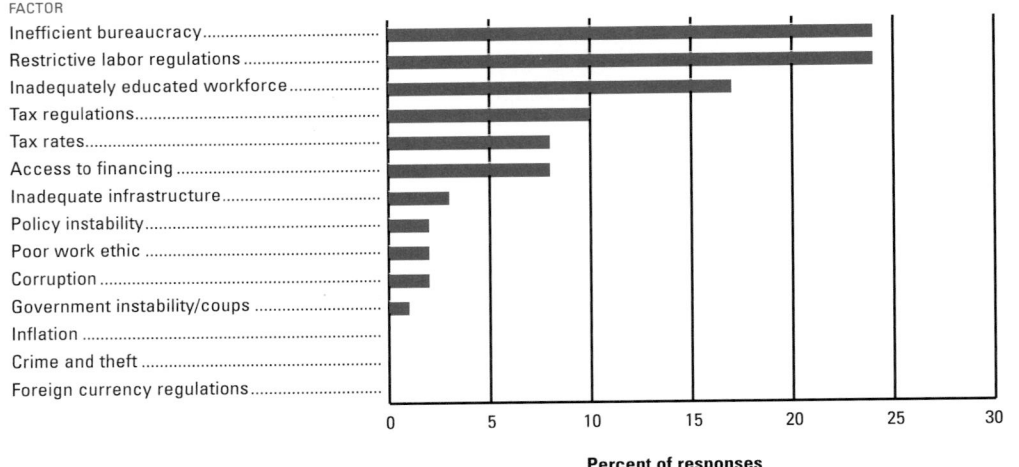

Note: From a list of 14 factors, respondents were asked to select the five most problematic for doing business in their country and to rank them between 1 (most problematic) and 5. The bars in the figure show the responses weighted according to their rankings.

Source: World Economic Forum, Executive Opinion Survey (2003)

National competitiveness balance sheet

NOTABLE COMPETITIVE ADVANTAGES	
Growth Competitiveness Index	**Rank/102**

Macroeconomic Environment

2.22	Interest rate spread, 2002	10
2.17	Country credit rating, 2003	21

Public Institutions

6.17	Organized crime	12
6.01	Judicial independence	14
7.02	Irregular payments in public utilities	21

Technology

3.04	Prevalence of foreign technology licensing	7
3.19	Cellular telephones, 2002	16
3.20	Internet users, 2002	22
3.18	Tertiary enrollment	24

NOTABLE COMPETITIVE DISADVANTAGES	
Growth Competitiveness Index	**Rank/102**

Macroeconomic Environment

2.01	Recession expectations	96
2.09	Access to credit	90
2.19	National savings rate, 2002	69
2.03	Extent of distortive government subsidies	54
2.20	Inflation, 2002	52
2.21	Real exchange rate, 2002	47
2.18	Government surplus/deficit, 2002	42
7.10	Public trust of politicians	27
7.08	Diversion of public funds	25

Public Institutions

7.03	Irregular payments in tax collection	37
6.03	Property rights	33
6.08	Favoritism in decisions of government officials	30
7.01	Irregular payments in exports and imports	30

Technology

3.02	Firm-level technology absorption	87
3.06	Company spending on research and development	61
3.01	Technological sophistication	57
3.14	Government prioritization of ICT	53
3.08	University/industry research collaboration	49
3.15	Government success in ICT promotion	48
3.16	Laws relating to ICT	44
3.17	Utility patents, 2002	40
3.23	Personal computers, 2002	37
3.13	Quality of competition in the ISP sector	35
3.21	Internet hosts, 2002	32
3.22	Telephone lines, 2002	29
3.03	FDI and technology transfer	28
3.12	Internet access in schools	26

333

Business Competitiveness Index	Rank/95

Sophistication of Company Operations and Strategy

10.15	Reliance on professional management	37
10.14	Extent of incentive compensation	38
10.02	Value chain presence	41

Quality of the National Business Environment

6.01	Judicial independence	14
2.14	Hidden trade barriers	15
3.19	Cellular telephones, 2002	16

Business Competitiveness Index	Rank/95

Sophistication of Company Operations and Strategy

10.01	Nature of competitive advantage	70
10.08	Degree of customer orientation	62
10.13	Willingness to delegate authority	59

Quality of the National Business Environment

4.03	Quality of math and science education	71
8.05	Administrative burden for startups	69
10.17	Efficacy of corporate boards	68

Other Indicators	Rank/102

4.05	Business impact of malaria	4
2.02	Business costs of terrorism	4
6.05	Freedom of the press	6
6.14	Business costs of crime and violence	10
3.11	Availability of mobile or cellular telephones	15
7.07	Irregular payments in judicial decisions	18
7.04	Irregular payments in public contracts	21
5.07	Postal efficiency	22
3.07	Subsidies and tax credits for firm-level research and development	24
8.08	Private sector employment of women	24

Other Indicators	Rank/102

10.22	Charitable causes involvement	93
8.11	Focus of trade and industry associations	85
10.21	Pay and productivity	85
11.12	Political context of environmental gains	82
10.18	Hiring and firing practices	78
4.11	Maternity laws' impact on hiring women	77
11.11	Effects of compliance on business	77
10.23	Company promotion of volunteerism	76
8.10	Regional disparities in quality of business environment	70
10.19	Flexibility of wage determination	70
2.15	Agricultural policy costs	68
6.07	Transparency of government policymaking	60
2.04	Extent of distortive government intervention	59
11.09	Flexibility of regulations	56
6.06	Burden of regulation	54

Note: The Business Competitiveness Index applies different criteria for selecting a country's competitive advantages and disadvantages. Please refer to the section "How Country Profiles Work" for further details.

Romania

Competitiveness Rankings

Growth Competitiveness Index Rank	75

Macroeconomic Environment Index Rank **81**
    Macroeconomic Stability Subindex Rank.............81
    Government Waste Subindex Rank.....................96
    Country Credit Rating Rank..................................66

Public Institutions Index Rank..**86**
    Contracts and Law Subindex Rank 83
    Corruption Subindex Rank....................................90

Technology Index Rank **55**
    Innovation Subindex Rank....................................56
    ICT Subindex Rank 54
    Technology Transfer Subindex Rank
      (out of 77 non-core innovators).........................38

Business Competitiveness Index Rank	73

**Sophistication of Company Operations
  and Strategy Rank**...**80**

**Quality of the National Business
  Environment Rank**...**68**

The Most Problematic Factors for Doing Business

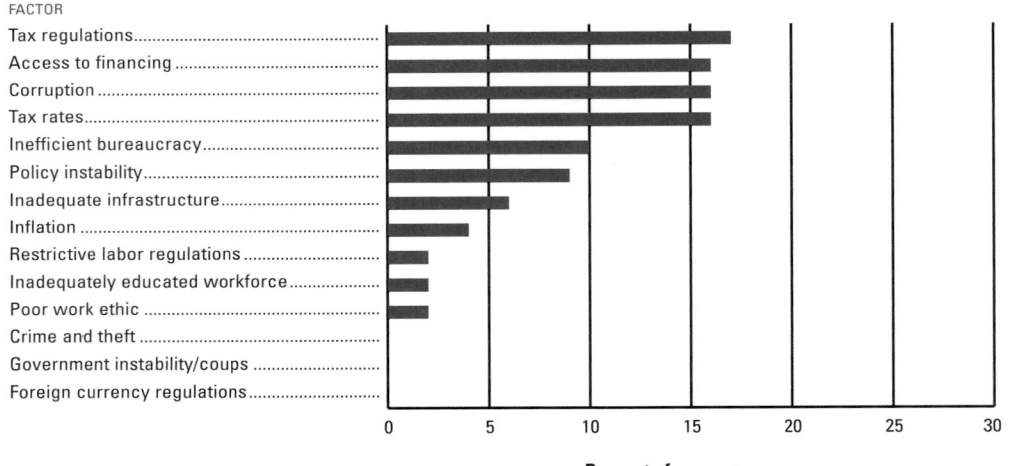

FACTOR

Tax regulations
Access to financing
Corruption
Tax rates
Inefficient bureaucracy
Policy instability
Inadequate infrastructure
Inflation
Restrictive labor regulations
Inadequately educated workforce
Poor work ethic
Crime and theft
Government instability/coups
Foreign currency regulations

Percent of responses

Note: From a list of 14 factors, respondents were asked to select the five most problematic for doing business in their country and to rank them between 1 (most problematic) and 5. The bars in the figure show the responses weighted according to their rankings.

Source: World Economic Forum, Executive Opinion Survey (2003)

National competitiveness balance sheet

NOTABLE COMPETITIVE ADVANTAGES		
Growth Competitiveness Index		**Rank/102**
	Macroeconomic Environment	
2.18	Government surplus/deficit, 2002	43
2.01	Recession expectations	47
	Technology	
3.03	FDI and technology transfer	32
3.04	Prevalence of foreign technology licensing	43
3.12	Internet access in schools	45
3.20	Internet users, 2002	48
3.15	Government success in ICT promotion	49
3.16	Laws relating to ICT	50

NOTABLE COMPETITIVE DISADVANTAGES		
Growth Competitiveness Index		**Rank/102**
	Macroeconomic Environment	
2.03	Extent of distortive government subsidies	102
2.20	Inflation, 2002	98
2.21	Real exchange rate, 2002	86
7.08	Diversion of public funds	86
7.10	Public trust of politicians	85
2.22	Interest rate spread, 2002	74
2.17	Country credit rating, 2003	66
2.09	Access to credit	60
2.19	National savings rate, 2002	53
	Public Institutions	
7.01	Irregular payments in exports and imports	98
6.08	Favoritism in decisions of government officials	93
7.02	Irregular payments in public utilities	86
6.01	Judicial independence	82
6.03	Property rights	79
7.03	Irregular payments in tax collection	70
6.17	Organized crime	67
	Technology	
3.06	Company spending on research and development	76
3.01	Technological sophistication	75
3.14	Government prioritization of ICT	73
3.13	Quality of competition in the ISP sector	72
3.02	Firm-level technology absorption	65
3.08	University/industry research collaboration	65
3.23	Personal computers, 2002	62
3.17	Utility patents, 2002	60
3.19	Cellular telephones, 2002	59
3.21	Internet hosts, 2002	55
3.22	Telephone lines, 2002	53
3.18	Tertiary enrollment	52

Business Competitiveness Index		**Rank/95**
	Sophistication of Company Operations and Strategy	
10.11	Breadth of international markets	64
10.03	Extent of branding	64
10.07	Extent of marketing	66
	Quality of the National Business Environment	
6.09	Extent of bureaucratic red tape	1
4.03	Quality of math and science education	12
6.12	Centralization of economic policymaking	24

Business Competitiveness Index		**Rank/95**
	Sophistication of Company Operations and Strategy	
10.08	Degree of customer orientation	86
10.01	Nature of competitive advantage	84
10.02	Value chain presence	83
	Quality of the National Business Environment	
2.03	Extent of distortive government subsidies	95
10.17	Efficacy of corporate boards	94
2.14	Hidden trade barriers	89

Other Indicators		**Rank/102**
10.19	Flexibility of wage determination	16
2.02	Business costs of terrorism	25
8.09	Wage equality of women in the workplace	38
11.07	Compliance with international agreements	41
11.11	Effects of compliance on business	42
10.21	Pay and productivity	42
10.18	Hiring and firing practices	44
5.07	Postal efficiency	45
4.07	Business impact of HIV/AIDS	48
4.05	Business impact of malaria	50

Other Indicators		**Rank/102**
6.11	Efficiency of the tax system	100
7.12	Policy consequences of legal political donations	99
7.05	Irregular payments in loan applications	99
11.12	Political context of environmental gains	98
2.04	Extent of distortive government intervention	98
2.15	Agricultural policy costs	97
6.06	Burden of regulation	97
7.13	Pervasiveness of money laundering through banks	97
7.14	Pervasiveness of money laundering through non-bank channels	96
7.06	Irregular payments in government policymaking	96
8.11	Focus of trade and industry associations	95
7.04	Irregular payments in public contracts	95
6.07	Transparency of government policymaking	93
2.10	Government intervention in corporate investment	93
4.09	Brain drain	93

335

Note: The Business Competitiveness Index applies different criteria for selecting a country's competitive advantages and disadvantages. Please refer to the section "How Country Profiles Work" for further details.

Russian Federation

Competitiveness Rankings

Growth Competitiveness Index Rank	70

Macroeconomic Environment Index Rank **61**
    Macroeconomic Stability Subindex Rank 61
    Government Waste Subindex Rank 76
    Country Credit Rating Rank 55

Public Institutions Index Rank...**81**
    Contracts and Law Subindex Rank 91
    Corruption Subindex Rank......................................75

Technology Index Rank **69**
    Innovation Subindex Rank....................................27
    ICT Subindex Rank 56
    Technology Transfer Subindex Rank
    (out of 77 non-core innovators) 69

Business Competitiveness Index Rank	65

Sophistication of Company Operations
  and Strategy Rank **68**

Quality of the National Business
  Environment Rank **63**

The Most Problematic Factors for Doing Business

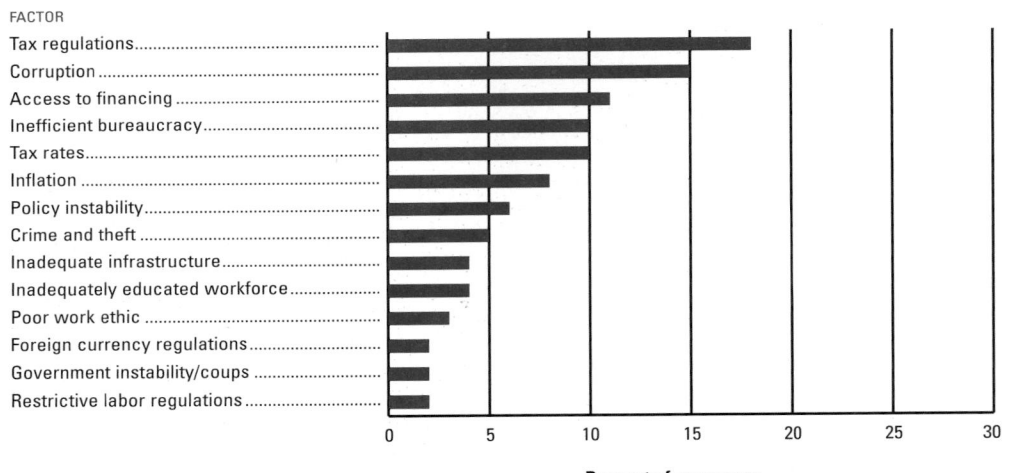

Note: From a list of 14 factors, respondents were asked to select the five most problematic for doing business in their country and to rank them between 1 (most problematic) and 5. The bars in the figure show the responses weighted according to their rankings.

Source: World Economic Forum, Executive Opinion Survey (2003)

National competitiveness balance sheet

NOTABLE COMPETITIVE ADVANTAGES

Growth Competitiveness Index		Rank/102
Macroeconomic Environment		
2.19	National savings rate, 2002	10
2.18	Government surplus/deficit, 2002	12
2.01	Recession expectations	34
2.09	Access to credit	49
Technology		
3.18	Tertiary enrollment	8
3.17	Utility patents, 2002	38
3.22	Telephone lines, 2002	46
3.23	Personal computers, 2002	42
3.21	Internet hosts, 2002	50

Business Competitiveness Index		Rank/95
Sophistication of Company Operations and Strategy		
10.04	Capacity for innovation	28
10.09	Control of international distribution	46
10.03	Extent of branding	47
Quality of the National Business Environment		
5.02	Railroad infrastructure development	17
9.09	Local availability of process machinery	18
4.03	Quality of math and science education	18

Other Indicators		Rank/102
10.18	Hiring and firing practices	11
10.19	Flexibility of wage determination	12
10.21	Pay and productivity	33
11.09	Flexibility of regulations	34

NOTABLE COMPETITIVE DISADVANTAGES

Growth Competitiveness Index		Rank/102
Macroeconomic Environment		
2.20	Inflation, 2002	93
2.03	Extent of distortive government subsidies	77
2.22	Interest rate spread, 2002	76
7.08	Diversion of public funds	76
7.10	Public trust of politicians	70
2.21	Real exchange rate, 2002	62
2.17	Country credit rating, 2003	55
Public Institutions		
6.03	Property rights	96
6.17	Organized crime	87
7.01	Irregular payments in exports and imports	87
6.01	Judicial independence	81
6.08	Favoritism in decisions of government officials	81
7.02	Irregular payments in public utilities	79
7.03	Irregular payments in tax collection	59
Technology		
3.15	Government success in ICT promotion	86
3.13	Quality of competition in the ISP sector	80
3.14	Government prioritization of ICT	78
3.16	Laws relating to ICT	76
3.03	FDI and technology transfer	71
3.06	Company spending on research and development	70
3.04	Prevalence of foreign technology licensing	68
3.19	Cellular telephones, 2002	67
3.02	Firm-level technology absorption	66
3.20	Internet users, 2002	64
3.01	Technological sophistication	61
3.12	Internet access in schools	61
3.08	University/industry research collaboration	56

Business Competitiveness Index		Rank/95
Sophistication of Company Operations and Strategy		
3.04	Prevalence of foreign technology licensing	86
10.02	Value chain presence	79
10.12	Extent of staff training	77
Quality of the National Business Environment		
10.24	Protection of minority shareholders' interests	94
10.26	Foreign ownership restrictions	93
6.09	Extent of bureaucratic red tape	89

Other Indicators		Rank/102
11.12	Political context of environmental gains	101
6.06	Burden of regulation	100
4.10	Maternity leave legislation	100
8.11	Focus of trade and industry associations	97
6.07	Transparency of government policymaking	97
6.11	Efficiency of the tax system	96
7.13	Pervasiveness of money laundering through banks	95
8.10	Regional disparities in quality of business environment	93
2.06	Soundness of banks	92
10.25	Availability of company financial information	91
6.16	Government effectiveness in reducing income inequality	90
6.15	Government effectiveness in reducing poverty	89
10.27	Strength of auditing and accounting standards	89
10.22	Charitable causes involvement	89
2.15	Agricultural policy costs	87

337

Note: The Business Competitiveness Index applies different criteria for selecting a country's competitive advantages and disadvantages. Please refer to the section "How Country Profiles Work" for further details.

Senegal

Competitiveness Rankings

Growth Competitiveness Index Rank	79

Macroeconomic Environment Index Rank **67**
   Macroeconomic Stability Subindex Rank 56
   Government Waste Subindex Rank 62
   Country Credit Rating Rank 76

Public Institutions Index Rank **75**
   Contracts and Law Subindex Rank 71
   Corruption Subindex Rank...................................78

Technology Index Rank **89**
   Innovation Subindex Rank...................................82
   ICT Subindex Rank 81
   Technology Transfer Subindex Rank
   (out of 77 non-core innovators) 64

Business Competitiveness Index Rank	82

**Sophistication of Company Operations
and Strategy Rank** **89**

**Quality of the National Business
Environment Rank** **79**

The Most Problematic Factors for Doing Business

FACTOR

Note: From a list of 14 factors, respondents were asked to select the five most problematic for doing business in their country and to rank them between 1 (most problematic) and 5. The bars in the figure show the responses weighted according to their rankings.

Source: World Economic Forum, Executive Opinion Survey (2003)

National competitiveness balance sheet

NOTABLE COMPETITIVE ADVANTAGES	
Growth Competitiveness Index	**Rank/102**

Macroeconomic Environment

2.20	Inflation, 2002	32
2.21	Real exchange rate, 2002	33
2.18	Government surplus/deficit, 2002	36
2.03	Extent of distortive government subsidies	43
2.01	Recession expectations	48

Technology

3.02	Firm-level technology absorption	12
3.14	Government prioritization of ICT	23
3.15	Government success in ICT promotion	36

NOTABLE COMPETITIVE DISADVANTAGES	
Growth Competitiveness Index	**Rank/102**

Macroeconomic Environment

2.09	Access to credit	86
2.19	National savings rate, 2002	77
2.17	Country credit rating, 2003	76
7.08	Diversion of public funds	75
2.22	Interest rate spread, 2002	67
7.10	Public trust of politicians	64

Public Institutions

7.03	Irregular payments in tax collection	82
6.03	Property rights	81
7.01	Irregular payments in exports and imports	74
7.02	Irregular payments in public utilities	71
6.01	Judicial independence	69
6.17	Organized crime	68
6.08	Favoritism in decisions of government officials	60

Technology

3.06	Company spending on research and development	89
3.18	Tertiary enrollment	87
3.13	Quality of competition in the ISP sector	86
3.22	Telephone lines, 2002	86
3.20	Internet users, 2002	85
3.21	Internet hosts, 2002	83
3.12	Internet access in schools	82
3.01	Technological sophistication	78
3.16	Laws relating to ICT	78
3.19	Cellular telephones, 2002	75
3.17	Utility patents, 2002	72
3.23	Personal computers, 2002	71
3.03	FDI and technology transfer	67
3.08	University/industry research collaboration	63
3.04	Prevalence of foreign technology licensing	57

Business Competitiveness Index	Rank/95

Sophistication of Company Operations and Strategy

10.01	Nature of competitive advantage	30
10.15	Reliance on professional management	51
10.11	Breadth of international markets	59

Quality of the National Business Environment

9.02	Local supplier quantity	26
10.26	Foreign ownership restrictions	27
8.05	Administrative burden for startups	30

Other Indicators	Rank/102

2.06	Soundness of banks	28
11.11	Effects of compliance on business	32
11.12	Political context of environmental gains	33
10.22	Charitable causes involvement	37
10.23	Company promotion of volunteerism	43
6.05	Freedom of the press	46
11.07	Compliance with international agreements	49

Business Competitiveness Index	Rank/95

Sophistication of Company Operations and Strategy

3.04	Prevalence of foreign technology licensing	95
10.06	Production process sophistication	94
10.08	Degree of customer orientation	93

Quality of the National Business Environment

9.06	State of cluster development	94
9.07	Extent of collaboration among clusters	94
10.20	Cooperation in labor-employer relations	94

Other Indicators	Rank/102

4.05	Business impact of malaria	93
3.11	Availability of mobile or cellular telephones	91
10.19	Flexibility of wage determination	90
6.06	Burden of regulation	89
8.10	Regional disparities in quality of business environment	87
4.06	Business impact of tuberculosis	87
4.04	Disparity in healthcare quality	87
2.15	Agricultural policy costs	86
7.05	Irregular payments in loan applications	86
11.13	Prevalence of environmental management systems	86
4.09	Brain drain	85
7.04	Irregular payments in public contracts	83
10.25	Availability of company financial information	81
11.01	Air pollution regulations	81
4.11	Maternity laws' impact on hiring women	80

339

Note: The Business Competitiveness Index applies different criteria for selecting a country's competitive advantages and disadvantages. Please refer to the section "How Country Profiles Work" for further details.

Serbia

Competitiveness Rankings

Growth Competitiveness Index Rank	77

Macroeconomic Environment Index Rank 87
    Macroeconomic Stability Subindex Rank 86
    Government Waste Subindex Rank 56
    Country Credit Rating Rank 93

Public Institutions Index Rank...**77**
    Contracts and Law Subindex Rank 77
    Corruption Subindex Rank 74

Technology Index Rank **66**
    Innovation Subindex Rank 62
    ICT Subindex Rank 55
    Technology Transfer Subindex Rank
    (out of 77 non-core innovators) 60

Business Competitiveness Index Rank	76

**Sophistication of Company Operations
  and Strategy Rank** **74**
**Quality of the National Business
  Environment Rank** **76**

The Most Problematic Factors for Doing Business

FACTOR

Percent of responses

Note: From a list of 14 factors, respondents were asked to select the five most problematic for doing business in their country and to rank them between 1 (most problematic) and 5. The bars in the figure show the responses weighted according to their rankings.

Source: World Economic Forum, Executive Opinion Survey (2003)

National competitiveness balance sheet

NOTABLE COMPETITIVE ADVANTAGES	
Growth Competitiveness Index	**Rank/102**

Macroeconomic Environment
| 2.21 | Real exchange rate, 2002 | 9 |
| 7.10 | Public trust of politicians | 43 |

Public Institutions
| 6.08 | Favoritism in decisions of government officials | 50 |

Technology
3.14	Government prioritization of ICT	45
3.19	Cellular telephones, 2002	48
3.22	Telephone lines, 2002	47

NOTABLE COMPETITIVE DISADVANTAGES	
Growth Competitiveness Index	**Rank/102**

Macroeconomic Environment
2.19	National savings rate, 2002	95
2.20	Inflation, 2002	95
2.17	Country credit rating, 2003	93
2.22	Interest rate spread, 2002	90
2.01	Recession expectations	77
2.03	Extent of distortive government subsidies	74
2.09	Access to credit	68
7.08	Diversion of public funds	66
2.18	Government surplus/deficit, 2002	65

Public Institutions
6.03	Property rights	87
7.02	Irregular payments in public utilities	82
6.01	Judicial independence	80
6.17	Organized crime	79
7.01	Irregular payments in exports and imports	78
7.03	Irregular payments in tax collection	63

Technology
3.01	Technological sophistication	96
3.13	Quality of competition in the ISP sector	91
3.02	Firm-level technology absorption	86
3.06	Company spending on research and development	80
3.08	University/industry research collaboration	70
3.17	Utility patents, 2002	72
3.12	Internet access in schools	72
3.23	Personal computers, 2002	68
3.16	Laws relating to ICT	65
3.04	Prevalence of foreign technology licensing	61
3.15	Government success in ICT promotion	57
3.21	Internet hosts, 2002	56
3.03	FDI and technology transfer	55
3.18	Tertiary enrollment	54
3.20	Internet users, 2002	53

Business Competitiveness Index	Rank/95

Sophistication of Company Operations and Strategy
10.09	Control of international distribution	51
10.01	Nature of competitive advantage	62
10.11	Breadth of international markets	63

Quality of the National Business Environment
3.10	Availability of scientists and engineers	31
2.16	Cost of importing foreign equipment	33
4.03	Quality of math and science education	33

Business Competitiveness Index	Rank/95

Sophistication of Company Operations and Strategy
10.08	Degree of customer orientation	79
10.02	Value chain presence	77
10.04	Capacity for innovation	77

Quality of the National Business Environment
10.24	Protection of minority shareholders' interests	93
8.05	Administrative burden for startups	91
5.06	Telephone infrastructure quality	87

Other Indicators	Rank/102
8.09	Wage equality of women in the workplace	26
10.19	Flexibility of wage determination	27
10.18	Hiring and firing practices	32
4.07	Business impact of HIV/AIDS	35
6.18	Informal sector	38
4.05	Business impact of malaria	39
2.15	Agricultural policy costs	41
6.07	Transparency of government policymaking	42
11.07	Compliance with international agreements	45
6.11	Efficiency of the tax system	46
4.08	Impact of HIV/AIDS on FDI	49

Other Indicators	Rank/102
4.09	Brain drain	100
2.06	Soundness of banks	95
7.05	Irregular payments in loan applications	93
7.12	Policy consequences of legal political donations	90
10.05	Ethical behavior of firms	88
6.05	Freedom of the press	86
10.25	Availability of company financial information	84
10.27	Strength of auditing and accounting standards	84
11.10	Consistency of regulation enforcement	84
10.22	Charitable causes involvement	84
6.06	Burden of regulation	81
7.07	Irregular payments in judicial decisions	81
7.13	Pervasiveness of money laundering through banks	81
8.11	Focus of trade and industry associations	81
3.11	Availability of mobile or cellular telephones	80

341

Note: The Business Competitiveness Index applies different criteria for selecting a country's competitive advantages and disadvantages. Please refer to the section "How Country Profiles Work" for further details.

Singapore

Competitiveness Rankings

The Most Problematic Factors for Doing Business

FACTOR

Factor	
Inadequately educated workforce	
Restrictive labor regulations	
Tax rates	
Poor work ethic	
Access to financing	
Inefficient bureaucracy	
Tax regulations	
Inadequate infrastructure	
Inflation	
Policy instability	
Foreign currency regulations	
Crime and theft	
Government instability/coups	
Corruption	

Percent of responses

Note: From a list of 14 factors, respondents were asked to select the five most problematic for doing business in their country and to rank them between 1 (most problematic) and 5. The bars in the figure show the responses weighted according to their rankings.

Source: World Economic Forum, Executive Opinion Survey (2003)

National competitiveness balance sheet

NOTABLE COMPETITIVE ADVANTAGES		
Growth Competitiveness Index		**Rank/102**

Macroeconomic Environment

2.03	Extent of distortive government subsidies	1
2.19	National savings rate, 2002	1
7.10	Public trust of politicians	1
7.08	Diversion of public funds	3
2.20	Inflation, 2002	6

Public Institutions

7.02	Irregular payments in public utilities	3
6.08	Favoritism in decisions of government officials	4
6.17	Organized crime	4
7.01	Irregular payments in exports and imports	4
6.03	Property rights	5
7.03	Irregular payments in tax collection	6

Technology

3.14	Government prioritization of ICT	1
3.15	Government success in ICT promotion	1
3.12	Internet access in schools	2
3.16	Laws relating to ICT	2
3.08	University/industry research collaboration	3
3.20	Internet users, 2002	4
3.02	Firm-level technology absorption	5
3.01	Technological sophistication	6
3.23	Personal computers, 2002	8
3.06	Company spending on research and development	10
3.17	Utility patents, 2002	10

Business Competitiveness Index		**Rank/95**

Sophistication of Company Operations and Strategy

10.12	Extent of staff training	8
3.06	Company spending on research and development	10
10.06	Production process sophistication	10

Quality of the National Business Environment

10.20	Cooperation in labor-employer relations	1
2.03	Extent of distortive government subsidies	1
3.09	Government procurement of advanced technology products	1

Other Indicators		**Rank/102**

6.07	Transparency of government policymaking	1
7.11	Prevalence of illegal political donations	1
6.14	Business costs of crime and violence	1
6.10	Effectiveness of law-making bodies	1
11.09	Flexibility of regulations	1
11.08	Clarity and stability of regulations	1
3.07	Subsidies and tax credits for firm-level research and development	1
11.11	Effects of compliance on business	1
8.10	Regional disparities in quality of business environment	1
11.12	Political context of environmental gains	1
8.11	Focus of trade and industry associations	1
6.06	Burden of regulation	1
7.12	Policy consequences of legal political donations	1
10.18	Hiring and firing practices	2
6.11	Efficiency of the tax system	2

NOTABLE COMPETITIVE DISADVANTAGES		
Growth Competitiveness Index		**Rank/102**

Macroeconomic Environment

2.01	Recession expectations	64
2.21	Real exchange rate, 2002	37
2.22	Interest rate spread, 2002	33
2.18	Government surplus/deficit, 2002	26
2.09	Access to credit	24
2.17	Country credit rating, 2003	17

Public Institutions

6.01	Judicial independence	27

Technology

3.18	Tertiary enrollment	32
3.22	Telephone lines, 2002	26
3.13	Quality of competition in the ISP sector	18
3.19	Cellular telephones, 2002	17
3.21	Internet hosts, 2002	16

Business Competitiveness Index		**Rank/95**

Sophistication of Company Operations and Strategy

10.09	Control of international distribution	28
10.04	Capacity for innovation	20
10.10	Extent of regional sales	18

Quality of the National Business Environment

6.12	Centralization of economic policymaking	78
8.02	Extent of locally based competitors	39
9.09	Local availability of process machinery	35

Other Indicators		**Rank/102**

6.05	Freedom of the press	96
2.02	Business costs of terrorism	74
4.05	Business impact of malaria	36
4.06	Business impact of tuberculosis	24
4.10	Maternity leave legislation	23
4.08	Impact of HIV/AIDS on FDI	21
10.22	Charitable causes involvement	18
4.07	Business impact of HIV/AIDS	17
4.09	Brain drain	15
4.04	Disparity in healthcare quality	14
10.19	Flexibility of wage determination	14
11.01	Air pollution regulations	12
11.03	Toxic waste disposal regulations	12
2.06	Soundness of banks	11
11.06	Compliance with environmental regulations	11

343

Note: The Business Competitiveness Index applies different criteria for selecting a country's competitive advantages and disadvantages. Please refer to the section "How Country Profiles Work" for further details.

Slovak Republic

Competitiveness Rankings

Growth Competitiveness Rank	**43**

Macroeconomic Environment Index Rank	**50**
Macroeconomic Stability Subindex Rank	44
Government Waste Subindex Rank	64
Country Credit Rating Rank	43
Public Institutions Index Rank	**51**
Contracts and Law Subindex Rank	70
Corruption Subindex Rank	40
Technology Index Rank	**33**
Innovation Subindex Rank	44
ICT Subindex Rank	37
Technology Transfer Subindex Rank (out of 77 non-core innovators)	16

Business Competitiveness Index Rank	**43**
Sophistication of Company Operations and Strategy Rank	**44**
Quality of the National Business Environment Rank	**43**

The Most Problematic Factors for Doing Business

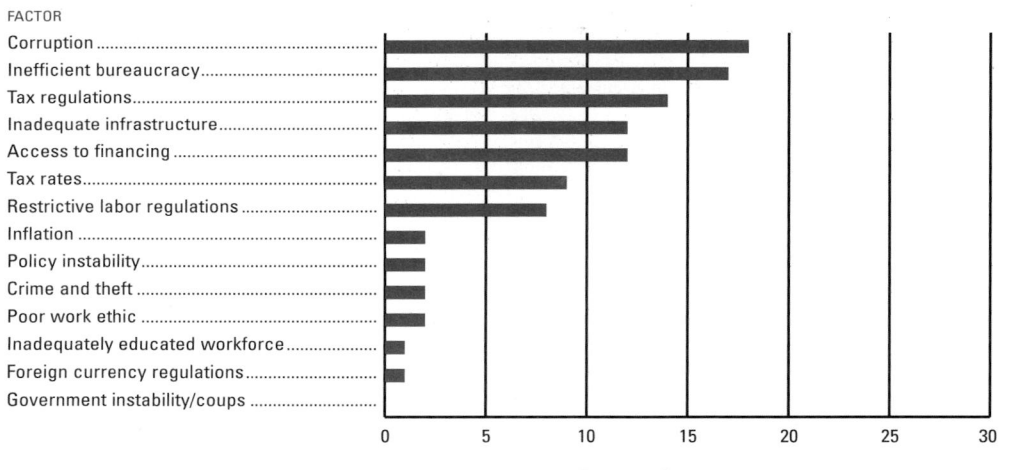

FACTOR

Corruption
Inefficient bureaucracy
Tax regulations
Inadequate infrastructure
Access to financing
Tax rates
Restrictive labor regulations
Inflation
Policy instability
Crime and theft
Poor work ethic
Inadequately educated workforce
Foreign currency regulations
Government instability/coups

Percent of responses

Note: From a list of 14 factors, respondents were asked to select the five most problematic for doing business in their country and to rank them between 1 (most problematic) and 5. The bars in the figure show the responses weighted according to their rankings.

Source: World Economic Forum, Executive Opinion Survey (2003)

344

National competitiveness balance sheet

NOTABLE COMPETITIVE ADVANTAGES		NOTABLE COMPETITIVE DISADVANTAGES	
Growth Competitiveness Index	**Rank/102**	**Growth Competitiveness Index**	**Rank/102**

	Macroeconomic Environment				**Macroeconomic Environment**	
2.09	Access to credit	9		2.18	Government surplus/deficit, 2002	82
2.22	Interest rate spread, 2002	23		2.21	Real exchange rate, 2002	74
2.01	Recession expectations	24		7.10	Public trust of politicians	71
2.19	National savings rate, 2002	37		7.08	Diversion of public funds	65
	Public Institutions			2.03	Extent of distortive government subsidies	55
7.02	Irregular payments in public utilities	34		2.20	Inflation, 2002	50
7.03	Irregular payments in tax collection	38		2.17	Country credit rating, 2003	43
	Technology				**Public Institutions**	
3.03	FDI and technology transfer	5		6.17	Organized crime	78
3.02	Firm-level technology absorption	26		6.08	Favoritism in decisions of government officials	76
3.23	Personal computers, 2002	29		6.01	Judicial independence	68
3.21	Internet hosts, 2002	31		6.03	Property rights	60
3.04	Prevalence of foreign technology licensing	32		7.01	Irregular payments in exports and imports	60
3.19	Cellular telephones, 2002	32			**Technology**	
3.20	Internet users, 2002	35		3.15	Government success in ICT promotion	78
3.17	Utility patents, 2002	36		3.14	Government prioritization of ICT	75
3.01	Technological sophistication	37		3.13	Quality of competition in the ISP sector	67
3.08	University/industry research collaboration	38		3.06	Company spending on research and development	54
3.12	Internet access in schools	38		3.16	Laws relating to ICT	47
				3.18	Tertiary enrollment	44
				3.22	Telephone lines, 2002	43

Business Competitiveness Index	**Rank/95**	**Business Competitiveness Index**	**Rank/95**

	Sophistication of Company Operations and Strategy				**Sophistication of Company Operations and Strategy**	
10.10	Extent of regional sales	33		10.01	Nature of competitive advantage	78
10.04	Capacity for innovation	34		10.14	Extent of incentive compensation	75
10.15	Reliance on professional management	34		10.09	Control of international distribution	59
	Quality of the National Business Environment				**Quality of the National Business Environment**	
4.03	Quality of math and science education	10		5.04	Air transport infrastructure quality	94
6.09	Extent of bureaucratic red tape	11		10.24	Protection of minority shareholders' interests	82
10.26	Foreign ownership restrictions	13		2.11	Local equity market access	75

Other Indicators	**Rank/102**	**Other Indicators**	**Rank/102**

6.18	Informal sector	7		8.10	Regional disparities in quality of business environment	98
10.23	Company promotion of volunteerism	10		7.12	Policy consequences of legal political donations	94
11.07	Compliance with international agreements	18		6.11	Efficiency of the tax system	91
4.07	Business impact of HIV/AIDS	19		6.06	Burden of regulation	86
11.02	Water pollution regulations	20		8.09	Wage equality of women in the workplace	83
11.04	Chemical waste regulations	20		8.11	Focus of trade and industry associations	82
11.03	Toxic waste disposal regulations	20		7.11	Prevalence of illegal political donations	81
11.01	Air pollution regulations	20		7.04	Irregular payments in public contracts	80
5.07	Postal efficiency	23		4.10	Maternity leave legislation	78
10.21	Pay and productivity	24		7.07	Irregular payments in judicial decisions	75
4.04	Disparity in healthcare quality	24		6.07	Transparency of government policymaking	75
3.11	Availability of mobile or cellular telephones	25		8.03	Extent of market dominance	74
10.19	Flexibility of wage determination	26		7.06	Irregular payments in government policymaking	74
11.10	Consistency of regulation enforcement	29		11.12	Political context of environmental gains	69
6.05	Freedom of the press	33		4.09	Brain drain	68

345

Note: The Business Competitiveness Index applies different criteria for selecting a country's competitive advantages and disadvantages.
Please refer to the section "How Country Profiles Work" for further details.

Slovenia

Competitiveness Rankings

Growth Competitiveness Index Rank	31

Macroeconomic Environment Index Rank **37**
    Macroeconomic Stability Subindex Rank 53
    Government Waste Subindex Rank 31
    Country Credit Rating Rank 29

Public Institutions Index Rank.......................................**35**
    Contracts and Law Subindex Rank 43
    Corruption Subindex Rank...................................32

Technology Index Rank **24**
    Innovation Subindex Rank 23
    ICT Subindex Rank 26
    Technology Transfer Subindex Rank
    (out of 77 non-core innovators).......................51

Business Competitiveness Index Rank	30

**Sophistication of Company Operations
and Strategy Rank** **27**

**Quality of the National Business
Environment Rank** **34**

The Most Problematic Factors for Doing Business

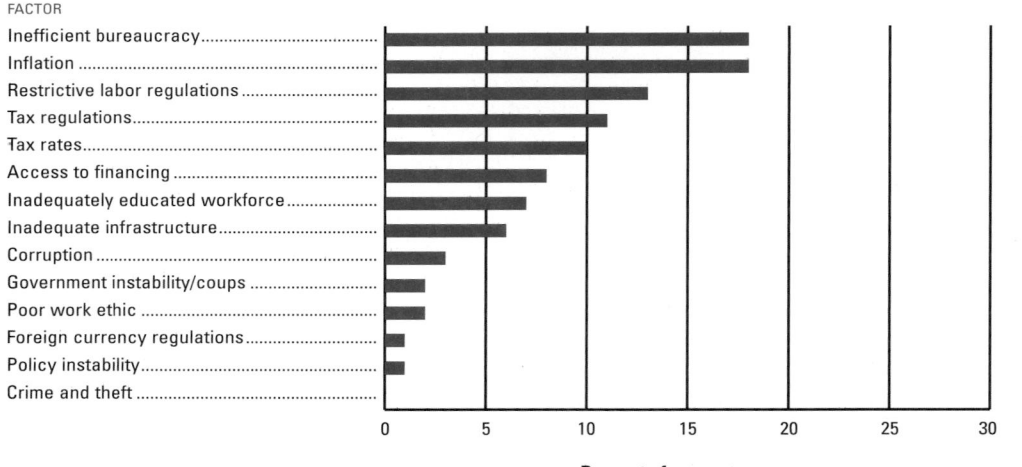

Note: From a list of 14 factors, respondents were asked to select the five most problematic for doing business in their country and to rank them between 1 (most problematic) and 5. The bars in the figure show the responses weighted according to their rankings.

Source: World Economic Forum, Executive Opinion Survey (2003)

National competitiveness balance sheet

NOTABLE COMPETITIVE ADVANTAGES	
Growth Competitiveness Index	**Rank/102**

Macroeconomic Environment

2.09	Access to credit	12
2.19	National savings rate, 2002	26
2.17	Country credit rating, 2003	29
7.08	Diversion of public funds	30

Public Institutions

7.03	Irregular payments in tax collection	29

Technology

3.18	Tertiary enrollment	11
3.19	Cellular telephones, 2002	13
3.20	Internet users, 2002	19
3.06	Company spending on research and development	20
3.12	Internet access in schools	21
3.16	Laws relating to ICT	23
3.23	Personal computers, 2002	23
3.17	Utility patents, 2002	26
3.21	Internet hosts, 2002	29
3.22	Telephone lines, 2002	30

NOTABLE COMPETITIVE DISADVANTAGES	
Growth Competitiveness Index	**Rank/102**

Macroeconomic Environment

2.20	Inflation, 2002	78
2.01	Recession expectations	56
7.10	Public trust of politicians	45
2.18	Government surplus/deficit, 2002	44
2.22	Interest rate spread, 2002	43
2.21	Real exchange rate, 2002	39
2.03	Extent of distortive government subsidies	31

Public Institutions

6.08	Favoritism in decisions of government officials	49
6.03	Property rights	46
6.01	Judicial independence	45
6.17	Organized crime	37
7.02	Irregular payments in public utilities	33
7.01	Irregular payments in exports and imports	31

Technology

3.03	FDI and technology transfer	63
3.13	Quality of competition in the ISP sector	59
3.14	Government prioritization of ICT	58
3.15	Government success in ICT promotion	55
3.02	Firm-level technology absorption	46
3.04	Prevalence of foreign technology licensing	38
3.01	Technological sophistication	33
3.08	University/industry research collaboration	33

Business Competitiveness Index	Rank/95

Sophistication of Company Operations and Strategy

3.06	Company spending on research and development	19
10.04	Capacity for innovation	22
10.09	Control of international distribution	24

Quality of the National Business Environment

3.19	Cellular telephones, 2002	12
3.20	Internet users, 2002	19
4.03	Quality of math and science education	19

Business Competitiveness Index	Rank/95

Sophistication of Company Operations and Strategy

10.15	Reliance on professional management	49
10.14	Extent of incentive compensation	41
10.07	Extent of marketing	33

Quality of the National Business Environment

10.26	Foreign ownership restrictions	84
8.02	Extent of locally based competitors	70
3.10	Availability of scientists and engineers	63

Other Indicators	Rank/102

4.07	Business impact of HIV/AIDS	6
4.06	Business impact of tuberculosis	15
4.05	Business impact of malaria	16
6.18	Informal sector	18
4.08	Impact of HIV/AIDS on FDI	18
5.07	Postal efficiency	20
11.04	Chemical waste regulations	21
3.11	Availability of mobile or cellular telephones	21
11.07	Compliance with international agreements	22
4.04	Disparity in healthcare quality	22
11.02	Water pollution regulations	23
11.01	Air pollution regulations	23
6.14	Business costs of crime and violence	23
11.03	Toxic waste disposal regulations	24
11.13	Prevalence of environmental management systems	24

Other Indicators	Rank/102

4.11	Maternity laws' impact on hiring women	101
10.18	Hiring and firing practices	80
10.19	Flexibility of wage determination	77
2.15	Agricultural policy costs	75
11.12	Political context of environmental gains	74
10.23	Company promotion of volunteerism	65
6.05	Freedom of the press	61
8.09	Wage equality of women in the workplace	60
4.10	Maternity leave legislation	58
10.22	Charitable causes involvement	58
6.06	Burden of regulation	55
2.06	Soundness of banks	54
6.10	Effectiveness of law-making bodies	52
7.12	Policy consequences of legal political donations	47
8.03	Extent of market dominance	46

347

Note: The Business Competitiveness Index applies different criteria for selecting a country's competitive advantages and disadvantages. Please refer to the section "How Country Profiles Work" for further details.

South Africa

Competitiveness Rankings

Growth Competitiveness Index Rank	42

Macroeconomic Environment Index Rank **40**
    Macroeconomic Stability Subindex Rank 41
    Government Waste Subindex Rank 37
    Country Credit Rating Rank 40

Public Institutions Index Rank...........................**43**
    Contracts and Law Subindex Rank 40
    Corruption Subindex Rank 48

Technology Index Rank **40**
    Innovation Subindex Rank 58
    ICT Subindex Rank 44
    Technology Transfer Subindex Rank
       (out of 77 non-core innovators).........................3

Business Competitiveness Index Rank	27

**Sophistication of Company Operations
  and Strategy Rank** **28**
**Quality of the National Business
  Environment Rank** **28**

The Most Problematic Factors for Doing Business

FACTOR

Inadequately educated workforce
Crime and theft
Restrictive labor regulations
Poor work ethic
Inefficient bureaucracy
Access to financing
Foreign currency regulations
Inflation
Tax rates
Corruption
Policy instability
Tax regulations
Inadequate infrastructure
Government instability/coups

Percent of responses

Note: From a list of 14 factors, respondents were asked to select the five most problematic for doing business in their country and to rank them between 1 (most problematic) and 5. The bars in the figure show the responses weighted according to their rankings.

Source: World Economic Forum, Executive Opinion Survey (2003)

National competitiveness balance sheet

NOTABLE COMPETITIVE ADVANTAGES		
Growth Competitiveness Index		**Rank/102**

Macroeconomic Environment

2.21	Real exchange rate, 2002	4
2.01	Recession expectations	9
2.03	Extent of distortive government subsidies	18
2.09	Access to credit	28
2.18	Government surplus/deficit, 2002	32
7.10	Public trust of politicians	35
2.17	Country credit rating, 2003	40

Public Institutions

6.01	Judicial independence	15
6.03	Property rights	31
7.03	Irregular payments in tax collection	41

Technology

3.04	Prevalence of foreign technology licensing	2
3.06	Company spending on research and development	21
3.08	University/industry research collaboration	21
3.03	FDI and technology transfer	23
3.16	Laws relating to ICT	24
3.17	Utility patents, 2002	31
3.15	Government success in ICT promotion	34
3.14	Government prioritization of ICT	35
3.01	Technological sophistication	39
3.02	Firm-level technology absorption	39

Business Competitiveness Index		**Rank/95**

Sophistication of Company Operations and Strategy

3.04	Prevalence of foreign technology licensing	4
10.14	Extent of incentive compensation	11
10.15	Reliance on professional management	16

Quality of the National Business Environment

2.11	Local equity market access	8
10.17	Efficacy of corporate boards	9
8.02	Extent of locally based competitors	10

Other Indicators		**Rank/102**

2.15	Agricultural policy costs	8
10.22	Charitable causes involvement	10
10.25	Availability of company financial information	13
10.27	Strength of auditing and accounting standards	15
6.10	Effectiveness of law-making bodies	17
11.09	Flexibility of regulations	20
8.11	Focus of trade and industry associations	23
2.04	Extent of distortive government intervention	24
10.23	Company promotion of volunteerism	25
11.08	Clarity and stability of regulations	26
10.05	Ethical behavior of firms	26
6.16	Government effectiveness in reducing income inequality	26
2.06	Soundness of banks	26
6.11	Efficiency of the tax system	28
6.05	Freedom of the press	28

NOTABLE COMPETITIVE DISADVANTAGES		
Growth Competitiveness Index		**Rank/102**

Macroeconomic Environment

2.20	Inflation, 2002	84
2.19	National savings rate, 2002	71
7.08	Diversion of public funds	47
2.22	Interest rate spread, 2002	45

Public Institutions

6.17	Organized crime	81
7.02	Irregular payments in public utilities	61
7.01	Irregular payments in exports and imports	48
6.08	Favoritism in decisions of government officials	45

Technology

3.18	Tertiary enrollment	65
3.22	Telephone lines, 2002	65
3.20	Internet users, 2002	52
3.12	Internet access in schools	50
3.13	Quality of competition in the ISP sector	50
3.23	Personal computers, 2002	48
3.19	Cellular telephones, 2002	46
3.21	Internet hosts, 2002	44

Business Competitiveness Index		**Rank/95**

Sophistication of Company Operations and Strategy

10.01	Nature of competitive advantage	65
10.02	Value chain presence	52
10.08	Degree of customer orientation	48

Quality of the National Business Environment

4.03	Quality of math and science education	79
6.13	Reliability of police services	78
10.20	Cooperation in labor-employer relations	78

Other Indicators		**Rank/102**

4.08	Impact of HIV/AIDS on FDI	101
4.07	Business impact of HIV/AIDS	100
6.14	Business costs of crime and violence	96
4.06	Business impact of tuberculosis	92
10.18	Hiring and firing practices	91
10.19	Flexibility of wage determination	87
4.05	Business impact of malaria	83
4.04	Disparity in healthcare quality	74
8.09	Wage equality of women in the workplace	67
4.09	Brain drain	67
5.07	Postal efficiency	67
8.08	Private sector employment of women	64
8.10	Regional disparities in quality of business environment	63
6.18	Informal sector	62
10.21	Pay and productivity	56

349

Note: The Business Competitiveness Index applies different criteria for selecting a country's competitive advantages and disadvantages. Please refer to the section "How Country Profiles Work" for further details.

Spain

Competitiveness Rankings

Growth Competitiveness Index Rank	23

Macroeconomic Environment Index Rank 17
 Macroeconomic Stability Subindex Rank 35
 Government Waste Subindex Rank 22
 Country Credit Rating Rank 16

Public Institutions Index Rank 31
 Contracts and Law Subindex Rank 41
 Corruption Subindex Rank 17

Technology Index Rank 25
 Innovation Subindex Rank 25
 ICT Subindex Rank 31
 Technology Transfer Subindex Rank
 (out of 77 non-core innovators) 35

Business Competitiveness Index Rank	25

**Sophistication of Company Operations
 and Strategy Rank 25**
**Quality of the National Business
 Environment Rank 26**

The Most Problematic Factors for Doing Business

FACTOR

Restrictive labor regulations
Access to financing
Inefficient bureaucracy
Tax rates
Tax regulations
Inflation
Inadequately educated workforce
Inadequate infrastructure
Policy instability
Poor work ethic
Corruption
Crime and theft
Foreign currency regulations
Government instability/coups

Percent of responses

Note: From a list of 14 factors, respondents were asked to select the five most problematic for doing business in their country and to rank them between 1 (most problematic) and 5. The bars in the figure show the responses weighted according to their rankings.

Source: World Economic Forum, Executive Opinion Survey (2003)

National competitiveness balance sheet

NOTABLE COMPETITIVE ADVANTAGES

Growth Competitiveness Index — Rank/102

Macroeconomic Environment

2.22	Interest rate spread, 2002	7
2.17	Country credit rating, 2003	16
2.18	Government surplus/deficit, 2002	17
7.08	Diversion of public funds	20

Public Institutions

7.01	Irregular payments in exports and imports	15
7.03	Irregular payments in tax collection	19

Technology

3.18	Tertiary enrollment	14
3.19	Cellular telephones, 2002	15

Business Competitiveness Index — Rank/95

Sophistication of Company Operations and Strategy

10.14	Extent of incentive compensation	13
10.03	Extent of branding	18
10.02	Value chain presence	18

Quality of the National Business Environment

6.12	Centralization of economic policymaking	2
8.02	Extent of locally based competitors	2
6.09	Extent of bureaucratic red tape	6

Other Indicators — Rank/102

4.09	Brain drain	4
4.06	Business impact of tuberculosis	12
2.06	Soundness of banks	13
4.05	Business impact of malaria	13
6.16	Government effectiveness in reducing income inequality	16
6.15	Government effectiveness in reducing poverty	17
2.04	Extent of distortive government intervention	18
10.05	Ethical behavior of firms	19
4.04	Disparity in healthcare quality	20
7.05	Irregular payments in loan applications	21
4.07	Business impact of HIV/AIDS	21
6.10	Effectiveness of law-making bodies	22
2.10	Government intervention in corporate investment	22

NOTABLE COMPETITIVE DISADVANTAGES

Growth Competitiveness Index — Rank/102

Macroeconomic Environment

2.01	Recession expectations	55
2.20	Inflation, 2002	51
2.21	Real exchange rate, 2002	41
2.03	Extent of distortive government subsidies	39
2.09	Access to credit	36
2.19	National savings rate, 2002	33
7.10	Public trust of politicians	23

Public Institutions

6.01	Judicial independence	55
6.08	Favoritism in decisions of government officials	41
6.17	Organized crime	43
6.03	Property rights	30
7.02	Irregular payments in public utilities	23

Technology

3.13	Quality of competition in the ISP sector	48
3.15	Government success in ICT promotion	46
3.03	FDI and technology transfer	37
3.08	University/industry research collaboration	37
3.14	Government prioritization of ICT	37
3.21	Internet hosts, 2002	37
3.02	Firm-level technology absorption	36
3.04	Prevalence of foreign technology licensing	36
3.16	Laws relating to ICT	33
3.20	Internet users, 2002	33
3.06	Company spending on research and development	32
3.12	Internet access in schools	32
3.23	Personal computers, 2002	32
3.01	Technological sophistication	28
3.17	Utility patents, 2002	27
3.22	Telephone lines, 2002	27

Business Competitiveness Index — Rank/95

Sophistication of Company Operations and Strategy

10.10	Extent of regional sales	39
3.06	Company spending on research and development	31
10.12	Extent of staff training	31

Quality of the National Business Environment

2.11	Local equity market access	58
6.01	Judicial independence	52
10.20	Cooperation in labor-employer relations	51

Other Indicators — Rank/102

10.18	Hiring and firing practices	95
4.10	Maternity leave legislation	86
8.09	Wage equality of women in the workplace	72
4.11	Maternity laws' impact on hiring women	69
10.19	Flexibility of wage determination	68
10.22	Charitable causes involvement	64
6.06	Burden of regulation	61
6.14	Business costs of crime and violence	55
11.11	Effects of compliance on business	55
2.15	Agricultural policy costs	54
8.08	Private sector employment of women	53
10.21	Pay and productivity	50
2.02	Business costs of terrorism	47
7.11	Prevalence of illegal political donations	46
11.12	Political context of environmental gains	44

Note: The Business Competitiveness Index applies different criteria for selecting a country's competitive advantages and disadvantages. Please refer to the section "How Country Profiles Work" for further details.

Sri Lanka

Competitiveness Rankings

The Most Problematic Factors for Doing Business

FACTOR

- Access to financing
- Inadequate infrastructure
- Corruption
- Inefficient bureaucracy
- Policy instability
- Inflation
- Tax regulations
- Restrictive labor regulations
- Government instability/coups
- Poor work ethic
- Inadequately educated workforce
- Tax rates
- Foreign currency regulations
- Crime and theft

Percent of responses

Note: From a list of 14 factors, respondents were asked to select the five most problematic for doing business in their country and to rank them between 1 (most problematic) and 5. The bars in the figure show the responses weighted according to their rankings.

Source: World Economic Forum, Executive Opinion Survey (2003)

National competitiveness balance sheet

NOTABLE COMPETITIVE ADVANTAGES	
Growth Competitiveness Index	**Rank/102**

Macroeconomic Environment

2.22	Interest rate spread, 2002	13
2.01	Recession expectations	30
2.09	Access to credit	32
2.03	Extent of distortive government subsidies	42

Technology

3.03	FDI and technology transfer	30
3.04	Prevalence of foreign technology licensing	30
3.13	Quality of competition in the ISP sector	44
3.15	Government success in ICT promotion	44
3.14	Government prioritization of ICT	47

NOTABLE COMPETITIVE DISADVANTAGES	
Growth Competitiveness Index	**Rank/102**

Macroeconomic Environment

2.18	Government surplus/deficit, 2002	85
2.20	Inflation, 2002	82
2.21	Real exchange rate, 2002	66
2.17	Country credit rating, 2003	65
2.19	National savings rate, 2002	58
7.08	Diversion of public funds	57
7.10	Public trust of politicians	56

Public Institutions

7.02	Irregular payments in public utilities	77
7.03	Irregular payments in tax collection	76
6.03	Property rights	76
7.01	Irregular payments in exports and imports	75
6.01	Judicial independence	66
6.08	Favoritism in decisions of government officials	64
6.17	Organized crime	59

Technology

3.20	Internet users, 2002	86
3.18	Tertiary enrollment	82
3.19	Cellular telephones, 2002	78
3.22	Telephone lines, 2002	76
3.23	Personal computers, 2002	76
3.21	Internet hosts, 2002	75
3.12	Internet access in schools	69
3.16	Laws relating to ICT	69
3.01	Technological sophistication	66
3.08	University/industry research collaboration	66
3.17	Utility patents, 2002	65
3.02	Firm-level technology absorption	62
3.06	Company spending on research and development	53

353

Business Competitiveness Index	
	Rank/95

Sophistication of Company Operations and Strategy

10.15	Reliance on professional management	36
10.08	Degree of customer orientation	39
10.11	Breadth of international markets	44

Quality of the National Business Environment

9.06	State of cluster development	28
2.11	Local equity market access	33
8.05	Administrative burden for startups	35

Business Competitiveness Index	
	Rank/95

Sophistication of Company Operations and Strategy

10.06	Production process sophistication	71
10.07	Extent of marketing	63
10.12	Extent of staff training	59

Quality of the National Business Environment

3.20	Internet users, 2002	82
10.20	Cooperation in labor-employer relations	81
2.16	Cost of importing foreign equipment	79

Other Indicators	
	Rank/102

2.15	Agricultural policy costs	28
8.08	Private sector employment of women	29
6.11	Efficiency of the tax system	30
8.09	Wage equality of women in the workplace	33
2.04	Extent of distortive government intervention	37
10.22	Charitable causes involvement	39
4.10	Maternity leave legislation	43
6.06	Burden of regulation	44
8.10	Regional disparities in quality of business environment	46
3.07	Subsidies and tax credits for firm-level research and development	47
10.23	Company promotion of volunteerism	49

Other Indicators	
	Rank/102

2.02	Business costs of terrorism	97
10.21	Pay and productivity	86
4.09	Brain drain	86
7.05	Irregular payments in loan applications	85
11.08	Clarity and stability of regulations	83
6.05	Freedom of the press	83
11.07	Compliance with international agreements	80
11.06	Compliance with environmental regulations	80
4.08	Impact of HIV/AIDS on FDI	79
11.11	Effects of compliance on business	78
10.05	Ethical behavior of firms	77
4.11	Maternity laws' impact on hiring women	76
7.11	Prevalence of illegal political donations	76
11.09	Flexibility of regulations	76
11.04	Chemical waste regulations	75

Note: The Business Competitiveness Index applies different criteria for selecting a country's competitive advantages and disadvantages. Please refer to the section "How Country Profiles Work" for further details.

Sweden

Competitiveness Rankings

The Most Problematic Factors for Doing Business

FACTOR
- Tax rates
- Tax regulations
- Restrictive labor regulations
- Inefficient bureaucracy
- Access to financing
- Policy instability
- Inflation
- Inadequately educated workforce
- Poor work ethic
- Inadequate infrastructure
- Foreign currency regulations
- Corruption
- Government instability/coups
- Crime and theft

Percent of responses

Note: From a list of 14 factors, respondents were asked to select the five most problematic for doing business in their country and to rank them between 1 (most problematic) and 5. The bars in the figure show the responses weighted according to their rankings.

Source: World Economic Forum, Executive Opinion Survey (2003)

National competitiveness balance sheet

NOTABLE COMPETITIVE ADVANTAGES		
Growth Competitiveness Index		**Rank/102**

Macroeconomic Environment

| 7.08 | Diversion of public funds | 5 |

Public Institutions

6.08	Favoritism in decisions of government officials	3
6.17	Organized crime	5
7.01	Irregular payments in exports and imports	6
7.03	Irregular payments in tax collection	8
6.01	Judicial independence	9
7.02	Irregular payments in public utilities	10

Technology

3.20	Internet users, 2002	2
3.01	Technological sophistication	3
3.02	Firm-level technology absorption	3
3.23	Personal computers, 2002	3
3.06	Company spending on research and development	4
3.08	University/industry research collaboration	4
3.17	Utility patents, 2002	4
3.22	Telephone lines, 2002	4
3.12	Internet access in schools	5
3.18	Tertiary enrollment	5
3.19	Cellular telephones, 2002	7
3.21	Internet hosts, 2002	9

Business Competitiveness Index		Rank/95

Sophistication of Company Operations and Strategy

10.13	Willingness to delegate authority	1
10.04	Capacity for innovation	2
10.03	Extent of branding	2

Quality of the National Business Environment

3.20	Internet users, 2002	2
9.04	Presence of demanding regulatory standards	2
11.05	Stringency of environmental regulations	2

Other Indicators		Rank/102
4.10	Maternity leave legislation	1
10.25	Availability of company financial information	1
4.06	Business impact of tuberculosis	1
4.05	Business impact of malaria	1
11.06	Compliance with environmental regulations	1
11.07	Compliance with international agreements	1
11.13	Prevalence of environmental management systems	2
11.01	Air pollution regulations	2
11.02	Water pollution regulations	2
4.08	Impact of HIV/AIDS on FDI	2
6.05	Freedom of the press	2
11.08	Clarity and stability of regulations	2
3.11	Availability of mobile or cellular telephones	3
11.03	Toxic waste disposal regulations	3
11.04	Chemical waste regulations	3

NOTABLE COMPETITIVE DISADVANTAGES		
Growth Competitiveness Index		**Rank/102**

Macroeconomic Environment

2.01	Recession expectations	68
2.19	National savings rate, 2002	48
2.09	Access to credit	44
2.20	Inflation, 2002	28
2.21	Real exchange rate, 2002	26
2.22	Interest rate spread, 2002	26
2.03	Extent of distortive government subsidies	26
7.10	Public trust of politicians	14
2.17	Country credit rating, 2003	13
2.18	Government surplus/deficit, 2002	11

Public Institutions

| 6.03 | Property rights | 15 |

Technology

3.15	Government success in ICT promotion	19
3.14	Government prioritization of ICT	14
3.13	Quality of competition in the ISP sector	12
3.16	Laws relating to ICT	11

Business Competitiveness Index		Rank/95

Quality of the National Business Environment

2.11	Local equity market access	40
8.02	Extent of locally based competitors	34
2.03	Extent of distortive government subsidies	22

Other Indicators		Rank/102
10.22	Charitable causes involvement	94
10.19	Flexibility of wage determination	89
10.18	Hiring and firing practices	86
10.23	Company promotion of volunteerism	72
6.11	Efficiency of the tax system	67
8.03	Extent of market dominance	54
8.09	Wage equality of women in the workplace	49
10.21	Pay and productivity	37
2.15	Agricultural policy costs	32
3.07	Subsidies and tax credits for firm-level research and development	30
11.12	Political context of environmental gains	26
6.18	Informal sector	23
8.10	Regional disparities in quality of business environment	22
4.07	Business impact of HIV/AIDS	16
11.09	Flexibility of regulations	15

355

Note: The Business Competitiveness Index applies different criteria for selecting a country's competitive advantages and disadvantages. Please refer to the section "How Country Profiles Work" for further details.

Switzerland

Competitiveness Rankings

The Most Problematic Factors for Doing Business

Note: From a list of 14 factors, respondents were asked to select the five most problematic for doing business in their country and to rank them between 1 (most problematic) and 5. The bars in the figure show the responses weighted according to their rankings.

Source: World Economic Forum, Executive Opinion Survey (2003)

356

National competitiveness balance sheet

NOTABLE COMPETITIVE ADVANTAGES

Growth Competitiveness Index		Rank/102
Macroeconomic Environment		
2.17	Country credit rating, 2003	1
7.10	Public trust of politicians	6
7.08	Diversion of public funds	8
Public Institutions		
6.03	Property rights	1
7.02	Irregular payments in public utilities	7
7.03	Irregular payments in tax collection	7
6.08	Favoritism in decisions of government officials	9
6.17	Organized crime	9
7.01	Irregular payments in exports and imports	10
Technology		
3.22	Telephone lines, 2002	2
3.06	Company spending on research and development	5
3.17	Utility patents, 2002	5
3.23	Personal computers, 2002	5
3.01	Technological sophistication	9
3.02	Firm-level technology absorption	9
3.08	University/industry research collaboration	10
3.21	Internet hosts, 2002	10

Business Competitiveness Index		Rank/95
Sophistication of Company Operations and Strategy		
10.08	Degree of customer orientation	2
10.12	Extent of staff training	2
10.03	Extent of branding	3
Quality of the National Business Environment		
6.12	Centralization of economic policymaking	1
5.02	Railroad infrastructure development	1
10.20	Cooperation in labor-employer relations	2

Other Indicators		Rank/102
11.01	Air pollution regulations	3
5.07	Postal efficiency	3
11.09	Flexibility of regulations	3
11.12	Political context of environmental gains	3
10.18	Hiring and firing practices	3
11.08	Clarity and stability of regulations	4
6.06	Burden of regulation	4
11.02	Water pollution regulations	5
11.03	Toxic waste disposal regulations	5
11.04	Chemical waste regulations	5
11.10	Consistency of regulation enforcement	5
10.21	Pay and productivity	5
11.06	Compliance with environmental regulations	6
6.18	Informal sector	6
11.07	Compliance with international agreements	7

NOTABLE COMPETITIVE DISADVANTAGES

Growth Competitiveness Index		Rank/102
Macroeconomic Environment		
2.01	Recession expectations	76
2.03	Extent of distortive government subsidies	72
2.09	Access to credit	58
2.21	Real exchange rate, 2002	30
2.18	Government surplus/deficit, 2002	22
2.22	Interest rate spread, 2002	17
2.19	National savings rate, 2002	12
2.20	Inflation, 2002	11
Public Institutions		
6.01	Judicial independence	12
Technology		
3.14	Government prioritization of ICT	39
3.18	Tertiary enrollment	34
3.15	Government success in ICT promotion	28
3.16	Laws relating to ICT	25
3.20	Internet users, 2002	24
3.19	Cellular telephones, 2002	18
3.12	Internet access in schools	17
3.13	Quality of competition in the ISP sector	15

Business Competitiveness Index		Rank/95
Sophistication of Company Operations and Strategy		
10.14	Extent of incentive compensation	22
10.15	Reliance on professional management	18
Quality of the National Business Environment		
2.03	Extent of distortive government subsidies	66
8.01	Intensity of local competition	35
10.26	Foreign ownership restrictions	33

Other Indicators		Rank/102
2.15	Agricultural policy costs	82
8.09	Wage equality of women in the workplace	71
4.10	Maternity leave legislation	64
4.11	Maternity laws' impact on hiring women	46
8.08	Private sector employment of women	45
10.22	Charitable causes involvement	42
7.13	Pervasiveness of money laundering through banks	42
3.07	Subsidies and tax credits for firm-level research and development	41
2.04	Extent of distortive government intervention	32
4.07	Business impact of HIV/AIDS	28
7.14	Pervasiveness of money laundering through non-bank channels	28
10.25	Availability of company financial information	25
4.05	Business impact of malaria	24
10.19	Flexibility of wage determination	23
10.23	Company promotion of volunteerism	20

357

Note: The Business Competitiveness Index applies different criteria for selecting a country's competitive advantages and disadvantages. Please refer to the section "How Country Profiles Work" for further details.

Taiwan

Competitiveness Rankings

The Most Problematic Factors for Doing Business

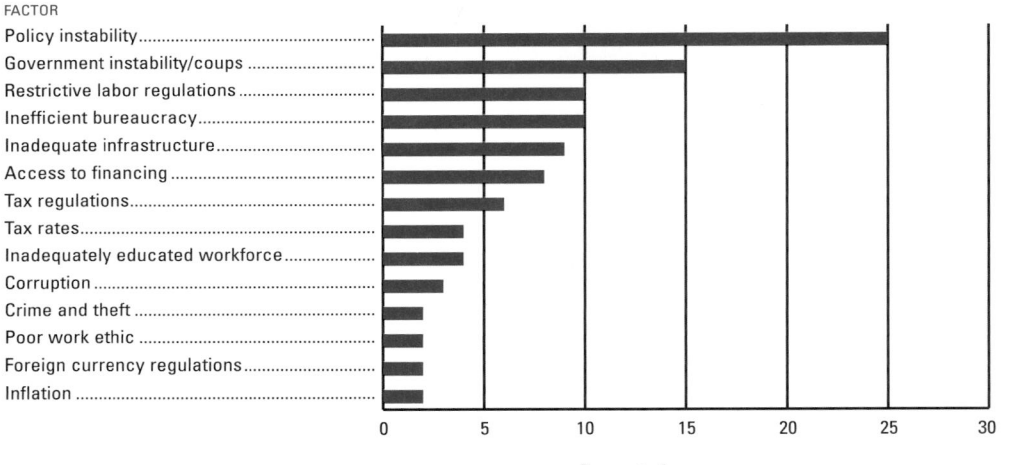

FACTOR

Percent of responses

Note: From a list of 14 factors, respondents were asked to select the five most problematic for doing business in their country and to rank them between 1 (most problematic) and 5. The bars in the figure show the responses weighted according to their rankings.

Source: World Economic Forum, Executive Opinion Survey (2003)

National competitiveness balance sheet

NOTABLE COMPETITIVE ADVANTAGES	
Growth Competitiveness Index	**Rank/102**

Macroeconomic Environment

2.09	Access to credit	3
2.20	Inflation, 2002	7

Technology

3.19	Cellular telephones, 2002	1
3.17	Utility patents, 2002	3
3.18	Tertiary enrollment	3
3.08	University/industry research collaboration	6
3.15	Government success in ICT promotion	6
3.14	Government prioritization of ICT	7
3.02	Firm-level technology absorption	8

NOTABLE COMPETITIVE DISADVANTAGES	
Growth Competitiveness Index	**Rank/102**

Macroeconomic Environment

2.18	Government surplus/deficit, 2002	79
2.01	Recession expectations	57
2.22	Interest rate spread, 2002	50
2.21	Real exchange rate, 2002	35
7.08	Diversion of public funds	28
2.17	Country credit rating, 2003	24
7.10	Public trust of politicians	24
2.03	Extent of distortive government subsidies	21
2.19	National savings rate, 2002	21

Public Institutions

6.01	Judicial independence	37
6.17	Organized crime	36
7.02	Irregular payments in public utilities	28
6.03	Property rights	23
7.01	Irregular payments in exports and imports	16
7.03	Irregular payments in tax collection	15
6.08	Favoritism in decisions of government officials	14

Technology

3.13	Quality of competition in the ISP sector	23
3.20	Internet users, 2002	20
3.01	Technological sophistication	17
3.16	Laws relating to ICT	17
3.23	Personal computers, 2002	15
3.06	Company spending on research and development	13
3.22	Telephone lines, 2002	12
3.12	Internet access in schools	11
3.21	Internet hosts, 2002	11

Business Competitiveness Index	Rank/95

Sophistication of Company Operations and Strategy

10.08	Degree of customer orientation	6
3.06	Company spending on research and development	13
10.11	Breadth of international markets	14

Quality of the National Business Environment

3.19	Cellular telephones, 2002	1
9.06	State of cluster development	3
3.17	Utility patents, 2002	3

Business Competitiveness Index	Rank/95

Sophistication of Company Operations and Strategy

10.07	Extent of marketing	28
10.10	Extent of regional sales	26
10.15	Reliance on professional management	24

Quality of the National Business Environment

8.07	Prevalence of mergers and acquisitions	55
10.26	Foreign ownership restrictions	53
6.09	Extent of bureaucratic red tape	40

Other Indicators	Rank/102

3.07	Subsidies and tax credits for firm-level research and development	2
10.21	Pay and productivity	4
8.11	Focus of trade and industry associations	4
10.18	Hiring and firing practices	6
11.11	Effects of compliance on business	6
6.06	Burden of regulation	7
8.03	Extent of market dominance	8
10.19	Flexibility of wage determination	8
11.12	Political context of environmental gains	9
11.13	Prevalence of environmental management systems	10

Other Indicators	Rank/102

2.06	Soundness of banks	73
4.08	Impact of HIV/AIDS on FDI	56
3.11	Availability of mobile or cellular telephones	54
4.05	Business impact of malaria	51
2.02	Business costs of terrorism	51
4.06	Business impact of tuberculosis	50
6.10	Effectiveness of law-making bodies	46
4.07	Business impact of HIV/AIDS	45
10.27	Strength of auditing and accounting standards	44
6.05	Freedom of the press	44
7.12	Policy consequences of legal political donations	43
6.16	Government effectiveness in reducing income inequality	39
10.22	Charitable causes involvement	38
7.13	Pervasiveness of money laundering through banks	37
6.15	Government effectiveness in reducing poverty	37

359

Note: The Business Competitiveness Index applies different criteria for selecting a country's competitive advantages and disadvantages. Please refer to the section "How Country Profiles Work" for further details.

Tanzania

Competitiveness Rankings

Growth Competitiveness Index Rank	69

Macroeconomic Environment Index Rank **76**
    Macroeconomic Stability Subindex Rank 79
    Government Waste Subindex Rank 43
    Country Credit Rating Rank 83

Public Institutions Index Rank **59**
    Contracts and Law Subindex Rank 46
    Corruption Subindex Rank...................................73

Technology Index Rank **81**
    Innovation Subindex Rank 90
    ICT Subindex Rank 90
    Technology Transfer Subindex Rank
    (out of 77 non-core innovators) 23

Business Competitiveness Index Rank	67

**Sophistication of Company Operations
  and Strategy Rank** 67
**Quality of the National Business
  Environment Rank** 65

The Most Problematic Factors for Doing Business

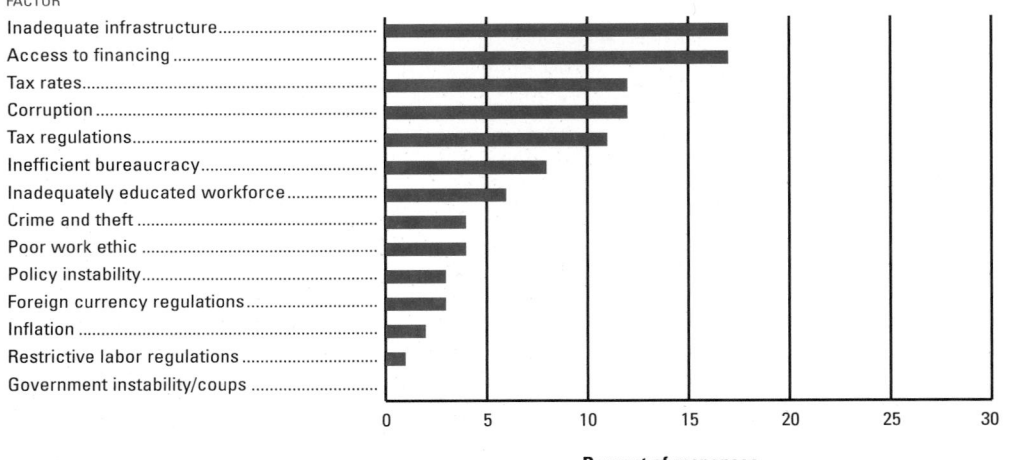

FACTOR

Inadequate infrastructure
Access to financing
Tax rates
Corruption
Tax regulations
Inefficient bureaucracy
Inadequately educated workforce
Crime and theft
Poor work ethic
Policy instability
Foreign currency regulations
Inflation
Restrictive labor regulations
Government instability/coups

Percent of responses

Note: From a list of 14 factors, respondents were asked to select the five most problematic for doing business in their country and to rank them between 1 (most problematic) and 5. The bars in the figure show the responses weighted according to their rankings.

Source: World Economic Forum, Executive Opinion Survey (2003)

National competitiveness balance sheet

NOTABLE COMPETITIVE ADVANTAGES

Growth Competitiveness Index		Rank/102

Macroeconomic Environment
2.01	Recession expectations	23
7.10	Public trust of politicians	32
2.03	Extent of distortive government subsidies	35
7.08	Diversion of public funds	49

Public Institutions
6.01	Judicial independence	38
6.08	Favoritism in decisions of government officials	44

Technology
3.04	Prevalence of foreign technology licensing	24
3.03	FDI and technology transfer	25
3.15	Government success in ICT promotion	27
3.14	Government prioritization of ICT	28
3.06	Company spending on research and development	46
3.02	Firm-level technology absorption	50
3.08	University/industry research collaboration	50

Business Competitiveness Index		Rank/95

Sophistication of Company Operations and Strategy
3.04	Prevalence of foreign technology licensing	35
10.15	Reliance on professional management	39
3.06	Company spending on research and development	45

Quality of the National Business Environment
3.09	Government procurement of advanced technology products	16
10.17	Efficacy of corporate boards	23
6.12	Centralization of economic policymaking	26

Other Indicators		Rank/102
8.09	Wage equality of women in the workplace	10
10.23	Company promotion of volunteerism	21
11.12	Political context of environmental gains	22
7.12	Policy consequences of legal political donations	26
10.22	Charitable causes involvement	27
6.15	Government effectiveness in reducing poverty	28
6.10	Effectiveness of law-making bodies	28
6.06	Burden of regulation	33
8.03	Extent of market dominance	34
4.11	Maternity laws' impact on hiring women	34
11.11	Effects of compliance on business	36
8.11	Focus of trade and industry associations	40
6.16	Government effectiveness in reducing income inequality	40
11.13	Prevalence of environmental management systems	41
7.11	Prevalence of illegal political donations	42

NOTABLE COMPETITIVE DISADVANTAGES

Growth Competitiveness Index		Rank/102

Macroeconomic Environment
2.19	National savings rate, 2002	91
2.22	Interest rate spread, 2002	86
2.17	Country credit rating, 2003	83
2.21	Real exchange rate, 2002	83
2.09	Access to credit	77
2.18	Government surplus/deficit, 2002	74
2.20	Inflation, 2002	63

Public Institutions
7.03	Irregular payments in tax collection	80
7.02	Irregular payments in public utilities	78
7.01	Irregular payments in exports and imports	62
6.03	Property rights	53
6.17	Organized crime	53

Technology
3.18	Tertiary enrollment	99
3.22	Telephone lines, 2002	99
3.19	Cellular telephones, 2002	93
3.20	Internet users, 2002	92
3.23	Personal computers, 2002	90
3.21	Internet hosts, 2002	87
3.12	Internet access in schools	84
3.01	Technological sophistication	82
3.17	Utility patents, 2002	72
3.13	Quality of competition in the ISP sector	56
3.16	Laws relating to ICT	55

Business Competitiveness Index		Rank/95

Sophistication of Company Operations and Strategy
10.14	Extent of incentive compensation	86
10.06	Production process sophistication	84
10.02	Value chain presence	78

Quality of the National Business Environment
5.05	Quality of electricity supply	88
2.16	Cost of importing foreign equipment	87
3.20	Internet users, 2002	87

Other Indicators		Rank/102
4.05	Business impact of malaria	97
4.07	Business impact of HIV/AIDS	96
4.06	Business impact of tuberculosis	95
2.02	Business costs of terrorism	94
4.08	Impact of HIV/AIDS on FDI	88
8.10	Regional disparities in quality of business environment	84
8.08	Private sector employment of women	83
6.05	Freedom of the press	80
3.11	Availability of mobile or cellular telephones	77
2.06	Soundness of banks	71
7.05	Irregular payments in loan applications	71
11.02	Water pollution regulations	69
6.14	Business costs of crime and violence	68
7.13	Pervasiveness of money laundering through banks	67
4.04	Disparity in healthcare quality	66

361

Note: The Business Competitiveness Index applies different criteria for selecting a country's competitive advantages and disadvantages. Please refer to the section "How Country Profiles Work" for further details.

Thailand

Competitiveness Rankings

The Most Problematic Factors for Doing Business

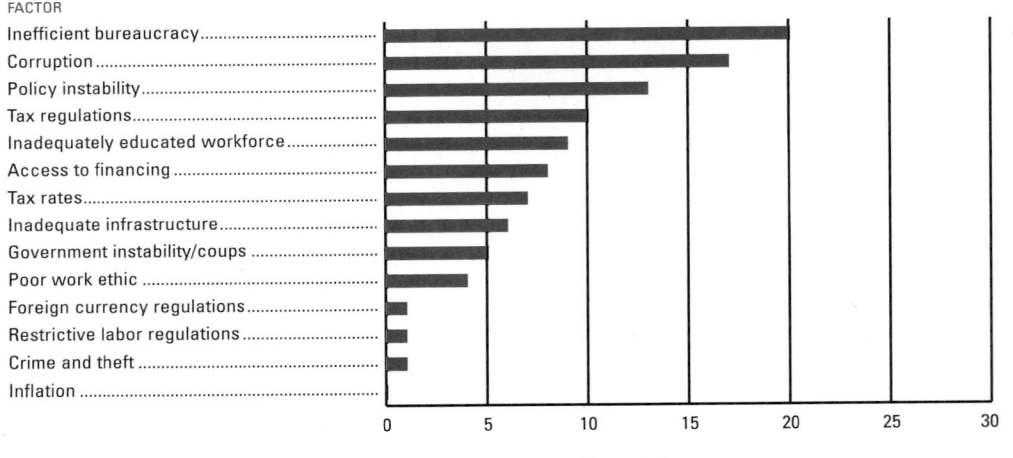

Note: From a list of 14 factors, respondents were asked to select the five most problematic for doing business in their country and to rank them between 1 (most problematic) and 5. The bars in the figure show the responses weighted according to their rankings.

Source: World Economic Forum, Executive Opinion Survey (2003)

National competitiveness balance sheet

NOTABLE COMPETITIVE ADVANTAGES	
Growth Competitiveness Index	Rank/102

Macroeconomic Environment

2.01	Recession expectations	2
2.03	Extent of distortive government subsidies	6
2.09	Access to credit	7
2.19	National savings rate, 2002	9
2.20	Inflation, 2002	10
2.21	Real exchange rate, 2002	15

Public Institutions

6.03	Property rights	24
6.08	Favoritism in decisions of government officials	27
6.17	Organized crime	31

Technology

3.04	Prevalence of foreign technology licensing	3
3.15	Government success in ICT promotion	14
3.14	Government prioritization of ICT	16
3.03	FDI and technology transfer	21
3.08	University/industry research collaboration	25
3.13	Quality of competition in the ISP sector	29
3.02	Firm-level technology absorption	30
3.12	Internet access in schools	30

Business Competitiveness Index		Rank/95

Sophistication of Company Operations and Strategy

3.04	Prevalence of foreign technology licensing	5
10.10	Extent of regional sales	21
10.08	Degree of customer orientation	22

Quality of the National Business Environment

2.03	Extent of distortive government subsidies	5
9.06	State of cluster development	10
10.20	Cooperation in labor-employer relations	13

Other Indicators		Rank/102

8.09	Wage equality of women in the workplace	5
8.08	Private sector employment of women	7
4.09	Brain drain	12
4.11	Maternity laws' impact on hiring women	14
2.10	Government intervention in corporate investment	14
10.21	Pay and productivity	15
10.18	Hiring and firing practices	17
2.02	Business costs of terrorism	17
6.15	Government effectiveness in reducing poverty	19
11.13	Prevalence of environmental management systems	19
2.04	Extent of distortive government intervention	19
6.14	Business costs of crime and violence	19
8.03	Extent of market dominance	21
2.15	Agricultural policy costs	21
8.11	Focus of trade and industry associations	22

NOTABLE COMPETITIVE DISADVANTAGES	
Growth Competitiveness Index	Rank/102

Macroeconomic Environment

7.08	Diversion of public funds	43
2.22	Interest rate spread, 2002	42
2.17	Country credit rating, 2003	41
7.10	Public trust of politicians	40
2.18	Government surplus/deficit, 2002	33

Public Institutions

7.01	Irregular payments in exports and imports	59
7.03	Irregular payments in tax collection	44
7.02	Irregular payments in public utilities	36
6.01	Judicial independence	34

Technology

3.22	Telephone lines, 2002	66
3.21	Internet hosts, 2002	60
3.23	Personal computers, 2002	58
3.20	Internet users, 2002	49
3.19	Cellular telephones, 2002	47
3.17	Utility patents, 2002	46
3.16	Laws relating to ICT	43
3.18	Tertiary enrollment	41
3.01	Technological sophistication	36
3.06	Company spending on research and development	36

Business Competitiveness Index		Rank/95

Sophistication of Company Operations and Strategy

10.06	Production process sophistication	47
10.09	Control of international distribution	47
10.15	Reliance on professional management	47

Quality of the National Business Environment

6.09	Extent of bureaucratic red tape	75
10.26	Foreign ownership restrictions	69
6.12	Centralization of economic policymaking	65

Other Indicators		Rank/102

2.06	Soundness of banks	82
4.07	Business impact of HIV/AIDS	80
10.19	Flexibility of wage determination	66
4.05	Business impact of malaria	65
4.06	Business impact of tuberculosis	65
7.14	Pervasiveness of money laundering through non-bank channels	64
4.08	Impact of HIV/AIDS on FDI	63
6.05	Freedom of the press	62
7.11	Prevalence of illegal political donations	54
3.11	Availability of mobile or cellular telephones	51
7.13	Pervasiveness of money laundering through banks	51
11.02	Water pollution regulations	48
6.18	Informal sector	47
11.04	Chemical waste regulations	46
11.10	Consistency of regulation enforcement	46

363

Note: The Business Competitiveness Index applies different criteria for selecting a country's competitive advantages and disadvantages. Please refer to the section "How Country Profiles Work" for further details.

Trinidad and Tobago

Competitiveness Rankings

Growth Competitiveness Index Rank	49

Macroeconomic Environment Index Rank **47**
   Macroeconomic Stability Subindex Rank 34
   Government Waste Subindex Rank 69
   Country Credit Rating Rank 42

Public Institutions Index Rank...**56**
   Contracts and Law Subindex Rank 51
   Corruption Subindex Rank....................................59

Technology Index Rank **47**
   Innovation Subindex Rank....................................75
   ICT Subindex Rank 50
   Technology Transfer Subindex Rank
   (out of 77 non-core innovators).........................14

Business Competitiveness Index Rank	53

**Sophistication of Company Operations
and Strategy Rank** **54**
**Quality of the National Business
Environment Rank** **53**

The Most Problematic Factors for Doing Business

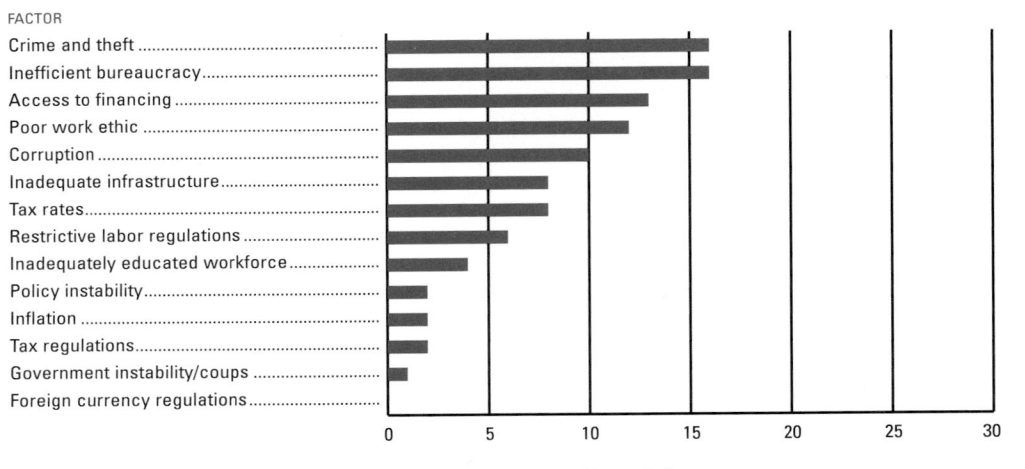

Note: From a list of 14 factors, respondents were asked to select the five most problematic for doing business in their country and to rank them between 1 (most problematic) and 5. The bars in the figure show the responses weighted according to their rankings.

Source: World Economic Forum, Executive Opinion Survey (2003)

National competitiveness balance sheet

NOTABLE COMPETITIVE ADVANTAGES	
Growth Competitiveness Index	**Rank/102**

Macroeconomic Environment
2.01	Recession expectations	10
2.09	Access to credit	19
2.18	Government surplus/deficit, 2002	21
2.19	National savings rate, 2002	22
2.17	Country credit rating, 2003	42

Public Institutions
| 6.01 | Judicial independence | 24 |

Technology
3.03	FDI and technology transfer	7
3.04	Prevalence of foreign technology licensing	28
3.20	Internet users, 2002	43
3.01	Technological sophistication	45
3.19	Cellular telephones, 2002	45
3.21	Internet hosts, 2002	45
3.22	Telephone lines, 2002	45
3.23	Personal computers, 2002	46
3.02	Firm-level technology absorption	47

| **Business Competitiveness Index** | **Rank/95** |

Sophistication of Company Operations and Strategy
10.10	Extent of regional sales	27
10.06	Production process sophistication	33
10.15	Reliance on professional management	38

Quality of the National Business Environment
6.01	Judicial independence	23
2.11	Local equity market access	26
8.05	Administrative burden for startups	32

Other Indicators	**Rank/102**
6.11	Efficiency of the tax system	14
10.22	Charitable causes involvement	16
2.06	Soundness of banks	19
8.10	Regional disparities in quality of business environment	20
4.11	Maternity laws' impact on hiring women	22
2.10	Government intervention in corporate investment	29
10.27	Strength of auditing and accounting standards	31
4.10	Maternity leave legislation	36
10.18	Hiring and firing practices	37
6.06	Burden of regulation	42
7.07	Irregular payments in judicial decisions	42
8.11	Focus of trade and industry associations	45
2.04	Extent of distortive government intervention	46
10.25	Availability of company financial information	46
6.05	Freedom of the press	47

NOTABLE COMPETITIVE DISADVANTAGES	
Growth Competitiveness Index	**Rank/102**

Macroeconomic Environment
2.21	Real exchange rate, 2002	92
7.08	Diversion of public funds	72
7.10	Public trust of politicians	69
2.03	Extent of distortive government subsidies	64
2.22	Interest rate spread, 2002	62
2.20	Inflation, 2002	53

Public Institutions
6.17	Organized crime	77
6.08	Favoritism in decisions of government officials	75
7.01	Irregular payments in exports and imports	64
7.02	Irregular payments in public utilities	62
7.03	Irregular payments in tax collection	57
6.03	Property rights	52

Technology
3.13	Quality of competition in the ISP sector	98
3.16	Laws relating to ICT	80
3.18	Tertiary enrollment	80
3.14	Government prioritization of ICT	76
3.12	Internet access in schools	74
3.17	Utility patents, 2002	72
3.15	Government success in ICT promotion	70
3.06	Company spending on research and development	60
3.08	University/industry research collaboration	55

| **Business Competitiveness Index** | **Rank/95** |

Sophistication of Company Operations and Strategy
10.01	Nature of competitive advantage	75
10.04	Capacity for innovation	75
10.08	Degree of customer orientation	71

Quality of the National Business Environment
10.20	Cooperation in labor-employer relations	95
6.12	Centralization of economic policymaking	91
8.06	Effectiveness of antitrust policy	82

Other Indicators	**Rank/102**
7.14	Pervasiveness of money laundering through non-bank channels	93
11.10	Consistency of regulation enforcement	86
7.13	Pervasiveness of money laundering through banks	85
11.01	Air pollution regulations	84
11.06	Compliance with environmental regulations	84
6.14	Business costs of crime and violence	84
11.07	Compliance with international agreements	83
2.15	Agricultural policy costs	83
11.03	Toxic waste disposal regulations	82
7.12	Policy consequences of legal political donations	82
4.07	Business impact of HIV/AIDS	81
11.02	Water pollution regulations	81
11.04	Chemical waste regulations	81
3.11	Availability of mobile or cellular telephones	72
11.13	Prevalence of environmental management systems	72

365

Note: The Business Competitiveness Index applies different criteria for selecting a country's competitive advantages and disadvantages. Please refer to the section "How Country Profiles Work" for further details.

Tunisia

Competitiveness Rankings

Growth Competitiveness Index Rank	38

Macroeconomic Environment Index Rank **32**
　Macroeconomic Stability Subindex Rank 31
　Government Waste Subindex Rank 11
　Country Credit Rating Rank..................................45

Public Institutions Index Rank...**32**
　Contracts and Law Subindex Rank 22
　Corruption Subindex Rank...................................42

Technology Index Rank **57**
　Innovation Subindex Rank....................................50
　ICT Subindex Rank 59
　Technology Transfer Subindex Rank
　　(out of 77 non-core innovators).......................31

Business Competitiveness Index Rank	33

**Sophistication of Company Operations
　and Strategy Rank** **38**

**Quality of the National Business
　Environment Rank** **29**

The Most Problematic Factors for Doing Business

FACTOR

Access to financing ....
Poor work ethic ....
Inefficient bureaucracy.....................................
Restrictive labor regulations ....
Tax regulations...
Foreign currency regulations............................
Inadequate infrastructure.................................
Inadequately educated workforce...................
Tax rates...
Corruption ....
Inflation ....
Policy instability...
Government instability/coups ....
Crime and theft ....

Percent of responses

Note: From a list of 14 factors, respondents were asked to select the five most problematic for doing business in their country and to rank them between 1 (most problematic) and 5. The bars in the figure show the responses weighted according to their rankings.

Source: World Economic Forum, Executive Opinion Survey (2003)

National competitiveness balance sheet

NOTABLE COMPETITIVE ADVANTAGES		
Growth Competitiveness Index		**Rank/102**
	Macroeconomic Environment	
2.03	Extent of distortive government subsidies	4
7.10	Public trust of politicians	11
7.08	Diversion of public funds	21
2.09	Access to credit	29
2.19	National savings rate, 2002	30
2.21	Real exchange rate, 2002	34
	Public Institutions	
6.08	Favoritism in decisions of government officials	11
6.17	Organized crime	21
6.03	Property rights	28
6.01	Judicial independence	33
7.01	Irregular payments in exports and imports	37
	Technology	
3.15	Government success in ICT promotion	3
3.14	Government prioritization of ICT	5
3.04	Prevalence of foreign technology licensing	19
3.16	Laws relating to ICT	19
3.02	Firm-level technology absorption	23
3.08	University/industry research collaboration	31
3.06	Company spending on research and development	33
3.12	Internet access in schools	33

Business Competitiveness Index		**Rank/95**
	Sophistication of Company Operations and Strategy	
10.02	Value chain presence	23
10.12	Extent of staff training	25
3.04	Prevalence of foreign technology licensing	29
	Quality of the National Business Environment	
2.03	Extent of distortive government subsidies	3
3.09	Government procurement of advanced technology products	5
4.03	Quality of math and science education	9

Other Indicators		**Rank/102**
6.16	Government effectiveness in reducing income inequality	3
8.09	Wage equality of women in the workplace	3
6.15	Government effectiveness in reducing poverty	3
2.15	Agricultural policy costs	4
11.11	Effects of compliance on business	5
8.08	Private sector employment of women	6
3.07	Subsidies and tax credits for firm-level research and development	7
11.12	Political context of environmental gains	7
11.09	Flexibility of regulations	7
7.14	Pervasiveness of money laundering through non-bank channels	8
7.12	Policy consequences of legal political donations	9
7.13	Pervasiveness of money laundering through banks	9
6.06	Burden of regulation	10
2.04	Extent of distortive government intervention	10
8.03	Extent of market dominance	10

NOTABLE COMPETITIVE DISADVANTAGES		
Growth Competitiveness Index		**Rank/102**
	Macroeconomic Environment	
2.20	Inflation, 2002	47
2.22	Interest rate spread, 2002	46
2.17	Country credit rating, 2003	45
2.18	Government surplus/deficit, 2002	40
2.01	Recession expectations	38
	Public Institutions	
7.03	Irregular payments in tax collection	48
7.02	Irregular payments in public utilities	47
	Technology	
3.21	Internet hosts, 2002	88
3.19	Cellular telephones, 2002	77
3.23	Personal computers, 2002	65
3.17	Utility patents, 2002	62
3.13	Quality of competition in the ISP sector	60
3.22	Telephone lines, 2002	60
3.18	Tertiary enrollment	57
3.20	Internet users, 2002	55
3.01	Technological sophistication	42
3.03	FDI and technology transfer	41

Business Competitiveness Index		**Rank/95**
	Sophistication of Company Operations and Strategy	
10.15	Reliance on professional management	61
10.08	Degree of customer orientation	55
10.04	Capacity for innovation	54
	Quality of the National Business Environment	
3.19	Cellular telephones, 2002	79
8.02	Extent of locally based competitors	68
8.01	Intensity of local competition	65

Other Indicators		**Rank/102**
10.19	Flexibility of wage determination	93
6.05	Freedom of the press	87
3.11	Availability of mobile or cellular telephones	76
4.05	Business impact of malaria	65
4.06	Business impact of tuberculosis	56
2.06	Soundness of banks	56
10.25	Availability of company financial information	53
7.05	Irregular payments in loan applications	52
4.07	Business impact of HIV/AIDS	46
8.10	Regional disparities in quality of business environment	42
4.09	Brain drain	41
10.21	Pay and productivity	38

367

Note: The Business Competitiveness Index applies different criteria for selecting a country's competitive advantages and disadvantages. Please refer to the section "How Country Profiles Work" for further details.

Turkey

Competitiveness Rankings

Growth Competitiveness Index Rank	65

Macroeconomic Environment Index Rank **82**
 Macroeconomic Stability Subindex Rank 94
 Government Waste Subindex Rank 75
 Country Credit Rating Rank 63

Public Institutions Index Rank **63**
 Contracts and Law Subindex Rank 52
 Corruption Subindex Rank 69

Technology Index Rank **54**
 Innovation Subindex Rank 68
 ICT Subindex Rank 51
 Technology Transfer Subindex Rank
 (out of 77 non-core innovators) 39

Business Competitiveness Index Rank	52

**Sophistication of Company Operations
 and Strategy Rank** **51**

**Quality of the National Business
 Environment Rank** **55**

The Most Problematic Factors for Doing Business

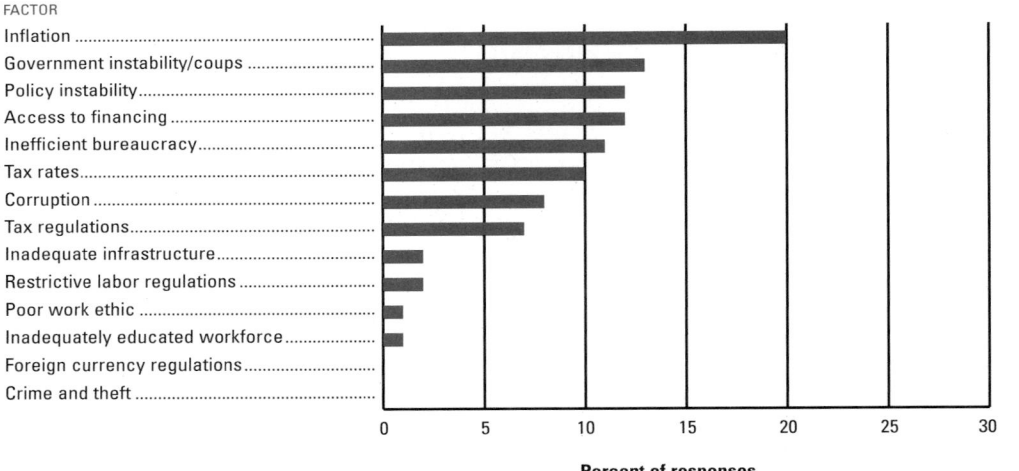

Note: From a list of 14 factors, respondents were asked to select the five most problematic for doing business in their country and to rank them between 1 (most problematic) and 5. The bars in the figure show the responses weighted according to their rankings.

Source: World Economic Forum, Executive Opinion Survey (2003)

National competitiveness balance sheet

Note: The Business Competitiveness Index applies different criteria for selecting a country's competitive advantages and disadvantages. Please refer to the section "How Country Profiles Work" for further details.

369

Uganda

Competitiveness Rankings

Growth Competitiveness Index Rank	80

Macroeconomic Environment Index Rank 71
    Macroeconomic Stability Subindex Rank 58
    Government Waste Subindex Rank 60
    Country Credit Rating Rank 85

Public Institutions Index Rank **84**
    Contracts and Law Subindex Rank 73
    Corruption Subindex Rank....................................93

Technology Index Rank **77**
    Innovation Subindex Rank....................................86
    ICT Subindex Rank 89
    Technology Transfer Subindex Rank
    (out of 77 non-core innovators) 22

Business Competitiveness Index Rank	n/a

**Sophistication of Company Operations
and Strategy Rank** ....n/a

**Quality of the National Business
Environment Rank**...n/a

370

The Most Problematic Factors for Doing Business

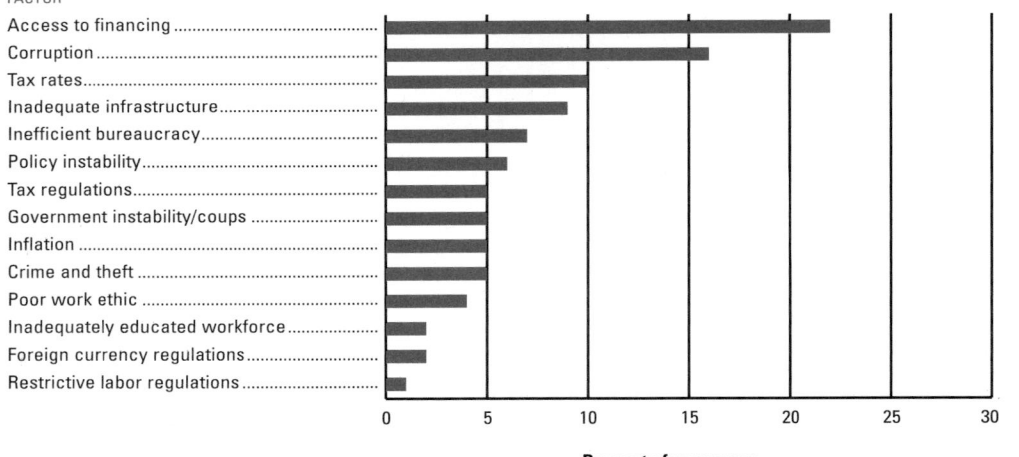

Note: From a list of 14 factors, respondents were asked to select the five most problematic for doing business in their country and to rank them between 1 (most problematic) and 5. The bars in the figure show the responses weighted according to their rankings.

Source: World Economic Forum, Executive Opinion Survey (2003)

National competitiveness balance sheet

NOTABLE COMPETITIVE ADVANTAGES	
Growth Competitiveness Index	**Rank/102**

Macroeconomic Environment

2.20	Inflation, 2002	3
2.21	Real exchange rate, 2002	12
2.03	Extent of distortive government subsidies	17
2.01	Recession expectations	33

Technology

3.03	FDI and technology transfer	20
3.15	Government success in ICT promotion	25
3.04	Prevalence of foreign technology licensing	26
3.14	Government prioritization of ICT	39
3.08	University/industry research collaboration	43

NOTABLE COMPETITIVE DISADVANTAGES	
Growth Competitiveness Index	**Rank/102**

Macroeconomic Environment

2.18	Government surplus/deficit, 2002	98
2.19	National savings rate, 2002	94
7.08	Diversion of public funds	90
2.22	Interest rate spread, 2002	88
2.17	Country credit rating, 2003	85
2.09	Access to credit	69
7.10	Public trust of politicians	61

Public Institutions

7.01	Irregular payments in exports and imports	95
7.03	Irregular payments in tax collection	93
7.02	Irregular payments in public utilities	92
6.17	Organized crime	82
6.08	Favoritism in decisions of government officials	79
6.03	Property rights	75
6.01	Judicial independence	58

Technology

3.22	Telephone lines, 2002	101
3.20	Internet users, 2002	96
3.23	Personal computers, 2002	93
3.18	Tertiary enrollment	91
3.19	Cellular telephones, 2002	89
3.01	Technological sophistication	86
3.21	Internet hosts, 2002	78
3.12	Internet access in schools	75
3.16	Laws relating to ICT	66
3.17	Utility patents, 2002	66
3.02	Firm-level technology absorption	60
3.13	Quality of competition in the ISP sector	53
3.06	Company spending on research and development	51

371

Other Indicators		**Rank/102**
10.19	Flexibility of wage determination	6
10.18	Hiring and firing practices	9
2.15	Agricultural policy costs	13
8.09	Wage equality of women in the workplace	31
7.12	Policy consequences of legal political donations	34
8.03	Extent of market dominance	38
6.15	Government effectiveness in reducing poverty	39
6.06	Burden of regulation	41
11.10	Consistency of regulation enforcement	42
6.10	Effectiveness of law-making bodies	44
3.07	Subsidies and tax credits for firm-level research and development	48
7.11	Prevalence of illegal political donations	48

Other Indicators		**Rank/102**
2.02	Business costs of terrorism	98
7.05	Irregular payments in loan applications	97
10.21	Pay and productivity	96
4.05	Business impact of malaria	94
6.05	Freedom of the press	93
4.06	Business impact of tuberculosis	93
4.08	Impact of HIV/AIDS on FDI	91
2.06	Soundness of banks	90
7.04	Irregular payments in public contracts	90
4.07	Business impact of HIV/AIDS	90
8.08	Private sector employment of women	90
4.10	Maternity leave legislation	88
11.02	Water pollution regulations	87
5.07	Postal efficiency	85
10.05	Ethical behavior of firms	83

Note: This country is not included in the coverage of the Business Competitiveness Index 2003–2004.

Ukraine

Competitiveness Rankings

Growth Competitiveness Index Rank	84

Macroeconomic Environment Index Rank **70**
    Macroeconomic Stability Subindex Rank 42
    Government Waste Subindex Rank 85
    Country Credit Rating Rank 78

Public Institutions Index Rank **94**
    Contracts and Law Subindex Rank 94
    Corruption Subindex Rank 89

Technology Index Rank **84**
    Innovation Subindex Rank 36
    ICT Subindex Rank 70
    Technology Transfer Subindex Rank
    (out of 77 non-core innovators) 71

Business Competitiveness Index Rank	71

**Sophistication of Company Operations
  and Strategy Rank** **71**
**Quality of the National Business
  Environment Rank** **74**

The Most Problematic Factors for Doing Business

Note: From a list of 14 factors, respondents were asked to select the five most problematic for doing business in their country and to rank them between 1 (most problematic) and 5. The bars in the figure show the responses weighted according to their rankings.

Source: World Economic Forum, Executive Opinion Survey (2003)

National competitiveness balance sheet

NOTABLE COMPETITIVE ADVANTAGES

Growth Competitiveness Index	Rank/102

Macroeconomic Environment

2.20	Inflation, 2002	12
2.18	Government surplus/deficit, 2002	13
2.19	National savings rate, 2002	17

Technology

3.18	Tertiary enrollment	33
3.08	University/industry research collaboration	36
3.17	Utility patents, 2002	47

NOTABLE COMPETITIVE DISADVANTAGES

Growth Competitiveness Index	Rank/102

Macroeconomic Environment

2.03	Extent of distortive government subsidies	97
2.21	Real exchange rate, 2002	96
2.22	Interest rate spread, 2002	94
7.10	Public trust of politicians	81
2.17	Country credit rating, 2003	78
7.08	Diversion of public funds	73
2.09	Access to credit	64
2.01	Recession expectations	51

Public Institutions

6.03	Property rights	100
7.01	Irregular payments in exports and imports	94
6.17	Organized crime	91
7.03	Irregular payments in tax collection	89
6.01	Judicial independence	83
6.08	Favoritism in decisions of government officials	82
7.02	Irregular payments in public utilities	74

Technology

3.16	Laws relating to ICT	85
3.20	Internet users, 2002	84
3.15	Government success in ICT promotion	82
3.06	Company spending on research and development	81
3.19	Cellular telephones, 2002	81
3.12	Internet access in schools	77
3.13	Quality of competition in the ISP sector	75
3.03	FDI and technology transfer	74
3.23	Personal computers, 2002	73
3.04	Prevalence of foreign technology licensing	69
3.14	Government prioritization of ICT	69
3.01	Technological sophistication	68
3.02	Firm-level technology absorption	67
3.21	Internet hosts, 2002	57
3.22	Telephone lines, 2002	51

Business Competitiveness Index — Advantages

Business Competitiveness Index	Rank/95

Sophistication of Company Operations and Strategy

10.09	Control of international distribution	21
10.04	Capacity for innovation	31
10.03	Extent of branding	39

Quality of the National Business Environment

5.02	Railroad infrastructure development	19
9.09	Local availability of process machinery	22
9.08	Local availability of components and parts	23

Other Indicators	Rank/102

10.18	Hiring and firing practices	13
11.09	Flexibility of regulations	26
2.02	Business costs of terrorism	30
10.21	Pay and productivity	39

Business Competitiveness Index — Disadvantages

Business Competitiveness Index	Rank/95

Sophistication of Company Operations and Strategy

10.12	Extent of staff training	89
3.04	Prevalence of foreign technology licensing	87
10.15	Reliance on professional management	87

Quality of the National Business Environment

10.24	Protection of minority shareholders' interests	95
2.12	Regulation of securities exchanges	94
8.05	Administrative burden for startups	94

Other Indicators	Rank/102

7.13	Pervasiveness of money laundering through banks	102
7.12	Policy consequences of legal political donations	102
6.05	Freedom of the press	101
4.10	Maternity leave legislation	101
8.11	Focus of trade and industry associations	101
6.11	Efficiency of the tax system	98
2.10	Government intervention in corporate investment	98
6.07	Transparency of government policymaking	98
6.18	Informal sector	97
7.14	Pervasiveness of money laundering through non-bank channels	97
10.25	Availability of company financial information	96
3.11	Availability of mobile or cellular telephones	96
4.11	Maternity laws' impact on hiring women	96
10.05	Ethical behavior of firms	95
6.16	Government effectiveness in reducing income inequality	95

373

Note: The Business Competitiveness Index applies different criteria for selecting a country's competitive advantages and disadvantages. Please refer to the section "How Country Profiles Work" for further details.

United Kingdom

Competitiveness Rankings

Growth Competitiveness Index Rank	15

Macroeconomic Environment Index Rank **12**
    Macroeconomic Stability Subindex Rank 54
    Government Waste Subindex Rank 12
    Country Credit Rating Rank 5

Public Institutions Index Rank **12**
    Contracts and Law Subindex Rank 10
    Corruption Subindex Rank......................................12

Technology Index Rank **16**
    Innovation Subindex Rank 13
    ICT Subindex Rank 16

Business Competitiveness Index Rank	6

Sophistication of Company Operations
  and Strategy Rank **8**
Quality of the National Business
  Environment Rank **6**

The Most Problematic Factors for Doing Business

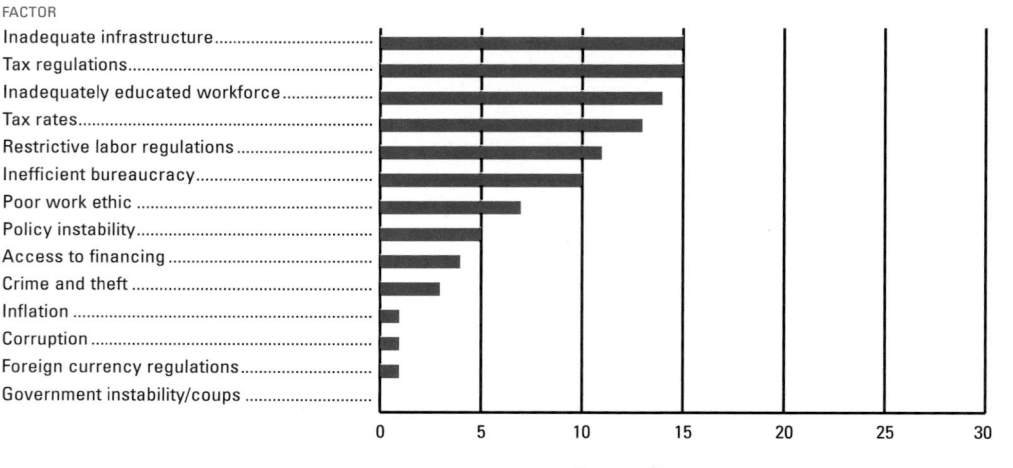

FACTOR

Note: From a list of 14 factors, respondents were asked to select the five most problematic for doing business in their country and to rank them between 1 (most problematic) and 5. The bars in the figure show the responses weighted according to their rankings.

Source: World Economic Forum, Executive Opinion Survey (2003)

National competitiveness balance sheet

NOTABLE COMPETITIVE ADVANTAGES		NOTABLE COMPETITIVE DISADVANTAGES	
Growth Competitiveness Index	**Rank/102**	**Growth Competitiveness Index**	**Rank/102**

	Macroeconomic Environment			**Macroeconomic Environment**	
2.22	Interest rate spread, 2002	1	2.19	National savings rate, 2002	83
2.17	Country credit rating, 2003	5	2.21	Real exchange rate, 2002	77
7.08	Diversion of public funds	10	2.01	Recession expectations	73
	Public Institutions		2.09	Access to credit	55
6.03	Property rights	8	2.20	Inflation, 2002	32
6.01	Judicial independence	10	2.18	Government surplus/deficit, 2002	31
7.03	Irregular payments in tax collection	10	7.10	Public trust of politicians	16
6.08	Favoritism in decisions of government officials	12	2.03	Extent of distortive government subsidies	15
7.01	Irregular payments in exports and imports	12		**Public Institutions**	
	Technology		6.17	Organized crime	23
3.08	University/industry research collaboration	8	7.02	Irregular payments in public utilities	17
3.13	Quality of competition in the ISP sector	8		**Technology**	
3.16	Laws relating to ICT	8	3.15	Government success in ICT promotion	47
3.01	Technological sophistication	10	3.02	Firm-level technology absorption	34
3.06	Company spending on research and development	11	3.14	Government prioritization of ICT	25
3.19	Cellular telephones, 2002	11	3.23	Personal computers, 2002	21
3.22	Telephone lines, 2002	11	3.17	Utility patents, 2002	18
3.18	Tertiary enrollment	13	3.20	Internet users, 2002	18
3.12	Internet access in schools	14	3.21	Internet hosts, 2002	15

Business Competitiveness Index	**Rank/95**	**Business Competitiveness Index**	**Rank/95**

	Sophistication of Company Operations and Strategy			**Sophistication of Company Operations and Strategy**	
10.14	Extent of incentive compensation	2	10.10	Extent of regional sales	22
10.15	Reliance on professional management	2		**Quality of the National Business Environment**	
10.07	Extent of marketing	3	6.12	Centralization of economic policymaking	46
	Quality of the National Business Environment		6.09	Extent of bureaucratic red tape	44
10.17	Efficacy of corporate boards	1	4.03	Quality of math and science education	42
2.05	Financial market sophistication	1			
8.07	Prevalence of mergers and acquisitions	1			

Other Indicators	**Rank/102**	**Other Indicators**	**Rank/102**

10.27	Strength of auditing and accounting standards	1	2.02	Business costs of terrorism	87
10.05	Ethical behavior of firms	3	8.09	Wage equality of women in the workplace	56
10.25	Availability of company financial information	3	4.07	Business impact of HIV/AIDS	40
2.06	Soundness of banks	4	2.15	Agricultural policy costs	39
10.23	Company promotion of volunteerism	5	6.06	Burden of regulation	38
6.10	Effectiveness of law-making bodies	6	6.14	Business costs of crime and violence	37
10.22	Charitable causes involvement	7	4.11	Maternity laws' impact on hiring women	36
11.10	Consistency of regulation enforcement	8	6.11	Efficiency of the tax system	35
7.04	Irregular payments in public contracts	8	4.06	Business impact of tuberculosis	33
11.13	Prevalence of environmental management systems	8	4.08	Impact of HIV/AIDS on FDI	32
11.12	Political context of environmental gains	8	4.04	Disparity in healthcare quality	32
10.21	Pay and productivity	9	8.11	Focus of trade and industry associations	30
7.05	Irregular payments in loan applications	10	4.05	Business impact of malaria	29
7.13	Pervasiveness of money laundering through banks	10	6.15	Government effectiveness in reducing poverty	24
7.06	Irregular payments in government policymaking	11	5.07	Postal efficiency	24

Note: The Business Competitiveness Index applies different criteria for selecting a country's competitive advantages and disadvantages. Please refer to the section "How Country Profiles Work" for further details.

United States

Competitiveness Rankings

Growth Competitiveness Index Rank	2

Macroeconomic Environment Index Rank **14**
    Macroeconomic Stability Subindex Rank 52
    Government Waste Subindex Rank 16
    Country Credit Rating Rank 3

Public Institutions Index Rank **17**
    Contracts and Law Subindex Rank 17
    Corruption Subindex Rank 24

Technology Index Rank **1**
    Innovation Subindex Rank 1
    ICT Subindex Rank 5

Business Competitiveness Index Rank	2

**Sophistication of Company Operations
and Strategy Rank** 2
**Quality of the National Business
Environment Rank** 2

The Most Problematic Factors for Doing Business

FACTOR

Percent of responses

Note: From a list of 14 factors, respondents were asked to select the five most problematic for doing business in their country and to rank them between 1 (most problematic) and 5. The bars in the figure show the responses weighted according to their rankings.

Source: World Economic Forum, Executive Opinion Survey (2003)

National competitiveness balance sheet

377

Note: The Business Competitiveness Index applies different criteria for selecting a country's competitive advantages and disadvantages.
Please refer to the section "How Country Profiles Work" for further details.

Uruguay

Competitiveness Rankings

Growth Competitiveness Index Rank	50

Macroeconomic Environment Index Rank **89**
    Macroeconomic Stability Subindex Rank 102
    Government Waste Subindex Rank 33
    Country Credit Rating Rank 70

Public Institutions Index Rank **29**
    Contracts and Law Subindex Rank 33
    Corruption Subindex Rank 26

Technology Index Rank **51**
    Innovation Subindex Rank 46
    ICT Subindex Rank 42
    Technology Transfer Subindex Rank
    (out of 77 non-core innovators) 56

Business Competitiveness Index Rank	69

**Sophistication of Company Operations
and Strategy Rank** 76
**Quality of the National Business
Environment Rank** 66

The Most Problematic Factors for Doing Business

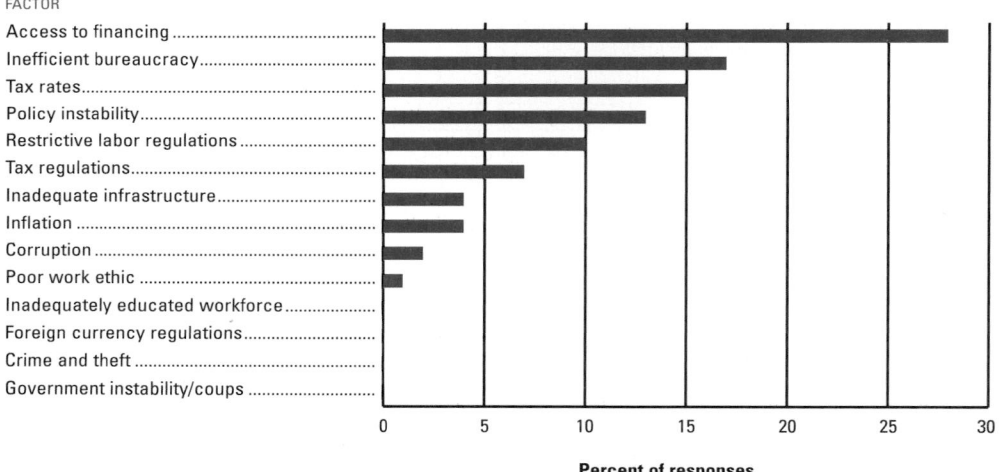

FACTOR

Access to financing
Inefficient bureaucracy
Tax rates
Policy instability
Restrictive labor regulations
Tax regulations
Inadequate infrastructure
Inflation
Corruption
Poor work ethic
Inadequately educated workforce
Foreign currency regulations
Crime and theft
Government instability/coups

Percent of responses

Note: From a list of 14 factors, respondents were asked to select the five most problematic for doing business in their country and to rank them between 1 (most problematic) and 5. The bars in the figure show the responses weighted according to their rankings.

Source: World Economic Forum, Executive Opinion Survey (2003)

National competitiveness balance sheet

NOTABLE COMPETITIVE ADVANTAGES		
Growth Competitiveness Index		**Rank/102**
	Macroeconomic Environment	
2.21	Real exchange rate, 2002	11
7.08	Diversion of public funds	27
7.10	Public trust of politicians	29
	Public Institutions	
6.17	Organized crime	17
7.01	Irregular payments in exports and imports	22
7.02	Irregular payments in public utilities	24
6.01	Judicial independence	31
7.03	Irregular payments in tax collection	34
6.08	Favoritism in decisions of government officials	35
	Technology	
3.21	Internet hosts, 2002	26
3.23	Personal computers, 2002	38
3.18	Tertiary enrollment	39
3.22	Telephone lines, 2002	39
3.20	Internet users, 2002	41
3.17	Utility patents, 2002	42

NOTABLE COMPETITIVE DISADVANTAGES		
Growth Competitiveness Index		**Rank/102**
	Macroeconomic Environment	
2.22	Interest rate spread, 2002	102
2.09	Access to credit	101
2.01	Recession expectations	97
2.20	Inflation, 2002	90
2.19	National savings rate, 2002	89
2.17	Country credit rating, 2003	70
2.03	Extent of distortive government subsidies	68
2.18	Government surplus/deficit, 2002	67
	Public Institutions	
6.03	Property rights	57
	Technology	
3.02	Firm-level technology absorption	96
3.06	Company spending on research and development	84
3.15	Government success in ICT promotion	79
3.16	Laws relating to ICT	79
3.08	University/industry research collaboration	73
3.14	Government prioritization of ICT	71
3.01	Technological sophistication	65
3.13	Quality of competition in the ISP sector	64
3.03	FDI and technology transfer	58
3.19	Cellular telephones, 2002	55
3.04	Prevalence of foreign technology licensing	51
3.12	Internet access in schools	51

Business Competitiveness Index		Rank/95
	Sophistication of Company Operations and Strategy	
10.10	Extent of regional sales	37
10.06	Production process sophistication	60
10.08	Degree of customer orientation	66
	Quality of the National Business Environment	
7.09	Business costs of corruption	23
5.06	Telephone infrastructure quality	24
6.01	Judicial independence	29

Business Competitiveness Index		Rank/95
	Sophistication of Company Operations and Strategy	
10.14	Extent of incentive compensation	87
10.15	Reliance on professional management	85
10.12	Extent of staff training	80
	Quality of the National Business Environment	
2.11	Local equity market access	94
2.08	Venture capital availability	93
8.06	Effectiveness of antitrust policy	88

Other Indicators		Rank/102
2.02	Business costs of terrorism	1
4.05	Business impact of malaria	9
4.08	Impact of HIV/AIDS on FDI	11
4.06	Business impact of tuberculosis	16
4.07	Business impact of HIV/AIDS	20
7.07	Irregular payments in judicial decisions	21
7.04	Irregular payments in public contracts	23
10.19	Flexibility of wage determination	25
7.11	Prevalence of illegal political donations	26
6.05	Freedom of the press	27
8.10	Regional disparities in quality of business environment	29
7.14	Pervasiveness of money laundering through non-bank channels	29
10.05	Ethical behavior of firms	31
7.05	Irregular payments in loan applications	33
7.06	Irregular payments in government policymaking	33

Other Indicators		Rank/102
8.11	Focus of trade and industry associations	99
2.06	Soundness of banks	99
10.23	Company promotion of volunteerism	98
10.25	Availability of company financial information	94
8.03	Extent of market dominance	93
10.22	Charitable causes involvement	92
2.10	Government intervention in corporate investment	91
2.04	Extent of distortive government intervention	87
8.09	Wage equality of women in the workplace	84
3.07	Subsidies and tax credits for firm-level research and development	84
10.18	Hiring and firing practices	84
10.21	Pay and productivity	82
6.07	Transparency of government policymaking	80
6.11	Efficiency of the tax system	78
4.09	Brain drain	78

Note: The Business Competitiveness Index applies different criteria for selecting a country's competitive advantages and disadvantages. Please refer to the section "How Country Profiles Work" for further details.

Venezuela

Competitiveness Rankings

Growth Competitiveness Rank	82

Macroeconomic Environment Index Rank **94**
    Macroeconomic Stability Subindex Rank 95
    Government Waste Subindex 102
    Country Credit Rating Rank 72

Public Institutions Index Rank **89**
    Contracts and Law Subindex Rank 100
    Corruption Subindex Rank 66

Technology Index Rank **58**
    Innovation Subindex Rank 51
    ICT Subindex Rank 60
    Technology Transfer Subindex Rank
    (out of 77 non-core innovators) 32

Business Competitiveness Index Rank	80

**Sophistication of Company Operations
and Strategy Rank** 73
**Quality of the National Business
Environment Rank** 82

The Most Problematic Factors for Doing Business

FACTOR

Foreign currency regulations
Policy instability
Access to financing
Government instability/coups
Inefficient bureaucracy
Inflation
Corruption
Crime and theft
Restrictive labor regulations
Tax rates
Inadequately educated workforce
Inadequate infrastructure
Poor work ethic
Tax regulations

Percent of responses

Note: From a list of 14 factors, respondents were asked to select the five most problematic for doing business in their country and to rank them between 1 (most problematic) and 5. The bars in the figure show the responses weighted according to their rankings.

Source: World Economic Forum, Executive Opinion Survey (2003)

National competitiveness balance sheet

NOTABLE COMPETITIVE ADVANTAGES	
Growth Competitiveness Index	**Rank/102**

Macroeconomic Environment
2.19 National savings rate, 2002 23

Public Institutions
7.02 Irregular payments in public utilities 40

Technology
3.04 Prevalence of foreign technology licensing 34
3.03 FDI and technology transfer..38
3.17 Utility patents, 2002 39
3.18 Tertiary enrollment 49
3.19 Cellular telephones, 2002..49

NOTABLE COMPETITIVE DISADVANTAGES	
Growth Competitiveness Index	**Rank/102**

Macroeconomic Environment
7.08 Diversion of public funds 102
2.01 Recession expectations 101
2.09 Access to credit 98
2.20 Inflation, 2002 97
2.03 Extent of distortive government subsidies 96
7.10 Public trust of politicians 96
2.21 Real exchange rate, 2002 87
2.17 Country credit rating, 2003 72
2.22 Interest rate spread, 2002...61
2.18 Government surplus/deficit, 2002 55

Public Institutions
6.01 Judicial independence...101
6.08 Favoritism in decisions of government officials.............99
6.17 Organized crime 92
7.03 Irregular payments in tax collection 92
6.03 Property rights...89
7.01 Irregular payments in exports and imports 85

Technology
3.15 Government success in ICT promotion 99
3.14 Government prioritization of ICT 93
3.06 Company spending on research and development 82
3.02 Firm-level technology absorption 74
3.08 University/industry research collaboration 73
3.12 Internet access in schools 70
3.01 Technological sophistication...62
3.13 Quality of competition in the ISP sector 62
3.22 Telephone lines, 2002 62
3.21 Internet hosts, 2002...61
3.16 Laws relating to ICT 58
3.20 Internet users, 2002 56
3.23 Personal computers, 2002 51

Business Competitiveness Index	Rank/95

Sophistication of Company Operations and Strategy
3.04 Prevalence of foreign technology licensing 49
10.07 Extent of marketing..50
10.15 Reliance on professional management..........................58

Quality of the National Business Environment
6.09 Extent of bureaucratic red tape.....................................29
3.17 Utility patents, 2002 38
3.19 Cellular telephones, 2002..47

Other Indicators	Rank/102
8.08 Private sector employment of women 30
10.23 Company promotion of volunteerism 35
4.06 Business impact of tuberculosis 41
4.07 Business impact of HIV/AIDS 42
3.11 Availability of mobile or cellular telephones 42
8.09 Wage equality of women in the workplace 43
8.10 Regional disparities in quality of business environment ...49

Business Competitiveness Index	Rank/95

Sophistication of Company Operations and Strategy
10.02 Value chain presence 85
10.03 Extent of branding..85
10.08 Degree of customer orientation 81

Quality of the National Business Environment
6.02 Efficiency of legal framework 95
2.14 Hidden trade barriers..94
6.01 Judicial independence...94

Other Indicators	Rank/102
2.10 Government intervention in corporate investment.......102
2.04 Extent of distortive government intervention 102
10.18 Hiring and firing practices 102
6.06 Burden of regulation..102
6.15 Government effectiveness in reducing poverty............102
6.16 Government effectiveness in reducing income inequality ...102
5.07 Postal efficiency 102
6.10 Effectiveness of law-making bodies 101
11.07 Compliance with international agreements 101
2.15 Agricultural policy costs 101
6.14 Business costs of crime and violence 101
6.07 Transparency of government policymaking...................100
11.10 Consistency of regulation enforcement..........................99
4.04 Disparity in healthcare quality 99
7.11 Prevalence of illegal political donations..........................99

381

Note: The Business Competitiveness Index applies different criteria for selecting a country's competitive advantages and disadvantages.
Please refer to the section "How Country Profiles Work" for further details.

Vietnam

Competitiveness Rankings

The Most Problematic Factors for Doing Business

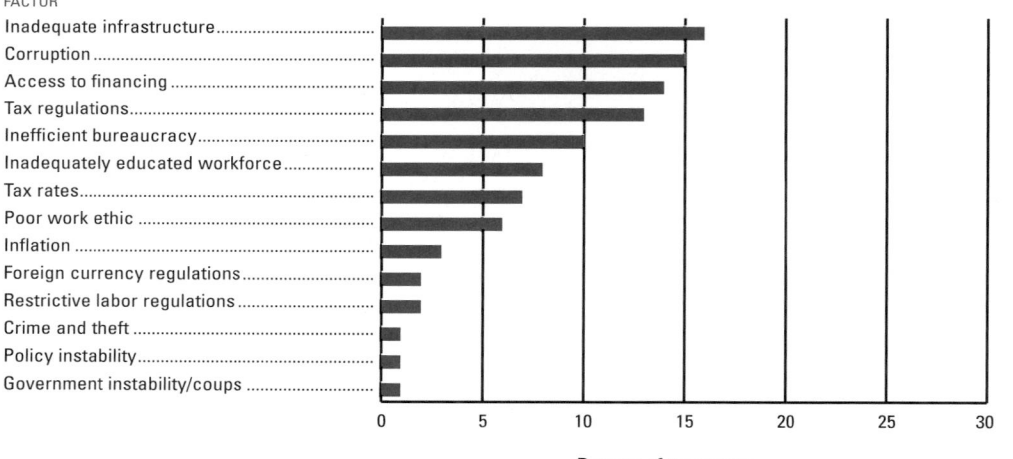

Note: From a list of 14 factors, respondents were asked to select the five most problematic for doing business in their country and to rank them between 1 (most problematic) and 5. The bars in the figure show the responses weighted according to their rankings.

Source: World Economic Forum, Executive Opinion Survey (2003)

National competitiveness balance sheet

NOTABLE COMPETITIVE ADVANTAGES

Growth Competitiveness Index — Rank/102

Macroeconomic Environment

2.01	Recession expectations	1
2.19	National savings rate, 2002	7
2.22	Interest rate spread, 2002	11
2.09	Access to credit	21
7.10	Public trust of politicians	25
2.03	Extent of distortive government subsidies	27

Public Institutions

6.08	Favoritism in decisions of government officials	31

Technology

3.02	Firm-level technology absorption	15
3.15	Government success in ICT promotion	15
3.03	FDI and technology transfer	17
3.06	Company spending on research and development	30
3.14	Government prioritization of ICT	34
3.08	University/industry research collaboration	40
3.04	Prevalence of foreign technology licensing	44

Business Competitiveness Index — Rank/95

Sophistication of Company Operations and Strategy

10.04	Capacity for innovation	27
3.06	Company spending on research and development	29
10.03	Extent of branding	32

Quality of the National Business Environment

8.05	Administrative burden for startups	5
3.09	Government procurement of advanced technology products	10
9.05	Decentralization of corporate activity	18

Other Indicators — Rank/102

10.23	Company promotion of volunteerism	2
2.15	Agricultural policy costs	6
10.21	Pay and productivity	8
6.15	Government effectiveness in reducing poverty	8
7.11	Prevalence of illegal political donations	10
4.11	Maternity laws' impact on hiring women	16
10.19	Flexibility of wage determination	17
7.12	Policy consequences of legal political donations	18
8.11	Focus of trade and industry associations	21
10.18	Hiring and firing practices	21
8.09	Wage equality of women in the workplace	22
6.16	Government effectiveness in reducing income inequality	22
8.03	Extent of market dominance	24
10.22	Charitable causes involvement	25
7.13	Pervasiveness of money laundering through banks	25

NOTABLE COMPETITIVE DISADVANTAGES

Growth Competitiveness Index — Rank/102

Macroeconomic Environment

2.18	Government surplus/deficit, 2002	71
2.17	Country credit rating, 2003	67
2.20	Inflation, 2002	56
7.08	Diversion of public funds	55
2.21	Real exchange rate, 2002	52

Public Institutions

7.01	Irregular payments in exports and imports	76
7.02	Irregular payments in public utilities	64
7.03	Irregular payments in tax collection	64
6.03	Property rights	62
6.17	Organized crime	61
6.01	Judicial independence	53

Technology

3.21	Internet hosts, 2002	95
3.13	Quality of competition in the ISP sector	85
3.19	Cellular telephones, 2002	85
3.23	Personal computers, 2002	81
3.22	Telephone lines, 2002	77
3.20	Internet users, 2002	76
3.18	Tertiary enrollment	75
3.17	Utility patents, 2002	72
3.01	Technological sophistication	71
3.12	Internet access in schools	71
3.16	Laws relating to ICT	54

Business Competitiveness Index — Rank/95

Sophistication of Company Operations and Strategy

10.07	Extent of marketing	84
10.15	Reliance on professional management	76
10.01	Nature of competitive advantage	73

Quality of the National Business Environment

2.12	Regulation of securities exchanges	84
3.19	Cellular telephones, 2002	81
6.09	Extent of bureaucratic red tape	81

Other Indicators — Rank/102

6.05	Freedom of the press	97
4.07	Business impact of HIV/AIDS	93
4.06	Business impact of tuberculosis	86
11.06	Compliance with environmental regulations	85
3.11	Availability of mobile or cellular telephones	85
4.08	Impact of HIV/AIDS on FDI	84
11.02	Water pollution regulations	82
7.05	Irregular payments in loan applications	81
4.05	Business impact of malaria	81
10.27	Strength of auditing and accounting standards	78
11.04	Chemical waste regulations	78
11.01	Air pollution regulations	76
2.02	Business costs of terrorism	75
11.03	Toxic waste disposal regulations	72
10.25	Availability of company financial information	72

383

Note: The Business Competitiveness Index applies different criteria for selecting a country's competitive advantages and disadvantages. Please refer to the section "How Country Profiles Work" for further details.

Zambia

Competitiveness Rankings

Growth Competitiveness Index Rank	88

Macroeconomic Environment Index Rank **97**
    Macroeconomic Stability Subindex Rank 96
    Government Waste Subindex Rank 84
    Country Credit Rating Rank 95

Public Institutions Index Rank **69**
    Contracts and Law Subindex Rank 56
    Corruption Subindex Rank..................................82

Technology Index Rank **90**
    Innovation Subindex Rank...................................92
    ICT Subindex Rank 87
    Technology Transfer Subindex Rank
    (out of 77 non-core innovators)........................55

Business Competitiveness Index Rank	79

**Sophistication of Company Operations
  and Strategy Rank** **78**

**Quality of the National Business
  Environment Rank** **80**

The Most Problematic Factors for Doing Business

FACTOR

Percent of responses

Note: From a list of 14 factors, respondents were asked to select the five most problematic for doing business in their country and to rank them between 1 (most problematic) and 5. The bars in the figure show the responses weighted according to their rankings.

Source: World Economic Forum, Executive Opinion Survey (2003)

National competitiveness balance sheet

NOTABLE COMPETITIVE ADVANTAGES	
Growth Competitiveness Index	**Rank/102**

Macroeconomic Environment

2.19	National savings rate, 2002	4

NOTABLE COMPETITIVE DISADVANTAGES	
Growth Competitiveness Index	**Rank/102**

Macroeconomic Environment

2.18	Government surplus/deficit, 2002	100
2.22	Interest rate spread, 2002	98
2.20	Inflation, 2002	96
2.17	Country credit rating, 2003	95
2.09	Access to credit	92
7.10	Public trust of politicians	83
2.01	Recession expectations	82
7.08	Diversion of public funds	81
2.21	Real exchange rate, 2002	71
2.03	Extent of distortive government subsidies	71

Public Institutions

7.02	Irregular payments in public utilities	89
7.03	Irregular payments in tax collection	72
7.01	Irregular payments in exports and imports	67
6.03	Property rights	64
6.08	Favoritism in decisions of government officials	62
6.01	Judicial independence	56
6.17	Organized crime	52

Technology

3.18	Tertiary enrollment	92
3.19	Cellular telephones, 2002	91
3.22	Telephone lines, 2002	90
3.20	Internet users, 2002	89
3.02	Firm-level technology absorption	88
3.12	Internet access in schools	88
3.08	University/industry research collaboration	84
3.01	Technological sophistication	83
3.23	Personal computers, 2002	82
3.14	Government prioritization of ICT	79
3.13	Quality of competition in the ISP sector	78
3.21	Internet hosts, 2002	76
3.16	Laws relating to ICT	72
3.17	Utility patents, 2002	72
3.06	Company spending on research and development	71
3.15	Government success in ICT promotion	67
3.03	FDI and technology transfer	52
3.04	Prevalence of foreign technology licensing	52

Business Competitiveness Index	Rank/95

Sophistication of Company Operations and Strategy

10.01	Nature of competitive advantage	33
10.15	Reliance on professional management	53
10.04	Capacity for innovation	61

Quality of the National Business Environment

10.26	Foreign ownership restrictions	10
10.24	Protection of minority shareholders' interests	34
8.05	Administrative burden for startups	39

Other Indicators	Rank/102

4.10	Maternity leave legislation	11
8.09	Wage equality of women in the workplace	12
4.11	Maternity laws' impact on hiring women	15
6.07	Transparency of government policymaking	21
2.02	Business costs of terrorism	22
6.11	Efficiency of the tax system	26
10.18	Hiring and firing practices	28
6.10	Effectiveness of law-making bodies	38
11.11	Effects of compliance on business	38
10.19	Flexibility of wage determination	39
8.11	Focus of trade and industry associations	41
11.09	Flexibility of regulations	43
11.10	Consistency of regulation enforcement	43

Business Competitiveness Index	Rank/95

Sophistication of Company Operations and Strategy

10.02	Value chain presence	93
10.03	Extent of branding	92
10.07	Extent of marketing	83

Quality of the National Business Environment

2.07	Ease of access to loans	93
9.03	Local supplier quality	93
2.03	Extent of distortive government subsidies	91

Other Indicators	Rank/102

4.06	Business impact of tuberculosis	101
4.07	Business impact of HIV/AIDS	99
4.09	Brain drain	99
4.05	Business impact of malaria	96
4.08	Impact of HIV/AIDS on FDI	95
7.13	Pervasiveness of money laundering through banks	90
3.11	Availability of mobile or cellular telephones	88
10.21	Pay and productivity	87
3.07	Subsidies and tax credits for firm-level research and development	86
10.23	Company promotion of volunteerism	85
7.14	Pervasiveness of money laundering through non-bank channels	83

Note: The Business Competitiveness Index applies different criteria for selecting a country's competitive advantages and disadvantages.
Please refer to the section "How Country Profiles Work" for further details.

385

Zimbabwe

Competitiveness Rankings

Growth Competitiveness Index Rank	97

Macroeconomic Environment Index Rank **102**
   Macroeconomic Stability Subindex Rank 101
   Government Waste Subindex Rank 100
   Country Credit Rating Rank 100

Public Institutions Index Rank...**90**
   Contracts and Law Subindex Rank 93
   Corruption Subindex Rank...................................84

Technology Index Rank **75**
   Innovation Subindex Rank...................................87
   ICT Subindex Rank 80
   Technology Transfer Subindex Rank
   (out of 77 non-core innovators) 41

Business Competitiveness Index Rank	75

**Sophistication of Company Operations
  and Strategy Rank** **69**

**Quality of the National Business
  Environment Rank** **78**

The Most Problematic Factors for Doing Business

FACTOR
- Inflation
- Foreign currency regulations
- Policy instability
- Corruption
- Government instability/coups
- Inefficient bureaucracy
- Crime and theft
- Restrictive labor regulations
- Inadequate infrastructure
- Access to financing
- Poor work ethic
- Tax regulations
- Tax rates
- Inadequately educated workforce

Percent of responses (0, 5, 10, 15, 20, 25, 30)

Note: From a list of 14 factors, respondents were asked to select the five most problematic for doing business in their country and to rank them between 1 (most problematic) and 5. The bars in the figure show the responses weighted according to their rankings.

Source: World Economic Forum, Executive Opinion Survey (2003)

National competitiveness balance sheet

NOTABLE COMPETITIVE ADVANTAGES	
Growth Competitiveness Index	**Rank/102**

Macroeconomic Environment

2.09	Access to credit	30

Technology

3.04	Prevalence of foreign technology licensing	25

NOTABLE COMPETITIVE DISADVANTAGES	
Growth Competitiveness Index	**Rank/102**

Macroeconomic Environment

2.01	Recession expectations	102
2.20	Inflation, 2002	102
2.21	Real exchange rate, 2002	102
2.03	Extent of distortive government subsidies	101
2.17	Country credit rating, 2003	100
7.10	Public trust of politicians	97
2.22	Interest rate spread, 2002	96
2.18	Government surplus/deficit, 2002	95
7.08	Diversion of public funds	94
2.19	National savings rate, 2002	92

Public Institutions

6.01	Judicial independence	97
6.08	Favoritism in decisions of government officials	94
6.03	Property rights	93
7.02	Irregular payments in public utilities	93
7.01	Irregular payments in exports and imports	84
6.17	Organized crime	64
7.03	Irregular payments in tax collection	56

Technology

3.14	Government prioritization of ICT	99
3.15	Government success in ICT promotion	97
3.13	Quality of competition in the ISP sector	87
3.18	Tertiary enrollment	86
3.22	Telephone lines, 2002	85
3.19	Cellular telephones, 2002	84
3.16	Laws relating to ICT	82
3.12	Internet access in schools	81
3.02	Firm-level technology absorption	80
3.08	University/industry research collaboration	77
3.06	Company spending on research and development	72
3.21	Internet hosts, 2002	71
3.01	Technological sophistication	69
3.17	Utility patents, 2002	63
3.20	Internet users, 2002	62
3.03	FDI and technology transfer	53
3.23	Personal computers, 2002	53

Business Competitiveness Index	Rank/95

Sophistication of Company Operations and Strategy

10.14	Extent of incentive compensation	20
10.15	Reliance on professional management	29
10.12	Extent of staff training	34

Quality of the National Business Environment

2.11	Local equity market access	2
8.07	Prevalence of mergers and acquisitions	17
10.24	Protection of minority shareholders' interests	27

Other Indicators	Rank/102

4.10	Maternity leave legislation	18
10.25	Availability of company financial information	20
10.27	Strength of auditing and accounting standards	28
6.11	Efficiency of the tax system	33
10.22	Charitable causes involvement	33
8.10	Regional disparities in quality of business environment	39
11.12	Political context of environmental gains	45
7.12	Policy consequences of legal political donations	48

Business Competitiveness Index	Rank/95

Sophistication of Company Operations and Strategy

10.01	Nature of competitive advantage	92
10.09	Control of international distribution	89
10.02	Value chain presence	87

Quality of the National Business Environment

2.03	Extent of distortive government subsidies	94
10.26	Foreign ownership restrictions	94
6.12	Centralization of economic policymaking	93

Other Indicators	Rank/102

4.06	Business impact of tuberculosis	102
4.07	Business impact of HIV/AIDS	102
4.04	Disparity in healthcare quality	102
6.05	Freedom of the press	102
2.15	Agricultural policy costs	102
4.09	Brain drain	101
10.21	Pay and productivity	101
8.03	Extent of market dominance	101
2.04	Extent of distortive government intervention	101
2.10	Government intervention in corporate investment	100
10.18	Hiring and firing practices	100
6.16	Government effectiveness in reducing income inequality	99
10.19	Flexibility of wage determination	99

Note: The Business Competitiveness Index applies different criteria for selecting a country's competitive advantages and disadvantages. Please refer to the section "How Country Profiles Work" for further details.

3.3: Data Tables

How data tables work

The following pages provide detailed data for all 102 economies included in the *Global Competitiveness Report 2003–2004*. The data are organized into eleven categories:

I   Aggregate Country Performance Indicators

II   Macroeconomic Environment

III   Technology: Innovation and Diffusion

IV   Human Resources: Education, Health, and Labor

V   General Infrastructure

VI   Public Institutions: Contracts and Law

VII   Public Institutions: Corruption

VIII   Domestic Competition

IX   Cluster Development

X   Company Operations and Strategy

XI   Environment

Two types of variables are presented in these tables: (1) average country responses to questions included in the World Economic Forum's Executive Opinion Survey, conducted in the early months of 2003; and (2) "hard data" obtained from a variety of sources.

❶ Survey data

Data yielded from the Executive Opinion Survey are presented with blue-colored bar graphs. In sections including both hard and Survey data, the Survey data are presented first. For each Survey variable, the original question is included in the description at the top of the page, with minor abbreviations made in some instances due to space constraints. As outlined in Chapter 3.1 of this *Report*, in most cases questions asked for responses on a scale of 1 to 7, where an answer of 1 corresponds to one end of a spectrum of responses and an answer of 7 corresponds to the other end. We report the average response for each country. Variable 2.01, for example, asks about respondents' recession expectations at the time of the Survey, with higher scores corresponding to a lower perceived likelihood of recession. The score noted for Vietnam is 5.2, indicating the arithmetic mean of responses to this question from executives in Vietnam, and a relatively low average expectation of recession.

❷ A dotted line on the graph indicates the mean score across the sample of 102 countries. We report country responses rounded to a single decimal point, but use the exact figures to determine rankings and for graphs. In the case of variable 2.01, for example, Vietnam's average score was 5.211, Thailand's was 5.177, Latvia's was 5.163, and Australia's was 5.150. These economies are therefore ranked first through fourth respectively, even though they are all listed with the same rounded score of 5.2. In other cases, ties are true, so shared rankings are indicated accordingly. For example, still in the case of variable 2.01, the average scores for Greece and Tunisia are the same down to 14 decimal points, so here both countries are ranked 38th.

❸ Just to the right of each country's mean score, we have also included the standard deviation of the responses. This gives an indication of how closely or widely the individual responses are spread around the mean country score. In other words, this provides information on the extent of agreement or disagreement on the question within the given country. Still looking at variable 2.01, we see that the standard deviation of the responses from Vietnam is 1.0, a measure of the fluctuation of the responses around the mean score of 5.2.

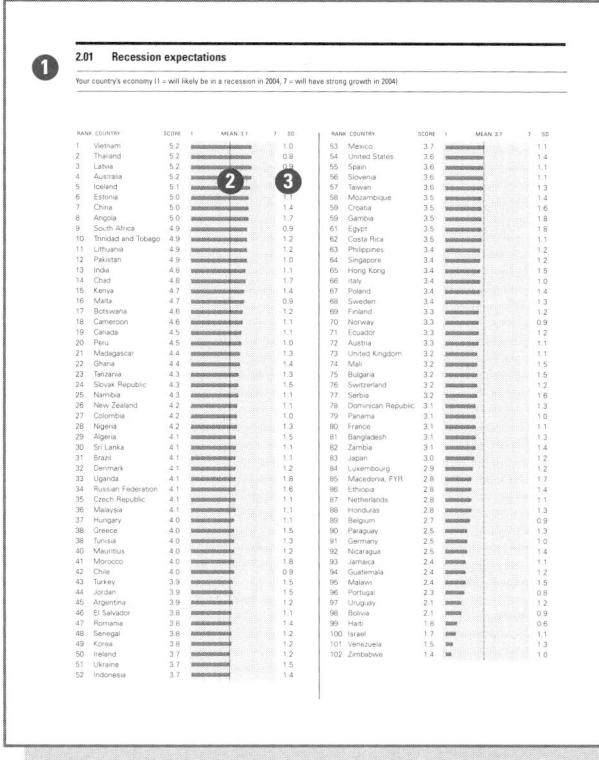

Hard data

Data originating not from the Executive Opinion Survey but from other publicly available sources are presented in black bar graphs and are followed on each page with a brief reference to the source from which they were obtained. More detailed citation information can be found in the Technical Notes and Sources section at the end of the *Report*. Here again, true ties are indicated by shared rankings where relevant.

Many of these variables, although presented as hard data, still depend to a great extent on surveying techniques. Indeed, even GDP statistics rely heavily on surveying methodologies.

Index of tables

1.01 Total GDP, 2002

Gross Domestic Product in billions of US Dollars, 2002

RANK	COUNTRY	HARD DATA		RANK	COUNTRY	HARD DATA
1	United States	10,445.63		53	Morocco	37.15
2	Japan	3,992.22		54	Vietnam	34.08
3	Germany	1,990.26		55	Ecuador	24.51
4	United Kingdom	1,557.24		56	Slovak Republic	23.69
5	France	1,422.94		57	Dominican Republic	21.82
6	China	1,237.15		58	Tunisia	21.25
7	Italy	1,187.96		59	Croatia	21.22
8	Canada	727.78		60	Slovenia	21.21
9	Spain	655.11		61	Luxembourg	20.60
10	Mexico	641.53		62	Guatemala	19.65
11	India	502.42		63	Zimbabwe	19.30
12	Korea	461.48		64	Costa Rica	16.92
13	Brazil	448.67		65	Sri Lanka	16.43
14	Netherlands	419.85		66	Bulgaria	16.23
15	Australia	399.09		67	El Salvador	14.51
16	Russian Federation	346.57		68	Serbia	13.00
17	Taiwan	281.51		69	Lithuania	12.68
18	Switzerland	267.48		70	Kenya	11.76
19	Belgium	246.79		71	Angola	11.63
20	Sweden	240.31		72	Panama	11.24
21	Austria	206.20		73	Uruguay	9.88
22	Norway	189.74		74	Tanzania	9.39
23	Poland	189.16		75	Jordan	9.30
24	Turkey	182.83		76	Cameroon	9.04
25	Indonesia	173.22		77	Trinidad and Tobago	9.03
26	Denmark	172.38		78	Iceland	8.67
27	Hong Kong SAR	162.98		79	Latvia	8.40
28	Greece	133.24		80	Bolivia	8.07
29	Finland	132.23		81	Jamaica	7.78
30	Thailand	126.41		82	Paraguay	7.14
31	Portugal	122.10		83	Honduras	6.58
32	Ireland	121.80		84	Estonia	6.07
33	South Africa	104.77		85	Ghana	6.06
34	Argentina	103.01		86	Ethiopia	5.99
35	Israel	102.71		87	Uganda	5.87
36	Malaysia	95.16		88	Senegal	5.11
37	Venezuela	94.34		89	Botswana	5.04
38	Singapore	90.24		90	Mauritius	4.53
39	Egypt	85.55		91	Madagascar	4.48
40	Philippines	77.05		92	Malta	3.92
41	Colombia	71.22		93	Mozambique	3.92
42	Czech Republic	70.12		94	Macedonia, FYR	3.80
43	Pakistan	65.14		95	Zambia	3.74
44	Chile	64.45		96	Haiti	3.59
45	Hungary	64.00		97	Mali	3.09
46	New Zealand	58.35		98	Namibia	2.87
47	Peru	54.82		99	Nicaragua	2.57
48	Algeria	54.15		100	Chad	1.94
49	Bangladesh	46.91		101	Malawi	1.93
50	Romania	42.83		102	Gambia	0.35
51	Nigeria	42.73				
52	Ukraine	41.41				

SOURCE: IMF World Economic Outlook Database, April 2003

1.02 Total population, 2002

Population in millions, 2002

RANK	COUNTRY	HARD DATA		RANK	COUNTRY	HARD DATA
1	China	1,294.4		53	Malawi	11.8
2	India	1,041.1		54	Zambia	10.9
3	United States	288.5		55	Greece	10.6
4	Indonesia	217.5		56	Serbia*	10.5
5	Brazil	174.7		57	Belgium	10.3
6	Pakistan	148.7		57	Czech Republic	10.3
7	Russian Federation	143.8		59	Portugal	10.0
8	Bangladesh	143.4		60	Hungary	9.9
9	Japan	127.5		60	Senegal	9.9
10	Nigeria	120.0		62	Tunisia	9.7
11	Mexico	101.8		63	Sweden	8.8
12	Germany	82.0		64	Bolivia	8.7
13	Vietnam	80.2		65	Dominican Republic	8.6
14	Philippines	78.6		66	Chad	8.4
15	Egypt	70.3		66	Haiti	8.4
16	Turkey	68.6		68	Austria	8.1
17	Ethiopia	66.0		69	Bulgaria	7.8
18	Thailand	64.3		70	Switzerland	7.2
19	France	59.7		71	Hong Kong SAR	7.0
19	United Kingdom	59.7		72	Honduras	6.7
21	Italy	57.4		73	El Salvador	6.5
22	Ukraine	48.7		74	Israel	6.3
23	Korea	47.4		75	Paraguay	5.8
24	South Africa	44.2		76	Slovak Republic	5.4
25	Colombia	43.5		77	Denmark	5.3
26	Spain	39.9		77	Nicaragua	5.3
27	Poland	38.5		79	Finland	5.2
28	Argentina	37.9		79	Jordan	5.2
29	Tanzania	36.8		81	Croatia	4.7
30	Kenya	31.9		82	Norway	4.5
31	Algeria	31.4		83	Costa Rica	4.2
32	Canada	31.3		83	Singapore	4.2
33	Morocco	31.0		85	Ireland	3.9
34	Peru	26.5		86	New Zealand	3.8
35	Venezuela	25.1		87	Lithuania	3.7
36	Uganda	24.8		88	Uruguay	3.4
37	Malaysia	23.0		89	Panama	2.9
38	Taiwan	22.5		90	Jamaica	2.6
39	Romania	22.3		91	Latvia	2.4
40	Ghana	20.2		92	Macedonia, FYR	2.1
41	Australia	19.5		93	Slovenia	2.0
42	Sri Lanka	19.3		94	Namibia	1.8
43	Mozambique	19.0		95	Botswana	1.6
44	Madagascar	16.9		96	Estonia	1.4
45	Netherlands	16.0		96	Gambia	1.4
46	Chile	15.6		98	Trinidad and Tobago	1.3
47	Cameroon	15.5		99	Mauritius	1.2
48	Angola	13.9		100	Luxembourg	0.4
49	Ecuador	13.1		100	Malta	0.4
49	Zimbabwe	13.1		102	Iceland	0.3
51	Guatemala	12.0				
51	Mali	12.0				

SOURCE: UNFPA *State of the World Population 2002*

*Value for Serbia and Montenegro

1.03   GDP per capita (PPP), 2002

Gross Domestic Product per capita in US dollars, measured at Purchasing Power Parity, 2002

RANK	COUNTRY	HARD DATA		RANK	COUNTRY	HARD DATA
1	Luxembourg	56,546		53	Tunisia	6,579
2	Norway	36,047		54	Namibia	6,410
3	United States	35,158		55	Romania	6,326
4	Ireland	32,960		56	Macedonia, FYR	6,262
5	Denmark	29,975		57	Dominican Republic	6,197
6	Iceland	29,614		58	Turkey	6,176
7	Canada	28,699		59	Colombia	6,068
8	Austria	28,611		60	Panama	5,972
9	Switzerland	28,359		61	Algeria	5,536
10	Australia	27,756		62	Venezuela	5,226
11	Netherlands	27,275		63	Peru	4,924
12	Belgium	26,695		64	Ukraine	4,714
13	Germany	26,324		65	El Salvador	4,675
14	Hong Kong SAR	26,235		66	China	4,475
15	France	26,151		67	Paraguay	4,419
16	Finland	25,859		68	Jordan	4,106
17	United Kingdom	25,672		69	Philippines	4,021
18	Japan	25,650		70	Guatemala	3,927
19	Italy	25,570		71	Jamaica	3,774
20	Sweden	25,315		72	Morocco	3,767
21	Taiwan	23,420		73	Egypt	3,701
22	Singapore	23,393		74	Sri Lanka	3,447
23	Spain	20,697		75	Ecuador	3,357
24	New Zealand	20,455		76	Serbia	3,270
25	Israel	19,382		77	Indonesia	3,138
26	Greece	18,184		78	India	2,571
27	Portugal	17,808		79	Honduras	2,520
28	Slovenia	17,748		80	Nicaragua	2,510
29	Malta	17,344		81	Bolivia	2,360
30	Korea	16,465		82	Vietnam	2,240
31	Czech Republic	15,148		83	Angola	2,053
32	Hungary	13,129		84	Ghana	2,050
33	Slovak Republic	12,426		85	Pakistan	2,014
34	Uruguay	12,118		86	Zimbabwe	1,993
35	Estonia	11,712		87	Bangladesh	1,736
36	Argentina	10,594		88	Gambia	1,723
37	Mauritius	10,530		89	Cameroon	1,712
38	Poland	10,187		90	Haiti	1,578
39	South Africa	10,132		91	Senegal	1,535
40	Lithuania	10,015		92	Uganda	1,354
41	Croatia	9,967		93	Mozambique	1,237
42	Chile	9,561		94	Chad	1,008
43	Trinidad and Tobago	9,114		95	Kenya	992
44	Latvia	8,965		96	Mali	878
45	Malaysia	8,922		97	Nigeria	851
46	Mexico	8,707		98	Zambia	806
47	Costa Rica	8,470		99	Madagascar	735
48	Botswana	8,244		100	Ethiopia	724
49	Russian Federation	7,926		101	Malawi	586
50	Brazil	7,516		102	Tanzania	557
51	Bulgaria	6,909				
52	Thailand	6,788				

SOURCES: International Comparison Program (ICP) of The World Bank, Economist Intelligence Unit, and authors' calculations

1.04 Change in GDP per capita relative to the United States, 1995 to 2002

Average annual percentage change in ratio of GDP per capita (PPP) relative to US GDP per capita from 1995 to 2002

RANK	COUNTRY	HARD DATA
1	Mozambique	6.63
2	Ireland	5.76
3	Estonia	5.35
4	Latvia	5.20
5	Lithuania	5.20
6	Luxembourg	4.93
7	China	4.24
8	Croatia	4.19
9	Uruguay	2.77
10	Poland	2.65
11	Vietnam	2.52
12	Macedonia, FYR	2.23
13	Slovak Republic	2.00
14	Norway	1.89
15	Dominican Republic	1.81
16	Botswana	1.76
17	India	1.47
18	Mauritius	1.45
19	Hungary	1.35
20	Taiwan	1.32
21	Greece	1.25
22	Uganda	1.19
23	Bangladesh	1.12
24	Finland	1.09
25	Slovenia	1.07
26	Spain	1.06
27	Tunisia	0.92
28	Malta	0.85
29	Mali	0.53
30	Portugal	0.52
31	Netherlands	0.51
32	United Kingdom	0.48
33	Trinidad and Tobago	0.46
34	Ethiopia	0.44
35	Australia	0.42
36	Denmark	0.29
37	Iceland	0.18
38	Austria	0.16
39	Egypt	0.11
40	Costa Rica	0.03
41	United States	0.00
42	France	−0.08
43	Sri Lanka	−0.12
44	Sweden	−0.13
45	Ukraine	−0.13
46	Chile	−0.17
47	Ghana	−0.28
48	Italy	−0.28
49	Canada	−0.31
50	Chad	−0.35
51	Bulgaria	−0.37
52	Czech Republic	−0.40

RANK	COUNTRY	HARD DATA
53	Singapore	−0.46
54	Mexico	−0.49
55	Morocco	−0.50
56	Korea	−0.60
57	Germany	−0.62
58	Namibia	−0.63
59	Malaysia	−0.65
60	Gambia	−0.69
61	Cameroon	−0.71
62	Senegal	−0.72
63	Tanzania	−0.80
64	Algeria	−0.81
65	South Africa	−0.86
66	Hong Kong SAR	−0.87
67	Belgium	−0.94
68	New Zealand	−1.05
69	El Salvador	−1.16
70	Panama	−1.19
71	Guatemala	−1.22
72	Nicaragua	−1.31
73	Pakistan	−1.34
74	Haiti	−1.55
75	Brazil	−1.61
76	Peru	−1.61
77	Israel	−1.68
78	Philippines	−1.69
79	Russian Federation	−1.79
80	Switzerland	−1.89
81	Thailand	−2.00
82	Indonesia	−2.10
83	Malawi	−2.10
84	Bolivia	−2.16
85	Zambia	−2.21
86	Japan	−2.25
87	Ecuador	−2.52
88	Turkey	−2.54
89	Honduras	−2.56
90	Jordan	−2.56
91	Nigeria	−2.70
92	Angola	−3.06
93	Jamaica	−3.12
94	Colombia	−3.46
95	Argentina	−3.56
96	Romania	−3.58
97	Paraguay	−3.66
98	Kenya	−3.69
99	Madagascar	−4.27
100	Venezuela	−5.06
101	Zimbabwe	−6.41
	Serbia	n/a

SOURCES: International Comparison Program (ICP) of The World Bank, Economist Intelligence Unit, and authors' calculations

2.01 Recession expectations

Your country's economy (1 = will likely be in a recession in 2004, 7 = will have strong growth in 2004)

RANK	COUNTRY	SCORE	1 MEAN: 3.7 7	SD	RANK	COUNTRY	SCORE	1 MEAN: 3.7 7	SD
1	Vietnam	5.2		1.0	53	Mexico	3.7		1.1
2	Thailand	5.2		0.8	54	United States	3.6		1.4
3	Latvia	5.2		0.9	55	Spain	3.6		1.1
4	Australia	5.2		1.0	56	Slovenia	3.6		1.1
5	Iceland	5.1		1.3	57	Taiwan	3.6		1.3
6	Estonia	5.0		1.1	58	Mozambique	3.5		1.4
7	China	5.0		1.4	59	Croatia	3.5		1.6
8	Angola	5.0		1.7	59	Gambia	3.5		1.8
9	South Africa	4.9		0.9	61	Egypt	3.5		1.8
10	Trinidad and Tobago	4.9		1.2	62	Costa Rica	3.5		1.1
11	Lithuania	4.9		1.2	63	Philippines	3.4		1.2
12	Pakistan	4.9		1.0	64	Singapore	3.4		1.2
13	India	4.8		1.1	65	Hong Kong SAR	3.4		1.5
14	Chad	4.8		1.7	66	Italy	3.4		1.0
15	Kenya	4.7		1.4	67	Poland	3.4		1.4
16	Malta	4.7		0.9	68	Sweden	3.4		1.3
17	Botswana	4.6		1.2	69	Finland	3.3		1.2
18	Cameroon	4.6		1.1	70	Norway	3.3		0.9
19	Canada	4.5		1.1	71	Ecuador	3.3		1.2
20	Peru	4.5		1.0	72	Austria	3.3		1.1
21	Madagascar	4.4		1.3	73	United Kingdom	3.2		1.1
22	Ghana	4.4		1.4	74	Mali	3.2		1.5
23	Tanzania	4.3		1.3	75	Bulgaria	3.2		1.5
24	Slovak Republic	4.3		1.5	76	Switzerland	3.2		1.2
25	Namibia	4.3		1.1	77	Serbia	3.2		1.6
26	New Zealand	4.2		1.1	78	Dominican Republic	3.1		1.3
27	Colombia	4.2		1.0	79	Panama	3.1		1.0
28	Nigeria	4.2		1.3	80	France	3.1		1.1
29	Algeria	4.1		1.5	81	Bangladesh	3.1		1.3
30	Sri Lanka	4.1		1.1	82	Zambia	3.1		1.4
31	Brazil	4.1		1.1	83	Japan	3.0		1.2
32	Denmark	4.1		1.2	84	Luxembourg	2.9		1.2
33	Uganda	4.1		1.8	85	Macedonia, FYR	2.8		1.7
34	Russian Federation	4.1		1.6	86	Ethiopia	2.8		1.4
35	Czech Republic	4.1		1.1	87	Netherlands	2.8		1.1
36	Malaysia	4.1		1.1	88	Honduras	2.8		1.3
37	Hungary	4.0		1.1	89	Belgium	2.7		0.9
38	Greece	4.0		1.5	90	Paraguay	2.5		1.3
38	Tunisia	4.0		1.3	91	Germany	2.5		1.0
40	Mauritius	4.0		1.2	92	Nicaragua	2.5		1.4
41	Morocco	4.0		1.8	93	Jamaica	2.4		1.1
42	Chile	4.0		0.9	94	Guatemala	2.4		1.2
43	Turkey	3.9		1.5	95	Malawi	2.4		1.5
44	Jordan	3.9		1.5	96	Portugal	2.3		0.8
45	Argentina	3.9		1.2	97	Uruguay	2.1		1.2
46	El Salvador	3.8		1.1	98	Bolivia	2.1		0.9
47	Romania	3.8		1.4	99	Haiti	1.8		0.6
48	Senegal	3.8		1.2	100	Israel	1.7		1.1
49	Korea	3.8		1.2	101	Venezuela	1.5		1.3
50	Ireland	3.7		1.2	102	Zimbabwe	1.4		1.0
51	Ukraine	3.7		1.5					
52	Indonesia	3.7		1.4					

2.02   Business costs of terrorism

The threat of terrorism in your country (1 = imposes significant costs on business, 7 = does not impose significant costs on business)

RANK	COUNTRY	SCORE	1 MEAN: 4.9 7	SD
1	Uruguay	6.6		0.9
2	Finland	6.3		1.3
3	Estonia	6.3		1.5
4	Portugal	6.2		1.3
5	Sweden	6.1		1.4
6	Denmark	6.0		1.1
7	Dominican Republic	5.9		1.4
8	Hungary	5.9		1.4
9	Luxembourg	5.8		1.3
10	Iceland	5.8		2.0
11	Chile	5.7		1.7
12	Switzerland	5.7		1.3
13	Lithuania	5.7		1.7
14	Hong Kong SAR	5.7		1.6
15	Argentina	5.7		1.7
16	Gambia	5.6		2.1
17	Thailand	5.6		1.4
18	Malta	5.6		1.9
19	Tunisia	5.6		1.9
20	Costa Rica	5.6		1.8
21	Brazil	5.6		1.7
22	Zambia	5.6		1.7
23	Austria	5.5		1.6
24	Paraguay	5.5		1.7
25	Romania	5.5		1.8
26	Latvia	5.4		1.3
27	Jordan	5.4		1.7
28	Botswana	5.4		2.0
29	Belgium	5.4		1.5
30	Ukraine	5.4		1.9
31	Mauritius	5.4		1.6
32	South Africa	5.4		1.6
33	Slovenia	5.4		1.6
34	Madagascar	5.4		1.8
35	Norway	5.3		1.9
35	Malaysia	5.3		1.6
37	Jamaica	5.3		1.9
38	Ireland	5.3		1.7
39	Slovak Republic	5.3		1.8
40	Netherlands	5.3		1.5
41	Mozambique	5.2		1.8
42	New Zealand	5.2		1.8
43	Mexico	5.2		1.6
44	Nigeria	5.2		1.8
45	Mali	5.1		2.2
46	Ghana	5.1		2.0
47	Spain	5.1		1.9
48	Namibia	5.1		1.7
49	Greece	5.1		1.8
50	Poland	5.1		1.8
51	Taiwan	5.1		1.9
52	France	5.1		1.5

RANK	COUNTRY	SCORE	1 MEAN: 4.9 7	SD
53	Croatia	5.1		2.2
54	Panama	5.1		1.9
55	Korea	5.1		1.7
56	Nicaragua	5.0		1.9
57	Morocco	5.0		2.2
57	Italy	5.0		1.5
59	Malawi	5.0		2.0
60	Czech Republic	4.9		1.6
61	Bolivia	4.9		2.0
62	Turkey	4.9		1.7
63	Angola	4.9		2.2
64	Peru	4.9		1.6
65	China	4.8		1.8
66	Canada	4.7		1.6
67	Ecuador	4.7		1.6
68	Russian Federation	4.6		1.9
69	Trinidad and Tobago	4.6		1.6
70	Bulgaria	4.5		1.7
71	Ethiopia	4.5		2.1
72	Senegal	4.5		1.9
73	Honduras	4.5		1.9
74	Singapore	4.5		1.7
75	Vietnam	4.5		1.7
76	Haiti	4.5		2.2
77	Serbia	4.4		2.1
78	Cameroon	4.4		2.2
79	India	4.3		1.5
80	El Salvador	4.3		2.1
81	Zimbabwe	4.2		2.1
82	Australia	4.2		1.4
83	Venezuela	4.1		1.7
84	Indonesia	4.1		1.6
85	Japan	4.0		1.5
86	Germany	4.0		1.6
87	United Kingdom	4.0		1.7
88	Pakistan	3.9		1.7
89	Egypt	3.8		2.1
90	Bangladesh	3.8		2.1
91	Guatemala	3.7		1.9
92	Chad	3.6		2.1
93	United States	3.5		1.5
94	Tanzania	3.5		1.9
95	Algeria	3.4		1.8
96	Kenya	3.1		1.7
97	Sri Lanka	3.1		1.5
98	Uganda	3.0		1.7
99	Macedonia, FYR	2.7		1.8
100	Philippines	2.5		1.2
101	Colombia	2.1		1.4
102	Israel	1.7		0.9

2.03 Extent of distortive government subsidies

Government subsidies to business in your country (1 = keep uncompetitive industries alive artificially, 7 = improve productivity of industries)

RANK	COUNTRY	SCORE	1 MEAN: 3.4 7	SD		RANK	COUNTRY	SCORE	1 MEAN: 3.4 7	SD
1	Singapore	5.5		1.0		53	Lithuania	3.3		1.2
2	Luxembourg	5.1		1.2		54	Portugal	3.3		1.1
3	Finland	5.0		1.2		55	Slovak Republic	3.3		1.4
4	Tunisia	4.6		1.7		56	Peru	3.3		1.2
5	Latvia	4.4		1.4		57	Norway	3.3		1.4
6	Thailand	4.4		1.0		58	Pakistan	3.2		1.4
7	Denmark	4.4		1.0		59	Dominican Republic	3.2		1.2
8	Netherlands	4.4		1.2		60	Kenya	3.2		1.4
9	Australia	4.3		1.3		61	Cameroon	3.2		1.4
10	Chile	4.3		1.3		62	Madagascar	3.2		1.4
11	Estonia	4.3		1.4		63	Nicaragua	3.1		1.3
12	Hong Kong SAR	4.3		1.4		64	Trinidad and Tobago	3.1		1.4
13	Israel	4.3		1.1		65	France	3.1		1.3
14	Hungary	4.2		1.3		66	Mali	3.1		1.5
15	United Kingdom	4.1		1.0		67	India	3.0		1.4
16	Iceland	4.1		1.1		68	Uruguay	3.0		1.3
17	Uganda	4.1		1.8		69	Mozambique	3.0		1.5
18	South Africa	4.1		1.4		70	Guatemala	3.0		1.2
19	Gambia	4.1		2.0		71	Zambia	2.9		1.3
20	Ghana	4.0		1.5		72	Switzerland	2.9		1.4
21	Taiwan	4.0		1.1		73	Nigeria	2.9		1.5
22	Morocco	4.0		1.7		74	Serbia	2.9		1.5
23	Korea	4.0		1.0		75	Bolivia	2.9		1.2
24	Malaysia	4.0		1.4		76	Argentina	2.9		1.1
25	Brazil	4.0		1.2		77	Russian Federation	2.9		1.4
26	Sweden	4.0		1.2		78	Philippines	2.8		1.2
27	Vietnam	3.9		1.6		79	Malawi	2.8		1.4
28	Jordan	3.9		1.4		80	Czech Republic	2.8		1.2
29	China	3.8		1.4		81	Panama	2.8		1.3
30	Indonesia	3.8		1.7		82	Chad	2.8		1.5
31	Slovenia	3.8		1.4		83	Croatia	2.8		1.4
32	Ireland	3.8		1.4		84	Jamaica	2.7		1.3
33	United States	3.8		1.3		85	Poland	2.7		1.4
34	New Zealand	3.7		1.4		86	Haiti	2.7		1.3
35	Tanzania	3.7		1.4		87	Turkey	2.7		1.1
36	Austria	3.7		1.3		88	Ecuador	2.7		1.2
37	Italy	3.7		1.1		89	Bulgaria	2.6		1.2
38	Botswana	3.6		1.6		90	Japan	2.6		1.4
39	Spain	3.6		1.1		91	Ethiopia	2.6		1.4
40	Egypt	3.6		1.6		92	Bangladesh	2.6		1.3
41	Malta	3.5		1.5		93	Paraguay	2.5		1.4
42	Sri Lanka	3.5		1.4		94	Honduras	2.5		1.3
43	Senegal	3.5		0.9		95	Algeria	2.5		1.3
44	El Salvador	3.5		1.2		96	Venezuela	2.5		1.1
45	Mauritius	3.5		1.3		97	Ukraine	2.4		1.1
46	Costa Rica	3.4		1.3		98	Angola	2.4		1.3
47	Colombia	3.4		1.3		99	Macedonia, FYR	2.4		1.6
48	Canada	3.4		1.3		100	Germany	2.3		1.2
49	Greece	3.4		1.4		101	Zimbabwe	2.2		1.2
50	Belgium	3.4		1.2		102	Romania	2.0		1.3
51	Namibia	3.4		1.5						
52	Mexico	3.4		1.4						

2.04   Extent of distortive government intervention

The impact of government intervention on fair competition in your economy is (1 = distorting, 7 = not distorting)

RANK	COUNTRY	SCORE	1 MEAN: 3.6 7	SD
1	Luxembourg	5.3		1.2
2	Denmark	5.1		1.3
3	Finland	5.1		1.5
4	Singapore	4.9		1.4
5	Iceland	4.9		1.3
6	Netherlands	4.8		1.4
7	Australia	4.8		1.5
8	United States	4.8		1.6
9	Estonia	4.7		1.5
10	Tunisia	4.7		1.5
11	Hong Kong SAR	4.7		1.8
12	United Kingdom	4.6		1.5
13	Chile	4.6		1.6
14	Sweden	4.5		1.6
15	El Salvador	4.3		1.7
16	Taiwan	4.3		1.2
17	Jordan	4.3		1.5
18	Spain	4.3		1.5
19	Thailand	4.2		1.2
20	Ghana	4.2		1.6
21	Latvia	4.2		1.3
22	Botswana	4.2		1.6
23	Malta	4.2		1.4
24	South Africa	4.1		1.4
25	Israel	4.1		1.2
26	Gambia	4.1		2.0
27	New Zealand	4.1		1.6
28	Malaysia	4.1		1.4
29	Lithuania	4.0		1.6
30	Hungary	4.0		1.4
31	Vietnam	4.0		1.4
32	Switzerland	4.0		1.6
33	Mexico	4.0		1.5
34	Brazil	4.0		1.3
35	Slovenia	3.9		1.3
36	Morocco	3.9		1.8
37	Sri Lanka	3.9		1.3
38	Colombia	3.9		1.5
39	Italy	3.9		1.3
40	Korea	3.9		1.2
41	Austria	3.9		1.5
41	Norway	3.9		1.6
43	France	3.8		1.6
44	Ireland	3.8		1.2
45	Belgium	3.8		1.4
46	Trinidad and Tobago	3.8		1.4
47	Namibia	3.8		1.6
48	Peru	3.7		1.6
49	China	3.7		1.5
50	Canada	3.7		1.4
51	Tanzania	3.7		1.4
52	Uganda	3.7		1.9

RANK	COUNTRY	SCORE	1 MEAN: 3.6 7	SD
53	Mozambique	3.6		1.7
54	India	3.6		1.4
55	Costa Rica	3.6		1.7
56	Cameroon	3.6		1.8
57	Dominican Republic	3.6		1.6
57	Mali	3.6		1.9
59	Portugal	3.6		1.5
60	Greece	3.5		1.4
61	Egypt	3.5		1.7
62	Indonesia	3.4		1.4
63	Czech Republic	3.4		1.4
64	Slovak Republic	3.4		1.5
65	Malawi	3.3		1.5
66	Senegal	3.3		1.6
67	Kenya	3.3		1.6
68	Mauritius	3.3		1.2
69	Zambia	3.3		1.7
70	Croatia	3.3		1.7
71	Nicaragua	3.3		1.7
72	Jamaica	3.3		1.2
73	Germany	3.2		1.5
74	Haiti	3.2		2.1
75	Pakistan	3.2		1.4
76	Panama	3.2		1.4
77	Madagascar	3.1		1.5
78	Russian Federation	3.1		1.5
79	Serbia	3.1		1.7
80	Bolivia	3.1		1.6
81	Poland	3.0		1.3
82	Philippines	2.9		1.5
83	Ecuador	2.9		1.4
84	Ukraine	2.9		1.6
85	Macedonia, FYR	2.9		1.9
86	Bulgaria	2.9		1.5
87	Uruguay	2.8		1.5
88	Japan	2.8		1.2
89	Honduras	2.8		1.4
90	Nigeria	2.8		1.5
91	Argentina	2.8		1.3
91	Paraguay	2.8		1.6
93	Algeria	2.7		1.4
94	Turkey	2.7		1.3
95	Bangladesh	2.7		1.4
96	Chad	2.7		1.5
97	Guatemala	2.4		1.4
98	Romania	2.3		1.3
99	Ethiopia	2.2		1.4
100	Angola	2.1		1.2
101	Zimbabwe	1.7		0.9
102	Venezuela	1.6		1.0

405

2.05   Financial market sophistication

The level of sophistication of financial markets in your country is (1 = lower than international norms, 7 = higher than international norms)

RANK	COUNTRY	SCORE	SD		RANK	COUNTRY	SCORE	SD
1	United Kingdom	6.7	0.7		53	Peru	3.8	1.2
2	United States	6.7	0.9		54	Tunisia	3.8	1.2
3	Switzerland	6.5	0.9		55	Slovenia	3.7	1.1
4	Australia	6.3	0.6		56	Philippines	3.7	1.3
5	Hong Kong SAR	6.3	1.1		57	Pakistan	3.7	1.3
6	Canada	6.1	0.8		57	Poland	3.7	1.0
7	Sweden	6.1	0.7		59	Argentina	3.6	1.3
8	Finland	6.0	0.8		60	Botswana	3.5	1.2
9	Luxembourg	5.9	1.3		61	Slovak Republic	3.4	1.4
10	Singapore	5.9	0.9		62	Egypt	3.4	1.7
11	New Zealand	5.8	1.0		63	Indonesia	3.4	1.0
12	Netherlands	5.8	1.0		64	Kenya	3.4	1.3
13	Germany	5.7	1.0		65	Morocco	3.4	1.8
14	Denmark	5.7	1.0		66	Guatemala	3.4	1.2
15	Belgium	5.7	1.1		67	Uruguay	3.3	1.4
16	South Africa	5.6	1.1		68	Sri Lanka	3.3	1.2
17	Israel	5.5	1.1		69	Venezuela	3.3	1.2
18	France	5.4	1.1		70	Czech Republic	3.3	1.3
19	Brazil	5.4	1.2		71	Nigeria	3.2	1.4
20	Spain	5.3	1.0		72	China	3.1	1.4
21	Malaysia	5.2	0.8		73	Croatia	3.1	1.4
22	Chile	5.2	0.9		74	Mali	3.0	2.1
23	Ireland	5.2	1.3		75	Ghana	3.0	1.2
24	Italy	5.1	1.3		76	Ecuador	2.9	1.3
25	Iceland	4.9	0.8		77	Tanzania	2.9	1.4
26	Norway	4.9	1.1		78	Paraguay	2.9	1.2
27	Panama	4.9	1.4		79	Serbia	2.9	1.3
28	Estonia	4.9	1.3		80	Zambia	2.8	1.2
29	Taiwan	4.7	1.0		81	Malawi	2.7	1.4
30	Latvia	4.7	1.3		82	Vietnam	2.7	1.2
31	Portugal	4.7	1.3		83	Bolivia	2.7	1.2
32	Mexico	4.5	1.1		84	Romania	2.7	1.2
33	Korea	4.5	1.1		85	Senegal	2.7	1.6
34	Austria	4.5	1.5		86	Madagascar	2.7	1.9
35	Hungary	4.5	1.3		87	Russian Federation	2.6	1.1
36	Japan	4.4	1.6		88	Nicaragua	2.5	1.2
37	India	4.4	1.2		89	Mozambique	2.5	1.4
38	El Salvador	4.3	1.6		90	Uganda	2.5	1.5
39	Thailand	4.3	1.1		91	Cameroon	2.4	1.3
40	Jamaica	4.3	1.4		92	Honduras	2.4	1.2
41	Namibia	4.2	1.4		93	Ukraine	2.4	1.1
42	Greece	4.1	1.2		94	Bulgaria	2.3	1.2
43	Malta	4.1	1.4		95	Gambia	2.3	1.4
44	Turkey	4.0	1.6		96	Bangladesh	2.3	1.0
45	Colombia	4.0	1.2		97	Macedonia, FYR	2.1	1.1
45	Costa Rica	4.0	1.1		98	Angola	2.0	1.0
45	Trinidad and Tobago	4.0	1.3		99	Algeria	1.7	1.1
48	Jordan	4.0	1.3		100	Ethiopia	1.6	1.1
49	Dominican Republic	3.9	1.3		101	Haiti	1.5	0.8
50	Lithuania	3.9	1.1		102	Chad	1.4	1.1
51	Mauritius	3.9	1.4					
52	Zimbabwe	3.8	1.2					

2.06 Soundness of banks

Banks in your country are (1 = insolvent and may require government bailout, 7 = generally healthy with sound balance sheets)

RANK	COUNTRY	SCORE	1 MEAN: 5.2 7	SD
1	Australia	6.9		0.4
2	New Zealand	6.7		0.5
3	Canada	6.7		0.5
4	United Kingdom	6.6		0.7
5	Netherlands	6.6		0.6
6	Ireland	6.6		0.7
7	Denmark	6.6		0.7
8	Finland	6.6		0.6
9	Luxembourg	6.5		0.5
10	Switzerland	6.5		0.7
11	Singapore	6.5		0.6
12	United States	6.5		0.8
13	Spain	6.5		0.6
14	Sweden	6.4		0.6
15	Hong Kong SAR	6.4		1.3
16	Botswana	6.4		0.8
17	Chile	6.4		0.7
18	Malta	6.4		0.7
19	Trinidad and Tobago	6.3		0.7
20	Malawi	6.3		0.8
21	Belgium	6.3		0.7
22	Estonia	6.3		0.7
23	Iceland	6.3		0.8
24	France	6.2		0.8
25	Brazil	6.2		0.9
26	South Africa	6.1		0.7
27	Panama	6.1		0.8
28	Senegal	6.0		1.1
29	Dominican Republic	6.0		0.8
30	Austria	6.0		0.9
31	Norway	6.0		0.9
32	El Salvador	5.9		0.7
33	Madagascar	5.8		1.2
33	Portugal	5.8		1.0
35	Namibia	5.8		1.2
36	Malaysia	5.6		0.8
37	Slovak Republic	5.6		0.9
38	Gambia	5.6		1.3
39	Haiti	5.5		1.0
40	Greece	5.5		0.9
41	Mali	5.5		1.4
42	Israel	5.5		0.9
43	Italy	5.5		0.8
44	Lithuania	5.4		1.1
45	Jordan	5.4		1.1
46	Latvia	5.4		0.9
47	Morocco	5.4		1.6
48	Mauritius	5.4		1.1
49	Costa Rica	5.3		1.1
50	Peru	5.3		1.0
51	Pakistan	5.3		1.2
52	Jamaica	5.2		1.2
53	Ghana	5.2		1.3
54	Slovenia	5.2		1.1
55	Germany	5.2		1.1
56	Tunisia	5.1		1.3
57	Mexico	5.1		1.3
58	Sri Lanka	5.1		1.3
59	Cameroon	5.0		1.3
60	Vietnam	5.0		1.2
61	Poland	4.9		1.1
62	Zambia	4.9		1.5
63	Colombia	4.9		1.2
64	Hungary	4.9		1.3
65	Bulgaria	4.9		1.4
66	Croatia	4.9		1.6
67	Venezuela	4.9		1.0
68	India	4.7		1.2
69	Philippines	4.7		1.2
70	Korea	4.7		1.1
71	Tanzania	4.7		1.3
72	Zimbabwe	4.6		1.4
73	Taiwan	4.6		1.1
74	Nigeria	4.6		1.3
75	Guatemala	4.6		1.2
76	Kenya	4.6		1.3
77	Bolivia	4.6		1.1
78	Czech Republic	4.5		1.4
79	Ethiopia	4.5		1.7
80	Romania	4.5		1.4
81	Chad	4.5		2.0
82	Thailand	4.4		1.2
83	Mozambique	4.3		1.3
84	Bangladesh	4.2		1.5
85	Nicaragua	4.2		1.4
86	Paraguay	4.1		1.3
87	Algeria	4.1		1.9
88	Egypt	4.0		1.7
89	Angola	4.0		1.6
90	Uganda	4.0		1.6
91	Ukraine	3.9		1.3
92	Russian Federation	3.8		1.3
93	China	3.7		1.2
94	Macedonia, FYR	3.7		1.7
95	Serbia	3.6		1.5
96	Honduras	3.5		1.4
97	Indonesia	3.4		1.4
98	Ecuador	3.3		1.3
99	Uruguay	3.3		1.2
100	Turkey	3.1		1.5
101	Argentina	2.8		1.2
102	Japan	2.3		1.1

2.07   Ease of access to loans

How easy is it to obtain a bank loan in your country with only a good business plan and no collateral? (1 = impossible, 7 = easy)

RANK	COUNTRY	SCORE	1 MEAN: 3.2 7	SD
1	Finland	5.2		1.3
2	United Kingdom	5.1		1.3
3	Denmark	5.1		1.4
4	Ireland	5.0		1.4
5	Luxembourg	4.9		1.5
6	Australia	4.8		1.5
7	Sweden	4.8		1.5
8	Iceland	4.8		1.5
9	Lithuania	4.7		1.6
10	Norway	4.7		1.5
11	New Zealand	4.6		1.4
12	United States	4.6		1.7
13	Taiwan	4.5		1.6
14	Latvia	4.5		1.5
15	Hong Kong SAR	4.4		1.5
16	Netherlands	4.4		1.6
17	Singapore	4.3		1.7
18	Belgium	4.2		1.5
19	France	4.2		1.5
20	Canada	4.1		1.7
21	Chile	4.0		1.8
22	Panama	3.9		1.8
23	Switzerland	3.9		1.6
24	Mauritius	3.9		1.5
25	Portugal	3.9		1.5
26	Greece	3.8		1.6
27	Spain	3.8		1.6
28	Slovenia	3.8		1.7
29	Tunisia	3.8		1.5
30	Estonia	3.8		1.7
31	Malaysia	3.8		1.2
32	Korea	3.7		1.5
33	Namibia	3.7		1.5
34	South Africa	3.7		1.6
35	Israel	3.7		1.6
36	Dominican Republic	3.7		1.8
37	Austria	3.7		1.6
38	India	3.7		1.5
39	El Salvador	3.6		1.9
40	Italy	3.5		1.4
41	Sri Lanka	3.5		1.5
42	Germany	3.5		1.3
42	Slovak Republic	3.5		1.9
44	Brazil	3.4		1.6
45	Thailand	3.4		1.4
46	Serbia	3.4		1.7
47	Indonesia	3.3		1.4
48	Egypt	3.3		1.9
49	Botswana	3.3		1.8
50	Poland	3.3		1.4
51	Malta	3.3		1.7
52	Hungary	3.3		1.5

RANK	COUNTRY	SCORE	1 MEAN: 3.2 7	SD
53	Romania	3.2		1.7
54	Jordan	3.1		1.7
55	Zimbabwe	3.1		1.6
56	Colombia	3.1		1.8
57	Trinidad and Tobago	3.0		1.4
58	Croatia	2.9		1.8
59	Gambia	2.9		1.7
60	Philippines	2.8		1.2
61	Uganda	2.8		1.8
62	Morocco	2.8		1.8
63	Costa Rica	2.8		1.6
64	Bulgaria	2.7		1.6
65	Czech Republic	2.7		1.4
66	Turkey	2.7		1.4
67	Haiti	2.6		1.5
68	Tanzania	2.6		1.7
69	Peru	2.6		1.3
70	Ghana	2.5		1.4
71	Pakistan	2.5		1.6
72	Japan	2.5		1.3
73	Vietnam	2.5		1.6
74	China	2.5		1.4
75	Russian Federation	2.4		1.4
76	Guatemala	2.4		1.2
77	Kenya	2.4		1.5
78	Jamaica	2.4		1.3
79	Venezuela	2.4		1.1
80	Malawi	2.3		1.7
81	Mexico	2.3		1.1
82	Nigeria	2.3		1.3
83	Paraguay	2.2		1.4
84	Cameroon	2.2		1.7
85	Algeria	2.2		1.5
86	Ecuador	2.2		1.3
87	Ukraine	2.1		1.3
88	Nicaragua	2.1		1.5
89	Angola	2.1		1.3
90	Honduras	2.1		1.4
91	Bangladesh	2.1		1.4
92	Uruguay	2.0		1.1
93	Zambia	2.0		1.1
94	Mozambique	2.0		1.3
95	Senegal	1.9		1.5
96	Ethiopia	1.8		1.4
97	Bolivia	1.8		0.9
98	Macedonia, FYR	1.8		1.1
99	Mali	1.8		1.2
100	Argentina	1.7		0.8
101	Madagascar	1.6		1.1
102	Chad	1.5		0.9

2.08 Venture capital availability

Entrepreneurs with innovative but risky projects can generally find venture capital in your country (1 = not true, 7 = true)

RANK	COUNTRY	SCORE	1 MEAN: 3.2 7	SD
1	Finland	5.4		1.0
2	United Kingdom	5.3		1.3
3	United States	5.3		1.5
4	Israel	5.0		1.2
5	Luxembourg	4.9		1.2
6	Netherlands	4.9		1.6
7	Sweden	4.8		1.2
7	Australia	4.8		1.7
9	Ireland	4.7		1.4
10	Norway	4.6		1.5
11	Canada	4.6		1.5
12	Singapore	4.5		1.4
13	Denmark	4.5		1.6
14	France	4.4		1.5
15	Hong Kong SAR	4.4		1.4
16	Korea	4.4		1.3
17	New Zealand	4.4		1.4
18	Taiwan	4.4		1.1
19	Latvia	4.4		1.6
20	Iceland	4.3		1.3
21	Belgium	4.2		1.4
22	Lithuania	4.1		1.3
23	Spain	4.1		1.4
24	Malaysia	4.0		1.3
25	Tunisia	3.9		1.6
26	Switzerland	3.9		1.6
27	Estonia	3.9		1.4
28	India	3.8		1.5
29	Italy	3.8		1.3
30	Germany	3.7		1.5
31	Mauritius	3.6		1.3
32	South Africa	3.6		1.6
33	Portugal	3.6		1.4
34	Panama	3.6		1.6
35	Greece	3.5		1.4
36	Macedonia, FYR	3.5		2.2
37	Chile	3.4		1.5
38	Czech Republic	3.4		1.6
39	Thailand	3.4		1.3
40	Sri Lanka	3.4		1.4
41	Hungary	3.3		1.6
42	Botswana	3.3		1.6
42	Poland	3.3		1.3
44	Egypt	3.3		1.9
45	Japan	3.2		1.3
46	Namibia	3.2		1.3
47	Austria	3.2		1.5
48	Dominican Republic	3.2		1.8
49	Indonesia	3.2		1.4
50	El Salvador	3.1		1.4
51	Serbia	3.1		1.7
52	Zimbabwe	3.1		1.6

RANK	COUNTRY	SCORE	1 MEAN: 3.2 7	SD
53	Morocco	3.1		1.7
54	Brazil	3.0		1.3
55	Slovak Republic	3.0		1.3
56	Malta	3.0		1.3
57	Uganda	3.0		1.9
58	China	3.0		1.2
58	Vietnam	3.0		1.6
60	Trinidad and Tobago	3.0		1.4
61	Slovenia	3.0		1.2
62	Jordan	2.9		1.4
63	Russian Federation	2.9		1.5
64	Romania	2.9		1.6
65	Croatia	2.8		1.6
66	Nigeria	2.7		1.5
67	Guatemala	2.7		1.6
68	Costa Rica	2.7		1.5
69	Colombia	2.7		1.3
70	Tanzania	2.7		1.4
71	Philippines	2.6		1.2
72	Ghana	2.6		1.5
73	Ukraine	2.6		1.3
74	Jamaica	2.5		1.6
75	Bulgaria	2.4		1.3
76	Mexico	2.4		1.3
77	Kenya	2.4		1.4
78	Cameroon	2.4		1.5
79	Gambia	2.4		1.6
80	Pakistan	2.4		1.3
81	Ecuador	2.4		1.6
82	Madagascar	2.3		1.5
83	Nicaragua	2.3		1.5
84	Turkey	2.2		1.2
85	Peru	2.2		1.2
86	Zambia	2.1		1.2
87	Mozambique	2.1		1.3
88	Bolivia	2.1		1.3
89	Haiti	2.1		1.2
90	Ethiopia	2.1		1.7
91	Honduras	2.0		1.3
92	Senegal	2.0		1.0
93	Venezuela	2.0		1.1
94	Bangladesh	2.0		1.3
95	Mali	2.0		1.5
96	Paraguay	2.0		1.4
97	Angola	1.9		1.4
98	Argentina	1.9		1.1
99	Malawi	1.9		1.2
100	Uruguay	1.8		1.1
101	Algeria	1.8		1.3
102	Chad	1.5		1.1

2.09   Access to credit

During the past year, obtaining credit for your company has become (1 = more difficult, 7 = easier)

RANK	COUNTRY	SCORE	1 MEAN: 4.1 7	SD
1	Pakistan	5.8		1.3
2	Iceland	5.8		1.2
3	Taiwan	5.7		1.4
4	India	5.6		1.2
5	Estonia	5.6		1.1
6	El Salvador	5.5		1.5
7	Thailand	5.4		1.4
8	Lithuania	5.4		1.5
9	Slovak Republic	5.2		1.7
10	Latvia	5.2		1.1
11	Finland	5.2		1.3
12	Slovenia	5.1		1.4
13	Australia	5.0		1.3
14	New Zealand	5.0		1.2
15	Croatia	4.9		1.8
16	Korea	4.8		1.4
17	Greece	4.8		1.6
18	Ireland	4.8		1.5
19	Trinidad and Tobago	4.8		1.6
20	Botswana	4.8		1.7
21	Vietnam	4.7		1.4
22	Hong Kong SAR	4.6		1.8
23	Colombia	4.6		1.9
24	Singapore	4.6		1.5
25	Hungary	4.6		1.3
26	Czech Republic	4.6		1.6
27	Morocco	4.6		1.8
28	South Africa	4.5		1.2
29	Tunisia	4.5		1.5
30	Zimbabwe	4.5		1.7
31	Canada	4.4		1.5
32	Sri Lanka	4.4		1.5
33	Haiti	4.4		1.6
34	Denmark	4.4		1.5
35	Malaysia	4.4		1.3
36	Spain	4.4		1.6
37	Chile	4.4		1.7
38	United States	4.3		1.6
39	Italy	4.3		1.4
40	Luxembourg	4.3		1.0
41	Namibia	4.3		1.6
42	Jordan	4.3		1.6
43	Philippines	4.2		1.8
44	Sweden	4.2		1.5
45	Austria	4.2		1.4
46	Bangladesh	4.2		1.8
47	Norway	4.2		1.4
48	Peru	4.1		1.9
49	Russian Federation	4.1		1.6
50	Jamaica	4.1		1.5
51	Costa Rica	4.1		1.6
52	France	4.1		1.5

RANK	COUNTRY	SCORE	1 MEAN: 4.1 7	SD
53	Mexico	4.1		1.7
54	Mauritius	4.1		1.3
55	United Kingdom	4.0		1.1
56	Gambia	4.0		1.8
57	Malta	4.0		1.3
58	Switzerland	4.0		1.8
59	Indonesia	3.9		1.4
60	Romania	3.9		1.6
61	Guatemala	3.9		1.8
62	Malawi	3.9		1.4
63	China	3.9		1.6
64	Ukraine	3.8		1.3
65	Nigeria	3.8		1.5
66	Israel	3.8		1.5
67	Japan	3.8		1.3
68	Serbia	3.8		1.7
69	Uganda	3.8		1.8
70	Brazil	3.8		1.6
71	Dominican Republic	3.7		1.5
71	Ghana	3.7		1.6
73	Poland	3.7		1.4
74	Algeria	3.6		2.0
75	Bulgaria	3.6		1.6
76	Netherlands	3.6		1.3
77	Tanzania	3.6		1.6
78	Egypt	3.6		1.8
79	Turkey	3.6		1.7
80	Kenya	3.5		1.7
81	Honduras	3.5		1.9
82	Germany	3.5		1.3
83	Panama	3.5		1.8
84	Angola	3.5		1.7
85	Belgium	3.3		1.5
86	Senegal	3.3		1.8
87	Mozambique	3.3		1.6
88	Nicaragua	3.3		1.7
89	Macedonia, FYR	3.3		2.0
90	Portugal	3.3		1.5
91	Ecuador	3.3		1.7
92	Zambia	3.0		1.7
93	Bolivia	3.0		1.7
94	Madagascar	2.9		1.7
95	Ethiopia	2.9		1.7
96	Cameroon	2.8		1.8
97	Chad	2.7		1.8
98	Venezuela	2.6		1.3
99	Mali	2.6		1.9
100	Paraguay	2.5		1.8
101	Uruguay	1.6		0.9
102	Argentina	1.3		0.6

2.10 Government intervention in corporate investment

The effect of government intervention on corporate investment is (1 = distorting, 7 = free from government intervention)

RANK	COUNTRY	SCORE	1 MEAN: 4.2 7	SD
1	Finland	6.3		1.0
2	Hong Kong SAR	5.9		1.4
3	Denmark	5.7		1.2
4	Iceland	5.6		1.2
5	United States	5.4		1.3
6	Australia	5.4		1.0
7	Netherlands	5.4		1.2
8	Gambia	5.4		1.6
9	Singapore	5.3		1.4
10	Sweden	5.3		1.5
11	Luxembourg	5.2		1.2
12	Switzerland	5.2		1.4
13	United Kingdom	5.2		1.4
14	Thailand	5.2		1.3
15	New Zealand	5.1		1.2
16	Tunisia	5.1		1.5
17	Estonia	5.0		1.5
18	El Salvador	5.0		1.5
19	Malta	5.0		1.3
20	Botswana	4.8		1.5
21	Jordan	4.8		1.4
22	Spain	4.8		1.3
23	Chile	4.7		1.5
24	Taiwan	4.7		1.4
25	Belgium	4.7		1.2
26	Ghana	4.6		1.7
27	Czech Republic	4.6		1.4
28	Latvia	4.6		1.2
29	Trinidad and Tobago	4.6		1.4
30	Mauritius	4.6		1.3
31	Slovenia	4.6		1.3
32	Austria	4.5		1.4
33	Japan	4.5		1.7
34	India	4.5		1.3
35	South Africa	4.5		1.4
36	France	4.5		1.5
37	Mexico	4.5		1.5
38	China	4.5		1.4
39	Canada	4.5		1.3
40	Italy	4.4		1.3
41	Lithuania	4.4		1.4
42	Namibia	4.4		1.3
43	Brazil	4.4		1.4
44	Norway	4.4		1.3
45	Hungary	4.3		1.4
46	Zambia	4.3		1.8
47	Vietnam	4.3		1.5
48	Malawi	4.3		1.6
49	Korea	4.3		1.3
50	Tanzania	4.3		1.5
51	Portugal	4.2		1.4
52	Israel	4.2		1.2

RANK	COUNTRY	SCORE	1 MEAN: 4.2 7	SD
53	Slovak Republic	4.2		1.6
54	Mali	4.2		2.1
55	Costa Rica	4.2		1.6
56	Dominican Republic	4.2		1.7
57	Sri Lanka	4.1		1.4
58	Malaysia	4.1		1.2
59	Uganda	4.1		1.9
60	Ireland	4.0		1.4
61	Greece	4.0		1.5
62	Morocco	4.0		1.5
63	Poland	4.0		1.3
64	Senegal	4.0		1.9
65	Jamaica	3.9		1.6
66	Egypt	3.9		1.8
67	Kenya	3.9		1.6
68	Germany	3.7		1.5
69	Colombia	3.7		1.6
70	Philippines	3.7		1.5
71	Haiti	3.7		2.2
72	Cameroon	3.6		1.7
73	Pakistan	3.6		1.5
74	Russian Federation	3.6		1.5
75	Mozambique	3.6		1.7
76	Serbia	3.6		1.7
77	Turkey	3.5		1.7
78	Bangladesh	3.5		1.8
78	Indonesia	3.5		1.4
80	Madagascar	3.5		1.5
81	Peru	3.5		1.5
82	Nigeria	3.5		1.7
83	Paraguay	3.5		1.8
84	Bulgaria	3.4		1.4
85	Croatia	3.4		1.3
86	Macedonia, FYR	3.4		1.7
87	Panama	3.4		1.5
88	Nicaragua	3.4		1.8
89	Algeria	3.3		1.8
90	Honduras	3.3		1.6
91	Uruguay	3.1		1.5
92	Chad	3.1		2.0
93	Romania	3.1		1.8
94	Ecuador	3.0		1.4
95	Bolivia	2.9		1.6
96	Angola	2.9		1.7
97	Ethiopia	2.9		1.6
98	Ukraine	2.9		1.4
99	Argentina	2.8		1.6
100	Zimbabwe	2.6		1.6
101	Guatemala	2.5		1.3
102	Venezuela	1.9		1.4

2.11   Local equity market access

Raising money by issuing shares on the local stock market is (1 = nearly impossible, 7 = quite possible for a good company)

RANK	COUNTRY	SCORE	1 MEAN: 4.6 7	SD
1	Australia	6.5		1.0
2	Zimbabwe	6.4		0.7
3	Hong Kong SAR	6.3		1.1
4	France	6.2		1.0
5	Pakistan	6.1		1.1
6	Iceland	6.0		1.3
7	Germany	6.0		1.1
8	South Africa	6.0		1.2
9	Japan	6.0		1.3
10	Singapore	6.0		1.0
11	New Zealand	5.9		1.3
12	Malta	5.9		1.1
13	Jamaica	5.9		1.3
14	Taiwan	5.8		1.2
15	Switzerland	5.8		1.3
16	Malaysia	5.8		0.8
17	Nigeria	5.8		1.3
18	United Kingdom	5.8		1.5
19	United States	5.8		1.5
20	Finland	5.8		1.5
21	Thailand	5.8		1.4
22	Botswana	5.7		1.3
23	Luxembourg	5.7		1.4
24	Canada	5.7		1.5
25	Austria	5.6		1.5
26	India	5.6		1.5
27	Trinidad and Tobago	5.6		1.5
28	Estonia	5.5		1.3
29	Korea	5.4		1.3
30	Ireland	5.4		1.7
31	Tunisia	5.4		1.3
32	Kenya	5.3		1.4
33	Sri Lanka	5.3		1.4
34	Jordan	5.3		1.3
35	Bangladesh	5.3		1.5
36	Norway	5.3		1.4
37	Namibia	5.3		1.3
38	Netherlands	5.3		1.9
39	Ghana	5.2		1.6
40	Mauritius	5.2		1.4
41	Senegal	5.1		1.6
42	Sweden	5.1		1.7
43	Morocco	5.1		1.7
44	China	5.0		1.4
45	Hungary	5.0		1.5
46	Slovenia	5.0		1.4
47	Greece	5.0		1.6
48	Lithuania	5.0		1.4
49	Israel	5.0		1.9
50	Vietnam	4.9		1.6
51	Malawi	4.9		1.8
52	Denmark	4.8		1.9

RANK	COUNTRY	SCORE	1 MEAN: 4.6 7	SD
53	Chile	4.8		1.7
54	Portugal	4.8		1.8
55	Turkey	4.7		1.5
56	Zambia	4.7		2.0
57	Italy	4.7		1.5
58	Latvia	4.7		1.4
59	Belgium	4.6		1.8
60	Spain	4.6		1.7
61	Tanzania	4.5		1.8
62	Mexico	4.5		1.8
63	Poland	4.5		1.6
64	Peru	4.5		1.7
65	Brazil	4.4		1.6
66	Egypt	4.4		1.7
67	Panama	4.4		1.6
68	Colombia	4.4		1.7
69	Romania	4.3		1.9
70	Macedonia, FYR	4.2		2.2
71	Indonesia	4.2		1.4
72	Philippines	4.1		1.9
73	Russian Federation	4.1		1.8
74	Costa Rica	4.1		1.7
75	Uganda	4.0		2.1
76	Croatia	4.0		1.7
77	Serbia	3.9		1.8
78	El Salvador	3.9		1.9
79	Dominican Republic	3.8		1.6
80	Slovak Republic	3.6		1.7
81	Bolivia	3.6		1.8
82	Ukraine	3.5		1.5
83	Gambia	3.3		2.0
84	Czech Republic	3.2		1.9
85	Ecuador	3.0		1.7
86	Guatemala	3.0		1.7
86	Mozambique	3.0		1.8
86	Venezuela	3.0		1.4
89	Nicaragua	2.9		1.9
90	Bulgaria	2.8		1.6
91	Haiti	2.7		1.7
92	Mali	2.6		1.9
93	Cameroon	2.6		1.7
94	Algeria	2.3		1.7
95	Argentina	2.3		1.1
96	Madagascar	2.1		1.6
97	Ethiopia	1.9		1.5
98	Paraguay	1.8		1.2
99	Chad	1.8		1.3
100	Honduras	1.7		1.2
101	Uruguay	1.7		1.0
102	Angola	1.3		0.9

2.12 Regulation of securities exchanges

The regulation of securities exchanges in your country is (1 = nontransparent, ineffective, and subject to excessive industry and government influences, 7 = transparent, effective, and independent of excessive industry and government influences)

RANK	COUNTRY	SCORE	MEAN: 4.8	SD
1	Australia	6.7		0.5
2	United Kingdom	6.6		0.8
3	Denmark	6.3		0.7
4	Singapore	6.2		0.8
5	Finland	6.2		0.8
6	Germany	6.2		0.8
7	Switzerland	6.1		1.0
8	New Zealand	6.1		0.7
9	Ireland	6.1		0.8
10	Sweden	6.0		0.7
11	United States	6.0		1.1
12	South Africa	6.0		1.0
13	Luxembourg	5.9		0.8
14	Iceland	5.9		0.7
15	Netherlands	5.9		0.9
16	France	5.9		1.0
17	Hong Kong SAR	5.9		1.1
18	Chile	5.7		1.0
19	Malawi	5.7		1.2
20	Israel	5.6		0.9
21	Belgium	5.6		1.0
22	Malta	5.6		1.0
23	Jordan	5.6		0.9
24	Norway	5.6		1.1
25	Canada	5.6		1.1
26	Austria	5.6		1.2
27	Estonia	5.5		1.0
28	Malaysia	5.5		0.9
29	Thailand	5.4		0.9
30	Gambia	5.4		1.5
31	Pakistan	5.4		1.2
32	Taiwan	5.3		1.2
33	Portugal	5.3		1.2
34	Spain	5.3		1.2
35	Mexico	5.3		1.3
36	India	5.3		1.1
37	Italy	5.2		1.2
38	Brazil	5.2		1.0
39	Jamaica	5.2		1.3
40	Hungary	5.2		1.3
41	Tunisia	5.2		1.2
42	Botswana	5.2		1.4
43	Mauritius	5.1		1.3
44	Ghana	5.1		1.3
45	Namibia	5.0		1.4
46	Panama	5.0		1.4
47	Korea	5.0		1.1
48	Costa Rica	5.0		1.2
49	Zambia	5.0		1.5
50	El Salvador	4.9		1.3
51	Poland	4.9		1.3
52	Latvia	4.9		1.1
53	Peru	4.8		1.3
54	Dominican Republic	4.8		1.1
55	Nigeria	4.8		1.6
56	Colombia	4.8		1.2
57	Greece	4.8		1.4
58	Slovenia	4.8		1.0
59	Senegal	4.7		0.9
60	Lithuania	4.7		1.1
61	Tanzania	4.6		1.2
62	Uganda	4.6		1.6
63	Kenya	4.6		1.3
64	Turkey	4.6		1.3
65	Japan	4.6		1.4
66	Argentina	4.6		1.3
67	Bolivia	4.6		1.3
68	Morocco	4.5		1.7
69	Zimbabwe	4.5		1.4
70	Trinidad and Tobago	4.4		1.4
71	Slovak Republic	4.4		1.3
72	Cameroon	4.4		1.4
73	Czech Republic	4.4		1.3
74	Uruguay	4.4		1.3
75	Macedonia, FYR	4.3		1.8
76	Nicaragua	4.2		1.4
77	Sri Lanka	4.2		1.4
78	Egypt	4.2		1.5
79	Venezuela	4.2		1.6
80	Philippines	4.2		1.3
81	Croatia	4.1		1.5
82	Mali	4.0		1.4
83	Romania	4.0		1.7
84	Mozambique	4.0		1.3
85	Guatemala	3.9		1.4
86	Ecuador	3.7		1.4
87	China	3.7		1.3
88	Bangladesh	3.6		1.6
89	Serbia	3.6		1.5
90	Indonesia	3.6		1.3
91	Bulgaria	3.6		1.4
92	Vietnam	3.5		1.4
93	Russian Federation	3.3		1.3
94	Algeria	3.3		1.6
95	Madagascar	3.2		1.3
96	Paraguay	3.1		1.5
97	Haiti	2.9		1.0
98	Chad	2.9		1.4
99	Honduras	2.8		1.2
100	Ethiopia	2.7		1.6
101	Ukraine	2.6		1.1
102	Angola	2.2		1.6

413

2.13   Effectiveness of bankruptcy law

In your country, laws governing bankruptcies, especially protection of creditors, are (1 = nonexistent and poorly enforced, 7 = well defined and strictly enforced in an orderly manner)

RANK	COUNTRY	SCORE	SD	RANK	COUNTRY	SCORE	SD
1	Denmark	6.7	0.6	53	Malta	4.3	1.7
2	United Kingdom	6.6	0.8	54	India	4.3	1.6
3	Sweden	6.5	0.6	55	Mexico	4.2	1.6
4	Australia	6.5	0.5	56	Lithuania	4.2	1.3
5	Finland	6.3	0.8	57	Poland	4.2	1.3
6	Germany	6.3	0.7	58	Uganda	4.1	1.8
7	Singapore	6.3	0.7	59	Trinidad and Tobago	4.1	1.4
8	Netherlands	6.3	1.0	60	Zambia	4.1	1.7
9	United States	6.3	0.9	61	Algeria	4.1	1.7
10	Austria	6.2	0.8	62	Philippines	4.1	1.5
11	New Zealand	6.1	0.9	63	Cameroon	4.1	1.6
12	Switzerland	6.0	1.2	64	Czech Republic	4.0	1.5
13	Canada	6.0	1.1	65	Jamaica	4.0	1.5
14	Hong Kong SAR	6.0	1.1	66	Indonesia	3.9	1.6
15	France	5.9	1.1	67	Egypt	3.9	1.7
16	Norway	5.8	0.6	68	Sri Lanka	3.9	1.3
17	Malaysia	5.8	1.0	69	Mali	3.8	1.7
18	Belgium	5.8	1.2	70	Nigeria	3.8	1.8
19	Ireland	5.8	1.4	71	Kenya	3.8	1.5
20	Iceland	5.7	1.4	72	Turkey	3.8	1.4
21	Chile	5.6	1.1	73	Uruguay	3.7	1.5
22	Israel	5.6	0.8	74	Vietnam	3.7	1.6
23	Luxembourg	5.5	1.3	75	Slovak Republic	3.5	1.5
24	Tunisia	5.5	1.4	76	Ethiopia	3.5	2.0
25	South Africa	5.3	1.4	77	Romania	3.4	1.7
26	Taiwan	5.2	1.1	78	Venezuela	3.4	1.3
27	Japan	5.2	1.3	79	Argentina	3.4	1.5
28	Estonia	5.2	1.2	80	Dominican Republic	3.4	1.5
29	Zimbabwe	5.2	1.3	81	Macedonia, FYR	3.3	1.9
30	Thailand	5.1	1.1	82	Bulgaria	3.3	1.4
31	Colombia	5.1	1.1	83	Pakistan	3.3	1.7
32	Malawi	5.1	1.4	84	Paraguay	3.3	1.5
33	Spain	5.0	1.5	85	Chad	3.3	1.9
34	Italy	5.0	1.1	86	Croatia	3.3	1.6
35	Korea	5.0	1.2	87	Panama	3.2	1.6
36	Jordan	5.0	1.5	88	China	3.2	1.3
37	Gambia	4.9	2.0	89	Russian Federation	3.2	1.4
38	Hungary	4.9	1.4	90	Madagascar	3.2	1.6
39	Greece	4.8	1.3	91	Serbia	3.1	1.5
40	Brazil	4.8	1.2	92	El Salvador	3.0	1.5
41	Botswana	4.7	1.7	93	Nicaragua	3.0	1.4
42	Namibia	4.7	1.5	94	Mozambique	2.8	1.2
43	Peru	4.7	1.4	95	Bolivia	2.8	1.4
44	Latvia	4.6	1.2	96	Bangladesh	2.7	1.4
45	Portugal	4.5	1.4	97	Guatemala	2.7	1.4
46	Morocco	4.5	1.7	98	Ukraine	2.7	1.0
47	Slovenia	4.5	1.6	99	Ecuador	2.6	1.3
48	Mauritius	4.4	1.7	100	Honduras	2.5	1.3
49	Tanzania	4.4	1.4	101	Angola	2.2	1.5
50	Ghana	4.3	1.7	102	Haiti	2.0	0.9
51	Costa Rica	4.3	1.5				
52	Senegal	4.3	1.6				

MEAN: 4.4

2.14   Hidden trade barriers

In your country, hidden import barriers (that is, barriers other than published tariffs and quotas) are (1 = an important problem, 7 = not an important problem)

RANK	COUNTRY	SCORE	1 MEAN: 4.5 7	SD
1	Finland	6.6		0.7
2	Denmark	6.3		1.1
3	New Zealand	6.3		1.1
4	Sweden	6.3		0.9
5	Hong Kong SAR	6.2		1.3
6	Singapore	6.2		1.1
7	Chile	6.1		1.0
8	United Kingdom	6.0		1.0
9	Netherlands	5.9		1.2
10	Luxembourg	5.9		1.1
11	Australia	5.9		1.0
12	Belgium	5.9		1.1
13	Iceland	5.9		1.1
14	Germany	5.9		1.2
15	Austria	5.8		1.3
16	Portugal	5.8		1.2
17	Switzerland	5.7		1.3
18	Estonia	5.7		1.3
19	Ireland	5.6		1.4
20	France	5.6		1.3
21	Israel	5.6		1.3
22	Taiwan	5.5		1.2
23	Canada	5.4		1.4
24	Spain	5.4		1.4
25	Botswana	5.4		1.0
26	Slovenia	5.3		1.3
27	Slovak Republic	5.3		1.4
28	Greece	5.2		1.5
29	Gambia	5.2		1.7
30	Hungary	5.2		1.7
31	Jordan	5.2		1.5
32	South Africa	5.1		1.4
33	United States	5.1		1.5
34	Malta	5.1		1.5
35	Malaysia	5.0		1.2
36	Czech Republic	5.0		1.3
37	Italy	5.0		1.3
38	Uruguay	4.9		1.6
39	Malawi	4.8		1.7
40	Latvia	4.7		1.3
41	Norway	4.7		1.5
42	Peru	4.7		1.7
43	Korea	4.7		1.4
44	Mauritius	4.7		1.6
45	El Salvador	4.7		1.4
46	Trinidad and Tobago	4.6		1.4
47	Pakistan	4.6		1.8
48	Tunisia	4.6		1.5
49	Mexico	4.6		1.6
50	Lithuania	4.5		1.4
51	Brazil	4.4		1.5
52	Thailand	4.4		1.5

RANK	COUNTRY	SCORE	1 MEAN: 4.5 7	SD
53	Zambia	4.3		1.6
54	India	4.3		1.8
55	Poland	4.3		1.3
56	Namibia	4.3		1.4
57	Dominican Republic	4.2		1.4
58	Turkey	4.2		1.9
59	Colombia	4.2		1.5
60	Jamaica	4.1		1.8
61	Panama	4.1		1.6
62	Costa Rica	4.1		1.6
63	Croatia	4.1		1.8
64	Sri Lanka	4.0		1.5
65	China	4.0		1.1
66	Haiti	4.0		1.9
67	Argentina	4.0		1.5
68	Vietnam	3.9		1.3
69	Bangladesh	3.9		1.9
70	Angola	3.9		2.2
71	Bolivia	3.8		1.8
72	Ghana	3.8		1.6
73	Serbia	3.8		1.6
74	Morocco	3.7		1.8
75	Japan	3.7		1.7
76	Egypt	3.7		1.7
77	Honduras	3.7		1.6
78	Algeria	3.7		1.8
79	Tanzania	3.6		1.6
80	Kenya	3.6		1.4
81	Russian Federation	3.6		1.5
82	Guatemala	3.6		1.8
83	Senegal	3.6		1.2
84	Ethiopia	3.6		1.9
85	Bulgaria	3.6		1.6
86	Uganda	3.6		1.8
87	Paraguay	3.6		2.1
88	Philippines	3.5		1.7
89	Indonesia	3.5		1.3
90	Ecuador	3.4		1.6
91	Nicaragua	3.4		1.6
92	Mozambique	3.3		1.8
93	Macedonia, FYR	3.3		2.0
94	Madagascar	3.3		1.5
95	Ukraine	3.3		1.3
96	Romania	3.3		1.7
97	Zimbabwe	3.2		1.4
98	Mali	3.0		1.8
99	Cameroon	3.0		1.7
100	Nigeria	2.9		1.5
101	Venezuela	2.8		1.6
102	Chad	2.1		1.4

415

2.15   Agricultural policy costs

The cost of agricultural policy in your country is (1 = excessively burdensome, 7 = balances all economic agents' interests)

RANK	COUNTRY	SCORE	1 MEAN: 3.7 7	SD
1	New Zealand	5.7		1.1
2	Malaysia	5.2		0.9
3	Singapore	5.1		1.3
4	Tunisia	5.0		1.4
5	Australia	4.9		1.3
6	Vietnam	4.7		1.1
7	Hong Kong SAR	4.6		1.5
8	South Africa	4.6		1.2
9	Brazil	4.5		1.2
10	Ghana	4.4		1.4
11	China	4.4		1.2
12	Chile	4.4		1.3
13	Uganda	4.4		1.7
14	Taiwan	4.3		1.4
15	Luxembourg	4.3		1.2
16	Latvia	4.3		1.4
17	Cameroon	4.3		1.4
18	Gambia	4.3		1.8
19	Estonia	4.3		1.4
20	Austria	4.3		1.6
21	Thailand	4.3		1.3
22	Malta	4.2		1.2
23	Bangladesh	4.2		1.5
24	Mauritius	4.1		1.3
25	Canada	4.1		1.4
26	Malawi	4.0		1.3
27	United States	4.0		1.5
28	Sri Lanka	4.0		1.3
29	Namibia	4.0		1.4
30	Jordan	4.0		1.3
31	Argentina	4.0		1.5
32	Sweden	4.0		1.3
33	Costa Rica	4.0		1.2
34	Denmark	4.0		1.6
35	Italy	3.9		1.1
36	Uruguay	3.9		1.6
37	Dominican Republic	3.8		1.2
38	Finland	3.8		1.6
39	United Kingdom	3.8		1.4
40	Egypt	3.8		1.5
41	Serbia	3.8		1.5
42	Morocco	3.8		2.1
43	Mali	3.8		2.0
44	Zambia	3.8		1.6
45	Botswana	3.8		1.4
46	Netherlands	3.7		1.5
47	Algeria	3.7		1.7
48	France	3.7		1.7
49	Paraguay	3.7		1.6
50	El Salvador	3.7		1.2
51	Slovak Republic	3.7		1.2
52	Czech Republic	3.7		1.4

RANK	COUNTRY	SCORE	1 MEAN: 3.7 7	SD
53	Madagascar	3.6		1.4
54	Spain	3.6		1.3
55	Israel	3.6		1.1
56	Indonesia	3.6		1.4
57	Tanzania	3.6		1.6
58	Colombia	3.6		1.3
59	Macedonia, FYR	3.6		1.9
60	Korea	3.5		1.1
61	Chad	3.5		1.6
62	Greece	3.5		1.3
63	Bolivia	3.5		1.4
64	Honduras	3.5		1.3
65	Hungary	3.5		1.2
66	Belgium	3.5		1.5
67	Jamaica	3.4		1.1
68	Portugal	3.4		1.2
69	Panama	3.4		1.2
70	Philippines	3.3		1.2
71	Pakistan	3.3		1.3
72	Haiti	3.3		1.3
73	Mexico	3.3		1.3
74	Nicaragua	3.3		1.3
75	Slovenia	3.3		1.2
76	Ecuador	3.3		1.3
77	Nigeria	3.3		1.4
78	Mozambique	3.2		1.6
79	Kenya	3.2		1.5
80	Lithuania	3.2		1.3
81	Peru	3.2		1.1
82	Switzerland	3.1		1.4
83	Trinidad and Tobago	3.1		1.2
84	Iceland	3.1		1.6
85	India	3.1		1.6
86	Senegal	3.0		1.2
87	Russian Federation	3.0		1.4
88	Guatemala	3.0		1.3
89	Ireland	3.0		1.3
90	Germany	3.0		1.3
91	Croatia	2.9		1.4
92	Norway	2.9		1.4
93	Poland	2.8		1.5
94	Bulgaria	2.8		1.4
95	Ukraine	2.8		1.3
96	Angola	2.6		1.5
97	Romania	2.6		1.3
98	Turkey	2.5		1.2
99	Ethiopia	2.4		1.4
100	Japan	2.3		1.0
101	Venezuela	2.1		1.1
102	Zimbabwe	1.5		1.2

2.16 Cost of importing foreign equipment

When your firm needs to import foreign equipment, the combined effect of import tariffs, license fees, bank fees, and the time required for administrative red tape raises the cost by (approximately) (1 = less than 10%, 2 = 11–20%, 3 = 21–30%, 9 = greater than 80%)

RANK	COUNTRY	SCORE	1 MEAN: 2.6 9	SD
1	Luxembourg	1.1		0.3
2	Hong Kong SAR	1.1		0.3
3	Singapore	1.1		0.4
4	Australia	1.2		0.4
5	New Zealand	1.3		0.6
6	Denmark	1.3		1.1
7	Belgium	1.3		0.6
8	Sweden	1.3		0.7
9	United States	1.3		0.5
10	Finland	1.3		0.7
11	Estonia	1.3		0.6
12	Taiwan	1.4		0.7
13	United Kingdom	1.4		0.6
14	Netherlands	1.4		0.8
15	Switzerland	1.4		0.7
16	Germany	1.5		0.7
17	Spain	1.5		0.8
18	Ireland	1.5		0.9
19	Portugal	1.5		0.8
20	Greece	1.5		0.9
21	Austria	1.5		0.8
22	Lithuania	1.6		0.9
23	Japan	1.6		1.2
24	Chile	1.6		0.8
25	Hungary	1.6		0.9
26	Slovak Republic	1.7		0.8
27	Iceland	1.7		1.2
28	France	1.7		0.9
29	Malaysia	1.8		1.1
30	Canada	1.8		1.1
31	Slovenia	1.8		1.0
32	Italy	1.8		1.2
33	Malta	1.9		1.2
34	Czech Republic	1.9		1.1
35	Israel	2.0		1.9
36	Botswana	2.0		1.1
37	Vietnam	2.0		1.4
38	Korea	2.1		1.2
39	El Salvador	2.1		1.1
40	South Africa	2.2		1.2
41	Philippines	2.2		1.3
42	Mexico	2.3		1.4
43	Bulgaria	2.3		1.4
44	Gambia	2.3		1.6
45	Serbia	2.3		1.2
46	Honduras	2.3		1.2
47	Poland	2.4		1.2
47	Thailand	2.4		1.4
49	Tunisia	2.5		1.5
50	Norway	2.5		1.4
51	Trinidad and Tobago	2.5		1.5
52	Jordan	2.6		1.7
53	Guatemala	2.6		1.3
54	Panama	2.6		1.5
55	Croatia	2.6		1.2
56	Dominican Republic	2.6		1.6
57	Nicaragua	2.7		1.4
58	Pakistan	2.7		1.5
59	Costa Rica	2.8		1.5
60	Latvia	2.8		1.6
61	Indonesia	2.8		1.5
62	Mauritius	2.9		2.4
63	Peru	2.9		1.4
64	Namibia	2.9		2.1
65	Jamaica	3.0		1.7
66	Ukraine	3.0		1.7
67	Macedonia, FYR	3.0		2.1
68	Paraguay	3.1		1.9
69	Turkey	3.1		2.1
70	India	3.1		1.8
71	Colombia	3.1		1.3
72	China	3.1		2.0
73	Uruguay	3.1		2.0
74	Bangladesh	3.2		1.8
75	Romania	3.3		1.8
76	Argentina	3.4		1.7
77	Russian Federation	3.4		1.6
78	Ghana	3.4		1.9
79	Venezuela	3.4		1.4
80	Ecuador	3.4		1.7
81	Sri Lanka	3.5		2.0
82	Ethiopia	3.5		2.2
83	Senegal	3.5		2.0
84	Mali	3.6		1.5
85	Zambia	3.6		1.9
86	Algeria	3.6		1.8
87	Morocco	3.6		2.0
88	Mozambique	3.7		2.1
89	Bolivia	3.7		1.4
90	Egypt	3.8		2.1
91	Haiti	3.9		2.0
92	Kenya	4.0		2.2
93	Tanzania	4.0		2.1
94	Angola	4.0		1.4
95	Zimbabwe	4.0		2.8
96	Uganda	4.0		2.0
97	Malawi	4.3		2.7
98	Nigeria	4.3		2.2
99	Chad	4.3		1.8
100	Brazil	4.4		2.0
101	Madagascar	5.1		2.0
102	Cameroon	5.2		1.6

417

2.17 Country Credit Rating, 2003

Institutional Investor Country Credit Rating, March 2003

RANK	COUNTRY	RATING		RANK	COUNTRY	RATING
1	Switzerland	95.3		53	Egypt	43.8
2	Luxembourg	94.3		54	Philippines	43.4
3	United States	93.3		55	Russian Federation	41.7
4	Netherlands	93.2		56	El Salvador	41.5
5	Norway	92.8		57	Bulgaria	39.6
5	United Kingdom	92.8		57	Namibia	39.6
7	Germany	92.3		59	Jordan	38.6
8	France	92.2		60	Colombia	37.5
9	Austria	90.6		61	Peru	36.3
10	Denmark	90.3		62	Brazil	36.1
11	Canada	89.9		63	Dominican Republic	34.9
11	Finland	89.9		63	Turkey	34.9
13	Sweden	89.1		65	Sri Lanka	34.8
14	Belgium	88.3		66	Romania	33.9
15	Ireland	86.9		67	Vietnam	33.5
16	Spain	86.1		68	Algeria	33.4
17	Singapore	85.6		69	Guatemala	33.0
18	Italy	84.3		70	Uruguay	31.6
19	Australia	83.3		71	Bolivia	30.7
20	Japan	82.0		72	Venezuela	29.6
21	Portugal	81.6		73	Jamaica	29.4
22	New Zealand	79.9		74	Paraguay	28.6
23	Greece	74.6		75	Bangladesh	28.2
24	Taiwan	74.3		76	Senegal	27.6
25	Iceland	73.2		77	Honduras	25.9
26	Hong Kong SAR	68.6		78	Ukraine	25.5
27	Korea	68.2		79	Ghana	25.2
28	Malta	67.3		80	Indonesia	25.0
29	Slovenia	66.4		81	Ecuador	23.2
30	Hungary	65.4		82	Kenya	22.1
31	Chile	64.7		83	Macedonia, FYR	22.0
32	Czech Republic	63.7		83	Tanzania	22.0
33	Poland	60.6		85	Uganda	21.4
34	China	60.0		86	Pakistan	20.5
35	Malaysia	59.2		87	Cameroon	20.0
36	Estonia	59.1		87	Nigeria	20.0
37	Mexico	58.5		89	Mozambique	19.8
38	Botswana	56.3		90	Malawi	19.4
39	Israel	56.1		91	Mali	18.9
40	South Africa	52.4		92	Nicaragua	18.2
41	Thailand	52.2		93	Serbia*	17.5
42	Trinidad and Tobago	51.4		94	Haiti	16.3
43	Slovak Republic	51.2		95	Angola	15.7
44	Latvia	51.1		95	Zambia	15.7
45	Tunisia	50.7		97	Chad	15.2
46	Lithuania	50.6		98	Ethiopia	14.7
46	Mauritius	50.6		99	Argentina	14.5
48	India	49.4		100	Zimbabwe	10.8
49	Croatia	46.7			Gambia	n/a
50	Morocco	46.1			Madagascar	n/a
51	Panama	44.7				
52	Costa Rica	44.0				

SOURCE: Institutional Investor, available online at http://www.institutionalinvestor.com/platinum/rr/countrycredit/ccr/2003.asp © Institutional Investor, 2003. No further copying or transmission of this material is allowed without the express permission of Institutional Investor (publisher@institutionalinvestor.com).

*Value for Yugoslavia

2.18   Government surplus/deficit, 2002

Government fiscal suplus/deficit as a percentage of GDP, 2002

RANK	COUNTRY	HARD DATA
1	Norway	12.79
2	Korea	5.96
3	Finland	4.74
4	Cameroon	3.00
5	Luxembourg	2.57
6	Algeria	2.20
7	Denmark	1.76
8	Canada	1.31
9	New Zealand	1.29
10	Estonia	1.21
11	Sweden	1.06
12	Russian Federation	0.60
13	Ukraine	0.50
14	Iceland	0.25
15	Dominican Republic	0.10
16	Belgium	0.01
17	Spain	−0.07
18	Guatemala	−0.10
19	Australia	−0.13
20	Ireland	−0.29
21	Trinidad and Tobago	−0.30
22	Switzerland	−0.40
23	Austria	−0.57
24	Bulgaria	−0.68
25	Chile	−0.80
26	Singapore	−1.11
27	Netherlands	−1.14
28	Mexico	−1.17
29	Lithuania	−1.20
30	Greece	−1.24
31	United Kingdom	−1.29
32	South Africa	−1.40
33	Thailand	−1.50
34	Indonesia	−1.60
35	Morocco	−2.00
36	Senegal	−2.20
37	Paraguay	−2.28
38	Peru	−2.30
39	Italy	−2.46
40	Tunisia	−2.50
41	Latvia	−2.52
42	Portugal	−2.68
43	Romania	−2.90
44	Slovenia	−2.98
45	Namibia	−3.00
46	El Salvador	−3.10
47	France	−3.17
48	China	−3.20
48	Panama	−3.20
50	United States	−3.37
51	Haiti	−3.40
51	Kenya	−3.40

RANK	COUNTRY	HARD DATA
53	Nigeria	−3.60
54	Germany	−3.61
55	Venezuela	−3.70
56	Botswana	−4.00
56	Colombia	−4.00
56	Costa Rica	−4.00
56	Israel	−4.00
60	Bangladesh	−4.40
61	Czech Republic	−4.49
62	Angola	−4.50
62	Pakistan	−4.50
64	Philippines	−4.52
65	Serbia	−4.70
66	Macedonia, FYR	−4.80
67	Malaysia	−5.20
67	Malta	−5.20
67	Uruguay	−5.20
70	Hong Kong SAR	−5.40
71	Vietnam	−5.50
72	Poland	−5.74
73	Egypt	−5.90
74	Tanzania	−6.10
75	Ghana	−6.20
76	Honduras	−6.50
76	Mauritius	−6.50
78	Croatia	−6.60
79	Taiwan	−6.70
80	Ecuador	−6.90
81	Japan	−7.11
82	Slovak Republic	−7.16
83	Madagascar	−7.70
84	Jordan	−8.00
85	Sri Lanka	−8.20
86	Hungary	−8.36
87	Bolivia	−8.70
87	Brazil	−8.70
89	Jamaica	−9.30
89	Nicaragua	−9.30
91	Gambia	−9.40
92	Malawi	−9.90
93	India	−10.00
94	Argentina	−10.30
95	Mali	−10.50
95	Zimbabwe	−10.50
97	Chad	−11.00
98	Uganda	−12.60
99	Turkey	−13.00
100	Zambia	−14.40
101	Ethiopia	−14.90
102	Mozambique	−18.40

419

SOURCES: IMF Country Reports; OECD Economic Outlook, No. 73, June 2003; OECD African Economic Outlook 2002/03; Economist Intelligence Unit, and national sources

2.19 National savings rate, 2002

National savings rate as a percentage of GDP, 2002

RANK	COUNTRY	HARD DATA
1	Singapore	43.90
2	China	42.40
3	Hong Kong SAR	35.90
4	Zambia	34.40
5	Botswana	34.10
6	Algeria	32.60
7	Vietnam	32.40
8	Norway	31.96
9	Thailand	30.60
10	Russian Federation	30.52
11	Malaysia	30.30
12	Switzerland	29.60
13	Korea	29.43
14	Jordan	29.40
15	Luxembourg	28.10
16	Mauritius	28.00
17	Ukraine	27.60
18	Finland	27.30
19	Nigeria	27.10
20	Japan	26.60
21	Taiwan	26.40
22	Trinidad and Tobago	25.90
23	Venezuela	25.80
24	Morocco	25.40
24	Namibia	25.40
26	Slovenia	24.90
27	Honduras	24.20
28	Philippines	24.10
29	Belgium	24.09
30	Tunisia	24.00
31	Panama	23.90
32	Latvia	23.80
33	Spain	23.51
34	Bangladesh	23.30
35	India	23.20
36	Turkey	23.20
37	Ghana	23.10
37	Netherlands	23.10
37	Slovak Republic	23.10
40	Czech Republic	22.82
41	Denmark	22.70
42	Germany	22.10
43	Cameroon	21.80
44	Ecuador	21.75
45	Ireland	21.60
46	Canada	21.50
47	France	21.04
48	Sweden	20.90
49	Paraguay	20.70
50	Austria	20.60
51	Croatia	20.16
52	Hungary	20.10
53	Romania	19.70
54	Dominican Republic	19.60
55	Argentina	19.40
55	Chile	19.40
55	Italy	19.40
58	Estonia	19.30
58	Sri Lanka	19.30
60	Pakistan	19.20
61	Iceland	19.10
62	Malta	18.75
63	Australia	18.70
64	Jamaica	18.40
65	Haiti	18.20
66	Israel	18.18
67	Indonesia	18.10
67	Mexico	18.10
69	Portugal	17.90
70	Lithuania	17.70
71	Greece	17.50
71	South Africa	17.50
73	Egypt	17.20
74	New Zealand	17.10
75	Brazil	17.00
75	Mozambique	17.00
77	Senegal	16.50
78	Peru	16.38
79	Poland	15.67
80	Bulgaria	15.34
81	Gambia	15.10
82	Costa Rica	14.60
83	United Kingdom	14.54
84	Angola	13.60
85	El Salvador	13.20
85	Mali	13.20
87	Kenya	12.90
88	Colombia	12.10
89	Uruguay	11.80
90	Guatemala	11.70
91	Tanzania	11.50
92	Zimbabwe	11.40
93	United States	10.48
94	Uganda	10.00
95	Serbia*	9.90
96	Bolivia	9.70
97	Macedonia, FYR	8.40
98	Madagascar	6.40
99	Malawi	6.20
100	Ethiopia	4.30
101	Chad	3.30
102	Nicaragua	−1.20

SOURCES: Economist Intelligence Unit, IMF Country Reports, and national sources

*Value for Serbia and Montenegro

2.20   Inflation, 2002

Percentage change in consumer price index, 2002

RANK	COUNTRY	HARD DATA	
1	Ethiopia	−7.2	▪
2	Hong Kong SAR	−3.0	▪
3	Uganda	−2.0	▪
4	Japan	−0.9	▪
5	China	−0.8	▪
6	Singapore	−0.4	▪
7	Taiwan	−0.2	▪
8	Peru	0.2	▪
9	Lithuania	0.3	▪
10	Thailand	0.6	▪
11	Switzerland	0.7	▪
12	Ukraine	0.8	▪
13	Bolivia	0.9	▪
14	Panama	1.0	▪
15	Germany	1.3	▪
15	Norway	1.3	▪
17	Algeria	1.4	▪
18	Belgium	1.6	▪
18	United States	1.6	▪
20	Austria	1.8	▪
20	Czech Republic	1.8	▪
20	Jordan	1.8	▪
20	Malaysia	1.8	▪
24	El Salvador	1.9	▪
24	France	1.9	▪
24	Latvia	1.9	▪
24	Poland	1.9	▪
28	Canada	2.0	▪
28	Kenya	2.0	▪
28	Sweden	2.0	▪
31	Luxembourg	2.1	▪
32	Croatia	2.2	▪
32	Finland	2.2	▪
32	Malta	2.2	▪
32	Senegal	2.2	▪
32	United Kingdom	2.2	▪
37	Bangladesh	2.4	▪
37	Denmark	2.4	▪
37	Macedonia, FYR	2.4	▪
40	Chile	2.5	▪
40	Egypt	2.5	▪
42	Italy	2.6	▪
43	New Zealand	2.7	▪
44	Korea	2.8	▪
44	Morocco	2.8	▪
46	Australia	3.0	▪
47	Pakistan	3.1	▪
47	Philippines	3.1	▪
47	Tunisia	3.1	▪
50	Slovak Republic	3.3	▪
51	Spain	3.6	▪
52	Portugal	3.7	▪

RANK	COUNTRY	HARD DATA	
53	Trinidad and Tobago	3.8	▪
54	Greece	3.9	▪
54	Netherlands	3.9	▪
56	Vietnam	4.0	▪
57	Estonia	4.3	▪
57	India	4.3	▪
59	Nicaragua	4.4	▪
60	Cameroon	4.5	▪
60	Chad	4.5	▪
60	Madagascar	4.5	▪
63	Ireland	4.7	▪
63	Tanzania	4.7	▪
65	Iceland	4.8	▪
66	Mali	4.9	▪
67	Mexico	5.0	▪
68	Dominican Republic	5.2	▪
69	Hungary	5.3	▪
70	Botswana	5.5	▪
71	Israel	5.7	▪
72	Bulgaria	5.8	▪
73	Mauritius	6.0	▪
74	Colombia	6.3	▪
74	Guatemala	6.3	▪
76	Jamaica	6.5	▪
77	Gambia	7.1	▪
78	Slovenia	7.5	▪
79	Honduras	7.7	▪
80	Brazil	8.4	▪
81	Haiti	8.7	▪
82	Sri Lanka	8.8	▪
83	Costa Rica	9.1	▪
84	South Africa	10.0	▪
85	Paraguay	10.5	▪
86	Namibia	11.3	▪
87	Indonesia	11.9	▪
88	Ecuador	12.6	▪
89	Nigeria	12.9	▪
90	Uruguay	14.0	▪
91	Malawi	14.1	▪
92	Ghana	14.5	▪
93	Russian Federation	16.0	▪
94	Mozambique	16.8	▪
95	Serbia	21.3	▪
96	Zambia	22.2	▪
97	Venezuela	22.4	▪
98	Romania	22.5	▪
99	Argentina	25.9	▪
100	Turkey	45.0	▪
101	Angola	108.9	▪
102	Zimbabwe	140.0	▪

SOURCE: IMF World Economic Outlook Database, April 2003

2.21 Real exchange rate, 2002

2002 period average real exchange rate relative to the United States (1995 = 100). Values greater (less) than 100 indicate depreciation (appreciation) relative to the United States.

RANK	COUNTRY	HARD DATA		RANK	COUNTRY	HARD DATA
1	Argentina	291.8		53	Iceland	130.0
2	Nigeria	275.2		54	Peru	129.3
3	Brazil	226.0		55	Bangladesh	127.3
4	South Africa	202.3		56	Norway	127.2
5	Gambia	200.0		57	Mozambique	127.1
6	Macedonia, FYR	194.6		58	Bolivia	126.9
7	Namibia	190.3		59	Italy	125.5
8	Paraguay	190.2		60	Malta	121.7
9	Serbia*	182.7		61	Egypt	120.6
10	Ireland	181.6		62	Russian Federation	119.2
11	Uruguay	176.1		63	Canada	118.2
12	Uganda	171.7		64	Hong Kong SAR	116.6
13	Ghana	169.0		65	Nicaragua	115.4
14	Ethiopia	162.5		66	Sri Lanka	113.9
15	Thailand	161.7		67	India	113.5
16	Japan	157.6		68	Ecuador	112.5
17	Botswana	156.5		69	Malawi	111.5
18	Germany	154.2		70	Kenya	111.4
19	Philippines	153.6		71	Zambia	111.1
20	Indonesia	153.0		72	Panama	109.9
21	Austria	152.8		73	Turkey	109.7
22	Finland	151.8		74	Slovak Republic	109.4
23	Belgium	151.7		75	Chad	108.2
24	Luxembourg	151.4		76	Costa Rica	107.2
25	Pakistan	150.5		77	United Kingdom	105.0
26	Sweden	150.4		78	Hungary	104.1
27	Chile	150.2		79	Dominican Republic	102.8
28	France	149.7		80	Poland	101.4
29	Malaysia	148.6		81	Jordan	100.5
30	Switzerland	147.4		82	United States	100.0
31	New Zealand	147.4		83	Tanzania	99.7
32	Korea	147.4		84	Estonia	98.7
33	Senegal	145.8		85	Czech Republic	98.5
34	Tunisia	144.6		86	Romania	97.4
35	Taiwan	143.8		87	Venezuela	96.2
36	Netherlands	142.8		88	Latvia	94.8
37	Singapore	141.7		89	Guatemala	94.7
38	Denmark	141.5		90	Madagascar	93.1
39	Slovenia	138.3		91	Bulgaria	93.1
40	Colombia	137.8		92	Trinidad and Tobago	93.1
41	Spain	137.7		93	El Salvador	92.3
42	Algeria	137.6		94	China	91.9
43	Mali	137.3		95	Haiti	91.6
44	Australia	136.1		96	Ukraine	90.2
45	Greece	136.0		97	Honduras	82.6
46	Israel	135.9		98	Jamaica	82.2
47	Portugal	135.0		99	Angola	77.9
48	Cameroon	135.0		100	Lithuania	73.6
49	Mauritius	134.4		101	Mexico	66.2
50	Morocco	134.2		102	Zimbabwe	37.6
51	Croatia	132.0				
52	Vietnam	131.9				

SOURCES: IMF World Economic Outlook Database, April 2003, IMF International Financial Statistics, June 2003, national sources, and authors' calculations

*1997 = 100 for Serbia

2.22   Interest rate spread, 2002

Average interest rate spread, 2002 (difference between typical lending and deposit rates)

RANK	COUNTRY	HARD DATA		RANK	COUNTRY	HARD DATA
1	United Kingdom	1.00		53	Namibia	6.03
2	Netherlands	1.18		54	Mexico	6.52
3	Japan	1.36		55	Bulgaria	6.58
4	Canada	1.56		56	Jordan	6.66
5	Norway	1.61		57	Germany	7.05
6	Malta	1.74		58	Mozambique	7.22
7	Spain	1.81		59	Colombia	7.38
8	Korea	1.81		60	Pakistan	7.42
9	Luxembourg	1.98		61	Venezuela	7.58
10	Portugal	2.40		62	Trinidad and Tobago	7.80
11	Vietnam	2.61		63	Bangladesh	7.83
12	Hungary	2.73		64	Nigeria	8.00
13	India	2.90		65	Macedonia, FYR	8.30
13	Indonesia	2.90		66	Honduras	8.90
13	Sri Lanka	2.90		67	Senegal	9.00
16	United States	2.95		68	Ecuador	9.04
17	Switzerland	3.03		69	Morocco	9.20
18	Malaysia	3.19		70	Dominican Republic	9.52
19	Algeria	3.20		71	Jamaica	9.90
20	China	3.30		72	Guatemala	10.00
21	Finland	3.33		73	Iceland	10.07
22	France	3.60		74	Romania	10.11
23	Slovak Republic	3.60		75	Peru	10.54
24	El Salvador	3.73		76	Russian Federation	10.70
25	Ireland	3.73		77	Croatia	10.95
26	Sweden	3.76		78	Bolivia	11.03
27	Czech Republic	3.80		79	Mauritius	11.12
28	Austria	3.87		80	Mali	11.31
29	Israel	3.90		81	Ghana	11.40
30	Chile	3.96		82	Gambia	11.50
31	Estonia	3.97		83	Kenya	12.45
32	Italy	4.34		84	Cameroon	13.00
33	Singapore	4.46		84	Chad	13.00
34	New Zealand	4.48		86	Tanzania	13.14
35	Egypt	4.50		87	Madagascar	13.30
36	Philippines	4.53		88	Uganda	13.39
37	Ethiopia	4.55		89	Argentina	13.72
38	Denmark	4.60		90	Serbia*	14.00
38	Greece	4.60		91	Turkey	14.51
40	Hong Kong SAR	4.70		92	Costa Rica	14.96
41	Latvia	4.74		93	Nicaragua	15.90
42	Thailand	4.90		94	Ukraine	17.42
43	Slovenia	4.93		95	Haiti	17.43
44	Australia	4.93		96	Zimbabwe	18.30
45	South Africa	4.98		97	Malawi	19.50
46	Tunisia	5.00		98	Zambia	21.90
47	Belgium	5.11		99	Paraguay	29.24
48	Lithuania	5.14		100	Brazil	43.52
49	Panama	5.43		101	Angola	49.51
50	Taiwan	5.62		102	Uruguay	81.10
51	Botswana	5.66				
52	Poland	6.00				

SOURCES: IMF International Financial Statistics, June 2003; Economist Intelligence Unit, and national sources

*Value for Serbia and Montenegro

Section III: Technology: Innovation and Diffusion

3.01 Technological sophistication

Your country's position in technology (1 = generally lags behind most other countries, 7 = is among those of the world leaders)

RANK	COUNTRY	SCORE	MEAN: 3.7	SD	RANK	COUNTRY	SCORE	MEAN: 3.7	SD
1	Finland	6.6		0.6	53	Botswana	3.5		1.3
2	United States	6.3		1.4	54	Indonesia	3.5		1.6
3	Sweden	6.3		0.7	55	Jamaica	3.4		1.2
4	Israel	6.2		0.9	56	Lithuania	3.4		1.2
5	Japan	6.2		0.7	57	Portugal	3.4		1.2
6	Singapore	5.8		0.9	58	Colombia	3.3		1.1
7	Denmark	5.7		0.9	59	Turkey	3.3		1.1
8	Iceland	5.7		1.0	60	Mauritius	3.3		1.4
9	Switzerland	5.6		1.0	61	Russian Federation	3.3		1.5
10	United Kingdom	5.5		1.0	62	Venezuela	3.3		1.3
11	Canada	5.3		1.4	63	Greece	3.2		1.3
12	Australia	5.3		1.1	64	Morocco	3.2		1.7
13	Norway	5.2		1.1	65	Uruguay	3.2		1.5
14	France	5.2		1.3	66	Sri Lanka	3.2		1.2
15	Korea	5.2		1.0	67	Peru	3.1		1.3
16	Germany	5.2		1.3	68	Ukraine	3.0		1.4
17	Taiwan	5.0		1.0	69	Zimbabwe	3.0		1.5
18	New Zealand	5.0		1.1	70	Philippines	3.0		1.4
19	Hong Kong SAR	4.9		1.1	71	Vietnam	2.9		1.2
20	Belgium	4.9		1.5	72	Kenya	2.9		1.2
21	Ireland	4.8		1.4	73	Pakistan	2.8		1.1
22	Malaysia	4.7		1.1	74	Ghana	2.7		1.3
23	Netherlands	4.7		1.4	75	Romania	2.7		1.2
24	Estonia	4.6		1.1	76	Guatemala	2.6		1.2
25	India	4.6		1.4	77	Ecuador	2.6		1.2
26	Luxembourg	4.5		1.4	78	Senegal	2.6		1.4
27	Panama	4.4		1.1	79	Bulgaria	2.6		1.1
28	Spain	4.4		1.3	80	Croatia	2.6		1.5
29	Chile	4.4		1.2	81	Paraguay	2.5		1.1
30	Malta	4.3		1.4	82	Tanzania	2.4		1.3
31	Latvia	4.3		1.4	83	Zambia	2.4		1.1
32	Austria	4.3		1.3	84	Nigeria	2.4		1.3
33	Slovenia	4.1		1.1	85	Madagascar	2.4		1.2
34	Costa Rica	4.1		1.3	86	Uganda	2.3		1.3
35	Italy	4.1		1.4	87	Gambia	2.3		1.3
36	Thailand	4.1		1.3	88	Macedonia, FYR	2.3		1.6
37	Slovak Republic	4.1		1.4	89	Algeria	2.3		1.1
38	Czech Republic	4.1		1.2	90	Cameroon	2.3		1.4
39	South Africa	4.0		1.4	91	Bangladesh	2.2		1.2
40	Brazil	4.0		1.3	92	Nicaragua	2.2		1.1
41	Namibia	4.0		1.2	93	Malawi	2.2		1.4
42	Tunisia	4.0		1.2	94	Bolivia	2.0		1.0
43	Dominican Republic	4.0		0.9	95	Mozambique	2.0		1.2
44	Jordan	4.0		1.3	96	Serbia	2.0		1.2
45	Trinidad and Tobago	3.9		1.3	97	Honduras	1.9		1.0
46	Argentina	3.8		1.2	98	Mali	1.8		1.0
47	Hungary	3.8		1.1	99	Angola	1.8		0.9
48	China	3.7		1.2	100	Chad	1.7		1.2
49	El Salvador	3.6		1.2	101	Haiti	1.7		0.6
50	Poland	3.6		1.4	102	Ethiopia	1.5		0.8
51	Mexico	3.6		1.3					
52	Egypt	3.6		1.6					

3.02 Firm-level technology absorption

Companies in your country are (1 = not interested in absorbing new technology, 7 = aggressive in absorbing new technology)

RANK	COUNTRY	SCORE	1 MEAN: 4.9 7	SD
1	Finland	6.4		0.6
2	Japan	6.3		0.6
3	Sweden	6.3		0.7
4	Israel	6.2		0.8
5	Singapore	6.1		0.8
6	United States	6.1		1.4
7	Iceland	6.0		0.6
8	Taiwan	5.9		1.1
9	Switzerland	5.8		1.1
10	Korea	5.8		1.0
11	Germany	5.7		1.0
12	Senegal	5.7		1.3
13	Denmark	5.7		0.6
14	Malaysia	5.6		0.8
15	Vietnam	5.5		1.3
16	Australia	5.5		0.6
17	Costa Rica	5.4		1.1
18	Canada	5.4		1.0
19	Estonia	5.4		1.0
20	Luxembourg	5.4		1.0
21	Norway	5.4		0.8
22	New Zealand	5.3		0.9
23	Tunisia	5.3		1.2
24	Chile	5.3		1.0
25	Lithuania	5.3		0.9
26	Slovak Republic	5.3		1.1
27	France	5.3		0.9
28	Hong Kong SAR	5.3		1.2
29	Ireland	5.3		1.0
30	Thailand	5.2		1.0
31	India	5.2		1.1
32	Panama	5.1		1.1
33	Dominican Republic	5.1		1.1
34	United Kingdom	5.1		1.0
35	Croatia	5.1		1.5
36	Spain	5.1		1.1
37	Austria	5.1		1.2
38	Latvia	5.1		0.9
39	South Africa	5.1		1.0
40	Brazil	5.1		1.1
41	Belgium	5.0		1.1
42	Gambia	5.0		1.5
43	Morocco	5.0		1.7
44	Mexico	5.0		1.1
45	Malta	5.0		1.0
46	Slovenia	5.0		1.0
47	Trinidad and Tobago	4.9		1.0
48	Jordan	4.9		1.3
49	Nigeria	4.9		1.3
50	Tanzania	4.9		1.3
51	Netherlands	4.8		1.2
52	El Salvador	4.8		1.4

RANK	COUNTRY	SCORE	1 MEAN: 4.9 7	SD
53	Czech Republic	4.8		1.2
54	Poland	4.8		1.1
54	Turkey	4.8		1.2
56	Madagascar	4.8		1.4
57	Ghana	4.7		1.6
58	China	4.7		1.5
59	Colombia	4.7		1.2
60	Uganda	4.7		1.8
61	Italy	4.7		1.3
62	Sri Lanka	4.7		1.4
63	Mauritius	4.7		0.9
64	Mozambique	4.6		1.4
65	Romania	4.6		1.4
66	Russian Federation	4.6		1.4
67	Ukraine	4.6		1.3
68	Hungary	4.6		0.9
69	Botswana	4.6		1.2
70	Argentina	4.5		1.2
71	Egypt	4.5		1.6
72	Philippines	4.5		1.1
73	Jamaica	4.5		1.2
74	Venezuela	4.5		1.3
75	Namibia	4.5		1.2
76	Algeria	4.5		1.7
77	Kenya	4.5		1.2
78	Greece	4.4		1.2
79	Peru	4.4		1.3
80	Zimbabwe	4.4		1.2
81	Guatemala	4.3		1.3
82	Pakistan	4.3		1.2
83	Bangladesh	4.3		1.5
84	Cameroon	4.3		1.6
85	Angola	4.3		1.8
86	Serbia	4.3		1.3
87	Portugal	4.2		1.2
88	Zambia	4.2		1.4
89	Haiti	4.2		1.4
90	Ecuador	4.1		1.4
91	Nicaragua	4.1		1.7
92	Malawi	4.1		1.5
93	Macedonia, FYR	4.0		1.8
94	Mali	4.0		1.9
95	Bulgaria	4.0		1.2
96	Indonesia	4.0		1.5
96	Uruguay	4.0		1.0
98	Ethiopia	4.0		1.6
99	Chad	4.0		2.1
100	Paraguay	3.8		1.3
101	Honduras	3.8		1.4
102	Bolivia	3.7		1.3

427

3.03   FDI and technology transfer

Foreign direct investment (FDI) in your country (1 = brings little new technology, 7 = is an important source of new technology)

RANK	COUNTRY	SCORE	1 MEAN: 4.8 7	SD
1	Ireland	6.4		0.6
2	Singapore	6.3		0.9
3	Malta	5.8		1.0
4	Malaysia	5.8		0.9
5	Estonia	5.7		0.9
6	Czech Republic	5.6		1.3
7	Slovak Republic	5.6		1.6
8	Hungary	5.6		1.1
9	Trinidad and Tobago	5.6		1.2
10	Brazil	5.6		1.1
11	Panama	5.5		1.3
12	Dominican Republic	5.5		1.2
13	Mexico	5.5		1.3
14	Philippines	5.4		1.4
15	Costa Rica	5.4		1.1
16	Argentina	5.4		1.4
17	Jamaica	5.3		1.3
18	Chile	5.3		1.1
19	Vietnam	5.3		1.4
20	Nigeria	5.3		1.6
21	Kenya	5.3		1.4
22	Australia	5.3		1.2
23	Uganda	5.2		1.9
24	Thailand	5.2		1.1
25	Peru	5.2		1.4
26	South Africa	5.2		1.3
27	Taiwan	5.2		1.1
28	Poland	5.2		1.2
29	Tanzania	5.1		1.5
30	Mozambique	5.1		1.6
31	India	5.1		1.4
32	New Zealand	5.1		1.2
33	Portugal	5.1		1.2
34	Latvia	5.1		1.2
35	United Kingdom	5.1		1.1
36	Sri Lanka	5.1		1.6
37	Belgium	5.0		1.4
38	Luxembourg	5.0		1.3
39	Honduras	5.0		1.6
40	Romania	5.0		1.8
41	Morocco	5.0		1.6
42	Ghana	4.9		1.7
43	Malawi	4.9		1.8
44	El Salvador	4.9		1.6
45	Canada	4.9		1.5
46	Spain	4.9		1.3
47	Venezuela	4.9		1.5
48	Botswana	4.9		1.6
49	Lithuania	4.8		1.6
50	Tunisia	4.8		1.4
51	China	4.8		1.5
52	Guatemala	4.8		1.6

RANK	COUNTRY	SCORE	1 MEAN: 4.8 7	SD
53	Israel	4.8		1.5
54	Gambia	4.7		2.1
55	Colombia	4.7		1.6
56	Italy	4.7		1.2
57	Egypt	4.7		1.8
58	Korea	4.7		1.3
59	Hong Kong SAR	4.7		1.7
60	Greece	4.7		1.3
61	Netherlands	4.7		1.3
62	Namibia	4.7		1.5
63	Iceland	4.7		1.4
63	Norway	4.7		1.2
65	Jordan	4.7		1.6
66	France	4.6		1.3
67	Denmark	4.6		1.1
68	Nicaragua	4.6		1.8
69	Pakistan	4.6		1.6
70	Austria	4.6		1.2
71	Zambia	4.6		1.9
72	Japan	4.6		1.2
73	Zimbabwe	4.5		2.1
74	Angola	4.5		2.0
75	Sweden	4.5		1.3
76	Serbia	4.5		2.0
77	Bangladesh	4.5		1.9
78	United States	4.5		1.5
79	Germany	4.5		1.4
80	Turkey	4.4		1.7
81	Uruguay	4.4		1.4
82	Macedonia, FYR	4.4		2.1
83	Ecuador	4.4		1.8
84	Finland	4.4		1.4
85	Indonesia	4.4		1.5
86	Mauritius	4.3		1.3
87	Slovenia	4.3		1.4
88	Croatia	4.2		1.9
89	Switzerland	4.2		1.6
90	Cameroon	4.2		1.9
91	Bolivia	4.2		1.7
92	Senegal	4.2		1.7
93	Paraguay	4.1		1.8
94	Madagascar	4.0		1.5
95	Bulgaria	4.0		1.8
96	Russian Federation	4.0		1.9
97	Mali	3.9		2.1
98	Ethiopia	3.9		2.4
99	Ukraine	3.7		1.5
100	Chad	3.5		1.9
101	Haiti	2.8		1.5
102	Algeria	2.7		1.5

428

In your country, licensing foreign technology is (1 = uncommon, 7 = a common means of acquiring new technology)

RANK	COUNTRY	SCORE	1 MEAN: 4.5 7	SD
1	Singapore	5.7		1.1
2	Malaysia	5.6		0.9
3	Australia	5.6		1.0
4	South Africa	5.6		0.8
5	Thailand	5.5		1.1
6	India	5.5		1.4
7	Brazil	5.3		1.4
8	Mexico	5.2		1.4
9	Portugal	5.2		1.2
10	Greece	5.2		1.4
11	Costa Rica	5.2		1.4
12	Botswana	5.1		1.6
13	Jordan	5.1		1.5
14	Taiwan	5.1		1.6
15	Italy	5.1		1.2
16	Denmark	5.1		1.2
17	Czech Republic	5.1		1.3
18	Latvia	5.1		1.2
19	Korea	5.1		1.4
20	Israel	5.1		1.1
21	Croatia	5.0		1.7
22	Iceland	5.0		1.2
23	Philippines	5.0		1.3
23	Turkey	5.0		1.4
23	United States	5.0		1.3
26	Panama	5.0		1.4
27	Japan	5.0		1.5
28	Kenya	5.0		1.7
29	Tunisia	4.9		1.3
30	Chile	4.9		1.4
31	Dominican Republic	4.9		1.4
32	New Zealand	4.9		1.3
33	Namibia	4.9		1.4
34	Nigeria	4.9		1.7
35	Tanzania	4.9		1.6
36	Netherlands	4.9		1.4
37	Hong Kong SAR	4.8		1.7
38	Germany	4.8		1.4
39	Zimbabwe	4.8		1.5
40	Uganda	4.8		2.0
41	Estonia	4.8		1.3
42	Trinidad and Tobago	4.8		1.6
43	Poland	4.7		1.4
44	Sri Lanka	4.7		1.7
45	Malta	4.7		1.6
46	Luxembourg	4.7		1.5
47	Finland	4.7		1.5
48	Slovak Republic	4.7		1.6
49	Argentina	4.7		1.5
50	Venezuela	4.6		1.4
51	Mauritius	4.6		1.3
52	Canada	4.6		1.6

RANK	COUNTRY	SCORE	1 MEAN: 4.5 7	SD
53	Belgium	4.6		1.7
54	Ireland	4.6		1.5
55	France	4.6		1.2
55	Spain	4.6		1.7
57	United Kingdom	4.6		1.7
58	El Salvador	4.6		1.5
58	Switzerland	4.6		1.6
60	Slovenia	4.6		1.2
61	Pakistan	4.6		1.6
62	Norway	4.6		1.2
63	Sweden	4.5		1.6
64	Egypt	4.5		1.7
65	Hungary	4.5		1.5
66	Lithuania	4.5		1.5
67	Romania	4.5		1.6
68	Vietnam	4.4		1.7
69	Morocco	4.4		1.9
70	China	4.4		1.6
71	Ghana	4.3		1.7
72	Peru	4.3		1.5
73	Jamaica	4.2		1.6
74	Austria	4.2		1.5
75	Colombia	4.1		1.6
76	Uruguay	4.0		1.5
77	Zambia	3.9		1.8
78	Macedonia, FYR	3.9		2.2
79	Malawi	3.9		1.9
80	Ecuador	3.8		1.5
81	Indonesia	3.8		1.4
82	Senegal	3.8		2.1
83	Bangladesh	3.8		1.9
84	Mozambique	3.8		1.9
85	Nicaragua	3.8		1.5
86	Serbia	3.8		1.9
87	Guatemala	3.7		1.8
88	Cameroon	3.7		1.9
89	Honduras	3.7		1.6
90	Gambia	3.6		2.1
91	Bulgaria	3.6		1.6
92	Algeria	3.3		2.0
93	Russian Federation	3.3		1.6
94	Ukraine	3.3		1.5
95	Bolivia	3.1		1.5
96	Angola	3.1		1.8
97	Paraguay	2.9		1.3
98	Madagascar	2.8		1.7
99	Ethiopia	2.8		1.7
100	Chad	2.7		1.9
101	Haiti	2.6		1.7
102	Mali	2.6		1.8

429

3.05   Quality of scientific research institutions

Scientific research institutions in your country (eg, university laboratories, government laboratories) are (1 = nonexistent, 7 = the best in their fields)

RANK	COUNTRY	SCORE	1 MEAN: 4.0 7	SD
1	United States	6.2		1.4
2	Israel	5.9		0.8
3	Switzerland	5.8		1.0
4	Finland	5.8		0.6
5	United Kingdom	5.7		1.0
6	Sweden	5.6		0.7
7	Denmark	5.5		0.7
8	France	5.5		0.9
9	Australia	5.5		0.8
10	Singapore	5.4		0.9
11	Japan	5.4		1.0
12	Germany	5.4		0.8
13	Canada	5.3		1.0
14	Ireland	5.2		1.0
15	Belgium	5.2		1.1
16	Netherlands	5.1		1.1
17	New Zealand	5.1		1.0
18	Taiwan	5.0		1.1
19	Norway	4.9		1.1
20	India	4.9		1.4
21	Iceland	4.9		0.9
22	Hungary	4.8		1.1
23	Austria	4.7		1.0
24	South Africa	4.7		1.2
25	Russian Federation	4.7		1.5
26	Korea	4.7		1.1
27	Kenya	4.6		1.3
28	China	4.6		1.1
29	Slovenia	4.5		1.0
30	Costa Rica	4.5		1.2
31	Estonia	4.5		1.1
32	Tanzania	4.5		1.4
33	Uganda	4.4		1.6
34	Czech Republic	4.4		1.3
35	Vietnam	4.4		1.3
36	Malaysia	4.3		1.0
37	Jamaica	4.3		1.2
38	Lithuania	4.3		1.3
39	Hong Kong SAR	4.3		1.3
40	Ghana	4.2		1.5
41	Portugal	4.2		1.0
42	Croatia	4.2		1.3
43	Thailand	4.2		1.0
44	Italy	4.2		1.4
45	Tunisia	4.2		1.3
46	Jordan	4.2		1.3
47	Latvia	4.1		1.3
48	Chile	4.1		1.3
49	Brazil	4.1		1.1
50	Cameroon	4.0		1.5
51	Spain	4.0		1.2
52	Mexico	3.9		1.3

RANK	COUNTRY	SCORE	1 MEAN: 4.0 7	SD
53	Botswana	3.9		1.4
54	Poland	3.9		1.2
55	Greece	3.9		1.2
56	Sri Lanka	3.9		1.4
57	Ukraine	3.9		1.3
58	Serbia	3.8		1.5
59	Slovak Republic	3.8		1.3
60	Egypt	3.8		1.7
61	Trinidad and Tobago	3.7		1.1
62	Indonesia	3.7		1.3
63	Luxembourg	3.7		1.3
64	Colombia	3.7		1.3
65	Ethiopia	3.7		1.5
66	Morocco	3.7		1.6
67	Senegal	3.7		1.9
68	Malawi	3.6		1.5
69	Romania	3.6		1.6
70	Bulgaria	3.6		1.4
71	Malta	3.6		1.4
72	Zimbabwe	3.6		1.4
73	Argentina	3.5		1.4
74	Uruguay	3.5		1.3
75	Mali	3.5		1.8
76	Zambia	3.5		1.4
77	Venezuela	3.5		1.3
78	Mauritius	3.5		1.3
79	Turkey	3.4		1.1
80	Namibia	3.4		1.3
81	Nigeria	3.4		1.4
82	Panama	3.3		1.3
83	Dominican Republic	3.2		1.4
84	Macedonia, FYR	3.2		1.6
85	Bangladesh	3.2		1.3
86	Madagascar	3.2		1.3
87	Gambia	3.1		1.9
88	Algeria	3.1		1.2
89	Philippines	3.0		1.3
90	Pakistan	3.0		1.3
91	Peru	3.0		1.1
92	Mozambique	2.9		1.4
93	Guatemala	2.9		1.3
94	Ecuador	2.8		1.3
95	Honduras	2.6		1.3
96	El Salvador	2.5		1.1
97	Nicaragua	2.5		1.2
98	Bolivia	2.4		1.1
99	Angola	2.4		1.2
100	Chad	2.4		1.5
101	Paraguay	2.2		1.0
102	Haiti	1.6		0.7

3.06 Company spending on research and development

Companies in your country (1 = do not spend money on research and development, 7 = spend heavily on research and development relative to international peers)

RANK	COUNTRY	SCORE	1 MEAN: 3.4 7	SD
1	United States	5.9		1.3
2	Finland	5.8		0.8
3	Japan	5.6		0.9
4	Sweden	5.6		0.8
5	Switzerland	5.6		1.2
6	Germany	5.4		1.0
7	Israel	5.1		0.8
8	Denmark	5.1		0.8
9	France	4.9		0.9
10	Singapore	4.8		1.1
11	United Kingdom	4.8		1.0
12	Korea	4.7		1.1
13	Taiwan	4.7		1.1
14	Canada	4.6		1.2
15	Netherlands	4.6		1.2
16	Iceland	4.5		1.2
17	Belgium	4.5		1.1
18	Luxembourg	4.4		1.2
19	Ireland	4.4		1.2
20	Slovenia	4.3		1.0
21	South Africa	4.2		0.9
22	Norway	4.1		1.1
23	Australia	4.0		1.3
24	Latvia	4.0		1.3
25	Malaysia	4.0		1.1
26	Brazil	3.9		1.2
27	Costa Rica	3.9		1.2
28	Hong Kong SAR	3.8		1.3
29	China	3.8		1.3
30	Vietnam	3.7		1.4
31	Austria	3.7		1.1
32	Spain	3.7		1.0
33	Tunisia	3.6		1.6
34	New Zealand	3.6		1.1
35	Indonesia	3.6		1.4
36	Thailand	3.6		1.3
37	Italy	3.6		1.5
38	Morocco	3.6		1.8
39	India	3.5		1.2
40	Lithuania	3.5		1.3
41	Kenya	3.5		1.4
42	Czech Republic	3.4		1.2
43	Namibia	3.4		1.3
44	Estonia	3.4		1.2
45	Poland	3.4		1.1
46	Tanzania	3.4		1.6
47	Greece	3.3		1.2
48	Jamaica	3.3		1.2
49	Chile	3.3		1.1
50	Colombia	3.3		1.2
51	Uganda	3.3		1.5
52	Egypt	3.3		1.8

RANK	COUNTRY	SCORE	1 MEAN: 3.4 7	SD
53	Sri Lanka	3.2		1.2
54	Slovak Republic	3.2		1.3
55	Malta	3.2		1.2
56	Ghana	3.2		1.5
57	Croatia	3.2		1.4
58	Mexico	3.1		1.2
59	Dominican Republic	3.1		1.3
60	Trinidad and Tobago	3.1		1.1
61	Portugal	3.1		1.1
62	Malawi	3.1		1.3
63	Argentina	3.0		1.0
64	Botswana	3.0		1.3
65	Jordan	3.0		1.3
66	Panama	3.0		1.2
67	Hungary	3.0		1.1
68	Philippines	2.9		1.1
69	Nigeria	2.9		1.3
70	Russian Federation	2.9		1.4
71	Zambia	2.9		1.5
72	Zimbabwe	2.9		1.2
73	Mauritius	2.9		1.1
74	Turkey	2.9		0.9
75	Cameroon	2.9		1.6
76	Romania	2.9		1.3
77	El Salvador	2.9		1.1
78	Guatemala	2.8		1.1
79	Bulgaria	2.7		1.1
80	Serbia	2.7		1.3
81	Ukraine	2.7		1.2
82	Venezuela	2.6		1.0
83	Macedonia, FYR	2.6		1.5
84	Uruguay	2.6		1.1
85	Peru	2.6		0.9
86	Madagascar	2.5		1.1
87	Algeria	2.5		1.3
88	Ecuador	2.5		1.0
89	Senegal	2.5		1.1
90	Pakistan	2.3		1.0
91	Honduras	2.3		1.0
92	Mozambique	2.3		1.1
93	Bangladesh	2.3		1.1
94	Nicaragua	2.2		1.0
95	Mali	2.1		1.2
96	Gambia	2.1		1.6
97	Bolivia	2.0		0.9
98	Paraguay	2.0		1.0
99	Chad	2.0		1.3
100	Haiti	1.9		0.9
101	Ethiopia	1.9		0.9
102	Angola	1.9		1.0

431

3.07 Subsidies and tax credits for firm-level research and development

For firms conducting research and development (R&D) in your country, direct government subsidies to individual companies or R&D tax credits
(1 = never occur, 7 = are widespread and large)

RANK	COUNTRY	SCORE		SD
1	Singapore	5.8		0.8
2	Taiwan	5.3		1.1
3	Luxembourg	5.2		1.4
4	Israel	5.0		0.9
5	Canada	5.0		1.3
6	Finland	4.8		1.1
7	Tunisia	4.8		1.5
8	France	4.6		1.2
9	Malaysia	4.6		1.0
10	Japan	4.6		1.4
11	Ireland	4.5		1.2
12	United States	4.5		1.5
13	Australia	4.4		1.2
14	Austria	4.3		1.3
15	Korea	4.3		1.2
16	Norway	4.3		1.3
17	Belgium	4.3		1.3
18	Netherlands	4.2		1.4
19	Germany	4.2		1.3
19	United Kingdom	4.2		1.2
21	India	4.1		1.4
22	China	3.9		1.3
23	Spain	3.8		1.1
24	Portugal	3.8		1.3
25	Thailand	3.8		1.5
26	Greece	3.7		1.4
27	Latvia	3.7		1.6
28	Indonesia	3.7		1.5
29	Slovenia	3.6		1.4
30	Sweden	3.6		1.6
31	Iceland	3.5		1.4
32	Denmark	3.5		1.5
33	Italy	3.5		1.2
34	Vietnam	3.5		1.4
35	Brazil	3.5		1.3
36	Morocco	3.5		1.6
37	Hungary	3.5		1.2
38	Malta	3.5		1.5
39	South Africa	3.4		1.2
40	Turkey	3.3		1.4
41	Switzerland	3.2		1.6
42	Czech Republic	3.2		1.2
43	Poland	3.2		1.3
44	Chile	3.2		1.3
45	Egypt	3.2		1.8
46	Lithuania	3.1		1.2
47	Sri Lanka	3.1		1.4
48	Uganda	3.1		1.7
49	Cameroon	3.1		1.6
50	Mauritius	3.0		1.6
51	Mexico	3.0		1.4
52	Croatia	3.0		1.5

RANK	COUNTRY	SCORE		SD
53	Hong Kong SAR	3.0		1.4
54	Jordan	3.0		1.4
55	Estonia	3.0		1.4
56	Tanzania	2.9		1.4
57	Romania	2.9		1.3
58	Botswana	2.9		1.5
59	Algeria	2.9		1.6
60	Senegal	2.9		1.7
61	Russian Federation	2.9		1.4
62	Ghana	2.8		1.5
63	Mali	2.8		1.9
64	Nigeria	2.8		1.5
65	Trinidad and Tobago	2.8		1.2
66	Ukraine	2.8		1.1
67	Slovak Republic	2.8		1.3
68	Namibia	2.8		1.4
69	Kenya	2.6		1.4
70	Jamaica	2.6		1.2
71	Colombia	2.5		1.1
72	New Zealand	2.5		1.3
73	Panama	2.4		1.3
74	Serbia	2.4		1.2
75	Costa Rica	2.4		1.3
76	Zimbabwe	2.4		1.4
77	Bulgaria	2.3		1.1
78	Philippines	2.3		1.0
79	Macedonia, FYR	2.2		1.4
80	Dominican Republic	2.2		1.2
81	Pakistan	2.2		1.3
82	Argentina	2.1		1.0
83	Chad	2.1		1.5
84	Uruguay	2.0		1.1
85	Venezuela	2.0		0.9
86	Zambia	2.0		1.3
87	Madagascar	2.0		1.4
88	Honduras	2.0		1.2
89	Gambia	2.0		1.6
90	Ethiopia	2.0		1.2
91	Mozambique	1.9		1.2
92	Ecuador	1.8		0.8
93	Malawi	1.8		1.0
94	Bangladesh	1.8		1.2
95	Nicaragua	1.6		0.9
96	Angola	1.6		0.9
97	Peru	1.6		0.8
98	Guatemala	1.5		0.9
99	Bolivia	1.4		0.7
100	El Salvador	1.4		0.7
101	Haiti	1.4		0.6
102	Paraguay	1.3		0.6

MEAN: 3.1

In its R&D activity, business collaboration with local universities is (1 = minimal or nonexistent, 7 = intensive and ongoing)

RANK	COUNTRY	SCORE	1 MEAN: 3.3 7	SD
1	Finland	5.9		0.6
2	United States	5.4		1.4
3	Singapore	5.3		1.1
4	Sweden	5.3		1.2
5	Germany	5.1		1.3
6	Taiwan	5.0		1.0
7	Canada	5.0		1.2
8	United Kingdom	4.9		1.3
9	Israel	4.8		1.0
10	Switzerland	4.7		1.5
11	Ireland	4.7		1.3
12	Belgium	4.6		1.4
13	Denmark	4.6		1.3
14	Iceland	4.6		1.4
15	Japan	4.5		1.5
16	Netherlands	4.4		1.4
17	Norway	4.3		1.3
18	Korea	4.3		1.3
19	France	4.2		1.3
20	China	4.2		1.4
21	South Africa	4.2		1.4
22	Australia	4.2		1.1
23	Austria	4.1		1.3
24	Hong Kong SAR	4.1		1.3
25	Thailand	4.0		1.3
26	Malaysia	4.0		1.2
27	New Zealand	4.0		1.2
28	Indonesia	3.9		1.5
29	Brazil	3.9		1.4
30	Italy	3.9		1.8
31	Tunisia	3.8		1.7
32	Latvia	3.7		1.5
33	Slovenia	3.7		1.3
34	Czech Republic	3.7		1.5
35	Greece	3.6		1.4
36	Ukraine	3.6		2.1
37	Spain	3.6		1.7
38	Slovak Republic	3.5		1.5
39	Cameroon	3.5		1.8
40	Vietnam	3.5		1.7
41	Estonia	3.5		1.2
42	Poland	3.4		1.4
43	Uganda	3.4		1.8
44	Chile	3.4		1.5
45	Mexico	3.3		1.5
46	Croatia	3.3		1.7
47	Lithuania	3.3		1.4
48	Jamaica	3.3		1.4
49	Portugal	3.3		1.3
50	Tanzania	3.2		1.4
51	India	3.2		1.3
52	Colombia	3.2		1.4

RANK	COUNTRY	SCORE	1 MEAN: 3.3 7	SD
53	Morocco	3.2		1.6
54	Egypt	3.2		1.8
55	Trinidad and Tobago	3.1		1.3
56	Russian Federation	3.1		2.1
57	Ghana	3.1		1.6
58	Costa Rica	3.1		1.6
59	Jordan	3.0		1.5
60	Kenya	3.0		1.6
61	Hungary	3.0		1.9
62	Malta	2.9		1.2
63	Senegal	2.9		1.7
64	Luxembourg	2.9		1.8
65	Romania	2.9		1.7
66	Sri Lanka	2.9		1.2
67	Turkey	2.8		1.3
68	Botswana	2.8		1.4
69	Argentina	2.8		1.5
70	Serbia	2.8		1.5
71	Namibia	2.8		1.4
72	Philippines	2.7		1.3
73	Dominican Republic	2.7		1.3
73	Uruguay	2.7		1.2
73	Venezuela	2.7		1.3
76	Nigeria	2.7		1.4
77	Mauritius	2.7		1.4
77	Zimbabwe	2.7		1.2
79	Panama	2.6		1.4
80	Bulgaria	2.6		1.2
81	Guatemala	2.5		1.2
82	Macedonia, FYR	2.5		1.3
83	Malawi	2.5		1.3
84	Zambia	2.4		1.6
85	Madagascar	2.4		1.4
86	Peru	2.4		1.1
87	Ecuador	2.3		1.2
88	Mozambique	2.3		1.3
89	Algeria	2.2		1.3
90	Mali	2.1		1.5
91	Nicaragua	2.0		1.1
92	Ethiopia	1.9		1.2
93	Honduras	1.8		1.0
94	Bangladesh	1.8		1.2
95	Bolivia	1.8		0.9
96	Pakistan	1.8		0.9
97	Chad	1.8		1.1
98	Paraguay	1.8		1.3
99	El Salvador	1.7		0.9
100	Haiti	1.7		0.5
101	Gambia	1.7		1.1
102	Angola	1.4		0.8

3.09 Government procurement of advanced technology products

Government purchase decisions for the procurement of advanced technology products are (1 = based solely on price, 7 = based on technology and encourage innovation)

RANK	COUNTRY	SCORE	1	MEAN: 3.6	7	SD
1	Singapore	5.4				1.2
2	Malaysia	5.2				1.0
3	Taiwan	5.0				1.0
4	Finland	5.0				0.9
5	Tunisia	4.9				1.5
6	France	4.8				1.1
7	Israel	4.8				1.1
8	Luxembourg	4.8				1.0
9	China	4.7				1.3
10	United States	4.7				1.1
11	Vietnam	4.5				1.6
12	Korea	4.5				1.2
13	Denmark	4.5				1.3
14	Germany	4.4				1.3
15	Japan	4.4				1.3
16	Canada	4.3				1.5
17	Tanzania	4.2				1.5
18	Ireland	4.2				1.1
19	Ghana	4.2				1.6
20	Switzerland	4.2				1.4
21	Iceland	4.1				1.5
22	Cameroon	4.1				1.8
23	Latvia	4.1				1.5
24	Sweden	4.0				1.1
25	Botswana	4.0				1.7
26	Hong Kong SAR	4.0				1.4
27	Indonesia	4.0				1.4
27	Norway	4.0				1.1
27	Senegal	4.0				1.4
27	Australia	4.0				1.1
31	Spain	3.9				1.3
32	Nigeria	3.9				1.5
33	Estonia	3.9				1.4
34	Hungary	3.9				1.4
35	Jamaica	3.9				1.4
36	Thailand	3.9				1.3
37	Netherlands	3.8				1.3
38	South Africa	3.8				1.1
39	Trinidad and Tobago	3.8				1.1
40	Italy	3.8				1.3
41	Uganda	3.8				1.9
42	United Kingdom	3.8				1.4
43	Austria	3.8				1.5
44	Slovenia	3.8				1.3
45	Jordan	3.8				1.5
46	Costa Rica	3.8				1.5
47	Lithuania	3.7				1.3
48	Egypt	3.7				1.8
49	Slovak Republic	3.7				1.4
50	New Zealand	3.7				1.1
51	Czech Republic	3.7				1.2
52	Algeria	3.6				1.5
53	Brazil	3.6				1.2
54	Malta	3.6				1.4
55	Chile	3.6				1.3
56	Belgium	3.6				1.3
57	El Salvador	3.5				1.4
58	Morocco	3.5				1.8
59	Mexico	3.5				1.5
60	Poland	3.5				1.4
61	Macedonia, FYR	3.4				1.9
62	Serbia	3.4				1.6
63	Dominican Republic	3.4				1.6
64	Colombia	3.4				1.2
65	Sri Lanka	3.4				1.5
66	Mauritius	3.4				1.3
67	Kenya	3.4				1.6
67	Portugal	3.4				1.2
69	Namibia	3.3				1.6
70	Zambia	3.3				1.6
71	India	3.3				1.2
72	Mali	3.3				1.9
73	Mozambique	3.3				1.4
74	Croatia	3.3				1.6
75	Madagascar	3.3				1.7
76	Greece	3.2				1.2
77	Russian Federation	3.2				1.5
78	Pakistan	3.1				1.4
79	Bulgaria	3.1				1.5
80	Malawi	3.1				1.5
81	Gambia	3.1				1.9
82	Ukraine	3.1				1.5
83	Turkey	3.0				1.2
84	Philippines	3.0				1.3
85	Romania	2.9				1.5
86	Nicaragua	2.9				1.4
87	Venezuela	2.9				1.1
88	Uruguay	2.9				1.2
89	Argentina	2.8				1.1
90	Zimbabwe	2.8				1.0
91	Panama	2.8				1.5
92	Peru	2.8				1.3
93	Haiti	2.7				1.2
94	Ecuador	2.7				1.3
95	Ethiopia	2.7				1.5
96	Angola	2.6				1.6
97	Bangladesh	2.6				1.5
98	Honduras	2.5				1.3
99	Chad	2.5				1.7
100	Guatemala	2.5				1.3
101	Bolivia	2.3				1.1
102	Paraguay	2.1				1.1

3.10   Availability of scientists and engineers

Scientists and engineers in your country are (1 = nonexistent or rare, 7 = widely available)

RANK	COUNTRY	SCORE	1 MEAN: 4.7 7	SD
1	Israel	6.5		0.7
2	Finland	6.5		0.6
3	India	6.3		0.8
4	France	6.2		1.0
5	Canada	6.1		0.9
6	Iceland	6.1		0.8
7	Switzerland	6.0		0.9
8	United States	6.0		0.9
9	Japan	6.0		0.8
10	Sweden	5.9		1.0
11	Denmark	5.9		0.8
12	Jordan	5.8		1.0
13	Tunisia	5.8		1.1
14	Australia	5.8		1.2
15	Slovak Republic	5.7		1.1
16	Singapore	5.7		0.9
17	Taiwan	5.6		1.1
18	Germany	5.6		0.9
19	Greece	5.6		1.1
20	Ireland	5.6		1.3
21	Romania	5.5		1.4
22	Belgium	5.5		1.0
23	Algeria	5.5		1.4
24	Hungary	5.5		1.1
25	Norway	5.4		1.1
26	Austria	5.4		1.2
27	Russian Federation	5.4		1.4
28	Lithuania	5.4		1.1
29	Italy	5.3		1.3
30	Spain	5.3		1.2
31	Bulgaria	5.3		1.3
32	Vietnam	5.3		1.3
33	Czech Republic	5.3		1.2
34	Costa Rica	5.1		1.2
35	Poland	5.1		1.4
36	Cameroon	5.1		1.4
37	United Kingdom	5.1		1.2
38	Serbia	5.1		1.6
39	Chile	5.1		1.2
40	Korea	5.0		1.2
41	Argentina	5.0		1.3
42	Macedonia, FYR	5.0		1.8
43	Croatia	5.0		1.3
44	Uruguay	5.0		1.4
45	Ukraine	4.9		1.5
46	Brazil	4.9		1.4
47	Turkey	4.9		1.4
48	Portugal	4.8		1.1
49	Netherlands	4.8		1.4
50	New Zealand	4.7		1.2
51	Hong Kong SAR	4.7		1.5
52	Estonia	4.7		1.1

RANK	COUNTRY	SCORE	1 MEAN: 4.7 7	SD
53	Morocco	4.6		1.8
54	Kenya	4.6		1.4
55	Nigeria	4.6		1.5
56	Trinidad and Tobago	4.5		1.3
57	Egypt	4.5		1.7
58	Malta	4.5		1.3
59	Sri Lanka	4.5		1.3
60	Madagascar	4.5		1.5
61	Latvia	4.5		1.3
62	Bangladesh	4.5		1.4
63	Thailand	4.4		1.3
64	Slovenia	4.4		1.2
65	Malaysia	4.4		1.4
66	Mauritius	4.3		1.1
67	Venezuela	4.3		1.4
68	China	4.2		1.3
69	Luxembourg	4.2		1.3
70	Malawi	4.1		1.6
71	Peru	4.1		1.5
72	Philippines	4.1		1.6
73	Tanzania	4.1		1.5
74	Colombia	4.1		1.5
74	South Africa	4.1		1.3
76	Jamaica	4.1		1.2
77	Uganda	4.0		1.5
78	Zambia	4.0		1.6
79	Mali	4.0		2.0
80	Ghana	4.0		1.6
81	Pakistan	4.0		1.4
82	Mexico	3.9		1.4
83	Panama	3.9		1.4
84	Senegal	3.8		1.4
85	Indonesia	3.7		1.4
86	Ecuador	3.5		1.5
87	Botswana	3.5		1.3
88	Zimbabwe	3.5		1.4
89	Guatemala	3.4		1.6
90	Dominican Republic	3.3		1.5
91	Bolivia	3.2		1.4
92	Nicaragua	3.1		1.6
93	Namibia	3.1		1.2
94	Haiti	3.1		1.2
95	Honduras	3.1		1.4
96	Ethiopia	3.0		1.4
97	El Salvador	2.9		1.3
98	Paraguay	2.9		1.3
99	Chad	2.7		1.5
100	Gambia	2.6		1.6
101	Mozambique	2.6		1.1
102	Angola	2.1		1.2

3.11   Availability of mobile or cellular telephones

Mobile or cellular telephones for your business are (1 = not available, 7 = as accessible and affordable as in the world's most technologically advanced countries)

RANK	COUNTRY	SCORE	1 MEAN: 5.9 7	SD
1	Finland	7.0		0.0
2	Israel	7.0		0.2
3	Denmark	6.9		0.3
3	Sweden	6.9		0.3
5	Germany	6.9		0.3
6	Austria	6.9		0.4
7	Singapore	6.9		0.4
8	Iceland	6.9		0.4
9	Hong Kong SAR	6.9		0.5
10	Chile	6.8		0.4
11	Switzerland	6.8		0.5
12	France	6.8		0.4
13	Netherlands	6.8		0.4
14	Australia	6.8		0.4
15	Portugal	6.8		0.5
16	Czech Republic	6.8		0.5
17	Japan	6.8		0.5
18	United States	6.7		0.5
19	Canada	6.7		0.5
20	Estonia	6.7		0.7
21	Slovenia	6.7		0.7
22	United Kingdom	6.7		0.7
23	Norway	6.7		0.6
24	Lithuania	6.7		0.6
25	Slovak Republic	6.7		0.5
26	Belgium	6.7		0.6
27	El Salvador	6.6		0.6
28	Spain	6.6		0.6
29	Jordan	6.6		0.6
30	Korea	6.6		0.7
31	Hungary	6.6		0.6
32	New Zealand	6.6		0.6
33	Italy	6.6		0.8
34	Dominican Republic	6.6		0.7
35	South Africa	6.6		0.6
36	Malaysia	6.6		0.7
37	Turkey	6.5		0.6
38	Philippines	6.5		0.6
39	Greece	6.5		0.8
40	Luxembourg	6.5		0.7
41	Brazil	6.5		0.7
42	Venezuela	6.4		0.9
43	Uruguay	6.4		0.9
44	India	6.4		0.9
45	Guatemala	6.4		1.0
46	Peru	6.4		0.8
47	Jamaica	6.3		0.8
48	Croatia	6.3		1.1
49	Poland	6.3		1.0
50	Malta	6.2		0.8
51	Thailand	6.2		1.0
52	Mauritius	6.2		0.8

RANK	COUNTRY	SCORE	1 MEAN: 5.9 7	SD
53	Ireland	6.1		1.0
54	Taiwan	6.1		1.1
55	Mexico	6.1		1.1
56	Bolivia	6.1		1.0
57	Panama	6.1		1.3
58	Paraguay	6.0		1.2
59	Gambia	6.0		1.3
60	Nicaragua	6.0		1.3
61	Sri Lanka	6.0		1.0
62	Colombia	5.9		1.0
63	Pakistan	5.9		0.9
64	Botswana	5.9		1.0
65	Romania	5.9		1.3
66	Namibia	5.8		1.2
67	Argentina	5.8		1.3
68	Morocco	5.8		1.9
69	Latvia	5.7		1.2
70	Russian Federation	5.7		1.2
71	Bangladesh	5.6		1.0
72	Trinidad and Tobago	5.5		0.8
73	Bulgaria	5.5		1.5
74	Haiti	5.5		0.8
75	Uganda	5.5		1.4
76	Tunisia	5.4		1.4
77	Tanzania	5.3		1.2
78	Kenya	5.3		1.2
79	Egypt	5.3		1.7
80	Serbia	5.3		1.5
81	Malawi	5.2		1.0
82	Honduras	5.2		1.6
83	Nigeria	5.2		1.1
84	Macedonia, FYR	5.2		1.5
85	Vietnam	5.2		1.2
86	Ecuador	5.1		1.5
87	Ghana	5.1		1.4
88	Zambia	5.1		1.1
89	China	5.0		1.5
90	Madagascar	5.0		1.4
91	Senegal	5.0		1.9
92	Indonesia	4.7		1.2
93	Cameroon	4.5		2.1
94	Algeria	4.5		1.7
95	Mozambique	4.4		1.2
96	Ukraine	4.4		1.4
97	Costa Rica	4.1		1.9
98	Zimbabwe	3.8		1.4
99	Angola	3.6		1.5
100	Ethiopia	3.0		1.3
101	Mali	2.9		1.6
102	Chad	2.9		2.0

3.12   Internet access in schools

Internet access in schools is (1 = very limited, 7 = pervasive—most children have frequent access)

RANK	COUNTRY	SCORE	MEAN: 3.7	SD
1	Finland	6.6		0.6
2	Singapore	6.6		0.6
3	Iceland	6.6		0.6
4	Korea	6.4		1.0
5	Sweden	6.3		1.0
6	Canada	6.2		0.9
7	Australia	6.2		0.8
8	Denmark	6.0		0.9
9	Hong Kong SAR	6.0		1.1
10	United States	6.0		1.3
11	Taiwan	6.0		0.8
12	Austria	5.9		1.1
13	Estonia	5.9		1.1
14	United Kingdom	5.8		0.9
15	Israel	5.8		0.9
16	New Zealand	5.7		0.9
17	Switzerland	5.7		1.2
18	Netherlands	5.7		1.3
19	Malta	5.7		1.0
20	Luxembourg	5.6		1.1
21	Slovenia	5.6		1.0
22	Norway	5.5		1.5
23	Germany	5.3		1.3
24	Japan	5.1		1.3
25	Belgium	5.0		1.2
26	Portugal	4.8		1.2
27	Hungary	4.8		1.4
28	Latvia	4.7		1.2
29	Czech Republic	4.6		1.5
30	Thailand	4.6		1.5
31	France	4.6		1.7
32	Spain	4.6		1.5
33	Tunisia	4.5		1.5
34	Ireland	4.5		1.7
35	Lithuania	4.5		1.6
36	Chile	4.4		1.3
37	Malaysia	4.3		1.4
38	Slovak Republic	4.1		1.7
39	Poland	4.1		1.5
40	Brazil	4.0		1.3
41	Jordan	4.0		1.4
42	Egypt	3.9		1.7
43	Croatia	3.9		1.8
44	Italy	3.9		1.3
45	Romania	3.8		1.6
46	Namibia	3.8		1.5
47	Greece	3.8		1.4
48	India	3.8		1.5
49	Mauritius	3.7		1.6
50	South Africa	3.6		1.6
51	Uruguay	3.6		1.5
52	Indonesia	3.6		1.3

RANK	COUNTRY	SCORE	MEAN: 3.7	SD
53	Philippines	3.5		1.6
54	China	3.5		1.7
55	Turkey	3.5		1.6
56	Mexico	3.4		1.6
57	Panama	3.4		1.6
58	Costa Rica	3.3		1.6
59	Bulgaria	3.3		1.6
60	Argentina	3.3		1.3
61	Russian Federation	3.2		1.6
62	Peru	3.2		1.6
63	Macedonia, FYR	3.2		1.9
64	Jamaica	3.1		1.4
65	Colombia	3.0		1.3
66	Dominican Republic	3.0		1.6
67	El Salvador	3.0		1.5
67	Pakistan	3.0		1.5
69	Sri Lanka	2.9		1.5
70	Venezuela	2.9		1.6
71	Vietnam	2.9		1.5
72	Serbia	2.8		1.6
73	Morocco	2.6		1.8
74	Trinidad and Tobago	2.6		1.4
75	Uganda	2.6		1.6
76	Botswana	2.5		1.4
77	Ukraine	2.4		1.4
78	Gambia	2.4		1.7
79	Guatemala	2.3		1.4
80	Bolivia	2.2		1.2
81	Zimbabwe	2.2		1.2
82	Senegal	2.1		1.5
83	Ecuador	2.1		1.2
84	Tanzania	2.1		1.5
85	Ghana	1.9		1.3
86	Kenya	1.9		1.3
87	Nicaragua	1.8		1.2
88	Zambia	1.8		1.3
89	Paraguay	1.8		1.0
90	Nigeria	1.8		1.0
91	Honduras	1.8		1.1
92	Malawi	1.8		1.3
93	Bangladesh	1.8		1.3
94	Algeria	1.7		1.1
95	Cameroon	1.6		1.0
96	Haiti	1.6		0.8
97	Mozambique	1.5		0.9
98	Madagascar	1.5		0.9
99	Ethiopia	1.5		1.0
100	Mali	1.4		0.8
101	Angola	1.3		0.6
102	Chad	1.1		0.6

3.13 Quality of competition in the ISP sector

Is there sufficient competition among Internet Service Providers (ISPs) in your country to ensure high quality, infrequent interruptions, and low prices?
(1 = no, 7 = yes, equal to the best in the world)

RANK	COUNTRY	SCORE	1 MEAN: 4.2 7	SD
1	Korea	6.1		1.0
2	United States	6.1		1.2
3	Iceland	6.0		1.0
4	Hong Kong SAR	5.9		1.1
5	Estonia	5.9		1.3
6	Finland	5.9		1.3
7	Israel	5.9		1.0
8	United Kingdom	5.8		1.2
9	Denmark	5.7		1.6
10	Canada	5.7		1.6
11	Germany	5.5		1.4
12	Sweden	5.5		1.4
13	Chile	5.5		1.3
14	Japan	5.4		1.4
15	Switzerland	5.4		1.5
16	Australia	5.4		1.5
17	Netherlands	5.3		1.5
18	Singapore	5.3		1.4
19	Jordan	5.2		1.1
20	Italy	5.2		1.5
21	Austria	5.2		1.3
22	New Zealand	5.2		1.4
23	Taiwan	5.2		1.4
24	France	5.1		1.6
25	Norway	5.1		1.3
26	Brazil	5.1		1.5
26	India	5.1		1.5
28	Argentina	4.9		1.4
29	Thailand	4.8		1.4
30	Luxembourg	4.8		1.3
31	Belgium	4.8		1.5
32	Jamaica	4.7		1.6
33	Egypt	4.7		1.5
34	Malta	4.7		1.5
35	Portugal	4.6		1.5
36	Malaysia	4.5		1.5
37	Panama	4.5		1.8
38	Pakistan	4.5		1.4
39	Greece	4.4		1.5
40	Latvia	4.4		1.4
41	Philippines	4.4		1.3
42	Dominican Republic	4.4		1.7
43	El Salvador	4.4		1.5
44	Sri Lanka	4.3		1.5
45	Colombia	4.3		1.3
46	Gambia	4.3		2.1
47	Czech Republic	4.3		1.7
48	Spain	4.2		1.6
49	Mexico	4.2		1.7
50	South Africa	4.2		1.8
51	Guatemala	4.2		1.6
52	China	4.2		1.3

RANK	COUNTRY	SCORE	1 MEAN: 4.2 7	SD
53	Uganda	4.1		1.6
54	Turkey	4.1		1.5
55	Malawi	4.1		1.7
56	Tanzania	4.1		1.6
57	Bolivia	4.1		1.5
58	Lithuania	4.1		1.5
59	Slovenia	4.1		1.5
60	Tunisia	4.0		1.7
61	Namibia	4.0		1.7
62	Venezuela	3.9		1.4
63	Bangladesh	3.9		1.8
64	Uruguay	3.8		1.8
65	Ghana	3.8		1.8
66	Peru	3.8		1.5
67	Slovak Republic	3.8		1.7
68	Cameroon	3.8		2.0
69	Indonesia	3.8		1.4
70	Bulgaria	3.8		1.5
71	Poland	3.7		1.6
72	Romania	3.7		1.8
73	Kenya	3.7		1.8
74	Morocco	3.7		1.9
75	Ukraine	3.6		1.4
76	Macedonia, FYR	3.6		2.0
77	Nigeria	3.6		1.8
78	Zambia	3.6		1.7
79	Madagascar	3.6		1.8
80	Russian Federation	3.5		1.8
81	Paraguay	3.5		1.6
82	Nicaragua	3.5		1.5
83	Croatia	3.4		1.8
84	Mali	3.4		1.9
85	Vietnam	3.3		1.5
86	Senegal	3.3		2.0
87	Zimbabwe	3.2		1.6
88	Haiti	3.2		1.4
89	Honduras	3.1		1.4
90	Ecuador	3.1		1.6
91	Serbia	3.1		1.5
92	Mozambique	3.1		1.5
93	Botswana	2.9		1.5
94	Hungary	2.9		1.5
95	Angola	2.7		1.5
96	Algeria	2.7		1.8
97	Ireland	2.7		1.5
98	Trinidad and Tobago	2.3		1.7
99	Mauritius	1.9		1.1
100	Costa Rica	1.9		1.3
101	Chad	1.6		1.2
102	Ethiopia	1.4		1.0

3.14 Government prioritization of ICT

Information and communication technologies (ICT) are an overall priority for the government (1 = strongly disagree, 7 = strongly agree)

RANK	COUNTRY	SCORE	1 MEAN: 4.4 7	SD
1	Singapore	6.4		0.8
2	Malaysia	6.3		0.7
3	Finland	5.9		1.0
4	Mauritius	5.8		1.2
5	Tunisia	5.8		1.1
6	Malta	5.7		1.2
7	Taiwan	5.6		0.9
8	Korea	5.6		1.2
9	Japan	5.6		1.2
10	Denmark	5.5		1.0
11	Jordan	5.4		1.3
12	India	5.4		1.3
13	Gambia	5.3		1.8
14	Sweden	5.3		1.2
15	United States	5.3		1.3
16	Thailand	5.3		1.3
17	Ghana	5.3		1.5
18	Estonia	5.2		1.3
19	Canada	5.2		1.4
20	Iceland	5.1		1.3
21	Mali	5.1		1.6
22	Hong Kong SAR	5.1		1.3
23	Luxembourg	5.0		1.3
23	Senegal	5.0		1.7
25	United Kingdom	5.0		1.2
26	France	4.9		1.1
27	Jamaica	4.9		1.6
28	Tanzania	4.9		1.4
29	Pakistan	4.9		1.4
30	Australia	4.9		1.2
31	Ireland	4.8		1.6
32	China	4.8		1.6
33	Chile	4.8		1.3
34	Vietnam	4.8		1.6
35	South Africa	4.8		1.4
36	Botswana	4.8		1.4
37	Spain	4.8		1.4
38	Germany	4.7		1.3
39	Switzerland	4.6		1.2
39	Uganda	4.6		1.8
41	Mexico	4.6		1.4
42	Egypt	4.6		1.5
43	Bangladesh	4.6		1.7
44	Madagascar	4.6		1.7
45	Serbia	4.6		1.7
46	Cameroon	4.5		2.1
47	Sri Lanka	4.5		1.5
48	Norway	4.5		1.1
49	Croatia	4.4		1.7
50	Hungary	4.4		1.5
51	New Zealand	4.4		1.5
52	Latvia	4.4		1.3

RANK	COUNTRY	SCORE	1 MEAN: 4.4 7	SD
53	Portugal	4.4		1.3
54	Lithuania	4.4		1.6
55	Mozambique	4.4		1.8
56	Austria	4.3		1.5
57	Colombia	4.3		1.5
58	Israel	4.3		1.6
58	Slovenia	4.3		1.3
60	Belgium	4.3		1.6
61	Philippines	4.3		1.8
62	Czech Republic	4.2		1.5
63	Morocco	4.2		1.8
64	Netherlands	4.2		1.5
65	Italy	4.2		1.2
66	Brazil	4.1		1.4
67	Nigeria	4.1		1.8
68	Greece	4.1		1.3
69	Ukraine	4.1		1.7
70	Namibia	4.0		1.6
71	Uruguay	4.0		1.5
72	El Salvador	4.0		1.5
73	Romania	3.9		1.7
74	Dominican Republic	3.9		1.7
75	Slovak Republic	3.9		1.5
76	Trinidad and Tobago	3.9		1.5
77	Costa Rica	3.8		1.5
78	Russian Federation	3.8		1.7
79	Zambia	3.8		1.6
80	Algeria	3.8		1.7
81	Kenya	3.7		1.7
82	Peru	3.7		1.5
83	Indonesia	3.7		1.3
84	Poland	3.6		1.2
85	Macedonia, FYR	3.5		2.1
86	Ethiopia	3.5		2.0
87	Nicaragua	3.5		1.7
88	Bulgaria	3.5		1.7
89	Malawi	3.5		1.6
90	Turkey	3.4		1.3
91	Panama	3.3		1.5
92	Honduras	3.0		1.5
93	Venezuela	3.0		1.6
94	Bolivia	3.0		1.5
95	Ecuador	2.9		1.5
96	Chad	2.8		2.1
97	Angola	2.8		1.5
98	Argentina	2.8		1.4
99	Zimbabwe	2.5		1.3
100	Haiti	2.5		1.3
101	Paraguay	2.3		1.3
102	Guatemala	2.2		1.4

439

3.15   Government success in ICT promotion

Government programs promoting the use of information and communication technologies (ICT) are (1 = not very successful, 7 = highly successful)

RANK	COUNTRY	SCORE	MEAN: 3.8	SD
1	Singapore	5.9		0.9
2	Malaysia	5.3		0.9
3	Tunisia	5.3		1.2
4	Korea	5.3		1.1
5	Finland	5.2		0.9
6	Taiwan	5.2		1.2
7	Malta	5.1		1.3
8	Jordan	4.9		1.3
9	Gambia	4.9		1.6
10	Denmark	4.8		1.1
11	Iceland	4.8		1.3
12	Estonia	4.8		1.1
13	Mauritius	4.8		1.0
14	Thailand	4.6		1.2
15	Vietnam	4.6		1.3
16	India	4.6		1.3
17	Canada	4.6		1.6
18	United States	4.6		1.3
19	Sweden	4.4		1.4
20	Ireland	4.4		1.5
21	Israel	4.4		1.6
22	Ghana	4.4		1.6
23	Luxembourg	4.3		1.2
24	China	4.3		1.4
25	Uganda	4.3		1.9
26	France	4.3		1.2
27	Tanzania	4.2		1.6
28	Switzerland	4.2		1.4
29	Botswana	4.2		1.2
30	Japan	4.1		1.3
31	Hong Kong SAR	4.1		1.4
32	Morocco	4.1		1.6
33	Pakistan	4.1		1.4
34	South Africa	4.0		1.3
35	Egypt	4.0		1.5
36	Senegal	4.0		1.7
37	Germany	4.0		1.3
38	Brazil	4.0		1.3
39	Nigeria	3.9		1.8
40	Austria	3.9		1.4
41	Chile	3.9		1.3
42	Norway	3.9		1.2
43	Latvia	3.9		1.4
44	Sri Lanka	3.9		1.4
45	Australia	3.9		0.9
46	Spain	3.8		1.3
47	United Kingdom	3.8		1.3
48	Portugal	3.8		1.1
49	Romania	3.8		1.5
50	Madagascar	3.8		1.5
51	Mexico	3.7		1.5
52	Lithuania	3.7		1.4
53	Mozambique	3.7		1.5
54	Netherlands	3.7		1.3
55	Slovenia	3.7		1.3
56	Colombia	3.7		1.3
57	Serbia	3.7		1.4
58	Italy	3.7		1.3
59	New Zealand	3.6		1.3
60	Jamaica	3.6		1.3
61	Belgium	3.6		1.5
62	El Salvador	3.6		1.2
63	Costa Rica	3.6		1.4
64	Croatia	3.6		1.5
65	Hungary	3.6		1.5
66	Namibia	3.6		1.3
67	Zambia	3.6		1.6
68	Philippines	3.6		1.5
69	Indonesia	3.5		1.2
70	Trinidad and Tobago	3.5		1.3
71	Mali	3.5		1.6
72	Greece	3.5		1.3
73	Cameroon	3.4		1.6
74	Dominican Republic	3.4		1.5
75	Kenya	3.4		1.5
76	Malawi	3.3		1.3
77	Czech Republic	3.3		1.4
78	Slovak Republic	3.2		1.3
79	Uruguay	3.2		1.3
80	Panama	3.2		1.4
81	Poland	3.1		1.4
82	Peru	3.1		1.4
82	Ukraine	3.1		1.4
84	Ethiopia	3.1		1.5
85	Bulgaria	3.0		1.3
86	Russian Federation	2.9		1.3
87	Turkey	2.9		1.1
88	Bangladesh	2.8		1.3
89	Macedonia, FYR	2.8		1.7
90	Angola	2.8		1.3
91	Algeria	2.8		1.2
92	Nicaragua	2.8		1.3
93	Bolivia	2.6		1.3
94	Ecuador	2.5		1.3
95	Honduras	2.4		1.2
96	Argentina	2.4		1.2
97	Zimbabwe	2.4		1.3
98	Chad	2.3		1.6
99	Venezuela	2.2		1.2
100	Haiti	2.0		1.0
101	Guatemala	1.9		1.0
102	Paraguay	1.8		1.1

3.16 Laws relating to ICT

Laws relating to information and communication technologies (ICT) (electronic commerce, digital signatures, consumer protection) are
(1 = nonexistent, 7 = well developed and enforced)

RANK	COUNTRY	SCORE	1 MEAN: 3.7 7	SD
1	Finland	5.9		0.9
2	Singapore	5.8		0.9
3	Australia	5.6		0.9
4	Denmark	5.5		1.1
5	United States	5.5		1.1
6	Estonia	5.5		1.1
7	Malaysia	5.4		1.1
8	United Kingdom	5.4		1.2
9	Iceland	5.1		1.0
10	New Zealand	5.1		1.1
11	Sweden	5.0		1.0
12	Korea	5.0		1.1
13	France	5.0		1.2
14	Germany	5.0		1.4
15	Norway	4.8		1.2
16	Canada	4.8		1.6
17	Taiwan	4.7		1.1
18	Hong Kong SAR	4.7		1.3
19	Tunisia	4.7		1.5
20	Luxembourg	4.7		1.2
21	Israel	4.7		1.1
22	Ireland	4.6		1.3
23	Slovenia	4.6		1.2
24	South Africa	4.6		1.1
25	Switzerland	4.6		1.5
26	Netherlands	4.5		1.2
27	Japan	4.4		1.3
28	Latvia	4.3		1.5
29	Malta	4.3		1.4
30	Chile	4.3		1.3
31	Austria	4.3		1.5
32	Mauritius	4.3		1.1
33	Spain	4.2		1.1
34	Italy	4.2		1.4
35	Czech Republic	4.2		1.2
36	India	4.1		1.5
37	Brazil	4.1		1.3
38	Jordan	4.0		1.5
39	Belgium	4.0		1.3
40	Dominican Republic	4.0		1.3
41	Colombia	3.9		1.3
42	Panama	3.8		1.6
43	Thailand	3.8		1.3
44	Portugal	3.8		1.3
45	Lithuania	3.7		1.3
46	Poland	3.7		1.3
47	Slovak Republic	3.7		1.2
48	Indonesia	3.7		1.3
49	Hungary	3.7		1.3
50	Romania	3.6		1.5
51	China	3.6		1.3
52	Philippines	3.6		1.3
53	Ghana	3.6		1.7
54	Vietnam	3.5		1.5
55	Tanzania	3.5		1.7
56	Mexico	3.5		1.3
57	Morocco	3.5		1.7
58	Venezuela	3.5		1.3
59	Jamaica	3.4		1.4
60	Peru	3.4		1.4
61	Croatia	3.4		1.5
62	Costa Rica	3.4		1.5
63	Egypt	3.4		1.8
64	Greece	3.3		1.4
65	Serbia	3.3		1.4
66	Uganda	3.3		1.9
67	Kenya	3.2		1.4
68	Namibia	3.2		1.5
69	Sri Lanka	3.2		1.4
70	Bulgaria	3.2		1.4
71	Argentina	3.2		1.2
72	Zambia	3.2		1.4
73	Botswana	3.1		1.4
74	El Salvador	3.1		1.4
75	Nigeria	3.1		1.5
76	Russian Federation	3.0		1.4
77	Pakistan	3.0		1.2
78	Senegal	3.0		1.9
79	Uruguay	3.0		1.3
80	Trinidad and Tobago	3.0		1.3
81	Ecuador	3.0		1.3
82	Zimbabwe	2.8		1.4
83	Gambia	2.8		1.9
84	Macedonia, FYR	2.8		1.6
85	Ukraine	2.8		1.3
86	Turkey	2.8		1.2
87	Cameroon	2.7		1.6
88	Nicaragua	2.7		1.3
89	Mozambique	2.7		1.4
90	Malawi	2.6		1.6
91	Honduras	2.5		1.3
92	Guatemala	2.5		1.3
93	Chad	2.3		1.5
94	Madagascar	2.3		1.3
95	Bolivia	2.3		1.3
96	Mali	2.2		1.5
97	Angola	2.2		1.2
98	Paraguay	2.1		1.3
99	Bangladesh	2.1		1.2
100	Algeria	2.0		1.2
101	Ethiopia	1.9		1.2
102	Haiti	1.5		0.9

3.17   Utility patents, 2002

US utility patents (ie, patents for invention) granted per million population, 2002

RANK	COUNTRY	HARD DATA
1	United States	301.48
2	Japan	273.40
3	Taiwan	241.38
4	Sweden	190.34
5	Switzerland	189.44
6	Israel	165.08
7	Finland	155.58
8	Germany	137.52
9	Canada	109.62
10	Singapore	97.62
11	Netherlands	86.94
12	Luxembourg	82.59
13	Denmark	80.38
14	Korea	79.87
15	Belgium	70.10
16	France	67.59
17	Austria	65.43
18	United Kingdom	64.29
19	Norway	53.78
20	Iceland	45.94
21	Australia	44.00
22	New Zealand	36.84
23	Ireland	33.85
24	Hong Kong SAR	33.29
25	Italy	30.49
26	Slovenia	8.00
27	Spain	7.59
28	Hungary	4.85
29	Estonia	2.86
30	Czech Republic	2.82
31	South Africa	2.58
32	Croatia	2.55
33	Malta	2.54
34	Malaysia	2.39
35	Greece	1.89
36	Slovak Republic	1.48
37	Argentina	1.42
38	Russian Federation	1.39
39	Venezuela	1.20
40	Portugal	1.10
41	Mexico	0.92
42	Uruguay	0.88
43	Jamaica	0.77
44	Costa Rica	0.71
45	Chile	0.71
46	Thailand	0.68
47	Ukraine	0.55
48	Brazil	0.55
49	Lithuania	0.54
50	Bulgaria	0.38
51	Panama	0.34
52	Honduras	0.30

RANK	COUNTRY	HARD DATA
53	Poland	0.29
54	India	0.24
55	China	0.22
56	Turkey	0.22
57	Jordan	0.19
58	Philippines	0.18
59	Colombia	0.14
60	Romania	0.13
61	Dominican Republic	0.12
62	Tunisia	0.10
63	Zimbabwe	0.08
64	Egypt	0.07
65	Sri Lanka	0.05
66	Uganda	0.04
67	Peru	0.04
68	Nigeria	0.03
69	Indonesia	0.03
70	Kenya	0.03
71	Pakistan	0.01
72	Algeria	0.00
72	Angola	0.00
72	Bangladesh	0.00
72	Bolivia	0.00
72	Botswana	0.00
72	Cameroon	0.00
72	Chad	0.00
72	Ecuador	0.00
72	El Salvador	0.00
72	Ethiopia	0.00
72	Gambia	0.00
72	Ghana	0.00
72	Guatemala	0.00
72	Haiti	0.00
72	Latvia	0.00
72	Macedonia, FYR	0.00
72	Madagascar	0.00
72	Malawi	0.00
72	Mali	0.00
72	Mauritius	0.00
72	Morocco	0.00
72	Mozambique	0.00
72	Namibia	0.00
72	Nicaragua	0.00
72	Paraguay	0.00
72	Senegal	0.00
72	Serbia	0.00
72	Tanzania	0.00
72	Trinidad and Tobago	0.00
72	Vietnam	0.00
72	Zambia	0.00

SOURCE: US Patent and Trademark Office, February 2003

3.18   Tertiary enrollment

Gross tertiary enrollment rate, 2000 or most recent year available

RANK	COUNTRY	HARD DATA
1	Finland	83.31
2	Korea	77.62
3	Taiwan	77.12
4	United States	72.62
5	Sweden	70.04
6	Norway	70.01
7	New Zealand	69.24
8	Russian Federation	64.09
9	Australia	63.26
10	Latvia	63.11
11	Slovenia	60.55
12	Canada	59.99
13	United Kingdom	59.53
14	Spain	59.36
15	Denmark	58.86
16	Austria	57.71
17	Estonia	57.55
18	Belgium	56.99
19	Poland	55.54
20	Netherlands	55.01
21	France	53.58
22	Israel	52.67
23	Lithuania	52.48
24	Portugal	50.20
25	Italy	49.88
26	Greece	49.87
27	Iceland	48.66
28	Argentina	47.96
29	Japan	47.70
30	Ireland	47.53
31	Germany	46.30
32	Singapore	43.82
33	Ukraine	43.30
34	Switzerland	42.14
35	Bulgaria	40.82
36	Hungary	40.01
37	Egypt	39.00
38	Chile	37.52
39	Uruguay	36.10
40	Bolivia	35.66
41	Thailand	35.27
42	Panama	34.90
43	Philippines	31.21
44	Slovak Republic	30.32
45	Czech Republic	29.84
46	Croatia	29.04
47	Peru	28.84
48	Jordan	28.62
49	Venezuela	28.50
50	Malaysia	28.16
51	Hong Kong SAR	27.42
52	Romania	27.32

RANK	COUNTRY	HARD DATA
53	Macedonia, FYR	24.45
54	Serbia*	24.21
55	Colombia	23.33
56	Dominican Republic	23.08
57	Tunisia	21.71
58	Malta	21.49
59	Mexico	20.71
60	El Salvador	18.20
61	Ecuador	17.61
62	Brazil	16.51
63	Jamaica	16.44
64	Costa Rica	16.04
65	South Africa	15.24
66	Turkey	14.99
67	Algeria	14.98
68	Honduras	14.73
69	Indonesia	14.58
70	Nicaragua	11.85
71	Mauritius	11.38
72	India	10.49
73	Morocco	10.30
74	Paraguay	10.15
75	Vietnam	9.73
76	Luxembourg	9.27
77	Guatemala	8.38
78	China	7.45
79	Bangladesh	6.61
80	Trinidad and Tobago	6.48
81	Namibia	5.94
82	Sri Lanka	5.32
83	Cameroon	4.93
84	Botswana	4.65
85	Nigeria	4.02
86	Zimbabwe	3.93
87	Senegal	3.75
88	Pakistan	3.55
89	Ghana	3.30
90	Kenya	3.00
91	Uganda	2.98
92	Zambia	2.47
93	Madagascar	2.16
94	Mali	1.91
95	Gambia	1.86
96	Ethiopia	1.58
97	Haiti	1.24
98	Chad	0.88
99	Tanzania	0.69
100	Angola	0.67
101	Mozambique	0.57
102	Malawi	0.31

443

SOURCES: UNESCO Institute for Statistics; World Bank World Development Indicators 2002; and national sources

*Value for Yugoslavia

3.19   Cellular telephones, 2002

Cellular mobile subscribers per 100 inhabitants, 2002

RANK	COUNTRY	HARD DATA
1	Taiwan	106.45
2	Luxembourg	101.34
3	Israel	95.45
4	Hong Kong SAR	92.98
5	Italy	92.65
6	Iceland	88.89
7	Sweden	88.50
8	Czech Republic	84.88
9	Greece	84.54
10	Finland	84.50
11	United Kingdom	84.49
12	Norway	84.33
13	Slovenia	83.52
14	Denmark	83.33
15	Spain	82.28
16	Portugal	81.94
17	Singapore	79.14
18	Switzerland	78.75
19	Belgium	78.63
20	Austria	78.62
21	Ireland	75.53
22	Netherlands	74.71
23	Germany	71.67
24	Malta	69.91
25	Korea	67.95
26	Estonia	65.02
27	France	64.70
28	Hungary	64.64
29	Australia	63.97
30	Japan	63.61
31	New Zealand	61.84
32	Slovak Republic	54.36
33	Jamaica	53.48
34	United States	48.81
35	Lithuania	47.16
36	Croatia	47.03
37	Chile	42.83
38	Latvia	39.38
39	Malaysia	37.94
40	Canada	37.72
41	Poland	36.26
42	Turkey	34.75
43	Mauritius	28.91
44	Paraguay	28.83
45	Trinidad and Tobago	27.81
46	South Africa	26.58
47	Thailand	26.04
48	Serbia**	25.66
49	Venezuela	25.55
50	Mexico	25.45
51	Botswana	24.13
52	Jordan	22.89

RANK	COUNTRY	HARD DATA
53	Morocco	20.91
54	Brazil	20.06
55	Uruguay	19.26
56	Bulgaria*	19.12
57	Philippines	17.77
58	Argentina	17.76
59	Romania*	17.17
60	Panama*	16.40
61	China	16.09
62	Dominican Republic*	14.65
63	El Salvador	13.76
64	Guatemala	13.15
65	Costa Rica	12.75
66	Ecuador	12.06
67	Russian Federation	12.05
68	Macedonia, FYR*	10.92
69	Colombia	10.62
70	Bolivia	10.46
71	Peru	8.60
72	Namibia	8.00
73	Gambia	7.29
74	Egypt	6.85
75	Senegal	5.65
76	Indonesia	5.52
77	Tunisia	5.13
78	Sri Lanka	4.92
79	Honduras	4.86
80	Nicaragua	4.47
81	Ukraine*	4.42
82	Kenya	4.15
83	Cameroon	3.57
84	Zimbabwe	3.03
85	Vietnam	2.34
86	Ghana	1.87
87	Haiti	1.69
88	Mozambique	1.63
89	Uganda	1.59
90	Nigeria	1.36
91	Zambia	1.30
92	Algeria	1.28
93	Tanzania*	1.27
94	India	1.22
95	Madagascar	1.02
96	Angola	0.93
97	Malawi	0.82
98	Pakistan	0.82
99	Bangladesh	0.81
100	Mali	0.50
101	Chad	0.43
102	Ethiopia	0.07

SOURCE: International Telecommunication Union, July 2003

*2001
**Value for Yugoslavia

3.20   Internet users, 2002

Internet users per 10,000 inhabitants, 2002

RANK	COUNTRY	HARD DATA
1	Iceland	6,076.39
2	Sweden	5,730.74
3	Korea	5,518.91
4	Singapore	5,396.64
5	United States	5,375.06
6	Netherlands	5,304.11
7	Finland	5,089.30
8	Norway	5,048.29
9	New Zealand	4,843.75
10	Canada	4,838.61
11	Denmark	4,651.81
12	Japan	4,485.22
13	Hong Kong SAR	4,309.46
14	Australia	4,272.03
15	Germany	4,237.29
16	Estonia	4,132.84
17	Austria	4,093.64
18	United Kingdom	4,061.74
19	Slovenia	4,008.02
20	Taiwan	3,825.09
21	Luxembourg	3,674.83
22	Portugal	3,554.62
23	Belgium	3,286.29
24	Switzerland	3,261.79
25	France	3,138.32
26	Malaysia	3,077.55
27	Israel	3,014.05
28	Italy	3,010.77
29	Ireland	2,709.23
30	Malta*	2,525.51
31	Czech Republic	2,464.51
32	Chile	2,375.36
33	Spain	1,931.03
34	Croatia	1,628.82
35	Slovak Republic	1,604.38
36	Hungary	1,576.04
37	Greece	1,547.41
38	Mauritius	1,487.00
39	Lithuania	1,445.09
40	Latvia	1,331.04
41	Uruguay*	1,190.12
42	Argentina	1,120.22
43	Trinidad and Tobago	1,060.32
44	Poland*	983.72
45	Costa Rica*	933.63
46	Bulgaria	897.32
47	Brazil	822.41
48	Romania	806.09
49	Thailand	775.61
50	Peru*	766.49
51	Turkey	728.39
52	South Africa	682.01

RANK	COUNTRY	HARD DATA
53	Serbia**	597.01
54	Jordan	576.09
55	Tunisia	515.03
56	Venezuela	503.73
57	El Salvador	464.58
58	China	460.09
59	Colombia	457.84
60	Mexico	457.74
61	Philippines	437.60
62	Zimbabwe	429.75
63	Panama*	413.94
64	Russian Federation	409.32
65	Ecuador	388.92
66	Jamaica*	384.71
67	Indonesia	377.16
68	Macedonia, FYR*	342.47
69	Guatemala	333.42
70	Bolivia	323.70
71	Honduras	297.97
72	Botswana*	297.47
73	Namibia*	246.33
74	Egypt	228.51
75	Dominican Republic*	214.53
76	Vietnam	184.62
77	Paraguay	172.95
78	Morocco	168.67
79	Nicaragua	167.60
80	Algeria	159.78
80	Kenya*	159.78
82	India	159.14
83	Gambia*	134.63
84	Ukraine*	119.29
85	Senegal	107.12
86	Sri Lanka	105.56
87	Pakistan	100.82
88	Haiti	96.41
89	Zambia	49.01
90	Madagascar	34.57
91	Mali	30.11
92	Tanzania*	29.77
93	Angola	29.42
94	Cameroon*	29.19
95	Malawi	25.87
96	Uganda*	25.18
97	Ghana*	19.36
98	Chad	19.06
99	Mozambique*	16.99
100	Nigeria	16.66
101	Bangladesh	15.32
102	Ethiopia	7.42

445

SOURCE: International Telecommunication Union, July 2003

*2001
**Value for Yugoslavia

3.21   Internet hosts, 2002

Internet hosts per 10,000 inhabitants, 2002

RANK	COUNTRY	HARD DATA		RANK	COUNTRY	HARD DATA
1	United States*	3,728.74		53	Turkey	22.98
2	Iceland	2,370.17		54	Costa Rica*	20.79
3	Finland	2,343.12		55	Romania	18.35
4	Netherlands	1,937.14		56	Serbia**	15.83
5	Denmark	1,556.74		57	Ukraine	14.30
6	Australia	1,304.16		58	Colombia*	13.41
7	New Zealand	1,099.13		59	Macedonia, FYR*	12.69
8	Canada*	963.20		60	Thailand*	11.75
9	Sweden	949.54		61	Venezuela*	9.18
10	Switzerland	770.34		62	Jordan	7.72
11	Taiwan*	764.34		63	Botswana*	7.57
12	Hong Kong SAR*	576.47		64	Guatemala*	5.67
13	Norway	561.33		65	Jamaica*	5.52
14	Japan*	559.22		66	Peru*	5.18
15	United Kingdom	485.03		67	Paraguay*	4.80
16	Singapore*	479.18		68	Nicaragua*	4.20
17	Estonia	467.63		69	Gambia	4.14
18	Austria	450.95		70	Philippines*	3.94
19	Ireland	347.21		71	Zimbabwe*	3.04
20	Belgium	325.35		72	Ecuador*	2.63
21	Germany	314.08		73	Indonesia*	2.18
22	Luxembourg*	314.08		74	Bolivia*	1.84
23	France	232.86		75	Sri Lanka*	1.22
24	Czech Republic	223.21		76	Zambia*	1.03
25	Israel	221.22		77	Kenya	0.93
26	Uruguay*	210.93		78	Uganda	0.91
27	Hungary	191.59		79	Morocco	0.90
28	Malta	185.73		80	India*	0.81
29	Slovenia	179.31		81	El Salvador*	0.80
30	Poland	170.30		82	Pakistan*	0.78
31	Slovak Republic	159.91		83	Senegal	0.78
32	Portugal	158.24		84	China*	0.68
33	Lithuania	157.82		85	Honduras*	0.49
34	Latvia	152.39		86	Egypt	0.47
35	Korea*	148.37		87	Tanzania*	0.44
36	Greece	145.97		88	Tunisia	0.35
37	Spain	145.02		89	Cameroon	0.28
38	Argentina*	128.47		90	Algeria	0.26
39	Italy	119.13		91	Madagascar*	0.15
40	Brazil*	95.71		92	Mali	0.15
41	Mexico*	91.49		93	Ghana	0.14
42	Chile*	79.68		94	Nigeria	0.09
43	Croatia	61.20		95	Vietnam*	0.06
44	South Africa*	53.51		96	Malawi*	0.02
45	Trinidad and Tobago*	52.86		97	Chad	0.01
46	Dominican Republic*	48.17		98	Mozambique*	0.01
47	Bulgaria	42.28		99	Ethiopia*	0.01
48	Malaysia*	31.10		100	Angola*	0.01
49	Mauritius	28.60			Bangladesh	n/a
50	Russian Federation	27.92			Haiti	n/a
51	Panama*	26.99				
52	Namibia*	25.36				

SOURCE: International Telecommunication Union, July 2003

*2001
**Value for Yugoslavia

3.22 Telephone lines, 2002

Main telephone lines per 100 inhabitants, 2002

RANK	COUNTRY	HARD DATA
1	Luxembourg*	77.99
2	Switzerland	73.27
3	Norway	72.98
4	Sweden	72.02
5	Denmark	69.58
6	United States	65.89
7	Germany	65.04
8	Canada	63.55
9	Iceland	62.74
10	Netherlands	61.75
11	United Kingdom	59.48
12	Taiwan	58.33
13	France	56.89
14	Hong Kong SAR	56.74
15	Japan	55.79
16	Finland	54.73
17	Australia	53.86
18	Greece*	52.92
19	Malta	52.34
20	Ireland	50.24
21	Belgium	49.61
22	Austria	48.88
23	Korea	48.86
24	Italy	48.62
25	Israel	46.72
26	Singapore	46.36
27	Spain	45.98
28	New Zealand	44.81
29	Portugal	41.90
30	Slovenia	40.65
31	Croatia	38.79
32	Czech Republic*	37.76
33	Bulgaria	37.46
34	Hungary	36.12
35	Estonia	35.06
36	Latvia	30.11
37	Poland*	29.51
38	Turkey	28.12
39	Uruguay	27.96
40	Lithuania	27.05
41	Mauritius	27.03
42	Macedonia, FYR*	26.35
43	Slovak Republic	26.08
44	Costa Rica	25.05
45	Trinidad and Tobago	24.98
46	Russian Federation	24.22
47	Serbia**	23.26
48	Chile	23.04
49	Brazil	22.32
50	Argentina	21.88
51	Ukraine*	21.21
52	Malaysia	19.16

RANK	COUNTRY	HARD DATA
53	Romania*	18.38
54	Colombia	17.94
55	Jamaica	17.19
56	China	16.69
57	Mexico	14.67
58	Panama*	12.99
59	Jordan	12.90
60	Tunisia	11.70
61	Egypt	11.32
62	Venezuela	11.23
63	Ecuador	11.02
64	Dominican Republic*	11.02
65	South Africa	10.77
66	Thailand	10.50
67	El Salvador	10.34
68	Botswana*	8.48
69	Peru*	7.75
70	Guatemala	7.05
71	Bolivia	6.76
72	Namibia*	6.43
73	Algeria	6.10
74	Honduras	4.80
75	Paraguay	4.73
76	Sri Lanka	4.66
77	Vietnam	4.51
78	Philippines	4.17
79	India	3.98
80	Morocco	3.80
81	Indonesia	3.65
82	Nicaragua	3.20
83	Gambia	2.80
84	Pakistan	2.48
85	Zimbabwe	2.47
86	Senegal	2.29
87	Haiti	1.57
88	Ghana*	1.16
89	Kenya	1.03
90	Zambia	0.83
91	Malawi	0.70
92	Cameroon*	0.66
93	Angola	0.61
94	Nigeria	0.58
95	Ethiopia	0.55
96	Bangladesh	0.51
97	Mozambique*	0.51
98	Mali	0.47
99	Tanzania*	0.44
100	Madagascar	0.37
101	Uganda	0.22
102	Chad	0.15

SOURCE: International Telecommunication Union, July 2003

*2001
**Value for Yugoslavia

3.23 Personal computers, 2002

Personal computers per 100 inhabitants, 2002

RANK	COUNTRY	HARD DATA
1	United States*	62.50
2	Denmark	57.68
3	Sweden*	56.12
4	Korea	55.58
5	Switzerland*	53.83
6	Luxembourg*	51.73
7	Australia*	51.58
8	Singapore*	50.83
9	Norway*	50.80
10	Canada	48.70
11	Iceland	45.14
12	Finland	44.17
13	Germany	43.49
14	Netherlands*	42.84
15	Taiwan	39.57
16	New Zealand*	39.26
17	Ireland*	39.07
18	Hong Kong SAR*	38.66
19	Japan	38.19
20	Austria	36.93
21	United Kingdom*	36.62
22	France	34.71
23	Slovenia	30.06
24	Israel*	24.59
25	Belgium	24.16
26	Italy	23.07
27	Malta*	22.96
28	Estonia	21.03
29	Slovak Republic	18.04
30	Latvia	17.17
31	Costa Rica*	17.02
32	Spain*	16.82
33	Croatia	15.69
34	Malaysia	14.77
35	Czech Republic*	14.67
36	Chile	11.93
37	Portugal*	11.74
38	Uruguay*	11.01
39	Lithuania	10.98
40	Hungary	10.84
41	Mauritius*	10.83
42	Russian Federation	8.87
43	Poland*	8.54
44	Argentina	8.20
45	Greece*	8.12
46	Trinidad and Tobago	7.95
47	Brazil	7.48
48	South Africa	7.26
49	Mexico*	6.87
50	Namibia*	5.47
51	Venezuela*	5.28
52	Bulgaria	5.19

RANK	COUNTRY	HARD DATA
53	Zimbabwe	5.16
54	Jamaica*	5.00
55	Colombia	4.93
56	Peru*	4.79
57	Turkey*	4.07
58	Thailand	3.98
59	Botswana*	3.87
60	Panama*	3.79
61	Jordan	3.75
62	Romania*	3.57
63	Paraguay	3.46
64	Ecuador	3.11
65	Tunisia	3.06
66	Nicaragua	2.79
67	Philippines	2.75
68	Serbia**	2.71
69	Bolivia	2.28
70	El Salvador*	2.19
71	Senegal	2.04
72	China*	1.90
73	Ukraine*	1.83
74	Egypt	1.71
75	Morocco*	1.37
76	Sri Lanka	1.32
77	Guatemala*	1.28
78	Gambia*	1.27
79	Honduras*	1.22
80	Indonesia*	1.10
81	Vietnam	0.98
82	Zambia	0.75
83	Algeria*	0.71
84	Nigeria*	0.68
85	India*	0.58
86	Kenya*	0.56
87	Pakistan*	0.41
88	Mozambique*	0.40
89	Cameroon*	0.39
90	Tanzania*	0.36
91	Bangladesh	0.34
92	Ghana*	0.33
93	Uganda*	0.29
94	Madagascar*	0.26
95	Angola	0.19
96	Chad*	0.16
97	Ethiopia	0.15
98	Mali*	0.13
99	Malawi*	0.13
	Dominican Republic	n/a
	Haiti	n/a
	Macedonia, FYR	n/a

SOURCE: International Telecommunication Union, July 2003

*2001
**Value for Yugoslavia

Human Resources: Education, Health, and Labor

4.01 Quality of the educational system

The educational system in your country prepares for coping with the needs of a competitive economy (1 = clearly no, 7 = clearly yes)

RANK	COUNTRY	SCORE	1 MEAN: 3.5 7	SD
1	Finland	6.0		1.1
2	Singapore	6.0		0.9
3	Iceland	5.8		0.8
4	Switzerland	5.6		1.0
5	Belgium	5.6		1.1
6	Canada	5.5		1.4
7	Australia	5.5		1.4
8	Denmark	5.3		1.2
9	Taiwan	5.3		1.1
10	Ireland	5.3		1.7
10	Sweden	5.3		1.4
12	Israel	5.2		0.8
13	France	5.1		1.5
14	Austria	5.1		1.4
15	Tunisia	5.1		1.5
16	Malta	4.9		1.3
17	Netherlands	4.9		1.4
18	United States	4.7		1.7
19	Latvia	4.6		1.3
20	Norway	4.6		1.5
21	Spain	4.5		1.3
22	Malaysia	4.5		1.2
23	New Zealand	4.4		1.6
24	Costa Rica	4.4		1.4
25	United Kingdom	4.3		1.5
26	Slovenia	4.3		1.4
27	Jordan	4.3		1.4
28	Italy	4.3		1.5
29	Estonia	4.3		1.3
30	Romania	4.3		2.0
31	Hong Kong SAR	4.2		1.7
32	Czech Republic	4.2		1.5
33	Lithuania	4.2		1.3
34	Luxembourg	4.2		1.5
35	Hungary	4.1		1.6
36	India	4.0		1.7
37	Botswana	4.0		1.6
38	Bulgaria	3.9		1.7
39	Russian Federation	3.9		1.5
40	Ukraine	3.9		1.6
41	Thailand	3.8		1.2
42	Slovak Republic	3.7		1.6
43	Uruguay	3.7		1.5
44	Poland	3.7		1.3
45	Gambia	3.7		1.9
46	Germany	3.6		1.6
47	Korea	3.6		1.4
48	Japan	3.6		1.7
49	Indonesia	3.6		1.6
50	China	3.5		1.4
51	Mauritius	3.5		1.3
52	Trinidad and Tobago	3.5		1.7
53	Greece	3.4		1.4
54	Macedonia, FYR	3.4		2.2
55	Croatia	3.4		1.9
56	Serbia	3.4		1.7
57	Ghana	3.3		1.7
58	Portugal	3.3		1.3
59	Zimbabwe	3.3		1.5
60	Kenya	3.3		1.8
61	Colombia	3.3		1.5
62	Vietnam	3.2		1.7
63	Uganda	3.2		1.7
64	Namibia	3.0		1.2
65	Philippines	3.0		1.4
66	Chile	3.0		1.4
67	Egypt	3.0		1.9
68	South Africa	2.9		1.5
69	Malawi	2.9		1.7
70	Jamaica	2.9		1.5
71	Morocco	2.9		1.9
72	Brazil	2.9		1.4
73	Cameroon	2.9		1.6
74	Mexico	2.8		1.4
75	Turkey	2.8		1.2
76	Tanzania	2.8		1.6
77	Argentina	2.6		1.2
78	Dominican Republic	2.6		1.5
79	Nigeria	2.5		1.5
80	Sri Lanka	2.5		1.3
81	El Salvador	2.5		1.4
82	Zambia	2.4		1.3
83	Panama	2.4		1.3
84	Senegal	2.4		1.4
85	Ethiopia	2.3		1.3
86	Algeria	2.2		1.2
87	Pakistan	2.1		1.0
88	Bangladesh	2.1		1.1
89	Madagascar	2.1		1.3
90	Peru	2.0		1.1
91	Mozambique	2.0		1.2
92	Mali	1.9		1.4
93	Nicaragua	1.9		1.1
94	Ecuador	1.8		1.1
95	Bolivia	1.8		1.0
96	Paraguay	1.7		0.8
97	Venezuela	1.7		0.9
98	Honduras	1.6		0.9
99	Guatemala	1.5		0.7
100	Chad	1.5		0.8
101	Haiti	1.5		1.2
102	Angola	1.4		0.7

The public (free) schools in your country are (1 = of poor quality, 7 = equal to the best in the world)

RANK	COUNTRY	SCORE	1	MEAN: 3.8	7	SD
1	Finland	6.7				0.6
2	Iceland	6.4				0.6
3	Singapore	6.3				0.8
4	Switzerland	6.2				0.9
5	Austria	6.1				0.9
6	Canada	6.0				1.0
7	Belgium	6.0				1.2
8	Netherlands	5.9				1.1
9	France	5.8				1.2
10	Australia	5.8				1.2
11	Denmark	5.7				0.9
12	Ireland	5.7				1.4
13	Italy	5.7				1.4
14	Sweden	5.6				1.2
15	New Zealand	5.6				1.0
16	Israel	5.5				0.7
17	Estonia	5.5				1.0
18	Taiwan	5.5				1.1
19	Czech Republic	5.4				1.1
20	Slovenia	5.3				1.2
21	Slovak Republic	5.3				1.3
22	Tunisia	5.3				1.5
23	Norway	5.3				1.3
24	Luxembourg	5.2				1.1
25	United States	5.0				1.5
26	Hungary	5.0				1.3
27	Japan	5.0				1.4
28	Romania	4.9				1.8
29	Malaysia	4.8				1.1
30	Hong Kong SAR	4.8				1.3
31	Spain	4.8				1.5
32	Latvia	4.7				1.2
33	Malta	4.7				1.3
34	Korea	4.7				1.3
35	United Kingdom	4.7				1.2
36	Lithuania	4.7				1.4
37	Germany	4.6				1.1
38	Portugal	4.5				1.4
39	Poland	4.5				1.3
40	Bulgaria	4.4				1.6
41	Croatia	4.4				1.6
42	Russian Federation	4.2				1.6
43	Uruguay	4.1				1.4
44	Trinidad and Tobago	4.1				1.7
45	Costa Rica	4.1				1.4
46	Ukraine	4.0				1.4
47	Thailand	4.0				1.4
48	Jordan	4.0				1.3
49	Botswana	3.9				1.4
50	Mauritius	3.8				1.3
51	Greece	3.7				1.3
52	Namibia	3.7				1.4

RANK	COUNTRY	SCORE	1	MEAN: 3.8	7	SD
53	Sri Lanka	3.6				1.5
54	Serbia	3.5				1.7
55	Indonesia	3.5				1.4
56	Vietnam	3.4				1.4
57	Gambia	3.4				1.5
58	China	3.4				1.5
59	Macedonia, FYR	3.3				1.9
60	South Africa	3.3				1.4
61	Jamaica	3.2				1.4
62	Egypt	3.2				1.8
63	Argentina	3.1				1.4
64	Morocco	3.0				1.6
65	Turkey	2.9				1.0
66	Chile	2.9				1.1
67	Colombia	2.8				1.3
68	Algeria	2.7				1.3
69	Mexico	2.6				1.2
70	Kenya	2.6				1.4
71	India	2.6				1.2
72	Zimbabwe	2.6				1.3
73	Panama	2.6				1.3
74	Uganda	2.5				1.4
75	Tanzania	2.5				1.5
76	Cameroon	2.5				1.4
77	El Salvador	2.4				1.0
78	Brazil	2.3				0.9
79	Senegal	2.3				1.2
80	Ghana	2.2				1.3
81	Philippines	2.2				1.2
82	Mali	2.1				1.2
83	Mozambique	2.1				1.2
84	Dominican Republic	2.1				1.3
85	Malawi	2.1				1.3
86	Paraguay	2.0				1.1
87	Ethiopia	2.0				1.2
88	Madagascar	1.9				0.8
89	Zambia	1.9				1.0
90	Chad	1.9				1.0
91	Peru	1.9				0.9
92	Bangladesh	1.9				1.0
93	Ecuador	1.8				0.9
94	Pakistan	1.8				1.0
95	Angola	1.8				0.9
96	Nigeria	1.8				1.0
97	Bolivia	1.7				0.9
98	Honduras	1.7				0.9
99	Venezuela	1.6				0.7
100	Nicaragua	1.6				0.9
101	Haiti	1.6				0.9
102	Guatemala	1.5				0.6

4.03   Quality of math and science education

Math and science education in your country's schools (1 = lag far behind that of most other countries, 7 = are among the best in the world)

RANK	COUNTRY	SCORE	1 MEAN: 4.1 7	SD	RANK	COUNTRY	SCORE	1 MEAN: 4.1 7	SD
1	Singapore	6.5		0.6	53	Germany	4.1		1.5
2	Belgium	6.1		1.0	54	Turkey	4.0		1.6
3	France	6.1		1.0	55	Norway	4.0		1.8
4	Finland	5.9		0.9	56	Uruguay	3.9		1.5
5	Romania	5.9		1.5	57	Vietnam	3.9		1.5
6	Switzerland	5.9		1.1	58	Colombia	3.9		1.5
7	Austria	5.8		1.0	59	Botswana	3.8		1.4
8	Hungary	5.7		1.1	60	Zimbabwe	3.8		1.5
9	Australia	5.7		1.2	61	Cameroon	3.7		1.6
10	Tunisia	5.6		1.1	62	Indonesia	3.7		1.4
11	Slovak Republic	5.6		1.0	63	Madagascar	3.7		1.3
12	Taiwan	5.6		1.1	64	Kenya	3.7		1.5
13	Canada	5.5		1.3	65	Argentina	3.7		1.2
14	India	5.5		1.2	66	Egypt	3.6		1.6
15	Estonia	5.5		0.9	67	Chile	3.6		1.3
16	Hong Kong SAR	5.5		1.1	68	Uganda	3.6		1.5
17	Czech Republic	5.5		1.3	69	Zambia	3.5		1.5
18	Russian Federation	5.4		1.4	70	Ghana	3.5		1.7
19	Slovenia	5.3		1.2	71	Malawi	3.4		1.6
20	Ireland	5.3		1.4	72	Jamaica	3.4		1.5
21	Israel	5.3		0.8	73	Algeria	3.3		1.5
21	Sweden	5.3		1.2	74	Tanzania	3.3		1.5
23	Lithuania	5.2		1.2	75	Brazil	3.3		1.3
24	Japan	5.2		1.2	76	Portugal	3.2		1.3
25	Netherlands	5.2		1.4	77	Panama	3.2		1.4
26	Iceland	5.1		0.9	78	Senegal	3.1		1.4
27	Ukraine	5.1		1.3	79	Mali	3.1		1.6
28	Denmark	5.1		1.1	80	Mexico	3.1		1.4
29	Bulgaria	5.0		1.5	81	El Salvador	3.1		1.4
30	Malta	4.9		1.3	82	Namibia	3.0		1.4
31	Jordan	4.9		1.2	83	Gambia	3.0		1.8
32	Latvia	4.8		1.1	84	Dominican Republic	2.9		1.2
33	Spain	4.8		1.2	85	Ethiopia	2.8		1.3
34	Croatia	4.8		1.6	86	South Africa	2.8		1.4
35	Korea	4.7		1.5	87	Bangladesh	2.8		1.4
36	Poland	4.7		1.4	88	Bolivia	2.8		1.2
37	United States	4.7		1.6	89	Philippines	2.8		1.3
38	Greece	4.6		1.3	90	Nicaragua	2.8		1.2
39	Macedonia, FYR	4.6		1.9	91	Nigeria	2.7		1.5
40	Italy	4.6		1.3	92	Ecuador	2.7		1.3
41	Luxembourg	4.5		1.1	93	Peru	2.7		1.1
42	Thailand	4.5		1.2	94	Venezuela	2.6		1.1
43	United Kingdom	4.5		1.3	95	Pakistan	2.6		1.1
44	New Zealand	4.5		1.4	96	Mozambique	2.6		1.3
45	Serbia	4.4		1.8	97	Paraguay	2.3		1.1
46	China	4.4		1.5	98	Haiti	2.3		1.2
47	Malaysia	4.4		1.3	99	Honduras	2.1		1.1
48	Costa Rica	4.3		1.2	100	Chad	2.1		1.2
49	Trinidad and Tobago	4.3		1.6	101	Guatemala	2.0		1.0
50	Morocco	4.2		1.9	102	Angola	1.9		1.0
51	Mauritius	4.2		1.1					
52	Sri Lanka	4.2		1.6					

The difference in the quality of the health care available to rich and poor people in your country is (1 = large, 7 = small)

RANK	COUNTRY	SCORE	MEAN: 3.0	SD
1	Iceland	6.6		0.6
2	Denmark	6.2		0.9
3	Luxembourg	6.1		0.8
4	Norway	6.0		1.1
5	Netherlands	5.9		1.1
6	Canada	5.9		1.4
7	Finland	5.9		1.2
8	Sweden	5.6		1.3
9	Switzerland	5.5		1.4
10	Belgium	5.5		1.5
11	Japan	5.4		1.5
12	Malta	5.4		1.5
13	France	5.3		1.4
14	Singapore	5.3		1.4
15	Czech Republic	5.2		1.6
16	Australia	5.1		1.4
17	Taiwan	5.0		1.5
18	Austria	4.8		1.7
19	Hong Kong SAR	4.8		1.7
20	Spain	4.8		1.6
21	Germany	4.6		1.6
22	Slovenia	4.4		1.8
23	Estonia	4.3		1.7
24	Slovak Republic	4.2		2.0
25	Korea	4.2		1.5
26	Tunisia	4.2		1.7
27	New Zealand	3.9		1.5
28	Israel	3.9		1.4
29	Italy	3.9		1.6
30	Malaysia	3.8		1.5
31	Latvia	3.7		1.8
32	United Kingdom	3.7		1.8
33	Gambia	3.6		2.2
34	Costa Rica	3.6		1.7
35	Croatia	3.6		1.9
36	Botswana	3.5		1.7
37	Jordan	3.2		1.5
38	Indonesia	3.2		1.6
39	China	3.2		1.7
40	United States	3.1		1.7
41	Macedonia, FYR	3.0		2.0
42	Portugal	3.0		1.5
43	Thailand	3.0		1.5
44	Ireland	2.9		1.6
45	Mauritius	2.9		1.4
46	Hungary	2.9		1.6
47	Vietnam	2.8		1.7
48	Algeria	2.8		1.6
49	Namibia	2.8		1.6
50	Uruguay	2.8		1.5
51	Egypt	2.7		2.1
52	Sri Lanka	2.7		1.4

RANK	COUNTRY	SCORE	MEAN: 3.0	SD
53	Lithuania	2.6		1.6
54	Greece	2.6		1.5
55	Bulgaria	2.6		1.4
56	Poland	2.6		1.4
57	Colombia	2.4		1.6
58	Serbia	2.4		1.5
59	Ghana	2.4		1.6
60	Romania	2.4		1.8
61	Ethiopia	2.3		1.7
62	Panama	2.3		1.5
63	Trinidad and Tobago	2.1		1.4
64	Malawi	2.1		1.3
65	Uganda	2.1		1.5
66	Tanzania	2.0		1.2
67	Chile	1.9		1.1
68	Jamaica	1.9		1.1
69	El Salvador	1.9		1.1
70	Russian Federation	1.9		1.3
71	Mexico	1.9		1.0
72	Turkey	1.8		0.9
73	Dominican Republic	1.8		1.2
74	South Africa	1.8		1.0
75	Peru	1.8		1.1
76	Morocco	1.8		1.2
77	Ukraine	1.7		1.2
78	India	1.7		0.9
79	Zambia	1.6		0.8
80	Pakistan	1.6		1.2
81	Philippines	1.6		0.8
82	Honduras	1.6		1.2
83	Argentina	1.6		0.8
84	Bangladesh	1.6		1.2
85	Nigeria	1.6		0.9
86	Mali	1.6		0.8
87	Senegal	1.6		0.9
88	Bolivia	1.5		1.0
89	Guatemala	1.5		1.0
90	Cameroon	1.5		0.8
91	Brazil	1.5		0.8
92	Ecuador	1.4		0.8
93	Nicaragua	1.4		0.8
94	Chad	1.4		1.3
95	Mozambique	1.4		0.8
96	Kenya	1.4		0.8
97	Haiti	1.4		1.1
98	Angola	1.3		0.8
99	Venezuela	1.3		1.1
100	Madagascar	1.3		0.7
101	Paraguay	1.3		0.5
102	Zimbabwe	1.3		0.5

4.05 Business impact of malaria

The current and future impact of malaria on your company is (1 = extremely serious, 7 = not a problem)

RANK	COUNTRY	SCORE	MEAN: 5.6	SD
1	Sweden	7.0		0.0
2	Belgium	7.0		0.1
3	Denmark	7.0		0.2
4	Portugal	6.9		0.2
5	Iceland	6.9		0.3
6	Austria	6.9		0.3
7	New Zealand	6.9		0.3
8	Israel	6.9		0.3
9	Estonia	6.9		0.4
9	Uruguay	6.9		0.8
11	Czech Republic	6.9		0.5
12	Germany	6.9		0.6
13	Spain	6.9		0.5
14	Luxembourg	6.9		0.4
15	Norway	6.9		0.5
16	Slovenia	6.9		0.7
17	Ireland	6.9		0.6
17	Australia	6.9		0.4
19	Canada	6.8		0.8
20	Finland	6.8		1.0
21	Hungary	6.8		0.9
22	Netherlands	6.8		0.7
23	Chile	6.8		0.8
24	Switzerland	6.8		0.7
25	Greece	6.8		0.8
26	Malta	6.8		0.7
27	Italy	6.7		0.6
28	Macedonia, FYR	6.7		1.2
29	United Kingdom	6.7		0.9
30	France	6.6		1.1
31	Argentina	6.6		1.0
32	Mauritius	6.6		0.8
33	United States	6.6		0.9
34	Mexico	6.5		1.1
35	Jordan	6.5		1.2
36	Singapore	6.5		1.0
37	Korea	6.5		1.0
38	Costa Rica	6.5		1.3
39	Serbia	6.5		1.2
40	Latvia	6.4		1.0
41	Turkey	6.4		1.2
42	Brazil	6.4		1.0
43	Bulgaria	6.4		1.3
44	Croatia	6.4		1.6
45	Slovak Republic	6.4		1.4
46	Hong Kong SAR	6.4		1.1
47	Lithuania	6.3		1.4
48	Poland	6.3		1.2
49	Malaysia	6.3		1.1
50	Romania	6.3		1.6
51	Taiwan	6.3		1.3
52	Japan	6.3		1.4

RANK	COUNTRY	SCORE	MEAN: 5.6	SD
53	Dominican Republic	6.3		1.2
54	El Salvador	6.3		1.3
55	Venezuela	6.2		1.3
56	Jamaica	6.1		1.5
57	Russian Federation	6.0		1.7
58	Peru	6.0		1.4
59	Algeria	6.0		1.8
60	Guatemala	6.0		1.4
61	Trinidad and Tobago	6.0		1.4
62	Paraguay	5.9		1.8
63	Colombia	5.9		1.8
64	Bolivia	5.9		1.8
65	Thailand	5.8		1.6
65	Tunisia	5.8		2.0
67	Panama	5.7		2.0
68	Honduras	5.6		1.7
69	Philippines	5.6		1.6
70	Egypt	5.6		2.0
71	Ecuador	5.5		1.8
72	Ukraine	5.3		2.2
73	Sri Lanka	5.3		1.7
74	Botswana	5.2		1.8
75	Morocco	5.2		2.3
76	Pakistan	5.2		1.8
77	India	5.1		1.9
78	Bangladesh	5.0		1.7
79	Nicaragua	4.9		2.2
80	China	4.6		2.0
81	Vietnam	4.6		1.7
82	Indonesia	4.0		1.5
83	South Africa	3.9		1.8
84	Haiti	3.8		2.0
85	Namibia	3.6		1.6
86	Nigeria	3.5		2.1
87	Zimbabwe	3.4		1.9
88	Madagascar	3.3		1.7
89	Kenya	3.2		1.9
90	Ghana	3.1		1.8
91	Malawi	3.0		1.6
92	Ethiopia	2.9		2.1
93	Senegal	2.8		1.8
94	Uganda	2.5		1.7
95	Mozambique	2.3		1.7
96	Zambia	2.3		1.7
97	Tanzania	2.2		1.5
98	Mali	2.2		1.3
99	Cameroon	2.2		1.5
100	Angola	2.1		1.2
101	Chad	2.1		1.6
102	Gambia	2.0		1.5

4.06　Business impact of tuberculosis

The current and future impact of tuberculosis on your company is (1 = extremely serious, 7 = not a problem)

RANK	COUNTRY	SCORE	1　MEAN: 5.4　7	SD
1	Sweden	7.0		0.0
2	Denmark	6.9		0.3
3	Germany	6.9		0.3
4	Iceland	6.9		0.3
5	Belgium	6.9		0.3
6	Australia	6.9		0.4
7	Finland	6.8		1.0
8	Austria	6.7		0.7
9	Chile	6.7		0.8
10	Switzerland	6.7		0.7
11	Malta	6.7		0.6
12	Spain	6.7		1.0
13	Netherlands	6.7		0.8
14	Israel	6.7		0.5
15	Slovenia	6.7		0.9
16	Uruguay	6.7		1.1
17	New Zealand	6.6		1.0
18	Norway	6.6		0.9
19	Luxembourg	6.6		0.7
20	Italy	6.6		0.9
21	Canada	6.6		1.0
22	Mauritius	6.6		0.9
23	France	6.5		1.1
24	Singapore	6.5		0.9
25	Costa Rica	6.5		1.3
26	Greece	6.5		1.1
27	Hungary	6.5		1.2
28	Czech Republic	6.4		1.3
29	Mexico	6.4		1.1
30	Ireland	6.4		1.3
31	Argentina	6.4		1.2
32	Jordan	6.4		1.3
33	United Kingdom	6.4		1.2
34	Macedonia, FYR	6.3		1.4
35	Malaysia	6.3		1.1
36	Portugal	6.3		1.0
37	Brazil	6.3		1.1
38	Korea	6.3		1.1
39	Dominican Republic	6.3		1.2
40	United States	6.2		1.2
41	Venezuela	6.2		1.3
42	Hong Kong SAR	6.2		1.2
43	Colombia	6.1		1.7
44	El Salvador	6.1		1.3
44	Japan	6.1		1.4
46	Croatia	6.1		1.8
47	Turkey	6.1		1.2
48	Slovak Republic	6.0		1.6
49	Guatemala	6.0		1.5
50	Taiwan	5.9		1.7
51	Jamaica	5.9		1.7
52	Latvia	5.9		1.5

RANK	COUNTRY	SCORE	1　MEAN: 5.4　7	SD
53	Estonia	5.9		1.3
54	Bulgaria	5.8		1.7
55	Serbia	5.8		1.7
56	Tunisia	5.8		1.9
57	Poland	5.8		1.4
58	Panama	5.8		1.8
59	Honduras	5.7		1.7
60	Lithuania	5.7		1.6
61	Ecuador	5.7		1.7
62	Paraguay	5.6		1.8
63	Trinidad and Tobago	5.6		1.6
64	Algeria	5.6		1.8
65	Thailand	5.5		1.5
66	Romania	5.5		2.0
67	Bolivia	5.5		2.0
68	Peru	5.4		1.7
69	Sri Lanka	5.3		1.6
70	India	5.2		1.9
71	Egypt	5.2		2.1
72	Nicaragua	5.1		2.2
73	Russian Federation	4.9		2.0
74	Bangladesh	4.9		1.8
75	Pakistan	4.9		2.0
76	Morocco	4.8		2.3
77	China	4.5		1.9
78	Philippines	4.4		1.9
79	Nigeria	4.0		2.0
80	Indonesia	4.0		1.5
81	Ukraine	3.9		2.0
82	Madagascar	3.9		1.9
83	Mali	3.8		2.2
84	Ghana	3.8		1.8
85	Botswana	3.8		1.9
86	Vietnam	3.6		1.8
87	Kenya	3.5		1.7
87	Senegal	3.5		2.2
89	Namibia	3.4		1.5
90	Mozambique	3.2		1.9
91	Gambia	3.2		1.9
92	South Africa	3.2		1.9
93	Uganda	3.1		1.8
94	Haiti	3.1		1.7
95	Tanzania	3.0		1.9
96	Angola	3.0		1.7
97	Ethiopia	2.8		1.8
98	Malawi	2.6		1.7
99	Cameroon	2.6		1.6
100	Chad	2.4		1.7
101	Zambia	2.3		1.5
102	Zimbabwe	2.1		1.3

4.07 Business impact of HIV/AIDS

The current and future impact of HIV/AIDS on your company is (1 = extremely serious, 7 = not a problem)

RANK	COUNTRY	SCORE	1 MEAN: 4.8 7	SD
1	Finland	6.5		1.0
2	Austria	6.4		0.8
3	Belgium	6.4		0.6
4	Denmark	6.4		1.1
5	Hungary	6.4		1.2
6	Slovenia	6.4		1.1
7	Israel	6.4		0.9
8	Germany	6.4		1.1
9	Iceland	6.3		1.0
10	Jordan	6.2		1.4
11	Norway	6.2		1.0
12	Malta	6.2		1.2
13	New Zealand	6.2		1.1
14	Luxembourg	6.2		1.1
15	Australia	6.2		1.2
16	Sweden	6.1		1.2
17	Singapore	6.1		1.2
18	Chile	6.0		1.3
19	Slovak Republic	6.0		1.5
20	Uruguay	6.0		1.3
21	Spain	6.0		1.4
22	Czech Republic	6.0		1.5
23	Italy	5.9		1.2
24	Macedonia, FYR	5.9		1.8
25	Netherlands	5.9		1.2
26	Ireland	5.9		1.6
27	Malaysia	5.9		1.5
28	Switzerland	5.8		1.4
29	Greece	5.8		1.6
30	Latvia	5.8		1.6
31	France	5.8		1.4
32	Turkey	5.8		1.6
33	Mauritius	5.7		1.3
34	Korea	5.7		1.4
35	Serbia	5.7		1.6
36	Bulgaria	5.7		1.8
37	Costa Rica	5.7		1.6
38	Croatia	5.7		2.0
39	Hong Kong SAR	5.6		1.6
40	United Kingdom	5.6		1.5
41	Portugal	5.6		1.5
42	Venezuela	5.6		1.5
43	Lithuania	5.6		1.6
44	Argentina	5.6		1.5
45	Taiwan	5.5		1.7
46	Tunisia	5.5		2.0
47	Mexico	5.5		1.6
48	Romania	5.4		2.1
49	Canada	5.4		1.5
50	Poland	5.4		1.4
51	Japan	5.4		1.9
52	Egypt	5.3		2.2
53	El Salvador	5.3		1.8
54	Estonia	5.3		1.7
55	Colombia	5.3		1.9
56	Pakistan	5.3		2.1
57	Peru	5.3		1.8
58	Brazil	5.3		1.5
59	Guatemala	5.2		1.8
60	Ecuador	5.2		1.8
61	Bangladesh	5.2		1.7
62	Algeria	5.2		2.1
63	Bolivia	5.2		2.1
64	Sri Lanka	5.2		1.7
65	Panama	5.0		2.2
66	Russian Federation	4.9		2.1
67	Philippines	4.9		1.7
68	Paraguay	4.9		2.0
69	Nicaragua	4.8		2.3
70	United States	4.7		1.9
71	Dominican Republic	4.5		2.0
72	Morocco	4.5		2.5
73	China	4.4		2.2
74	India	4.3		2.0
75	Honduras	4.3		2.3
76	Ukraine	4.2		2.0
77	Indonesia	4.0		1.4
78	Madagascar	3.6		1.9
79	Senegal	3.5		2.1
80	Thailand	3.5		1.7
81	Trinidad and Tobago	3.3		2.0
82	Nigeria	3.2		2.1
83	Gambia	3.1		2.0
84	Jamaica	3.0		1.8
85	Angola	3.0		1.8
86	Ghana	2.7		1.7
87	Mali	2.7		2.0
88	Haiti	2.5		1.7
89	Mozambique	2.4		1.8
90	Uganda	2.3		1.7
91	Kenya	2.2		1.4
92	Namibia	2.1		1.3
93	Vietnam	2.0		1.5
94	Ethiopia	2.0		1.5
95	Malawi	2.0		1.5
96	Tanzania	2.0		1.5
97	Cameroon	1.9		1.4
98	Botswana	1.9		1.4
99	Zambia	1.8		1.2
100	South Africa	1.7		1.0
101	Chad	1.6		1.2
102	Zimbabwe	1.4		0.6

4.08   Impact of HIV/AIDS on FDI

In the last five years, the current and future impact of HIV/AIDS on your country affected the country's access to foreign direct investment (FDI)
(1 = significantly, 7 = not at all)

RANK	COUNTRY	SCORE	1 MEAN: 6.0 7	SD
1	Denmark	7.0		0.0
2	Sweden	7.0		0.2
3	Australia	6.9		0.2
4	Iceland	6.9		0.3
5	Malta	6.9		0.3
6	Finland	6.9		0.5
7	Norway	6.9		0.3
8	New Zealand	6.8		0.6
9	Belgium	6.8		0.5
10	Luxembourg	6.8		0.4
11	Uruguay	6.8		0.5
12	Germany	6.8		0.6
13	Switzerland	6.8		0.6
14	Austria	6.8		0.7
14	Ireland	6.8		0.7
16	Malaysia	6.7		0.5
17	Netherlands	6.7		0.7
18	Slovenia	6.7		0.7
19	Greece	6.7		0.6
20	Hong Kong SAR	6.7		0.6
21	Singapore	6.7		0.7
22	Czech Republic	6.7		0.9
23	Spain	6.7		0.6
24	Canada	6.7		0.7
25	Chile	6.7		0.6
26	France	6.6		0.8
27	Israel	6.6		1.1
28	Jordan	6.6		0.8
29	Hungary	6.6		0.8
30	Portugal	6.6		1.0
31	Turkey	6.6		0.8
32	United Kingdom	6.6		1.1
33	Mauritius	6.6		0.8
34	Croatia	6.6		1.0
35	United States	6.6		0.9
36	Tunisia	6.5		0.8
37	Slovak Republic	6.5		1.2
38	Italy	6.5		0.9
39	Brazil	6.4		1.1
40	Mexico	6.4		0.9
41	Argentina	6.4		1.1
42	Bangladesh	6.4		1.1
43	India	6.3		0.9
44	Bulgaria	6.3		1.2
45	Pakistan	6.3		1.3
46	Algeria	6.3		1.6
47	Macedonia, FYR	6.3		1.5
48	Colombia	6.3		1.1
49	Serbia	6.2		1.4
50	Egypt	6.2		1.4
51	Peru	6.2		1.1
52	Japan	6.2		1.2

RANK	COUNTRY	SCORE	1 MEAN: 6.0 7	SD
53	Costa Rica	6.2		1.1
54	Philippines	6.2		0.9
55	Estonia	6.2		1.1
56	Taiwan	6.2		1.2
57	El Salvador	6.2		1.0
58	Venezuela	6.2		1.2
59	Paraguay	6.1		1.3
60	Dominican Republic	6.1		1.0
61	Nicaragua	6.1		1.3
62	Bolivia	6.0		1.2
63	Thailand	6.0		1.0
64	Latvia	5.9		1.5
65	Senegal	5.9		1.1
66	Panama	5.9		1.3
67	Trinidad and Tobago	5.9		1.2
68	Jamaica	5.9		1.4
69	Gambia	5.8		1.6
70	Poland	5.8		1.3
71	Korea	5.8		1.3
72	Ecuador	5.8		1.4
73	Madagascar	5.8		1.3
74	Morocco	5.8		1.5
75	Russian Federation	5.7		1.5
76	Guatemala	5.7		1.1
77	Lithuania	5.7		1.6
78	Mali	5.6		1.4
79	Sri Lanka	5.6		1.5
80	Angola	5.5		1.6
81	Ukraine	5.4		1.5
82	Nigeria	5.3		1.3
83	Ghana	5.1		1.6
84	Vietnam	5.0		1.3
85	Cameroon	5.0		1.7
86	Romania	4.9		2.0
87	Malawi	4.9		1.6
88	Tanzania	4.7		1.5
89	Honduras	4.7		1.5
90	China	4.7		1.8
91	Uganda	4.6		1.8
92	Namibia	4.5		1.6
93	Zimbabwe	4.5		1.7
94	Mozambique	4.5		1.3
95	Zambia	4.4		1.6
96	Chad	4.4		1.9
97	Kenya	4.4		1.4
98	Ethiopia	4.4		1.8
99	Botswana	4.2		1.6
100	Indonesia	4.2		1.3
101	South Africa	4.1		1.7
102	Haiti	3.7		2.0

4.09 Brain drain

Your country's talented people (1 = normally leave to pursue opportunities in other countries, 7 = almost always remain in the country)

RANK	COUNTRY	SCORE	1 MEAN: 3.5 7	SD
1	United States	6.3		1.1
2	Finland	5.6		1.2
3	Chile	5.6		1.1
4	Spain	5.4		1.3
5	Norway	5.4		1.0
6	Netherlands	5.3		1.1
7	Switzerland	5.3		1.1
8	Japan	5.3		1.1
9	Costa Rica	5.2		1.4
10	Iceland	5.1		0.9
11	Sweden	5.1		1.2
12	Thailand	5.0		1.1
13	United Kingdom	5.0		1.1
14	Luxembourg	5.0		1.1
15	Singapore	4.9		1.2
16	Taiwan	4.8		1.0
17	Botswana	4.8		1.6
18	Israel	4.8		1.0
19	Belgium	4.8		1.4
20	Ireland	4.7		1.2
21	Hong Kong SAR	4.7		1.3
22	Brazil	4.6		1.4
23	Austria	4.6		1.4
24	Denmark	4.6		1.3
25	Panama	4.4		1.5
26	Canada	4.4		1.5
27	Portugal	4.3		1.3
28	Germany	4.3		1.6
29	Malta	4.3		1.3
30	Australia	4.3		1.1
31	Mexico	4.2		1.4
32	Korea	4.2		1.4
33	Dominican Republic	4.2		1.6
34	Slovenia	4.1		1.4
35	Czech Republic	4.1		1.4
36	Latvia	4.1		1.5
37	Malaysia	4.0		1.1
38	Estonia	3.9		1.1
39	Mozambique	3.8		1.8
40	France	3.8		1.5
41	Tunisia	3.8		1.5
42	Greece	3.8		1.3
43	Vietnam	3.8		1.6
44	Poland	3.7		1.3
45	Indonesia	3.6		1.2
46	Hungary	3.6		1.3
47	Namibia	3.6		1.3
48	Trinidad and Tobago	3.6		1.3
49	El Salvador	3.6		1.4
50	Italy	3.5		1.4
51	China	3.4		1.3
52	Turkey	3.3		1.2

RANK	COUNTRY	SCORE	1 MEAN: 3.5 7	SD
53	Guatemala	3.3		1.3
54	Egypt	3.3		1.8
55	New Zealand	3.2		1.0
56	Russian Federation	3.1		1.4
57	Angola	3.1		1.4
58	Colombia	3.0		1.3
59	Paraguay	3.0		1.4
60	Honduras	3.0		1.3
61	Nicaragua	3.0		1.6
62	Mauritius	3.0		1.2
63	Jordan	2.9		1.3
64	Tanzania	2.9		1.5
65	India	2.8		1.2
66	Chad	2.8		1.6
67	South Africa	2.8		1.2
68	Slovak Republic	2.8		1.2
69	Lithuania	2.8		1.3
70	Peru	2.7		1.2
71	Croatia	2.7		1.4
72	Malawi	2.7		1.1
73	Argentina	2.7		1.1
74	Ukraine	2.6		1.3
75	Ecuador	2.6		1.3
76	Bolivia	2.6		1.1
77	Madagascar	2.5		1.3
78	Uruguay	2.5		1.3
79	Jamaica	2.5		1.0
80	Cameroon	2.5		1.5
81	Pakistan	2.5		1.3
82	Kenya	2.5		1.4
83	Uganda	2.5		1.5
84	Venezuela	2.3		1.1
85	Senegal	2.3		1.3
86	Sri Lanka	2.3		1.1
87	Philippines	2.2		1.1
88	Algeria	2.2		1.2
89	Gambia	2.2		1.4
90	Morocco	2.1		1.4
91	Bulgaria	2.1		1.1
92	Ethiopia	2.1		1.3
93	Romania	2.1		1.1
94	Mali	2.1		1.3
95	Bangladesh	2.0		1.0
96	Ghana	2.0		1.0
97	Nigeria	2.0		1.0
98	Macedonia, FYR	1.9		1.3
99	Zambia	1.9		1.1
100	Serbia	1.9		0.9
101	Zimbabwe	1.8		1.1
102	Haiti	1.6		0.7

4.10 Maternity leave legislation

In your country, government policies on maternity leave are (1 = insufficient and impede re-entry into the workforce, 7 = sufficient and facilitate re-entry into the workforce)

RANK	COUNTRY	SCORE	1 MEAN: 5.2 7	SD
1	Sweden	6.7		0.6
2	Canada	6.4		0.7
3	Denmark	6.4		0.8
4	Iceland	6.4		0.8
5	Luxembourg	6.4		0.8
6	Norway	6.3		0.7
7	Finland	6.3		1.0
8	Botswana	6.3		0.9
9	Malawi	6.3		1.2
10	Malaysia	6.2		0.8
11	Zambia	6.2		1.1
12	France	6.0		1.0
13	Belgium	6.0		1.1
14	Philippines	6.0		1.1
15	Israel	5.9		1.0
16	Jamaica	5.9		1.2
17	Gambia	5.9		1.6
18	Zimbabwe	5.8		1.3
19	United Kingdom	5.8		1.1
20	Taiwan	5.8		1.4
21	Malta	5.8		1.0
22	New Zealand	5.8		1.1
23	Singapore	5.8		1.0
24	Jordan	5.8		1.1
25	Hong Kong SAR	5.8		1.4
26	Germany	5.7		1.3
27	Netherlands	5.7		1.2
28	Costa Rica	5.7		1.1
29	Cameroon	5.7		1.3
30	Thailand	5.7		1.3
31	Tunisia	5.6		1.3
32	Macedonia, FYR	5.6		1.7
33	Vietnam	5.6		1.3
34	Dominican Republic	5.6		1.2
35	Panama	5.6		1.4
36	Trinidad and Tobago	5.6		1.1
37	Uruguay	5.5		1.3
38	Portugal	5.5		1.2
39	Nigeria	5.5		1.5
40	Italy	5.5		1.6
41	South Africa	5.5		1.1
42	Ethiopia	5.5		1.7
43	Sri Lanka	5.4		1.3
44	Algeria	5.4		1.5
45	Ghana	5.4		1.5
46	Mauritius	5.4		1.2
47	Tanzania	5.4		1.6
48	India	5.4		1.5
49	Mali	5.4		1.7
50	Ireland	5.4		1.7
51	Greece	5.3		1.3
52	United States	5.3		1.4
53	Namibia	5.2		1.5
54	Austria	5.2		1.5
55	Morocco	5.1		1.6
56	Australia	5.1		1.3
57	Colombia	5.1		1.4
58	Slovenia	5.0		1.6
59	Egypt	5.0		2.0
60	Chile	5.0		1.5
61	Turkey	4.9		1.6
62	Chad	4.9		1.7
63	Peru	4.9		1.4
64	Switzerland	4.9		1.6
65	Czech Republic	4.8		1.7
66	Brazil	4.8		1.4
67	Bangladesh	4.8		1.6
68	Honduras	4.8		1.6
69	Madagascar	4.8		1.6
70	Nicaragua	4.7		1.6
71	Serbia	4.7		1.8
72	Mexico	4.7		1.5
73	Argentina	4.7		1.4
74	Mozambique	4.7		1.7
75	Venezuela	4.6		1.5
76	El Salvador	4.6		1.6
77	Senegal	4.6		1.7
78	Slovak Republic	4.6		1.7
79	Kenya	4.6		1.6
80	Haiti	4.6		1.8
81	Angola	4.6		1.8
82	Romania	4.5		1.8
83	Hungary	4.5		1.5
84	Latvia	4.5		1.5
85	Pakistan	4.5		1.5
86	Spain	4.5		1.7
87	Lithuania	4.4		1.8
88	Uganda	4.4		1.9
89	Bolivia	4.4		1.7
90	Ecuador	4.3		1.7
91	China	4.3		1.6
92	Paraguay	4.3		1.6
93	Poland	4.3		1.6
94	Japan	4.2		1.6
95	Guatemala	4.1		1.6
96	Bulgaria	4.0		2.0
97	Korea	3.9		1.4
98	Indonesia	3.9		1.4
99	Estonia	3.8		1.5
100	Russian Federation	3.8		1.9
101	Ukraine	3.5		1.8
102	Croatia	3.4		1.9

459

4.11   Maternity laws' impact on hiring women

In your country, maternity laws affect hiring women (1 = negatively, 7 = have no impact)

RANK	COUNTRY	SCORE	1 MEAN: 5.0 7	SD
1	Botswana	6.2		0.9
2	Iceland	6.2		1.0
3	Sweden	6.1		1.2
4	Malaysia	6.1		0.9
5	Singapore	6.1		0.9
6	Gambia	6.0		1.5
7	Canada	6.0		1.2
8	Malawi	5.9		1.5
9	United States	5.8		1.3
10	Israel	5.7		0.7
11	Tunisia	5.7		1.3
12	Dominican Republic	5.7		1.5
13	Hong Kong SAR	5.7		1.4
14	Thailand	5.6		1.4
15	Zambia	5.6		1.5
16	Vietnam	5.6		1.3
17	Algeria	5.6		1.5
18	Philippines	5.6		1.5
19	Cameroon	5.5		1.4
20	Taiwan	5.5		1.4
21	Netherlands	5.5		1.2
22	Trinidad and Tobago	5.5		1.3
23	Jamaica	5.5		1.4
24	Finland	5.5		1.3
25	India	5.4		1.3
26	Turkey	5.4		1.4
27	Jordan	5.4		1.2
28	Mexico	5.3		1.4
29	Norway	5.3		1.5
30	France	5.3		1.5
31	Denmark	5.3		1.2
32	Chad	5.3		1.8
32	Ethiopia	5.3		1.6
34	Tanzania	5.3		1.6
35	New Zealand	5.3		1.5
36	United Kingdom	5.3		1.5
37	Nigeria	5.2		1.5
38	China	5.2		1.4
39	Ireland	5.2		1.7
40	Australia	5.2		1.5
41	Morocco	5.2		1.7
42	El Salvador	5.2		1.5
43	Ghana	5.2		1.5
44	Malta	5.2		1.4
45	South Africa	5.2		1.3
46	Switzerland	5.2		1.5
47	Luxembourg	5.1		1.5
48	Panama	5.1		1.5
49	Haiti	5.1		1.5
50	Costa Rica	5.1		1.5
51	Macedonia, FYR	5.1		2.0
52	Belgium	5.1		1.5

RANK	COUNTRY	SCORE	1 MEAN: 5.0 7	SD
53	Mauritius	5.0		1.3
54	Uganda	5.0		1.8
55	Mali	5.0		2.1
55	Nicaragua	5.0		1.7
57	Serbia	5.0		1.7
58	Uruguay	5.0		1.6
59	Angola	5.0		1.8
60	Namibia	4.9		1.6
61	Honduras	4.9		1.6
62	Peru	4.9		1.6
63	Slovak Republic	4.9		1.5
64	Hungary	4.8		1.5
65	Czech Republic	4.8		1.5
66	Latvia	4.8		1.3
66	Madagascar	4.8		1.5
68	Pakistan	4.8		1.4
69	Spain	4.8		1.6
70	Kenya	4.8		1.6
71	Argentina	4.8		1.6
72	Egypt	4.8		1.9
73	Japan	4.7		1.4
74	Guatemala	4.7		1.6
75	Bangladesh	4.7		1.5
76	Sri Lanka	4.7		1.6
77	Portugal	4.7		1.6
78	Greece	4.6		1.5
79	Colombia	4.6		1.6
80	Senegal	4.6		1.9
81	Austria	4.6		1.6
82	Russian Federation	4.6		1.8
83	Mozambique	4.6		1.8
84	Estonia	4.5		1.3
85	Romania	4.5		1.7
86	Italy	4.4		1.8
87	Bolivia	4.4		1.6
88	Brazil	4.3		1.5
89	Ecuador	4.3		1.7
90	Paraguay	4.3		1.6
91	Venezuela	4.2		1.4
92	Zimbabwe	4.2		1.6
93	Bulgaria	4.2		1.8
94	Chile	4.2		1.6
95	Korea	4.1		1.4
96	Ukraine	4.0		1.7
97	Germany	4.0		1.5
98	Croatia	3.9		2.0
99	Poland	3.7		1.4
100	Indonesia	3.6		1.4
101	Slovenia	3.6		1.9
102	Lithuania	2.9		1.5

5.01 Overall infrastructure quality

General infrastructure in your country is (1 = poorly developed and inefficient, 7 = among the best in the world)

RANK	COUNTRY	SCORE	1 MEAN: 3.9 7	SD	RANK	COUNTRY	SCORE	1 MEAN: 3.9 7	SD
1	Singapore	6.8		0.4	53	Gambia	3.5		1.5
2	Switzerland	6.7		0.8	54	Turkey	3.5		1.3
3	Denmark	6.7		0.6	55	China	3.5		1.2
4	Germany	6.6		0.8	56	Jamaica	3.4		1.2
5	Finland	6.6		0.7	57	Slovak Republic	3.4		1.4
6	France	6.5		0.7	58	Hungary	3.3		1.2
7	Sweden	6.4		0.7	59	Ukraine	3.3		1.5
8	United States	6.3		1.1	60	Russian Federation	3.3		1.3
9	Australia	6.3		0.7	61	Tanzania	3.2		1.3
10	Hong Kong SAR	6.3		1.1	62	Venezuela	3.2		1.3
11	Iceland	6.2		0.6	63	Zimbabwe	3.2		1.3
12	Malaysia	6.1		0.7	64	Ireland	3.2		1.3
13	Austria	6.1		1.1	65	Morocco	3.1		1.3
14	Canada	6.0		1.1	66	Colombia	3.1		1.0
15	Luxembourg	6.0		0.8	67	Sri Lanka	3.1		1.3
16	Netherlands	6.0		1.2	68	Pakistan	3.0		1.3
17	Belgium	5.9		0.9	69	Algeria	3.0		1.1
18	Japan	5.6		1.3	70	India	2.9		1.3
19	South Africa	5.2		1.0	71	Ghana	2.9		1.2
20	Namibia	5.2		1.0	72	Costa Rica	2.9		1.1
21	Korea	5.2		1.0	73	Poland	2.8		1.1
22	New Zealand	5.2		1.2	74	Bulgaria	2.8		1.2
23	Jordan	5.2		0.9	75	Guatemala	2.8		1.2
24	Spain	5.0		0.9	76	Vietnam	2.7		1.2
25	Israel	5.0		0.9	77	Romania	2.7		1.5
26	United Kingdom	5.0		1.3	78	Ecuador	2.7		0.9
27	Taiwan	5.0		1.0	79	Malawi	2.7		1.3
28	Botswana	4.9		1.2	80	Uganda	2.6		1.3
29	Thailand	4.9		1.1	81	Croatia	2.6		1.2
30	Portugal	4.8		0.9	82	Zambia	2.6		1.2
31	Chile	4.8		0.8	83	Peru	2.5		1.1
32	Estonia	4.8		1.0	84	Cameroon	2.5		1.0
33	Tunisia	4.7		1.1	85	Macedonia, FYR	2.5		1.3
34	Norway	4.7		1.5	86	Honduras	2.5		1.0
35	Mauritius	4.6		1.1	87	Senegal	2.4		1.0
36	Slovenia	4.6		1.0	88	Kenya	2.3		1.0
37	Latvia	4.4		1.2	89	Philippines	2.3		1.0
38	Czech Republic	4.3		1.3	90	Bangladesh	2.1		0.9
39	Lithuania	4.2		1.3	91	Mali	2.1		1.0
40	Italy	4.2		1.4	92	Mozambique	2.0		1.0
41	Trinidad and Tobago	4.0		1.2	93	Ethiopia	2.0		1.0
42	Malta	4.0		1.2	94	Serbia	1.9		0.9
43	Egypt	3.9		1.4	95	Nicaragua	1.9		0.9
44	Dominican Republic	3.9		1.1	96	Madagascar	1.9		0.9
45	Argentina	3.9		1.3	97	Paraguay	1.9		0.9
46	Panama	3.8		1.2	98	Bolivia	1.9		0.8
47	Brazil	3.8		1.2	99	Nigeria	1.8		0.9
48	Uruguay	3.8		1.1	100	Angola	1.5		0.6
49	Greece	3.8		1.1	101	Haiti	1.3		0.6
50	El Salvador	3.8		1.1	102	Chad	1.2		0.6
51	Indonesia	3.7		1.3					
52	Mexico	3.6		1.2					

5.02   Railroad infrastructure development

Railroads in your country are (1 = underdeveloped, 7 = as extensive and efficient as the world's best)

RANK	COUNTRY	SCORE	1 MEAN: 3.1 7	SD
1	Switzerland	6.7		1.0
2	Japan	6.7		0.7
3	France	6.6		0.8
4	Germany	6.2		0.8
5	Denmark	6.2		0.8
6	Hong Kong SAR	6.1		1.1
7	Finland	6.1		0.8
8	Singapore	5.7		1.4
9	Sweden	5.5		0.9
10	Belgium	5.5		1.1
11	Korea	5.4		1.0
12	Netherlands	5.1		1.6
13	Canada	5.1		1.8
14	Australia	5.1		1.3
15	Austria	5.0		1.4
16	Taiwan	4.9		1.0
17	Russian Federation	4.9		1.5
18	Malaysia	4.9		1.1
19	Ukraine	4.8		1.3
20	India	4.7		1.5
21	United States	4.7		1.7
22	Luxembourg	4.5		1.2
23	Latvia	4.5		1.4
24	South Africa	4.5		1.4
25	Spain	4.4		1.4
26	Slovak Republic	4.4		1.2
27	Czech Republic	4.2		1.4
28	Namibia	4.2		1.3
29	Italy	4.0		1.4
30	United Kingdom	3.9		1.5
31	New Zealand	3.9		1.4
32	Portugal	3.9		1.3
33	Botswana	3.8		1.3
34	Lithuania	3.7		1.2
35	Bulgaria	3.7		1.3
36	Tunisia	3.7		1.4
37	China	3.7		1.1
38	Thailand	3.7		1.3
39	Estonia	3.7		1.4
40	Poland	3.6		1.5
41	Norway	3.6		1.6
42	Slovenia	3.4		1.2
43	Romania	3.4		1.8
44	Israel	3.4		1.4
45	Hungary	3.4		1.4
46	Egypt	3.3		1.7
47	Indonesia	3.2		1.4
48	Morocco	3.2		1.4
49	Pakistan	3.0		1.3
50	Tanzania	2.9		1.4
51	Vietnam	2.8		1.4
52	Zimbabwe	2.7		1.2

RANK	COUNTRY	SCORE	1 MEAN: 3.1 7	SD
53	Sri Lanka	2.6		1.3
54	Greece	2.6		1.1
55	Argentina	2.5		1.4
55	Iceland	2.5		2.1
57	Mexico	2.4		1.3
58	Algeria	2.3		1.0
58	Panama	2.3		1.3
60	Macedonia, FYR	2.3		1.3
61	Turkey	2.3		1.1
62	Bangladesh	2.3		1.2
63	Chile	2.2		1.0
64	Brazil	2.2		1.1
65	Ireland	2.2		1.0
66	Malawi	2.1		1.3
67	Croatia	2.1		1.1
68	Jordan	2.0		1.3
69	Zambia	1.9		1.0
70	Kenya	1.8		0.9
71	Gambia	1.8		1.3
72	Peru	1.7		0.9
73	Uganda	1.7		1.1
74	Cameroon	1.7		1.0
75	Serbia	1.7		0.7
76	Mozambique	1.7		0.8
77	Dominican Republic	1.6		1.3
78	Malta	1.6		1.1
79	Ghana	1.6		1.0
80	Uruguay	1.5		0.8
81	Bolivia	1.5		0.7
82	Senegal	1.5		0.8
83	Philippines	1.5		0.8
84	Nigeria	1.4		0.7
85	Trinidad and Tobago	1.4		1.0
86	Colombia	1.4		0.9
86	Guatemala	1.4		0.8
88	Ethiopia	1.4		0.6
89	Chad	1.3		1.0
90	Honduras	1.3		0.6
91	Mali	1.3		0.6
92	Angola	1.3		0.5
93	Jamaica	1.2		0.5
94	Mauritius	1.2		0.7
95	Costa Rica	1.2		0.8
96	Madagascar	1.2		0.4
97	Venezuela	1.1		0.4
98	Haiti	1.1		0.7
99	Ecuador	1.1		0.5
100	El Salvador	1.1		0.4
101	Nicaragua	1.1		0.3
102	Paraguay	1.0		0.2

463

5.03 Port infrastructure quality

Port facilities and inland waterways in your country are (1 = underdeveloped, 7 = as developed as the world's best)

RANK	COUNTRY	SCORE	1 MEAN: 3.9 7	SD
1	Singapore	6.8		0.5
2	Netherlands	6.6		0.7
3	Hong Kong SAR	6.6		0.8
4	Denmark	6.6		0.6
5	Finland	6.4		0.6
6	Germany	6.3		0.8
7	Malaysia	6.1		0.8
8	Belgium	6.1		0.9
9	Australia	6.0		0.8
10	United States	6.0		1.3
11	Sweden	6.0		0.6
12	Canada	5.9		1.1
13	New Zealand	5.9		0.8
14	Iceland	5.9		0.8
15	France	5.8		1.1
16	Japan	5.6		1.2
17	Panama	5.4		1.3
18	Korea	5.3		1.0
19	Estonia	5.3		1.3
19	Israel	5.3		0.9
21	Mauritius	5.2		0.9
22	Taiwan	5.1		1.2
23	Malta	5.1		1.2
24	United Kingdom	5.1		1.2
25	Norway	5.1		1.5
26	Switzerland	4.9		1.5
27	Namibia	4.9		1.3
28	Latvia	4.8		1.2
29	Jamaica	4.7		1.6
30	Spain	4.7		1.4
31	Jordan	4.7		1.3
32	South Africa	4.6		1.2
33	Slovenia	4.6		1.3
34	Chile	4.6		1.1
35	Portugal	4.5		1.1
36	Thailand	4.5		1.2
37	Tunisia	4.5		1.3
38	Trinidad and Tobago	4.4		1.3
39	Luxembourg	4.4		1.0
40	Italy	4.4		1.2
41	Greece	4.4		1.3
42	Austria	4.4		1.4
43	Russian Federation	4.3		1.4
44	Gambia	4.1		1.7
45	Lithuania	4.1		1.3
46	Romania	4.0		1.7
47	Uruguay	4.0		1.3
48	Sri Lanka	3.9		1.5
49	Egypt	3.9		1.6
50	Turkey	3.7		1.5
51	Morocco	3.7		1.5
52	Argentina	3.7		1.4
53	Indonesia	3.7		1.6
54	China	3.7		1.1
55	Poland	3.7		1.4
56	Bulgaria	3.7		1.4
57	Slovak Republic	3.5		1.4
58	Senegal	3.5		1.4
59	Pakistan	3.5		1.2
60	Dominican Republic	3.4		1.4
61	Ukraine	3.4		1.3
62	Honduras	3.4		1.5
63	Brazil	3.3		1.2
64	Ireland	3.3		1.4
65	Mexico	3.3		1.3
66	Czech Republic	3.2		1.4
67	Ghana	3.2		1.6
68	Tanzania	3.2		1.2
69	India	3.2		1.2
70	Venezuela	3.1		1.6
71	Vietnam	3.1		1.2
72	Algeria	3.0		1.2
73	Botswana	3.0		1.5
74	Kenya	2.9		1.3
75	Ecuador	2.8		1.1
76	Colombia	2.6		1.3
77	El Salvador	2.6		1.5
78	Guatemala	2.6		1.2
79	Cameroon	2.6		1.4
80	Hungary	2.5		1.1
81	Nigeria	2.5		1.3
82	Croatia	2.5		1.2
83	Philippines	2.4		1.2
84	Peru	2.3		1.0
85	Paraguay	2.3		1.2
86	Mozambique	2.2		1.1
87	Uganda	2.1		1.5
88	Bangladesh	2.1		1.1
89	Costa Rica	2.1		1.1
90	Madagascar	2.1		1.0
91	Serbia	2.0		0.8
92	Angola	2.0		1.0
93	Malawi	1.8		1.2
94	Macedonia, FYR	1.8		1.5
95	Zimbabwe	1.8		1.1
96	Zambia	1.7		0.8
97	Nicaragua	1.7		0.8
98	Bolivia	1.4		0.6
99	Ethiopia	1.4		0.8
99	Haiti	1.4		0.6
101	Chad	1.3		1.0
102	Mali	1.2		0.6

5.04   Air transport infrastructure quality

Air transport in your country is (1 = infrequent and inefficient, 7 = as extensive and efficient as the world's best)

RANK	COUNTRY	SCORE	1 MEAN: 4.5 7	SD
1	Singapore	6.9		0.3
2	Germany	6.7		0.5
3	Hong Kong SAR	6.7		0.8
4	United States	6.7		0.8
5	Denmark	6.6		0.7
6	Australia	6.6		0.6
7	Finland	6.4		0.6
8	Netherlands	6.3		1.2
9	Malaysia	6.2		0.8
10	United Kingdom	6.2		0.9
11	France	6.2		0.9
12	South Africa	6.0		0.8
13	New Zealand	5.9		0.9
14	Austria	5.9		1.0
15	Iceland	5.9		1.2
16	Israel	5.9		0.9
17	Sweden	5.8		0.7
18	Canada	5.8		1.3
19	Korea	5.7		1.0
20	Thailand	5.6		0.9
21	Jordan	5.6		0.9
22	Belgium	5.5		0.9
23	Switzerland	5.5		1.3
24	Jamaica	5.4		1.2
25	Norway	5.4		1.3
26	Mauritius	5.4		0.8
27	Chile	5.4		1.0
28	Turkey	5.4		1.0
29	Taiwan	5.3		1.0
30	Portugal	5.3		0.9
31	Japan	5.3		1.4
32	Malta	5.2		1.1
33	Czech Republic	5.1		1.2
34	Spain	5.1		1.0
35	Brazil	5.1		1.2
36	Luxembourg	5.1		1.0
37	Italy	5.0		1.4
38	El Salvador	5.0		1.3
38	Ethiopia	5.0		1.4
40	Greece	5.0		1.1
41	Trinidad and Tobago	5.0		0.9
42	Estonia	5.0		1.3
43	Panama	4.9		1.2
44	Gambia	4.9		1.5
45	Tunisia	4.9		1.2
46	Namibia	4.8		1.1
47	India	4.8		1.1
48	Kenya	4.7		1.1
49	Latvia	4.7		1.2
50	Pakistan	4.7		1.1
51	Dominican Republic	4.6		1.4
52	Mexico	4.6		1.2

RANK	COUNTRY	SCORE	1 MEAN: 4.5 7	SD
53	Ireland	4.5		1.5
54	Slovenia	4.5		1.2
55	Sri Lanka	4.4		1.4
56	Botswana	4.3		1.1
57	Morocco	4.3		1.6
58	Senegal	4.3		1.2
59	Russian Federation	4.3		1.4
60	Lithuania	4.2		1.2
61	Colombia	4.2		1.2
62	Romania	4.1		1.8
63	Costa Rica	4.1		1.2
64	Poland	4.1		1.2
65	Indonesia	4.1		1.2
66	Egypt	4.0		1.4
67	Philippines	3.9		1.2
68	China	3.9		1.2
69	Argentina	3.9		1.3
70	Venezuela	3.9		1.2
71	Vietnam	3.9		1.4
72	Croatia	3.8		1.7
73	Guatemala	3.7		1.2
74	Ghana	3.5		1.7
75	Malawi	3.5		1.3
76	Zambia	3.5		1.7
77	Hungary	3.5		1.4
78	Nigeria	3.5		1.3
79	Tanzania	3.4		1.3
80	Bolivia	3.3		1.1
81	Ukraine	3.3		1.2
82	Mozambique	3.2		1.2
83	Uganda	3.2		1.5
84	Serbia	3.2		1.4
85	Zimbabwe	3.1		1.2
86	Nicaragua	3.0		1.1
87	Ecuador	3.0		1.2
88	Algeria	3.0		1.2
89	Peru	3.0		1.2
90	Uruguay	3.0		1.3
91	Honduras	2.9		1.4
92	Madagascar	2.9		1.3
93	Haiti	2.9		1.1
94	Cameroon	2.9		1.4
95	Mali	2.8		1.3
96	Macedonia, FYR	2.7		1.6
97	Angola	2.7		1.3
98	Bangladesh	2.7		1.2
99	Bulgaria	2.7		1.3
100	Paraguay	2.7		1.1
101	Slovak Republic	2.2		0.9
102	Chad	1.7		1.1

465

5.05 Quality of electricity supply

The quality of electricity supply in your country (in terms of lack of interruptions and lack of voltage fluctuations) is (1 = worse than in most other countries, 7 = equal to the highest in the world)

RANK	COUNTRY	SCORE	1 MEAN: 4.6 7	SD
1	Iceland	7.0		0.2
2	Denmark	6.9		0.3
3	Germany	6.9		0.3
4	Switzerland	6.9		0.4
5	Sweden	6.8		0.5
6	Finland	6.8		0.5
7	France	6.8		0.5
8	Japan	6.8		0.6
9	Austria	6.7		0.7
10	Singapore	6.7		0.6
11	Hong Kong SAR	6.7		0.8
12	Australia	6.7		0.6
13	Belgium	6.6		0.6
14	United Kingdom	6.6		0.6
15	Netherlands	6.6		0.7
16	Canada	6.6		0.6
17	Norway	6.5		0.6
18	Israel	6.4		0.6
19	United States	6.4		1.1
20	Luxembourg	6.4		0.7
21	Korea	6.1		1.0
22	Czech Republic	6.0		1.0
23	Ireland	6.0		1.2
24	South Africa	6.0		0.9
25	Jordan	5.9		0.9
26	Malaysia	5.9		0.8
27	Slovak Republic	5.9		1.3
28	Italy	5.8		1.3
29	Slovenia	5.8		1.1
30	New Zealand	5.8		1.2
31	Tunisia	5.6		1.0
32	Portugal	5.5		1.3
33	Taiwan	5.5		1.2
34	Chile	5.5		1.1
35	Namibia	5.5		1.1
36	Uruguay	5.4		1.3
37	Botswana	5.4		1.1
38	Estonia	5.4		1.1
39	Lithuania	5.4		1.2
40	Morocco	5.3		1.5
41	Thailand	5.3		1.2
42	Spain	5.3		1.3
43	Hungary	5.2		1.2
44	Latvia	5.1		1.1
45	Poland	5.1		1.4
46	Trinidad and Tobago	5.1		1.2
47	Mauritius	5.1		1.0
48	Argentina	5.0		1.3
49	Greece	4.7		1.5
50	Brazil	4.7		1.5
51	Croatia	4.6		1.7
52	Costa Rica	4.6		1.4

RANK	COUNTRY	SCORE	1 MEAN: 4.6 7	SD
53	Peru	4.5		1.2
54	Malta	4.5		1.4
55	Colombia	4.5		1.3
56	Egypt	4.4		1.6
57	Venezuela	4.3		1.6
58	Bulgaria	4.3		1.5
59	Panama	4.3		1.6
60	China	4.2		1.2
61	Bolivia	4.2		1.3
62	Macedonia, FYR	4.1		1.8
63	Turkey	4.1		1.4
64	El Salvador	4.1		1.2
65	Jamaica	4.0		1.2
66	Algeria	4.0		1.3
67	Mexico	3.9		1.5
68	Russian Federation	3.9		1.5
69	Serbia	3.9		1.5
70	Zambia	3.8		1.6
71	Romania	3.8		1.8
72	Guatemala	3.7		1.4
73	Philippines	3.6		1.3
74	Indonesia	3.6		1.2
75	Paraguay	3.5		1.5
76	Vietnam	3.4		1.5
77	Sri Lanka	3.2		1.3
78	Ghana	3.2		1.5
79	Nicaragua	3.1		1.4
80	Ukraine	3.1		1.2
81	Ecuador	3.1		1.3
82	Kenya	3.0		1.2
83	Honduras	3.0		1.4
84	Uganda	3.0		1.6
85	India	3.0		1.4
86	Ethiopia	2.8		1.3
87	Zimbabwe	2.7		1.4
88	Mali	2.6		1.4
89	Malawi	2.6		1.4
90	Pakistan	2.6		1.1
91	Mozambique	2.4		1.3
92	Tanzania	2.4		1.3
93	Madagascar	2.3		1.1
94	Dominican Republic	2.3		1.6
95	Gambia	2.3		1.2
96	Senegal	2.2		1.0
97	Bangladesh	1.9		1.0
98	Cameroon	1.7		0.9
99	Nigeria	1.6		0.9
100	Angola	1.4		0.6
101	Haiti	1.2		0.5
102	Chad	1.1		0.4

5.06 Telephone infrastructure quality

New telephone lines for your business are (1 = scarce and difficult to obtain, 7 = widely available and highly reliable)

RANK	COUNTRY	SCORE	MEAN: 5.2	SD
1	Finland	6.9		0.3
2	Singapore	6.9		0.3
3	Switzerland	6.9		0.4
4	Iceland	6.9		0.3
5	Israel	6.9		0.4
6	Japan	6.8		0.4
7	Sweden	6.8		0.4
8	Denmark	6.8		0.7
9	France	6.8		0.6
10	Germany	6.8		0.4
11	Hong Kong SAR	6.8		0.7
12	Canada	6.7		0.6
13	Netherlands	6.7		0.6
14	Australia	6.7		0.5
15	Chile	6.7		0.7
16	New Zealand	6.6		0.6
17	Austria	6.6		0.9
18	United States	6.6		1.1
19	Belgium	6.5		0.8
19	Luxembourg	6.5		0.7
21	Norway	6.5		1.0
22	United Kingdom	6.5		1.1
23	Korea	6.5		0.8
24	Portugal	6.5		0.7
25	Uruguay	6.4		0.9
26	El Salvador	6.4		0.9
27	Estonia	6.3		1.2
28	Taiwan	6.3		1.0
29	Jordan	6.3		0.9
30	Slovenia	6.3		0.7
31	Dominican Republic	6.3		1.1
32	Malta	6.3		0.9
33	Morocco	6.3		1.2
34	Brazil	6.3		0.9
35	Slovak Republic	6.2		1.0
36	Spain	6.2		0.9
37	Peru	6.2		0.9
38	Lithuania	6.2		0.9
39	Greece	6.1		1.0
40	Hungary	6.1		1.2
41	Thailand	6.1		0.8
42	Croatia	6.1		1.2
43	Ireland	6.0		1.3
44	Malaysia	6.0		0.8
45	Czech Republic	6.0		1.2
45	India	6.0		1.0
47	Italy	5.9		1.3
48	Colombia	5.7		1.0
49	Tunisia	5.7		1.3
50	Guatemala	5.7		1.2
51	Argentina	5.7		1.2
52	Mauritius	5.6		0.9

RANK	COUNTRY	SCORE	MEAN: 5.2	SD
53	Mexico	5.6		1.5
54	Venezuela	5.6		1.2
55	Macedonia, FYR	5.5		1.4
56	Bolivia	5.5		1.4
57	China	5.4		1.5
58	Panama	5.4		1.3
59	Namibia	5.4		1.4
60	Turkey	5.4		1.6
61	Latvia	5.3		1.2
62	Senegal	5.2		1.7
63	Jamaica	5.1		1.5
64	Egypt	5.1		2.0
65	Pakistan	5.1		1.4
66	South Africa	5.1		1.4
67	Gambia	5.1		1.8
68	Poland	5.0		1.5
69	Sri Lanka	5.0		1.6
70	Vietnam	4.9		1.6
71	Philippines	4.8		1.6
72	Bulgaria	4.8		1.5
73	Uganda	4.7		1.9
74	Russian Federation	4.6		1.5
75	Romania	4.6		1.7
76	Tanzania	4.6		1.7
77	Botswana	4.6		1.6
78	Mozambique	4.3		1.5
79	Trinidad and Tobago	4.1		1.7
80	Ukraine	4.1		1.3
81	Indonesia	3.9		1.3
82	Zambia	3.7		1.6
83	Nigeria	3.7		1.9
84	Malawi	3.6		1.6
85	Serbia	3.5		1.9
86	Paraguay	3.3		1.6
87	Ecuador	3.2		1.6
88	Nicaragua	3.2		1.9
89	Madagascar	3.2		1.7
90	Algeria	3.2		1.7
91	Ghana	3.2		1.7
92	Costa Rica	3.1		1.7
93	Kenya	2.8		1.4
94	Ethiopia	2.8		1.6
95	Chad	2.7		1.8
96	Angola	2.6		1.5
97	Zimbabwe	2.6		1.4
98	Cameroon	2.3		1.7
99	Mali	2.2		1.4
100	Bangladesh	2.0		1.1
101	Haiti	1.8		1.3
102	Honduras	1.4		0.7

5.07   Postal efficiency

Do you trust your country's postal system sufficiently to have a friend mail a small package worth US$ 100 to you? (1 = not at all, 7 = yes, trust the system entirely)

RANK	COUNTRY	SCORE	MEAN: 4.4	SD
1	Iceland	6.9		0.4
2	Finland	6.8		0.5
3	Japan	6.8		0.5
3	Switzerland	6.8		0.6
5	Singapore	6.7		0.7
6	Germany	6.6		0.6
7	Denmark	6.6		0.8
8	Australia	6.6		0.5
9	Israel	6.5		0.6
10	Hong Kong SAR	6.5		1.0
11	Luxembourg	6.5		0.8
12	New Zealand	6.4		0.8
13	Netherlands	6.4		1.1
13	Sweden	6.4		0.9
15	United States	6.3		1.4
16	Norway	6.3		0.8
17	Taiwan	6.3		0.8
18	France	6.3		1.3
19	Canada	6.2		1.4
20	Slovenia	6.2		1.2
21	Ireland	6.0		1.2
22	Portugal	5.9		1.2
23	Slovak Republic	5.9		1.1
24	United Kingdom	5.8		1.4
25	Korea	5.8		1.2
26	Botswana	5.7		1.5
27	Estonia	5.6		1.6
28	Tunisia	5.6		1.5
29	Malta	5.5		1.4
30	Brazil	5.5		1.6
31	Spain	5.5		1.6
32	Morocco	5.4		1.9
33	Belgium	5.3		1.5
34	Jordan	5.3		1.7
35	Hungary	5.2		1.8
36	Malaysia	5.2		1.3
37	Italy	5.2		1.6
38	Thailand	5.1		1.3
39	Greece	5.1		1.6
40	Austria	5.0		2.0
41	Czech Republic	5.0		1.7
42	Croatia	4.9		2.0
43	Lithuania	4.9		1.8
44	Vietnam	4.7		1.6
45	Romania	4.7		1.7
46	Latvia	4.7		1.6
47	China	4.7		1.8
48	Chile	4.5		1.9
49	Turkey	4.4		1.8
50	Egypt	4.4		2.0
51	India	4.3		1.9
52	Poland	4.3		1.7

RANK	COUNTRY	SCORE	MEAN: 4.4	SD
53	Serbia	4.2		2.1
54	Trinidad and Tobago	4.2		1.9
55	Mauritius	4.1		1.9
56	Macedonia, FYR	4.1		2.2
57	Uruguay	3.9		1.8
58	Tanzania	3.9		1.9
59	Argentina	3.9		1.9
60	Russian Federation	3.8		1.9
61	Ukraine	3.6		1.6
62	Ghana	3.6		2.0
63	Bulgaria	3.6		1.9
64	Senegal	3.6		2.0
65	Malawi	3.5		2.0
66	Namibia	3.5		1.9
67	South Africa	3.5		1.8
68	Indonesia	3.4		1.3
69	Ethiopia	3.4		1.8
70	Sri Lanka	3.4		1.8
71	Bolivia	3.3		2.0
72	Costa Rica	3.3		1.9
73	Zambia	3.2		1.8
74	Gambia	3.2		2.0
75	Nicaragua	3.2		2.1
76	Haiti	3.1		1.9
77	Guatemala	3.1		1.8
78	Panama	3.0		1.8
79	Colombia	3.0		1.8
80	El Salvador	3.0		1.8
81	Pakistan	3.0		1.8
82	Algeria	3.0		1.8
83	Jamaica	3.0		1.9
84	Peru	2.8		1.7
85	Uganda	2.8		1.8
86	Mali	2.8		1.8
87	Mexico	2.7		1.9
88	Cameroon	2.7		2.0
89	Kenya	2.6		1.5
90	Bangladesh	2.5		1.7
91	Angola	2.4		1.8
92	Ecuador	2.4		1.7
93	Madagascar	2.4		1.6
94	Zimbabwe	2.3		1.7
95	Chad	2.2		2.0
96	Mozambique	2.0		1.6
97	Philippines	2.0		1.2
98	Dominican Republic	1.9		1.6
99	Honduras	1.8		1.2
100	Nigeria	1.8		1.2
101	Paraguay	1.7		1.4
102	Venezuela	1.3		0.6

6.01 Judicial independence

The judiciary in your country is independent from political influences of members of government, citizens, or firms (1 = no, heavily influenced, 7 = yes, entirely independent)

RANK	COUNTRY	SCORE	1 MEAN: 4.0 7	SD
1	Finland	6.6		0.8
2	Israel	6.5		1.1
3	Australia	6.4		0.8
4	Denmark	6.4		1.4
5	Netherlands	6.3		1.1
6	Iceland	6.3		0.9
7	New Zealand	6.3		0.8
8	Germany	6.1		1.1
9	Sweden	6.0		1.3
10	United Kingdom	6.0		1.2
11	Botswana	5.9		1.3
12	Switzerland	5.9		1.3
13	United States	5.7		1.4
14	Portugal	5.7		1.1
15	South Africa	5.6		1.2
16	Norway	5.6		1.6
17	Hong Kong SAR	5.6		1.7
18	Luxembourg	5.5		1.3
19	Austria	5.5		1.6
20	Canada	5.5		1.8
21	Malta	5.3		1.6
22	Estonia	5.3		1.5
23	Jordan	5.2		1.4
24	Trinidad and Tobago	5.2		1.4
25	India	5.2		1.5
26	Ireland	5.2		1.7
27	Singapore	5.2		1.6
28	Belgium	5.0		1.4
29	Hungary	4.9		1.6
30	Gambia	4.8		1.8
31	Uruguay	4.8		1.7
32	Namibia	4.8		1.5
33	Tunisia	4.8		1.5
34	Thailand	4.8		1.7
35	Greece	4.7		1.6
36	Japan	4.7		1.7
37	Taiwan	4.7		1.3
38	Chile	4.6		1.6
38	Tanzania	4.6		1.7
40	Malawi	4.6		1.9
41	Malaysia	4.5		1.4
42	France	4.4		1.7
43	Italy	4.4		1.7
44	Mauritius	4.4		1.7
45	Slovenia	4.3		1.6
46	Czech Republic	4.2		1.5
47	Latvia	4.2		1.7
48	Jamaica	4.2		1.7
49	Korea	4.1		1.4
50	Ghana	4.1		1.8
51	Poland	3.9		1.6
52	Brazil	3.9		1.4

RANK	COUNTRY	SCORE	1 MEAN: 4.0 7	SD
53	Vietnam	3.9		1.4
54	Costa Rica	3.8		1.7
55	Spain	3.8		1.5
56	Zambia	3.8		1.7
57	Turkey	3.7		1.9
58	Uganda	3.7		1.9
59	Egypt	3.7		1.9
60	Dominican Republic	3.6		1.8
61	Nigeria	3.5		1.6
62	China	3.4		1.6
63	Mali	3.4		2.2
64	Mexico	3.3		1.6
65	Lithuania	3.3		1.5
66	Sri Lanka	3.2		1.5
67	Indonesia	3.2		1.4
68	Slovak Republic	3.2		1.7
69	Senegal	3.1		1.8
70	Colombia	3.1		1.4
71	Morocco	3.1		1.9
72	Cameroon	3.0		2.0
73	Philippines	2.9		1.2
74	Bangladesh	2.9		1.5
75	El Salvador	2.9		1.5
76	Algeria	2.8		1.6
77	Pakistan	2.8		1.4
78	Bulgaria	2.7		1.4
79	Croatia	2.7		1.7
80	Serbia	2.7		1.4
81	Russian Federation	2.5		1.4
82	Romania	2.4		1.6
83	Ukraine	2.4		1.4
84	Kenya	2.4		1.4
85	Mozambique	2.4		1.4
86	Madagascar	2.4		1.4
87	Ethiopia	2.3		1.5
88	Macedonia, FYR	2.3		1.6
89	Panama	2.2		1.2
90	Guatemala	2.2		1.3
91	Angola	2.0		1.2
92	Peru	1.9		1.1
93	Honduras	1.9		1.1
94	Ecuador	1.9		1.2
95	Argentina	1.8		1.1
96	Chad	1.8		1.4
97	Zimbabwe	1.7		1.1
98	Bolivia	1.7		1.0
99	Nicaragua	1.6		1.0
100	Paraguay	1.4		0.7
101	Venezuela	1.2		0.5
102	Haiti	1.1		0.3

6.02 Efficiency of legal framework

The legal framework in your country for private businesses to settle disputes and challenge the legality of government actions and/or regulations (1 = is inefficient and subject to manipulation, 7 = is efficient and follows a clear, neutral process)

RANK	COUNTRY	SCORE	1 MEAN: 3.9 7	SD
1	Finland	6.3		0.9
2	Denmark	6.2		1.0
3	Hong Kong SAR	6.0		1.2
4	New Zealand	6.0		0.8
5	United Kingdom	6.0		1.0
6	Switzerland	6.0		1.1
7	Germany	6.0		1.1
8	Netherlands	6.0		1.1
9	Iceland	5.9		1.1
10	Australia	5.9		1.1
11	Singapore	5.8		1.2
12	Israel	5.8		1.3
13	Austria	5.8		1.3
14	Sweden	5.7		1.5
15	United States	5.6		1.0
16	Botswana	5.6		1.4
17	Luxembourg	5.5		1.1
18	Norway	5.3		1.4
19	Malaysia	5.3		1.1
20	South Africa	5.2		1.3
21	Tunisia	5.1		1.4
22	Malawi	5.0		1.7
23	France	4.9		1.5
24	Canada	4.9		1.8
25	Ireland	4.8		1.6
26	Gambia	4.8		1.8
27	Namibia	4.7		1.2
28	Belgium	4.7		1.5
29	Jordan	4.7		1.5
30	Estonia	4.7		1.4
31	Taiwan	4.6		1.3
32	Thailand	4.5		1.4
33	Mauritius	4.5		1.5
34	Malta	4.5		1.6
35	India	4.4		1.7
36	Chile	4.4		1.6
37	Portugal	4.3		1.6
38	Italy	4.2		1.5
39	Slovenia	4.2		1.4
40	Greece	4.1		1.5
41	Korea	4.1		1.1
42	Hungary	4.1		1.6
43	Tanzania	4.0		1.6
44	Latvia	4.0		1.4
45	Ghana	4.0		1.8
46	Spain	4.0		1.4
47	Trinidad and Tobago	4.0		1.7
48	Uruguay	3.9		1.6
49	Japan	3.9		1.6
50	China	3.9		1.2
51	Brazil	3.9		1.4
52	Costa Rica	3.9		1.4

RANK	COUNTRY	SCORE	1 MEAN: 3.9 7	SD
53	Vietnam	3.9		1.3
54	Morocco	3.8		1.6
55	Jamaica	3.7		1.5
56	Zambia	3.6		1.9
57	Uganda	3.6		1.9
58	Indonesia	3.6		1.5
59	Colombia	3.5		1.5
60	Dominican Republic	3.4		1.6
61	Senegal	3.4		1.6
62	Egypt	3.4		1.9
63	Mexico	3.4		1.5
64	El Salvador	3.4		1.3
65	Poland	3.3		1.5
66	Lithuania	3.3		1.4
67	Czech Republic	3.3		1.5
68	Algeria	3.2		1.6
69	Sri Lanka	3.2		1.4
70	Mali	3.2		1.8
71	Slovak Republic	3.1		1.5
72	Nigeria	3.1		1.6
73	Cameroon	3.1		1.8
74	Turkey	3.1		1.4
75	Serbia	2.8		1.4
76	Croatia	2.8		1.4
77	Madagascar	2.8		1.4
78	Pakistan	2.7		1.3
79	Bangladesh	2.7		1.4
80	Panama	2.6		1.2
81	Bulgaria	2.6		1.3
82	Kenya	2.6		1.5
83	Macedonia, FYR	2.6		1.7
84	Mozambique	2.5		1.4
85	Russian Federation	2.5		1.2
86	Philippines	2.5		1.5
87	Ethiopia	2.5		1.5
88	Zimbabwe	2.5		1.6
89	Ukraine	2.5		1.1
90	Peru	2.4		1.4
91	Romania	2.4		1.4
92	Chad	2.3		1.7
93	Guatemala	2.2		1.2
94	Honduras	2.2		1.2
95	Ecuador	2.2		1.1
96	Angola	2.1		1.1
97	Bolivia	2.1		0.9
98	Nicaragua	2.1		1.2
99	Argentina	2.0		0.9
100	Paraguay	1.8		0.9
101	Haiti	1.8		1.0
102	Venezuela	1.3		0.5

6.03 Property rights

Financial assets and wealth (1 = are poorly delineated and not protected by law, 7 = are clearly delineated and well protected by law)

RANK	COUNTRY	SCORE	1 MEAN: 4.6 7	SD
1	Switzerland	6.5		0.7
2	Finland	6.5		0.7
3	Austria	6.5		0.8
4	Hong Kong SAR	6.4		1.0
5	Singapore	6.4		0.7
6	Denmark	6.4		1.1
7	Australia	6.4		0.7
8	United Kingdom	6.3		0.9
9	United States	6.2		1.0
10	Iceland	6.2		0.9
11	Germany	6.2		1.1
12	Luxembourg	6.2		0.8
13	New Zealand	6.2		0.8
14	Netherlands	6.1		1.1
15	Sweden	6.0		1.0
16	Jordan	6.0		1.0
17	Malaysia	5.8		1.0
18	Malta	5.8		1.0
19	Chile	5.7		1.1
20	France	5.7		1.1
21	Botswana	5.7		1.2
22	Norway	5.6		1.2
23	Taiwan	5.5		1.1
24	Belgium	5.5		1.2
24	Thailand	5.5		1.2
26	Ireland	5.5		1.3
27	Canada	5.5		1.4
28	Tunisia	5.5		1.4
29	Israel	5.5		1.2
30	Spain	5.4		1.1
31	South Africa	5.4		1.2
32	Estonia	5.3		1.2
33	Portugal	5.2		1.1
34	Gambia	5.2		1.7
35	Italy	5.2		1.3
36	Korea	5.2		1.2
37	Hungary	5.2		1.3
38	Costa Rica	5.2		1.2
39	Japan	5.2		1.5
40	Mauritius	5.1		1.4
41	Greece	5.1		1.3
42	El Salvador	5.1		1.4
43	India	5.1		1.2
44	Brazil	4.9		1.4
45	Namibia	4.8		1.4
46	Slovenia	4.8		1.3
47	Mexico	4.8		1.4
48	Latvia	4.7		1.2
49	Colombia	4.7		1.3
50	Malawi	4.7		1.5
51	Lithuania	4.6		1.5
52	Trinidad and Tobago	4.6		1.4

RANK	COUNTRY	SCORE	1 MEAN: 4.6 7	SD
53	Tanzania	4.6		1.5
54	Dominican Republic	4.6		1.5
55	Jamaica	4.5		1.5
56	Morocco	4.5		2.0
57	Uruguay	4.5		1.8
58	Egypt	4.4		1.7
59	Panama	4.4		1.4
60	Slovak Republic	4.3		1.4
61	Ghana	4.3		1.8
62	Vietnam	4.2		1.6
63	Peru	4.1		1.5
64	China	4.1		1.3
64	Zambia	4.1		1.6
66	Turkey	4.1		1.7
67	Kenya	4.0		1.5
68	Philippines	4.0		1.7
69	Poland	3.9		1.4
70	Algeria	3.9		1.8
71	Pakistan	3.9		1.5
72	Czech Republic	3.9		1.4
73	Indonesia	3.8		1.2
74	Bangladesh	3.7		1.5
75	Uganda	3.7		1.8
76	Sri Lanka	3.7		1.3
77	Bolivia	3.6		1.5
78	Mozambique	3.5		1.4
79	Romania	3.5		1.6
80	Nicaragua	3.4		1.4
81	Senegal	3.4		1.5
82	Nigeria	3.4		1.5
83	Ethiopia	3.4		1.8
84	Guatemala	3.3		1.4
85	Ecuador	3.3		1.4
86	Honduras	3.2		1.3
87	Serbia	3.2		1.5
88	Cameroon	3.1		1.6
89	Venezuela	3.0		1.4
90	Croatia	3.0		1.5
91	Paraguay	2.9		1.4
92	Bulgaria	2.9		1.2
93	Zimbabwe	2.8		1.8
94	Mali	2.8		1.5
95	Angola	2.7		1.5
96	Russian Federation	2.7		1.4
97	Madagascar	2.6		1.3
98	Chad	2.5		2.0
99	Macedonia, FYR	2.5		1.6
100	Ukraine	2.3		1.1
101	Haiti	2.2		1.1
102	Argentina	2.1		1.2

6.04   Intellectual property protection

Intellectual property protection in your country (1 = is weak or nonexistent, 7 = is equal to the world's most stringent)

RANK	COUNTRY	SCORE	1 MEAN: 3.8 7	SD
1	Denmark	6.2		1.1
2	United States	6.2		1.1
3	United Kingdom	6.1		0.9
4	Germany	6.1		1.0
5	Finland	6.1		1.2
6	Australia	6.1		0.7
7	Sweden	6.0		1.1
8	Singapore	5.9		0.9
9	Netherlands	5.9		1.1
10	Switzerland	5.9		1.1
11	France	5.8		1.0
12	Iceland	5.7		1.0
13	New Zealand	5.6		1.0
14	Israel	5.5		1.2
15	Canada	5.4		1.4
16	Austria	5.4		1.3
17	Belgium	5.3		1.4
18	Hong Kong SAR	5.3		1.4
19	Luxembourg	5.2		1.0
20	Norway	5.0		1.1
21	Taiwan	5.0		1.2
22	Jordan	4.9		1.2
23	Malaysia	4.9		1.3
24	South Africa	4.7		1.5
25	Spain	4.7		1.3
26	Ireland	4.7		1.5
27	Japan	4.7		1.5
28	Tunisia	4.7		1.4
29	Portugal	4.7		1.2
30	Italy	4.6		1.6
31	Slovenia	4.6		1.3
32	Estonia	4.6		1.3
33	Korea	4.5		1.3
34	Hungary	4.2		1.4
35	Thailand	4.2		1.5
36	Chile	4.1		1.4
37	Greece	4.1		1.4
38	Latvia	4.0		1.5
39	Morocco	3.9		2.0
40	Panama	3.9		1.3
41	Namibia	3.9		1.5
42	Mexico	3.8		1.4
43	Brazil	3.8		1.4
44	Egypt	3.7		1.8
45	El Salvador	3.7		1.3
46	Uruguay	3.7		1.4
47	Senegal	3.7		1.5
48	Slovak Republic	3.7		1.5
49	Mauritius	3.7		1.5
50	Costa Rica	3.7		1.4
51	Czech Republic	3.6		1.5
52	Dominican Republic	3.6		1.4

RANK	COUNTRY	SCORE	1 MEAN: 3.8 7	SD
53	Poland	3.5		1.4
54	India	3.5		1.3
55	Indonesia	3.5		1.5
56	Colombia	3.4		1.3
57	Cameroon	3.4		1.6
58	China	3.4		1.3
59	Lithuania	3.4		1.3
60	Botswana	3.3		1.5
61	Malawi	3.3		1.8
62	Malta	3.3		1.5
63	Ghana	3.3		1.6
64	Trinidad and Tobago	3.3		1.4
65	Algeria	3.1		1.5
66	Zimbabwe	3.1		1.4
67	Jamaica	3.1		1.3
68	Sri Lanka	3.1		1.3
69	Gambia	3.0		2.0
70	Tanzania	3.0		1.6
71	Argentina	2.9		1.2
72	Madagascar	2.8		1.3
73	Romania	2.8		1.6
74	Zambia	2.8		1.5
75	Turkey	2.8		1.3
76	Croatia	2.8		1.4
77	Philippines	2.8		1.3
78	Bulgaria	2.7		1.3
79	Nicaragua	2.7		1.3
80	Ecuador	2.7		1.2
81	Vietnam	2.7		1.3
82	Uganda	2.7		1.6
83	Kenya	2.7		1.3
84	Peru	2.6		1.3
85	Nigeria	2.6		1.4
86	Guatemala	2.5		1.2
87	Pakistan	2.5		1.1
88	Honduras	2.5		1.2
89	Macedonia, FYR	2.4		1.6
90	Mali	2.4		1.5
91	Ukraine	2.4		0.9
92	Russian Federation	2.3		1.2
93	Serbia	2.3		1.1
94	Venezuela	2.3		1.1
95	Mozambique	2.2		1.0
96	Paraguay	2.1		1.0
97	Bangladesh	2.1		1.0
98	Angola	2.0		1.2
99	Chad	1.9		1.1
100	Ethiopia	1.8		1.1
101	Haiti	1.7		1.1
102	Bolivia	1.7		0.9

473

6.05 Freedom of the press

In your country, can newspapers publish stories of their choosing without fear of censorship or retaliation? (1 = no, 7 = yes, whatever they want)

RANK	COUNTRY	SCORE	1 MEAN: 5.3 7	SD	RANK	COUNTRY	SCORE	1 MEAN: 5.3 7	SD
1	Denmark	7.0		0.2	53	Jamaica	5.5		1.8
2	Sweden	6.9		0.3	54	Argentina	5.4		1.6
3	Netherlands	6.8		0.8	55	Botswana	5.4		1.5
4	Germany	6.8		0.6	56	Algeria	5.4		1.6
5	Australia	6.8		0.4	57	Bolivia	5.3		1.6
6	Portugal	6.7		0.6	58	Korea	5.3		1.4
7	United States	6.7		0.5	59	Latvia	5.2		1.3
8	Finland	6.6		1.2	60	Dominican Republic	5.2		1.6
9	Belgium	6.6		0.7	61	Slovenia	5.2		1.6
10	Switzerland	6.6		0.7	62	Thailand	5.1		1.7
11	Austria	6.5		0.9	63	Panama	5.1		1.7
12	Iceland	6.5		0.8	64	Nigeria	5.1		1.8
13	New Zealand	6.5		0.8	65	Namibia	5.0		1.7
14	Norway	6.4		1.2	65	Pakistan	5.0		1.8
15	United Kingdom	6.4		1.1	67	Honduras	5.0		1.8
16	Philippines	6.4		1.1	68	Madagascar	5.0		1.7
17	Brazil	6.4		0.9	69	Paraguay	5.0		1.9
18	Luxembourg	6.3		0.8	70	Turkey	4.9		1.8
19	Canada	6.3		1.2	71	Gambia	4.9		1.8
20	Estonia	6.3		1.1	72	Guatemala	4.8		1.9
21	Costa Rica	6.2		1.4	73	Malawi	4.8		2.1
22	Israel	6.2		1.5	74	Croatia	4.7		2.0
23	Spain	6.2		1.0	75	Bangladesh	4.7		1.9
24	Greece	6.2		1.1	76	Romania	4.7		2.1
25	France	6.2		1.2	77	Zambia	4.6		2.0
26	India	6.2		1.0	78	Bulgaria	4.6		1.8
27	Uruguay	6.2		1.1	79	Kenya	4.6		1.9
28	South Africa	6.2		1.2	80	Tanzania	4.6		1.8
29	El Salvador	6.1		1.2	81	Mozambique	4.4		1.8
30	Chile	6.1		1.1	82	Russian Federation	4.3		1.8
31	Japan	6.1		1.2	83	Sri Lanka	4.2		1.9
32	Czech Republic	6.0		1.2	84	Haiti	4.1		1.8
33	Slovak Republic	5.9		1.4	85	Jordan	4.1		1.6
34	Italy	5.9		1.5	86	Serbia	4.1		2.0
35	Malta	5.8		1.4	87	Tunisia	4.0		1.8
36	Mali	5.8		1.8	88	Venezuela	3.8		1.9
37	Lithuania	5.8		1.4	89	Indonesia	3.8		1.3
38	Nicaragua	5.8		1.8	90	Egypt	3.8		2.0
39	Hong Kong SAR	5.8		1.7	91	Morocco	3.5		2.0
40	Mexico	5.8		1.2	92	Cameroon	3.5		1.9
41	Mauritius	5.8		1.5	93	Uganda	3.4		2.1
42	Hungary	5.8		1.4	94	Ethiopia	3.4		2.0
43	Ghana	5.8		1.5	95	Chad	3.3		2.4
44	Taiwan	5.7		1.2	96	Singapore	3.2		1.7
45	Peru	5.7		1.5	97	Vietnam	3.1		1.5
46	Senegal	5.7		1.3	98	Malaysia	3.1		1.6
47	Trinidad and Tobago	5.7		1.5	99	China	3.0		1.4
48	Ireland	5.6		1.8	100	Angola	3.0		2.0
49	Colombia	5.6		1.2	101	Ukraine	2.9		1.6
50	Poland	5.6		1.3	102	Zimbabwe	2.8		2.0
51	Ecuador	5.5		1.5					
52	Macedonia, FYR	5.5		2.0					

6.06 Burden of regulation

Administrative regulations in your country are (1 = burdensome, 7 = not burdensome)

RANK	COUNTRY	SCORE	1 MEAN: 2.9 7	SD	RANK	COUNTRY	SCORE	1 MEAN: 2.9 7	SD
1	Singapore	5.1		1.4	53	Brazil	2.8		1.4
2	Hong Kong SAR	5.0		1.3	54	Portugal	2.8		1.2
3	Finland	4.7		1.5	55	Slovenia	2.8		1.1
4	Switzerland	4.2		1.4	56	Netherlands	2.7		1.2
5	Iceland	4.2		1.3	57	Czech Republic	2.7		1.3
6	Estonia	4.2		1.3	58	Hungary	2.7		1.3
7	Taiwan	4.1		1.3	59	Haiti	2.7		1.8
8	Gambia	4.1		2.1	60	New Zealand	2.7		1.1
9	Jordan	3.9		1.5	61	Mali	2.7		1.6
10	Tunisia	3.8		1.5	61	Spain	2.7		1.2
11	Sweden	3.8		1.5	63	Kenya	2.6		1.4
12	Austria	3.7		1.4	64	Colombia	2.6		1.2
13	Latvia	3.7		1.6	65	Bulgaria	2.5		1.3
14	Denmark	3.6		1.5	66	Turkey	2.5		1.2
15	Indonesia	3.6		1.5	67	India	2.5		1.2
16	Malaysia	3.6		1.2	68	Ethiopia	2.5		1.5
17	Luxembourg	3.6		1.6	69	Macedonia, FYR	2.4		1.7
18	Ireland	3.4		1.5	70	Honduras	2.4		1.3
19	United States	3.4		1.6	71	Panama	2.4		1.3
20	Malawi	3.4		1.3	72	Ukraine	2.4		1.2
21	China	3.3		1.3	73	Italy	2.4		1.3
22	Australia	3.3		1.6	74	Uruguay	2.4		1.2
23	Korea	3.2		1.3	75	Greece	2.4		1.3
24	Germany	3.2		1.5	76	Nigeria	2.3		1.4
25	Thailand	3.2		1.4	77	Mozambique	2.3		1.4
26	Botswana	3.1		1.7	78	Nicaragua	2.3		1.2
27	Ghana	3.1		1.6	79	Cameroon	2.3		1.4
28	Costa Rica	3.1		1.4	80	Bolivia	2.3		1.2
29	El Salvador	3.1		1.3	81	Serbia	2.3		1.3
30	Chile	3.1		1.4	82	Mexico	2.3		1.1
31	Israel	3.0		1.6	83	Pakistan	2.3		1.2
32	Norway	3.0		1.5	84	Guatemala	2.3		1.2
33	Tanzania	3.0		1.5	85	Croatia	2.2		1.2
34	Canada	3.0		1.5	86	Slovak Republic	2.2		1.0
35	Angola	3.0		2.0	87	Mauritius	2.2		1.3
36	Morocco	3.0		2.1	88	Ecuador	2.2		1.2
37	Namibia	3.0		1.5	89	Senegal	2.2		1.4
38	United Kingdom	3.0		1.4	90	France	2.1		1.2
39	Malta	2.9		1.3	91	Peru	2.1		1.1
40	Vietnam	2.9		1.6	92	Jamaica	2.1		1.1
41	Uganda	2.9		1.7	93	Belgium	2.1		1.2
42	Trinidad and Tobago	2.9		1.4	94	Zimbabwe	2.1		1.1
43	Chad	2.9		2.2	95	Argentina	2.0		1.1
44	Paraguay	2.9		1.6	96	Bangladesh	2.0		1.1
44	Sri Lanka	2.9		1.3	97	Romania	2.0		1.2
46	Dominican Republic	2.9		1.7	98	Philippines	2.0		1.0
47	Zambia	2.9		1.5	99	Algeria	1.9		1.1
48	South Africa	2.9		1.2	100	Russian Federation	1.9		1.2
49	Egypt	2.8		2.1	101	Madagascar	1.8		1.0
50	Japan	2.8		1.4	102	Venezuela	1.6		1.0
51	Poland	2.8		1.3					
52	Lithuania	2.8		1.1					

475

6.07 Transparency of government policymaking

Firms in your country are usually informed clearly and transparently by the government on changes in policies and regulations affecting your industry
(1 = never informed, 7 = always fully and clearly informed)

RANK	COUNTRY	SCORE	1 MEAN: 3.9 7	SD	RANK	COUNTRY	SCORE	1 MEAN: 3.9 7	SD
1	Singapore	6.2		0.8	53	Belgium	3.9		1.6
2	Australia	5.6		0.9	54	Uganda	3.9		1.8
3	Finland	5.5		1.3	55	Japan	3.9		1.7
4	Hong Kong SAR	5.4		1.2	56	Italy	3.9		1.5
5	Iceland	5.3		1.1	57	Norway	3.8		1.4
6	Luxembourg	5.3		1.1	58	Macedonia, FYR	3.8		2.0
7	Switzerland	5.3		1.4	59	Lithuania	3.8		1.5
8	New Zealand	5.2		1.3	60	Portugal	3.7		1.4
9	Sweden	5.2		1.5	61	Mexico	3.7		1.5
10	Denmark	5.2		1.2	62	Sri Lanka	3.7		1.3
11	Taiwan	5.1		1.1	63	Philippines	3.7		1.7
12	Botswana	5.1		1.7	64	Indonesia	3.6		1.2
13	Tunisia	5.1		1.6	65	Brazil	3.6		1.3
14	Malaysia	5.0		1.1	66	Algeria	3.6		1.6
15	United Kingdom	5.0		1.4	67	Greece	3.6		1.5
16	United States	4.9		1.4	68	Kenya	3.6		1.6
17	Malta	4.8		1.4	69	Mali	3.5		1.9
18	Netherlands	4.8		1.3	70	Nigeria	3.5		1.7
19	Gambia	4.7		2.0	71	Czech Republic	3.5		1.4
20	Canada	4.5		1.5	72	Madagascar	3.5		1.6
21	Zambia	4.5		1.7	73	Pakistan	3.5		1.5
22	Mauritius	4.5		1.3	74	Jamaica	3.5		1.5
23	Chile	4.5		1.3	75	Slovak Republic	3.4		1.3
24	Germany	4.5		1.7	76	Dominican Republic	3.4		1.6
25	Korea	4.4		1.2	77	Mozambique	3.4		1.5
26	Cameroon	4.4		1.9	78	Turkey	3.4		1.3
27	France	4.4		1.6	79	Egypt	3.4		1.9
28	Jordan	4.4		1.6	80	Uruguay	3.3		1.4
29	Ghana	4.3		1.7	81	Croatia	3.1		1.5
30	South Africa	4.3		1.4	82	Bolivia	3.0		1.5
31	Thailand	4.3		1.5	83	Bangladesh	3.0		1.6
32	Vietnam	4.3		1.6	84	Ethiopia	3.0		1.4
33	China	4.2		1.4	85	Peru	2.9		1.4
34	Israel	4.2		1.1	86	Honduras	2.9		1.5
35	Estonia	4.2		1.4	87	Nicaragua	2.9		1.5
36	Slovenia	4.2		1.3	88	Poland	2.9		1.4
37	Namibia	4.2		1.5	89	Panama	2.8		1.2
38	Spain	4.2		1.4	90	Bulgaria	2.7		1.4
39	Morocco	4.2		1.8	91	Haiti	2.7		1.7
40	Ireland	4.2		1.8	92	Zimbabwe	2.6		1.5
41	India	4.1		1.5	93	Romania	2.6		1.4
42	Serbia	4.1		1.8	94	Ecuador	2.5		1.3
43	Tanzania	4.1		1.7	95	Angola	2.5		1.2
44	Latvia	4.1		1.5	96	Chad	2.5		1.9
45	Austria	4.0		1.6	97	Russian Federation	2.5		1.3
46	El Salvador	4.0		1.3	98	Ukraine	2.2		1.1
47	Malawi	4.0		1.6	99	Paraguay	2.2		1.2
48	Colombia	4.0		1.5	100	Venezuela	2.1		1.3
49	Trinidad and Tobago	3.9		1.5	101	Argentina	2.0		0.9
50	Hungary	3.9		1.3	102	Guatemala	2.0		1.2
51	Costa Rica	3.9		1.4					
52	Senegal	3.9		2.1					

6.08 Favoritism in decisions of government officials

When deciding upon policies and contracts, government officials (1 = usually favor well-connected firms and individuals, 7 = are neutral among firms and individuals)

RANK	COUNTRY	SCORE	1 MEAN: 3.3 7	SD
1	Denmark	5.7		1.3
2	Finland	5.7		1.5
3	Sweden	5.4		1.3
4	Singapore	5.3		1.3
5	New Zealand	5.3		1.4
6	Australia	5.1		1.7
7	Iceland	4.8		1.4
8	Germany	4.8		1.4
9	Switzerland	4.7		1.6
10	Netherlands	4.7		1.6
11	Tunisia	4.7		1.4
12	United Kingdom	4.6		1.6
13	Luxembourg	4.5		1.5
14	Taiwan	4.4		1.4
15	Hong Kong SAR	4.4		1.8
16	Norway	4.4		1.4
17	Botswana	4.4		1.6
18	Korea	4.2		1.3
19	United States	4.1		1.6
20	Gambia	4.1		2.1
21	France	4.0		1.6
22	Belgium	4.0		1.6
22	Jordan	4.0		1.5
24	Latvia	3.8		1.6
25	Algeria	3.8		1.5
26	Egypt	3.8		1.8
27	Thailand	3.7		1.5
28	Austria	3.7		1.7
29	Estonia	3.7		1.4
30	Portugal	3.7		1.5
31	Vietnam	3.7		1.7
32	Chile	3.6		1.6
33	Indonesia	3.6		1.3
34	Malta	3.6		1.3
35	Uruguay	3.6		1.5
36	Japan	3.6		1.5
37	Canada	3.6		1.6
38	Lithuania	3.6		1.3
39	Brazil	3.5		1.2
40	Ireland	3.5		1.8
41	Spain	3.5		1.6
42	Mauritius	3.5		1.3
43	China	3.5		1.5
44	Tanzania	3.4		1.5
45	South Africa	3.4		1.6
46	El Salvador	3.4		1.5
47	Mexico	3.4		1.6
48	Malaysia	3.4		1.6
49	Slovenia	3.4		1.5
50	Serbia	3.4		1.7
51	Italy	3.4		1.3
52	Pakistan	3.3		1.5

RANK	COUNTRY	SCORE	1 MEAN: 3.3 7	SD
53	Israel	3.3		1.4
54	Namibia	3.2		1.6
55	Ghana	3.2		1.8
56	Morocco	3.2		1.6
57	India	3.2		1.4
58	Costa Rica	3.2		1.4
59	Cameroon	3.2		1.8
60	Senegal	3.2		1.5
61	Turkey	3.2		1.5
62	Zambia	3.1		1.8
63	Mali	3.1		1.9
64	Sri Lanka	3.0		1.5
65	Malawi	3.0		1.6
66	Ethiopia	3.0		1.8
67	Hungary	2.9		1.2
68	Czech Republic	2.9		1.2
69	Poland	2.9		1.4
70	Greece	2.9		1.4
71	Peru	2.8		1.2
72	Colombia	2.7		1.2
73	Croatia	2.7		1.4
74	Dominican Republic	2.7		1.8
75	Trinidad and Tobago	2.6		1.3
76	Slovak Republic	2.6		1.3
77	Kenya	2.6		1.5
78	Macedonia, FYR	2.6		1.7
79	Uganda	2.6		1.6
80	Madagascar	2.6		1.2
81	Russian Federation	2.5		1.4
82	Ukraine	2.4		1.3
83	Mozambique	2.4		1.2
84	Philippines	2.3		1.1
85	Jamaica	2.3		1.1
86	Nicaragua	2.3		1.2
87	Bulgaria	2.3		1.2
88	Bangladesh	2.2		1.2
89	Angola	2.1		1.6
90	Honduras	2.1		1.2
91	Nigeria	2.1		1.2
92	Panama	2.0		1.1
93	Romania	2.0		1.3
94	Zimbabwe	2.0		1.3
95	Bolivia	1.9		1.0
96	Ecuador	1.9		1.0
97	Chad	1.9		1.3
98	Argentina	1.9		0.9
99	Venezuela	1.8		1.0
100	Guatemala	1.8		0.8
101	Haiti	1.7		1.0
102	Paraguay	1.6		0.8

477

6.09 Extent of bureaucratic red tape

How much time does your firm's senior management spend dealing/negotiating with government officials (as a percentage of work time)?
(1 = 0%, 2 = 1–10%, 3 = 11–20%, 8 = 81–100%)

RANK	COUNTRY	SCORE	SD	RANK	COUNTRY	SCORE	SD
1	Hungary	1.9	0.7	53	Portugal	2.7	1.3
2	Panama	2.1	1.3	54	Dominican Republic	2.7	1.4
3	Guatemala	2.1	1.2	55	Tunisia	2.7	1.4
4	Japan	2.1	0.8	56	Canada	2.7	1.5
5	Spain	2.1	1.0	57	Malaysia	2.7	1.2
6	Switzerland	2.1	0.9	58	Brazil	2.7	1.5
7	Norway	2.2	0.9	59	Lithuania	2.7	1.4
8	Croatia	2.2	1.4	60	Mali	2.7	1.4
9	El Salvador	2.2	1.0	61	South Africa	2.7	1.1
10	Slovak Republic	2.2	0.8	62	Estonia	2.8	1.4
11	Iceland	2.2	0.9	63	Gambia	2.8	1.6
12	Romania	2.2	1.7	64	India	2.8	1.0
13	Paraguay	2.2	1.2	65	Uruguay	2.8	1.6
14	United States	2.3	1.1	66	Morocco	2.8	1.5
15	Belgium	2.3	1.1	67	Poland	2.8	1.5
16	New Zealand	2.3	0.9	68	Finland	2.9	1.5
17	Luxembourg	2.3	0.9	69	Turkey	2.9	1.4
18	Italy	2.3	0.9	70	Ghana	2.9	1.7
19	Sweden	2.3	1.4	71	Mauritius	2.9	1.1
20	Philippines	2.3	0.9	72	Namibia	3.0	1.6
20	Haiti	2.3	1.5	73	Mexico	3.0	1.6
22	Jamaica	2.4	1.3	74	Mozambique	3.0	1.4
23	Chile	2.4	1.1	75	Kenya	3.0	1.4
24	France	2.4	1.2	76	Nicaragua	3.0	1.7
25	Australia	2.4	0.9	77	Jordan	3.1	1.5
26	Germany	2.4	1.1	78	Sri Lanka	3.1	1.4
27	Singapore	2.4	1.0	79	Thailand	3.1	1.3
28	Argentina	2.4	1.2	80	Zimbabwe	3.1	1.2
29	Malta	2.4	1.0	81	Ukraine	3.1	1.1
30	Venezuela	2.4	1.3	82	Latvia	3.2	1.2
31	Peru	2.4	1.4	83	Madagascar	3.2	1.5
32	Ireland	2.4	1.0	84	Bangladesh	3.2	1.5
33	Austria	2.5	1.1	85	Vietnam	3.3	1.4
34	Greece	2.5	1.1	86	Bolivia	3.3	2.0
35	Colombia	2.5	1.3	87	Pakistan	3.3	1.1
36	Costa Rica	2.5	1.6	88	Botswana	3.3	1.7
37	Korea	2.5	1.0	89	Tanzania	3.3	1.7
38	Macedonia, FYR	2.5	1.7	90	Malawi	3.4	1.3
39	Honduras	2.5	1.6	91	Bulgaria	3.4	1.5
40	Netherlands	2.5	1.2	92	Russian Federation	3.4	1.6
41	Hong Kong SAR	2.6	1.2	93	Cameroon	3.5	1.8
42	Taiwan	2.6	1.3	94	Zambia	3.5	1.8
43	Denmark	2.6	1.1	95	Egypt	3.5	1.5
44	Ecuador	2.6	1.5	96	Ethiopia	3.5	1.9
45	United Kingdom	2.6	1.3	97	Indonesia	3.6	1.2
46	Chad	2.6	1.4	98	Nigeria	3.6	1.9
47	Senegal	2.7	1.3	99	Uganda	3.7	1.9
48	Trinidad and Tobago	2.7	1.2	100	Angola	3.7	1.7
49	Israel	2.7	1.3	101	Algeria	3.9	1.7
50	Czech Republic	2.7	1.1	102	China	3.9	1.6
51	Serbia	2.7	1.3				
52	Slovenia	2.7	1.0				

MEAN: 2.7

6.10   Effectiveness of law-making bodies

How effective is your national Parliament/Congress as a law-making and oversight institution? (1 = very ineffective, 7 = very effective, equal to the best in the world)

RANK	COUNTRY	SCORE	1 MEAN: 3.4 7	SD
1	Singapore	6.3		0.7
2	Australia	5.8		1.1
3	Malaysia	5.5		1.3
4	Denmark	5.4		1.1
5	Iceland	5.3		0.7
6	United Kingdom	5.3		1.4
7	Finland	5.3		0.9
8	United States	5.2		1.6
9	Luxembourg	5.1		1.1
10	Malta	4.8		1.1
11	Sweden	4.8		1.4
12	Estonia	4.8		1.1
13	Switzerland	4.7		1.4
14	Ghana	4.6		1.5
15	Botswana	4.6		1.5
16	Canada	4.6		1.4
17	South Africa	4.5		1.3
18	New Zealand	4.5		1.5
19	France	4.4		1.6
20	Netherlands	4.4		1.5
21	Tunisia	4.4		1.4
22	Spain	4.4		1.2
23	Mauritius	4.3		1.3
24	Norway	4.3		1.5
25	Thailand	4.2		1.2
26	China	4.2		1.4
27	Gambia	4.2		1.8
28	Tanzania	4.2		1.4
29	Latvia	4.1		1.5
30	Vietnam	4.1		1.4
31	India	4.0		1.5
32	Namibia	4.0		1.4
33	Ireland	4.0		1.5
34	Hungary	3.9		1.3
35	Portugal	3.9		1.2
36	Austria	3.8		1.3
37	Greece	3.8		1.2
38	Zambia	3.8		1.7
39	Kenya	3.7		1.4
40	Egypt	3.7		1.7
41	Jordan	3.6		1.6
42	Germany	3.6		1.7
43	Belgium	3.6		1.6
44	Uganda	3.6		1.6
45	Japan	3.6		1.5
46	Taiwan	3.6		1.5
47	Malawi	3.5		1.6
48	Hong Kong SAR	3.5		1.5
49	Indonesia	3.5		1.6
50	Turkey	3.4		1.2
51	Brazil	3.4		1.3
52	Slovenia	3.4		1.2

RANK	COUNTRY	SCORE	1 MEAN: 3.4 7	SD
53	Chile	3.4		1.3
54	Israel	3.4		1.2
55	Morocco	3.3		1.7
56	Korea	3.3		1.4
57	Italy	3.3		1.2
58	Sri Lanka	3.3		1.3
59	Mali	3.2		1.6
59	Lithuania	3.2		1.3
61	Trinidad and Tobago	3.2		1.4
62	Serbia	3.1		1.5
63	Jamaica	3.1		1.4
64	Slovak Republic	2.9		1.2
65	Nigeria	2.9		1.5
66	Russian Federation	2.8		1.4
67	Czech Republic	2.8		1.3
68	Macedonia, FYR	2.8		1.5
69	Ukraine	2.8		1.3
70	Poland	2.8		1.3
71	Cameroon	2.8		1.3
72	Uruguay	2.7		1.2
73	Croatia	2.7		1.5
74	Senegal	2.7		1.2
75	Mozambique	2.7		1.2
76	Pakistan	2.7		1.2
77	Dominican Republic	2.6		1.4
78	Colombia	2.6		1.2
79	Algeria	2.6		1.4
80	Bangladesh	2.5		1.3
81	Angola	2.5		0.9
82	Mexico	2.5		1.2
83	Madagascar	2.4		1.1
84	Costa Rica	2.4		1.1
85	Bulgaria	2.4		1.2
86	Honduras	2.4		1.1
87	El Salvador	2.3		1.2
88	Philippines	2.3		1.3
89	Romania	2.2		1.2
90	Ethiopia	2.2		1.4
91	Peru	2.2		1.0
92	Panama	2.2		1.2
93	Chad	2.0		1.4
94	Bolivia	1.9		0.9
95	Zimbabwe	1.9		1.2
96	Nicaragua	1.7		1.0
97	Ecuador	1.7		0.8
98	Guatemala	1.6		0.8
99	Argentina	1.4		0.7
100	Paraguay	1.4		0.9
101	Venezuela	1.3		0.6
102	Haiti	1.1		0.3

6.11 Efficiency of the tax system

Your country's tax system is (1 = highly complex and distortive on business decisions, 7 = simple and transparent)

RANK	COUNTRY	SCORE	1 MEAN: 3.3 7	SD
1	Hong Kong SAR	6.3		1.3
2	Singapore	5.8		1.0
3	Botswana	5.4		1.2
4	Estonia	5.4		1.4
5	Malaysia	5.3		1.0
6	Iceland	5.2		1.1
7	Luxembourg	5.1		1.1
8	Malta	5.0		1.1
9	El Salvador	4.8		1.3
10	Mauritius	4.7		1.2
11	Taiwan	4.7		1.4
12	Finland	4.6		1.6
13	Gambia	4.6		2.1
14	Trinidad and Tobago	4.6		1.4
15	New Zealand	4.5		1.5
16	Switzerland	4.4		1.4
17	Namibia	4.4		1.4
18	Tunisia	4.3		1.5
19	Chile	4.3		1.5
20	Ireland	4.2		1.5
20	Jordan	4.2		1.3
22	Ghana	4.0		1.6
23	Netherlands	4.0		1.3
24	Latvia	3.9		1.6
25	Spain	3.9		1.3
26	Zambia	3.8		1.8
27	Thailand	3.8		1.3
28	South Africa	3.8		1.3
29	China	3.7		1.2
30	Sri Lanka	3.6		1.5
31	Morocco	3.5		1.9
32	Malawi	3.5		1.7
33	Zimbabwe	3.5		1.8
34	Paraguay	3.5		1.5
35	United Kingdom	3.5		1.4
36	Indonesia	3.4		1.3
37	Korea	3.4		1.1
38	Croatia	3.4		1.8
39	Slovenia	3.4		1.4
40	Australia	3.4		1.8
41	Costa Rica	3.3		1.5
42	Bolivia	3.3		1.5
43	Haiti	3.3		1.6
44	Dominican Republic	3.2		1.6
45	United States	3.2		1.4
46	Serbia	3.2		1.7
47	Portugal	3.1		1.3
48	Macedonia, FYR	3.1		2.0
49	Kenya	3.1		1.4
50	Panama	3.1		1.4
51	Mozambique	3.1		1.6
52	Nigeria	3.1		1.6
53	Canada	3.1		1.5
54	Algeria	3.0		1.6
55	Tanzania	3.0		1.8
56	Norway	3.0		1.4
57	Egypt	3.0		1.8
58	Mali	2.9		1.7
59	India	2.9		1.2
60	Hungary	2.9		1.4
61	Vietnam	2.9		1.3
62	Philippines	2.9		1.5
63	Senegal	2.9		1.4
64	Jamaica	2.9		1.4
64	Uganda	2.9		1.7
66	Peru	2.9		1.2
67	Sweden	2.9		1.5
68	Honduras	2.8		1.5
69	Austria	2.8		1.4
70	Angola	2.8		1.4
71	Madagascar	2.7		1.4
72	Colombia	2.7		1.4
73	Cameroon	2.7		1.3
74	Nicaragua	2.7		1.3
75	Czech Republic	2.7		1.3
76	Ethiopia	2.6		1.5
77	Israel	2.6		1.1
78	Uruguay	2.6		1.2
79	France	2.6		1.2
80	Denmark	2.6		1.2
81	Japan	2.6		1.1
82	Lithuania	2.5		1.1
83	Bangladesh	2.5		1.1
84	Italy	2.4		1.1
85	Ecuador	2.4		1.2
86	Belgium	2.4		1.3
87	Poland	2.4		1.3
88	Greece	2.3		1.1
89	Bulgaria	2.3		1.2
90	Mexico	2.2		1.1
91	Slovak Republic	2.2		1.1
92	Venezuela	2.2		1.1
93	Pakistan	2.2		1.1
94	Turkey	2.2		1.0
95	Guatemala	2.1		1.2
96	Russian Federation	2.1		1.2
97	Chad	2.1		1.5
98	Ukraine	1.8		1.0
99	Argentina	1.8		0.8
100	Romania	1.7		1.1
101	Brazil	1.7		0.8
102	Germany	1.5		0.6

6.12   Centralization of economic policymaking

Economic policymaking in your country is (1 = centralized at the national level, 7 = decentralized at the state and city level)

RANK	COUNTRY	SCORE	1 MEAN: 3.0 7	SD
1	Switzerland	6.1		0.9
2	Spain	5.4		1.1
3	Germany	5.1		1.5
4	Belgium	5.0		1.3
5	Austria	4.9		1.4
6	United States	4.9		1.6
7	Iceland	4.8		1.6
8	India	4.4		1.5
9	Denmark	4.4		1.8
10	Canada	4.3		1.8
11	Italy	4.3		1.5
12	Latvia	4.1		1.5
13	Estonia	4.0		1.4
14	Indonesia	4.0		1.3
15	Finland	4.0		1.6
16	Netherlands	3.9		1.6
17	Hong Kong SAR	3.9		2.2
18	Czech Republic	3.7		1.4
19	Vietnam	3.7		1.7
20	Sweden	3.6		1.6
21	Brazil	3.6		1.7
22	Taiwan	3.6		1.7
23	Australia	3.6		1.9
24	Norway	3.5		1.6
25	Tanzania	3.5		2.1
26	Poland	3.5		1.4
27	China	3.4		1.3
28	Slovenia	3.4		1.5
29	Hungary	3.4		1.4
30	New Zealand	3.4		1.5
31	Uganda	3.3		2.1
32	El Salvador	3.3		1.8
33	Russian Federation	3.2		1.5
34	South Africa	3.2		1.6
35	Mexico	3.2		1.7
36	Ghana	3.1		1.8
37	Croatia	3.1		1.7
38	Slovak Republic	3.1		1.4
39	France	3.1		1.6
40	Lithuania	3.1		1.5
41	Namibia	3.0		1.5
42	Chile	3.0		1.6
43	Romania	3.0		1.6
44	Egypt	3.0		2.0
45	Korea	3.0		1.4
46	Morocco	2.9		1.7
47	Colombia	2.9		1.5
48	United Kingdom	2.9		1.6
49	Philippines	2.9		1.6
50	Jordan	2.8		1.6
51	Serbia	2.8		1.7
52	Luxembourg	2.8		1.9

RANK	COUNTRY	SCORE	1 MEAN: 3.0 7	SD
53	Ukraine	2.8		1.2
54	Bulgaria	2.7		1.4
55	Bolivia	2.7		1.5
56	Tunisia	2.7		1.6
57	Sri Lanka	2.7		1.4
58	Portugal	2.7		1.4
59	Nigeria	2.7		1.7
60	Mozambique	2.6		1.4
61	Ethiopia	2.6		1.6
62	Costa Rica	2.6		1.5
63	Gambia	2.6		1.8
64	Greece	2.6		1.5
65	Botswana	2.5		1.4
66	Peru	2.5		1.5
67	Mali	2.5		1.6
68	Madagascar	2.5		1.4
69	Thailand	2.5		1.6
70	Israel	2.5		1.2
71	Argentina	2.5		1.2
72	Mauritius	2.4		1.6
73	Honduras	2.4		1.3
74	Malaysia	2.4		1.2
75	Malta	2.4		1.8
76	Nicaragua	2.3		1.3
77	Macedonia, FYR	2.3		1.6
78	Kenya	2.3		1.2
79	Senegal	2.3		1.3
80	Malawi	2.3		1.5
81	Pakistan	2.2		1.3
82	Ecuador	2.2		1.1
83	Dominican Republic	2.2		1.4
84	Singapore	2.1		1.7
85	Panama	2.1		1.1
86	Jamaica	2.1		1.2
87	Uruguay	2.1		1.3
88	Japan	2.1		1.1
89	Zambia	2.1		1.4
90	Paraguay	2.0		1.1
91	Turkey	2.0		1.1
92	Guatemala	1.9		1.1
93	Algeria	1.9		1.3
94	Ireland	1.9		1.1
95	Angola	1.8		1.1
96	Cameroon	1.7		1.1
97	Bangladesh	1.7		1.0
98	Trinidad and Tobago	1.7		1.0
99	Chad	1.6		1.1
100	Zimbabwe	1.4		0.9
101	Venezuela	1.4		0.8
102	Haiti	1.3		0.5

6.13 Reliability of police services

Police services (1 = cannot be relied upon to protect businesses from criminals, 7 = can be relied upon to protect businesses from criminals)

RANK	COUNTRY	SCORE	1 MEAN: 4.2 7	SD
1	Singapore	6.5		0.7
2	Denmark	6.5		0.7
3	Finland	6.3		1.1
4	Hong Kong SAR	6.3		0.8
5	Iceland	6.3		0.6
6	Australia	6.3		0.6
7	Jordan	6.2		1.0
8	Switzerland	6.0		1.1
9	United States	6.0		1.2
10	Israel	5.9		0.7
11	Sweden	5.9		1.5
12	Canada	5.8		1.2
13	Germany	5.8		1.1
14	New Zealand	5.8		1.1
15	Austria	5.7		1.3
16	Luxembourg	5.7		1.1
17	Tunisia	5.6		1.3
18	United Kingdom	5.6		1.2
19	Malaysia	5.6		0.9
20	Portugal	5.5		1.1
21	Norway	5.5		1.6
22	France	5.5		1.3
23	Korea	5.3		1.3
24	Malta	5.2		1.3
25	Taiwan	5.2		1.0
26	Netherlands	5.2		1.5
27	Italy	5.2		1.5
28	Ireland	5.2		1.7
29	Japan	5.1		1.4
30	Chile	5.1		1.4
31	Thailand	4.9		1.4
32	Morocco	4.9		1.9
33	Gambia	4.9		2.1
34	Botswana	4.8		1.6
35	Belgium	4.7		1.6
36	Spain	4.7		1.5
37	Vietnam	4.6		1.8
38	Greece	4.6		1.4
39	Latvia	4.5		1.5
40	Algeria	4.5		1.7
41	Uruguay	4.5		1.6
42	Egypt	4.5		1.9
43	Estonia	4.4		1.6
44	Senegal	4.4		2.0
45	Colombia	4.4		1.4
46	Ghana	4.3		1.7
47	Turkey	4.3		1.5
48	China	4.2		1.5
49	Panama	4.1		1.6
50	Dominican Republic	4.1		1.6
51	Hungary	4.1		1.6
52	India	4.1		1.6
53	Ethiopia	4.0		1.9
54	Slovenia	4.0		1.7
55	El Salvador	3.9		1.6
56	Serbia	3.9		1.8
57	Malawi	3.9		1.8
58	Czech Republic	3.8		1.5
59	Mauritius	3.8		1.5
60	Mali	3.8		1.9
61	Nicaragua	3.7		1.6
62	Costa Rica	3.7		1.5
63	Tanzania	3.7		1.8
64	Zambia	3.6		1.8
65	Macedonia, FYR	3.6		2.0
66	Angola	3.6		1.6
67	Croatia	3.5		1.8
68	Sri Lanka	3.5		1.5
69	Indonesia	3.5		1.3
70	Poland	3.4		1.2
71	Lithuania	3.3		1.4
72	Uganda	3.3		1.8
73	Cameroon	3.3		1.7
74	Jamaica	3.2		1.5
75	Honduras	3.2		1.5
76	Namibia	3.2		1.5
77	Romania	3.2		1.9
78	Peru	3.2		1.4
79	Slovak Republic	3.1		1.6
80	Bulgaria	3.1		1.5
81	Brazil	3.1		1.4
82	Mexico	3.1		1.6
83	Bolivia	3.0		1.5
84	Mozambique	3.0		1.6
85	Madagascar	2.9		1.3
86	South Africa	2.9		1.3
87	Trinidad and Tobago	2.9		1.5
88	Russian Federation	2.8		1.6
89	Kenya	2.8		1.4
90	Ecuador	2.7		1.3
91	Paraguay	2.6		1.4
92	Ukraine	2.6		1.5
93	Nigeria	2.6		1.4
94	Argentina	2.6		1.3
95	Philippines	2.5		1.4
96	Pakistan	2.4		1.4
97	Chad	2.3		1.6
98	Zimbabwe	2.3		1.4
99	Venezuela	2.1		0.9
100	Guatemala	2.1		1.1
101	Bangladesh	2.1		1.2
102	Haiti	1.4		0.8

6.14 Business costs of crime and violence

Common crime and violence (eg, street muggings, firms being looted) (1 = impose significant costs on businesses, 7 = do not impose significant costs on businesses)

RANK	COUNTRY	SCORE	1 MEAN: 4.3 7	SD
1	Singapore	6.6		0.9
2	Finland	6.6		0.7
3	Denmark	6.5		0.9
4	Israel	6.5		0.7
5	Hong Kong SAR	6.5		0.8
6	Jordan	6.4		0.8
7	Germany	6.3		0.9
8	Iceland	6.3		1.0
9	Switzerland	6.3		1.0
10	Portugal	6.3		0.9
11	Australia	6.2		1.2
12	Austria	6.1		1.3
13	Luxembourg	6.1		1.1
14	Sweden	6.1		1.2
15	Norway	6.0		1.4
16	Malaysia	6.0		1.0
17	Malta	6.0		1.1
18	Turkey	5.7		1.3
19	Thailand	5.7		1.2
20	Taiwan	5.7		1.2
21	Tunisia	5.6		1.4
22	New Zealand	5.6		1.5
23	Slovenia	5.6		1.4
24	Greece	5.5		1.4
25	India	5.5		1.3
26	United States	5.5		1.7
27	Gambia	5.4		2.0
28	Japan	5.4		1.5
29	Canada	5.4		1.5
30	Korea	5.4		1.5
31	Mali	5.4		1.7
32	Botswana	5.2		1.4
33	Morocco	5.0		2.0
34	Belgium	5.0		1.6
35	France	4.9		1.5
36	Uruguay	4.9		1.6
37	United Kingdom	4.9		1.4
38	Mauritius	4.9		1.5
39	Hungary	4.8		1.6
40	Estonia	4.8		1.5
41	Chile	4.8		1.5
42	Italy	4.8		1.4
43	Dominican Republic	4.8		1.3
44	Egypt	4.7		1.9
45	Ethiopia	4.7		2.1
46	Netherlands	4.7		1.7
47	Algeria	4.7		1.8
48	Czech Republic	4.7		1.7
49	Slovak Republic	4.6		1.6
50	Latvia	4.6		1.4
51	Ireland	4.5		1.9
52	China	4.3		1.5

RANK	COUNTRY	SCORE	1 MEAN: 4.3 7	SD
52	Croatia	4.3		2.0
54	Malawi	4.3		1.6
55	Spain	4.3		1.7
56	Vietnam	4.2		1.9
57	Ghana	4.1		2.0
58	Sri Lanka	4.0		1.5
59	Romania	4.0		1.8
60	Serbia	4.0		1.7
61	Lithuania	3.9		1.7
62	Poland	3.9		1.4
63	Bolivia	3.8		1.7
64	Ukraine	3.8		1.7
65	Nicaragua	3.7		2.0
66	Zambia	3.7		1.9
67	Indonesia	3.7		1.4
68	Tanzania	3.6		1.7
69	Panama	3.6		1.5
70	Costa Rica	3.5		1.6
71	Russian Federation	3.5		1.8
72	Madagascar	3.4		1.6
73	Pakistan	3.3		1.6
74	Zimbabwe	3.2		1.7
75	Philippines	3.2		1.4
76	Senegal	3.2		1.7
77	Uganda	3.2		1.8
78	Namibia	3.1		1.7
79	Peru	3.1		1.7
80	Colombia	2.9		1.6
81	Nigeria	2.9		1.8
82	Macedonia, FYR	2.9		1.9
83	Chad	2.9		2.0
84	Trinidad and Tobago	2.8		1.5
85	Bangladesh	2.8		1.5
86	Bulgaria	2.8		1.5
87	Ecuador	2.8		1.4
88	Angola	2.7		1.8
89	Mexico	2.7		1.5
90	Cameroon	2.6		1.6
91	Brazil	2.5		1.6
92	El Salvador	2.5		1.5
93	Argentina	2.5		1.2
94	Mozambique	2.5		1.4
95	Paraguay	2.5		1.2
96	South Africa	2.4		1.2
97	Kenya	2.2		1.3
98	Haiti	2.0		1.4
99	Honduras	2.0		1.2
100	Jamaica	1.9		1.2
101	Venezuela	1.9		0.9
102	Guatemala	1.7		0.7

6.15   Government effectiveness in reducing poverty

In your country, the government's efforts to reduce poverty are (1 = ineffective, 7 = effective)

RANK	COUNTRY	SCORE		SD
1	Denmark	6.2		1.1
2	Singapore	6.1		0.8
3	Tunisia	6.1		0.9
4	Malta	6.0		0.9
5	Malaysia	6.0		1.0
6	Sweden	5.9		0.9
7	Luxembourg	5.7		1.1
8	Vietnam	5.6		1.2
9	Netherlands	5.6		1.1
10	Switzerland	5.5		1.1
11	Australia	5.5		1.1
12	Iceland	5.4		1.2
13	Finland	5.2		1.3
14	Norway	5.2		1.2
15	Belgium	5.0		1.3
16	Gambia	5.0		1.8
17	Spain	4.9		1.2
18	Canada	4.9		1.5
19	Thailand	4.9		1.3
20	China	4.9		1.3
21	Austria	4.8		1.6
22	New Zealand	4.8		1.3
23	Germany	4.7		1.7
24	United Kingdom	4.7		1.3
25	Botswana	4.6		1.5
26	Japan	4.6		1.4
27	Hong Kong SAR	4.6		1.6
28	Tanzania	4.6		1.6
29	United States	4.5		1.3
30	Italy	4.5		1.4
31	Morocco	4.5		2.0
32	Portugal	4.5		1.0
33	Mauritius	4.5		0.9
34	France	4.5		1.5
35	Ireland	4.5		1.4
36	Jordan	4.4		1.3
37	Taiwan	4.4		1.4
38	Korea	4.3		1.3
39	Uganda	4.2		1.8
40	Ghana	4.1		1.8
41	Greece	4.1		1.3
42	South Africa	4.1		1.3
43	Latvia	4.0		1.6
44	Slovenia	4.0		1.5
45	Chile	4.0		1.5
46	Brazil	3.8		1.4
47	India	3.8		1.4
48	Egypt	3.8		1.8
49	Namibia	3.7		1.3
50	Malawi	3.7		1.6
51	Indonesia	3.7		1.4
52	Czech Republic	3.7		1.6
53	El Salvador	3.6		1.4
54	Sri Lanka	3.6		1.4
55	Bangladesh	3.6		1.7
56	Estonia	3.5		1.4
57	Costa Rica	3.5		1.2
58	Senegal	3.4		1.5
59	Colombia	3.4		1.5
60	Mozambique	3.4		1.4
61	Hungary	3.3		1.4
62	Cameroon	3.3		1.6
63	Serbia	3.3		1.6
64	Madagascar	3.3		1.3
65	Dominican Republic	3.2		1.6
66	Slovak Republic	3.2		1.6
67	Trinidad and Tobago	3.1		1.5
68	Algeria	3.1		1.4
69	Kenya	3.1		1.4
70	Uruguay	3.0		1.3
71	Pakistan	3.0		1.3
72	Lithuania	3.0		1.3
73	Mexico	3.0		1.3
74	Mali	2.9		1.7
75	Zambia	2.9		1.6
76	Israel	2.9		1.1
77	Panama	2.8		1.4
78	Ethiopia	2.8		1.7
79	Turkey	2.8		1.2
80	Croatia	2.8		1.4
81	Poland	2.8		1.3
82	Macedonia, FYR	2.7		1.9
83	Jamaica	2.7		1.3
84	Honduras	2.7		1.3
85	Peru	2.6		1.2
86	Angola	2.6		1.3
87	Philippines	2.5		1.2
87	Romania	2.5		1.4
89	Russian Federation	2.4		1.3
90	Argentina	2.4		1.3
91	Nigeria	2.4		1.5
92	Nicaragua	2.4		1.4
93	Bulgaria	2.3		1.3
94	Bolivia	2.3		1.0
95	Ukraine	2.3		1.2
96	Ecuador	2.1		1.1
97	Chad	2.1		1.7
98	Zimbabwe	1.9		1.2
99	Guatemala	1.7		0.9
100	Paraguay	1.6		0.7
101	Haiti	1.5		0.7
102	Venezuela	1.2		0.5

MEAN: 3.8

In your country, the government's efforts to address income inequality are (1 = ineffective, 7 = effective)

RANK	COUNTRY	SCORE	1　MEAN: 3.4　7	SD
1	Denmark	6.3		1.1
2	Finland	5.5		1.4
3	Tunisia	5.4		1.0
4	Iceland	5.4		1.1
5	Netherlands	5.3		1.3
6	Malta	5.3		1.1
7	Norway	5.3		1.2
8	Sweden	5.3		1.5
9	Malaysia	5.2		1.0
10	Singapore	5.2		1.1
11	Belgium	5.1		1.4
12	Switzerland	4.9		1.2
13	Luxembourg	4.8		1.3
14	Canada	4.8		1.4
15	China	4.8		1.2
16	Spain	4.7		1.2
17	Australia	4.6		1.5
18	New Zealand	4.5		1.3
19	Germany	4.5		1.6
20	United Kingdom	4.4		1.4
21	Japan	4.4		1.7
22	Vietnam	4.3		1.6
23	Gambia	4.2		1.9
24	Thailand	4.2		1.5
25	Italy	4.1		1.4
26	South Africa	4.1		1.1
27	Mauritius	4.1		1.1
28	France	4.1		1.6
29	Latvia	4.0		1.8
30	Korea	4.0		1.2
31	Portugal	4.0		1.1
32	United States	4.0		1.4
33	Austria	3.9		1.6
34	Ireland	3.9		1.5
35	Jordan	3.9		1.3
36	Morocco	3.9		1.9
37	Namibia	3.9		1.2
38	Botswana	3.9		1.4
39	Taiwan	3.8		1.4
40	Tanzania	3.8		1.7
41	Greece	3.7		1.2
42	Hong Kong SAR	3.7		1.6
43	Slovenia	3.6		1.3
44	Egypt	3.6		2.0
45	Indonesia	3.5		1.3
46	Costa Rica	3.4		1.2
47	Chile	3.4		1.3
48	Ghana	3.4		1.6
49	El Salvador	3.3		1.4
50	India	3.3		1.4
51	Mali	3.3		1.6
52	Czech Republic	3.3		1.4

RANK	COUNTRY	SCORE	1　MEAN: 3.4　7	SD
53	Trinidad and Tobago	3.2		1.5
54	Uganda	3.2		1.9
55	Colombia	3.2		1.4
56	Hungary	3.2		1.3
57	Estonia	3.2		1.4
58	Slovak Republic	3.2		1.6
59	Uruguay	3.1		1.3
60	Poland	3.1		1.5
61	Israel	3.0		1.3
62	Serbia	3.0		1.4
63	Sri Lanka	3.0		1.2
64	Senegal	3.0		1.4
65	Brazil	3.0		1.4
66	Algeria	2.9		1.3
67	Croatia	2.9		1.3
68	Malawi	2.8		1.4
69	Dominican Republic	2.8		1.3
70	Lithuania	2.8		1.3
71	Cameroon	2.8		1.7
72	Macedonia, FYR	2.8		1.7
73	Madagascar	2.7		1.2
74	Kenya	2.7		1.4
75	Mexico	2.7		1.2
76	Mozambique	2.6		1.3
77	Bangladesh	2.6		1.5
78	Jamaica	2.6		1.2
79	Zambia	2.5		1.4
80	Turkey	2.5		1.2
81	Pakistan	2.5		1.1
81	Panama	2.5		1.3
83	Honduras	2.5		1.2
84	Peru	2.4		1.1
85	Ethiopia	2.4		1.3
86	Romania	2.3		1.2
87	Philippines	2.3		1.1
88	Bulgaria	2.2		1.2
89	Nigeria	2.2		1.3
90	Russian Federation	2.2		1.1
91	Nicaragua	2.1		1.1
92	Bolivia	2.1		0.9
93	Angola	2.0		1.1
94	Ecuador	2.0		1.0
95	Ukraine	2.0		1.0
96	Argentina	2.0		1.0
97	Chad	2.0		1.4
98	Guatemala	1.8		0.9
99	Zimbabwe	1.7		1.0
100	Haiti	1.5		0.7
101	Paraguay	1.4		0.7
102	Venezuela	1.1		0.3

485

6.17   Organized crime

Organized crime (eg, mafia-oriented racketeering, extortion) in your country (1 = imposes significant costs on businesses, 7 = does not impose significant costs on businesses)

RANK	COUNTRY	SCORE	1 MEAN: 4.7 7	SD
1	Iceland	6.9		0.3
2	Denmark	6.7		0.5
3	Finland	6.7		0.6
4	Singapore	6.6		0.8
5	Sweden	6.6		0.8
6	Jordan	6.6		0.6
7	Australia	6.6		0.5
8	Malta	6.4		1.1
9	Switzerland	6.4		0.8
10	New Zealand	6.4		1.1
11	Israel	6.4		0.8
12	Portugal	6.3		1.1
13	Hong Kong SAR	6.2		1.0
14	Luxembourg	6.2		1.0
15	Austria	6.1		1.2
16	Malaysia	6.1		1.1
17	Uruguay	6.1		1.4
18	Gambia	6.1		1.6
19	Germany	6.0		1.1
20	Norway	5.9		1.3
21	Tunisia	5.8		1.3
22	Greece	5.8		1.1
23	United Kingdom	5.8		1.2
24	Botswana	5.8		1.3
25	Chile	5.7		1.3
26	France	5.7		1.4
27	Mauritius	5.7		1.1
28	Mali	5.6		1.8
29	United States	5.5		1.5
30	Netherlands	5.5		1.3
31	Thailand	5.5		1.3
32	Malawi	5.5		1.5
33	Belgium	5.5		1.5
34	Korea	5.4		1.5
35	Canada	5.4		1.4
36	Taiwan	5.4		1.6
37	Slovenia	5.3		1.4
38	Ireland	5.3		1.6
39	Ethiopia	5.3		2.0
40	Dominican Republic	5.3		1.2
41	Estonia	5.2		1.3
42	Turkey	5.2		1.4
43	Spain	5.1		1.6
44	India	5.1		1.3
45	Egypt	5.1		1.9
46	Hungary	5.1		1.4
47	Morocco	5.1		2.1
48	Algeria	4.9		1.6
49	Japan	4.8		1.7
50	Ghana	4.7		1.8
51	Latvia	4.7		1.3
52	Zambia	4.7		2.0

RANK	COUNTRY	SCORE	1 MEAN: 4.7 7	SD
53	Tanzania	4.6		1.6
54	Bolivia	4.6		1.7
55	Costa Rica	4.5		1.6
56	Panama	4.4		1.7
57	Nicaragua	4.4		2.2
58	Namibia	4.4		1.6
59	Sri Lanka	4.3		1.6
60	China	4.3		1.6
61	Vietnam	4.3		2.0
62	Czech Republic	4.2		1.6
63	Angola	4.2		2.1
64	Zimbabwe	4.1		1.6
65	Lithuania	4.1		1.6
66	Ecuador	4.0		1.6
67	Romania	3.9		1.8
68	Senegal	3.9		2.0
69	Peru	3.9		1.6
70	Indonesia	3.9		1.3
71	Croatia	3.9		1.9
72	Madagascar	3.8		1.7
73	Pakistan	3.8		1.8
74	Poland	3.7		1.4
75	Nigeria	3.7		1.9
76	Italy	3.7		1.5
77	Trinidad and Tobago	3.6		1.8
78	Slovak Republic	3.6		1.5
79	Serbia	3.6		1.8
80	Philippines	3.6		1.6
81	South Africa	3.5		1.7
82	Uganda	3.4		1.9
83	Kenya	3.4		1.6
84	Argentina	3.4		1.4
85	Brazil	3.4		1.7
86	Mozambique	3.3		1.6
87	Russian Federation	3.3		1.5
88	Mexico	3.3		1.7
89	El Salvador	3.2		1.7
90	Paraguay	3.2		1.7
91	Ukraine	3.1		1.3
92	Venezuela	3.1		1.5
93	Bulgaria	2.9		1.5
94	Bangladesh	2.9		1.4
95	Cameroon	2.8		1.7
96	Honduras	2.8		1.5
97	Chad	2.7		1.9
98	Haiti	2.6		1.7
99	Macedonia, FYR	2.6		1.7
100	Jamaica	2.5		1.2
101	Colombia	2.1		1.4
102	Guatemala	2.1		0.9

6.18 Informal sector

What percentage of businesses in your country would you guess are unofficial or unregistered? (1 = less than 5% of all businesses, 2 = 6–10%, 3 = 11–20%, 9 = more than 70%)

RANK	COUNTRY	SCORE	1 MEAN: 3.8 9	SD
1	Luxembourg	1.2		0.4
2	Australia	1.3		0.5
3	Singapore	1.4		1.0
4	France	1.4		1.0
5	Finland	1.5		0.7
6	Switzerland	1.6		0.7
7	Slovak Republic	1.6		1.0
8	Iceland	1.6		0.7
9	Japan	1.7		1.3
10	Netherlands	1.8		0.9
11	Hong Kong SAR	1.8		1.2
12	New Zealand	1.8		0.9
13	Malaysia	1.9		0.9
14	Norway	1.9		1.0
15	Germany	1.9		1.0
16	Denmark	2.0		1.1
17	United States	2.0		1.4
18	Slovenia	2.0		1.2
19	Austria	2.1		1.0
20	United Kingdom	2.1		1.0
21	Tunisia	2.1		1.3
22	Estonia	2.1		1.3
23	Sweden	2.3		1.2
24	Jordan	2.3		1.6
25	Hungary	2.3		1.2
26	Ireland	2.3		1.3
27	Canada	2.4		1.6
28	Lithuania	2.4		1.4
29	Chile	2.4		1.0
30	Vietnam	2.4		1.4
31	Belgium	2.6		1.3
32	Israel	2.6		0.8
33	Taiwan	2.6		1.4
34	Czech Republic	2.6		1.2
35	Korea	2.8		1.6
36	Botswana	2.8		1.6
37	Spain	2.9		1.2
38	Serbia	2.9		1.7
39	Algeria	2.9		1.7
40	Malta	3.0		1.3
41	Portugal	3.0		0.9
42	Mauritius	3.3		1.6
43	Indonesia	3.4		1.8
44	Greece	3.5		1.5
45	Italy	3.5		0.9
46	Latvia	3.6		1.3
47	Thailand	3.7		1.6
48	Poland	3.7		1.2
49	China	3.8		1.9
50	Gambia	3.9		2.3
51	Panama	3.9		1.4
52	Trinidad and Tobago	3.9		1.8

RANK	COUNTRY	SCORE	1 MEAN: 3.8 9	SD
53	Morocco	3.9		1.8
54	Croatia	4.0		1.4
55	Egypt	4.2		2.0
56	Namibia	4.2		1.8
57	Uruguay	4.2		1.3
58	Dominican Republic	4.3		1.8
59	Mali	4.4		2.6
60	Sri Lanka	4.4		1.9
61	Tanzania	4.4		2.0
62	South Africa	4.5		1.6
63	Costa Rica	4.5		1.5
64	Colombia	4.5		1.6
65	India	4.6		2.1
66	Brazil	4.6		1.3
67	Cameroon	4.7		2.2
68	Malawi	4.7		1.9
69	Uganda	4.8		2.2
70	Senegal	4.9		2.6
71	Philippines	4.9		2.0
72	El Salvador	5.0		1.3
73	Mexico	5.0		1.3
74	Ecuador	5.1		1.3
75	Ghana	5.1		2.2
76	Ethiopia	5.1		1.9
77	Zambia	5.1		2.0
78	Bulgaria	5.2		1.6
79	Chad	5.2		2.1
80	Bangladesh	5.2		2.1
81	Kenya	5.2		1.9
82	Argentina	5.3		1.1
83	Zimbabwe	5.5		1.8
84	Romania	5.5		2.1
85	Macedonia, FYR	5.6		1.7
86	Russian Federation	5.6		1.6
87	Jamaica	5.6		1.3
88	Honduras	5.7		1.5
89	Turkey	5.7		1.4
90	Nicaragua	5.8		1.5
91	Madagascar	5.9		2.3
92	Guatemala	6.0		1.4
93	Peru	6.0		1.6
94	Nigeria	6.1		2.0
95	Venezuela	6.1		1.7
96	Pakistan	6.1		1.7
97	Ukraine	6.2		1.8
98	Mozambique	6.2		1.9
99	Angola	6.6		1.7
100	Bolivia	6.8		1.5
101	Paraguay	7.0		1.3
102	Haiti	7.3		1.5

7.01 Irregular payments in exports and imports

In your industry, how commonly would you estimate that firms make undocumented extra payments or bribes connected with export and import permits? (1 = common, 7 = never occurs)

RANK	COUNTRY	SCORE	1 MEAN: 4.7 7	SD
1	Denmark	6.8		0.4
2	Iceland	6.8		0.6
3	New Zealand	6.6		0.6
4	Singapore	6.6		0.7
5	Finland	6.5		1.0
6	Sweden	6.5		0.7
7	Australia	6.5		0.7
8	Chile	6.4		1.0
9	Hong Kong SAR	6.3		1.2
10	Switzerland	6.3		0.9
11	Israel	6.3		0.7
12	United Kingdom	6.2		0.9
13	Germany	6.2		1.1
14	Netherlands	6.1		1.1
15	Spain	6.1		1.1
16	Taiwan	6.0		1.5
17	Ireland	6.0		1.3
18	Japan	6.0		1.4
19	Luxembourg	5.9		1.2
20	Austria	5.9		1.4
21	United States	5.9		1.3
22	Uruguay	5.9		1.3
23	France	5.9		1.4
24	Norway	5.9		1.6
25	Malta	5.8		1.4
26	Canada	5.8		1.3
27	Estonia	5.7		1.3
28	Jordan	5.7		1.3
29	Belgium	5.7		1.1
30	Portugal	5.6		1.4
31	Slovenia	5.6		1.3
32	El Salvador	5.6		1.5
33	Hungary	5.5		1.5
34	Korea	5.4		1.5
35	Bulgaria	5.3		2.0
36	Malawi	5.3		1.3
37	Tunisia	5.3		1.4
38	Botswana	5.1		1.7
39	Greece	5.1		1.5
40	Lithuania	5.0		1.6
41	Czech Republic	5.0		1.7
42	Colombia	5.0		1.9
43	China	5.0		1.9
44	Peru	5.0		2.0
45	Italy	4.8		1.7
46	Gambia	4.6		1.8
47	Mexico	4.6		2.0
48	South Africa	4.6		1.4
49	Malaysia	4.6		1.6
50	Algeria	4.5		1.9
51	Latvia	4.5		1.5
52	Poland	4.5		1.8
53	Namibia	4.4		1.7
54	Egypt	4.4		2.1
55	Costa Rica	4.4		1.9
56	Brazil	4.4		1.7
57	Croatia	4.3		1.8
58	Pakistan	4.3		1.9
59	Thailand	4.3		1.8
60	Slovak Republic	4.3		1.8
61	Ethiopia	4.3		1.9
62	Tanzania	4.2		1.7
63	Nicaragua	4.2		2.1
64	Trinidad and Tobago	4.0		1.8
65	Panama	4.0		1.9
66	Guatemala	4.0		1.9
67	Zambia	4.0		1.9
68	Ecuador	4.0		2.1
69	Ghana	3.9		1.9
70	Paraguay	3.9		2.3
71	Bolivia	3.8		2.0
72	India	3.8		1.9
73	Dominican Republic	3.8		1.9
74	Senegal	3.8		1.7
75	Sri Lanka	3.7		1.6
76	Vietnam	3.7		1.9
77	Jamaica	3.7		1.6
78	Serbia	3.7		1.7
79	Mauritius	3.7		1.7
80	Argentina	3.7		1.9
81	Indonesia	3.6		1.4
82	Morocco	3.6		1.6
83	Turkey	3.6		1.9
84	Zimbabwe	3.5		1.6
85	Venezuela	3.5		2.5
86	Madagascar	3.5		1.9
87	Russian Federation	3.5		1.9
88	Kenya	3.4		1.9
89	Mali	3.4		2.0
90	Angola	3.4		1.8
91	Macedonia, FYR	3.3		2.1
92	Cameroon	3.3		1.7
93	Mozambique	3.3		1.6
94	Ukraine	3.2		1.4
95	Uganda	3.2		1.8
96	Haiti	3.1		1.8
97	Honduras	3.1		1.7
98	Romania	3.0		1.9
99	Philippines	2.9		1.7
100	Nigeria	2.8		1.7
101	Bangladesh	2.3		1.5
102	Chad	2.3		1.5

7.02 Irregular payments in public utilities

In your industry, how commonly would you estimate that firms make undocumented extra payments or bribes when getting connected to public utilities (eg, telephone or electricity)? (1 = common, 7 = never occurs)

RANK	COUNTRY	SCORE	1 MEAN: 5.0 7	SD
1	Denmark	6.9		0.4
2	Iceland	6.8		0.6
3	Singapore	6.8		0.4
4	Finland	6.7		0.6
5	Germany	6.7		0.6
6	New Zealand	6.7		0.5
7	Switzerland	6.7		0.6
8	Australia	6.6		0.6
9	Netherlands	6.5		0.7
10	Sweden	6.5		0.9
11	Israel	6.5		0.6
12	Hong Kong SAR	6.5		1.0
13	Austria	6.4		1.1
14	Luxembourg	6.4		0.9
15	Chile	6.4		1.1
16	France	6.4		1.2
17	United Kingdom	6.3		0.9
18	Malta	6.3		1.1
19	Norway	6.3		1.0
20	Canada	6.2		1.3
21	Portugal	6.2		1.1
22	Ireland	6.2		1.1
23	Spain	6.2		1.2
24	Uruguay	6.1		1.3
25	Japan	6.1		1.3
26	Belgium	6.1		0.9
27	United States	6.1		1.4
28	Taiwan	6.1		1.4
29	El Salvador	6.0		1.3
30	Hungary	6.0		1.3
31	Estonia	6.0		1.4
32	Lithuania	6.0		1.3
33	Slovenia	5.9		1.3
34	Slovak Republic	5.9		1.4
35	Jordan	5.9		1.3
36	Thailand	5.8		1.2
37	Peru	5.8		1.5
38	Korea	5.7		1.4
39	Czech Republic	5.6		1.6
40	Venezuela	5.6		1.7
41	Botswana	5.6		1.4
42	Greece	5.5		1.5
43	Malaysia	5.4		1.3
44	Bulgaria	5.4		1.9
45	Colombia	5.3		1.7
46	Italy	5.3		1.7
47	Tunisia	5.3		1.7
48	Costa Rica	5.2		1.6
49	Latvia	5.2		1.3
50	Brazil	5.1		1.6
51	Mexico	5.1		1.9
52	Bolivia	5.1		1.8

RANK	COUNTRY	SCORE	1 MEAN: 5.0 7	SD
53	Croatia	5.0		1.8
54	Argentina	4.9		1.8
55	Namibia	4.9		1.9
56	Malawi	4.9		1.7
57	Poland	4.9		1.8
58	Dominican Republic	4.8		2.0
59	Mauritius	4.8		1.6
60	China	4.8		1.9
61	South Africa	4.7		1.5
62	Trinidad and Tobago	4.7		1.6
63	Guatemala	4.7		2.0
64	Vietnam	4.6		1.8
65	Panama	4.5		1.9
66	Jamaica	4.4		1.8
67	Turkey	4.4		1.7
68	Nicaragua	4.3		2.1
69	Philippines	4.3		1.8
70	Ecuador	4.3		2.1
71	Senegal	4.3		1.7
72	Mozambique	4.3		1.7
73	Gambia	4.2		2.1
74	Ukraine	4.2		1.3
75	Morocco	4.1		2.3
76	Macedonia, FYR	4.1		2.3
77	Sri Lanka	4.0		1.6
78	Tanzania	4.0		1.8
79	Russian Federation	4.0		2.0
80	Algeria	3.9		2.0
81	Ethiopia	3.9		2.0
82	Serbia	3.9		1.7
83	India	3.9		1.9
84	Egypt	3.8		2.1
85	Paraguay	3.8		2.2
86	Romania	3.8		2.2
87	Ghana	3.7		1.8
88	Indonesia	3.7		1.2
89	Zambia	3.5		1.9
90	Angola	3.5		1.9
91	Pakistan	3.5		1.8
92	Uganda	3.3		1.8
93	Zimbabwe	3.3		1.6
94	Madagascar	3.3		1.7
95	Honduras	3.1		1.6
96	Kenya	3.0		1.7
97	Mali	3.0		1.5
98	Nigeria	2.8		1.5
99	Cameroon	2.7		1.6
100	Chad	2.7		1.9
101	Haiti	2.6		1.5
102	Bangladesh	1.8		1.1

7.03   Irregular payments in tax collection

In your industry, how commonly would you estimate that firms make undocumented extra payments or bribes connected with annual tax payments?
(1 = common, 7 = never occurs)

RANK	COUNTRY	SCORE	1 MEAN: 4.8 7	SD
1	Iceland	6.8		0.5
2	Denmark	6.8		0.6
3	Finland	6.8		0.6
4	New Zealand	6.8		0.5
5	Australia	6.8		0.4
6	Singapore	6.7		0.6
7	Switzerland	6.7		0.6
8	Sweden	6.6		0.7
9	Netherlands	6.5		0.7
10	United Kingdom	6.5		0.8
11	Hong Kong SAR	6.5		1.0
12	Luxembourg	6.3		0.9
13	Germany	6.3		1.1
14	Austria	6.3		1.1
15	Taiwan	6.2		1.4
16	Malta	6.1		1.0
17	Chile	6.1		1.2
18	Norway	6.1		1.3
19	Spain	6.1		1.1
20	Israel	6.0		1.2
21	United States	6.0		1.5
22	Hungary	6.0		1.3
23	Japan	6.0		1.4
24	Ireland	6.0		1.3
25	Canada	5.9		1.5
26	Estonia	5.9		1.1
27	Malaysia	5.9		1.1
28	France	5.8		1.4
29	Slovenia	5.8		1.4
30	Botswana	5.8		1.3
31	Bulgaria	5.8		1.7
32	El Salvador	5.7		1.5
33	Belgium	5.7		1.2
34	Uruguay	5.7		1.3
35	Jordan	5.6		1.3
36	Lithuania	5.6		1.5
37	Portugal	5.6		1.4
38	Slovak Republic	5.5		1.6
39	Mexico	5.3		1.6
40	Peru	5.3		1.7
41	South Africa	5.3		1.3
42	Mauritius	5.3		1.4
43	Malawi	5.2		1.7
44	Thailand	5.1		1.5
45	Colombia	5.0		1.7
45	Czech Republic	5.0		1.7
47	Korea	5.0		1.5
48	Tunisia	5.0		1.8
49	Poland	4.9		1.6
50	Latvia	4.8		1.4
51	Costa Rica	4.8		1.6
52	China	4.8		1.8

RANK	COUNTRY	SCORE	1 MEAN: 4.8 7	SD
53	Italy	4.7		1.7
54	Croatia	4.7		1.8
55	Namibia	4.6		1.9
56	Zimbabwe	4.5		1.6
57	Trinidad and Tobago	4.5		1.7
58	Turkey	4.4		1.7
59	Russian Federation	4.4		1.9
60	Brazil	4.4		1.6
61	Gambia	4.4		2.2
62	Jamaica	4.4		1.7
63	Serbia	4.3		1.6
64	Vietnam	4.3		1.8
65	Ecuador	4.3		2.0
66	Egypt	4.2		2.2
67	Panama	4.2		1.9
68	Nicaragua	4.1		2.1
69	Ghana	3.9		1.8
70	Romania	3.9		2.2
71	India	3.9		1.9
72	Zambia	3.9		1.9
73	Argentina	3.8		1.7
74	Macedonia, FYR	3.8		2.3
75	Greece	3.8		1.8
76	Sri Lanka	3.8		1.5
77	Pakistan	3.8		1.8
78	Mozambique	3.8		1.7
79	Angola	3.7		1.8
80	Tanzania	3.7		1.8
81	Guatemala	3.7		1.8
82	Indonesia	3.6		1.4
82	Senegal	3.6		1.6
84	Dominican Republic	3.6		2.2
85	Morocco	3.6		1.6
86	Ethiopia	3.5		2.1
87	Algeria	3.5		1.7
88	Paraguay	3.4		2.0
89	Ukraine	3.4		1.5
90	Bolivia	3.4		1.9
91	Honduras	3.4		1.5
92	Venezuela	3.3		2.2
93	Kenya	3.2		1.7
93	Uganda	3.2		1.9
95	Cameroon	3.1		1.7
96	Madagascar	3.0		1.5
97	Philippines	3.0		1.6
98	Nigeria	2.8		1.6
99	Chad	2.6		2.0
100	Mali	2.5		1.3
101	Haiti	2.2		1.1
102	Bangladesh	2.0		1.2

In your industry, how commonly would you estimate that firms make undocumented extra payments or bribes connected with public contracts (investment projects)? (1 = common, 7 = never occurs)

RANK	COUNTRY	SCORE	1 MEAN: 3.9 7	SD
1	Iceland	6.6		0.6
2	Denmark	6.5		0.8
3	New Zealand	6.5		0.7
4	Singapore	6.4		0.8
5	Finland	6.3		1.1
6	Sweden	6.0		0.9
7	Australia	6.0		1.0
8	United Kingdom	5.9		1.1
9	Switzerland	5.8		1.0
10	Hong Kong SAR	5.7		1.2
11	Germany	5.6		1.5
12	Norway	5.6		1.5
13	Luxembourg	5.6		1.3
14	Israel	5.6		1.2
15	United States	5.5		1.5
16	Austria	5.5		1.5
17	Taiwan	5.5		1.6
18	Netherlands	5.3		1.3
19	Jordan	5.0		1.5
20	Belgium	4.9		1.5
21	Portugal	4.9		1.4
22	France	4.8		1.7
23	Uruguay	4.8		1.7
24	Canada	4.8		1.7
25	El Salvador	4.8		1.5
26	Malta	4.7		1.9
27	Ireland	4.7		1.9
28	Spain	4.7		1.7
29	Slovenia	4.6		1.6
30	Tunisia	4.6		1.8
31	Korea	4.5		1.5
32	Botswana	4.5		1.7
33	Japan	4.5		2.0
34	Bulgaria	4.5		2.2
35	Egypt	4.5		1.9
36	China	4.5		2.0
37	Estonia	4.4		1.6
38	Latvia	4.3		1.8
39	Chile	4.3		1.7
40	Lithuania	4.2		2.0
41	Thailand	4.1		1.7
42	Italy	4.0		1.6
43	Mexico	4.0		1.8
44	Hungary	4.0		1.7
45	Brazil	3.9		1.7
46	Gambia	3.8		2.0
47	Vietnam	3.8		1.9
48	Peru	3.8		1.7
49	Malaysia	3.8		1.6
50	Costa Rica	3.8		1.7
51	South Africa	3.8		1.6
52	Colombia	3.7		2.0

RANK	COUNTRY	SCORE	1 MEAN: 3.9 7	SD
53	Indonesia	3.6		1.6
54	Namibia	3.6		1.7
55	Malawi	3.6		2.0
55	Tanzania	3.6		1.7
57	Pakistan	3.6		1.5
58	Croatia	3.5		1.8
59	Poland	3.5		1.8
60	Algeria	3.5		1.7
61	Ukraine	3.5		1.5
62	Ghana	3.5		1.9
63	Ethiopia	3.4		1.9
64	Russian Federation	3.4		1.9
65	Greece	3.4		1.6
66	Nicaragua	3.3		2.1
67	Zambia	3.2		1.7
68	Trinidad and Tobago	3.2		1.8
69	Mauritius	3.2		1.5
70	Panama	3.2		1.9
71	Czech Republic	3.1		1.7
72	Dominican Republic	3.1		1.8
73	Morocco	3.0		1.8
74	Sri Lanka	3.0		1.5
75	Serbia	3.0		1.6
76	Ecuador	3.0		2.0
77	Paraguay	3.0		2.1
78	Jamaica	2.9		1.6
79	Turkey	2.9		1.4
80	Slovak Republic	2.9		1.5
81	Mozambique	2.9		1.7
82	India	2.8		1.5
83	Senegal	2.8		1.6
84	Angola	2.8		1.6
85	Mali	2.7		1.5
86	Honduras	2.7		1.6
87	Macedonia, FYR	2.7		1.8
88	Cameroon	2.7		1.6
89	Zimbabwe	2.6		1.6
90	Uganda	2.6		1.8
91	Venezuela	2.6		2.2
92	Haiti	2.6		1.4
93	Argentina	2.5		1.5
94	Madagascar	2.5		1.4
95	Romania	2.5		1.7
96	Kenya	2.4		1.4
97	Bolivia	2.3		1.6
98	Guatemala	2.2		1.4
99	Chad	2.2		1.7
100	Nigeria	2.2		1.3
101	Philippines	2.1		1.4
102	Bangladesh	2.1		1.2

7.05 Irregular payments in loan applications

In your industry, how commonly would you estimate that firms make undocumented extra payments or bribes connected with loan applications?
(1 = common, 7 = never occurs)

RANK	COUNTRY	SCORE	MEAN: 4.9	SD
1	Denmark	6.8		0.5
2	Iceland	6.8		0.5
3	Finland	6.8		0.6
4	Australia	6.7		0.5
5	New Zealand	6.7		0.6
6	Sweden	6.7		0.5
7	Singapore	6.5		0.6
8	Switzerland	6.5		0.7
9	Germany	6.4		0.9
10	United Kingdom	6.4		0.8
11	Luxembourg	6.4		0.9
12	Netherlands	6.3		0.9
13	Austria	6.3		1.1
14	Israel	6.2		1.0
15	United States	6.1		1.1
16	Taiwan	6.0		1.4
17	Malta	6.0		1.3
18	Chile	6.0		1.4
18	France	6.0		1.3
18	Norway	6.0		1.1
21	Spain	6.0		1.2
22	El Salvador	6.0		1.4
23	Hong Kong SAR	5.9		1.1
24	Belgium	5.8		1.2
25	Estonia	5.8		1.2
26	Ireland	5.8		1.5
27	Portugal	5.8		1.2
28	Jordan	5.7		1.2
29	Japan	5.7		1.6
30	Slovenia	5.6		1.4
31	Canada	5.6		1.6
32	Colombia	5.5		1.5
33	Uruguay	5.5		1.4
34	Botswana	5.5		1.5
35	Lithuania	5.4		1.6
36	Mexico	5.4		1.6
37	Thailand	5.3		1.4
38	Peru	5.3		1.6
39	Greece	5.3		1.4
40	Bulgaria	5.2		2.0
41	Italy	5.2		1.6
42	Mauritius	5.2		1.4
43	Hungary	5.1		1.6
43	Slovak Republic	5.1		1.6
45	Malawi	5.1		1.7
46	Malaysia	5.1		1.4
47	Korea	5.1		1.4
48	South Africa	5.1		1.5
49	Latvia	5.0		1.3
50	Dominican Republic	5.0		1.7
51	Costa Rica	4.9		1.6
52	Tunisia	4.8		1.8
53	Pakistan	4.8		1.6
54	Brazil	4.8		1.5
55	Guatemala	4.7		1.8
56	Ecuador	4.7		1.8
57	Trinidad and Tobago	4.7		1.6
58	Nicaragua	4.7		2.0
59	Philippines	4.7		1.6
60	Panama	4.6		1.7
61	Gambia	4.6		2.1
62	Jamaica	4.6		1.6
63	Namibia	4.5		1.7
64	China	4.5		1.8
65	Poland	4.5		1.5
66	Czech Republic	4.5		1.9
67	Bolivia	4.4		1.9
68	Egypt	4.4		2.1
69	India	4.3		1.7
70	Croatia	4.3		2.0
71	Tanzania	4.3		1.7
72	Argentina	4.1		1.8
73	Zambia	4.1		1.9
74	Zimbabwe	4.1		1.8
75	Venezuela	4.1		2.4
76	Kenya	4.1		1.5
77	Russian Federation	4.1		1.8
78	Madagascar	4.0		1.8
79	Paraguay	4.0		2.2
79	Turkey	4.0		1.5
81	Vietnam	3.9		1.8
82	Ghana	3.9		1.7
83	Haiti	3.8		1.9
84	Angola	3.8		1.8
85	Sri Lanka	3.7		1.7
86	Senegal	3.7		1.6
87	Honduras	3.7		1.7
88	Ukraine	3.7		1.4
89	Indonesia	3.6		1.4
90	Mozambique	3.6		1.7
91	Algeria	3.6		1.8
92	Ethiopia	3.5		1.9
93	Serbia	3.5		1.7
94	Macedonia, FYR	3.4		2.2
95	Nigeria	3.4		1.6
96	Morocco	3.3		1.9
97	Uganda	3.2		1.7
98	Cameroon	3.1		1.7
99	Romania	3.1		2.0
100	Chad	2.9		2.0
101	Mali	2.8		1.7
102	Bangladesh	2.5		1.4

In your industry, how commonly would you estimate that firms make undocumented extra payments or bribes connected with influencing laws and policies, regulations, or decrees to favor selected business interests? (1 = common, 7 = never occurs)

RANK	COUNTRY	SCORE	1 MEAN: 4.2 7	SD
1	Denmark	6.5		0.8
2	Iceland	6.4		0.8
3	Singapore	6.4		0.8
4	Finland	6.4		0.8
5	New Zealand	6.3		0.9
6	Sweden	6.2		1.0
7	Switzerland	6.0		1.1
8	Germany	6.0		1.1
9	Luxembourg	5.9		1.2
10	Hong Kong SAR	5.9		1.0
11	United Kingdom	5.8		1.1
12	Austria	5.8		1.4
12	Australia	5.8		1.3
14	Netherlands	5.8		1.1
15	Norway	5.8		1.4
16	Malta	5.6		1.5
17	Israel	5.4		1.4
18	France	5.3		1.4
19	Tunisia	5.3		1.4
20	Taiwan	5.3		1.5
21	Botswana	5.2		1.4
22	Jordan	5.2		1.4
23	Canada	5.2		1.5
24	United States	5.1		1.5
25	Portugal	5.1		1.3
26	Spain	5.0		1.5
27	Malaysia	5.0		1.2
28	Belgium	5.0		1.5
29	Slovenia	4.9		1.5
30	Malawi	4.8		1.7
31	Estonia	4.8		1.5
32	Chile	4.8		1.5
33	Uruguay	4.7		1.5
34	Bulgaria	4.6		2.2
35	Korea	4.6		1.3
36	Gambia	4.6		1.9
37	Ireland	4.5		1.9
38	Japan	4.5		2.0
39	Hungary	4.5		1.6
40	China	4.5		1.9
41	Thailand	4.4		1.5
42	Lithuania	4.4		1.8
43	South Africa	4.3		1.6
44	Egypt	4.3		2.0
45	Latvia	4.2		1.5
46	Mexico	4.2		1.8
47	Ghana	4.2		1.7
48	Namibia	4.2		1.6
49	El Salvador	4.2		1.5
50	Morocco	4.1		1.8
51	Algeria	4.1		1.7
52	Tanzania	4.1		1.4

RANK	COUNTRY	SCORE	1 MEAN: 4.2 7	SD
53	Mauritius	4.1		1.6
54	Vietnam	4.0		1.6
55	Croatia	3.9		1.8
56	Greece	3.9		1.5
57	Czech Republic	3.8		1.5
58	Poland	3.8		1.6
59	Brazil	3.8		1.7
60	Trinidad and Tobago	3.8		1.6
61	Italy	3.8		1.8
62	Zambia	3.8		1.6
63	Indonesia	3.7		1.4
64	Ethiopia	3.7		1.8
65	Colombia	3.7		1.8
66	Senegal	3.7		1.5
67	Jamaica	3.7		1.6
68	Costa Rica	3.7		1.4
69	Pakistan	3.6		1.6
70	Cameroon	3.6		1.5
71	Sri Lanka	3.5		1.4
72	Peru	3.4		1.6
73	Turkey	3.4		1.3
74	Slovak Republic	3.4		1.3
75	Macedonia, FYR	3.4		1.8
76	Ukraine	3.3		1.4
77	Russian Federation	3.3		1.8
78	India	3.3		1.5
79	Mozambique	3.3		1.5
80	Serbia	3.3		1.5
81	Zimbabwe	3.2		1.8
82	Uganda	3.2		1.9
83	Venezuela	3.2		2.2
84	Kenya	3.1		1.3
85	Nicaragua	3.1		2.0
86	Madagascar	3.0		1.6
87	Mali	3.0		1.8
88	Panama	3.0		1.7
89	Nigeria	3.0		1.7
90	Dominican Republic	3.0		1.5
91	Bangladesh	2.7		1.4
92	Ecuador	2.7		1.5
93	Paraguay	2.7		1.9
94	Bolivia	2.6		1.5
95	Philippines	2.6		1.2
96	Romania	2.5		1.4
97	Angola	2.5		1.4
98	Honduras	2.5		1.4
99	Guatemala	2.4		1.2
100	Argentina	2.3		1.4
101	Haiti	2.3		1.4
102	Chad	2.1		1.5

7.07   Irregular payments in judicial decisions

In your industry, how commonly would you estimate that firms make undocumented extra payments or bribes connected with getting favorable judicial decisions? (1 = common, 7 = never occurs)

RANK	COUNTRY	SCORE	MEAN: 4.5	SD
1	Iceland	6.8		0.5
2	Denmark	6.8		0.7
3	Finland	6.7		0.7
4	New Zealand	6.7		0.7
5	Germany	6.6		0.8
6	Australia	6.6		0.5
7	Israel	6.6		0.8
8	Singapore	6.5		0.8
9	Netherlands	6.5		0.9
10	Sweden	6.5		0.7
11	Austria	6.5		1.1
12	United Kingdom	6.4		0.9
13	Switzerland	6.4		0.9
14	Hong Kong SAR	6.3		1.1
15	Norway	6.1		1.1
16	Luxembourg	6.1		1.0
17	Botswana	5.9		1.1
18	Portugal	5.9		1.1
19	Canada	5.8		1.5
20	Japan	5.8		1.4
21	Uruguay	5.8		1.4
22	Belgium	5.7		1.0
23	United States	5.7		1.5
23	France	5.7		1.3
25	Ireland	5.6		1.7
25	Jordan	5.6		1.2
27	Malta	5.6		1.6
28	Spain	5.5		1.4
29	South Africa	5.5		1.3
30	Slovenia	5.5		1.4
31	Estonia	5.4		1.3
32	Taiwan	5.4		1.5
33	Tunisia	5.4		1.3
34	Hungary	5.3		1.5
35	Malaysia	5.3		1.2
36	Malawi	5.2		1.8
37	Korea	5.1		1.3
38	Chile	5.1		1.5
39	Mauritius	5.1		1.4
40	Gambia	5.1		1.8
41	Thailand	5.0		1.4
42	Trinidad and Tobago	5.0		1.5
43	Egypt	4.8		2.1
44	Greece	4.8		1.5
45	Namibia	4.8		1.5
46	Costa Rica	4.8		1.5
47	Bulgaria	4.7		2.2
48	Vietnam	4.6		1.6
49	Czech Republic	4.5		1.5
50	China	4.5		1.8
51	Italy	4.5		1.6
52	India	4.5		1.6

RANK	COUNTRY	SCORE	MEAN: 4.5	SD
53	Lithuania	4.4		1.8
54	Jamaica	4.4		1.7
55	Ghana	4.2		1.7
56	Latvia	4.2		1.6
57	Zambia	4.2		1.7
58	Poland	4.2		1.5
59	Colombia	4.1		1.9
60	Turkey	4.1		1.5
61	Brazil	4.1		1.6
62	Mexico	4.1		2.0
63	Croatia	4.0		1.8
64	Sri Lanka	3.9		1.6
65	Tanzania	3.9		1.6
66	Pakistan	3.9		1.5
67	Morocco	3.8		2.1
68	Zimbabwe	3.8		1.6
69	El Salvador	3.7		1.5
70	Indonesia	3.6		1.2
71	Algeria	3.6		1.7
72	Ethiopia	3.6		1.6
73	Senegal	3.5		1.4
74	Dominican Republic	3.5		1.8
75	Slovak Republic	3.4		1.5
76	Nigeria	3.4		1.5
77	Russian Federation	3.4		1.7
78	Uganda	3.3		1.8
79	Macedonia, FYR	3.3		1.8
80	Panama	3.3		1.7
81	Serbia	3.3		1.6
82	Bangladesh	3.2		1.5
83	Ukraine	3.0		1.3
84	Cameroon	3.0		1.3
85	Angola	2.9		1.4
86	Argentina	2.9		1.6
87	Romania	2.8		1.5
88	Mozambique	2.8		1.4
89	Kenya	2.7		1.5
90	Venezuela	2.7		2.1
91	Peru	2.7		1.6
92	Madagascar	2.5		1.4
93	Nicaragua	2.5		1.9
94	Philippines	2.5		1.2
95	Ecuador	2.5		1.6
96	Paraguay	2.5		1.8
97	Guatemala	2.3		1.2
98	Mali	2.3		1.3
99	Honduras	2.2		1.5
100	Bolivia	2.1		1.5
101	Haiti	2.0		1.1
102	Chad	2.0		1.4

In your country, diversion of public funds to companies, individuals, or groups due to corruption (1 = is common, 7 = never occurs)

RANK	COUNTRY	SCORE	1 MEAN: 3.7 7	SD
1	Denmark	6.7		0.5
2	Finland	6.5		0.8
3	Singapore	6.4		0.7
4	Australia	6.3		0.5
5	Sweden	6.3		0.5
6	New Zealand	6.2		0.7
7	Iceland	6.2		0.7
8	Switzerland	6.0		0.9
9	Hong Kong SAR	5.9		1.1
10	United Kingdom	5.9		0.8
11	Norway	5.8		0.9
12	Netherlands	5.8		0.9
13	Luxembourg	5.7		1.0
14	Austria	5.7		1.1
15	Germany	5.4		1.3
16	United States	5.3		1.3
17	Israel	5.2		1.0
18	Jordan	5.2		1.3
19	Canada	5.2		1.4
20	Spain	5.1		1.2
21	Tunisia	5.0		1.3
22	Belgium	5.0		1.2
23	Malta	4.9		1.5
24	Botswana	4.8		1.4
25	Portugal	4.8		1.2
26	Ireland	4.8		1.5
27	Uruguay	4.8		1.4
28	Taiwan	4.8		1.2
29	Gambia	4.7		1.8
30	Slovenia	4.6		1.4
31	France	4.6		1.6
32	Korea	4.5		1.4
33	El Salvador	4.4		1.6
34	Estonia	4.3		1.3
35	Malaysia	4.2		1.3
36	Japan	4.0		1.6
37	Chile	3.9		1.4
38	Latvia	3.9		1.5
39	Egypt	3.9		1.9
40	Costa Rica	3.8		1.4
41	Hungary	3.7		1.3
42	Greece	3.7		1.4
43	Thailand	3.7		1.3
44	Croatia	3.6		1.6
45	Indonesia	3.6		1.7
46	Italy	3.6		1.2
47	South Africa	3.6		1.4
48	Namibia	3.6		1.4
49	Tanzania	3.5		1.4
50	Ghana	3.4		1.5
51	China	3.4		1.6
52	Ethiopia	3.4		1.6

RANK	COUNTRY	SCORE	1 MEAN: 3.7 7	SD
53	Algeria	3.3		1.5
54	Morocco	3.3		1.7
55	Vietnam	3.3		1.4
56	Mexico	3.3		1.4
57	Sri Lanka	3.2		1.3
58	Poland	3.2		1.4
59	Dominican Republic	3.2		1.7
59	Mauritius	3.2		1.5
61	Lithuania	3.2		1.3
62	Malawi	3.2		1.6
63	Brazil	3.1		1.3
64	Pakistan	3.1		1.4
65	Slovak Republic	3.0		1.3
66	Serbia	3.0		1.2
67	India	3.0		1.4
68	Peru	2.9		1.3
69	Czech Republic	2.9		1.4
70	Turkey	2.9		1.2
71	Macedonia, FYR	2.9		1.6
72	Trinidad and Tobago	2.9		1.2
73	Ukraine	2.7		0.9
74	Panama	2.7		1.5
75	Senegal	2.7		1.2
76	Russian Federation	2.6		1.3
77	Jamaica	2.6		1.2
78	Bangladesh	2.5		1.4
79	Bulgaria	2.4		1.2
80	Colombia	2.4		1.3
81	Zambia	2.3		1.3
82	Nicaragua	2.3		1.7
83	Angola	2.3		1.3
84	Mozambique	2.2		1.2
85	Honduras	2.2		1.1
86	Romania	2.2		1.3
87	Madagascar	2.1		1.0
88	Philippines	2.1		1.1
89	Ecuador	2.1		1.1
90	Uganda	2.1		1.3
91	Argentina	2.1		1.1
92	Mali	2.1		1.0
93	Kenya	2.0		1.0
94	Zimbabwe	2.0		1.0
95	Cameroon	1.9		1.0
96	Chad	1.9		1.2
97	Nigeria	1.8		1.1
98	Haiti	1.7		1.0
99	Bolivia	1.7		0.8
100	Paraguay	1.6		0.8
101	Guatemala	1.5		0.7
102	Venezuela	1.2		0.6

7.09 Business costs of corruption

Do other firms' illegal payments to influence government policies, laws, or regulations impose costs or otherwise negatively affect your firm?
(1 = impose large costs, 7 = impose no costs/not relevant)

RANK	COUNTRY	SCORE	1 MEAN: 3.9 7	SD
1	Denmark	6.7		0.8
2	Iceland	6.6		0.8
3	Finland	6.6		0.9
4	New Zealand	6.6		0.9
5	Sweden	6.4		1.0
6	Singapore	6.1		1.4
7	Netherlands	5.8		1.5
8	Australia	5.8		1.4
9	Switzerland	5.6		1.5
10	United Kingdom	5.6		1.6
11	Norway	5.5		1.7
12	Hong Kong SAR	5.5		1.5
13	Belgium	5.4		1.2
14	Austria	5.4		1.5
15	Germany	5.3		1.5
16	Luxembourg	5.2		1.7
17	Ireland	5.1		1.7
18	United States	5.1		1.8
19	Canada	5.1		1.6
20	Estonia	5.0		1.5
21	France	4.9		1.7
22	Israel	4.9		1.8
23	Jordan	4.8		1.5
24	Uruguay	4.8		1.7
25	Portugal	4.8		1.8
26	South Africa	4.7		1.8
27	Malta	4.7		1.8
28	Malaysia	4.6		1.4
29	Botswana	4.5		1.8
30	Tunisia	4.5		2.0
31	Taiwan	4.4		1.5
32	Japan	4.4		2.0
33	Spain	4.4		2.0
34	Korea	4.3		1.4
35	Slovenia	4.2		1.6
36	Chile	4.1		1.7
37	Latvia	4.1		1.5
38	Thailand	4.0		1.4
39	Brazil	4.0		1.6
40	Egypt	4.0		1.8
41	Italy	3.9		1.5
42	Hungary	3.9		1.6
43	China	3.9		1.6
44	Gambia	3.8		1.4
45	Mexico	3.8		1.8
46	Indonesia	3.8		1.5
47	Pakistan	3.7		1.4
48	Malawi	3.7		1.9
49	Algeria	3.7		1.5
50	India	3.7		1.5
51	Costa Rica	3.7		1.8
52	Poland	3.6		1.3

RANK	COUNTRY	SCORE	1 MEAN: 3.9 7	SD
53	Czech Republic	3.6		1.5
54	Ghana	3.6		1.7
55	Lithuania	3.5		1.5
56	Russian Federation	3.5		1.7
57	Greece	3.5		1.4
58	Namibia	3.5		1.3
59	Turkey	3.5		1.5
60	El Salvador	3.4		1.5
61	Zimbabwe	3.4		1.4
62	Slovak Republic	3.4		1.4
63	Vietnam	3.3		1.6
64	Trinidad and Tobago	3.3		1.3
65	Dominican Republic	3.2		1.4
66	Morocco	3.2		1.5
67	Sri Lanka	3.2		1.2
68	Mauritius	3.2		1.2
69	Jamaica	3.2		1.4
70	Zambia	3.1		1.9
71	Ethiopia	3.1		1.7
72	Cameroon	3.1		1.6
73	Tanzania	3.0		1.2
74	Serbia	3.0		1.4
75	Colombia	3.0		1.5
75	Senegal	3.0		1.6
77	Uganda	3.0		1.7
78	Argentina	3.0		1.3
79	Croatia	3.0		1.5
80	Peru	3.0		1.3
81	Mozambique	2.9		1.5
82	Philippines	2.9		1.3
83	Ukraine	2.9		1.1
84	Angola	2.8		1.5
85	Ecuador	2.8		1.4
85	Nigeria	2.8		1.4
87	Mali	2.8		1.6
88	Bangladesh	2.7		1.2
89	Panama	2.7		1.3
90	Haiti	2.6		1.4
91	Bolivia	2.6		1.3
92	Bulgaria	2.6		1.2
93	Nicaragua	2.6		1.4
94	Honduras	2.6		1.4
95	Romania	2.5		1.3
96	Macedonia, FYR	2.5		1.6
97	Kenya	2.5		1.4
98	Madagascar	2.4		0.9
99	Venezuela	2.4		1.1
100	Guatemala	2.4		1.3
101	Paraguay	2.2		1.3
102	Chad	2.1		1.4

Public trust in the financial honesty of politicians is (1 = very low, 7 = very high)

RANK	COUNTRY	SCORE	1 MEAN: 2.7 7	SD
1	Singapore	6.5		0.8
2	Denmark	5.8		1.5
3	Finland	5.8		1.5
4	Luxembourg	5.5		1.0
5	Iceland	5.3		1.4
6	Switzerland	5.2		1.3
7	Netherlands	5.1		1.4
8	Australia	5.0		1.4
9	Botswana	4.7		1.5
10	Norway	4.7		1.6
11	Tunisia	4.6		1.5
12	New Zealand	4.6		1.7
13	Hong Kong SAR	4.4		1.7
14	Sweden	4.3		1.8
15	United States	4.3		1.5
16	United Kingdom	4.2		1.5
17	Austria	4.0		1.7
18	Jordan	3.9		1.5
19	Malaysia	3.8		1.2
20	China	3.8		1.4
21	Canada	3.7		1.6
22	Malta	3.7		1.5
23	Spain	3.7		1.2
24	Taiwan	3.6		1.3
25	Vietnam	3.5		1.7
26	Germany	3.5		1.7
27	Portugal	3.3		1.3
28	Gambia	3.3		1.8
29	Uruguay	3.3		1.4
30	Belgium	3.3		1.5
31	Latvia	3.3		1.8
32	Tanzania	3.2		1.5
33	Estonia	3.2		1.3
34	Namibia	3.1		1.3
35	South Africa	3.1		1.4
36	Morocco	3.1		1.7
37	France	3.1		1.4
38	Indonesia	3.1		1.4
39	Israel	3.0		1.4
40	Thailand	2.9		1.4
41	Egypt	2.9		1.5
42	Korea	2.9		1.3
43	Serbia	2.8		1.5
44	Greece	2.8		1.4
45	Slovenia	2.8		1.2
46	Ghana	2.8		1.5
47	Hungary	2.7		1.4
48	Chile	2.7		1.3
49	Italy	2.4		1.1
50	Costa Rica	2.3		1.3
51	Japan	2.3		1.2
52	El Salvador	2.3		1.2

RANK	COUNTRY	SCORE	1 MEAN: 2.7 7	SD
53	Algeria	2.3		1.2
54	Cameroon	2.3		1.4
55	Mexico	2.3		1.2
56	Sri Lanka	2.2		1.2
57	Ireland	2.2		1.2
58	Ethiopia	2.2		1.5
59	Poland	2.2		1.3
60	Lithuania	2.2		1.0
61	Uganda	2.2		1.4
62	Brazil	2.1		1.0
63	Croatia	2.0		1.2
64	Senegal	2.0		1.3
65	Czech Republic	2.0		1.0
66	Mali	2.0		1.5
67	Kenya	2.0		1.2
68	Malawi	2.0		1.2
69	Trinidad and Tobago	2.0		1.0
70	Russian Federation	1.9		1.2
71	Slovak Republic	1.8		1.0
72	Pakistan	1.8		0.9
72	Turkey	1.8		0.9
74	Dominican Republic	1.8		1.6
75	Macedonia, FYR	1.8		1.1
75	Mauritius	1.8		1.0
77	Colombia	1.8		1.0
78	Mozambique	1.8		1.0
79	Bulgaria	1.8		1.0
80	Madagascar	1.7		0.9
81	Ukraine	1.7		0.8
82	India	1.7		0.9
83	Zambia	1.7		1.0
84	Jamaica	1.7		0.9
85	Romania	1.7		0.9
86	Peru	1.6		0.9
87	Chad	1.5		1.0
88	Angola	1.5		0.9
89	Nigeria	1.5		0.9
90	Bangladesh	1.5		0.8
91	Panama	1.5		0.7
92	Honduras	1.4		0.7
93	Nicaragua	1.4		0.8
94	Philippines	1.4		0.7
95	Ecuador	1.3		0.6
96	Venezuela	1.2		0.5
97	Zimbabwe	1.2		0.5
98	Argentina	1.1		0.4
99	Bolivia	1.1		0.3
100	Guatemala	1.1		0.3
101	Paraguay	1.0		0.2
102	Haiti	1.0		0.2

7.11 Prevalence of illegal political donations

How common are illegal donations to political parties in your country? (1 = common, 7 = never occurs)

RANK	COUNTRY	SCORE	1 MEAN: 3.6 7	SD
1	Singapore	6.4		0.9
2	Denmark	6.3		1.2
3	Finland	6.1		1.1
4	Netherlands	6.0		0.8
5	Australia	5.9		0.9
6	Sweden	5.9		1.1
7	Hong Kong SAR	5.9		1.3
8	New Zealand	5.8		1.3
9	Norway	5.7		0.9
10	Vietnam	5.7		1.5
11	Iceland	5.7		1.5
12	United Kingdom	5.5		1.3
13	Jordan	5.5		1.4
14	Switzerland	5.4		1.3
15	Tunisia	5.3		1.5
16	Luxembourg	5.2		1.2
17	Austria	5.0		1.4
18	China	5.0		1.7
19	United States	4.8		1.5
20	Belgium	4.6		1.5
21	Canada	4.6		1.5
22	Botswana	4.5		1.6
23	Gambia	4.4		1.9
24	France	4.4		1.7
25	Algeria	4.3		1.9
26	Uruguay	4.3		1.9
27	Egypt	4.2		1.9
28	Taiwan	4.1		1.3
29	El Salvador	4.0		1.3
30	Namibia	4.0		1.6
31	Pakistan	3.9		1.6
32	Malta	3.9		1.8
33	Israel	3.9		1.5
34	Japan	3.8		1.7
35	Morocco	3.8		1.8
36	Malawi	3.8		1.8
37	Slovenia	3.8		1.5
38	Germany	3.7		1.3
39	South Africa	3.6		1.5
40	Ethiopia	3.6		1.9
41	Latvia	3.6		1.8
42	Tanzania	3.6		1.7
43	Korea	3.6		1.3
44	Malaysia	3.6		1.3
45	Indonesia	3.5		1.4
46	Spain	3.5		1.4
47	Hungary	3.4		1.3
48	Uganda	3.4		1.8
49	Estonia	3.4		1.4
50	Mali	3.3		1.8
51	Lithuania	3.3		1.3
52	Greece	3.2		1.6

RANK	COUNTRY	SCORE	1 MEAN: 3.6 7	SD
53	Portugal	3.2		1.4
54	Thailand	3.2		1.4
55	Mozambique	3.1		1.6
56	Poland	3.1		1.4
57	Ireland	3.1		1.5
58	Senegal	3.1		1.5
59	Italy	3.1		1.3
60	Serbia	3.1		1.5
61	Croatia	3.0		1.4
62	Ghana	3.0		1.6
63	Dominican Republic	3.0		1.8
64	Chad	3.0		1.8
65	Czech Republic	3.0		1.3
66	Trinidad and Tobago	2.9		1.6
67	Panama	2.9		1.5
68	Haiti	2.9		1.8
69	Costa Rica	2.8		1.2
70	Brazil	2.8		1.3
71	Chile	2.7		1.4
72	Colombia	2.7		1.3
73	Mexico	2.7		1.4
74	Peru	2.7		1.5
75	Bulgaria	2.7		1.4
76	Sri Lanka	2.6		1.4
77	Angola	2.6		1.8
78	Zambia	2.6		1.6
79	Macedonia, FYR	2.6		1.7
80	Kenya	2.6		1.4
81	Slovak Republic	2.5		1.2
82	Turkey	2.5		1.3
83	Cameroon	2.5		1.4
83	Zimbabwe	2.5		1.2
85	Jamaica	2.4		1.5
86	Russian Federation	2.4		1.3
87	Honduras	2.4		1.4
88	Madagascar	2.3		1.2
89	Ecuador	2.3		1.3
90	Nicaragua	2.3		1.4
91	Mauritius	2.3		1.0
92	Romania	2.2		1.3
93	Ukraine	2.2		1.2
94	India	2.2		1.1
95	Nigeria	2.1		1.3
96	Argentina	2.1		1.1
97	Guatemala	2.0		1.3
98	Bolivia	1.9		1.1
99	Venezuela	1.9		1.3
100	Philippines	1.9		1.0
101	Bangladesh	1.8		1.0
102	Paraguay	1.5		0.7

7.12 Policy consequences of legal political donations

To what extent do legal contributions to political parties have a direct influence on specific public policy outcomes? (1 = very close link between donations and policy, 7 = little direct influence on policy)

RANK	COUNTRY	SCORE	SD
1	Singapore	6.0	1.1
2	Netherlands	6.0	1.1
3	Finland	5.8	1.4
4	Denmark	5.7	1.4
5	Sweden	5.5	1.7
6	Hong Kong SAR	5.4	1.4
7	New Zealand	5.3	1.3
8	Iceland	5.2	1.5
9	Tunisia	5.2	1.5
10	Luxembourg	5.2	1.5
11	Jordan	5.1	1.5
12	Switzerland	4.7	1.7
13	United Kingdom	4.7	1.5
14	Haiti	4.7	1.9
15	Germany	4.6	1.6
16	Botswana	4.6	1.5
17	China	4.6	1.6
18	Vietnam	4.6	1.2
19	Australia	4.6	1.5
20	Belgium	4.6	1.5
21	France	4.6	1.7
22	Pakistan	4.6	1.4
23	Gambia	4.5	1.7
24	Norway	4.4	1.7
25	Israel	4.4	1.5
26	Tanzania	4.4	1.4
27	Malaysia	4.4	1.2
28	Malta	4.4	1.5
29	South Africa	4.4	1.4
30	Namibia	4.4	1.6
31	Austria	4.2	1.5
32	Canada	4.2	1.5
33	Chile	4.2	1.6
34	Uganda	4.2	2.0
35	Algeria	4.1	1.6
36	Korea	4.1	1.2
37	India	4.1	1.7
38	Spain	4.0	1.5
39	Malawi	4.0	1.6
40	Portugal	4.0	1.5
41	Egypt	3.9	1.7
42	Ethiopia	3.9	1.9
43	Taiwan	3.9	1.4
44	Latvia	3.9	1.6
45	Thailand	3.9	1.4
46	Indonesia	3.9	1.3
47	Slovenia	3.8	1.3
48	Zimbabwe	3.8	1.7
49	Morocco	3.8	1.4
50	Estonia	3.8	1.5
51	Japan	3.8	1.6
52	Senegal	3.8	1.3
53	Angola	3.7	2.3
54	Ghana	3.7	1.6
55	Bangladesh	3.7	1.8
56	Uruguay	3.7	1.6
57	Mexico	3.7	1.6
58	Hungary	3.7	1.5
59	El Salvador	3.6	1.6
60	Zambia	3.6	1.7
61	Sri Lanka	3.6	1.6
62	Greece	3.6	1.6
63	Kenya	3.5	1.5
64	Czech Republic	3.5	1.4
65	Mali	3.5	1.5
66	Cameroon	3.5	1.7
67	Italy	3.5	1.2
68	Brazil	3.5	1.4
69	Costa Rica	3.3	1.3
70	Macedonia, FYR	3.3	1.8
71	Lithuania	3.3	1.3
72	Mozambique	3.3	1.6
73	Turkey	3.3	1.6
74	Dominican Republic	3.3	1.9
75	Poland	3.3	1.6
76	Chad	3.2	1.6
77	Mauritius	3.2	1.3
78	Ireland	3.2	1.3
79	Jamaica	3.2	1.4
80	Croatia	3.1	1.6
81	Nigeria	3.1	1.7
82	Trinidad and Tobago	3.0	1.3
83	Madagascar	3.0	1.4
84	Bulgaria	3.0	1.5
85	United States	3.0	1.4
86	Russian Federation	3.0	1.7
87	Argentina	2.9	1.5
88	Colombia	2.9	1.2
89	Guatemala	2.8	1.5
90	Serbia	2.8	1.4
91	Peru	2.8	1.4
92	Bolivia	2.8	1.5
93	Philippines	2.7	1.2
94	Slovak Republic	2.7	1.4
95	Venezuela	2.7	1.6
96	Panama	2.6	1.2
97	Paraguay	2.6	1.8
98	Nicaragua	2.6	1.4
99	Romania	2.5	1.7
100	Ecuador	2.4	1.2
101	Honduras	2.3	1.4
102	Ukraine	2.3	1.2

MEAN: 3.8

7.13 Pervasiveness of money laundering through banks

Money laundering through the banking system in your country is (1 = pervasive, 7 = extremely rare)

RANK	COUNTRY	SCORE		SD
1	Finland	6.7		0.6
2	Iceland	6.7		0.6
3	Denmark	6.6		1.0
4	New Zealand	6.5		0.8
5	Australia	6.3		0.9
6	Singapore	6.2		0.9
7	Sweden	6.2		0.9
8	Jordan	6.1		1.2
9	Tunisia	6.0		1.2
10	United Kingdom	5.9		0.9
11	France	5.8		1.1
12	Netherlands	5.8		1.1
13	Germany	5.8		1.2
14	Belgium	5.7		0.9
15	Malawi	5.6		1.1
16	Gambia	5.6		1.7
17	Canada	5.6		1.1
18	Japan	5.6		1.4
19	Israel	5.6		1.1
20	Chile	5.5		1.1
21	United States	5.5		1.4
22	Estonia	5.5		1.2
23	Norway	5.5		1.2
24	Malaysia	5.5		1.2
25	Vietnam	5.4		1.4
26	Botswana	5.4		1.4
27	El Salvador	5.4		1.1
28	Malta	5.3		1.3
29	Ireland	5.3		1.6
30	Portugal	5.3		1.3
31	Slovenia	5.3		1.2
32	Spain	5.2		1.4
33	Hong Kong SAR	5.2		1.3
34	Luxembourg	5.2		1.4
35	Namibia	5.1		1.1
36	Ethiopia	5.1		1.9
37	Taiwan	5.0		1.3
38	Greece	5.0		1.4
39	Croatia	4.9		1.6
40	Austria	4.9		1.4
41	Korea	4.9		1.3
42	Switzerland	4.9		1.4
43	Egypt	4.9		1.8
44	Hungary	4.8		1.6
45	Morocco	4.8		1.6
46	Pakistan	4.8		1.4
47	Ghana	4.7		1.6
48	South Africa	4.7		1.3
49	Uruguay	4.7		1.6
50	India	4.6		1.4
51	Thailand	4.6		1.4
52	Algeria	4.5		1.6

MEAN: 4.6

RANK	COUNTRY	SCORE		SD
53	Italy	4.5		1.2
54	Slovak Republic	4.5		1.1
55	Mali	4.5		1.6
56	Lithuania	4.5		1.2
57	Dominican Republic	4.4		1.4
58	Latvia	4.4		1.4
59	Macedonia, FYR	4.3		1.9
60	Chad	4.3		1.8
61	China	4.3		1.1
62	Madagascar	4.3		1.4
63	Mauritius	4.3		1.5
64	Brazil	4.3		1.3
65	Sri Lanka	4.2		1.4
66	Senegal	4.2		1.6
67	Tanzania	4.2		1.4
68	Cameroon	4.2		1.3
69	Turkey	4.1		1.5
70	Peru	4.1		1.3
71	Czech Republic	4.1		1.5
72	Poland	4.1		1.4
73	Nicaragua	4.1		1.6
74	Jamaica	4.1		1.2
75	Mexico	4.0		1.5
76	Costa Rica	4.0		1.4
77	Indonesia	4.0		1.4
78	Uganda	4.0		1.6
79	Haiti	3.9		1.6
80	Bulgaria	3.9		1.6
81	Serbia	3.9		1.5
82	Panama	3.9		1.6
83	Bolivia	3.9		1.2
84	Zimbabwe	3.8		1.2
85	Trinidad and Tobago	3.7		1.4
86	Ecuador	3.7		1.4
87	Bangladesh	3.7		1.5
88	Kenya	3.6		1.3
89	Honduras	3.5		1.4
90	Zambia	3.5		1.7
91	Argentina	3.5		1.3
92	Colombia	3.5		1.3
93	Nigeria	3.4		1.5
94	Angola	3.4		1.9
95	Russian Federation	3.3		1.5
96	Venezuela	3.3		1.5
97	Romania	3.3		1.8
98	Mozambique	3.2		1.5
99	Philippines	3.2		1.0
100	Paraguay	2.9		1.4
101	Guatemala	2.8		1.3
102	Ukraine	2.6		1.3

MEAN: 4.6

7.14 Pervasiveness of money laundering through non-bank channels

Money laundering through non-bank channels (eg, exchange or retail shops, exports/imports, gems, real estate) is (1 = pervasive, 7 = extremely rare)

RANK	COUNTRY	SCORE	1 MEAN: 4.0 7	SD
1	Iceland	6.5		0.6
2	Finland	6.2		0.9
3	New Zealand	6.2		0.9
4	Denmark	6.0		1.3
5	Australia	5.9		0.8
6	Sweden	5.8		1.2
7	Singapore	5.8		1.1
8	Tunisia	5.6		1.4
9	Jordan	5.6		1.4
10	Germany	5.5		1.2
11	United Kingdom	5.5		1.2
12	Japan	5.2		1.6
13	Luxembourg	5.1		1.3
14	France	5.1		1.2
15	United States	5.0		1.4
16	Gambia	5.0		1.8
17	Chile	5.0		1.3
18	Malaysia	5.0		1.4
19	Canada	5.0		1.3
20	Taiwan	4.9		1.3
21	Austria	4.9		1.4
22	Israel	4.8		1.5
23	Ireland	4.8		1.3
24	Norway	4.8		1.2
25	Netherlands	4.8		1.3
26	Portugal	4.7		1.2
27	Botswana	4.6		1.6
28	Switzerland	4.6		1.4
29	Uruguay	4.6		1.7
30	Malawi	4.6		1.6
31	Hong Kong SAR	4.5		1.4
32	Belgium	4.5		1.5
33	Slovenia	4.5		1.4
34	Spain	4.5		1.6
35	Vietnam	4.4		1.6
36	Korea	4.3		1.3
37	El Salvador	4.3		1.5
38	Malta	4.3		1.4
39	Egypt	4.3		1.8
40	Ethiopia	4.2		1.9
41	Greece	4.2		1.2
42	Ghana	4.2		1.6
43	Morocco	4.2		1.7
44	Estonia	4.2		1.4
45	Latvia	4.1		1.4
46	Hungary	4.1		1.5
47	Namibia	4.1		1.3
48	China	4.1		1.1
49	South Africa	3.9		1.3
50	Indonesia	3.9		1.5
51	Lithuania	3.8		1.3
52	Italy	3.8		1.4

RANK	COUNTRY	SCORE	1 MEAN: 4.0 7	SD
53	Mauritius	3.8		1.6
54	Croatia	3.8		1.6
55	Dominican Republic	3.7		1.7
56	Mali	3.7		1.7
57	Slovak Republic	3.7		1.2
58	Uganda	3.6		1.4
59	Panama	3.6		1.5
60	Pakistan	3.6		1.4
61	Poland	3.6		1.2
62	Tanzania	3.6		1.2
63	Nicaragua	3.6		1.4
64	Thailand	3.5		1.1
65	Sri Lanka	3.5		1.2
66	Brazil	3.5		1.5
67	Cameroon	3.4		1.6
68	Kenya	3.3		1.2
69	Senegal	3.3		1.4
70	Chad	3.3		1.6
71	Peru	3.3		1.4
72	Macedonia, FYR	3.3		1.8
73	India	3.3		1.6
74	Turkey	3.2		1.3
75	Costa Rica	3.2		1.3
76	Czech Republic	3.2		1.1
77	Serbia	3.2		1.5
78	Ecuador	3.1		1.2
79	Mexico	3.1		1.5
80	Russian Federation	3.1		1.5
81	Algeria	3.0		1.4
82	Honduras	3.0		1.4
83	Zambia	3.0		1.4
84	Madagascar	3.0		1.3
85	Philippines	2.9		1.0
86	Bulgaria	2.9		1.4
87	Bolivia	2.9		1.3
88	Nigeria	2.9		1.4
89	Argentina	2.9		1.2
90	Jamaica	2.8		1.3
91	Angola	2.8		1.7
92	Venezuela	2.8		1.6
93	Trinidad and Tobago	2.7		1.1
94	Bangladesh	2.7		1.4
95	Zimbabwe	2.6		1.2
96	Romania	2.6		1.5
97	Ukraine	2.5		1.2
98	Colombia	2.4		1.3
99	Paraguay	2.4		1.1
100	Haiti	2.3		1.0
101	Guatemala	2.3		1.2
102	Mozambique	2.0		1.1

8.01 Intensity of local competition

Competition in the local market is (1 = limited in most industries and price-cutting is rare, 7 = intense in most industries as market leadership changes over time)

RANK	COUNTRY	SCORE	1 MEAN: 4.7 7	SD
1	United Kingdom	6.0		0.8
2	United States	5.9		1.1
3	Taiwan	5.7		0.9
4	New Zealand	5.7		0.9
5	Hong Kong SAR	5.6		1.2
6	Netherlands	5.6		1.0
7	Chile	5.6		1.0
8	Israel	5.6		0.7
9	Belgium	5.6		0.9
10	India	5.6		1.0
11	Japan	5.5		1.0
12	Spain	5.5		0.9
13	Germany	5.5		1.0
13	Sweden	5.5		1.3
15	Denmark	5.5		1.3
16	Canada	5.5		1.0
17	France	5.4		1.0
18	Australia	5.4		0.9
19	Finland	5.4		1.2
20	Singapore	5.4		1.2
21	Italy	5.3		1.3
22	Korea	5.3		1.1
23	Malaysia	5.3		0.8
24	China	5.3		1.3
25	Thailand	5.3		0.8
26	Iceland	5.3		1.2
27	Estonia	5.3		1.2
28	South Africa	5.3		1.1
29	Kenya	5.2		1.1
30	Jordan	5.2		1.0
31	Brazil	5.2		1.1
32	Ireland	5.2		1.3
33	Norway	5.1		1.2
34	Austria	5.1		1.2
35	Switzerland	5.1		1.3
36	Lithuania	5.1		1.3
37	Czech Republic	5.1		1.2
38	Greece	5.1		1.2
39	Pakistan	5.0		1.3
40	Malta	5.0		1.4
41	Philippines	5.0		1.1
42	El Salvador	5.0		1.2
43	Portugal	5.0		1.1
44	Latvia	5.0		1.0
45	Jamaica	4.9		1.2
46	Hungary	4.9		1.3
47	Mexico	4.9		1.5
48	Slovenia	4.9		1.1
49	Vietnam	4.9		1.4
50	Mauritius	4.9		1.2
51	Poland	4.8		1.2
52	Bangladesh	4.8		1.4
53	Trinidad and Tobago	4.8		1.3
54	Nigeria	4.7		1.5
55	Slovak Republic	4.7		1.4
56	Turkey	4.7		1.4
57	Tanzania	4.7		1.3
58	Sri Lanka	4.7		1.4
59	Costa Rica	4.7		1.4
60	Colombia	4.6		1.2
61	Bulgaria	4.6		1.4
62	Croatia	4.6		1.8
63	Peru	4.6		1.5
64	Tunisia	4.5		1.2
65	Dominican Republic	4.5		1.4
66	Panama	4.5		1.6
67	Egypt	4.4		1.7
68	Morocco	4.4		1.8
69	Namibia	4.4		1.6
70	Argentina	4.4		1.4
71	Luxembourg	4.4		1.3
72	Uganda	4.4		1.7
73	Senegal	4.3		1.8
74	Ghana	4.3		1.6
75	Macedonia, FYR	4.3		1.9
76	Uruguay	4.3		1.4
77	Malawi	4.2		1.6
78	Madagascar	4.2		1.6
79	Gambia	4.2		1.9
80	Botswana	4.1		1.5
81	Cameroon	4.1		2.0
82	Zambia	4.1		1.7
83	Paraguay	4.1		1.7
84	Ukraine	4.1		1.6
85	Guatemala	4.1		1.4
86	Serbia	4.1		1.7
87	Indonesia	4.0		1.2
88	Haiti	4.0		1.3
89	Russian Federation	4.0		1.6
90	Bolivia	3.8		1.5
91	Mali	3.8		1.7
92	Venezuela	3.8		1.4
93	Ethiopia	3.6		1.7
94	Romania	3.6		1.6
95	Chad	3.6		2.1
96	Zimbabwe	3.6		1.3
97	Ecuador	3.5		1.5
98	Algeria	3.5		1.6
99	Honduras	3.4		1.7
100	Mozambique	3.2		1.6
101	Nicaragua	3.2		1.6
102	Angola	2.4		1.2

8.02   Extent of locally based competitors

Competition in the local market (1 = comes primarily from imports, 7 = comes primarily from local firms or local subsidiaries of multinationals)

RANK	COUNTRY	SCORE	1 MEAN: 4.2 7	SD
1	India	5.7		1.1
2	Spain	5.6		1.1
3	Japan	5.6		1.3
4	Germany	5.5		1.2
5	United States	5.5		1.3
6	Austria	5.4		1.3
7	China	5.4		1.2
8	Brazil	5.4		1.2
9	Italy	5.4		1.3
10	South Africa	5.2		1.1
11	France	5.2		1.5
12	Korea	5.2		1.1
13	Malaysia	5.2		1.4
14	Taiwan	5.1		1.4
15	Canada	5.1		1.5
16	Portugal	5.1		1.3
17	Switzerland	5.1		1.5
18	Turkey	5.1		1.5
19	United Kingdom	5.0		1.4
20	Iceland	5.0		1.6
21	Thailand	5.0		1.5
22	Denmark	5.0		1.5
23	Australia	4.9		1.2
23	Netherlands	4.9		1.4
25	Colombia	4.9		1.4
26	Finland	4.8		1.5
27	New Zealand	4.8		1.3
28	Belgium	4.8		1.7
29	Greece	4.7		1.5
30	Argentina	4.7		1.3
31	Vietnam	4.7		1.6
32	Chile	4.7		1.6
33	Hong Kong SAR	4.7		1.8
34	Sweden	4.7		1.5
35	Latvia	4.7		1.4
36	Ireland	4.7		1.7
37	Czech Republic	4.6		1.5
38	Estonia	4.6		1.5
39	Singapore	4.6		1.7
40	Pakistan	4.6		1.3
41	Ukraine	4.5		1.5
42	Mexico	4.5		1.5
43	Costa Rica	4.4		1.5
44	Lithuania	4.4		1.4
45	Poland	4.4		1.4
46	Norway	4.3		1.3
47	Russian Federation	4.3		1.7
48	Philippines	4.3		1.7
49	Indonesia	4.3		1.3
50	Israel	4.2		1.4
51	Luxembourg	4.2		1.7
52	Venezuela	4.2		1.7
53	Hungary	4.1		1.6
54	Panama	4.1		1.7
55	Egypt	4.1		1.7
56	Uganda	4.1		1.9
57	Morocco	4.1		2.0
58	Nigeria	4.0		1.8
59	Dominican Republic	4.0		1.4
59	El Salvador	4.0		1.5
59	Mauritius	4.0		1.5
59	Namibia	4.0		1.8
59	Zimbabwe	4.0		1.5
64	Peru	4.0		1.7
65	Kenya	4.0		1.8
66	Jordan	4.0		1.6
67	Slovak Republic	3.9		1.8
68	Romania	3.9		1.8
69	Trinidad and Tobago	3.9		1.8
70	Cameroon	3.9		1.9
71	Guatemala	3.9		1.3
72	Tunisia	3.8		1.5
73	Sri Lanka	3.8		1.8
74	Slovenia	3.8		1.6
75	Botswana	3.8		2.0
76	Serbia	3.7		1.8
77	Bulgaria	3.7		1.7
78	Honduras	3.6		1.7
79	Croatia	3.6		2.0
80	Ghana	3.6		1.8
81	Uruguay	3.5		1.5
82	Senegal	3.5		2.2
83	Malta	3.5		1.7
84	Paraguay	3.5		1.7
85	Tanzania	3.5		1.9
86	Jamaica	3.4		1.6
87	Macedonia, FYR	3.4		1.9
88	Bangladesh	3.4		1.7
89	Ecuador	3.4		1.6
90	Gambia	3.4		2.3
91	Zambia	3.3		1.9
92	Chad	3.3		2.5
93	Nicaragua	3.3		1.8
94	Malawi	3.1		1.6
95	Bolivia	2.8		1.5
96	Haiti	2.8		1.7
97	Mozambique	2.8		1.8
98	Ethiopia	2.8		1.7
99	Madagascar	2.7		1.7
100	Algeria	2.5		1.6
101	Mali	2.2		1.7
102	Angola	1.8		1.0

8.03 Extent of market dominance

Market dominance by a few enterprises is (1 = common in key industries, 7 = rare)

RANK	COUNTRY	SCORE	SD
1	Germany	4.8	1.6
2	Luxembourg	4.2	1.5
3	Latvia	4.0	1.5
4	United States	3.9	1.7
5	Japan	3.9	1.6
6	Netherlands	3.9	1.6
7	Belgium	3.9	1.7
8	Taiwan	3.9	1.6
9	Jordan	3.7	1.5
10	Tunisia	3.7	1.3
11	Singapore	3.7	1.6
12	Estonia	3.6	1.6
13	Denmark	3.6	1.3
14	Indonesia	3.6	1.3
15	United Kingdom	3.6	1.6
16	India	3.6	1.5
17	Egypt	3.5	1.7
18	Switzerland	3.5	1.5
19	Canada	3.5	1.5
20	Pakistan	3.5	1.3
21	Thailand	3.5	1.5
22	China	3.4	1.4
23	Austria	3.4	1.4
24	Vietnam	3.4	1.5
25	Ethiopia	3.3	1.9
26	Israel	3.3	1.1
26	Spain	3.3	1.5
28	Bulgaria	3.3	1.5
29	Italy	3.3	1.4
30	Finland	3.3	1.4
31	Brazil	3.2	1.3
32	Lithuania	3.2	1.4
33	France	3.2	1.3
34	Tanzania	3.2	1.3
35	Poland	3.2	1.3
36	Chile	3.2	1.4
37	New Zealand	3.1	1.2
38	Uganda	3.1	1.7
39	Korea	3.1	1.5
40	Portugal	3.1	1.3
41	Australia	3.1	1.2
42	Hong Kong SAR	3.1	1.7
43	Ghana	3.1	1.5
44	Ireland	3.1	1.3
45	Colombia	3.0	1.3
46	Slovenia	3.0	1.2
47	Greece	3.0	1.1
48	Gambia	3.0	2.0
49	Norway	3.0	1.1
50	Hungary	3.0	1.3
51	Costa Rica	3.0	1.2
52	Macedonia, FYR	3.0	1.9
53	Croatia	3.0	1.5
54	Sweden	3.0	1.3
55	South Africa	2.9	1.2
56	Algeria	2.9	1.5
57	Malta	2.9	1.4
58	Czech Republic	2.9	1.2
59	Morocco	2.9	1.6
60	El Salvador	2.9	1.5
61	Serbia	2.9	1.4
62	Russian Federation	2.8	1.4
63	Turkey	2.8	1.3
64	Ukraine	2.8	1.4
65	Mali	2.8	1.7
66	Sri Lanka	2.8	1.3
67	Malaysia	2.8	1.0
68	Jamaica	2.7	1.4
69	Bolivia	2.7	1.4
70	Trinidad and Tobago	2.7	1.1
71	Mauritius	2.7	1.0
72	Bangladesh	2.7	1.2
73	Kenya	2.6	1.3
74	Slovak Republic	2.6	1.3
75	Senegal	2.6	1.2
76	Iceland	2.6	1.2
77	Namibia	2.6	1.2
78	Argentina	2.6	1.0
79	Dominican Republic	2.6	1.1
80	Panama	2.6	1.3
81	Nigeria	2.5	1.2
82	Zambia	2.5	1.3
83	Philippines	2.5	1.0
84	Paraguay	2.5	1.1
85	Guatemala	2.5	1.3
86	Malawi	2.4	1.1
87	Romania	2.4	1.3
88	Mozambique	2.4	1.5
89	Mexico	2.4	1.1
90	Venezuela	2.4	1.3
91	Peru	2.4	1.1
92	Cameroon	2.3	1.3
93	Uruguay	2.3	1.0
94	Botswana	2.3	1.0
95	Honduras	2.2	1.2
96	Chad	2.2	1.7
97	Madagascar	2.2	0.9
98	Haiti	2.2	0.9
99	Ecuador	2.1	0.9
100	Angola	2.1	1.3
101	Zimbabwe	2.1	0.7
102	Nicaragua	2.1	1.2

8.04 Sophistication of local buyers' products and processes

Buyers in your country are (1 = slow to adopt new products and processes, 7 = actively seeking the latest products, technologies, and processes)

RANK	COUNTRY	SCORE	1 MEAN: 4.5 7	SD
1	Iceland	6.2		0.6
2	United States	6.1		1.2
3	Hong Kong SAR	6.1		0.8
4	Sweden	6.0		0.7
5	Australia	6.0		0.8
6	Finland	5.9		1.0
7	United Kingdom	5.9		0.9
8	Singapore	5.9		0.9
9	New Zealand	5.8		0.7
10	Israel	5.7		0.9
11	Canada	5.7		1.0
12	Denmark	5.7		1.0
13	Japan	5.7		1.4
14	Taiwan	5.7		1.0
15	Luxembourg	5.6		1.0
16	Korea	5.5		1.1
17	Norway	5.5		0.9
18	Belgium	5.5		1.1
19	France	5.4		1.0
20	Netherlands	5.4		1.1
21	Malaysia	5.3		1.0
22	Switzerland	5.3		1.3
23	Italy	5.2		1.4
24	Estonia	5.1		1.1
25	Thailand	5.1		1.1
26	Ireland	5.1		1.5
27	Germany	5.0		1.2
28	Spain	5.0		1.0
29	South Africa	5.0		1.2
30	Tunisia	4.9		1.2
31	Slovenia	4.9		1.1
32	Latvia	4.9		1.1
33	Brazil	4.9		1.1
34	Slovak Republic	4.9		1.1
35	Malta	4.8		1.2
36	Turkey	4.8		1.4
37	Czech Republic	4.8		1.3
38	Portugal	4.8		1.1
39	Chile	4.7		1.2
40	India	4.7		1.1
41	Vietnam	4.7		1.4
42	Greece	4.6		1.3
43	Morocco	4.6		1.7
44	Austria	4.6		1.1
45	Costa Rica	4.6		1.2
46	Algeria	4.5		1.5
47	Lithuania	4.5		1.2
48	Hungary	4.5		1.2
49	Poland	4.5		1.2
50	Colombia	4.3		1.2
51	Ukraine	4.3		1.3
52	Trinidad and Tobago	4.3		1.3

RANK	COUNTRY	SCORE	1 MEAN: 4.5 7	SD
53	Jamaica	4.3		1.3
54	Mexico	4.3		1.3
55	Jordan	4.3		1.4
56	Panama	4.2		1.3
57	Mauritius	4.2		1.4
58	Russian Federation	4.2		1.5
59	Philippines	4.2		1.4
60	Zambia	4.2		1.6
61	Ghana	4.1		1.8
62	Croatia	4.1		1.6
63	Dominican Republic	4.1		1.4
64	China	4.1		1.3
65	Cameroon	4.1		1.6
66	Argentina	4.1		1.3
67	Madagascar	4.1		1.4
68	El Salvador	4.1		1.3
69	Egypt	4.0		1.7
70	Nigeria	4.0		1.7
71	Uganda	4.0		1.8
72	Chad	4.0		1.9
73	Kenya	4.0		1.6
74	Botswana	3.9		1.5
75	Senegal	3.9		1.3
76	Namibia	3.9		1.3
77	Sri Lanka	3.8		1.4
78	Venezuela	3.8		1.2
79	Serbia	3.8		1.5
80	Pakistan	3.8		1.5
81	Zimbabwe	3.8		1.3
82	Indonesia	3.8		1.3
83	Malawi	3.7		1.3
84	Tanzania	3.7		1.5
85	Bulgaria	3.7		1.3
86	Bangladesh	3.7		1.5
87	Gambia	3.6		1.8
88	Romania	3.6		1.7
89	Peru	3.5		1.2
90	Guatemala	3.5		1.3
91	Macedonia, FYR	3.3		1.7
92	Uruguay	3.3		1.3
93	Mali	3.2		1.8
94	Ecuador	3.2		1.3
95	Honduras	3.1		1.3
96	Paraguay	2.9		1.3
97	Nicaragua	2.9		1.4
98	Bolivia	2.8		1.1
99	Mozambique	2.8		1.3
100	Haiti	2.8		1.3
101	Ethiopia	2.7		1.5
102	Angola	2.7		1.5

509

8.05 Administrative burden for startups

Starting a new business in your country is generally (1 = extremely difficult and time consuming, 7 = easy)

RANK	COUNTRY	SCORE	1 MEAN: 4.1 7	SD
1	Hong Kong SAR	6.2		1.1
2	Iceland	6.1		0.8
3	United States	5.8		1.3
4	Estonia	5.8		1.0
5	Vietnam	5.7		1.1
6	Singapore	5.6		1.2
7	Finland	5.6		1.3
8	Australia	5.6		1.3
9	Switzerland	5.5		1.4
10	Malaysia	5.5		1.0
11	New Zealand	5.4		1.1
12	Taiwan	5.4		1.2
13	Luxembourg	5.4		1.0
14	Tunisia	5.4		1.4
15	Canada	5.4		1.3
16	United Kingdom	5.3		1.3
17	Gambia	5.3		1.9
18	Jordan	5.3		1.3
19	Hungary	5.2		1.5
20	Israel	5.1		1.2
20	Sweden	5.1		1.5
22	Netherlands	5.0		1.4
23	Thailand	4.8		1.5
24	Malta	4.8		1.5
25	Denmark	4.7		1.4
26	Ireland	4.7		1.4
27	Latvia	4.6		1.4
28	Namibia	4.6		1.5
29	Norway	4.6		1.3
30	Austria	4.5		1.6
31	Mauritius	4.5		1.3
32	Zambia	4.5		1.7
33	Cameroon	4.4		1.8
34	South Africa	4.4		1.4
35	Uganda	4.4		1.8
36	Trinidad and Tobago	4.4		1.6
37	El Salvador	4.3		1.7
38	Germany	4.3		1.7
39	Sri Lanka	4.3		1.5
40	China	4.2		1.5
41	Slovenia	4.2		1.5
42	Senegal	4.2		1.8
43	Malawi	4.2		1.7
44	Dominican Republic	4.2		1.7
45	Korea	4.2		1.3
46	Belgium	4.1		1.8
47	Slovak Republic	4.1		1.5
47	Spain	4.1		1.5
49	Philippines	4.1		1.4
50	Botswana	4.1		1.7
51	Chile	4.0		1.4
52	India	4.0		1.4

RANK	COUNTRY	SCORE	1 MEAN: 4.1 7	SD
53	Panama	3.9		1.5
54	Costa Rica	3.9		1.4
54	Mali	3.9		2.1
56	Croatia	3.8		1.8
57	Poland	3.8		1.4
58	Zimbabwe	3.8		1.6
59	Morocco	3.7		2.0
60	Guatemala	3.7		1.5
61	Egypt	3.7		1.7
62	Brazil	3.6		1.6
63	Turkey	3.6		1.4
64	Indonesia	3.6		1.4
65	Jamaica	3.5		1.7
66	Lithuania	3.5		1.6
67	Italy	3.5		1.4
68	Czech Republic	3.5		1.6
69	Madagascar	3.4		1.7
70	Tanzania	3.4		1.6
71	Ghana	3.4		1.8
72	Pakistan	3.4		1.7
73	Greece	3.4		1.5
74	Paraguay	3.3		1.5
75	Algeria	3.3		1.9
76	Portugal	3.3		1.5
77	Bangladesh	3.3		1.8
78	Nigeria	3.3		1.8
79	Peru	3.3		1.6
80	Argentina	3.3		1.6
81	Kenya	3.3		1.5
82	France	3.2		1.4
83	Ethiopia	3.2		1.7
84	Uruguay	3.1		1.5
85	Colombia	3.1		1.3
86	Macedonia, FYR	3.1		2.0
87	Japan	3.1		1.4
88	Chad	3.1		2.5
89	Ecuador	3.1		1.4
90	Mexico	3.1		1.4
91	Russian Federation	3.0		1.7
92	Nicaragua	3.0		1.5
93	Bolivia	3.0		1.6
94	Romania	2.8		1.6
95	Haiti	2.8		1.3
96	Angola	2.7		1.7
97	Serbia	2.7		1.4
98	Venezuela	2.7		1.4
99	Honduras	2.6		1.3
100	Mozambique	2.4		1.4
101	Ukraine	2.4		1.6
102	Bulgaria	2.3		1.2

Anti-monopoly policy in your country is (1 = lax and not effective at promoting competition, 7 = effective and promotes competition)

RANK	COUNTRY	SCORE	1 MEAN: 4.0 7	SD
1	Finland	6.1		0.9
2	United Kingdom	6.1		0.9
3	Australia	6.0		0.9
4	United States	5.8		1.2
5	Germany	5.8		1.0
6	Denmark	5.8		1.1
7	Sweden	5.7		1.0
8	New Zealand	5.7		1.0
9	Israel	5.6		0.8
10	Belgium	5.6		0.9
11	Netherlands	5.6		1.1
12	Iceland	5.4		1.1
13	France	5.4		1.2
14	Canada	5.4		1.2
15	South Africa	5.3		1.2
16	Taiwan	5.1		1.2
17	Luxembourg	5.1		1.0
18	Ireland	5.0		1.3
19	Singapore	5.0		1.3
20	Norway	5.0		1.3
21	Chile	4.9		1.2
22	Italy	4.9		1.3
23	Austria	4.9		1.4
24	Korea	4.9		1.2
25	Spain	4.7		1.3
26	Brazil	4.7		1.3
27	Switzerland	4.7		1.6
28	Japan	4.7		1.4
29	Tunisia	4.6		1.3
30	Malaysia	4.5		1.4
31	Portugal	4.5		1.2
32	Estonia	4.4		1.4
33	Czech Republic	4.4		1.4
34	Slovenia	4.4		1.2
35	Latvia	4.4		1.4
36	Jordan	4.4		1.4
37	India	4.3		1.3
38	Mexico	4.2		1.6
39	Greece	4.2		1.3
40	Malta	4.2		1.4
41	Jamaica	4.1		1.3
42	Thailand	4.1		1.5
43	Hungary	4.1		1.5
44	Lithuania	4.0		1.3
45	Slovak Republic	4.0		1.4
46	Poland	3.9		1.3
47	Gambia	3.9		1.9
48	Tanzania	3.9		1.4
49	Morocco	3.9		1.5
50	Uganda	3.8		1.8
51	Ghana	3.8		1.6
52	China	3.8		1.4

RANK	COUNTRY	SCORE	1 MEAN: 4.0 7	SD
53	Colombia	3.7		1.3
54	Panama	3.7		1.4
55	Namibia	3.7		1.3
56	Turkey	3.7		1.4
57	Mali	3.7		1.7
58	Egypt	3.6		1.6
59	Zimbabwe	3.6		1.2
60	Hong Kong SAR	3.6		1.7
60	Zambia	3.6		1.6
62	Indonesia	3.6		1.3
63	Kenya	3.5		1.5
64	Costa Rica	3.5		1.4
65	Pakistan	3.4		1.5
66	Sri Lanka	3.4		1.4
67	Mauritius	3.4		1.3
68	Algeria	3.4		1.7
69	Croatia	3.4		1.4
70	Peru	3.4		1.3
71	Senegal	3.3		1.0
72	Vietnam	3.3		1.4
73	Cameroon	3.3		1.3
74	Venezuela	3.2		1.1
75	Philippines	3.2		1.5
76	Botswana	3.2		1.5
77	Dominican Republic	3.2		1.5
78	Malawi	3.2		1.5
79	Bulgaria	3.1		1.3
80	Russian Federation	3.1		1.3
81	Serbia	3.1		1.4
82	Argentina	3.1		1.2
83	Romania	3.1		1.6
84	Bangladesh	3.0		1.5
85	Nigeria	3.0		1.6
86	Ukraine	2.9		1.3
87	Macedonia, FYR	2.9		1.8
88	Bolivia	2.9		1.3
89	El Salvador	2.9		1.2
90	Trinidad and Tobago	2.8		1.4
91	Chad	2.7		1.5
92	Madagascar	2.7		1.4
93	Ethiopia	2.7		1.3
94	Nicaragua	2.6		1.4
95	Ecuador	2.5		1.0
96	Uruguay	2.5		1.3
97	Paraguay	2.5		1.0
98	Guatemala	2.4		1.1
99	Haiti	2.3		1.2
100	Mozambique	2.3		1.1
101	Honduras	2.2		1.3
102	Angola	1.9		1.0

8.07 Prevalence of mergers and acquisitions

In your country, mergers and acquisitions—particularly hostile takeovers—are (1 = rare and face serious legal impediments, 7 = common and allowed by law)

RANK	COUNTRY	SCORE	1　　MEAN: 3.9　　7	SD
1	United Kingdom	6.5		0.8
2	United States	6.1		1.1
3	Australia	6.0		1.3
4	New Zealand	5.7		1.1
5	Denmark	5.3		1.2
6	Ireland	5.3		1.1
7	Hong Kong SAR	5.1		1.3
8	Sweden	5.1		1.4
9	Canada	5.1		1.4
10	France	5.0		1.3
11	Finland	5.0		1.3
12	Singapore	5.0		1.3
13	Latvia	5.0		1.1
14	Switzerland	4.9		1.4
15	South Africa	4.8		1.4
16	Norway	4.8		1.4
17	Zimbabwe	4.8		1.1
18	Italy	4.6		1.2
19	Iceland	4.6		1.1
20	Morocco	4.6		1.9
21	Belgium	4.6		1.5
22	Malaysia	4.6		1.2
23	Spain	4.5		1.4
24	Germany	4.5		1.5
25	Poland	4.5		1.1
26	Lithuania	4.3		1.1
27	Slovak Republic	4.3		1.4
28	Estonia	4.3		1.2
29	Egypt	4.2		1.7
30	Russian Federation	4.2		1.5
31	Austria	4.1		1.6
32	Greece	4.1		1.5
33	Korea	4.1		1.4
34	Thailand	4.1		1.6
35	Panama	4.1		1.6
36	Namibia	4.1		1.4
37	Luxembourg	4.0		1.6
38	Chile	4.0		1.6
39	Netherlands	4.0		1.7
40	Czech Republic	4.0		1.3
41	Ukraine	4.0		1.2
42	Slovenia	4.0		1.4
43	Romania	4.0		1.4
44	Israel	3.9		1.5
45	Brazil	3.9		1.4
46	Vietnam	3.9		1.5
47	Japan	3.9		1.5
48	Tunisia	3.9		1.7
49	Argentina	3.8		1.6
50	Hungary	3.8		1.2
51	Venezuela	3.7		1.4
52	Indonesia	3.7		1.3

RANK	COUNTRY	SCORE	1　　MEAN: 3.9　　7	SD
53	Dominican Republic	3.7		1.6
54	India	3.7		1.5
55	Botswana	3.7		1.4
56	Jordan	3.7		1.5
57	Taiwan	3.7		1.7
58	Cameroon	3.7		1.7
59	China	3.7		1.3
60	Bulgaria	3.7		1.4
61	Trinidad and Tobago	3.6		1.3
62	Mauritius	3.6		1.2
63	Senegal	3.6		1.4
64	Portugal	3.6		1.3
65	Mozambique	3.6		1.6
66	Mexico	3.5		1.5
67	Peru	3.5		1.4
68	Sri Lanka	3.5		1.3
69	Turkey	3.5		1.4
70	Tanzania	3.5		1.5
71	Philippines	3.4		1.5
72	Honduras	3.4		1.7
73	Jamaica	3.4		1.4
74	Costa Rica	3.4		1.5
75	Kenya	3.4		1.5
76	Croatia	3.4		1.4
77	Mali	3.3		1.7
78	Colombia	3.3		1.3
79	Paraguay	3.3		1.5
80	Ghana	3.3		1.5
81	El Salvador	3.3		1.6
82	Malawi	3.3		1.7
83	Uganda	3.2		1.8
84	Macedonia, FYR	3.2		1.7
85	Nigeria	3.2		1.6
86	Uruguay	3.2		1.4
87	Guatemala	3.1		1.6
88	Malta	3.1		1.3
89	Zambia	3.1		1.4
90	Nicaragua	3.1		1.6
91	Serbia	3.0		1.3
92	Pakistan	2.9		1.6
93	Ecuador	2.9		1.3
94	Madagascar	2.9		1.4
95	Bolivia	2.8		1.2
96	Chad	2.8		1.7
97	Angola	2.7		1.6
98	Algeria	2.3		1.3
99	Ethiopia	2.3		1.3
100	Gambia	2.3		1.6
101	Haiti	2.2		1.3
102	Bangladesh	2.2		1.4

In your country, private-sector employment of women is (1 = scarce and limited to less important jobs, 7 = similar to private-sector employment of men)

RANK	COUNTRY	SCORE	1 MEAN: 4.6 7	SD
1	Hong Kong SAR	6.0		1.1
2	Finland	6.0		0.8
3	Singapore	5.9		0.9
4	Canada	5.8		1.0
5	Denmark	5.8		1.1
6	Tunisia	5.8		1.2
7	Malaysia	5.6		1.0
7	Thailand	5.6		1.0
9	Iceland	5.6		1.0
10	Morocco	5.5		1.8
11	United States	5.5		1.0
12	Sweden	5.5		0.9
13	Macedonia, FYR	5.4		1.7
14	Panama	5.4		1.2
15	Israel	5.2		1.1
16	United Kingdom	5.2		1.2
17	Norway	5.2		0.9
18	Luxembourg	5.2		1.3
19	Philippines	5.2		1.5
20	New Zealand	5.2		1.2
21	Ireland	5.2		1.2
22	Turkey	5.2		1.4
23	Botswana	5.2		1.5
24	Belgium	5.1		1.3
24	Portugal	5.1		1.4
26	Latvia	5.1		1.2
27	Haiti	5.1		1.4
28	Jamaica	5.1		1.6
29	Sri Lanka	5.0		1.5
30	Venezuela	5.0		1.3
31	Taiwan	5.0		1.5
32	Costa Rica	5.0		1.2
33	Dominican Republic	4.9		1.4
34	Estonia	4.9		1.4
35	France	4.9		1.3
36	Colombia	4.9		1.4
37	Bulgaria	4.8		1.7
38	Czech Republic	4.8		1.5
39	Australia	4.8		1.1
40	Greece	4.8		1.3
41	Jordan	4.8		1.4
42	Nigeria	4.7		1.6
43	Netherlands	4.7		1.4
44	Madagascar	4.7		1.7
45	Switzerland	4.6		1.4
46	Slovenia	4.6		1.5
47	Croatia	4.6		1.7
48	Argentina	4.6		1.5
48	Trinidad and Tobago	4.6		1.5
50	Vietnam	4.6		1.7
51	Brazil	4.5		1.4
52	Romania	4.5		2.0
53	Spain	4.5		1.2
54	Gambia	4.5		1.9
54	Germany	4.5		1.5
56	Slovak Republic	4.5		1.5
57	Uruguay	4.4		1.4
58	Cameroon	4.4		1.8
59	Malta	4.4		1.6
60	Poland	4.4		1.5
61	Mauritius	4.4		1.3
62	Egypt	4.4		1.9
63	Namibia	4.4		1.5
64	South Africa	4.4		1.3
65	Serbia	4.3		1.9
66	Algeria	4.3		1.7
67	Hungary	4.3		1.5
68	El Salvador	4.3		1.6
69	Zambia	4.2		1.7
70	Russian Federation	4.2		1.7
71	Nicaragua	4.2		1.6
72	Lithuania	4.2		1.8
73	Chile	4.2		1.3
74	Austria	4.2		1.5
75	Ghana	4.2		1.7
76	Mali	4.2		2.1
77	Peru	4.2		1.4
78	Malawi	4.1		1.5
79	Ecuador	4.0		1.7
80	Senegal	4.0		2.0
81	India	4.0		1.7
82	Zimbabwe	4.0		1.3
83	Tanzania	4.0		1.5
84	Chad	4.0		2.1
85	Honduras	4.0		1.4
86	Kenya	4.0		1.5
87	Italy	4.0		1.5
88	Mexico	3.9		1.4
89	Ukraine	3.9		1.6
90	Uganda	3.9		2.0
91	China	3.8		1.6
92	Guatemala	3.7		1.3
93	Indonesia	3.6		1.1
94	Japan	3.6		1.5
95	Paraguay	3.6		1.5
96	Mozambique	3.4		1.4
97	Ethiopia	3.4		1.8
98	Bolivia	3.3		1.2
99	Angola	3.3		1.7
100	Korea	3.3		1.4
101	Bangladesh	3.2		1.5
102	Pakistan	2.8		1.1

513

8.09   Wage equality of women in the workplace

In your country, for similar work, wages for women are (1 = significantly below those of men, 7 = equal to those of men)

RANK	COUNTRY	SCORE	1 MEAN: 4.6 7	SD		RANK	COUNTRY	SCORE	1 MEAN: 4.6 7	SD
1	Macedonia, FYR	6.3		1.2		53	Dominican Republic	4.6		1.5
2	Botswana	6.0		1.4		53	Israel	4.6		1.0
3	Tunisia	5.9		1.2		55	Jamaica	4.6		1.4
4	Cameroon	5.8		1.5		56	United Kingdom	4.6		1.4
5	Thailand	5.7		1.2		57	Trinidad and Tobago	4.5		1.7
6	Nigeria	5.7		1.5		58	Belgium	4.5		1.2
7	Singapore	5.7		1.1		59	Estonia	4.5		1.5
8	Hong Kong SAR	5.7		1.4		60	Slovenia	4.5		1.7
9	Chad	5.6		1.8		61	Germany	4.5		1.4
10	Tanzania	5.5		1.5		61	India	4.5		1.7
11	Mali	5.5		1.8		63	Kenya	4.5		1.7
12	Zambia	5.5		1.7		64	Haiti	4.5		1.7
13	Malaysia	5.5		1.2		65	Panama	4.4		1.5
14	Ghana	5.4		1.6		66	Lithuania	4.4		1.6
15	Croatia	5.4		1.6		67	South Africa	4.4		1.5
16	Gambia	5.4		1.9		68	Netherlands	4.4		1.6
17	Australia	5.4		1.3		69	El Salvador	4.4		1.4
18	Malta	5.4		1.5		70	Russian Federation	4.3		1.8
19	Philippines	5.4		1.4		71	Switzerland	4.3		1.4
20	Canada	5.4		1.2		72	Spain	4.3		1.4
21	Algeria	5.3		1.7		73	Senegal	4.3		1.7
22	Vietnam	5.2		1.4		74	Ecuador	4.3		1.6
23	Turkey	5.2		1.6		75	Peru	4.2		1.6
24	Morocco	5.2		2.0		76	Mozambique	4.2		1.7
25	Costa Rica	5.2		1.3		77	Colombia	4.2		1.4
26	Serbia	5.2		1.8		78	Ukraine	4.2		1.7
27	Finland	5.1		1.2		79	Honduras	4.1		1.5
28	Malawi	5.1		2.2		80	Pakistan	4.1		1.8
29	Taiwan	5.1		1.3		81	Mauritius	4.1		1.6
30	Jordan	5.1		1.5		82	Japan	4.0		1.6
31	Uganda	5.1		2.0		83	Slovak Republic	4.0		1.5
32	Denmark	5.0		1.2		84	Uruguay	4.0		1.3
33	Sri Lanka	5.0		1.5		85	Mexico	4.0		1.5
34	Norway	5.0		1.4		86	Italy	3.9		1.5
35	Latvia	4.9		1.3		87	Guatemala	3.9		1.4
36	Portugal	4.9		1.3		88	Argentina	3.9		1.4
37	Ireland	4.9		1.6		89	Poland	3.9		1.5
38	Romania	4.8		1.8		90	Korea	3.9		1.4
39	Bulgaria	4.8		1.7		91	Hungary	3.8		1.4
40	Egypt	4.8		2.0		92	Paraguay	3.8		1.6
41	Iceland	4.8		1.3		93	Czech Republic	3.7		1.5
42	China	4.7		1.6		94	Indonesia	3.7		1.4
43	Venezuela	4.7		1.6		95	Brazil	3.7		1.4
44	Madagascar	4.7		1.7		96	France	3.6		1.4
45	Ethiopia	4.7		2.0		97	Chile	3.6		1.2
46	New Zealand	4.6		1.5		98	Bolivia	3.5		1.4
47	Luxembourg	4.6		1.4		99	Bangladesh	3.5		1.6
48	Greece	4.6		1.4		100	Nicaragua	3.5		1.6
49	Sweden	4.6		1.3		101	Angola	3.4		1.8
50	Namibia	4.6		1.6		102	Austria	3.0		1.2
51	United States	4.6		1.3						
52	Zimbabwe	4.6		1.5						

8.10 Regional disparities in quality of business environment

Differences among regions within your country in the quality of the business environment (human resources, infrastructure, and other factors) are (1 = large and persistent, 7 = modest)

RANK	COUNTRY	SCORE	MEAN: 3.4	SD		RANK	COUNTRY	SCORE	MEAN: 3.4	SD
1	Singapore	5.8		1.6		53	Czech Republic	3.2		1.6
2	Malta	5.5		1.3		54	Namibia	3.0		1.6
3	Hong Kong SAR	5.2		1.9		55	Bulgaria	3.0		1.5
4	United States	5.2		1.6		56	Bolivia	3.0		1.5
5	Luxembourg	5.1		1.5		57	Greece	3.0		1.4
6	Australia	5.1		1.9		58	Ghana	3.0		1.6
7	Netherlands	5.1		1.4		59	Lithuania	3.0		1.4
8	Austria	5.1		1.4		60	Nigeria	2.9		1.7
9	Denmark	5.0		1.6		61	Bangladesh	2.9		1.8
10	Israel	5.0		1.3		62	Malawi	2.9		1.5
11	New Zealand	4.9		1.6		63	South Africa	2.9		1.2
12	Germany	4.8		1.6		64	Nicaragua	2.9		1.6
13	Switzerland	4.7		1.4		65	Ecuador	2.9		1.4
14	Japan	4.5		1.8		66	Angola	2.8		1.9
15	Taiwan	4.5		1.6		67	Poland	2.8		1.3
16	Mauritius	4.4		1.6		68	Vietnam	2.8		1.4
17	United Kingdom	4.3		1.6		69	Zambia	2.8		1.8
18	Iceland	4.3		1.8		70	Portugal	2.8		1.2
19	Finland	4.3		1.7		71	Croatia	2.8		1.6
20	Trinidad and Tobago	4.3		1.6		72	Argentina	2.8		1.2
21	France	4.2		1.6		73	Colombia	2.8		1.1
22	Sweden	4.1		1.6		74	Pakistan	2.8		1.4
23	Thailand	4.1		1.6		75	Romania	2.8		1.3
24	Canada	4.1		1.7		76	Serbia	2.8		1.5
25	Jamaica	4.0		1.6		77	Cameroon	2.8		1.5
26	Spain	3.9		1.5		78	Kenya	2.8		1.2
27	Malaysia	3.9		1.6		79	Uganda	2.7		1.6
28	Norway	3.9		1.6		80	Algeria	2.7		1.5
29	Uruguay	3.9		1.6		81	Ukraine	2.7		1.6
30	Belgium	3.8		1.6		82	Estonia	2.7		1.2
31	Ireland	3.8		1.9		83	Guatemala	2.7		1.4
32	Korea	3.8		1.6		84	Tanzania	2.6		1.4
33	Botswana	3.8		1.7		85	Italy	2.6		1.4
34	Macedonia, FYR	3.7		2.0		86	Mexico	2.6		1.3
35	Costa Rica	3.7		1.5		87	Senegal	2.6		1.6
36	Indonesia	3.6		1.5		88	Mali	2.5		2.0
37	Latvia	3.6		1.9		89	Morocco	2.5		1.6
38	Egypt	3.6		1.8		90	Philippines	2.5		1.2
39	Zimbabwe	3.5		1.6		91	India	2.5		1.3
40	Honduras	3.5		1.7		92	Hungary	2.3		1.0
41	Gambia	3.4		2.0		93	Russian Federation	2.3		1.2
42	Tunisia	3.4		1.4		94	Chad	2.3		1.9
43	Jordan	3.4		1.4		95	Peru	2.2		1.3
44	Panama	3.4		1.5		96	Ethiopia	2.2		1.3
45	Slovenia	3.4		1.5		97	Turkey	2.2		1.2
46	Sri Lanka	3.4		1.6		98	Slovak Republic	2.2		1.0
47	Chile	3.3		1.4		99	Brazil	2.1		0.9
48	El Salvador	3.3		1.4		100	Mozambique	2.1		1.2
49	Dominican Republic	3.3		1.7		101	Madagascar	1.9		1.1
49	Venezuela	3.3		1.5		102	Haiti	1.5		1.3
51	China	3.3		1.5						
52	Paraguay	3.3		1.6						

515

8.11 Focus of trade and industry associations

Trade and industry associations in your country focus on (1 = government lobbying for financial support and lenient regulation, 7 = organize collective action to improve member firms' productivity levels)

RANK	COUNTRY	SCORE	1 MEAN: 3.8 7	SD
1	Singapore	5.3		1.2
2	Iceland	5.3		1.3
3	Finland	5.1		1.5
4	Taiwan	5.0		1.1
5	Luxembourg	4.9		1.5
6	Hong Kong SAR	4.7		1.4
7	Denmark	4.7		1.5
8	Korea	4.6		1.2
9	Switzerland	4.6		1.5
10	Sweden	4.6		1.3
11	Jordan	4.6		1.2
12	Netherlands	4.5		1.4
13	Latvia	4.5		1.4
14	Israel	4.5		1.2
15	New Zealand	4.5		1.4
16	Chile	4.5		1.3
17	Tunisia	4.4		1.4
18	Canada	4.4		1.4
19	Gambia	4.4		1.8
20	Belgium	4.4		1.3
21	Vietnam	4.4		1.3
22	Thailand	4.3		1.3
23	South Africa	4.2		1.2
24	China	4.2		1.2
25	Costa Rica	4.2		1.3
26	Norway	4.2		1.2
27	Mauritius	4.1		1.4
28	United States	4.1		1.7
29	Spain	4.1		1.4
30	United Kingdom	4.0		1.5
31	Kenya	4.0		1.5
32	France	4.0		1.3
33	Malta	4.0		1.6
33	Namibia	4.0		1.3
35	Japan	4.0		1.3
36	Egypt	4.0		1.6
37	Ghana	3.9		1.7
38	Germany	3.9		1.5
39	Slovenia	3.9		1.3
40	Tanzania	3.9		1.5
41	Zambia	3.9		1.9
42	El Salvador	3.9		1.4
43	Austria	3.9		1.3
44	Greece	3.9		1.4
45	Trinidad and Tobago	3.9		1.3
46	Dominican Republic	3.9		1.5
47	Guatemala	3.9		1.4
48	Brazil	3.8		1.3
49	Botswana	3.8		1.4
50	Italy	3.8		1.3
51	India	3.8		1.5
52	Malaysia	3.8		1.6

RANK	COUNTRY	SCORE	1 MEAN: 3.8 7	SD
53	Colombia	3.8		1.2
54	Senegal	3.8		1.4
55	Morocco	3.7		1.4
56	Haiti	3.7		1.5
57	Ethiopia	3.7		1.6
58	Nigeria	3.7		1.7
59	Panama	3.7		1.3
60	Jamaica	3.7		1.1
61	Australia	3.6		1.4
62	Mexico	3.6		1.3
63	Estonia	3.6		1.3
64	Chad	3.6		1.4
65	Malawi	3.5		1.4
65	Zimbabwe	3.5		1.3
67	Indonesia	3.5		1.5
68	Cameroon	3.5		1.3
69	Sri Lanka	3.5		1.5
70	Ireland	3.4		1.5
71	Turkey	3.4		1.2
72	Peru	3.4		1.4
73	Uganda	3.4		1.8
74	Bulgaria	3.4		1.3
75	Mali	3.4		1.8
76	Venezuela	3.4		1.3
77	Lithuania	3.3		1.2
78	Nicaragua	3.3		1.5
79	Poland	3.3		1.2
80	Madagascar	3.3		1.6
81	Serbia	3.3		1.2
82	Slovak Republic	3.3		1.4
83	Czech Republic	3.3		1.2
84	Croatia	3.3		1.2
85	Portugal	3.3		1.2
86	Honduras	3.3		1.4
87	Macedonia, FYR	3.3		1.6
88	Philippines	3.2		1.2
89	Ecuador	3.2		1.2
90	Pakistan	3.2		1.4
91	Hungary	3.2		1.2
92	Angola	3.1		1.7
93	Algeria	3.1		1.4
94	Mozambique	3.1		1.3
95	Romania	3.1		1.7
96	Bolivia	3.0		1.1
97	Russian Federation	3.0		1.3
98	Paraguay	2.9		1.2
99	Uruguay	2.9		1.3
100	Bangladesh	2.8		1.3
101	Ukraine	2.7		1.0
102	Argentina	2.6		1.0

9.01 Buyer sophistication

Buyers in your country are (1 = unsophisticated and make choices based on the lowest price, 7 = knowledgeable and demanding and buy based on superior performance attributes)

RANK	COUNTRY	SCORE	1 MEAN: 3.9 7	SD
1	Luxembourg	6.0		1.0
2	United Kingdom	5.8		1.1
2	United States	5.8		1.3
4	Switzerland	5.8		0.9
5	Denmark	5.8		1.1
6	Hong Kong SAR	5.8		1.1
7	Australia	5.8		0.7
8	Japan	5.7		1.0
9	Finland	5.6		1.1
10	France	5.6		1.0
11	Singapore	5.6		1.0
12	Germany	5.6		1.3
13	New Zealand	5.5		1.1
14	Canada	5.5		1.2
15	Sweden	5.4		1.1
16	Taiwan	5.4		1.0
17	Belgium	5.4		1.1
18	Israel	5.3		1.2
19	Italy	5.3		1.4
20	Malaysia	5.3		1.2
21	Netherlands	5.2		1.3
22	Austria	5.1		1.4
23	Iceland	5.1		1.4
24	Korea	4.9		1.1
25	South Africa	4.8		1.2
26	Ireland	4.8		1.6
27	Slovenia	4.7		1.4
28	Tunisia	4.7		1.5
29	Estonia	4.5		1.4
30	Norway	4.5		1.3
31	Malta	4.5		1.2
32	Vietnam	4.4		1.6
33	Spain	4.4		1.5
34	India	4.4		1.6
35	Greece	4.3		1.4
36	Latvia	4.3		1.4
37	Thailand	4.3		1.2
38	Brazil	4.2		1.4
39	Mauritius	4.1		1.4
40	Chile	4.1		1.4
41	Morocco	4.0		1.8
42	China	3.9		1.4
43	Costa Rica	3.9		1.5
44	Czech Republic	3.9		1.4
45	Poland	3.8		1.3
46	Trinidad and Tobago	3.8		1.6
47	Portugal	3.8		1.2
48	Jordan	3.8		1.5
49	Mexico	3.7		1.4
50	Jamaica	3.7		1.4
51	Sri Lanka	3.6		1.4
52	Slovak Republic	3.6		1.5
53	Indonesia	3.6		1.4
54	Zimbabwe	3.6		1.4
55	Ghana	3.6		1.8
56	Algeria	3.6		1.7
57	Turkey	3.6		1.4
58	Philippines	3.6		1.6
59	Hungary	3.5		1.4
60	Dominican Republic	3.5		1.5
61	Panama	3.5		1.6
62	El Salvador	3.5		1.5
63	Namibia	3.5		1.5
64	Argentina	3.5		1.3
65	Colombia	3.4		1.4
66	Lithuania	3.4		1.4
67	Nigeria	3.4		1.8
68	Croatia	3.4		1.7
69	Ukraine	3.4		1.4
70	Russian Federation	3.4		1.6
71	Egypt	3.3		1.7
72	Botswana	3.3		1.5
72	Bulgaria	3.3		1.7
74	Pakistan	3.2		1.4
75	Romania	3.2		1.7
76	Kenya	3.2		1.5
77	Venezuela	3.1		1.3
78	Zambia	3.1		1.6
79	Malawi	3.1		1.6
80	Uganda	3.0		1.7
81	Uruguay	3.0		1.2
82	Guatemala	2.9		1.1
83	Bangladesh	2.8		1.4
84	Senegal	2.8		1.5
85	Peru	2.8		1.2
86	Serbia	2.8		1.5
87	Cameroon	2.7		1.7
88	Gambia	2.7		1.9
89	Tanzania	2.7		1.4
90	Macedonia, FYR	2.6		1.5
91	Honduras	2.5		1.2
92	Mali	2.5		1.5
93	Ecuador	2.5		1.0
94	Madagascar	2.3		1.3
95	Nicaragua	2.3		1.2
96	Paraguay	2.2		0.9
97	Mozambique	2.2		1.3
98	Angola	2.2		1.2
99	Bolivia	2.0		1.1
100	Ethiopia	2.0		1.0
101	Chad	1.9		1.5
102	Haiti	1.8		0.9

9.02   Local supplier quantity

Local suppliers in your country are (1 = largely nonexistent, 7 = numerous and include the most important materials, components, equipment, and services)

RANK	COUNTRY	SCORE	1 MEAN: 4.7 7	SD
1	Japan	6.3		1.0
2	Germany	6.1		1.1
3	United States	6.0		0.9
4	France	6.0		1.0
5	United Kingdom	5.9		1.1
6	Italy	5.8		1.0
7	Canada	5.7		1.0
8	India	5.7		1.0
9	Switzerland	5.7		1.1
10	Denmark	5.6		1.1
11	Australia	5.6		0.8
12	Taiwan	5.6		1.0
13	Israel	5.6		0.7
14	Belgium	5.5		1.1
15	Finland	5.5		1.0
16	Sweden	5.5		0.9
17	Netherlands	5.5		1.3
18	Austria	5.4		1.2
19	Korea	5.4		1.0
20	Lithuania	5.4		1.0
21	South Africa	5.4		0.9
22	Iceland	5.4		1.4
23	Spain	5.4		1.2
24	Hong Kong SAR	5.3		1.6
25	Brazil	5.3		1.1
26	New Zealand	5.2		1.2
27	Czech Republic	5.2		1.1
28	Thailand	5.2		1.0
29	Chile	5.2		1.1
30	Tunisia	5.1		1.3
31	China	5.1		1.0
32	Singapore	5.1		1.2
33	Vietnam	5.0		1.2
34	Morocco	5.0		1.4
35	Turkey	5.0		1.5
36	Ireland	5.0		1.4
36	Malaysia	5.0		1.1
36	Norway	5.0		1.3
39	Luxembourg	4.9		1.4
40	Slovak Republic	4.9		1.3
41	Dominican Republic	4.9		1.1
42	Cameroon	4.9		1.6
43	Kenya	4.9		1.2
44	Mexico	4.8		1.2
45	Latvia	4.8		1.2
46	Hungary	4.8		1.3
47	Greece	4.7		1.2
48	Portugal	4.7		1.1
49	Costa Rica	4.7		1.3
50	Mauritius	4.7		1.2
51	Estonia	4.7		1.2
52	Russian Federation	4.7		1.3

RANK	COUNTRY	SCORE	1 MEAN: 4.7 7	SD
53	Poland	4.7		1.1
54	Chad	4.6		2.1
55	Croatia	4.6		1.6
56	Malta	4.6		1.5
57	Jordan	4.6		1.3
58	Trinidad and Tobago	4.6		1.3
59	Pakistan	4.6		1.1
60	Colombia	4.6		1.2
61	Sri Lanka	4.5		1.1
62	Ghana	4.5		1.6
63	Bulgaria	4.5		1.4
64	Slovenia	4.5		1.2
65	Philippines	4.4		1.3
66	Ukraine	4.4		1.4
67	Egypt	4.4		1.4
68	Senegal	4.4		1.5
69	Romania	4.4		1.3
70	El Salvador	4.3		1.4
71	Panama	4.3		1.3
72	Peru	4.3		1.2
73	Uganda	4.3		1.6
74	Tanzania	4.2		1.4
75	Mali	4.2		2.0
76	Nigeria	4.2		1.7
77	Zimbabwe	4.2		1.3
78	Madagascar	4.1		1.5
79	Jamaica	4.1		1.2
79	Macedonia, FYR	4.1		1.8
81	Serbia	4.1		1.6
82	Guatemala	4.1		1.3
83	Argentina	4.0		1.2
84	Algeria	4.0		1.6
85	Indonesia	3.9		1.3
86	Zambia	3.9		1.4
87	Bangladesh	3.9		1.3
88	Venezuela	3.9		1.1
89	Ecuador	3.8		1.2
90	Namibia	3.8		1.5
91	Gambia	3.8		2.1
92	Uruguay	3.8		1.1
93	Malawi	3.8		1.4
94	Ethiopia	3.7		1.6
95	Honduras	3.4		1.3
96	Botswana	3.3		1.3
97	Nicaragua	3.2		1.4
98	Paraguay	3.1		1.2
99	Mozambique	3.1		1.4
100	Bolivia	2.7		1.0
101	Haiti	2.7		1.3
102	Angola	2.7		1.3

519

9.03 Local supplier quality

The quality of local suppliers in your country is (1 = poor, as they are inefficient and have little technological capability, 7 = very good, as they are internationally competitive and assist in new product and process development)

RANK	COUNTRY	SCORE	1 MEAN: 4.3 7	SD
1	Japan	6.1		1.0
2	Germany	6.1		0.8
3	United States	6.0		1.0
4	Finland	6.0		0.8
5	Denmark	6.0		0.8
6	Sweden	5.9		0.8
7	Switzerland	5.9		0.9
8	United Kingdom	5.8		0.9
9	Australia	5.8		0.7
10	Netherlands	5.8		1.0
11	France	5.8		1.1
12	Canada	5.8		0.9
13	Italy	5.7		1.1
14	New Zealand	5.7		0.9
15	Belgium	5.6		1.1
16	Austria	5.6		0.9
17	Israel	5.6		0.7
18	Iceland	5.6		1.2
19	Hong Kong SAR	5.4		1.2
20	Ireland	5.4		1.2
21	Singapore	5.3		1.0
22	Taiwan	5.3		1.1
23	Spain	5.3		1.1
24	Korea	5.3		1.0
25	South Africa	5.1		1.0
26	Norway	5.1		0.8
27	Thailand	5.1		1.1
28	Chile	5.0		1.1
29	Luxembourg	5.0		1.0
30	Brazil	5.0		1.2
31	Czech Republic	4.9		1.1
32	Turkey	4.9		1.2
33	Estonia	4.8		1.0
34	Latvia	4.7		1.1
35	Slovenia	4.7		1.1
36	Malaysia	4.7		1.2
37	India	4.6		1.3
38	Mexico	4.6		1.2
39	Lithuania	4.6		1.2
40	Portugal	4.5		1.0
41	Costa Rica	4.5		1.1
42	Greece	4.5		1.1
43	Tunisia	4.4		1.3
44	Mauritius	4.4		1.3
45	Vietnam	4.3		1.2
46	China	4.3		1.0
47	Colombia	4.3		1.1
48	Slovak Republic	4.3		1.3
49	Malta	4.3		1.2
50	Jordan	4.2		1.2
51	Poland	4.2		1.2
52	Trinidad and Tobago	4.2		1.3

RANK	COUNTRY	SCORE	1 MEAN: 4.3 7	SD
53	Ukraine	4.2		1.3
54	Jamaica	4.2		1.2
55	Namibia	4.2		1.3
56	Hungary	4.2		1.2
57	Panama	4.1		1.2
58	Kenya	4.1		1.3
59	Morocco	4.0		1.5
60	Egypt	4.0		1.3
61	Sri Lanka	3.9		1.2
62	Bulgaria	3.9		1.3
63	El Salvador	3.9		1.4
64	Argentina	3.9		1.1
65	Croatia	3.8		1.3
66	Dominican Republic	3.7		1.4
67	Guatemala	3.7		1.3
68	Philippines	3.7		1.3
69	Russian Federation	3.7		1.4
70	Senegal	3.7		1.4
71	Ghana	3.7		1.6
72	Zimbabwe	3.7		1.2
73	Peru	3.7		1.1
74	Uruguay	3.6		1.2
75	Tanzania	3.6		1.3
76	Indonesia	3.5		1.3
77	Pakistan	3.5		1.1
78	Romania	3.5		1.3
78	Venezuela	3.5		1.1
80	Malawi	3.4		1.3
81	Serbia	3.3		1.4
82	Uganda	3.3		1.6
83	Madagascar	3.3		1.2
84	Botswana	3.3		1.2
85	Macedonia, FYR	3.3		1.6
86	Cameroon	3.3		1.6
87	Mali	3.3		1.6
88	Gambia	3.2		1.7
89	Bangladesh	3.2		1.1
90	Algeria	3.2		1.3
91	Nigeria	3.1		1.4
92	Ecuador	3.0		1.1
93	Zambia	3.0		1.3
94	Ethiopia	2.9		1.4
95	Nicaragua	2.9		1.3
96	Honduras	2.8		1.1
97	Bolivia	2.7		1.0
98	Haiti	2.7		1.1
99	Mozambique	2.6		1.3
100	Paraguay	2.5		1.0
101	Chad	2.3		1.1
102	Angola	2.0		0.9

9.04 Presence of demanding regulatory standards

Standards for product/service quality, energy, and other regulations (outside environmental regulations) in your country are (1 = lax or nonexistent, 7 = among the world's most stringent)

RANK	COUNTRY	SCORE	MEAN: 4.2	SD
1	Germany	6.5		0.6
2	Sweden	6.2		0.6
3	Finland	6.2		0.7
4	Japan	6.1		0.9
5	Switzerland	6.1		0.8
6	United States	6.1		1.0
7	Austria	6.1		0.9
8	Denmark	6.0		0.7
9	Belgium	6.0		0.9
10	Australia	5.9		0.6
11	United Kingdom	5.9		0.9
12	Singapore	5.9		0.8
13	France	5.9		0.9
14	Netherlands	5.9		1.0
15	Canada	5.8		1.0
16	New Zealand	5.7		0.9
17	Iceland	5.6		0.8
18	Luxembourg	5.5		0.8
19	Israel	5.4		0.9
20	Slovak Republic	5.4		1.1
21	Hong Kong SAR	5.4		1.2
22	Norway	5.4		0.8
23	Ireland	5.4		1.2
24	Italy	5.3		1.2
25	Taiwan	5.3		1.0
26	Czech Republic	5.3		1.1
27	Spain	5.2		0.9
28	Korea	5.1		0.9
29	Slovenia	5.1		0.8
30	Hungary	5.0		1.3
31	Malaysia	5.0		0.9
32	South Africa	4.9		1.2
33	Tunisia	4.8		1.3
34	Latvia	4.8		1.0
35	Chile	4.8		0.9
36	Thailand	4.8		1.0
37	Estonia	4.8		1.1
38	Portugal	4.7		1.0
39	Brazil	4.7		0.9
40	Lithuania	4.6		1.2
41	Poland	4.4		1.2
42	Jordan	4.3		1.3
43	Mexico	4.3		1.1
44	Colombia	4.3		0.9
45	Greece	4.2		1.1
46	Costa Rica	4.2		1.3
47	Mauritius	4.2		1.2
48	Morocco	4.1		1.5
49	Jamaica	4.1		1.1
50	India	4.0		1.3
51	Russian Federation	4.0		1.5
52	Turkey	4.0		1.2

RANK	COUNTRY	SCORE	MEAN: 4.2	SD
53	China	4.0		1.1
54	Egypt	3.9		1.4
55	Malta	3.9		1.3
56	Namibia	3.9		1.2
57	Malawi	3.9		1.3
58	Argentina	3.9		1.1
59	Ukraine	3.9		1.3
60	Croatia	3.8		1.4
61	Tanzania	3.8		1.3
62	Uruguay	3.8		1.1
63	Ghana	3.7		1.5
64	Trinidad and Tobago	3.7		1.3
65	Panama	3.7		1.1
66	Peru	3.6		1.2
67	Bulgaria	3.6		1.2
68	Venezuela	3.6		1.1
69	Senegal	3.6		1.5
70	Serbia	3.6		1.5
71	Zimbabwe	3.5		1.4
72	Kenya	3.5		1.2
73	Vietnam	3.5		1.3
74	El Salvador	3.4		1.0
75	Indonesia	3.4		1.3
76	Sri Lanka	3.4		1.1
77	Botswana	3.4		1.2
78	Uganda	3.4		1.5
79	Macedonia, FYR	3.3		1.5
80	Philippines	3.3		1.2
81	Romania	3.2		1.6
82	Algeria	3.2		1.3
83	Dominican Republic	3.2		1.3
84	Nigeria	3.2		1.3
85	Cameroon	3.1		1.6
86	Gambia	3.1		1.5
87	Pakistan	3.0		1.1
88	Zambia	3.0		1.2
89	Guatemala	3.0		1.0
90	Ethiopia	2.9		1.3
91	Bolivia	2.9		1.1
92	Ecuador	2.8		1.1
93	Bangladesh	2.8		1.0
94	Honduras	2.7		1.0
95	Mali	2.6		1.5
96	Nicaragua	2.6		1.1
97	Paraguay	2.5		1.1
98	Madagascar	2.5		1.2
99	Mozambique	2.3		1.1
100	Angola	1.8		0.8
101	Chad	1.5		0.7
102	Haiti	1.5		0.7

9.05 Decentralization of corporate activity

Corporate activity in your country is (1 = dominated by a few business groups, 7 = spread among many firms)

RANK	COUNTRY	SCORE	1	MEAN: 3.9	7	SD		RANK	COUNTRY	SCORE	1	MEAN: 3.9	7	SD
1	Germany	6.3				0.8		53	Senegal	3.7				1.8
2	United States	6.1				1.1		54	Lithuania	3.6				1.2
3	United Kingdom	5.9				0.9		55	Ghana	3.6				1.7
4	Japan	5.8				1.2		56	Malta	3.6				1.3
5	Finland	5.7				1.3		57	Dominican Republic	3.5				1.6
6	Netherlands	5.6				1.2		58	Portugal	3.5				1.3
6	Switzerland	5.6				1.3		59	Tanzania	3.5				1.5
8	Taiwan	5.6				1.1		60	Zimbabwe	3.5				1.4
9	Austria	5.5				1.2		61	Turkey	3.5				1.5
10	Denmark	5.5				1.3		62	Mali	3.5				1.9
11	Canada	5.4				1.3		63	Macedonia, FYR	3.4				1.8
12	Sweden	5.4				1.4		64	Zambia	3.4				1.7
13	Belgium	5.3				1.1		65	Croatia	3.4				1.4
14	Australia	5.2				1.5		66	Kenya	3.4				1.5
15	Singapore	5.2				1.4		67	Mexico	3.4				1.4
16	Luxembourg	5.1				1.1		68	Jamaica	3.4				1.4
17	France	5.1				1.5		69	Namibia	3.3				1.4
18	Spain	4.8				1.4		70	Sri Lanka	3.3				1.4
19	Vietnam	4.8				1.2		71	Serbia	3.3				1.4
20	Tunisia	4.8				1.5		72	Panama	3.3				1.5
21	New Zealand	4.8				1.4		73	Cameroon	3.2				1.5
22	Brazil	4.7				1.4		74	Uganda	3.2				1.9
23	Malaysia	4.6				1.4		75	El Salvador	3.2				1.5
24	India	4.6				1.6		76	Trinidad and Tobago	3.2				1.5
25	China	4.6				1.3		77	Botswana	3.2				1.3
26	Ireland	4.5				1.5		78	Gambia	3.2				2.1
27	Thailand	4.5				1.4		79	Romania	3.2				1.5
28	Norway	4.4				1.2		80	Uruguay	3.1				1.4
29	Latvia	4.4				1.4		81	Russian Federation	3.1				1.4
30	Jordan	4.3				1.4		82	Madagascar	3.0				1.6
31	Costa Rica	4.3				1.3		83	Ukraine	3.0				1.2
32	Hong Kong SAR	4.2				2.0		84	Argentina	3.0				1.1
33	Italy	4.2				1.6		84	Colombia	3.0				1.3
34	Slovenia	4.2				1.5		86	Philippines	3.0				1.4
35	Morocco	4.2				1.8		87	Venezuela	3.0				1.0
36	Algeria	4.2				1.8		88	Peru	3.0				1.2
37	Israel	4.1				1.3		89	Guatemala	3.0				1.4
38	Hungary	4.1				1.4		90	Mauritius	2.9				1.2
39	Korea	4.1				1.5		91	Haiti	2.9				1.6
40	Chile	4.1				1.6		92	Ethiopia	2.9				1.4
41	Iceland	4.1				1.8		93	Malawi	2.7				1.1
42	Slovak Republic	4.0				1.6		94	Chad	2.6				2.1
43	Estonia	4.0				1.3		95	Mozambique	2.6				1.6
44	Greece	4.0				1.3		96	Paraguay	2.6				1.2
45	Bulgaria	3.9				1.7		97	Bangladesh	2.6				1.3
46	Nigeria	3.9				1.8		98	Bolivia	2.4				1.1
47	Egypt	3.9				1.7		99	Honduras	2.4				1.3
48	South Africa	3.9				1.5		100	Ecuador	2.3				1.1
49	Poland	3.8				1.4		101	Angola	2.1				1.3
50	Czech Republic	3.8				1.4		102	Nicaragua	2.1				1.2
51	Pakistan	3.8				1.5								
52	Indonesia	3.8				1.3								

How common are clusters in your country? (1 = limited and shallow, 7 = common and deep)

RANK	COUNTRY	SCORE	1 MEAN: 3.2 7	SD
1	Finland	6.0		1.1
2	Italy	5.8		1.3
3	Taiwan	5.5		1.2
4	Singapore	5.2		1.4
5	Japan	5.1		1.3
6	United States	4.9		1.4
7	Ireland	4.8		1.4
8	Korea	4.8		1.2
9	Hong Kong SAR	4.6		1.8
10	Thailand	4.4		1.2
11	Denmark	4.4		1.3
12	Canada	4.3		1.4
13	Pakistan	4.2		1.6
14	United Kingdom	4.2		1.3
15	Sweden	4.2		1.6
16	Germany	4.1		1.6
17	India	4.1		1.6
18	Switzerland	4.0		1.6
19	Austria	4.0		1.6
19	France	4.0		1.4
19	Netherlands	4.0		1.3
22	Nigeria	4.0		1.9
23	Norway	4.0		1.7
24	Malaysia	3.9		1.2
25	Brazil	3.9		1.4
26	Egypt	3.9		1.7
26	Israel	3.9		1.6
28	South Africa	3.8		1.5
29	Sri Lanka	3.8		1.5
30	China	3.7		1.3
31	Mauritius	3.6		1.5
32	Turkey	3.6		1.4
33	Indonesia	3.5		1.3
34	Australia	3.5		1.2
35	Spain	3.5		1.4
36	Luxembourg	3.5		1.6
37	Iceland	3.4		1.7
38	Belgium	3.4		1.5
39	Latvia	3.4		1.6
40	Morocco	3.3		1.6
41	Portugal	3.3		1.4
42	Kenya	3.3		1.7
43	Philippines	3.3		1.3
44	New Zealand	3.3		1.4
45	Vietnam	3.3		1.5
46	Lithuania	3.3		1.3
47	Mexico	3.2		1.4
48	Romania	3.2		1.6
49	Poland	3.2		1.3
50	Bangladesh	3.2		1.8
51	Uganda	3.2		1.8
52	Jordan	3.1		1.6
53	Trinidad and Tobago	3.1		1.5
54	Slovak Republic	3.1		1.5
55	Ghana	3.1		1.7
56	Russian Federation	3.0		1.3
57	Panama	3.0		1.4
58	Colombia	3.0		1.2
59	Botswana	2.9		1.7
60	Zimbabwe	2.9		1.5
61	Greece	2.9		1.4
62	Jamaica	2.9		1.6
63	Tunisia	2.9		1.4
64	Costa Rica	2.8		1.3
65	Chile	2.8		1.4
66	Namibia	2.8		1.5
66	Slovenia	2.8		1.2
68	Gambia	2.8		2.0
69	Zambia	2.8		1.7
70	Tanzania	2.8		1.5
71	Ecuador	2.7		1.7
72	Hungary	2.7		1.5
73	Serbia	2.7		1.7
74	Estonia	2.7		1.5
75	Malawi	2.7		1.6
76	Czech Republic	2.7		1.4
77	Bulgaria	2.7		1.5
78	Croatia	2.7		1.6
79	Malta	2.6		1.4
80	Venezuela	2.5		1.4
81	Guatemala	2.5		1.2
82	Dominican Republic	2.5		1.6
83	Argentina	2.4		1.0
84	Honduras	2.4		1.4
85	Peru	2.3		1.3
86	Ethiopia	2.3		1.5
87	El Salvador	2.3		1.1
88	Ukraine	2.3		1.1
89	Chad	2.2		1.5
90	Uruguay	2.2		1.2
91	Mali	2.2		1.6
92	Madagascar	2.2		1.3
93	Bolivia	2.1		1.1
94	Cameroon	2.0		1.3
95	Macedonia, FYR	2.0		1.2
96	Senegal	2.0		1.1
97	Algeria	1.9		1.2
98	Nicaragua	1.9		1.2
99	Paraguay	1.9		1.1
100	Mozambique	1.8		1.1
101	Haiti	1.7		1.1
102	Angola	1.6		1.2

523

9.07 Extent of collaboration among clusters

Collaboration in your clusters with suppliers and partners is (1 = almost nonexistent, 7 = extensive and involves suppliers, local customers, and local research institutions)

RANK	COUNTRY	SCORE	MEAN: 3.6	SD
1	Finland	6.0		1.1
2	Japan	5.7		1.0
3	United States	5.5		1.4
4	Italy	5.4		1.3
4	Taiwan	5.4		1.0
6	Germany	5.3		1.4
7	Singapore	4.9		1.4
8	Canada	4.9		1.1
9	Sweden	4.8		1.3
10	Denmark	4.8		1.4
11	Austria	4.8		1.3
12	Ireland	4.7		1.2
13	Korea	4.7		1.1
14	Croatia	4.7		1.3
15	France	4.7		1.2
16	Netherlands	4.6		1.4
17	Switzerland	4.5		1.5
18	China	4.5		1.3
19	Hong Kong SAR	4.5		1.4
20	South Africa	4.4		1.3
21	Norway	4.4		1.4
22	United Kingdom	4.4		1.3
23	Israel	4.3		1.4
24	Romania	4.3		1.6
25	Slovak Republic	4.2		1.6
26	Malaysia	4.2		1.1
27	Thailand	4.2		1.1
28	New Zealand	4.1		1.2
29	Latvia	4.1		1.3
30	Brazil	4.1		1.2
31	Iceland	4.0		1.4
32	Poland	4.0		1.3
33	Egypt	4.0		1.3
34	Belgium	4.0		1.5
35	Australia	4.0		1.1
36	Estonia	3.9		1.4
37	India	3.9		1.4
38	Spain	3.9		1.4
39	Luxembourg	3.8		1.7
40	Russian Federation	3.7		1.3
41	Czech Republic	3.7		1.4
42	Vietnam	3.7		1.2
43	Turkey	3.7		1.3
44	Lithuania	3.7		1.2
45	Jordan	3.6		1.4
46	Sri Lanka	3.6		1.2
47	Indonesia	3.6		1.2
48	Mauritius	3.6		1.5
49	Uganda	3.6		1.7
50	Slovenia	3.6		1.3
51	Portugal	3.5		1.2
52	Ghana	3.5		1.6

RANK	COUNTRY	SCORE	MEAN: 3.6	SD
53	Philippines	3.5		1.4
54	Mexico	3.5		1.3
55	Pakistan	3.5		1.1
56	Morocco	3.4		1.4
57	Chile	3.4		1.5
58	Tunisia	3.4		1.5
59	Ukraine	3.4		1.4
60	Kenya	3.3		1.6
61	Greece	3.3		1.4
62	Bulgaria	3.3		1.6
63	Nigeria	3.3		1.6
64	Costa Rica	3.3		1.2
65	Serbia	3.2		1.6
66	Panama	3.2		1.4
67	Colombia	3.2		1.2
68	Trinidad and Tobago	3.1		1.3
69	Hungary	3.1		1.5
70	Zimbabwe	3.1		1.4
71	Jamaica	3.1		1.3
72	Tanzania	3.1		1.4
73	Namibia	3.0		1.3
74	Argentina	3.0		1.3
75	Guatemala	3.0		1.3
76	Macedonia, FYR	3.0		1.7
77	Zambia	2.9		1.5
78	Botswana	2.9		1.3
79	Malta	2.9		1.6
80	Bangladesh	2.8		1.4
81	Malawi	2.8		1.6
82	Peru	2.7		1.3
83	Madagascar	2.7		1.5
84	Gambia	2.6		1.8
85	El Salvador	2.6		1.2
86	Ecuador	2.5		1.2
87	Dominican Republic	2.5		1.5
88	Senegal	2.5		1.4
89	Cameroon	2.5		1.4
90	Honduras	2.4		1.2
91	Uruguay	2.4		1.3
92	Venezuela	2.3		1.3
93	Ethiopia	2.3		1.3
94	Haiti	2.3		1.2
95	Algeria	2.2		1.3
96	Nicaragua	2.2		1.4
97	Bolivia	2.2		1.2
97	Paraguay	2.2		1.0
99	Chad	2.1		1.5
100	Mozambique	2.0		1.2
101	Mali	2.0		1.4
102	Angola	1.6		0.9

9.08 Local availability of components and parts

In your industry, how are components and parts obtained? (1 = almost always imported, 7 = almost always sourced locally)

RANK	COUNTRY	SCORE	1 MEAN: 3.2 7	SD
1	Japan	5.9		1.0
2	Italy	5.5		1.5
3	United States	5.3		1.4
4	Germany	5.1		1.1
5	Finland	5.1		1.3
6	China	5.0		1.4
7	Spain	4.9		1.5
8	Canada	4.7		1.3
9	Sweden	4.7		1.3
10	Denmark	4.7		1.4
11	Korea	4.5		1.2
12	United Kingdom	4.5		1.4
13	France	4.5		1.2
14	India	4.4		1.6
15	Switzerland	4.3		1.3
16	Austria	4.3		1.1
17	Thailand	4.2		1.5
18	Russian Federation	4.2		1.6
19	Taiwan	4.1		1.7
20	Brazil	4.1		1.4
21	Czech Republic	4.1		1.5
22	Netherlands	4.0		1.5
23	Ukraine	3.9		1.5
24	Egypt	3.9		1.7
25	Belgium	3.8		1.6
26	Lithuania	3.8		1.6
27	South Africa	3.8		1.4
28	Singapore	3.8		1.7
29	Australia	3.7		1.3
30	Norway	3.7		1.6
31	Mexico	3.7		1.5
32	Poland	3.6		1.4
33	Latvia	3.6		1.5
34	Indonesia	3.6		1.3
35	Ireland	3.6		1.6
36	Romania	3.5		1.5
37	Portugal	3.5		1.4
38	Bulgaria	3.5		1.7
39	Slovak Republic	3.5		1.3
40	Slovenia	3.4		1.2
41	Turkey	3.4		1.4
42	Chile	3.4		1.6
43	New Zealand	3.4		1.4
44	Hungary	3.3		1.5
45	Vietnam	3.3		1.4
46	Malaysia	3.3		1.4
47	Israel	3.3		1.1
48	Argentina	3.3		1.5
49	Costa Rica	3.3		1.6
50	Croatia	3.3		1.5
51	Hong Kong SAR	3.3		1.8
52	Colombia	3.2		1.4
53	Greece	3.1		1.2
54	Iceland	3.0		1.4
55	Estonia	3.0		1.2
56	Guatemala	2.9		1.5
57	Macedonia, FYR	2.9		1.8
58	Sri Lanka	2.9		1.4
59	Tunisia	2.9		1.2
60	Kenya	2.8		1.6
61	Serbia	2.8		1.5
62	Peru	2.8		1.3
63	Mauritius	2.8		1.4
64	Pakistan	2.8		1.2
65	Ghana	2.8		1.7
66	Jordan	2.7		1.5
67	Philippines	2.6		1.2
68	Dominican Republic	2.6		1.7
69	Morocco	2.6		1.5
70	El Salvador	2.5		1.4
71	Uganda	2.5		1.6
72	Nigeria	2.5		1.5
73	Namibia	2.5		1.5
74	Panama	2.4		1.5
75	Luxembourg	2.4		1.2
76	Tanzania	2.4		1.4
77	Ecuador	2.3		1.2
78	Uruguay	2.3		1.4
79	Malawi	2.3		1.5
80	Bangladesh	2.3		1.4
81	Trinidad and Tobago	2.3		1.2
82	Gambia	2.2		1.7
83	Bolivia	2.2		1.2
84	Zambia	2.1		1.6
85	Paraguay	2.1		1.2
86	Honduras	2.1		1.3
87	Malta	2.1		1.2
88	Botswana	2.0		1.4
89	Nicaragua	2.0		1.4
90	Jamaica	2.0		1.3
91	Zimbabwe	1.9		0.9
92	Ethiopia	1.8		1.1
93	Venezuela	1.8		0.9
94	Madagascar	1.7		1.2
95	Algeria	1.7		0.8
96	Cameroon	1.6		0.9
97	Mozambique	1.6		1.0
98	Senegal	1.5		0.7
99	Chad	1.5		1.3
100	Angola	1.3		0.8
101	Mali	1.3		0.7
102	Haiti	1.1		0.3

9.09 Local availability of process machinery

In your industry, how is process machinery obtained? (1 = almost always imported, 7 = almost always available locally from world-class suppliers)

RANK	COUNTRY	SCORE	1 MEAN: 2.8 7	SD
1	Japan	5.8		1.1
2	Italy	5.6		1.4
3	Germany	5.3		1.1
4	United States	5.2		1.6
5	Finland	4.9		1.4
6	China	4.6		1.4
7	Canada	4.5		1.2
8	Korea	4.5		1.1
9	Denmark	4.4		1.5
10	Sweden	4.3		1.3
11	Spain	4.3		1.6
11	Switzerland	4.3		1.6
13	France	4.2		1.2
14	Austria	4.1		1.6
15	United Kingdom	4.0		1.5
16	Netherlands	4.0		1.6
17	Taiwan	3.9		1.7
18	Russian Federation	3.9		1.6
19	Czech Republic	3.8		1.8
20	India	3.8		1.7
21	Belgium	3.7		1.6
22	Ukraine	3.7		1.4
23	Brazil	3.6		1.3
24	Poland	3.5		1.4
25	Indonesia	3.4		1.4
26	Latvia	3.4		1.7
27	Bulgaria	3.4		1.7
28	Lithuania	3.4		1.6
29	Egypt	3.3		1.9
30	Romania	3.3		1.5
31	Turkey	3.3		1.4
32	South Africa	3.3		1.3
33	Ireland	3.2		1.6
34	Norway	3.2		1.4
35	Thailand	3.2		1.6
36	Singapore	3.2		1.8
37	New Zealand	3.1		1.3
38	Israel	3.0		1.1
39	Hungary	3.0		1.5
40	Vietnam	3.0		1.2
41	Hong Kong SAR	2.9		1.8
42	Croatia	2.9		1.5
43	Argentina	2.9		1.4
44	Portugal	2.8		1.4
45	Chile	2.8		1.6
46	Greece	2.8		1.4
47	Mexico	2.8		1.5
48	Slovenia	2.7		1.2
49	Sri Lanka	2.7		1.5
50	Australia	2.7		0.9
51	Slovak Republic	2.7		1.4
52	Luxembourg	2.7		1.5

RANK	COUNTRY	SCORE	1 MEAN: 2.8 7	SD
53	Iceland	2.7		1.2
53	Morocco	2.7		1.6
55	Costa Rica	2.7		1.7
56	Pakistan	2.6		1.2
57	Colombia	2.6		1.1
58	Malaysia	2.5		1.4
59	Macedonia, FYR	2.5		1.7
60	Tunisia	2.5		1.2
61	Uganda	2.4		1.7
62	Estonia	2.4		1.0
63	Serbia	2.4		1.4
64	Namibia	2.4		1.4
65	Ghana	2.3		1.6
66	Jordan	2.3		1.3
67	Kenya	2.3		1.4
68	Nigeria	2.2		1.4
69	Mauritius	2.2		1.3
70	Guatemala	2.2		1.1
71	Peru	2.2		1.1
72	Philippines	2.2		1.1
73	Tanzania	2.1		1.2
74	Dominican Republic	2.0		1.1
74	El Salvador	2.0		1.3
74	Gambia	2.0		1.4
77	Panama	2.0		1.3
78	Uruguay	1.9		1.3
79	Malta	1.9		1.3
80	Malawi	1.9		1.4
81	Ecuador	1.9		1.1
82	Trinidad and Tobago	1.8		1.0
83	Botswana	1.8		1.1
84	Jamaica	1.8		1.2
85	Paraguay	1.8		1.1
86	Zambia	1.8		1.1
87	Honduras	1.8		1.1
88	Bolivia	1.8		1.1
89	Nicaragua	1.7		1.3
90	Senegal	1.7		1.1
91	Bangladesh	1.7		1.2
92	Madagascar	1.7		1.1
93	Algeria	1.6		0.8
94	Ethiopia	1.6		0.9
95	Zimbabwe	1.6		0.6
96	Venezuela	1.5		0.6
97	Mozambique	1.4		0.9
98	Chad	1.3		1.0
99	Cameroon	1.2		0.6
100	Mali	1.2		0.5
101	Angola	1.2		0.8
102	Haiti	1.1		0.3

9.10 Local availability of specialized research and training services

In your industry, specialized research and training services are (1 = not available in the country, 7 = available from world-class local institutions)

RANK	COUNTRY	SCORE	1 MEAN: 4.1 7	SD
1	United States	6.4		0.9
2	Japan	6.0		0.9
3	Finland	6.0		0.8
4	United Kingdom	5.9		0.9
5	Germany	5.9		1.0
6	Israel	5.7		1.2
7	Switzerland	5.7		1.2
8	Sweden	5.6		0.9
9	Canada	5.6		0.8
10	Netherlands	5.6		1.1
11	Denmark	5.6		0.9
12	France	5.5		1.2
13	Austria	5.4		1.5
14	Australia	5.4		0.9
15	Belgium	5.2		1.2
16	Italy	5.1		1.4
17	Singapore	5.0		1.5
18	New Zealand	5.0		1.0
19	Korea	4.9		1.0
20	Ireland	4.8		1.3
21	South Africa	4.7		1.3
22	Taiwan	4.7		1.1
23	Estonia	4.7		1.3
24	Iceland	4.7		1.3
25	Spain	4.7		1.2
26	India	4.7		1.3
27	Norway	4.6		1.2
28	Poland	4.6		1.3
29	Hong Kong SAR	4.6		1.6
30	Brazil	4.6		1.3
31	Slovenia	4.5		1.2
32	Chile	4.5		1.4
33	Russian Federation	4.5		1.4
34	Czech Republic	4.5		1.3
35	Croatia	4.4		1.4
36	Mexico	4.4		1.2
37	Costa Rica	4.4		1.5
38	Romania	4.3		1.7
39	China	4.3		1.3
40	Tunisia	4.3		1.7
41	Latvia	4.3		1.2
42	Lithuania	4.3		1.1
43	Portugal	4.3		1.4
44	Argentina	4.2		1.5
45	Jordan	4.2		1.5
46	Ghana	4.1		1.7
47	Kenya	4.1		1.6
48	Bulgaria	4.1		1.3
49	Jamaica	4.1		1.7
50	Hungary	4.0		1.2
51	Dominican Republic	4.0		1.3
52	Morocco	4.0		1.7
53	Ukraine	4.0		1.5
54	Greece	4.0		1.2
55	Slovak Republic	4.0		1.3
56	Vietnam	4.0		1.1
57	Thailand	3.9		1.4
58	Egypt	3.9		1.6
59	Colombia	3.8		1.2
60	Uruguay	3.8		1.3
61	Uganda	3.8		1.8
62	Mauritius	3.8		1.7
63	Malaysia	3.8		1.2
64	Malta	3.7		1.6
65	Turkey	3.7		1.3
66	Trinidad and Tobago	3.7		1.6
67	Venezuela	3.7		1.5
68	Serbia	3.6		1.4
69	Panama	3.6		1.5
70	Indonesia	3.6		1.4
71	Sri Lanka	3.6		1.4
72	Nigeria	3.6		1.7
73	Peru	3.5		1.7
74	Luxembourg	3.5		1.8
75	Guatemala	3.4		1.4
76	Macedonia, FYR	3.4		1.7
77	Tanzania	3.4		1.6
78	Malawi	3.3		1.6
79	Zambia	3.3		1.7
80	Zimbabwe	3.2		1.3
81	Cameroon	3.2		2.1
82	Ecuador	3.2		1.6
83	Philippines	3.1		1.2
84	Namibia	3.1		1.4
85	El Salvador	3.1		1.4
86	Senegal	3.0		2.0
87	Botswana	3.0		1.6
88	Honduras	3.0		1.5
89	Algeria	2.9		1.7
90	Madagascar	2.9		1.8
91	Nicaragua	2.8		1.6
92	Bolivia	2.8		1.4
93	Haiti	2.7		1.6
94	Pakistan	2.7		1.2
95	Gambia	2.7		1.8
96	Paraguay	2.6		1.4
97	Mali	2.5		1.8
98	Ethiopia	2.5		1.3
99	Mozambique	2.4		1.3
100	Bangladesh	2.2		1.1
101	Angola	1.9		0.9
102	Chad	1.8		1.5

10.01   Nature of competitive advantage

Competitiveness of your country's companies in international markets is primarily due to (1 = low cost or local natural resources, 7 = unique products and processes)

RANK	COUNTRY	SCORE	1 MEAN: 3.5 7	SD
1	Japan	6.3		0.9
2	Finland	6.2		0.7
3	Germany	6.2		0.8
4	Denmark	6.2		0.7
5	Switzerland	6.0		1.0
6	Sweden	5.9		0.7
7	United Kingdom	5.9		0.8
8	Israel	5.9		0.9
9	France	5.7		0.8
10	United States	5.6		1.5
11	Luxembourg	5.6		0.8
12	Belgium	5.4		1.2
13	Netherlands	5.4		1.2
14	Austria	5.3		1.2
15	Italy	5.3		1.2
16	Singapore	5.2		1.2
17	Taiwan	5.2		0.8
18	Norway	5.0		1.3
19	Hong Kong SAR	4.9		1.5
20	Ireland	4.7		1.3
21	Korea	4.7		1.1
22	Iceland	4.6		1.4
23	Jamaica	4.3		1.6
24	Canada	4.1		1.5
25	Slovenia	4.0		1.2
26	Latvia	4.0		1.5
27	Spain	3.9		1.2
28	Costa Rica	3.9		1.4
29	New Zealand	3.7		1.3
30	Botswana	3.7		1.6
31	Malta	3.7		1.3
32	Namibia	3.6		1.7
33	Egypt	3.5		1.6
34	Thailand	3.5		1.4
35	El Salvador	3.5		1.5
36	Mauritius	3.5		1.2
37	Australia	3.5		1.4
38	Indonesia	3.4		1.5
39	Zambia	3.4		1.9
40	Panama	3.4		1.3
41	Kenya	3.4		1.5
42	Greece	3.4		1.2
43	Senegal	3.4		1.4
44	Croatia	3.3		1.5
45	Czech Republic	3.3		1.4
46	Sri Lanka	3.3		1.6
47	Lithuania	3.2		1.4
48	Poland	3.2		1.2
49	Malaysia	3.2		1.3
50	Malawi	3.2		1.6
51	Ghana	3.2		1.7
52	Tunisia	3.2		1.3

RANK	COUNTRY	SCORE	1 MEAN: 3.5 7	SD
52	Uganda	3.2		1.9
54	Philippines	3.2		1.5
55	Hungary	3.1		1.4
56	Dominican Republic	3.1		1.3
57	Colombia	3.1		1.1
58	Jordan	3.1		1.1
59	China	3.0		1.4
60	Nigeria	3.0		1.6
61	Ukraine	3.0		1.2
62	Tanzania	3.0		1.3
63	Ecuador	3.0		1.5
64	Guatemala	2.9		1.3
65	Mexico	2.9		1.3
66	Brazil	2.9		1.1
67	South Africa	2.9		1.2
68	Estonia	2.9		1.2
69	Morocco	2.8		1.7
70	Uruguay	2.8		1.4
71	Gambia	2.8		1.5
72	India	2.8		1.2
73	Portugal	2.8		0.9
74	Chile	2.7		1.2
75	Bulgaria	2.7		1.3
76	Vietnam	2.7		1.4
77	Russian Federation	2.7		1.3
78	Trinidad and Tobago	2.7		1.3
79	Turkey	2.7		1.2
80	Peru	2.6		1.3
81	Slovak Republic	2.6		0.9
82	Romania	2.6		1.4
83	Nicaragua	2.5		1.3
84	Ethiopia	2.5		1.8
85	Venezuela	2.5		1.2
86	Honduras	2.5		1.3
87	Serbia	2.5		1.6
88	Pakistan	2.4		1.1
89	Argentina	2.4		1.1
90	Chad	2.4		1.6
91	Mozambique	2.4		1.5
92	Haiti	2.3		1.6
93	Madagascar	2.2		1.1
94	Cameroon	2.2		1.5
95	Bolivia	2.2		1.2
96	Paraguay	2.2		1.1
97	Zimbabwe	2.2		1.4
98	Mali	2.2		1.2
99	Macedonia, FYR	2.1		1.4
100	Algeria	2.1		1.0
101	Bangladesh	2.1		0.9
102	Angola	2.0		1.4

10.02   Value chain presence

Exporting companies in your country are (1 = primarily involved in resource extraction or production, 7 = not only produce but also perform product design, marketing sales, logistics, and after-sales services)

RANK	COUNTRY	SCORE	1 MEAN: 3.8 7	SD
1	Finland	6.4		0.6
2	Japan	6.4		0.7
3	Germany	6.4		0.9
4	Switzerland	6.3		0.7
5	Denmark	6.3		1.0
6	Sweden	6.3		0.8
7	France	6.2		0.9
8	United Kingdom	6.2		0.9
9	United States	6.1		1.0
10	Hong Kong SAR	5.9		1.1
11	Belgium	5.9		1.2
12	Italy	5.9		1.2
13	Luxembourg	5.8		0.9
14	Netherlands	5.7		1.1
15	Singapore	5.7		1.2
16	Austria	5.6		1.2
17	Israel	5.6		1.4
18	Ireland	5.3		1.4
19	Spain	5.2		1.1
20	Taiwan	5.1		1.2
21	Korea	5.1		1.2
22	Mauritius	4.8		1.1
23	Norway	4.7		1.5
24	Tunisia	4.7		1.4
25	Iceland	4.6		1.4
26	Lithuania	4.6		1.3
27	India	4.4		1.4
28	Czech Republic	4.4		1.3
29	Slovenia	4.4		1.3
30	Canada	4.3		1.6
31	Costa Rica	4.2		1.3
32	Malta	4.2		1.5
33	Egypt	4.1		1.5
34	Turkey	4.1		1.2
35	Latvia	4.1		1.4
36	Mexico	4.1		1.5
37	Poland	4.0		1.2
38	Hungary	4.0		1.6
39	Thailand	4.0		1.4
40	Malaysia	3.9		1.4
41	New Zealand	3.9		1.4
42	Portugal	3.9		1.2
43	Philippines	3.8		1.6
44	El Salvador	3.8		1.5
45	Brazil	3.7		1.3
46	Jordan	3.7		1.4
47	Greece	3.7		1.4
48	Colombia	3.7		1.4
49	Estonia	3.6		1.4
50	Sri Lanka	3.6		1.5
51	Morocco	3.5		1.8
52	Croatia	3.5		1.4

RANK	COUNTRY	SCORE	1 MEAN: 3.8 7	SD
53	South Africa	3.5		1.5
54	Indonesia	3.5		1.4
55	China	3.5		1.4
56	Romania	3.5		1.8
57	Vietnam	3.4		1.7
58	Slovak Republic	3.4		1.4
59	Dominican Republic	3.3		1.3
60	Panama	3.3		1.5
61	Ukraine	3.3		1.5
62	Chile	3.2		1.3
63	Jamaica	3.2		1.5
64	Ghana	3.2		1.7
65	Kenya	3.1		1.5
66	Macedonia, FYR	3.1		1.7
67	Guatemala	3.1		1.3
68	Pakistan	3.0		1.4
69	Malawi	3.0		1.6
70	Australia	3.0		1.0
71	Bulgaria	2.9		1.4
72	Uruguay	2.9		1.2
73	Trinidad and Tobago	2.9		1.4
74	Senegal	2.9		1.6
75	Uganda	2.9		1.7
76	Bangladesh	2.9		1.4
77	Namibia	2.8		1.6
78	Gambia	2.8		1.6
79	Cameroon	2.8		1.7
80	Honduras	2.8		1.4
81	Madagascar	2.7		1.5
82	Haiti	2.7		1.3
83	Argentina	2.7		1.2
84	Peru	2.6		1.3
85	Tanzania	2.6		1.5
86	Russian Federation	2.6		1.3
87	Botswana	2.5		1.4
88	Nicaragua	2.5		1.4
89	Mali	2.5		1.5
90	Ecuador	2.5		1.2
91	Nigeria	2.4		1.5
92	Serbia	2.4		1.3
93	Venezuela	2.4		1.4
94	Zimbabwe	2.3		1.4
95	Zambia	2.3		1.3
96	Mozambique	2.2		1.4
97	Ethiopia	2.1		1.0
98	Chad	2.1		1.4
99	Paraguay	2.0		1.2
100	Bolivia	2.0		0.9
101	Algeria	1.9		1.2
102	Angola	1.4		0.8

531

10.03 Extent of branding

Companies in your country that sell internationally (1 = sell into commodity markets or to other companies that handle marketing, 7 = have well-developed international brands and sales organizations)

RANK	COUNTRY	SCORE	1 MEAN: 3.5 7	SD
1	Germany	6.5		0.6
2	Sweden	6.4		0.7
3	Switzerland	6.3		0.7
4	France	6.2		0.9
5	United Kingdom	6.2		0.9
6	United States	6.2		0.9
7	Japan	6.1		1.0
8	Finland	5.9		0.6
9	Denmark	5.8		0.9
10	Netherlands	5.8		1.1
11	Italy	5.5		1.2
12	Belgium	5.3		1.3
13	Austria	5.3		1.1
14	Luxembourg	5.2		1.4
15	Singapore	5.1		1.3
16	Ireland	5.0		1.5
17	Hong Kong SAR	4.9		1.6
18	Israel	4.8		1.3
19	Spain	4.7		1.0
20	Korea	4.7		1.1
21	Iceland	4.7		1.4
22	Canada	4.5		1.5
22	Taiwan	4.5		1.2
24	Norway	4.2		1.5
25	Slovenia	4.1		1.2
26	New Zealand	4.0		1.4
27	Mauritius	4.0		1.4
28	Latvia	3.9		1.5
29	Hungary	3.9		1.5
30	Mexico	3.9		1.5
31	China	3.8		1.4
32	Czech Republic	3.8		1.3
33	Vietnam	3.8		1.4
34	Poland	3.7		1.2
35	Malaysia	3.6		1.2
36	Malta	3.6		1.5
37	Thailand	3.6		1.4
38	Tunisia	3.6		1.4
39	Ukraine	3.5		1.4
40	Egypt	3.5		1.6
41	Morocco	3.5		1.7
42	Brazil	3.5		1.2
43	Lithuania	3.5		1.3
44	Slovak Republic	3.4		1.3
45	Jamaica	3.4		1.6
46	South Africa	3.4		1.4
47	Greece	3.4		1.3
48	Russian Federation	3.4		1.4
49	Croatia	3.4		1.3
50	Indonesia	3.4		1.5
51	Costa Rica	3.3		1.2
52	Australia	3.3		1.0
53	Sri Lanka	3.3		1.6
54	Senegal	3.3		1.7
55	Portugal	3.2		1.0
56	Colombia	3.2		1.2
57	India	3.2		1.2
58	Philippines	3.2		1.4
59	Panama	3.2		1.5
60	Jordan	3.1		1.3
61	Turkey	3.1		1.2
62	El Salvador	3.0		1.4
63	Chile	3.0		1.2
64	Trinidad and Tobago	3.0		1.3
65	Dominican Republic	3.0		1.3
66	Estonia	2.9		1.2
67	Romania	2.9		1.6
68	Ghana	2.8		1.5
69	Kenya	2.8		1.4
70	Uruguay	2.8		1.1
71	Madagascar	2.8		1.4
72	Bulgaria	2.7		1.3
73	Guatemala	2.7		1.2
74	Pakistan	2.7		1.3
75	Serbia	2.6		1.3
76	Namibia	2.6		1.2
77	Mali	2.6		1.7
78	Uganda	2.5		1.7
79	Argentina	2.5		1.2
80	Macedonia, FYR	2.5		1.4
81	Gambia	2.5		1.5
82	Botswana	2.5		1.3
83	Algeria	2.5		1.4
84	Tanzania	2.5		1.2
85	Malawi	2.4		1.3
86	Cameroon	2.4		1.5
87	Peru	2.3		1.0
88	Ecuador	2.3		0.9
89	Honduras	2.3		1.1
90	Zambia	2.3		1.2
91	Nigeria	2.3		1.3
92	Haiti	2.3		1.2
93	Nicaragua	2.3		1.2
94	Venezuela	2.2		1.2
95	Zimbabwe	2.2		1.1
96	Bangladesh	2.2		1.2
97	Mozambique	2.1		1.2
98	Bolivia	2.0		0.8
99	Chad	2.0		1.3
100	Ethiopia	1.9		1.0
101	Paraguay	1.8		1.0
102	Angola	1.6		0.9

532

10.04 Capacity for innovation

Companies obtain technology (1 = exclusively from licensing or imitating foreign companies, 7 = by conducting formal research and pioneering their own new products and processes)

RANK	COUNTRY	SCORE		SD	RANK	COUNTRY	SCORE		SD
1	Finland	6.1		0.6	53	Ghana	3.2		1.6
2	Sweden	6.0		0.8	54	Mauritius	3.2		1.2
3	Germany	5.9		0.7	55	Morocco	3.2		1.7
4	Japan	5.8		0.8	56	Turkey	3.1		1.5
5	Switzerland	5.8		0.7	57	Romania	3.1		1.5
6	France	5.8		0.9	58	Tunisia	3.1		1.3
7	United States	5.7		1.2	59	Malta	3.0		1.2
8	United Kingdom	5.5		1.0	60	Chile	3.0		1.1
9	Denmark	5.5		0.9	61	Malawi	3.0		1.6
10	Israel	5.3		1.3	62	Dominican Republic	2.9		1.3
10	Netherlands	5.3		1.0	63	Philippines	2.9		1.2
12	Belgium	5.1		1.1	64	Senegal	2.9		1.2
13	Canada	5.0		1.2	65	Jamaica	2.9		1.3
14	Luxembourg	4.9		1.2	66	Namibia	2.9		1.3
15	Austria	4.9		0.9	67	Zambia	2.8		1.2
16	Korea	4.7		1.0	68	Jordan	2.8		1.3
17	Italy	4.7		1.0	69	Kenya	2.8		1.1
18	Norway	4.7		1.2	70	Uruguay	2.7		1.2
19	Ireland	4.6		1.3	71	Macedonia, FYR	2.7		1.6
20	Taiwan	4.6		1.3	72	Argentina	2.7		1.1
21	Singapore	4.5		1.3	73	Tanzania	2.7		1.3
22	Iceland	4.5		1.2	74	Guatemala	2.7		1.2
23	Slovenia	4.3		1.0	75	Uganda	2.7		1.6
24	New Zealand	4.3		0.9	76	Bulgaria	2.7		1.2
25	Spain	4.2		1.0	76	El Salvador	2.7		1.3
26	China	4.0		1.4	78	Panama	2.7		1.2
27	Latvia	4.0		1.5	79	Cameroon	2.6		1.5
28	Vietnam	3.8		1.4	80	Gambia	2.6		1.7
29	Russian Federation	3.8		1.2	81	Peru	2.6		1.1
30	Australia	3.8		1.0	82	Trinidad and Tobago	2.6		1.1
31	Indonesia	3.8		1.6	83	Ecuador	2.6		1.0
32	Ukraine	3.8		1.2	83	Serbia	2.6		1.1
33	Hungary	3.7		1.2	85	Venezuela	2.5		1.0
34	Czech Republic	3.7		1.2	86	Botswana	2.5		1.2
35	Slovak Republic	3.7		1.1	87	Madagascar	2.5		1.3
36	India	3.7		1.3	88	Pakistan	2.4		1.1
37	Estonia	3.6		1.3	89	Nigeria	2.4		1.3
38	Brazil	3.6		1.0	90	Ethiopia	2.4		1.2
39	Costa Rica	3.6		1.3	91	Honduras	2.2		1.0
40	Lithuania	3.5		1.1	92	Mozambique	2.2		1.4
41	Poland	3.5		1.1	93	Zimbabwe	2.2		0.9
42	South Africa	3.5		1.1	94	Bangladesh	2.2		1.0
43	Hong Kong SAR	3.5		1.3	94	Nicaragua	2.2		1.1
44	Egypt	3.4		1.6	96	Algeria	2.1		1.2
45	Croatia	3.4		1.4	97	Paraguay	2.1		1.0
46	Portugal	3.3		1.0	98	Haiti	2.1		1.0
47	Malaysia	3.2		1.2	99	Bolivia	2.1		0.9
48	Thailand	3.2		1.2	100	Chad	1.9		1.2
49	Greece	3.2		1.2	101	Mali	1.9		1.0
50	Sri Lanka	3.2		1.3	102	Angola	1.8		1.1
51	Colombia	3.2		1.2					
52	Mexico	3.2		1.2					

10.05 Ethical behavior of firms

The corporate ethics (ethical behavior in interactions with public officials, politicians, and other enterprises) of your country's firms in your industry are (1 = among the world's worst, 7 = among the world's best)

RANK	COUNTRY	SCORE	MEAN: 4.3	SD
1	Finland	6.5		0.7
2	Denmark	6.3		0.8
3	United Kingdom	6.2		0.9
4	Singapore	6.2		0.8
5	New Zealand	6.2		0.7
6	Sweden	6.1		0.6
7	Iceland	6.0		0.9
8	Australia	6.0		0.8
9	Netherlands	5.9		0.8
10	Canada	5.9		1.0
11	Switzerland	5.8		0.8
12	Luxembourg	5.8		0.8
13	United States	5.8		1.0
14	Germany	5.8		0.9
15	Austria	5.7		1.0
16	France	5.6		0.9
17	Norway	5.6		1.1
18	Belgium	5.5		0.9
19	Spain	5.4		0.9
20	Hong Kong SAR	5.2		1.1
21	Israel	5.1		0.8
22	Taiwan	5.0		0.9
23	Chile	5.0		0.9
24	Ireland	4.9		1.3
25	Malaysia	4.9		0.9
26	South Africa	4.9		1.2
27	Japan	4.8		1.3
28	Tunisia	4.7		1.2
29	Italy	4.6		0.9
30	Portugal	4.6		1.1
31	Uruguay	4.6		0.9
32	Morocco	4.6		1.6
33	Korea	4.6		1.1
34	Estonia	4.6		1.0
35	Latvia	4.5		1.1
36	Costa Rica	4.5		1.0
37	Botswana	4.5		1.0
38	Slovenia	4.5		1.0
39	Malta	4.5		1.1
40	Jordan	4.4		1.0
41	Mexico	4.4		1.3
42	Thailand	4.3		1.1
43	Brazil	4.3		1.3
44	Jamaica	4.3		1.0
45	El Salvador	4.3		1.1
46	Namibia	4.2		1.2
47	China	4.2		1.1
48	Colombia	4.2		1.1
49	Hungary	4.2		1.1
49	Lithuania	4.2		0.9
51	Gambia	4.2		1.2
52	Slovak Republic	4.2		1.2
53	Mali	4.1		1.0
54	Czech Republic	4.1		1.2
55	Trinidad and Tobago	4.1		1.3
56	Ghana	4.1		1.3
57	Poland	4.1		1.2
58	Tanzania	4.0		1.1
59	Malawi	4.0		1.2
60	Greece	4.0		1.3
61	Mauritius	4.0		1.3
62	Egypt	4.0		1.2
63	Senegal	3.9		1.3
64	Dominican Republic	3.9		1.4
65	Panama	3.9		1.2
66	Cameroon	3.9		0.9
67	Zimbabwe	3.8		1.1
68	Chad	3.8		1.4
69	Madagascar	3.8		1.0
70	Vietnam	3.8		1.2
71	Algeria	3.8		1.1
72	Pakistan	3.8		1.0
73	Zambia	3.8		1.2
74	India	3.7		1.3
75	Bulgaria	3.7		1.3
76	Philippines	3.6		1.3
77	Sri Lanka	3.6		1.0
78	Turkey	3.6		1.2
79	Peru	3.6		1.0
80	Argentina	3.5		1.1
81	Kenya	3.5		1.2
82	Croatia	3.5		1.1
83	Uganda	3.5		1.3
84	Ethiopia	3.5		1.4
85	Indonesia	3.5		1.3
86	Nigeria	3.5		1.4
87	Russian Federation	3.4		1.4
88	Serbia	3.4		1.0
89	Venezuela	3.4		1.6
90	Guatemala	3.4		1.1
91	Romania	3.4		1.4
92	Nicaragua	3.3		1.1
93	Ecuador	3.3		1.2
94	Macedonia, FYR	3.3		1.1
95	Ukraine	3.3		1.3
96	Haiti	3.2		0.9
97	Mozambique	3.1		1.2
98	Honduras	3.1		1.2
99	Bolivia	3.1		1.2
100	Bangladesh	2.8		1.3
101	Angola	2.7		0.9
102	Paraguay	2.6		1.1

10.06   Production process sophistication

Production processes use (1 = labor-intensive methods or previous generations of process technology, 7 = the world's best and most efficient process technology)

RANK	COUNTRY	SCORE	1 MEAN: 3.8 7	SD
1	Finland	6.4		0.6
2	Japan	6.3		0.7
3	Sweden	6.2		0.7
4	Germany	6.1		0.8
5	United States	6.0		1.1
6	Denmark	6.0		0.8
7	France	5.9		0.9
8	Switzerland	5.9		1.0
9	Belgium	5.8		1.0
10	Singapore	5.8		0.9
11	Netherlands	5.7		0.9
12	Australia	5.6		0.9
13	United Kingdom	5.6		0.8
14	Iceland	5.6		1.1
15	Canada	5.5		0.8
16	Luxembourg	5.5		0.9
17	Israel	5.5		1.0
18	Austria	5.4		1.3
19	Ireland	5.4		1.1
20	Taiwan	5.3		1.0
21	New Zealand	5.1		0.7
22	Norway	5.1		1.3
23	Italy	5.0		1.4
24	Spain	5.0		0.9
25	Korea	4.9		0.9
26	Hong Kong SAR	4.7		1.2
27	Chile	4.4		1.0
28	Malta	4.3		1.1
29	Latvia	4.3		1.3
30	Estonia	4.3		1.1
31	Slovenia	4.3		1.0
32	Brazil	4.2		1.0
33	Costa Rica	4.1		1.1
34	Trinidad and Tobago	4.1		1.5
35	Mauritius	4.1		1.2
36	Malaysia	4.1		1.2
37	Greece	4.0		1.2
38	Mexico	4.0		1.4
39	South Africa	3.9		1.3
40	Hungary	3.9		1.1
41	Argentina	3.8		1.1
42	Slovak Republic	3.8		1.2
43	Lithuania	3.8		1.2
44	Egypt	3.8		1.4
45	Tunisia	3.7		1.4
46	Czech Republic	3.7		1.1
47	China	3.7		1.4
48	Thailand	3.7		1.2
49	Turkey	3.7		1.2
50	Poland	3.7		1.1
51	Botswana	3.6		1.4
52	Jordan	3.6		1.3

RANK	COUNTRY	SCORE	1 MEAN: 3.8 7	SD
53	Panama	3.6		1.1
54	Vietnam	3.5		1.3
55	India	3.5		1.2
56	Portugal	3.5		1.0
57	Colombia	3.5		1.1
58	Dominican Republic	3.4		1.1
59	El Salvador	3.4		1.3
59	Jamaica	3.4		1.1
61	Uruguay	3.4		1.1
62	Morocco	3.4		1.6
63	Russian Federation	3.3		1.3
64	Indonesia	3.3		1.6
65	Peru	3.2		1.2
66	Croatia	3.2		1.4
67	Pakistan	3.1		1.1
68	Philippines	3.1		1.2
69	Namibia	3.0		1.4
70	Romania	3.0		1.4
71	Macedonia, FYR	3.0		1.5
72	Guatemala	3.0		1.0
73	Sri Lanka	3.0		1.2
74	Senegal	2.9		1.7
75	Venezuela	2.9		1.0
76	Ghana	2.8		1.4
77	Ukraine	2.8		1.1
78	Algeria	2.8		1.4
79	Angola	2.8		1.6
80	Ecuador	2.7		0.9
81	Cameroon	2.7		1.5
82	Serbia	2.7		1.4
83	Kenya	2.7		1.1
84	Bulgaria	2.7		1.2
85	Honduras	2.6		1.1
86	Nigeria	2.6		1.2
87	Malawi	2.6		1.3
88	Tanzania	2.6		1.1
89	Zambia	2.5		1.2
90	Paraguay	2.5		1.2
91	Uganda	2.4		1.4
92	Zimbabwe	2.4		0.9
93	Nicaragua	2.4		1.0
94	Bolivia	2.3		1.1
95	Madagascar	2.2		1.1
96	Bangladesh	2.2		1.0
97	Mozambique	2.2		1.2
98	Gambia	2.1		1.3
99	Mali	1.9		1.0
100	Ethiopia	1.8		1.0
101	Chad	1.8		1.2
102	Haiti	1.5		1.0

535

10.07 Extent of marketing

The extent of marketing in your country is (1 = limited and primitive, 7 = extensive and employs the world's most sophisticated tools and techniques)

RANK	COUNTRY	SCORE		SD	RANK	COUNTRY	SCORE		SD
1	United States	6.3		1.2	53	Tunisia	4.2		1.4
2	Germany	6.3		0.7	54	Colombia	4.1		1.0
3	United Kingdom	6.2		0.8	55	Turkey	4.1		1.3
4	France	6.1		0.8	56	Malta	4.1		1.3
5	Sweden	6.0		0.7	57	Kenya	4.1		1.4
6	Australia	6.0		0.7	58	Botswana	4.0		1.4
7	Switzerland	6.0		0.9	59	El Salvador	4.0		1.4
8	Netherlands	5.9		0.9	60	Hungary	3.9		1.2
9	Canada	5.9		0.9	61	Namibia	3.9		1.2
10	Japan	5.8		0.8	62	Nigeria	3.9		1.5
11	Belgium	5.8		1.0	63	Indonesia	3.8		1.3
12	Hong Kong SAR	5.7		1.1	64	Sri Lanka	3.8		1.2
13	Austria	5.7		1.0	65	Egypt	3.8		1.5
14	Singapore	5.6		0.8	66	Peru	3.7		1.2
15	Finland	5.6		0.8	67	Croatia	3.7		1.4
16	Denmark	5.6		1.0	68	Zimbabwe	3.7		1.3
17	Israel	5.5		0.8	69	Uruguay	3.7		1.3
18	Iceland	5.4		1.0	70	Ghana	3.7		1.5
19	Spain	5.4		1.0	71	Pakistan	3.6		1.3
20	New Zealand	5.3		0.9	72	Cameroon	3.6		1.8
21	Italy	5.3		1.0	73	Jordan	3.6		1.4
22	Brazil	5.3		1.0	74	Guatemala	3.6		1.5
23	Luxembourg	5.2		1.0	75	China	3.5		1.2
24	Ireland	5.2		1.4	76	Ecuador	3.5		1.2
25	South Africa	5.2		1.2	77	Romania	3.4		1.6
26	Korea	5.0		1.0	78	Russian Federation	3.4		1.3
27	Norway	5.0		1.2	79	Tanzania	3.3		1.4
28	Chile	5.0		1.1	80	Zambia	3.3		1.2
29	Taiwan	5.0		1.1	81	Madagascar	3.3		1.4
30	India	4.9		1.1	82	Honduras	3.3		1.2
31	Greece	4.8		1.0	83	Macedonia, FYR	3.2		1.5
32	Czech Republic	4.8		1.2	84	Malawi	3.2		1.4
33	Thailand	4.8		1.1	85	Senegal	3.2		1.4
34	Slovenia	4.7		1.2	86	Ukraine	3.2		1.3
35	Mexico	4.7		1.2	87	Bulgaria	3.2		1.2
36	Costa Rica	4.6		1.2	88	Serbia	3.1		1.4
37	Malaysia	4.6		1.1	89	Vietnam	3.0		1.3
38	Mauritius	4.6		1.0	90	Bangladesh	2.9		1.1
39	Dominican Republic	4.6		1.1	91	Paraguay	2.9		1.0
40	Latvia	4.6		1.3	92	Uganda	2.8		1.3
41	Slovak Republic	4.5		1.2	93	Bolivia	2.7		1.2
42	Estonia	4.5		1.2	94	Gambia	2.7		1.6
43	Poland	4.5		1.3	95	Nicaragua	2.7		1.2
44	Philippines	4.5		1.3	96	Algeria	2.5		1.2
45	Argentina	4.5		1.1	97	Haiti	2.5		1.3
46	Jamaica	4.5		1.2	98	Mozambique	2.4		1.2
47	Morocco	4.4		1.7	99	Angola	2.2		1.0
48	Trinidad and Tobago	4.3		1.2	100	Mali	2.2		1.4
49	Panama	4.3		1.4	101	Ethiopia	2.1		0.9
50	Lithuania	4.3		1.2	102	Chad	1.5		1.0
51	Venezuela	4.3		1.3					
52	Portugal	4.2		1.1					

MEAN: 4.2

10.08   Degree of customer orientation

Firms in your country (1 = generally treat their customers badly, 7 = are highly responsive to customers and customer retention)

RANK	COUNTRY	SCORE	1 MEAN: 4.6 7	SD
1	Japan	6.2		0.9
2	Switzerland	6.0		0.9
3	United States	6.0		1.2
4	Sweden	6.0		0.7
5	Denmark	5.9		1.1
6	Taiwan	5.8		0.8
7	Belgium	5.8		0.7
8	Finland	5.8		0.8
9	Iceland	5.7		0.6
10	Canada	5.7		1.1
11	Singapore	5.6		1.1
12	Netherlands	5.6		1.0
13	Hong Kong SAR	5.6		1.1
14	United Kingdom	5.6		1.1
15	Germany	5.6		1.4
16	Austria	5.5		1.2
17	New Zealand	5.5		0.8
18	Australia	5.5		0.8
19	Spain	5.5		0.9
20	France	5.4		1.1
21	Korea	5.4		0.9
22	Thailand	5.4		0.8
23	Norway	5.3		0.9
24	Malaysia	5.3		1.1
25	Luxembourg	5.3		1.1
26	Slovenia	5.2		1.1
27	Israel	5.2		0.9
28	Italy	5.1		1.1
29	Lithuania	5.1		1.1
30	Ireland	5.1		1.6
31	Colombia	5.0		1.1
32	Latvia	5.0		1.1
33	Estonia	5.0		1.1
34	Chile	4.9		1.3
35	Brazil	4.8		1.0
36	Gambia	4.8		1.7
37	Egypt	4.8		1.9
38	Dominican Republic	4.8		1.2
39	Greece	4.7		1.1
40	Mauritius	4.7		1.1
41	Sri Lanka	4.7		1.1
42	Mexico	4.7		1.3
43	Turkey	4.7		1.2
44	Vietnam	4.7		1.5
45	Jordan	4.7		1.2
46	Czech Republic	4.6		1.2
47	El Salvador	4.6		1.4
48	Morocco	4.6		1.8
49	Costa Rica	4.6		1.3
50	South Africa	4.5		1.4
51	Jamaica	4.5		1.2
52	China	4.5		1.4

RANK	COUNTRY	SCORE	1 MEAN: 4.6 7	SD
53	Kenya	4.5		1.5
54	Philippines	4.5		1.3
55	Poland	4.5		1.2
56	Panama	4.5		1.4
57	Tunisia	4.4		1.5
58	Bulgaria	4.4		1.5
59	Ghana	4.4		1.6
60	Malta	4.4		1.1
61	Slovak Republic	4.4		1.2
62	Russian Federation	4.4		1.5
63	Bangladesh	4.3		1.4
64	Tanzania	4.3		1.3
65	Zambia	4.3		1.3
66	Portugal	4.3		1.1
67	Malawi	4.3		1.5
68	Hungary	4.3		1.3
69	Nigeria	4.2		1.6
70	Uruguay	4.2		1.0
71	Peru	4.2		1.5
72	India	4.1		1.1
73	Pakistan	4.1		1.3
74	Ukraine	4.1		1.3
75	Trinidad and Tobago	4.1		1.3
76	Croatia	4.0		1.4
77	Senegal	4.0		1.7
78	Macedonia, FYR	4.0		1.6
79	Argentina	4.0		1.2
80	Uganda	3.9		1.6
81	Paraguay	3.9		1.4
82	Guatemala	3.9		1.4
83	Ethiopia	3.8		1.6
84	Mozambique	3.8		1.6
85	Namibia	3.7		1.1
86	Venezuela	3.7		1.3
87	Serbia	3.7		1.5
88	Botswana	3.6		1.3
89	Zimbabwe	3.6		1.3
90	Romania	3.6		1.8
91	Madagascar	3.5		1.6
92	Indonesia	3.5		1.0
93	Cameroon	3.4		1.7
94	Nicaragua	3.4		1.4
95	Honduras	3.3		1.4
96	Chad	3.3		1.9
97	Angola	3.2		1.5
98	Ecuador	3.1		1.4
99	Algeria	3.0		1.5
100	Haiti	3.0		1.4
101	Mali	3.0		1.8
102	Bolivia	2.9		1.4

537

10.09 Control of international distribution

International distribution and marketing from your country (1 = takes place through foreign companies, 7 = is owned and controlled by local companies)

RANK	COUNTRY	SCORE	1 MEAN: 3.9 7	SD
1	France	5.7		1.1
2	United States	5.7		0.9
3	Japan	5.6		1.1
4	Finland	5.2		1.1
5	Germany	5.2		1.2
6	Iceland	5.2		1.3
7	Sweden	5.1		1.1
8	Netherlands	5.1		1.0
9	United Kingdom	5.0		1.1
10	Denmark	5.0		1.0
11	Luxembourg	5.0		1.3
12	Austria	5.0		1.3
13	Switzerland	4.9		1.3
14	Korea	4.8		1.3
15	Canada	4.7		1.4
16	Taiwan	4.7		1.4
17	Mauritius	4.6		1.2
18	Norway	4.5		0.8
19	Hong Kong SAR	4.5		1.3
20	New Zealand	4.5		1.2
21	Spain	4.5		1.3
22	Ukraine	4.5		1.5
23	Belgium	4.4		1.1
24	Ireland	4.4		1.5
25	Slovenia	4.4		1.2
26	China	4.3		1.4
27	Australia	4.3		1.3
28	Singapore	4.2		1.4
29	Egypt	4.2		1.4
30	Italy	4.2		1.3
31	Israel	4.2		1.2
32	Lithuania	4.1		1.2
32	Morocco	4.1		1.9
34	Croatia	4.1		1.5
35	Macedonia, FYR	4.1		1.7
36	South Africa	4.0		1.2
37	India	4.0		1.3
38	Jordan	4.0		1.4
39	Malaysia	4.0		1.1
40	Tunisia	4.0		1.7
41	Latvia	4.0		1.4
42	Brazil	3.9		1.1
43	Poland	3.9		1.1
44	Greece	3.9		1.3
45	Hungary	3.9		1.4
46	Ghana	3.9		1.7
47	Portugal	3.9		1.1
48	Chile	3.8		1.3
49	Russian Federation	3.8		1.5
50	Gambia	3.8		1.9
51	Thailand	3.8		1.3
52	Turkey	3.8		1.5

RANK	COUNTRY	SCORE	1 MEAN: 3.9 7	SD
53	Romania	3.8		1.4
54	Mexico	3.7		1.4
55	Serbia	3.7		1.6
56	Panama	3.7		1.4
57	Sri Lanka	3.7		1.4
58	Costa Rica	3.7		1.4
59	Indonesia	3.7		1.3
60	Malawi	3.7		1.5
61	Cameroon	3.7		1.8
62	Algeria	3.6		2.0
63	Namibia	3.6		1.3
64	Trinidad and Tobago	3.6		1.5
65	Slovak Republic	3.6		1.3
66	Tanzania	3.6		1.4
67	Bulgaria	3.5		1.3
68	El Salvador	3.5		1.6
68	Pakistan	3.5		1.5
70	Vietnam	3.5		1.4
71	Colombia	3.5		1.4
72	Czech Republic	3.5		1.3
73	Estonia	3.5		1.4
74	Ethiopia	3.5		2.0
75	Jamaica	3.4		1.3
76	Zambia	3.4		1.4
77	Dominican Republic	3.4		1.6
77	Venezuela	3.4		1.3
79	Philippines	3.4		1.2
80	Senegal	3.4		1.8
81	Guatemala	3.4		1.6
82	Kenya	3.3		1.4
83	Malta	3.3		1.4
84	Uganda	3.3		1.7
85	Nigeria	3.2		1.5
86	Argentina	3.2		1.3
87	Ecuador	3.2		1.5
88	Mali	3.2		1.9
89	Uruguay	3.2		1.4
90	Bangladesh	3.0		1.6
91	Peru	3.0		1.3
92	Mozambique	2.9		1.4
93	Honduras	2.9		1.5
94	Botswana	2.9		1.2
95	Madagascar	2.9		1.6
96	Haiti	2.9		1.6
97	Zimbabwe	2.8		1.4
98	Nicaragua	2.8		1.5
99	Bolivia	2.8		1.5
100	Paraguay	2.7		1.3
101	Angola	2.5		1.4
102	Chad	2.5		1.9

10.10   Extent of regional sales

Exports from your country to neighboring countries are (1 = limited, 7 = substantial and growing)

RANK	COUNTRY	SCORE	MEAN: 4.5	SD		RANK	COUNTRY	SCORE	MEAN: 4.5	SD
1	Germany	6.4		0.8		53	Latvia	4.7		1.1
2	Finland	6.3		0.7		54	Poland	4.6		1.3
3	Netherlands	6.2		0.7		55	Guatemala	4.6		1.3
4	Belgium	6.2		0.8		56	Hungary	4.5		1.4
5	Ireland	6.2		0.8		57	Paraguay	4.4		1.6
6	Mexico	6.1		1.0		58	Tanzania	4.3		1.6
7	France	6.1		0.8		59	Sri Lanka	4.3		1.5
8	Switzerland	6.1		0.7		60	Mauritius	4.3		1.6
9	Canada	6.1		1.1		61	Philippines	4.2		1.4
10	Iceland	6.0		0.9		62	Russian Federation	4.1		1.5
10	Sweden	6.0		0.8		63	India	4.1		1.5
12	Japan	6.0		1.1		64	Uganda	4.1		2.0
13	Australia	6.0		0.9		65	Ghana	4.0		1.7
14	Denmark	5.9		1.1		66	Indonesia	4.0		1.3
15	Austria	5.9		1.3		67	Nigeria	4.0		1.8
16	United States	5.8		1.4		68	Venezuela	3.9		1.2
17	New Zealand	5.8		0.8		69	Morocco	3.9		2.0
18	Singapore	5.8		1.2		70	Zimbabwe	3.9		1.4
19	Hong Kong SAR	5.7		1.3		71	Egypt	3.7		1.5
20	South Africa	5.7		1.0		72	Bulgaria	3.7		1.4
21	Thailand	5.7		1.0		73	Honduras	3.7		1.2
22	United Kingdom	5.7		1.1		74	Gambia	3.7		2.3
23	Luxembourg	5.6		1.1		74	Namibia	3.7		1.5
24	Korea	5.6		1.0		76	Romania	3.7		1.6
25	Italy	5.6		1.0		77	Dominican Republic	3.6		1.4
26	Malaysia	5.6		0.8		78	Macedonia, FYR	3.6		1.7
27	Taiwan	5.5		1.1		79	Senegal	3.6		1.6
28	Trinidad and Tobago	5.5		1.1		80	Peru	3.6		1.2
29	Czech Republic	5.4		1.2		81	Ecuador	3.5		1.2
30	Norway	5.4		0.9		82	Croatia	3.5		1.5
31	Kenya	5.3		1.1		83	Jamaica	3.5		1.3
32	Slovenia	5.3		1.3		84	Panama	3.4		1.4
33	Greece	5.3		1.2		85	Malawi	3.3		1.5
34	Slovak Republic	5.2		1.1		86	Serbia	3.3		1.6
35	Brazil	5.2		1.1		87	Zambia	3.3		1.7
36	Costa Rica	5.2		1.1		88	Ukraine	3.2		1.2
37	Jordan	5.1		1.4		89	Pakistan	3.2		1.5
38	Estonia	5.1		1.1		90	Botswana	3.1		1.6
38	Uruguay	5.1		0.9		91	Mozambique	3.1		1.7
40	Spain	5.1		1.2		92	Madagascar	3.1		1.5
41	Cameroon	5.1		1.5		93	Mali	2.9		1.9
42	El Salvador	5.1		1.2		94	Nicaragua	2.8		1.4
43	Malta	5.0		1.2		95	Bolivia	2.8		1.4
44	Argentina	5.0		1.2		96	Ethiopia	2.5		1.5
45	Colombia	4.9		1.1		97	Bangladesh	2.3		1.3
46	Tunisia	4.9		1.5		98	Chad	2.1		1.6
47	Lithuania	4.9		1.3		99	Algeria	2.1		1.3
48	Vietnam	4.9		1.3		100	Israel	1.9		0.9
49	Portugal	4.8		1.3		101	Haiti	1.8		1.1
50	Turkey	4.8		1.5		102	Angola	1.8		1.0
51	China	4.8		1.3						
52	Chile	4.8		1.3						

539

10.11 Breadth of international markets

Exporting companies from your country sell (1 = primarily in a small number of foreign markets, 7 = in virtually all international country markets)

RANK	COUNTRY	SCORE	1 ... MEAN: 3.8 ... 7	SD		RANK	COUNTRY	SCORE	1 ... MEAN: 3.8 ... 7	SD
1	Japan	6.3		0.7		53	Malta	3.5		1.5
2	Germany	6.3		1.1		54	Estonia	3.4		1.3
3	Switzerland	6.3		1.0		55	Kenya	3.4		1.4
4	United Kingdom	6.2		1.0		56	Russian Federation	3.4		1.4
5	Sweden	6.2		1.1		57	Egypt	3.4		1.6
6	United States	6.2		1.2		58	Mexico	3.4		1.8
7	Finland	6.2		0.9		59	Argentina	3.4		1.3
8	Hong Kong SAR	6.0		1.3		60	Colombia	3.3		1.3
9	Netherlands	5.9		1.1		61	Pakistan	3.2		1.2
10	Denmark	5.9		1.1		62	Namibia	3.2		1.3
11	Singapore	5.7		1.2		63	Trinidad and Tobago	3.2		1.5
12	France	5.5		1.5		64	Senegal	3.2		1.9
13	Italy	5.5		1.1		65	Panama	3.1		1.5
14	Taiwan	5.5		1.2		66	Romania	3.1		1.6
15	Korea	5.4		1.1		67	Zimbabwe	3.1		1.5
16	Australia	5.4		1.6		68	Tanzania	3.0		1.4
17	Chile	5.4		1.4		69	Peru	3.0		1.2
18	Belgium	5.2		1.4		70	El Salvador	3.0		1.4
19	Malaysia	5.2		1.2		70	Uruguay	3.0		1.5
20	Israel	5.1		1.4		72	Guatemala	3.0		1.2
21	New Zealand	5.0		1.4		73	Ghana	2.9		1.5
22	Thailand	5.0		1.2		74	Jamaica	2.9		1.4
23	Ireland	4.9		1.8		75	Cameroon	2.8		1.7
24	Austria	4.8		1.9		76	Bulgaria	2.8		1.3
25	Turkey	4.7		1.3		77	Gambia	2.8		1.9
26	Norway	4.7		1.5		78	Ukraine	2.8		1.0
26	Spain	4.7		1.5		79	Nigeria	2.7		1.4
28	Czech Republic	4.7		1.3		80	Venezuela	2.7		1.4
29	Brazil	4.6		1.3		81	Macedonia, FYR	2.7		1.6
30	Iceland	4.6		1.6		82	Dominican Republic	2.7		1.4
31	Canada	4.4		1.9		83	Ecuador	2.6		0.9
32	Slovenia	4.4		1.5		84	Malawi	2.6		1.3
33	Luxembourg	4.3		1.7		85	Croatia	2.6		1.3
34	China	4.3		1.4		86	Serbia	2.6		1.4
35	South Africa	4.3		1.5		87	Uganda	2.5		1.6
36	Lithuania	4.3		1.6		88	Botswana	2.5		1.3
37	India	4.1		1.5		89	Ethiopia	2.4		1.4
38	Hungary	4.1		1.5		90	Bangladesh	2.4		1.4
39	Slovak Republic	4.0		1.5		91	Madagascar	2.4		1.2
40	Latvia	4.0		1.5		92	Paraguay	2.3		1.1
41	Indonesia	3.9		1.2		93	Zambia	2.3		1.3
42	Poland	3.9		1.2		94	Honduras	2.2		0.9
43	Vietnam	3.9		1.6		95	Mali	2.2		1.4
44	Greece	3.9		1.4		96	Mozambique	2.2		1.3
45	Sri Lanka	3.8		1.5		97	Nicaragua	2.1		1.0
46	Mauritius	3.8		1.3		98	Algeria	1.9		1.2
47	Portugal	3.8		1.3		99	Bolivia	1.9		0.7
48	Costa Rica	3.7		1.6		100	Angola	1.7		0.9
49	Philippines	3.7		1.5		101	Chad	1.7		1.2
50	Morocco	3.7		1.9		102	Haiti	1.5		0.8
51	Jordan	3.6		1.4						
52	Tunisia	3.6		1.6						

10.12 Extent of staff training

The general approach of companies in your country to human resources is (1 = to invest little in training and employee development, 7 = to invest heavily to attract, train, and retain employees)

RANK	COUNTRY	SCORE	1 MEAN: 3.9 7	SD
1	Denmark	6.0		0.7
2	Switzerland	6.0		0.9
3	Sweden	5.9		0.9
4	Germany	5.9		0.9
5	United States	5.9		1.1
6	Japan	5.8		1.0
7	Finland	5.8		0.8
8	Singapore	5.7		1.0
9	Netherlands	5.5		1.0
10	Belgium	5.5		1.0
11	United Kingdom	5.4		1.1
12	Australia	5.3		1.0
13	Luxembourg	5.3		1.1
14	Iceland	5.3		1.1
15	France	5.2		1.0
16	Austria	5.2		1.1
17	Canada	5.2		1.1
18	Malaysia	5.1		1.2
19	Taiwan	5.1		1.0
20	New Zealand	5.0		1.1
21	Korea	4.9		1.2
22	Norway	4.9		1.0
23	Ireland	4.9		1.5
24	Israel	4.6		1.2
25	South Africa	4.5		1.2
26	Tunisia	4.5		1.5
27	Brazil	4.5		1.2
28	Hong Kong SAR	4.4		1.3
29	Slovenia	4.4		1.2
30	Costa Rica	4.4		1.4
31	Mauritius	4.3		1.0
32	Spain	4.3		1.3
33	Italy	4.3		1.2
34	Thailand	4.3		1.3
35	Zimbabwe	4.2		1.3
36	Chile	4.2		1.2
37	Latvia	4.2		1.3
38	Malta	4.2		1.3
39	Slovak Republic	4.1		1.3
40	Estonia	4.0		1.4
41	Philippines	3.9		1.2
42	Mexico	3.9		1.3
43	Dominican Republic	3.9		1.4
44	Trinidad and Tobago	3.8		1.2
45	India	3.8		1.3
46	Greece	3.8		1.2
47	Indonesia	3.7		1.5
48	Jamaica	3.7		1.1
49	El Salvador	3.7		1.3
50	Czech Republic	3.7		1.3
51	Morocco	3.7		1.8
52	Colombia	3.7		1.0
53	Namibia	3.7		1.1
54	Poland	3.6		1.2
55	China	3.6		1.2
56	Portugal	3.6		1.0
57	Argentina	3.6		1.0
58	Turkey	3.6		1.2
59	Panama	3.6		1.2
60	Sri Lanka	3.5		1.4
61	Botswana	3.5		1.5
62	Jordan	3.5		1.4
63	Kenya	3.5		1.4
64	Vietnam	3.5		1.4
65	Hungary	3.5		1.2
66	Egypt	3.4		1.5
67	Lithuania	3.4		1.4
68	Nigeria	3.4		1.6
69	Malawi	3.3		1.4
70	Macedonia, FYR	3.3		1.9
71	Venezuela	3.3		1.3
72	Ghana	3.2		1.5
73	Tanzania	3.1		1.4
74	Croatia	3.1		1.4
75	Guatemala	3.1		1.2
76	Pakistan	3.0		1.1
77	Uganda	3.0		1.7
78	Peru	3.0		1.2
79	Russian Federation	3.0		1.4
80	Senegal	2.9		1.3
81	Zambia	2.9		1.3
82	Gambia	2.9		1.8
83	Mozambique	2.9		1.5
84	Uruguay	2.9		1.2
85	Cameroon	2.8		1.5
86	Madagascar	2.8		1.3
87	Algeria	2.7		1.5
88	Serbia	2.7		1.3
89	Romania	2.7		1.5
90	Ecuador	2.7		1.0
91	Bulgaria	2.6		1.2
92	Honduras	2.6		1.2
93	Angola	2.5		1.4
94	Nicaragua	2.5		1.1
95	Ukraine	2.5		1.2
96	Paraguay	2.4		0.9
97	Chad	2.4		1.6
98	Bangladesh	2.3		1.0
99	Haiti	2.3		1.2
100	Bolivia	2.3		0.9
101	Ethiopia	2.1		1.1
102	Mali	2.1		1.4

541

10.13 Willingness to delegate authority

Willingness to delegate authority to subordinates is (1 = low; top management controls all important decisions, 7 = high; authority is mostly delegated to business unit heads and other lower-level managers)

RANK	COUNTRY	SCORE	1 MEAN: 3.7 7	SD
1	Sweden	6.4		0.7
2	Denmark	6.1		1.0
3	Finland	5.9		1.0
4	Germany	5.7		1.1
5	Netherlands	5.7		1.0
6	Switzerland	5.7		1.0
7	United States	5.5		1.3
8	Norway	5.5		0.9
9	United Kingdom	5.5		1.0
10	New Zealand	5.4		0.9
11	Australia	5.4		1.1
12	Iceland	5.3		0.8
13	Canada	5.3		1.1
14	Belgium	5.2		1.2
15	Ireland	5.0		1.5
16	Luxembourg	5.0		1.2
17	Taiwan	4.9		1.1
18	Singapore	4.9		1.3
19	Malaysia	4.9		1.4
20	Japan	4.7		1.3
21	Austria	4.6		1.4
22	France	4.6		1.6
23	Spain	4.6		1.2
24	Israel	4.2		1.4
25	Korea	4.2		1.3
26	Latvia	4.1		1.4
27	Hong Kong SAR	4.0		1.6
28	Costa Rica	4.0		1.5
29	Slovenia	3.9		1.2
30	Estonia	3.9		1.3
31	South Africa	3.9		1.4
32	Italy	3.9		1.4
33	Thailand	3.8		1.5
34	Mauritius	3.8		1.2
35	Brazil	3.8		1.3
35	Chile	3.8		1.3
37	Namibia	3.8		1.2
38	Philippines	3.7		1.3
39	Tunisia	3.7		1.5
40	Mexico	3.7		1.5
41	Indonesia	3.6		1.5
42	Slovak Republic	3.6		1.3
43	Colombia	3.6		1.4
44	China	3.5		1.3
45	Lithuania	3.5		1.3
45	Zimbabwe	3.5		1.2
47	Dominican Republic	3.5		1.3
48	Jamaica	3.5		1.3
49	Botswana	3.5		1.6
50	Ukraine	3.5		1.4
51	Poland	3.5		1.3
52	Panama	3.5		1.4
53	Morocco	3.5		1.8
54	India	3.4		1.4
55	Czech Republic	3.4		1.4
56	Sri Lanka	3.4		1.6
57	Malta	3.4		1.4
58	Argentina	3.4		1.0
59	Tanzania	3.3		1.4
60	Portugal	3.3		1.1
61	Egypt	3.3		1.8
62	Greece	3.3		1.2
63	Macedonia, FYR	3.3		1.7
64	El Salvador	3.3		1.5
65	Croatia	3.2		1.6
66	Kenya	3.2		1.5
67	Hungary	3.2		1.2
68	Trinidad and Tobago	3.2		1.3
69	Gambia	3.2		1.8
70	Turkey	3.2		1.4
71	Nigeria	3.1		1.6
72	Vietnam	3.1		1.4
73	Ghana	3.1		1.6
74	Malawi	3.1		1.6
75	Jordan	3.1		1.5
76	Venezuela	3.1		1.4
77	Romania	3.1		1.6
78	Guatemala	3.1		1.3
79	Uganda	3.0		1.8
80	Peru	3.0		1.3
81	Russian Federation	2.9		1.4
82	Serbia	2.7		1.5
83	Chad	2.7		1.8
84	Uruguay	2.7		1.0
85	Zambia	2.6		1.2
86	Bulgaria	2.6		1.3
87	Senegal	2.6		1.7
88	Ecuador	2.6		1.0
89	Honduras	2.6		1.2
90	Algeria	2.5		1.4
91	Pakistan	2.5		1.0
92	Madagascar	2.5		1.2
93	Ethiopia	2.4		1.4
94	Nicaragua	2.4		1.1
95	Mozambique	2.4		1.1
96	Cameroon	2.4		1.3
97	Bolivia	2.3		1.1
98	Paraguay	2.3		0.9
99	Bangladesh	2.1		1.1
100	Angola	2.1		1.2
101	Mali	1.9		1.0
102	Haiti	1.8		0.9

10.14 Extent of incentive compensation

Cash compensation of management (1 = is based exclusively on salary, 7 = includes bonuses and stock options, representing a significant portion of overall compensation)

RANK	COUNTRY	SCORE	1 MEAN: 4.0 7	SD
1	United States	6.1		1.2
2	United Kingdom	6.0		0.9
3	Germany	5.9		1.0
4	Australia	5.8		1.2
5	Netherlands	5.6		0.9
6	Canada	5.5		1.1
7	Finland	5.5		1.0
8	France	5.4		1.1
9	Sweden	5.4		1.0
10	Singapore	5.3		1.1
11	South Africa	5.2		1.1
12	Belgium	5.2		1.0
13	Spain	5.1		1.0
14	Ireland	5.1		1.4
15	Austria	5.1		1.6
16	Luxembourg	5.0		1.3
17	Norway	5.0		0.9
18	Denmark	5.0		1.3
19	Italy	4.9		1.2
20	Israel	4.9		1.3
21	Zimbabwe	4.9		1.2
22	Brazil	4.9		1.2
23	Switzerland	4.8		1.8
24	New Zealand	4.8		1.1
25	Taiwan	4.8		1.2
26	Hong Kong SAR	4.8		1.6
27	Korea	4.6		1.2
28	Iceland	4.6		1.0
29	Czech Republic	4.6		1.5
30	Dominican Republic	4.5		1.1
31	Malaysia	4.5		1.4
32	Latvia	4.5		1.2
33	Estonia	4.5		1.2
34	Poland	4.4		1.5
35	Greece	4.3		1.2
36	Chile	4.3		1.2
37	Thailand	4.2		1.4
38	Philippines	4.2		1.3
39	Portugal	4.2		1.1
40	Panama	4.2		1.4
41	Mauritius	4.2		1.1
42	Slovenia	4.1		1.3
43	Mexico	4.1		1.3
44	Hungary	4.1		1.3
45	Trinidad and Tobago	4.1		1.4
46	India	4.1		1.4
47	Costa Rica	4.0		1.5
48	Ukraine	3.9		1.4
49	China	3.9		1.4
50	Argentina	3.9		1.2
51	Namibia	3.8		1.4
52	Vietnam	3.8		1.5

RANK	COUNTRY	SCORE	1 MEAN: 4.0 7	SD
53	El Salvador	3.8		1.4
53	Tunisia	3.8		1.3
55	Japan	3.8		1.4
56	Sri Lanka	3.7		1.4
57	Jamaica	3.7		1.4
58	Morocco	3.7		1.8
59	Venezuela	3.6		1.4
60	Russian Federation	3.6		1.5
61	Botswana	3.6		1.5
62	Nigeria	3.6		1.6
63	Malawi	3.6		1.8
64	Indonesia	3.5		1.1
65	Egypt	3.5		1.6
66	Colombia	3.5		1.3
67	Croatia	3.4		1.6
68	Romania	3.4		1.9
69	Malta	3.4		1.4
70	Guatemala	3.4		1.4
71	Turkey	3.3		1.4
72	Ghana	3.3		1.5
73	Lithuania	3.3		1.3
74	Mozambique	3.3		1.7
75	Slovak Republic	3.3		1.3
76	Angola	3.2		1.8
77	Kenya	3.2		1.4
78	Bulgaria	3.2		1.6
79	Chad	3.1		1.9
80	Honduras	3.1		1.5
81	Uganda	3.1		1.6
82	Zambia	3.1		1.6
83	Nicaragua	3.0		1.6
84	Ecuador	3.0		1.3
85	Pakistan	3.0		1.3
86	Gambia	3.0		1.9
87	Jordan	2.9		1.3
88	Peru	2.9		1.1
89	Tanzania	2.9		1.4
90	Serbia	2.8		1.5
91	Uruguay	2.8		1.1
92	Senegal	2.7		1.6
93	Bangladesh	2.7		1.2
94	Macedonia, FYR	2.7		1.7
95	Cameroon	2.7		1.2
96	Madagascar	2.7		1.4
97	Paraguay	2.7		1.2
98	Bolivia	2.6		1.2
99	Haiti	2.5		1.4
100	Mali	2.3		1.6
101	Ethiopia	2.3		1.3
102	Algeria	2.2		1.3

543

10.15   Reliance on professional management

Senior management positions in your country are (1 = usually held by relatives, 7 = held by professional managers chosen based on superior qualification)

RANK	COUNTRY	SCORE	1 MEAN: 4.7 7	SD
1	Australia	6.7		0.5
2	United Kingdom	6.5		0.6
3	Finland	6.5		0.7
4	Sweden	6.5		0.6
5	New Zealand	6.4		0.6
6	Germany	6.4		0.9
7	United States	6.3		1.0
8	Netherlands	6.2		0.7
9	Austria	6.2		1.2
10	Denmark	6.0		0.9
11	Canada	6.0		0.8
12	Ireland	6.0		0.9
13	Belgium	5.8		0.9
14	Singapore	5.8		0.9
15	France	5.7		0.9
16	South Africa	5.7		1.0
17	Malaysia	5.7		0.9
18	Switzerland	5.7		1.6
19	Iceland	5.7		0.7
19	Luxembourg	5.7		0.9
21	Israel	5.7		0.8
22	Japan	5.6		1.1
23	Botswana	5.5		1.0
24	Norway	5.4		0.9
25	Taiwan	5.3		1.1
26	Chile	5.3		1.1
27	Spain	5.2		1.0
28	Estonia	5.2		1.2
29	Malawi	5.2		1.5
30	Zimbabwe	5.1		1.3
31	Czech Republic	5.1		1.2
32	Latvia	5.1		1.0
33	Brazil	5.1		1.1
34	Hong Kong SAR	5.0		1.4
35	Gambia	5.0		1.7
36	Slovak Republic	5.0		1.1
37	Jamaica	4.9		1.2
38	Ghana	4.9		1.6
39	Sri Lanka	4.9		1.2
40	Portugal	4.9		0.8
41	Trinidad and Tobago	4.9		1.3
42	Tanzania	4.8		1.4
43	Zambia	4.8		1.6
44	Hungary	4.8		1.1
45	Nigeria	4.8		1.5
46	Argentina	4.7		1.2
47	Korea	4.7		1.2
48	India	4.7		1.3
49	Colombia	4.7		1.3
50	Costa Rica	4.7		1.2
51	Thailand	4.6		1.3
52	Kenya	4.6		1.4

RANK	COUNTRY	SCORE	1 MEAN: 4.7 7	SD
53	Slovenia	4.6		1.1
54	China	4.6		1.1
55	Philippines	4.5		1.1
56	Italy	4.5		1.4
57	Mauritius	4.5		1.1
58	Namibia	4.4		1.3
59	Venezuela	4.4		1.2
60	Poland	4.3		1.2
61	Mexico	4.3		1.3
62	Tunisia	4.3		1.5
63	Lithuania	4.3		1.2
64	Algeria	4.2		1.6
65	Malta	4.2		1.4
66	Senegal	4.2		1.7
67	El Salvador	4.2		1.5
68	Croatia	4.1		1.5
69	Morocco	4.1		1.9
70	Egypt	4.1		1.4
71	Greece	4.1		1.3
72	Madagascar	4.1		1.6
73	Pakistan	4.0		1.6
74	Mozambique	4.0		1.6
75	Cameroon	4.0		1.5
76	Serbia	4.0		1.5
77	Russian Federation	4.0		1.5
78	Peru	4.0		1.4
79	Dominican Republic	3.9		1.4
80	Vietnam	3.9		1.5
81	Turkey	3.9		1.4
82	Jordan	3.8		1.5
83	Macedonia, FYR	3.7		1.8
84	Ethiopia	3.7		1.7
85	Bangladesh	3.7		1.6
86	Romania	3.7		1.8
87	Chad	3.7		1.9
88	Panama	3.7		1.5
89	Indonesia	3.6		1.3
90	Uruguay	3.6		1.2
91	Uganda	3.6		1.9
92	Guatemala	3.5		1.5
93	Ukraine	3.5		1.1
94	Bulgaria	3.5		1.5
95	Ecuador	3.4		1.3
96	Nicaragua	3.3		1.7
97	Angola	3.2		1.3
98	Bolivia	3.1		1.4
99	Honduras	2.9		1.4
100	Mali	2.9		2.0
101	Paraguay	2.8		1.2
102	Haiti	2.4		1.2

10.16 Quality of management schools

Management or business schools in your country are (1 = limited or of poor quality, 7 = the best in the world)

RANK	COUNTRY	SCORE	MEAN: 4.2	SD		RANK	COUNTRY	SCORE	MEAN: 4.2	SD
1	United States	6.5		0.9		53	Japan	4.1		1.4
2	France	6.3		1.0		54	Senegal	4.1		1.4
3	Canada	6.2		0.6		55	Turkey	4.1		1.4
4	Switzerland	6.0		0.8		56	Pakistan	4.1		1.2
5	United Kingdom	5.9		0.7		57	Greece	4.1		1.3
6	Finland	5.8		0.6		58	Malta	4.1		1.3
7	Sweden	5.8		0.6		59	Ghana	4.0		1.5
8	India	5.7		1.0		60	Jordan	3.9		1.5
9	Singapore	5.7		0.8		61	Russian Federation	3.9		1.5
10	Israel	5.7		0.7		62	Romania	3.9		1.6
11	Spain	5.6		0.8		63	Dominican Republic	3.9		1.4
12	Norway	5.6		0.8		64	El Salvador	3.9		1.4
13	Australia	5.6		1.1		65	Ukraine	3.8		1.3
14	Netherlands	5.5		1.0		66	Guatemala	3.7		1.2
15	Belgium	5.5		0.9		67	Panama	3.7		1.2
16	Ireland	5.5		1.3		68	Malawi	3.6		1.5
17	Chile	5.4		0.9		69	Mauritius	3.6		1.2
18	South Africa	5.4		1.0		70	Uganda	3.6		1.3
19	Germany	5.3		0.7		71	Indonesia	3.6		1.6
20	New Zealand	5.3		1.0		72	China	3.6		1.3
21	Iceland	5.3		1.0		73	Kenya	3.6		1.3
22	Austria	5.2		1.2		74	Madagascar	3.5		1.3
23	Denmark	5.2		0.8		75	Egypt	3.5		1.5
24	Tunisia	5.1		1.0		76	Cameroon	3.5		1.4
25	Argentina	5.1		0.9		77	Nigeria	3.5		1.4
26	Costa Rica	5.1		0.9		78	Nicaragua	3.4		1.3
27	Italy	5.0		1.2		79	Croatia	3.3		1.4
28	Estonia	4.9		1.0		80	Zambia	3.3		1.5
29	Taiwan	4.9		1.0		81	Tanzania	3.3		1.5
30	Hong Kong SAR	4.8		1.3		82	Paraguay	3.3		1.2
31	Slovenia	4.8		1.1		83	Botswana	3.3		1.4
32	Philippines	4.8		1.1		84	Serbia	3.2		1.2
33	Latvia	4.7		1.1		85	Vietnam	3.2		1.3
34	Brazil	4.7		1.1		86	Algeria	3.2		1.2
35	Mexico	4.6		1.1		87	Bulgaria	3.2		1.2
36	Portugal	4.6		0.9		88	Gambia	3.1		1.6
36	Thailand	4.6		1.3		89	Zimbabwe	3.1		1.2
38	Jamaica	4.6		1.3		90	Ecuador	3.1		1.1
39	Uruguay	4.5		1.0		91	Macedonia, FYR	3.0		1.6
40	Hungary	4.5		1.1		92	Namibia	3.0		1.4
41	Colombia	4.5		1.0		93	Bangladesh	3.0		1.3
42	Morocco	4.4		1.9		93	Luxembourg	3.0		1.6
43	Trinidad and Tobago	4.3		1.2		95	Bolivia	2.9		1.1
44	Czech Republic	4.3		1.3		96	Mali	2.8		1.3
45	Korea	4.2		1.1		97	Ethiopia	2.8		1.3
46	Malaysia	4.2		1.2		98	Honduras	2.8		1.2
47	Peru	4.2		1.1		99	Mozambique	2.6		1.2
48	Slovak Republic	4.2		1.2		100	Haiti	2.5		0.8
49	Lithuania	4.2		1.2		101	Chad	2.0		1.2
50	Venezuela	4.1		1.5		102	Angola	1.9		0.9
51	Poland	4.1		1.2						
52	Sri Lanka	4.1		1.3						

10.17   Efficacy of corporate boards

Corporate boards in your country are (1 = controlled by management, 7 = powerful and represent outside shareholders)

RANK	COUNTRY	SCORE	1 MEAN: 4.5 7	SD
1	United Kingdom	6.1		0.9
2	Australia	6.0		1.0
3	New Zealand	5.8		0.7
4	United States	5.8		0.9
5	Denmark	5.8		1.0
6	Finland	5.7		0.9
7	Singapore	5.5		0.9
8	Canada	5.5		1.1
9	South Africa	5.3		1.0
10	Germany	5.3		1.1
11	Sweden	5.3		1.2
12	Luxembourg	5.2		1.1
13	Netherlands	5.2		1.0
14	Belgium	5.2		1.0
15	Malaysia	5.2		1.1
16	Iceland	5.1		0.9
16	Norway	5.1		0.9
18	Ireland	5.1		1.3
19	Taiwan	5.0		1.2
20	Austria	5.0		1.2
21	Latvia	5.0		1.1
22	Israel	5.0		1.0
23	Switzerland	5.0		1.2
24	Tanzania	4.9		1.3
25	Ghana	4.9		1.4
26	Gambia	4.8		1.8
27	Estonia	4.8		1.2
28	France	4.8		1.4
29	Zambia	4.8		1.4
30	Botswana	4.7		1.4
30	Cameroon	4.7		1.5
32	Hong Kong SAR	4.7		1.2
33	Jamaica	4.7		1.0
34	Chile	4.7		1.2
35	Hungary	4.7		1.2
36	Zimbabwe	4.6		1.2
37	Nigeria	4.6		1.4
38	Kenya	4.6		1.3
39	Spain	4.6		1.2
40	Italy	4.6		1.2
41	Malawi	4.6		1.4
42	Trinidad and Tobago	4.6		1.0
43	Malta	4.6		1.2
44	Lithuania	4.5		1.1
45	Mauritius	4.5		1.1
46	Namibia	4.5		1.1
47	Philippines	4.5		1.1
48	Korea	4.4		1.2
49	Bulgaria	4.4		1.4
50	Thailand	4.4		1.2
51	China	4.4		1.3
52	Japan	4.4		1.5

RANK	COUNTRY	SCORE	1 MEAN: 4.5 7	SD
53	Czech Republic	4.4		1.5
54	Slovak Republic	4.4		1.4
55	Costa Rica	4.4		1.4
56	Egypt	4.3		1.5
57	Ethiopia	4.3		1.8
58	Poland	4.3		1.3
59	Slovenia	4.3		1.3
60	Jordan	4.3		1.3
61	Colombia	4.3		1.1
62	El Salvador	4.3		1.3
63	Tunisia	4.3		1.4
64	Sri Lanka	4.3		1.1
65	Greece	4.3		1.3
66	Mexico	4.2		1.5
67	Macedonia, FYR	4.2		1.9
68	Ukraine	4.2		1.2
69	India	4.2		1.3
69	Russian Federation	4.2		1.3
71	Vietnam	4.2		1.7
72	Pakistan	4.2		1.3
73	Portugal	4.2		1.0
74	Uganda	4.1		1.8
75	Madagascar	4.1		1.6
76	Peru	4.1		1.4
77	Morocco	4.1		1.7
78	Croatia	4.1		1.6
79	Mozambique	4.0		1.6
80	Panama	4.0		1.3
81	Algeria	4.0		1.6
82	Brazil	4.0		1.1
83	Guatemala	3.9		1.6
84	Dominican Republic	3.9		1.5
85	Venezuela	3.9		1.2
86	Senegal	3.9		1.7
87	Chad	3.8		1.8
88	Serbia	3.7		1.4
89	Argentina	3.7		1.3
90	Honduras	3.7		1.5
91	Bangladesh	3.7		1.6
92	Ecuador	3.7		1.4
93	Nicaragua	3.6		1.5
94	Turkey	3.6		1.5
95	Mali	3.6		1.7
96	Romania	3.5		1.6
97	Uruguay	3.5		1.5
98	Indonesia	3.4		1.5
99	Haiti	3.3		1.6
100	Bolivia	3.2		1.4
101	Paraguay	3.2		1.4
102	Angola	3.0		1.5

10.18 Hiring and firing practices

Hiring and firing of workers is (1 = impeded by regulations, 7 = flexibly determined by employers)

RANK	COUNTRY	SCORE	1 MEAN: 3.5 7	SD
1	Hong Kong SAR	5.7		1.4
2	Singapore	5.6		1.2
3	Switzerland	5.5		1.4
4	United States	5.4		1.5
5	Denmark	5.3		1.9
6	Taiwan	5.1		1.3
7	Nigeria	5.1		1.7
8	Iceland	5.0		1.4
9	Uganda	5.0		1.7
10	Chad	4.8		1.9
11	Russian Federation	4.7		1.7
12	Haiti	4.7		1.5
13	Ukraine	4.6		1.5
14	Kenya	4.5		1.6
15	Gambia	4.4		1.9
16	Latvia	4.4		1.4
17	Thailand	4.3		1.5
18	Ghana	4.3		1.8
19	Canada	4.3		1.8
20	United Kingdom	4.3		1.8
21	Vietnam	4.3		1.6
22	Bangladesh	4.2		1.9
23	Estonia	4.2		1.4
24	Bulgaria	4.2		1.7
25	Malawi	4.2		1.7
26	China	4.2		1.7
27	Finland	4.1		1.7
28	Zambia	4.1		2.1
29	Czech Republic	4.0		1.8
30	Tunisia	4.0		1.7
31	Brazil	4.0		1.6
32	Serbia	4.0		1.8
33	Turkey	3.9		1.6
34	Jamaica	3.9		1.7
35	Israel	3.9		1.8
36	Hungary	3.8		1.6
37	Trinidad and Tobago	3.8		1.5
38	Australia	3.8		1.7
39	Mali	3.8		2.0
40	Ireland	3.7		1.6
41	Jordan	3.7		1.6
42	Madagascar	3.7		1.6
43	Indonesia	3.7		1.5
44	Romania	3.7		2.1
45	Egypt	3.7		1.9
46	Cameroon	3.6		1.4
47	Luxembourg	3.5		1.7
48	Pakistan	3.5		1.6
49	Slovak Republic	3.5		1.7
50	Algeria	3.4		1.7
51	Austria	3.4		1.8
52	El Salvador	3.4		1.7
53	Tanzania	3.4		1.5
54	Poland	3.4		1.5
55	New Zealand	3.4		1.8
56	Korea	3.4		1.4
57	Malaysia	3.3		1.6
58	Nicaragua	3.3		2.0
59	Croatia	3.3		1.7
60	Ethiopia	3.3		1.6
61	Macedonia, FYR	3.3		1.9
62	Lithuania	3.2		1.6
63	Guatemala	3.1		1.7
64	Bolivia	3.1		1.9
65	Botswana	3.0		1.3
66	Malta	3.0		1.6
67	Sri Lanka	2.9		1.4
68	Morocco	2.9		1.6
69	Namibia	2.9		1.4
69	Philippines	2.9		1.5
71	Dominican Republic	2.9		1.8
72	Costa Rica	2.9		1.9
73	Peru	2.9		1.5
74	Italy	2.8		1.0
75	Mexico	2.8		1.6
76	Chile	2.7		1.5
77	Colombia	2.7		1.5
78	Portugal	2.7		1.2
79	Senegal	2.7		1.4
80	Slovenia	2.6		1.3
81	Greece	2.6		1.0
81	Mauritius	2.6		1.4
83	Netherlands	2.6		1.2
84	Uruguay	2.6		1.3
85	Angola	2.6		1.5
86	Sweden	2.5		1.4
87	Japan	2.5		1.3
88	Paraguay	2.4		1.5
89	Panama	2.3		1.4
90	Mozambique	2.3		1.5
91	South Africa	2.3		1.2
92	Honduras	2.3		1.5
93	Ecuador	2.3		1.2
94	Norway	2.3		1.0
95	Spain	2.3		1.2
96	India	2.2		1.2
97	France	2.2		1.3
98	Belgium	1.9		1.1
99	Argentina	1.9		1.0
100	Zimbabwe	1.8		1.0
101	Germany	1.8		1.0
102	Venezuela	1.6		0.7

10.19 Flexibility of wage determination

Wages in your country are (1 = set by a centralized bargaining process, 7 = up to each individual company)

RANK	COUNTRY	SCORE	1 MEAN: 4.8 7	SD
1	Hong Kong SAR	6.5		0.7
2	Estonia	6.2		0.8
3	United States	6.0		1.0
4	Chad	6.0		1.5
5	Peru	6.0		0.9
6	Uganda	5.9		1.4
7	Chile	5.9		1.1
8	Taiwan	5.9		1.0
9	Nicaragua	5.9		1.5
10	Lithuania	5.9		1.2
11	El Salvador	5.8		1.0
12	Russian Federation	5.8		1.3
13	New Zealand	5.8		0.8
14	Singapore	5.8		1.2
15	Japan	5.8		1.4
16	Romania	5.8		1.4
17	Vietnam	5.8		1.1
18	Haiti	5.8		1.4
19	Gambia	5.7		1.5
20	Bolivia	5.7		1.4
21	Ethiopia	5.7		1.5
22	Bulgaria	5.7		1.4
23	Switzerland	5.7		1.2
24	United Kingdom	5.7		1.2
25	Uruguay	5.7		1.2
26	Slovak Republic	5.6		1.4
27	Serbia	5.6		1.5
28	Canada	5.6		1.4
29	Malaysia	5.6		0.9
30	Latvia	5.6		1.1
31	Czech Republic	5.5		1.2
32	Jordan	5.5		1.3
33	Macedonia, FYR	5.5		1.8
34	Jamaica	5.4		1.4
35	China	5.4		1.3
36	Malawi	5.4		1.6
37	Bangladesh	5.4		1.4
38	Morocco	5.3		1.9
39	Zambia	5.3		1.8
40	Pakistan	5.3		1.4
41	Hungary	5.2		1.1
42	Egypt	5.2		2.0
43	Poland	5.2		1.1
44	Turkey	5.2		1.4
45	Madagascar	5.2		1.6
46	India	5.1		1.4
47	Malta	5.0		1.3
48	Trinidad and Tobago	5.0		1.4
49	Nigeria	4.9		1.8
50	Botswana	4.9		1.8
51	Mexico	4.9		1.5
52	Ukraine	4.9		1.8
53	Sri Lanka	4.8		1.5
54	Korea	4.8		1.3
55	Tanzania	4.8		1.7
56	Kenya	4.8		1.6
57	Colombia	4.8		1.8
58	Namibia	4.8		1.2
59	Angola	4.7		2.1
60	Australia	4.7		1.0
61	Croatia	4.7		1.7
62	Cameroon	4.6		2.0
63	France	4.6		1.6
64	Panama	4.5		2.0
65	Dominican Republic	4.5		1.8
66	Thailand	4.5		1.6
67	Ecuador	4.5		1.8
68	Spain	4.4		1.5
69	Luxembourg	4.4		1.7
70	Portugal	4.4		1.5
71	Israel	4.4		1.4
72	Argentina	4.4		1.5
73	Iceland	4.3		1.4
74	Costa Rica	4.3		1.9
75	Brazil	4.2		1.4
76	Denmark	4.2		1.3
77	Slovenia	4.1		1.6
78	Philippines	4.1		1.8
79	Guatemala	4.1		2.0
80	Algeria	4.1		2.0
81	Ghana	4.1		2.0
82	Mali	4.1		2.2
83	Venezuela	3.9		1.6
84	Honduras	3.8		2.1
85	Paraguay	3.8		2.1
86	Mozambique	3.8		2.0
87	South Africa	3.8		1.7
88	Indonesia	3.7		1.5
89	Sweden	3.6		1.6
90	Senegal	3.6		2.0
91	Greece	3.5		1.6
92	Netherlands	3.5		1.5
93	Tunisia	3.2		1.7
94	Mauritius	3.2		1.5
95	Norway	3.1		1.1
96	Ireland	3.1		1.8
97	Belgium	3.0		1.5
98	Italy	2.8		1.2
99	Zimbabwe	2.8		1.6
100	Austria	2.7		1.5
101	Finland	2.3		1.1
102	Germany	2.1		1.1

10.20   Cooperation in labor-employer relations

Labor-employer relations in your country are (1 = generally confrontational, 7 = generally cooperative)

RANK	COUNTRY	SCORE	1 MEAN: 4.5 7	SD
1	Singapore	6.3		0.7
2	Switzerland	6.1		0.8
3	Denmark	6.0		1.0
4	Hong Kong SAR	5.8		0.9
5	Sweden	5.8		0.8
6	Iceland	5.8		0.8
7	Netherlands	5.8		0.8
8	Austria	5.7		1.0
9	Luxembourg	5.7		0.8
10	Malaysia	5.6		0.9
11	Costa Rica	5.5		0.8
12	Finland	5.5		1.2
13	Taiwan	5.5		0.8
14	Japan	5.4		1.1
14	Thailand	5.4		0.9
16	Malawi	5.4		1.2
17	Dominican Republic	5.3		1.0
18	United States	5.2		1.2
19	Gambia	5.2		1.6
20	El Salvador	5.1		1.1
21	Botswana	5.0		1.2
22	Vietnam	5.0		1.1
23	Estonia	5.0		1.1
23	United Kingdom	5.0		1.1
25	Ireland	5.0		1.6
26	Canada	4.9		1.5
27	Norway	4.9		1.3
28	Jordan	4.9		1.2
29	Latvia	4.8		1.1
30	Hungary	4.8		1.1
31	Slovak Republic	4.7		1.1
32	Germany	4.7		1.4
33	Mexico	4.7		1.2
34	Chile	4.7		1.1
35	Chad	4.7		2.0
36	New Zealand	4.7		1.1
37	Tunisia	4.6		1.4
38	Tanzania	4.6		1.2
39	Australia	4.5		1.3
39	Czech Republic	4.5		1.1
41	Ukraine	4.5		1.2
42	Colombia	4.5		1.2
43	Russian Federation	4.4		1.4
44	Mali	4.4		1.8
45	Haiti	4.4		1.0
46	Portugal	4.4		1.2
47	Nicaragua	4.4		1.4
48	Malta	4.3		1.4
49	Egypt	4.3		1.4
50	Israel	4.3		1.3
51	China	4.3		1.3
52	Brazil	4.3		1.2

RANK	COUNTRY	SCORE	1 MEAN: 4.5 7	SD
53	Guatemala	4.3		1.3
54	Ghana	4.3		1.6
55	Spain	4.3		1.1
56	Turkey	4.3		1.3
57	Slovenia	4.2		1.2
58	Lithuania	4.2		1.1
59	Mauritius	4.2		1.2
60	Belgium	4.2		1.6
61	Pakistan	4.1		1.2
62	Uganda	4.1		1.6
63	Zambia	4.1		1.5
64	Greece	4.1		1.3
65	Namibia	4.1		1.3
66	Angola	4.1		1.4
67	Bulgaria	4.0		1.3
68	Zimbabwe	4.0		1.4
69	Ethiopia	4.0		1.4
70	Mozambique	4.0		1.5
71	Panama	4.0		1.3
72	Ecuador	4.0		1.3
73	Madagascar	4.0		1.4
74	Argentina	4.0		1.3
75	India	4.0		1.3
76	Peru	3.9		1.2
77	Morocco	3.9		1.8
78	Jamaica	3.9		1.4
79	Algeria	3.9		1.4
80	Bolivia	3.8		1.3
81	Italy	3.8		1.2
82	Romania	3.8		1.8
83	Bangladesh	3.8		1.5
84	Serbia	3.8		1.4
85	South Africa	3.8		1.4
86	Macedonia, FYR	3.7		1.8
87	Senegal	3.7		1.8
88	Paraguay	3.7		1.4
89	Sri Lanka	3.7		1.2
90	Philippines	3.7		1.3
91	Indonesia	3.7		1.6
92	Uruguay	3.7		1.1
93	Korea	3.6		1.4
94	Kenya	3.6		1.4
95	Poland	3.6		1.3
96	Honduras	3.5		1.2
97	Croatia	3.5		1.5
98	Cameroon	3.5		1.8
99	France	3.5		1.4
100	Venezuela	3.5		1.3
101	Nigeria	3.5		1.6
102	Trinidad and Tobago	3.2		1.3

549

10.21   Pay and productivity

Pay in your country is (1 = not related to worker productivity, 7 = strongly related to worker productivity)

RANK	COUNTRY	SCORE	1 MEAN: 3.9 7	SD		RANK	COUNTRY	SCORE	1 MEAN: 3.9 7	SD
1	United States	5.9		0.9		53	Namibia	3.8		1.6
2	Hong Kong SAR	5.7		1.1		54	Turkey	3.8		1.2
3	Singapore	5.7		0.9		55	Chad	3.8		2.1
4	Taiwan	5.4		0.9		56	South Africa	3.7		1.3
5	Switzerland	5.3		1.0		57	Tanzania	3.7		1.7
6	Malaysia	5.1		1.3		58	Argentina	3.6		1.3
7	Latvia	5.1		1.2		59	Mexico	3.6		1.5
8	Vietnam	5.1		1.4		60	Haiti	3.6		1.3
9	United Kingdom	5.0		1.0		61	Malta	3.6		1.5
10	Estonia	4.9		1.4		62	Greece	3.6		1.4
11	Czech Republic	4.8		1.1		63	Germany	3.6		1.5
12	Australia	4.8		1.1		64	Trinidad and Tobago	3.5		1.2
13	Iceland	4.7		1.2		65	Senegal	3.5		1.8
14	New Zealand	4.7		1.0		66	Madagascar	3.5		1.5
15	Thailand	4.7		1.2		67	Kenya	3.5		1.5
16	Denmark	4.7		1.3		68	Malawi	3.4		1.8
17	China	4.7		1.6		69	Serbia	3.4		1.7
18	Luxembourg	4.6		1.1		70	Italy	3.4		1.2
19	Canada	4.6		1.5		71	Belgium	3.4		1.5
20	Hungary	4.5		1.3		72	Colombia	3.4		1.5
21	Gambia	4.5		1.7		73	India	3.3		1.2
22	Lithuania	4.4		1.5		74	Jamaica	3.3		1.2
23	Chile	4.4		1.4		75	Croatia	3.3		1.5
24	Slovak Republic	4.4		1.4		76	Norway	3.3		1.2
25	Slovenia	4.4		1.2		77	Algeria	3.3		1.7
26	Dominican Republic	4.4		1.5		78	Pakistan	3.3		1.5
27	El Salvador	4.4		1.3		79	Mauritius	3.2		1.1
28	Israel	4.3		1.2		80	Bolivia	3.2		1.6
29	Ireland	4.3		1.6		81	Panama	3.2		1.7
30	Finland	4.3		1.4		82	Uruguay	3.2		1.2
31	Bulgaria	4.3		1.7		83	Botswana	3.1		1.5
32	Poland	4.3		1.2		84	Ghana	3.1		1.6
33	Russian Federation	4.3		1.6		85	Portugal	3.1		1.1
34	Japan	4.3		1.3		86	Sri Lanka	3.1		1.3
35	Korea	4.2		1.3		87	Zambia	3.1		1.5
36	Jordan	4.2		1.5		88	Philippines	3.0		1.2
37	Sweden	4.1		1.0		89	Nigeria	3.0		1.4
38	Tunisia	4.1		1.7		90	Guatemala	3.0		1.5
39	Ukraine	4.1		1.6		91	Angola	3.0		1.9
40	Morocco	4.1		2.0		92	Bangladesh	2.9		1.4
41	Nicaragua	4.1		1.5		93	Honduras	2.9		1.6
42	Romania	4.1		1.9		94	Ecuador	2.8		1.4
43	France	4.0		1.4		95	Venezuela	2.8		1.4
44	Costa Rica	4.0		1.7		96	Uganda	2.8		1.6
45	Austria	4.0		1.5		97	Paraguay	2.7		1.4
46	Indonesia	3.9		1.4		98	Ethiopia	2.7		1.5
47	Brazil	3.9		1.3		99	Mozambique	2.6		1.6
48	Macedonia, FYR	3.9		2.0		100	Cameroon	2.6		1.6
49	Egypt	3.9		1.6		101	Zimbabwe	2.5		1.4
50	Spain	3.9		1.3		102	Mali	2.4		1.5
51	Peru	3.8		1.6						
52	Netherlands	3.8		1.3						

10.22   Charitable causes involvement

In your country, individuals and companies that contribute to charitable causes are (1 = not prevalent, 7 = prevalent)

RANK	COUNTRY	SCORE	1 MEAN: 4.6 7	SD
1	United States	6.3		1.1
2	Canada	6.0		0.9
3	Malawi	5.8		0.9
4	Malta	5.7		1.1
5	Australia	5.7		1.3
6	Iceland	5.7		1.4
7	United Kingdom	5.7		1.3
8	Ireland	5.6		1.2
9	Gambia	5.6		1.6
10	South Africa	5.6		1.2
11	Botswana	5.5		1.0
12	Malaysia	5.5		1.0
13	Hong Kong SAR	5.4		1.2
14	Morocco	5.4		1.6
15	Panama	5.4		1.2
16	Trinidad and Tobago	5.4		1.1
17	New Zealand	5.4		1.0
18	Singapore	5.4		1.3
19	Jamaica	5.4		1.3
20	El Salvador	5.4		1.4
21	India	5.3		1.4
22	Austria	5.3		1.7
23	Ghana	5.3		1.6
24	Luxembourg	5.3		1.5
25	Vietnam	5.2		1.4
26	Israel	5.2		1.7
27	Tanzania	5.2		1.3
28	Tunisia	5.2		1.5
29	Namibia	5.2		1.1
30	Germany	5.2		1.6
31	Kenya	5.2		1.4
32	Thailand	5.1		1.3
33	Zimbabwe	5.1		1.1
34	Slovak Republic	5.1		1.5
35	Chile	5.1		1.4
36	Netherlands	5.1		1.3
37	Senegal	5.1		1.7
38	Taiwan	5.0		1.4
39	Sri Lanka	5.0		1.3
40	Mauritius	5.0		1.3
41	Pakistan	5.0		1.2
42	Switzerland	4.9		1.4
43	Egypt	4.9		1.8
44	Costa Rica	4.9		1.3
45	Zambia	4.9		1.6
46	Turkey	4.8		1.2
47	Jordan	4.8		1.2
48	Philippines	4.8		1.7
49	Argentina	4.8		1.5
50	Brazil	4.8		1.4
51	Venezuela	4.7		1.2
52	Guatemala	4.7		1.6

RANK	COUNTRY	SCORE	1 MEAN: 4.6 7	SD
53	Nigeria	4.7		1.6
54	Norway	4.6		0.9
55	Madagascar	4.6		1.6
56	Dominican Republic	4.6		1.7
57	Colombia	4.5		1.4
58	Slovenia	4.5		1.2
59	Algeria	4.5		1.8
60	Cameroon	4.5		1.7
61	Latvia	4.5		1.3
62	Greece	4.5		1.4
63	Nicaragua	4.4		1.7
64	Spain	4.4		1.7
65	France	4.4		1.7
66	Italy	4.4		1.5
67	Mexico	4.4		1.6
68	Ethiopia	4.3		1.8
69	Belgium	4.3		1.5
70	Korea	4.3		1.4
71	Bangladesh	4.2		1.6
72	Honduras	4.2		1.7
73	Uganda	4.2		1.6
74	Haiti	4.1		1.6
75	Poland	4.1		1.3
76	Indonesia	4.1		1.4
77	Finland	3.9		1.5
78	Mali	3.9		2.0
79	Japan	3.9		1.6
80	Romania	3.8		1.9
81	Hungary	3.8		1.5
82	Lithuania	3.8		1.4
83	Ecuador	3.8		1.6
84	Serbia	3.8		1.7
85	Chad	3.8		2.3
86	Ukraine	3.7		1.3
87	Czech Republic	3.7		1.5
88	Mozambique	3.7		1.6
89	Russian Federation	3.7		1.5
90	Peru	3.7		1.6
91	Paraguay	3.7		1.5
92	Uruguay	3.7		1.4
93	Portugal	3.6		1.4
94	Sweden	3.5		1.6
95	China	3.5		1.4
96	Croatia	3.4		1.7
97	Denmark	3.4		1.6
98	Angola	3.3		1.7
99	Estonia	2.9		1.2
100	Bolivia	2.7		1.4
101	Macedonia, FYR	2.7		1.6
102	Bulgaria	2.4		1.0

10.23   Company promotion of volunteerism

Companies in your country encourage workers to volunteer for social causes and have incentives that facilitate that involvement (1 = never, 7 = common)

RANK	COUNTRY	SCORE	1 MEAN: 3.2 7	SD
1	United States	5.3		1.3
2	Vietnam	4.9		1.5
3	Malaysia	4.6		1.3
4	Canada	4.5		1.7
5	United Kingdom	4.5		1.3
6	Singapore	4.4		1.4
7	Australia	4.3		1.3
8	Brazil	4.1		1.4
9	Netherlands	4.0		1.5
10	Slovak Republic	4.0		1.8
11	China	4.0		1.4
12	Hong Kong SAR	4.0		1.6
13	Latvia	4.0		1.6
14	Korea	4.0		1.3
15	Luxembourg	4.0		1.6
16	Tunisia	3.9		1.7
17	Gambia	3.9		2.1
18	Norway	3.9		1.3
19	Taiwan	3.8		1.5
20	Switzerland	3.8		1.4
21	Tanzania	3.8		1.7
22	Iceland	3.8		1.6
22	Indonesia	3.8		1.4
24	Morocco	3.7		2.0
25	South Africa	3.7		1.4
26	Thailand	3.7		1.5
27	Malta	3.7		1.6
28	Germany	3.7		1.6
29	Chile	3.6		1.4
30	Costa Rica	3.6		1.6
31	Israel	3.6		1.2
32	Spain	3.5		1.5
33	Japan	3.5		1.6
34	Panama	3.5		1.4
35	Venezuela	3.4		1.5
36	Mauritius	3.4		1.1
37	Belgium	3.4		1.3
38	Argentina	3.3		1.4
39	Ghana	3.3		1.5
40	Colombia	3.3		1.3
41	Austria	3.3		1.5
42	Dominican Republic	3.3		1.5
43	Senegal	3.3		1.5
44	El Salvador	3.2		1.3
45	Jordan	3.2		1.4
46	Botswana	3.2		1.5
47	Egypt	3.2		1.8
48	Italy	3.2		1.4
49	Sri Lanka	3.2		1.3
50	Finland	3.2		1.5
51	New Zealand	3.2		1.3
52	Namibia	3.2		1.3

RANK	COUNTRY	SCORE	1 MEAN: 3.2 7	SD
53	Philippines	3.2		1.4
54	Uganda	3.1		1.6
55	Kenya	3.1		1.6
56	Denmark	3.1		1.3
57	Jamaica	3.0		1.3
58	Ukraine	3.0		1.5
59	Ireland	3.0		1.4
60	Poland	2.9		1.3
61	India	2.9		1.4
62	Greece	2.9		1.3
63	Russian Federation	2.9		1.7
64	Estonia	2.9		1.4
65	Slovenia	2.8		1.3
66	Mexico	2.8		1.4
67	Trinidad and Tobago	2.8		1.2
68	Mozambique	2.8		1.3
69	Guatemala	2.8		1.2
70	Cameroon	2.8		1.8
71	Macedonia, FYR	2.7		1.7
72	Sweden	2.7		1.5
73	Lithuania	2.7		1.2
74	Turkey	2.7		1.4
75	Nicaragua	2.7		1.2
76	France	2.7		1.4
76	Portugal	2.7		1.1
78	Nigeria	2.7		1.5
79	Serbia	2.6		1.3
80	Czech Republic	2.6		1.3
81	Peru	2.6		1.3
82	Malawi	2.6		1.5
83	Chad	2.6		1.7
84	Algeria	2.5		1.6
85	Zambia	2.5		1.3
86	Romania	2.5		1.6
87	Honduras	2.5		1.2
88	Ecuador	2.5		1.3
89	Croatia	2.4		1.4
90	Bangladesh	2.4		1.4
91	Zimbabwe	2.4		1.3
92	Hungary	2.4		1.2
93	Ethiopia	2.4		1.3
94	Pakistan	2.3		1.3
95	Mali	2.3		1.6
96	Bolivia	2.3		1.1
97	Angola	2.2		1.1
98	Uruguay	2.2		1.0
99	Paraguay	2.2		1.1
100	Madagascar	2.2		1.2
101	Bulgaria	2.2		1.1
102	Haiti	1.9		1.1

10.24 Protection of minority shareholders' interests

Law protection of minority shareholders' interests in your country is (1 = nonexistent and seldom recognized by majority shareholders, 7 = total and actively enforced)

RANK	COUNTRY	SCORE	1 MEAN: 4.5 7	SD
1	Australia	6.4		0.8
2	United Kingdom	6.4		1.0
3	Finland	6.2		1.4
4	Denmark	6.1		1.1
5	New Zealand	6.0		1.0
6	Germany	5.9		1.1
7	United States	5.9		1.0
8	Sweden	5.9		1.0
9	Israel	5.8		1.2
10	Canada	5.8		1.4
11	Singapore	5.8		1.1
12	Norway	5.7		0.9
13	Iceland	5.6		1.3
14	Belgium	5.6		1.0
15	South Africa	5.5		1.1
16	Gambia	5.4		1.6
17	Tunisia	5.4		1.4
18	Hong Kong SAR	5.4		1.3
19	Jordan	5.4		1.4
20	Ireland	5.3		1.5
21	Chile	5.2		1.5
22	Malaysia	5.1		1.2
23	Senegal	5.1		1.4
24	France	5.1		1.4
25	Malta	5.1		1.4
26	Greece	5.1		1.3
27	Austria	5.0		1.5
28	Netherlands	5.0		1.5
29	Zimbabwe	5.0		1.6
30	Taiwan	4.9		1.2
31	Portugal	4.9		1.5
32	Thailand	4.9		1.3
33	Morocco	4.9		1.9
33	Switzerland	4.9		1.6
35	Botswana	4.8		1.2
36	India	4.8		1.6
37	Algeria	4.8		1.7
38	Dominican Republic	4.8		1.7
38	Malawi	4.8		1.7
40	Ghana	4.7		1.6
41	Brazil	4.7		1.4
42	Namibia	4.6		1.5
43	Egypt	4.6		1.8
44	Spain	4.6		1.6
45	Jamaica	4.6		1.5
46	Slovenia	4.6		1.6
47	Japan	4.5		1.6
48	Tanzania	4.5		1.4
49	Costa Rica	4.5		1.7
50	Pakistan	4.4		1.8
51	Zambia	4.4		1.8
52	Peru	4.4		1.6

RANK	COUNTRY	SCORE	1 MEAN: 4.5 7	SD
53	Hungary	4.4		1.6
54	Uruguay	4.4		1.6
55	Latvia	4.4		1.5
56	Ethiopia	4.4		1.9
57	Mexico	4.4		1.7
58	Nigeria	4.3		1.7
59	Vietnam	4.3		1.6
60	Italy	4.3		1.6
61	Mauritius	4.3		1.7
62	Korea	4.3		1.3
63	Trinidad and Tobago	4.2		1.4
64	Colombia	4.2		1.5
65	Poland	4.2		1.4
66	El Salvador	4.2		1.7
67	Cameroon	4.2		1.4
68	Estonia	4.1		1.5
69	Philippines	4.1		1.5
70	Luxembourg	4.1		1.9
71	Mozambique	4.1		1.5
72	Mali	4.0		2.0
73	Panama	3.9		1.7
74	Sri Lanka	3.9		1.6
75	Czech Republic	3.9		1.7
76	Angola	3.9		1.8
77	Ecuador	3.9		1.7
78	Uganda	3.8		1.7
79	Venezuela	3.8		1.6
80	Bangladesh	3.8		1.9
81	Turkey	3.8		1.6
82	Argentina	3.7		1.5
83	China	3.7		1.6
84	Indonesia	3.7		1.3
85	Kenya	3.7		1.5
86	Paraguay	3.6		1.7
87	Slovak Republic	3.6		1.8
88	Nicaragua	3.5		1.6
89	Madagascar	3.5		1.7
90	Croatia	3.5		1.7
91	Lithuania	3.4		1.5
92	Romania	3.4		1.7
93	Chad	3.4		2.0
94	Guatemala	3.3		1.6
95	Macedonia, FYR	3.3		2.0
96	Honduras	3.2		1.8
97	Bolivia	3.2		1.7
98	Bulgaria	3.0		1.6
99	Serbia	3.0		1.6
100	Haiti	2.6		1.5
101	Russian Federation	2.6		1.4
102	Ukraine	2.5		1.3

553

10.25 Availability of company financial information

Access to reliable and timely information regarding company financial performance is (1 = often insufficient, delayed, and difficult to obtain, 7 = regular and easy)

RANK	COUNTRY	SCORE	SD
1	Sweden	6.7	0.5
2	Australia	6.7	0.5
3	United Kingdom	6.6	0.6
4	Finland	6.5	0.8
5	Denmark	6.2	1.0
6	New Zealand	6.2	0.8
7	United States	6.1	1.0
8	Canada	6.0	1.1
9	Singapore	6.0	0.9
10	Netherlands	6.0	1.0
11	Israel	5.9	0.9
12	Norway	5.9	0.9
13	South Africa	5.9	1.1
14	Iceland	5.9	1.2
15	Belgium	5.8	1.1
16	Germany	5.7	1.1
17	Hong Kong SAR	5.7	1.3
18	Chile	5.7	1.1
19	Taiwan	5.6	1.0
20	Zimbabwe	5.5	1.2
21	France	5.5	1.3
22	Ireland	5.5	1.6
23	Malaysia	5.4	1.1
23	Pakistan	5.4	1.5
25	Switzerland	5.3	1.5
26	Jordan	5.1	1.4
27	Malta	5.1	1.3
28	Greece	5.1	1.3
29	India	5.1	1.4
30	Italy	5.1	1.5
31	Luxembourg	5.0	1.6
32	Portugal	5.0	1.3
33	Namibia	5.0	1.2
34	Thailand	4.9	1.3
35	Jamaica	4.9	1.4
36	Japan	4.9	1.5
37	Colombia	4.9	1.1
38	Korea	4.9	1.4
39	Mauritius	4.9	1.5
40	Spain	4.8	1.6
41	Slovenia	4.8	1.5
42	Austria	4.8	1.6
43	Brazil	4.8	1.5
44	Estonia	4.7	1.5
45	Gambia	4.7	1.8
46	Trinidad and Tobago	4.7	1.5
47	Mexico	4.7	1.7
48	Latvia	4.7	1.3
49	Botswana	4.7	1.5
50	Egypt	4.6	1.8
51	Lithuania	4.5	1.6
52	Turkey	4.5	1.4

RANK	COUNTRY	SCORE	SD
53	Tunisia	4.5	1.6
54	Costa Rica	4.5	1.5
55	Poland	4.4	1.4
56	Bulgaria	4.4	1.8
57	Peru	4.3	1.5
58	Malawi	4.3	1.6
59	Zambia	4.3	1.8
60	Tanzania	4.3	1.6
61	Philippines	4.3	1.6
62	Slovak Republic	4.2	1.8
63	Kenya	4.2	1.6
64	Macedonia, FYR	4.2	2.1
65	Morocco	4.1	1.9
66	Nigeria	4.0	1.7
67	Sri Lanka	4.0	1.6
68	Ghana	4.0	1.6
69	Hungary	4.0	1.6
70	Panama	3.9	1.5
71	China	3.9	1.5
72	Vietnam	3.9	1.7
73	El Salvador	3.9	1.6
74	Indonesia	3.9	1.4
75	Uganda	3.8	1.9
76	Mozambique	3.8	1.7
77	Croatia	3.8	1.6
78	Czech Republic	3.7	1.6
79	Dominican Republic	3.6	1.7
80	Argentina	3.6	1.5
81	Senegal	3.5	1.6
82	Ethiopia	3.4	1.8
83	Venezuela	3.4	1.6
84	Serbia	3.3	1.8
85	Nicaragua	3.2	1.6
86	Romania	3.2	1.5
87	Bangladesh	3.2	1.5
88	Honduras	3.2	1.5
89	Ecuador	3.1	1.4
90	Guatemala	3.1	1.3
91	Russian Federation	3.0	1.6
92	Algeria	2.9	1.6
93	Cameroon	2.8	1.4
94	Uruguay	2.8	1.2
95	Bolivia	2.7	1.2
96	Ukraine	2.7	1.4
97	Angola	2.6	1.5
98	Paraguay	2.4	1.2
99	Madagascar	2.4	1.2
100	Haiti	2.4	1.1
101	Mali	2.3	1.4
102	Chad	2.3	1.9

10.26 Foreign ownership restrictions

Foreign ownership of companies in your country is (1 = rare, limited to few cases, and prohibited in key sectors, 7 = prevalent and encouraged)

RANK	COUNTRY	SCORE	1 — MEAN: 5.0 — 7	SD
1	United Kingdom	6.3		1.0
2	Hong Kong SAR	6.3		1.1
2	Ireland	6.3		0.6
4	Luxembourg	6.2		0.7
5	Singapore	6.1		1.0
6	Sweden	6.0		0.8
7	Finland	6.0		0.9
8	New Zealand	5.9		0.9
9	United States	5.9		1.1
10	Chile	5.8		0.9
11	Germany	5.8		1.0
12	Hungary	5.7		1.0
13	Slovak Republic	5.7		1.2
14	Gambia	5.7		1.4
15	Denmark	5.6		1.1
16	Jamaica	5.6		1.0
17	Malawi	5.6		1.2
18	Belgium	5.6		0.9
19	France	5.6		1.0
20	Austria	5.6		1.0
21	Dominican Republic	5.6		1.2
21	Nigeria	5.6		1.3
23	Israel	5.6		1.2
24	Netherlands	5.5		1.1
25	Botswana	5.5		1.1
26	Mexico	5.5		1.2
27	Spain	5.5		0.9
28	Zambia	5.5		1.3
29	Estonia	5.5		1.0
30	South Africa	5.5		1.1
31	Morocco	5.5		1.5
32	Uganda	5.5		1.7
33	Costa Rica	5.4		1.1
34	Ghana	5.4		1.4
35	Czech Republic	5.4		1.0
36	Switzerland	5.4		1.2
37	Malta	5.4		1.3
38	Argentina	5.4		1.0
39	Australia	5.4		1.2
40	Tunisia	5.3		1.5
41	India	5.3		1.3
42	Brazil	5.3		0.9
43	Latvia	5.2		0.9
44	Senegal	5.2		1.2
45	Panama	5.2		1.2
46	Pakistan	5.2		1.5
47	Jordan	5.2		1.3
48	Kenya	5.2		1.3
49	Cameroon	5.2		1.2
50	El Salvador	5.2		1.4
51	Poland	5.2		1.2
52	Tanzania	5.2		1.5
53	Mali	5.1		1.5
54	Greece	5.1		1.3
55	Canada	5.1		1.4
56	Sri Lanka	5.1		1.4
57	Peru	5.1		1.2
58	Taiwan	5.1		1.3
59	Portugal	5.1		1.2
60	Angola	5.0		1.6
61	Bangladesh	5.0		1.8
62	Mozambique	5.0		1.4
63	Lithuania	4.9		1.2
64	Trinidad and Tobago	4.9		1.3
65	Nicaragua	4.9		1.5
66	Turkey	4.8		1.5
67	Malaysia	4.8		1.4
68	Korea	4.8		1.2
69	Norway	4.8		0.9
70	Egypt	4.7		1.7
71	Uruguay	4.7		1.5
72	Italy	4.7		1.0
73	Namibia	4.7		1.4
74	Madagascar	4.7		1.5
75	Thailand	4.6		1.5
76	Venezuela	4.6		1.5
77	Romania	4.6		1.6
78	Honduras	4.5		1.6
79	Colombia	4.5		1.3
80	Paraguay	4.5		1.7
81	China	4.5		1.6
82	Bolivia	4.4		1.4
83	Philippines	4.3		1.7
84	Vietnam	4.3		1.7
85	Japan	4.3		1.2
86	Macedonia, FYR	4.2		1.7
87	Mauritius	4.2		1.4
88	Guatemala	4.1		1.3
89	Ukraine	4.0		1.2
90	Slovenia	4.0		1.0
91	Ecuador	4.0		1.4
92	Croatia	4.0		1.4
93	Iceland	4.0		1.7
94	Bulgaria	3.9		1.3
95	Indonesia	3.9		1.3
96	Algeria	3.9		1.8
97	Chad	3.8		2.0
98	Haiti	3.8		1.6
99	Russian Federation	3.7		1.4
100	Serbia	3.6		1.4
101	Zimbabwe	3.4		1.3
102	Ethiopia	3.3		1.9

10.27　Strength of auditing and accounting standards

Financial auditing and accounting standards in your country are (1 = extremely weak, 7 = extremely strong, among the best in the world)

RANK	COUNTRY	SCORE	1　MEAN: 4.8　7	SD
1	United Kingdom	6.6		0.7
2	Australia	6.4		0.6
3	Denmark	6.3		0.7
4	Israel	6.2		0.4
5	New Zealand	6.2		0.7
6	Canada	6.2		0.7
7	France	6.2		0.7
8	Sweden	6.1		0.7
9	Singapore	6.1		0.7
10	Finland	6.1		0.6
11	Germany	6.1		0.9
12	Netherlands	6.1		0.7
13	Luxembourg	6.1		0.7
14	Austria	6.0		0.8
15	South Africa	6.0		0.7
16	Ireland	6.0		0.8
17	Iceland	6.0		0.7
18	Hong Kong SAR	6.0		1.0
19	Belgium	5.9		0.7
20	Switzerland	5.8		0.9
21	Malta	5.8		1.0
22	United States	5.8		1.1
23	Norway	5.7		1.0
24	Malaysia	5.7		0.7
25	Malawi	5.7		0.9
26	Estonia	5.6		0.8
27	Tunisia	5.5		1.3
28	Zimbabwe	5.5		1.0
29	Jamaica	5.4		1.1
30	Namibia	5.4		1.1
31	Trinidad and Tobago	5.4		1.2
32	Spain	5.3		0.9
33	Italy	5.3		0.9
34	Chile	5.3		1.0
35	Portugal	5.3		0.9
36	India	5.2		1.2
37	Slovenia	5.2		1.2
38	Botswana	5.2		1.2
39	Jordan	5.2		1.2
40	Brazil	5.1		0.9
41	Pakistan	5.1		1.1
42	Hungary	5.1		0.9
43	Thailand	5.1		1.0
44	Taiwan	5.0		0.9
45	Latvia	5.0		1.1
46	Costa Rica	5.0		1.1
47	Mauritius	4.9		1.4
48	Slovak Republic	4.9		1.0
49	Greece	4.8		1.1
50	Japan	4.8		1.4
51	Mexico	4.8		1.1
52	Kenya	4.7		1.3
53	Korea	4.7		1.1
54	Philippines	4.7		1.1
55	Poland	4.7		1.1
56	Gambia	4.7		1.7
57	Czech Republic	4.7		1.3
58	Senegal	4.6		1.7
59	El Salvador	4.6		1.2
60	Lithuania	4.6		1.2
61	Tanzania	4.6		1.2
62	Colombia	4.6		1.2
63	Sri Lanka	4.6		1.3
64	Morocco	4.6		1.7
65	Zambia	4.6		1.3
66	Ghana	4.5		1.5
66	Peru	4.5		1.0
68	Egypt	4.5		1.4
69	Panama	4.5		1.4
70	Dominican Republic	4.4		1.1
71	Turkey	4.3		1.4
72	Croatia	4.3		1.4
73	Bulgaria	4.3		1.1
74	Macedonia, FYR	4.3		1.5
75	Nigeria	4.2		1.5
76	Uruguay	4.2		1.3
77	Madagascar	4.1		1.4
78	Vietnam	4.0		1.2
79	Uganda	3.9		1.6
80	Ecuador	3.9		1.2
81	Argentina	3.9		1.4
82	Venezuela	3.9		1.3
83	Cameroon	3.8		1.5
84	Serbia	3.8		1.4
85	Algeria	3.8		1.5
86	Romania	3.7		1.5
87	Guatemala	3.6		1.2
88	Ukraine	3.6		1.3
89	Russian Federation	3.6		1.3
90	Indonesia	3.6		1.3
91	Mali	3.5		1.6
92	Ethiopia	3.5		1.5
93	Bangladesh	3.5		1.4
94	Nicaragua	3.5		1.3
95	China	3.5		1.1
96	Bolivia	3.5		1.2
97	Mozambique	3.5		1.3
98	Honduras	3.4		1.3
99	Haiti	3.4		1.3
100	Paraguay	2.8		1.2
101	Angola	2.7		1.3
102	Chad	2.3		1.5

11.01　Air pollution regulations

The air pollution regulations in your country are (1 = lax compared with those of most other countries, 7 = among the world's most stringent)

RANK	COUNTRY	SCORE	1　MEAN: 3.8　7	SD		RANK	COUNTRY	SCORE	1　MEAN: 3.8　7	SD
1	Germany	6.7		0.6		53	Indonesia	3.5		1.5
2	Sweden	6.6		0.6		54	Ukraine	3.4		1.6
3	Switzerland	6.5		0.6		55	Egypt	3.3		2.0
4	Finland	6.5		0.5		56	Uruguay	3.2		1.4
5	Denmark	6.5		0.6		57	Turkey	3.2		1.2
6	Netherlands	6.2		0.8		58	Argentina	3.2		1.4
7	Norway	6.2		0.7		59	Zambia	3.2		1.6
8	Austria	6.1		0.9		60	Botswana	3.1		1.3
9	Luxembourg	6.1		0.7		61	Tanzania	3.0		1.5
10	Belgium	5.9		1.0		62	Ghana	3.0		1.6
11	Japan	5.9		1.1		63	Russian Federation	3.0		1.5
12	Singapore	5.8		1.0		64	Malawi	2.9		1.6
13	Iceland	5.8		1.0		64	Morocco	2.9		1.4
14	United Kingdom	5.7		1.1		66	Panama	2.9		1.2
15	France	5.7		0.9		67	Philippines	2.9		1.7
16	Canada	5.7		1.1		68	El Salvador	2.8		1.3
17	Australia	5.7		1.1		69	Sri Lanka	2.8		1.3
18	New Zealand	5.6		0.9		70	Dominican Republic	2.8		1.5
19	United States	5.4		1.4		71	Serbia	2.8		1.4
20	Slovak Republic	5.3		1.2		72	Algeria	2.7		1.4
21	Taiwan	5.2		0.9		73	Jamaica	2.7		1.1
22	Czech Republic	5.0		1.3		74	Pakistan	2.7		1.4
23	Slovenia	5.0		1.0		75	Bangladesh	2.7		1.3
24	Italy	5.0		1.3		76	Vietnam	2.7		1.2
25	Estonia	4.7		1.3		77	Romania	2.7		1.5
26	Portugal	4.7		1.0		78	Uganda	2.6		1.5
27	Tunisia	4.6		1.3		79	Cameroon	2.6		1.6
28	Hungary	4.6		1.5		80	Bulgaria	2.6		1.4
29	Chile	4.5		1.4		81	Senegal	2.5		1.3
30	Spain	4.5		1.2		82	Peru	2.5		1.1
31	Malaysia	4.4		1.2		83	Venezuela	2.5		1.4
32	Lithuania	4.4		1.4		84	Trinidad and Tobago	2.4		1.2
33	Korea	4.4		1.3		85	Honduras	2.4		1.2
34	Ireland	4.4		1.8		86	Kenya	2.4		1.3
35	Latvia	4.3		1.5		87	Ecuador	2.3		1.2
36	Brazil	4.2		1.4		88	Malta	2.3		1.3
37	Greece	4.2		1.3		89	Mozambique	2.3		1.3
38	South Africa	4.2		1.3		90	Nicaragua	2.2		1.2
39	Israel	4.1		1.4		91	Macedonia, FYR	2.2		1.4
40	Mexico	4.1		1.6		92	Madagascar	2.2		1.2
41	Hong Kong SAR	4.0		1.7		93	Zimbabwe	2.2		1.1
42	Thailand	4.0		1.2		94	Guatemala	2.2		1.0
43	Mauritius	4.0		1.4		95	Mali	2.1		1.1
44	Poland	4.0		1.3		96	Ethiopia	2.1		1.3
45	Jordan	4.0		1.4		97	Nigeria	2.1		1.1
46	Costa Rica	3.8		1.3		98	Bolivia	2.1		1.0
47	India	3.8		1.5		99	Chad	2.0		1.2
48	Croatia	3.7		1.7		100	Paraguay	2.0		1.0
49	Colombia	3.7		1.4		101	Angola	1.5		0.7
50	Namibia	3.6		1.6		102	Haiti	1.3		0.7
51	Gambia	3.5		2.0						
52	China	3.5		1.3						

11.02   Water pollution regulations

The water pollution regulations in your country are (1 = lax compared with those of most other countries, 7 = among the world's most stringent)

RANK	COUNTRY	SCORE	1 MEAN: 3.9 7	SD
1	Germany	6.7		0.6
2	Sweden	6.6		0.9
3	Finland	6.6		0.6
4	Denmark	6.6		0.6
5	Switzerland	6.6		0.6
6	Netherlands	6.5		0.7
7	Austria	6.4		0.7
8	Norway	6.4		0.6
9	Iceland	6.1		1.0
10	Singapore	6.1		0.9
11	Australia	6.1		0.9
12	Luxembourg	6.0		0.7
13	New Zealand	5.9		0.9
14	Belgium	5.9		1.0
15	United Kingdom	5.9		1.1
16	Canada	5.8		1.1
17	Japan	5.8		1.2
18	France	5.8		1.0
19	United States	5.7		1.3
20	Slovak Republic	5.4		1.2
21	Taiwan	5.1		1.1
22	Tunisia	5.1		1.4
23	Slovenia	5.0		1.1
24	Italy	5.0		1.3
25	Czech Republic	4.9		1.4
26	Portugal	4.8		1.0
27	Estonia	4.8		1.3
28	Spain	4.7		1.2
29	Hungary	4.6		1.5
30	Chile	4.6		1.3
31	Mauritius	4.5		1.3
32	South Africa	4.5		1.3
33	Lithuania	4.5		1.4
34	Latvia	4.5		1.4
35	Ireland	4.5		1.7
36	Korea	4.5		1.3
37	Greece	4.4		1.5
38	Malaysia	4.3		1.3
39	Israel	4.3		1.4
40	Jordan	4.3		1.4
41	Brazil	4.3		1.5
42	Hong Kong SAR	4.3		1.6
43	Namibia	4.0		1.6
44	Croatia	4.0		1.8
45	Costa Rica	4.0		1.7
46	Poland	3.9		1.3
47	Uruguay	3.9		1.4
48	Thailand	3.9		1.4
49	Mexico	3.8		1.6
50	Botswana	3.7		1.3
51	Colombia	3.7		1.5
52	Gambia	3.6		1.9

RANK	COUNTRY	SCORE	1 MEAN: 3.9 7	SD
53	Indonesia	3.6		1.4
54	Egypt	3.5		1.9
55	India	3.5		1.6
56	China	3.4		1.4
57	Jamaica	3.4		1.4
58	Argentina	3.4		1.6
59	Zambia	3.3		1.6
60	Dominican Republic	3.2		1.3
61	Ghana	3.2		1.7
62	Turkey	3.1		1.3
63	El Salvador	3.1		1.5
64	Malawi	3.1		1.6
65	Panama	3.1		1.4
66	Ukraine	3.1		1.5
67	Morocco	3.1		1.4
68	Russian Federation	3.0		1.5
69	Tanzania	3.0		1.5
70	Sri Lanka	3.0		1.4
71	Philippines	2.9		1.5
72	Algeria	2.9		1.6
73	Senegal	2.9		1.4
74	Venezuela	2.9		1.5
75	Pakistan	2.8		1.6
76	Malta	2.8		1.3
77	Serbia	2.7		1.5
78	Peru	2.7		1.2
79	Romania	2.7		1.5
80	Honduras	2.7		1.3
81	Trinidad and Tobago	2.7		1.2
82	Vietnam	2.6		1.3
83	Zimbabwe	2.6		1.3
84	Bulgaria	2.6		1.4
85	Ecuador	2.6		1.2
86	Cameroon	2.6		1.5
87	Uganda	2.5		1.4
88	Macedonia, FYR	2.5		1.5
89	Madagascar	2.4		1.3
90	Kenya	2.3		1.1
91	Bangladesh	2.3		1.4
92	Nicaragua	2.3		1.2
93	Mozambique	2.3		1.2
94	Nigeria	2.2		1.2
95	Ethiopia	2.1		1.3
96	Mali	2.1		1.4
97	Guatemala	2.1		1.1
98	Bolivia	2.1		1.0
99	Paraguay	2.1		1.2
100	Chad	1.8		1.0
101	Angola	1.5		0.8
102	Haiti	1.3		0.7

11.03   Toxic waste disposal regulations

The toxic waste disposal regulations in your country are (1 = lax compared with those of most other countries, 7 = among the world's most stringent)

RANK	COUNTRY	SCORE	1 MEAN: 3.9 7	SD
1	Germany	6.8		0.5
2	Finland	6.7		0.5
3	Denmark	6.6		0.6
3	Sweden	6.6		0.6
5	Switzerland	6.6		0.6
6	Netherlands	6.5		0.6
7	Austria	6.4		0.7
8	Norway	6.4		0.6
9	Belgium	6.3		0.9
10	Australia	6.3		0.6
11	Iceland	6.2		1.0
12	Singapore	6.2		0.8
13	New Zealand	6.1		0.9
14	Luxembourg	6.0		0.9
15	United States	5.9		1.2
16	France	5.9		0.9
17	Canada	5.9		1.3
18	United Kingdom	5.8		1.1
19	Japan	5.7		1.2
20	Slovak Republic	5.4		1.3
21	Taiwan	5.2		0.9
22	Italy	5.1		1.3
23	Tunisia	5.1		1.3
24	Slovenia	5.0		1.4
25	Spain	4.8		1.2
26	Estonia	4.8		1.4
27	Czech Republic	4.7		1.5
28	Ireland	4.6		1.9
29	Korea	4.6		1.3
30	South Africa	4.6		1.4
31	Hong Kong SAR	4.6		1.6
32	Malaysia	4.6		1.4
33	Portugal	4.6		1.2
34	Latvia	4.5		1.4
35	Hungary	4.5		1.5
36	Israel	4.4		1.7
37	Chile	4.3		1.4
38	Greece	4.3		1.4
39	Brazil	4.3		1.5
40	Lithuania	4.3		1.4
41	Jordan	4.2		1.4
42	Mauritius	4.2		1.4
43	Costa Rica	3.9		1.6
44	Poland	3.9		1.4
45	Thailand	3.9		1.4
46	Mexico	3.9		1.7
47	Namibia	3.8		1.7
48	Croatia	3.7		1.9
49	Uruguay	3.7		1.3
50	Indonesia	3.7		1.4
51	Gambia	3.6		2.1
52	Botswana	3.6		1.4

RANK	COUNTRY	SCORE	1 MEAN: 3.9 7	SD
53	Colombia	3.5		1.5
54	Egypt	3.5		2.0
55	Argentina	3.5		1.5
56	Zambia	3.4		1.4
57	China	3.4		1.4
58	India	3.3		1.5
59	Turkey	3.2		1.2
60	Ghana	3.2		1.6
61	Malawi	3.2		1.5
62	Ukraine	3.1		1.4
63	Russian Federation	3.1		1.6
64	Jamaica	3.1		1.1
65	Tanzania	3.0		1.5
66	Algeria	3.0		1.6
67	Dominican Republic	3.0		1.5
68	Serbia	2.9		1.6
69	El Salvador	2.9		1.5
70	Morocco	2.9		1.4
71	Romania	2.9		1.7
72	Vietnam	2.9		1.3
73	Sri Lanka	2.9		1.4
74	Uganda	2.8		1.7
75	Panama	2.8		1.2
76	Pakistan	2.8		1.4
76	Senegal	2.8		1.3
78	Philippines	2.8		1.5
79	Zimbabwe	2.8		1.2
80	Peru	2.7		1.2
81	Bulgaria	2.7		1.6
82	Trinidad and Tobago	2.7		1.2
83	Malta	2.7		1.4
84	Venezuela	2.7		1.4
85	Cameroon	2.6		1.6
86	Kenya	2.5		1.1
87	Madagascar	2.5		1.4
88	Honduras	2.5		1.2
89	Macedonia, FYR	2.4		1.5
90	Nigeria	2.4		1.3
91	Nicaragua	2.4		1.4
92	Ecuador	2.3		1.2
93	Bangladesh	2.3		1.4
94	Mali	2.3		1.3
95	Paraguay	2.3		1.2
96	Guatemala	2.2		1.2
97	Mozambique	2.2		1.3
98	Bolivia	2.2		1.1
99	Ethiopia	2.2		1.3
100	Chad	2.0		1.5
101	Haiti	1.6		0.8
102	Angola	1.4		0.7

11.04 Chemical waste regulations

The regulations concerning chemicals used in manufacturing in your country are (1 = lax compared with those of most other countries, 7 = among the world's most stringent)

RANK	COUNTRY	SCORE	1 MEAN: 3.9 7	SD		RANK	COUNTRY	SCORE	1 MEAN: 3.9 7	SD
1	Germany	6.7		0.5		53	Gambia	3.5		1.9
2	Finland	6.7		0.5		54	Argentina	3.5		1.4
3	Sweden	6.6		0.6		55	Malawi	3.5		1.6
4	Denmark	6.5		0.6		56	Indonesia	3.4		1.2
5	Switzerland	6.5		0.7		57	Colombia	3.4		1.4
6	Netherlands	6.4		0.7		58	Turkey	3.4		1.2
7	Norway	6.3		0.7		59	India	3.4		1.5
8	Australia	6.3		0.6		60	Ghana	3.4		1.5
9	Austria	6.2		0.8		61	Egypt	3.3		1.8
10	Belgium	6.1		0.9		62	Ukraine	3.3		1.4
11	Singapore	6.1		0.8		63	Jamaica	3.2		1.1
12	Luxembourg	6.0		0.7		64	Russian Federation	3.2		1.6
13	Iceland	6.0		1.0		65	Tanzania	3.1		1.4
14	New Zealand	6.0		1.0		66	Dominican Republic	3.1		1.4
15	Canada	5.9		1.2		67	Morocco	3.1		1.5
16	France	5.8		0.8		68	El Salvador	3.1		1.5
17	United Kingdom	5.8		1.2		69	Senegal	3.0		1.3
18	United States	5.8		1.3		70	Algeria	3.0		1.6
19	Japan	5.7		1.1		71	Malta	2.9		1.4
20	Slovak Republic	5.2		1.3		72	Uganda	2.9		1.6
21	Slovenia	5.2		1.1		73	Pakistan	2.9		1.4
22	Taiwan	5.1		1.1		74	Panama	2.9		1.2
23	Italy	5.1		1.2		75	Sri Lanka	2.9		1.2
24	Tunisia	5.0		1.3		76	Serbia	2.9		1.5
25	Spain	4.9		1.1		77	Philippines	2.8		1.3
26	Estonia	4.8		1.2		78	Vietnam	2.8		1.2
27	Ireland	4.8		1.6		79	Zimbabwe	2.8		1.2
28	Portugal	4.6		1.0		80	Romania	2.8		1.6
29	Czech Republic	4.6		1.5		81	Trinidad and Tobago	2.7		1.2
30	Korea	4.6		1.2		82	Venezuela	2.7		1.5
31	Hong Kong SAR	4.6		1.5		83	Peru	2.7		1.2
32	South Africa	4.6		1.4		84	Cameroon	2.7		1.5
33	Hungary	4.5		1.5		85	Bulgaria	2.7		1.3
34	Malaysia	4.4		1.3		86	Kenya	2.6		1.1
35	Chile	4.4		1.2		87	Madagascar	2.6		1.5
36	Latvia	4.3		1.3		88	Honduras	2.6		1.3
37	Greece	4.3		1.4		89	Nicaragua	2.5		1.4
38	Brazil	4.3		1.5		90	Macedonia, FYR	2.5		1.5
38	Mauritius	4.3		1.4		91	Nigeria	2.4		1.3
40	Lithuania	4.3		1.3		92	Mali	2.4		1.4
41	Israel	4.3		1.3		93	Guatemala	2.4		1.2
42	Jordan	4.2		1.4		94	Bangladesh	2.3		1.2
43	Poland	4.1		1.3		95	Ethiopia	2.3		1.3
44	Mexico	4.0		1.5		96	Ecuador	2.3		1.2
45	Costa Rica	4.0		1.6		97	Paraguay	2.2		1.2
46	Thailand	3.9		1.5		98	Mozambique	2.2		1.3
47	Namibia	3.8		1.6		99	Bolivia	2.1		0.9
48	Uruguay	3.7		1.3		100	Chad	2.0		1.2
49	Croatia	3.7		1.8		101	Haiti	1.4		0.5
50	Zambia	3.6		1.4		102	Angola	1.3		0.6
51	China	3.6		1.4						
52	Botswana	3.6		1.4						

11.05 Stringency of environmental regulations

How stringent is your country's overall environmental regulation? (1 = lax compared with that of most other countries, 7 = among the world's most stringent)

RANK	COUNTRY	SCORE	1	MEAN: 4.0	7	SD
1	Germany	6.7				0.5
2	Sweden	6.5				0.7
3	Denmark	6.5				0.6
4	Finland	6.5				0.6
5	Austria	6.4				0.7
6	Switzerland	6.3				0.8
7	Netherlands	6.3				0.8
8	Belgium	6.2				0.9
9	New Zealand	6.1				0.7
10	Norway	6.1				1.0
11	Luxembourg	6.0				0.7
12	Iceland	6.0				0.8
13	Canada	5.9				1.2
14	Australia	5.9				0.7
15	United Kingdom	5.8				0.8
16	Singapore	5.8				0.9
17	France	5.6				0.9
18	United States	5.6				1.4
19	Japan	5.6				1.0
20	Taiwan	5.3				1.0
21	Slovak Republic	5.1				1.2
22	Slovenia	5.0				1.1
23	Tunisia	4.9				1.3
24	Italy	4.9				1.2
25	Portugal	4.9				1.0
26	Czech Republic	4.9				1.3
27	Malaysia	4.7				1.1
28	Chile	4.7				1.1
29	Estonia	4.6				1.2
30	Spain	4.6				1.0
31	Korea	4.5				1.2
32	South Africa	4.5				1.5
33	Costa Rica	4.5				1.3
34	Hungary	4.5				1.3
35	Brazil	4.5				1.4
36	Israel	4.4				1.2
37	Ireland	4.4				1.6
38	Latvia	4.4				1.4
39	Mauritius	4.3				1.3
40	Hong Kong SAR	4.3				1.5
41	Lithuania	4.3				1.4
42	Jordan	4.3				1.2
43	Thailand	4.2				1.3
44	Greece	4.1				1.2
45	Poland	4.0				1.4
46	Croatia	4.0				1.8
47	Mexico	3.9				1.5
48	Namibia	3.9				1.6
49	Colombia	3.8				1.4
50	India	3.8				1.7
51	Indonesia	3.8				1.4
52	Gambia	3.7				1.7

RANK	COUNTRY	SCORE	1	MEAN: 4.0	7	SD
53	Egypt	3.7				1.8
54	Panama	3.6				1.4
55	Tanzania	3.6				1.2
56	Uruguay	3.6				1.2
57	China	3.5				1.3
58	Senegal	3.5				1.4
59	Zambia	3.4				1.3
60	Morocco	3.4				1.5
61	Botswana	3.4				1.2
62	Ghana	3.4				1.5
63	El Salvador	3.4				1.4
64	Argentina	3.3				1.4
65	Sri Lanka	3.3				1.3
66	Turkey	3.3				1.2
67	Ukraine	3.2				1.4
68	Dominican Republic	3.2				1.5
69	Jamaica	3.2				1.2
70	Cameroon	3.2				1.5
71	Philippines	3.2				1.4
72	Uganda	3.2				1.5
73	Malawi	3.1				1.4
74	Vietnam	3.1				1.3
75	Russian Federation	3.1				1.6
76	Madagascar	3.1				1.3
77	Kenya	3.0				1.3
78	Pakistan	2.9				1.2
79	Bangladesh	2.9				1.4
80	Algeria	2.9				1.4
81	Serbia	2.9				1.5
82	Peru	2.9				1.3
83	Romania	2.9				1.6
84	Trinidad and Tobago	2.9				1.3
85	Bulgaria	2.8				1.5
86	Honduras	2.8				1.4
87	Zimbabwe	2.8				1.3
88	Venezuela	2.7				1.6
89	Mali	2.7				1.3
90	Ecuador	2.7				1.2
91	Malta	2.6				1.2
92	Guatemala	2.5				1.0
93	Nigeria	2.5				1.3
94	Bolivia	2.4				1.3
95	Nicaragua	2.4				1.3
96	Mozambique	2.4				1.2
97	Macedonia, FYR	2.2				1.3
98	Paraguay	2.2				1.1
99	Ethiopia	2.1				1.1
100	Chad	2.0				1.2
101	Angola	1.6				0.8
102	Haiti	1.6				0.8

11.06 Compliance with environmental regulations

Your country normally enacts environmental regulations (1 = much later than other countries, 7 = ahead of most other countries)

RANK	COUNTRY	SCORE	1 MEAN: 3.7 7	SD
1	Sweden	6.5		0.9
2	Germany	6.4		0.8
3	Denmark	6.4		0.8
4	Netherlands	6.3		0.7
5	Finland	6.3		0.8
6	Switzerland	6.2		0.8
7	Norway	6.0		0.9
8	Austria	5.9		1.0
9	New Zealand	5.8		1.0
10	Canada	5.6		1.1
11	Singapore	5.5		1.0
12	United Kingdom	5.4		1.3
13	Belgium	5.4		1.3
14	Australia	5.4		0.7
15	Iceland	5.3		1.1
16	Japan	5.3		1.2
17	United States	5.2		1.4
18	Luxembourg	5.2		1.2
19	France	5.1		1.1
20	Malaysia	4.7		1.3
21	Taiwan	4.7		1.0
22	Italy	4.7		1.2
23	Tunisia	4.6		1.4
24	Spain	4.4		1.1
25	Brazil	4.4		1.2
26	Costa Rica	4.3		1.3
27	Portugal	4.3		1.2
28	Slovenia	4.3		1.1
29	Estonia	4.3		1.1
30	Czech Republic	4.3		1.3
31	Korea	4.3		1.2
32	Latvia	4.1		1.3
33	Chile	4.1		1.3
34	Israel	4.1		1.2
35	Hungary	4.1		1.1
36	Slovak Republic	4.1		1.2
37	Jordan	4.0		1.3
38	South Africa	3.9		1.2
39	Lithuania	3.9		1.1
40	Ireland	3.9		1.5
41	Thailand	3.8		1.2
42	Gambia	3.8		1.7
43	Poland	3.6		1.2
44	Hong Kong SAR	3.6		1.4
45	Greece	3.6		1.3
46	Indonesia	3.6		1.3
47	Croatia	3.5		1.5
48	Namibia	3.5		1.4
49	Egypt	3.5		1.7
50	Colombia	3.5		1.4
50	Mauritius	3.5		1.0
52	Ghana	3.5		1.4
53	Mexico	3.4		1.3
54	China	3.4		1.1
55	Zambia	3.3		1.4
56	Botswana	3.3		1.3
57	Cameroon	3.3		1.6
58	India	3.2		1.5
59	Tanzania	3.2		1.3
60	Uganda	3.2		1.6
61	Philippines	3.1		1.3
62	Senegal	3.1		1.6
63	Turkey	3.0		1.1
64	Malawi	3.0		1.2
65	Argentina	3.0		1.3
66	Uruguay	3.0		1.2
67	Ukraine	3.0		1.1
68	Panama	2.9		1.3
69	Jamaica	2.9		1.1
70	Madagascar	2.9		1.4
71	Dominican Republic	2.9		1.6
72	Morocco	2.9		1.6
73	Mali	2.9		1.3
74	Kenya	2.8		1.1
75	El Salvador	2.8		1.3
76	Russian Federation	2.7		1.3
77	Bulgaria	2.7		1.1
78	Serbia	2.6		1.1
79	Pakistan	2.6		1.1
80	Sri Lanka	2.6		1.1
81	Romania	2.6		1.3
82	Peru	2.6		1.0
83	Honduras	2.6		1.3
84	Trinidad and Tobago	2.6		1.0
85	Vietnam	2.5		1.1
86	Algeria	2.5		1.2
87	Zimbabwe	2.5		1.2
88	Nigeria	2.5		1.1
89	Venezuela	2.4		1.3
90	Bangladesh	2.4		1.2
91	Malta	2.4		1.1
92	Macedonia, FYR	2.4		1.3
93	Mozambique	2.3		1.2
94	Ecuador	2.2		1.0
95	Ethiopia	2.2		1.3
96	Nicaragua	2.2		1.3
97	Guatemala	2.2		0.9
98	Bolivia	2.2		1.1
99	Paraguay	2.2		1.1
100	Chad	2.2		1.3
101	Angola	1.7		0.9
102	Haiti	1.3		0.5

563

11.07 Compliance with international agreements

Compliance with international environmental agreements is a high priority in your country's government (1 = strongly disagree, 7 = strongly agree)

RANK	COUNTRY	SCORE	1 MEAN: 4.3 7	SD
1	Sweden	6.6		0.6
2	Germany	6.5		0.7
3	Finland	6.4		0.7
4	Netherlands	6.3		0.8
5	New Zealand	6.3		0.9
6	Denmark	6.2		1.2
7	Switzerland	6.2		0.8
8	Norway	6.1		1.1
9	Austria	6.0		1.0
10	Singapore	6.0		0.9
11	Iceland	5.9		1.0
12	Canada	5.8		1.2
13	Japan	5.7		1.2
14	Luxembourg	5.7		1.1
15	United Kingdom	5.6		1.2
16	Belgium	5.6		1.0
17	France	5.6		1.2
18	Slovak Republic	5.4		1.2
18	Tunisia	5.4		1.4
20	Taiwan	5.3		1.2
21	Estonia	5.3		1.2
22	Slovenia	5.2		1.1
23	Malaysia	5.1		1.1
24	Hungary	5.1		1.3
25	Gambia	5.1		1.8
26	Czech Republic	5.1		1.2
27	Portugal	4.9		1.2
28	Italy	4.9		1.3
29	China	4.8		1.4
30	Spain	4.8		1.3
31	Korea	4.7		1.1
32	Costa Rica	4.7		1.4
33	Jordan	4.7		1.4
34	Chile	4.7		1.2
35	South Africa	4.7		1.3
36	Lithuania	4.6		1.4
37	Mauritius	4.6		1.2
38	Latvia	4.6		1.2
39	Brazil	4.6		1.4
40	Australia	4.6		1.8
41	Romania	4.5		1.7
42	Hong Kong SAR	4.5		1.6
42	Thailand	4.5		1.4
44	Ghana	4.5		1.6
45	Serbia	4.4		1.8
46	Vietnam	4.4		1.4
47	Ireland	4.4		1.5
48	Croatia	4.4		1.8
49	Senegal	4.4		1.7
50	Botswana	4.4		1.3
51	Malawi	4.3		1.5
52	Colombia	4.3		1.5

RANK	COUNTRY	SCORE	1 MEAN: 4.3 7	SD
53	Namibia	4.3		1.4
54	Poland	4.3		1.2
55	Tanzania	4.3		1.3
56	Madagascar	4.3		1.5
57	Greece	4.2		1.4
58	Mexico	4.2		1.3
59	Cameroon	4.1		1.8
60	United States	4.1		1.7
61	Israel	4.0		1.4
62	Malta	4.0		1.7
63	Algeria	3.9		1.7
64	Ukraine	3.9		1.7
65	Zambia	3.9		1.7
66	Egypt	3.9		1.8
67	Mali	3.8		1.9
68	Indonesia	3.8		1.4
69	Morocco	3.8		1.8
70	Uruguay	3.8		1.2
71	Russian Federation	3.7		1.7
72	Honduras	3.7		1.7
73	Jamaica	3.7		1.3
74	Uganda	3.6		1.8
75	India	3.6		1.4
76	Bulgaria	3.6		1.7
77	Bangladesh	3.6		1.7
78	El Salvador	3.6		1.5
79	Kenya	3.5		1.6
80	Sri Lanka	3.5		1.5
81	Mozambique	3.5		1.7
82	Macedonia, FYR	3.5		2.0
83	Trinidad and Tobago	3.4		1.3
84	Turkey	3.4		1.4
85	Dominican Republic	3.4		1.7
86	Panama	3.3		1.4
87	Pakistan	3.2		1.4
88	Chad	3.2		2.1
89	Peru	3.2		1.3
90	Nigeria	3.1		1.5
91	Argentina	3.0		1.4
92	Philippines	3.0		1.5
93	Ethiopia	2.9		1.8
94	Zimbabwe	2.8		1.5
95	Ecuador	2.8		1.4
96	Nicaragua	2.7		1.6
97	Bolivia	2.6		1.3
98	Angola	2.5		1.6
99	Guatemala	2.3		1.2
100	Paraguay	2.2		1.1
101	Venezuela	2.0		1.0
102	Haiti	1.3		0.6

11.08 Clarity and stability of regulations

Environmental regulations in your country are (1 = confusing and frequently changing, 7 = transparent and stable)

RANK	COUNTRY	SCORE	1 — MEAN: 4.1 — 7	SD
1	Singapore	6.1		0.8
2	Sweden	5.9		1.1
3	Finland	5.9		1.0
4	Switzerland	5.9		0.9
5	Austria	5.7		1.0
6	Denmark	5.7		1.1
7	Germany	5.6		1.2
8	Iceland	5.5		1.3
9	Gambia	5.4		1.5
10	Canada	5.3		1.3
11	France	5.3		1.1
12	Norway	5.3		1.4
13	Tunisia	5.2		1.3
14	Taiwan	5.2		1.3
15	Netherlands	5.2		1.4
16	Malaysia	5.1		1.1
17	United Kingdom	5.0		1.4
18	Japan	5.0		1.2
19	Luxembourg	4.9		1.6
20	Australia	4.9		1.4
21	Estonia	4.9		1.1
22	New Zealand	4.9		1.3
23	Hong Kong SAR	4.8		1.4
24	Slovenia	4.8		1.0
25	Spain	4.7		1.1
26	South Africa	4.6		1.2
27	Czech Republic	4.6		1.2
28	Ghana	4.5		1.4
29	Italy	4.5		1.1
30	Israel	4.5		1.1
31	United States	4.5		1.6
32	Korea	4.4		1.1
33	Latvia	4.4		1.1
34	Ireland	4.4		1.2
35	Botswana	4.4		1.2
36	Jordan	4.4		1.3
37	Malawi	4.4		1.3
37	Mauritius	4.4		1.2
39	Thailand	4.3		1.3
40	Namibia	4.3		1.3
41	Brazil	4.3		1.4
42	Mexico	4.2		1.3
43	Slovak Republic	4.2		1.3
44	Lithuania	4.2		1.3
45	Zambia	4.2		1.6
46	Tanzania	4.2		1.4
47	Hungary	4.2		1.3
48	Portugal	4.2		1.2
49	Chile	4.1		1.3
50	Costa Rica	4.1		1.3
51	Poland	4.1		1.2
52	Greece	4.1		1.3
53	Belgium	4.0		1.5
53	China	4.0		1.3
53	Colombia	4.0		1.3
56	Jamaica	4.0		1.1
57	Croatia	3.9		1.6
58	Senegal	3.9		1.5
59	Trinidad and Tobago	3.8		1.1
60	Vietnam	3.8		1.3
61	Uruguay	3.8		1.0
62	Malta	3.8		1.3
63	Indonesia	3.8		1.3
64	India	3.8		1.5
65	Madagascar	3.8		1.4
66	Zimbabwe	3.7		1.3
67	Egypt	3.7		1.7
68	Mali	3.7		1.4
69	Uganda	3.6		1.7
70	Panama	3.6		1.4
71	Serbia	3.5		1.4
72	Russian Federation	3.5		1.5
73	Romania	3.5		1.5
74	Mozambique	3.5		1.4
75	El Salvador	3.5		1.2
76	Chad	3.4		1.7
77	Ukraine	3.4		1.3
78	Cameroon	3.4		1.7
79	Algeria	3.4		1.5
80	Kenya	3.4		1.3
81	Pakistan	3.4		1.2
82	Morocco	3.4		1.6
83	Sri Lanka	3.3		1.3
84	Bulgaria	3.3		1.4
85	Turkey	3.3		1.2
86	Dominican Republic	3.3		1.4
87	Peru	3.3		1.2
88	Argentina	3.3		1.3
89	Nigeria	3.2		1.4
90	Macedonia, FYR	3.2		1.9
91	Ethiopia	3.2		1.6
92	Bangladesh	3.2		1.4
93	Bolivia	3.1		1.2
94	Venezuela	3.1		1.3
95	Honduras	3.1		1.2
96	Philippines	3.1		1.2
97	Paraguay	2.9		1.1
98	Nicaragua	2.8		1.5
99	Ecuador	2.7		1.2
100	Angola	2.7		1.6
101	Guatemala	2.6		1.1
102	Haiti	1.6		1.0

565

11.09   Flexibility of regulations

Environmental regulations in your country (1 = offer no options for achieving compliance, 7 = are flexible and offer many options for achieving compliance)

RANK	COUNTRY	SCORE	1 MEAN: 4.0 7	SD
1	Singapore	5.4		1.2
2	Austria	5.3		1.1
3	Switzerland	5.2		1.2
4	Germany	5.2		1.1
5	France	5.1		0.9
6	Iceland	5.0		1.0
7	Tunisia	5.0		1.2
8	Finland	4.9		1.2
9	Denmark	4.9		1.3
10	Canada	4.8		1.3
11	Luxembourg	4.8		1.3
12	Malaysia	4.8		1.1
13	Gambia	4.7		1.8
14	Australia	4.7		1.0
15	Sweden	4.6		1.5
16	United Kingdom	4.6		1.3
17	Taiwan	4.6		1.3
18	Norway	4.5		1.4
19	United States	4.5		1.3
20	South Africa	4.5		1.0
21	Netherlands	4.5		1.4
22	New Zealand	4.5		1.3
23	Italy	4.5		1.1
24	Spain	4.4		0.9
25	Jordan	4.4		1.1
26	Ukraine	4.4		1.6
27	Ghana	4.4		1.4
28	Latvia	4.4		1.2
29	Japan	4.4		1.1
30	Israel	4.4		1.0
31	Hong Kong SAR	4.3		1.4
32	Korea	4.3		1.0
33	Czech Republic	4.3		1.0
34	Russian Federation	4.3		1.4
35	Ireland	4.2		1.3
36	Uruguay	4.2		1.0
37	Slovenia	4.2		1.1
38	Estonia	4.2		1.2
39	Colombia	4.1		1.2
40	Poland	4.1		1.0
41	Botswana	4.1		1.0
42	Vietnam	4.1		1.2
43	Zambia	4.1		1.5
44	Costa Rica	4.1		1.4
45	Thailand	4.1		1.0
46	Brazil	4.1		1.1
47	Slovak Republic	4.1		1.2
48	Mexico	4.0		1.3
49	Jamaica	4.0		1.1
50	Namibia	4.0		1.3
51	China	4.0		1.2
52	Tanzania	4.0		1.3

RANK	COUNTRY	SCORE	1 MEAN: 4.0 7	SD
53	Malawi	4.0		1.2
53	Mauritius	4.0		1.2
55	Chile	3.9		1.3
56	Portugal	3.9		1.0
57	Greece	3.8		1.1
58	Dominican Republic	3.8		1.2
59	Malta	3.8		1.3
60	Croatia	3.8		1.4
61	Zimbabwe	3.8		1.3
62	Indonesia	3.8		1.5
63	Egypt	3.7		1.6
64	Cameroon	3.7		1.8
65	Hungary	3.7		1.1
66	Mali	3.7		1.5
67	Uganda	3.7		1.6
68	Lithuania	3.7		1.1
69	Serbia	3.6		1.4
70	Belgium	3.6		1.3
71	Trinidad and Tobago	3.6		1.1
72	Macedonia, FYR	3.6		1.8
73	Bangladesh	3.6		1.5
74	Senegal	3.6		1.6
75	El Salvador	3.5		1.3
76	Sri Lanka	3.5		1.3
77	Turkey	3.5		1.4
78	Madagascar	3.5		1.4
79	Romania	3.5		1.4
80	Nigeria	3.5		1.5
81	Algeria	3.5		1.5
82	Panama	3.5		1.4
83	India	3.4		1.3
84	Argentina	3.4		1.3
85	Peru	3.4		1.4
86	Mozambique	3.4		1.5
87	Morocco	3.3		1.5
88	Kenya	3.3		1.4
89	Honduras	3.2		1.3
90	Pakistan	3.2		1.2
91	Bulgaria	3.1		1.2
92	Venezuela	3.1		1.3
93	Guatemala	3.0		1.4
94	Philippines	3.0		1.2
95	Chad	3.0		1.6
96	Nicaragua	3.0		1.6
97	Bolivia	2.9		1.3
98	Ecuador	2.9		1.4
99	Ethiopia	2.9		1.3
100	Paraguay	2.9		1.5
101	Angola	2.4		1.4
102	Haiti	2.1		1.3

11.10 Consistency of regulation enforcement

Environmental regulations in your country are (1 = not enforced or enforced erratically, 7 = enforced consistently and fairly)

RANK	COUNTRY	SCORE	MEAN: 3.8	SD	RANK	COUNTRY	SCORE	MEAN: 3.8	SD
1	Germany	6.1		0.9	53	Botswana	3.6		1.4
2	Finland	6.1		1.0	54	Ukraine	3.6		1.0
3	Singapore	6.0		0.8	55	Vietnam	3.6		1.5
4	Sweden	6.0		0.8	56	Cameroon	3.6		1.7
5	Switzerland	5.9		0.9	57	Senegal	3.6		1.4
6	Denmark	5.9		0.8	58	Mexico	3.6		1.4
7	Luxembourg	5.6		0.9	59	Malawi	3.6		1.3
8	United Kingdom	5.6		1.1	60	Egypt	3.6		1.7
9	Austria	5.6		1.0	61	Namibia	3.6		1.5
10	Australia	5.5		1.0	62	Uruguay	3.5		1.2
11	Netherlands	5.5		1.0	63	India	3.5		1.3
12	Norway	5.5		0.9	64	Russian Federation	3.5		1.4
13	Canada	5.5		1.1	65	Romania	3.4		1.5
14	Iceland	5.4		1.1	66	Indonesia	3.4		1.4
15	New Zealand	5.3		1.2	67	Turkey	3.3		1.2
16	United States	5.3		1.2	68	Jamaica	3.2		1.2
17	Taiwan	5.2		1.2	69	Croatia	3.2		1.6
18	France	5.1		1.2	70	Morocco	3.2		1.6
19	Tunisia	5.1		1.3	71	Sri Lanka	3.1		1.4
20	Belgium	5.1		1.3	72	Bulgaria	3.1		1.3
21	Japan	4.9		1.1	73	Madagascar	3.1		1.3
22	Korea	4.7		1.1	74	Bangladesh	3.1		1.4
23	Hong Kong SAR	4.6		1.5	74	Panama	3.1		1.3
24	Gambia	4.6		1.9	76	Algeria	3.0		1.6
25	Slovenia	4.6		1.1	77	Zimbabwe	3.0		1.6
26	Lithuania	4.5		1.0	78	Macedonia, FYR	3.0		1.6
27	Portugal	4.5		1.0	79	Argentina	2.9		1.3
28	Estonia	4.5		1.3	80	Dominican Republic	2.9		1.4
29	Slovak Republic	4.4		1.3	81	Malta	2.9		1.3
29	Spain	4.4		1.1	82	El Salvador	2.9		1.2
31	Czech Republic	4.4		1.3	83	Nigeria	2.9		1.5
32	Latvia	4.3		1.2	84	Serbia	2.8		1.3
33	Italy	4.3		1.1	85	Kenya	2.8		1.4
34	Brazil	4.2		1.3	86	Trinidad and Tobago	2.7		1.3
35	Jordan	4.2		1.3	87	Pakistan	2.7		1.2
36	Chile	4.2		1.3	88	Honduras	2.7		1.2
37	Poland	4.2		1.2	89	Mali	2.7		1.4
38	Israel	4.1		1.2	90	Philippines	2.6		1.2
39	Ghana	4.1		1.5	91	Peru	2.6		1.3
40	Malaysia	4.1		1.4	92	Ethiopia	2.6		1.3
41	Ireland	4.1		1.6	93	Chad	2.4		1.5
42	Uganda	4.0		1.8	94	Guatemala	2.4		1.1
43	Zambia	4.0		1.8	95	Mozambique	2.3		1.1
44	South Africa	4.0		1.3	96	Bolivia	2.3		1.1
45	Greece	4.0		1.2	97	Nicaragua	2.3		1.2
46	Thailand	4.0		1.2	98	Ecuador	2.2		1.0
47	Tanzania	4.0		1.3	99	Venezuela	2.1		1.2
48	China	3.9		1.3	100	Angola	1.9		1.0
49	Mauritius	3.8		1.5	101	Paraguay	1.9		0.9
50	Costa Rica	3.7		1.4	102	Haiti	1.3		0.4
51	Colombia	3.7		1.2					
52	Hungary	3.7		1.2					

11.11 Effects of compliance on business

Complying with environmental standards in your country (1 = hurts competitiveness, 7 = helps long-term competitiveness by prompting companies to improve products and processes)

RANK	COUNTRY	SCORE	MEAN: 4.4	SD
1	Singapore	5.9		0.9
2	Finland	5.6		1.3
3	Iceland	5.5		1.0
4	Denmark	5.4		1.3
5	Tunisia	5.4		1.1
6	Taiwan	5.4		1.0
7	Sweden	5.3		0.9
8	France	5.3		1.2
9	Japan	5.3		1.4
10	Switzerland	5.2		1.2
11	Netherlands	5.0		1.2
12	Canada	5.0		1.3
12	Malaysia	5.0		0.9
14	Austria	4.9		1.4
15	Norway	4.9		1.0
16	Gambia	4.9		1.5
17	Australia	4.9		1.1
18	Hong Kong SAR	4.9		0.9
19	Germany	4.9		1.5
20	Italy	4.9		1.1
21	Luxembourg	4.8		1.5
22	Ghana	4.8		1.2
23	United Kingdom	4.8		1.3
24	Korea	4.8		1.1
25	United States	4.7		1.4
26	Mali	4.7		1.4
27	China	4.7		1.4
28	Namibia	4.7		1.2
29	Jordan	4.6		1.2
30	Latvia	4.6		1.2
31	Cameroon	4.6		1.2
32	Jamaica	4.6		1.3
32	Senegal	4.6		1.4
34	Thailand	4.6		1.1
35	Israel	4.6		1.1
36	Tanzania	4.6		1.3
37	Brazil	4.6		1.2
38	Zambia	4.6		1.3
39	Slovenia	4.5		1.1
40	Madagascar	4.5		1.2
41	Croatia	4.5		1.5
42	Romania	4.5		1.7
43	Vietnam	4.5		1.4
44	Botswana	4.5		0.9
44	Estonia	4.5		1.2
46	Malawi	4.5		1.2
47	Slovak Republic	4.5		1.4
48	Ethiopia	4.5		1.8
49	South Africa	4.5		1.1
50	Chad	4.5		1.6
50	Ireland	4.5		1.4
52	Costa Rica	4.5		1.2

RANK	COUNTRY	SCORE	MEAN: 4.4	SD
53	Czech Republic	4.5		1.1
54	Lithuania	4.4		1.1
55	Spain	4.4		1.0
56	Malta	4.4		1.3
57	Mauritius	4.3		1.2
58	Chile	4.3		1.3
59	Algeria	4.3		1.5
60	Egypt	4.3		1.5
61	Uganda	4.2		1.8
62	India	4.2		1.1
63	New Zealand	4.2		1.5
64	Hungary	4.2		1.3
65	Greece	4.2		1.2
66	Uruguay	4.2		0.9
67	Kenya	4.2		1.5
68	Nigeria	4.2		1.4
69	Macedonia, FYR	4.1		1.8
70	Trinidad and Tobago	4.1		1.3
71	Belgium	4.1		1.3
72	Mexico	4.1		1.3
73	Bangladesh	4.1		1.3
74	Poland	4.0		1.2
75	Serbia	4.0		1.5
76	Russian Federation	4.0		1.4
77	Portugal	4.0		1.0
78	Sri Lanka	4.0		1.3
78	Zimbabwe	4.0		1.0
80	Morocco	4.0		1.5
81	Colombia	4.0		1.2
82	Dominican Republic	3.9		1.3
83	Peru	3.9		1.2
84	Bulgaria	3.9		1.5
85	Ukraine	3.9		1.2
86	Panama	3.8		1.2
87	Mozambique	3.7		1.2
88	El Salvador	3.7		1.3
89	Argentina	3.7		1.2
89	Pakistan	3.7		1.2
91	Venezuela	3.6		1.3
92	Indonesia	3.5		1.3
93	Honduras	3.5		1.4
94	Turkey	3.5		1.4
95	Nicaragua	3.5		1.5
96	Philippines	3.5		1.3
97	Ecuador	3.4		1.4
98	Bolivia	3.4		1.3
99	Haiti	3.3		1.3
100	Guatemala	3.3		1.3
101	Angola	3.2		1.7
102	Paraguay	3.1		1.3

11.12   Political context of environmental gains

Environmental gains in your country are achieved through (1 = adversarial and legal means, 7 = government-business cooperation and voluntary corporate action)

RANK	COUNTRY	SCORE	1 MEAN: 4.2 7	SD
1	Singapore	5.8		1.1
2	Austria	5.7		0.9
3	Switzerland	5.7		0.7
4	Germany	5.4		1.0
5	Japan	5.3		1.2
6	Finland	5.3		1.3
7	Tunisia	5.2		1.0
8	United Kingdom	5.1		1.1
9	Taiwan	5.1		1.4
10	Malawi	5.0		1.0
11	Luxembourg	5.0		1.3
12	Australia	5.0		1.0
13	Canada	4.9		1.4
14	Mali	4.9		1.2
15	Malaysia	4.9		0.9
16	Netherlands	4.9		1.2
17	Botswana	4.8		1.3
18	Denmark	4.8		1.5
19	Mauritius	4.8		1.3
20	Norway	4.8		1.2
21	Iceland	4.7		1.3
22	Tanzania	4.7		1.3
23	New Zealand	4.6		1.2
24	Ghana	4.6		1.4
25	Ireland	4.6		1.5
26	Sweden	4.6		1.5
27	Namibia	4.6		1.2
28	South Africa	4.6		1.3
29	Italy	4.5		1.1
30	France	4.5		1.3
31	United States	4.5		1.5
32	Costa Rica	4.5		1.3
33	Senegal	4.5		1.3
34	Hong Kong SAR	4.4		1.2
35	Brazil	4.4		1.1
36	Korea	4.4		1.2
37	Latvia	4.4		1.2
38	Cameroon	4.4		1.6
39	Jamaica	4.4		1.1
40	Gambia	4.4		1.8
41	Malta	4.4		1.4
42	Jordan	4.4		1.1
43	Chile	4.3		1.3
44	Spain	4.3		1.1
45	Zimbabwe	4.3		1.1
46	·Thailand	4.3		1.2
47	Mozambique	4.3		1.6
48	Madagascar	4.3		1.3
49	Croatia	4.3		1.4
50	Vietnam	4.3		1.7
51	Zambia	4.2		1.5
52	Colombia	4.2		1.2

RANK	COUNTRY	SCORE	1 MEAN: 4.2 7	SD
53	Mexico	4.2		1.3
54	Uganda	4.2		1.6
55	Indonesia	4.2		1.3
56	Nigeria	4.1		1.4
57	El Salvador	4.1		1.4
58	Algeria	4.1		1.5
58	Greece	4.1		1.1
60	Kenya	4.1		1.6
61	Uruguay	4.0		1.4
62	Haiti	4.0		1.4
63	Belgium	4.0		1.3
64	Sri Lanka	4.0		1.3
65	Dominican Republic	3.9		1.7
66	Morocco	3.9		1.5
67	Venezuela	3.9		1.2
68	Panama	3.9		1.4
69	Slovak Republic	3.9		1.3
70	Trinidad and Tobago	3.9		1.2
71	Lithuania	3.9		1.2
72	Philippines	3.9		1.4
73	Czech Republic	3.8		1.4
74	Slovenia	3.8		1.2
75	Angola	3.8		2.0
76	Argentina	3.8		1.3
77	Poland	3.8		1.2
78	Serbia	3.8		1.6
79	Bulgaria	3.8		1.4
80	Israel	3.8		1.2
81	India	3.7		1.4
82	Portugal	3.7		0.9
83	Guatemala	3.7		1.5
84	Egypt	3.7		1.9
85	Bangladesh	3.7		1.5
86	Pakistan	3.7		1.3
87	Peru	3.6		1.3
88	Estonia	3.6		1.3
89	Ukraine	3.6		1.4
90	Ethiopia	3.6		1.6
91	Turkey	3.6		1.4
92	Macedonia, FYR	3.5		1.6
93	Nicaragua	3.4		1.6
94	Chad	3.4		1.4
95	China	3.4		1.5
96	Bolivia	3.4		1.4
97	Honduras	3.4		1.6
98	Romania	3.3		1.6
99	Ecuador	3.3		1.4
100	Paraguay	3.3		1.7
101	Russian Federation	3.2		1.5
102	Hungary	3.0		1.1

11.13   Prevalence of environmental management systems

How many companies in your country utilize environmental management systems such as ISO 14000? (1 = almost no companies, 7 = most companies)

RANK	COUNTRY	SCORE	MEAN: 3.4	SD
1	Finland	5.5		1.0
2	Sweden	5.4		1.2
3	Japan	5.3		1.1
4	Germany	5.3		1.3
5	Singapore	5.1		1.1
6	Italy	5.0		1.3
7	United States	4.8		1.6
8	United Kingdom	4.8		1.3
9	Denmark	4.7		1.0
10	Taiwan	4.7		1.3
11	Netherlands	4.7		1.4
12	Korea	4.7		1.1
13	Norway	4.6		1.4
14	Australia	4.5		1.1
15	Malaysia	4.4		1.1
16	Austria	4.3		1.5
17	Canada	4.3		1.5
18	Switzerland	4.3		1.4
19	Thailand	4.2		1.1
20	Ghana	4.2		1.7
21	Belgium	4.2		1.2
22	Brazil	4.1		1.4
23	Iceland	4.1		1.4
24	Slovenia	4.1		1.1
25	New Zealand	4.1		1.1
26	Ireland	4.1		1.3
27	France	4.0		1.4
28	Luxembourg	4.0		1.6
29	Gambia	4.0		2.2
30	Spain	4.0		1.1
31	South Africa	3.9		1.2
32	Czech Republic	3.9		1.4
33	Israel	3.8		0.9
34	Tunisia	3.8		1.5
35	Lithuania	3.7		1.2
36	China	3.7		1.5
37	India	3.7		1.3
38	Indonesia	3.7		1.3
39	Slovak Republic	3.7		1.2
40	Hong Kong SAR	3.7		1.3
41	Tanzania	3.7		1.4
42	Vietnam	3.7		1.2
43	Egypt	3.7		1.3
44	Zambia	3.7		1.7
45	Poland	3.6		1.2
46	Malawi	3.6		1.7
47	Nigeria	3.6		1.5
48	Estonia	3.5		1.2
49	Hungary	3.5		1.1
50	Portugal	3.5		1.1
51	Jordan	3.5		1.4
52	Costa Rica	3.4		1.3

RANK	COUNTRY	SCORE	MEAN: 3.4	SD
53	Uganda	3.4		1.7
54	Jamaica	3.4		1.3
55	Mauritius	3.4		1.2
56	Greece	3.3		1.2
57	Namibia	3.3		1.5
58	Philippines	3.3		1.3
59	Zimbabwe	3.3		1.4
60	Sri Lanka	3.3		1.3
61	Mexico	3.3		1.2
62	Latvia	3.3		1.5
63	Colombia	3.2		1.1
64	Kenya	3.2		1.3
65	Morocco	3.2		1.5
66	Chile	3.1		1.1
67	Argentina	3.1		1.2
68	Turkey	3.1		1.2
69	Croatia	3.1		1.3
70	Botswana	3.1		1.6
71	Romania	2.9		1.3
72	Trinidad and Tobago	2.9		1.0
73	Dominican Republic	2.8		1.3
74	Uruguay	2.8		1.1
75	Russian Federation	2.8		1.3
76	Serbia	2.8		1.2
77	Panama	2.7		1.3
78	Pakistan	2.7		1.0
79	Macedonia, FYR	2.6		1.5
80	Bulgaria	2.4		1.1
81	Guatemala	2.4		1.2
82	Peru	2.4		0.9
83	Cameroon	2.3		1.7
84	Ecuador	2.3		0.9
85	Ukraine	2.3		1.4
86	Senegal	2.3		1.2
87	Malta	2.3		1.1
88	Venezuela	2.3		1.2
89	Honduras	2.1		1.0
90	Ethiopia	2.1		1.4
91	Bangladesh	2.1		1.1
92	Mozambique	2.1		1.3
93	Algeria	2.1		1.2
94	Bolivia	2.0		1.0
95	Mali	1.9		1.2
96	Nicaragua	1.9		1.0
97	El Salvador	1.9		1.0
98	Chad	1.8		1.3
99	Madagascar	1.7		0.9
100	Paraguay	1.6		0.7
101	Haiti	1.5		1.0
102	Angola	1.3		0.7

Technical Notes and Sources

The data used in this *Report* represent the best available estimates from various national authorities, international agencies, and private sources at the time the *Report* was prepared (July/August 2003). It is possible that some data will have been revised or updated by national sources after publication. Throughout the statistical tables in this publication, "n/a" denotes that the value is not available.

The following outlines some notes on sources for specific variables listed in the Data Tables of this *Report*. All of these variables are related to the Growth Competitiveness Index or the Business Competitiveness Index.

Section 1. Aggregate country performance indicators

1.01 Total GDP, 2002. Source: Gross domestic product (GDP) in current US dollars was taken from the International Monetary Fund's *World Economic Outlook Database, April 2003*. Available online at http://www.imf.org/external/pubs/ft/weo/2003/01/data/index.htm

1.02 Total population, 2002. Source: Population data were taken from the United Nations Population Fund's (UNFPA) *State of the World Population 2002*. Available online at http://www.unfpa.org/swp/2002/english/indicators/pdf/pdf2.pdf

1.03 GDP per capita (PPP), 2002. Source: Per capita GDP adjusted for purchasing power across countries was obtained from the International Comparison Program (ICP) of the World Bank. For three countries with missing values (Nicaragua, Serbia, and Taiwan), data from the Economist Intelligence Unit were used. Missing values for four additional countries (Israel, Malta, Mozambique, and Zimbabwe) were calculated as follows: 2001 GDP per capita (PPP) figures from either the ICP or from the World Bank's *World Development Indicators 2003* were multiplied by the real per capita growth rate from 2001 to 2002. These values were in turn scaled by the 2001 to 2002 US GDP implicit price deflator, as calculated by the US Department of Commerce's Bureau of Economic Analysis.

1.04 Change in GDP per capita relative to the United States, 1995 to 2002. Source: This variable is calculated as follows: first, GDP per capita relative to the United States for 2002 is calculated using the data from variable 1.03, showing GDP as a proportion of that of the United States rather than at an absolute level. Then, the same calculation is made for 1995 using data from the World Bank's *World Development Indicators 2003*. Using these two variables, average annual growth rates from 1995 to 2002 were calculated.

Section 2. Macroeconomic Environment

2.17 Country Credit Rating, 2003. Source: Institutional Investor, March 2003. Available online at http://www.institutionalinvestor.com/platinum/rr/countrycredit/ccr/2003.asp © Institutional Investor, 2003. No further copying or transmission of this material is allowed without the express permission of Institutional Investor (publisher@institutionalinvestor.com).

2.18 Government surplus/deficit, 2002. Source: IMF Country Reports; OECD Economic Outlook, No.73, June 2003; OECD African Economic Outlook 2002/03; Economist Intelligence Unit and national sources.

2.19 National savings rate, 2002. Source: Economist Intelligence Unit, IMF Country Reports, and national sources.

2.20 Inflation, 2002. IMF *World Economic Outlook Database, April 2003*.

2.21 Real exchange rate, 2002. Using consumer price index data and period average annual (nominal) exchange rate data from the IMF's *International Financial Statistics, June 2003*, and national sources, this variable was created by setting the average real exchange in 1995 to 100 (in some cases missing consumer price values were reconstructed using the IMF's *World Economic Outlook Database, April 2003* inflation data). The results thus show the relative appreciation (for numbers less than 100), or (depreciation for numbers greater than 100), of each currency relative to the US dollar up to 2002. The basis of the real exchange rate calculation was:

$$\left(\begin{array}{c} \text{Period average exchange rate} \\ \text{(in national currency per US\$)} \end{array} \right) \times \left(\frac{\text{US Consumer Price Index}}{\text{National Consumer Price Index}} \right)$$

2.22 Interest rate spread, 2002. Source: The IMF's *International Financial Statistics, June 2003*, Economist Intelligence Unit, and national sources. This variable is equal to the difference between the typical short-term lending and deposit rates over the 2002 period.

Section 3: Technology: Innovation and Diffusion

3.17 Utility patents, 2002. Source: United States Patent and Trademark Office. *Patent Counts by Country/State and Year, Utility Patents.* February 2003. Available online at: http://www.uspto.gov. Utility patents (ie, patents for invention) are recorded such that the origin of the patent is determined by the first-named inventor at the time of the grant. Patents per million population are calculated by dividing the number of patents granted to a country in 2002 by that country's population in the same year.

3.18 Tertiary enrollment. Sources: UNESCO Institute for Statistics *Gross Enrollment Ratio at Tertiary Level of Education by Country and Gender*, World Bank, *World Development Indicators 2002* and national sources. According to the *World Development Indicators*, the gross tertiary enrollment rate is the ratio of total enrollment, regardless of age, to the population of the age group that officially corresponds to the level of education shown. Tertiary education, whether or not leading to an advanced research qualification, normally requires, as a minimum condition of admission, the successful completion of education at the secondary level. Also according to the *World Development Indicators*, "in 1998, ISCED97 was introduced and UNESCO's data collection program and country reporting of education statistics were adjusted to this new classification. This was to facilitate the international compilation and comparison of educational statistics, as well as to take into account new types of learning opportunities and activities available for both children and adults. Thus the time series up to 1997 are not consistent with the data for 1998 and after." The revision to the classification had an important impact on the tertiary enrollment ratio of some countries covered by the *Report*, the most notable case being Australia, which dropped by approximately 16 percentage points following the revision. Note that this year UNESCO tertiary enrollment data are available for the year 2000 for a number of countries, as compared with last year when the most recent data available were for 1998. As this table contains data from 2000 or the most recent year available for all countries, the possible difference between the most recent and least recent data has also increased.

3.19 Cellular telephones, 2002. Source: International Telecommunications Union, July 2002. Some data are available online at http://www.itu.int/ITU-D/ict/statistics/

3.20 Internet users, 2002. Source: International Telecommunications Union, July 2002. Some data are available online at http://www.itu.int/ITU-D/ict/statistics/

3.21 Internet hosts, 2002. Source: International Telecommunications Union, July 2002. Some data are available online at http://www.itu.int/ITU-D/ict/statistics/

3.22 Telephone lines, 2002. Source: International Telecommunications Union, July 2002. Some data are available online at http://www.itu.int/ITU-D/ict/statistics/

3.23 Personal computers, 2002. Source: International Telecommunications Union, July 2002. Some data are available online at http://www.itu.int/ITU-D/ict/statistics/

573

The World Economic Forum would like to thank FedEx and KPMG for their support in making this *Report* possible.

FedEx Corp.

FedEx Corp. is the premier global provider of transportation, e-commerce, and supply chain management services. With a worldwide network that serves customers in 215 countries, FedEx offers integrated business solutions through its independently operating subsidiaries, including: FedEx Express, the world's largest express transportation company; FedEx Ground, North America's second largest provider of small-package ground delivery service; FedEx Freight, the largest U.S. provider of regional less-than-truckload freight services; FedEx Custom Critical, North America's largest provider of expedited time-critical shipments; and FedEx Trade Networks, North America's largest customs broker and a provider of international freight forwarding and trade facilitation services.

FedEx Express, the largest subsidiary, connects areas that generate more than 90 percent of the world's gross domestic product in 24 to 48 hours. The company delivers nearly 3.1 million packages every day through its unparalleled global network.

A fervent and vocal champion of global free trade, FedEx Corp. is proud to be a part of the World Economic Forum and its *Global Competitiveness Report 2003–2004*.

KPMG International

KPMG is the global network of professional services firms whose aim is to turn understanding of information, industries, and business trends into value. With nearly 100,000 people worldwide, KPMG member firms provide assurance, tax and legal, and financial advisory services from more than 750 cities in 150 countries.

Fundamental to KPMG's approach is its focus on industry sectors. KPMG believes it can add value for its clients by truly understanding their business. This is why KPMG invests in continuously improving its knowledge of the industries it serves.

KPMG is best defined by its strong commitment to quality. Accountancy—together with other advisory services—is still a profession of integrity and independence. KPMG embraces a set of core values that emphasizes qualities such as responsive leadership and personal accountability—all aimed at best serving clients and retaining the public's trust.

On a global basis, KPMG coordinates its national and local resources—people, ideas, skills, technologies and knowledge—through three operating regions, offering clients flexibility, responsiveness, and critical mass in a host of problem-solving disciplines.